SOCIOLOGY

Principles of Sociology with an Introduction to Sociological Thought

SOCIOLOGY

Principles of Sociology with an Introduction to Sociological Thought

C N SHANKAR RAO

Lecturer in Sociology

Canara Pre-University College

Mangalore, Karnataka

S Chand And Company Limited

(ISO 9001 Certified Company)

RAM NAGAR, NEW DELHI - 110 055

S Chand And Company Limited

(ISO 9001 Certified Company)

Head Office: 7361, RAM NAGAR, QUTAB ROAD, NEW DELHI - 110 055

Phone: 23672080-81-82, 66672000 Fax: 91-11-23677446

www.**schandpublishing.com**; e-mail: **info@schandpublishing.com**

Branches:

Ahmedabad : Ph: 27541965, 27542369, ahmedabad@schandpublishing.com
Bengaluru : Ph: 22268048, 22354008, bangalore@schandpublishing.com
Bhopal : Ph: 4209587, bhopal@schandpublishing.com
Chandigarh : Ph: 2625356, 2625546, 4025418, chandigarh@schandpublishing.com
Chennai : Ph: 28410027, 28410058, chennai@schandpublishing.com
Coimbatore : Ph: 2323620, 4217136, coimbatore@schandpublishing.com (Marketing Office)
Cuttack : Ph: 2332580, 2332581, cuttack@schandpublishing.com
Dehradun : Ph: 2711101, 2710861, dehradun@schandpublishing.com
Guwahati : Ph: 2738811, 2735640, guwahati@schandpublishing.com
Hyderabad : Ph: 27550194, 27550195, hyderabad@schandpublishing.com
Jaipur : Ph: 2219175, 2219176, jaipur@schandpublishing.com
Jalandhar : Ph: 2401630, jalandhar@schandpublishing.com
Kochi : Ph: 2809208, 2808207, cochin@schandpublishing.com
Kolkata : Ph: 23353914, 23357458, kolkata@schandpublishing.com
Lucknow : Ph: 4065646, lucknow@schandpublishing.com
Mumbai : Ph: 22690881, 22610885, 22610886, mumbai@schandpublishing.com
Nagpur : Ph: 2720523, 2777666, nagpur@schandpublishing.com
Patna : Ph: 2300489, 2260011, patna@schandpublishing.com
Pune : Ph: 64017298, pune@schandpublishing.com
Raipur : Ph: 2443142, raipur@schandpublishing.com (Marketing Office)
Ranchi : Ph: 2361178, ranchi@schandpublishing.com
Sahibabad : Ph: 2771235, 2771238, delhibr-sahibabad@schandpublishing.com

First Edition 1990

Subsequent Editions and Reprints 1991, 93 (Twice), 95, 97, 98, 99, 2000, 2001, 2002, 2003, 2004, 2005, 2006 (Twice), 2007 (Twice), 2008 (Twice), 2009, 2010, 2011 (Twice), Seventh Edition 2012, Reprints 2013 (Twice), 2014 (Thrice), 2015 (Twice), 2016 (Thrice), 2017 (Twice), 2018 (Twice)

Reprint 2019

ISBN: 978-81-219-1036-1

PRINTED IN INDIA

By Vikas Publishing House Pvt. Ltd., Plot 20/4, Site-IV, Industrial Area Sahibabad, Ghaziabad-201010
and Published by S. Chand And Company Limited, 7361, Ram Nagar, New Delhi -110 055.

PREFACE TO THE SEVENTH EDITION

I am happy to present the *Seventh Revised and Updated Edition* of this book within a year.

Two chapters, viz., "Women in Society" and "Social Work, Social Security and Social Welfare: Conceptual Overviews" have been added to make this book more meaningful to its readers. Existing chapter on "Population Problem and Beggary" has been replaced by the "Problem of Overpopulation in India".

I hope the present expansion of the book will serve the needs of many people, especially the students of undergraduate and postgraduate levels. Constructive suggestions and criticisms to further improve the book are always appreciated.

Mangalore, Karnataka **C N Shankar Rao**

PREFACE

As a teaching subject Sociology is becoming quite popular at present not only at degree level but also at pre-degree level. Hence a large number of students have taken up sociology for study at college level. But these students are faced with the problem of binding good and exhaustive textbooks to help guide them in their studies. I will be very much contented if they feel that this book can reduce their problem a little. The encouraging reception which the readers have given to my previous books, has further inspired me to produce and present this book. I do hope that this book will also be able to win their favour and get a warm reception.

This book mainly intends to meet the needs of degree students of Sociology of all the six Universities of Karnataka who in their three year degree course study one paper in common namely: "*Principles of Sociology*" or "*General Sociology*", or "*Principles of Sociology and Social Thought*". This book is designed to cover a wide range of topics and hence it can serve as a basic textbook for the degree students of sociology of the other Indian Universities. The two-year Pre-University students of Karnataka can also take the benefit of this book for it includes all the topics of their syllabi. The book, I am sure, is helpful to all those who want to have a glimpse of sociology at a stretch.

This book consists of 39 chapters in which the last two chapters are devoted for social thought and all the others concentrate on the fundamental concepts and principles of sociology. The basic sociological concepts are introduced in a simple language to enable the students to grasp them without any difficulty. I have also tried to maintain a simple and lucid style. I very sincerely hope that students as well as a teachers will find this book quite useful and interesting and appreciate my strenuous efforts in the task of producing a relatively standard textbook.

In writing this book, I have referred to and drawn much material from the works of a number of writers, to whom I am extremely grateful. In order to be objective in the explanation of sociological concepts I have profusely quoted sentences and statements of various sociologists for whom I am greatly indebted. Hence as an author I do not wish to claim any originality to many of the ideas and descriptions contained in the book. But with all humility I can say that I have presented the matter in my own way.

It is my duty to express my gratitude to all those who have helped me in preparing this book. My thanks are due to my fellow-teachers and student-readers without whose encouragement the book would not have appeared. I am indebted to all those friends and well-wishers of mine who have given valuable suggestions in this venture. I thank my wife Saraswathi S. Rao who has co-operated with me in the preparation of manuscripts.

I thank M/s S. Chand & Co. Ltd. and particularly, their Bangalore Branch Manager Sri Balaraman, for having shown interest in the publication of this book and in bringing it out at the right time.

Readers are most welcome to offer valuable suggestions which will be of great help in improving the book in its next edition.

C N Shankar Rao

CONTENTS

PART FOUR
Social Inequality

PART FIVE
Social Institutions

PART SIX
Social Control

PART SEVEN
Social Change

PART EIGHT
Collective Behaviour and Social Movements

PART NINE
Social Disorganisation and Social Problems

Additional Chapter on
Contemporary Social Issues
available on the website. Scan the QR code →

PART ONE

Introducing Sociology

1. Introduction
2. Definition, Scope and Uses of Sociology
3. Some Branches of Sociology
4. Methods of Sociology
5. Social Research: Its Methods and Techniques
6. Sociology and Other Social Sciences
7. The Study of Human Society

1

INTRODUCTION

CHAPTER OUTLINE

Sociology is the youngest of the Social Sciences. Its major concern is society, and hence it is popularly known as the "Science of Society". But, if we are to understand the entire scope of the subject, how it is to be studied, what sociologists do, how they do, what methods they follow, what problems they face in their studies, it is necessary to know the meaning of *Science* and the classification of sciences into *physical* and *social*.

SCIENCE IS KNOWLEDGE

Science is concerned with knowledge. It refers to the body of knowledge systematically arranged. Knowledge is its purpose and system refers to the method that has to be followed for the acquisition of knowledge. Exploring the different horizons of knowledge is not only a challenge but also a matter of great intellectual delight to a scientist. Knowledge is as vast as an ocean. The more a scientist acquires it, the more it remains to be acquired. Not only a scientist is more interested in acquiring knowledge but also he is better equipped to do so.

CLASSIFICATION OF SCIENCES

It is humanly impossible for any individual to master the whole of knowledge with all its complexity and diversity. One can only attempt to understand more about one or the other branch of knowledge. There are different sciences to deal with different branches of knowledge. These sciences are of two kinds: (*i*) *Physical Sciences*, and (*ii*) *Social Sciences*.

Physical Sciences

The physical sciences deal mostly with the natural inanimate objects. They are regarded as more precise, exact and less dubious. Ex: Mathematics, Physics, Chemistry, Geology, Geography, Astronomy, etc.

The physical scientists make use of the scientific method in order to acquire knowledge in their respective fields. They can conduct experiments to verify the facts. Theories and laws of universal validity are established more easily and accurately in physical sciences. They provide less scope for doubt and uncertainty. Prediction is not only possible, but also easy and accurate. The problem of objectivity can be overcome easily. The relationship between cause and effects is relatively more clear here.

Social Sciences

The term *Social Science* is often loosely applied to any kind of study which is concerned with man and society. But, in the strict sense, it refers to "the application of scientific methods of the study of intricate and complex network of human relationships and the forms of organization desired to enable peoples to live together in societies". As *Young* and *Mack* say, "*By Social Science we mean those bodies of knowledge compiled through the use of scientific method which deal with the forms and contents of man's interaction*". Ex: History, Political Science, Economics, Sociology, Anthropology, Psychology etc.

To be social is to interact, to participate in group life. All human beings are social. People interact with other people in order to survive. All human beings live in society, that is to say, every person is a member of the same human group or some social environment. The physicist, the chemist, the astronomer and the biologist study the universe, in which we live and the elements of which it is composed, in an attempt to understand our physical environment. Similarly, the social scientist studies the environment in which we live in, and attempts to understand human society and to predict how people will interact in a given set of circumstances.

Social Sciences are Less Exact

When compared with the physical sciences, the social sciences are less exact and less precise. The social scientists face many difficulties while making their studies. Scientific method, with all its established procedures, cannot be strictly used in social investigations, because experiments of laboratory conditions are difficult to be arranged in the social field. Controlled experiments are almost impossible here. The whole society constitutes the laboratory for the social scientist. Since the social scientists have to deal with man who is more complex and everchanging, their studies become less precise though not completely dubious. Complexity of social data, interdependence of cause and effect, problems of objectivity and prediction etc., have made social science comparatively less exact.

The Necessity for Social Sciences

The two global wars of the 20th century have created new anxieties and new fears for the mankind. These wars the world had to bear with before it could properly maintain its balance which was previously disturbed by the process of Industrial Revolution of the 18th and 19th centuries. The scientists, philosophers, administrators, politicians and many other thoughtful observers have been warning human beings for many years of the dangers of the increasing imbalance in their culture. The recent scientific advances in physical sciences culminating in the atomic bomb, hydrogen bomb, germ warfare and even the tragedy of Hiroshima, have at last awakened even the innocent people all over the world to the need for comparable competence in social sciences.

The science has shown that it is capable of organising the forces of the atom to cause the destruction of the entire world by a single explosion. It has posed a challenge whether it is possible to organise the forces inherent in human beings and in human society to make such destruction impossible. Hence the necessity of social science. This need, the humanity is obliged to fulfil in mutual self-defense.

It is an irony that the material resources like coal, iron, oil, forest, soil and minerals are better organised than human resources like human energy, intelligence, inherent goodness of man etc. Today governments are busily engaged in armament race. Every country spends millions for inventing or possessing destructive weapons on agencies. But no country spends even a fraction of it to stop such dangerous and suicidal works.

Fortunately, realisation has dawned. It is now felt that the imbalance between the physical and social sciences is to be set right. Advancement in physical sciences alone cannot bring man happiness. Social sciences are equally important in promoting human welfare. Social sciences help in understanding and controlling social interactions. "The anthropologist is the astronomer of the social sciences", as has been said by the UNESCO in 1954. The U.N.O., UNESCO, W.H.O. are organisations which attempt for the solution of the modern world problems on sociological knowledge.

In conclusion, it can be said that a medical doctor has a basic doctrine that he should prevent disease and save life. Similarly, the social scientist has a basic doctrine that he should prevent friction and violence in human relations and that he should save lives and help in establishing peaceful and self-respecting relations between man and man.

SOCIOLOGY AS A SOCIAL SCIENCE

Sociology is one of the members of the family of Social Sciences. As a young social science, it has acquired a distinct status for itself. Its importance and practical usefulness are widely recognised today.

Like all other social sciences, sociology also is concerned with the life and activities of man. It studies the nature and character of human society, and also its origin, and development, structure and functions. It analyses the group life of man and examines the bonds of social unity.

Sociology tries to determine the relationship and inter-dependence between different elements of social life; between the moral and the religious, the economic and political, the intellectual and the philosophical and the artistic and the aesthetic, the scientific and the technological, and non-material and so on.

Sociology also discovers the fundamental conditions of social stability and social change. It analyses the influence of economic, political, technological, cultural and other forces and factors on man and his life. It endeavours to examine the influence of biological and geographic factors on man also. It throws more light on various social problems like poverty, beggary, over-population, crime, unemployment, etc.

EMERGENCE OF SOCIAL SCIENCES: A BRIEF HISTORICAL BACKGROUND

The beginning of the tradition of social sciences has been one of the major developments of the 19th century. Social sciences such as economics, political science and history though have a long story of their own, could get the recognition as "*social sciences*" only in the 19th century. Thinkers and writers such as **Herodotus** [known as the "*Father of History*"]; **Aristotle** [often known as the "*Father of political science*"]; **Manu**, the great law giver; **Kautilya**, an authority on "*Arthashastra*", and many others had written good treatises on different areas of social sciences more than 2000 years ago. The political and social atmosphere of ancient Greece, Rome and India also favoured this kind of intellectual exercises. Due to historical reasons these countries could not maintain the same tempo during the Middle Age. [500 A.D. to 1550 A.D.] But during 17th and 18th centuries the processes of Renaissance, and Enlightenment gave a big impetus to the continuation of the tradition of reasoning. This change in the intellectual atmosphere favoured the development of sciences which came to be called "*social sciences*".

Impact of Twin Revolutions: The French Revolution and the Industrial Revolution

It is often said that social sciences in the 19th century are mostly understood as responses to the problem of order that was created in men's minds by the weakening of the old order under the twin blows of the *French Revolution* and *the Industrial Revolution*. The European society was hard hit by these twin Revolutions. The old social order that rested on kinship, land social class, religion, local community, and monarchy became very shaky. Thinkers were more concerned about finding ways and means of reconsolidating these elements of social order. Hence the history of 19th century politics, industry, and trade is basically about *the practical efforts of human beings to reconsolidate these elements*. Thus, it is obvious that the history of the 19th century social thought is about theoretical efforts to reconsolidate them - that is, *to give them new contents and meaning.*

"In terms of the immediacy and sheer massiveness of the impact on human thought and values, it would be difficult to find revolutions of comparable magnitude in human history. The political, social and cultural changes that began in France and England at the very end of the 18th century spread almost immediately through Europe and the America in the 19th century and then on to Asia, Africa, and Oceania in the 20th. The effects of the two revolutions, the one overwhelmingly democratic in the thrust, the other industrial capitalist, have been to undermine, shake, or topple institutions that had endured for centuries, even millennia, and with them systems of authority, status, belief and community".[1]

New Intellectual and Philosophical Tendencies and their Impact on the Development of Social Sciences

The twin revolutions, [the French Revolution and the Industrial Revolution of Britain] that took place in the 18th century in Europe let loose a new intellectual and philosophical wave. Intellectual currents in the form of socio-political ideologies were also witnessed. For example, the ideologies of *individualism, socialism, utilitarianism, utopianism* etc. *took their birth. It became fashionable* for *intellectuals and thinkers to float new ideologies and spread novel ideas.*

Of the various types of intellectual influences, the impact of *positivism, humanitarianism* and *evolutionism on social sciences was considerable.*

[1] *Encyclopedia Britannica*, Vol. 27, p. 367.

Positivism

Positivism implied *not merely an appeal to science* but *almost reverence for science*. The positivist appeal of science was to be seen everywhere. The 19th century saw the virtual institutionalisation of the ideal of science. The great aim was that of dealing with moral values, institutions, and all social phenomena through the same fundamental methods that could be used so successfully in such areas as physics or biology.

Prior to the 19th century, no very clear distinction had been made between philosophy and science. But now the distinction between philosophy and science became very clear. It was also felt that every area of man's thought and behaviour could be put to scientific investigation. More than anyone else, it was Auguste Comte who heralded the idea of the scientific treatment of social behaviour. His book "Positive Philosophy" [original French name: "*Cours de philosophie Positive*"] published in six volumes between 1830 and l842, sought to demonstrate the necessity of the science of man in society. He coined the word "*sociology*" to name such a science. He argued that this science called "sociology" would do for "man the social being" exactly what biology had already done for "man the biological animal". Comte was not alone to argue and to think in this manner. He was supported by many thinkers of the day.

Humanitarianism

Humanitarianism, though a very distinguishable current of thought, it was closely related to the idea of "science of society". Humanitarianism is an ideology committed to the cause of human welfare or societal welfare. The ultimate purpose of social science was also thought by almost everyone to be the welfare society. Humanitarianism entered the sphere of "*social consciousness*" and made the people to realise *the need for doing something for the improvement of the poor and needy*.

Due to the influence of humanitarianism, several social service organisations, orphanages, poor houses, child protective laws came in. Great concern was shown towards the poor in the artistic, literary, religious and political communities. Hospitals and sanitaria sprang up in many cities. Making provisions for drinking water facilities, educational opportunities, economic assistance etc. for the benefit of the needy, became a part of the local administrative bodies. The need for more "*social philosophising*" was called for. A genuine application of the science of human understanding was needed. It is clear from the above, that humanitarianism and social science were *reciprocally related in their purposes*. All that helped the cause of the one could be seen as helpful to the other.

Evolutionism

The third of the intellectual influences is that of evolution,[2] It affected everyone of the social sciences each of which was concerned with the idea of "*development*". It was believed that the idea of evolution would help people to understand the *development* in social structures or societies as it had helped the biologists to understand the development in the structure of animals.

The impact of **Charles Darwin's** "*origin of Species*", published in 1859, was of course great and further enhanced the appeal of the evolutionary view of things. It should be noted that even before the publication of Darwin's work, **Comte, Spencer** and **Marx** had already given shape to the idea of evolution in their literary works. "The important point, in any event, is that the idea or the philosophy of evolution was in the air throughout the century, as profoundly contributory to the establishment of sociology as a systematic discipline in the 1830s as to such fields as geology, astronomy, and biology. Evolution was as permeative an idea as the Trinity had been in medieval Europe".[3]

Development of Different Social Sciences

Among the disciplines that formed the social sciences, two contrary, but powerful tendencies at first dominated them, (*i*) *The first was the drive towards unification, that is towards a single, master social science*. Some thinkers felt that it was better to have a single science of society [that would take its place in the hierarchy of sciences] than to have a plurality of social sciences. In the 1820s itself Auguste Comte wrote calling for a new science, the one to study man as a social animal. Comte, Spencer, Marx, Bentham and many others to join them, saw the study of society as a unified enterprise. Since society is an indivisible thing, the study of society must be a unified one. This was their basic belief.

---

[2] Evolution: Evolution means "*to develop*" or "*to unfold*". It implies continuous change that takes place especially in some structure. Social thinkers like Comte and others borrowed the term from biological science and replaced it with "social evolution". The term "*social evolution*" was used by them to explain the evolution of human society from one stage to another, from simplicity to complexity.

[3] *Encyclopedia Britannico,* Vol. 27, p. 369.

(*ii*) *The second tendency was towards specialisation of individual social sciences*. It was this opposite tendency of specialisation or differentiation that won out. In spite of the dreams of Comte, Spencer, Marx and others, there were to be found at the end of the 19th century not one, but several distinct, competitive social sciences. Development of colleges and universities throughout Europe and America very strongly supported this process. These formal educational institutions in fact, started the "*age of specialisation*". This began first in Germany and later on spread to England, America, France and other countries. The philosophy of specialisation became so fascinating that no major field of study could escape the lure of specialisation.

Different Social Sciences: A Glimpse

As it has already been said earlier social sciences refer to a related group of disciplines that study various aspects of human behaviour. The main social sciences are—sociology, economics, political science, anthropology and psychology. History is also included in this category. Human behaviour, of course, does not come in such neat compartments. In reality the boundaries between, the social sciences are very vague and constantly shifting. Each one of these sciences has different historical origins and each science is trying to preserve its distinctness. In spite of the specialisation found among the social sciences, they are interrelated and interdependent. Nobody could possibly be an expert in all of them. Because, social scientists are aware that their sciences overlap. This awareness has been responsible for the development of what is known as an "interdisciplinary approach". This approach stresses the idea that each science is necessarily related to, and sometimes dependent on the other. This approach gives them a free hand to "invade" each other's territory whenever it seems useful to do so.

Economics

Economics studies the production, distribution and consumption of goods and services. Wealth constitutes the central problem of economics. It studies man as a wealth-getter and wealth-disposer. Economics is in many ways the most advanced of the social sciences. Its subject-matter is often more easily measured than that of the other disciplines. But the economy is also a part of society: goods and services do not produce, distribute and consume themselves. The economic processes depend upon Society. The social aspects of economic life are the subject matter of "*sociology of economics*", one of the major branches of sociology.

Political Science

Political science is the science of state and government. Traditionally it has focused on two main areas. Political philosophy and actual forms of government. Political science has close links with sociology. In the recent years political science has been very strongly influenced by one of the branches of sociology, known as "*political sociology*". Political sociology analyses political behaviour and studies the social interaction involved in the process of government. The interests of political scientists and political sociologists have been gradually converging and in many instances they now overlap.

Anthropology

Anthropology is a science of man and his works. Sociology and anthropology are "twin sisters". Both are mutually helpful and supportive. Anthropology has two main branches: (*i*) Physical anthropology and (*ii*) cultural anthropology. Physical anthropology deals with human evolution and studies the physical characteristics of man. Cultural anthropology deals with the cultural evolution. It studies the ways of life of different communities, particularly, the primitive ones.

Anthropology differs from sociology in that it usually focuses on the simple, small-scale, primitive societies. Anthropology studies the society as "whole". Sociology concentrates more on group processes within larger modern complex societies.

Psychology

Psychology is the science of human behaviour. This science, more than any other social science, focuses on the individual. Psychology shares one major field of interest with sociology, namely social psychology. Social psychology is the science of the behaviour of the individual in society. It studies the way in which personality and behaviour are influenced by the social context.

History

History according to some belongs more to the category of humanities than to the group of social sciences. But for all practical purposes it is also treated as one among the social sciences. History is a systematic record of human past. "*It is the story of the experience of mankind*". History is a storehouse of records, a treasury of knowledge. It supplies useful information and facts to the social sciences including sociology. Sociology is also useful to history for it provides the social background for the study of history.

Sociology

Sociology joined the family of social sciences relatively at a later stage *i.e.* in the 19th century, for it had no independent existence before.

In fact, sociology began to emerge as an independent and separate discipline only around the middle of the 19th century. It took almost fifty years before the subject began to assume scientific character that it has today. Prior to the middle of the 18th century, the study of society was domi- nated by social philosophers rather than by social scientists. These philosophers were less concerned about what society actually is like, than what they thought it ought to be like. But in a relatively short period this emphasis was completely reversed. Hence study of society became more scientific than philosophical.

THE BEGINNINGS OF SOCIOLOGY

Sociology before Auguste Comte

Sociology has a long past but only a short history. Sociology which is known as the science of society, is one of the youngest as well as one of the oldest of the social sciences. It is one of the youngest sciences because only recently it came to be established as a distinct branch of knowledge with its own distinct set of concepts and its own methods of inquiry.

Sociology is also one of the oldest of the sciences. Since the dawn of civilisation, society has been a subject for speculation and inquiry along with other phenomena which have agitated the restless and inquisitive mind of man. Even centuries ago men were thinking about society and how it should be organised, and held views on man and his destiny, the rise and fall of peoples and civilisations. Though they were thinking in sociological terms they were called philosophers, historians, thinkers, law-givers or seers. Thus, "*Broadly it may be said that sociology has had a fourfold origin: in political philosophy, the philosophy of history, biological theories of evolution and the movements for social and political reforms...*"

There was Social Thought during the Ancient Age

Though sociology came to be established as a separate discipline in the 19th century due to the efforts of the French philosopher Auguste Comte, it is wrong to suppose that there existed no social thought before him. For thousands of years men have reflected upon societies in which they lived. In the writings of philosophers, thinkers and law-givers of various countries of various epochs we find ideas that are sociological. For instance, in the writings of Plato, Aristotle, Manu, Kautilya, Confucius, Cicero and others we find major attempts to deal methodically with the nature of society, law, religion, philosophy etc. Plato's *Republic*, Aristotle's *Politics*, *Kautilya's Arthashastra*, the *Smriti* of Manu, Confucius' *Analects*, Cicero's "*On Justice*" are some of the ancient sources of social thought.

During the middle ages and early modern times the teachings of the church dominated the human mind and hence most part of the human thinking remained as metaphysical speculation far away from the scientific inquiry. Intellectuals became more active since the l6th century onwards. Their quest for an understanding human society, its nature, socio-political system and its problems now received new impetus. The literary works of some prominent intellectuals of this period clearly reveals this urge to understand and interpret man's socio-political system.

Machiavelli's "*The Prince*", Thomas Hobbes' "*Leviathan*", Rosseau's "*Social Contract*", Montesquieu's "The Spirit of Laws", Adam Smith's "*Wealth of Nations*", Condorcet's "*Historical Sketch of the Progress of the Human mind*" serve as examples of such literary works. Thinkers like Sir Thomas More in his "*Utopia*", Thomasso Campanella in his "*City of the Sun*", Sir Francis Bacon in his "*New, Atlantis*", James Harrington in his "*Common Wealth of Oceana*", H.G. Wells in his "*A Modern Utopia*" - had made attempts to project a picture of an ideal society free from all shortcomings.

However, it was only in the l9th century that systematic attempts were made by Auguste Comte, Spencer, Durkheim, Weber and others to study society and to establish a science of society called "**sociology**".

Characteristics of Early Sociology

The science of sociology was taking its shape to emerge as a distinct science in the second half of the 19th century and the early part of the 20th century. According to T.B. Bottomore[4] early sociology assumed the following characteristics:

[4] T.B. Bottomore in *Sociology: A Guide to Problems and Literature*, 1971, p. 20.

(*i*) Early sociology was encyclopedic in character. It was "*concerned with the whole social life of man and with the hole of human history*".

(*ii*) Early sociology, which was under the influence of philosophy of history and the biological theory of evolution, was largely evolutionary in nature.

(*iii*) It was generally regarded as a positive science similar in character to the natural sciences.' "*Sociology in the l9th century was modelled upon biology*". This fact could be ascertained from the widely used conceptions of society as an organisation and from the attempts to formulate general laws of social evolution.

(*iv*) Sociology was virtually recognised above all, "a science of the new industrial society." Even though sociology claimed itself to be a general science, it dealt particularly with social problems arising from the political and economic revolutions of the 18th century.

(*v*) Sociology as "*an ideological as well as scientific character*". Various conservative and radical idea entered into its formation, gave rise to conflicting theories, and provoked controversies which continue to the present day.

Factors Contributing to the Emergence of Sociology

Sociology came to be established as an independent and a separate social science in the middle of the l9th century. Various factors paved the way for its emergence. **Ian Robertson** in his book "*Sociology*", [Pages: 11-12] has mentioned of three factors that hastened the process of the establishment of sociology as a separate science. They may be briefed here.

Industrial Revolution and Industrialisation

Industrial Revolution that took place first in England during the l8th century brought about sweeping changes throughout Europe. Never before in history did social changes take place on such a massive scale. Sociology emerged in the context of the sweeping changes.

Factory system of production and the consequent mechanisation and industrialisation brought turmoils in society. New industries and technologies change the face of the social and physical environment. The simple rural life and small-scale home industries were replaced by complex urban life and mass production of goods. Industrialisation changed the direction of civilisation. It destroyed, or radically altered, the medieval customs, beliefs and ideals.

Industrialisation led to urbanisation. Peasants left rural areas and flocked to the towns, where they worked as industrial labourers under dangerous conditions. Cities grew at an unprecedented rate providing an anonymous environment for people. Social problems became rampant in the fast, developing cities. Aristocraties and monarchies crumbled and fell. Religion began to lose its force as a source of moral authority. "*For the first time in history, rapid social change became the normal rather than an abnormal state of affairs, and people could no longer expect that their children would live much the same lives as they had done. The direction of social change was unclear, and the, stability of the social order seemed threatened. An understanding of what was happening was urgently needed*" [**Robertson's**' "*Sociology*" Page: 11]

It is clear from the above that sociology was born out of the attempt to understand the transformations that seemed to threaten the stability of European society. Social thinkers like Comte, Spencer and others argued that there was an urgent need to establish a separate science of society. They believed that such a science would be of great help in understanding the nature and problems of society and to find out solutions for the same.

Inspiration from the Growth of Natural Sciences

Nineteenth century was a period in which natural sciences had made much progress. The success attained by the natural scientists inspired and even tempted good number of social thinkers to emulate their example. If their methods could be successful in the physical world to understand physical or natural phenomena, could they not be applied successfully to the social world to understand social phenomena? As an answer to this question Comte, Spencer, Durkehim, Weber and others successfully demonstrated that these methods could be used to study the social world.

Inspiration Provided by the Radically Diverse Societies and Cultures of the Colonial Empires

The colonial powers of Europe were exposed to different types of societies and cultures in the colonial empires. Their exposure to such diversities in societies and cultures provided an intellectual challenge for the social scientist of the day. Information about the widely contrasting social practices of these distant peoples raised fresh questions about society: *Why some societies were more advanced than others? What lessons could the European countries learn from comparisons of various societies?* Why the rate of social change was not the same everywhere? The new science of society called "*sociology*" had emerged as an independent science in an attempt to find convincing answers to these questions.

ESTABLISHMENT OF SOCIOLOGY AS A SCIENCE

Contributions of Comte and Spencer

The credit for having established sociology into an independent and a separate science and to obtain for sociology a respectable position in the family of social sciences, goes to Comte and Spencer. Both of them championed the cause of sociology. In addition to Comte and Spencer, other thinkers such as Durkheim, Marx and Weber also took a leading role in making sociology a science. Hence these five thinkers are often called the "*pioneers*" or "*founding fathers of sociology*".

Auguste Comte (1798—1857)–The Founding Father of Sociology

Auguste Comte, the French Philosopher, is traditionally considered the "*Father of Sociology*". Comte who invented the term "Sociology" was the first man to distinguish the subject-matter of sociology from all the other sciences. He worked out in a series of books, a general approach to the study of society. Comte is regarded as the "Father of Sociology" not because of any significant contributions to the science as such, but because of the great influence he had upon it. It would be more appropriate to regard him as a *philosopher of science rather than as a sociologist*.

Comte introduced the word "*sociology*" for the first time in his famous work "*Positive Philosophy*" at about 1839. The term "**Sociology**" is derived from the Latin word **Socius**, meaning companion or associate, and the Greek word **logos**, meaning *study* or *science*. Thus, the etymological meaning of sociology is the *science of society*. He defined sociology as the science of social phenomena "*subject to natural and invariable laws, the discovery of which is the object of investigation*".

Comte devoted his main efforts to an inquiry into the nature of human knowledge and *tried to classify all knowledge* and to analyse the methods of achieving it. He concentrated his efforts to determine the nature of human society and the laws and principles underlying its growth and development. He also laboured to establish the methods to be employed in studying social phenomena.

Comte believed that the sciences follow one another in a definite and logical order and that all inquiry goes through certain stages (namely, the *theological*, the *metaphysical* and the '*positive* or *scientific* or *empirical*). Finally, they arrive at the last or scientific stage or as he called the positive stage. In the positive stage, objective observation is substituted for speculation. Social phenomena like physical phenomena, he maintained, can be studied objectively by making use of the positive method. He thought that it was time for inquiries into social problems and social phenomena to enter into this last stage. So, he recommended that the study of society be called the *science of society, i.e.*, '**sociology**'.

Comte proposed sociology to be studied in two main parts: (*i*) *the social statics* and (*ii*) *the social dynamics*. These two concepts represent a basic division in the subject-matter of sociology. The social statics deals with the major institutions of society such as family, economy or polity. Sociology is conceived of as the study of inter-relations between such institutions. In the words of Comte, "the Statical study of sociology consists in the investigations of laws of action and reaction of different parts of the social system". He argued that the parts of a society cannot be studied separately, "as if they had an independent existence."

If *Statics examines* how the parts of societies are interrelated, *social dynamics* focuses on whole societies as the unit of analysis and reveals how they developed and changed through time. "We must remember that the laws of social dynamics are most recognisable when they relate to the largest societies", he said. Comte was convinced that all societies moved through certain fixed stages of development and that progressed towards ever increasing perfection. He felt that the comparative study of societies as "*wholes*" was a major subject for sociological analysis.

Contributions of Comte to the development of sociology as a science

1. Comte gave to '*sociology*' its name and laid its foundation so that it could develop into an independent and a separate science.
2. Comte's insistence on *positive approach*, *objectivity* and *scientific attitude* contributed to the progress of social sciences in general.
3. Comte, through his "*Law of Three Stages*" clearly established the close association between *intellectual evolution and social progress*.
4. Comte's *classification of sciences* drives home the fact that *sociology depends heavily on the achievements of other sciences*. The 'interdisciplinary approach' of the modern times is in tune with the Comtean view.
5. Comte gave maximum *importance to the scientific method*. He criticised the attitude of the armchair social philosophers and stressed the need to follow the method of science.

6. Comte divided the study of sociology into two broad areas: "*social statics*" and "*social dynamics*". Present day sociologists have retained them in the form of '*social structure and function*' and '*social change and progress*'.
7. Comte had argued that sociology was not just a "*pure*" science, but an "*applied*" science also. He believed that sociology should help to solve the problems of society. This insistence on the practical aspect of sociology led to the development of various applied fields of sociology such as "*social work*", "*social welfare*", etc.
8. Comte also contributed to the *development of theoretical sociology*.
9. Comte upheld the '*moral order*' in the society. The importance which he attached to morality highly impressed the later writers such as *Arnold Toynbee* and *Pitirim A. Sorokin*.
10. Comte's famous books (*i*) '*Positive Philosophy*' [in 6 volumes] and, (*ii*) "*Positive polity*" [in 4 volumes] are a memorable contribution to the development of sociological literature.

Herbert Spencer (1820-1903)

An English scholar, Herbert Spencer, known as one of the most brilliant intellects of modern times, contributed a great deal to the establishment of sociology as a systematic discipline. His three volumes of "*Principles of Sociology*", published in 1877 were the first systematic study devoted mainly to the sociological analysis. He was much more precise then Comte in specifying the topics or special fields of sociology.

According to Spencer, *the fields of sociology are*: *the family, politics, religion, social control* and *industry* or *work*. He also mentioned the sociological study of associations, communities, the division of labour, social differentiation and stratification, the sociology of knowledge and of science, and the study of arts and aesthetics.

Spencer stressed the obligation of sociology to deal with the inter-relations between the different elements of society, to give an account of *how the parts influence the whole and are in turn reacted upon*. He insisted that sociology should take the whole society as its unit for analysis. He maintained that the parts of society were not arranged unsystematically. The parts bore some constant relation and this made society as such *a meaningful* 'entity', a fit subject for scientific inqurity.

Spencer's another contribution is his famous organic analogy, in which society is compared with the human organism. Spencer was influenced by the theory of organic evolution of his contemporary, Charles Darwin. Even L.F. Ward, Sumner and Giddings were highly influenced by the organismic theory of society advocated by Spencer.

Contributions of Spencer to the development of sociology:

1. Spencer very strongly supported the views of Comte who insisted on *the need to establish a separate science of society*.
2. Spencer stressed upon the *interdependence of different parts of society*. Spencer argued, the various parts of society, such as the state and the economy, are also interdependent and work to ensure the stability and survival of the entire system.
3. Spencer through his "*theory of Organic Analogy*" contributed to the *development of the tradition of comparative studies* in sociology. Though this theory has its own limitations it influenced **Ward, Sumner, Giddings** and other later writers.
4. Spencer emphasised the "*laws of evolution*" and tried to universalise them. According to **L.A. Coser**, the laws of evolution popularised by Spencer could be taken as *his contribution to the philosophy of sociology rather than to the science of sociology*.
5. Spencer's theories had a special appeal for two reasons: (*i*) they satisfied the desire for unifying knowledge; and (*ii*) *they stressed the need for the* "*principle of free enterprise*" [or "laissezfaire principle"]. Spencer was a supporter of the principle of "*individualism*". The policy of *free thinking advocated by him supported the cause of the development of the new science of sociology*.
6. Spencer's works such as- "*Social Statics*", "*First Principle*", "*The Study of Sociology*", "*Principles of Ethics*", "*Principles of Sociology*", "*The Man Versus The State*" have been a great contribution to the enrichment of sociological literature.

Contributions of Marx, Durkheim and Weber

It is relevant here to make a brief mention of the contributions of other founding fathers such as Marx, Durkheim and Weber to the development of sociology.

Karl Marx (1818–1883)

Karl Marx was one of the most important thinkers of the 19th century. He wrote brilliantly on subjects such as *philosophy, political science, economics* and *history*. *He never called himself a sociologist*, but his work is very rich in sociological insights. Hence he is regarded as one of most profound and original sociological thinkers. His influence has been tremendous. Millions of people throughout the world accept his theories with almost religious fervour.

Marx believed that the task of the social scientist was *not merely to describe the world, it was to change it.* Whereas **Spencer** saw social harmony and the inevitability of progress, Marx saw social conflict and the inevitability of revolution. *The key to history, he believed is class conflict*—the bitter struggle between the capitalists and the labourers or between those who own the means of producing wealth and those who do not. Marx also believed that the historic struggle would end only with the overthrow of the ruling exploiters, and the establishment of a free, harmonious, classless society. *Marx placed too much emphasis on the economic base of society*. Marx believed that the economic base of society influences the general character of all other aspects of culture and social structure, such as law, religion, education, government etc.

Modern sociologists though reject many of the ideas of Marx, do generally recognise the fundamental influence of the economy on other areas of society. The '*conflict approach*' to the study of social phenomena developed by Marx is still in currency. Later sociologists and social thinkers could hardly escape the influence of Marxian ideas and theories. Good number of writers and thinkers still subscribe to his views and theories.

Emile Durkheim (1858–1917)

Prof. Durkheim, the French thinker, like Spencer, considered societies as such to be important units of sociological analysis. He stressed the importance of studying different types of society comparatively. "Comparative Sociology is not a particular branch of sociology; it is sociology itself," he maintained.

In Durkheim's theory the ultimate social reality is the group, not the individual. Social life has to be analysed in terms of '*social facts*', according to him. Social facts are nothing but collective ways of thinking, feeling and acting which though coming from the individual, "are external" to him and exert an external "constraint" or pressure on him. These social facts are the proper study of sociology and to them all social phenomena should be reduced, he opined. Further, each social fact, he felt, must be related "*to a particular social milieu, to a definite type of society*".

Durkheim also mentioned various fields of sociological inquiry such as—*General Sociology, Sociology of Religion, Sociology of Law and Morals*, including sub-sections on political organisations, social organisation, marriage and family; *The sociology of Crime, Economic Sociology* including sub-sections on measurement of value and occupational groups; *Demography*, including studies on urban and rural communities; and Sociology of *Aesthetics*. His major works are: *The Division of Labour in Society, The Rules of Sociological Method, Suicide, The Elementary Forms of the Republic Life.*

Max Weber (1864–1920)

Max Weber's approach is almost contrary to that of Durkheim. For Weber, the *individual* is the basic unit of society. He opines that the finding of sociological laws is but a means to understand man. In his system, sociological laws are "empirically established probabilities or statistical generalisations of the course of social behaviour of which an interpretation can be given in terms of typical motives and intentions. Sociological method is a combination of inductive or statistical generalisation with *verstchen* (understanding) interpretation by the aid of an ideal type of behaviour, that is, assumed to be rationally or purposefully determined".

Weber devoted much of his efforts to expound a special method called the *method of understanding* (verstchen) for the study of social phenomena. He stressed the importance of maintaining objectivity and neutrality of value-judgements in social sciences. He wrote much on such topics as religion; various aspects of economic life, including money and the division of labour, political parties and other forms of political organisation and authority; bureaucracy and other varieties of large-scale organisation; class and caste; the city; and music. His influence on contemporary sociologists especially those of analytic school is rapidly increasing. His major works are: *Economics* and *Society*, *The Protestant Ethic and the Spirit of Capitalism*, *The City, Bureaucracy* and various other books and essays.

What these four pioneers of sociology did in common? These "four founding fathers" – Comte, Spencer, Durkheim and Weber – it seems, agreed upon the proper subject-matter of Sociology.

1. *Firstly,* all of them urged the sociologists to study a wide range of institutions from the family to the state.

2. *Secondly*, they agreed that a unique subject-matter for sociology is found in the inter-relations among different institutions.
3. *Thirdly*, they came to the common consensus on the opinion that society as a whole can be taken as a distinctive unit of sociological analysis. They assigned sociology the task of explaining wherein and why societies are alike or different.
4. *Finally*, they insisted that sociology should focus on '*social acts*' or '*social relationships*' regardless of their institutional setting. This view was most clearly expressed by Weber.

DEVELOPMENT OF SOCIOLOGY IN THE 20TH CENTURY

In the second half of the 19th and in the beginning of the 20th centuries a large number of sociologists and social thinkers contributed a great deal to the development of sociology. Karl Marx 1818–1883, Lester F. Ward 1841–1913, George Simmel 1858–1918, Alfred Vierkandt 1867–1953, Gabrial Tarde 1843–1904, Small 1854–1926, Giddings 1855–1931, C.H. Cooley 1864–1929, James Ward 1843–1925, Lloyd Morgan 1852–1932, L.T. Hobhouse 1864–1929, E.A. Westermarck 1862–1939. Pareto 1848–1923, Charles A. Elwood 1873–1946, Benjamin Kidd 1858–1916, E.B. Tylor 1832–1917, J.G. Frazer 1854–1941, B. Malinowski 1884–1942 and others are some of them.

Sociology experienced a rapid development in the 20th century, most notably in France, Germany, the United States and England. Recently famous sociologists like P.A. Sorokin, Talcott Parsons, R.K. Merton, R.M. MacIver, M. Ginsberg, Kingsley Davis, W.F. Ogburn, A.W. Green, Kimball Young, P.G. Murdock, W.I.H. Sprott, E.A. Ross, Wilbert Moore, Karl Manheim, M.N. Srinivas, G.S. Ghurye and a host of others have further enriched the subject by their social investigations and writings. Today, sociology is firmly established as a discipline. The developments of the 20th century provided a great stimulus for the study of social sciences in general, and sociology in particular. All major universities in the world, now offer instruction in the subject. Even in the U.S.S.R. sociology is a legitimate discipline now. "It is not yet in many respects, a mature science and the student will find in it therefore, more divergent points of view and rather less systematic agreement than in such other sciences as physics, astronomy and biology". **(Robert Bierstedt)**

SOCIOLOGY IN INDIA

Sociology was introduced to India as an academic discipline only after World War I. Since then, being closely allied with anthropology, it is forging ahead in India. The sociological movement has gained some momentum in Bombay with its mouthpiece "Sociological Bulletin" and in Agra with its organ "Journal of Social Sciences." Some prominent sociologists of our country like G.S. Ghurye, R.K. Mukherjee, D.P. Mukherjee, Humayun Kabir, K.M. Kapadia, R.N. Saxena, Mrs. Iravati Karve, Benoy K. Sarkar, A. Aiyappan, D.N. Majumdar, M.N. Srinivas, M.S. Gore, S.C. Dube, P.N. Prabhu, A.R. Desai and others have contributed their mite to the enrichment of the discipline. India with its diverse cultural peculiarities provides wonderful opportunities for sociological researches and studies. Sociology is now taught in many universities as one of the major disciplines. It is becoming more and more popular at the level of students also. Compared with the English-speaking countries, the sociological movement has not much flourished in India to the extent which it should have been.

THE ULTIMATE GOALS OF SOCIOLOGY

The immediate goal of sociology is to acquire knowledge about society like all the sciences. However, sociology is not content with descriptions, exhibitions and analysis. It has a more remote and ultimate purpose. *Robert Bierstedt's* views are meaningful in this regard. He says: "The final questions to which sociology addresses itself are those that have to do with the nature of human experience and this earth and the succession of societies over the long centuries of human existence...........What are the factors responsible for the disintegration of one social structure, like that of the medieval world, and the coming into being of another? Do human societies like the individuals who comprise them, grow old after a while, and wery and finally disappear from the face of the earth? Is there an ebb and a flow in the affairs of men, a systole and diastole of human history? These too are problems of sociology ... But some day, if sociology, through its intimate analysis of the dynamics of society, can achieve some understanding of problems of this kind, and contribute to their resolution, it will fulfil its initial promise and its ultimate destiny. In brief, as *Samuel Koenig* has pointed out the ultimate aim of sociology is "*to improve man's adjustment to life by developing objective knowledge concerning social phenomena which can be used to deal effectively with social problems*."

REVIEW QUESTIONS

1. Write an essay on the emergence of social sciences.
2. Sociology is popularly known as the "Science of Society." Discuss.
3. Is Sociology a social science? Critically analyse.
4. Social sciences are less exact. Discuss.
5. Assess the contributions of different sociologists to the development of Sociology as a science.
6. How did the French and Industrial Revolutions play an important role in the emergence of Sociology?
7. Write a detailed note on the development of Sociology in the twentieth century.
8. Discuss the factors which affect the development of Sociology.
9. Define Sociology. Can Sociology be called a science?
10. Analyse the impact of Industrial and French Revolutions on the emergence of Sociology.
11. Discuss the contributions of Spencer, Weber and Marx to the development of Sociology.
12. Assess the impact of new intellectual and philosophical tendencies on the development of social sciences.
13. Write short notes on the following:
    (a) Goal of Sociology
    (b) Development of different social sciences
    (c) Characteristics of early Sociology
    (d) Positivism
    (e) Humanitarianism
    (f) Evolutionism

⌘⌘⌘⌘⌘⌘⌘⌘⌘⌘⌘

2

DEFINITION, SCOPE AND USES OF SOCIOLOGY

CHAPTER OUTLINE

SOCIOLOGY: THE SCIENCE OF SOCIETY

"In all ages and human times, ever since our erect and restless species appeared upon the planet, men have been living with others of their kind in something called *Societies*. Wherever these societies may be and whatever their chapter of history–whether primitive Polynesian or ancient Egyptian, classical Chinese or contemporary Russian, medieval English or modern American–*they all exhibit common elements and constant features*. These are the elements that give to society its form and shape, that constitute its structure and that, in a word, comprise the social order. It is the, task of general sociology to discover these constants, to describe them with an economy of concepts, and to delineate their inter-relations".

Sociology is the science of society. No other science endeavours to study it in its entirely. *Economics* studies man as a wealth-getter and wealth-disposer and inquires into the relations of wealth and welfare. *History* deals with the human past in accordance with the time order. *Cultural Anthropology* studies man, particularly the primitive man and it concentrates more on the primitive communities and their cultures. *Psychology* studies the man as a behaving individual. *Social psychology*, as a branch of psychology, is concerned with the ways in which the individual reacts to his social conditions. *Political Science* studies man as a citizen, as a ruler and as being ruled. *Religion* deals with man as a spiritual being and inquires into his faith in the supernatural power. *Sociology* alone studies social relationships, society itself, Thus the '*focus*' of no other social science is identical with that of sociology. Indeed, it is the focus of interest that distinguishes one social science from another.

Sociology is interested in social relationships not because they are economic or political or religious or legal or educational but because they are at the same time, social. "*Society*", as *MacIver* says, "is the marvellously intricate and ever-changing pattern of the totality of these relationships". Further, in sociology we do not study everything that happens "in society" or under social conditions. But we study culture, for example, only for the light it throws on social relationships. Similarly, we do not study religion as religion or art as art or inventions as inventions. We study social relationships, their specific forms, varieties and patternings. We study how the relations combine, how they build up smaller or greater systems, and how they respond to changes and changing demands or needs. Hence our study of society is essentially analytical.

DEFINITION OF SOCIOLOGY

'Sociology' which had once been treated as social philosophy, or the philosophy of history, emerged as, an independent social science in the 19th century. *Auguste Comte*, a Frenchman, is traditionally considered to be the father of sociology. Comte is accredited with the coining of the term *sociology* (in 1839). "Sociology" is composed of two words: *socius*, meaning companion or associate; and 'logos' meaning science or study. The etymological meaning of "sociology" is thus the *science of society*. *John Stuart Mill*, another social thinker and philosopher of the 19th century, proposed the word *ethology* for this new science. *Herbert Spencer* developed his systematic study of society and adopted the word "sociology" in his works. With the contributions of Spencer and others it (sociology) became the permanent name of the new science.

The question '*what is sociology*' is, indeed, a question pertaining to the definition of sociology. No student can rightfully be expected to enter on a field of study which is totally undefined or unbounded. At the same time, it is not an easy task to set some fixed limits to a field of study. It is true in the case of sociology. Hence it is difficult to give a brief and a comprehensive definition of sociology.

Sociology has been defined in a number of ways by different sociologists. No single definition has yet been accepted as completely satisfactory. In fact, there are as many definitions of sociology as there are sociologists. For our purpose of study a few definitions may be cited here.

1. *Auguste Comte*, the founding father of "Sociology, defines sociology as the science of social phenomena "subject to natural and invariable laws, the discovery of which is the object of investigation".
2. *Kingsley Davis* says that "sociology is a general science of society".
3. *Harry M. Johnson* opines that "sociology is the science that deals with social groups".
4. *Emile Durkheim* defines sociology as the "science of social institutions".
5. *Park* regards sociology as "the science of collective behaviour".
6. *Small* defines sociology as "the science of social relations".
7. *Marshal Jones* defines sociology as "the study of man-in-relationship-to-men".
8. *Ogburn* and *Nimkoff* define sociology as "the scientific study of social life".
9. *Franklin Henry Giddings* defines sociology as "the science of social phenomena".
10. *Henry Fairchild* defines sociology as " the study of man and his human environment in their relations to each other".
11. *Max Weber* defines sociology as "the science which attempts the interpretative understanding of social action in order there by to arrive at a casual explanation of its course and effects".
12. Alex Inkeles says, "sociology is the study of systems of social action and of their interrelations".
13. *Kimball Young and Raymond W. Mack* define sociology as "the scientific study of the social aspects of human life".
14. *Morris Ginsberg*: Of the various definitions of sociology the one given by Morris Ginsberg seems to be more satisfactory and comprehensive. He defines sociology in the following ways: "*In the broadest sense, sociology is the study of human interactions and inter-relations, their conditions and consequences*".

A careful examination of various definitions cited above, makes it evident that sociologists differ in their opinion about the definition of sociology. Their divergent views about the definition of sociology only reveal their distinct approaches to its study. However, the common idea underlying all the definitions mentioned above is that sociology is concerned with man, his social relations and his society.

NATURE OF SOCIOLOGY

Sociology, as a branch of knowledge, has its own unique characteristics. It is different from other sciences in certain respects. An analysis of its internal logical characteristics helps one to understand what kind of science it is. The following are the main characteristics of sociology as enlisted by Robert Bierstedt in his book "*The Social Order*".

1. Sociology is an Independent Science

Sociology has now emerged into an independent science. It is not treated and studied as a branch of any other science like philosophy or political philosophy or history. As an independent science it has its own field of study, boundary and method.

2. Sociology is a Social Science and not a Physical Science

Sociology belongs to the family of social sciences and not to the family of physical sciences. As a social science it concentrates its attention on man, his social behaviour, social activities and social life. As a member of the family of social sciences it is intimately related to other social sciences like history, political science, economics, psychology, anthropology etc. The fact that sociology deals with the *Social universe* distinguishes it from astronomy, physics, chemistry, geology, mathematics and other physical sciences.

3. Sociology is a Categorical and not a Normative Discipline

Sociology "confines itself to statements about *what is*, not *what should be or ought to be*". As a science, sociology is necessarily silent about questions of value. It does not make any kind of value judgements. Its approach is neither moral nor immoral but amoral. It is *ethically neutral*. It cannot decide the directions in which sociology ought to go. It makes no recommendations on matters of social policy or legislation or programme. But it does not mean that sociological knowledge is useless and serves no purpose. It only means that sociology as a discipline cannot deal with problems of good and evil, right and wrong, and moral or immoral.

4. Sociology is a Pure Science and not an Applied Science

A distinction is often made between *pure* sciences and *applied* sciences. The main aim of pure sciences is the acquisition of knowledge and it is not bothered whether the acquired knowledge is useful or can be put to use. On the other hand, the aim of applied science is to apply the acquired knowledge into life and to put it to use. Each pure science may have its own applied field. For example, physics is a pure science and engineering is its applied field. Similarly, the pure sciences such as *economics, political science, history,* etc., have their applied fields like *business, politics, journalism* respectively. Sociology as a *pure* science has its applied field such as *administration, diplomacy, social work* etc.Each pure science may have more than one application.

Sociology is a pure science, because the immediate aim of sociology is the acquisition of knowledge about human society, not the utilisation of that knowledge. Sociologists never determine questions of public policy and do not recommend legislators what laws should be passed or repealed. But the knowledge acquired by a sociologist is of great help to the administrator, the legislator, the diplomat, the teacher, the foreman, the supervisor, the social worker and the citizen. But sociologists themselves do not apply the knowledge to life and use, as a matter of their duty and profession.

5. Sociology is Relatively an Abstract Science and not a Concrete Science

This does not mean that sociology is an art and not a science. Nor does it mean, it is unnecessarily complicated and unduly difficult. It only means that sociology is not interested in concrete manifestations of human events. It is more concerned with the *form* of human events and their *patterns*. For example, sociology is not concerned with particular wars and revolutions but with war and revolution in general, as social phenomena, as types of social conflict. Similarly, sociology does not confine itself to the study of this society or that particular society or social organization, or marriage, or religion, or group and so on. It is in this simple sense that sociology is an abstract not a concrete science.

6. Sociology is a Generalising and not a Particularising or Individualising Science

Sociology tries to find out the general laws or principles about human interaction and association, about the nature, form, content and structure of human groups and societies. It does not study each and every event that takes place in society. It is not possible also. It tries to make generalisations on the basis of the study of some selected events. For example, a sociologist makes generalisations about the nature of secondary groups. He may conclude that secondary groups are comparatively bigger in size, less stable, not necessarily spatially limited, more specialised, and so on. This, he does, not by examining all the secondary groups but by observing and studying a few.

7. Sociology is a General Science and not a Special Social Science

The area of inquiry of sociology is general and not specialised. It is concerned with human interaction and human life in general. Other social sciences like political science, history, economics etc., also study man and human interaction, but not all about human interaction. They concentrate their attention on certain aspects of human interaction and activities and specialise themselves in those fields. Accordingly, economics specialises itself in the study of economic activities, political science concentrates on political activities and so on. Sociology, of course, does not investigate economic, religious, political, legal, moral or any other special kind of phenomena in relation to human life and activities as such. It only studies human activities in a general way. This does not, however, mean that sociology is the basic social science nor does it imply sociology is the general social science. Anthropology and social psychology often claim themselves to be *general social sciences*.

8. Finally, Sociology is Both a Rational and an Empirical Science

There are two broad ways of approach to scientific knowledge. One, known as empiricism, is the approach that emphasises experience and the facts that result from observation and experimentation. The other, known as rationalism, stresses reason and the theories that result from logical inference.

The empiricist collects facts; the rationalist co-ordinates and arranges them. Theories and facts are required in the construction of knowledge. In sociological inquiry both are significant. A theory unsubstantiated by hard, solid facts is nothing more than an opinion Facts, by themselves, in their isolated character, are meaningless and useless. As *Immanuel Kant* said, "*theories without facts are empty and facts without theories are blind*". All modern sciences, therefore, avail themselves of both empirical and rational resources. Sociology is not an exception.

It is clear from the above that sociology is *an independent, a social, a categorical, o pure, an abstract, a generalising, both a rational and an empirical and a general social science*.

SUBJECT-MATTER AND SCOPE OF SOCIOLOGY

Major Concerns of Sociology (Subject-Matter of Sociology)

Ever since the beginning of sociology, sociologists have shown a great concern in man and in the dynamics of society. The emphasis has been oscillating, between and society. "Sometimes the emphasis was on *man* in society, at other times, it was on man in *society*. But at no stage of its development, *man as an individual was its focus of attention*. On the contrary, sociology concentrated heavily on society and its major units and their dynamics. It has been striving to analyse the dynamics of society in terms of organised patterns of social relations. It may be said that sociology seeks to find explanations for three basic questions: *How and why societies emerge? How and why societies persist? How and why societies change*?

An all-embracive and expanding science like sociology is growing at a fast rate no doubt. It is quite natural that sociologists have developed different approaches from time to time in their attempts to enrich its study. Still it is possible to identify some topics which constitute the subject matter of sociology on which there is little disagreement among the sociologists. Such topics and areas broadly constitute the field of sociology. A general outline of the fields of sociology on which there is considerable agreement among sociologists could be given here.

Firstly, the major concern of sociology is *sociological analysis*. It means the sociologist seeks to provide an analysis of human society and culture with a sociological perspective. He evinces his interest in the evolution of society and tries to reconstruct the major stages in the evolutionary process. An attempt is also made "to analyse the factors and forces underlying historical transformations of society". Due importance is given to the scientific method that is adopted in the sociological analysis.

Secondly, sociology has given sufficient attention *to the study of primary units of social life*. In this area, it is concerned with social acts and social relationships, individual personality, groups of all varieties, communities (urban, rural and tribal), associations, organisations and populations.

Thirdly, sociology has been concerned with the *development*, *structure and function of a wide variety of basic social institutions* such as the family and kinship, religion and property, economic, political, legal, educational and scientific, recreational and welfare, aesthetic and expressive institutions.

Fourthly, no sociologist can afford to ignore the *fundamental social processes* that play a vital role. The social processes such as co-operation and competition, accommodation and assimilation, social conflict including war and revolution; communication including opinion formation' expression and change; social differentiation and stratification, socialisation and indoctrination, social control and deviance including crime, suicide, social integration and social change assume prominence in sociological studies.

Fifthly, sociology has placed high premium on *the method of research* also. Contemporary sociology has tended to become more and more rational and empirical rather than philosophical and idealistic. Sociologists have sought the application of scientific method in social researches. Like a natural scientist, sociologist senses a problem for investigation. He then tries to formulate it into a researchable proposition. After collecting the data he tries to establish connections between them. He finally arrives at meaningful concepts, propositions and generalisations.

Sixthly, sociologists are concerned with the task of "*formulating concepts, propositions and theories*". "Concepts are abstracted from concrete experience to represent a class of phenomena".For example, terms such as social stratification, differentiation, conformity, deviance etc., represent concepts. A proposition "seeks to reflect a relationship between different categories of data or concepts". For example "lower-class youths are more likely to commit crimes than middle-class youths". This proposition is debatable. It may be proved to be false. To take another example, it could be said that "taking advantage of opportunities of higher education and occupational mobility leads to the weakening of the ties of kinship and territorial loyalties". Though this proposition sounds debatable, it has been established after careful observations, inquiry and collection of 'relevant data. Theories go beyond concepts and propositions. "Theories represent systematically related propositions that explain social phenomena". Sociological theories are mostly rooted in factual than philosophical. The sociological perspective becomes more meaningful and fruitful when one tries to derive insight from concepts. propositions and theories.

Finally, in the present era of explosion of knowledge *sociologists have ventured to make specialisations* also. Thus, today good number of specialised fields of inquiry are emerging out.Sociology of knowledge, sociology of history, sociology of literature, sociology of culture, sociology of religion, sociology of family etc., represent such specialised fields., The field of sociological inquiry is so vast that any student of sociology equipped with genius and rich sociological imagination can add new dimensions to the discipline of sociology as a whole.

SCOPE OF SOCIOLOGY

Every science has its own areas of study or fields of inquiry. It becomes difficult for anyone to study a science systematically unless its boundaries are demarcated and scope determined precisely.Unfortunately, there is no consensus on the part of sociologist with regard to the scope of sociology. *V.F. Calberton* comments, "since sociology is so elastic a science. it is difficult to determine just where its boundaries begin and end, where sociology becomes social psychology and where social psychology becomes sociology, or where economic theory becomes sociological doctrine or biological theory becomes sociological theory something, which is impossible to decide".

However, there are two main schools of thought regarding the scope of sociology: (l) The specialistic or formalistic school and (2) the synthetic school.

1. The Specialistic or Formalistic School

This school of thought is led by the German sociologist *George Simmel*. The other main advocates of this school are *Vierkandt, Max Weber, Small, Von Wiese and Tonnies*.

Simmel and others are of the opinion that sociology is a *pure* and an *independent science*. As a pure science it has a *limited scope*. Sociology should confine itself to the study of certain aspects of human relationship only. Further, it should study only the '*forms*' of social relationships but not their contents. Social relationship such as competition, sub-ordination, division of labour etc., are expressed in different fields of social life such as economic, political, religious, moral, artistic etc. Sociology should disentangle the forms of social relationships and study them in abstraction. Sociol-ogy as a specific social science describes, classifies and analyses the forms of social relationships.

Vierkandt says that sociology concerns itself with the ultimate form of mental or psychic relationship which links men to one another in society. He maintains that in dealing with culture, sociology should not concern itself with the actual contents of cultural evolution but it should confine itself to only the discovery of the fundamental forces of change and persistence. It should refrain itself from making a historical study of concrete societies.

Max Weber opines that the aim of sociology is to interpret or understand social behaviour. But social behaviour does not cover the whole field of human relations. He further says that sociology should make an analysis and classification of types of social relationships.

Small insisted that sociology has only a limited field. Von Wiese and Tonnies expressed more or less the same opinion.

Criticism: The views of the Formalistic School are widely criticised. Some critical remarks may be cited here:

Firstly, the formalistic school has unreasonably narrowed the field of sociology. Sociology should study not only the general forms of social relationships but also their concrete contents.

Secondly, the distinction between the forms of social relations and their contents is not workable. Social forms cannot be abstracted from the content at all, since social forms keep on changing when the contents change. *Sorokin* writes, "we may fill a glass with wine, water or sugar without changing its form, but I cannot conceive of a social institution whose form would not change when its members change".

Thirdly, sociology is not the only science that studies the forms of social relationships. Other sciences also do that. The study of international law, for example, includes social relations like conflict, war, opposition, agreement, contract etc. Political Science, Economics also study social relationships.

Finally, the establishment of *pure sociology* is impractical. No sociologist has been able to develop a pure sociology so far. No science can be studied in complete isolation from the other sciences. In fact, today more emphasis is laid on *inter-disciplinary approach*.

2. The Synthetic School

The synthetic school of thought conceives of sociology as a *synthesis* of the social sciences. It wants to make sociology a general social science and not a *pure* or *special* social science. In fact, the school has made sociology synoptic or encyclopedic in character. *Durkheim*, *Hob House*. *Ginsberg* and *Sorokin* have been the chief exponents of this school.

The main argument of this school is that all parts of social life are intimately inter-related. Hence the study of one aspect is not sufficient to understand the entire phenomenon. Hence sociology should study social life as a whole. This opinion has contributed to the creation of a general and systematic sociology.

The views of Emile Durkheim: *Durkheim*, one of the stalwarts of this school of thought, says that sociology has three main divisions or fields of inquiry. They are as follows: *Social Morphology*, *Social Physiology* and *General Sociology*.

1. ***Social morphology:*** Social morphology studies the territorial basis of the life of people and also the problems of population such as volume and density, local distribution etc.
2. ***Social physiology:*** Social physiology has different branches such as sociology of religion, of morals, of law, of economic life and of language etc.
3. ***General sociology:*** General Sociology can be regarded as the philosophical part of sociology. It deals with the general character of the social facts. Its function is the formulation of general social laws.

The views of morris ginsberg: *Ginsberg*, another advocate of the synthetic school, says that the main task of sociology can be categorised into four branches: *Social Morphology*, *Social Control*, *Social Processes* and *Social Pathology*.

1. ***Social morphology:*** 'Social Morphology' deals with the quantity and quality of population.It studies the social structure, social groups and institutions.
2. ***Social control:*** 'Social Control' studies–formal as well as informal–means of social control such as custom, tradition, morals, religion, convention, and also law, court, legislation etc. It deals with the regulating agencies of society.
3. ***Social processes:*** 'Social processes' tries to make a study of different modes of interaction such as cooperation, competition, conflict, accommodation, assimilation, isolation, integration, differentiation, development, arrest and decay.
4. ***Social pathology:*** 'Social Pathology' studies social mal-adjustment and disturbances. It also includes studies on various social problems like poverty, beggary, unemployment, over-population, prostitution, crime etc.

Ginsberg has summed up the chief functions of sociology as follows:

(*i*) Sociology seeks to provide a classification of types and forms of social relationships.

(*ii*) It tries to determine the relation between different factors of social life. For example, the economic and political, the moral and the religious, the moral and the legal, the intellectual and the social elements.

(*iii*) It tries to disentangle the fundamental conditions of social change and persistence and to discover sociological principles governing social life.

The scope of sociology is, indeed, very vast. It studies all the social aspects of society such as social processes, social control, social change, social stratification, social system, social groups, social pathology etc. Actually, it is neither possible nor essential to delimit the scope of sociology, because, it would be, as Sprott puts it, "*A brave attempt to confine an enormous mass of slippery material into a relatively simple system of pigeonholes*".

USES OF SOCIOLOGY

Of the various social sciences, sociology seems to be the youngest. It is gradually developing. Still it has made remarkable progress. Its uses are recognised widely today. In modern times, there is a growing realisation of the importance of the scientific study of social phenomena and the means of promoting what *Prof. Giddings* calls *human adequacy* (human welfare).

The study of sociology has a great value especially in modem complex society. Some of the uses of sociology are as follows:

1. *Sociology studies society in a scientific way.* Before the emergence of sociology, there was no systematic and scientific attempt to study human society with all its complexities. Sociology has made it possible to study society in a scientific manner. This scientific knowledge about human society is needed in order to achieve progress in various fields.
2. *Sociology throws more light on the social nature of man.* Sociology delves deep into the social nature of man. It tells us why man is a social animal, why he lives in groups, communities and societies. It examines the relationship between individual and society, the impact of society on man and other matters.
3. *Sociology improves our understanding of society and increases the power of social action.* The science of society assists an individual to understand himself, his capacities, talents and limitations. It enables him to adjust himself to the environment. Knowledge of society, social groups, social institutions, associations, their functions etc., helps us to lead an effective social life.'
4. *The study of sociology helps us to know not only our society and men but also others, their motives, aspirations, status, occupations, traditions, customs, institutions, culture etc.* In a huge industrialised society our experience is comparatively limited. We can hardly have a comprehensive knowledge of our society and rarely have an idea regarding other societies. But we must have some insight into an appreciation of the motives by which others live and the conditions under which they exist. Such an insight we derive from the study of sociology.
5. *The contribution of sociology is not less significant in enriching culture.* Sociology has given training to us to have rational approach to questions concerning ourselves, our religion, customs, mores, institutions, values, ideologies, etc. It has made us to become more objective, rational, critical and dispassionate. The study of societies has made people to become more broad minded. It has impressed upon its students to overcome their prejudices, misconceptions, egoistic ambitions, and class and religious hatreds. It has made our life richer, fuller and meaningful.
6. *Another aspect of the practical side of sociology is the study of great social institutions and the relations of individuals of each one of them.* The home and family, the school and education, the state and government, industry and work, religion and morality, marriage and family, law and legislation, property and government, etc. are some

of the main institutions, through which our society functions. More than that, they condition our life in countless ways. Knowledge of sociology may help to strengthen them to serve man better.

7. *Sociology is useful as a teaching subject too*. Sociology is a profession in which technical competence brings its own rewards. Sociologists, especially those trained in research procedures, are in increasing demand in business, government, industry, city planning, race relations, social work, social welfare, supervision, advertising, communications, administration, and many other areas of community life. A few years ago, sociologists could only teach sociology in schools and colleges. But *sociology has now become practical* enough to be practiced outside of academic halls. Careers apart from teaching are now possible in sociology. The various areas of applied sociology are coming more and more into prominence in local, state, national and international levels.
8. *The need for the study of sociology is greater especially in underdeveloped countries*. Sociologists have now drawn the attention of economists regarding the social factors that have contributed to the economic backwardness of a few countries. Economists have now realised the importance of sociological knowledge in analysing the economic affairs of a country.
9. *The study of society is of paramount importance in solving social problems*. The present world is beset with several social problems of great magnitude like poverty, beggary, unemploy-ment, prostitution, over-population, family disorganisation, community disorganisation, racial problems, crime, juvenile delinquency, gambling, alcoholism, youth unrest, untouchability etc. A careful analysis of these problems is necessary in order to solve them. Sociology provides such an analysis.
10. *Sociological knowledge is necessary for understanding and planning of society*. Social planning has been made easier by sociology. Sociology is often considered a vehicle of social reform and social reorganisation. It plays an important role in the reconstruction of society.
11. *The practical utility of sociological techniques*: The techniques developed by the sociologists and other social scientists are adopted by others. Let us think the example of social survey. Developed and used mainly by sociologists and statisticians, it has become an essential tool of market research and political polling. In the same way, sociologists provide a *great deal of information that is helpful in making decisions on social policy*.
12. Study of society has helped several governments to promote the welfare of the tribal people. Not only the civilised societies, but even the tribal societies are faced with several socio-economic and cultural problems. Studies conducted by sociologists and anthropologists regarding tribal societies and problems have helped many governments in undertaking various social welfare measures to promote the welfare of the tribal people. Efforts are now being made to treat the tribals on par with the rest of the civilised people.
13. *Sociology has drawn our attention to the intrinsic worth and dignity of man*. Sociology has been greatly responsible in changing our attitudes towards fellow human beings. It has helped people to become catholic in outlook and broadminded in spirit. It has made people to become tolerant and patient towards others. It has minimised the mental distance and reduced the gap between different peoples and communities.
14. *Sociology is of great practical help in the sense, it keeps us up-to-date on modern social situations and developments*. Sociology makes us to become more alert towards the changes and developments that take place around us. As a result, we come to know about our changed roles and expectations and responsibilities.
15. Finally, as *Prof. Giddings* has pointed out "*Sociology tells us how to become what we want to be*".

In conclusion, it can be said that the question of '*value of sociology*' is not a question whether or not we should study a subject. But it is a simple question of how it is actually to be used. Sociology, in short, has both individual and social advantages.

THREE MAJOR THEORETICAL PERSPECTIVES OF SOCIOLOGY

The Concept of "Theoretical Perspective"

Sociologists view society differently. They have their own way of understanding society and its dynamics in a theoretical manner. For example:

1. Some see the social world basically as a stable and an ongoing unity. They are impressed with the endurance of the family, organized religion and other social institutions. [This represents the "*functionalist perspective*"]
2. Some other sociologists see society as composed of many groups in conflict, competing for scarce resources. [This denotes the "*conflict perspective*".]
3. To other sociologists, the most interesting aspects of the social world are the everyday life, routine interactions among individuals that we sometimes take for granted. [This signifies the "*interactionist perspective*"]

It is clear from the above, that the same society or social phenomenon can be approached or viewed or studied from different theoretical perspectives". The theoretical perspectives refer to "*broad assumptions about society and social behaviour that provide a point of view for the study of specific problems*" [Ian Robertson - Page: 16.]

Types of Major Perspective in Sociology

Our sociological imagination may help us to employ any of a number of theoretical perspectives or approaches in order to study human behaviour. From these approaches sociologists develop theories to explain specific types of behaviour. There are three of these general perspectives in modem sociology. They are (1) *the functionalist*, (2) *the conflict, and* (3) *the interactionist perspectives*. Let us look at each in turn.

1. The Functionalist Perspective

The functionalist perspective draws its original inspiration from the work of Herbert Spencer and Durkheim. In the view of functionalists, society is like living organism in which each part of the organism contributes to its survival. Therefore, the functionalist perspective emphasises the way that parts of a society are structured to maintain its stability.

Spencer compared societies to living organisms. Any organism has a structure, that is, it consists of number of interrelated parts, such as a head, limbs, heart, blood veins, nervous system, and soon. Each of these parts has a *function* to play in the life of the total organism. Spencer further argued that in the same way, a society has a structure - it also further argued that in the same way, a society has a structure, it also consists of interrelated parts, such as the family, religion, state, education, economy, and so on. Each of these components also has a function that contributes to the overall stability of the social system. Modern structural-functionalism [which is usually referred to as *functionalism*] does not insist much on the analogy between a society and an organism. However, the general idea of society as a system of interrelated parts, persists even now.

Emile Durkheim's analysis of religion represented a critical contribution to the development of functionalism. Durkheim focused on the role of religion in reinforcing feelings of solidarity and unity within group life.

The work of Durkheim, Max Weber and other European sociologists greatly influenced **Talcott Parsons (1902-1979)**, a Harvard University sociologist. For over four decades, Parsons dominated American sociology with his advocacy of functionalism. He saw society as a network of connected parts, each of which contributes to the maintenance of the system as a whole. "*Under the functionalist approach, if an aspect of social life does not serve some identifiable useful function or promote value consensus among members of a society - it will not be passed on from one generation to the next*".

The functionalist theory assumes that society tends to be an organized, stable, well-integrated system, in which most members agree on basic values.

In the functionalist view, a society has an underlying tendency to be in equilibrium or balance. Social change is therefore, believed to be disruptive unless it takes place in a slow and gradual manner. Because changes in one part of the system normally brings about changes elsewhere in the system.

Functionalism presumes that a given element in the social system may have its own functions or dysfunctions. The proper '*functions*' *add to the stability of the order, whereas the dysfunctions* may disrupt the social equilibrium.

Functionalism makes a distinction between '*manifest functions*', that is, those that are obvious and intended, and "*latent functions*" that is, those that are unrecognized unintended.

An important criticism of the functional perspective is that it tends to be inherently conservative. This theory, it is said, fails to pay sufficient importance to the changes that take place in the system. Further, it is commented that this perspective ignores the element of conflict and its role in the social system.

2. The Conflict Perspective

The conflict perspective derives its strength and support from the work of Karl Marx, who saw the struggle between the social classes as the major fact of history. In contrast to functionalists' emphasis on stability and consensus, conflict sociologists see the social world in continual struggle.

The conflict theorists assume that societies are in a constant state of change, in which conflict is a permanent feature. Conflict does not necessarily imply outright violence. It includes tension, hostility, severe competition, and disagreement over goals and values. Conflict is not deemed here as an occasional event that disturbs the smooth functioning of the system. It is regarded as *a constant process and an inevitable part of social life.*

Karl Marx viewed struggle between social classes as inevitable because of the exploitation of workers under capitalism. Expanding on Marx's work sociologists and other social scientists have come to see conflict not merely as a class phenomenon but as a part of everyday life in all societies. Thus in studying any culture, organisation, or social group, sociologists want to know "*who benefits, who suffers, and who dominates at the expense of others*". They are concerned with conflicts between women and men, parents and children, cities and villages, rich and the poor, upper castes and the lower castes and so on. In studying such questions conflict theorists are interested in how society's institutions - including the family, government, religion, education, and the media, may help to maintain the privileges of some groups and keep others in a subservient position.

The conflict perspective dominated the Western European sociology and was largely neglected in American sociology until the sixties. Modern conflict theory, which is associated with such sociologists as C. Wright Mills (1956) and Lewis Coser (1956), does not focus, as Marx did, on class conflict. It sees conflict between many other groups such as the Whites and Negroes, Asians and the Europeans, and so on.

Conflict theorists are primarily concerned with the kinds of changes that conflict can bring about, whereas functionalists look for stability and consensus.

The conflict perspective is viewed as more "*radical*" and "*activist*". This is because of its emphasis on social change and redistribution of resources. The functionalist perspective, on the other hand, because of its focus on the stability of society, is generally seen as more "*conservative*". At present, the conflict perspective is accepted within the discipline of sociology as one valid way to gain insight into a society.

One important contribution of conflict theory is that it has encouraged sociologists to view society through the eyes of those people who rarely influence decision-making. Example, the Blacks in America and South Africa, the untouchables in India, the Hindu minorities in Pakistan, and so on. Similarly, feminist scholarship in sociology has helped us to have a better understanding of social behaviour. Thus a family's social standing is also now considered from the woman's point of view and not solely from the husband's position or income. Feminist scholars have also argued for a gender-balanced study of society in which women's experiences and contributions are visible as those of men.

The conflict perspective has its own limitations. It is also criticized. "*By focusing so narrowly on issues of competition and change, it fails to come to grips with the more orderly, stable, and less politically controversial aspects of social reality*". (Ian Robertson. Page 19)

3. The Interactionist Perspective

The functionalist and conflict perspectives both analyse society at the macro-level. These approaches attempt to explain society—wide patterns of behaviour. However, many contemporary sociologists are more interested in understanding society as a whole through an examination of social interactions at the micro-level small groups, two friends casually talking with one another, a family, and so forth. This is the interactionist perspective. This perspective generalizes about fundamental or everyday forms of social interaction. From these generalizations, interactionists seek to explain both micro and macro-level behaviour.

The interactionist perspective in sociology was initially influenced by Max Weber. He had emphasized the importance of understanding the social world from the viewpoint of the individuals who act within it. Later developments in this theory have been strongly influenced by social psychology and by the work of early leaders in the Chicago School of Sociology, particularly George Herbert Mead.

"*The interactionist perspective focuses on social behaviour in everyday life. It tries to understand how people create and interpret the situations they experience, and it emphasizes how countless instances of social interaction produce the larger structure of society - government, the economy and other institutions*". This perspective presumes that it is only through these social behaviour of the people that society can come into being. Society is ultimately created, maintained, and changed by the social interaction of its members.

The interactionist perspective has a number of loosely linked approaches.

(*i*) **Erving Goffman (1959),** for example, takes a "dramaturgical" approach to social interaction. He sees social life as a form of theatre, in which people play different parts/roles and "stage manage" their lives and the impressions they create on others.

(*ii*) **George Homans (1961)** prefers to have an "*exchange*" approach. He stresses on the way people control one another's behaviour by exchanging various forms of rewards and punishments for approved or disapproved behaviour.

(*iii*) **Harold Garfinkel (1967)** adopts what he calls an "*ethno methodological*" approach. This is only *an attempt to find out how people themselves understand the routines of daily life*. This approach focuses on how people view, describe, and explain shared meanings underlying everyday social life and social routines.

(*iv*) **Blumer and his Symbolic Interaction (1969)**. Blumer preferred to stress on the symbolic interaction approach laid down by G.H. Mead in the thirties. *Symbolic interaction is the interaction that takes place between people through symbols - such as signs, gestures, shared rules, and most important, written and spoken language*. Much of this interaction takes place on a face-to-face basis, but it can also occur in other forms. For example, symbolic interaction is taking place between the author of this book and the readers who read the sentences here. Interaction occurs whenever we obey [or even disobey] a traffic signal, or a "*Stick no Bills*" notice. The essential point is that people do not respond to that meaning. For example, the words or sentences of this book, the red light of a traffic signal have no meaning in themselves. People learn to attach symbolic meaning to these things, and they order their lives on the basis of these meanings. We live in a symbolic as well as in a physical world. Our social life involves a constant process of interpreting the meanings of our own acts and those of others.

The interactionist perspective, in general, invites the sociologist to ask specific kinds of question: *What kinds of interaction are taking place between people, how do they understand and interpret what is happening to them, and why do they act toward others as they do?* Those who follow this perspective usually focus on the more minute, personal aspects of everyday life. For example, by what process an individual becomes a beggar or a prostitute or a criminal? How does someone learn to experience cigarette smoking as pleasurable? What tactics are used by a college lecturer to have class control? What strategies are resorted to by a political leader to convince the angry mob about a political decision taken by his party on an issue that would affect their interests? What happens, and why, if we stand too close to someone during a conversation? and so on.

The interactionist perspective provides a very interesting insight into the basic mechanics of everyday life. It has the advantage of revealing fundamental social processes that other perspectives normally ignore.

This *perspective is also open to criticism*. It neglects larger social institutions and societal processes, which have powerful effects on social interaction and on our personal experience.

An Evaluation of These Three Perspectives

These three perspectives - *functionalist*, *conflict* and the *interactionist* - represent three different ways of understanding the same reality, that is social phenomenon. Each of these perspectives starts from different assumptions, each leads the investigator to ask different kinds of questions, and each viewpoint is therefore likely to produce different types of conclusions. These perspectives seem to be contradictory also. But we cannot say that one is "*better*" than the other two, or even that they are always incompatible.

Each of these perspectives focuses on a different aspect of reality: (*i*) *functionalism*, primarily on social order and stability, (*ii*) *conflict theory*, primarily on tension and change, and (*iii*) *interactionism*, primarily on ordinary experiences of everyday life. Each of the perspectives has a part to play in the analysis of society.

All these three perspectives could be applied, *for example, to the study of education*, although each would focus on a different aspect of the institution. A *functionalist approach would emphasis the functions that education plays in maintaining the social system as a whole*. A conflict approach would emphasise that education is believed to be an important avenue to social and financial success in life. It stresses on the social class background of the pupil affecting his academic achievement. An *interactionist approach* would emphasise the daily activities within school. It would point to the forms of interaction between teachers and pupils, the influence of the student peer group over its individual members. None of these approaches can claim itself to be the only "*true*" one. Because, taken together they provide a broader and deeper understanding of the entire institution of education.

Sociology makes use of all the three perspectives since each offers unique insights into the same problem being studied. These perspectives overlap as their interests overlap.

REVIEW QUESTIONS

1. What is Sociology? Write its origin and characteristic features.
2. Discuss the meaning, scope and importance of Sociology.
3. Define Sociology. Is Sociology the science of society? Comment.
4. Write the definitions of Sociology as given by different sociologists. Discuss its nature.
5. What is the subject matter of Sociology? Write its scope and limitations.
6. What are the three major perspectives of Sociology? Discuss each in detail.
7. "Sociology is relatively an abstract science and not a concrete science." Analyse.
8. "Sociology is the science of society." Elaborate on this statement in the light of scope of Sociology.
9. Define Sociology and discuss its subject matter, nature and scope.
10. Discuss the relationship of sociology with any three social science disciplines.
11. Write short notes on the following:
    (a) Major concerns of Sociology
    (b) Social morphology
    (c) Uses of Sociology
12. What are the two main schools of thought? Discuss each in detail.

⌘⌘⌘⌘⌘⌘⌘⌘⌘⌘⌘

3

SOME BRANCHES OF SOCIOLOGY

CHAPTER OUTLINE

- Historical Sociology
- Sociology of Knowledge
- Sociology of Law
- Social or Human Ecology
- Sociology of Education
- Political Sociology
- Sociology of Economic Life
- Sociology of Occupation
- Sociology of Religion
- Rural Sociology
- Industrial Sociology
- Urban Sociology.

Sociology is a fast growing discipline. Sociologists are at work to bring into its range of study almost all aspects of man's social life. Sociology has a tendency to break down into an endless list of specialities. Thus it has several specialised areas of inquiry each of which may employ its own approach and techniques. Here is a small attempt to introduce some of the main branches or specialised areas of study.

HISTORICAL SOCIOLOGY

Historical sociology has emerged as one of the branches of sociology. In a sense, all sociological research is historical for the sociologists normally go into the records pertaining to the events that have happened or have been observed. "The term historical sociology is, however, usually applied to the study of social facts which are more than fifty or so years old".

In actual practice, historical sociology has become a particular kind of comparative study of social groups. It is a study of social groups, their composition, their interrelationships and the social conditions that support or undermine them. If the social anthropologist looks at these things in con- temporary simple societies, the historical sociologist examines them in comparison with the records of earlier societies and their cultures.

Some historians such as *Rostovtzer*, *G.G. Coullon* and *Jacob Burkhardt*, have written *social history*. "Social history is history which deals with human relations, social patterns, mores and customs and important institutions other than monarchy and army." Social history has become "*The history of people with the politics left out*". "It has now become the history of men and women in their social relationships and groupings".

Social history has yet to establish itself as a separate discipline. Only a handful of people are busy with teaching it in British Universities. On the other hand, social history has gained much acceptance by sociologists. They have become aware of the significance of the past in the interpretation of the present. Social history has been acknowledged as 'historical sociology' by sociologists. It is today one of the standard special fields of sociology. *Sigmund Diamond*, *Robert Bellah* and *Norman Brinbaum* may be pointed out as important contemporary practitioners of historical sociology.

SOCIOLOGY OF KNOWLEDGE

'*Sociology of knowledge*' is one of the recently emerged branches of sociology. This branch pre-supposes the idea "*that our knowledge is in some measure a social product*." Thinkers had recognised long back the importance of economic, religious, political and other interests in shaping human beliefs and ideas. Of late, the view that even human society and its very structure can influence knowledge, gained sufficient recognition. The history of Greece and Rome in particular has strongly supported this view. In his book "*New Science*" (1725) *Vico tried* to show how heroic literature constituted the thought mode of a specific kind of society.

The problem of the relationship between society and knowledge has been raised by *Marxism*, and it has offered a solution to it also. "According to Marx and Engels, all knowledge has been distorted, directed and conditioned by the interests conscious and unconscious, of conflicting exploited and exploiting classes". In the light of contemporary sociological information, this view is found to be untenable as a total sociology of knowledge.

Durkheim tried to approach this problem in his own way. In "*The Elementary Forms of the Religious Life*" *1912* and "*Sociology and Philosophy" 1952* (essays translated) he argued that our perception and experience are derived from and constitute a part of social structure. This view may be alright for simpler societies and not for complex societies. Even Comte's three stages of social evolution had been regarded as stages of forms of thought of which the last stage, that is, the positivist stage is alone objective.

The foundations of the sociology of knowledge will have to be found in *Karl Manheim's* "*Ideology and Utopia*" *1936* and "*Essays on the Sociology of Knowledge*", *1952*. Manheim tried to face "The problem of sociology of knowledge with great philosophical learning and methodological ingenuity". A number of sociologists are attracted by the subject of sociology of knowledge but the problems it raises are unsolved.

SOCIOLOGY OF LAW

'*Sociology of Law*' looks at law and legal systems as a part of society and also as social institutions related to other institutions and changing with them. It regards law as one means of social control. Hence law is often made to be related to a moral order, to a body of customs and ideas about society. From this point of view, sociology of law is itself related to jurisprudence. Still it is not like jurisprudence. Sociology of law requires an understanding of the system of law no doubt. But it is still wider in scope. It seeks "to perceive the relationship of systems of law to other social subsystems like the economy, the nature and distribution of authority, and the structure of family and kinship relationships". In Britain, some social anthropologists have examined the systems of law and courts in relatively simple societies and tried to determine their relationships to the other aspects of the social system.

The study of 'Sociology of Law' is well known in Europe but not in America and Britain. In fact, sociologists have hardly turned their attention towards sociology of law in modern societies. Previously, Durkheim (through his classification of law into retributive and restitutive) and Max Weber (through his "Law in Economy and Society" — Translated work) had made some initial studies in this field. Austrian scholar E. Ehrlich published one of the most outstanding works on sociology of law in 1913 which was translated into English under the title "*Fundamental Principles of the Sociology of Law*" *in 1936*. Another famous work is that of *Georges Gurvitch's* '*Sociology of Law*' *1942*. Due to the work of some jurists in America considerable interest is now being shown to sociology of law. Due to this growing interest only a number of sociologists and lawyers have made a joint venture to produce an interesting work entitled "*Society and the Law*: *New Meanings for an old Profession" 1962*.

SOCIAL OR HUMAN ECOLOGY

Ecology is a branch of biology and has been largely concerned with the environment of the lower animals and plants. It refers to the influence of the environment upon animal ecology. The sociologists who adopted the approach of these natural scientists in their study of the community refer to their field as "*human ecology*" or "*social ecology*". The botanists also supplied the sociologists with fundamental principles, concepts, and terminology.

The study of human ecology is nothing but the logical extension of the ecological point of view. Human ecology is that part of sociology which studies human beings' adjustments to their environments which include not only the physical conditions of their geographic environment but also other organisms such as other fellow human beings, plants and animals. Man, the subject of human ecology is less restricted by his physical environment. With the help of culture that man possesses, he can live almost anywhere on the planet. He can grow and produce different kinds of food, wear clothings of various types, construct houses, bridges and dams, create tools and implements which have different uses, kill beasts that are dangerous, destroy harmful insects with pesticides and so on.

Social ecologists have focused their attention on the community. The ecological factors can more easily and more productively be studied when the community is the unit of observation. Ecology studies community in relation to environment. Culture modifies the influence of natural environment, and as culture changes, communities change.

The *Ecological Approach*: The ecological approach to the study of communities had been used, so far, mainly by American sociologists. *Park and Burgess* were the pioneers in the study of human ecology. They and their student *Mckenzie* formulated its basic principles. They made it a field of study within sociology. Later this approach was very usefully employed by sociologists other than those of the "*Chicago School*".

Sociologists who study communities from the ecological point of view consider a village, town or city sociological rather than a legal or an administrative unit. It needs not confine itself to the boundaries set by law. "A community, from the ecological point of view, includes a focal area plus the surrounding territory. Its size is determined by the extent of its economic and social influence". This ecological conception is used by the sociologists in their study of the community. Even economists, social workers, businessmen, and social planning agencies make use of this approach.

SOCIOLOGY OF EDUCATION

Sociology of education is one of the specialised fields of sociological inquiry. It analyses the institutions and organisations of education. It studies the functional relationship between education and the other great institutional orders of society such as the economy, the polity, religion and kinship. It concentrates on educational system or subsystem or individual school or college.

'Sociology of education' studies 'education' as an agent of transmission of culture. It studies the functional importance of education also. It makes studies of school organisation and the relation between schools and social structure, especially social class, family and neighbourhood. The interaction of these social forces with the internal organisation of the school is explored in order to find out the social determinants of educability. Studies have shown that social class and its correlates have a systematic effect on educability and educational selection. For example, in Britain, the chances of achieving a university degree are six times better for a middle class than for a working-class child. The social determinants of academic success remain powerful even in modern educational systems in spite of the provision of equal opportunities for all. The theoretical notion of "*meritocracy*", i.e., rule by the educated and talented persons, has to be understood within this context. Sociological studies of higher education have increased since 1950.

Sociology of education stresses upon the social importance of education. The social importance of education is widely recognised today, especially in modern industrialised societies. In such societies education has become one of the means of acquiring social and technical skills. Education has come to be not only a way of training people to work in different fields but also a qualification for jobs in certain fields. It fits people for increasingly specialised roles

More than that, education has become an essential need today to register progress in scientific and technological fields. As such, it is a means of promoting economic prosperity. Education, as a means of bringing about social change, is no less significant. It promotes social mobility, that is, movement of people from one social status to another. It influences social stratification. Education is often made use of in totalitarian and communist countries as an instrument to propagate some **chauvinist** and communist ideologies.

The famous writer, *Newman* said that the main practical purpose of a university is to produce socially responsible people. President Truman of America, stressing the importance of education, once remarked that man with wide experience, practical vision of things, intellectual depth and capacity to take right decisions at right time should be given the reins of administration to rule the country. *Dr. S Radhakrishnan* said that the main objective of education was to give training to students to undertake occupations effectively and to become proper leaders in various social fields in which they happen to work. *Dr. Kothari Commission*, appointed by the Government of India to recommend suitable educational reforms declares in the very beginning of its very comprehensive report that, "*The destiny of India is being shaped in her class-rooms today*".

POLITICAL SOCIOLOGY

Ever since the time of *Aristotle*, thinkers have been making systematic study of concrete political phenomena. They have been observing how political phenomena influence and get influenced by the rest of the social structure and culture. In this regard, Aristotle's '*Politics*' may be taken as a work of political sociology. *Ferguson*, *Montesquieu* and *Tocqueville* were all engaged in what today would be called *political sociology*. The classical sociologists like *Weber* (his essay '*Politics as Vocation*') and *Pareto* (his work "*The Mind and Society*') were pioneers in including a political sociology in their work. Further, *Karl Marx* in Germany, *Mosca* in Italy and *Graham Wallas* in England advanced so essentially sociological theories of *political elites* and of the processes of consensus and dissent. Also *Andre Siegfried* of pre-1914 France made a detailed study of this social group and interests in voting behaviour. The phrase '*Political Sociology*' to describe this tradition only came into general use after 1945.

Ever since the birth of sociology, the analysis of political processes and institutions has been one of its most important concerns. Sociologists argue and many political scientists agree that it is difficult to study political processes except as special cases of more general psychological and sociological relationships. The term "*Political Sociology*" has come to be accepted both within sociology and political science as encompassing the overlap between the two sciences. However, the *political scientist* is primarily concerned with the dimension of power and the factors affecting its distribution. The *sociologist*, on the other hand, is more concerned with social control, with the way in which the values and norms of a society regulate relations. His emphasis is on social ties, rather than on formal structures and legal definitions.

As *Smelser N.J.* says, "*Political Sociology can be defined as the study of the interrelationship between society and polity, between social structures and political institutions*". Political sociology is not solely the study of the social factors that condition the political order.

Political sociology employs the methods of sociological research, including those of attitude research to investigate the content of political behaviour. It treats political institutions, both formal or constitutional and informal, as parts of the social system. It has concentrated attention on '*elites*' and their membership, on the expression and regulation of conflict, on formal pressure groups, on the formation of political opinion. Political sociologists have been concerned with political parties as social institutions and with the phenomena of despotic and totalitarian regimes. It is an integral part of sociology which has progressively transformed political science in the direction of a wider attention to empirical reality.

SOCIOLOGY OF ECONOMIC LIFE OR ECONOMIC SOCIOLOGY

Sociology of Economic Life or *Economic Sociology* is a new branch of sociology. As *Neil J. Smelser* defines, economic sociology is "the application of the general frame of reference, variables, and explanatory models of sociology to that complex of activities concerned with the production, distribution, exchange, and consumption of scarce goods and services."

The *first focus* of economic sociology is on *economic activities* alone. The economic sociologist studies how these activities are structured into roles and collectivities. He inquires by what values these activities are legitimised, by what norm is and sanctions they are regulated, and how these sociological factors or variables interact.

The *second focus* of economic sociology is on the *relations between sociological variables or factors as they manifest themselves in the economic as well as non-economic contexts*. For example, how do familial roles associate with occupational role of a local community and the control of its political structure? This focus includes both situations in which economic and non-economic structures are integrated with one another.

This interplay of sociological variables or factors in the economic and non-economic fields can be observed in two ways: – (*i*) *Within concrete economic units*. For example, in the industrial firm, the economic sociologist studies the status systems, power and authority relations deviance, cliques and coalitions, and the relations among these phenomena. In fact, '*industrial sociology*' concentrates more on this point. (*ii*) *Between economic units and their social environment*. At one level, the economic sociologist studies the relations between economic interests and other interests (legal, political, familial, religious) in both the community and the larger society. At a higher level he studies the relation between the economy (considered as an analytic system of society) and the other systems. "This inter-unit focus leads to the "*larger issues*" of economic sociology – *e.g.*, public policy, labour-management conflict, and the relations between economic classes-that lie in the tradition of Marxian and Weberian thought". Finally, the economic sociologist studies the distinctively sociological aspects of the central economic variables themselves – *money as one of many types of sanctions in social life*.

Sub-divisions of Economic Sociology: Economic sociology has its own sub-divisions. Among these can be mentioned – (*a*) Occupational Sociology, (*b*) The Sociology of Work, (*c*) The Sociology of Complex Organisations (at least that part which deals with economic bureaucracies), (*d*) Industrial Sociology, (*e*) Plant Sociology, (*f*) the Sociology of Consumption and so on.

SOCIOLOGY OF OCCUPATION

'*Sociology of Occupations*' is one of the new branches of sociology. It deals with the problem of examining how the occupational structure and particular occupations associate with other segments of society like the family, the economy, the educational system, the political system and the system of social stratification. Its investigations concentrate upon the following themes: (*i*) the division of labour, its causes and consequences, (*ii*) The study of specific occupations of the people like the prostitute, the dockworkers, the clerk, the architect, the physician, etc. (*iii*) The function and meaning of work and related phenomena such as leisure, unemployment and retirement. (*iv*) Researches are also undertaken on such topics as the amount and method of remuneration, recruitment and training, career patterns, conflicts inherent in the role, the relation between personality and occupation, interpersonal relations at work, the public image of the occupation, and the distribution of power and prestige within the occupation, etc.

SOCIOLOGY OF RELIGION

The phenomenon of religion attracted the attention of the sociologists because of its great human importance. No society is free from the influence of religion. In established societies, religion is one of the most important institutional structures making up the total social system. A special branch of sociology has now emerged in order to analyse the religious behaviour of men from a sociological point of view. "The sociology of religion is but one aspect of the study of the relationship between ideas and ideals embodied in movements and institutions, and the social situations of their origin, development, flourishing and decline". *Thomas F.O' Dea*.

The early sociological studies of religion had three distinctive methological characteristics – *Evolutionist*, *Positivist* and *Psychological*. Ex: The works of *Comte*, *Tylor* and *Spencer*. But *Emile Durkheim* in his "*Elementary Forms of the Religious Life*", 1912, made a different approach to the study of religion. He argued that in all societies, a distinction is made between the '*sacred*' and the '*profane*'. He emphasised the collective aspects of religion. He was of the opinion that the function of religious rituals is to affirm the moral superiority of the society over its individual members and thus to maintain the solidarity of the society. *Durkheim's* emphasis on ritual as against belief, later influenced many anthropologists to undertake functionalist investigations of religion. *B. Malinowski* and *A.R. Radcliffe-Brown* and other anthropologists were also influenced by the views of *Durkheim*.

In the study of religion in civilised societies, *Durkheim's* theory has proved less useful. Here, religion not only unites people but also divides. In modem societies, beliefs and doctrines have more importance than ritual. Here, the sociological study of religion differs from that of anthropology. It is more influenced by the ethical doctrines of the world religions. This approach can be witnessed in the works of *L.T. Hobhouse* and *Max Weber*. *Hobhouse*, in discussing religion in his major work "*Morals in Evolution*",–1907, gave more importance to moral codes of the major religions and particularly of Christianity.

Max Weber's treatment of religious beliefs differs in important respects. *Firstly*, it is not based on an evolutionary scheme. *Secondly*, it is mainly concerned with one major aspect of religious ethics. That is, he wanted to examine the influence of particular religious doctrines upon economic behaviour; and the relations between the position of groups in the economic order and types of religious beliefs. He is less concerned with ethical doctrines as such. His famous work, "*The Protestant Ethic and the Spirit of Capitalism*" is an example of such an approach.

Comparatively, nothing more has been added to the theoretical development of a Sociology of Religion since the work of *Weber* and *Durkheim*. *Weber's* influence has contributed to two main lines of study; (*i*) The characteristics, doctrines and social significance of religious sects, and (*ii*) the interlink between social classes and religious sects. *Ernst Troeltsch's* "*The Social Teachings of the Christian Churches*", 1912, *HR. Niebuhr's* "*The Social Sources of Denominationalism, 1929*; and *Brian Wilson's* '*Seats and Society*', 1961, can be mentioned here as examples carrying weber's influence.

The Sociology of Religion seeks to offer a scientific explanation to religion. As *Kingsley Davis* says this "*task is not easy. No societal phenomenon is more resistant than religion to scientific explanation*". Two factors seem to be responsible for this— first an *emotional* and second a '*rational bias*'. "The emotional bias springs from the fact that religion by its very nature involves ultimate values, making it almost impossible to view with a disinterested attitude". The '*rational bias*' would also create problems. Religion which involves transcendental ends, strong sentiments, deep-rooted beliefs, and symbolic instruments may appear to be fallacious to a "*rationalist*". He may attribute religion simply to ignorance and error and assume that when these are removed there will emerge the completely '*rational*' man. Some hold that religion is an expression of instinctive emotions. These views are equally false, "*The very non-rationality of religious behaviour is the thing that gives religion its vitalily in human life*".

RURAL SOCIOLOGY

Rural Sociology is a specialised field of sociology. As the name indicates, it deals with the society of village or rural society. It is a systematic and scientific study of rural society. The majority of the people on the earth live in villages and rural areas. They follow patterns of occupation and life somewhat different from those living in urban areas. Their behaviour, way of life, and beliefs are conditioned and deeply influenced by their rural environment. A specialised branch of sociology called, Rural Sociology, has, therefore, emerged to study the rural society.

Definition of Rural Sociology

Different sociologists have defined rural sociology in different ways. A few definitions may be examined here.

1. *Sanderson* says that "Rural sociology is the sociology of rural life in the rural environment".
2. *Bertand* says that in its broadest sense, "Rural sociology is that study of human relationships in rural environment".
3. *F. Stuard Chopin* defines rural sociology as follows: "The sociology of rural life is a study of the rural population, rural social organisation and the social processes comparative, in rural society".
4. *A.R. Desai* says that "Rural sociology is the science of rural society... It is the science of laws of the development of rural society".

It is clear from the above-mentioned definitions that rural sociology studies the social interactions, institutions and activities and social changes that take place in the rural society. It studies the rural social organisations, structure and set up. It provides us that knowledge about the rural social phenomena which can help us in making contribution to the development of rural society.

Origin of Rural Sociology

Rural sociology is comparatively a new branch of sociology. It was first originated in the United States of America. It has taken more than half a century to become established as a distinct academic field or professional study. The main contributors to the development of rural sociology are – *Charles Sanderson, Burthefield, Ernest Burnholme, John Morris Gillin, Franklin H. Giddings, and Thomas Nixon Carver*. It was President Roosevelt who, through the appointment of 'Country Life Commission' gave a good encouragement to the development of the rural sociology in 1908. The report of this Commission encouraged the studies of rural society.

In 1917 the Department of Rural Sociology was set up by the American Sociological Society. In 1919, a '*Rural Sociology Department*" was established under the chairmanship of *Dr. CJ. Galpin*. The Great Depression of 1930 provided another stimulus to the growth of rural sociology. In 1937, '*Rural Sociological Society*' was formed. It started publishing a professional journal '*Rural Sociology*' containing results of rural sociological research. C.J. Galpin of the University of Wisconsin developed techniques for defining and delimiting the rural community. His approach is still popular today.

The Great Second World War gave yet another fillip to the growth of rural sociology. The destruction caused by the war demanded reconstruction. The reconstruction work brought further encouragement to the science. By 1958 there were about 1000 professional rural sociologists in America. Rural sociology crossed the boundaries of America and became popular in Europe. A European society for Rural Sociology was formed in 1957, and a similar organisation was started in Japan also. In developing countries, the role of the rural sociologist is primarily in the applied field of more effective planning and operation of rural community development programmes.

Scope or Subject-Matter of Rural Sociology

The scope or the subject-matter of rural sociology is basically the study of rural society with all its complexities. According to *Lawry* and *Nelson*, '*The subject-matter of rural sociology is the description and analysis of the progress of various groups as they exist in the rural environment.*'

The main tasks of *rural sociology* can be mentioned here. They are as follows:

1. ***Rural community and rural problems:*** This includes the characteristics and nature of rural community and its problems.
2. ***Rural social life:*** This includes various aspects of the rural people.
3. ***Rural social organisation:*** This includes the study of various rural social organisations and institutions including family and marriage.

4. ***Rural social institutions and structure:*** This includes the study of dogmas, customs, traditions, values, morals, conventions, practices and various political, economic, religious and cultural institutions.
5. ***Rural planning and reconstruction:*** Rural sociology has great practical applications. Hence rural planning and reconstruction are also the main tasks of rural sociology to be dealt with.
6. ***Social change and social control in rural social set up:*** It is here we study the impact of city on rural life. The mechanisms of social control of the rural society are also examined here.
7. ***Religion and culture in rural society:*** Religion plays an important role in a rural set up. Culture of rural society exhibits striking peculiarities. These come within the domain of rural sociology.
8. ***Rural social processes:*** Different social processes such as cooperation, competition, integration, isolation, differentiation etc., that take place in rural society are also studied in rural sociology.
9. ***Differences between urban and rural society:*** The study of rural society includes the differences between urban and rural society also.

Importance of Rural Sociology

The practical value of the study of rural sociology is widely recognised today. As long as the villages and the rural society assume importance, the rural sociology shall continue to acquire importance. The value of rural sociology can be understood by the following points:

1. ***Rural population is in majority:*** The world's population is more rural than urban. More than two-third of the people of the world live in villages. In India alone more than 50 crores people (more than 75 per cent of the total population) live in more than 5 lakh villages. It is the village that forms the basis of society. Rural sociology is inevitable for the study of the majority of the population.
2. ***Intimate relationship between the land and man*:** Man is born out of land and his entire culture depends on it. Land has been the pan and parcel of human life. Progress starts from the village. The type of land partially conditions the type of society and the opportunities for human development. This close relationship between man and land has also been recognised by the economists and political scientists.
3. ***Villages and rural life form the source of population:*** Cities normally grow out of towns and villages. No city can come into existence all of a sudden without having a rural background. A village, when improved and thickly populated, becomes a town or a city. Thus it is the village population that forms the source of urban life.
4. ***Psychological approach to the rural life:*** Rural progress, rural reconstruction or improve- ment of rural societies is possible only when the people have correct idea about the rural way of life and problems. Rural sociology touches upon the rural psychology and provides a good understanding of the rural people and their society.

INDUSTRIAL SOCIOLOGY

The Industrial Revolution that took place in England in the 18th century changed the course of human history. The Revolution, though essentially took place in the economic field, its effects were never confined to the economic field alone. It brought down the cost of production, improved quality and maximised output. More than that, it changed the pattern of human relations. It eased human life, and provided more comforts and luxuries to man. At the same time, it altered human outlook and attitudes. It brought about radical changes in the very structure of the society.

Industrial revolution, in course of time resulted in the continuous process of *industrialisation.* Industrialisation is a phenomenon of world significance today. Development in the field of science and technology further added to the volume and speed of the process. Agricultural economy turned into industrial economy. Industrial area developed into towns and cities. The process of *urbanisation* began. People from rural areas started flocking towards cities. Capitalist economy was born. Social classes with class-hatreds emerged. Social institutions and values underwent changes. New prob- lems and new fears and new anxieties were invariably the results of it. The very face of the society changed. These developments necessitated the birth of a new branch of sociology called "*Industrial Sociology*' which essentially deals with the industrial society with all its complexities.

Definition of Industrial Sociology

1. 'Industrial sociology is the application of the sociological approach to the reality and problems of industry'.

—P. Gisbert

2. Industrial sociology centres its attention on the social organisation of factory, the store, and the office. This focus includes not only the interactions of people playing roles in these organisations but also the ways in which their work roles are interrelated with other aspects of their life". — Charles B. Spaulding

3. Industrial sociology is the sociology of industrial relations and industrial activities of man.

Development of Industrial Sociology

As a specialised branch of sociology, industrial sociology is yet to become mature. In fact, *Durkheim* and *Max Weber* in their classical styles have made some analysis of industrial institutions. But systematic research in the field has developed only in recent decades. It gained importance about the middle of the present century. The famous experiments at the *Hawthorne Works in Chicago*, of the *Western Electric Company*, conducted by *George Elton Mayo* and his associates during the last twenties and in the early thirties, provided the fillip to the development of industrial sociology.

Industrial sociology gained the grounds comparatively on a wider scale in America. Various factors contributed to the development of industrial sociology in the U.S.A. The development of corporate industry, the achievement of scientific management, the unemployment of the depressed 1930s, the labour legislation of the New Deal (Economic Policy), the rise of '*human relations*', the manpower shortages and enforced restrictions of wartime, the great awakening of the trade unions, the continued emigration of the population from the American farm, the new technology and mechanisation, the desire for a higher standard of living, the occasional labour strikes involving thousands of workers, the investigation of the Congress, the legislative programme of the Kennedy Administration–and other factors contributed to the growth of this branch in America.

In the beginning, in Industrial Sociology much of the work was limited to the analysis of rather restricted problems. But today industrial sociologist's field of study is developing. It now includes the analysis of industrial institutions and organisation. It also studies the relation between them. It examines the links between industrial phenomena and institutions of the wider society. Theoretically, this is correct. But practically much remains to be done. As regards many of the internal problems of industrial organisations, our systematic knowledge is still fragmentary and inadequate. In respect of the links between industrial and other institutions our knowledge is scattered.

The Concept of Industry

The key term to be explained here is '*industry*'. '*Industry*' may be defined as '*the application of complex and sophisticated methods to the production of economic goods and services*'. In order to improve the quality of production, reduce the cost and maximise the production, the complex methods, that is, the machines were used. This process of mechanisation of production originated during the Industrial Revolution in the 18th century.

Man, in some way or the other, has always been '*industrial*'. He has always used tools to obtain food and satisfy his needs. Advanced industry consists in the use of tools and machines that are far more complicated than the digging stick, the hoe, or the bow and arrow, used by the early stone age man to obtain his daily food. In fact, the original Latin word for industry is '*industria*', which means *skill* and *resourcefulness*. The term 'industry' is applied to the modem sophisticated system of procuring goods and services which began in the Industrial Revolution.

The Sociological Approach

A complex reality like '*industry*' can be studied from various points of view – technological, physical, psychological, economic, sociological etc. Sociology is essentially a science of society, of social relationships, associations and institutions. It analyses the social relations, their forms, contents and the systems they assume. Its method is scientific. Its approach is rational and empirical.

Industrial sociology is that branch of sociology which concerns mainly with the *industrial relations of man*. It examines the various industrial organisations and institutions, their interrelations and links with the other institutions and organisations of the wider society.

Scope of Industrial Sociology

Industrial sociology is an applied discipline. It is concerned with the study of human relations as they grow and operate in the field of industries. It deals with the sociological concepts that have relevance to industry. It concentrates upon the social organisations of the work place or industry. It studies the patterns of interaction between people in terms of their roles in industrial organisations.

Industrial organisations are also studied by other disciplines such as–*industrial management, industrial engineering, industrial psychology* and *economics*. But they study the phenomena of industry in different ways. Their studies sometimes may overlap.

Industrial engineering deals with the design of products and equipments. *Industrial management* is more an art than a science. *Industrial psychology* studies–the selection of personnel, job satisfaction, motivation and incentive to work, team spirit, accident proneness and such other personal matters and behavioural problems. *Economics* concentrates on such matters as–prices, wages, profits, full employment, finance, monopoly, marketing, taxation, etc. But none of these sciences focuses its attention on the social or human aspects of industrial organisations. This task is done only by industrial sociology.

Industrial sociology studies industrial organisation not as a technological or economic organisation, but more than that, as a social or human organisation. It stresses upon the social or interactional factors in industrial relations, formal and informal organisation, team work, communication etc. "When interaction among two or more persons is affected by the fact that one of them is a doctor, a teacher, a plumber, a factory worker, a stenographer, a boss, an employee, a union leader, or an unemployed person, we have before us the raw material of industrial sociology".— Charles B. Spaulding

The industrial sociology deals with the total organisation of the workplace. It also deals with three different organisations which may be conceived of as distinguishable but interrelated: namely, (*a*) *management organisation*, (*b*) *informal organisation of workers,* and (*c*) *union organisation*.

(*a*) '*Management organisation*' refers to the relations between management and the workers. It also includes policies, programmes-structure and the functioning of the management. Its main emphasis is on the formal relations developed by the workers with the management.

(*b*) '*Informal organisation*' *of workers* consists of informal relations developed voluntarily by the workers themselves. Such relations are established by the individuals and small groups within the factory or industry. Such organisations assume the forms of cliques, gangs, friendship groups, bands etc. These organisations develop their own informal norms to control the activities of the members.

(*c*) '*Union organisation*' refers to the role of trade unions and the participation or involvement of workers in union activities. Trade unions are playing a vital role in creating industrial unrest and maintaining industrial peace. They also control the formal and informal relations of the workers.

These three organisations of the industry are affected by the physical conditions of the work place, fashions in management thinking, governmental and other social control, the personalities of employees and their experiences in playing roles in other organisations.

Importance of Industrial Sociology

Industrial sociology is of great practical importance.

1. Industrial sociology has been of great help in finding solutions to many of the industrial disputes and instances of industrial unrest.
2. It has reduced the gap between industrial management and industrial workers. It has also helped both to develop friendly relations.
3. Industrial Sociology has stressed upon the important role of trade unions in settling industrial disputes.
4. It has thrown light upon the problems of industrial workers. It has suggested ways and means of improving the living conditions of workers.
5. Various industrial sociological studies have impressed upon the management and the government the need to undertake social security measures for promoting labour welfare.
6. Industrial sociology studies the relations between man's industrial activities on the one hand, and his political, economic, educational and other activities, on the other.
7. Industrial sociology also analyses the processes of industrialisation and urbanisation, their magnitude and their mutual interaction.
8. Finally, industrial sociology plays a vital role in contributing to planned industrial growth.

URBAN SOCIOLOGY

Our modern industrial civilisation is dominated by cities. '*Urbanisation*' or the growth of cities is a phenomenon of recent years. It is '*an extremely new phenomenon in human history, so recent that its rapid growth and full potentialities are not yet thoroughly understood or realised.*' Not only the existing cities of the world are growing today but also new cities are emerging. Urban sociology is born to study cities and their unprecedented growth.

Definition of Urban Sociology

1. 'Urban Sociology' is that branch of sociology which deals with the city or the urban community, with urbanisation and urbanism.
— J.A. Quinn
2. Urban Sociology is the sociology of urban life and activities.

Urbanisation and Urban Sociology

The city is not a phenomenon limited to civilised life, for it has existed in some preliterate cultures. However, the first small urban centres appeared only some 5 to 6 thousand years ago. True urbanisation, however, is much more recent than that. The earliest urban centres such as Memphis, Thebes, Babylon, Athens, Rome, Carthage, Pataliputra, Ujjian, were of course, called 'cities'. But in modern context they would be called "*towns*". "They were mere urban islands in a vast sea of rurality".

'*Urbanisation*' refers to the growth of cities. It also indicates an enormous increase in the size of population in urban centres. "Urbanisation covers the movement of people permanently or temporarily from village to city; it refers to the effect upon village manners of city habits..."

Urbanisation became a world phenomenon only in the 19th century. In 1800 there were only 21 cities in the world each with a population of not less than one lakh. They were all in Europe. By 1950 their number increased to 858 and their total population exceeded 313 million. The populations of the major cities ranged from one million to about twelve million. The population of New York, Tokyo and Shanghai has already exceeded one crore. Some countries became more urbanised than others. America, England, Germany and Israel became the most urbanised countries of the world. In these countries more than 50 per cent of the people live in towns and cities today. This increase in proportion in cities is what we mean by 'urbanisation'.

Importance of cities is today widely recognised. But cities are more often studied with '*moralistic*' rather than '*scientific*' approach. Some have highlighted the significance of city, past and present, and its dominant role in the building of civilisation. They have argued that cities have led in the creation of art, advancement of science and the spread of knowledge. They have also stated that without huge cities the modem complex and industrial civilisation could not have developed.

On the contrary, some other scholars have condemned cities '*as abnormal seed-beds of sin, scepticism, greed, misery, filth and congestion*'. The cities are branded as centres of '*corruption, vice and misery*'. They further maintained that "the urban way of life inevitably encourages attitudes of selfish pleasure-seeking, exploitation of one's fellowmen, and indifference to human suffering."

Whether in condemnation or in praise, these scholars have implicitly paid great tributes '*to the human significance of the city*'. Although a more detached point of view is emerging, the scientific study and literature on cities are very much lacking.

Origin of Urban Sociology

The phenomenal growth of cities or what we call the phenomenon of '*Urbanisation*' with all its attendant merits and demerits necessitated a systematic and a scientific study of the urban communities of cities. Accordingly was born that branch of sociology called '*Urban Sociology*'. Though studies of cities were made even earlier, urban sociology, as a systematic discipline came into being in the 20th century only. As it is in the case of Rural Sociology, maximum work in the field of Urban Sociology has been done in the specialised fields of urban sociology today. For example, many books have appeared on classification of towns, citizenship, development of towns, urban environment, social disorganisation in cities, demographic trends, community life and its impact on personality, family, marriage and divorce in cities etc. Intensive research has also been made regarding the mechanism of social welfare, proper use of leisure, religious, cultural and educational institutions in cities, town planning and rehabilitation and such other topics.

Scope of Urban Sociology

The scope of urban sociology is really vast. In addition to the study of the general principles of urban sociology, it deals with the development of towns, social disorganisation, problems of urban life and town planning. It studies the interaction between the urban environment and the development of human personality. It studies the structure and functions of urban family, its role and changing patterns. It deals with the institution of marriage in urban context, and the recent trends in it. It studies the class structure and class struggle in urban societies. It concentrates on such features of social disorganisation, such as–crimes, juvenile delinquency, prostitution, beggary, unemployment, diseases, environment pollution, slums, gambling, alcoholism and night life. It analyses the factors and causes of social and personal disorganisation. It undertakes an investigation of industries and industrial relations, the causes of disharmony between the labour and the management and the ways and means of bringing about harmony between the two.

Urban sociology makes its study with its basic assumption that the city is '*not a static phenomenon*, *but a series of dynamic inter-relationships*'. "In the ever-changing modem city institutions are altered; old problems change or disappear and new ones arise. Likewise, new methods for solving these problems are constantly being tried in urban sociology. It gives suggestions for urban planning and control. Hence, it not only studies the facts of urban life but also evaluates the facts in order to understand their causes and means of improvement. Though the immediate task of urban sociology is to make an analytical study of the structure and functioning of the urban community, in doing so, it gives suggestions to overcome the problems of city life, which are of great practical importance.

Value of Urban Sociology

The value of urban sociology is widely recognised today. The process of urbanisation has been greatly hastened in advanced countries due to industrialisation and technological changes. The cities today '*embrace in one way or another nearly everything in life*'. The studies on urban society and urban life have also been diverse and many. They may deal with "urban traffic or urban housing, with municipal govemment or finance, with fire protection or park maintenance, with juvenile delinquency or commercialised vice." Urban sociology seeks to find ways of solving some of the difficulties, nuisances, dangers and derelictions of city life.

As a result of urbanisation there is a change in personal tendencies and trends. The norms and standards of marriage and family have undergone considerable changes. It has given rise to various social, economic and sanitary problems. It is in this context that the need of urban sociology is strongly felt. An urban sociologist is a social doctor who is busily engaged in diagnosing the social diseases. "The emphasis on problems is natural and necessary because the close-packing of thousands and millions of people in small space inevitably creates conditions universally regarded as unfortunate." Some of these conditions are so new that there are no traditional modes of handling them. They can be dealt with only by investigating, by inventing new institutional arrangements. The value of urban sociology under these conditions can hardly be exaggerated.

Rural Sociology and Urban Sociology Interrelations

Various branches of sociology study the different aspects of the same reality, that is, society. It is but natural that all the branches are interrelated. Accordingly, rural sociology and urban sociology too have interconnections.

Rural sociology studies the village and urban sociology deals with the city. The city life depends on the village and what it produces. Similarly, the village is very much influenced by the city. Due to the pressures from within and attractions from outside people are flocking towards the cities from the villages. The economic necessity and social deficiency are '*pushing*' the people out of the village, while the attractions of the city are '*pulling*' them towards their centres. This has resulted in phenomenon known as 'urbanisation'. Both rural sociology and urban sociology are interested in studying this phenomenon.

Rural sociology and urban sociology are mutually contributory. Rural sociology is helpfull to urban sociology in studying such matters as–the causes for the growth of population in cities, the nature of urban problems and their solution, the reasons for the laxity of urban social institutions, rural trends in urban centres, the phenomenon of "loss of community", etc. Similarly urban sociology is helpful to rural sociology in studying such matters as–the limitations of rural life, the urban impact on the village, the 'rush' of people towards the city, rural change, rural problems, rural development, rural reconstruction, etc.

Rural sociology and urban sociology are so interrelated that one cannot be separated from the other. Just as it is difficult to draw a line of demarcation between the urban society and rural society, it is equally difficult to draw a hard and fast line of difference between urban sociology and rural sociology. Urban trends are found in rural societies and rural tendencies are often continued in urban societies. In small cities and towns and also in sub-urban centres we find the intermixture of rural urban trends and features which is often described in terms of 'rural-urban convergence".

A rural sociologist must have a basic understanding of urban sociology and similarly an urban sociologist must know the fundamental principles of rural sociology. There is no city in the world which does not have its rural background and similarly almost all the villages are influenced by the cities in one way or the other. This fact further emphasises the inter-relationship between urban sociology and rural sociology.

Interconnections between Urban Sociology and Industrial Sociology

Urban sociology and industrial sociology are interconnected and interdependent. Their interdependence is such that one is often looked upon as the branch of another.

Urban sociology studies the origin of the city, its growth, the city life, the problems of the city and their solutions, urban reconstruction, the city planning, etc. Industrial sociology studies the industrial system, industrial relations, industrial problems, industrialisation etc. Industrialisation and urbanisation often go together. The growth of cities is associated with the growth of industries. Similarly, the growth of industries accelerates the growth of cities. It is from this point of view we can say that the city life has its reliance on industrial growth, and industrial life has its roots in city life. Industrial sociology and urban sociology coincide on this point.

Urban sociology has a vast scope. Industrial life is often treated as a part of urban life. It is not possible for one to study industrial sociology without basic knowledge of urban sociology. Topics of interest for industrial sociology such as– industrial environment, industrial advancement, slums, industrial relations, industrial unrest, labour welfare etc.–are also studied in a general manner by urban sociology. On the contrary, industrial sociology which has a narrow field of study, concentrates more on the industrial behaviour of man. It gives practical suggestions for urban sociology in matters such as urban development, city planning, urban problems, etc.

OTHER BRANCHES

In addition to the fields of inquiry cited above, sociologists have explored a few other fields also. They are:

- Medical Sociology
- Folk Sociology
- Sociology of Art
- Sociology of Sexual Behaviour
- Sociology of Aesthetics
- Sociology of Racial and Ethnic Relations
- Sociology of Social Structure
- Sociology of Group Relations
- Sociology of the Community and Locality Relations
- Sociology of Complex Organisations
- Sociology of International Relations
- Sociology of Mass Society
- Statistics and Quantitative Sociology
- Social Psychology
- Social Disorganisation or Pathology
- Military Sociology
- Criminology
- Sociology of Small Groups
- Sociology of Culture
- Sociology of Communication and Opinion
- Sociology of Popular Culture and Recreation
- Sociological Methodology
- Sociology of Differentiation and Stratification
- Sociology of the Graphic and Plastic Arts
- Sociology of Planning for Development in Underdeveloped Areas
- Sociology of Collective Behaviour
- Sociology of Age Statuses (i.e. Adolescence Middle Age Old Age)
- Sociology of Action [Welfare].
- Social Psychiatry
- Sociological Theory

Sociology has already made intensive studies in fields like social stratification, mass media of communication, public opinion and bureaucracy. The horizons of sociology are expanding gradually. Its scope is becoming wider and wider to encompass all the realms of man's social life.

REVIEW QUESTIONS

1. What are the main branches of Sociology? Describe their origins and importance.
2. Write a detailed note on Historical Sociology.
3. Throw light on the scope and subject matter of Rural Sociology.
4. What are the main tasks of Rural Sociology?
5. Define Industrial Sociology. Discuss the 'concept of industry'.
6. Discuss the development, scope and importance of Industrial Sociology.
7. Assess the interrelations between Rural Sociology and Urban Sociology.
8. Write short notes on the following:
   (a) Sociology of Knowledge
   (b) Sociology of Occupation
   (c) Urbanisation and Urban Sociology
   (d) Value of Urban Sociology
   (e) Relationship between Urban Sociology and Industrial Sociology

⌘⌘⌘⌘⌘⌘⌘⌘⌘⌘⌘

4

METHODS OF SOCIOLOGY

CHAPTER OUTLINE

- The Comparative Method
- The Historical Method
- The Statistical Method
- The Case Study Method
- The Functional Method
- The Scientific Method
- Limitations of the Scientific Method
- The Scientific View Point
- Sociology as a Science
- The Sociological Point of View

Sociology as a social science has been trying to develop its own method of study. In comparison with other social sciences sociology has to face greater problems in evolving a satisfactory method. Though sociology is in its extreme infancy it tries to touch upon various aspects of man's social life in as precise a manner as possible. Man's social life is complex and multi-faceted. It is highly a challenging task for sociologists to collect, analyse, synthesise and finally generalise social data which are too numerous, complex and illusive. They are seeking out all the avenues of collecting and interpreting social data. Hence it has become quite natural for them to employ various methods in their study. A brief survey of some of these methods is given below.

THE COMPARATIVE METHOD

In order to tackle the problems of society effectively and to make fruitful discoveries, sociology has to employ precise and well-tested methods of investigation. The comparative method is one such method. This method is as old as Aristotle for it is known that he had made use of this method in his study of political systems. But it became "*the method par excellence of sociology*" only in the 19th century. Sociologists and social investigators like Comte, Durkheim, Tylor, J.G. Frazer, Weber, Hobhouse, Wheeler, Ginsberg, Gouldner, G.P. Murdock, S.F. Nadel, S.M. Lipset and R. Bendix, ER. Leach, and others have not only used this method in their studies but also made it sufficiently popular.

The comparative method refers to "*the method of comparing different societies or groups within the same society to show whether and why they are similar or different in certain respects*". By such comparisons of differences as well as similarities found in the ways of life of peoples of different groups and societies, one can find clues to man's social behaviour.

The comparative method is not specifically a sociological method but is a method quite known in logic, and as such it is applicable to all the sciences. In the 18th century, philologists made use of this method in their study of different languages. In the 19th century, this method was used by the social investigators to find out similarities in social institutions so as to trace their common origins. Both Montesquieu and Comte used and recommended this method in the 19th century to establish and explain both differences and similarities between societies.

Throughout the 19th century there was a strong link between the use of the comparative method and the evolutionist approach. Durkheim set out clearly the significance of this method in his "*The Rules of Sociological Method*". According to him, the sociological explanation consists entirely in the establishment of causal connections'. In the case of natural sciences, the causal connections could be more easily established because of facility of experiment. Since such direct experiments are out of question in sociology, we are compelled to use the method of indirect experiment, *i.e.*, comparative method—says Durkheim.

Durkheim in his work "*Division of Labour in Society*" compared the legal systems of different societies at the same time and at different levels of development. In that he used law as an index of the moral character of society. By comparison "he tested his hypothesis that an increase in the division of labour is accompanied by a change in the nature of social integration or solidarity".

Further, Durkheim in his study of "*Suicide*" aimed to discover the social causes of suicide by relating the rates of suicide in different social groups to characteristics of the groups. He showed that "the suicide rates varied inversely with the degree of social cohesion and with the degree of stability of moral norms".

Tylor used this method in the study of institutions connected with the family among primitive people and was able to show that the practice of mother-in-law avoidance was correlated with the system of matrilocal residence.

Recently, *S.M. Lipset* and *R. Bendix* have compared "rates of social mobility in different industrial societies to show that these rates are governed largely by the stage or degree of industrialisation."

Thus, by employing this method it may be possible to explain the significance of a custom or practice, though it varies from one society to another, by studying the motives behind it.

By adopting this method it is quite possible to establish correlations between crime and urbanisation, between family size and social mobility, between social class and educational attainment, between urban living and divorce or delinquency rates, etc. Studies of this kind have resulted in a number of generalisations also.

It is true that *the comparative method has its own limitations*. Critics have pointed out that "what appear superficially to be similar institutions may, in fact, be very different in the societies being considered". Further, "an institution detached from the context of the whole society in which it functions may easily be misunderstood". These comments denote practical difficulties involved in the application of the method. As Bottomore has suggested these difficulties could be minimised by limiting the range of comparisons to societies which are broadly similar.

In spite of its deficiencies, the comparative method has been widely used today in sociological studies. E.A. Freeman claimed that "the establishment of the comparative method of study has been the greatest intellectual achievement of our time." As Durkheim said, in the absence of experimental method comparative method is the only method available to the sociological disciplines. Due to the success attained by employing this method in small-scale studies in particular societies, sociologists are encouraged to make comparisons between societies. Such higher-level comparisons between societies and nations are necessary to verify the conclusions of the small-scale studies.

THE HISTORICAL METHOD

The historical method refers to, "*a study of events, processes, and institutions of past civilisations, for the purpose of finding the origins or antecedents of contemporary social life and thus understanding its nature and working*." This method is based on the idea that our present forms of social life, our customs and traditions, beliefs and values, and our ways of living as such have their roots in the past and that one can best explain them by tracing them back to their origins.

The utility and wide acceptance of the historical method have resulted in one of the fields of sociology known as "*historical sociology*." "Historical sociology studies societies of the remote as well as of recent past to discover origins of, and find explanations for, our present ways of life."

In a way, all types of sociological researches are historical for the sociologists make use of the records relating to the things that have happened or have been observed. But generally, the term "historical sociology" is applied to the study of social facts which are more than fifty or so years old. It means all the social facts relating to the 19th and early phase of 20th centuries are referred to as "historical."

In practice, "historical sociology is a particular kind of comparative study of social groups; their compositions, their interrelationships and the social conditions which support or undermine them." The social anthropologist examines these things in contemporary simple societies. But the historical sociologist examines them in the records of societies and cultures prior to his own.

The historical approach has taken two main forms. (*i*) The first one is highly influenced by the *biological theory of evolution*, and (*ii*) the second one by the *economic interpretation*.

(*i*) In the first approach concentration is made on the issues such as the origins, development and transformation of societies and social institutions. This is actually concerned with the entire span of human history. Comte, Spencer and Hobhouse used this approach to study the development of the whole society. But E. Westermarck and F. Oppenheimer followed this method to study the development of institutions such as marriage and state in their famous studies of "*History of Human Marriage*" and "*The State*" respectively.

(*ii*) The *second approach* was characteristic of the works of Max Weber and his followers. Weber strongly criticised Mark's materialist conception of history and his "formula for the causal explanation of historical reality". He advocated the idea of economic 'interpretation' of history. Weber applied this approach in his studies of the origins of Capitalism, the development of modem bureaucracy, and the economic influence of the world religions. In these studies particular historical changes of social structures are investigated and interpreted. Very recently *C. Wright Mills* and *Raymond Aron* also came under the influence of Weber's methodology in their studies.

THE STATISTICAL METHOD

From the 17th Century onwards statistical methods have become essential in analysing vital statistics concerning people or things. The term "*statistics*" may be used in two ways: (*i*) to refer to the application of statistical methods to social or non-social problems, and (*ii*) to refer to the actual numerical data collected in relation to these problems.

The term '*social statistics*' or '*statistical method*' refers to the method that is used to measure social phenomena mathematically. It may be regarded as "the method of collecting, analysing and interpreting numerical information about social aggregates". As Bogardus has pointed out "Social statistics is mathematics applied to human facts".

The statistical method is of great help in some cases in order to disclose the relationship between different aspects of social phenomena. It also helps to arrive at generalisations regarding their nature, occurrence, and meaning. It is an important tool in research in the sense it can be effectively used in issues or problems which involve measurement or numerals. For example, this method can be very effectively used in studies relating to rates of birth and death, divorce and marriage, crime and suicide. Useful information can be obtained by the application of this method in studies pertaining to migration, economic conditions, standard of living, human ecology, public opinion, and so on.

The statistical method reveals certain distinctive features when applied to the study of social phenomena. *Firstly*, collection of numerical information about social issues or problems cannot always be done by direct observation. It has to be done through questionnaires and surveys which have their own limitations. *Secondly*, a social statistician is concerned with the problems of interviews also. In interviews some respondents may *refuse* to provide the information which they have been asked for. If such respondents are selected out of sampling, the problem of refusal becomes a significant deficiency in the whole process. *Thirdly*, social statisticians are often interested in the analysis of data, which can be *ordered* but not measured. (Ex: the provision of medical facilities being classified into—good, fair, indifferent and poor).

Sociologists like Comte, Prof. Giddings and others have emphasised the importance of this method in sociological research. It is true that most of the data dealt with in sociology are qualitative and not quantitative in nature. Still sociologists are struggling to reduce more and more of such data to quantitative terms so that they can be studied statistically.

THE CASE STUDY METHOD

The '*Case study*' is a practice derived from legal studies. In legal studies a '*case*' refers to an event or set of events involving legal acts. In sociology case study method is a holistic treatment of a subject. This method provides for the qualitative analysis of the issues. This is an in-depth study of an individual or a situation or an organisation or an institution or a family or a group or a small community. The idea behind this method is that any case being studied is representative of many similar cases (if not all) and, hence, will make generalisations possible. This method involves the minute study of all the information and data collected regarding the object or case under study. Hence *Burgess* called this method "*social microscope*."

The case study may make use of various techniques such as interviews, questionnaires, schedules, life histories, relevant documents of all kinds and also 'participant observation' for collecting information about the case under study. This method is essential in obtaining an insight into the problems of the alcoholic, drug addict, the criminal, the juvenile delinquent, the social deviant, or the immigrant. Thomas and Znaniecki's "*Polish Peasant in Europe and America*"–(1922) is a classic work in the field of case study.

This method is often criticised by the social statisticians. According to them, this method can- not provide methodologically precise results of a general nature. Still, it could be used as a valuable preliminary approach in order to discover the significant variables that speak of human behaviour. These variables may lead to the formulation of hypotheses which could be tasted by making references to a large number of instances.

THE FUNCTIONAL METHOD (FUNCTIONALISM)

The functional method or functionalism has been given greater emphasis during recent times in sociological studies. This method, in sociology and social anthropology, appeared in the beginning almost as a reaction against the method of the evolutionists. In comparison with other methods such as scientific method, comparative method, etc., functionalism can be more understood as a method of analysis and interpretation than as a method of investigation.

Functionalism refers "*to the study of social phenomena from the point of view of the functions that particular institutions or social structures, such as class, serve in a society.*" This method is based on the assumption that the total social system of the society is made up of parts which are interrelated and interdependent. Each part performs a function necessary to the life of the group. These parts could be understood only in relations to the functions that they perform or the needs they meet with. Since this method, presupposes the interdependence of parts, we can understand and study any one part of the social system only in its relationships with other parts as well as with the whole system. For example, the institution of religion in society has to be understood by means of its relationship with other institutions such as morality, family, state, law, etc., and in its relationship with the entire social system. As this method presupposes, religion has its own function to perform or need to fulfil, (and it may be the expression and reinforcement of social solidarity as Durkheim spoke of).

The 19th Century sociologists such as Auguste Comte and Herbert Spencer had actually laid the foundations for this functional approach. But it was Durkheim who first gave a rigorous concept of social function in his "*The Division of Labour in Society*" and in "*The Rules of Sociological Method.*" Functionalism became quite popular at the hands of Radcliffe Brown and Malinowski. The extreme form of functionalism was propagated by B. Malinowski whose influence pervaded amongst a good number of social anthropologists. He spoke in terms of the functional integration of every society and its institutions. He dogmatically asserted that "*every social activity had function by virtue of its existence, and every activity was so completely integrated with all the others.*"

During the recent years the concept of functionalism has been put to a very novel use by American sociologists such as R.K. Merton and Talcott Parsons. Because of their greater emphasis on social structures, or institutions, functionalism at their hands came to be known as '*structural functional method.*' R.K. Merton has made functionalist approach less dogmatic and less exclusive. He has presented it as one possible approach to the study of social behaviour. He has made a distinction between "*function and dysfunction*", and also between "*latent and manifest functions.*" These new qualities indicate that any social institution may have several functions any one of which may be of greater importance in a particular society. As *Bottomore* has pointed out "what is most valuable in the functionalist approach is the greater emphasis and clarity given to the simple idea that in every particular society the different social activities are interconnected".

THE SCIENTIFIC METHOD

The basis of study of any science or discipline is its methods. Sciences in general and natural science in particular follow the scientific method. The scientific method has added much to their credibility and objectivity. The scientific method consists of certain steps or procedures which are to be followed precisely. A glance of these steps or procedures is given below.

1. ***Formulation of the problem:*** A 'problem' is a gap in knowledge, something not understood. It may be simple or complex. But this problem is to be defined properly. Otherwise, we may miss the direction and efforts may be wasted. A casual observation and an idea regarding the existing amount of knowledge on that particular issue may help one to define the problem properly.
2. ***Formulation of hypothesis:*** When the problem to be tackled is known we must have some idea to the new aspects that are likely to be discovered. These primary ideas which may guide us in our study may be termed as hypothesis. It is a *tentative explanation of a phenomenon*. It is a provisional supposition which is not yet proved but is anticipated to be correct.
3. ***Observation and collection of data:*** The formulated hypothesis will have to be tested. This requires observation and collection of facts. In social investigations we collect data by interview, schedules, questionnaires, field observations, etc. The methods of collecting data depend upon the nature of the research and the resources at our disposal.
4. ***Analysis and synthesis:*** After the data have been collected they must be processed and analysed in order to draw proper inferences. This requires the *classification of the data*. Classification means arranging the data in different groups or classes according to their similarities or dissimilarities.
5. ***Generalisation:*** After the data have been collected, processed, and analysed, we have to draw broad inferences or conclusions or generalisations.
6. ***Formulation of theory and law:*** When a scientist has succeeded in describing and explaining the relation between various facts, he has formulated a *theory*. When these facts have been tested and accepted by the scientist as invariably true the theory may be properly regarded as a *law*.

Hypothesis—Theory—and Law. At this point it is necessary to distinguish between hypothesis, theory and law. A hypothesis is generally formulated before the facts are observed properly. It deals with comparatively narrower range of facts. A *theory is a tested hypothesis* and deals with wide range of facts. Theory is sometimes regarded as an elaborate hypothesis. When a theory is well established and found to be correct invariably, it is regarded as a law.

We should note that we encounter some difficulties in applying scientific method to the study of social phenomena. Scientific method has a few limitations in sociology. Still, with some modifications the scientific method is being followed even in social investigations.

Limitations of the Scientific Method

Science is defined as a systematic body of knowledge. Here the word '*system*' refers to the method that is followed. This method is the scientific method. It is commonly followed in the case of physical sciences. A sociologist encounters some difficulties in applying this method in social researches. Scientific method has few limitations in sociology. This is due to the very nature of its subject-matter.

1. ***Difficulty in the use of experimental method:*** The laboratory of a sociologist is the world of everyday living. The sociologist does not have much control over the subjects of his investigation, that is, people. Here the people are not only conscious of, but also have their own motives, incentives, emotions, feelings, ideas values etc., which may affect the investigation very much. Social phenomena cannot be reproduced artificially at our will.
2. ***Interdependence of cause and effect:*** In social investigations it is often difficult to deter- mine which is the cause and which is the effect. Whether poverty is due to beggary, or beggary is due to poverty, we cannot be sure. Causation is reciprocal here. Further, one effect may have several causes. There is plurality of causation also.
3. ***Intangibility of social phenomena:*** The social phenomena are not external tangible things that can be identified directly by our senses. We cannot see or touch relations. We cannot isolate our units in a laboratory. Customs cannot be handled and institutions cannot be measured, religion cannot be preserved in a museum and values cannot be demonstrated.
4. ***Complexity of social data:*** The social research is about man and his social behaviour and activities. Human behaviour is influenced by many factors: physical, social, psychological, etc., and the observer is simply confused with the complexity of data. No two persons are exactly alike. Hence generalisations are difficult to make.
5. ***Unpredictability:*** Social behaviour is irregular and unpredictable. Society is dynamic. It is an ongoing process. Therefore, we cannot formulate laws that hold good for all societies and for all times and circumstances. Predictions are hence difficult to make.
6. ***Problem of objectivity***: In social sciences the observer is a part of his data. He may have his own ideas, opinion, prejudices which are difficult to control. Hence objectivity is difficult to maintain.

Hence, sociology, in addition to the scientific method makes use of other methods such as the comparative method, the statistical method, the social survey method, the case study method, questionnaire and interview methods and the functional method in order to obtain more reliable knowledge about phenomena.

THE SCIENTIFIC VIEWPOINT

Scientific outlook is very essential for a learner of a discipline like sociology. A man of science yearns to *know*. The scientist has to make use of all the available sources and means for the search of knowledge. The scientific outlook or view point refers mainly to the way in which an individual looks at the things. A scientist, to be called a scientist, must have the scientific outlook or perspective. To have this scientific outlook or view point or perspective he must have certain qualities and follow certain basic norms. Some of them may be mentioned:

1. *The scientist likes and loves truth*. He is after facts. He is clear in his vision and careful in his statement of facts.
2. *The scientist maintains objectivity*. He tries to separate his own wishes and values from the process of observation. He tries to control his likes and dislikes that may affect his inquiry.
3. The scientist follows the *amoral approach*. He is ethically neutral. He never studies things as they *ought to be*. He deals with them *as they are*. He never makes value-judgments.
4. The scientist is free *from prejudices* or preconceived notions. He is not swayed by the opinions or views of others. He cultivates the habit of dispassionate thinking and precise expression.
5. The scientist is a *man of courage*. He is ever ready to face the facts. He never rejects the facts just because they are disliked by others. He never accepts the views which only cater to his prejudices. Failures cannot discourage him, for he is an unselfish seeker of truth. He is not afraid of facing truth under any circumstances.
6. The scientist generally *assumes that knowledge is worthwhile*. He does not assume that only facts about people are more important and that facts about animals are not. As a scientist, he knows the importance of giving mankind more knowledge than it previously possessed.

7. The scientist is *broadminded in spirit*. He never confines himself to the narrow religious, or racial or national and other kind of cell at the cost of facts and naked truths. He is uncompromising as far as truth is concerned.
8. The scientist is always analytical. He delves deep into the problems and tries to find answers for questions like – *what*? *why*? *how*? He is *rationalistic too*.

SOCIOLOGY AS A SCIENCE

There is a controversy about the nature of sociology as a science. '*Is sociology a science*?'– is an issue which is highly debated and discussed. A correct answer to this question cannot be divided, into two categories, '*Yes*' or '*No*'. But the correct answer should be in terms of degree, the degree to which sociology is a science. Some critics argue that sociology cannot claim to be a science. Some others assert that sociology is very much a science like other social sciences such as Political Science, Economics and Psychology.

W.F. Ogburn, an American sociologist, is of the opinion that sociology is a science. According to him, a science is to be judged by three criteria:

1. *The reliability of its body of knowledge.*
2. *Its organisation, and*
3. *Its method.*

The question whether sociology is a science or not, can be better answered if this question is thought over in the light of these criteria.

1. *The reliability of knowledge:* Science depends upon reliable knowledge. In this regard sociology has made a promising beginning. Sociological studies of population, the family, group behaviour, the evolution of institutions, the process of social change and such other topics are re- garded as considerably reliable.

Science assumes that all phenomena show uniformities and regularities. It seeks to establish *generalisations that are universal*. But sociological generalisations are restricted to time and space unlike the generations of Physics or Chemistry. Social data change too much and too fast. Sociology mainly deals with the human material and this human material is irregular and illusive. Social relations are not fixed but flexible. It is difficult to control the variable, and there are many variables in social data.

In spite of the difficulties, sociologists have tried to establish generalisations, which have had great success. For instance, it is a sociological generalisation that societies always regulate marriages in such a way as to prevent incest. Much of the sociological knowledge is becoming reliable.

A very good test of the reliability of knowledge is *the test of prediction and control*. Predications are difficult to be made in sociology, if not impossible, so also the control. For instance, there are many causes for juvenile delinquency like, unhappy parents, broken home and crowded cities. To test the effect of only one factor, i.e. broken home on juvenile delinquency, we should control the other variables like crowded cities. This is almost an impossible task.

Not in all areas of sociological study, knowledge can be obtained easily. On some areas, mea- surement cannot be made. Areas such as religion, art, morality etc. are not very much amenable to scientific method.

Further, many publications are made under the title of sociology and some of them consist of only ideas, not knowledge. These are essays, ethical discussions, wise pronouncements, interpretations, theories, programmes, valuations etc. Their practical importance may be even greater than that of science.

2. *The organisation of knowledge:* Disjointed collection of facts cannot be a science. The science should be organised. The organisation of a science rests upon the relationship, which the parts of knowledge bear to each other. The value of organisation lies not in a symmetry, but in its value for the discovery of more knowledge.

As regards the organisation of knowledge, sociology is not disappointing. In sociology there are many inter-relationships which are enough to encourage more discoveries though inadequate to provide a proper synthesis for the whole field. A larger collection of knowledge, it is expected, will eventually provide such a synthesis.

3. *Method:* A branch of knowledge can be called science if it follows the *scientific method* in its studies and investigations. Scientific method starts with a hypothesis. This hypothesis is verified through experimentation. But an experimentation of laboratory situation is difficult in sociology.

The *laboratory experiment*, which has been a great aid to many natural scientists, is not very common in sociology, because there are some limitations in the experimental method as related to human conduct. One limitation is that people who become aware of the fact that they are being studied, may render the experimental situation impossible. Further, the experimenter himself may have his own bias or prejudices against his subjects of experimentation.

Experimental method requires a fixed static situation. But it is difficult in sociology. Social life is actually dynamic and not static. *Strictly speaking, laboratory experiment is not possible in sociology*. However, in sociology we can measure the relationships of two variables by employing statistical method. For example, if we want to know whether families with low income have more infant deaths, we can collect the statistics. We must have two groups of families with the same type of feeding, same customs etc. By studying and varying the factor of income and by keeping other factors constant, we can establish a relation between the rate of infant mortality and income.

Sociology has quite a number of other methods besides the experimental method. The historical method, case study method, social survey method, functional method, the statistical method, etc. can be cited here as examples. These methods are often found to be fruitful in sociological studies Sociology has shown itself a growing science. Of course, sociology as a science is not as accurate as Physics or Chemistry. It is true that *social phenomena are hard to measure*. Still there is a relative orderliness and approximate predictability in certain classes of social phenomena. With those who charge that experimentation is impossible in sociology and experimentation is the only criterion of science, we may argue that many of the facts and generalisations even in physical sciences are not based on experiments at all. But their facts are mostly gathered through observations and not through experiments.

To conclude, we may say that '*science*', after all, is a method to discover the truth. Experimental method is not the only method of realising the truth. There are many methods and techniques in sociology and if these are properly applied, sociology will have definitely the characteristics of a genuine science. Right application of different methods in the spirit of objectivity will certainly yield fruitful results.

THE SOCIOLOGICAL POINT OF VIEW

The generally accepted meaning of sociology is that it is the science of society. But sociology is not the only science that deals with the human society and social phenomena. Different social sciences such as Economics, History, Political Science, Psychology, etc., also select one or the other aspect of society for their study. For example, Economics may study man's attempts to make his living; political science, his power relations; history, his "significant past life", psychology, his behaviour as such, and sociology, his 'society' and 'social behaviour'. What accounts for their differences? It is not the difference in concrete subject-matter, for these "social disciplines are all studying the same external phenomena–the facts of social life". As *K. Davis* points out, "It is rather a difference in the point of view or focus of attention", that accounts for their real differences.

Then what is the sociological point of view ? The student of sociology must learn the sociological perspective or point of view for "sociology is first and foremost a way of looking at the social world". The sociologist must see into and through man's daily round of activities. — *David Popenoe*

An untrained eye sees simply the routine that underlies daily social interactions. "Every one has become so accustomed to the fact that he kisses his children, greets warmly friends and relatives, waves hands to his neighbours, shakes hands when he meets a stranger, etc., and these actions are virtually invisible". The primary task of a sociologist is to teach himself to notice these social relationship with fresh eyes, with as much wonder as if they were exotic rites performed by some far-off jungle tribe. "The sociologist specialises in seeing those things to which familiarity has made most of us blind." — *David Popenoe*

A sociologist learns that a number of social transactions like these make up the fabric of human social life. Now he must ask himself questions – why do people do all these? Say, for example, why a male child is still preferred to a female child in the Indian family? Why wife prostrates before the husband and not vice versa? Why the kissing act of adults in public is still looked with disapproval amongst the Indians and not so amongst their Western counterpart? Why people go to the temples in bigger number on the occasion of festival, etc.

No sociological training is, of course, required to answer these questions. Ordinarily people may give an answer—*it is the* '*right*' *thing to do*. But a sociologist goes beyond these and tries to find an answer through traditions or morality. He asks questions why some practices become traditional?

How people know that certain practices are right? Who or what conferred this "*rightfulness*" upon them? He may point out that an action which is, one society's sacred custom, may be another's immoral vice.

In other words, sociologist will look beyond the generally accepted explanations for social behaviour and seek more scientific answers. This is what *Peter Berger* calls the "*debunking*" function of sociology. When sociologists "*debunk*" or remove traditional explanations many of their explanations or answers become public controversy because people may be upset with their explanations.

Example: Why do people go to temples or churches? The ordinary explanation is people go to temples due to their utmost religiosity. But a sociologist might say, in addition to the above-mentioned '*manifest*' function, the church-going behaviour may serve some "*latent*" functions such as—to enhance one's social standing, to exhibit one's new clothes, to parade one's jewellery, to demonstrate one's religiosity, and so on. Sociologists must be ready to face the charge that is made against them as "*unrespectable*".

The sociological perspective is quite different from the ordinary way of looking at things and events as it is stated above. The following example of the class-room will further clarify this point.

Example of class-room: During their very first class the college students will be having their own assumptions relating to professor's looks, dress, knowledge, language, expression, style of performance, class command etc. Students evaluation of the class is based on personal reactions to a particular professor. But a sociologist focuses on social relationships rather than on individual behaviour. He observes power relations, rules of conduct, and class characteristics.

A sociologist observes unequal distribution of power in the class-room, the teacher having the power to talk, discipline, punish and to determine grades. He observes that the teacher has the insti- tutional support at his command in disciplining the students, denying library and laboratory facility, etc. Still, teacher is not having absolute power. Students may also use their power as a sharp reaction and may refuse to keep quiet, boycott classes, stage strikes, etc. Further, the sociologist observes that there are certain unspoken rules and expectations that every one more or less follows. It is known that combing in class-room is inappropriate.

The sociologist observes that the class as a unit has its own characteristics which are not the properties of any individual in the class. The class meets in a room, has a size, has a specific average age of students, has a specific number of men and women in it, has lower-upper-class people, etc. Each of these features belongs to the class as a whole, and individual in that class.

These observations of a class of students are sociological observations. They concern patterns and regularities that will occur regardless of the individuals who occupy that class-room. A doctor or a photographer or an artist, or an educationalist, or a social reformer, or an administrator, or a parent, etc., looks at the classroom from various other points of view. "The sociological perspective trains us to pay attention to those details that are regular and patterned, details that are not unique to a particular situation or to particular people in those situations"—*Donald Light Jr* and *Suzanne Keller*.

As *Kingsley Davis* has pointed out that "our interest lies in societies as systems (that is, as going concerns) and in *social relationship* regardless of their type". This does not mean that sociology is purely encyclopedic in its approach summing up everything that the other social sciences include, but rather "a special discipline devoted to the way in which *societies achieve their unity and continuity* and *the way in which they change*". This sort of analysis is usually called sociology.

REVIEW QUESTIONS

1. What are the important methods of sociological studies? Discuss in detail.
2. Write a detailed note on the comparative and historical methods of Sociology.
3. The case study method of Sociology is called "social microscope." Discuss.
4. What is functionalism? Analyse the salient features of functionalism.
5. Discuss the procedure and limitations of the scientific method of Sociology.
6. Scientific outlook is very essential for Sociology. Comment.
7. Is Sociology a science? Analyse

⌘⌘⌘⌘⌘⌘⌘⌘⌘⌘⌘

5

SOCIAL RESEARCH: ITS METHODS AND TECHNIQUES

CHAPTER OUTLINE

- SOCIAL RESEARCH: MEANING, DEFINITION AND IMPORTANCE
- DIFFICULTIES OR PROBLEMS INVOLVED IN SOCIOLOGICAL RESEARCH
- METHODS AND TECHNIQUES OF SOCIAL RESEARCH.
- *OBSERVATION:* — MEANING AND DEFINITION — TYPES OF OBSERVATION — NON-CONTROLLED PARTICIPANT OBSERVATION: NON-CONTROLLED NON-PARTICIPANT OBSERVATION — SYSTEMATIC CONTROLLED OBSERVATION— MERITS AND LIMITATIONS OF OBSERVATION.
- QUESTIONNAIRE: MEANING AND DEFINITION — QUESTIONNAIRE, SCHEDULE AND INTERVIEW GUIDE — TYPES OF QUESTIONNAIRE: STRUCTURED QUESTIONNAIRES AND UNSTRUCTURED QUESTIONNAIRES — FORMATION OR CONSTRUCTION OF QUESTIONNAIRES —ADVANTAGE AND LIMITATIONS OF QUESTIONNAIRE.
- INTERVIEW: MEANING AND DEFINITION — THE OBJECTIVE AND THE PROCESS OF INTERVIEW — TYPES OF INTERVIEW: THE NON-DIRECTIVE INTERVIEW, THE DIRECTIVE INTERVIEW, THE FOCUSED INTERVIEW, THE REPEATED INTERVIEW AND THE DEPTH INTERVIEW — CRUCIAL POINTS IN THE INTERVIEW — ADVANTAGES, DISADVANTAGES LIMITATIONS OF INTERVIEW.
- SOCIAL SURVEYS: MEANING AND DEFINITION — PROCEDURAL WAYS OF SOCIAL SURVEY — SAMPLE SURVEYS AND RANDOM SAMPLE — OTHER KINDS OF SAMPLE: SYSTEMATIC SAMPLE, STRATIFIED SAMPLE AND CLUSTER SAMPLE.
- OTHER METHODS: SOCIOMETRY — THE EXPERIMENTAL METHOD — THE HAWTHORN EFFECTS — THE VERSTCHEN APPROACH

SOCIAL RESEARCH: MEANING, DEFINITION AND IMPORTANCE

What is Research?

Research is an attempt to know new things, facts, information, etc. in a scientific manner. Its main purpose is to diffuse knowledge and establish theories on the basis of the believable facts. As *L. V. Redman* and *A. V. H. Mory* have said, "*systematised effort to gain new knowledge we call research*".

A research scientist makes an untiring effort to collect new facts, information and knowledge about things or phenomena. He may not become, always successful in all his efforts to collect new facts. But the desire to know new things persists in him. Hence F.A. Ogg has pointed out "*Research may or may not come to success; it may or may not add anything to what is already known. It is sufficient that its objective be held knowledge or at least a new mode or orientation of knowledge*".

The method that is followed in order to carry on research is "*scientific method*". In general terms it can be said that 'research' is the aim and the scientific method is the means of attaining it. Research in whatever science it is carried on, follows the same scientific method. As *C.R. Kothari*[1] pointed out ".... *the philosophy common to all research methods and techniques, although they may vary considerably from one science to another, is usually given the name of scientific method.*"

The basic purpose of science is to establish the systematic relationship between facts. Hence all the sciences are bound to follow the "*scientific method*" which is dedicated to provide us the truth or ultimate reality. *Karl Pearson* has rightly said

---

[1] C.R. Kothari in *Research Methodology—Methods and Techniques*, 1993, p. 11.

that "*the scientific method is one and the same in the branches of (science) and that method is the method of all logically trained minds... the unity of all sciences consists alone in its methods, not its material, the man who classifies the facts of any kind whatever, who sees their mutual relation and describes these sequences, is applying the scientific method and is a man of science.*"[2]

Meaning of Social Research

Not only in the field of physical science but also in the realm of social sciences researches are taking place. The youngest of the social sciences that is sociology is also doing a lot of research work. "Sociological research is highly interesting and exciting. Research in sociology is really a kind of systematic detective work. It faces innumerable puzzles and suspicions, withstands disappointments and discouragements, challenges blind faith and hearsays and finally becomes successful in unraveling the mystery that clouds the truth."

Research today has become a part of sociology. Research in sociology is where the real action takes place. In fact, there are two sides to the sociological enterprise: *theory* and *research*. Both are essential, and each depends on the other and each hinges on the other. Facts without theory are utterly meaningless. Theories without facts are unproved speculations of little use to anybody, because there is no way to tell whether they are correct. Theory and research thus go together. A theory inspires research that can be used to verify or disprove it, and the findings of research are used to confirm, reject or modify the theory, or even to provide the basis of new theories. This process recurs endlessly.

Definition of Social Research

1. According to *Pauline V. Young, "... social research is a systematic method of exploring, analysing and conceptualising social life in order to "extend, correct, or verify knowledge, whether that knowledge aids in the construction of a theory or in the practice of an art."*
2. Stating it still differently, *social research seeks to find explanations to unexplained social phenomena to clarify the doubtful and correct the misconceived fact of social life.*
3. *Pauline V. Young has also said that "social research may be defined as a scientific undertaking which, by means of logical and systematised techniques aims to (1) discover new facts or verify and test old facts. (2) analyse their sequences, interrelationships, and causal explanations ... (3) develop new scientific tools, concepts and theories which would facilitate reliable and valid study of human behaviour".*
4. According to Wallace and Wallace, "*Sociological research refers to the structural observation of social behaviour*".

Importance of Social Research

Research is carried on in the social field not just with academic interests. It has both academic and non-academic purposes and importance. Importance of research can be briefly stated here.

1. Research is essential to diffuse knowledge and to expand its horizon.
2. Research helps us to verify or disprove, confirm or reject, modify and re-assert the existing theories and to establish new ones.
3. Research provides practical clues, to undertake measures that leads to social improvement, social change and social progress.
4. Research by probing into the perplexing problems of the day... provides new insight regarding their nature. Research helps us to know the nature and the magnitude of the problems.
5. Researches have commercial importance also. Industries, business firms and commercial establishments can get lot of information and clues about their endeavours in society.
6. Research can provide all the required data and facts to the administrators to adopt and undertake appropriate policies, plans and programmes.
7. Research has educational importance. It is mainly an intellectual activity. Information obtained through research may have their educational importance.
8. Research motivates interdisciplinary studies. It stresses the interdependence of different sciences. It thus strengthens the "*interdisciplinary approach*" which is emerging out these days.
9. Other uses and Importance

   (*i*) Those working in the academic field can obtain a new degree known as Ph.D. [Doctor of Philosophy] by successfully carrying out research as per the stipulated rules.

[2] Karl Pearson as quoted by C.R. Kothari, p. 11.

(ii) Those working in the research department attached to industries, other types of establishments have made research their profession and obtain salary for their service. It provides job opportunities for a few intellectuals.

(iii) For the philosophers and scientists research can be intellectually delighting and mentally satisfying, and

(iv) Those who are in the field of literature, art, architecture, etc., can seek to establish new styles and trends through research.

DIFFICULTIES OR PROBLEMS INVOLVED IN SOCIOLOGICAL RESEARCH

Unlike in the physical sciences, conducting research in the field of sociology is problematic. The sociologist's subject-matter presents some difficult research problems of a kind that natural scientists rearely have to deal with. Sociologists are dealing with human beings and not inanimate objects or unreflecting animals. They are people who have self-awareness and complex individual personalities. They are capable of choosing their own course of action for both rational and irrational reasons. The fact that the sociologist is studying human beings poses some major problems to research methodology.

1. ***The mere act of investigating social behaviour may alter the very behaviour that is being observed:*** When people come to know that they are being closely watched and observed they may not behave in their usual way. The presence, personality and actions of the observer can disrupt the behaviour that is being investigated.
2. ***People — unlike flies or worms, mountains or aeroplanes — have emotions, motives, and other highly individual personality characteristics:*** They may give false information deliberately or unintentionally or by ignorance. They may fail to understand a question put to them or they may misinterpret it. They may cancel certain facts for reasons of their own. They may also behave in unpredictable ways for a variety of peculiar reasons of their own. It is for this reason sociological explanations and predictions are often less precise than those of the physical sciences.
3. ***The origins of social behaviour are almost always extremely complex, involving many social, psychological, historical and other foctors:*** Establishing the cause-and-effect relationship is highly problematic here. It is relatively easy to establish why water boils and how fire burns and bomb explodes. It is much more difficult to establish why people fall in love, why do they kill, why do they lie, etc. The causes of social behaviour are usually innumerable and intricate.
4. ***For ethical reasons it becomes difficult to perform certain kinds of experiments on human beings:*** These moral questions do not disturb the physical scientists who are experimenting with water, gas, rays, minerals, etc. In the human world, the dignity and privacy of human beings must be respected. We can not deliberately make the young boys to stay with young girls separately for a couple of days or weeks just to test or assess the intensity of sex-morals, which have already been taught to them. Similarly, we can not make husbands to divorce their wives to study the impact of divorce on children. Ethical considerations place severe limitations on the methods the sociologists can use.
5. ***The sociologists, unlike the physical scientist, is part of the very subject he or she is studying:*** It is therefore very difficult for a sociologist to maintain objectivity or detached attitude towards his own study. An astronomer may look at and observe the heavenly bodies without being disturbed emotionally. On the contrary, the sociologist who is studying issues such as communal riots, race relations, ethnic conflicts, etc. can become passionately involved in the outcome of the research. The researcher may identify strongly with the problems and experiences of the subjects. As a result, the process of investigation and interpretation get distorted.

Sociologists are aware of these problems involved in their research work. In spite of these problems they aim to make sociology as exact and precise a science as possible. Most of the sociologists probably accept the viewpoint expressed by *Max Weber* many decades ago. "*Weber believed that sociology must model itself as far as possible on the natural sciences, but its subject-matter, being so different, sometimes also calls for an interpretative, subjective approach.*"[3]

As Ian Robertson has pointed out "subjective interpretation — which Weber called 'Verstehen'. or sympathetic understanding—is in no sense a substitute for the scientific method. Wherever possible, the conclusions drawn from subjective interpretation must be verified by the scientific method".

METHODS AND TECHNIQUES OF SOCIAL RESEARCH

Social research is systematic and scientific. It is not just guesswork and imaginative work. Guesswork, intuition, and common sense all have an important part to play in sociological research, but they cannot produce reliable evidence on their own. Reliable evidence can be produced only by using a research methodology.

[3] In Robertson in his *Sociology*, p. 34.

"*A methodology is a system of rules, principles and procedures, that guides scientific investigation*".[4]

The sociologist is interested in what happens in social world and why it happens. Research methodology provides guidelines for collecting evidence about what takes place and for explaining why it takes place. These findings can be checked and verified by other researchers.

The heart of the research process constitutes the actual procedures that sociologists use to collect their facts. Sociologists use a variety of research methods, systematic techniques for gathering and analysing facts about theories or new phenomena. The following section gives us an overview and examples of the four most common research methods used in sociology today: (*i*) *Observation*, (*ii*) *Questionnaire*, (*iii*) *Interview*, and (*iv*) *The Social Survey Method*. Each of these has its advantages and its drawbacks, and the success of the research project depends largely on the researcher's choice of an appropriate method.

OBSERVATION

Observation is one of the principal techniques of research in social sciences. Some of the difficulties arising out of the use of interviewing in sociological data-collection can be overcome by combining observation with interviewing, or perhaps by using observation alone. In fact, observation is essential for any scientific study or research. Science begins with observation and must ultimately return to observation for its final validation. Observation may take many forms and is at once the most primitive and the most modern of research techniques. It includes the most casual uncontrolled experiences as well as the most exact firm records of laboratory experimentation. There are many observational techniques and each has its own uses.

Definition of Observation

1. ***P.G. Gisbert***: "*Observation consists in the application of our mind and its cognitive powers to the phenomena which we are studying*".
2. ***Ian robertson***: "*Observational studies usually involve an intensive examination of a particular group, event, or social process. The researcher does not attempt to influence what happens in any way but aims instead at an accurate description and analysis of what takes place.*"
3. ***Wallace and wallace***: "*In an observational study the researcher actually witnesses social behaviour in its natural setting*".
4. In general, we can say that *observation is a systematic, direct, definite and deliberate ex- amination of the spontaneous occurrences at the time of their occurrence.*

Hypothesis and Observation

The basis for selecting a particular aspect for study is guided by the nature, scope and objectives of the inquiry. Generally, the formulated hypothesis is the guiding element in the immediate observation. *For example*, we are interested in the problem of juvenile delinquency and have tentatively formulated a hypothesis that juvenile delinquency is caused by broken homes and careless child rearing. Then, to test this, we concentrate our attention on broken homes and observe it as a cause of juvenile delinquency. If our observation demands the rejection of that hypothesis, then a new hypothesis is found in its place.

Observation and Experiment

Observation and experiment as representing two techniques of scientific research are being used in all the sciences. Both the techniques intend to trace the cause-and-effect relationships in the phenomena at study. But the procedures of using these techniques vary according to the material being studied.

"Observational studies are like experiments in all respects except one. *In an experiment the scientist arranges for something to happen in order to observe what follows, whereas in an observational study the scientist observes something which happens, or has already happened.* Both rely upon systematic observation under controlled conditions in a search for verifiable sequences and relationships".

— *Horton and Hunt*

Like the experiment, the observational study can be conducted in the laboratory or in the field. *In a laboratory observation*, for example, the sociologist might bring a group of subjects together and present them with a problem in order to observe the processes by which leaders emerge and decisions are made. The researcher may make use of instruments such as tape-recorder, camera etc., to record the interaction and to watch. *In the field observation*, sociologist studies something that is happening or has happened without attempting to structure the conditions of observation. Most observational studies take place in the field only.

---

[4] *Ibid*., p. 29.

Types of Observation

Observation may be of three broad types:

1. Non-Controlled Participant Observation
2. Non-Controlled Non-participant Observation
3. Systematic Controlled Observation

1. Non-Controlled Participant Observation

This procedure or type is made use of when the observer can so disguise himself as to be accepted as a member of the group under study. The degree of participation of the observer depends largely upon the nature of the study and the practical demands of the situation. The observer must identify himself closely with the group studied, since the subject matter is quite new and requires intensive study.

The sociologist need not carry out exactly the same activities as others in order to be a participant observer. He may find a role in the group *which will not disturb the usual patterns of behaviour*. This participant observation may vary from complete membership in the group to a part-time membership in the group.

It can be taken for granted that if the members are unaware of the scientist's purpose, their behaviour is least likely to be affected. Thus, we may be able to record the natural behaviour of the group. The observer has access to a body of information, which could not easily be obtained by merely looking on in a disinterested fashion.

Some examples of participant observational studies:

(*a*) **William Whyte** (1943) took the role of a participant observer in an Italian slum neighbourhood of an American city, that is, Boston. Whyte learnt Italian language and participated in all the activities of the gang such as—gambling, drinking alcohol, bowling, etc. The gang knew Whyte as some one who was writing a book. Sociologists had previously presumed that such a slum community would not be highly organised. Whyte showed that it was, although not in tune with the middle-class values.

(*b*) **Erving Goffman** (1961), an American social psychologist spent many months as an observer in mental hospital. His description gives us an idea as to how the organisation of an asylum systematically depersonalises the patients and may even aggravate their problems.

(*c*) **Leo Festinger** (1966) and his associates wanted to study a very exclusive cult whose members believed that the end of the world was to come on a certain specified day. Festinger with his associates took part in its meetings by pretending to be believers.

Challenges of participant observation:

Participant observation has its own challenges. Participant observation brings on the sociologist heavy obligations:

(*i*) The identities of the informants must be protected

(*ii*) Systematic notes must be kept each day and memory must be maintained afresh

(*iii*) The observer must be careful not to influence the behaviour that he or she is observing

(*iv*) Gaining access to the group and winning the confidence of its members is highly challenging

(*v*) This method relies heavily on the skills and subjective interpretations of the observer. Hence the observer must have sufficient competence and experience.

Limitations and disadvantages of participant observation:

Participant observation has its own limitations.

(*i*) The observing *researcher has no control over what happens and may have difficulty in putting the observations into systematic form in order to draw conclusions*.

(*ii*) The number of subjects or people the researcher can observe is small. There are often *service problems in gaining entry into a natural setting*. Many potential subjects, for example, the very wealthy and the very deviant, do not want to be subjects for the benefit of social science research.

(*iii*) The *participant observer may become so emotionally involved as to lose objectivity*. Instead of keeping himself as a neutral observer he may become a dedicated partisan. Or the participant observer may over generalise—that is, assume that what is found in the group studied is also true of all other groups. For example, in the first example cited previously, *William Whyte* in his study of the Italian slum neighbourhood had eventually become so absorbed with his life as a gang member that he stopped his observation as an impassionate researcher. But Whyte was aware of what was happening in him. He commented: "*I began as a non-ost a non-observing participator*". [*Ref.* quoted by *Peter Worsely* in his "*Introducing Sociology*" Page 95].

(iv) In participant observation *one may have to sacrifice scientific precision to some extent*. The observer may misinterpret events, may unwillingly ignore some important things that are very much relevant. He may focus on unimportant things and may become emotionally involved with the lives of the subjects.

(v) Another disadvantage is that the findings of *single observational study cannot be generalised to all apparently similar cases*. The phenomenon that has been studied may have been an exceptional one. Hence its findings cannot be uncritically applied to parallel situations.

(vi) To become a participant observer *one must at least share sufficient cultural background with the actors involved* in the phenomenon under study. Only then he is able to construe their behaviour meaningfully. It would be pointless, for example, for him to attempt to study the behaviour of some quite unknown people merely by observation.

(vii) As it is in the case of the interviewer, *the observer's role is conditioned by his age, sex and possibly by his caste, ethnic or racial status*. A man will find much of the behaviour of women beyond his observation and vice versa. Similarly, a young researcher may find it virtually impossible to associate with the old in order to see what they do and what they talk about and vice versa.

(viii) As *Horton* and *Hunt* have pointed out this method of observation gives rise to *some ethical questions also. "It is ethical to pretend to be a loyal member of a group in order to study it? Is such a deception justifiable*?" Is he sure, that his role as an observer does not harm the interest of the members of the group under study? The best answer though it is difficult to practice is that a reputable scientist will be careful not to injure the people being studied.

(ix) The eyewitness account of the participant observer has definitely its own limitations. *Many of the happenings and events are beyond its purview*. How do people behave after a disaster, say, an earthquake, or a bomb explosion? What happens at a religious revival, riot, a famine? Rarely we find a visiting sociologist with a pen in hand really to record the event.

Relative merits of participant observation:

Participant Observation has certain advantages or merits also. Some of them may be pointed out here.

(i) Since the observer is not a stranger but a known person, *it is possible to observe the natural behaviour of the group*;

(ii) This type *facilitaties gathering quantitatively more and qualitatively better information* about the people or events;

(iii) It is also possible *to get better insights into the inner dynamics of the phenomena* since the observer happens to be an insider;

(iv) Even the so called *secret behaviour* (relating to sex, crime, business tactics, etc.,) *can be observed* through this method;

(v) The *dependability of the data collected through this method is believed to be greater* because it is gathered first-hand.

(ii) Non-Controlled Non-Participant Observation

The non-participant observation is difficult to conduct. We have no standard set of relationship or role patterns for the non-member who is always present but never participating. Both the group and the outsider are likely to feel uncomfortable. In many research situations, an outsider cannot become a genuine participant. The sociologist, for example, cannot become a criminal in order to study a criminal gang. Neither can he become a true member of the criminal gang.

On the other hand, it is possible for the observer to take part in many activities of the group so as to avoid the awkwardness of complete non-participation. This has been a classic pattern in social research. It was used by *Leplay* a century ago in his study of European working families. In such studies, the investigators have lived as members of the family as participants in community activities taking part in games and dances or even in study groups. They nevertheless made clear that their purpose was to gather facts.

Non-participant observation is usually "*quasi-participant*" observation. What is necessary here is a good plan for entering the group. If the observer is good at observation, then, he can establish good contact with the group members. Here, the observer is a stranger and hence is less involved emotionally with the social situation. True members of the group may thus feel relatively free to talk over even delicate matters which they would not discuss with their own inmates. The observer is also a good listener and is like a pupil eager to learn.

Merits of non-participant observation

(i) This type *contributes to a higher degree of objectivity* on the part of the observer. There is no need for him to become emotionally involved in the event.

(ii) Since the observer observes the events with an "open mind" he is able to collect more information.

(iii) The people who are being observed can also be *more free* with the observer for he is an outsider.

Demerits of non-participant observation:

(*i*) Observation in this category is *mostly limited to formal occasions and Organisations*. It fails to provide information regarding many aspects of our social life.

(*ii*) Since the observer is an outsider *he may fail to understand the behaviour of the observed* in its entirity. The observer may not get insights into different aspects of behaviour.

3. Systematic Controlled Observation

Here the observer tries to systematise the process of observation and does not try to limit the activities of the observed individuals. This is most useful in exploratory studies. The observer makes use of the carefully drawn schedules and questionnaires and better techniques of observation. He tries to check his own biases, his selective perception, and the vagueness of his senses. He makes use of standardised instruments like camera, tape-records, maps, sociometric scales etc. to record his observation with more precision.

The sociologist in this controlled observation is often in the position of a zoologist or a psychologist or an astronomer attempting to study the lives of animals or objects in their natural habitat. Hence it is difficult to control the object under investigation. Instead of that the observer must at least put controls on himself. By this he increases precision and at the same time he protects his work from later attacks.

Controlled observation may also be directed towards situations which are natural, but in which the subjects are aware that they are being observed. Systematic observation limits the bias of the individual observer partly by making the subjects feel the situation as natural and partly by the application of controls on the observer in the form of mechanical devices like films, photographs, recordings etc. Here, the controls are applied to both the observer and the observed.

Merits of Observation

(*i*) Observation, whether of participant or non-participant type, has, it is to be acknowledged, its own advantages. As *Robertson* has pointed out "Observational studies have the advantage that *they come to grips with real-life situations* and so offer insights that years of experimenting and surveying might overlook".

(*ii*) "The great advantage of the observational study is that the research is accomplished *by directly observing subject's behaviour*, as opposed to a survey or an analysis of existing sources in which the researcher must rely of others' observations and reports. Observational techniques are also greatly superior to either the survey or the document study in providing information about non—verbal behaviour" — (*Ref.:* **Wallace** and **Wallace** in their "*Sociology*" Page - 30).

(*iii*) Observational techniques allow the researcher "*to observe the subject in a natural setting*, and they provide for the study of the subject *over a time rather than at one point, as a survey usually does*".

(*iv*) Though there is the danger of an observer getting himself absorbed with the group under study, it has a peculiar strength of its own. As *Peter Worsley* points out, "*the peculir strength of participant observation demands not complete detachment, but the involvement of the research worker in the lives of the people he is studying... This gives him a deeper insight into the behaviour of the people he is studying*".

Limitations of Observation

(*i*) One of the limitations of observation is that the *data collected through observation cannot always be quantified.*

(*ii*) Observation is essentially the study of occurrences at the time they occur. Hence it is very much *limited by the duration of the event.* Events do not wait for the conveniences of the observer.

(*iii*) Observation *cannot always be effectively used to study the private and secret behaviour of the individuals. For example*, observing the criminal behaviour of a so called "decent person", is not an easy task.

(*iv*) There is no guarantee that the observer studies the phenomenon in an impartial manner and without prejudice. Hence, *there is scope for the danger of bias, especially hidden bias.*

Conclusion

Observation is one of the effective methods of collecting reliable information about the social behaviour of man though it has its own limitations. In this method the role of the observer is very significant. The effectiveness of the method depends to a great exent on the efficiency of the observer.

The observer is a mediator between the actual situation and the data. The researcher must keep in mind the *role of the observer* while making observations. All scientific study depends ultimately upon the observer, especially, in our field. The observer, however, is always a variable to be taken into account. In case of sociology, much information must be gathered before a genuine experiment can be designed and both participant and non-participant observation types are used for this purpose. We cannot do away with the influence of the observer, hut we can limit it to a great extent.

QUESTIONNAIRE

Questionnaires and schedules are very much used in gathering a variety of data. They have been used for the collection of personal preferences, social beliefs, attitudes, opinions, behaviour patterns, group practices, habits and other kinds of data. The increasing use of schedules and questionnaires is probably due to increased emphasis by social scientists on quantitative measurement of uniformly accumulated data.

A questionnaire is a tool for data collection. It consists of a number of questions printed or typed in a definite order on a form or a set of forms. It is administered to a respondent either personally or through mail. The respondent answers the questions on his own without being aided.

Questionnaires are now widely used collecting data, particularly when data are to be collected from a large number of people who are scattered over a wide area. They are used both as independent and separate method of collecting data. They are also used as an additional device to check data gathered through observation and personal interview.

Definition of Questionnaire

1. "*A questionnaire is a means of gathering information by having the respondents fill in answers to printed questions*" — **Wallace and Wallace**
2. "*Fundamentally, the questionnaire is a set of stimuli to which literate people are exposed in order to observe their verbal behaviour under these stimuli*" — **Lundberg**
3. **Good** and **Hate** define questionnaire as *a device for securing answers to questions using a form which the respondent fills in himself.*
4. Questionnaire studies are systematic ways of asking questions under scientific controls. *A questionaire is a device in which the respondents fill in their responses in specified manner personally.*

Questionnaire, Schedule and Interview Guide

The questionnaire is designed to collect data from large, diverse and widely scattered groups of people. The questionnaire is generally sent through the mail to the informants to be answered as specified in a covering letter and without further assistance from the sender. The schedule, on the other hand, is generally filled out by the researcher who can interpret questions when necessary.

Questionnaire. The word "*Questionnaire*" refers to a device for securing anwers to questions by using a form which the respondent fills in himself.

Schedule or Interview Schedule. "*Schedule*" or "*interview schedule*" is the name usually applied to a set of questions which are asked and filled in by an interviewer in a face-to-face situation with another person. In its *form and content, a schedule is similar to the questionnaire*. Like the questionnaire, it can be structured and unstructured. As in questionnaire, here also the wording of the questions is the same for all the respondents.

The main difference between the questionnaire and schedule is that— the *questionnaire* is filled in by the respondent on his own, whereas the *schedule* is filled in by the interviewer.

Interview Guide. An '*interview guide*' on the other hand, is a list of points or topics which the interviewer must cover during the interview. In this case, flexibility may be allowed as to the manner, order and language in which the interviewer asks the questions. The interview guides are also referred to "*unstructured questionnaires.*" The interview guide permits the interviewer to ask a fresh question in order to make the previous answer more meaningful.

Ways of Obtaining Response through the Questionnaire Method

There are two ways through which the responses of the informants could be collected. Responses of the informants could be collected through questionnaire method (*i*) *by mailing the questionnaires to the selected people under study*, or (*ii*) *by asking the questions to them directly in an interview*. Mailed questionnaires have some advantage over interviews, including *saving money and time, convenience to the respondents who can reply at will*. There is greater assurance for them that *the respondents will remain anonymous*; and that *questions will not be put in various tricky ways*; and that the respondents are *not biased by the interviewer*. Further there is greater chance for the respondents to *find time to consult other sources before responding*. There is greater ease of access to the people who are widely separated geographically. (*Ref*.: **Bailey** 1978, as stated by **Wallace** and **Wallace**).

Types of Questionnaire

Questionnaires can be classified into two broad types:

1. Structured Questionnaires, and
2. Unstructured Questionnaires.

1. Structured Questionnaires

Structured questionnaires are those which pose definite, concrete and prepared questions. It means the questions are prepared in advance and not constructed on the spot during the questioning period. Additional questions may be used only when need arises to clarify vague or inadequate replies by informants. This structured questionnaire may be of two broad types:

(*a*) Closed-Form or Poll Type or Selective Type Questionnaire, and

(*b*) Open-End or Inventive Type Questionnaire.

(*a*) ***Closed-form questionnaire:*** In closed-form questionnaire, a number of alternative answers are provided at the end of each question and the task is, the informant has to choose one of them. This is also called "*Poll-Type*" or "*Selective-Type*" of questionnaire for the informant has to select one among the answers supplied by the investigator himself. His choice of giving his own answer is not permitted and hence it is a "*closed-type*". "*Example*: *Where do you wish to live in?* (*i*) *City,* (*ii*) *Suburb*, (*iii*) *Village*?

(*b*) ***Open-end type or inventive type:*** In this type, questions are not followed by any readymade answers. The informant has to think of the answer himself and he is free to answer as he likes. The open-end responses are free and spontaneous expressions on the part of the informant who is not limited in his replies to a particular question posed to him. This is also called "*inventive type*" for the respondent has to think of or invent the answer for himself. The respondent may be asked to write a descriptive essay and express his viewpoints, describe his relationships, attitudes, indicate his problems, and report on details and events without restrictions imposed as in the type of closed questions.

Structured questionnaires are used in a wide range of projects which may pertain to studies of economic or social problems, measurement of public opinion on public issues or events, studies of administrative policies, studies on cost of living, consumer expenditures, child welfare, public health and numerous other issues.

In the "*closed-form*" questions, the responses may be easily tabulated and statistical measures can be easily applied, because, the number of possible answers to each question is fixed. Its disadvantage is that it may often suggest answers that may not be there in the mind of the informant. This may defeat the very purpose of the study. Another defect is, the informant has to confine his answers to the points given in the questionnaire itself. He cannot go out of it and express his true opinion on a particular issue.

The merit of the "*open-end*" type is that it gives wide chance to the informant to give his own answer to the questions. He is not bound by rules and can be free. Its demerit is that it poses some problems of classification and analysis. But this open-end question has been employed successfully where the primary information to be collected is qualitative in nature.

2. Unstructured Questionnaires

Unstructured questionnaires, frequently referred to as "*interview guides*", also aim at precision and contain definite subject-matter areas. *Flexibility is its main advantage*. It is designed to obtain view—points, opinions, attitudes, and to show relationships and interconnections between data which might escape notice under more mechanical types of interrogation. The object is to give the respondent maximum opportunity to reveal how he had arrived at or developed his world of experience. Free responses of the respondents are solicited and no limitations are imposed and no predetermined responses are provided.

This form of questionnaire is used for intensive studies, but generally for a limited number of selected cases. It has been applied to studies of family group cohesiveness, to studies of personal experiences, beliefs and attitudes. The chief *disadvantage* of unstructured questionnaires stems from the danger that *non-additive and non-comparable data will be accumulated when no structuring is imposed.*

Formation or Construction of a Questionnaire

The effectiveness of questionnaire as a tool of obtaining information also depends on the construction or formation of a questionnaire. It is not an easy task to prepare a good questionnaire. Hence attention must be paid to the following aspects in preparing a questionnaire.

1. ***Physical format:*** The physical format of a good questionnaire must be such that it must evoke spontaneous interest from respondents.

2. ***Question content:*** Questions must be specific and unambiguous rand seek responses on a definite topic.
3. ***Question wording:*** The wording of the questions and the language used must be simple, direct and unambiguous. Questions and key words carrying dual meaning must be avoided.
4. ***Question sequence:*** Questions in a questionnaire must be ordered in a definite sequence. In addition to these, the following suggestions may also be considered in preparing and using the questionnaire.

Main points to be Noted in Preparing and Using the Questionnaire

1. Any questionnaire must be limited in its length and scope. In interviews especially the questionnaire should not require more than 30 minutes to be completed.
2. When the questioner and the interviewee possess a more detailed experience with the subject of the inquiry, many questions become unnecessary and can be avoided.
3. The questioner should try to know as much as possible about his subject-matter before he begins to formulate questions.
4. Sufficient care should be taken to include all the important questions on the subject. Each and every item of the questionnaire must be relevant and related with central problem.
5. There must be logical connection between the questions and they can be thought of as moving from the inside to outward.
6. Care must be taken to avoid ambiguous, too personal and embarrassing questions.
7. Care must be taken to ask questions which include all the possible alternatives on a particular issue at study.
8. Wordings of the questionnaire should be simple, and unambiguous.
9. Likert's Scale [or Five Point Scale] can be made use of when "*yes*" or "*no*" answer cannot be given to a question. This includes five points or responses to a question among which one can be accepted by the respondent:

   (*i*) I strongly approve. (*ii*) I approve.

   (*iii*) I am undecided. (*iv*) I disapprove.

   (*v*) I strongly disapprove.
10. Further, there must be a unity in the construction of a questionnaire or schedule. The questions should be so designed to awaken the interest of the respondent and must proceed from simplicity to complexity. Embarrassing questions should be avoided and the personal information should not be sought. The questions should proceed from one frame of reference to another instead of jumping back and forth.

Advantages of Questionnaire

1. Questionnaire is relatively *economical* and *inexpensive*. It is possible to cover a large number of people scattered over a wide area.
2. This method *saves time*. Instead of meeting people personally it is possible to approach them in a larger number through the mailed questionnaire. Analysis and interpretation can be done quickly.
3. Questionnaire *ensures anonymity*. The respondent is free to express his views and opinions.
4. Questionnaire is said to be more *suitable for eliciting information regarding some personal and private affairs* such as sex habits, marital relations, etc., because of the anonymity that it maintains.
5. Questionnaire *does not put much pressure on the respondent's emotionality*. It provides sufficient leisure time to answer the questions in a relaxed mood.
6. In questionnaire, the *collected answers can be processed and analysed in a simpler and a faster manner*. Uniformity of answers helps the standardisation of the recording procedure.

Disadvantages and Limitations of Questionnaire

1. Questionnaire method *cannot be administered in the case of illiterate and uneducated persons*.
2. Questionnaire is *not suitable when a spontaneous answer is very much required.*
3. There is *no way of checking misinterpretations* and unintelligible replies by the respondents.
4. *Proportion of returns, especially of mailed questionnaire*, can be very low, as low as 10%. This does not give a comprehensive picture of the situation.

5. In spite of their advantage *questionnaires lack the flexibility of interviews*. Generally, they have lower response rates, since it is easier for the respondents not to respond. They permit the measurement of verbal behaviour only, without allowing the researcher to make observations. Furthermore, *mailed questionnaires enable the respondent to skip questions*.

INTERVIEW

Interview is one of the important methods of collecting data in social research. Literally, interview means mutual view of each other. *It is called a conversation with a purpose*. But it is not a simple conversation or verbal exchange. Its objective is to exchange ideas, elicit information regarding a wide area in which the interviewee may *wish to recollect the past, interpret the present and advocate his future course of action or plan*.

An interview is a means of gathering information in which one person asks another either in person directly, or indirectly. Interview, is an effective, informal verbal or non-verbal conversation, initiated for specific purposes and focused on certain planned content areas.

Definition of Interview

1. According to **Young**, as the very term implies, "*interviewing is an interactional process*".
2. According to **Gopal**, "*The interview is conversation with a purpose and, therefore, is more than a mere oral exchange of information.*"
3. In general, it can be said that *an interview is face-to-face verbal interchange in which one person, i.e., the interviewer, attempts to elicit some information or expressions of opinion from another person or persons regarding a particular issue*.

Interview is Not Just Conversation

"Interviewing is not a simple two-way conversation between an interrogator and informant. Gestures, glances, facial expressions, pauses often reveal subtle feelings. Voice, inflictions and halting statement can be as much a part of the interplay between the conversing persons and their questions and answers." Much can be understood by means of verbal expressions and also from the use of sounds. Furthermore, not only reaction to a statement but also attitudes can be learned from a blush, nervous laugh, sudden palor or undue embarrassment. This behaviour is in itself important data for the interviewer.

The interaction that takes place in an interview is highly complex. A minute change of facial expression, a slight tensing of a muscle, the flick of an eye, a trace of a change in emphasis, a slight change in one's rate of speaking, one's choice of words, and other involuntary reactions that may not involve spoken words can be comprehended by a shrewd interviewer. Every interview has its own balance of revelation and of withholding of information.

Major Objectives of Interview

The objective of an interviewer in any interview is to know the mind, opinion, attitudes and feelings of an interviewee with regard to a particular object or situation. The objectives of the interview may be *exchange of ideas and experiences, eliciting of information pertaining to a wide range of data in which the interviewee may wish to rehearse his past, define his present and canvass his future possibilities*. The task of the interviewer is to penetrate the outer and inner life of persons and groups.

As *T. W. Adorn* points out, it is the task of an interviewer "to ascertain opinions, attitudes, values that (are) on the surface... ideological trends that (are) more or less, inhibited and reach the surface only in indirect manifestations; and explore personality forces in the subject's unconsciousness."

Process of Interview

A systematic interview may consist of the following stages:

1. At the beginning of the interview, *the interviewer has to introduce himself to the interviewee* in a very polite manner to win over his confidence.
2. The very *nature and purpose of the interview must be made known ta the interviewee* so as to dispel the undesirable anxiety and tension.
3. The *interviewer may ask some serious questions in the beginning* and later on talk freely with the interviewee.
4. The *interviewer may also assist the interviewee* in eliciting information from him and must prompt here and there depending upon the need.

5. *Questions must be put in a systematic manner* and in a lucid language.
6. The interviewer *must encourage the interviewee to talk freely* and can jot down points during brief pauses.
7. The interview *must not be closed suddenly* and abruptly.
8. The interviewer *must be very careful in working the report.* He must also make observations about the feelings, emotions, facial expressions, and gestures of the interviewee and must give due weightage for them.

Types of Interview

There are different classifications of interview on the basis of different criteria. Interviews may be classified in various ways - *according to their function* (diagnostic, treatment, research, sample interviews), or *according to the number of persons participating* (group or individual interviews) or *length of contact* (short or long contact) or *type of approach* (directive or non-directive, structured or unstructured). Types of interviews are based chiefly on the respective roles assumed in them by interviewer and interviewee. The following types of interviews may be noted:

1. The Non-Directive Interview
2. The Directive Interview
3. The Focused Interview
4. The Repeated Interview
5. The Depth Interview

1. The Non-Directive Interview or Unstructured Interview

This type of interview is also known as *uncontrolled* or *unguided or unstructured interview*. In this kind of interview, interviewer does not follow a system or list of predetermined questions. Interviewees are encouraged to relate their concrete experiences with no or little direction from interviewer, to provide their own definitions of their social situations, report their own foci of attention, reveal their attitudes and opinions as they see fit.

The unstructured interview is much more flexible and "open-ended". The researcher puts more general questions to the respondents, allows them to answer freely, and follows up on their comments. This approach allows the researcher to get insights that a structural interview may ignore.

Limitations: The unstructured interview has its own limitations. During a free-flowing interview, the non-directive interviewer at times is *at a loss to know how actively he should participate during the course of the discussion*. As long as pertinent facts are being related and the informant shows no signs of lack of interest, the interviewer need only round out discussion by raising additional questions, if need be.

The unstructured interview approach has its other disadvantages. The answers are often extremely difficult to compare. If people are asked, for example, "*Do you intend to vote at the next parliamentary elections*?", they will give such answers as - "*May be*" "*I might, if I feel like it*", "*Depends on who contests*", "*I suppose so*", "*I have not decided yet*", and so on.

The researcher also *has to be on guard against influencing the respondents' answers by such subtle signals as choice of words, tone of voice, and facial expressions*. He has to put questions in *straight forward and unemotional language* which must be phrased in such a manner that all respondents will understand them in the same way. The question "*Are you religious*"?- for example, is absurd, in the sense, it will be interpreted in different ways by different people. It is on the other hand, necessary to ask specific questions about - attending temples or churches, belief in rituals, God, and so on. Further, questions must be put in a very natural and neutral manner.

Unstructured interview essentially *demands the training of the interviewer*. A mere training in the social skill of keeping a conversation going on a topic which the respondent may not be very interested, is not sufficient. He must have the sensitivity to link the responses of his respondents to the theoretical topic that he is pursuing, wherever it is possible. This means unstructred inverviews can only be carried out by people trained in sociological theory.

An illustrative example of unstructured interview: *Elizabeth Bott's* (Bott-l957) study of twenty London families can be cited here as a good example of unstructured interviewing. Bott was interested in the way in which husbands and wives divided the domestic tasks between themselves, and wanted to relate this division of labour to the structure of friendships the couple had with others. A structured interview could hardly be successful on a topic as delicate as this. Even if Bott were to resort to observation method, she would have had to combine herself solely to those families with whom she was able to live, and not with all the twenty families. On the average, Bott conducted 13 interviews with each family and each such interview lasted for more than 80 minutes. The interviews tended to be a friendly exchange of information rather than a matter of question and answer. Needless to say, a seasoned interviewer such as Bott was a great success in her study of those families. [*Ref.:* "*Introducing Sociology*" by **Peter Worsley**, Page 90-91].

2. The Directive Interview or Structured Interview

This interview uses a highly standardised technique and a set of predetermined questions. It is especially useful for administrative and market research of various types.

In a structured interview the researcher has a checklist of questions and puts them to the respondents in exactly the same form and exactly the same order. The respondent is asked to choose between several predetermined answers such as "Yes/no/don't know", or "very likely/likely/unlikely/ very unlikely". This type of interview is very inflexible.

Merits and Limitation: The structured interview method has its own merits. Since the interviewer follows a predetermined set of procedure there will be less scope for interference by the interviewer himself. By asking the predetermined questions he can maintain his objectivity. This will force the interviewer to confine himself to the topic only rather than asking about some irrelevant questions.

The main merit of the structured interview is that it helps the researcher to make careful tabulations and comparisons of the answers. If other information about the respondents is included, such as income, geographic location, or age, all these variables can be fed into a computer, and correlations between them can be extracted within seconds. The object of using structured interviews is to standardise the interviewer's personal approach or biases may have upon the results. If proper training is given to the interviewer it would further ensure the reliability and validity of the results.

The limitation of this interview is that, we cannot use this type of interview in all situations. Further, the questions that are used here may fail to elicit the real opinions of the informant.

3. The Focused Interview

This is differentiated from other types of interviews by the following characteristics.

(*i*) It takes place with persons known to have been involved in particular concrete situation.(These persons have seen a particular film, heard a particular broadcast, or have participated in a particular ceremony.)

(*ii*) It refers to situations which have been analysed prior to the interview.

(*iii*) It proceeds on the basis of an interview guide which outlines the major areas of the inquiry and the hypotheses which locate pertinence of data to be secured in the interview.

(*iv*) It is focused on the subjective experiences-attitudes and emotional responses regarding the particular concrete situations under study.

In this type of interview the interviewee is given considerable freedom to express his definition of a situation that is presented to him. Therefore, *focused interview is considered as semi-standardised.*

The focused interview is based on the assumptions that through it, *it is possible to secure precise details of personal reactions, specific emotions, definite mental associations provoked by a certain stimulus and the like*. The focused interview is not being used as widely as its merits deserve probably because it requires extreme care in preparation and exceptionally sophisticated handling by skillful interviewers.

4. The Repeated Interview

This type of interview is *particularly useful in attempts to trace the specific developments of social or psychological process* (that is, the progressive actions, factors or attitudes which determine a given behaviour pattern or social situation).

Paul Lazarsfield and his associates made extensive use of this repeated interview technique in their study of how the voter makes up his mind in a presidential campaign. These interviews secured the progressive reactions of the voter and also helped to know about the influence of various factors entering into the choice of a president.

The repeated interview technique is expensive in time and energy and money but it offers the advantage of studying the progressive actions and events as they actually occur.

The data secured through focuses as well as repeated interviews lend themselves to quantitative interpretation. Because, they are consistent and specific and aim at realisation of details which can be differentiated, tabulated and ultimately measured.

5. The Depth Interview

This kind of *interview aims to elicit unconscious as well as other types of material relating especially to personality dynamics and motivations*. It is generally a lengthy procedure designed to encourage free expression of information charged with emotions. It may be used along with special devices such as free association and projective techniques. When used carefully by an interviewer having specialised training the depth interview can reveal important aspects of psycho-social relations which are otherwise not readily available. Unless the researcher has specialised training, it is better not to attempt depth interviewing.

Crucial Points in Interview

There are certain critical points which need special attention in interviewing:

1. The *appearances of the interviewer must not be too strange or remote.* He must dress and try to act in a similar way with that of the other people.
2. *He must establish a good rapport with the interviewees* and try to be friendly with them.
3. *He must not impose his own will on the interviewees* to get information since the interviewed has the right to deny giving answers.
4. Interviewer must, as far as possible, *avoid arguments, insults and ambiguous and confusing terms.* Double-barreled questions such as "*Do you think that mercy-killing and corporal punishment be legalised?*"- necessarily create confusions in the minds of the respondents. Because, people may have different opinions about two subjects.
5. Questions must not be asked immediately about the subject in which the interviewer is interested.
6. He *must take down the responses of the respondents without approval or disapproval.*
7. The interviewer *must have patience* to hear the interviewee.
8. If the interviewer wants to get the personal views of opinions of the interviewee, then *he must assure him that his expressed views will be kept in secret.*
9. The interviewer must understand that his object is to elicit the opinions of the interviewee and *not to exhibit his intelligence or shrewdness.*
10. The interviewer who conducts the interview will be benefited *if he himself goes through an interview with others who are good in interviewing.*

Advantages of Interview

1. Through interview *it is possible to secure relatively dependable information* about issues, peoples and events.
2. Interview *may help us to obtain in-depth knowledge* of social issues.
3. It is possible *to secure information about the past, present and also about future course* or plans in somewhat a detailed manner.
4. The *active and intelligent role of the interviewer can add to the high rate of response.*
5. The interview method can be used to obtain information from almost *all types of persons.*

Disadvantages and Limitations of Interview

1. Many disadvantages of this method *arise due to the incapability of the interviewer.*
2. *Prejudices or bias developed* knowingly or unknowingly by the interviewer *may completely mislead the outcome of interview.*
3. The interviewer *may fail to select a "right" person* (due to defective sampling procedure) to obtain information.
4. Possibilities of the interviewer and the interviewee having diving divergent, often antagonistic, views and outlook cannot be overlooked. This situation may *create confusion* in the course of the interview or it may spoil its outcome.
5. *Interviewing is a difficult skill* and it needs an intense and time-consuming training.
6. *Interview by itself is incomplete* and needs to be supplemented with other methods such as observation.
7. *There is no guarantee that the interviewee gives his honest opinions* on the issues referred to him. Hence his information may mislead the outcome of the interview.
8. One major danger with interview is that when people are asked to report on their own behaviour *they may tend merely to mention the formal rules of social behaviour, rather than recount exactly how they actually behave.* Bott found this in her study. She knew that one woman held strong views about the desirability of easy divorce. Yet in a meeting of women's association, the same woman spoke out against easy divorce. This she did, probably because she felt it necessary to stress the "*respectable*" norm of the sanctity of marriage even though her personal, or private opinions were just contrary to that. The same thing can happen in interviews also. Particularly in face-to-face interviews, respondents may give false information. People may deny their racist views or caste mindedness or communal bias, because, they know that these views are not "*respectable*".

SOCIAL SURVEYS

The social survey technique seems to be very popular in sociology. In fact, the man in the street particularly associates the social survey with sociologists. This he does, probably because, this he thinks to be the only available technique that sociologists have for collecting information. This is especially so in the Western context. The social survey is certainly a very important way of assembling data, but *it is by no means the only way.*

Meaning and Definition of Social Survey

1. **Duncan Mitchell's** "*Dictionary of Sociology*" defines social survey this way: "*The social survey is a systematic collection of facts about people living in a specific geographic, cultural, or administrative area*".
2. **Bogardus.** "*A social survey is the collection of data concerning the living and working conditions, broadly speaking, of the people, in a given community*".
3. **Ian Robertson.** "*Surveys are frequently used in sociological research, either simply for the purpose of gathering facts (such as the political opinions of college students,) or for finding out about the relationship between facts (such as how sex, parental opinions, or social class, influence students' political views)*".
4. **E.W. Burgess.** "*A social survey of a community is the scientific study of its conditions and needs for the purpose of presenting a constructive programme of social advance*".

Social surveys are usually for dealing with many related aspects of a social problem. *They provide the data for administration*, rather than for the illustrative or descriptive material. They are generally *quantitative* and the history of the social survey is intimately bound up with the develop- ment of statistics.

"The early ancestors of the social survey are—'the Doomsday Book,' '*Stow's Survey of London,*' 'Camden's Britannia,' the essays of 17th and 18th Century demographers, Arthur Young's reports to the Board of Agriculture, and the two Statistical Accounts of Scotland"—(Ref.: **Duncan Mitchell's** "*Dictionary of Sociology*").

The modern social survey is said to be the product of the intellectual response of the urban middle classes to the social condition of town life in the 19th Century. In the modern period, three kinds of social surveys are often differentiated: (*a*) *The Poverty Survey* (originating in the work of Booth, Rowntree and Bowley, (*b*) *The Ecological Survey* (developed by Ratzel, Redus, Le Play and the Geddes; and (*c*) *The Functional Study of the city* (stemmed out of the works of Sherwell, the Chicago School, the Lynds, Warner and Lunt and Others).

Procedural Ways of Social Survey

The social survey method has the *ultimate goal of seeking social facts*. It normally involves the following steps: *Enunciating the object or purpose of the survey; definition of the problem under study; the delimitation of the area or scope of study; examination of the available evidences or sources relating to the problem; preparation of questionnaire schedule; field work to collect data; arrangement, tabulation and satistical analysis of the data; interpretation of results; deduction and graphic expression.*

The social survey is concerned with the collection of data relating to some problems of great social importance with a view to find out an effective solution for it. The survey is normally limited to a fixed geographic area or confined to a defined population. The basic procedure is that people are asked a number of questions focused on that aspect of behaviour in which the sociologist is interested. The focal point could be — "*students' participation in politics*", or "*Opinions of highly educated scheduled caste and scheduled tribe people regarding reservation*", or "*Ayodya Problem*" or any such topic or issue of social interest.

The total group of people whose attitudes, opinions or behaviour , the sociologist is interested in, is called the "*population*". The people are carefully selected so that they become representative of the population being studied. They are asked to answer exactly the same questions, so that the replies of different categories of respondents, may be examined for differences. In some cases, it is possible to survey the entire population, but time and expense make their procedure impracticable unless the population is a small one and confined to limited area. In most cases it is necessary to survey a "*sample*", a small number of individuals drawn from the larger population. This type of survey is often called "*sample survey*". The sample must exactly represent the population in question. If it does not, then any conclusions are valid only for the actual people who were surveyed (that is, the respondents) and cannot be applied to the entire population from which the sample was drawn.

One of the major virtues of the survey is that a large number of respondents can be included in it. For the very same reason both the method of getting the questionnaires completed, and the formulation of the questions to be asked, must be very carefully worked out.

Survey can be Conducted in Various Ways

1. One type of survey lies on contacting the respondents by letter and asking them to complete the questionnaires themselves before returning it.
2. Another variation in the procedure is that, an assistant of the survey or delivers the questionnaires to the respondents, requests them to complete it, and makes an arrangement to pick them up later.

3. Sometimes questionnaires are not completed by individuals separately but by people in a group under the direct supervision of the research worker. *For example*, a class of students in a college or a group of women at a meeting of the "*Mahila Samaj*" and so on, may be asked to respond to the questionnaire together.
4. In some other surveys a trained interviewer asks the questions and records the responses on a schedule for each respondent. It should be noted, these alternative procedures have different strengths and weaknesses.

Social surveys, as it is clear from the above, may depend either on questionnaires which are self-administered, or on schedules which are completed by trained interviewers, or by the research worker personally. Social surveys involves same amount of home work or office work. *For example*, schedules must be prepared with sample identifications (example, the addresses of houses or firms). If a mail questionnaire is to be used, the envelopes have to be addressed, stamped and posted. If the enquiry is based on interviews, the interviewers will have to be very carefully briefed. When the schedules are completed and returned they are processed in such a manner that they could be provided for computer analysis.

Some Main Forms of Social Surveys

Depending upon the purpose and the nature of study, social surveys assume different forms, Some form of social surveys are as follows: (*i*) *Official, semi-official or private surveys*, (*ii*) *wide spread or limited surveys*; (*iii*) *census survey or sample surveys*, (*iv*) *general or specialised surveys*; (*v*) *postal or personal surveys*, (*vi*) *public or confidential surveys*; (*vii*) *initial or repetitive surveys*; (*viii*) *regional or adhoc surveys*, etc.

Controversies Relating to Social Surveys

Though social surveys provide very useful information about our social life, its intricacies and problems, there has been a good deal of controversy about (1) *The reliability and validity of results obtained from social surveys*. (2) Another objection is regarding *the extent to which individual characteristics may be assumed to relate to social properties*. (3) Yet another doubt is concerning the *validity of the replies to questions which are obtained in social surveys*.

Though these objections have an element of truth in them, sociologists are trying their level best to make social surveys free from these controversies. They use different means to collect data to suit the sort of information they require for their study. While mail-questionnaires are perfectly alright to collect information relating to some straight forward topics, other topics may require the help of an expert interviewer.

Sample Surveys and Random Sample

Most of the sociological surveys are sample surveys. "*A sample survey is a systematic means of gathering data on people's behaviour, attitudes, or opinions by questioning a representative group*'– **(N.J. Smelser)**. It has three basic units: *elements*, *a population*, and *a sample*.

1. **Elements** are units of analysis. These units are mostly people. They can also be households, castes, cities or even societies. '
2. **Population.** The elements in a survey constitute the "population". They could be, for example, all the members of a particular caste or cult, all the registered voters of a university senate etc.
3. **Sample.** A sample is any portion of a population. But this sample is expected to be repre- sentative of the population. It means, it should precisely represent or reflect its elements. In fact, it is designed to be a precise reflection of population.

Sampling is an important aspect of social survey. Sampling, that is, selection of the relevant units of inquiry for the collection of data, must be done in a scientific manner. To ensure that the units he selects really reflect the characteristics of the population, the researcher may resort to different devices such as "*quota sampling*" or "*random sampling*".

Random Sample

Is a sample, the *real representative* of the total population? Whether its *size* has anything to do with its representative character? These are pertinent questions in the sample survey. The answer is equally simple. A sample could be more approximately representative even if its size is very small. *For example*, in a nation like India, a representative sample of 10,000 people could be used to predict the outcome of the parliamentary elections. The standard method of ensuring that the sample is representative is to make a random selection of subjects from the population concerned. *This selection has to be done in such a way that every member of the population should get an equal chance of being selected.*

Thus, "*a random sample is one that is chosen in such a way that every element* (*or every combination of elements*) *in the population has an equal chance of being included in the sample*". (Ref.: **N.J. Smelser** in his "*Sociology*" - 1993 Page 407)

In this particular context, random does not mean "*haphazard*". On the other hand, it denotes "*equal probability of occurrence*". The process of creating a random sample usually begins with a complete listing of the population. *For example*, students' attendance register lists the undergraduate population of a college. Next all the names in the list are numbered. The sample is then selected from this list, say every 10th or 15th person from the population would be selected.

Another method of obtaining a random sample is to assign a number to each member of the population and then to select the sample by using random numbers produced by a computer. This method seems to be more reliable because it eliminates most sources of human error.

The basic features of random sampling are straight forward, but random sampling is not often in sociological research. The main reason for this is that adequate population lists (such as, *the list of all the higher educated scheduled tribe and scheduled caste people, or the list of all the divorced persons etc.*) are not always available. Further, many projects study populations for which there is no list or directory in existence. (For example, the reliable list of households that possess television in India is not available.) It might be possible to make lists of such populations, but this would probably require more work than the study itself.

Where population lists do exist, they must be used with great care because they may be biased towards certain portions of the population. A list of doctors, for example, may include only registered medical practitioners, and it naturally excludes relatively good number of traditional medical practitioners including even some Ayurvedic doctors and Homeopathic doctors.

Other Kinds of Sample

The random sample has served as a good model for designing other models of sampling. Some of them can be mentioned here.

1. **Systemate (Pseudo-random) Sample.** The ratio of sample size to population size (say, 1 to 15) is used to derive a "*skip*" interval (K). Then every K*th* element in a population is included in the sample. **For example**, *every 15th student who registers himself or herself in the college office and who is regularly attending the classes might be included in the sample*.
2. **Stratified Sample.** This mode entails dividing the population into segments or strata, and then sampling within each stratum. This technique ensures that the different segments or strata will be represented in the sample in precisely the same proportion as they occur in the population. *For example, if in the category of scheduled castes higher educated people constitute 10%, then, they will constitute 10% of the sample.*
3. **Cluster Sample.** This mode entails grouping elements of a population into geographic units. **For example**, *student population of a University Campus could be sampled in clusters based on the different hostels in which they stay.*

Sampling has been used for a considerable period of time. But controlled methods of sampling started in social research only in the beginning of this century. In England and Wales, *Professor A.L. Bowley* was one of the first investigators to use sampling methods in his five town-surveys. These he did before the First World War. Afterwards, sampling methods have been applied in many branches of social investigation, in public opinion surveys, the assessment of social mobility, in the study of performances in intelligence tests, and so on. Sampling Techniques are being used by the official statisticians also.

OTHER METHODS

1. Sociometry

"*Sociometry*" is one of the techniques of social research in sciences such as psychology, sociology, and so on. The term was coined by *Jacob L. Moreno*, an Austrian psychiatrist who migrated to the United States of America. Being in charge of a refugee camp as an administrator soon after the First World War, he took interest to develop techniques to find out the ways in which people group themselves according to their own choices. He developed this as a small group therapeutic and research techniques.

"Sociometry" refers to a set of techniques to measure in quantitative and diagrammatic terms attractions and repulsions in interpersonal relations.

"The practice of 'sociometry' consists of the administration of a questionnaire in which the subject chooses five other people in rank order of their attractiveness as associates, either generally or in relation to some specific activity". It was later extended to cover negative choices. The results are plotted on paper in diagrammatic form hence the term "sociogram"—(*Ref.*: **Duncan Mitchell** in "*Dictionary of Sociology*").

The technique of sociometry is a very simple one and is applicable for the study of small group structures, personality traits and social status. It gives an insight relating to the feelings people have for one another and provides various indexes or measures of interaction. Within its limitation it has been found to be very useful. It can be particularly *helpful in the assignment of personnel to work groups in such a way as to achieve a maximum of interpersonal harmony and a minimum of inter- personal friction.*

Moreno's original exposition of this technique is found in his book "*Who Shall Survive*" 1934, and in the journal he founded, called "*Sociometry*". But Moreno himself does not appear to have used this technique much in small group experimental investigations. His theoretical approach seems to be very vague and too general. In spite of that, good number of other people, engaged in research have made use of this approach (including Helen H. Jennigs who used it in detailed studies of women in correctional institutions in America).

Sociometry aroused considerable interest because once it has been decided what is implied in interpersonal choices recorded in this manner it is possible to present the results quantitatively. This technique is, in a sense, a *combination of ideal type analysis and statistics*. Though in the beginning psychologists were more attracted by this technique, in course of time, the sociologists also got enthused with it particularly to study the different dimensions of interpersonal relations. The technique is now found to be simple, reliable and more useful in the study of interpersonal relations.

2. The Experimental Method

All sciences use experiments. The experimental method provides a reliable way of studying the relationship between two variables under carefully controlled conditions. Experiments can be conducted either in the laboratory or in the field. It means the experiment method is of two types: (*a*) *Laboratory experiments*, and (*b*) *Field experiments*.

(*a*) ***Laboratory experiments:*** In a laboratory experiment the people and any necessary materials are brought into an artificial experiment that can be carefully regulated by a researcher. In laboratory experiments with people, people are recruited, assembled; and sometimes even paid for engaging in the experiment. This type of experiment is more appropriate when the researcher wants to control the situation in minute detail.

(*b*) ***Field experiment:*** The field experiment takes research out to people instead of bringing people to the research laboratory. It takes place outside the laboratory under somewhat less artificial conditions, say in a prison, hospital, college, or factory. The field experiment is more suitable when the researcher wants to minimise the possibility that people will change their typical behaviour in the artificial laboratory experiment.

Ways of Experimental Method

The concept of any experiment is very simple. The researcher has to hold all variables constant, except one, has to vary it and see what happens. In a typical experiment, an independent variable is introduced into a carefully designed situation and its influence on a dependent variable is recorded. This can be illustrated with the help of an example.

Example. Let us say, *the researcher is interested in the effects of communal integration in school on Muslim students' attitudes* and decides to run a small experiment on the subject. The researcher must first measure the Muslim students' attitudes, then introduce Hindu and Christian students into the class, and then, after a suitable period, measure the Muslim students' attitudes again to find out whether any change has taken place. But actually this procedure is not sufficient to establish a causal link between the two variables. Any changes in the students' attitudes might have been caused by the coincidental factors—say, *communal disturbances in the neighbourhood or probably, a mass media campaign against communal illwill or disharmony*,-that happened to take place while the experiment was in progress.

The researcher therefore, has to control the situation in such a way that other possible influences can be discounted. The standard method of doing this would be to *divide the Muslim students into two groups whose members are similar in all relevant aspects*. Both groups are then tested on their communal attitudes, but only one group called the experimental group, is exposed to classroom integration. The other group called, *the control group*, is not subjected to this variable, but its experience is the same in all other respects. Finally, both groups are again tested on their communal attitudes, and any difference between the groups is assumed to be the result of the independent Variable.

The "Hawthorne Effects"

The experimental method cannot be easily administered in the sociological field. It involves some subtle problems. Controlling the situation is not always easier. The researcher is dealing with people who have their mind, thinking, feeling and their own ways of reacting. One of the best known experiments in sociology known as "*The Hawthorne Experiment*", too had recorded some of the problems of experiment.

Elton Mayo and his associates had conducted an experiment before World War II at the *Hawthorne plant of the Western Electric Company*. The management was anxious to improve productivity and wanted to know what kind of incentives would encourage the workers to increase output. Researcher Mayo separated a group of women from the other workers and started varying the conditions systematically to find out how the changes would influence productivity. *Each change that was introduced, say providing for better lighting, coffee breaks, lunch hours, new methods of payment, etc., contributed to an improvement in the productivity. With each change, production rose*. Mayo and his associates were delighted in the beginning. When they found that productivity rose no matter which Variables were involved, they became suspicious. Finally, the researchers returned the group to their original conditions and production rose to even greater heights.

The experiment revealed that, something was seriously wrong with the researchers' assumptions. Whatever had caused the change in the dependent Variable, that is, productivity, it was not the independent Variables that the experimenters had introduced. Actually, from this point of view, the experiment was a failure. But the reasons for the experiment's failure have taught sociologists a great deal. It appears *that production rose because the women enjoyed all the attention they were getting*. They had formed a close-knit primary group highly co-operative in nature. They had established their own norms for productivity; they knew what effects the sociologists were trying to produce and they had decided to co-operate with them to increase the output. They did their best to please the sociologists. This phenomenon-*the contamination of the experiment by the subjects' assumptions about what the sociologist is attempting to prove*-is still known as "*the Hawthorne effect*". The "Hawthorne effect" reveals one main limitation of the experimental method, *when people realise that they are experimental subjects, they begin to act differently and the experiment may be spoiled.*

Planned experiments upon human beings are most reliable when these subjects do not know the true object of the experiment. They may be given a rationale, a reasonable explanation of what the experiment is doing. This rationale may be a harmless one but it is a necessary deception which conceals the true purpose of the experiment. As Kelman points out, the use of deception in social research poses *the ethical question of distinguishing between harmless deception and intellectual dishonesty*, and it may even produce errors in the outcome-(subjects may detect the deception and may begin to act intelligently).

The experimental method has a few other disadvantages also. It can be used only for very narrowly defined issues. Further people may behave very differently in the artificial experimental situation, than they would, in the normal situations. Experimenters, may, sometimes, unwittingly produce the effect that they are looking for.

Because of all these limitations, social sciences, excepting of course, psychology, make limited use of planned experiments. We still use them wherever practical. We cannot completely do away with it. It allows the sociologist to investigate specific topics that often cannot be systematically examined under everyday conditions where so many other influences might conceal or distort the processes involved. Though sociologists often make use of this method, they depend more heavily on other techniques.

3. "The Verstehen Approach" (The Method of Understanding)

The "*Verstehen approach*" is often used in sociological researches. The German word "*Verstehen*" means "*understanding*" or '*comprehension*' of sociological issues or problems. German sociologist Max Weber developed this method, or approach.

Weber believed that sociology must model itself as far as possible on the natural sciences. Since the subject-matter of sociology is vitally different from those of other sciences it calls for an *interpretative, subjective approach*. This subjective interpretation Weber called "*Verstehen*" or "*sympathetic understanding*". But it is in *no sense a substitute* for the scientific method. Wherever possible, the conclusions drawn from subjective interpretation must be verified by the scientific method.

The advocates of this method have maintained that the observed facts are of little significance unless they are evaluated through discovery of their inner meaning. The intuitive understanding of social behaviour as insisted upon by this method, has its own importance. Weber himself used "Verstehen" in his famous study of "*the Protestant Ethic and the Spirit of Capitalism*". He used this method when he was trying to prove causal link between the beliefs of early Puritans and the development of capitalism. Weber believed that the Puritan Ethic (or the Protest Ethic) was more favourable for the development of Capitalism than the ethics of other religions such as Catholicism, Islam, Buddhism, or even Hinduism. Because of the intrinsic support given by the Puritan Ethic, the Protestants accumulated and reinvested wealth instead of immediately spending it, as others were prone to do. By this, they unintentionally created modern capitalism. This argument of Weber, seems plausible, but there is no way to prove it scientifically because we cannot know whether the Puritans really did experience the so called "*salvation panic*". Weber's method was to put himself in the place of Puritan's shoes in order to understand their real feelings and motives. Thus, as **Ian Robertson** has pointed out, "By *combining his subjective interpretations of Puritan psychology with a rigorous analysis of the development of capitalism, he enhanced the richness (but not necessarily the reliability) of his study*".

It is clear from the above that the nature of this approach is that *it can be used only by such persons who have a greater capacity of comprehensions and a high level of intelligence and education*. It may yield better results if it is used along with the scientific method.

REVIEW QUESTIONS

1. What is social research? Write its importance.
2. Define social research. What problems are involved in sociological research?
3. Throw light on the methods and techniques of social research.
4. Give the definition of observation. Discuss its types, merits, demerits and limitations.
5. Define questionnaire. Describe the types, advantages, disadvantages and limitations of questionnaire.
6. Define interview. Discuss the process, types, advantages, disadvantages and limitations of interview.
7. What are the main forms of social surveys? Differentiate between the sample survey and the random sample?
8. Explain how role and status are related to one another.
9. Write short notes on the following:
   (a) Kinds of sample
   (b) Sociometry
   (c) Hawthorne effects
   (d) Verstehen approach

6

Sociology and Other Social Sciences

Chapter Outline

- Sociology and History
- Sociology and Political Science
- Sociology and Anthropology
- Sociology and Social Psychology
- Sociology and Economics
- Sociology and Education
- Sociology and Philosophy
- Sociology and Ecology
- Sociology and Criminology.

Social Sciences deal with the social universe or phenomena in general. They deal with forms and contents of man's interaction. They study human groups, society and social environment. The social phenomena which they study are as natural as the phenomena of magnetism, gravitation and electricity, and a modem city is as natural as an ocean.

Different social sciences deal with the different aspects of the social life of man. Accordingly, History, Anthropology, Social Psychology, Economics, Political Science, etc. study the various facets of the same reality, *i.e.* the social milieu. Naturally, these social sciences are then very much interrelated. Sociology, as social science, has joined the family of social sciences very recently. It was born at a time when there was no other social science to study the human society in its entirety with all its complexity.

It is essential for a student of sociology to know in what respect his subject differs from the other social sciences and in what ways it is related to them. However, this is not an easy task. It is more difficult to distinguish sociology from the various social sciences, because the same content or area of investigation is sometimes studied by different social sciences with different degrees of emphasis.

Further, some of the relationships between sociology and other social sciences have been matters of controversy. For example, there are some thinkers, like *Comte*, *Spencer, Hobhouse*, who would say that sociology is the *basic* or the *sole* social science and all the others are its subdivisions. There are others like *Giddings* who would argue that sociology is not the '*sole*' science, not the *mother* of other social sciences, but only their common *sister*. Some others regard sociology as a specialised science of social phenomena; as specialised in its interests as are economics and political science. Again, some sociologists profess to see the closest relations between sociology and psychology on the one hand, and sociology and anthropology on the other. Still some others say that sociology and history are more interrelated than others.

In the field of social sciences interdisciplinary approach is gaining more currency today. Understanding of one social science requires some amount of understanding of the other. Further, sociology as a young science, has borrowed many things from other sciences. In return, it has enriched other sciences by its highly useful sociological knowledge. In this context, it becomes essential for us to know the interrelation between *sociology* and *history*, *economics*, *political science.*

anthropology, social psychology and *education*.

SOCIOLOGY AND HISTORY

Sociology and History are very much interrelated. Like political science, sociology is becoming one of the most genuine fruits of history to which it is intimately connected. The two sciences are so close that some writers like *G. Von Bulow* refused to accept sociology as a science different from history.

History: History is the reconstruction of man's past. It is the story of the experience of mankind. It is a record of the human past. It is a systematic record of man's life and achievements from the dim past to the present. The historian studies the significant events of man in the order of time. The historian is interested in what happened at a particular time in the past.

Further, a historian is not satisfied, however, with mere description. He seeks to learn the causes of these events to understand the past—not only how it has been but also how it came to be. Nevertheless, he is, in a sense, interested in events for their own sake. "He wants to know everything there is to know about them and to describe them in all their unique individuality". The historian concentrates only on the past. He is not interested in the present and is unwilling to look to the future Still history provides the connecting link for the present and the future. It is said that history is the microscope of the past, the horoscope of the present and the telescope of the future.

Sociology: Sociology as a science of society, on the other hand is interested in the present. It tries to analyse human interactions and interrelations with all their complexity and diversity. It also studies the historical development of societies. It studies various stages of human life, modes of living, customs, manners and their expression in the form of social institutions and associations. Sociology has thus to depend upon history for its material. History with its record of various social events of the past offers data and facts to sociologists.

History Supplies Information to Sociology

History is a storehouse of records, a treasury of knowledge. It supplies materials to various social sciences including sociology. History contains records even with regard to social matters. It contains information about the different stages of human life, modes of living, customs and manners, social institutions, etc. This information about the past is of great help to a sociologist. A sociologist has to make use of the historical records. For example, if he wants to study marriage and family as social institutions. he must study their historical development also. Similarly, if he wants to know the impact of Islamic culture on the Hindu culture, he has to refer to the Muslim conquests of India, for which he has to depend on history.

A sociologist is, no doubt, concerned with the present-day society. But the present-day society can he better understood from the knowledge of its past because what people are today is because of what they had been in the past. Further, sociologists often make use of comparative method in their studies for which they depend on history for data. Historical sociology, one of the fields of sociological inquiry, depends very much on historical data. It is true that the sociologist must sometimes be his own historian, amassing information from all the available sources.

Sociology Helps History Too

Historian also uses sociology. Until recently it was perhaps from philosophy that the historian took his clues to important problems and Historical concepts and ideas. But now these are drawn increasingly from sociology. Indeed, we can see that modern historiography and increasingly sociology have both been influenced in similar ways by the philosophy of history.

Further sociology provides the *social background* for the study of history. History is now being studied and read from the sociological point of view. It is said that history would be meaningless without the appreciation of socially significant events. Further, it is often remarked that history would be boring, monotonous, prosaic and uninteresting unless the social events are narrated. Historical facts without reference to socially important matters would be like a body with flesh, blood and bone, but without life.

Some Opinions on the Relation Between the Two Sciences

The mutual dependence of history and sociology has made *G.E. Howard* to remark that '*History is past Sociology, and Sociology is present History'. Peter Worsley says that 'the best history is in fact sociology: the sociology of the past'. T.B. Bottomore*' has pointed out that "it is of the greatest importance for the development of the social sciences that the two subjects should be closely related and that each should borrow extensively from the other, as they are increasingly inclined to do." *Robert Bierstedit Comments*. "If the past is of as a continuous cloth unrolling through the centuries, history is interested in the individual threads and strands that make it up; sociology in the patterns it exhibits".

Differences between History and Sociology

The two social sciences History and Sociology, are different. The points of difference between the two may be noted.

	Sociology	*History*
1.	Sociology is interested in the study of the *present* social phenomena with all their complexity.	History deals with the past events of man. It is silent regarding the present.
2.	Sociology is relatively a *young social science*. It has a very short history of its own. It is not even two centuries old.	History is an *age-old social science*. It has a long story of 2000 years or even more.
3.	Sociology is an *analytical* science.	History is a *descriptive science*.
4.	Sociology is *abstract* in nature. It studies mostly regular, the recurrent and the universal. *For example*, the sociologist does not study all the wars or battles waged by the mankind. But he is interested in war itself as a social phenomenon, as one kind of conflict between two groups.	History is *concrete*. The historian is interested in the unique, the particular and the, individual. *For example*, the historian studies all the wars waged by mankind in the past—the Wars, the World Wars, the Indo-Pak War, etc. For him, each war is unique and significant.
5.	Sociology is a *generalising science*. Socio- logy seeks to establish generalisations after a careful study of the social pheno-mena.	History is an individualising science. History rarely makes generalisations. It seeks to establish the sequence in which events occurred.
6.	Sociology follows the sociological approach. It studies human events from the sociological point of view. i.e., from the view point of *social relationships involved.*	History studies human events in accordance with the *time order*. Its approach is historical.

SOCIOLOGY AND POLITICAL SCIENCE

Political Science and Sociology are very closely related. This intimate relationship between the two social sciences may be examined here.

Political Science. Political Science deals with the political activities of man. It studies social groups organised under the sovereignty of the state. It studies man as a ruler and being ruled. *Laski*, *Gettell* and *Gilchrist*, the eminent political scientists, are of the opinion that the scope of political science embraces the study of both State and Government.

Political Science has its own topics such as the origin, evolution and functions of state, the forms of government, types of constitution, administration, law, legislation, international relations, methods of political representation, elections, voting, political movements, political ideologies, etc. "Political science is an historical investigation of *what the state has been*, an analytical study of *what the state is*, and a politico-ethical discussion of *what the state should be*".

Sociology Has its Roots in Politics

Morris Ginsberg writes: "Historically, sociology has its main roots in politics and philosophy of history". The main works on social subjects such as *Plato's Republic, the Politics of Aristotle, Arthhastra of Kautilya, The Laws and Republic of Cicero* and other classical works were treated to be complete works on political science. Only recently distinction between the two has been clearly made.

Relationship between Sociology and Political Science

Political Science and Sociology are so intimately connected as *Garner* said that the "political is embedded in the social that if political science remains distinct from sociology, it will be because of the breadth of the field calls for the specialist, not because there are any well-defined boundaries marking it off from sociology". Both the sciences are mutually helpful. In fact, political activity is only a part of social activity. Thus political science appears to be a branch of sociology. However, we cannot say that political science is just *Political sociology*.

Political activity influences and is influenced by the social life of man. In fact, political activities will have no meaning outside the social context. Politics is after all the reflection of society. This is made clear by the common saying, that '*people have the government which they deserve*'. Political science gives sociology facts about the organisation and functions of the state and government. Political science derives from sociology a knowledge of the origin of the political authority.

Political science is concerned with the state. But sociology also studies state *as one of the human associations*. The state, in its early form, was more a social institution than a political one.

Moreover, a political scientist must also be a sociologist. The laws of the state have a great influence upon society. These laws are largely based on customs, traditions, conventions and usages. But these customs, traditions, etc., are the concern of sociology. The institution of family, for example, is an element in social life. It is the concern of sociology. But the laws of marriage, made to regulate the family, fall within the field of political science.

Common Foci of Attention

There are some common topics of interest for both sociologists and political scientists. Such topics as war, mass movements, revolutions, government control, public opinion, propaganda, leadership. elections, voting, political minorities, social legislations like civil code and the like may be cited here as examples.

Further, many of the social problems are also deep political problems. Communal riots, (*clashes between Muslims and Christians, Hindus and Muslims, Protestants and Christians etc.*), racial tensions between Whites and Negroes, Asians and Europeans, etc., border disputes between different states, caste conflicts, etc., are problems that have political as well as social implications. It has become quite common to use political instruments to solve such social problems like beggary, unemployment, prostitution, poverty, crime, etc.

Views of Various Thinkers on the Relation between Sociology and Political Science

The interrelationship of political science and sociology has been stressed by some thinkers. *Prof. Giddings* says that "to teach the theory of the state to men who have not learnt the first principles of sociology is like teaching astronomy or thermodynamics to men who have not learnt the Newtonian Laws of Motion". *F.G. Wilson* remarks that "it must be admitted, of course. that it is often difficult to determine, whether a particular writer should be considered a sociologist, political theorist or philosopher". According to *Comte* and *Spencer*, there is no difference whatsoever between the two. *G.E.C. Catlin* has remarked that political science and sociology are two facets or aspects of the same figure.

Differences between Sociology and Political Science

Political Science and Sociology are however, different from each other. The differences may be cited below:

	Sociology	*Political Science*
1.	Sociology is a science of society.	Political Science is a science of state and government.
2.	Sociology studies *all* kinds of societies, organised as well as unorganised.	Political Science studies *only* the politically organised societies.
3.	Sociology has a *wider* scope.	Political Science has *a narrower field.*
4.	Sociology studies man as fundamentally a *social animal.*	Political Science studies man as a *political animal.*
5.	Sociology is a *general social science*. Hence it studies all kinds or forms of social relations in a general way.	Political Science is a *special social science*, because it concentrates only on the human relationships which are political in character.
6.	The approach of sociology is *sociological.* It follows its own methods in addition to the scientific method, in its investigations.	The approach of political science is *Political*. It has its own methods of study like the historical method, philosophical method, comparative method, statistical method, etc.
7.	Finally, sociology is quite *young*. It is not even two centuries old.	Political science is an *older science* comparatively. It has centuries of history of its own right from days of Plato or Cicero.

SOCIOLOGY AND ANTHROPOLOGY

The relation between Sociology and Anthropology is widely recognised today. In fact, anthropologist *Kroeber* pointed out that the two sciences are twin sisters. *Robert Redfield* writes that "viewing the whole United States, one sees that the relations between sociology and anthropology are closer than those between Anthropology and Political Science, that is partly due to greater similarity in ways of work".

Anthropology. Anthropology is a general science like sociology. The word *Anthropology* is derived from two Greek words—*Anthropos* meaning 'man' and *logos* meaning 'study'. Thus, the etymological meaning of 'Anthropology' is the study of man. More precisely, it is declined by Kroeber as '*the science of man and his works and behaviour*'. Anthropology is "concerned not with particular man but with man in groups, with races and peoples and their happenings and doings".

Though the youngest of the traditional social sciences, it has developed and gone ahead of many of them. It has made outstanding contributions to the study of man. Sociology, in particular, has been immensely enriched by the anthropological studies.

Anthropology seems to be the broadest of all the social sciences. It studies man both as a member of the animal kingdom and as a member of the human society. It studies the biological as well as the cultural developments of man. Anthropology has a wide field of study. *Kroeber* mentions two broad divisions of anthropology: 1. *Organic* or *Physical Anthropology* and 2. *the Socio-cultural Anthropology*.

1. ***Physical anthropology:*** Physical Anthropology studies man as a biological being, that is, as a member of the animal kingdom. Here, anthropology accepts and uses the general principles of biology; the laws of heredity and the doctrines of cell development and evolution. Also, it makes use of all the findings of anatomy, physiology, zoology, palaeontology and the like. Its business has been to ascertain how far these principles apply to man, what forms they take in his particular case.

   Physical Anthropology is concerned with the evolution of man, his bodily characteristics, racial features, and the influence of environment and heredity on the physical characteristics of man. It has two main branches: (*i*) *Human palaeontology* which concentrates on the study of fossils, and (*ii*)*Somatology* which deals with the human body in particular.

2. ***Socio-cultural anthropology:*** Socio-cultural Anthropology, more often referred to as 'Cultural Anthropology', studies man as a social animal. This branch of anthropology which is concerned with the more-than-merely-organic aspects of human behaviour seems to be more interested in ancient and savage and exotic and extinct peoples. The main reason for this is a desire to understand better all civilisations, irrespective of time and place, in the abstract, or as generalised principles as possible. (Social Anthropology and Cultural Anthropology are often treated as two separate branches).

   Socio-cultural Anthropology's main concern is, of course, culture. It deals with the origin and development of man's culture. It also studies various social institutions of primitive communities of the past as well as that of the present. It has three sub-divisions:

   (*i*) *Ethnology—the science of peoples* and their cultures and life histories as groups, irrespective of their degree of advancement.

   (*ii*) *Archaeology—the science of what is old* in the career of humanity, especially as revealed by the excavations of prehistorical importance, and

   (*iii*) *Linguistics—the study of language* in its widest sense, in every aspect and in all its varieties, but with its main accent on the languages of the primitive peoples.

Relationship between Sociology and Anthropology

According to *Hoebel*, "Sociology and Social Anthropology are, in their broadest sense one and the same". *Evans Pritchard* considers social anthropology a branch of sociology. Sociology is greatly benefited by anthropological studies. Sociologists have to depend upon anthropologists to understand the present-day social phenomena from our knowledge of the past which is often provided by anthropology. The studies made by famous anthropologists like *Radcliffe Brown*, *B. Malinowski*, *Ralph Linton*, *Lowie*, *Raymond Firth*, *Margaret Mead*, *Evans Pritchard* and others, have been proved to be valuable in sociology.

Sociological topics such as the origin of family, the beginning of marriage, private property, the genesis of religion, etc., can better be understood in the light of anthropological knowledge. The anthropological studies have shown that there is no correlation between anatomical characteristics and mental superiority. The notion of racial superiority has been disproved by anthropology.

Further, sociology has borrowed many concepts like cultural area, culture traits, interdependent traits, cultural lag, culture patterns, culture configuration etc., from socio-cultural anthropology. The knowledge of anthropology, physical as well as socio-cultural, is necessary for a sociologist. An understanding of society can be gained by comparing various cultures, particularly, the modern with the primitive.

Anthropology as a discipline is so closely related to sociology that the two are frequently indistinguishable. Both of them are fast growing. The socio-cultural anthropologists, today are also making a study of the present peoples and their societies. In a number of universities anthropology and sociology are administratively organised into one department.

The conclusions drawn by sociologists have also helped the anthropologists in their studies. For example, anthropologists like *Morgan* and his followers have come to the conclusion regarding the existence of primitive communism from the conception of private property in our modern society.

Differences between Sociology and Anthropology

Sociology and Anthropology differ from each other in certain respects. According to *Klukhon*, "The sociological attitude had tended towards the practical and present, the anthropological towards the pure understanding and the past". Differences between the two subjects may be mentioned here.

	Sociology	*Anthropology*
1.	Sociology studies the modern, *civilised* and *complex* societies.	Anthropology concerns itself with the *simple, uncivilised* or primitive and non-literate societies.
2.	Sociologists more often study *parts* of a society and generally specialise in institutions such as family, marriage, or processes, such as social change, social mobility.	Anthropologists tend to study societies in all their aspects, as *wholes*. They concentrate their studies in a given "culture area", such as Melanesia or Negaland.
3.	Sociologists study 'small' as well as 'large' societies.	Anthropologists usually concentrate on small societies such as those of Naga, Rengma Naga, Khasis, Gond, Bhil, etc.
4.	Sociology makes use of observation, interview, social survey, questionnaires and other methods and techniques in its investigations.	Anthropologists directly go and live in the communities they study. They make use of direct observations and interviews.

SOCIOLOGY AND SOCIAL PSYCHOLOGY

Sociology and Psychology are contributory sciences. Psychology has been defined as *the study of human behaviour*. In the words of *Thouless*, "Psychology is the positive science of human experience and behaviour".

The problem of relation between sociology and psychology is still disputed. According to *Durkheim*, sociology should study *social facts* and not psychological facts. Social facts, according to him, are something *external* to the individual and exercise an *external constraint* on the individual. On the other hand, writers like *Ginsberg* hold the opinion that many sociological explanations could be made firmly established by being related to general psychological laws or explanations. As such, psychological phenomenon is the result of social interaction.

Social Psychology. Psychology, as the science of behaviour, occupies itself principally and primarily with the individual. It is interested in his intelligence and his learning, his hopes and his fears and the order and the disorder of his mind: Social psychology serves as a bridge between psychology and sociology. As *Krech* and *Crutchfield* define, "*Social psychology is the science of the behaviour of the individual in society*". Social psychology deals with the mental processes of man, considering him as a social being. It attempts to determine the character of his social behaviour. It involves various aspects of social behaviour: social interaction, interaction between an individual and a group, and interaction between one group of individuals and another group of individuals. It studies the individual in his relation to his fellow-men. It also studies how an individual's personality is a function both of his basic physiological and temperamental equipment and of the social and cultural influences to which he is exposed.

The relationship between social psychology and sociology is so close that *Karl Pearson* asserts that the two are not separate sciences. *McDaugall* and *Freud* expressed the view that the whole of the social life could be reduced finally to psychological forces. In that case, sociology would be reduced to a mere branch of psychology. This view is not an acceptable one. Social behaviour of man is affected by political, economic, biological and geographic factors also. Social life of man should not be studied exclusively with the methods of psychology. The mutual dependence of social psychology and sociology should not be interpreted to mean that one is either identical with or is the branch of the other.

Interdependence of Sociology and Social Psychology

Social psychology has to depend on sociology to understand properly human nature and behaviour as it is sociology which provides the necessary material regarding the structure, organisation and culture of societies to which individuals belong. Similarly, the sociologists have taken the assistance from social psychology. They have recognised the importance of psychological factors in understanding the changes in social structure.

Common Topics of Interest for Both Sociology and Social Psychology

Sociologists and social psychologists may have to study together certain common topics such as–individual disorganisation, crime, juvenile delinquency, social disorganisation, public opinion, propaganda, leadership, war conflicts, socialisation, suggestion, imitation, fashion and so on.

Social Psychology Helps to Face Social Problems

Social psychology helps us a great deal in facing several social problems. Problems such as racial conflict, religious prejudices, communal tensions, crimes, juvenile delinquency, prostitution, gambling and alcoholism are not totally isolated cases in the society. As they are inseparable from normal social processes and normal social behaviour, the knowledge of social psychology should be brought to bear on the solution of these problems. Deviant patterns such as stealing, suicide, divorce and prostitution are also normal consequences of our social institutions. As social behaviour and misbehaviour are very closely interrelated, applied social psychologist must be an expert in the details of the practical problems. Of course, the social psychologist must know his limitations in curing these social evils. He cannot be 'master-fixer' of solutions to social problems.

The Expressed Views of Some Thinkers on the Mutual Relationship of the Two Sciences

Emphasising the close relation between sociology and social psychology, *Lapiere* writes that "Social psychology is to sociology and psychology as Bio-chemistry is to Biology and Chemistry". *MacIver* says that "Sociology in special gives aid to psychology, just as psychology gives special aid to sociology". To quote *Murphy*, "social psychology is the study of the way in which the individual becomes member of and functions in a social group".

T.B. Bottornore says that "Social Psychology is that part of general psychology which has a particular relevance to social phenomena, or which deals with the psychological aspects of social life". *Robert Bierstedt* says that "Social psychology, serves as a bridge between psychology and sociology". *Macilver* and *Page* have said: "When we study the nature of the individual consciousness which expresses itself in social relationships. We are taking the psychological point of view. When we study the relationships themselves we take the sociological point of view. Both sciences are concerned with different aspects of an indivisible reality. Individuals cannot be understood apart from their relations with one another; the relations cannot be understood apart from the units of the relationship."

Differences between Sociology and Social Psychology

	Sociology	*Social Psychology*
1.	Sociology studies society and *social groups*. It has no primary interest in the individual, not in his personality nor in his individual behaviour.	Social psychology studies the *behaviour of individual* in group situation or in society. Its focus of interest is individual and not the society as such.
2.	Sociology analyses *social processes*.	Social psychology analyses *mental processes* of man.
3.	Sociology is interested in the social forms and structures within which the behaviour of man takes place.	Psychology and social psychology are primarily concerned with the behaviour of individuals as such.
4.	Sociology studies the groups themselves and the larger social structure within which both individual and group processes occur.	Psychology studies the individual and social psychology the individual in his social groups.
5.	Sociology studies society from the sociolo-gical view point.	Social psychology studies the individual's behaviour from the viewpoint of psychological factors involved.

SOCIOLOGY AND ECONOMICS

Sociology and economics as social sciences have close relations. Relationship between the two is so close that one is often treated as the branch of the other. According to *Thomas*, "*Economics is, in fact, but one branch of the comprehensive science of sociology.....*". In the words of *Silverman*, "It may be regarded for ordinary purposes, as an offshoot of the parent science of sociology, which studies the general principles of all social relations". But this does not mean that economics is a branch of sociology.

Economics: Economics deals with the economic activities of man. *Dr. Alfred Marshall* defines economics as "On the one side the study of wealth and on the other and more important side a part of the study of man". *Prof. Lionel Robbins* defines economics as "*the sciences of human behaviour in its relations with ends and scarce means which have alternative uses*". It can also be understood as the science of wealth in its three stages namely: production, distribution and consumption.

Economics studies man as a wealth-getter and a wealth disposer. Wealth constitutes the central problem of economics. It studies the interrelations of purely economic factors and forces: the relations of price and supply, money flows, input-output ratios and the like. It studies the structure and function of economic organisations like banks, factories, markets, business firms, corporations, transport, etc. Recently economists have shown more interest in motivation behind man's economic action.

Sociology and Economics are Mutually Helpful

Economics and sociology are helpful to each other. Economic relationships bear a close relation to social activities. At the same time social relationships are also affected by economic activities. Because of this close relation *Thomas* regarded economics as the branch of Sociology. But this is an extreme view. Economics, it may be specified here, is an independent science.

Social Interpretation of Economic Changes

Some economists, like *Sombart, Max Weber, Pareto, Oppenheimer, Schumpeter* have explained economic change as an aspect of social change. According to them, the study of economics would be incomplete without an understanding of human society. Economic system is embedded in the social structure as a part of it. The society, its structures, its organisations, its institutions, its strength and weaknesses etc., are bound to affect the economic activities of its people. That is why a celebrated modern economist has said that "Economics must be made the handmaid of sociology".

Max Weber, a German sociologist, made classical attempt to show how social factors, and particularly, religious beliefs and practical ethics influence the economic activities of people. He made this clear in his celebrated book *The Protestant Ethic and the Spirit of Capitalism*. His contention is that the progressive protestant ethic provided the stimulus to the rapid growth of capitalism in the West, whereas Hinduism and Buddhism, with their so called fatalistic approach, failed to stimulate the growth of capitalism in the East.

Economic Interpretations of Social Changes

At the other end, there are environmentalists like *Karl Marx* and *Veblen* according to whom social phenomena are determined by economic forces. According to them social reality or social change can be explained in terms of economic forces. According to *Marx*, the infrastructure of a society is nothing but the economic relations among its people. However, there is a growing awareness among social scientists about the mutual interplay between the economic and non-economic forces of society.

Sociologists have contributed to the study of different aspects of economic organisation. Knowledge of property system, division of labour, occupations, industrial organisation, etc., is provided by a sociologist to an economist. Such matters as labour relations, standard of living, employer employee relations, social classes, socio-economic planning, socio-economic reforms, etc., are common to both economists and sociologists.

The area of co-operation between sociology and economics is widening. Economists are now analysing the social factors influencing economic growth. Economists are working with the sociologists in their study of the problems of economic development in underdeveloped countries. Economists are more and more making use of the sociological concepts and generalisations in the study of economic problems.

Further, there are certain socio-economic problems of greater importance to be studied by both economists and sociologists. Such problems like poverty, beggary, unemployment, over-population, unregulated industrialisation have both social and economic implications. Combined studies of both the experts in this regard may be of great practical help in meeting the challenges.

Differences between Sociology and Economics

In spite of the inter-relationship between the two sciences, they are different. Points of differences between the two are mentioned here.

	Sociology	*Economics*
1.	Sociology studies all kinds of social relationships.	But economics deals with only those social relationships which are economic in character.
2.	Sociology is a *general* social science.	Economics is a *special* social science.
3.	The scope of sociology seems to be *wider*. It has a comprehensive viewpoint.	The scope of economics is *narrower*. It does not have a comprehensive viewpoint.
4.	Sociology is a science of recent emergence.	Economics has attained an advanced degree of maturity.
5.	Sociology is *abstract* in nature and less precise also. Social variables are very difficult to measure and to quantify.	Economics is *concrete* in nature. It is more precise. Economic variables can be measured and quantified more easily and accurately.

SOCIOLOGY AND EDUCATION

Sociology and Education, as two branches of knowledge, concerned essentially with man and his life, are intimately related. Education has come to be one of the basic activities of human societies everywhere. The continued existence of a society depends upon the transmission of its heritage to the young. It is essential that the young be trained according to the ways and expectations of the group so that they will behave in a desired way. All societies have their own ways and means of meeting this need. 'Education' as a process has come to stay as an effective means of meeting this need.

Education

The term education comes from the Latin word "*educare*" which means to *bring up* and is connected with the verb "*educere*" which means to *bring forth*. Education, in its widest sense, can mean everything that is learned by an individual in society. *Durkheim* conceived of education as the '*socialisation of the younger generation*'. It is a process of transmission of social heritage. Education consists in "an attempt on the part of the adult members of human society to shape the development of the coming generation in accordance with its own ideals of life".

Education and sociology are intimately related. Education is one of the major institutions of society. It is the creation of society itself. Educational activities constitute a part of the social activities of man. In this way 'education' appears as a branch of sociology.

Sociology of Education

The bridge between sociology and education is probably '*sociology of education*', a recently emerged branch of sociology. It analyses the institutions and organisation of education. It studies the functional relationship between education and the other great institutional orders of society such as the economy, the polity, religion and kinship. It concentrates on educational system or subsystem or individual school or college.

'Sociology of education' studies 'education' as an agent of transmission of culture. It studies the functional importance of education also. It makes studies of school organisation and the relation between schools and social structure, especially social class, family and neighbourhood. The inter- action of these social forces with the internal organisation of the school is explored in order to find out the social determinants of educability. Studies have shown that social class and its correlates have a systematic effect on educability and educational selection.

Social Importance of Education

The social importance of education is widely recognised today, especially in modern industrialised societies. In such societies education has become one of the means of acquiring social and technical skills. Education has come to be not only a way of training people of work in different fields but also a qualification for jobs in certain fields. It fits people for increasingly specialised roles.

More than that, education has become an essential need today to register progress in scientific and technological fields. As such, it is a means of promoting economic prosperity. Education, as a means of bringing about social change, is no less significant. It promotes social mobility, that is, movement of people from one social status to another. It influences social stratification. Education is often made use of in totalitarian and communist countries as an instrument to propagate some *chauvinist* and communist ideologies.

The famous writer, *Newman* said that the main practical purpose of a university is to produce socially responsible people. President *Truman* of America, stressing the importance of education, once remarked that man with wide experience, practical vision of things, intellectual depth and capacity to take right decisions at right time should be given the reins of administration to rule the country. *Dr. S. Radhakrishnan* said that the main objective of education was to give training to students to undertake occupations effectively and to become proper leaders in various social fields in which they happen to work. *Dr. Kothari Commission*, appointed by the Government of India to recommend suitable educational reforms declares in the very beginning of its very comprehensive report that, *The destiny of India is being shaped in her classrooms today*.

Sociology and Education are not, however, one and the same. Sociology studies all kinds of social relationship including the educational. Hence its scope is wider. Education, on the other hand, deals with only the educational activities of man and hence has smaller field of study. Sociology is a general social science, whereas education, as a branch of knowledge, specialises itself in only one kind of human activity, that is, educational.

SOCIOLOGY AND PHILOSOPHY

Historically, sociology has its closest relationship with philosophy. Sociology was once called one of the branches of philosophy, i.e., at a time when philosophy was regarded as the *mother* of all the sciences. In the 19th century, psychology, or the science of human behaviour; and sociology, or the science of human society, emerged out of philosophy as independent sciences. What had once been called the *mental philosophy*, or the *philosophy of mind*, became the science of *sociology*; and what had once been *social philosophy*, or the *philosophy of history*, became the science of sociology.

The word '*philosophy*' is derived from Greek language and it literally means '*love of wisdom*'. Philosophy is concerned with the task of acquiring knowledge regarding the causes and laws of all things. Sociology can be said to have originated with some *philosophical ambitions*–to provide an account of the course of human history, to explain the social crisis of the (European) 19th century, to seek out the avenues for social welfare and social reform. As Bottomore has pointed out whether the philosophical ambitions or aims of sociology are still alive or died out, one could find connections between sociology and philosophy in three respects which are explained below.

Three Connections between Sociology and Philosophy

1. ***Philosophy of sociology:*** Any science has a philosophy of its own in the sense it is committed to acquire knowledge relevant to its field in its own legitimate ways. Sociology is ever vigilant in its examination of the methods, concepts and arguments. This philosophical scrutiny is more urgently felt in sociology than in the natural sciences because of the very nature of sociology.
2. ***Sociology entertains philosophical thoughts:*** More than any other social science, sociology raises to a greater extent philosophical problems in its studies. Hence a sociologist at studies is bound to consider the philosophical issues which are always in the background of sociological problems. *For example*, Marxism could invite and stimulate a lot of social research for it represents not only a sociological theory but also a "*Philosophical world view*" and a "*revolutionary doctrine*".

"Both Durkheim and Manheim seemed to claim that sociology can make a direct contribution to philosophy, in the sense of settling philosophical questions. Durkheim, for instance, wrote– "I believe that sociology, more than any other science, has a contribution to make to the renewal of philosophical questions..... sociological reflection is bound to prolong itself by a natural progress in the form of philosophical reflection". In his own study of religion Durkheim transgressed the field of sociological thought and stepped into epistemological discussion.

Intimate Relationship between Sociology and Social Philosophy

Social Philosophy seems to be the meeting point of sociology and philosophy. Its role in the social sciences is "the study of the fundamental principles and concerned of social life in their epistemological and axiological aspects ..." The *epistemological* aspect is concerned with the question of knowledge; and the *axiological* aspect deals with the questions of value. The *former* deals with the fundamental principles and concepts of social life such as man, society, justice, happiness, etc. It also delves deep into the validity of the assumptions, principles and inferences of the social sciences. It also tries to synthesise its results with those of the other sciences that deal with man. The *latter* (i.e. the axiological aspect) deals with the ultimate values of social life and the means of attaining them. It thus tries to interpret and estimate the social phenomena in terms of ethical principles. The object of social philosophy is, therefore, the attainment of *social good* itself.

The study of society is inextricably mixed up with moral values. Because the subject-matter of sociology is human behaviour which is directed and guided by values on the one hand and impulses and interests, on the other. Thus the sociologist is bound to study values and human valuations, as facts. To do this, he must have some knowledge of values in their own context, that is, in moral and social philosophy. *For example*, he must know the role and influence of '*dharma*' in the making of Indian institutions, and that of individualism and liberalism in the making of American institutions. Here the concepts such as '*dharma*', *individualism and liberalism* are mostly ethical in nature, but they are studied as objects of knowledge. Only a sociologist who is capable of distinguishing between questions of fact and value questions, can make such studies more objective. As Bottomore writes, "Only by some training in social philosophy can the sociologist become competent to distinguish the different issues, and at the same time to see their relationships to each other".

In conclusion, we can say that a philosopher who is well acquainted with the social sciences and a sociologist who is sufficiently grounded in philosophy could become, more competent in their respective fields. As *Vierkandt* says, "Sociology is productive only when it has a philosophical basis". In the absence of such a basis sociology can pile together facts and investigations and achieve no final meaning or end. Social sciences may deal with means, but social philosophy deals with ends without disregarding the means. As *Ginsberg* says, "Social philosophy is bound to be the golden crown of the social sciences."

SOCIOLOGY AND ECOLOGY

Meaning of Ecology

The term "ecology" was coined by the l9th century German biologist Ernst Haeckel. He used the term to refer to study of the influence of the environment upon animals. As a branch of biology, ecology studies the relations between organisms or groups of organisms and their environment. Ecology is the study of plants or of animals, or of peoples and institutions in relation to their environment. Zoologists and botanists started using the term ecology in their researches and at their hands it came to be known as '*animal ecology*' and '*plant ecology*' respectively. Sociologists have borrowed this ecological approach of these natural scientists and applied the same in their studies of communities. At their hands it came to be known as '*human ecology*' or '*social ecology*'. The ecological studies of botanists, rather than those of Zoologists influenced the studies of sociologists.

The ecological point of view stresses the idea that every living organism, human and non-human, is incessantly making adjustments to the environmental conditions. "The life of an organism.... is inescapably bound up with the conditions of environment, which comprise not only topography, climate, drainage, etc., but their organisms and their activities as well"

—*A.H. Hawley*

Social or Human Ecology

The study of human ecology is nothing but the logical extension of the ecological point of view. Human ecology is that part of sociology which studies human beings' adjustments to their environments which include not only the physical conditions of their geographic environment but also other organisms such as the fellow human beings, plants and animals. Man, the subject of human ecology, is less restricted by his physical environment. With the help of culture that man possesses, he can live almost anywhere on the planet. He can grow and produce different kinds of food, wear clothing of various types, construct houses, bridges and dams, create tools and implements which have different uses, kill beasts that are dangerous, destroy harmful insects with pesticides, and so on.

It is true that natural environment does set its own limits to human habitations. The size and spatial distribution of peoples are, in part, a function of natural environment. Human happiness and welfare have to do with the size of the communities and the spatial distribution of the population.

Studies in human ecology stress upon its four interrelated aspects: "A group of people (*i.e., a population*) adapting to an environment by means of a *technology* and a *social organisation*. Technology and social organisation only represent a part of culture. But ecology does not focus on all aspects of culture. It focuses on such aspects of technology and social organisation as contribute to man's sustenance or are a consequent adaptation to the environment.

Ecology's Focus on the Community

Social ecologists have focused on the community. The ecological factors can more easily and more productively be studied when the community is the unit of observation and study. A sociologist with ecological orientation considers the community – city, town or agricultural village – as a sociological unit and not as a legal or administrative unit. Ecologists are interested in the spatial distribution of any social phenomenon: What part of the community is more vulnerable to crimes and suicides? Where the areas of high and low economic status groups are located? Where minorities live? Where the regular churchgoers are found? and so on. "The ecologist regards spatial relations as an index of social relations. He is interested in the spatial structuring of human activities in order to learn about the social structure." —*Young* and *Mack*. A community, from the ecological point of view, includes a focal area plus the surrounding territory. Its size is determined by the extent of its economic and social influence. This kind of ecological approach is now well appreciated and used not only by the sociologists but also by economists, social workers, businessmen, and social planning agencies.

American sociologists made much popular the ecological approach to the study of communities. C.J. Galpin is said to have been the first to throw light on this approach in his study of a Wisconsin agricultural village. Such studies are now extended to include modern urban societies. The studies are mainly concerned with the social relationships of people in relation to the limitations and opportunities of the urban environment, and in relation to the environment of industry, its location, the limits it imposes on domestic and local relationships. Park and Burgess made some pioneering works in the field of social ecology. Later on, Mckenzie formulated the basic principles of social ecology and made it one of the specialised fields of study within sociology. This ecological approach could become popular even outside the circle of the "*Chicago School*" in due course.

SOCIOLOGY AND CRIMINOLOGY

Meaning of Criminology

Criminology refers to "the study of criminal behaviour" of man. The French anthropologist *P. Topinard* seems to be the first man to use the term criminology in his writings towards the end of the 19th, century. However several studies in penology and the treatment of offenders had been made still earlier. Even studies on crime were also made earlier.

"Scientific study of law breaking and serious attempts to uncover the causes of criminality has usually taken place within an area of study called "criminology", which is concerned with the objective analysis of crime as a social phenomenon. Criminology includes within its scope inquiry into the process of making laws, breaking laws, and reacting to the breaking of laws"— *Don C. Gibbons*

Tasks of Criminology

As *G.B. Trasler* has pointed out in "*A Dictionary of Sociology*" edited by *D. Mitchell* criminology embraces the studies of:

1. The nature, forms and incidence of criminal acts, and of their social, temporal and geographic distribution;
2. The physical and psychological characteristics, histories and social origins of criminals and of the relations between criminality and other abnormalities of behaviour;
3. The characteristics of victims of crime;
4. Non-criminal and anti-social behaviour, (particularly, the acts such as homosexual conduct, adultery, prostitution, etc., that are regarded as criminal in some societies and not in others);
5. The procedures of the police and of the criminal courts including the social influences upon the decisions of the judges;
6. Methods of punishing, training and treating offenders;
7. The social structure and organisation of penal institutions;
8. Methods of preventing and controlling crime (The last four fields of study are commonly grouped under the general name penology).

Some writers have even included within the domain of criminology the *science of criminalistics*, *i.e.*, of methods of identifying crimes and detecting offenders. In the same way, studies of the origins and development of the criminal law and of public attitudes to crime and criminals – are also included in it.

Criminology has its Roots in Sociology

The terms "*Criminology*" and "*Criminologist*" are most commonly used in the study of criminality as a form of social behaviour. Those sociologists who specialise in this topic are called "*Criminologists*". Sociologists interested in the study of law-violation as a form of social behaviour have made lot of sociological propositions and collected research evidence about criminality.

Historically, in the U.S.A., a relatively small, specialised group of sociologists inquired into criminology. Today, there is good deal of interest in criminological topics, as witnessed in the works of students of deviance, large scale organisations and sociology of law. That is, the social origin of law and societal reactions to it are being studied in a number of areas within sociology. Sociologists continue to evince interest in the phenomenon of criminality and public responses to it. They are trying to throw more light on the different facts of criminality.

Criminology has its roots in the disciplines of sociology, psychology, psychiatry and law. It is also indebted to economics, political science and other sciences. Criminologists have drawn upon. the varied contributions of these established sciences in order to pose economic, political, legal, sociological, psychological and other kinds of questions about crime and responses to it. Criminology borrows heavily from the work of sociologist. Because a good deal of theoretical and research work that has been done on causes of criminality and the organisation of criminal justice agencies and processes has been carried on by sociologists, many of whom call themselves "*Criminologists*". Further, the sociologists have had much to say about rehabilitation efforts and treatment programmes.

Sociology of Criminality

Criminal behaviour is similar to any other social behaviour in the sense it springs from the same social set up or environment. *No individual is born as a criminal*, but he may become one because of the provocative social set up. Still, all those who live in such a kind of set up never invariably turn out to be criminals. Hence the discovery of the causes of crime including juvenile delinquency has been the principal task of criminologist-sociologist. His major aim is to develop a body of generalisations or propositions accounting for criminality. This task is a many faceted one. Two main aspects of this task a sociologist has to do: (1) The first has to do with the development of explanations for the *kinds and degree of criminality* observed in society. "Sociological studies of neighbourhoods in which there are high rates of delinquency, have thrown light on environmental correlates of delinquency and crime." (2) The other centre about discovery of the processes involved in the *acquisition of criminal behaviour patterns by specific individuals*. The field of sociology of criminality has become quite interesting and challenging in the wake of modern civilisation.

Sociology and Criminology are Mutually Supportive

It is made abundantly clear from the above explanation that sociology and criminology are mutually contributory. Criminology, which can be called a branch of sociology, concentrates on only a part of the social life of man, that is, the criminal life. A criminologist is basically a sociologist. He looks at criminal behaviour mainly from the social point of view. He makes use of sociological concepts and techniques in his inquiry. Criminological studies have influenced the sociological view towards crime, criminal and rehabilitation of criminals. Criminological studies have convincingly proved the sociological view that criminality is basically a social product. Crime, the subject matter of criminology, is after all, a social phenomenon. As *Durkheim stated we do not disapprove of an action because it is crime, but it is a crime because society disapproves of it*.

REVIEW QUESTIONS

1. What is the interrelation between Sociology and History? Differentiate between these two.
2. Examine the intimate relationship between Sociology and Political Science. How are these different from each other?
3. The relation between Sociology and Anthropology is widely recognised. Comment.
4. The relation between Sociology and Psychology is disputed. Critically examine.
5. Write the views of thinkers on the mutual relationship of Sociology and Social Psychology.
6. What are the differences between Sociology and Social Psychology?
7. Economics and Sociology are helpful to each other. Discuss.

8. Explain the relationship between Sociology and Education. Evaluate the social importance of Education.
9. Discuss the relationship between Sociology and Philosophy.
10. What is the meaning of the term 'Ecology'? Who Coined this term? Discuss how Sociology and Ecology are related to each other.
11. Write short notes on the following:
    (a) Differences between Sociology and Anthropology
    (b) Differences between Sociology and Economics
    (c) Social or Human Ecology
12. Criminology has its roots in Sociology. Discuss.
13. Throw light on the tasks of Criminology. Write a note on the Sociology of Criminality.
14. Define Sociology. Discuss its relation with any two other social sciences.

⌘⌘⌘⌘⌘⌘⌘⌘⌘⌘⌘

7

THE STUDY OF HUMAN SOCIETY

CHAPTER OUTLINE

- Basic Features of Society
- Societal Needs
- Bio-Social Systems

In comparison with other animals human beings stand out as distinct species. This uniqueness of human beings or men as such has been attributed to various factors. But man's uniqueness does not stem out from his physical traits. As human beings claim man alone has a soul, has higher level of intelligence, has a speaking ability, has sociability and hence civilized from the sociological point of view this uniqueness can be attributed to the sole factor of *culture*. All the other differences stem out from culture itself. It adds an extra dimension to human existence.

Culture includes all modes of thought and behaviour and all kinds of material or non-material achievement of man that are handed down from one generation to another through language. The possession of culture makes not only man but his society unique. The addition of culture has made the humanoid to stem out of primates with all the difference.

The study of human society, thus, necessarily involves the study of culture. The impact of culture is there on all the parts of society. If we study, for example, the family patterns, then they are understood as cultural patterns; their variations from time to time and place, as cultural variations. The difference between marriage and mating; legitimacy and illegitimacy; authority and dominance can he understood only with cultural interpretations. Culture is equally significant in providing explanations for economic, religious, legal, political, educational and other organisations.

The analysis of human society can be made on the cultural level. But the content of culture is so diverse that it includes art, architecture, music, literature, science, technology, philosophy, religion and such other millions of things. No single discipline can set out to study culture in all its infinite details.

Most of the sciences of man (the so called humanistic science) are actually the science of culture. A social scientist is interested in culture to the extent to which culture is related to the social life of man. He selects for his study those aspects of culture which throw light on social organisation and behaviour. Of the social scientists, a sociologist or social anthropologist is more interested in culture for it contributes to the complexity and continuity of human society. He takes more interest in those aspects of culture, that condition the patterns of social interaction, that is, the folkways, mores, customs, values, law and institutions that govern conduct.

It is true that the cultural element is so pervasive in human society that no behaviour is free from its influence. Man's political, economic, educational, occupational and such other activities are all influenced by culture. Still it cannot be said that a social scientist is primarily or exclusively interested in culture as such. He is concerned primarily with society, and with culture insofar as it influences man's life in society.

The social sciences are devoted to the study of mental and not physical phenomena. The physical objects that constitute the parts of physical phenomena are the outcome of ideas and techniques which are included in social heritage. "From the sociological point of view such physical objects are products made possible only by transmission of principles and ideas from person to person". What is more important here is the meaningful interaction between different individuals. Such things as–social solidarity, economic exchange, technological production, political organisation, kinship identification etc., involve mutual awareness and symbolic communication. They would exist because of the contact of mind with mind. Thus, the social phenomena must essentially be construed as mental phenomena.

BASIC FEATURES OF SOCIETY

Man is a social animal and he always lives in society. Like him some other creatures such as ants, termites, birds, monkeys, apes, etc., also live in societies. Human society, in comparison with other societies, is unique in several respects. Still some of the characteristics are common to all kinds of societies whether they are animal or human.

1. As *Kingsley Davis* has pointed out, any society involves *a certain level of association*. But this association is more intricate than a mere aggregation and less complex than an organism. (*ii*) Further, the units that the societies bring together at the level of association are not cells or organs, but individuals. The terms '*aggregation*' and '*organism*' are to be understood to know the real nature of societies.
2. An *aggregation* refers to collection of individuals who are subjected to the same external conditions. For example, a flood may bring together accidentally a collection of animals or insects. In the same manner temperature, moisture or light may draw together to a common place some creatures which are responsive to such stimuli. Similarly, animals often come to common water hole or tank to quench their thirst. In these instances, they are *not actually drawn towards one another* to have some relationship. Such collections or aggregations have no resemblance to society as such. Sometimes, the animals and insects in the aggregate *may help one another* to satisfy their appetite, to quench their thirst or to protect themselves from external danger. A pack of wolves may be able to kill the game that could not otherwise be killed. A group of ants may kill and carry an earthworm. Thus, when the individual organisms are welded together into a *network of mutual stimulus and response* the basis of an association is laid down. In the absence of mutual responsiveness the '*aggregation*' may disappear as Soon as the external stimulus disappears. Thus, when the flood is over, the animals which have come to common spot because of that may disappear. The aggregation cannot perpetuate itself nor can it have an internal unity of its own.
3. It is true that the Organisms who are stimulating each other contribute to the making of society. Still society cannot be understood just by studying its constituent individuals. The following explanation would clarify this point.

A living organism is made up of cells which are interrelated. It has a unity and a structure of its own which the cells cannot decide. The cells may live and die but the organism survives for a longer period. The organism is subjected to the different stages of growth, maturity, decay and death. It has the primary needs such as: nutrition, protection and reproduction. All these needs are interdependent the satisfaction of which contributes to the perpetuation of the organism.

Society too has a system of relations. These are only the relations between organisms and not between cells. Society has its own structure. The parts of this structure fulfil functions and contribute to its existence as a whole. This existence is a continuous one and is independent of its constituent individuals. Society is like a building which is composed of bricks, cement, sand, iron, nails, wood. etc. But these materials alone cannot help us to understand the building. It has its own structure and a function as a building.

For a few organisms life in society serves as one mode of adjustment of the environment. It provides for the associated individuals the satisfaction of their needs for nutrition, protection and reproduction. The *societal mode of existence* has a great *survival value* for those species which have become adapted to such a mode of existence. Man who belongs to the *Homo sapiens* has been a social animal from the very beginning. He cannot exist apart from his own peculiar kind of society, for he has inherited this quality of living in society from his animal ancestors. In fact, *we do not find a single species that belongs to the category of mammals and which is living without the help of society*. Society, thus, has become a biological necessity for man. It has emerged in the line of descent and hence is capable of affecting the direction of organic change.

The emergence of society can be considered to be a great step in organic evolution. But it is a step taken by *only some* species and not by all. It is associated with the emergence of the multicellu- lar organism and with the vertebrate system. It is an example of what is called '*emergent evolution*'. It is called so, because society is different from the organisms of which it is composed. Previously, it was fashionable for some to use the analogy between organism and society to emphasise the idea that social system is, after all a system. This analogy had its own limitations. For example, the cells of the organisms are too rigidly fixed in their mutual relations and are completely subordinated to the organism. They are too specialised to be called members of a society. Like the individual members they are not so spatially detached and independently mobile. Further, the organism has got a 'sensorium' and consciousness which no society possesses. The society does not have the characteristic of the fixed life story of the organism. Society may be subjected to the stages of growth, maturity, and decay. But due to the lesser unity of society they are not as properly defined as the organic stages. The types of organisms are also clear and they can be easily classified than the types of societies. Thus *the analogy must be understood only as on analogy and not as an identity*. In this way the society is different from the organisms that compose it. It must be a new quality or thing added to these. It is a new emergent.

SOCIETAL NEEDS

Irrespective of their types all the societies have certain common needs which must be fulfilled. These needs which may be regarded as "primary needs" define the necessary conditions for the existence of any society. According to *Kingsley Davis*, these societal needs may be classified into four major categories — the needs for *population, specialisation, solidarity,* and *continuity.*

1. ***The need for population:*** Society is composed of separate organisms without whom no society could exist. Societies of all kinds whether insect, animal, or human, must make provision for fulfilling the three basic needs of their members. These needs of the organisms are (*a*) *the need for nutrition or nourishment*, (*b*) *the need for protection and* (*c*) *the need for reproduction*. These needs are felt by all the species. A social system has to make provision for the satisfaction of these needs through group interaction of some kind. The very introduction of group co-operation may however create new needs for the maintenance of the social system if not for the individual organisms.
2. ***The need for specialisation:*** Group co-operation among members presupposes the idea of division of labour and specialisation. The group members must have some mode of dividing work among themselves. The degree of specialisation may differ from society to society. It may be very slight in the case of a herd of cattle or it may be very great as it is in ant community.
3. ***The need for solidarity:*** Societies must guarantee some mode of contact between the members and provide for some motivation for such contact. Added to this, the members must have the spirit of tolerance and must be able to distinguish themselves from other non-members. The individual members must have some means of identifying themselves with the group. They must have some means of resisting the outsiders and the outside influence. Only then, social solidarity or cohesiveness in the group would be found.
4. ***The need for reproduction:*** The society or the group must be able to perpetuate its structure, and character. There must be provision for the continuity of the social system even beyond the life-span of any one individual or generation. This is possible only when there is provision for the members to reproduce their kind.

It is clear from the above, that any kind of society requires certain conditions for its existence. The members of a group or society may not realise them always and strive for their requirements. It is not implied here that the members must always realise the societal needs and strive for their fulfilment. What could be stressed here is that societies require certain conditions before they can exist. We are, of course, interested in understanding various kinds of mechanisms that have been evolved to supply these conditions.

BIO-SOCIAL SYSTEMS

According to *Kingsley Davis*, societies may be classified into two broad types depending upon the nature of social patterns. Social patterns are determined by heredity or culture. Societies that have patterns fixed by '*heredity*' may be called '*bio-social*', and those fixed by '*culture*' may be called '*socio-cultural*'. All social species except man exhibit the 'bio-social system' and man alone exhibits the socio-cultural system. Thus, the term '*bio-social system*' *stands for animal society* whereas the expression '*socio-cultural system*' *represents human society*.'

Heredity: The Main Trait of Bio-social System

The non-human social system meets its basic needs mainly through the mechanisms that are determined by *heredity*. The individuals respond to the social situations mostly instinctively. It does not mean that all the members react in the same way always. Because the physical characteristic of the individuals differ in predetermined ways. Here the continuation of the social system is accomplished through the *transmission of the genes*. Here a change in the social order is possible only from the change in the germ plasm. *The society is in the grip of organic evolution. It is biological in character and hence the name 'bio-social system*'. In order to help the organism to adapt itself to life in society the hereditary structure gets modified in the case of bio-social species.

All non-human societies that are called 'bio-social' are not alike. For instance, between a termite and a bird society we find wide differences. The termites have an elaborate division of labour, a tight cohesiveness and a well constructed social environment. On the contrary, the birds have minimum of these qualities. A greater amount of flexibility is found in their individual behaviour. But the social actions of termites and birds are essentially inherited.

The bio-social systems are thus largely hereditary in character. Each kind of such society whether of termites or of birds, or of bees, is characteristic of the species as a whole. It means the species as a whole reveal the same characteristics throughout the world. In the case of human society, such uniformity is not found. Though all the human beings belong to the same species—the '*homo sapiens*'– their social patterns differ from place to place and time to time. These social patterns are not determined by heredity, but by cultural transmission.

Kingsley Davis has carried on his discussion of bio-social system and socio-cultural system at three levels: (*i*) In the first level he makes a *comparison between the mammalian and other non- mammalian societies.* (*ii*) At the second level, he *compares the primates, the highest kind of mammals, with the lower mammals on the one hand, and with the human beings on the other; and* (*iii*) At the third level; *he concentrates on the human society which represents the socio-cultural system.*

1. The Mammalian vs Non-Mammalian Society

The addition of the element of culture to the social system at the level of human beings has contributed to the widespread differences between human beings and other mammalian societies including those of primates. Between the mammalian societies and other non-mammalian societies also we find lot of differences. Such differences may be noted here.

Differences

(*a*) *Less bodily differentiation between males and females among mammalians*: In the mammalian social groups we find very *less bodily differentiation* among the members than those of insects. However, some amount of bodily specialisation is found along the sex lines. Even this is very less. We find very less differences in size, strength and shape between a cow and a bull, a tomcat and a female cat, a male Chimpanzee and a female Chimpanzee, and a man and a woman. On the contrary, vast bodily differences are observed between males and females at the level of insects. Further, each sex may have its own castes or divisions. The female ants, for example, are divided into queens and workers. Among the Carebara ants, the queen is several thousand times larger than the workers. Only the queen is endowed with the structural requirement for reproduction. Among the mammalians, there is no queen endowed with such a special quality. Here each female is capable of both working and reproducing. Hence *sex need has much to do with the mammalians and it has a limited role to play among the insects*. Further, *the mammalian family is also quite smaller* than that of any insect. The ant queen for example, if once mated, can carry for a lifetime store of sperms in her spermatheca and produce eggs when the need arises.

(*b*) *Learnt social responses:* In the mammalian groups, *social responses are learnt rather than inherited*. The higher non-human mammals are capable of a good deal of learning. This learning is not cultural for it involves no symbolic communication. It is direct experience and is very much limited in scope and importance than cultural learning. For instance, the Chimpanzee mother may encourage its infant "to walk, climb, to run about and to play". But she cannot give instructions symbolically. She cannot tell the infant what kind of Chimpanzee he *should* be when he grows up.

(*c*) *More flexible social behaviour:* The mammalian social behaviour is more flexible. They have greater capacity for modification. They have a long life-span and an extended period of infancy. During its slow maturation the organism gradually learns the social patterns through trial-and-error method. Hence '*play*' *is important for learning* in the mammalian childhood. The mammalian social groups thus do not have the fixed innate patterns of social behaviour as it is found in the insect society. The insects have some compensatory advantage against this supremacy of the mammals. The insects are smaller and can exist in great numbers. They are short-lived but have greater capacity for fast breeding. The insect mortality is also very high, the turn-over of generations is very rapid. Their hereditary mechanisms can change very rapidly. For them, heredity provides a flexible instrument for environmental adaptation. But the mammals have to depend more on learnt responses.

2. Primate Society vs. Non-primate Mammalian Society

The Primates such as monkeys, apes, chimpanzees, gorillas, men represent the highest order of mammals. They all exhibit certain bio-social traits that are common to all mammals. But these traits in primates exhibit a difference also. This difference has the effect of producing a more complex society especially in the case of man. The following explanation reveals this fact.

(*a*) ***The role of sex in primate society:*** The mammals in general *are not separated into anatomically separate castes*. Physical specialisation within the same sex is also not found in them. But the sexes-females and males are not sharply different. Further, we find in them almost an equal *sex* ratio at birth. Because of this all mature members of the society get a chance to participate in reproduction. *Sex is therefore an important element in group cohesion among the mammals*. In comparison with other mammals, the primates have gone a step further in this regard. The primates do not have a definite mating season as such. Among them the female like the male is capable of sexual intercourse at all times. Hence they are constantly tied to one another. *The sex is thus made a continual and a pervasive basis of group cohesion*.

(*b*) ***Primates have a better sensori-motor equipment:*** In comparison with lower mammals the *primates possess a more complex sensori-motor equipment*. They have keener eyes, more developed brains and more flexible behaviour. Since they have neural complexity and prolonged infancy they have a greater chance of being conditioned within the group environment.

(*c*) ***The role of the principle of 'Dominance':*** "Dominance" characterises all mammalian social groups. But the primates exhibit it to a greater extent. In the primate group the relationship of each with his fellows is mostly determined by the principle of dominance. The degree of dominance determines how his bodily appetites will be satisfied, the number of females he will possess, the amount of food he will eat, the freedom from attack that he will enjoy, etc. Here, each member, male or female, adapts himself to his competitive social system partly through sexual reactions. For example, if a weaker baboon secures the food and if he is attacked by a stronger one at that time, he can swallow the food by presenting himself sexually to the attacker.

(*d*) ***Durable relationship between mother and the child:*** In the lower mammalian family we find relationship only between mother and children. This tie is also short lived for it lasts only until the child becomes self-sufficient. Among the primates, due to the prolonged infancy we find relatively *long lasting relationship between the mother and the child*. Due to the constant sexual attraction the male is made to live along with the female. The family group of the primates is smaller for the female can have only one offspring at a time.

(*e*) ***Primates have a better communicative mechanism:*** The primates reveal, in comparison with other mammals, a *better communicative mechanism*. They show a wide range of vocalisation, facial expression, bodily posture and manual exploration. They are able to *learn* some particular sounds or movements coming from another monkey or ape. All the mammals can do this but *primates can do it better*. They can learn to respond in an appropriate way to social situations when they get vocal, gestural, postural, or all these kinds of cues. *Still they do not have the facility of language.* Symbolic communication in its purest sense, is absent among the primates such as apes, monkeys, etc. Hence they cannot transmit their acquired knowledge and attitudes to the next generation. Each generation must make a fresh attempt to understand things by its own actual participation and experience in situations. Infant apes or monkeys cannot be told without seeing a snake that snakes are dangerous. They cannot be told about gods, spirits, and ghosts, about morality, truthfulness, democracy etc.

Culture: The Creator of Gulf between Human Beings and Primates

The *Homo sapiens*, the highminded type of primate has a clear edge over other primates for it has the facility of culture. The emergence of culture at their level has created a tremendous gulf between the human society and the society of the rest of the primates. The presence of culture together with the remaining traits of primate society at the level of the human beings made the human society a distinctive one. Strictly speaking this new kind of society is bio-socio-cultural. It can be briefly referred to as '*socio-cultural*' or in simply as 'human society'.

3. Human Society or Socio-Cultural System vs. Non-Human Society or Bio-Social System

According to *Kingsley Davis*, culture provides the sole explanation for the marked differences that we find between human society on the one hand and non-human society, on the other. Hence he calls the human social system "*socio-cultural system*". The mammals, including primates and human beings have established their supremacy over the non-mammalian social beings because of superior biological traits or qualities. But from the sociological point of view, the uniqueness and the supremacy of human beings over all the other animals including primates are to be sought through the phenomenon of culture. The primates that represent the highest order mammals too have their own limitations in comparison with man. Still, it is true that the human groups exhibit certain traits that are common to all primates. But any modification of these general traits takes place on a physiological basis in the case of primate group, but it takes place on a cultural basis in the case of human groups. The following explanations clarify the dominant role of culture in the socio-cultural system.

Dominant Role of Culture in the Socio-Culture System

1. ***Division of labour based on culture:*** Human beings like all primates and mammals are structurally homogeneous. All the women are born with the same anatomical features and so the case with men. Unlike the termites they are not born with different anatomical characteristics suited to their caste functions. But in human society we find vast division of labour. Here culture plays its role. It is possible to train people for specific tasks through culture. Human society in this way is capable of creating its own occupational groups which are not based on organic peculiarities.
2. ***Continuous sexuality conditioned by culture:*** Human beings possess the same reproduc- tive physiology as those of anthropoids. But human society has continuous sexuality. We find constant association of men and women. This is possible because of the conditioning of this sexuality which is, different from that of a 'system of dominance' found among the apes and monkeys. The phenomena of repression and sublimation, of marriage, adultery, incest, prostitution can describe the cultural conditioning of sexuality at the level of human beings.
3. ***Symbolic communication:*** Human beings have greater neural complexity and hence have greater capacity for learning than the primates. Man has evolved a system of arbitrary symbolic communication through which knowledge, attitudes, skills etc., can be transmitted from one generation to the next. In the case of apes and monkeys learning must take place in the actual situation and the range of their learning is also very much limited. The possession of language is a boon to the human beings through which one can convey to the others a clear idea of situations which are not present and of the behaviour appropriate to such situations.
4. ***The speed of learning:*** Cultural learning can speed up the process of learning to a great extent. One can profit from the failures and successes in the learning of another. Though there is still the element of trial-and-error it can be reduced to the minimum. The techniques adopted and the experience gained by the previous generation can provide guidance for the learning of present generation. Culture has been assisting man as a short-hand method of acquiring knowledge.
5. ***The volume of learning:*** The system of symbolic communication, a product of culture has increased not only the speed of learning but also the volume of things learnt. The human beings capacity to learn techniques, devices, principles, rules, beliefs, rituals, ideas, attitudes, theories etc., is beyond compare. The primates or mammals are no match to them in this regard, Culture accumulates. Each generation adds its own to the cultural heritage. Hence human beings can learn more and learn better knowledge.
6. ***Division of labour in learning:*** Still even under cultural conditions, the quantum of one person's learning in his lifetime is very much limited. Further, it is not necessary for all the members of the group to learn the total culture in order to get

its profit. Through the social arrangement of the division of labour it is possible to make different people to learn different things with mutual benefit.

7. ***Social survival depends on culture:*** Culture belongs to the society and not to the individual. Hence survival does not depend upon the strength and talents of particular individuals. It depends upon the culture of the group as a whole. Since different human groups possess different cultures conflict would take place among them. In this cultural struggle the group that is the most efficiently organised and has the most advanced techniques would dominate over others. The Spaniards, for example, could conquer and impose most of their culture on the Indians of South America by means of their cultural superiority and not by their biological superiority.

8. ***The cultural invention of writing:*** With the invention of writing the cultural transmission has become quite easier. Writing, in contrast to verbal communication, allows ideas to be 'stored' apart from the immediate communicating situation. By fixing ideas to writing it is possible to spread communication far and wide. Through writing men can insure that the great contributions will be incorporated into cultural heritage. Writing can add to and intensify the degree of specialisation. Writing extends the effectiveness of symbolic communication in human society. Other inventions such as printing, radio and telephone, television etc., may do the same.

9. ***Normative control of behaviour:*** The symbolic communication has given rise to what is known as 'legitimacy' or the 'normative' in the human society. This peculiarity is not present among the monkeys and apes. Any human situation has two aspects: the facts and the attitude or sentiment toward facts. Attitude is conveyed as a part of cultural heritage, It is there before the presence of the actual situations. Particularly, the attitudes and, sentiments relating to what 'ought to be' and 'ought not to be' are very powerful. We are more prone to approve or disapprove of the facts, particularly the actual behaviour of the individuals on the basis of these received judgements or sentiments. This trend adds a new dimension to our social existence which is of tremendous importance in exercising control over individual conduct. The normative ideas exist in the minds of the individuals. They are communicated as judgements on conduct and they influence the course of external events. For example, a man can talk, play, work, eat, drink, write, sleep, or do anything legitimately or illegitimately, depending upon the kind of social situation that is defined. His behaviour, including his sexual behaviour is defined normatively and not biologically.

10. ***The moral order of the human society:*** As against the animal society the human society has not only a factual order but also a moral order. These two are causally interdependent. In the human society, the normative control exists because the individuals are always responsive to the judgements of others. Since they are subjected to the transmission of attitudes and ideas they are bound to be responsive, to the judgements of others. These received judgements of others become in course of time their own judgements about themselves. They approve or disapprove of their own acts and those of their fellow members. The concepts of 'conscience' and 'feelings of guilt' confirm this tendency of the people. An assessment of success or failure in one's endeavour to attain ends is also mostly influenced by the opinions of other. An individual is thus motivated to the esteem of his fellows.

11. ***The normative factor modifies bio-social traits:*** Further, the presence of the normative factor complicates every bio-social trait that we have inherited from our anthropoid ancestors. For example, the system of dominance, has been greatly modified by the cultural definition of legitimate and illegitimate dominance. In human society, we find a system of normatively sanctioned power called 'authority'. This often overrules other bases of power such as strength, ability, personality, etc. Further, persons in authority may use their legitimate power even in, illegitimate ways. Thus, it is clear that in the study of human society we must take into account not only facts but also the normative attitude toward facts. Both are included in the reality which is called socio-cultural.

REVIEW QUESTIONS

1. Bring out the basic features of society.
2. What are the societal needs? How are these societal needs classified?
3. Write a detailed note on the bio-social systems. Differentiate between the mamalian and non-mammalian societies.
4. Give an account of the characteristic features of the primate and non-primate mammalian societies.
5. Write a detailed note on the human society vs non-human society.
6. Critically examine the role of culture in the socio-culture system.
7. Write short notes on the following:
   (a) Heredity
   (b) Mammalian social groups
   (c) Socio-cultural system

⌘⌘⌘⌘⌘⌘⌘⌘⌘⌘⌘⌘

PART TWO

BASIC SOCIOLOGICAL TERMS

We use various [illegible] [illegible] more clearly [illegible] the basic soci[illegible] [illegible]

SOCIETY

Meaning and Nature of Society

The term [illegible] the sociologi[illegible] [illegible]

[illegible] the word 'society' [illegible] sociability [illegible] dictates that [illegible] lives in [illegible] his living [illegible] human life and social [illegible] together.

Definition of Society

1. "A society is a collection of [illegible] which mark them off from others who do not [illegible] behaviour." — *Morris Ginsberg*

8

SOME BASIC CONCEPTS

CHAPTER OUTLINE

- SOCIETY: MEANING, NATURE AND CHARACTERISTICS
- COMMUNITY: MEANING, DEFINITION ELEMENTS AND OTHER ASPECTS
- SOCIETY AND COMMUNITY
- ASSOCIATION: DEFINITION AND CHARACTERISTICS
- ASSOCIATION AND COMMUNITY
- INSTITUTION: DEFINITION AND CHARACTERISTICS—PRIMARY AND SECONDARY INSTITUTIONS
- DIFFERENCES BETWEEN FUNCTIONS OF SOCIAL INSTITUTIONS
- DIFFERENCES BETWEEN ASSOCIATIONS AND INSTITUTIONS
- SOCIAL SYSTEM: MEANING, DEFINITION, CHARACTERISTICS ELEMENTS AND MECHANISMS
- SOCIAL ACTION: ELEMENTS, TYPOLOGY AND IMPORTANCE

We use very often certain words like *society, community, association, institution, social organisation, social system, folkways, mores, values, customs*, etc., in our study of society. These are not merely words, they are concepts. They carry some precise meaning. Every science has its own terms or concepts. These terms help a student of a science to understand it more clearly. The student of sociology also should have a clear vision and correct understanding of its basic terms. Some of the basic sociological terms may be examined here.

SOCIETY

Meaning and Nature of Society

The term '*Society*' is the most fundamental one in sociology. But still it is one of the most vague and general concepts in the sociologist's vocabulary. We speak of—*The Co-operative Society, The Agricultural Society, The Friendly Society, The Society of Jesus, The Theosophical Society*, etc. In these examples, "Society" means no more than an association. Sometimes, we may say, '*I enjoy his society*', '*I like the society of artists*', '*I move in high society*'. These three uses of the word '*society*' here indicate company or fellowship. The term *society* is also used to mean an *urban society*, or a *rural society*, a modem *industrial society* or a *primitive society*, an *open* society or a *closed* society, and so on. Then what do we mean by society ?

The term '*society*' is derived from the Latin word '*socius*', which means companionship or friendship. Companionship means sociability. As *George Simmel* pointed out, it is this element of sociability which defines the true essence of society. It indicates that man always lives in the com- pany of other people. '*Man is a social animal*', said *Aristotle* centuries ago. Man lives in towns, cities, tribes, villages, but never alone. Loneliness brings him boredom and fear. Man needs society for his living, working and enjoying life. Society has become an essential condition for human life to arise and to continue. Human life and society always go together.

Definition of Society

1. "A society is a collection of individuals united by certain relations or mode of behaviour which mark them off from others who do not enter into these relations or who differ from them in behaviour". — *Morris Ginsberg*

2. "Society is the complex of organised associations and institutions with a community". — *G.D.M. Cole*
3. "Society is the union itself, the organisation, the sum of formal relations in which associating individuals are bound together." — *Prof. Giddings*
4. "The term society refers not to group of people, but to the complex pattern of the norms of interaction, that arise among and between them". —*Lapiere*
5. Society is "a web of social relationship". — *Muclver*

Characteristics of Society

The basic characteristics of society are as follows:

1. ***Society consists of people:*** Society is composed of people. Without the students and the teachers there can be no college and no university. Similarly, without people there can be no society, no social relationships, and no social life at all.
2. ***Mutual interaction and mutual awareness:*** Society is a group of people in continuous interaction with each other. It refers to the reciprocal contact between two or more persons. It is '*a process whereby men interpenetrate the minds of each other*'. An individual is a member of society so long as he engages in relationship with other members of society. It means that individuals are in continuous interaction with other individuals of society. The limits of society are marked by the limits of social interactions.

   Social interaction is made possible because of *mutual awareness*. Society is understood as a network of social relationships. But not all relations are social relations. Social relationships exist only when the members are *aware* of each other. Society exists only where social beings '*behave*' towards one another in ways determined by their recognition of one another. Without this awareness there can be no society. A social relationship, thus implies mutual awareness.
3. ***Society depends on likeness:*** The principle of likeness is essential for society. It exists among those who resemble one another in some degree, in body and in mind. Likeness refers to the similarities. People have similarities with regards to their needs, works, aims, ideals, values, outlook towards life, and so on. Just as the '*birds of the same feather flock together*', men belonging to the same species called '*Homo sapiens*', have many things in common. Society, hence, rests on what *F.H. Giddings* calls *consciousness of kind*. "Comradeship, intimacy, association of any kind or degree would be impossible without some understanding of each by the other and that understanding depends on the likeness which each apprehends in the other" Society in brief, exists among *like beings and likeminded.*
4. ***Society rests on difference too:*** Society also implies difference. A society based entirely on likeness and uniformities is bound to be loose in socialities. If men are exactly alike, their social relationships would be very much limited. There would be little give-and-take, little reciprocity They would contribute very little to one another. More than that, life becomes boring, monotonous and uninteresting, if differences are not there.

   Hence, we find difference in society. Family for example, rests on the biological difference between the sexes. People differ from one another in their looks, personality, ability, talent, attitude, interest, taste, intelligence, faith and so on. People pursue different activities because of these differences. Thus we find farmers, labourers, teachers, soldiers, businessmen, bankers, engineers, doctors, advocates, writers, artists, scientists, musicians, actors, politicians, bureaucrats and others working in different capacities, in different fields in society. However, difference alone cannot create society. It is subordinate to likeness.
5. ***Co-operation and division of labour:*** Primarily likeness and secondarily difference create the division of labour. Division of labour involves the assignment to each unit or group a specific share of a common task. For example, the common task of producing cotton clothes is shared by a number of people like the farmers who grow cotton, the spinners, and weavers, the dyers, and the merchants. Similarly, at home work is divided and shared by the father, mother and children. Division of labour leads to specialisation. Division of labour and specialisation are the hallmarks of modem complex society.

   Division of labour is possible because of *co-operation*. Society is based on co-operation. It is the very basis of our social life. As *C.H. Cooley* says, 'co-operation arises when men realise that they have common interests'. It refers to the mutual working together for the attainment of a common goal. Men satisfy many of their desires and fulfil interests through joint efforts. People may have direct or indirect co-operation among them. Thus co-operation and division of labour have made possible social solidarity or social cohesion.

6. ***Society implies interdependence also:*** Social relationships are characterised by interdependence. Family, the most basic social group, for example, is based upon the interdependence of man and woman. One depends upon the 'other for the satisfaction of one's needs. As society advances, the area of interdependence also grows. Today, not only individuals are interdependent upon one another, but even, communities, social groups, societies and nations are also interdependent.
7. ***Society is dynamic:*** Society is not static; it is dynamic. Change is ever present in society. Changeability is an inherent quality of human society. No society can ever remain constant for any length of time. Society is like water in a stream or river that forever flows. It is always in flux. Old men die and new ones are born. New associations and institutions and groups may come into being and old ones may die a natural death. The existing ones may undergo changes to suit the demands of time or they may give birth to the new ones. Changes may take place slowly and gradually or suddenly and abruptly.
8. ***Social control:*** Society has its own ways and means of controlling the behaviour of its members. Co-operation, no doubt exists in society. But, side by side, competitions, conflicts, tensions, revolts, rebellions and suppressions are also there. They appear and re-appear off and on. Clash of economic or political or religious interests is not uncommon. Left to themselves, they may damage the very fabric of society. They are to be controlled. The behaviour or the activities of people are to be regulated. Society has various formal as well as informal means of social control. It means, society has customs, traditions, conventions and folkways, mores, manners, etiquettes and the *informal* means of social control. Also it has law, legislation, constitution, police, court, army and other *formal* means of social control to regulate the behaviour of its members.
9. ***Culture:*** Each society is distinct from the other. Every society is unique because it has its own way of life, called culture. Culture refers to, as *Linton says, the social heritage of man*. It includes the whole range of our life. It includes our attitudes, judgements, morals, values, beliefs, ideas, ideologies and our institutions: political, legal, economic; our sciences and philosophies. Culture is the expression of human nature in our ways of living and thinking, in behaving, and acting as members of society.

   Culture and society go together. What distinguishes one society from the other is culture. Culture is a thing which only human beings possess. It is not found at the level of animals. Culture is not society, but an element of society. As *Gillin* and *Gillin* say, "*Culture is the cement binding together into a society its component individuals; ... human society is people interacting; culture is the patterning of their behaviour*".
10. There is yet another attribute on which society depends. It is the *gregarious nature of man. Aristotle* said that "*man is a social animal*". Psychologists like *McDougall*, say that man is social because of the basic human instinct called the *gregarious instinct*. Gregariousness refers to the tendency of man to live in groups. Man always lives amidst men. He cannot live without it. This internal nature of man has forced him to establish social groups and societies and to live in them.

Human life and society almost go together. Man is born in society and bred up in society, nourished and nurtured in society. From childhood to adolescence, from adolescence to youth, from youth to maturity, from maturity to old age, from old age up to death, man lives in society. He depends on society for protection and comfort, for nurture and education. Participation in society is necessary for the development of personality. Various cases show that *man can become man only among men*.

Society makes our life livable. It is the nurse of youth, the arena of manhood and womanhood. Society is, therefore, as *MacIver* puts it, more than our environment. It is within us as well as around us. Society not only liberates the activities of men, but it limits their activities also. It controls their behaviour in countless ways. It shapes our attributes, our beliefs, our morals and our ideals. Emotional development, intellectual maturity, satisfaction of physical needs and material comforts are unthinkable without society. Society is a part of our mental equipment and we are a part of society. It stimulates the growth of our personality. It liberates and controls our talents and capacities.

COMMUNITY

Different Meanings of the Term 'Community'

The term *Community* is very loosely used. It is given different interpretations and used in different ways to mean different things. In their casual talks, people often use the term community to refer to a racial community, or a religious community or a national community or a caste community or a linguistic community or a professional community or sometimes, to refer to the entire mankind in a restricted sense, it is used to mean an association or group, and in wider sense, it is used to refer to the entire humanity.

Definition of Community

1. Community is "a social group with some degree of "we-feeling" and living in a given area"

— Bogardus

2. Community is "the smallest territorial group that can embrace all aspects of social life".

— Kingsley Davis

3. Community is "an area of social living marked by some degree of social coherence".

— R.M. MacIver

4. "A community is a group or collection of groups that inhabits a locality".

— Ogbum and Nimkoff

5. Community is "any circle of people who live together and belong together in such a way that they do not share this or that particular interest only, but a whole set of interests".

— Manheim

Community is, therefore, a geographic area having common centres of interests and activities. A community is essentially an area of social living. It is marked by some degree of social coherence. Thus community is a circle in which common life is living. 'Community' is an all-inclusive term. It includes in itself all our social relationships. It includes a variety of associations and institutions. Within the range of a community the members may carry on their economic, religious, political, educational and other activities. Hence community is the total organisation of social life within limited space. Examples: village, town, tribe, city, district.

Elements of Community

The main bases of community are: 1. *locality*, and 2. *community sentiment.*

1. Locality

A community is a territorial group. It always occupies some geographic area. Locality is the physical basis of community. Even the wandering tribe or a nomad community, for example, has a locality, though changing habitation. A group of people forms community only when it begins to reside a definite locality. In contrast with society, a community is more or less locally limited.

Living together facilitates people to develop social contacts, gives protection, safety and security. It help the members to promote and fulfil their common interests. Further, the very physical conditions may influence social life to a great extent. Most communities are settled and derive from the conditions of their locality a strong bond of solidarity.

Locality continues to be a basic factor of community life. However, in modern times the local bond of community is weakened by the development of the means of transport and communication. In fact, the extension of communication is itself the condition of a larger but still territorial community.

The physical factors such as fertile soil, minerals, forests, fisheries, water resources, vegetation, weather, climate, etc., are included in the locality. These factors condition or influence the lives of community members in several ways. They have a close bearing on their economic activities in particular.

2. Community Sentiment

Locality alone cannot make a group, a community. Sometimes, people residing in the same area may not have any contacts and communications. For example, people living in different extensions of a city may lack sufficient social contacts. They may not have common outlook and share no common interests. A community is essentially an area of common living with a feeling of belonging. There must be the common living with its *awareness* of sharing a way of life as well as the common earth.

Community Sentiment means a feeling of belonging together. The members must be aware of their staying together and sharing common interests. The members develop a sense of *we-feeling*. It means a kind of identification with the group. Without a sense of identification, a sense of awareness, a sense of living and sharing some common interests in life, there cannot be any community.

OTHER ASPECTS OF COMMUNITY

1. ***Stability:*** A community has not only locality and community sentiment, but also has stability. It is not a temporary group like a crowd or a mob. It is relatively stable. It includes a permanent group life in a definite place.

2. ***Naturalness:*** Communities normally become established in a natural way. They are not deliberately created. They are not made or created by an act of will or by planned efforts. Individuals become its members by birth itself. Membership, hence, is not voluntary. Communities are spontaneous in their origin and development. Of course, they cannot come into being suddenly and automatically.
3. ***Size of the community:*** Community involves the idea of size. A community may be big or small. A small community may be included in a wider community. A city and a village may be included in a wider community called the district. Hence, there are communities within communities. District, as a big community may enclose small communities like villages, towns, cities, tribes, etc. Thus the term community is used in a relative sense.
4. ***Regulation of relations:*** Every community develops in course of time, a system of traditions, customs, morals, practices; a bundle of rules and regulations to regulate the relations of its members. The sense of what they have in common memories and traditions, customs and institutions shapes and defines the general need of man to live together.

However, in modern times, the nature of community sentiment is gradually changing. Today, the interests of men are diverse and complex. Their attachment towards their community is gradually fading. In modern highly industrialised urban communities, the spirit of community sentiment is very much lacking.

DIFFERENCES BETWEEN SOCIETY AND COMMUNITY

The terms *society* and *community* are relative terms. The terms are clearly distinguished in sociology. The following table clarifies the difference between society and community.

Society	*Community*
1. Society is a web of social relationships.	Community consists of a group of individuals living in a particular area with some degree of 'we-feeling'.
2. A definite geographic area is not an essential aspect of society.	Community always denotes a definite locality or geographic area.
3. Society is abstract.	Community is concrete.
4. 'Community sentiment' or a sense of 'we-feeling' may be present or may not be present in society.	'Community sentiment' is an essential element of community. There can be no community in its absence.
5. Society is wider. There can be more than one community in a society.	Community is smaller than society.
6. The objectives and interests of society are more extensive and varied.	The objectives and interests of a community are comparatively less extensive and varied.
7. Society involves both likeness and difference. Common interests as well as diverse interests are present in society.	Likeness is more important than difference in community. There is common agreement of interests and objectives on the part of members.

ASSOCIATION

We use the words *association* and *institution* very commonly in our daily talks. Sometimes, these words are used interchangeably to mean one and the same. But these words are used in a specific way in sociology. Hence it is necessary for us to know the meaning and nature of and difference between these two terms.

Association as a Means of Pursuing Ends

Men have diverse needs, desires and interests and ends which demand their satisfaction. They have three ways of fulfilling their ends. *Firstly*, they may act independently, each in his own way without bothering about others. This is unsocial and has its own limitations. *Secondly*, men may seek their ends through conflicts with one another. One may clash with another or others to snatch things or objects which one wants from others. *Finally*, men may try to fulfil their ends through co-operation and mutual assistance. On the basis of this co-operative effort each individual will be contributing to the ends of his fellow-men. This co-operative pursuit has a reference to *association*. When a group or collection of individuals organises itself expressly for the purpose of pursuing certain of its interests together on a co-operative pursuit, an association is said to be born.

Definition of Association

1. An association is "an organisation deliberately formed for the collective pursuit of some interest, or a set of interests, which its members share". — *R.M. MacIver*
2. An association is "a group of social beings related to one another by the fact that they possess or have instituted in common an organisation with a view to securing a specific end or specific ends". — *Morris Ginsberg*
3. An association is a group of people organised for the achievement of a particular interest or interests.
4. An association is "a group organised for the pursuit of an interest or group of interests in common".

Men have several interests. Hence they establish different associations to fulfil them. They have a number of associations of different kinds. Some examples may be cited here.

Examples of Association

(1) *Political Associations*. The Bharatiya Janata Party, The Congress Party, The Communist Party, The Bharatiya Janata Yuva Morcha, etc. (2) *Religious Associations*: The Vishwa Hindu Parishad, The Ramakrishan Mission, The Arya Samaj, The Society of Jesus, etc. (3) *Students ' Associations*: The Akhil Bharatiya Vidyarthi Parishad, Delhi University Students' Association, The National Students Union of India, Chhatra Yuva-Sangharsh Vahini, etc. (4) *Labourers 'Associations*: Bharatiya Mazdoor Sangha, The Hind Mazdoor Panchayat, Indian National Trade Union Congress, All India Trade Union Congress, etc. (5) *Professional Associations*: Karnataka State College Teachers' Association, Indian Medical Association, The Indian Bar Council. (6) *Economic Associations* or *Business Organisations*: Business Corporations, Hotels Owners' Association, Chamber of Commerce, The Consumers' Co-operative Society, etc. (7) *International Associations*: The Rotary Club, The Lions' Club, The Y.M.C.A., Y.W.C.A., The Amnesty International, Friends of Indian Society.

The Associations may be found in different fields. No single association can satisfy all the interests of the individual or individuals. Since man has a bundle of interests, he organises various associations for the purpose of fulfilling his varied interests. It follows then that a man may belong to more than one association. He may be member of a political association, religious association, a professional association, a cultural association, an entertainment club, a sports club, a rotary club, and so on.

Main Characteristics of Association

The main characteristics of association are as follows:

1. ***Association – A human group:*** An association is formed or created by people . It is basically a social group. Without people there can be no association. However, all groups are not associations, because, an association is basically an organised group. An unorganised group like crowd or mob cannot be an association.
2. ***Common interest or interests:*** An association is not merely a collection of individuals. It consists of those individuals who have more or less the same interests. Accordingly, those who have political interests may join political associations, and those who have religious interests may join religious associations, and so on.
3. ***Co-operative spirit:*** An association is based on the co-operative spirit of its members. People work together to achieve some definite purposes. For example, a political party has to work together as a united group on the basis of co-operation in order to fulfil its objective of coming to power.
4. ***Organisation:*** Association denotes some kind of organisation. An association is known essentially as an organised group. Organisation gives stability and proper shape to an association. Organisation refers to the way in which the statuses and roles are distributed among the members.
5. ***Regulation of relations:*** Every association has its own ways and means of regulating the relations of its members. Organisation depends on this element of regulation. They may assume written or unwritten forms.
6. ***Association as agencies:*** Associations are means or agencies through which their members seek to realise their similar or shared interests. Such social organisations necessarily act not merely through leaders, but through officials or representatives, as agencies. Associations normally act through agents who are responsible for and to the association. This fact gives association a distinctive character and its peculiar legal status. Further, association may have its own *methods* of operation peculiar to it as an association.
7. ***Durability of association:*** An association may be permanent or temporary. There are some long-standing associations like the state, family, religious associations etc. Some associations may be purely temporary in nature. Ex.

Associations that are established to felicitate some great writers, scientists, and religious leaders and associations created for performing some social, religious or other ceremony or fair on a grand scale.

It is clear from the above, that an association is not merely a group, it is something more than that. It is a group *expressly organised* around a particular interest. The qualification "expressly organised", helps us to distinguish between associations and other social groups. Social groups like class, crowd, mob, public, etc., in this way, are not associations.

In modem society, the number of associations is on the increase. Not only their numbers is increasing, but their varieties are also increasing. In almost all the fields of our social life we have associations. The rapid changes that are taking place in different fields of our social life have necessitated the birth of a large number of associations. In modern democratic countries associations have a distinct role to play. Their role in strengthening the democratic set-up can hardly be exaggerated. The modern age today, is really an age of organisations or associations. Man's life is, today, to a very great extent, lived and controlled by the *larger association* (The state).

ASSOCIATION AND COMMUNITY

An association is established for the purpose of fulfilling some common but definite need or needs of the people. It is hence *deliberately created*. On the other hand, community is a *natural organisation*. Its objectives are common but not specific. Man is born in a community but he enters into different associations to fulfil his specific interests or needs. An association is *not* a community, but an organisation *within* the community. We can call a city a community, but not a church or a trade union or a political party. We can call a country a community but not the political parties of the country. They are associations. The interests of a community are wider than those of an association. Hence an association is *partial*, whereas a community is *integral*. A community is more comprehensive than an association. Community is therefore, *more free and wider* than even the greatest associations. Within a community there may exist not only numerous associations but also antagonistic associations, Ex. Political parties of the communists and democrats. Since an association is organised for a particular interest, *we belong to it* by virtue of this interest. Membership in an association has only limited significance.

The following table makes clear the difference between association and community:

Association	*Community*
1. Membership of an association is voluntary. Individuals are at liberty to join them.	By birth itself individuals become members of community. In this way membership is rather compulsory.
2. An association has some specific interest or interests.	A community has some general interests.
3. An association does not necessarily imply the spatial aspects.	A community is marked by a locality.
4. An association may be stable and long-lasting or it may not be so.	A community is relatively more stable and permanent.
5. Associations may have their legal status.	A community has no legal status.
6. Associations may have their own rules and regulations to regulate the relations of their members. They may have written or unwritten rules.	A community regulates the behaviour of its members by means of customs, traditions, etc. It does not have written rules or laws.
7. Association is partial. It may be regarded as a part of the community.	Community is integral. It may have within its boundary, several associations.

INSTITUTION

The concept of *institution* is one of the most important in the entire field of sociology. Unfortunately, it is a concept that has not been consistently used by sociologist. The importance of understanding the concept of institution in order to understand society is, at the same time, recognised by all the sociologists. In fact, *Durkheim* has gone to the extent of defining sociology as *the science of social institutions. Sumner and Keller* have said, "Folkways are to society what cells are to the biological organism; institutions are its bones and tissues". *F.H. Giddings* regards institutions as "the organs that conserve what is best in the past of human race".

The term *institution* has been given various interpretations. Some sociologists have used it in a vague manner also. Commenting on this, *Harry M. Johnson* writes, " ..... both laymen and sociologists often speak of schools, churches, business organisations, prisons, and the like as the institutions of the community. This usage is so frequent that we should be foolish to condemn it".

Definition of Institution

1. ***Ginsberg:*** Institutions "may be described as recognised and established usages governing the relations between individuals and groups".
2. ***MacIver and Page:*** Institutions may be defined as the "established forms or conditions of procedure characteristic of group activity".
3. ***Kingsley Davis:*** Institution can be defined as "a set of interwoven folkways, mores, and laws built around one or more functions".
4. ***H.E. Barnes:*** Institutions represent "the social structure and the machinery through which human society organises, directs and executes the multifarious activities required to satisfy human needs".
5. ***C.A. Ellwood:*** Institutions may be defined as "the habitual ways of living together which have been sanctioned, systematised and established by the authority of communities".

Characteristics of Institution

The main characteristics of social institutions may be described here.

1. ***Social in nature:*** Institutions come into being due to the collective activities of the people. They are essentially social in nature. After all, institutions are the products of the secular and repetitive forms of social relationships of the individuals.
2. ***Universality:*** Social institutions are ubiquitous. They exist in all the societies and existed at all the stages of social development. The basic institutions like family, religion, property and some kind of political institutions are observed even in the tribal or primitive societies.
3. ***Institutions are standardised norms:*** An institution must be understood as standardised procedures and norms. They prescribe the ways of doing things. They also prescribe rules and regulations that are to be followed. *Marriage*, as an institution, for example, governs the relations between the husband and wife. Similarly, the school or college has its own rules and procedures.
4. ***Institutions as means of satisfying needs:*** Institutions are established by men themselves. They cater to the satisfaction of some basic and vital needs of man. These basic needs are – (1) the need for self-preservation, (2) the need for self-perpetuation, and (3) the need for self-expression.
5. ***Institutions are the controlling mechanisms:*** Institutions like religion, morality, state, government, law, legislation, etc., control the behaviour of men. These mechanisms preserve the social order and give stability to it. Institutions are like wheels on which human society marches on towards the desired destination.
6. ***Relatively permanent:*** Institutions normally do not undergo sudden or rapid changes. Changes take place slowly and gradually in them. Many institutions are rigid and enduring. They, in course of time, become the conservative elements in society. Ex: caste, religion, etc. But under the pressure of circumstances they also undergo changes.
7. ***Abstract in nature:*** Institutions are not external, visible or tangible things. They are abstract. Thus *marriage* cannot be kept in a museum, *religion* cannot be rated or quantified; *war* cannot be weighed and law cannot be brought to the laboratory experiments and so on.
8. ***Oral and written traditions:*** Institutions may persist in the form of oral and/or written traditions. For the primitive societies they may be largely oral. But in modem complex societies they may be observed in written as well as unwritten forms. There may be written institutional forms like constitutions, sacred text books, syllabus, governmental orders, business contracts, examination system, etc., relating to political, religious, educational and economic institutions and so on.
9. ***Synthesising symbols:*** Institutions may have their own symbols, material or non-material. Ex. the state has flag emblem, national anthem as its symbols, religion may have its own symbols like crucifix, crescent, star, swastika; the school may have its own flag or school prayer, marriage may have its own wedding ring or *mangala-sutra*, and so on.
10. ***Institutions are interrelated:*** Institutions, though diverse, are interrelated. Understanding of one institution requires the understanding of the other related institutions. The religious, moral, educational, political, economic and other types of institutions are essentially interlinked.

Primary and Secondary Institutions

Institutions are often classified into (*i*) primary institutions and (*ii*) secondary institutions. The most basic institutions which are found even in primitive societies like religion, family, marriage, property, some kind of political system, are *primary* in character. As societies grew in size and complexity, institutions became progressive and more differentiated. Accordingly, a large number of institutions are evolved to cater to the secondary needs of people. They may be called secondary institutions. Ex. education, examination, law, legislation, constitution, parliamentary procedure, business, etc.

Sumner makes a distinction between the *crescive* and the *enacted* institutions. Those that evolved or developed naturally, unconsciously and even spontaneously are called by him *crescive*. Those institutions that are consciously and purposefully and in a planned way established are referred to by him as *enacted*. The *crescive* ones are more akin to primary institutions whereas the enacted ones resemble secondary institutions.

FUNCTIONS OF SOCIAL INSTITUTIONS

Institutions have great functional importance. Their main functions are as follows:

1. ***Institutions cater to the satisfaction of needs:*** Institutions contribute to the fulfilment of the fundamental human needs such as (*i*) The need for self-perpetuation, (*ii*) perpetuation, and (*iii*) self-expression. They provide and prescribe the ways and means of fulfilling them.
2. ***Institutions control human behaviour:*** Institutions organize and regulate the system of social behaviour. Through the institutions the unexpected, spontaneous, and irregular behaviour of people is replaced by expected, patterned, systematic, regular and predictable behaviour. Thus, the interpersonal relationships of the individuals are regulated by institutions. They make clear for the members what is allowed and what is not; what is desirable and what is undesirable. This is particularly true of the governmental institutions.
3. ***Institution simplify actions for the individual:*** Since the institutions prescribe a particular way of behaviour for the fulfilment of our basic needs, they save much of our energy and also time. They avoid confusion and uncertainties and contribute to a system and order in society.
4. ***Institutions assign roles and statuses to the individual:*** Institutionalisation of the social behaviour consists of the establishment of definite norms. These norms assign status positions and role-functions in connection with such behaviour. Institutions such as family, marriage, education, property, division of labour, caste, religion, etc. provide some social standing for the individual concerned.
5. ***Institutions contribute to unity and uniformity:*** Institutions which regulate the relations between individuals have largely been responsible for unity and uniformity that are found in a society.
6. ***Manifest functions of institutions:*** Every institution has two types of manifest functions (*i*) the pursuit of its objectives or interests, and (*ii*) the preservation of its own internal cohesion so that it may survive. For example, the state must serve its citizens and protect its boundaries. At the same time, the state must escape the danger of internal revolution and external conquests.
7. ***The negative functions of institutions:*** Institutions may cause harmful effects also. They do not undergo changes easily and quickly even if the circumstances demand change. When they become too conservative they retard progress. They even hamper the growth of personalities of the people. Religion and caste can be mentioned here as examples to show how they often discourage people to do achievements or adventures.

DIFFERENCES BETWEEN ASSOCIATION AND INSTITUTION

The terms *association* and *institution* are commonly used by people to mean one and the same thing. But the difference between the two terms is of great importance in sociology.

When men create associations they must also create institutions to get their desires satisfied. Men form an association to satisfy their need or needs. But these needs are fulfilled through institutions. Every association has its own institutions. For example, *family*, as an association has its institutions like marriage, the property system, the system of inheritance, the home, the family-meal, etc. A *state*, as an association may have its institutions like government, legislative procedures, parliament, etc. Institutions are impossible without associations. Institutions may be established by community as well as by association. The table below makes clear the difference between association and institution.

	Association	Institution
1.	An association is a group of people organised for the purpose of fulfilling a need or needs.	Institution refers to the organised way of doing things. It represents common procedure.
2.	Association denotes membership. We belong to associations, to political parties, trade unions, youth clubs, families, etc.	Institution denotes only a mode or means of service. We do not belong to institution. We do not belong to marriage, property, education or law.
3.	Associations consist of individuals.	Institutions consist of laws, rules, and regulations.
4.	Associations are *concrete*.	Institutions are *abstract*.
5.	An association has a location; it makes sense to ask where it is. Thus, a family can be located in space.	An institution does not have locations. The question where it is, makes no sense at all. Thus, we cannot locate examination, education, marriage, etc.
6.	Associations are mostly *created* or *estab-lished*.	Institutions are primarily *evolved*.
7.	An association may have its own distinctive name.	Institution does not possess specific names, but has a structure and may have *symbol*.
8.	Associations may be temporary or perma-nent.	Institutions are relatively more durable.

SOCIAL SYSTEM

Meaning of System

The term 'social system' is popularly used in sociology today. It is necessary for us to know the meaning of the word "system" before we start our venture to understand the term 'social system'.

(*i*) According to *Oxford Dictionary*, the term 'system' represents "a group of things or parts working together in a regular relation".

(*ii*) As *Robert A. Dahl* says, "Any collection of real objects that interact in some way with one another can be considered a system: a galaxy, a football team, a legislature, a political party".

(*iii*) "A system is any collection of interrelated pans, objects, things or organisms".

Five Points about Any System

The term 'system' denotes the following points or factors:

(*a*) *A System indicates an orderly arrangement of parts*. It has parts which are interrelated.

These parts may have their specific functions.

(*b*) *A system may have its own boundaries*. In order to determine what lies within a particular system and what lies outside it, it is necessary to specify the boundaries of that system.

(*c*) *One system can be an element or a subsystem in another*. For example, city is a sub-system in the thaluk and thaluk is a sub-system in the district which happens to be a sub-system in the province, and so on.

(*d*) *To call something a system is an abstract or an analytical way of looking at concrete things*. A system is merely an aspect of things abstracted from reality for purpose of analysis.

(*e*) *The concept of system is applicable to the study of organic as well as inorganic realities*. The term 'system' is used to refer to the organic realities such as the human digestive system, circulatory system, nervous system, etc. It is also used in the study of inorganic realities such as political system, economic system, industrial system, educational system, social system, etc.

Example of the Human Body as a System

The human body is an excellent example of system. It helps us to know the concept of 'system' and how system represents an orderly arrangement of its various parts.

There are different organs and systems in the human body with various functions to perform. There are organs with which we take food, breathe air, and excrete waste. There are organs of sight, hearing, taste and smell. The circulatory system supplies blood to different parts of the body. The nervous system stimulates and controls the activity of the various parts and of the 'whole'. The digestive system digests the food consumed. In the same way, different glandular systems have their distinctive functions to perform. What is to be noted here is that every organ in the human body is connected with every other, and true it is in the case of different systems and functions. There is interrelation and interdependence. As a result, the human body maintains its unity and balance, and an equilibrium among all the organs and systems. These relationships of the parts of the body are in a systematic arrangement or, in other words, they constitute a system.

Origin of the Concept of 'Social System'

Biological thought has inspired many sociologists. *Herbert Spencer*, who was highly influenced by the views of *Charles Darwin* has given an *organic analogy* in which society is compared with the human organism. Even from classical times right through the Middle Ages, writers were fascinated by this organic analogy. Studies on human physiology and anatomy made by the scientists have also impressed upon many sociologists. Studies made by *Walter B. Canon* and *L.J. Henderson* and others revealed the importance of interrelationship of parts or organs in the human body. This idea inspired many sociologists to think of society as a "system".

As *A.R. Radcliffe-Brown* has pointed out it was *Montesquieu* who formulated and used the concept of "Social system" for the first time towards the middle of the l8th century. The theory of Montesquieu states that "*all the features of social life are united into a coherent whole*". As a student of jurisprudence, Montesquieu was concerned with the study of laws. He sought to show that the laws of a society are connected with the political constitution, the economic life, the religion, the climate, the size of the population, the manners and customs and what he called the '*general spirit*' (*esprit general*). His study suggests that if we investigate systematically the *interconnections amongst features of social life*, we can advance our understanding of human societies.

The leading social analysts of the 19th century such as *Comte*, *Karl Marx*, *Herbert Spencer* and *Emile Durkheim* had their own conceptions of the social system and the relationship between social units. But they never used '*social system*' as a key term in their works.

Meaning of Social System

Human society is a network of human interactions and interrelations. The interaction of individuals takes place under such conditions that such a process of interaction may be called a system. System refers to the orderly arrangement of parts. *Social system* refers to the orderly arrangement of parts or components of society namely; human interactions. Individuals in their process of interaction influence each other. Their interrelationship and interaction assume a definite pattern which is called '*social system*'.

The concept is not however limited to interpersonal interaction alone. It also refers to the analysis of groups, institutions, societies and inter-societal entities. it may, for example, be employed in the analysis of the university, or the state, or the U.N.O. as social systems which have structures of interrelated parts.

As *David Popenoe* has pointed out "*social system can refer to any kind of social grouping, from a group of two friends to a large complex society*". It is widely used in sociology because it makes us to think of the way in which social units fit together into a whole, and the basic similarities among all forms of social interaction. We can look at the social system of a high school and see how it compares with the social system of a business firm or we can compare family with a football team.Each is a social unit in which people are pursuing a special set of goals, depending upon one another in various ways, and sharing a sense of common identity as a group.

The concept of "*social system*" has been used most explicitly, and self-consciously in modern '*functionalism*'. But it was implicit as much in 19th century social thought. "A social theory which treats social relations, groups or societies as a set of interrelated parts which function to maintain some boundary or unity of the parts is based explicitly or implicitly on the concept of social system".

The chief exponent of the most modern theory- of 'social system' has been *Talcott Parsons*. Persons have tried to give a more scientific and a rational explanation to the concept of social system in his books "*The Structure of Social Action*", and "*An Outline of the Social System*".

Definitions of Social System

1. According to *David Popenoe*, "A social system is a set of persons or groups who interact with one another; the set is conceived of as a social unit distinct from the particular persons who compose it".
2. "A social system is the system constituted by the interaction of a plurality of individual actors whose relations to each other are mutually oriented...[*i.e.*, are defined and mediated by a system of culturally structural and shared expectations]"–Source: "*A Dictionary of Social Sciences*" *By Julius Gould and William-L-Kolb*.

3. "A social system is defined in terms of two or more social actors engaged in more or less stable interaction within a bounded environment".
4. *W.F. Ogburn* has simplified *Talcott Parsons*' definition of social system in the following way: "*A social system may be defined as a plurality of individuals interacting with each other according to shared cultural norms and meanings*".
5. *Duncan Mitchell in his A Dictionary of Sociology writes*: "A social system basically consists of two or more individuals interacting directly or indirectly in a bounded Situation".

There may be physical or territorial boundaries, but the fundamental sociological point of reference is that the individuals are oriented, in a wide sense to a common focus or interrelated foci".

Characteristics of Social System

Our concept of social system consists of the following features:

1. Social system consists of two or more individuals among whom we find an established pattern of interaction.
2. Individuals in their actions take account of how the others are likely to act or behave.
3. Individuals in the system behave in accordance with their shared cultural norms and values.
4. Individuals in the system act together in pursuit of common goals or rewards,
5. "Social system" as a concept may represent the entire society or a number of sub-systems such as political system, educational system, economic system, judicial system, etc., that are found within the society.
6. A social system has its own boundary with the help of which it can be distinguished from other social systems.
7. The term 'social system' denotes a sociological concept that has been evolved to study society. In Weber's language it represents an 'ideal type'.

Elements of Social System

The social system is constituted by the actions of individuals. It involves participation of an actor in a process of interactive relationships. This participation has two main aspects: (*i*) *the positional aspect and the processional aspect*. The *positional* aspect indicates the location of the actor in social system which may be called his status. The *processional* aspect indicates the functional importance of the actor for the social system which may be called his role.

Thus, there are three elements of social system: 1. *The social act or action,* 2. *the actor*, and 3. *the role and status*.

1. ***The act:*** Social act or action is a process in the social system that motivates the individual or individuals in the case of a group. The orientation of action has a close relation with the attainment of satisfaction of the actor. The action is not an unexpected response to a particular situation or stimulus. It indicates that the actor has *a system of expectations relative to his own need-arrangements*. The need-arrangement system of the individual actor has two aspects: (*i*) the *gratificational* aspect, and (*ii*) the *orientational* aspect. The gratificational aspect refers to what the actor gets out of his interaction and what its costs are to him. The orientational aspect refers to the how he gets it. Both these aspects must be present in what is called a *social act*.
2. ***The actor:*** The actor is also a significant unit of social system. It is he who holds a status and performs a role. A social system must have a sufficient proportion of its actors. These actors *must be sufficiently motivated to act* according to the requirements of its role system. The social system *must also be adapted to the minimum needs* of the individual actor. The system *must secure sufficient participation of its actors* also. It means, it must motivate them sufficiently to the performances which are necessary for the social system to develop or to persist. The act and actor are complementary to each other. The actor has to act according to the roles assigned to him. This he learns through the process of *socialisation*. The social system limits and regulates the needs and also actions of the actor. This, the system does through *social control*.
3. ***The role and status:*** The social system involves the participation of actor in a process of interactive relationship. This participation has two aspects: (*i*) the role aspect, and (*ii*) the status aspect. *Role* denotes the functional significance of the actor for the social system. Status denotes the place of the actor in the social system.

An actor has a high or low status in a social system and he has a definite role to play. Different roles associated with the same status are properly integrated in the system. The actors are distributed between different roles. This process of distribution has been called by Parsons "*allocation*". Proper allocation of roles between actors minimises problems for the system. The allocation of roles is related to the problem of *allocation of facilities*. Problem of facilities is actually the problem of power because possession of facilities means to have power—economic or political.

Thus, a social system faces the problems of proper allocation of roles, proper allocation of facilities and rewards and proper allocation of economic and political power. If this allocation is properly made it may preserve itself, otherwise, it may disintegrate.

Mechanism of Social System

Social system is a system of interdependent action processes. But the tendencies of the individuals are such that they may alter the established status of social system. This may disturb the established interaction process of the system. It is, therefore, essential that some proper mechanisms are applied for maintaining the equilibrium between the various processes of social interaction. These mechanisms have been classified by *Persons* into two categories:

1. Mechanisms of socialisation, and 2. Mechanisms of social control.

1. ***Mechanisms of socialisation:*** Socialisation is a process whereby an individual learns to adjust with the conventional pattern of social behaviour. He learns to adjust himself with the social situations conforming with social norms, values, and standards. This process is not confined to the child alone. It goes on throughout life. Some of the principal aspects of socialisation are known as rearing, sympathy, identification, imitation, social teaching, suggestion, practice and punishment.
2. ***Mechanisms of social control:*** Social control consists of the mechanisms whereby the society moulds its members to conform to the approved pattern of social behaviour. According to Parsons, there are two types of elements which exist in every system. These are *integrative* and *disintegrative*. The function of social control is to eliminate those elements which bring disintegration and create problems for integration. Besides, in every society, there is a system of rewards for conformative behaviour and punishments for deviant behaviour. Deviant behaviour tendencies may also constitute one of the principal sources of change in the structure of the social system.

Levels of Systems

The term 'Social System' is used in sociological studies to denote different levels of systems. *GR. Leslie, R.F. Larson and B.L. Gorman* have spoken of four levels of systems. They are of the opinion that social systems differ according to the number of participants in them, and the kinds of relationships that exist among those participants. The four levels of systems are as follows:

1. ***Groups:*** Groups are social systems in which participants are conscious of their membership in the system. They are also aware of the boundaries of groups. It means they know who are members and who are not. They are conscious of interaction as it affects them and their co–participants. Finally, the members share values, goals towards which they strive. The groups act and have purposes or goals, just as individuals do.
2. ***Organisations:*** In some kinds of social systems larger than groups–the members are not necessarily conscious of the interaction among them. Further, the system itself may not have a consciousness as such. Such systems are called organisations.

   Ex. Two economic classes which are in conflict as constituting a system. Big business companies engaged in competition for getting the shares of the market as constituting a system, etc. Organisations may have members who are acting consciously and are enacting roles. But the organisation itself should not be personified. The organisation acts but it is not conscious.
3. ***Society:*** The largest and most nearly independent social systems are called 'societies'. Ideally, societies are substantial collections of people living in near isolation from other such collections of people (or societies). It is true that in reality no social system can be completely independent. The term 'society' has almost come to mean the 'nation state' – India, America, Japan, etc.
4. ***Supra-national systems:*** Above the national systems we find 'Supra-national systems'. In modern times, forces such as trade, war, travel, communication, politics are world-wide. The boundaries of formerly independent societies have become unclear. Supra-national systems are coming into existence. In sociological studies, the term social system is very rarely used to denote the 'supra-national systems'.

SOCIAL ACTION

The word '*action*', or '*behaviour*', is more a psychological category and it has been studied by many psychologists as a basic unit of their study. But the term "*social action*" is used by both social psychologists and sociologists. Many have regarded social action as the proper unit of observation in social sciences. In sociology it was Max Weber who explicitly used and emphasised social action as the basis for theory. Talcott Parsons has elaborately dealt with this concept in his famous work '*Structure of Social Action*.' A modified version of the Parsonian concept of social action has been provided by Kingsley Davis. It may be considered here.

"*Action is social when the actor behaves in such a manner that his action is intended to influence the actions of one or more other persons*". —*Duncan Mitchell*

Elements of Social Action

As mentioned by Kingsley Davis, Parsons speaks of four elements of action. In our analysis of the action of a single individual these four inseparable factors are to be kept in mind. They are: 1. *an actor*, 2. *an end*, 3. *a set of conditions*, and 4. *a set of means*. These four factors are only analytically distinct and no one can analyse a social action in its proper perspective without knowing these elements.

1. Actor

Social action presupposes the existence of an actor who initiates action. He is the agent of action. Here we refer to the '*ego*' or '*self*' of the actor concerned rather than to his body. The '*ego*' then is the subjective entity that possesses awareness and has experience. It makes decisions and holds together past events and imagines the future ones. To the self the body is only a condition for attaining ends. The self or 'ego' is an emergent quality characteristic of highly integrated organisms such as man. With his capacity for symbolic communication man can judge himself as others judge him.

Those who study human life must pay sufficient importance to the internal subjective experience which accompanies his behaviour. Not only the external events that affect the human body must be known but more than that, one must discover the way in which the individual *perceives* them. *"The way a person perceives his world, the way he feels and thinks, is an indispensable clue to his behaviour. True, it is the organism which behaves, but it is the ego which acts*". — *K. Davis*

2. End

The 'end' which motivates action is another important element. It has reference to the future, to a state of affairs which does not exist now. The end is "*that part of the future state of affairs which would not eventuate if the actor did not want it and did not exert himself to attain it.*"

The act comes to a finish when the end is attained. When one end is attained another end may crop up in its place which may initiate a new line of action. Thus each person's behaviour consists of an interrelated series of acts. The end may be conscious or unconscious. We cannot say that all. human activities are motivated invariably by some ends. But it could be said that all actions that are social in character have 'ends'.

An end is not just a resultant. If something is going to happen regardless of the actor's intervention, it cannot be called end. The end presupposes the desire to attain it and exertion for the same. *Example*: A local jeweller may want the price of the gold to go up suddenly. But whether or not the price will increase, is beyond his control. Hence the sudden increase in the price of the gold is not, from our point of view, his end. But if he starts hoarding gold immediately with the assumption that if its price increases he will get maximum profit, then it can be said that maximising the profit is his end. If things go as per his expectation, it is partly because, he has acted to attain his end.

The ends are *chosen* by the individual. The choice of ends is based on *values*. A value is that which is considered desirable, worthy of being pursued. The source of the value lies chiefly in the *sentiments*. In making the choice of the ends the actor is influenced partly by his sentiments, and partly by organic needs. The end is thus the particular application of a sentiment or value to a given situation as perceived by the actor.

3. Conditions

The presence of end cannot ensure that there will be no obstacles in the path of its realisation. The conditions that surround the individual will determine whether he will achieve the end or not. The conditions are actually the obstacles in the way of the realisation of an end. According to K. Davis, "the concept of action clearly implies that obstacles can be overcome." *The insuperable obstacles are called 'conditions*. 'They set the stage for action to take place. *Example*: If a Mangalorean wants to reach Bangalore he has to travel the distance. The distance as a given condition is unalterable. He cannot make a compromise with it. He cannot make an appeal to Bangalore to come near him. But he has to find out means for the realisation of his end.

The conditions imposed on the actor may be both *external* and *internal*. The physical environ- ment and society or social laws represent external conditions, whereas individual's inner capacity indicates internal condition. One's own personality may set a condition on what one can attain. Example: An individual may aspire to become a great singer, but his voice may not permit it. An- other person may aspire to have two wives, but the social laws may not permit it. In brief, the conditions that limit our attainment of ends stem from three sources: *physical environment, innate capacity,* and *society*.

4. Means

The end can be achieved only with the application of some means. Different situations may provide for different ends. In some situations simple means such as *speech* may be enough, while in some others, elaborate means such as educating the illiterate masses, may be required. Often the same end is attainable by more than one means, by providing the actor considerable choice. Due to this choice the actor may make an error, for the means chosen by him may not be most efficient ones. This may contribute to an element of uncertainty in action.

What appears to be a 'means' for one actor may prove to be a 'condition' for another. In the same situation, for example, one may feel privileged to tell a lie while another may feel obligated to tell the truth. For a city man who knows driving a vehicle may be useful *too* or *means* but for a primitive man, it may be an obstacle, that is, a *condition*. Whether or not a given part of a situation is a means or a condition depends much on the actor himself and not upon the part as such.

What is a means in one situation may be a goal in another. If a man intends to purchase a vehicle he may adopt the means of saving a part of his salary. Here, his saving money becomes an immediate goal and for reaching that goal budgeting the salary may be adopted as means. But actually his attempt at saving money is only a means towards the realisation of his final goal, that is, purchasing the vehicle. The actor's total behaviour is thus a complicated network of interrelated means and ends.

Typology of Social Action

The concept of '*Social Action*' is fundamental to Weberian sociological analyses. In fact, Weber conceived of sociology as a comprehensive science of social action. Human society is understood as a network of social actions. Weber has given a typology of social action which may be briefly examined here. Weber makes a distinction between four types of social action; namely:

1. Zweckrational action, or rational action in relation to a goal;
2. Wertrational action, or rational action in relation to a value;
3. Affective or emotional action, and
4. Traditional action.

1. ***Zweckrational action:*** This is actually a rational action in relation to a goal. It is comparable to Pareto's "logical action". In this type of action the actor conceives his goal clearly and combines means with the intention of attaning it. Weber here defines rationality only in terms of the knowledge of the actor and not in terms of the observer, as Pareto does. *Examples*: The action of the surgeon who is conducting an operation, the general of the army who wants to win a victory in war, the author who is writing to publish a book and so on.
2. ***Wertrational action:*** This is actually action in relation to a value. The action is rational not because it seeks to attain a goal, but because there is a value behind the goal. *Example*: The brave captain in a war goes down in water with his ship fighting the battle till the last. He is not prepared to abandon the sinking ship for he considers it as dishonourable. For the captain his action is rational because he wants to remain faithful to his own idea or value of honour.
3. ***Affective action:*** Affective action is one which is dictated immediately by the state of mind. In this type of action more than rationality emotions play a dominant role. *Example*: In a fit of anger the mother may beat the child, on hearing the news of his failure in examination the student may commit suicide, due to disappointment in love affairs one may take to drinking intoxicating drinks, etc. In these instances of action there is no reference to a goal or system of values.
4. ***Traditional action:*** This kind of action is dictated by customs and beliefs. One may become quite habituated to act in accordance with customary ways. In such customary ways of acting it is not necessary for the actor to imagine a goal, or be conscious of a value, or be stirred by an immediate emotion. The actor implicitly obeys his impulses that have become conditioned. *Example*: Students getting up impulsively from their seats to show respect to the teacher when he enters the classroom. The priest following the customary ways of worshipping in a temple in the presence of devotees.

Importance of the Typology

According to *Raymond Aron*, Weber's classification of social action is important for the following reasons:

1. Weber defined sociology as the science of social action. The typology of action is thus an *abstract conceptual tool*

to understand man's behaviour in the social world. His classification of types of authority (rational, legal, traditional and charismatic) is also based on this typology.

2. Weber has called sociology a comprehensive science of social action. He has placed much premium on *comprehension*. This is also reflected in his conception of social action and its typology. Weber's aim is to know the meaning each man gives to his own conduct, or action. He does not look at social action from observer's point of view, but from the subjective point of the actor himself.
3. His classification helps us to know *Weber 's interpretation of the contemporary era*. According to Weber, the modern society is tending towards more and more rationalisation. Modern economic enterprises, technological inventions and bureaucratisation, etc., indicate the same trend. "The society as a whole tends towards Zweckrational organisation.....".
4. Finally, the classification reveals the heart of *Weber's philosophical thought*. He was interested in "the relations of solidarity or independence between science and politics". For example, he was interested in the question, "What is ideal type of the political man? The ideal type of the scientist? How can one be both a politician and a professor?" The question was for him, as Aron points out, personal as well as philosophical. According to Weber, it could be said, that the scientific behaviour is combination of rational action in relation to a goal and also a value. "*The value is truth, the rationality is that of the rules of logic and research...*".

REVIEW QUESTIONS

1. What is the meaning of the term 'society'? Examine its nature.
2. Define society. Bring out the basic characteristics of society.
3. Define community. What are the main bases of community?
4. Point out the differences between society and community.
5. Give the definition of association. Discuss its characteristics and differentiate it from institution.
6. Explain the difference between society and community.
7. Define the term 'institution'. Describe the types and characteristics of social institutions.
8. Throw light on the functions of social institution.
9. Discuss the importance of education as a social institution.
10. The difference between association and institution is of great importance in Sociology. Discuss.
11. What is social system? Discuss its origin and characteristic features.
12. What are the elements of social system? Discuss its mechanism.
13. What do you mean by social action? Describe the typology and importance of social action.
14. Write short notes on the following:
    (a) Elements of Community
    (b) Levels of systems
15. Weber's classification of social action is important for various reasons. What are those reasons?

⌘⌘⌘⌘⌘⌘⌘⌘⌘⌘⌘

9

ROLE AND STATUS

CHAPTER OUTLINE

- Concept of Role: Meaning and Nature
- Social Status: Meaning, Definition and Nature—Orgainsation of Statuses
- Status and Office
- Prestige, Esteem and Rank
- Power and Position
- Ascribed and Achieved Statuses: Ascribed Status and its Bases: Sex, Ages, Kinship and Other Bases—Achieved Status
- Interrelationship of Ascribed and Achieved Statuses.

The human society exhibits an '*order*' because the social relations of its members and their activities are normally integrated. The varied needs of the members of society can be fulfilled only when they are prepared to work together by co-ordinating their energy talents, time and their strength and weaknesses. They realise by their common sense and experience that no one can satisfy all his ends and desires by himself. They also come to understand that no one in society can do the work of all and all are not prepared and equipped to do some particular task. Members of society occupy different places and discharge different responsibilities in the mutual interest of all. Thus the coordination of division of labour is achieved primarily through the assignment of duties and rights to positions or statuses. Society itself is a network of such statuses. Each status has a set of expected behaviours called '*roles*'. By providing for such 'roles' associated with each status, the many things which a society wants done will be distributed among people and groups in an agreed manner. This contributes to the orderliness in society. Thus, statuses and roles constitute an important element in social structure.

CONCEPT OF ROLE OR SOCIAL ROLE

Meaning of Role

1. According to *Young* and *Mack*, "A role is the function of a status".
2. Robert Biersted says that a "role is the dynamic or the behavioural aspect of status… . A role is what an individual does in the status he occupies".
3. *Duncan Mitchell* writes that "a social role is the expected behaviour associated with a social position.
4. For *Kingsley Davis* role refers to "the manner in which a person actually carries out the requirements of his position".

Nature of Role

An analysis of 'social role' would reveal to us the following things.

1. Every individual member of social group or society is bound to play social roles. It means *role-playing is obligatory* for all members. The number of roles that one plays depends on the statues that he assumes.
2. Some social roles are *shared* by a great many people. *Ex*: There are many adults, citizens, voters, authors, ministers, teachers, and so on.
3. Some social roles are enacted only by *one* or by comparatively a *few* individuals at a particular time in a particular place. *Ex*: In India, there can only a few governors at a time depending upon the number of states.

4. Some social roles may be assumed *voluntarily*. The individual may choose to enact or not enact certain roles. *Ex*: one may choose to live in city as city dweller, play as a bowler in a cricket team, join a voluntary association and play the role of its executive member or not.
5. The assumption of certain roles is largely involuntary. The enactment of many such roles has to take place continuously. *Example*: Females will have to continuously enact the roles of females, males of males, whites of whites, Harjijans of Harijans, and so on. They are unchangeable.

Interrelationship between Roles and Statuses

1. ***The terms 'role' and 'status' are interrelated:*** A status is simply a position' in society or in a group. A '*role*' is the behavioural aspect of status. Statuses are *occupied* and roles are *played*. A role is the manner in which a given individual fulfills the obligations of a status and enjoys its privileges and prerogatives. A position or status is simply the means of identifying a particular social role. The two terms are often used interchangeably. For example, the position of 'advocate' identifies a particular body of expected behaviour or the role of advocate. To define a social role is actually to define the essential or minimal features of the expected behaviour or role. Strictly, from the sociological point of view, to define a social position completely means to define or to indicate its (status) *entire* role prescriptions. In this way these two terms 'position' or status and role are only analytically separable.
2. ***Role is a relational term:*** An individual plays a role vis-a-vis another person's role which is attached to a '*counter-position*'. For example, an advocate plays his role as advocate in relation to the client's role. Role concept is relevant at the level of individual when he is in interaction. Because, its individuals, not organisations, institutions, or sub-systems, who play roles and occupy positions.
3. ***'Role' and 'status'—in a way point out the divergent interests of the two sciences—social psychology and sociology:*** Status is a sociological concept and a sociological phenomenon. On the contrary, role is a concept and a phenomenon of social psychology. Individual differences in personality, ability, talents and behaviour can alone explain as to why different individuals play different roles in the *same* status. For example, though the status of Prime Minister has been the same for Pandit Nehru, Lal Bahadur Shastri, Indira Gandhi and Rajiv Gandhi. They have played different roles in that status.
4. ***Both status and role are dynamic and constantly changing:*** Hence, role changes with each new incumbent in a status. The status changes as the norms attached to it are altered. It is quite likely that in course of time, new obligations and new responsibilities may be added to a status or old ones may be removed. Sometimes more rigorous role playing may expand the functions of a status. Similarly, these functions may change due to the newly felt needs of the system of which status is a part. For example, when an association increases in size, its office-bearers may acquire new duties, or new statuses may be established. Thus, both status and role are dynamic elements in the life of a society. But the statuses are cultural and roles are behavioural in nature.
5. Though statuses and roles are correlative phenomena, *it is possible to have one without the other*. A status without a role may simply denote an unfilled position in an association. For example, when the Vice Chancellor of a University resigns it may take some time to find a suitable successor for the post. During this time gap the duties of the Vice-Chancellor may be looked into by some of his assistants. These assistants can never enjoy privileges of the status of Vice-Chancellor.

   In the same manner, roles we often played without occupying a status. For example, a mother plays the role of nurse when a member of her family is ill. Nurse is a status in hospital, but in home it may be a role. Similarly, some are known as good practical jokers. Still they do not occupy the status of clown. Clown is a status only in the circus.
6. As *Robert Bierstedt* has pointed out, in a formal sociological language a *status may be called an institutionalised role*. It is a role that has become regularised, standardised, and formalised in the society at large or in any specific association with society. The structure of society consists of statuses and not roles, "It is statuses, together with norms, that give order, predictability and even possibility to social relations".

Role Behaviour

'*Role behaviour*' *refers to the way in which a certain individual fulfills the expectations of his role*. According to T.M. Newcomb, 'role behaviour' refers to *actual behaviour* as distinct from the role itself. T.R. Sarbin uses the term '*role enactment*' to refer to role behaviour. Example: The status of an engineer ranks above that of a foreman. The engineer's role includes the expectations that he tells the foreman what to do. But the role behaviour of engineers may vary considerably. Engineer Mr. Gupta gives specific orders and in a pleasant voice, while engineer Mr. Mehta gives very general instructions and in a harsh tone. The difference between them stems out from neither status nor role, but from *role behaviour*.

Role behaviour is influenced by some factors. It means some factors make an individual to do less or more than what is expected of him in a status. *Firstly*, role behaviour depends on the *efforts* that one puts in as an occupant of a status. He may or may not put proper efforts in that direction due to some or the other reason. *Secondly*, role behaviour depends on the *feeling of obligation* that one has towards the normative aspect of the status. For example, depending upon the strong or weak obligation that an individual may do his work and play his role as a father. *Thirdly*, role behaviour is also affected by *one's holding of other positions* or statuses with rights and obligations attached to them. The role requirements of different statuses make it almost impossible for the individual who assumes various statuses to do '*justice*' to all. Individuals who somehow try to lead a balanced life make lot of compromises with their obligations. Thus a labourer who is capable of showing a better performance will not do that because of his membership with the trade union which has advocated a go-slow policy. *Finally*, role behaviour differs with the capacity of the individuals which is determined by both *experience* and by *heredity*. Experience involves cumulative learning in previous situations and heredity influences the effect that experience has. For example, a mentally deficient person cannot ordinarily perform well the duties of husband, teacher, advocate or legislator. On the other hand, a talented person may perform them much better than an average man.

Role-taking

In the role analysis the concept of '*role-taking*' has assumed importance. Role-taking or taking the role of the other, means that a person responds by putting himself mentally or imaginatively in the role of the other person in order to regulate his own behaviour. This he does only in view of other's expectations and not necessarily in the direction of conformity. Sociologists used the term 'role-taking' in their discussion of 'social interaction', that is, when some behaviour is initiated by one actor and the reaction comes to it from other actors.

Role-taking is significant in the process of socialisation, that is, in the *learning* of social roles. The idea of role-taking is fundamental to the theory of 'social self' established by the social psychologist G.H. Mead. The child becomes a social being by playing roles and taking the roles of other individuals. Here the term 'self' is profusely used in role literature. The term 'self' would imply what ego thinks he is as a person, that is, how" he sees himself. As Mead has stated in the development of child's social self role-taking is of crucial importance at two stages: the earlier '*play*' stage and the later 'game' stage. In the former, the child takes the roles of other persons such as mother, father, teacher, milk man, bus driver, etc., and plays these roles *individually*. In the latter, the older child can put himself in the roles of a number of other positions simultaneously. For example, in playing a team game the child is able to play the game because of its ability to imagine the roles of all, the other players. Mead used the expression '*generalised other*' to refer to the other roles.

Role Conflict

Role conflict refers to the conflict experienced by the individual at the time of role playing. This maybe experienced by the individual at two levels: (*a*) *within his own body of roles, and* (*b*) *between his own roles and those of other actors*.

Firstly, an individual may experience conflict if there is a discrepancy between *his perception of his role* and his perception of *his actual role behaviour*. This conflict may have harmful effects upon his self-image. For example, if a person finds a vast difference between–how he should act as a husband and how he actually does behave–he may experience an inner conflict. In extreme cases, one may even become neurotic.

Secondly, an individual may experience conflicts within his own body of roles. An individual may perceive some incompatibility between the role-requirements of two or more roles when he is playing them together. For example, one's role as a doctor may come into clash with one's role as a husband or wife at home. The doctor is expected to serve the patients even during the non-working hours, if the need arises. It is equally expected of the same person as a husband or wife to pay attention to the needs of the family and family members at least during the non-working hours. Conflicts of this kind arise only when the occupants in the counter-positions perceive the role of the individual concerned in a different way. Thus, the doctor experiences a conflict because, the doctor's wife has a different perception of her husband's role. Similarly, a factory worker may experience conflict when his opinion of his duties and obligations as a worker differs from the opinions of both his employer and his union leader.

In a simple, culturally homogeneous and relatively 'immobile' society, there may be comparatively less role conflicts. But in a comparatively complex and heterogeneous social system role conflicts have increased a great deal. These have led to more and more group tensions as well as individual discomforts.

SOCIAL STATUS

Meaning of Social Status

Society is understood in terms of the network of social interaction and interconnection. In any interaction situation we cannot expect everyone to respond to the stimulus in the same manner. Because everyone has his own separate identity which is already there even before entering the social situation. *Example*: A husband expects sexual response from his wife, but other men have no such right to expect such a response from her. Similarly, patients expect treatment for their diseases from the doctors, students expect clarification for their doubts in lessons from their teachers, and so on. Thus, everyone enters a social situation with an identity. This identity refers to his *position* or *status*.

Definitions of Social Status

1. According to *Duncan Mitchell*, social status refers to "the position occupied by a person, family, or kinship group in a social system relative to others. This determines rights, duties and other behaviours, including the nature and extent of the relationships with persons of other statuses'.
2. *Ralph Linton* says that "status is the place in a particular system, which a certain individual occupies at a particular time".
3. *Robert Bierstedt* is of the opinion that "A status is simply a position in society or in a group....the status is the position afforded by group affiliation, group membership, or group organisation. It is 'set' in the structure of the group or of the society before a given individual comes along to occupy it".
4. *For Morris Ginsberg* "A status is a position in a social group or grouping, a relation to other positions held by other individuals in the group or grouping".

Nature of Status

1. ***External symbols to identify the status:*** As *Kingsley Davis* has said, a person's identity in a social situation reveals his status. Though not always certain external symbols help the identification of one's statuses in society. The style of dress is one such indicator. Soldiers and army officers, nurses, doctors, advocates, policemen, religious missionaries, priests wear different dresses. Their statuses could be understood by means of their dresses. The various badges the policemen, and the army officials wear further pin point their status. Sex status of men and women could be ascertained with the help of the dress that they wear. In some societies married and unmarried persons, the old and young, the merchants and craftsmen wear different costumes. This kind of identification has its limitations because some unauthorised persons may wear certain type of costumes for fun, fashion or for cheating.
2. ***Every status has its own rights, duties and obligations:*** The nature of these rights and duties is decided by the normative system of society. A right is a legitimate expectation that one can entertain as an occupant of a status in relation to the behaviour of a person in another position. From the viewpoint of another person their claim represents only an obligation. For example, it is the *right* of an employer to expect a particular behaviour from his employee and it is the *obligation* of the employee to behave in the so desired manner. Similarly, it is the right of an employee to expect some rewards for his labour from his employer, and it becomes the obligation; but it becomes a duty on the part of the employer to give the rewards to the employee. Thus, 'rights' and 'obligations' are only different definitions of the same relationship.
3. ***Social statuses are governed by norms:*** These norms vary with persons, situations and statuses, even though they are believed to be common to all. For example, the norms like '*be honest*', '*be truthful*' etc., are believed to be common to all. But in practice we know that a doctor cannot always tell the truth to the patient regarding the state of his disease. Similarly, a merchant cannot practice honesty always in his trade. Thus norms are always relative to situations. Which norms apply in a given case depends upon the relations between the statuses of the interacting persons and the situations in which they interact.
4. ***One individual may have several statuses:*** Since society can be understood as the network of statuses, it is quite natural that in every society we find a large number of groups which have many statuses. Every individual occupies many such statuses. His status will differ with the type of group.

   In a modern complex society each individual during the course of a single day may find himself in a large number of statuses. *Example*: A college student may be a student to his teachers, a customer to the shop owner, a depositor to his banker, a passenger to the bus driver, a brother to his sister, a son to his father and mother, a secretary to the members of the cricket club, a male to all females, a patient to his doctor, and so on. It means the individual occupies the statuses such as student, customer, depositor, passenger, brother, son, secretary of the cricket club, patient and many such statuses in the course of a single day. It becomes thus impossible to enlist all the statuses that each one is likely to occupy at one time or other in the course of his entire life. Of course, in smaller and simpler societies an individual can have only a fewer statuses.
5. ***Statuses exercise an influence upon the careers of individuals:*** The behaviour of individuals can be understood only by understanding the statuses that they assume in their respective groups or societies. For example, an Eskimo cannot think of becoming a nuclear physicist because such a status is not there in his society. Similarly, no American boy at present wants to become a witch-doctor because there is no such status in his society.
6. ***Statuses differ with their degree of importance:*** Some statuses are more important than others in deciding the position of an individual in society. Different societies have different criteria for deciding the importance of statuses. Sociologist *E. T. Hiller* has made use of the concept of '*key status*' to denote a man's position in society. In most of modern industrial societies, for example, '*occupational status*' has become the 'key status'. It mostly influences his

various other statuses. In some societies, kinship statuses, religious statuses or even political statuses may be more important and hence become 'key statuses'. In India, caste status and occupational status may be more important, Russians may attach more weightage to political status and so on. In primitive societies age, sex and kinship statuses are important than others.

7. ***Statuses add to social order and social stability:*** We are all born into a society in which the statuses are already there. They are the part of the structure of our society. We are not creating them afresh. The statuses of farmers, soldiers, teachers, clerks etc., are not our creations. In exceptional cases some may find out new ways and new paths of living and thus may create new statuses. Like other elements of culture, status, which is cultural item, is also dynamic. Some statuses, may, in course of time, become obsolete, and disappear from the social structure. But most of the individuals, in most of the cases occupy statuses that are already there established in the societies in which they are born. .

8. ***Social status has a hierarchical distribution also:*** All the statuses in society are not equally distributed among all. Thus a few persons occupy the highest positions while the majority assumes the so called 'ordinary' statuses. The theoretical assumption behind the distribution of the statuses is that the statuses are determined competitively by the possession of abilities relative to the demand for abilities in society. Thus, it could be said in the competitive struggle those who possess greater abilities and qualities assume higher statuses in society. But in actuality, the relation between the possession of abilities and the assumption of higher statuses has not been found to be invariable. The factors such as private property, inheritance, social services, etc., all modify the form of the distribution of statuses.

Organisation of Statuses

Every individual in society occupies many different statuses. As an occupant of these statuses he has to fulfil his obligations and duties towards others in the counter positions. Hence in the interest of the individual and the society it is essential that these statuses get integrated or organised properly.

Sometimes we recognise a particular individual as an occupant of a particular status even though he may be an occupant of several other statuses at the same time. We also speak of *the* status or *the* social position of a given individual by which we imply the *sum total* of his specific statuses and roles. *Example*: We may speak of Mr. X as a good advocate or Mrs. Y as a renowned dancer. Here we implicitly accept that the person concerned has many statuses and we are pointing out only one of them for a particular reference.

The statuses that an individual occupies and the roles that he plays constitute an essential element in his personality. The time, energy and ability that an individual has, are very much limited. He must achieve results and satisfy needs. For this the system of his statuses must be integrated to some extent. Otherwise, he may feel unhappy. His personal efficiency, confidence and contentment also depend on the integration of his various social positions.

From the societal point of view, the total system of statuses in the entire society or group must be integrated to some reasonable extent. The very existence of society depends on such an integration. Normally, occupational, familial, religious, political and other statuses are built in such a manner that they provide scope for such an integration through an interlocking system of rights and obligations. What is to be noted is that the system of statuses remains permanent while those who occupy these statuses may get changed. For example, in the economic system of a society; 'employer-employee' statuses and roles are designed by the society. In actuality, these-statuses and roles remain permanent though the occupants of these statuses may differ markedly. Thus, for the smooth functioning of the society it is essential that its innumerable statuses are properly organised or integrated.

STATUS AND OFFICE

The term '*status*' and '*office*' are interrelated. The term '*status*' designates a position in the general institutional system of a society. Since such an institutional system which is more evolved in nature is recognised and supported by the entire society and rooted in the folkways and mores, the status associated with it, is also well recognised. *Example*: In the institutional system of university we recognise the statuses of 'professor', 'dean of arts faculty', 'vice-chancellor', 'registrar' etc.

The term '*office*', on the other hand, designates a position in a purposefully created organisation. This organisation may be governed by specific rules in a limited group. The position in the organisation which is called '*office*' is generally achieved and not ascribed. *Example*: The 'master carpenter of Southern Timber Company', 'dean of the faculty of arts of the University of Mangalore', etc.

It is quite obvious that holding an office, may, at the same time, give an individual, a status. The kind of status it gives depends upon the importance of the organisation of which office is a part. The status also depends on the importance of this particular office within the organisation. *Example:* An inspector general of police and a circle inspector though both occupy a place in police department have wide difference in their ranking. Depending upon their rank their positions offer them different statuses.

It is also quite likely that an individual may acquire a certain office because of his access to a particular status. Statistics have proved that the sons of professional people and businessmen have a greater chance of securing high positions and offices than the sons of labour-class people.

These two kinds of social positions, that is, status and office, are necessarily interrelated and interdependent. For example, occupational position may be both a status and an office. It appears as a '*status*' from the standpoint of the general public, and sounds like an '*office*' from the viewpoint of the particular business company or agency.

PRESTIGE, ESTEEM AND RANK

People in every society have their own evaluation of the statuses. They may consider a status as 'good' or 'important' or 'difficult' or 'routine' or 'filthy' or 'criminal' and so on. They have some judgement based on the norms of society about the degree of desirability of the status. This evaluation of the status is called '*prestige*'. The evaluation of an individual's role behaviour in status which he occupies is called '*esteem*'.

People always tend to rank positions and attach an invidious value to them almost independent of their occupants. Most of the Indians may believe that the status of the mayor of a city corporation is more desirable than that of street sweeper. They do not take into account the particular person who is occupying the status nor the manner of his performance in that status. The judgement of the statuses is so important that some may feel hurt if their 'status' is not properly recognised. Because, people gives much importance to the prestige associated with status. For example, the office superin- tendent of a big college may feel insulted if he is mistaken for a second division clerk in the college. He cannot tolerate people who damage the prestige associated with his status.

The same people attach another kind of value to the individual depending upon the nature of his performance as an occupant of a particular status. This evaluation of his role is called '*esteem*'. A person may be in a status which has high prestige and earn high esteem by means of his role behaviour there. But prestige does not ensure esteem. The alcoholic advocate has low esteem even though he is in a status which has high prestige; the best clerk in an office may earn a high esteem even though he occupies a status which has low prestige. Esteem is always related to the expectations of a position. But it is not attached to the position itself but to the success or failure in carrying out the expectations of the position.

The esteem accruing collectively to individuals in a status can in course of time alter the prestige of that status. For example, if, over a period of years, only incompetent persons were made Vice chancellors of a University, the prestige of Vice-Chancellorship would suffer badly. Further, we have a tendency to speak proudly of highly esteemed persons who occupy the same status as we, because we feel that their presence raises the prestige of our position.

Ranking

Ranking actually refers to the ranking of social positions or statuses (particularly occupational statuses). We know by our common observation that all statuses are not ranked equally. Some sta- tuses come to rank higher than others. There are several causes for this:

Firstly, personal characteristics and skills which are required to adequately fill a status is one of the causes. *Example*: Status of a University professor is ranked relatively higher. Because, this status requires greater intelligence, the person in the status has to teach very complex subjects, has to control the students, etc.

Secondly, the amount of training that a status requires is another factor in ranking. The highest statuses (Example: the statuses of doctors, high court advocates, high army officials like major gen- eral, general etc., scientists etc.) that indicate high ranking, normally call for the greatest preparation or training.

Thirdly, the importance, the status has for the society is another factor in ranking. This is one reason why a judge holds a higher status and makes more money, than the clerk of the court. It is also a reason men have traditionally held a higher status than women.

Statuses which rank high in these three respects are usually rewarded with relatively large amounts of wealth, privilege, and power. Wealth and power in turn, become additional factors which the members of society use in ranking status and granting prestige.

POWER AND POSITION

Power plays an important part in human behaviour. As *Kingsley Davis* says power refers to "the determination of the behaviour of others in accordance with one's own end". According to *Weber*, power refers to "*the probability that one actor (individual or group) within a social relationship will be in a position to carry out his own will despite opposition.....*". Power, thus reflects one's ability to get one's wishes carried out despite opposition. It indicates one's ability to influence the behaviour of other person(s). But it is more than influence.

There is an intimate relationship between the distribution of power and distribution of statuses and office. Power is not only associated with the status of office but also with the individual independently of his position. An individual can acquire power through his position as well as through his role. *Example*: In the traditional Indian family the husband by virtue of his position has some supremacy over the wife. Hence, normally he exercises power over her. But in some cases intelligent and shrewd wives by virtue of their clever role performance have reversed the relations and forced their husbands to play the subordinate role. In the same manner, some parents may fail to exercise power over their own children in spite of their authority over their children. On the contrary, the children themselves may control them without any corresponding office or status.

Exertion of Power

We may make a distinction between 'structural power' or 'positional power' and all other kinds of power. The power that goes with authority becomes very evident when the behaviour is determined solely by one's status or office. *Example*: A father may exercise power over his son, a teacher over his students, a master over his servant, a prime minister over his cabinet colleagues, an army commander over soldiers, and so on. These indicate *positional power*. Other ways of exercising power without an approved status or position may be called *naked* or *unauthorised power*. *Example*: sometimes film actors, bogus religious leaders may exercise power over state leaders, or an office clerk may exercise power over the principal and so on.

Source of Power

Now it could be asked as to what is the *source* of a man's power in a given case. The answer is clear. A part of the source of power is the person's statuses and office itself. Another part lies in his roles in these statuses and office. The problem of the source of power leads to two other questions: (*i*) How does a particular individual occupy a given position and thus enjoy the authority and power associated with it? (*ii*) Why does the position carry the power that it does? These questions will take us to a discussion on the two types of statuses: namely: *ascribed statuses* and *achieved statuses*.

ASCRIBED AND ACHIEVED STATUSES

There are two ways in which an individual in society can get his status, that is, through '*ascription*' or '*achievement*'. Some statuses are inevitable for the individual while others can be selected by him more or less freely. *Linton* uses the concepts of 'ascribed' and 'achieved' to refer to this distinction of statuses. Some statuses are '*ascribed*' to individuals while others are achieved by them. It is possible to find in some societies more of ascribed statuses than achieved statuses and the converse may be true in some others. But strictly speaking, all the societies make use of both the principles–of ascription and achievement–in providing for the statuses of their members.

Ascribed Status

Ascribed statuses are those over which the individual has absolutely no choice. They are de- rived from membership in involuntary groups such as sex group, age group, racial group, etc. At the beginning stages of socialisation itself the new born individual derives such statuses. Virtually these statuses are 'ascribed' to the individual before knowing his potentialities. These statuses definitely "*determine and limit the range of statuses*" which he may subsequently achieve or try to achieve. Statuses are ascribed mostly on the basis of following considerations.

Sex

An individual's sex is a highly visible physiological fact. It appears at birth and remains fixed for life. Individuals are born as either males or females and remain so for life. This sex difference is taken as one of the bases of ascribing status to the individuals. Some of the achieved statuses are influenced by this factor of sex.

It is wrong to assume that the male-female division of statuses is mainly based on inherent traits of men and women. Because, biological attributes cannot explain the behaviour differences of men and women. Further, social differences themselves are not fixed but they change from one society to another and from one time to another. *Example*: Among the Tchambuli people, women are the bread-earners whereas men look after household work and spend time in combing hair, wearing different kinds of beads and other kinds of beautification. Among the Mundugumor people women and men are equally aggressive. Among the Trobriand Islanders, except for breast-feeding, all the other tasks of child nursing are done by the father. In some tribes, the father gives training to the son in the art of dancing. These differences cannot be explained by the biological attributes as such.

In reality, the assignment of '*female status*' to women is mainly due to her '*child-bearing function*'. Her physical weakness and limitation mainly spring from this fact. Woman is thus forced to carry the parasitic embryo in her body for a long time and nurse it later when it comes out of her womb. She is thus provided with some tasks that are compatible with reproduction. Usually, though not invariably, she is given tasks such as keeping house, cooking, gardening, sewing, making pots and baskets. These may fit in with her tasks of child-bearing and child-rearing. Very rarely women are assigned the tasks that take them away from their home for a long time, and those require heavy physical exertion, exposure to bodily injury and sheer physical strength. For this reason, female work is more uniform and localised than that of men.

In the modem complex societies the statuses assigned to women have changed greatly. Still some division of labour between the sexes persists. In the occupational sphere today though women are not excluded they are handicapped in competition against men in certain fields such as medicine, law, college teaching, factory work, defence, industry, etc. Certainly they are excluded in works such as coal mining, structural steel work, underwater tunneling, etc. It means for women, *their described statuses limit their attainment for achieved statuses*.

Age

All societies recognise differences in statuses and roles related to age. Like sex, it is a definite and highly visible physiological fact. Unlike sex, age cannot give rise to permanent lifetime statuses. Age represents not static but a steadily changing condition. The *age relationship* between given persons, that is, between father and son, younger brother arid elder brother, etc. remains fixed throughout life. But each living individual is subject to different age statuses during his life span. Most of the societies recognise five main age statuses such as: *infancy, childhood, adolescence, adulthood* and *old age*. In some societies the *unborn* and the *dead* too are recognised as two peculiar age-periods which have their own importance.

The *unborn* may be believed to be the spirits of departed ancestors. Hindus think of the unborn in a vague manner as the spirits of 'souls' of persons who lived in previous incarnations or 'janmas'. The transition from the status of the *unborn* to the status of the living is marked by some kind of ceremonies. Some taboos have surrounded the very event of birth. The Hindus, for example, observe pollution for 11 days from the day of birth of the child. Among the Chinese and Greeks the new born child is recognised as a member of the society only after the relevant ceremonies are held.

The transition from *infancy* to *childhood* is relatively smooth one and involves no social complication. But the change from childhood to *adolescent period* and then to *adulthood* is of tremen- dous importance. During this transitional period obvious physiological and mental changes do take place in the individual. The individual who has been absorbing culture now starts participating in it. The change to adulthood is widely recognised in *ceremony*, *custom* and *law*. In some communities '*puberty rites*' are observed, In some societies marriage takes place soon after this change, though in the civilized societies it takes place after a long time.

In the modern society, the transition from the childhood to adulthood involves great strains for the following reasons. *Firstly*, the child becomes an adult not when he is physiologically mature but socially mature. The physiological maturation takes place long before the individual is admitted socially as an adult. *Secondly*, man is not all at once considered socially as competent to take up any kind of activity. Physiological maturation does not guarantee that the person is fit for any kind of socially important tasks. *Thirdly*, there is no universally accepted and publicly expressed procedure or step as such to declare that an individual has become an adult. It becomes a matter of private definition in each family. *Fourthly*, there is a long time interval between sexual maturity and marriage. But this prolonged period of bachelorship and the disapproval of pre-marital sex relationship that introduce an element of sexual strain have further complicated the period of adolescence.

The passage of individuals from *adulthood to old age* is not very much visible. It varies with individuals also. Normally in old age mental and physical powers decline and dependence on others increases. Hence the range of thought and action of the old become very much limited. The roles assigned to the old also vary considerably from society to society. In some societies they are relieved of their work while in others they are made to work hard. The old may receive a high degree of reverence in some societies such as those of Indians, Chinese, Japanese, etc., while their counter- parts in the West may not enjoy that much of respect. In extreme cases, as it has been among the Eskimos, the old may even be abandoned and hence made to meet death. In some societies, the transition to old age status is socially distinguished. For example, in Japan, it was customary for the old father to hand over to the son his power in a formal manner to enter a period of voluntary retirement. The Hindu concept of '*Vanaprasthashrama*' also reveals the same thing. In settled cultures normally, an individual's power and prestige increases with age. The older persons seek to hold their power which they have enjoyed so far. Society too may expect their service especially for political and administrative purposes. They are able to hold their power because of a superiority which is based on knowledge and experience. The younger ones may appreciate this superiority or envy it. This superiority is definitely developed by the ascription of status on the basis of age in an organised society.

Not only the living individuals but also the *dead are given a status in society*. The main reason is the living are descended both physically and socially from the dead. The practice of ancestral worship clearly indicates the recognition of the status of the dead. Among the Hindus, there is the ritual of '*Shraddha*' in which the dead are given some offerings. In some societies the great deeds of the great men are remembered. In this case, their status would indicate an achieved status".

Finally, as *Ralph Linton* has pointed out, "In the case of age, as in that of sex, biological factors involved appear to be secondary to the cultural ones in determining the content of status."

Kinship

Kinship status reveals the individual's relation to his parents and siblings. The new born infant's status in the community is normally identified with that of the parents'. This ascription is highly arbitrary because there is no necessary relation between the capacities of the parents and those of the offspring. Stupid parents may have wise children and vice-versa. Still it is socially convenient to relate the child to the society through the parents. When the child is born the father and mother become responsible for it. *They* only socialise him in the initial stage. It is quite natural that the child's first status connection rests with the parents only.

The child may take the status of parents soon after its birth as it is in the case of caste or race. But sometimes it may acquire the parental status sometimes later as it is in the case of *succession* or *inheritance*. The latter one is often referred to as the process of "*delayed ascription*". Further, the child in its later life may seek to acquire some achieved statuses that are different from those of parents. The relative advantage or disadvantage that the child enjoys in securing these statuses is mostly provided by his parents. *Example*: the son of an upper-class man has greater advantages in making achievements in academic field than the son of a poor-class man. This is also true in the case of open-class occupational placement. This is often referred to as '*fluid ascription*". Here the element of achievement does not completely dismiss the element of ascription.

It is true that a number of important statuses of the child are dependent on the factor of kinship. The ascription of citizenship, religious affiliation, and community membership, for example, in most cases are, a matter of identification with parents. The class or the caste position is transmitted from parents to the child.

Due to kinship ties the child acquires not only a status in larger society but also a *position in the family*. The child acquires the status as a son or daughter. To his parents' kinsmen he may be a grandson, a nephew, a brother, a cousin and son. Mutual rights and obligations go along with kinship connections. Even in the modern society, if not extended kinship ties, the immediate family ties remain socially important. In some societies much of social life is governed by them.

Other Bases of Ascription

In addition to age, sex and kinship there are also other bases of status ascription. Since the individual manifests certain racial traits at the time of his birth itself, it is possible to ascribe him a *racial status*. An individual has no choice about his place of birth and hence his *regional* and *national statuses* are ascribed. Though these may be changed later, there is no initial choice. Similarly, we are born as Hindus, Christians, Muslims etc. for our *religious status* is ascribed at birth itself. A different religious status may, however be, acquired later. Our initial class-status is likewise ascribed. At birth, we take on the class position of our parents for we have no choice. We can however change it later. But our *caste status* which is ascribed at birth cannot be changed. Illegitimacy, for example prevents full identification with the parents. Similarly, the total number of children born in the family, the fact of adoption, the fact of the death of a parent, the occurrence of divorce all can affect the infant's status independently of his will. Thus, the "accident of birth" is universal and extremely important in society.

Achieved Status

The statuses about which the person has some choice, however much or little, are *achieved statuses*. All societies have some achieved statuses and no society depends completely on ascribed statuses. The proportion of the statuses in a social structure which are open to achievement varies widely around the world.

Even if a society is very particular about providing ascribed statuses to its members, there will be some individuals who will alter the place which they are assigned to occupy in the structure because they have special talents or ambitions. The history of all societies and all times is filled with their names, for they are the men who make history. In order to make use of their capacities for common social ends the society institutionalizes the achievement of status. By doing so, society can capitalize on the deviant instead of punishing him. Further, by making certain changes of status legitimate, a society may admit members with unusual abilities for statuses where average ability is not just enough. It can also prevent the filling of high positions by some incompetent persons. The leader of combat teams, the creator of artistic products, and the inventor are examples of statuses which a society might find it worthwhile to throw open to achievements rather than ascribing to a few on the basis of birth.

In primitive societies one can find that greater stress is laid on ascribed statuses. The civilized societies on the contrary, have placed high premium on achieved statuses. Factors such as the domi- nance of commercial activities, urban conditions of life, greater division of labour, and rapid social change have compelled the individuals to achieve their statuses on the basis of accomplishments in the modern societies. In urban centres and in commercial fields no mediocre person can thrive. They provide better opportunities for achievement also. Division of labour offers a chance to a talented man for a competitive advantage to work with efficiency to secure a status. Rapid change provides continually new statuses. Since they are new they cannot be filled by ascription.

As we know *all kinds of statuses are not thrown open to all* in all societies. Only some of them are thrown to achievement on some basis. *Firstly*, the statuses that require the possession of unusual talents are obviously thrown open. For example, no mediocre person can achieve the status of a great artist or a great physicist, or a great writer or a great actor, etc. *Secondly*, the statuses that depend on the informal and spontaneous approval of the people are predominantly achieved. For example, the sportsmen, singers, drama artists, film actors, public speakers and such men can achieve very high status in spite of their humble birth. *Finally*, the statuses that require long and costly education are normally achieved. For example, only through high level of education that one can attain the status of a doctor, psychiatrist, judge, advocate, engineer, etc.

In the modern civilized societies most of the *occupational statuses* are achieved. The existence of a number of secondary groups indicates that our *organisational membership* is an achieved status. *Marital status, parental status. educational status*, etc., are all achieved. Because one is not obliged to become a husband or a wife or a parent or an educated person.

The outstanding function of a social structure with many achieved statuses is that, it provides not for the isolation of roles but for their combination into a necessary interdependence. A structure characterised by achieved statuses enhances competition for those statuses, but the specialization of roles also necessitates co-operation.

Interrelationship of Ascribed and Achieved Statuses

Ascription and achievement of statuses go hand in hand in all the societies. Though opposite in principle, they are complementary in function and hence essential to society.

For the purpose of socialization, that is to introduce the culture of the group of the individual, he must be placed somewhere in the social structure at birth. This initial *placement* or *ascription* may be a matter of purely arbitrary social rules based on some external factors. But later, the individual's *achievements* must be recognised. It is quite likely that his initial placement itself may influence his later achievements.

If all statuses were achieved, some of them might not get filled. If all statuses were to be ascribed, there would be little scope for human creativity and talents. Ascribed statuses give a feeling of security that purely achieved statuses can never give. Our entire life cannot be thrown open for competition. One should not be made to face a life in which all his fellows are potential competitors for every bit of prestige and esteem which he may attain. On the other hand, the value of achieved status is that it not only places right individuals in the right place but it also stimulates efforts and accomplishments.

Within the framework of ascribed statuses are sets of achieved statuses. One can compete for some of these, but he does not have to compete for all of them. The ascribed status of male excuses one from competing for a number of statuses: nurse in a hospital, teacher in kindergarten, baby sitter, etc. The ascribed status of old man relieves one from competing for statuses that go with the youths. *Ascription thus can reduce some of the pressure in free choice*. Whereas the achieved statuses provide the individual some freedom in selecting a task of his choice and to do it well, it also contributes to the survival of social structure by motivating the people to seek statuses and ultimately fulfil their duties.

It may be pointed out that societies differ significantly in relation to the statuses. In the medieval society, for example, religious status, class status and even occupational statuses were ascribed. They could not be achieved. In the totalitarian societies, even in the 20th century political status is mostly ascribed. In some societies, the occupational statuses of all the members are functions of age, sex and kinship. In a caste society like India, Caste-status is a function of kinship. But in more 'mobile' societies with class-structure class-statuses are mostly achieved. In a 'free society' in which a wide variety of voluntary associations are found, achieved statuses are at their maximum.

REVIEW QUESTIONS

1. What is the meaning of the term 'role'? Discuss its nature.
2. Discuss the interrelationship between the role and status.
3. What do you mean by social status? Give its definitions.
4. Point out the different forms of social status.
5. Differentiate between ascribed and achieved statuses.
6. Throw light on the organisation of statuses.
7. Examine the interrelationship between the ascribed and achieved statuses.
8. Differentiate between status and role.
9. Define social status and social role.
10. Write short notes on the following:
    (a) Social role
    (b) Role behaviour
    (c) Role-taking
    (d) Role conflict
    (e) Power and position

⌘⌘⌘⌘⌘⌘⌘⌘⌘⌘⌘

10

POWER—AUTHORITY—STATUS

CHAPTER OUTLINE

- MEANING OF POWER
- AUTHORITY AND TYPES OF AUTHORITY
- AUTHORITY AND STATUS

POWER

Meaning of Power

Power is a fundamental entity of human society. It is a universal phenomenon. Society itself is built of power relations–the father exercising his power over his child, a master over his slave, a teacher over his student, a victor over the vanquished, an employer over his employee, an army commander over the soldiers and so on. All these are examples of social power. What then do we mean by power?

1. *Max Weber* defined power as "the ability to control the behaviour of others, even in the absence of their consent".
2. As *Ian Robertson* says, "power is the capacity to participate effectively in a decision making process".
3. According to *NJ. Demerath III* and *Gerald Marwell*, "power may be defined as the capacity to get things done despite obstacles and resistance".

It may be pointed out that there are many types of power and many ways of overcoming resistance. "One can threaten, cajole, influence, coerce, wheedle, persuade, beg, blackmail, inspire, etc., to get his things done. But power on a large scale is almost always embedded within organisational structures whether they be governments, political parties, business firms, schools, churches, or protest movements." "In each of these settings power involves a kind of gamble. Because there is always the risk that the people in power will betray the common trust". *— Demerath, and Marwell*

Power may be exercised blatantly or subtly, legally or illegally, justly or unjustly. It may derive from many sources, such as wealth, status, prestige, numbers, or organisational efficiency. Its ultimate basis, however, is the ability to compel obedience, if necessary through the threat or use of force.

Social power has been identified in different ways with prestige, influence, eminence, compe- tence, dominance, rights, strength, force, and authority.

1. ***Power and prestige are closely linked:*** As *Ross* said, "The class that has the most prestige will have the most power". It can be said that the powerful groups tend to be prestigious and prestigious groups powerful.
2. ***Knowledge, eminence, skill, and competence***—all contribute to prestige, but they need not necessarily accompany power. If at all power is accompanied by these factors then the association is only incidental.
3. ***Power and influence*** are more intimately connected. Still they are different. Influence is persuasive whereas power is coercive. We submit voluntarily to influence but power requires our submission. They are, so as to say, independent variables. Influence does not require power and power may dispense with influence.

4. ***Power and dominance*** are also to be distinguished. *Power is a* sociological, and *dominance* a psychological phenomenon. The locus of power is in both persons and groups, and in important cases it is in the latter. But dominance is a function of personality or of temperament. It is a personal trait. It is also possible to find dominant individuals playing roles in powerless groups and submis- sive individuals playing roles in powerful ones. Power is one thing and dominance quite another.
5. ***Power and rights:*** Rights are more closely associated with privileges and with authority than they are with power. A right is one of the prerequisites of power and not power itself. One may have a right without the power to exercise it. The man who has the power rarely waits for the right to use it. A right always requires some support in the social structure. No individual can successfully claim a right that is unrecognised in the law and non-existent in the mores. Rights in general, like privileges, duties, obligations, responsibilities, etc., are attached to the statuses. Whereas, power does not necessarily require the backing of the status.
6. ***Power, force and authority:*** Power is not force and power is not authority, but it is related to both. As Robert Bierstedt said, "Power is latent force; force is manifest power, and authority is institutionalized power." Power is the prior capacity that makes the use of force possible. Only groups that have power can threaten to use force and the threat itself is power. Power is the ability to employ force, not its actual employment. Power is always successful; when it is not successful, it ceases to be power. Power thus symbolises the force that may be applied in any social situation and supports the authority that is applied. "Power is thus neither force nor authority but it makes both force and authority possible." — *Robert Bierstedt.*

Weber's Views on Power

According to *Demerath* and *Marwell*, Weber, an authority on "power and authority", saw power more as a property of organisations and organisational roles than an attribute of individuals as such. This relationship between power and organisations, throws light on three theoretical innovations: *Firstly*, Weber provided rich and abundant demonstration that power relationships are not restricted to the realm of politics or the state but pervade the whole of everyday human relationship, *Secondly*, Weber pointed out "a conception of power involving only coercion or force, is all too narrow; it misses the subtlety and variety entailed in its other forms". *Thirdly*, Weber showed that it is very important "to understand the attitudes of the followers as well as the leaders in any organisational setting since the relationship between them is neither automatic nor unchanging'. An explanation of this third point would take us to a discussion of Weber's use of the term "*authority*" and its types.

AUTHORITY

The exercise of authority is a constant and pervasive phenomenon in the human society. Hu- man society maintains itself because of '*order*'—and it is the authority that serves as the foundation of social order. It is wrong to assume that 'authority' is purely a political phenomenon. In fact, in all kinds of organisations, political as well as non-political, authority appears. Every association in society whether it is temporary or permanent, small or big, has its own structure of authority.

Definitions of Authority

1. "Authority is that form of power which orders or articulates the actions of other actors through commands which are effective because those who are commanded regard the commands as legitimate" — By *E.A. Shils in Dictionary of Sociology.*
2. *Max Weber* used the term authority to refer to legitimate power.
3. In simple words, it can be said that authority refers to power which is regarded as legitimate in the minds of followers.

Weber's notion of authority does not imply that power is legitimate and that illegitimate power plays no role in society. "Weber only argued that legitimacy is a general condition for the most effective and enduring manifestations of power. Still this legitimacy may take different forms and different justifications." — *Demerath* and *Marwell*

As Ian Robertson has stated, "Power based on authority is usually unquestionably accepted by those to whom it is applied, for obedience to it has become a social norm. Power based on coercion, on the other hand, tends to be unstable, because people obey only out of fear and will disobey at the first opportunity. For this reason every political system must be regarded as legitimate by its participants if it is to survive." Most people must consider it desirable, workable, and better than alternatives. If the majority of the citizens in any society no longer consider their political system legitimate, it is doomed, because power that rests only on coercion will fail in the long run. The French, Russian and the American Revolutions, for example, have proved it. The authority of the respective monarchies was questioned, and their power which was based mainly on coercion rather than on loyalty inevitably crumbled. In these cases, the exercise of coercive control was in conflict with the exercise of legitimate authority.

"The legitimacy of authority is ultimately a matter of belief concerning the rightfulness of institutional system through which authority is exercised". It depends on "the rightfulness of the exerciser's incumbency in the authoritative role with the institutional system". It also depends on "the rightfulness of the command itself or of the mode of its promulgation'. Weber describes three '*ideal types*' of legitimation which correspond to three types of authority.

Types or Authority

Max Weber distinguished three basic types of legitimate authority: which also correspond to three types of *dominance* or *leadership*. Weber spoke of *traditional authority*, *legal-rational authority*, and *charismatic authority*. Each type of authority is legitimate because it rests on the implicit or explicit consent of the governed. One who can successfully claim any of these types of authority is regarded as having the right to compel obedience at least for some time.

1. Traditional Authority

Of all the legitimations of authority, the appeal to tradition is certainly the most common. People obey traditional authority because "*it has always been that way*". The right of the king to rule is not open to question. People obey a ruler because they know that doing so in past generations has given their society order and continuity. Thus it is not tradition alone here that is at issue, rather the stability of the social order that is being accepted for its own sake.

In a political system based on 'traditional authority' power is legitimated by ancient custom. The authority of the ruler is generally founded on unwritten laws and it has almost a sacred quality. Tribal leaders and monarchs have always relied on traditional authority. From the historical point of view it has been the most common source of legitimation of power.

Traditional authority tends to be more common in organisations which stress upon continuity with the past and the upholding of widely shared values and beliefs. *Example*: Established churches, the higher reaches of government, and the courts and familial organisations based on kinship ties. In each one of these settings, it is inconvenient for us to question the authority relationships involved. We tend to follow the tradition for it has always been followed, and doing any other thing would create more problems than it would solve.

2. Rational-legal Authority

In this kind of authority power is legitimated by explicit rules and procedures that define the rights and obligations of the rulers. Such rules and procedures are commonly found in a written constitution, and set of laws. Legal-rational authority stresses a "*government of laws, not of peoples*". Officials here can exercise power only within legally defined limits that have been formally set in advance. This kind of authority is commonly found in most of the political systems of modern societies.

In this kind of authority power is respected and complied with neither because the followers are fools nor because the exercise is endowed with extraordinary qualities as it is the charismatic case. Here, the legitimacy of authority is derived from the respect for the legality of power. Weber described such authority with reference to its most common organisational context, namely, bureaucracy, *Weber* writes—"Legal authority rests on enactment, its pure type is best represented by bureaucracy. The basic idea is that laws can be enacted and changed at pleasure by formally correct procedure. The governing body is either elected or appointed and constitutes as a whole and in all of its sections rational organisations....".

3. Charismatic Authority

"In a system based on charismatic authority, power is legitimated by the unusual, exceptional, or even supernatural qualities that people attribute to particular political, religious, or military leaders". Weber called this extraordinary quality '*Charisma*'. *Robert Bierstedt* calls this kind of authority, not authority at all, but *leadership*. Human history provides classical examples of such leaders with that quality of 'Charisma'. *Example*: Jesus Christ, M.K. Gandhi, Hitler, Napoleon, Mao, Castro, Julius Caesar, Alexander the Great, Churchill, and so on. "The charismatic leader is seen as a person of destiny who is inspired by unusual vision, by lofty principles or even by God. The charisma of these leaders is itself sufficient to make their authority seem legitimate to their followers". *-Ian Robertson*

In stressing the importance and sanctity of tradition, Weber never said that tradition is inviolable. He only said that tradition is the rule rather than an exception. There are exceptions also. Weber used the term "Charismatic authority" to refer to such exceptions (borrowing the term from the Christian theology). Weber writes: "Charismatic authority rests on affectual and personal devotion of the follower to the lord and his gifts of grace (Charisma). They comprise especially magical abilities, revelations of heroism, power of the mind and the speech.... The purest types are the rule of the prophet, the warrior hero, the great demagogue....".

The important thing in charismatic authority is that the leader is not magical, but he is believed to be so. Through various devices and tactics the leader creates an army of true believers to get the perpetual support of the people. Yet Charismatic authority is inherently unstable. It has no rules or traditions to guide conduct. Since it is based on the unique qualities of a particular individual, it is undermined if the leader fails or dies. Subsequent leaders may lack the reason and qualities. Hence systems based on charismatic authority are usually short – lived.

"Each of these forms of authority represents an "ideal type". In other words, each is an abstraction that is only approximated to a greater or lesser extent by any actual political system. In practice, political systems and political leaders may derive their authority from more than one source"

— *Ian Robertson*

AUTHORITY AND STATUS

Authority and status always go together. Though individuals exercise authority, it is always related to statuses and not to individuals, in normal cases. The exercise of authority is a function of norms that are themselves attached to statuses. An individual exercises the authority of a status as long as he occupies that status. He ceases to exercise it when he resigns, or when he is removed, or when his tenure of office is over. Authority is created in associations. Hence, the exercise of authority is wholly a function of associational status.

Authority comes to be well established in associations when they become more and more organised. Associations create authority where initially there was only leadership. Unless the roles are institutionalised into statuses associations suffer from the problem of instability and discontinuity. When once the roles are institutionalised no leader becomes indispensable for the association. Further, the leader may even be deposed from his position of authority.

The formal organisation of an association is constituted of norms and statuses. "The norms are attached to the statuses and not to the persons who occupy them. The norms involve rights, duties, obligations, responsibilities, privileges as they are attached to particular statuses. The right to exercise authority is now attached to certain statuses. This right receives the support of all those who belong to the association and who conform to its norms. The exercise of authority, however, is not only a right but also a duty'. — *Robbert Bierstedt*

Authority is never exercised except in a status relationship. Sometimes a person without having an appropriate status may try to influence or control the action of another. In this case, what actually influences is, the leadership of the person and not his authority. Authority does not make its appearance in the informal organisation. It is completely a function of the formal organisation of an association. Still the personal factors do enter into status relationships.

REVIEW QUESTIONS

1. Give the meaning of power. Discuss Weber's views on power.
2. Social power has been identified in different ways. Discuss.
3. Define authority. Explain its various types.
4. What is status? Comment on the relationship between the authority and status.
5. Write short notes on the following:
   (a) Power
   (b) Status
   (c) Authority
   (d) Charismatic authority
6. Authority is never exercised except in a status relationship. Examine.

⌘⌘⌘⌘⌘⌘⌘⌘⌘⌘⌘⌘

11

SOCIAL STRUCTURE AND FUNCTION

CHAPTER OUTLINE

- SOCIAL STRUCTURE
- ELEMENTS OF SOCIAL STRUCTURE
- SOCIAL STRUCTURE: AN ANTHROPOLOGICAL PERSPECTIVE
- CONCEPT OF FUNCTION
- FUNCTIONALISM OR FUNCTIONAL PERSPECTIVE
- FUNCTIONAL PRE-REQUISITES
- SOCIAL FUNCTIONS AND DYSFUNCTIONS
- MANIFEST AND LATENT FUNCTIONS.

The twin concepts of '*structure*' and '*function*' have assumed tremendous significance in the modern sociological literature. They are complementary concepts and the full understanding of either depends upon an understanding of the other.

These concepts of '*structure*' and '*function*' as applied in sociological studies draw their original inspiration from the works of *Herbert Spencer* and *Emile Durkheim*. Spencer compared societies to living organisms. Any organism has a '*structure*'–that is, it consists of a number of interrelated parts, such as a head, limbs, a heart, and so on. Each of these parts has a '*function*' to play in the life of the total organism. In the same way, Spencer argued, a society has a structure – it also consists of interrelated parts, such as the family, religion, the state and so on. Ideally, each of these components also has a function that contributes to the overall stability of the social system. Modern sociologists do not, of course, much press the analogy between a society and an organism. But they have retained the same general idea of society as a system of interrelated systems, each having its structure and function. This idea has been stressed much by the sociologists who are called "*functionalists*".

SOCIAL STRUCTURE

A number of sciences deal with the phenomenon of 'structure' in their own way mainly to discover the characteristics of "structure" of their interest. For example, *atomic physics* deals with the structure of atoms, *chemistry* with the structure of molecules, *crystallography* and *colloidal chemistry* with the structure of crystals and colloids, and *anatomy* and *physiology* with the structures of organisms. In sociological and social anthropological studies also the term 'social structure' is relevant because, the main task here is to discover the general characteristics of those 'social structures' the component parts of which are human beings.

'*Social Structure*' is one of the basic concepts of sociology. But it has not been used consistently or unambiguously. In the decade following the Second World War the concept 'Social Structure' became extremely fashionable in social anthropological studies. It became so general that it could be applied to almost any ordered arrangement of social phenomena.

The word '*structure*' in its original English meaning refers to "*building construction*" or "*arrangement of parts*", or "*manner of organisation*". But by the 16th century it was used to refer to the interrelations between the component parts of any whole. It was in this sense widely used in anatomical studies. The term became relatively popular in sociological studies with the works of *Herbert Spencer*, that is, after 1850. Spencer who was very much fascinated by his biological analogies (organic structure and evolution) applied the term-'structure' to his analysis of society and spoke of 'social structure'. Even Durkheim, Morgan, Marx and others gave their own interpretations to it.

At modern times, *George Murdock* in America, *A .R. Radcliffe-Brown* and his followers in Brit- ain and *Claude Levi-Strauss* in France used profusely this concept and popularised it. The usages of other writers are mostly the modified versions of these writers.

Murdock's use of term '*structure*' implies either a building analogy or a dead organic model dissected for demonstration. *Radcliffe-Brown* presumes that society may be compared to a living organism or a working mechanism. For Brown, society has a life of its own. Society is not an object but it is very much like a creature. Hence, the study of structure, that is, the inter-dependence of the component parts of the system–is invariably linked with the study of function. It means one has to study how the component parts of the system '*work*' in relation to each other and to the whole.

Definitions of Social Structure

The concept of social structure has been defined in different ways by different thinkers. We may consider some of these definitions:

1. *Radcliffe-Brown* defines social structure as "an arrangement of persons in institutionally controlled or defined relationships, (such as the relationship of King and subject, or that of husband and wife)".
2. In the *British social anthropological circles* the term social structure is used to refer to "a body of principles underlying social relations, rather than their actual content".
3. *Morris Ginsberg* regards social structure as "the complex of principal groups and institutions which constitute societies".
4. In current sociological usage the concept of social structure is applied to small groups as well as larger associations, communities and societies. Thus, *Ogburn* and *Nimkoff* are of the opinion that "In society, the organisation of a group of persons is the social structure. What the group does is the function." They use the terms 'social organisation' and 'social structure' almost interchangeably.
5. In a loose manner, the term 'social structure' is used to refer to any recurring pattern of social behaviour.
6. Many sociologists have used the term 'social structure' to refer to "the enduring, orderly and patterned relationships between elements of a society..." (But there is disagreement as to what would count as an "element". For example, according to *A.R. Brown*, general and regular kinds of relationships that exist between people, constitute the elements. For *S.F. Nadel*, the elements are roles. For most of the sociologists who are called 'functionalists', the elements of social structures are 'social institutions'. They consider these elements (that is, social institutions) as necessary because they are "functional pre-requisites". Without these institutions no society can survive.

Toward an Understanding of the Terms 'Structure' and 'Social Structure'

The term 'structure' refers to "some sort of ordered arrangements of parts or components". A musical composition has a structure, a sentence has a structure, a building has a structure, a molecule or an animal has a structure and so on. In all these we find ordered arrangement of different parts. *For example*, a building which has structure consists of various parts such as stones, sand, bricks, iron, cement, wood, glass, etc. A structure that can be called a building can be obtained only when these parts or components are properly ordered and arranged one in relationship with the other.

In the same way, society too has its own structure called 'social structure'. The components or units of social structure are "*persons*". A person is a human being and is considered not just as an organism but as occupying position in a social structure. Even though the persons are subject to change (due to change of membership, mobility or death) the structure as such maintains its continuity. A nation, tribe, a body such as Indian Institute of Technology, a political party, a religious body such as the Vishwa Hindu Parishad, can continue in existence as an arrangement of persons though the personnel of each changes from time to time. There is continuity of the structure, just as a human body maintains its structure. The components of human body are molecules. The human body preserves the continuity of its structure though the actual molecules out of which it is made, are continually changing. In the political structure of India, there must always be a Prime Minister, at one time it was Pandit Nehru, at another Indira Gandhi, and at present, it is Mr. Atal Bihari Vajpayee. Thus the structure as an arrangement remains continuous.

The Example of University as Having a Structure

University as an educational group or system has a structure of its own. Every year senior students depart and a new batch of freshmen enters. Some faculty members are replaced, new professors are appointed and new classes may be added to the curriculum. The administration agrees to include student representation in its planning sessions. Yet despite changes in personnel and policy, some things about university remain unchanged. Faculty members still design their courses, assign work to the students and evaluate their progress. The ways in which individual faculty members and students perform their roles vary, but the *general patterns* are much the same and fit together into an overall structure that we call a university. Although the structure itself remains invisible, it silently shapes our actions. Thus, analysing the form and influence of social structure gives sociology its distinctive power in understanding human affairs.

The Necessity and Universality of Social Structures

Human beings must be social to survive. Man is a member of social species, a species which cannot survive unless its members are organised into groups and societies. These, in turn, develop a culture to meet shared needs. It is these minimum needs–biological, economic, social, psychological, etc., which result in the universality of some basic structures. These structures lead to some general functions. Sociologists can therefore speak of a few kinds of structures or groups which will be present in all societies. These structures will exist in any society regardless of its ethos, its history, or any cultural variability. Because without the functions of these structures a human society could not survive.

Thus, a family may be monogamous or polygamous; a government may be democratic or totalitarian; an economy may be capitalist or socialist. The nature of the specific structure may vary from society to society but there is always *some* structure resulting in the function because, the functions are universal and essential.

Elements of Social Structure

According to H.M. Johnson, the main elements of social structure are as follows.

1. ***Sub-groups of various types:*** Society can be understood as a big group which consists of people. This big group or larger system consists of various sub-groups. Various political, economic, religious, educational, familial and other groups and associations represent such sub-groups. People who enact roles are organised in these sub-groups within the larger system. Some of these sub- groups persist longer than any particular members. *Example*: A particular family may continue to stay even after the death of the husband or wife. Many other sub-groups persist as '*types*' longer than any particular example of the type. *Example*: a family may perish due to the collapse of building in which its members lived, families as such are not going to perish. Social norms define the roles and the obligations of sub-groups.
2. ***Social structure consists of roles of various types:*** 'Social structure consists of not only sub-groups but also roles. Roles are found within the larger system and also within the sub-groups. The concepts of role and sub-group imply interrelationship. Role occupants are expected to fulfil obligations to other people (who are also role-occupants). *For example*, in family, the husband has obligations towards his Wife and children; in the college teacher has obligations towards students, principal and the management and vice versa. Further, the number of sub-groups that are there are not only interrelated but also subject to social norms. The political, economic, educational and other groups, *for example*, are interrelated through social norms.
3. ***Regulative norms governing sub-groups and roles:*** Sub-groups and roles are governed by social norms. Social norms are of two types: (*i*) *obligatory or relational*, and (*ii*) *permissive or regulative*.

   Some norms *specify positive obligations*. But they are not commonly applied to all the roles and sub-groups. *Example*: The positive obligations of a family is not the same as those of business firm. Similarly, the obligations of a father are not the same as those of a son. Norms of this kind are obligatory or relational in nature.

   Some other norms *specify the limit of permissible action*. A role-occupant of a sub-group in this case, '*must*' do certain things, 'may' do certain things, and '*must not*' do still others. They are called "regulative norms". They do not differentiate between roles and between sub-groups. *For example*, in our society, regardless of one's role, one must not seek to influence others by threats of violence or by violence itself.
4. ***Cultural values:*** Every society has its own cultural values. 'Values' refer to the measures of goodness or desirability. Individuals or groups are often found to be emotionally committed to val- ues. They help to integrate a personality or a system of interaction. They provide a means by which conflicts tend to be resolved. Still some conflicts persist, because no system of action is perfectly integrated. Values are closely related to norms, Infact, they may be regarded as "*higher-order norms*".

Any one of these element—a sub-group, a role, a social norm, or a value-may be called a "*partial structure*"

Social Structure: An Anthropological Perspective

In the field of social science social anthropology can be considered as a special science of structures and function of society. Anthropology is the science of small societies and hence it is comparatively easier to study the structure and function of primitive society. A number of thinkers and writers have enriched the fields of social anthropology and social structure by means of their studies and writings. We shall now confine ourselves to Radcliffe-Brown's conception of social structure.

Radcliffe Brown's Conception of Social Structure

According to Radcliffe-Brown, social structure "*denotes the network of actually existing relations*" between people. Culture is not a concrete reality, but only an abstraction. Hence what we observe concretely in society is not very much culture, but "*the acts of behaviour of the individuals*" who compose society. The human beings are connected by a complex network of social relations which itself could be social structure, according to Brown.

As Brown says, "social structures are just as real as are individual organisms". The physiological and psychological phenomena that we observe in the organisms are very much the result of the structure (made up of cells and interstitial fluids) in which they are united. Similarly, the social phenomena that are observed in human society are the result of social structure by which they are united.

Brown has made it clear that the study of social structures is not equivalent to the study of social relations as such. A particular relation between Tom and Ram, or Rekha and Ruth, is not studied here. But a wide network of social relations involving many other persons is the object of study. .

Parts of Social Structure

Brown considers as a part of the social structure (*i*) *all social relations of person to person*. For example, the kinship structure of any society consists of interpersonal relations between father and son, or a mother's brother and his sister's son, etc. (*ii*) Brown includes under social structure the different *social roles of* individuals. (*iii*) The differentiated *social positions* of men and women, of chiefs and commoners, of employers and employees etc., no doubt determine the different clans or nations, or groups to which they belong. But more than that they work as the determinants of social relations.

Actual Structure and Structural Form

Brown makes a clear distinction between "*actual structure*" and "*structural farm*". Actual structure refers to a set of actually existing social relations at a given moment of time. One can make direct observations of that. It is a *concrete* reality which any one can directly observe. But "structural form" is *abstract*. It refers to the *patterns* or *kinds of relations* which people maintain over a period of time. lt is relatively *stable*. But the actual structure, that is, the actual relations of persons and groups of persons *change* from year to year, or even from day to day. New members come, old members go, friends may become enemies, and enemy's friends, and, so on. Though the actual structure changes in this way, the structural form may remain constant for some time. Structural form may change gradually and sometimes suddenly due to war, revolutions, etc. Thus, *the conception of social structure, involves the idea of continuity*. But this continuity is "not static like that of a building, but a dynamic continuity, like that of the organic structure of a living body. The social life constantly renews the social structure as it is evidenced in the changes of social roles and positions of individuals.

Spatial Aspect. Brown is of the opinion that 'social structure' involves the *spatial* aspect also. Brown feels that it is convenient to study any network of social relations as confined to a locality of a suitable size. With this "we can observe, describe, and compare the systems of social structure of as many localities as we wish".

Social Structure and Social Personality

Brown's conception of social structure is essentially related to the conception of '*social personality*'. 'Social personality', according to Brown, refers to the position occupied by a human being in a social structure. This includes the complex of all his social relations with others. Thus every human being living in society is two things: (*i*) he is an *individual* and also a (*ii*) *person*. Human beings as individuals are subjects of study for physiologists and psychologists. "*The human being as a person is a complex of social relationships*". For example, he is a citizen of India, a husband, a father, a brother. a cricket player, a trade unionist, a parliamentarian, and so on. Each of these descriptions indicates a place in social structure. Since a person can change his place in social structure, social personality is subject to change during the course of life of the person. The human being as a person is the object of study for the social anthropologist and also sociologist. Hence Brown says "*we cannot study persons except in terms of social structure, nor can we study social structure except in terms of the persons who are the units of which it is composed*"

CONCEPT OF FUNCTION

The term '*function*' has different meanings in different contexts. Its ordinary dictionary meaning is – "*doing a thing*", or '*activity*' or '*performance*'. In mathematics, physiology and also in sociology the term is used in different ways. In *mathematics*, the term 'function' refers to "a quantity so connected with another that any change in the one produces a corresponding change in the other". In *physiology*, it is used as a technical term to refer to "the vital activity of organ, tissue, or cell". In physiology, the concept of organic function is one that is used to refer to the physiology, the concept of organic Function is one that is used to refer to the connection between the structure of an organism and the life process of that organism.

The concept of 'function' applied to human societies is based on an analogy between social life and organic life. The recognition of this analogy is quite old. Even during the 19th century, the analogy and the concept of and the word 'function' were used very commonly in social philosophy and sociology. But the systematic formulation of the concept of 'function' in the study of society can be said to have been made by Emile Durkheim in 1895 in his '*Rules of Sociological Method*'.

Definitions of Function

1. *Durkheim's* definition of function is that "the 'function' of a social institution is the correspondence between it and the needs of the social organism". (It may be noted that Radcliffe-Brown prefers to substitute for the term 'needs' the term—"necessary conditions of existence")
2. *R.K. Merton* defines function as "those observed consequences which make for the adapta- tion and adjustment of a given system".

Radcliffe-brown's Views Regarding 'Function'

The concept of 'function' has become quite popular in modern sociology due to the contributions of *Malinowski*, *A.R. Brown*, *Talcot Parsons*, *Robert K. Merton*, and *Kingsley Davis*. Durkheim's views of 'function' have deeply influenced the thoughts of all these writers. For the purpose of understanding the term 'function' as used in sociology, we shall briefly deal with Brown's views.

Analogy between Social and Organic Life

Brown frankly advocated the analogy between social life and organic life. He tried to avoid Durkheim's emphasis on the 'needs' of the social organism and hence spoke in terms of "*necessary conditions of existence*". This was because he wished to avoid teleological implications, (such as "the notion of some 'guiding spirit' or mysterious force in social life".)

As the analogy runs, a complex organism such as a human body, has a structure as an arrangement of organs, tissues and fluids. Even the single cellular organism has a structure of its own in the form of an arrangement of molecules. An organism has life which can be referred to as a '*process*'. The term '*organic function*' refers to the "*connection between the structure of an organism and its life process*". The life processes that go on within the living human body are dependent on the organic structure. For example, it is the function of the heart to pump blood throughout the body. The continued existence of the organic structure depends on the processes that make up the total life processes. If the heart fails to perform its function the life process comes to an end, and the living structure also comes to an end. *Process* is *dependent on structure and continuity of structure is dependent on process*.

In the study of social system also the concept of 'function' could be used in a scientific way as it is used in physiology. It could be used to refer to the interconnection between the social structure and the process of life. The three concepts–*process*, *structure* and *function* – are logically connected. They constitute the essential aspects of the theory of human social system.

In the field of social life, we find that every community whether it is Indian or African, or Australian, has a structure of its own, the individual human beings are its essential units. They are interconnected by set of social relations. The continuity of the social structure is not destroyed by changes in the units. It means individuals may die or go out of their society; and new members may enter in. The continuity of social structure is maintained by the process of social life. The '*process of social life*' refers to the activities and interactions of the individuals and of the organised groups, into which they are united. The social life of the community itself is understood as the '*functioning*' of the social structure. The *function* of any particular usage, institution, norm etc. (such as punishment of a crime, or a funeral ceremony) is the pan it plays in the social life as a whole. It is also its contribution to the maintenance of the structural continuity.

It is clear from the above explanation that according to Brown, the concept of function involves the notion of a 'structure'. Structure consists of a '*set of relations*' that exists amongst 'unit entities' namely individuals and groups. The '*continuity* of the structure is maintained by a 'life process' made up of the activities of the constituent units, that is; individuals and groups.

According to Brown, the term 'function' indicates "*the contribution which a partial activity makes to the total activity of which it is a part*". Thus, a social custom by means of its functioning contributes to the total social life, that is, to the functioning of the total social system. This view implies that a social system has a certain kind of unity, which Brown speaks of as a "*functional unity*". This functional unity is "*a condition in which all parts of the social system work together with a sufficient degree of harmony or internal consistency*". This idea of functional unity presupposes that the parts of the social system do not produce persistent conflicts which can neither be resolved nor regulated. Brown made it clear that this idea of functional unity of a social system is only hypothesis which could be tested by a systematic examination of the facts.

Brown who has made use of the organic analogy for his explanation of the concept of function is quite aware of its limitations also. *Firstly*, as he stated, "it is possible to observe the organic structure to some extent independent of its functioning". "But in human society the social structure as a whole can only be *observed* in its functioning". For example, the relations of father and son, buyer and seller, ruler and subject, cannot be observed except in the social activities, in which the relations are functioning. Thus, he states "a social morphology cannot be established independently of a social physiology".

Secondly, an animal organism does not in the course of its life, change its structural type. For example, a donkey does not become horse. But, a human society "in the course of its history can and does change its structural type without any breach of continuity".

Thirdly, in the case of organic life we find that an organism may function more or less efficiently. Here, there is a special science of pathology to deal with all phenomena of dysfunction. We distinguish in an organism very clearly what we call '*health*' and *disease*. Here, we find objective criteria by which we distinguish between ill-health and health, or between the pathological and normal. Disease is regarded as that which either threatens the organism with death or interferes with its organic activities. As far as human societies are concerned, they do not die in the manner in which the animals die. Hence, we cannot say, that if a particular '*dysnomia*' or *disorder* is not treated properly or checked, it would cause the death of a society; it need not. Further, unlike the organism, the society can change its structural type, if need arises.

Concept of Function–As a Working Hypothesis

Brown firmly believes that the concept of function constitutes a '*working hypothesis*' to understand human society and its working. It helps to formulate problems for investigation. No scientific inquiry is possible without some kind of a working hypothesis such as the concept of 'function'. But Brown here has cautioned us that no dogmatic assertion be made such as "*that everything in the life of every community has a function.* The assumption is, it *may have* one, and we can reasonably seek to discover it.

Further, as Brown has pointed out, it is quite likely, that "the same social usage in two societies may have different functions in the two". For example, belief in Supreme Being in a simple society is something different from such a belief in a modern civilised community.

Brown is quite aware of the fact that the acceptance of the functional hypothesis or point of view as stated above may lead to the recognition of a large number of problems. But he has suggested that the solutions for these could be found by making wide comparative studies of societies of many diverse types, and also intensive studies of as many single societies as possible. He is also of the opinion that the hypothesis leads to an attempt "to investigate directly the functional consistency or unity of a social system". It also helps to determine the nature of that unity.

FUNCTIONALISM OR FUNCTIONAL PERSPECTIVE

The concept of 'function' has been further elaborated by some of the sociologists which ultimately led them to establish a "*functionalist theory*" as such. The functionalist theory which is often referred to as '*functional approach*', or "*structural-functionalism*", or '*functionalist perspective*", or "*functionalism*" has been associated with the work of American sociologists such as Talcott Parsons, Robert K. Merton, and Kingsley Davis.

"The functionalist theory implies that society tends to be an organised, stable, well-integrated system, in which most members agree on basic values". Sociologists with a functional approach study the way in which each part of a society contributes to the functioning of the society as a Whole. They stress much the role of balance or equilibrium in society. They view society as a system of interrelated parts. They are mainly interested in the '*contributions*' or '*purposes*' these' parts serve for ongoing social life. They focus on the '*functions*' or '*consequences*', that a given element has in society. To make it more specific, the functionalists say that each group or institution persists because it is functional.

Examples: (*i*) In trying to explain why all human societies have a family system – the functionalists would ask what function (or need) does the family system fulfil for the larger society? The answer to this question will highlight the contributions that family systems make to the on-going life of societies. The family, for instance, *functions* to regulate sexual behaviour, to transmit social values to children, and to take care of young and aged people who could not otherwise survive. (*ii*) Economic activity, *functions* to provide the goods and services on which our society depends for its existence. It also gives people roles in life, enabling them to earn a living and to draw a sense of identity from the work that they do. (*iii*) The school *functions* to educate children, prepare workers, take children off their parents' hands for part of the day, etc.

In the functionalist view, a society has an underlying tendency to be in equilibrium, or balance. Social change is, therefore, likely to be disruptive unless it takes place relatively slowly. Because, changes in one part of the system usually provoke changes elsewhere in the system. *Example*: If the economy requires an increasing number of highly trained workers, the schools and colleges will adopt the policies and practices to supply them, and the state will sanction more money for education. But if the economy expands so rapidly that the other elements in the social system cannot "*catch up*", social disequilibrium will result.

From the functional point of view, if a particular social change promotes a harmonious equilib- rium it is seen as *functional*; if it disturbs the equilibrium it is *dysfunctional*; if it has no effects, it is *non-functional*. *Example*: In a democracy political parties are functional, while bombings, assassinations, and political terrorism are dysfunctional, and changes in political vocabulary or party symbols are non-functional.

Functionalists ask such questions as- "*How does this value, or practice, or institution help meet the needs of the society* "? "*How does it fit in with the other practices and institutions of the society"*? " *Would a proposed change make it more or less useful to society?*"

As *Donold Light Jr.* and *S.Killer* have pointed out. "By looking at the social world through a functional perspective, sociologists often develop convincing explanations for the existence of social phenomena that would otherwise be puzzling or incomprehensible". For example, *Kingsley Davis* has come up with some innovative and convincing explanation for the practice of prostitution which the society condemns and at the same time maintains. His functionalist explanations are as follows: (*i*) *Prostitution provides a sexual outlet for travellers, businessmen, salesmen, sailors etc., who will be unable to find stable partners*, (*ii*) *For those who do not have the will or energy to pursue more elaborate forms of courtship, it is required*, (*iii*) *For those whose stable partners are temporarily out of contact during separation, divorce, Widowhood*, (*iv*) *For those sexual perverts who cannot continue the long-term enduring sex relationships*, (*v*) *For those who are unable to compete in ordinary sexual market place, examples: the disfigured, handicapped, impotent.*

Assumptions of Functionalism

Functional theory is based on some assumptions. According to *Dahrendorf*, the main assump- tions of functionalism arc as follows:–

1. A society is a system of integrated parts.
2. Social systems tend to be stable because they have built-in mechanisms of control.
3. Dysfunctions exist, but they tend to resolve themselves or become institutionalised in the long run.
4. Change is usually gradual.
5. Social integration is produced by the agreement of most members of the society on a certain set of values. The value system is the most stable element of the social system. Functional theory and research represent a young but rapidly growing approach. Its accomplishments are promising but still tentative. "Functionalism is perhaps more promise than achievement. But it is an important promise." —*Prof. Timasheff*

FUNCTIONAL PRE-REQUISITES

The functional theory has to answer questions such as–"If social life is to persist what condi- tions must be met with by the group or social system?" Several of Parsons' students have compiled a list that they call the "*Functional pre-requisites*" of any social system. They can be grouped under four headings. In fact, they represent four recurrent functional problems which every social system must solve in its attempts to adapt itself to the basic facts of life. As mentioned by H.M. Johnson they are: (*i*) *pattern maintenance and tension management,* (*ii*) *adaptation,* (*iii*) *goal attainment, and (iv) integration.*

1. ***Pattern maintenance and tension management:*** A social system has its own patterns which must be maintained. The units of the system, that is, role-occupants or sub-groups, must learn these patterns and develop an attitude of respect towards them. Thus any social system must have *mechanisms of "socialisation"*. Through the process of socialisation the cultural patterns of the system become a part and parcel of the personalities of its members. After they are learnt the cultural patterns have to be renewed. They are renewed through appropriate rituals and other symbols.

   Tension management: A human group cannot endure if it fails to meet the individual human needs of its members. The units of any system, *i.e.*, individuals or sub-groups are subject to emo- tional disturbance and distractions. Man's emotional, spiritual, and cultural requirements are extremely complex. Still they must be met with or "*managed*" if the units are to be able to carry on effectively. All social systems provide for relaxation from tension by means of activities that allow a person to express his or her inner feelings. For example, dance and the arts do this task. All societies provide special structural arrangements for differences in sex and also for such crucial events as births and deaths. Wherever there is social life, there are structures or patterns of leisure and recreation, crafts, art, and some form of religion expressed in myths or elaborate ritual.

2. ***Adaptation:*** Any social system must be adapted to its social and non-social environment. For a society to survive it must have a technology adequate to provide food, shelter and clothing. The economy of the society meets this need. Every 'permanent' social system has its own division of labour. Because, for the production of goods and service, role differentiation becomes necessary. It is known that no one person can perform simultaneously all the tasks that have to be performed. The system must also provide care for the helpless young and protection against animal and human predators. Many of the structures existing in any society are designed to fulfil these essential functions.

3. ***Goal Attainment:*** Every social system has one or more goals to be attained, through cooperative effort. '*National security*'— can be cited here as the best example of a societal goal. Adaptation to the environment, social and non-social, is necessary if goals are to be attained. Further, in accordance with the specific nature of tasks of the system, the human and non-human resources must be mobilized in some effective way. For example, in any social system there must be a proper process for determining which persons will occupy what role at what time for what purpose. The problem of allocation of members within the social system will be solved by such a process. The rules regulating inheritance, for example, solve this problem in part.

   The allocation of members and the allocation of scarce resources are important for both adap- tation and goal attainment. The economy of a society as a sub-system produces goods and services for various purposes. The government in complex societies, mobilizes goods and services for the attainment of specific goals of the total society. *Example*: A business firm may have the goal of producing steel. The goal is *adaptive* for the society because steel can be used for many purposes, including the purposes of other business firms. The steel company faces the adaptive problem. It means, it had to adjust to the government and to competing firms and provides itself with the neces- sary raw materials for its productive goals.

4. ***Integration:*** Since they live in groups men and women must consider the needs of the group as well as their own needs. They must coordinate and integrate their actions. 'Integration' has to do with the interrelations of units of

social system, that is, individuals and groups. "To some extent, the members of a system must be loyal to one another and to the system as a whole. This is a problem of solidarity and morale". Morale is important for both integration and pattern maintenance. It is closely related to common values. It is the willingness to give oneself to specific undertakings. In the routine living, the goals and interests of the whole society are not very much interests of the whole society and are not very much present in the minds of most of its members. That way, the interests of sub-groups are always remembered. But during the period of crisis such as war or revolution the goal and interest must always dominate if the society is to survive an independent group.

In almost every social system, some participants, including whole sub-groups, violate the norms. Since the norms fulfil some social needs, their violations are a threat to the social system. Thus, the need for "*social control*" arises. It is essential to protect the integrity of the system. "Thus, the elaborate rules provide orderly procedures to determine who will occupy given sites, to control the use of force and fraud, to co-ordinate traffic, to regulate sexual behaviour, to govern the conditions of exchange, and so on".

Since the individual members are often motivated by "self-interests" chances of clashes taking place between them cannot be ruled out. Sometimes, even with best morale we find threats to inte- gration. Hence, there must be mechanism for restoring solidarity. Such mechanisms are normally operative most of the time. It must be noted that even with the well-institutionalized norms, instances of deviance do take place. The deviations may even become disruptive. Hence, there is the need for "secondary" mechanism of social control. *Example*: In the modern state, the whole apparatus of catching and rehabilitating the criminal represents such a kind of secondary mechanism.

SOCIAL FUNCTIONS AND DYSFUNCTIONS

The concepts of social functions and dysfunctions are essentially related to the functional theory: *RK. Merton* has drawn our attention to the fact that not all elements in the social system are *functional* at all times. On occasion some element may actually disrupt the social equilibrium and may therefore be *dysfunctional*.

As *H.M. Johnson* has explained, "Any partial structure–a type of sub-group, or a role, or a social norm, or a cultural value–is said to have a *function* if it contributes to the fulfilment of one or more of the social needs of a social system;–any partial structure is said to have a *dysfunction* if it hinders the fulfilment of one or more of these needs".

Thus, a cultural trait which helps the society in meeting its needs or requirements is called a *functional trait*, and one which hinders a society in achieving its needs or requirements, is called a *dysfunctional trait*.

Examples: (*i*) *Religion* is said to be functional when it helps in binding together members of a society. It is called dysfunctional when it promotes superstitious beliefs and 'meaningless' practices. (*ii*) A *political machine* is dysfunctional when it increases graft and corruption. It remains functional when it is able to protect the rights of minorities and assure equality to all. (*iii*) The *high birth rate* in the less developed countries of the world is very dysfunctional for those societies because, it has created a serious problem of overpopulation.

Sometimes, an element, in the social order can be functional in one respect and dysfunctional in another. Any industry in any modern society, for example, has the manifest function of providing the goods on which the way of life of the people depends. But it has also the latent function of polluting the environment and is therefore, dysfunctional in this sense. The full implication of any element in the social system therefore has to be carefully explored.

Not 'Purposes' but 'Functions'

As Merton has made it clear '*function*' of any element has to be distinguished from "*purpose*". A purpose is something *subjective* that is, something in the mind of the participant or participants in a social system. But a function of dysfunction is an *objective* consequence of action. When we attribute functions to sub-groups, roles, norms or any partial structure, we mean that its action has certain consequences for a social system irrespective of the motives of the actor or actors. Motives are important, no doubt, but they are not the same thing as functions or dysfunctions.

The Distinction is only Relative

It is to be noted that the distinction between "*function*" and "*dysfunction*" is only relative and not absolute. Sometimes, they may be complementary to one another also. Because, we often find both function and dysfunction in any single phenomenon simultaneously. It is difficult to draw a line of separation between the two. Whatever is functional to some may turn out to be dysfunctional for someone else. Hence the description of the two expressions often becomes subjective depending upon the social situations.

Further, the value or practice or norm, etc., which is functional at one time or place may become dysfunctional interfering with the smooth operation of society–at another time or place. *Example*: large families were desired' throughout most history. Death rates were high and large families helped to ensure some services. Especially, in America, with a big continent to fill, and with never enough hands to do the work, large families were functionally useful. They provided workers, compan–ionship, and old age security, and were good both for the individual and the society. But today, in a crowded World with a low death rate, large families are no longer a blessing. In other words, large families have become dysfunctional and 'threaten the welfare' of the society.

Functions and Dysfunctions as Eunomia and Dysnomia

The distinction between function and dysfunction can further be made clear by making use of the much fashionable organic analogy. In an organism we distinguish between health and ill-health or disease. Ancient Greeks thought that the ideas of health and disease could be applied to society to distinguish conditions of '*eunomia*' (which refers to good order or social health) from '*dysnomia*' (which denotes disorder or social ill-health). In brief, 'eunomia' refers to function and 'dysnomia' refers to dysfunctions. In the organic world, there is a special science called 'pathology' which studies ill-health or the phenomena of dysnomia or dysfunction. In the 19th century, *Durkheim* borrowed this concept of Pathology from the organic sciences and used it in his sociological studies of '*Suicide*' and "*Division of Labour in Society*". He called it "social pathology". In these two studies "he attempted to find out objective criteria by which to judge whether a given society at a given time is normal or pathological, eunomic or dysnomic". Durkheim preferred to use the term "*anomic conditions*" in place of '*dysnomic conditions*'.

With regard to the organic structures we can find strictly objective criteria by which we distin- guish disease from health, pathological from normal. Disease may either threaten the organism with death or interfere with its organic activities or functions. As far as the human societies are concerned, we cannot say that societies die in the manner in which the organism dies. Hence, we cannot define dysnomia as some conditions which lead, if not controlled, to the death of a society. Unlike an organism, a society can change its structural type, or it can become an integral part of a larger society. It is for this reason Brown says, "we cannot define dysnomia as a disturbance of the usual activities of a social type".

As far as the comparison between "*the health of an organism*" and "*the eunomia of a society*" is concerned, we find a striking congruence. In both the instances, it means a condition of the harmo- nious working together of the parts. Due to its organic unity the organism tries to maintain its health. Similarly, society too has a kind of unity which Brown calls "*functional unity*", or "inner consistency of a social system". Brown is confident that it may be possible to establish a purely objective crite- rion to determine the degree of functional unity of any particular society. But he has admitted that the infant science of society has not been able to establish such a kind of criterion at present.

MANIFEST AND LATENT AND MANIFEST FUNCTIONS

The functional theory presupposes that every element in a social system fulfils certain func- tions. But how does one determine what the functions of a given element in the social system are? The sociologist only asks what its consequences are–and not what its purposes are believed to be. The assumed purposes of some component in the social system do not necessarily tell us what its functions are. Because the component can have consequences other than those that were intended. This fact has made *R.K. Merton* to make a distinction between '*manifest functions*' and '*latent functions*'.

According to *Merton*, "*Manifest*" functions are those that are intended and recognised; "*latent*" functions are unrecognised and unintended".

Manifest Functions

These are "*intended and recognised*" functions. These are functions which people assume and expect the institutions to fulfil. *Examples*: (*i*) Schools are expected to educate the young in the knowledge and skills that they need. It is its manifest function. (*ii*) *Economic institutions* are expected to produce and distribute goods and direct the flow of capital wherever it is needed. (*iii*) *Dating* is expected to help the young men and women to find out their suitability for marriage. (*iv*) The *welfare system* has the manifest function of preventing the poor from starving. (*v*) Similarly, *incest taboos* are expected to prevent biological degeneration. These manifest functions are obvious, admitted, and generally applauded.

Latent Functions

These are "*unrecognised and unintended*" functions. These are the unforeseen consequences of institutions. *Examples:* (*i*) *Schools* not only educate youth, they also provide mass entertainment and keep the young out of employment market. (*ii*) *Economic institutions* not only produce and distribute goods, but also promote technological, political and educational changes, and even philanthropy. (*iii*) *Dating* not only selects marriage partners, but also supports a large entertainment industry. (*iv*) The welfare system not only protects the starving, but it also has the latent function of preventing a civil disorder that might result if millions of people had no source of income. (*v*) *Incest taboo* has the latent function of preventing conflicts within the family. It's another latent function is. it reinforces the sexual union between husband and wife.

Role of Latent Functions in Relation to Manifest Functions

Latent functions of an institution or partial structure may– 1. *support the manifest functions*, or 2. *be irrelevant to*, or 3. *may even undermine manifest functions*. These points may be clarified with examples.

1. ***Latent functions may support the manifest functions:*** *Example*: The latent functions of religious institutions in the modern society include–offering recreational activities and courtship opportunities to young people. All Church

leaders agree that these activities help Churches pursue their manifest functions.

2. ***Latent functions may be irrelevant to manifest functions:*** *Example*: It is very much doubtful that the sports spectacles staged by schools and colleges have much effect upon the manifest functions of promoting education. But, they seem to be largely irrelevant to this manifest function.

3. ***Latent functions sometimes undermine manifest functions:*** *Example*: The manifest function of civil service regulations is to secure a competent, dedicated staff of civil servants to make government more efficient. But the civil service system may have the latent function of establishing a rigid bureaucracy (consisting of bureaucrats with least concern) which may block the programme of an elected government. Such a bureaucracy may refuse to carry out the government programmes, which disturb the bureaucrats' routine procedures. This could be referred to as the 'dysfunctional' aspect of the civil service system.

Latent Dysfunctions

As it is clear, a particular or some latent functions of an element or a particular structure may prove to be dysfunctional for the system as such. *Example*: The manifest function of the regulation of drugs by the government is to protect consumers against injurious substances. Its latent function may be to delay the introduction of new, lifesaving drugs. This latent function, it is obvious, is dysfunctional for the social system. Similarly, the manifest function of Western health institutions has been to reduce illness, premature death and human misery; the latent function has been to promote a population explosion and massive famine in the underdeveloped countries. These latent functions are definitely 'dysfunctional' in nature.

There are, therefore, many instances in which latent functions might more precisely be called "latent dysfunctions". Because they tend to underline and weaken institution or to impede attainment its manifest functions.

Interlink between Manifest and Latent Functions

As *H.M. Johnson* has pointed out the distinction between manifest and latent functions is es- sentially relative and not absolute. A function may appear to be '*manifest*' for some participants in the social system and '*latent*' for others. But the individuals, many times, are not aware of the latent, or manifest dysfunctions of most of the partial structures of society. Still the distinction between them is of some importance.

Firstly, if the sociologist is not aware of the possibility of latent functions, he might often think that some partial structures have no function at all. Further, he might become quite contented with discovering manifest functions only. It is here, that the sociologist in his investigation, has got ample chance to go beyond his "*common sense*" to find out explanation for certain social element in terms of latent functions and dysfunctions.

Secondly, any social reformer must be sufficiently aware of the latent functions and dysfunctions of any partial structure which he wants to reform or change. His proposals for reform would become ineffective, if he is not conscious of these functions. In fact, "knowledge of the way in which society actually "works" is the only sound basis for social planning. Naive moralising can be not only ineffectual but wasteful and otherwise harmful". For example, mere launching a crusade against the so called '*corrupt*' political machines in a city or a province in a blind manner is of no use if one is ignorant of the latent functions of '*corruption*'.

Finally, the distinction will help one to know or estimate the effects of transformation of a previously latent function into a manifest function, the distinction also involves the problem of the role of knowledge in human behaviour and the problems of "*manipulation*" of human behaviour.

REVIEW QUESTIONS

1. What is social structure? Point out its elements.
2. Give the definitions of social structure as defined by different sociologists. Describe its characteristic features.
3. Discuss the social structure in an anthropological perspective.
4. Throw light on Brown's concept of social structure.
5. Bring out the relation between the social structure and social personality.
6. What do you mean by function? Discuss its functional perspective.
7. Clarify the concept of function. Discuss the views of Brown regarding the concept of function.
8. How do social functions differ from dysfunctions?
9. Write short notes on the following:
   (a) Functional pre-requisites
   (b) Latent and manifest functions
   (c) Latent dysfunctions
10. Assess the role of functions in relation to manifest functions.
11. The distinction between manifest and latent functions is essentially relative and not absolute. Comment.

⌘⌘⌘⌘⌘⌘⌘⌘⌘⌘⌘

PART THREE

Individual—Culture—Society

12

INDIVIDUAL AND SOCIETY

CHAPTER OUTLINE

Man is a social animal. He lives in social groups, in communities and in society. Human life and society almost go together. Man cannot live as man, without society. Solitary life is unbearable to him. Man is biologically and psychologically equipped to live in groups, in society. Society has become an essential condition for human life to arise and to continue. Society is more than our environment. It is within us as well as around us.

There is a vast literature on the questions such as the nature or the essence of man's social life, it's origin and sources. It is essential to study the deepest relations that exist between the individual and society. It is equally significant to know the nature of man's motives or impulses towards society.

THE 'SOCIALITY' OF MAN: THE CENTRAL PROBLEM OF SOCIOLOGY

It was Aristotle who said long back that man is a social animal. This proposition gives room to the central problem of sociology *i.e.*, the *sociability* or the *sociality of man*. The essential fact is that man always belongs to a society or a group of one kind or the other, and without it, he cannot exist. Several questions of great sociological importance arise in this regard. "In what sense man is a social animal? In what sense do we belong to society? In what sense society belongs to us ? What is the nature of our dependence upon it?" These questions take us to a more fundamental question of the relation between the individual and society,

The relationship between individual and society is ultimately one of the most profound of all the problems of social philosophy. It is, in fact, a philosophical rather than a sociological problem, because it involves the question of values. We see ourselves on one side and our society on the other the person and the group, the individual and the collectivity. What does each owe to the other? In what sense is the single individual a part of a whole that is greater than he? In what sense does the whole exist for the individual? When we accept the statement of Aristotle that man is a social animal, what does this proposition ultimately mean? These are some of the difficult questions. The sociologist cannot remain silent when confronted with these larger issues of human worth and human destiny.

MAN DEPENDS ON SOCIETY

It is a thing of common observation of every one that the individual is living, breathing, work- ing, playing, resting, praying, enjoying, suffering, sometimes sweating, sometimes swearing with millions like him in society. It is in the society that an individual is surrounded and encompassed by culture, a societal force. It is in the society again, that he has to conform to the norms, occupy statuses and become members of groups. Then, what is the role and responsibility of an individual to himself and to his society ? Is the individual lost in society, or is it only in society, that he can find himself.

It is a self-obvious fact that man has not only a capacity for social life but also an intrinsic need of it. Emotional development, intellectual maturity and a certain amount of material goods and comforts for the full exercise of his liberty and progress are unthinkable without society. No human being is known to have normally developed in isolation. A few instances like that of *Kasper Hauser*; the *wolf-children* of India called Kamala and her sister; the isolated, *illegitimate child Anna* and others have fortified the fact that man develops human qualities only in society. He can attain his real nature only in society. The psychological development of the social consciousness of the child is also a confirmation of the natural sociality of the human being. The biological potentiality of becoming social is inherent in the very social nature of man.

TWO THEORIES CONCERNING THE NATURE OF SOCIETY

The question of the relation between the individual and the society is the starting point of many social investigations. The question of the nature of society is closely connected with the question of the relationship of man and society. There are two main theories regarding the relationships of man and society which have been propounded by several thinkers and writers. They are 1. The Social Contract Theory and 2. Organismic Theory.

Social Contract Theory

The '*social contract theory*' throws light on the origin of the society. According to this theory, all men are born free and equal. Individual precedes society. Society came into existence because of an agreement entered into by the individuals. The classical representatives of this school of thought are *Thomas Hobbes*, *John Locke*, and *J.J. Rousseau*. The three of them thought in various ways that before the existence of civil society men lived in a sort of pre-social state, called *the state of nature*, and in virtue of a contract among themselves, society came into existence. The essence of their argument is as follows:

(*a*) Thomas Hobbes (1588-1679). Thomas Hobbes, an English thinker, was of the opinion that society came into being as a means for the protection of men against the consequences of their own nature. Man in the state of nature was in perpetual conflict with his neighbours on account of his essentially selfish nature. To quote Hobbes, the life of man was "*solitary poor, nasty, brutish and short*". Every man was an enemy to every other man.

Hobbes in his book "*Leviathan*" has made it clear that man in the state of nature was not at all social According to him, man found "*nothing but grief in the company of his fellows*"—all being almost equally "*selfish, self-seeking, cunning, egoistic, brutal and aggressive*". Thus, men in the state of nature were like hungry wolves each ready to pounce on the others with all its ferocity.

Since the conditions in the state of nature were intolerable and men longed for peace, the people entered into a kind of social contract to ensure for themselves security and certainty of life and property. By mutual agreement they decided to surrender their natural rights into the hands of a few or one with authority to command. The covenant or agreement was of each with all and of all with each. The covenant was, of course, a social contract and a governmental contract. The contract became binding on the whole community as a perpetual social bond. Thus, in order to protect himself against the evil consequences of his own nature man organised himself in society in order to live in peace with all.

(*b*) John Locke (1632-1704). John Locke, another English political philosopher, believed that man in the state of nature was enjoying an ideal liberty, free from all sorts of rules and regulations. The state of nature was a state of "*peace, goodwill, mutual assistance, and preservation*". But there was no recognised system of law and justice. Hence his peaceful life was often upset by the "*corruption and viciousness of degenerate men*". Man was forced to face such an "*ill condition*".

John Locke, the British writer who supported the cause of limited monarchy in England, main- tained in his "*On Civil Government*" that the "*ill condition*" in which men were forced to live was "*full of fears and continual dangers*". In order to escape from this and to gain certainty and security men made a contract to enter into civil society or the state. This contract Locke called 'social contract'. This contract put an end to the state of nature and substituted it by civil society. The social contract was no more than a surrender of certain rights and powers so that man's remaining rights would be protected and preserved. The contract was for limited and specific purposes, and what was given up or surrendered to the whole community and not to a man or to an assembly of men (as Hobbes said). Locke made it clear that the social contract later on contributed to the governmental control. The governmental contract was made by the society when it established a government and selected a ruler to remove the inconveniences of "ill-condition".

***(c)* Jean Jacques Rousseau** (1712-1778). J.J. Rousseau, the French writer of the 18th century, in his famous book "*The Social Contract*" (1762) wrote that man in the state of nature was a '*noble savage*' who led a life of "*primitive simplicity and idyllic happiness*". He was independent, contented, self-sufficient, healthy, fearless and good. It was only primitive instinct and sympathy which united him with others. He knew neither right nor wrong and was free from all notions of virtue and vice. Man enjoyed a pure, unsophisticated, innocent life of perfect freedom and equality in the state of nature, Rousseau argued. Men were free from the influence of civilisation, and sought their own happiness uncontrolled by social laws and social institutions.

But these conditions did not last long. Population increased and reason was dawned. Simplicity and idyllic happiness disappeared. Families were established, institution of property emerged and human equality was ended. Man began to think in terms of '*mine*' and '*thine*'. Difference between stronger and weaker, rich and poor, arose.

Emergence of Civil Society

When equality and happiness of the early state was lost, war, murder, conflicts, wretchedness, etc., became the order of the day. The escape from this was found in the formation of a civil society. Natural freedom gave place to civil freedom by a social contract. As a result of this contract a multitude of individuals became a collective unity—a civil society. Rousseau said that by virtue of this contract "*everyone while uniting himself to all, remains as free as before*".

General Will

There was only one contract according to Rousseau which was social as well as political. The individual surrendered himself completely and unconditionally to the will of the body of which he became a member. The body so created was a moral and collective body and Rousseau called it the '*general will*'. The unique feature of the general will was that it represented collective good as distinguished from the private interests of its members. The will was 'inalienable and indivisible' according to him.

Criticism

The theory of social contract has been widely criticised. Firstly, the historically, theory seems to be a mere fiction. There is nothing in the whole range of history to show that the society has ever been deliberately created as a result of voluntary agreement or contract. Nor can we suppose that man could ever think of entering into a contract with others when he lived under conditions of extreme simplicity, ignorance and even brutality.

Secondly, the theory is far away from the facts. Nothing like the state of nature has ever existed. The most primitive peoples that the anthropologists have described lived in some form of society or the other, however rudimentary or unorganised it may be. It is quite unhistorical to, suppose, that such men would resort to a contract.

Thirdly, the advocates of the theory hold that the early individuals entered into the contract for their individual safety and security of property. But history tells us the other way. Early law was more communal than individual, and the unit of society was not the individual but the family. Each man was born into his family, and into his status in society. "Society has moved from status to contract and not from contract to status" as the champions of the theory argued. Contract is not the beginning of society but the end of it, said Sir Henry Maine.

Fourthly, our own common sense tells us that there are always two parties to the contract. There cannot be a one-sided contract, as was conceived by Hobbes (Moreover, every contract lapses after the death of one of the contracting parties).

Fifthly, conception of natural rights and natural liberty, as is said to have existed in the state of nature, is illogical and fallacious. Liberty cannot exist in the state of nature. Law is the condition of liberty. Without restraint liberty is nothing short of licence, and condition of licence is anarchy. Rights, too, arise only in a society. If there is no society we cannot think of rights.

Finally, there can be no rights without a consciousness of common interest on the part of members of a society and common consciousness was conspicuous by its absence in the state of nature.

The Organismic Theory of Society

This view, at least as ancient as the contract idea, conceives society as a biological system, a greater organism, alike in its structure and its functions. This theory can even be dated back to *Plato* and *Aristotle*.

Plato compared society and state to a magnified human being. He divided society into three classes of *rulers*, the *warriors* and *artisans* based upon the three faculties of the human soul, that is wisdom, courage and desire. Aristotle drew a comparison between the symmetry of the state and symmetry of the body and firmly held that the individual is an intrinsic part of society.

The parallelism between an individual organism and social organism has been worked out to the minutest possible extent by *Bluntschli* and *Herbert Spencer* during the recent times.

The organic theory considers society as a unity similar to that which characterises a biological organism. The union of individuals forming the society has been described as similar to the union between the several parts of an animal body, wherein all parts are functionally related. Just as the body has a natural unity, so has a social group. The animal body is composed of cells, so is the society composed of individuals, and as is the "*relation of the hand to the body or the leaf to the tree, so is the relation of man to society. He exists in it and it in him*".

The ancient and medieval writers had merely drawn an analogy between the society and an organism. They held that the society resembled an organism. But the writers of the 19th century regarded the society as an organism. They tried to analyse the structure and function of society in comparison with those of an organism.

Views of Herbert Spencer

The English social philosopher Herbert Spencer has been the chief exponent of this theory. He said that society is an organism and it does not differ in essential principle from the other biological organisms. The attributes of an organism and the society, he maintained, are similar. Both exhibit the same process of development. The animal and social bodies, Spencer affirmed, begin as germs, all similar and simple in structure. As they grow and develop, they become unlike and complex in structure. Their process of development is the same, both moving from similarity and simplicity to dissimilarity and complexity. "*As the lowest type of animal is all stomach, respiratory surface, or limb, so primitive society is all warrior, all hunter, all builder, or all tool-maker. As society grows in complexity, division of labour follows...*".

In each case there is mutual dependence of parts. Just as the hand depends on the arm and the arm on the body and head, so do the parts of social organism depend on each other. Every organism depends for its life and full performance of its functions on the proper co-ordination and interrelation of the units. As the diseased condition of one organ affects the health and proper functioning of other organs, similarly, individuals who form society are inseparably connected with one another for the realisation of their best self. There is so much dependence of one on the other that the distress of one paralyses the rest of the society. The society and organism, it is pointed out are subject to wear and tear and then replacement. (Just as cell tissues and blood corpuscles in the animal organism, wear out and are replaced by new ones, in the same manner, old, infirm, and diseased persons die giving place to newly born persons).

Spencer gives striking structural analogies between society and organism. He says, society, too, has three systems corresponding to the 1. *sustaining system*. 2. *the distributary system*, and 3. the *regulating system in an organism*.

1. *The sustaining system* in an organism consists of mouth, gullet, stomach and intestines. It is by means of this system that food is digested and the whole organic machine is sustained. Society has its own sustaining system which refers to the productive system comprising the manufacturing districts and agricultural areas. The workers, *i.e.*, the men who farm the soil, work the mines and factories and workshops are the alimentary organs of a society.
2. *The distributary system* in an organism consists of the blood vessels, heart, arteries and veins and they carry blood to all parts of the body. Means of communication and transport and along with them the wholesalers, retailers, bankers, railway and steamshipmen and others may correspond to the distributary or vascular system of an organism. Society's Cells are individuals only. And what the arteries and veins mean to the human body, roads, railways, post and telegraph services, institu- tions and associations, mean to society.
3. Finally, *the regulating system* is the nerve-motor mechanism which regulates the whole body. Government in society, regulates and controls the activities of the individuals. The professional men–doctors, lawyers, engineers, rulers, priests, the thinkers, in short, perform the functions of the brain and the nervous system. Further, as Spencer opined society also passes through the organic processes of birth, youth, maturity, old age and death.

Murray sums up the points of resemblance between a society and an individual organism as noted by Spencer in the following ways:-

(*i*) Society as well as individual organism grow in size.

(*ii*) They grow from comparatively a simple structure to that of an increasingly complex one.

(*iii*) Increasing differentiation leads to increasing mutual dependence of the component parts. The life and normal functioning of each becomes dependent on the life of the whole.

(*iv*) The life of the whole becomes independent and lasts longer than the life of the component pans.

Spencer hence argued that society is a social organism. Individuals are the limbs of the society and behave as cells of the body whose activity and life are meant for the sake of the whole. Limbs separated from body have no life, and similarly individuals separated from society have no life. The individuals exist in and within society.

Criticism

1. The analogy used in the organic theory has, no doubt, useful purpose to serve as it stresses the unity of society. The society is not a mere aggregation of individuals. It is a social unity. Man cannot lead a life of isolation. Dependence is his very psychology, and individuals depend on one another and on society as a whole. The welfare of each is involved in the welfare of all. Every individual has obligations to himself, to his family, to his neighbours, and to the society of which he is a unit. He cannot be separated from society, just as a hand or a leg, without losing its utility cannot be separated from the body.
2. The analogy used here to compare society with an organism, has its own limitations. Even Spencer was aware of these. He himself noted some of the defects of this analogy such as the following:
   - A society has no specific form comparable to the body of an individual;
   - The units of a society, *i.e.*, individuals are not fixed in their respective positions like those of an individual organism;
   - The units of a society are dispersed persons and are not physically continuous like cells of the individual;
   - Society has no 'common sensorium', no central organ of perception and thought as an individual has.
3. The proposition that society is like an organism is acceptable with some reservations. But the assertion that society is an organism, is rather misleading.

   At many points the comparison between society and an organism is exceedingly superficial. There is no similarity between the cells of an organism and the individuals who compose society. The cells have no independent life of their own. Each cell is fixed in its place, "*having no power of thought or will, and existing solely to support and perpetuate the life of the whole*". The individuals, on the other hand, are independent, intellectual and moral human beings They do not act like a machine. Each has a physical life independent of the whole.

   It is true that man cannot be the best of himself independently of society, but he can live, if he so wishes, an independent life of his own. This is not possible in an organism.
4. It is true that the society has grown from similarity and simplicity to dissimilarity and complexity. But commonsense tells us that society is not subject to the same process of birth, growth and decay as an organism. An organism comes into existence by the union of two organisms. This is not the method of the birth of society.

The process of growth is also not similar. Organisms grow from within and internal adaptation. They grow "unconsciously independent of volition entirely dependent on its environment and the natural laws of the biological world". Society grows largely due to the conscious efforts of the members and it is "to a great extent self-directed".

An organism dies. But society is not liable to death. It is permanent, it endures. "Society does not originate or renew itself as a plant, or as an animal does". The theory is pregnant of dangerous results. Some writers have gone to the extent of justifying the unity of society even at the cost of sacrificing individual interests. The relation of man to society and the overemphasis on man's obligation to society, the world witnessed it in Hitler's-Germany, Mussolini's Italy, Communist countries like China and Russia repeat the same story. The theory has a little truth in it, but it has been exaggerated.

Limitations of the Theories

Both the theories have their own limitations. No sociologist subscribes to them today. Historically, the social contract theory seems to be a mere fiction. We have no evidence to prove that society came into being due to a deliberate contract or voluntary agreement among the early people.

The organismic theory is equally imaginary. Society is like an organism, but is not an organism. Society has no specific form, no fixed organs, no central organ of perception comparable to the body of an organism. This organic analogy is well appreciated, but the theory is almost rejected.

THE INSEPARABLE INDIVIDUAL AND THE SOCIETY

The relation or the type of unity between the part and the whole, between the individual and society is not merely a physical unity, or a functional unity, or organic or systematic unity, but it is something more than these. It is *sui generis* peculiar; of its own kind. It is simply *social*, that is, without the company of his fellowmen, the individual cannot live at all, nor develop his personality. Still, the individual has a life of his own; his autonomy and character which cannot be fused or confused with the lives of other men. Social values are in the ultimate analysis personal values. Even quality or powers which belong to society as such are realised only in its members, present or future. The life of society has no meaning except as an expression of the lives of individuals.

The truth is that society is not and *cannot* be an organism; it *is like* an organism. Society has no body; it is an organisation of minds for a common purpose. "Society is the sum of interacting individuals, and this interaction is, what differentiates society from the mere aggregation of individuals". Society is a reality of its own kind, itself unique, and different from every other natural object. Society gives us choices, inviting us to accept or decline, and in our selections we become ever more completely what we are.

MAN IN SOCIETY AND SOCIETY IN MAN

Everywhere and all the time we are members of groups. The isolated individual does not exist. The language we speak, the clothes we wear, the food that sustains us, the games we play, the goals we seek, and the ideals we cherish are all derived from our culture. Culture is a societal force. Society surrounds us in our infancy and follows us to our resting place. We depend upon society and its processes not only for our livelihood but for our very lives. "Society not only controls our movements, but shapes our identity, our thought and our emotions. The structures of society become the structures of our own consciousness."— *Peter L. Berger*. Society does not stop at the surface of our skins. Society penetrates us as much as it environs us. Our bondage to society is not simple but complex. Sometimes, indeed, we are crushed into submission. Much more frequently we are entrapped by our own social nature. As Peter L. Berger says, "The walls of our imprisonment were there before we appeared on the scene, but they are ever rebuilt by ourselves. We are betrayed into captivity with our own co-operation."

As *Durkheim* says society confronts us as an objective facticity. It is *there* something that cannot be denied and that must be reckoned with. Society is external to ourselves. It encompasses our entire life. We are in society, located in specific sectors of the social system. Our wishes are not taken into consideration in this matter of social location. The institutions of society *pattern* our actions and even *shape* our expectations. We are located in society not only in space but also in time. Our society is an historical entity that extends beyond the temporary life of any individual. "It was there before we were born and it will be there after we are dead. Our lives are but episodes in its majestic march through time. In sum, society is the walls of our imprisonment in history". — *Peter L. Berger*

SCOPE FOR INDIVIDUALITY

We need society in order to become persons. But society is no great an engine which we are merely a mechanical part. It is not a giant organism in which we are only a microscopic cell. Society is unique to itself. '*From it we receive the gift of individuality and in it we express our personality*'. —*Robert Bierstedt*. Even in society we are always, in some sense, alone. There is always a pan of us that we never share, a thought that is uncommunicated, a dream that stays in its private chamber. For it has also been written that '*the heart knoweth its own bitterness and a stranger intermeddleth not with its joy*.'

The same society and the same culture which limit the activities of man also liberate his energies and talents. No culture produces individuals who are like carbon copies. No two individuals are exactly alike. The same culture may produce men of marvellous genius and men of matchless stupidity. The utterly selfish persons and the completely selfless individuals may be found in the same society. Not even the twins are alike. Every individual is unique to himself and his society. Not only every society has a history of ' its own but every individual too has his own history. Different individuals may react to the same stimuli in different ways because of their individuality. This individuality is the gift of society. But individuals become individuals only in society.

REVIEW QUESTIONS

1. Bring out the relation between the individual and society.
2. Discuss the theories concerning the nature of society.
3. Man is a social animal. Comment.
4. The 'sociality' of man is the central problem of sociology. Explain.
5. Discuss the views of Herbert spencer regarding the organismic theory of society.
6. Throw light on the various systems of society.
7. What are the criticisms against the organismic theory of society?
8. Discuss the limitations of the social control theory and the organismic theory.
9. Write short notes on the following:
   (a) Inseparable individual and society
   (b) Scope of individuality
   (c) Man in society and society in man
   (d) Social contract theory

⌘⌘⌘⌘⌘⌘⌘⌘⌘⌘⌘

13

ENVIRONMENT AND HEREDITY

CHAPTER OUTLINE

- CAUSES OF DIFFERENCES IN HUMAN PERSONALITY
- ENVIRONMENT
- TYPES OF ENVIRONMENT
- INFLUENCE OF ENVIRONMENT ON PERSONALITY
- HEREDITY: MEANING AND MECHANISM OF HEREDITY
- ROLE OF GENES
- INFLUENCE OF HEREDITY
- CONTROLLED EXPERIMENTS TO STUDY THE RELATIVE ROLE OF HEREDITY AND ENVIRONMENT
- INTERPLAY BETWEEN HEREDITY AND ENVIRONMENT.

Human society is not only dynamic but also diverse. Differences are found between societies and within the same society among peoples and groups. In fact, society is based on the principle of difference. Society exhibits diversity because, people who constitute society themselves differ. As the popular saying "*all fingers are not equal*"–all people are not alike. They do differ. Human beings differ from one another in their physical development, in their mental make-up, in their moral, spiritual temperament, in their noble work, intellectual endeavours, criminal activity, and so on. The physical traits of people such as stature, skin, colour, height, weight, texture of hair and its colour, structure of eyes, perimeter of the chest and so on do differ. Their psychological qualities such as intelligence, ability, aptitude, interest, taste, attitude, temperament, mental health, etc., also differ significantly. Similarly, groups also differ. Individuals differ because they reveal different personalities. As G.W. Allport, a noted psychologist, says, *personality refers to "a person's patterns of habits, attitudes*, and *traits which determine his adjustment to his environment*". Differences between personalities are obvious because each individual represents a unique combination of these physical and psychological traits or qualities. What factors make every individual to develop his own physical and psychological traits? To make it more specific, what factors contribute to the development of human personality which is unique to every individual?

CAUSE OF DIFFERENCES IN HUMAN PERSONALITY

It is generally believed that the following factors contribute enormously to the formation and development of human personality. They are: biological inheritance, physical environment, culture, group experience and unique experience of the individual. These have often been reduced into only two factors namely; (*i*) *heredity*, and (*ii*) *environment*.

Can the differences in human personalities be explained by differences in heredity alone? Or, should they be explained in terms of environment? Or, in terms of both? Some have argued that heredity is more significant, while others have asserted that environment plays a dominant role in shaping different human personalities. This "*nature–nurture*", or *heredity versus environment* controversy is one of the most fascinating topics of inquiry in sociology. In fact, "this is one of the great problems of sociology, one of the unfinished sections on the sociological map". There has been a great deal of work done on it. However, sociologists, psychologists, biologists, anthropologists, statisticians and others have evinced much interest in this topic and have made considerable studies in this regard. Let us have a glimpse of some of these studies so as to find a relatively convincing answer for the perplexing issue of 'nature–nurture' controversy.

ENVIRONMENT: MEANING, TYPES AND INFLUENCE

Meaning of Environment

"*Environment'*, as the term itself indicates, is anything immediately surrounding an object and exerting a direct influence on it".–*P. Gisbert*. According to *Kimball Young*, environment refers to "those forces, situations or stimuli which influence the organism from outside". The role of environment is so great that it can affect our society and our behaviour. The environment is more than a "*conditioning*" factor of life. As *MacIver* says, "*It interpenetrates life everywhere. It directs or diverts, stimulates or depresses man's energies. It moulds his speech; it subtly changes his frame. Nay, more it lives within him. It is entirely inseparable from life*". "Life and environment are, in fact, correlates". "Furthermore, every change in a living creature involves some change in its relation to environment; and every change in the environment, some change in the response of the organic being". It is, indeed, a factor of great complexity. It consists of various aspects.

Types of Environment

Environment is a complex totality of many things. It has been divided into different types. (*i*) *MacIver* and *Page* have mentioned of two types of environment: (*a*) *Outer environment*, and (*b*) *Inner environment*. (*ii*) *Marshall Jones* has spoken of three kinds of environment: (*a*) *Physical Environment*, (*b*) *Social Environment*, and (*c*) *Cultural Environment*. (*iii*) *P. Gisbert* has divided environment into four types: (*a*) *Natural Environment*, (*b*) *Artificial Environment*, (*c*) *Social Environment*, and (*c*) *Psychological Environment*. (*iv*) *Kimbal Young* divided it into only two types: (*i*) *Geographic Environment*, and (*ii*) *Social-Cultural Environment*.

For our purpose of study we may speak of two types of environment namely: 1. Geographic Environment and 2. Man-made Environment.

1. Geographical Environment

This can be called '*natural environment*' for it consists of things that are provided by nature. This can also be called 'physical environment' for it includes the physical conditions of life. The geographic or physical conditions exist independently of man's existence. Man has limited and sometimes no control over them. This environment includes; the surface of the earth, natural resources, land and water, mountains and plains, fertile lands and deserts, oceans, storms and cyclones, weather and climatic factors, seasons, etc. It also includes biological conditions such as plants, animals with all their complexities.

2. Man-Made Environment

In order to control the conditions of his life man has created a new environment which can be called 'man-made environment' and some have called it '*socio-cultural environment* '. It can be sub- divided into two types: (*a*) *outer environment*, and (*b*) *inner environment*

(*a*) ***The outer environment:*** Man, through the introduction of science and technology has tried to modify the conditions of physical environment. It can be understood as '*outer environment*'. We, what we are today, is because of the modifications of physical environment introduced by man's technology. It includes our houses and cities, our means of transport and communication, our comforts and conveniences. It also includes the vast systems of industry and machinery created by man. It covers, in brief, the whole apparatus of our civilisation. Some anthropologists have called this part of socio-cultural environment, '*material culture*'.

(*b*) ***The inner environment:*** The inner environment is the society itself. It is the *social environment* and endures only so long as the society endures. It consists of the organisations and regulations, the traditions and institutions. It includes the folkways and mores and customs which every human 'group provides for man. This environment is also known as '*social heritage*', and sometimes referred to as the order of '*non-material culture*'. The social heritage is the necessary condition for human social life to arise and to continue. It has a profound influence on man's life.

The so-called '*artificial environment*' which refers to the modified form of physical environ- ment and the *economic environment*, which refers to all the things of human creation that have great economic value–can be understood as nothing but two aspects of the man-made environment.

In should be noted that man cannot Separate the outer environment as one order of the things from the social environment. The outer and the inner environments are blended. For example, the land which we bring under cultivation is more than a land; it is a form of property. It is often wor- shipped also, as the Hindus do. The houses are also homes that represent the institution of family. Thus the various factors of the total environment (the physical, the inner and the outer) are merged together in our experience.

Influence of Environment on Personality

Environment of both the types–geographic and social or natural and man-made has a tremendous bearing on human personality. The natural environment sets limits to the personality and also provides opportunities for its development. The social environment provides enough conditions for its proper expression. The family, school, neighbourhood, friends, various persons in contact, social customs, practices, values, institutions, etc., all affect an individual's personality. The status of the child, young man, and adult, and old man in the family and in society is not the same. As a result of this difference a man's temperament, attitudes, tendencies, ways of thinking, acting inclinations, and character, in brief, his personality is affected. In the same way, the status of the person in places like school, office, occupation, etc., affects his behaviour to a great extent.

The famous psycho-analyst *Sigmund Freud* has expressed the opinion that the personality of a person is fashioned in the first few years, the rest of the life being an expression of the tendencies already developed. The present psychologists also agree that the influence of environment of family upon the character, nature, mental tendencies, habits, behaviour of the individual is very great. This view has been verified by comparison of children brought up in families and those bred in govern- ment institutions. In childhood, parental love affects the stability of the emotions of the child. It has been observed that excessive love and care spoil the children and lack of affection leaves their feeling undeveloped which are then unnaturally expressed. *Alfred Adler*, a famous, psychologist, maintained that even the birth order of the child in the family affects its personality. This may be understood by remembering that in the family mother, father, husband, wife, elder and younger brother, elder and younger sister, loved child, and unwanted off springs all have their respective statuses which affect their personality.

Culture or the social environment provides lot of scope for variation in personality. It has been observed that the *Zuni* people are said to be emotionally more secure, and most *Alorese* insecure. Further, the Zuni people are known for their co-operative spirit. They are calm, gracious, non-competitive and maintain control even in the most exciting ceremonial dances. On the other hand, the *Kwakiutl Indians* (of the Pacific North West) are highly competitive in nature. They give more importance to prestige, rank and property and hence widespread competition is there to possess them. Similarly, the *Ba Thonga* people are crazy after women and beer. *Eskimos* are known for their skill and muscular strength. The *Dakota* people are known for their generosity, hospitality, bravery and fortitude (courage in pain or adversity).

As *Ogburn* and *Nimkoff* have stated, Russians appear to have a strong need for intensive interaction with others in immediate, direct, personal relationships. They have greater capacity for warm personal contact and enjoy such relationships more. They are not too anxiously concerned about others' opinion of them. Americans, on the contrary, emphasise achievement more and the need for approval and autonomy. They fear too close or intimate association because it limits free- dom. They desire recognition more and are more eager to be liked. The Russians are said to be more expressive, more highly aware of their impulses and more readily yield to the impulses and depend more on external controls applied by authority to keep in line. On the other hand, Americans rely more on self-control.

These differences in outlook, temperament, attitudes, tendencies, etc., found in various peoples as mentioned above, cannot be attributed to the hereditary factors. Rather they are more affected by environment, that too by the social or cultural environment. People tend to develop in them qualities in accordance with the values, goals, objectives set forth by their culture.

Individual differences arise not only between different societies, even within the society variations in personality may be found. How to account for these differences? The answer lies in differences in (*i*) *constitutional characteristics*, (*ii*) *emotional relationships with members of the family and other groups*, and (*iii*) *socialisation in distinctive sub*-cultures.

Culture varies *within* a society and not just between societies. It is a point of the first importance to recognise that culture is not a single massive die that cuts all the members of the group of precisely the same specifications. There is in every culture what may be called a division of learning according to social classification. Both sexes and all age groups learn certain things in common but in addition each sex and age group learn different things. Age-grading and sex-typing are perhaps the most important classifications for determining social roles. Occupation, education, income and family background are additional selective factors which are highly important in determining what aspects of the culture an individual will be exposed to. *All cultures accordingly produce variety as well as uniformity of personality*.

It is well to note that the same personality trait can often be produced by varying the environ- mental factors. A child who is not dominant naturally may be made more aggressive by increasing the domination at home or ridicule by the gang; that is, by varying interpersonal, or group, factors. Again a child who is normally not assertive may perhaps be rendered more energetic by environ- mental pressures, (such as the frequent prospects of famine or constant danger from attack by wild animals, as may be the case in primitive society) Finally, training or cultural experience may convert a submissive child into an assertive one.

To ascertain the influence of environment on personality, psychologists, sociologists and biologists studied identical and fraternal twins who were brought up in dissimilar environments. One particular case may be mentioned here.

'*Mildred*' and '*Ruth*' are so called 'identical twins' whose mother died when they were three months old and who were immediately adopted by two different families of relatives. Mildred became the foster daughter of a banker who was also the mayor of a small city. He was a well-educated man and made all facilities for Mildred to develop her-'self'. She read widely, studied music and played the violin in the high school orchestra. Further, she participated in various other social activities outside of the home.

Ruth, on the other hand, became the foster daughter of a foreman of labourers, a man of little education who lived in a fairly large city. Ruth's foster mother was not much educated and kept her closely confined to her home, where there were no books, no good music, and no intellectual activities.

Up to the age of l5 when these two girls were given extensive examinations their physical appearance and health records had been about the same. Their personalities, however, were vastly different. Mildred was a confident girl, expressive, talkative, without a lisp and happy in facial expression. Ruth, on the other hand, showed an inhibited personality–the different, silent, with lisping speech and an unhappy expression. Mentally there was also striking difference. Despite the fact that their formal educational opportunities had been about the same, Mildred had an I.Q. score on two different tests that was l5 points higher than Ruth's.

In the case of identical twins, Mildred and Ruth, the hereditary potential is assumed to have been the same. The hereditary factor is presumably held constant. The differences in I.Q. scores and other aspects of personalities of the two girls are clearly attributable to the cultural and unique factors in their respective social environments.

Most of the studies have revealed that environment and heredity both play an important role in determining human personality. If mental factors are much influenced by environment physical and physiological characteristics are more affected by heredity. Environment alone cannot determine an individual's personality. But it gives opportunities to the individuals to express themselves and to develop their personality. Environment brings out the hidden potentialities into a definite form. All the inherited qualities become actualities only within and under the conditions of environment. Different aspects of an individual's personality like interests, intelligence, skill, dexterity, attitudes, beliefs, faith, inspirations, etc., are very much influenced by the environment.

HEREDITY: MEANING, MECHANISM AND INFLUENCE

Meaning of Heredity

Heredity is one of the powerful factors that contribute to the formation c ̃human personality. It influences man's social behaviour too. It is through the process of heredity that children normally get some of the physical and psychological characteristics of their parents. *Heredity refers to the biological process of transmission of certain biological and psychological characteristics from parents to their children through what are known as genes*. Thus, the heredity of the child works through the genes which determine its physical and psychological characteristics. The great researches and observations made by *Mendel*, a priest with scientific insight, almost a century ago, have thrown much light on the phenomenon of heredity and its mechanism. Mendel's works also removed many of the misconceptions developed about the role of heredity in life.

Mechanism of Heredity

Man's biological heredity begins with the union of the sperm ejected by the male with the egg- cell in the mother's womb. This is the contribution of each parent to the formation of the first cell. This first cell called the '*germinal cell*' divides repeatedly into thousands and millions of cells. The first cell contains 23 pairs of chromosomes which correspond to the human species. Each parent has contributed one half to this cell. Every human cell has the same number of chromosomes except the reproductive cells. The reproductive cells which proceed from each parent for the procreation of the new being have only one half of this number, that is, 23 unpaired chromosomes. If there is a single special chromosome called 'Y' the offspring is going to be male; and if all chromosomes are 'X', the offspring is bound to be a female.

If, in the mother's womb, two egg-cells are fertilised by two sperms contributed by the father, twins will be born. These may be of the same sex or of different sex. 'Identical' or 'equal' twins are born when only one egg-cell is fertilised by the sperm which at the time of its first division breaks into two independent cells, which multiply as normally as the others. These identical twins are very much alike and they necessarily belong to the same sex.

Role of Genes

The chromosomes that are contributed by each parent contain thousands of ultramicroscopic particles called "genes". *These genes are the carriers of heredity*. They determine the physiological characteristics of the new being. Not all inherited characteristics appear at birth; many like baldness or deafness manifest themselves later in life. Intensive researches carried on by *Gregor Mendel, Thomas Hunt Morgan, Hugo de Vries* and others, have further confirmed the fact that the genes largely decide the heredity of the offspring.

It was previously believed that every physiological trait has a definite gene corresponding to it. Now it has been proved that some inherited qualities are due to the combination of a few genes. Experiments have shown that when two characteristics, one from each parent, combine, the offspring is a hybrid uniting in itself the two characteristics. Of these two characteristics, one is '*dominant*' and the other is '*recessive*' and the former always prevails over the latter. Thus, as Mendel showed in experiments on rats, mice, and most/fur-bearing animals, black is the dominant character over white; smooth hair over curly, and short over long hair. In the case of man, brown eyes are dominant over blue eyes. It may also happen that sometimes, some white complexioned parents may get a child with black complexion, and 'black' parents may get 'white' child. Because some genes which were recessive in the previous generation of those parents become dominant at that time and express qualities peculiar to themselves.

Still it cannot be said that every characteristic with which we are born is strictly inherited. Many of them are '*exageneous*' or due to environmental influences. Every characteristic in order to be '*endogeneous*' or inherited, must have its basis in the cell genes and be capable of being transmit- ted through them. According to H.S. Jennings, the following somatic characteristics may be strictly inherited.

"Sex, colour of eyes and hair, complexion, form of the features, form the distribution of hair, finger prints and palms and sole patterns, structure and form of the hands and feet, form of the body (stoutness, slenderness, stature, and the like), chemical composition of the blood, the blood types, the glandular types to which individuals belong, the senses and their efficiency, efficiency of the brain, vigour and weakness of constitution, susceptibility and immunity of various diseases, and many other physical and physiological peculiarities".

Recent investigations have revealed that even the genes undergo changes. "The changes occurring in the genes which may be transmitted by generation are called '*mutations*'. "These must be differentiated from '*variations*'. A variation refers to a change in the degree or intensity of a certain characteristic or trait. For example, in a group of short men some may be shorter than others; of two pairs of black eyes one may be more intense than the other. But a change from tallness to shortness, from blue to brown eyes, or from white to black colour, as may occur in the offspring, is the effect of a "*mutation*". *Variations are temporary* and they indicate changes in the individual. But *mutations are permanent*, and found in the species. It is only in terms of mutations the evolution of species can be understood. Hence the changes in skin colour, bodily features, or hair forms of a group have become perpetuated because of mutations in the genes.

It may be reiterated that *heredity is the living link or bridge between two generations*. What actually goes over the bridge are thousands of living microscopic particles packed away in the single cell which each of us received from each of our parents. These particles are the genes.

Influence of Heredity on Personality

Biological inheritance provides the raw materials of personality and these raw materials can be shaped in many different ways. All normal healthy human beings have certain biological similarities. Still every person's biological inheritance is unique. It means that no other person (except an identical twin) has exactly the same inherited physical characteristics. People believed for a very long time that a person's personality was nothing more than the unfolding of that person's biological inheritance. Such personality traits as–perseverance, ambition, honesty, criminality, intelligence, sex deviation, physical energy, and most other traits were believed to arise from inherited predispositions. Such an idea, of course, is rarely believed today.

The influence of heredity in shaping human personality and determining human behaviour has been highlighted by the supporters of heredity such as–*Francis Galton*, *Karl Pearson*; *William MC Dougall*, and others.

Francis Galton (1822-1911) in his book "*Hereditary Genius*" pointed out that human differences are inborn. In his opinion men who achieve greatness are naturally capable. He argues that human beings are fundamentally unequal. This inequality is due to two factors namely: heredity and environment, among which heredity is more dominant. He also gives evidences to support his views. According to him, an able father produces able children. Further, royal families produce more men of intelligence than the ordinary families. He says the environment has little to do with the achieve- ments of the people. He even tried to show that the children would be greatly gifted when the father was of higher intelligence. "*Nature prevails enormously over nurture*", he maintained. He, however, concluded that "*no man can achieve a very high reputation without being gifted with very high ability*".

Karl Pearson (1857) continued the works of Francis Galton. Pearson and his followers after making some studies concluded that "*man varies*; *that these variations favourable or unfavourable are inherited*". He tried to show that heredity is more than seven times more important than environment.

Evidences in Support of Heredity

Some supporters of heredity have based their investigations on the following evidences: 1. *Unequal intelligence levels of individuals of different occupational groups*; 2. *Unequal intelligence levels of different racial categories*; and 3. *The study of famous families of Edwards and degenerate families of Jukes*.

1. ***Unequal intelligence levels of individuals of different occupational groups:*** Some supporters of heredity have drawn our attention towards considerable differences between the intelligence levels of different occupational groups. For example, in one of the studies it has been observed that the children of professional parents had an average I.Q. (intelligence quotient) of 116; those of semi-professional and managerial classes 112; clerical skilled trades, and retail business 107.5; semi- skilled, minor clerical occupation and business 105; slightly skilled 98; and finally the children of labourers, urban and rural farmers, 96. These differences in I.Q. were attributed mainly to heredity.
2. ***Unequal intelligence levels of racial categories such as whites and negroes:*** In America, a number of psychological intelligence tests were administered to the Negroes and Whites. In these studies of comparative intelligence the Whites faired better than the Negroes. For example, the tests applied to army recruits during World War I had revealed the average mental age of Negroes as 10.4 years and of the Whites as 13.1 years.
3. ***The study of the families of edwards and jukes:*** The study of the families of Edwards and Jukes as an evidence in favour of heredity is quite fascinating. In America, towards the end of the l9th century, some 1391 descendants of Jonathan Edwards were identified out of which more than 295 were college graduates and among them 13 came to be college presidents or principals and one a vice-president of America. The records showed that there were no convicted criminals among them.

As against the above, in 1887, there were identified 1200 descendants of a certain 'Juke' who was born in New York in 1720. Of these, 440 were physically defective or diseased, 310 were paupers, 130 convicted of crime, and 7 condemned as murderers. It was concluded that heredity and not environment, was the decisive cause of the difference of behaviour in these families.

Comments

The conclusions drawn by the supporters of heredity are no doubt interesting. But they rather appear to be onesided, misleading and exaggerative. These thinkers and writers have not made any attempt to study the effect of environment. The question whether the individuals of different occupational groups or racial categories or family groups have had the same social environment and opportunities–is very important here. This was actually neglected by these thinkers.

With regard to the intelligence tests conducted to different groups, we have our own doubts. *Firstly*, the so called 'intelligence tests' were more knowledge tests and hence they could hardly assess the original intelligence of the individuals involved. *Secondly*, the cultural background of both the groups—Whites and Negroes, and those of different occupational groups was hardly the same. *Thirdly*, we are not sure whether the intelligence tests were administrated objectively. *Finally*, intelligence is not the outcome of heredity alone. Environment too plays its role in helping the individual to develop his intelligence. These studies had ignored environmental factors.

With regard to the studies of two different families also certain defects have been noticed. *Firstly*, there is no solid proof to ascertain that the Jukes and Edwards of the present generation are the same as those of 9 or 10 generations back. Biologically no succeeding generation can be a carbon copy of the preceding generation. *Secondly*, the studies are incomplete as all descendants on either side have not been taken into account. *Thirdly*, in a prejudiced manner, Jukes were searched for in Jails, orphanages, and in bad families, while the Edwards were searched for in respectable places. *Fourthly*, subsequent investigations on the Edwards families showed that a certain Elizabeth Tuttla, the grandmother of Jonathan Edwards, had been guilty of adultery and immorality, her sister murdered her own son and she herself was killed by her own brother. Champions of heredity cannot explain this startling fact. *Fifthly*, the supporters of heredity never studied the influence of respective environments in which Jukes and Edwards were brought up.

CONTROLLED EXPERIMENTS TO STUDY THE RELATIVE ROLE OF HEREDITY AND ENVIRONMENT

The '*nature-nurture*' controversy has been raging for centuries. Interest in the biological basis for individual differences in intelligence and behaviour is currently rising. At the same time equal attention is paid to ascertain the influence of environment. Hence some sociologists, psychologists and biologists in their studies have held one of the factors as constant and the other varied in order to find out the relative importance of both. Studies of identical twins are a favourite research approach in this regard. These twins are believed to possess more or less the same hereditary qualities. They have been reared apart to know the influence of environment on their personality. Some of the studies conducted with this approach may be cited here.

1. Francis Galton himself studied twins reared apart and came to the conclusion that heredity plays a more dominant role in determining an individual's personality.
2. One study of 2500 high school twins conducted in America concludes that "about half the variation among people in a broad spectrum of psychological traits is due to differences among people in genetic characteristics", while the other half is due to environment.
3. The most extensive twin study ever made was by the Medicogenetical Institute of Moscow which separated 1000 sets of identical twins at infancy. They were placed in controlled environ- ments for two years of observation. The findings supported strongly a hereditary basis for many characteristics, including intelligence differences. (This conclusion displeased Stalin who abolished the institute and executed its director).
4. *Miss Burks* made a study of children in foster homes and arrived at the conclusion that the role of heredity is about 80% and that of environment 20%.
5. *H.H. Newman*, a biologist; F. N. Freeman, a psychologist; and KJ. Holzinger, a statistician, made a study of 19 pairs of identical twins reared apart. They compared the data concerning 50 pairs of identical twins and 52 pairs of fraternal twins reared together. The authors concluded that physical characteristics are least affected by the environment and psychological characteristics are more subjected to environmental influence.
6. *F.N. Freeman* made a study of 671 children who were placed in Chicago foster homes. His study led him to conclude that I.Q. of the children placed in homes other than their own, would increase in proportion to the quality of the foster homes. It means the level of intelligence varies with the nature of environmental influence.
7. *H.M. Skeels* made a study of 150 illegitimate children at the State University of IOWA which led him to conclude that intelligence is more responsive to environmental changes.

Interplay between Heredity and Environment

The above-mentioned and several other studies do not tell us whether heredity or environment is the 'more' important factor. But they tell us why each is important. Individual differences in biological inheritance are real regardless of whether this fact makes one happy or unhappy. For some traits, biological inheritance is more important than others. While individual differences in I.Q. are more highly determined by heredity than by environment, other trait differences are almost entirely environmental. One recent study has revealed that certain qualities such as sociability, compulsiveness, and societal ease are said to be more influenced by heredity, while certain traits such as leader- ship, impulse control, attitudes and interests are believed to be more sensitive to environmental influence.

We may conclude that biological inheritance is important for some personality traits and unim- portant for others. In no case the respective influence of heredity and environment be precisely measured. But most scientists, agreed that the degree to which one's inherited potentials are fully developed is determined by one's social experience.

It is evident that those who study the influence of environment see only one side of the coin and those who study the effect of heredity see only the other side. They have failed to realise that they are inseparable. "*Neither can ever be eliminated and neither can ever be isolated*".

Environment is complex and changing, heredity is not completely known. Hence we must take into account the interaction of the two factors rather than the absolute action of any one factor. Heredity is what the new life starts with, and environment is what makes its maintenance and development possible. Both are equally essential.

Personality is the product of both environment and heredity. Heredity provides the potentialities and environment brings them out into a definite form. All the inherited qualities become actualities only within and under the conditions of environment. No amount of environment can turn a mediocre person into a genius. "*Heredity determines what we can do, and environment what we do do*".

Heredity is potentiality made actual within an environment. Hidden potentialities are revealed when the favourable opportunities are given. Man being the final product of evolution has greater capacity of adaptability and he can adjust himself with any environment. Hence heredity and environment are equally important. Each human trait requires both heredity and environment for its development. As *Lumley* said, "*It is not heredity* or *environment, but heredity* and *environment*". Both have been operating in determining human behaviour. As *MacIver* has pointed out, "Every phenomenon of life is the product of both, each is as necessary to the result as the other....." No society or no organism is the product of either heredity or environment.

We may conclude that "Nature and nurture are so obviously necessary and inseparable that the important question is not which is more important but rather how together they determine our qualities."

REVIEW QUESTIONS

1. Elucidate the role of factors in the formation and development of human personality.
2. Human society is not only dynamic but also diverse. Discuss.
3. What do you mean by environment. Discuss its types.
4. Assess the impact of environment on personality.
5. What is the meaning of heredity? Discuss its mechanism.
6. What is the role of genes in the mechanism of heredity? Elaborate.
7. Assess the influence of heredity on personality.
8. Give the evidences in support of heredity.
9. Throw light on the controlled experiments to study the relative role of heredity and environment.
10. Write short notes on the following:
    (a) Heredity
    (b) Environment
    (c) Types of environment
11. Comment on the relationship between heredity and environment.

⌘⌘⌘⌘⌘⌘⌘⌘⌘⌘⌘

14

TYPES OF SOCIETIES

CHAPTER OUTLINE

- Classification of Societies Based on the Mode of Subsistence or the Types of Technology
- Hunting and Gathering Societies and their Characteristics
- Herding or Pastoral Societies and their Characteristics
- Horticultural Societies and their Characteristics
- Agricultural or Agrarian Societies and their Characteristics
- Industrial Societies and their Characteristics
- Differences Between Pre-Industrial and Industrial or Pre-Modern and Modern Societies.

Human societies are not uniform. They differ from one another in several respects. Sociologists throw more light on the types of societies for they very often make comparisons between societies. In fact, macrosociology which refers to the study of large scale social systems, makes comparative analysis of societies. Such an analysis requires the classification of societies. Social thinkers' interest in classifying societies is not something new. Historians, social philosophers were inventing classification schemes centuries before sociology came to be established as an independent science. Sociologists also continued that tradition.

The classical sociologists of the late 19th and early 20th centuries made great efforts in developing "master social types". The classification schemes introduced by our early thinkers included strong value judgements and hence have their own limitations. Some examples of such classifications may be cited below.

1. *Morgan's classification*: Anthropologist **Lewis Henry Morgan** [1818-1881] in his last major work *"Ancient Society"* [1879] divided all societies into three groups - *savage, barbarian* and *civilised.* His argument, mostly in tune with the unilineal theory of evolution, was that *human societies progressed from savagery through barbarism to civilisation.*

2. *Comte's classification*: The French philosopher **Auguste Comte**, also presented a scheme of classification based on the assumption that *"all societies passed through distinct stages of belief or ideology, evolving from the lower to the higher stages"*. His scheme consisted of types of societies namely, (*i*) *military society,* (*ii*) *legal society,* and (*iii*) *industrial society,* which corresponded to three types of thinking namely, (*a*) *theological thinking,* (*b*) *metaphysical thinking* and (*c*) *positive thinking.*

3. *Spencer's classification*: Herbert Spencer also constructed two extremely dissimilar types or models to classify societies into two categories namely; (*i*) *militant societies,* and (*ii*) *industrial societies.* According to him, in the former, the *'regulating system'* was dominant and in the latter, the *"sustaining system"* [which stresses the importance of service] was much emphasised.

Classification schemes of societies such as the above, have their own weaknesses though they are important in giving a perspective from which to consider the overall workings of a society. A classification scheme which is in common use today is the one based on the mode of subsistence.

CLASSIFICATION OF SOCIETIES BASED ON THE MODE OF SUBSISTENCE OR THE TYPES OF TECHNOLOGY

Our social world consists of thousands of human societies. For the sake of comparison, and analysis, it is necessary for us to classify them on some basis. According to **Lenski** and **Lenski** [1970], these diverse societies which are existing at present can be classified into a limited number of basic types depending upon *the technologies or the subsistence strategies* that they use to exploit the natural environment. Different societies have used different subsistence strategies, and those societies that have found more productive strategies have tended to grow larger and more complex. These complex societies often enjoy their success at the expense of societies using more primitive technologies.

Speaking about the evolution of societies, it could be said that there has been a general historical trend of socio-cultural evolution, a process which is more or less similar to biological evolution. A society, like an organism, has to adapt to its environment in order to exploit food resources. In this process of socio-cultural evolution, some societies have evolved further and faster than others; some have become *"stuck"* at a particular level. In general, all have changed in ways that are unique to themselves.

Thus, it is on the basis of the level of technology or reliance on the basic type of subsistence strategy, societies can be generally classified into the following types:

(*i*) Hunting and Gathering Societies,

(*ii*) Herding or Pastoral Societies (Pastoralism),

(*iii*) Horticultural Societies,

(*iv*) Agricultural or Agrarian Societies, and

(*v*) Industrial Societies [which includes Pre-industrial Societies also.]

Social scientists have long recognised that core technology or subsistence strategy has a major impact on values, beliefs, and virtually all social structures, including the family, religion, the political and economic orders, and educational institutions. Because of the importance of core technology or subsistence strategy, we can form an important classification system of societies based on differences in core technology or subsistence strategy.

HUNTING AND GATHERING SOCIETIES

As **Gerhard Lenski** pointed out in his *"Human Societies"* (1970), the oldest and the simplest type of society is the *"Hunting and Gathering Society"*. Such a society is characterised by a small and sparse population; a nomadic way of life and a very primitive technology. They have the most primitive tools such as stone axes, spears and knives.

Hunter-gather society relies heavily on hunting wild animals and gathering food for its survival, as it grows naturally in the form of fruits, nuts and vegetables.

Hunting and gathering societies represent *"A mode of subsistence dependent on the exploitation of wild or non-domesticated food resources."*[1]

All societies used this subsistence strategy of hunting and gathering until only a two thousand years ago. Even today there are still a handful of isolated peoples who still continue this style of life. *Example:* (*i*) **Aranda** *of the Central Australian desert;* (*ii*) The **San people** *of Kalahari desert in Southern Africa.* (*iii*) **Itibamute Eskimos**. (*iv*) **Bushmen** *of Southwestern Africa*

Characteristics of Hunting and Gathering Societies

1. *Small in Size*: Hunting and gathering societies consist of very small but scattered groups. The environment in which they live cannot support a large concentration of people. They depend upon whatever food they can find or catch from one day to the next. They live in small primary groups and sometimes their number does not even exceed 40-50 members.

2. *Nomadic in Nature*: These people are constantly on the move because they have to leave one area as soon as they have exhausted its food resources.

3. *Not Desire to Acquire Wealth*: There is no strong desire among these people to acquire wealth for two main reasons: (*i*) ***Firstly,*** no individual can acquire wealth for there is no wealth to be acquired (*ii*) ***Secondly,*** *sharing is a norm in such societies.* Hence, people who do find a substantial food resources are expected to share it with the whole community. Sharing of food serves as a *"social insurance"* for it guarantees the one who shares his surplus today, some food tomorrow, from some one particularly when his collection is not good.

[1] *Oxford Dictionary of Sociology,* p. 291.

4. ***Family and kinship are the only defined institutions*:** Hunting and gathering people have the only interconnected social institutions which are somewhat well defined namely; *family* and *kinship*. **Family** is all in all for these people. Educating the young, economic production, protection of the members of the group and such functions [which are normally looked into by the specialised institutions in the other established societies] are performed by the family itself. **Kinship** is also important in the sense most of these groups are based on kinship, with most of their members being related by ancestry or marriage. The entire society is organised around kinship ties, which means the idea of individual families existing as distinct units within society is unknown.

5. ***Absence of political institution*:** In these institutions the difference between the ruler and the ruled is not there, because political institutions are not found here. Statuses in these societies are essentially equal and hence the difference between the leader and followers is not there. Most decisions are made through group discussion. Warfare is unknown to these people, partly because they have virtually no property and therefore have very little to fight out.

6. ***Limited Or no division of labour*:** There is no scope for division of labour in these societies except along the lines of age and sex. Men and women, young and old perform different roles, but there are no specialised occupational roles. *There is gender-based division of labour but there is no gender inequality as such.* Most people do much the same things most of the time. Hence they share common life experiences and values. Production is communal and co-operative and *the distribution system is based on sharing.*

7. Constant need to face danger: Some hunters and gatherers constantly face the danger of extinction in a struggle against adverse environments. Among the **Itibamute Eskimos**, for example, a family's fate rests in the hands of the father, who must find and catch the game, build the house and maintain the family. Hunting and gathering people in order to eke out their living in the natural set up, must command a complex knowledge of the plants, animals, environmental conditions, and seasonal changes in the environment.

8. ***Simple religious belief*:** Religion is not developed among these people into a complex institution. Their religion does not include a belief in a powerful god or gods who are active in human affairs. On the contrary, *they tend to see the world as populated by unseen spirits that must be taken into account but not necessarily worshipped.*

It is clear from the above description, though the hunting and gathering lifestyle seems alien to us, it appears to have been the most common form of society for most of the history of our human species.

HERDING OR PASTORAL SOCIETIES

The herding or the pastoral society is the one which *"relies on the domestication of animals into herds as a major means of support"*[2]

"Herding society refers to any form of society whose main subsistence comes from tending flocks and herds of domesticated animals. In practice, subsistence needs are often met by a combination of herding with hunting and gathering and other forms of agriculture"[3]

Around 10 to 12 thousand years ago, some hunting and gathering groups began to adopt a new subsistence strategy based on the domestication of herds of animals. Many people living in deserts or other regions which are not suited for cultivation, adopted this strategy and started taming animals such as goats or sheep which could be used as a source of food. Pastoral societies still exist today in the modern world, particularly in Africa, and in the Middle and Near East. ***Example: Bakhtiari of Western Iran.***

Characteristics of Herding Societies

1. Relatively larger in size: In comparison with the hunting and gathering societies, herding societies are larger in size and may have hundreds or even thousands of members, due to their technological *"invention"* of the domesticated animal which can be used for human food. The Bakhtiari of Iran, for example, who herd goats and sheeps in the **Zagros** mountains even today, number between 50,000 to 1,50,000.[4]

2. ***Pastoralism as a better productive strategy*:** Pastoralism has proved to be a better productive strategy than hunting and gathering for it provides an assured food supply and permits the accumulation of surplus resources. But herding is never practised as a sole means of support, and is linked with either hunting and gathering or a more advanced technology such as horticulture or agriculture. Such societies are usually adapted to heavy grasslands, mountains, deserts, or other land that would not readily support crops.

[2] Wallace and Wallace in *Sociology*, p. 86.

[3] *Collins Dictionary of Sociology,* p. 280.

[4] Wallace and Wallace, p. 86.

3. *Beginning of inequality:* Since pastoralism contributes to the accumulation of surplus resources, some individuals who have better access to surplus, become more powerful than others and pass on their status to their descendants. With this practice is born social inequality. Patterns of chieftainship begin to appear as powerful and wealthy families secure better social positions.

4. *Nomadism coupled with trading:* Herding people, like the hunters and gathers, are nomadic because of their seasonal need to find sufficient grazing areas for their herds. Their nomadic way of life often brings pastoralists into contact with their groups. This helps them to develop trading. Goats, sheep, tents, woven carpets, simple utensils etc., constitute their main objects of trading.

5. *Pastoralism and development of religious belief:* Pastoral people tend to develop their own religious beliefs. *"They commonly believe in a God or Gods who take an active interest in human affairs, and look after the people who worship them. This belief seems to have been suggested by the pastoralists experience of the relationship between themselves and their flocks.* [**Lenski** and **Lenski**, *1974*] *It is no coincidence that the few modern religions based on this view of the relationship between human beings and a god -* ***Judaism*** *and its offshoots,* ***Christianity*** *and* ***Islam*** *- originated among pastoral peoples."*[5]

6. *Herding technology leading to several changes:* Herding technology has led to several social changes among which the following may be noted

(*i*) The herding society tends to place a higher value on their temporary territories than do the hunting and gathering societies. Disputes over grazing rights with other herding societies sometimes result in warfare.

(*ii*) *Slavery,* unknown in hunting and gathering societies, makes its appearance as captives in war are put to work for their conquerors.

(*iii*) Since herds can be owned, *ideas about private property and inheritance of wealth* are likely to emerge.

(*iv*) *Patriarchal forms of social organisation tend to become popular* especially among, those who make use of horses for transportation and warfare.

(*v*) In general, in these pastoral societies, *populations become larger*, political and economic institutions begin to appear and *both social structure and culture become more complex.*

HORTICULTURAL SOCIETIES

- *"A horticultural society is a social system based on horticulture, a mode of production in which digging sticks are used to cultivate small gardens"*[6]
- *"A horticultural society produces its food through cultivation of the soil with hand tools"*[7]

Horticultural societies first came into existence in the middle east about 4000BC and subsequently spread to China and Europe; those that survive today are found mainly in sub-Saharan Africa. Horticultural society is associated with the elementary discovery that *plants can be grown from seeds*. While herding is common in areas with poor soil, horticulture is more common as a means of subsistence in regions with fertile soil. But the horticultural societies first appeared at about the same time as pastoral societies. Examples for horticultural societies: (*i*) **Gururumba** Tribe in New Guinea, (*ii*) **Masai** people of Kenya.

Characteristics of Horticultural Societies

1. *Domestication of plants*: Horticulturists specialise in the domestication of plants such as wheat, rice, etc. The simplest horticulturalists cultivate manually with hoes or digging sticks in relatively small gardens without using the metal tools and weapons. More advanced horticultural societies have metal tools and weapons and not ploughs. Like hunting-gathering societies, horticultural societies are just subsistence societies.

2. *Slash and burn technology*: The subsistence strategy of the horticulturists is typically based on a *"slash and burn"* technology. This is a type of strategy in which people clear areas of land, burn the trees and plants they have cut down, raise crops for 2 or 3 years until the soil is exhausted and then repeat the process elsewhere.

Horticulture is essentially an alternative to pastoralism and depending upon the environmental factors people select one or the other. If the soil and climate favour crop cultivation, horticulture is more likely to be adopted. It is found that many horticultural societies still exist in Africa, Asia, South America, and Australia.

[5] Ian Robertson in *Sociology*, pp. 83-84.

[6] Allan G. Johnson in his *The Blackwell Dictionary of Sociology*, 2000, p. 132.

[7] Wallace and Wallace in *Sociology*, p. 87.

3. ***Horticulturalists are better settled than pastoralists***: Unlike the pastoralists, horticulturalists, are relatively better settled, although periodically they must move short distances. They develop settlements that have larger populations and stay in one place longer before they migrate in search of better conditions.

4. ***Relatively more complex division of labour***: This society assures better food supply and the possibility of surplus. Existence of surplus leads to specialisation of roles. It means that some people no longer have to work at food production, and hence, specialised statuses and roles appear such as those of *Shaman* [religious leader] trader, or craft worker. Advanced horticultural societies sometimes consisting of as many as 5000 people [and sometimes even more], support specialists producing and trading with a variety of products such as boats, salt, volcanic glass, shells, pottery, war weapons, utensils and even textiles.

5. ***Emergence of political institutions***: The surplus production allows some wealthy individuals to become more powerful than others. This leads to the emergence of political institutions in the form of chieftainships. Warfare is more common in the horticultural societies. Since it is more convenient and easier to steal one's neighbour's goods or property than to produce one's own, giving protection to wealth and property becomes a necessity. This situation necessitated warfare. *In fact, horticultural societies are also the first known societies to support the institution of slavery.*

6. ***Creation of relatively elaborate cultural artefacts***: Since these people live in comparatively permanent settlements, they can create more elaborate cultural artefacts. These could consist of, for example, houses, thrones, or large stone sculptures. Their settled way of life also contributes to greater complexity in social structure and a more diverse and elaborate material culture.

7. ***Some rare practices***: One important feature of the horticultural societies is that some rare practices such as *cannibalism, headhunting,* and *human sacrifice* are found exclusively in a few horticultural societies, ***"Cannibalism** usually involves either eating one's deceased relatives as an act of piety or eating one's enemies skin as an act of ritual revenge. **The successful hunting of heads** is taken as evidence of the courage and skill of the warrior. The emergence of **human sacrifice** coincides with a change in the nature of religious beliefs."*[8]

In the more advanced horticultural societies, political and economic institutions become well developed as conquest and trade, link various villages together.

AGRICULTURAL OR AGRARIAN SOCIETIES

Around 3000 B.C [or 6000 years ago] the invention of the plough led to the beginning of the agrarian society. Agrarian societies first arose in ancient Egypt and were based on the introduction of the plough and the harnessing of animal power.

- *"An agricultural society focuses its mode of production primarily on agriculture and the cultivation of large fields."*[9]
- *Agricultural societies employ animal drawn ploughs to cultivate the land."*[10]
- Agrarian society refers to *"any form of society, especially so traditional societies, primarily based on agricultural and craft production rather than industrial production"*.[11]

The mode of production of the agrarian society, that is, cultivation distinguishes it from the hunter-gatherer society which produces none of its food, and the horticultural society which produces food in small gardens rather than big fields.

Characteristics of Agricultural Societies

1. ***Cultivation of land through the plough***: Based on the invention of the plough around 3000 B.C., the *"agrarian revolution"* marked its beginning. This invention enabled people to make a great leap forward in food production. Use of plough increases the productivity of the land. It brings to surface nutrients that have sunk out of reach of the roots of plants. It also returns weeds to the soil to act as fertilizers. The use of animal power to pull the plough enables a person to achieve great productivity.

- ***Combining irrigation techniques*** with the use of the plough increased productivity and made the increased yields more reliable. It also made it possible to work on land which had been previously useless for food production. The same land can be cultivated almost continuously, and full permanent settlements become possible.

- ***Introduction of plough in the cultivation of land increased food production enormously.*** One person with an animal drawn plough could do the work of many working with sticks and hand hoes. This increased production and ability to renew the soil allowed the development of some *of the first permanent residential settlements or cities, in human history.*

---

[8] Ian Robertson, p. 85.

[9] *The Blackwell Dictionary of Sociology*, p. 7.

[10] Wallace and Wallace in their *Sociology*, p. 89.

[11] *Collins Dictionary of Sociology*, p. 12

2. ***An Increase in the size of society***: Size of the agricultural societies is much greater than that of horticultural or pastoral communities. It relieves the burden of working in the field for a fairly large number of people who can engage themselves in other types of activities on full-time basis.

Appearance of Cities: The full-time specialists who engage themselves in non agricultural activities tend to concentrate in some compact places which ultimately led to the birth of cities. The society itself often consists of several such cities and their hinterlands loosely welded together.

3. ***Emergence of elaborate political institutions***: Agricultural societies, in course of time, lead to the establishment of more elaborate political institutions. Power is concentrated in the hands of a single individual. A hereditary monarchy tends to emerge. The monarch becomes powerful and literally has the power to take off the lives of his subjects. In well established agricultural societies, a formalised government bureaucracy emerges duly assisted by a legal system. Court system of providing justice also emerges. These developments make the state not only to become for the first time a separate institution but also the most powerful one.

4. ***Evolution of distinct social classes***: Agricultural societies produce relatively greater wealth which is unequally shared. As a result, a small minority enjoys a surplus produced by the working majority. Thus for the first time, two distinct social classes - *those who own the land and those who work on the land of others*- make their appearance. Land is the major source of wealth and is individually owned and inherited. This actually creates the major difference between the social strata. The old feudal system of Europe is an example of such differences between the strata.

5. ***Emergence of a clearly defined economic institution***: Agricultural societies provide the basis for the establishment of economic institutions. Trade becomes more elaborate and money is used here as a medium of exchange. Trade which takes place on an elaborate scale demands the maintenance of records of transaction, crop harvest, taxation, government rules and regulations. These developments provide an incentive for the enrichment of systematic writing which is found only in these societies and not in the previous ones.

6. ***Religion becomes a separate institution***: As societies become more and more complex, the religion also becomes more complex with the status of a separate institution. Religion requires full-time officials (priests, *shamans*, church officials and others) who often exercise considerable political influence. The religions of the agricultural societies often include a belief in a *"family of gods"*, of whom one becomes more powerful than the others. In some societies, a hierarchy of gods (higher gods, lesser gods , etc.,) is also found.

7. ***Warfare and empire building***: Agricultural societies constantly fight amongst themselves and hence warfare becomes a regular feature. These societies also engage themselves in systematic empire building. These developments necessitate the formation of an effective military organisation. For the first time, full-time permanent armies make their appearance. These armies require, like that of the traders, the development of proper roads and waterways. Such developments in the field of transport bring the previously isolated communities into contact with one another.

8. ***Enrichment of culture***: Since more food is produced than is necessary for subsistence, agricultural societies are able to support people whose sole purpose is to provide creative ideas to the culture. Hence, poets, writers, historians, artists, scientists, architects and such other talented people are encouraged to spend their days cultivating wisdom and beauty rather than fields. Surplus agricultural resources are now invested in new cultural artefacts such as paintings, statues, public buildings, monuments, palaces and stadiums.

"The ability to produce great surpluses and to support a complex division of labour brought with it an enormous expansion of knowledge, technology, population, trade and the size and performances of communities that could truly be called "cities".[12] *With these changes came major social institutions such as organised religion, the state, universities, and the military."*

9. ***Revolutionary transition in the social structure***: In comparison with many other less evolved types of societies (hunter-gatherer, herding or horticultural) the agricultural society has a far more complex social structure and culture. The transition from the previous social structures to the present one has been revolutionary. "*The number of statuses multiplies, population size increases, cities appear, new institutions emerge, social classes arise, political and economic inequality becomes built into the social structure, and culture becomes much more diversified and heterogeneous.*"[13]

INDUSTRIAL SOCIETIES

The industrial mode of production began in England about 250 years ago. It became a very successful one and has since spread all over the world. It has, in one way or the other, absorbed, transformed or destroyed all other types of society in

[12] *The Blackwell Dictionary of Sociology,* p. 7.

[13] Ian Robertson in his *Sociology,* pp. 86-87.

the process of its emergence. The very invention of machines to produce goods has proved to be an event of great historical importance.

Industrial societies have existed only in the very modern era, dating from the industrialisation of Great Britain in the late 18th century. The most advanced industrial societies today are found in North America, Europe and East Asia including Japan, Taiwan, Hongkong and South Korea. Countries such as India, Mexico, Brazil and some African countries have also become industrialised to a great extent.

- *"In the simplest sense, an industrial society is a social system whose mode of production focuses primarily on finished goods manufactured with the aid of machinery."*[14]
- ***"In industrial societies, the largest portion of the labour force is involved in mechanised production of goods and services"***[15]
- *"Industrial society refers to that form of society , or any particular society in which industrialisation and modernisation have occurred."*[16]

The general term ***"industrial societies"*** originates from **Saint-Simon** who chose it to reflect the emerging central role of manufacturing industry in the 18th century Europe, in contrast with previous pre-industrial and agrarian society.

Characteristics of Industrial Society

1. ***Industrial society is associated with industrial revolution and industrialism***: Industrial revolution spanning the late 18th to the early 19th centuries, is an event of great socio-economic and historical significance. *"It transformed much of Europe and the United States by replacing essentially agriculturally based societies with industrial societies based on the use of machines and non-animal sources of energy to produce finished goods"*.[17]

Industrialism is based on the application of scientific knowledge to the technology of production, enabling new energy sources to be harnessed . It permits machines to do the work that was previously done by people or animals. It is a highly efficient subsistence strategy. Because it allows a relatively small proportion of the population to feed the majority.

2. ***Technology initiating vast and rapid social changes:*** Technology based on modern scientific knowledge leads to higher rate of technological innovations. These innovations in turn, bring about a flood of social changes. *"New technologies" such as the steam engine, the internal combustion engine, electrical power, or atomic energy tend to bring about social changes as the economic and other institutions constantly adjust to altered conditions. Unlike other societies, therefore, industrial societies are in a continual state of rapid social change."*[18]

3. ***Larger societies with huge populations:*** The high levels of productivity of industrial societies further stimulates population growth with increasing members living in cities and metropolitan areas. Populations of these societies often run to tens or hundreds of millions. In all the highly advanced industrial societies a majority of the population prefers to live in urban areas, where most jobs are located. The growth rate of population increases very sharply in the early stages of industrialism. New medical technologies and improved living standards serve to extend life expectancy. But it is observed that population size tends to stabilise in the later stages of industrialism as the birth rate drops.

4. ***Large scale division of labour:*** As industrialism spreads and population grows, division of labour becomes highly complex. Industrial society creates tens of thousands of new specialised jobs. More and more statuses are achieved rather than ascribed. In the previous agricultural societies a person used to become a lord or peasant through circumstances beyond personal control . But, here in the industrial society, statuses as those of politicians, teachers, advocates, mechanics, technicians, chartered accountants, engineers, doctors, etc., could be achieved.

5. ***Losing importance of family and kinship:*** Family and kinship as social institutions tend to lose their importance. The ***family*** loses many of its functions. It no longer remains as a producing unit but has to be contented with as a unit of consumption. It loses the main responsibility of educating the younger ones. ***Kinship*** ties are also weakened. Kinship does not play an important role in unifying and controlling people. The immediate neighbours often become more important than the distant kins.

6. ***Religion losing its hold over the people:*** Religious institutions are no longer playing an important role in controlling the behaviour of the people. The influence of religious institutions as such shrinks markedly. People hold many different

[14] *The Blackwell Dictionary of Sociology* by Allan G. Johnson, p. 140.

[15] Wallace and Wallace in *Sociology,* p. 90.

[16] *Collins Dictionary of Sociology,* p. 340.

[17] *The Blackwell Dictionary of Sociology*, p. 139.

[18] Ian Robertson, p. 87.

and competing values and beliefs. The world no longer remains as *the god-centered world* for it is looked upon as *the man-centered one*. Various technological and scientific developments have made religion to lose its hold as an unquestioned source of moral authority.

7. ***Increasing importance of science and education:*** For the first time, science emerges out as a new and very important social institution. All technological innovations depend on the growth and refinement of scientific knowledge. Science is looked upon as a promising and an effective means of socio-economic progress. Similarly, ***education*** has evolved into an independent and distinct institution. Any industrial society for that matter, requires a literate population to understand and make use of the modern technological innovations. For the first time, formal education becomes a compulsory thing for majority of people rather than a luxury for the few.

8. ***Increasing important role of the state:*** Hereditary monarchies die out giving place to more democratic institutions. State which assumes the central power in the industrial society is more known for its welfare activities than for the regulative functions. State is increasingly involved in the economic, educational, medical, military and other activities. States are equipped with the war weapons to fight wars, but the actual outbreaks of war are relatively infrequent. *"One study of pre-industrial European societies found that over periods of several centuries, they were at war, on the average, almost every second year.* (**Sorokin**, 1937). *In contrast, most European societies have been at war only twice in the course of the century, and some have not been at war at all."*[19] Warfare can be ruinous for an advanced industrial society for it involves deadly war weapons and economic dislocations.

9. ***Widening gap between the rich and the poor:*** Industrialism, in its beginning stages, is normally associated with the emergence of the two social classes- *the rich and the poor*- between whom sharp inequalities are found. It also often widens the gap between the rich and the poor, referred to by **Marx** as *the haves* and *the have- nots*. The rich class which is also known as the *capitalist class* is branded as the exploiting class, and the poor class known as the *working class* is sympathised as the exploited class. According to Marx, these two classes are always at conflict. Phenomenal changes have taken place in the industrial world especially after the death of Marx. Most of his predictions have not come true. However, the general trend of industrial societies is towards a steady reduction in social inequalities, although, according to **Lenski** (1966), there are some notable exceptions.

10. Spread of heterogeneous culture: Industrial societies give rise to a number of *secondary groups* such as corporations, political parties, business houses, government bureaucracies, cultural and literary associations and special-purpose organisations of various kind. Primary groups tend to lose their importance and more and more social life takes place in the context of secondary groups. New life styles and values create a much more heterogeneous culture which spreads its influence far and wide.

The overall characteristics of industrial societies described above, tend to be broadly similar, partly as a result of the effects of global mass communications and partly because industrialism imposes certain basic requirements on social structure and culture. The industrial society is becoming more and more dominant in the modern world extending its influence on the other types of societies such as agricultural, horticultural, etc. It has become highly successful in exploiting the natural environment in an effective manner. But this success has caused "*a variety of problems as we witness in the form of -environment pollution, exhaustion of scarce resources, over population, the destruction of traditional communities, the disruption of kinship systems, mass anonymity, and a breakneck rate of social change that constantly threatens to disorganise the existing social structure*".[20]

INDUSTRIAL AND PRE-INDUSTRIAL SOCIETIES: COMPARATIVE DIFFERENCES

Striking differences do exist between what are known as *"traditional"*, or *"pre-modern"* or *"pre-industrial"* societies, and *"modern"* or *"industrial"* societies. Both these types of societies still exist in various regions of the world. Many sociologists and anthropologists have made attempts to clarify the differences in the quality of social life by distinguishing between the two extremes.

1. ***Durkheim's classification*:** The French sociologist **Emile Durkheim** in his book *"Division of Labour in Society"* [1893], distinguished societies based on two types of solidarity namely; (*i*) *mechanical solidarity*, and (*ii*) *organic solidarity.* The **former** one which corresponds to 'pre-modern' or traditional society serves as bonds of common activities and values. Here the society is held together by the fact that people perform the same tasks and share similar values. The **latter** [organic solidarity], which corresponds to modern society serves as bonds based on interdependence. Here the society is held together by the fact that people are highly specialised and are, therefore, mutually dependent on one another.

---

[19] *Ibid.*, p. 89.

[20] *Ibid.*, p. 89.

2. ***Ferdinand Tonnie's classification***: The German sociologist **Ferdinand Tonnie's** used the labels **Gemeinschaft** [*community*] and **Gesellschaft** [*association*] to describe similar differences between societies.

Gemeinschaft type of society, Tonnies argued, is characterised by intimate, face-to-face contact, strong feelings of social solidarity, and a commitment to tradition. The **Gesellschaft** type of society is characterised by impersonal contacts, individualism rather than group loyalty, and a decline of the traditional ties and values.

3. ***Robert Redfield's classification***: American anthropologist **Robert Redfield** draws a distinction between *"folk"* and *"urban"* societies. ***Folk society*** is small and bound by tradition and intimate personal links. The ***urban society***, on the contrary, represents a large scale social unit marked by impersonal relationships and a pluralism of values.

The classification mentioned above, make it evident that the same phenomena of the differences between the pre-modern and the modern, or the pre-industrial and the industrial societies are highlighted in several ways but in different words.

What then, are the fundamental differences between pre-industrial and industrial societies? Some outstanding differences which can be noticed easily and which are important, are the following:

Main Differences between Pre-Industrial and Industrial Society

1. Simple Versus Complex Social Structures

In the ***pre-industrial societies,*** social structure is comparatively simple. There is less scope for division of labour, which is mostly based on age and sex. Men normally go out of family for hunting or fishing or for cultivating the land while women confine themselves to home to raise children and sometimes go out to gather food or work in the field. There are, in general, fewer statuses and roles. Social institutions other than family and kinship, are either non-existent, or in a rudimentary stage, or very ineffective.

In the ***industrial societies,*** the social structure is more complex. There is vast scope for division of labour and specialization and it is more based on personal talents, abilities, efficiency, experience and preferences than age and sex. Vast number of statuses and roles emerges. The importance of family and kinship in the social structure tends to get reduced. A series of new institutions and organisations catering to the diverse needs of the people emerges.

2. Life in the Context of Primary Groups Versus Secondary Groups

In the ***pre-industrial societies***, we find the domination of primary groups such as family, kinship groups, small communities, etc. Life in the context of these groups is under the grip of social relationships which are conducted on an intimate and personal basis. In these simple societies, social relationships generally involve those who have known one another for their lifetime. Relations are personal, and individual emotions and needs are considered.

In the ***modern industrial societies***, on the contrary, social life occurs in the context of secondary groups and large anonymous urban communities. Here, social contact is often between relative strangers who have little or emotional involvement with each other. Social relationships take place mostly on an impersonal basis where there is no real emotional attachment, Workers in service positions do not particularly care who their clients are personally, for there is no personal and emotional involvement in this kind of relationship. Modern people may be treated as living material to be processed, in much the same way that raw material is treated in factories. This attitude which characterises the modern form of social bond is formal rather than informal, and non-intimate rather than intimate.

3. 'Ascribed' Versus 'Achieved' Statuses

Statuses in the case of the ***pre-industrial societies*** are normally *'ascribed'*, A person's *"station in life"*, so to say, is usually determined by the unchanging element of *birth.* Institutions such as family, kinship, race and religion rather fix the status of an individual on the basis of the birth of the individual. There is hardly any scope to change or improve it. Personal talents, capacities, efficiences do not help much an individual to improve his status.

In ***industrial or modern societies,*** many statuses can be *'achieved'.* There is scope for the individuals to achieve social mobility, that is, to move up and down the status scale. Availability of wide socio-economic, occupational and political opportunities helps individuals to take a chance to improve their statuses.

4. Homogeneous Versus Heterogeneous Cultures

Pre-industrial societies are characterised by a homogeneous culture in which striking resemblances are found in the ways of thinking, behaving, dressing, conversing, believing and so on. Unity and uniformity in social life are largely visible. Life is simple and smooth going with less tension and friction. There is general agreement among people on social values, opinions, morals, religious beliefs, community practices, and so on.

Industrial societies are mostly dominated by urban way of life and hence they are characterised by heterogeneous culture. Diversification of life - styles is very conspicuous. Life is complex and manysided. Differentiation is potent in modern societies. The wide range of different groups leads to a pluralism of values, outlooks, opinions and beliefs. Wide range of sub-cultures also make their appearance.

5. Social Control through Informal versus Formal Means

In ***pre-industrial societies,*** behaviour of the people is regulated by informal means such as social customs, traditions, folkways, mores and the like which are rarely questioned. People have a strong sense of belonging or identity with their group and hence they tend to think of themselves as members of their group first and as individuals next. In simple societies, violators of group norms are often taken to task first by the very witnesses to the offence, and only afterwards, they call the police, if needed.

The ***industrial societies*** attempt to control behaviour through more institutionalised means like laws, legislations, written contracts with specific penalties and procedures for dealing with offenders. In the event of any violation of the rules or norms, witnesses themselves would not pursue the offenders but would call the police. In these societies, custom and tradition lose much of their force, and people act primarily as individuals, often taking more account of their personal interests than the needs of the group.

6. Slow versus Rapid Rates of Social Change

In ***the pre-industrial societies,*** the rate of social change is usually very slow. People are normally not ready for sudden changes. They are for status quo, and hence change is regarded with suspicion. Their social life is routinised to such an extent that a small deviation from it is regarded as an unusual feature of social life.

In ***the industrial societies,*** rapid social change becomes a normal state of attires. People have a positive attitude towards social change. They expect change and sometimes even welcome it, for change is often identified with *"progress"* towards a better life. Rapid improvements in the fields of transport and communication, progress in the fields of science and technology, introduction of uniform legal and educational system and such other developments taking place in the industrial societies have added new dimensions to social change.

***Conclusion*:** The changes mentioned above, are entirely new in the history of the human species, and industrial societies are still in the difficult process of adjusting themselves to them. The terms such as pre-industrial and industrial, or pre-modern and modern, have been used to facilitate discussion. It is important to note, however, *"that societies actually exist on a continuum from pre-modern to modern rather than as purely one or the other. Furthermore, no modern society is modern throughout its territory. Social relations in some areas are more Gemeinschaft than Gesellschaft, more folk than urban and more characterised by mechanical than organic solidarity.... Generally, however, as societies move towards the modern end of the spectrum they experience increasing division of labour, fewer primary relations, greater reliance on non-family institutions and less reliance on custom to regulate behaviour"*[21]

REVIEW QUESTIONS

1. Given the classification of societies based on the mode of subsistence or the type of technology.
2. Highlight the characteristic features of hunting and gathering societies.
3. What do you mean by herding society? Write its characteristic features.
4. Write the salient features of horticultural and agrarian societies.
5. Explain the characteristic features of industrial society.
6. Give a comparative account of pre-industrial and modern societies.

⌘⌘⌘⌘⌘⌘⌘⌘⌘⌘⌘⌘

[21] Wallace and Wallace in *Sociology,* p. 94.

15

COMMUNITY AND INDIVIDUAL

CHAPTER OUTLINE

COMMUNITY AND INDIVIDUAL LIFE

Community plays an important role in the life of an individual. A community is the total organised social life of a locality. "*The mark of a community is that one's life may be lived wholly within it*". One cannot live wholly within a business organisation or a church; one can live wholly within a tribe or a city. The basic criterion of community, then, is that all of one's social relationships may be found within it.

Some communities are inclusive and independent on others. There are a few primitive communities like that of the *Yurok* tribes of California which are almost isolated. But modern communities have big population and are very much dependent on other communities. The character of the com- munity and the role of the individual in it depend much on its territorial size, size of the population, nature of the local government and the economic pursuits of the people.

Identification with the Community: One aspect of every community is its territorial base. People tend to develop attachment or sentimental identification with the area in which they live permanently. This gives rise to what is often called 'we-feeling'. This becomes evident, as MacIver says, when people say 'we' and 'ours'. The we-sentiment represents the common interests of the group. It is because of this strong sense of identification that people react sharply whenever their village, or town, or city, or nation, the community to which they belong, is criticised, or threatened by others. For an individual the community is "home of his home and flesh of his flesh".

Role-Playing: Further, every individual is conscious of the fact that he has to play his role, his own function to fulfil in his community. The role may be any role, a farmer, a shop-keeper, a teacher, a servant, a carpenter, a scavenger, and so on. This involves the sub-ordination of an individual to the group. This kind of attachment towards the group (community) on the one hand, and the realisation of the role that one has to play, the individual may develop through socialisation and "habituation in the daily discipline of life".

Dependence: Every member of the community feels that he is dependent upon, the community. This involves both physical dependence and psychological dependence. An individual is physically dependent on the community because many of his physical needs are satisfied with the community. He is psychologically dependent upon the community because it saves him from the fear of solitude and the boredom of isolation.

R.S. Lynd and *H.M. Lynd* in their "*Middletown: A Study in American Culture*" point out that we can find some common activities being performed by the people of a community despite infinite variations in detail. They write 'Whether in an Arunta village in Central Australia or in our own seemingly intricate institutional life of corporations, dividends coming-out of parties, prayer meet- ings, freshmen and Congress, human behaviour appears to consist of variations upon a few major lines of activity: getting the material necessities for food, clothing, shelter, mating, initiating the young into the group habits of thought and behaviour; and so on'. Lynd and Lynd have mentioned- six major kinds of human activities on which the impact of community (particularly the city) is comparatively great. They are: '(l) *Getting a living*, (2) *Making a home*, (3) *Training the young*, (4) *Using the leisure in various forms of play, art and so an*, (5) *Engaging in religious practices*, and (6) *Engaging in community activities*'. They have also pointed out that the character of these activities may go on changing in keeping with the changes that take place in the material as well as the non- material culture of the community.

Benefits of Community Life

The individual not only lives in a community but also reaps the benefits of community life. The individual makes achievements and registers progress due to the support given by the community.

1. The community life provides the individual the needed *protection and security*. There is strength in unity. The individual is better equipped to face dangers and overcome problems with the due assistance of the other members of the community than alone.
2. The community life *provides for co-operation* of the members. The individual in co-operation with others can work in the more efficient manner in the social, economic, cultural and other fields. The community plays a very important role especially in the economic field. Hence the community development projects are given high priority in India.
3. The community life *depends on some kind of communication system* among the members. Communication is the medium of interaction. It may take place through the senses, emotions, senti- ments and ideas. Language in its spoken and written form has made communication much easier. *Language has become the collective memory of mankind*. It has contributed to the advancement of civilisation and to the conservation of cultural values. Thus, community life which depends on lan- guage has contributed to its development.
4. The community life *provides the individual opportunities for the manifestation of his talents and abilities*. It helps him to develop nobler feelings of service-mindedness, selflessness, self-sacrifice, kindness, compassion, patience, perseverance, sublimity, benevolence towards each other and so on. The community has been reminding the individual of his social responsibilities and obligations and to become more human and less brutal in his approach. It has been helping him to move towards ever greater perfection.

The community life has its own conflicts and contradictions for the individual. It is not always smooth and free from tensions and clashes. Due to the greediness, selfishness, unsocial and anti social habits and tendencies of man, conflicts and clashes, tensions and tussles do take place in community. The community can manage with these only if it has an efficient system of social control.

Conclusion

Historically, the community has been an expression that emphasised the unity of the common life of a people or of mankind". Community has been "*generating a sense of belonging together*" all these days. But in the Wake of modern industrialisation, increasing mechanisation of living, phenomenal growth of urbanisation, widespread division of labour and specialisation, and vast socio-economic and political changes, the task of retaining the 'sense of belonging together' has become, as *MacIver* says, '*not less necessary but more difficult*'. As *Louis Wirth* observes, "In the transition from a type of social organisation based on kinship, status and a crude division of labour, to a type of social organisation characterised by rapid technological developments, mobility, the rise of special interest groups and formal social control, the community has acquired new meaning and has revealed new problems" One of the main problems mercilessly imposed by the modern complex urban community is the problem of the mental disorder. Cases of mental disorder are higher in cities. Even living in the midst of plenty people may often feel that they are alone. The sense of identification with the community may become weak. The loss of identification may lead to the "*loss of community*" which in turn may result in '*alienation*'. Alienation may even cause suicide. This made *Oswald Spengler to lament that "the wheel of destiny rolls or to its end, the birth of the city entails its death*"

RURAL AND URBAN COMMUNITIES

Communities are commonly divided into two general types—*rural* and *urban*. The line distin- guishing these two types is not definite. Writers do not agree in the use of criterion for defining them. Often locality is regarded as rural or urban by reference to its *population*. Other criterion employed are: density of population, legal limits, and legal status (i.e. whether the locality has been given the status of rural or urban). Some other writers have used occupations and social organisations, that is, the type of social and economic institutions, relationships, folkways as criterion.

P.A. Sorokin and *C. C. Zimmerman*, in "*Principles of Rural-Urban Sociology*", have stated that the factors distinguishing rural from urban communities include occupation, size, and density of population, as well as mobility, differentiation and stratification.

However, in many countries the distinction between rural and urban communities has been made on the basis of the size of the population. In Holland, a community containing more than 20,000 people is called urban. In Japan, the number is fixed at 30,000; in India at 5,000; and in U.S.A. at 2,500 and in France at 2000. *Mark Jefferson* says that a community with a density of 10,000 people or more per square mile should be considered a city. *Walter Willcox* suggested that a community with a population of more than 1,000 per square mile should be regarded as a city and less than 1,000 people as 'rural' community.

RURAL COMMUNITY

The social life of man has undergone different stages of development. The earliest human communities were perhaps the loosely organised aggregations of a few families who carried on mutually interdependent activities in gathering food and defending themselves against their enemies. These primitive bands were migratory. Gradually, man acquired skill and knowledge in agriculture. Then began the settled life of man. With the development of agriculture and the consequent stabilisation of the source of food, human communities became more permanent. These communities came to be known as *Village Communities*. The village is the oldest permanent community of man.

All early communities were basically rural in character. As *Kropotkin* points out, "We do not know one single human race of single nation which has not had its period of village communities." *Bogardus* says, "*Human society has been cradled in the rural group*".

Meaning and Definition of Rural Community

Rural society or the village community consists of people living in a limited physical area who have common interests and common ways of satisfying them. Psychological bonds play an important part in the rural community. Physical locality contributes to the integration and stability of the village community. Such proximity had developed a sociability and had encouraged solidarity and mutuality.

As the rural sociologist *Dwight Sanderson* has stated in his "*The Rural Community*", a rural community consists of people living "on dispersed farmsteads and in a hamlet or village which forms the centre of their common activities".

Rural community is often looked upon as an association in which there is "social interaction of people and their institutions in the local area". The relationships in the rural community tend to be what *Cooley* termed primary, that is, of the intimate nature. The rural localities are often referred to as "*country neighbourhood*".

The rural sociologists *J.H. Kolb and Brunner* defined a village as a population centre with 250 to 2500 persons and a hamlet as a somewhat smaller aggregation. A rural community may be defined as "a group of people permanently residing in a definite geographic area who, having developed a certain community consciousness and cultural, social and economic relations feel that they are separate from other communities".

The rural community has a long history of its own. It has become almost natural with the human life. No known community was started on purely urban character. Urban community is a phenomenon of recent development. Rural life has preceded the urban life. It is said that *God made the village and man built the city*. In spite of the growth of cities, the population of the world is largely rural. In India alone more than 50 crores of people live in villages. More than 70 per cent of Indians live in more than five lakh villages in India. The urban life still depends on the farm and what it produces.

Characteristics of Rural Community

1. ***The social homogeneity:*** The rural community is largely homogeneous. The rural social life is simple and smooth-going. Unity and uniformity in social life are largely visible. W/e find similarity in the ways of thinking, behaving, dressing, action and living. We also find agreement or consensus among people with regards to habits, opinions, morals, customs, values, religious beliefs, dress, etc.

2. ***Dominance of primary relations:*** A village community is often regarded as a *primary group*'. Hence the rural community is characterised by the primary relations. There exist face-to-face relations among people. Every person knows every other and hence everyone is interested in the welfare of all. The village community is relatively small in size. The members frequently meet and maintain regular contacts. The relationships are informal, personal and inclusive. Community spirit prevails over individual interests. People are free and frank in their expressions. A sense of belonging to the community holds them together.
3. ***Informal social control:*** Social control, that is, the control of social behaviour of people is relatively simpler and less problematic. Predominance of face-to-face relationship has made the task of regulating relations a simple one. Customs, traditions, group standards and morals are themselves effective as social pressures. Any kind of social disobedience is easily noticed and the disobedient is put to gossip and slander. Formal means of social control such as law, legislation, police, court, etc. are not resorted to in normal situations to maintain the social order'
4. ***Occupations:*** The rural community is marked by a predominant type of occupation, that is, *agriculture*. Agriculture is associated with different crafts like pottery, basket-making, spinning, weaving, carpentry, smithery, brick-making, shoe-making, tanning, curing hides, washing clothes, barbering, building houses and repairing, oil grinding, toy-making, etc. In contrast with the urban society there is less division of labour and specialisation in rural community. Even opportunities for specialisation are also limited. Neither the villager is equipped with sufficient qualification to pursue varied tasks. On the contrary, the villager at times performs the role of an all rounder. He is often called a jack of all trades, but master of none. Women assist their menfolk in various agricultural tasks.
5. ***Importance of family:*** The rural community is *built around the institution of family*. The rural family is very cohesive. It lives together as a unit, eats together and works together. The family circle provides the greatest part of the economic and social needs of its members. People are traditional and conservative. People are bound by family customs and traditions. *Rural women* are very much dependent on their menfolk. They are very much sentimental. They require the support of institutions like marriage and family for a living. Most of the time, the rural women engage themselves in indoor activities, but often they work in fields.

   In rural life, the *family* is the smallest unit and not the individual. Individual interests are sub- ordinated to the family interests. Status of the individual is mostly derived from his family. Property is considered as a possession of the family itself. Individual accepts the authority of the family in almost all fields. Marriage, religion, occupation, mode of living, etc. are all influenced by the tradition of the family. Generally, there is less individual question and rebellion in a family. Further, the rural family is mostly a *joint family*. Size of the family is normally big. Agricultural operation requires a large number of people. The rural joint family meets the need for large labour force.
6. ***Role of neighbourhood:*** '*Neighbourhood*' is a community in miniature. It is similar to a community, but it is a smaller area in which relationships tend to be primary, or more or less inti- mate. The neighbourhood is a part of the village, town or city, in which live a number of families among whom close relationships exist. A neighbourhood has been defined as–*an area in which the residents are personally well acquainted with each other and are in the habit of visiting one another, of exchanging articles and services and, in general of doing things together*.

   In, a village the neighbourhood is of great importance. Neighbours share the joys and sorrows together. They have the spirit of comradeship. There is not enough of individuality and speed in the life of the village to disregard the feeling, interests and expectations of the neighbours. They participate in all common ceremonies, functions and festivals. They assist one another in all important matters.
7. ***Faith in religion:*** The rural people are mostly religious in their outlook. They have deep faith in religion, in God. They have awe and reverence and, more than that fear of God. Their main occupation is agriculture which mainly depends on the mercy of Nature. The rural men believe that the Nature-Gods will have to be pleased by various means to help them in agricultural operations. The deep faith in religion and God has minimised their mental tension and disturbance.
8. ***Conservatism and dogmatism:*** The rural people are said to be highly conservative, tradi- tional and dogmatic in their approach. It is true that their social attitudes and behaviour pattems are dictated by traditions. They do not accept policies, plans, programmes, principles, projects, doctrines, etc. that the majority disapproached. They are basically skeptical in their attitude.
9. ***Rural community and social change:*** The villagers are generally simpletons. They cling firmly to their beliefs, traditions and ago-old practices. *Custom is their* '*Kin*'. They are not ready to go against it. Their behaviour is natural and not artificial. They are far away from the superficial manners and artificial gestures. They live a peaceful life.

They are free from mental tensions and conflicts. They dislike conflicts and quarrels. They are sincere, hardworking and hospitable. But their problem is that they cannot accept the urban people and their way of life readily. They are not ready for sudden change. They are for *status quo*. They are in a way far away from the rapidly changing urban civilised world. There is gap between the urban and the rural way of life. Of course nowadays the rural people are awakened to the need of the modem world. They are also modifying their behaviour patterns slowly and gradually.

The Industrial Revolution and the consequent industrialisation have brought far-reaching results to the rural community. Rapid improvements in the fields of transport and communication, progress in the fields of science and technology, introduction of uniform system of education, implementation of various community welfare programmes and projects, opening of small factories and industries even in rural areas, provision of modem civilised facilities like radio, electricity, telephone, television, post and telegraph, newspapers, introduction of various domestic electrical appliances, increasing political consciousness of the people, the liberation of women, etc., have all contributed to some radical changes in the rural life.

Types of Rural Communities

Sociologists have spoken of two types of rural communities: 1. *Agricultural Village Communities*, and 2. *Industrial Village Communities*.

1. ***Agricultural village community:*** Agricultural village is mainly built around agriculture even though trade may be carried on there in a small scale. Such a village is the trade and social centre for the surrounding farmers. In the U.S.A. typically, the farmers themselves do not live in a village, but out on the land. In most parts of the world, it is customary for farmers to live in the village, and to go out by day to cultivate their land, returning to their homes in the village centre at night. In the Indian villages, normally people build their houses near their land and live in it. The Indian farmers depend more on agriculture rather than on trade.
2. ***Industrial village community:*** It is wrong to assume that all the villages are invariably depending upon agriculture and the related crafts. In some villages, more than the agriculture some small industries have provided means of livelihood for a relatively bigger number of people. The people in such industrial villages gain most of their income from small industries located there. Industries such as cutting the tree and firewood, preparing charcoal, brick-making and baking, producing stones for building houses, fishing, rolling beedies, mining, etc., may be carried on there. The industrial village may also provide services for the surrounding farmers. But its chief economic endeavour is industry rather than farm service occupations. The nations which are undergoing the process of rapid industrialisation and the industrialised countries normally give birth to such industrial villages. Similarly, *mining villages* are found in some places. However, the employment potential of such villages has its own limitations.

Rural Economic Organisation

The rural economic organisation is simple and free from complexity. The scope for division of labour and specialisation is very much limited. The small size of the farm as the economic unit of production makes extreme specialisation of function impractical. The rural economic organisation in the Indian continent consists of the following aspects:

1. ***Agriculture:*** Agriculture is the backbone of the village life. The progress of the village depends much on the progress of agriculture. In some villages, agriculture is carried on in a scientific manner. But the sub-division and fragmentation of landholdings has made scientific farming impossible in some places. This has an adverse effect on production. Agriculture has been mechanised in some of the economically advanced countries of the world though not in India.
2. ***Cottage industries and crafts:*** Agriculture is normally associated with some home indus- tries and crafts. Mat-making, basket-making, brick-making, carpentry, fishing, animal husbandry, tailoring, oil grinding, toy-making, pottery, spinning, weaving, embroidery, smithery, shoe-making and other crafts are carried on along with agriculture.
3. ***Small-scale industries:*** In some of the villages small-scale industries are associated with agriculture. In some other villages small industries are the main means of livelihood of the people. Beedi industry, brick-making industry, mining industry, tile-making, agarbathi industry, and other types of industries have provided for people employment opportunities. In the western villages the farm economy is slowly becoming a money economy. There has developed a tendency among the Western farmers to give up their traditional economic functions. *For example*, in America, people are no more making butter and cheese for commercial purposes. Crops are raised to sell for money which the farmers have to pay for purchasing other goods.

The rapid growth of industrialisation has its own impact on the economic organisation of the villages. People are more attracted by the industrial occupations rather than the agricultural work. The farmers are also more interested in the commercial crops. There is a growing tendency among the rural people to depend more and more on the city and the factories for their daily needed com- modities than on the locally produced goods.

Rural Recreational Activities

The recreational activities of the rural communities are not only simple but also limited. The nature and the type of recreational activities of a village depend on its economic and social progress. The commercial types of recreational activities are not found in the villages.

Chit-chating, visiting relatives, arranging dinner parties for friends and relatives, conducting religious ceremonies and sacraments, observing festivals, singing and dancing in a group, worship- ping together, praying together in temples, hunting collectively, participating in community activi- ties such as fairs and festivals, playing some indoor as well as out-door games, etc., are some of the traditional recreational activities of the Indian villages.

During the recent years, the urban trends are very diffused in the rural areas. The urban means of recreation have entered the villages also. The rural people now listen to the radio, witness television-shows, read newspapers and magazines and discuss everyday politics and sports. The church picnics, family visits. community socials are diminishing. Especially in the West, the ruralities are habituated to Sunday outings. Still, the youths are not satisfied with the recreational amenities of the village. The lack of modem means of recreation is one of the factors that has contributed to the movement of people from the rural areas to the towns and cities.

Rural Problems

The rural communities are not free from problems. Though they are simple and less complex, they have their own social, economic, educational, medical and other problems.

1. ***Economic problems:*** Comparatively, the rural people are poorer. Increase in population, disintegration of joint families, subdivision and fragmentation of land holding, heavy load on land, traditional methods of cultivation, unemployment and other factors have been responsible for poverty in the rural areas especially in India. In India, more than 40% of the people are living below the line of poverty.
2. ***Lack of educational facilities:*** Sizeable number of people are uneducated and ignorant in the rural areas. In India, many villages do not have schools, and some of the existing schools do not have teachers, and some others are not in working conditions. Lack of education has contributed to the development of traditionalism, and superstitious beliefs among the ruralites. The ruralites also fail to get the jobs for their inability to get themselves qualified through the formal education.
3. ***Traditionalism:*** The ruralites are traditional and custom-bound. They are illiterate, ignorant and superstitious. They do not easily accept the change. They are sceptical regarding the developmental programmes of the government.
4. ***Lack of adequate civic amenities:*** In comparison with the cities, the villages are lacking in civic amenities. The necessary civic amenities such as—medical facilities, electricity, transport facilities, communication facilities, such as radio, television, newspaper, post and telegraph, tele- phone, etc., are not available to the satisfaction of the people. Sometimes it becomes difficult for the rural people to get the daily required necessities of life.
5. ***Defective rural administration:*** The ruralites are unorganised and politically not awak- ened. Their failure to understand the democratic methods of administration has contributed to the inefficient functioning of the rural administrative bodies. In India the rural administrative bodies such as the panchayats have been widely criticised as inefficient, defective, corrupt, selfish and full of communal and caste feelings. Inefficient rural administration can hardly serve the cause of the people.
6. ***Social problems:*** Due to ignorance, illiteracy and poverty, the rural people have become the victims of some evil habits and practices. Many of them are habituated to smoking, gambling, drinking liquors and prostitution. The evils of animosity, hatred, jealousy, fraud, cheating, etc, are also widespread among the ruralites. Many of them simply idle away much of their time in talking over useless topics. Their suspicious outlook makes them to doubt and discourage even the good intentions of the rural developmental programmes. This is especially true in the case of the Indian villages.

Rural Health and Welfare Activities

Rural Health

In comparison with the urban communities, the rural communities are lagging behind in mat- ters connected with health. Lack of medical facilities, non-availability of essential energising food, insanitation and ill health are normally found in the villages especially in the underdeveloped coun- tries. Hospitals, nursing homes, maternity homes, drug shops, clinics, clinical laboratories and such other modern medical amenities are rarely found in the villages. In many places people still follow the traditional methods of curing diseases. Two reasons may be cited here for the lack of enough medical facilities in the rural communities—(*i*) *the rural environment is naturally healthier than the urban, (ii) the stronger primary groups in rural environment have been able to take care of their own people in time of need, and especially, in times of disease.* Hence, the rural health programme has suffered.

An important factor in the rural health programme is the problem *of the lower income* of the rural people. *Economic distress, the burden of children, superstitious beliefs* and *practices, the difficulty of attracting the medical personnel to the rural areas* have further added to the rural health problem. The rural administrative bodies are giving more importance to rural health nowadays. Voluntary associations are also playing a vital role in this regard. The rural people have started realising the importance of the modern means of medical facilities during the recent years. Intensification of rural education has been a great help in this regard.

Rural Welfare Activities

More than 2/3 of the people of the world still live in villages. Rural Welfare activities consti- tute One of the powerful means of promoting the progress of ruralites. No nation can afford to ignore rural development and rural welfare. Some of the rural welfare activities are as follows:

1. ***Rural education:*** Rural education is given much importance nowadays. Kindergartens, nurseries, primary schools, secondary schools, adult education centres are being established even in villages now. Primary education has been made compulsory in some nations. Primary education has been made free and compulsory for the children below 14 years in India.
2. ***Rural economic development:*** Economically, the rural people are relatively poorer. Hence, various economic developmental programmes have been undertaken in rural areas. Agriculture, animal husbandry, poultry farming, fishing, rural crafts, cottage industries—and other rural economic tasks have been given more attention now. In India; through the Community Development Projects and National Extension Services the rural developmental work is taken in hand. The Five-Year Plans have been giving more importance to the rural economic development.
3. ***Provision of civic amenities:*** The rural communities are also provided with more and more civic facilities today. Transport and communication facilities, educational and medical facilities, entertainment facilities have been improved in the villages. Buses, trucks, taxies, cycles, motor cycles have now reached the village. Men and materials can move from one area to another. Post and telegraph facilities and radio, telephone and television facilities are found in the villages also. Good roads, bridges and railways are connecting the villages with the towns and cities. Electric facility has made the village life more interesting. Modern electric appliances have already reached the villages.
4. ***Other welfare activities:*** Various projects and schemes have been undertaken to promote the welfare of the children, women, unemployed persons, agricultural labourers and the weaker sections of the village. The unemployed young men are given maintenance allowance and old and needy people are given old-age pension. Various co-operative societies, agricultural banks and voluntary associations have come in to prevent the exploitation of the weaker sections. Attempts are made to maximise rural agricultural production and to develop the rural cottage industries. Special attention has been paid to take the maximum benefit of the human power. Rural youths have been encouraged to organise various cultural as well as economic activities. Various voluntary organisations have been working in the rural areas also to develop the right attitudes among the ruralites towards matters such as higher education, family planning, rural sanitation and health, communal harmony, cottage industries, civil rights and duties.

URBAN COMMUNITY

The City

The '*urban community*' means the city community. "The history of every civilisation is the history, not of its countryside, but of its cities and towns. Civilisation means the city, and the city means civilisation. Man originally built the city, and the city, in tum, civilised man." Man became a citizen when he became a member of a city-state. With the rise of the world-city, as *Spengler* tells us, "there were no longer noblessee and bourgeoisie, freemen and slaves, Hellenes and Barbarians, believers and nonbelievers, but only cosmopolitans and provincials. All other contrasts pale before this one, which dominates all events, all habits of life, all views of the world." The city is culture par excellence; it is the epitome of culture. It is mankind's greatest work of art–and of artifice–because it contains all others. Culture, a manufactured environment, surrounds the city man. "It is an environment of bricks and steel and mortar and cement, of bridges and tunnels, of sidewalks and streets, of monuments and buildings, of elevators and subway platforms." The city is the product of man and his own achievement. The city "has everything that is 'tawdry' and everything sublime. It holds both hope and despair. It encompasses millions of people, and it can be the loveliest place on earth... It is a vital centre of every civilised society... It is both a place and a state of mind."–*Robert Bierstedt*.

Meaning of Urban System of Community

By '*urban system*', we mean urban community. Urban Community life represents the city-life. Though the term '*urban*' is popularly used, it is not properly defined. There is no single all-inclusive definition of a city or urban community.

1. The urban sociologist *Hawrad Woolston*, in his '*Metropolis*', defined the city as a "limited geographic area, inhabited by a largely and closely settled population, having many common interests and institutions, under a local govemment authorised by the State."
2. *Park* in his "*The City*" says that the city far from being a mere collection of individuals and of social conveniences, is rather a "state of mind, a body of customs and traditions, and the organised attitudes and sentiments that inhere in these customs."
3. *James A. Quinn* in his "*Urban Sociology*", viewed the city as a "*phenomenon of specialisation*", as a population aggregate whose occupations are nonagricultural.
4. *Adna F. Weber in his* "*The Growth of Cities*" defined the city as any incorporated place with a minimum of 10,000 inhabitants.
5. *Lowis Wirth* in his essay "*Urbanism as a way of life*" writes: "For sociological purposes a city may be defined as a relatively large, dense and permanent settlement of socially heterogeneous individuals..."

Though some sociologists have tried to define the concept of '*urban*' no one has given a satisfactory definition so far. *Bergel* writes, "Everybody seems to know what a city is, but no one has given a satisfactory definition." *Kingsley Davis* writes, "Much ink has been wasted in trying to define urban". *MacIver* remarks, "But between the two (urban and rural communities) there is no sharp demarcation to tell where the city ends and country beings." Every village possesses some elements of the city while every city carries some features of the villages. Different criteria are used to decide a community as urban. Some of them are population, legal limits, types of occupations, social organisations.

Characteristics of Urban Community

1. ***Social heterogeneity:*** An urban society is heterogeneous. The city life is complex and many sided. Wide difference is found in the ways of living of the people. Uniformity and similarity are rarely found. It is more characterised by diversity. As *Louis Wirth* in his "*Urbanism as a way of life*", points out "the greater the number of individuals participating in a process of interaction, the greater the potential differentiation between them...." *Louis Wirth* further says that "*the city has been the melting-pot of races, peoples and cultures, and a most favourable breeding ground of new biological and cultural hybrids*." He also says that the city "has brought together people from the ends of the earth because they are different and thus useful to one another, rather than because they are homogeneous and likeminded." The ways of thinking, behaving, acting, the habits, morals, religious beliefs and practices, food and dress habits, occupations, etc., of the people differ significantly. Differentiation is potent in urban life.
2. ***Secondary relations:*** The urban community is characterised by secondary relations. A city by virtue of its size cannot be a primary group. It is a secondary group. People are indifferent towards one another. Face-to-face, friendly or intimate relations may not be observed among people. Mass media of communication such as telephone, radio, press, post and telegraph, etc. are often resorted to by the urbanites for contacts In cities people rarely take personal interests in others' concerns. Superficial form of politeness and manners are commonly found. Physical contact rarely results in intimacy and closeness. Even the neighbours are often found to be strangers. Private interests prevail over the common interests.
3. ***The anonymity of the city life:*** The city is an Ocean of strangers. Heavy concentration in a limited space makes it impossible for people to know one another. Every one appears to be a stranger for every other person. There prevails a state of namelessness in which the individual identities remain unknown. This kind of namelessness that is found in the city is often referred to as *anonymity of the city life*. The anonymity of the city life makes more complex the problem of social control.
4. ***Secondary control:*** Control of social behaviour is more difficult in a city. Predominance of secondary relations makes it more complex, the social control. The social behaviour of people is no more regulated by customs,

traditions, religion and group standards. Instances of social deviation are commonly found in a city. City is the ocean of strangers. Violations of standards of behaviour may pass unnoticed and unchecked. In this way, informal means of social control are not very effective. Regulation of social behaviour is largely done through the specialised agencies like law, legislation, police, court, etc. The larger the city, the greater becomes the problem of control and more complex the agencies of secondary regulation.

5. ***Large-scale division of labour and specialisation:*** An Urban community is known for its large-scale division of labour and specialisation. Specialisation is visible in every walk of life. The larger the city, the greater is the specialisation. Hence we find different people in society engaging themselves in different kinds of activities like mechanical, commercial, educational, political, recre- ational, artistic. literary, scientific and so on. There are skilled, unskilled and semi-skilled workers, the artisans, the technicians, the '*paper expert*', the '*white-collar*' employees, the financiers, the businessmen, administrators, the politicians, the artists and others in society specialising themselves in some particular kind of activity or the other. City depends on division of labour also. Work is divided among people on the basis of interests, talents, efficiency, opportunities, age, sex and so on. Division of labour and specialisation are possible because of co-operation.

6. ***Large-scale social mobility:*** An urban community is characterised by intense social mobil- ity. '*Social Mobility*' refers to the movement of people from one social status to another, from lower status to higher status or from poor position to rich position. An individual's position in an urban community is determined more by his achievements than by his birth. The status is not predetermined. High stress is laid on accomplishments. Urban life in this way is highly competitive. The city with its elaborate division of labour, its competitiveness, its impersonality, has a tendency to emphasise the achievements of people. A city judges status according to what the individual does and how he speaks and what he accomplishes.

   An urban society provides for social mobility in countless ways. It provides for occupational mobility and geographic mobility on the one hand, and horizontal social mobility and vertical social mobility on the other. Individuals are busily engaged in improving their "*career*". An element of chance is always present in city. *MacIver* and *Page* write– "An accident, a lucky contract, a sudden opportunity seized or missed, a change of style or fad, a happy or unhappy forecast of some event far beyond his control, may revolutionise his prospects in a day."

7. ***Individuation:*** In an urban community people are more individualistic in their attitudes. As Kingsley Davis points out, "The secondary and voluntary character of urban association, the multiplicity of opportunities and the social mobility all force the individual to make his own decisions and to plan his life as a career".

   The concentration of people in a limited space has the effect of emphasising individuality. The city dweller takes his independent decisions on such matters as education, marriage, occupation, enterprise, adventure, and so on. *He is more selective in his choice and more individualistic in his preferences* He is guided by his own whims and fancies. *He is detached except for the attachment of his own choice*. He is not tied to any particular relationship or any particular cause. As Davis points out, "The individual stands over against the whole city, never completely absorbed by any one social group." The city provides wide opportunities for the adventurous spirit of the individuals. Simmel observes, "The city person is free in behaviour, less restrained, more individualistic, more formal and less sympathetic, and less of a conformist than the country person."

8. ***Voluntary association:*** An urban community is the breeding centre of a number of voluntary associations. The size of the urban population, its close proximity, diversity, and easy contact, make it the proper ground for voluntary associations. "No matter what a person's hobby or vocation, national background of religion, age or colour, he can always find others with a similar basis of interest." As a result new kinds of groups arise, based on extremely specialised interests. The group must organise or its cause will perish. People normally become members of a number of associations which may be called '*secondary group*' in order to fulfil their varied interests.

9. ***Social tolerance:*** Social tolerance characterises city life. Diversity of population, imper- sonality of contacts and heterogeneity in living style make it almost inevitable for the city people to develop the spirit of tolerance. "*People rub elbows with and become indifferent, to extremes of all kinds–extremes of opinion and interest, extremes of poverty and wealth, extremes of education and background.*" The spirit of tolerance gives the strength of unity in diversity to the life in a city. "Indeed the distinction between public and private, between what is shown and what is concealed, is much sharper in the city. It is the public behaviour that the city regulates, the private behaviour that it ignores. Its control is impersonal and general, that of the country personal and particular."—*Kingsley Davis*.

10. ***Spatial segregation:*** Due to its very nature, the city is bound to be overcrowded. It attracts a large number of people from the village areas. It is found that various types of business tend to concentrate in different spots of the city. Occupational groups of people also prefer to live together in distinct zones of a city. That is to say, some kind of *functional segregation* is found there. Commercial activities in the form of big departmental stores, show rooms, fancy stores, legitimate theatres, fine hotels, jewellery stores, etc. are located in the centre. The same is true of high-priced professional services–*e.g.* clinics, law offices, accounting firms, government offices, etc. Retail grocery establishments, filling stations, cleaning and pressing shops, shoe repair shops, garages, drug stores, etc., may be found at the cross-roads of the entire city. In the city land is so costly that the buildings expand vertically, filling the centre of the city with skyscrapers.
11. ***Unstable family:*** It is said that the urban family is not firmly organised. Many of the traditional functions of the family are transferred to the external agencies. Family is no longer the economic, educational, protective, recreational and effective unit. Family has lost much of its control over its individual members. Individualism is developing even inside the family. Even the women are getting employed outside the family. Relations between the husband and wife, parents and children are strained to some extent. Some sociologists have even remarked that the urban family is much more disorganised.

Attractions of City Life

The city is a centre of attraction. From its very inception the city has been attracting a large number of people especially from the rural areas. After the outbreak of the Industrial Revolution in the 18th Century this trend has been intensified. Various factors have made the rural people to flock to the cities. Of these two factors are significant" (*i*) the '*push*' factor, and (*ii*) the '*pull*' factor. The '*pull*' factor refers to the *attractions* of the city.

The city is pulling people from various comers towards its nucleus. The rural people who are faced with various economic problems, burdened with a large number of children, bored with the monotony of the routine life, and attracted by the glamour of the city, have started moving towards the cities. The city is tempting the rural people with its employment opportunities, educational facilities, medical facilities, recreational facilities such as–movies, dramas, night clubs, cabarets, gambling centres, horse race, library, public parks, museums, orchestra, zoo, circus shows, etc.

In comparison with the village, the city provides ample opportunities for personal advancement. The city is a centre of brisk economic, commercial, artistic, literary, political, educational, technological, scientific and other activities. The rural people who come in contact with the city for a brief spell of time get themselves impressed by its appearance, glamour, comfort and luxuries. They are likely to develop rosy imaginations of the luxuries of the city life. They have come to believe that money-making is easier in the city. The city men and women, their dresses, fashions, habits, styles, tastes, interests, intelligence, talents, comforts, luxuries, etc., have great impact on the rural people. As a result, they have started flocking towards the cities in a big number. This has contributed to the process of urbanisation. Urbanisation resulted in urban concentration on the one hand and rural depopulation, on the other.

Urbanisation in India

An agrarian country like India is also undergoing the process of urbanisation. The number and the size of the cities are increasing in India. In 1901, there were only 25 cities in India each with a population of one lakh or over. By 1960 there were 107 such cities in our nation. In l97l, there were 768; major towns each with a population of 20,000 or over. At present, ll major cities are there in India each with a population of one million or over. Calcutta is the biggest city having a population of 92 lakhs (according to the 1981 census) followed by other cities such as Mumbai (82 Lakhs), Delhi (52 Lakhs), Chennai (43 Lakhs), Bangalore (29 Lakhs), Hyderabad (26 Lakhs), Ahmedabad (25 Lakhs), Kanpur (17 Lakhs), Pune (l7 Lakhs), Nagpur (13 Lakhs), Lucknow and Jaipur (10 Lakhs each). Bangalore is one of the fastest growing cities of the world.

Urban Problems

The process of industrialisation has added much to the phenomenal growth of cities. Due to the rapid industrialisation cities have grown in an unsystematic manner. Industrialisation and urbanisation have brought along with them many vices.

1. ***The problem of concentration:*** Concentration of people in a definite limited space is one of the problems of the urban society. Due to the attraction of city life ('*Pull-factors*') men have started flocking towards the cities. Lack of job opportunities in the rural societies ('*Push-factor*') also forced people to desert villages and start moving to the cities. This has led to urban concentration and rural depopulation.
2. ***The problem of facilities:*** Concentration of people has resulted in other problems such as overcrowding, congestion, housing problems, lack of water facility and fresh air, insanitation, etc.

3. ***The problem of slums:*** Increasing industrialisation and urbanisation have created slums in the city. The slum dwellers live in horrible areas. Their living conditions are really unfortunate. The low-paid workers live in these slum areas. The facilities that are found in the cities are not found in these places. Slums consist of sub-standard, ill-ventilated, *insanitary* and poorly lighted houses. They consist of houses which are unfit for human habitation.
4. ***The problem of privacy:*** Lack of privacy and intimacy are the natural outcome of the city life. Due to the indirect and impersonal relationships, closeness and intimacy will not develop. Life becomes mechanical, competitive and charmless.
5. ***The problem of vices:*** The city is a centre of economic insecurity, mental illness, gambling, prostitution, drunkenness, crimes, juvenile delinquency, alcoholism, environment pollution and such other vices. There is poverty in the midst of plenty. The city life endangers the physical, mental and moral health of the people.
6. ***The problem of lndividuation:*** The urban community encourages *individuation*. Individuals are moved by their own aspirations, ambitions, aims, and interests. They have become more and more *career-conscious*. They are invariably caught in the competitive race for a successful career. The competitiveness of the city, places one over against everyone else. The materialistic outlook that a city-dweller develops may often result in what is known as the '*loss of community*'. An individual may become '*alienated*' from his own community, his own people, It is own profession. This state, when it reaches the extreme, may drive a depressed and an 'alienated' man to commit suicide.

Advantages and Disadvantages of the City

Advantages or Merits

1. The city offers *opportunities* and *facilities* for making full use of One's abilities and talents. 2. It can make life *joyful* and *comfortable*. Major *service agencies are centralised* in the city to satisfy various interests of the people such as work, education, recreation and politics. 3. It *encourages new ideals and inventions*. 4. It *quickens social movements* and enlarges social contacts. Social mobility becomes easier. 5. There is less *social distance* being kept among people of different castes, races and religions. Hence there is *more tolerance* towards others. 6. The city is *dynamic*. This dynamism contributes to social changes. 7. The city has *liberated women* from the exclusiveness of domesticity. It has made women to stand on an equal footing with men. 8. The city provides various means of *recreation*. In a city there is *scope for personal advancement*. The multifarious associations of the city cater to the multiple needs, interests and tastes of the people. 9. That is why, as *Quinn* says, "*the great civilisations of antiquity–Mesopotamian, Egyptian, Greek, Roman,—were cradled in cities, that urban communities typically have led in the creation of art, the advancement of science, and the dissemination of learning*". 10. The city functions as a laboratory for human genius.

Disadvantages or Demerits

The city has its dark or the ugly side too. 1. The city makes life materialistic and mechanical. It takes away from man his human aspect. 2. *Secondary relations* are dominant in the city. People are *indifferent* towards one another. Superficial forms of politeness and manners are commonly found. There is lack of *intimacy* and *privacy* in the city. 3. The city has made the people to become *individualistic*, *selfish*, *rationalistic* and *calculative*. Relations are commercialised. All relations are means to means and to no final ends. 4. The city has posed a *challenge to family*. The urban family is in doldrums. Individualism is ripening within it. *Divorce*, *desertion* and *separation* are increasing. Joint family has disappeared. The family is cut to size. 5. *Social control is complex* and *less effective* in the city. Instances of *social deviance* are more in the city. 6. The city has made the life to become uncertain, insecure, and competitive. 7. The city is said to be the centre of economic insecurity, mental illness, gambling, prostitution, drunkenness, crime, juvenile delinquency, etc. 8. Concentration of people in the city creates problems of housing, water and electricity facility, overcrowdedness, insanitation, etc. 9. The cities are condemned as '*abnormal seed-beds of sin, scepticism, greed, crime, misery, filth and congestion*'. It is branded as the centre of '*corruption, vice and misery.*

Urban Influence on the Country

In the recent years it is evident everywhere that the city is growing in population at the expense of the village. It is also observed that urban culture is spreading to the rural areas. As *Davis* says that "*The city effects are wider than the city itself*" *McKenzie* has proved conclusively that "*the influence of a city varies with its size and that it tends to wane with distance outward*". The growing transport and communications, the increased urban newspaper circulation in rural areas, advancement in science and technology, etc., have gone a long way in diffusing a wide variety of urban attitudes, ideas and habits from the city to the village.

Some of the *facilities and the comforts* of the city like electricity, radio, newspapers, hotels, libraries, post offices, schools and even colleges, games and sports and various electrical appliances are now diffused to the rural areas. The newspapers carry the stories and editorial comments about politics, sports, prominent persons and a host of ideas about religious, civic, economic, artistic and other interests and events. As readers of these newspapers the country people share these interests.

Urbanism or the urban way of life, has affected the size and character of the rural family. The *size of the family* in the village is decreasing. Joint families are slowly disappearing. The family is losing its control over its members. The younger generation wants to enjoy more freedom like its counterpart in the city. The *rural people have acquired some of the evil habits of the city people*. Drunkenness, gambling, prostitution, smoking, crimes, etc. have made inroads into the village. Morality has fallen, costly fashions and expensive habits are acquired. Life in the country is slowly becoming more and more individualistic, materialistic, rationalistic and calculative.

The *modern means of transport and communications* are introduced in many villages. Cycles, scooters, motor cycles, taxis, are also found in many villages which are equipped with post and telegraph. Radios and transistors are commonly found in villages. Some villages have even phone connections. Further, rural occupations and agricultural operations are slowly being mechanised. The blacksmiths, goldsmiths, silversmiths, coppersmiths, barbers, carpenters and others are now adopting modern tools in their work. The city as a market for rural products, and as a centre of trade and financial control over the rural regions, provides for the increasing dominance over the village.

The *mode of rural recreation* has changed due to the urban influence. Radios and gramaphones and tape recorders have changed the tastes of rural people. Football, volleyball, cards, chess, and such other plays are becoming popular. The cricket is equally enthusiastic for the rural youth. The city has radically altered the *mode of living* of the rural people. Food and dress habits, fads and fashions, of the ruralites have changed. The rural youth are slowly becoming *career conscious*. Education is becoming popular among them. The rural people take interest in political and cultural activities. They look to the city for guidance and imitation. The '*push*' (mostly economic pressures) factors and the '*pull*' (the attractions of the city) factors have made the rural people to rush to the cities. This has resulted in *urban concentration* and *rural depopulation* in many places. The city has continued to absorb the people from the hinterland. The process will be faster, the more the city is linked with its hinterland.

It is true that the city continues to dominate the country. Even with respect to birth rate, death rate, age at marriage, infant mortality, divorce, suicide, church affiliation, etc., rural indices are moving nearer to urban indices. The dominance of the city over the country is regarded by some sociologists as a dangerous trend. *Oswals Spengler* in his "*Decline of the West*" points out that "the, city destroys the solidarity of the kin, the family, the 'blood', the nation and with its competitive stress fosters the disintegrating attitudes of individualism, socialism, rationalism and cosmopolitanism". However, sociologists like *MacIver* are of the opinion that there is no need to be pessimistic about the city as such. Man is gradually making the urban environment more suited to his needs. Inspite of the widespread urbanisation, more than two-third of the population of the world is rural in character.

URBAN-RURAL CONTRAST

The city and country (village), the town and the land, the capital and the province (this despite Sperigler's exaggeration) is one of the most widespread and important of all kinds of social differentiation to be found in all human societies except the most primitive, and in most of human history. "Soil and cement, the land and the pavement, the lane and the street–these are symbols of two different ways of life, two different cultures". "The city man and the country man do indeed have two different views of the world, have different rounds of activity, sustain in different ways the progression of the seasons, indulge in different kinds of work and play, and spend their span of life in different surroundings." The differences between the rural society and the urban society can be elaborated in the following way:-

	Rural Society	*Urban Society*
1.	The rural society is homogeneous. It is marked by unity and uniformity	The urban society is heterogeneous. It is known for its diversity and complexity.
2.	It is dominated by primary relations. It is hence more cohesive.	It is dominated by secondary relations. It is not united.
3.	People here are known for their simplicity and hospitality, frankness and generosity.	The urban people are known for their artificiality, narrow-mindedness and selfishness.

(*Contd.*)

	Rural Society	Urban Society
4.	Informal means of social control such as customs, mores, conventions are sufficient to regulate interpersonal relations.	Formal means of social control such as law, legislation, police, court, etc. are needed in addition to the informal means for regulating the behaviour of the people.
5.	It is less mobile. Opportunities for social movements are limited. Status is mostly 'ascribed'.	It is more mobile. It is an 'open' society. It provides more chances for social mobility. Here status is 'achieved'.
6.	The rural society provides limitted scope for division of labour and specialisation. Occupations are mostly unspecialiscd. Agriculture is the main occupation.	Here occupations are more specialised. There is a wide spread division of labour and specialisation opportunities for pursuing occupations are numerous.
7.	It is built of family units. Family is very influential and dominant institution. People are bound by family tradition.	Here, the family is said to be unstable. More than the family, individual is given importance. Joint families are comparatively less in number.
8.	Women are mostly tradition bound. They are passive, emmeek, submissive and obedient. They work in the field as well as in the kitchen. Women are not career-conscious. They cannot live with out family.	Women have almost an equal status with men. Many are employed outside the family. They ae more free, and have their individualistic ideas. They are very much career-conscious.
9.	Rural people are poorer, Still they are not class-conscious. Class-conflicts are unknown.	Chances are greater for people to become rich. People are more class-conscious. Class-conflicts often parlyse the city life.
10.	People are more conservative, orthodox and dogmatic. They are for *status quo*, not for change.	People are progressive. They welcome changes. They are exposed to the modern developments in the fields of science and technology.
11.	The rural community has a small number of people.	Urban community consists of a big number of people.
12.	It is a "simple unigroup society".	Urban community is a "Complex multigroup society"
13.	The rural community is know for its ethnocentrism and its corrective, suspicion towards outsiders.	Here, the growing contacts with outsiders make the people to become tolerant with them.
14.	It is free from conflicts, frictions and tensions. It is characterised by common consensus. The social organisation is well deined and there is little scope for metal illness and anomic (lawlessness).	The urban community replaced consensus by common dissensus. The social organisation is atomistic and illdefined. It is characterised by dis-organisation, mental illness and anomic.
15.	There is less stress on education in the rural system. Scantly formal education pervades the village. Education is largely informal.	Mass education is widespread in the city increasing democratisation of the organisation and institutions demand formal education.

RURAL-URBAN CONVERGENCE

Though the communities are normally divided into '*rural*' and '*urban*' the line of demarcation is not always clear as *MacIver* has remarked, between these two types of communities "*there is no sharp demarcation to tell where the city ends and country beings*". Every village possesses some elements of the city and every city carries some features of the village. The concept of '*rural-urban convergence*' refers to the striking similarities between the village and the town in some aspects of community life.

Cities are growing in number and size everywhere. It is true that urban culture is diffusing at a very fast rate in the rural areas. As *Kingsley Davis* has said, "*the city effects are wider than the city itself*". The influence of the city varies with its size also. The urban way of life can be carried far beyond the city boundaries and can thus characterise people who do not actually live in cities.

With the diffusion of urban culture to the rural areas, the extreme differences between rural and urban cultures have diminished. The growing transport and communications, the radio, press, television, telephone, etc., the growing circulation of the urban newspapers in the rural areas have changed the attitudes and outlook of the moralites. Medical, educational, commercial, recreational and other facilities are also being enjoyed by the rural people. The automobile has played an important role in the rural areas. It has ended the secluded life of the rural people. People prefer to stay near the highways now. Villages in a way are closely linked with the cities. Buses, trains, taxies and motor cycles, etc., have helped the city people to go out and stay in the fringes of the city.

Everywhere big cities are characterised by sub-centres or sub-urban areas. In structure and function they are like cities. Too much of concentration in the city contributes to an opposite process of decentralisation. The sub-centres or *sub-urban* areas resemble the city in several respects. A single city may have a number of small *sub-urban* areas. These sub-urban areas may retain in them some of the features of the city. They are like *satellite* cities built around a major city. *Sub-urban areas represent the rough amalgam of rural and urban ways of living*. Here, we may find the urban way of life being mixed with the rural way of life. In these areas we find the '*rural-urban convergence*'

RURAL-URBAN CONTINUUM

Some sociologists have used the concept of '*rural-urban continuum* to stress the idea that there are no sharp breaking points to be found in the degree or quantity of rural urban differences. The impact of urban life over rural life is evident in many ways. With regard to birthrate, age at marriage, infant mortality, church affiliations, divorce, suicide, etc., rural indices are moving to nearer urban indices. In this way, rural areas can become highly urbanised.

As the contacts of the city become closer as transportation and communication become more rapid, the rural community tends to assume more closely the urban social structure. We may even speak of different degrees of "*urbanness*" or "*ruralness*". One country can be demographically more urban and yet socially more rural than another. *Example*: Chile has a greater percentage of its population living in cities than does Canada, but its people, by almost all sets of indices, are less urban.

REVIEW QUESTIONS

1. What is community? Discuss its role in the life of an individual.
2. Explain the types of communities.
3. What are the benefits of community life?
4. Define rural community. Bring out its characteristic features.
5. Discuss the types of rural community.
6. What are the characteristic features of rural economic organisation?
7. Throw light on the problems of rural communities.
8. Write a detailed note on the rural health and welfare activities.
9. What do you mean by urban community? Explain its characteristic features.
10. Write an essay on urbanisation in India.
11. Discuss the advantages and disadvantages of city life.
12. Write short notes on the following:
    (a) Urban problems
    (b) Rural-urban convergence
    (c) Rural-urban continuum
13. Differentiate between rural and urban societies.
14. Define community. Explain the difference between society and community.

⌘⌘⌘⌘⌘⌘⌘⌘⌘⌘⌘

16

WOMEN IN SOCIETY

CHAPTER OUTLINE

It is customary everywhere to classify the human community on the basis of sex into groups of 'men' and 'women'. The biological fact of sex has created much difference between them. The aims and objectives, desires and aspirations, duties and responsibilities, dress styles and behavioural patterns, roles and statuses of men and women are different. No where in the history of humanity men and women were treated alike and assigned statuses alike. Women have not been able to lead a life exactly on par with men in spite of their urge for equality. This does not mean that men and women represent two different cultures as such. They represent one way of life, one culture and one heritage. This is also true of India and Indian women.

The type of the status assigned to women in any society reflects the nature of its cultural richness and the level of its civilisational standards. Hence **Swami Vivekananda** said, "*that country and that nation which did not respect women have never become great nor will ever in future*". The degree of Freedom and respectability given to women to move about and take part in public activities gives a good idea of the nature of the society to which they belong. The status accorded to women in society symbolises its level of progress. The spirit of a civilisation can be assessed by the way in which women are treated by the members of that civilisation.

Status of women is a topic of sociological studies and discussions, for it mirrors the position of about 50% of the population of any society. Study of the history of human society reveals that in no society of the world have women enjoyed absolute equality on par with men. Everywhere they were subjected to inequality, discrimination and exploitation. In some societies their position has been comparatively better than that of their counterparts in some other societies. Even in the same society the status accorded to women has never been the same all through. It has been changing in keeping with the changes in the general conditions of society.

SEX DIFFERENCES AND SEXUAL DISCRIMINATION IN SOCIETY

Society consists of men and women, that is, individuals of both the sex. The societal principle of difference also includes sex difference. All human societies attach great importance to sex differences. Though men and women have been living together from the very inception of human history, every society differentiates its members on the basis of sex, treating men and women in different ways and expecting different patterns of behaviour from them. This differentiation does not necessarily imply that one sex should have status superior to the other, but in practice, sexual differentiation is always translated into sexual inequality.

Sexual Inequality at Birth

The importance of sexual inequality is often felt at the instance of the birth of a child. The first question parents ask at the birth of a child, in all societies all over the world, is always the same - *"is it a boy or a girl ?" "In fact, the inequality of the sexes is probably the oldest form of structural social inequality; it certainly existed long before social castes or classes first appeared."*[1]

Stratification by Sex

Most societies have two universal criteria for ascribing status within a stratification system: sex and age. These attributes may be chosen because "*they are ascertainable at birth, making it possible to begin the training of the individual for his potential statuses and roles at once*."[2] It is a brute fact of society that in no society in the world men and women are treated alike, given the same status and guaranteed social equality' On the contrary, in every society known to us, certain rights and opportunities have been denied to women. A social rationale given for this discrimination is that the talents and potentials of the sexes are different in many respects. Throughout history the inferior status of women has been seen as a self-evident fact of nature. Both the men and women in each society tend to share this assumption which is passed on from generation to generation as a part of culture.

Differentiation based on gender seems to be a universal feature of the human society. Men have been traditionally considered the "*providers*" for the family, while women have been expected to assume almost every responsibility, to take care of the child and to attend to household duties. Most of the cultures view many forms of Work as "*women's work* " or "*men's work*" using as a basis sexual stereotypes. A person's gender becomes a means for categorising people into "*males*" or "*females*" and is given a distinct social significance.

Different Cultural Expectations about Males and Females

In almost all societies different cultural expectations have been woven around male-female differences. The following explanation highlights such expectations : "*Men should be competitive," women are supposed to be cooperative. Men can be impatient," women must have boundless 'patience. Men may be critical; women should always be accepting and supportive. Men can rush and be hurried," women are always supposed to have time for people, to sit and chat, to weave an effective network of mutual support and empathy. Men are expected to express anger," women should never be angry - at least they should certainly never show it. Men are supposed to gain gratification from the self-recognition of a job well done*."[3] The literary works of great writers, novelists and poets also highlight such cultural expectations about the gender roles of many societies of the past.[4] *It may thus be concluded that much of our behaviour as men and Women is subject to cultural definition*. "*If we are male, our society bends our conduct in one way; if we are female in another: How much of this difference is due to nature, how much due to culture society" This is the question* which the sociologists should explore by means of their studies, surveys and observations.

---

[1] Ian Robertson in Sociology, p. 289.

[2] Linton (1936) as quoted by Wallace and Wallace in Sociology, p. 346.

[3] as quoted by N.J. Smelser in Sociology, (1993), p. 204-205

[4] The following 19th century verse describes the "ideal", masculine and feminine roles in many societies of the past and some in the present: Man for the field and woman for the hearth: Man for the sword and for the needle she : Man with the head and woman with the heart: Man to command and women to obey; All else confusion Alfred Tennyson, from The princess as quoted by David Popenoe, p: 128.

TRADITIONAL BASES OF SEXUAL IDENTITY

Men and women are different, no doubt. But the differences between them are not simple, but complex. As **N.J. Smelser** has pointed out[5] sociologists have developed four important concepts to understand and analyse these differences. These concepts are : (*i*) *biological sex*, (*ii*) *gender identity*, (*iii*) *gender ideals*, and (*iv*) *sex roles*.

1. Biological Sex

On the basis of the *biological factor of sex*, human society is divided into two groups or communities [community of men and community of women] everywhere. Primary physical traits such as reproductive organs, body shape and secondary physical traits such as facial hair, muscular strength, etc., are helpful in making such a division or classification.

2. Gender Identity

The concept of "*gender identity*" refers to our sexual-image. Biological differences between men and women contribute to the development of "gender identity", which refers to the self-concepts of a person being male or female. Human beings learn this gender-identity at a very early age. Generally. a child learns that she is a girl or he is a boy between the ages of **18** months and **3** years.

3. Gender Ideals

The concept of '*gender ideals*' refers to the cultural expectations woven around male and female behaviour. Gender ideals reveal what men and women are supposed to be like in a particular context. For example, in our Indian society, men are expected to be actively engaged in some good job, confident, courageous, responsible, respectful, helpful, and so on. Similarly, women are expected to be very affectionate, tolerant, obedient, loyal, dutiful, hospitable, service minded, loving, more committed to family than to their personal career, and so on. These ideals, are of course, fast changing.

4. Sex Roles

The concept of '*sex roles*' which represents the fourth component of sexual identity, includes division of labour, rights and responsibilities according to sex. During the early days sex roles were clearly laid down. For example, men went out of their homes and worked for wages to support their family members. On the contrary, women confined themselves to homes, worked in them, looked after children and other domestic affairs. But today, like gender ideals, sex roles are also undergoing fast transformation.

Harmony Between These Four Components

As **N.J. Smelser** points out, the four components mentioned above usually function in a harmonious manner. ***For example***, a biological female feels like a Woman and her feelings may be in tune with the cultural definition of womanhood. The woman in this context, is prepared to take on the roles and responsibilities that have been traditionally associated with her sex. It is to be noted that this assumption may not hold true always. Sometimes, peoples' biological sex may not agree with their gender identity.

It is also possible that a person's gender identity may not often fit the gender ideal. An individual may feel comfortable as a biological male but uncomfortable behaving according to cultural expectations for men. Further. an individual's sex role [that is, his rights and responsibilities] may not often match the society's gender ideals. ***For example***, in modem times, it is not uncommon to find women working as police officers, military personnel, bus conductors, auto rickshaw drivers, firefighters, and so on. These sex roles do not fit traditional gender ideals.

ACTUAL DIFFERENCES BETWEEN THE SEXES

What are the real differences between the sexes ? This is a pertinent question in our discussion of male-female relations. An attempt to find an answer to this question gives rise to many other questions such as the following: *Are there any inborn differences between the sexes ? Are they really important ? Are sex roles completely flexible? Are there some natural and genetically determined qualities which do not permit any change of sex roles?*

In order to answer these questions in a satisfactory manner, sociologists have taken the help of other sciences by drawing relevant evidences from them. Sociologists, thus have drawn the evidences from biology which tells us about the physical and physiological differences between males and females; psychology which provides us information about the personality differences between the sexes; and anthropology, which is of great help in knowing the variations in sex roles that exist among the many cultures of the world. Let us go into greater details of these three kinds of evidences.

---

[5] N.J. Smelser in Sociology, p: 205

1. Biological Evidence

From the biological point of view, men and women differ in three respects, that is, (*a*) *anatomically,* (*b*) *genetically*, and (*c*) *hormonally*

(a) Anatomical differences: These differences are apparent in the physical structure arcl appearance of the sexes. Anatomical differences found in the reproductive systems of men and women are the most important ones. Men develop testes and women ovaries and these are called *primary sex characteristics*. Due to the impact of the hormones at puberty they develop *secondary sex characteristics* such as breasts and body hair in females, deeper voice, facial and body hair in men.

As a result of these anatomical differences, it is women who become pregnant and suckle children. This is a biological responsibility that places a number of restrictions on the social and economic activities of women. On the contrary, men are free from these restrictions. Other anatomical differences such as height, weight, amount of body hair, distribution of body fat, and musculature are socially important for they help others to recognise the sex of an individual. These characteristics also reveal that men are physically more powerful than women. This greater strength helps man to dominate women by force. This fact also helps to explain why in society men have political status superior to women.

(b) Genetic differences: Due to the genetic differences, individuals belonging to two sexes are born. Differences in the sexes are based on differences in the make up of their sex chromosomes. it is well known that females have two similar chromosomes [**x x**], while males have two different chromosomes [**x y**]. Scientists are still busy with their studies to know whether this difference affects the personalities or abilities of the sexes, But this difference is found to be having its biological effects. The males which lack the second **x** chromosomes are found to be weaker in some respects. Male infants are more likely than females to be still born or malformed. Over thirty hereditary disorders [such as haemophilia and webbing of the toes] are found only in men. Further, the death rate of men is found to be higher than that of women. Women are regarded as more resistant than men to most diseases and seem to have a greater tolerance for pain and malnutrition.

(c) The hormonal differences: A hormone is a chemical substance that is secreted by glands in the body, and it is known that hormones can influence both physical development and certain forms of behaviour. Both men and women have "*male*" as well as "*female*" hormones; but the proportion of '*male hormone*' is greater in men and the proportion of "*female hormone*"- is greater in women. Whether the hormones completely determine the characteristic male and female behaviour is a question still debated. Experiments conducted at the level of animals by means of injecting male hormones in females have revealed that hormones to a very great extent influence their behavioural pattern. But, at the level of human beings, culture and socialisation play a vital role in influencing behaviour. The natural and social scientists are of the opinion today that hormonal differences probably do have some influence on the behaviour of men and women but this influence is a minor one.

2. Psychological Evidence

The behavioural and personality patterns of adult men and women are clearly different. The question is whether these differences are inborn or learnt ? To find out a satisfactory answer to this question psychologists have focused much of their research on infants.

A number of studies of young infants has found sex-linked personality differences early in life. It is observed that even in the cradle, male babies are more active than female babies. On the other hand, female babies smile more readily and are more sensitive to warmth and touch than males. These are, however, only general tendencies. In actuality, many male babies show traits that are typical of female babies, and vice versa. 'It remains possible that even these early differences are learned. Children respond in ways depending upon the manner in which they are handled.

Findings of John Money's studies: **John Money** and his associates conducted some studies to find out the impact on the child and his behaviour if he is raised as a member of the opposite sex. *If a child is biologically a boy but is raised as girl, what happens*? If sex roles were determined by biological factors, it should be impossible to socialise a child into the "*wrong*" sex role. John Money's studies have shown that it is possible to raise a child as a member of the opposite sex. His studies have also pointed out that it is possible to do so before the child attains the age of three and after that it may put up some resistance. John Money concludes that the human species is "*psycho sexually neuter at birth*" and that sex roles are independent of biological sex.

3. Anthropological Evidences OR Cross Cultural Evidences

Are sex roles completely determined by inborn differences? If that were to be so, then we would expect the roles of men and women to be much the same in all cultures. On the contrary, if the sex roles vary a great deal from one culture to another, then they must be much more flexible than we have assumed it in the past.

The Classic Study Conducted by Margaret Mead

Anthropologists have reported a number of societies whose sex roles are different from our own. **Margaret Mead's** study [1935] in this field, relating to three New Guinea tribes is worth mentioning here.

1. ***The arapesh tribe :*** In this tribe, Mead found that both men and women conformed to a personality type that we would consider "*feminine*". Individuals of both the sexes are gentle, sober, passive and emotionally very warm. Men and women were believed to have identical sex drives and both were responsible for child care.
2. ***The mundugumor tribe :*** Tribes of this group are cannibalistic. These are head hunting people and they expected women and men to be violent and aggressive. Both men and women act in ways which we would call predominantly "*masculine*". Mundugumor women rarely showed what is known as "*maternal instinct*" common to women everywhere. These women dreaded pregnancy, disliked nursing their children, and were especially hostile towards their own daughters.
3. ***The tchambuli tribe :*** Sex roles in this community differed from the first two tribes. In this tribe, male and female roles are defined in a way that is quite contrary to our modern way. The women were domineering and energetic and wore no ornaments. They were the major economic providers of the family. They managed and did major tasks of the family. The men, on the other hand, are artistic, gossipy, expressive and looked after children.

The study of these communities made Mead conclude that '*gender traits of masculinity and femininity have no necessary connection to biological sex*.[6] Various other studies conducted by other anthropologists also confirmed the conclusion that "*In every culture children systematically socialised into acceptance of the prevailing sex roles.*"[7]

GENDER BASED DIVISION OF LABOUR

Division of labour on the basis of sex has been a universal feature of the human society. Women and men have been assigned different works and responsibilities everywhere. This division of labour is of more rigid and structured type especially in ancient and traditional societies.

Division of Labour in Ancient and Traditional Societies

In most of the traditional societies, child rearing and home maintenance are normally regarded as woman's task, while hunting and fighting are always reserved for man. Sexual division of labour seems to have a biological base especially in simple primitive societies. Thus, men are generally given tasks that require vigorous physical activity such as hunting, fishing in the deep sea, or herding. Women, on the other hand, are assigned tasks that do not require much of physical strength and can be performed close to home. Though this is a typical scene found in most of the societies, there is great cross-cultural variation in the kind of labour that is considered appropriate for men and women.

George P. Murdoek's Comparative Study on the Division of Labour by Sex

American anthropologist **George P. Murdock** once studied [1935] **224** traditional pre-industrial non-literate societies in an effort to discover regularities in the sexual division of labour. "*In these societies warfare, metal working, hunting and trapping, fishing, and trade are predominantly male activities. Cooking, the manufacture and repair of clothing, pottery making, and fire making and tending are predominantly female activities. Agriculture, on the contrary, which includes the preparation, planting, and cultivation of the soil, is an activity shared almost equally by the two sexes.*"[8] *Table No.* 1 [given in the next page] provides a cross-cultural comparison of the division of labour based on sex.

Cross-Cultural Variations in Division of Labour by Sex

Table No. 1 makes it clear that there is great cross-cultural variation in the tasks that are considered appropriate for men and women. In many societies, the division of labour is completely different from that of the one that we find in the modern societies. The general tendency, however, is for man to be responsible for tasks involving strenuous effort or great hardwork and for women to be responsible for tasks that can be performed near the home.

Gender Roles are Not Inborn

The *Table* reveals that the gender roles are not necessarily innate. Further, gender roles are not wholly determined by a society's relationship to its environment. Although all hunting-gathering societies sent men out to hunt While women cared for the home, in early agrarian societies there was a less rigid division of labour.

---

6 Ian Robertson in *Sociology*, p. 292.

7 Barry Bacon, and Child (1957) as quoted by Ian Robertson, p. 292.

8 Robert Bierstedt in *The Social Order* -pp. 377-378.

The table also shows that "*as societies evolve from hunting and gathering to agrarian production and the demands of pregnancy and child-rearing are less limiting, the division of labour by sex becomes more varied, although women tend to specialise in household tasks and men in tasks that take them outside home*" [9]

Influence of Culture on Gender Roles

The cross-cultural study of division of labour by sex makes it evident that gender roles are highly influenced by culture. Male and female roles are not necessarily fixed for all time even though the relationship of earlier societies to their natural environment often required a division of labour by sex. They can and do change as cultures adapt to new environmental and social conditions.

Table: The Division Of Labour by Sex: A Cross - Cultural Comparison

Activity	Number of Societies in Which Activity is Performed By:				
	Men Always	Men Usually	Either Sex Equally	Woman Usually	Women Always
Pursuing sea mammals	34	1	0	0	0
Hunting	166	13	0	0	0
Trapping small animals	128	13	4	1	2
Herding	38	8	4	0	5
Fishing	98	34	19	3	4
Clearing land for agriculture	73	22	17	5	13
Dairy operations	17	4	3	1	13
Preparing and planting saplings	31	23	33	20	37
Erecting and dismatching shelter	14	2	5	6	22
Tending fowl and small animals	21	4	8	1	39
Tending and harvesting crops	10	15	35	39	44
Gathering shellfish	9	4	8	7	35
Making and tending fire	18	6	25	22	62
Bearing burdens	12	6	35	20	57
Preparing drinks and narcotics	20	1	13	8	57
Gathering fruits, berries and nuts	12	3	15	13	63
Gathering fuel	22	1	10	19	89
Preserving meat and fish	8	2	10	14	74
Gathering herbs, roots, seeds, etc.	8	1	11	7	74
Cooking	5	1	9	28	158
Carrying water	7	0	5	7	119
Grinding grain	2	4	5	13	114

Source: George P. Murdock's Study of *Comparative Data on the Division of Labour by Sex* - as quoted by Ian Robertson in his *Sociology*, p. 293. The data in this table from a survey of 224 traditional pre-industrial societies.

Impact of Technology

As a result of advances in technology, the greater strength of males becomes less important, and it makes less sense to maintain the earlier divisions of labour. Infact, *the modern societies have demanded more involvement of women in a broader range of tasks*. This has given rise to a demand that women should not be excluded from access to any roles, including those that are associated with high levels of power and prestige.

SOCIAL CONSEQUENCES OF WOMEN'S EMPLOYMENT IN MODERN SOCIETY

Women are found in a large number in the work force today. The great Industrial Revolution and the consequent industrialisation opened the doors of employment for women. Women started availing themselves of the employment opportunities in almost all the civilised countries including India. Adult women are no longer associated solely with the role of 'homemaker' especially in the urban areas. Millions of women - married and single, with and without children - are

[9] William Kornblum in *Sociology in A Changing* World, p. 328.

working outside the home. A greater proportion of women are seeking and obtaining paid employment more than ever before. In America, for example, more than 55% of adult American women held jobs outside the home, as compared with only 43% in 1970. In India also the percentage of employed women is steadily increasing especially in the urban area.

Provision of employment opportunities for women on wage, salary or other type of remuneration basis outside the family has been a socio-economic development of great importance. Women's increasing involvement in paid labour force has led to a number of social consequences of which the following may be noted.

1. An Increase in the Social Status of Women

In the modern societies, women engaged in a job outside the family and obtaining good salary or income, are more respected than Women Without a gainful job. As far as Women are concerned, their self-esteem and power within the family too should increase as they move outside the home and function as productive wage-earners. Employment of women outside the home helps them become more confident and courageous. It gives scope for them to become career-conscious and inspires them to make accomplishments independent of family roles. It widens their vision and broadens their field of work. Women have now started their search for prestigious positions and occupations. Even though the number of women employed in high prestige-jobs is comparatively less, their overall self- esteem as working women, has increased.

2. A Gain in Power Both Inside and Outside the Family

In terms of power dynamics women clearly gain some degree of power within the family by earning their own incomes. Studies have revealed that when a woman provides sole financial support for her family, employment even in a low-status occupation has a positive effect on her self-esteem. During the recent years, women are also availing higher education which has increased their eligibility to get into high-level jobs and even power positions in economic pursuits. Though relatively in a smaller number, women are becoming bank managers, company directors, executive engineers, police officers, principals, judges, and so on. This situation has helped them gain more power even outside the family.

3. Increasing Instances of Divorces and Separations

Gainful job outside the family has boosted the morale of women. Thus, for married women income from employment can be an effective security in case of separation or divorce. The separated and the divorced women can lead economically a comfortable living provided they have a gainful job. Studies have revealed that in the Western societies, the rate of divorce is relatively higher at the level of employed women than at the level of women without jobs. In the past, many fulltime home-makers or housewives had little confidence in their ability to make a living. As a result, some remained in unsatisfying marriages, thinking that they had no alternative way to survive. This is still the case for a considerable number of women in most of the developing countries of the world. India is also not an exception.

WOMEN TO BEAR THE BRUNT OF "DOUBLE BURDEN"

As women become increasingly involved in employment outside the home, men will have an opportunity to become more involved in the care and socialisation of children. But, in actuality, as many studies have revealed, men find little time to devote for either socialisation of children or to share the family burden of their wives. For example, (*i*) **Freda Rebelsky and Cheryl Hanks**' [1973] studies conducted in the U.S.A. have revealed that "The average period of verbal interactions between father and baby was only 38 seconds per day." (*ii*) Psychologist **Wade Mackey** conducted in 1987 a cross-cultural study of 17 societies -including those in Morocco, Hongkong, Ireland, and Mexico and found that the limited father-child interactions were typical of all the societies surveyed.[10]

Many other studies[11] too confirmed the same result as mentioned above. Thus, **Longway** (1981) concluded : "*It remains difficult for men in two-parent households to deviate from their traditional occupational roles in order to become more involved in child rearing*. "These studies only reveal that employed women have been largely unable to get their husbands to assume a greater role in needed homemaking duties, including child care. As a result, increasing number of wives become subject to a "*double burden*" - long work weeks both at home and outside the home. Thus, Women's growing participation in the paid labour force is not bringing them greater freedom and power as it was expected.

---

[10] Richard Schaefer's *Sociology*, pp. 286-287.

[11] The New York State Study : Karthryn Walker and Margaret Woods (1976) studied 1296 dual-career families in New York State and found that, on an average, wives account for about 70 percent of the total family time spent on housework. Husbands provide about 15 percent, and children about 15 percent. In terms of the actual time involved. the full-time homemaker spends a minimum of 40 hours per week on housework, whereas the wife who works for wages spends a minimum of 30 hours each week." – Richard Schaefar, pp. 287.

5. Consequences on Society

Employment of women outside the family is to be considered as a phenomenon of no less significance. It has influenced a wide range of societal activities.

(*i*) It has hastened the emergence of *child-care facilities* on a very wide scale. As a result, number of baby-sitting centres, kindergartens, creches, '*anganawadis*', '*balawadis*', etc., have come in.

(*ii*) It has led to the *rise of fast food chains in society*. Since many women, especially in urban areas, are no longer at home and cooking during the day time, the fast food producing industry received a great fillip.

(*iii*) Employment of women has been a big boon to many of the entrepreneurs for *female labour is found to be much cheaper* Easy availability of female labour has also led to the *exploitation and harassment of women*.

(*iv*) Pre-occupation of women with jobs outside the family has its *adverse consequences on the maintenance and continuation of the family traditions and religious customs*. Employed parents, are no longer able to give cultural training to their children in family traditions and religious practices.

(*v*) Employment of women outside the family has contributed much to the *economic betterment of the family as such*. At the same time, the inability of employed women to spare enough time for their children has often resulted in *emotional and psychic problems*.

In conclusion, it could be said that an ever increasing number of women are entering the world of employment. The processes of modernisation, industrialisation, urbanisation and universalisation of education have provided new opportunities for women to earn wealth as wage-earners, salaried professionals and individual entrepreneurs. This new trend has added greater momentum to the processes of social change and social mobility which have been taking place in the society.

ARE WOMEN EXCEPTIONALLY DELICATE AND WEAK?

The belief that women represent the weaker sex has been there since a long time. The belief continues even today in the modern societies. Since they are considered weak, they are usually not permitted to undertake certain strenuous tasks such as–carrying heavy weight, working in deep mines and under the sea, driving heavy vehicles, working in armies as soldiers, and so on. There have been laws in many countries restricting women from taking up some of these professions. The USA has laws restricting the amount of weight a woman may carry at work. In India also there are laws preventing women from taking up deep mining, driving heavy trucks, and so on.

Contrary to the prevailing above mentioned beliefs and practices in the modem civilised world, the bearing of heavy burdens is often considered a woman's job in several traditional societies. For example, in most of the sub-Saharan Africa, labouring in agricultural field is considered unsuitable for a man's talents. In these regions, husbands do not work in the fields but travel on horseback while their wives walk on foot bearing all burden on their heads. In several traditional societies, men are entitled to beat their wives, deny food for some time and drive them away from the house if they displease them or disobey their order. In modem societies, on the contrary, such a behaviour would be regarded as uncivilised and brutish.

In the western world, the concept that the female is a delicate creature and requires protection and assistance, was developed particularly among the upper-classes in the 12th century Europe. This concept has persisted in various forms ever since. Traces of this medieval concept or belief are still found, especially in the male practice of taking of hats, giving up seats, and opening doors for females and so on.

In the Indian context, though women enjoyed relatively equal status on par with men, their status started declining continuously from the time of *Puranas* and *Dharmashastras* and the trend continued throughout the medieval period. Women were required to be protected and taken care of especially due to foreign attacks on India. The incessant foreign invasions that were taking place in India further strengthened the views of *shastrakara* **Manu** who had said that "*women must be carefully guarded at all stages in their lives.*" Since then, the view that women represent the weaker sex and require protection, has continued to prevail.

Attempt to Equalise Sex Roles

In most of the civilised societies of the world the general belief that males are relatively aggressive and dominant, while females are weak and submissive, continues to prevail. Only in the socialist countries of Eastern Europe and Asia some formal attempts have been made to equalise the statuses of men and women. In spite of these attempts, sex roles in these societies, however, are not very different from the rest of the societies. In the soviet Russia, women are encouraged to take up independent careers and they have entered many professions which were previously dominated by men. About **3/4** of Soviet doctors are women. But their entry into this profession in a large number has led to the decline in the status of the doctors for they earn less than **2/3** of the salaries of skilled non-professionals. About 42% of the Soviet Scientists are women. But in the 204 members of the prestigious Soviet Academy of Scientists, there are only **2** female members.

Further, high political positions are very much a male prerogative, and the Soviet woman still has the main responsibility of house work.[12]

In conclusion, it could be said that male-dominance is the norm everywhere, although there are many societies whose sex-role arrangements are unlike our own. It is also observable that sex-roles like any other learnt behaviour, are highly flexible it seems unlikely to equalise the male-female roles by means of legislations. Societies may struggle to minimise the difference between male-female roles but establishing absolute equality between the two is almost an impossibility.

SOCIALISATION INTO SEX ROLES OR SOCIAL CONSTRUCTION OF GENDER

In modern societies, gender and age interact to determine the roles open to a person throughout life. Before puberty, boys and girls everywhere normally tend to associate in sex-segregated peer groups. Due to the influence of different role-behaviours that they observe in their own home and in the social environment around them, boys and girls come to know about the type of behaviour expected of them. Accordingly, girls spend more of their time playing domestic roles than boys do. Meanwhile, boys tend to play outside the home more than girls do. These patterns are changing at different rates in different social classes. Even now, these patterns continue to be the accepted norms of behaviour. They have important social consequences also. It is through socialisation that men and women come to know about their *gender roles*, - that is, "*feminine roles*", and "*masculine roles*".

Socialisation and the Gender Roles

Sex roles are not inborn, but learnt. Sex roles are learnt in the course of the socialisation process like any other roles. A major goal of socialisation is to teach people to behave appropriately and to define themselves in ways which are consistent with their statuses. If their status is male, they will be trained for masculine behaviour, and if their status is female, they will be trained for feminine behaviour. Thus, the basic patterns of behaviour expected of the sexes are learnt in the family environment very early in life. They are further strengthened in the schools, in peer groups, through the mass media, and in many other specific agencies, ranging from sports teams to work places. Let us consider the role of the family, the schools, and the media in the sex-role socialisation of new born individuals.

1. The Family and Family Influence

Parents and family are, the most important people who constitute the dominant influence in shaping gender identity. Children are given a gender label from the beginning and are treated according to the label. As the child grows, gender identity is established through four processes namely; (*i*) *moulding or reinforcement*, (*ii*) *opportunities*, (*iii*) *role modelling*, and (*iv*) *explicit verbal instruction*.

(*i*) ***Reinforcement or moulding :*** Parents at home treat their children differently depending on their sex. Boys are normally given more freedom while girls are treated protectively. Girls are expected to be mild, gentle, pleasing, shy and not very competitive. Boys are given much more rigorous sex-role training. Any "*effeminate*" behaviour on the part of the boy is highly discouraged, and if such tendencies continue they are regarded as "*psychological disturbances*." As a result of this training, children learn their sex roles quickly and effectively.

(*ii*) ***Opportunities :*** Boys and girls in the family are provided with different opportunities. Although girls may sometimes wear jeans, boys are not allowed to wear female dresses such as skirts, sarees, or *chudidhar*. From this point of view the masculine role seems to be more restrictive than the feminine. Similarly, girls are less likely to get toy guns, trucks, trains, or bats and balls. Boys are less likely to receive dolls and carriages. Girls are permitted to wear their mothers' old jewellery, dresses and high-heeled shoes, snow, powder, lipstick, nail polish, and so on. Male children are strongly discouraged by their own mothers to use or play with such things. Boys, mostly go along with the 'masculine' way. They often play with their fathers' things such as - pens, diaries, calculators, torches, keybunch, documents, cooling glass, etc. The boys are expected to help their fathers, while the daughters are expected to be of some help to the mothers in the kitchen.

(*iii*) ***Role modelling :*** Role modelling is a major mechanism of gender socialisation. Children come to know of their masculine and feminine roles much before they realise the sexual basis for gender labelling. By the age of three, nearly all children know whether they are male or female, and by the age of four, they have very definite ideas of what masculinity and femininity should involve. Hence, they accept their categorisation as 'a boy or girl. A male child usually identifies with his father and a female child usually wants to be like her mother. As a result, boys become interested in tools, vehicles, and sports, and they try to be assertive and exhibit more courageous behaviour. Girls, on the contrary, are interested in fashionable dresses, hairstyles, jewels, make-up and cooking. They develop

[12] Ian Robertson's *Sociology*, pp. 294

the passive, submissive, mild and gentle side of their personalities. Role modelling is more effective when the child has a strong and warm relationship with the role model.

(iv) ***Explicit verbal instruction :*** Sometimes, in the process of socialisation into gender roles the child is often told that certain behaviour is, or is not, a pan of the gender role : "*Boys are stronger than girls* ", "*Ladies first, gents next*", "*Girls make the house beautiful* "*Boys do not cry like girls* ", "*Girls are supposed to wear modest dresses*." "*Girls are not supposed to play rough like boys do.* " Providing different opportunities is probably more important than these verbal instructions. Verbal instructions too have their importance particularly when the individual has not already begun to identify with the proper role model

2. The Schools

In the modem societies, schools constitute an important agent of gender socialisation. The school continues the sex roles training for the children which the family has already begun. The school continues the lesson by teaching boys and girls appropriate behaviour in the wider outside world.

(a) ***Textbooks :*** Textbooks are a major means through which students come to know about the world outside their families and classrooms. Textbooks, of course, do not directly address the children as to how they should behave as boys and girls. These text books comment on gender roles through the characters that figure in the lessons. Female and male characters in the lessons provide models for young people who are forming self-identities.

School textbooks also encourage acceptance of the traditional sex roles. Several recent studies have shown that the literature for children, from pre-school onwards, suggests as to how children and adults as belonging to male or female sex, should behave.[13]

Examples : (*i*) "In a study of picture books that had been awarded as prizes for "*excellence*" by the "*American Library Association*", **Lenore Weitzman** and her associates (1972) found that one third of the books had no female characters at all. In the total sample of books, males outnumbered females in a ratio of **11: 1**... The ratio of titles featuring males and females was **8:3**. Throughout the books boys were presented as active and girls as passive ".

(*ii*) In another study of school textbooks, **Marjorie U'Ren** (1971) found that only **15%** of the illustrations that featured people, included women. As she points out, "*we tend to forget the simple fact that the female sex is half the human species, that women are not merely a ladies' auxiliary to the human species*" - [**Ian Robertson** - Page: 305.] **U'Ren** *summarises school book gender differentiation with regard to personalities. "The emphasis on masculine strength extends beyond physical qualities. Males of all ages are pictured as having greater mental perseverance and moral strength than females. Not only are females more often described as lazy and incapable of independent thinking or direct action, but they are also shown as giving up more easily They collapse into tears, they betray secrets, they are more likely to act upon petty or selfish motives.*"[14]

(b) ***Leisure reading :*** What the children read during their leisure time also influences their gender role assumptions. Children's literature everywhere has been found to contain stereotypic behaviour which describes traditional male and female gender roles. Normally, in all typical social stories the father of a family is pictured as a person who goes out for work while the mother who does not go out for work confines herself to the home and mostly to the kitchen work. Again the girls in the family are depicted as younger females assisting their mother to carry on household drudgery while the boys are presented as persons taking part in adventurous activities. **Florence Howe** (1971) has strongly criticised this type of a domesticated, home-loving mother.[15]

(c) ***Course segregation :*** Academic courses and sports activities which the students opt for in schools are distinctly gender -'segregated. Physical education classes have traditionally been segregated by gender. Certain classes such as sewing, embroidery, home science, are meant for girls. Courses such as carpentry, plumbing, garage work, etc., are rarely chosen by females. Many sports such as - wrestling, football, field hockey, cricket, volleyball, etc., are restricted to male sex.

3. The Mass Media

As it is well-known, the mass-media which includes films, books, magazines, comics, television,' radio, and records -

---

[13] It is quite interesting to note that many studies especially in America, have pointed out that textbook materials are not prepared in a balanced manner for they are prejudiced against 'females.

[14] Wallace and Wallace, p. 359-360.

[15] According to Florence Howe, this type of presentation of American family even at the fag end of the 20th century is totally inaccurate. As she says, in the American context, "nine out of ten married women work outside the home at some point in their lives and over n third of mothers with children are currently at work" - Ian Robertson, p. 305.

are a powerful agency for socialisation. Although some media address factual matters, most material selected is presented for entertainment. What is transmitted, therefore, is not a realistic portrayal but an exaggerated version of social life. Gender images are often caricatures of either the audience's or the sponsor's ideal people. Thus, an audience's ideal male is not just brave he is ridiculously brave; he is not just an honest idealist but is prepared to risk his life to pose himself to be so; Further, he is incredibly good-looking and lucky. The female ideal is a superhuman who is beautiful, tolerant but cunning and properly fulfils the male's adolescent sex fantasies.

Advertising : Advertisers normally present the images of men and women in such a manner so as to impress the intended consumers. Sponsors may also portray the genders in ways which are appealing to the opposite sex. The image of women is presented variously and sometimes vulgarly in magazines and television advertising. Women, for example, are either portrayed as sex objects in an attempt to market various products to men, or as domesticated housewives, in order to market home maintenance products to women. Advertisers have found out one of the most effective devices of reaching a male audience and that is to associate their product with a seductively smiling female. The sexuality of women is thus exploited. Women writers have strongly criticised this type of exploitation of female gender for commercial purposes.[16] "*Advertising legitimizes the ideal, stereotyped roles of woman as a temptress, wife, mother, and sex object, and portrays women as less intelligent and more dependent than men. It makes women believe that their chief role is to please men and that their fulfilment will be as wives, mothers, and homemakers. It makes women feel unfeminine if they. are not pretty enough and guilty if they do not spend most of their time in desperate attempts to imitate gourmet cooks It makes women believe that their own lives, talents, and interests ought to be secondary to the needs of their husbands*."[17] What is important is that the media do not transmit a unified image of male and female gender roles. Often one sees traditional roles, frequently one witnesses fantasy roles and sometimes one sees the modern egalitarian roles.

4. ROLE OF CULTURE

Our definitions of appropriate gender role behaviour are influenced by our culture also. Socially accepted ideas of how men and women should behave are circulated among people in different ways. Language that we speak and the institutions through which we work also influence the circulation of such ideas.

(a) ***Rule of language :*** Differences between the sexes are reflected through language. We cannot speak of the other person without making reference to the other person's gender. In fact, in every discussion of a person, gender is revealed, but not age, race, ethnic background, religion, or social status. This constant reminder of who is male and who is female contributes to gender socialisation. The use of language is one means by which people learn what males and females should not be. Name-calling provides strong social control.

(b) ***Influence of interaction in institutions on gender socialisatian*** : Men and women's participation in institutions too has its influence on gender socialisation. In most of the societies today women play very minor role in the major social institutions such as-government, religion, economy legal institution, and to a certain extent, in education. In many societies, Women voters outnumber men, but their direct participation in political institutions is far from satisfactory. The proportion of female members in religious, legal and political organisations is comparatively low. The number of women in the paid work-force area is slowly increasing but not their leadership positions in the areas such as government, politics, industry, business, education, religion, etc. Women still constitute a minority in occupying" the positions of formal power and prestige. For example, not a single woman has assumed the office of the President of America or the President of India. In neither of these countries, has a woman assumed the office of the Chief Justice of the Supreme Court. Male and female children observe this and assume future roles for themselves.

As far as the institution of family is concerned, women are still socially central and dominant. They only organise and take lead in most of the family activities . Women usually look alter children, cook, wash clothes, clean or supervise the cleaning. "*In order to come to parity with men in the other institutions, women must achieve cooperation within the family that will free their energies to work elsewhere if they choose to do so.* "[18]

It is clear from the above, that through many different agents people are socialised into gender roles. Families give the earliest reinforcement for acting appropriately according to one's gender, and the environment continues to teach what is

---

[16] Lucy Komisnar's (1971) Comments on Advertising.

[17] As quoted by Ian Robertson, p. 306

[18] Wallace and Wallace, p. 366.

acceptable and what is not for men and for women. Gender roles are demonstrated and reinforced in almost every aspect of one's social life.

THEORIES OF SEX-ROLE DIFFERENTIATION: A SOCIOLOGICAL ANALYSIS OR STRATIFICATION BY GENDER

It is a universally observed fact that males and females are constantly assigned two different social roles. As **N.J. Smelser** [Page : 220] points out "There are '*boy*' activities and '*girl*' activities, '*man's* work and *woman's*' work, behaviour that is *just like a man*' or '*just like a woman*'. "Nowhere they are treated alike or given similar status, responsibilities and positions. At the same time, the available evidences have made it clear that "*anatomy is not destiny*". It means, the unalterable biological factor of sex difference cannot satisfactorily explain the sex-role differentiation. Human beings can be socialised into a very wide range of sex roles with their associated gender characteristics.

A sociological analysis of "*sex-roles in society*" always leads to a question - as to why sex-role differentiation is observed in society and how it could be explained best. Sociologists have turned to all the major theoretical perspectives to understand how and why social distinctions between males and females are established. Each approach focuses on culture, rather than biology as the principle cause of gender differences. But, in other respects, there are wide disagreements between advocates of these sociological perspectives.

Arguments of two major sociological perspectives, (*a*) *functionalist perspective*, and (*b*) *conflict perspective*; - relating to sex-role differentiation may be considered here.

(*a*) A Functionalist Theory or Explanation

The functionalist view maintains that the sex role differentiation was highly functional in traditional and pre-industrial societies, for men and women were to play very different roles. It stresses that a society functions more efficiently if there is a division of tasks and responsibilities and if its members are socialised to play specific roles. Though this division of labour need not necessarily take place along the sex lines, it could also be done on the basis of sexual differences. The functionalists also maintain that gender differentiation has contributed to overall social stability.

Are the traditional sex roles still functional in a modem industrial society? **Tacott Parsons** and **Robert Bales**, two functional sociologists have suggested a positive function of sex-role differentia- tion. They have claimed that the modem family needs two adults who will specialise in particular roles. The father assumes the "*instrumental role*", which focuses on the relationship between the family and the outside world. This role is also concerned with job and money-making or income-generating activities. The mother assumes the "*expressive role* " which focuses on relationships within the family. The mother is also responsible for providing the love and support that is needed to hold the family together. This role includes the task of maintenance of harmony and the internal emotional affairs of the family.

The functionalists have thus concluded that "*the male's instrument rule requires that he be dominant and competent; the female 's expressive role requires that she be passive and nurturant. The family unit functions more effectively than it would if the roles were not so sharply defined.*" [**Ian Robertson** - 294.]

Criticisms Against the Functionalist Theory

Functionalist theory has been bitterly criticised. A few of the main points of criticism can be mentioned below.

1. Some sociologists have argued that this theory oversimplifies the complexities of contemporary sex-roles.
2. This theory only defends the status quo relating to the traditional sex roles.
3. Critics have said that the traditional sex roles may have been functional in traditional societies but they make no sense in a diversified modern society. In these societies, the daily activities of men and women are far removed from these primitive origins.
4. The theory is silent about the strains that the traditional roles place on women who want to play an "*instrumental*" role in society, or on men who would prefer to play an "*expressive role*".
5. The theory also says nothing about the dysfunctions to society of preventing half of the population from participating fully in economic life.

(b) A Conflict Theory or Explanation

A functionalist can explain how sex-role inequalities arose, but a conflict analysis may offer a better explanation of why they persist. These theorists do not deny the presence of a differentiation by gender. In fact, they argue that the relationship between males and females has been one of unequal power, with men in a dominant position over women. Previously, men might have become powerful in pre-industrial times because their size, physical strength and freedom from child-bearing duties allowed them to dominate women physically. But, in present day societies, such considerations are not that important. Yet, cultural beliefs about the sexes are now long established. *Such beliefs support a social structure which places males in controlling positions*.

Conflict theorists always see gender differences *as a reflection of the subjugation of one group (women) by another group (men)*. A few opinions expressed by some of these theorists may be considered here.

Letly Cottin Pogrebin (1981), a feminist author, suggests that the two crucial messages of gender-role stereotypes are that - "*boys are better*" and "*girls are meant to be mothers*". The system in order to maintain male dominance makes arrangements to socialise children to accept traditional gender role divisions as natural and just.

Barbara Bovee Polk [1974], a sociologist, while describing the "*conflicting cultures approach*" to gender differences, observes that "*masculine values have higher status and constitute the dominant and visible culture of the society. They ...... provide the standard for adulthood and normality.*" *According to this view, "women are oppressed because they constitute an alternative subculture which deviates from the prevailing masculine value system* "[19]

Helen Hacker (1951) has argued that women can be regarded as a minority group in society, in much the same as racial or other minorities that suffer from discrimination. She draws a number of convincing comparisons between the situation of women and the situation of Blacks in America. She has also shown that both groups are at a disadvantage as a result of a status ascribed to them on the unalterable grounds of sex or race.

Randall Collins (1971), yet another conflict theorist, argues that sexual inequalities, like any other structure, social inequality, are based on a conflict of interests between the dominant and subordinate group. Because of the sexual inequalities, women who constitute the lower-status group, are not able to make use of their best talents. This naturally gives a chance to the males who constitute the superior status group, to make use of the best in them. Men may not hatch any deliberate conspiracy to take this advantage. It only means that the existing arrangements benefit the dominant group and hence it may not get any motivation to change them "*Since the cultural arrangements of any society always reflect the interests of the dominant group, sex roles continue to reinforce the pattern of male dominance.*"[20]

Conclusion

Each of these theories has its own argument but none of them explains every kind of sex-role differentiation. At the same time, these two theories are not found to be contradictory always, especially on the issue of sex roles. There are functional theorists who would also accept that traditional sex roles are becoming dysfunctional in the modern world. Similarly, there are conflict theorists who would accept that sex inequalities may have arisen because they were functional then, even if they are no longer functional now. What is more important is that both perspectives agree on one point: *the existing sex-role patterns are primarily social in origin, not biological*.

SEXISM AND ITS CONSEQUENCES

The Concept of Sexism

Human societies have various types of inequalities - such as social, economic, racial, ethnic, and so on. Sexual inequality is also one of such inequalities. These inequalities are often justified by one or the other kind of ideology. For example, *racisms*[21] is an ideology which helps the dominant race to impose its will on the weaker ones. The ideology of racism is often used by the Whites to victimise the Blacks. Similarly, ***sexism*** is an ideology which is used by men to victimise women.

- "*Sexism is the ideology that one sex is superior to the other The term is generally used to refer to male prejudice and discrimination against women.* " - **Richard Schaefer**[22]
- Sexism refers to "*any attitudes and actions which overtly or covertly discriminate against women or men on the grounds of their sex or gender* " - ***Collins Dictionary of Sociology***[23]

Sexism is thus unfair discrimination on the basis of sex. In sexism, one sex is discriminated against another [normally men discriminating against women], but it is not always done openly and in the presence of all. Many a time, it is practised secretly, silently and in an undeclared manner.

---

[19] Richard T. Schaefer in *Sociology*, p. 277.

[20] Ian Robertson, p. 296.

[21] Racism : *Racism is a phenomenon in which a group that is seen as inferior or different is exploited and oppressed by a dominant group.* Blauner

[22] Richard Schaefer in *Sociology* – International Edition, p. 280.

[23] Collins Dictionary of Sociology, p. 589.

Sexism in modern societies is reflected in attitudes that reinforce the sub-ordinated status of Women. It is an ideology that justifies prejudice or discrimination based on sex. It results in the channeling of women into statuses considered appropriate for women and their 'exclusion from statuses considered appropriate for men. Sexist attitudes also tend to "objectify" women, which means they treat women as objects of sex. They do not consider women as individuals worthy of a full measure of respect and equal treatment in social institutions.

Institutional Discrimination and Sexism

Institutional discrimination refers to the "denial of opportunities and equal rights to individuals or groups which result from the normal operations of a society."[24] In the same way, it could be said that women suffer from both individual acts of sexism and from institutional sexism.

It is quite known that in almost all the modern civilised countries, particular men are prejudiced in their treatment of women. Even the major institutions of our society such as - *armed forces, large business establishments, police force, courts, the media, transport system, heavy industries*, etc., are controlled by men. These institutions, in their 'normal' day-to-day operations, often discriminate against women and perpetuate sexism. In the Indian context also, there are a number of instances in which helpless women who go to police station seeking justice, are often cheated there. The media continue to represent women even today in a vulgar manner.

Why is There Sexism

Why is sexism practised ? Why do males, and male-dominated institutions discriminate against women ? Questions like these naturally arise in any discussion of sexism. **Barbara Bovee Polk** [1974] has stated that men in their own interest to maintain power and privilege over women, are practising sex differentiation. It is, indeed, a power game in which men want to establish their supremacy over women. **B.B. Polk** writes : "*power over women in personal relationships gives men what they want, whether that be sex, smiles, chores, admiration, increased leisure, or control itself Men occupy and actively exclude women from positions of economic and political power in society These positions give men a heavily disproportionate share of the rewards of society, especially economic rewards*."[25]

CONSEQUENCES OF SEXISM

(a) consequences of Sexism

(i) ***The talents of women go unutilised*** : The practice of 'sexism 'has made society pay a heavy economic and psychological price for it. Due to the justification of the ideology of sexism and its practice, the society is not in a position to make use of the talents of half of its population, that is, female population.

(ii) ***Provision of very limited opportunities for women*** : Sexism places serious limitations on the options and opportunities for women, because of these limitations women are not able to assume many of the responsibilities and statuses even though they have the needed capacities and qualifications. Men on the contrary, do not suffer from these limitations. **Sandra** and **Daryl Bem's** [1970] views are worth mentioning here: " ...... *when a boy is born, it is difficult to predict what he will be doing twenty-five years later. We cannot say, whether he will be an artist or a doctor or a college professor, because he will be permitted to develop and fulfil his own identity. But if the newborn child is a girl, we can predict with almost complete certainty how she will be spending her time twenty-five years later'. Her individuality does not have to be considered," it is irrelevant*."[26]

COSTS OF THE PRACTICE OF SEXISM

1. Economic Costs of Sexism

In comparison with men, the economic costs to women are greater. Even though women have equal qualifications on par with men, in many business establishments they are paid less than what men in the same profession get. In fact, there are legislations such as "*The Equal Remuneration Act, 1976*." [passed in India] which remove wage discrimination between male and female workers. But in actuality, these legislations remain in majority of the instances as dead letters. Studies have proved that families that rely on female breadwinners are found to be poorer than the ones which have male breadwinners.

Any society that ascribes low status to some of its members on such arbitrary grounds as race, caste, or sex is artificially restricting the economic contribution of part of the population. To be fully efficient, a modem industrial economy must allow social mobility on the grounds of merit, and not restrict it on the grounds of an irrational ascribed status.

---

[24] Richard T. Schaefer in Sociology, p. 280.

[25] Barbara Bovee Polk as quoted by Richard Schaefer in Sociology, p. 280.

[26] Sandra and Daryl Bern as quoted by Ian Robertson in "Sociology", p. 306.

2. The Psychological Costs of Sexism

(a) Women being treated as thoughtless objects and not subjects **:** Sexism involves psychological costs also for women. Unlike other species, human beings are said to possess greater creative ability, capacity to act on and shape the external environment. But in reality. this basic human experience is largely restricted to men only. Women experience it only second hand, that is, through their supportive role of the men who act, and shape the world. Women's experience becomes passive rather than active. More than that, they tend to be treated as thoughtless objects and not subjects in the social environment.

(b) Pressures of role-conflicts for women **:** Since women are to bear the brunt of mother- hood, they are forced to forego many educational, political, cultural and economic opportunities, and are made to accept the feminine ideal - *a thing of beauty, and perfect housewife*. If they accept these stereotypes or expectations they must give up the idea of exploring their talents. If they dare to reject them, then they risk severe role-conflicts. They may even be accused of being "*unfeminine.*"

(c) The challenges of ageing specially haunt women **:** Added to the role-conflicts, women have yet another psychological problem. The female self-concept depends much on physical appearance and a motherhood role. The process of ageing disturbs this self-concept. Many women face this process with distaste and even shame. On the contrary, growing old is not a big trial for men. A man in his forties and fifties may still hope to attract younger women. His job also helps him to obtain continuous source of identity that is denied to a mother when her children mature and leave home. Women especially ir1 the Western context, may find the last 2/3 of their lives something of a challenge as their youth and their children are slowly lost to them.

(d) Strains and pressure experienced by men as a result of the practice of sexism **:** Due to the vast socio-economic and technological changes, the male role is undergoing heavy stresses and strains. The available data especially regarding the western society, cautions about the outcome of these **strains**. Some of the alarming facts about these outcomes[27] are mentioned below:

(*i*) *The available data have revealed that men are* ***5*** *times more likely than women to commit suicide*;

(*ii*) *Men are* ***3*** *times more likely to suffer from severe mental disorders.*

(*iii*) *Men are* ***14*** *times more likely to become alcoholics and the majority of narcotic addicts are found to be males.*

(*iv*) *Men are likely to suffer more than women from all stress-related diseases such as ulcers, asthama, hypertension, and heart disease.*

(*v*) *Men commit* ***8*** *times as many murders as women do and are also responsible for* ***95%*** *of violent crimes.*

(*vi*) *It is generally known that men are far more frequently involved in acts of violence than women.*

(*e*) ***The costs of emotionally insensitive roles*** **:** Men often find it embarrassing to reveal or show too much of affection for other men. They are unprepared for the emotional closeness that is increasingly expected of a lover or husband. Their frequent assumption that women are in some ways inferior makes truly meaningful relationships with women very difficult for them. As a result, many men are virtually incapable of showing tenderness to the opposite sex. Some others, play a different role treating females as commodities and avoiding personal involvement with them, and the main emphasis is on sexually manipulating women. "*The male's nurturant potential as a husband and father is undermined by his continual need to strive, compete, and achieve.*"[28]

WOMEN'S LIBERATION MOVEMENT OR FEMINIST MOVEMENT

The Concept of Feminism or Women's Liberation

Men and women are born equal and they should always be treated so. There should be no sexual discrimination. Treating women as inferior especially to men and considering them individuals of the "*second sex*", is not fair. When one speaks of women's duties, one should show equal respect to women's rights. Providing equal rights, opportunities and statuses to women on par with men is essential and morally mandatory. A powerful advocacy and justification of views such as these, is known as "*feminism*". A social movement launched in support of these views under the leadership of women, can be regarded as '*feminist movement*' or '*women's movement*', or '*women's liberation movement*' [and briefly as '*women's lib movement*'.]

Definition of 'Feminism' or 'Feminist Movement'

(*i*) **N. abercrombie :** "*Feminism is a doctrine suggesting that women are systematically disadvantaged in modern society and advocating equal opportunities for men and women.*"

(*ii*) **The New Encyclopaedia Britannica [Vol. 12. Page: 733] :** "*Women's liberation movement also called feminist movement refers to a social movement that seeks equal rights for women, giving them equal status with men and freedom to decide their own careers and life-partners.*"

---

[27]Ian Robertson, pp. 306 - 307.

[28]Ian Robertson, p. 307.

(*iii*) **Collins Dictionary of Sociology :** *Feminism refers to "a holistic theory concerned with the nature of woman's global oppression and subordination to men."*

- Feminism is also referred to as "*a sociopolitical theory and practice which aims to free all women from male supremacy and exploitation.*"

Feminist Movement Not A Powerful Social Movement as Yet

The feminist movement of the Western origin, generally has followed the spread of the Industrial Revolution and the associated breakdown of traditional norms and the attainment of economic independence by women. Although feminist movements existed much earlier in America, [that is, in 1850s referred to as the *first phase of the movement*] they lost most of their impetus after the voting right was granted to Women. "*In the West today, feminism having achieved its original objectives, has become more of a psychological state - a constellation of certain attitudes held by individual women than a social movement. It remains a social movement in its traditional form in certain currently industrialising nations, particularly those in which women have traditionally held a subordinate position.*"[29]

A GLANCE OF THE GROWTH OF FEMINISM

The First Wave of Feminism

Feminism as a social movement took its origins in the 18th century England which sought to achieve equality between the sexes by extension of rights to women. In the 1890s, radical women and men with liberal outlook campaigned for votes for women and Women's access to education and professions. After the achievement of the voting rights [in 1920 in the USA and 1928 in England] the vigour of the movement was lost. Feminists then devoted much of their attention to assert their objective of equal rights with men in the public sphere, and to enhance their position in the private sphere of the family. The development is referred to as "*the first wave*" in the feminist movement.

The Second Wave of Feminism

The second wave "of feminism emerged in the 1960: - 1970s onwards has many different strands. This has persisted as a social movement into the present. The structured inequality of the sexes, [which refers to the non-biological differences of gender, that is, notions of "*masculinity*" and '*femininity*" so long taken for granted is now being vigorously challenged. What was once regarded as an unalterable fact of life is now seen by millions of people to be nothing more than a cultural product of human society. Although women still occupy a sub-ordinate status in almost all areas of the Western social life, there is a growing consensus that this situation is irrational and unjust.

In the American context, the second wave of feminism was inspired by the publication of the two pioneering books in defence of women's rights : (*i*) **Simone de Beauvoir's** book "*The Second Sex*", and (*ii*) **Betty Friedan's** book "*The Feminine Mystique*". In addition, the general political activism of the 1960s - 1970s [a period in which many American women were working for Black Civil Rights, or against the war in Vietnam] made many women decide that they needed to establish their own movement for "*women's liberation.*"

Further, studies of gender inequality conducted by social scientists like **Alice Rossi** (1964) and **Jessi Bernard** (1964), played a major part in creating an awareness among women. At the same time, another less formal network of women was developing. Women who were experiencing sexism within other social movements - *the anti-war movement, the civil rights movement, the environmental protection movement, and the labour movement* - began to form small "*consciousness-raising*" groups.

Social awareness among women started growing in America especially regarding the gender discrimination. More and more women became aware of sexist attitudes and practices [including attitudes they themselves had accepted through socialisation into traditional gender roles] and began to challenge male dominance. A sense of "sisterhood" [much like "class- consciousness" about which **Karl Marx** had spoken of] became evident. Individual women identified their interests with those of the collectivity of women. Women made it known that they could no longer be happy in "*submissive, and subordinate roles*" [comparable to '*false consciousness*" in Marxist terms].

Women for the first time developed a new sense of group solidarity. As a result, loyalty was fostered within feminist consciousness raising groups. Women started sharing their personal feelings, experiences, and conflicts. Many discovered that their '*individual*' problems were shared by other women. Such awareness of common oppression is a pre-condition for social change. Consciousness or awareness is essential in mobilising a group for collective action.

[29] **William. P. Scott** in "*Dictionary of Sociology*" - Page : 154.

The rising consciousness among the American women gave the feminist movement there a new strength. They became successful in bringing an amendment to the legislation on equal rights; obtaining greater representation for women in government; better facilities for the women of the minority groups; they also became successful in making federal governments to outlaw sex discrimination in education and obtained the right to legal abortions. Feminists have also condemned the forced sterilisation of poor and minority women, sexist advertising, pornography and violence against women within and outside the family.

Creation of New Consciousness among Women by the Feminist Movement

The feminist movement in the West is comparatively strong. A large number of women have now become aware of the sexist attitudes and practices of men. They have protested against the attempt to impose upon them through socialisation either traditional sex roles or male domination. Women, especially in the urban set up, remain no more as individuals but as a united force. A new type of unity and solidarity is slowly growing among them. In many urban centres in the West, the feminist movement still continues to be a big force.

Varied Purposes of the Movement

The feminist movement has not been able to get open support everywhere. In fact, men in some places and women in some others have often opposed it. The very purposes of the movement have also not been the same everywhere. ***For example;*** In some part of **Africa** its purpose may be to fight for the removal of the practice of paying heavy bride-price. In **Middle Asia**, the movement may aim at obtaining greater freedom to women in dress matters. In some other nations, the movement may have to fight against a legal condition imposed on women which insists on obtaining the prior permission of their husbands to fight any legal battle in a Court. In **Western Europe**, these feminists are busy in fighting against the misrepresentation of women in the media. **In industrialising societies**, the leaders of this movement may put forward a demand for paying equal remuneration for equal work. In a nation like **India**, leaders of this movement may have to fight for social freedom and equal social status for women, and the establishment of socio-economic environment free from exploitation of all kinds.

The Feminist Campaign : Five Basic Approaches Proposed by Barbara Bovee Polk

In connection with the feminist campaign for social change, Barbara Bovee Polk (1974) spoke of some basic approaches among which the following may be noted.

1. Attempts by women to resocialize themselves and overcome traditional gender-role conditioning.
2. Efforts to change day-to-day personal interactions with men and other women and to avoid, conventional sexist patterns.
3. Use of the media and academic world to combat sexism and resocialize others to more egalitarian values and greater respect for women.
4. Challenges to male dominance of social institutions through demonstrations, boycotts, lawsuits, and other tactics.
5. Creation of alternative institutions, such as women's self-help medical clinics, publishing houses, and communes.[30]

WOMEN IN THE INDIAN SOCIETY

Nowhere in the history of humanity men and women were treated alike and assigned statuses alike. Women have not been able to lead a life exactly on par with men in spite of their urge for equality. But women in ancient India, particularly during the Vedic period, enjoyed a position which was on the whole much more satisfactory than in the later periods. Women underwent almost a kind of servitude during the Medieval period and their position Went on improving during the British period and after independence. Today, Indian women are almost assigned an equal status with men. All their political, economic, educational and other disabilities have been removed legally.

STATUS OF WOMEN IN INDEPENDENT INDIA

The status of Indian woman has radically changed since independence. Both the structural and cultural changes provided equality of opportunities to women in education, employment and political participation. With the help of these changes exploitation of women, to a great extent, was reduced. More freedom and better orientation were provided to the women's organizations to pursue their interests. Importance of researches, national policies and programmes focused on women came

[30]Barabara Bovee Polk as quoted by Richard T. Schaefer in *Sociology*, p. 290.

to be increasingly realised. Several commissions were appointed by the Central and State governments to study the causes of low status of women and to protect their rights in various fields. The celebration of "***International Women's Year***" in 1975 and the activities of **UNESCO** also created awareness of the problems of women.

The improvement in the status of Indian women especially after independence can be analysed in the light of the major changes that have taken place in areas such as *legislations, education, economic* and *employment sector, political participation and awareness of their rights on the part of women*, etc.

1. Constitution and Legislation in Support of Women's Cause

• ***Constitutional provision for equality to women:*** The constitution of India does not discriminate between men and women. All the men and women of India are equally entitled to individual freedom, fundamental rights including the right to participate in social, cultural, religious, educational, economic and political activities. The constitution provides for equality of sex and offers protection to women against exploitation. It has given the voting right to women and in no way treats women as second grade citizens.

• ***Social legislations safeguarding women's interests:*** The Government of Independent India undertook a number of legislative measures to safeguard the interests of women. Some of them may be noted here.

(i) **The Hindu Marriage Act, 1955** which prohibits polygamy, polyandry and child marriage and concedes equal rights to women to divorce and to remarry.

(ii) **The Hindu Succession Act, 1956** which provides for women the right to parental property.

(iii) ***The Hindu Adoption and Maintenance Act, 1956*** which gives a childless woman the right to adopt a child and to claim maintenance from the husband if she is divorced by him.

(iv) ***The Special Marriage Act, 1954*** which provides rights to women on par with men for intercaste marriage, love marriage and registered marriage. The Act has also fixed the minimum age of marriage at **21** for males and **18** for females.

(v) ***The Dowry Prohibition Act, 1961*** which declares the taking of dowry an unlawful activity and thereby prevents the exploitation of Women.

(vi) ***Other Legislations:***

(*a*) ***The Suppression of Immoral Traffic of Women and Girls Act, 1956*** which gives protection to women from being kidnapped and being compelled to become prostitutes.

(*b*) ***The Medical Termination of Pregnancy Act, 1971*** which legalises abortion conceding the right of a woman to go for abortion on the ground of physical and mental health.

(*c*) ***The Criminal Law Amendment Act, 1983*** which seeks to stop various types of crimes against women.

(*d*) ***The Family Court Act, 1984***, which seeks to provide justice to women who get involved in family disputes.

(*e*) ***The Indecent Representation of Women [Prohibition] Act, 1986*** which prohibits the vulgar presentation of women in the media such as - newspapers, cinema, T.V., etc.

(*f*) ***The 73rd and 74th Constitution Amendment Acts, 1993*** which empower women and seek to secure greater participation of women at all the levels of the *Panchayat System*.

2. Women in the Field of Education

After Independence, women of India took to education in a relatively larger number. ***For example***, in 1901, the literacy level of the females in India was just 0.6%; it increased to 54.16% in 2001. This brought down the gap between male and female literacy rates from 28.84% in 1991 to 21.70% in 2001. Various benefits such as freeship, scholarship, loan facility, hostel facility etc. are being given to women who go for higher education. By making use of the new opportunities, a large number of girl students go for higher education today. *For example*, in 1950-51 the percentage of girl students pursuing higher education was 10.9% [that is, out of the total enrollment] and this increased to 32.0% in 1992.[31] In fact, the ***National Educational Policy 1986***, has been in favour of empowering woman through education. It gave a call to remove the gender prejudices by the inclusion of relevant lessons in the curriculum. It promoted the opening of women study centres in colleges and universities.

• ***Separate schools and colleges for girls :*** In many towns and cities, educational institutions meant only for female children have been established. ***For example***, in 1958-59 there were 146 colleges meant exclusively for women and the

[31] UGC Reports as quoted by Shamim Aleem in Women's Development Problems and Prospects [1996], pp. 88-89.

number increased to 824 colleges in 1992. The educational performance of girl students at high school and college levels, is proving to be better than that of boys especially after 1990s. This performance of girls makes it evident that intellect is not the monopoly of men alone.

• ***Women universities*** : The nation has gone much ahead in the field of female education and we have today some universities exclusively meant for women. ***Examples***: (*i*) *SNDT* [Shrimathi Nathibai Damodar Thackersey] *University for Women* [Poona]; (*ii*) *Padmavathi University For Women* [Tirupati]; (*iii*) *Mother Teresa University for Women* [Kodai Kenal, Tamil Nadu]. (*iv*) *Women's University, Bijapur* [Kamataka]. Girl students are getting admitted on merit basis to the prestigious engineering and medical colleges in relatively a bigger number during the recent years. Women have now realised that education makes a lot of difference in the social status of the individual whether they are men or women. It must be noted here that even though city women are quite conscious of education and its importance, more than 60% of our rural women are still illiterate and only a negligible number of them develop their educational career.

3. Women in the Economic and Employment Fields

In both villages and cities there has been a remarkable increase in the number of women going out of the four walls of the household and becoming workers. In the '*employment market*', they are giving a tough competition to the menfolk. In some fields, the number of women employees is steadily increasing. *For example*, women working as teachers, college professors, doctors, nurses, advocates, judges, managers, administrators, police officers, bank employees, clerks, typists, telephone operators, receptionists, personal assistants and so on, are to be found in almost all major cities. In big cities, women do not hesitate to work as bus conductors and drivers, police constables, autoriksha drivers and so on. Since 1991, they are being recruited into the three wings of the armed forces namely, military, air force and naval force. In urban areas, women white -collar workers are on the increase since 1970. On seeing the rise of these "*new women*", **M.N. Srinivas** had exclaimed long back that "*it is nothing short of a revolution*".

4. Awareness of Women Regarding Their Rights

Women in independent India have more rights than their counterparts in many other countries of the world. But most of our women are not very conscious of these rights. Uneducated rural women do not have any awareness of their rights. **Prof. Ram Ahuja** conducted a study[32] a few years ago in eight villages of a district in Rajasthan among 753 women belonging to different age-groups. His intention was to assess the degree of awareness and measure the level of satisfaction among women about the rights sanctioned by the Constitution of India. He concluded that the level of awareness of rights by women depends upon the following four aspects.

(*i*) ***Individual background of women*** which refers to their educational level, aspiration level and personal needs.

(*ii*) ***Social environment of women*** which includes the social expectations of kins, husband's values and family members' perceptions.

(*iii*) ***Economic base of women*** which refers to the level of class-membership, that is, whether they belong to lower class, middle class or upper class, and

(*iv*) ***Subjective perception of women*** which refers to women's own feeling and assessment of their - statuses and roles.

In 'Prof. Ahuja's study more than 75% of women were unaware of their rights; 20% of them did not have any awareness of their political rights; less than 1/3 of women had the chance of inheriting their husband's property and only 0.5% of them got a share of the father's property.

On the basis of the above study and some other general observations made by experts, it could be concluded that even today majority of our women are being identified *not as independent individuals but only as daughters, wives, mothers or as family members. Women are also not ready for their separate or independent identification*. Hence, women are still regarded as belonging to the "*weaker section*".

It can also be said that majority of our women [surely more than 50%] are happy with their family life and do not cherish any ambition relating to political and public life. Those earning women members also do not have the full freedom to spend their money in accordance with their own will and wish. Most of the women do not prefer to take decisions on important matters but leave them to their menfolk's discretion. Thus, our women are not completely free from the hold of the customs. In the unorganised sector, exploitation of women continues, for they are illiterate, ignorant and unorganised. In most of the homes male-children are still being preferred to female children. It appears that the societal approach towards women, their role and status has not radically changed. Hence, bringing about more and more legislations to ensure better opportunities to grant more rights and concessions, is of no benefit *unless there is a basic change in the people's attitude towards women and women's role in society*.

---

[32] Ram Ahuja's *Indian Social System*, pp. 111-112.

PROBLEMS OF WOMEN IN MODERN INDIA

Women in independent India are comparatively in a more respectable position. Some of the problems which had been haunting the community of women for centuries are not found now. Problems such as child marriage, practice of '*sati*', prohibition on widow remarriage, exploitation of widows, *devadasi* system, *purdah* system, etc. have almost disappeared. *Development in the field of science and technology; universalisation of education, socio-political movements, modernisation* and similar developments have changed the approach of people towards women to a certain extent. These developments boosted the morale and self-confidence of women. As a result, Indian women now feel that they too have their own individuality, personality, self-respect, talent, capacity and efficiency. Many of those women who could grab the opportunities extended to them have proved that they are capable of discharging the responsibilities assigned to them on par with men. The nation which neglected almost 50% of its population for several centuries has now understood the necessity of giving equal rights and opportunities to its womenfolk.

The Constitution of India provides equal rights and opportunities to women. It does not make any discrimination on the grounds of sex. Indian women are also responding positively to this changed socio-political situation. This does not mean that our women are completely free from problems. On the contrary, the changing situation is causing them new problems. They are now beset with new stresses and strains. Some of the major problems haunting the modern women may briefly be analysed here.

1. Increasing Violence Against Women

• ***Violence is almost universal :*** Most societies exhibit violence in one way or another. Violence against men or women is a social problem because, a large number of people are affected by it almost every day. Each of us is affected in countless ways by the climate of violence. Violence disrupts society. Every society creates institutions designed to achieve certain ends. Violence cuts short normal institutional functions. Every act of violence, from assault to armed revolution, detracts to some degree from the authority normally vested in society.

• ***Women as victims of violence*** : Who is most likely to be victimised by violent crime? Women are less likely to be victimised by violent crime than men, though for some crimes and among some groups of women, victimisation is higher than men. Violence against women is not a new phenomenon in India. "*Women in Indian society have been victims of ill-treatment, humiliation, torture, and exploitation for as long as written records of social organisation and family life are available. These records are replete with incidents of abduction, rape, murder, and torture of women. But, regretfully, female victims of violence have not been given much attention in the literature on social problems or in the literature on criminal violence.*"[33]

• ***Increasing crimes against women*** : Crime against women is an ever-increasing problem. This problem has been growing more and more acute in India during the recent years. Crimes against women include *violence against women, rape, molestation, dowry harassment, wife-battering, kidnapping female children to be sold into brothel homes, forcible embracement, forcible religious conversion. cheating young women with a promise to marry them or fetch them a job and various types of sexual harassments and abuse of women including eve teasing.*

As per the report [1994] of the "*Crime Record Bureau*" of the Central Home Ministry,[34] crimes against women increased to a great extent in the year 1993-94. As per this report, in India on an average, (*i*) every day for every 6 minutes one atrocity is committed against woman; (*ii*) for every 44 minutes a woman is kidnapped; (*iii*) for every 47 minutes a woman is raped; (*iv*) every day 17 dowry deaths take place. The same report says that crimes against women increased two times in the last 10 years: instances of rape by 400% in the last two decades; instances of kidnapping and blackmailing women by 30% between 1974 and 1993. In 1993 alone about 82,818 instances of crimes against women were registered. Many cases are not registered. It is said that only 10% of the rape cases are reported.

Violence Against Women Within and Outside Family

In a male dominated society like India violences against women are unfortunately increasing at an alarming rate. Such violences can be grouped into two types 1 (*a*) *violence against women within the family*, and (*b*) *violence against women outside the family*.

(*a*) ***Violence against women within the family or domestic violence*** : Women are often subject to violence within the family, a place which is expected to protect their dignity and assure their safety. This type of violence includes crimes such as – *dowry related harassments including death, wife-battering, marital rape, sexual abuse of female children and women of one's own family, deprivation of sufficient food to female members, committing incestuous*

[33] Prof. Ram Ahuja in *Violence Against Women* 1998, p. 11.

[34] Report in *Udayavani,* Kannada Daily, dated Feb 27th, 1994.

offences, inducing female members of the family to resort to sex-trade, female genital mutilation, abusing female servants of the family, and so on.

(b) ***Violence against aomen outside the family or social violence*** **:** Kidnapping, raping and murdering women are very serious offences. The society at large itself is to be blamed for many types of violences that are committed against women especially outside the family. Such violences include – *compelling women for abortion and to undergo tubectomy operation, eve-teasing, kidnapping girls of pre-matured age and forcing them to marry, sexual harassment of women employees in work place, immoral trafficking in women and girls, forced prostitution, kidnapping and mutilating the organs [such as hands, legs, ears, nose, etc.] of female children to use them for the purpose of begging, resorting to forcible religious conversion of young women, blackmailing of women, throwing acid at the faces of girls who refuse to marry, the police and the jail personnel committing sexual crimes against female prisoners, the police, armed forces and the border security forces committing sex crimes against the female citizens in the border areas and so on.*

2. Gender Discrimination

Gender discrimination refers to "the practice whereby one sac is given preferential treatment over the others."[35] The practice of giving social importance to the biological differences between men and women is there everywhere. In some societies, these differences are very much pronounced while in others, they are given less importance. Even the Indian society is not an exception to this.

Different Faces of the Practice" of "Gender Discrimination"

In comparison with some other social problems, "gender discrimination" does not "appear" to be a serious problem in India. It "appears" to be so because, it has not been made a very big social issue so far. But in reality, it has weakened the strength of the female community of India. Though constitutionally men and women are equal, socially men are given priority and importance sometimes to the disadvantage of women. There are various areas wherein this discrimination is apparent.

(i) ***Discrimination in socialisation*** **:** In our socialisation process female children are becoming victims of discrimination. In the Indian social context even today male children are preferred to female children. Hence, female children are subject to discriminatory treatment. Male preference and female negligence has almost become a working policy especially in the rural areas. Discrimination between male and female children is made in matters relating to food, dress, health, education, domestic work etc. The policy of male preference and female negligence has led to what is known as "*female disadvantages*". In India, mothers show preferences for male children. They give them importance because - *males are wanted during their old age to offer protection, males have greater scope than women and occupational avenues are also wider for males than for females*. This male preference has led to the abuse of advanced technology. The sophisticated scanning and supersonographic equipments are being misused to find out the sex of the child; that is to go for abortion if the child is found to be an unwanted female child. These medical tests which would cost between ₹ 80 to 800 are within the reach of the middle class and even the upper-lower class resulting in the killing of the female foetuses in large number. Between 1978 and 1982 more than 78,000 foetuses were killed mainly because of these medical tests.[36] .

(ii) ***Discrimination in the distribution of power and work*** **:** Most of the Indian families are patriarchal. Hence, the philosophy of equality of sex is not acceptable to them. Domestic works such as cooking, looking after the children, washing clothes and vessels, keeping the house neat and clean, looking after the domesticated animals, serving family members like a nurse on all days and especially when they fall sick, etc., are branded as "*women's work*". Very rarely men do these works. But when the question of exercising power comes, it is always the man who dominates. His decisions are final and his orders are ultimate. The female voice is always suppressed.

(iii) ***Women's health is ignored*** **:** Women suffer from some distinctive health problems from which men are free. Women have to undergo the distinctive biological process of pregnancy, or child bearing, delivering, nursing, feeding, child-caring or rearing etc. These are their maternal functions. But the insistence on the family planning has posed many health hazards. The use of contraceptives, Copper-T, sterilisation, abortion and hormonal drugs has an adverse effect on health. Those who make use of them suffer from problems such as *bodily weakness, bloodlessness, high bleeding, fatness, problems in uterus discomfort in breast, chronic backpain*, etc. As **Neera Desai** and **Vibhuti Patel** have criticised, the advocates of family planning do not seem to bother much about these problems.

---

[35] **David Jury** and **July Jary** in "*Collins Dictionary of Sociology*" - **Page** : 588.

[36] *Source : Times of India, Editorial June 1982.*

• ***Women Neglecting their Own Health:*** Studies have revealed that our Women themselves are neglecting their own health. Normally Indian women consume less food [that is, on an average 100 calories a day] and spend more energy on work. Women toil for the good of the family and children even at the cost of neglecting their own health. Women very rarely complain about their ill-health because of their virtue of "*self-denial*". The records in the health centres reveal that women are lagging behind men [that is, 1:3, meaning one woman taking medical help for every 3 men] even in matters of availing of medical help.

• ***Women have their own reasons to neglect their health:*** *Not finding free time to go to health centres because of heavy work at home; non-availability of proper medical facility to test the health or ill-health of the mother and the child especially in the primary health centres; inability to walk a long distance to reach a well equipped health centre in the absence of proper transportation facility; non-availability of female doctors in the nearby health centres,* etc., are some such excuses.

(iv) ***Decline in the female population*** : Normally, in the population of any country, male female ratio remains more or less the same, that is, 50:50. In India as the census reports reveal female population has been steadily declining ever since 1901. It is for this reason **Neera Desai** and **Vibhuti Patel** raised the point whether the womenfolk in India represent a "*declining sex*". According to 2001 Census, there is a deficit of **35** million women as compared to **3** million in 1901. For every 1000 men, we have only **933** women at present as against **972** women in 1901. The male preference has led to the abuse of technology. Thousands of "unwanted female" children are killed at the stage of foetus itself. It is said that in India, out of **12** million female children born every year, around 25% of them die before they attain the age of 15. Of the children which die every year, about 3 lakh female children, that is, more than the number of male children, die for one or the other reason. Of the children which die every year in India, the 6th child dies due to gender discrimination.[37]

(v) ***Gender discrimination in occupations and public life*** : Women workers are paid less than' the male workers for the same type of work. Much labour is extracted from women by giving them very minimum wages. In matters of giving treatment, promotion. increment, facilities, etc., discrimination is normally made. In ***public life*** also men are given priority. Excepting the glamorous film actresses and politicians, in all other fields, women are not given importance on par with men. Government officials also practise this discriminatory treatment in dealing with the people.

3. Problems of Female Education

Social reformers and social thinkers believe that in a nation like India giving education to women in as large a number as possible can prove to be a panacea for many of the problems of women. Accordingly, much attention is paid to the education of women after independence. The female literacy level is also increasing steadily. It has increased from 18.7% in 1971 to 39.42% in 1991 and to **64%** in 2001. In spite of this change in the trend towards literacy, some problem have cropped up. We find glaring differences between the level of education of men and women. *For example,*

• It is found ***that girls are being discouraged*** to go for higher education and also for professional and technical education.

• ***There are regional imbalances also.*** In states like Kerala, Karnataka and Maharashtra, female education is encouraged and given almost equal importance. Whereas in states like Bihar, Orissa, Madhya Pradesh etc. education of girls is neglected even today.

• ***Increasing drop-out of female children*** from schools is another problem. Though female children are getting admitted to primary, middle and high schools in a substantial number, many of them drop out of the school in the middle without completing the course. *For example*, as per the data furnished by the Ministry of Education [New Delhi], in 1984-85 the number of female children enrolled at primary school crossed the figure of 34.2 million, and at middle school level the enrolment crossed 9.2 million. More than 74% of these female children, between the age-groups of 6-14 years, quit schools and lapsed into ignorance.

• ***Admission to School*** : Even in the matter of admitting children to school at elementary level, female children are discriminated against male children. *For example*, in 1984-85, the admission of male children to school was around 90%, the percentage of female children was only 66.2. It means complete awareness is not there among people regarding female education.

4. Problems Relating to Employment and Unemployment of Women

In the economic field the situation is such that majority of women who are ready to work are not finding suitable work to their satisfaction. Those who are in the employment sector are becoming the objects of exploitation and harassment.

[37] Dr. R. Indira in, her *Mahile - Samaja Mattu Samskriti*, p. 93.

Though an increase in the female literacy level and extensions of employment opportunities for women in the non-agricultural sector, have added to the trend in favour of female employment, these two problems continue to exist.

• ***Large number of employed women are illiterate*** : Of every 100 women employed, 52.59% of them are illiterate and 28.56% of them have studied only up to elementary level. Of every 100 women working in the rural areas, 88.11% are illiterate. These illiterate women in the unorganised sector are totally exploited by their employers. Women working in factories, mining industries, building construction process, in dams, bridges and road repair or construction work are not only paid less but also made to work in unhealthy surroundings.

• ***Decreasing economic participation of women*** : Technological development seems to have a negative effect on employment opportunities of women. Studies conducted between 1975-85 have revealed this fact. Application of new technology in agrarian sector, textiles, mines, jute, pharmaceuticals, small scale industries like coir, handloom, weaving, spinning, cashew, fisheries, tobacco, animal husbandry, fruits and vegetable processing etc. rendered many women jobless. Computerisation has also adversely affected the job prospects of women as clerks, typists and accountants.

5. Harassment of Women at Work Place

Women constitute an important labour force in all the countries. During the recent years there is an increasing number of women especially in the Indian context, who are working outside the family to get more income for the family. In fact, "*the term working woman*" *refers to one who works outside the home for a wage or salary*".[38]

Nearly **1/3** of our labour force [32%] consists of women. Working women constitute 16.43% of the female population of the country. As per 1991 Census, the number of working women was around **278.35** million, representing a growth rate of 26.12% over the previous decade. The percentage increase of working women during the last decade was double that of male workers. The main problem with these female workers, is that they are harassed in work place in different ways. "*Harassment*" *refers to the basic violation of an individual's rights*. Not only the rights of working women are violated, they are often sexually harassed also.

• ***Economic exploitation*** : Women workers are given much work but are paid less wages or salary especially in the unorganised sector. "*Equal pay for equal work*" remains only a slogan. "***Equal Remuneration Act, 1976*** has proved to be a dead letter in this regard. There are also sufficient instances of such exploitation even in the organised sector.

• ***Threat of removal from job :*** In the Indian context, majority of women go for work not for fun but out of necessity. Some are compelled to work because of poor family conditions. Employers who are aware of the helplessness of these female employees exploit them in all the possible ways. They do not tolerate any type of opposition or protest from the side of the female workers. Due to the fear of losing the job, women bear all the exploitations, and do not protest.

• ***Women are given more work*** : Women normally work with devotion, seriousness and sincerity. This commitment to work is proving to be a big disadvantage for them Hence, every time they are given more and more work which is not duly rewarded.

• ***Discrimination in giving opportunities*** : In spite of the hard work which women do, many employers consider these working women as "*non serious workers*". They are also regarded as "*non- permanent employees*" especially in the case of unmarried female workers. They are discriminated with regard to recruitment, promotion, increment, training, over-time allowance, facilities at work place, and so on. Male workers are given preference in these matters.

• ***Sexual harassment of women*** : *Sexual harassment of women at workplace refers to giving indecent treatment to women workers by violating all the norms of modesty*. Many female workers have complained of such harassments during the recent years. This harassment by men includes - continuous staring at women, making women the targets of lewd remarks, dirty jokes, repeated invitation to meals and outings, offers to drop them home, making unwanted comments about dressings, making "accidental" touches and dashes, making them stay back in the Work spot even after the working hours, male bosses calling smart female employees to their chambers and making unwanted "advances" towards them, molesting women workers and so on.[39]

6. Exploitation of Women in the Media

The mass media such as the radio, television, news papers and the cinema play a vital role in social change and social development especially in the modem societies. But unfortunately, the media has not been playing a positive role in the case of women. The media is even condemned of exploiting and misrepresenting women.

---

[38] Anjann Maitra Sinha in *Women in a Changing Society,* 1993, p. 105

[39] In 1998, the *National Commission for Women* conducted a survey in five States consisting of 1211 female workers in order to assess the extent of harassment of female workers in the work spot. The survey reported that 68% of women were mentally harassed by men, 26% of them physically tortured, and 38% of them had become the victims of gender discrimination. – Out look English Weekly Dated : April 19, 1999, p. 66.

(*i*) ***Journalism as print media and women*** **:** Newspapers, weeklies, monthlies or other types of magazines seem to be interested in increasing their circulation by rousing the cheap emotions of the people. "*They target the woman's body to get their things done.*" Papers no doubt give due publicity to some unfortunate events under the captions such as "*Atrocity Against Women*", "*Dowry Costs A Woman's Life". Mass Rape of a Woman', 'Sexual Harassment of Women'*, etc. But in doing so they give the least information about the culprit of the crime. On the contrary, they take more interest in weaving stories about the victim of the event which often amounts to character assassination.

(*ii*) ***Visual media and women*** : Since about 35% of the people in our society are illiterate, visual media such as television and the cinema have a greater impact on people. The Indian visual media is a failure in playing a positive role in educating people and enriching their knowledge Like the newspapers, they also exhibit the female body and make it their main capital to mint money. Modern movies believe in achieving success by portraying more and more sex, violence and murder. Women are shown as targets of attack, sex, rape and such other exploitations.

Unfortunately, our T.V. is also following the example of the movies. With the invasion of our skies with a number of T.V. channels, the choice of T.V. viewers has greatly expanded. T.V. channels such as the Star Plus, MTV, Asian TV Network, Zee TV, and other Cable channels, are promoting a lifestyle which is totally alien to us. As usual women are presented in these channels in an indecent manner. Indian movies and T.V. serials are playing havoc with our values and morals.

(*iii*) ***Advertisements and women*** **:** Advertisements whether in newspapers or T.V. play no less an important role in debasing women. Advertisement firms also make use of female body in a cheap manner to get publicity for things.

(*iv*) ***Media and women movements*** **:** Media has an important role to play in strengthening women's position. While pronouncing women's weaknesses, it must also emphasise their strength. It must awaken women from the slumber of centuries, inform them, mobilise them and motivate them Whenever required. It must give due publicity to women's struggle for justice, equality and fairplay. This will help them in regenerating power. The present role of the media in this regard is not that encouraging, but disappointing.

• *Legislation to Regulate the Media :* The Government had passed as early as in 1986 a legislation namely; "***The Indecent Representation of Woman [Prohibition] Act, (1986)*** in order to prevent the media from misrepresenting the women. Any attempt to degrade and discredit women, insult and humiliate them, assassinate the character of women, and present them in an indecent manner is declared punishable. The provisions of this Act are applicable to all the means of the mass media and also to advertisements, books, handbills, posters, etc. Violation of this Act is liable for punishment, which amounts to ₹ 2000 fine and 2 years imprisonment.

7. Divorce and Desertion

During the recent years, instances of desertion and divorce are increasing making the lives of many women very miserable.

(*a*) ***The hardship of desertion*** : Desertion is defined as "*deliberate abandonment of conjugal relationships*." As a matter of fact, desertion may take place at the behest of any one of the two, or both together. In actuality, in the Indian context, it is mostly the husband who goes away from the family leaving the wife and children at home to fend for themselves.

Desertion causes lot of hardships especially for women. It immediately drives a woman to a state of uncertainty and helplessness. Deserted women belonging to poor families all of a sudden become orphans especially when they are disowned by their own parents. Some of them may resort to immoral activity, some others fall prey into the hands of anti-social elements, while a few of them may commit suicide.

(*b*) ***The agony of divorce*** : Divorce is "*...an institutional arrangement for terminating marital relationship...*"[40]

Causes of divorce are many. Sociologists like **Damle, Fonseca** and **Chaudhary** together conducted a study in India which revealed the following causes of divorce : *marital disharmony, sexual conflicts, maladjustments between husband and wife, marital desertion, husband's cruelty, prostitution on the part of wife, sexual impotency, severe and unmanageable clashes with the in-laws, mother-in-law's harassment, including dowry harassment, illicit sex relationship on the part of either the husband or the wife, irreparable health hazards, mutual distrust, total irresponsibility of the husband or wife towards the family matters and so on.*

Divorce causes lot of hardships especially for the women. It damages the social image of the wife. It becomes a permanent stigma in her life. Many sensitive women find it difficult to come out of the shock of divorce. The impact of divorce on children is also very severe. The burden of protecting and rearing of children also lies on the wife.

---

[40] W.P. Scott in Dictionary of Sociology.

Jobless and resourceless divorced women find themselves in a big economic crisis. Young and beautiful divorced women find it difficult to suppress their sex urge. They are often forced to resort to illicit ways of satisfying it. It usually leads to family disintegration.

8. The Problem of Dowry

Dowry is both a practice and a problem associated with the Indian marriage. Though it was more in practice among the Hindus, it has now spread to almost all the religious communities of India.

• Dowry refers to "*.... the property, money, ornaments or any other form of wealth which a man or his family receives from his wife or her family at the time of marriage.*"

The age-old practice of dowry has now assumed the form of a social evil because the bride's family is compelled to give some dowry as a price for marriage. It has become a social bane and a kind of bargain. It has caused unhappiness, misery and ruin of the bride's family. Huge amount of money is demanded at the time of marriage and the failure to give the promised amount would make the bride to suffer the consequences at the hands of her in-laws and also the husband.

• ***Dowry harassments are many:*** Women are ill-treated, disrespected, man-handled, tortured and subject to all sorts of cruelties in the name of dowry. Very often, our daily papers flash news about the tragic results of the dowry system, in which the newly married girls are always the victims of harassment, violence, murder and suicide. Dowry is demanded as though it is a fundamental right of the bridegroom. Violence against women who bring less dowry or no dowry include – wife battering, emotional neglect / torture, verbal abuse, refusal of sufficient food, imposition of heavy physical work, severe physical harassments to the extent of killing the victim, and so on.

In spite of the legislation against the practice of dowry, it persists. Demands for dowry have even caused dowry deaths. According to an estimate, as many as 4148 dowry deaths were reported in the year 1990 and it increased to 4366 in the year 1993, and to 6205 in the year 1994, that is, at the rate of one dowry death for every 17 minutes.

• ***Dowry leads to the degradation of women:*** Prevalence of the practice of dowry reflects the inferior status of women in society. It makes a girl a great liability on her family's resources. Some unscrupulous and money minded young men contract more than one marriage just for money. It disturbs the normal relationship between the married women and her in—laws in the husbands family. Some poor parents who cannot pay a huge amount as dowry, are often compelled to arrange the marriage of their daughters with old men, or physically or mentally handicapped persons. Such marriages prove to be miserable for women.

As early as in **1961** itself, ***The Dowry Prohibition Act*** was passed in order to prevent the practice of dowry. It was amended in 1986 to make its provisions more severe and stringent. In spite of this Act, the practice continues to be in vogue.

9. Decline in the Political Participation of Women

Participation of women who constitute 50% of our total population in politics and public life is very much negligible in India. We find only a negligible number of women in prestigious positions like those of Central and State cabinet ministers, governors, secretaries and legal advisers to the governments, ambassadors to other countries, IPS, IAS, IFS officers, judges in courts, mayors of big cities, office bearers of all-India parties, etc. No political party of India has given position to women in accordance with their number in the total population. In some areas seats are reserved for women as we find in Gram Panchayat, Jilla Panchayat, University Senate, etc. Even in these areas women have not constituted themselves into a "*pressure group*". Hence in our political life, we have caste lobbies, linguistic lobbies, capitalist lobbies, minority lobby, etc. but we do not have "*women lobby*" to bring pressure on the government.

• ***Increasing violence and terrorism in politics:*** Political corruption, criminalisation of politics, erosion of political values, disappearance of political decency, instability, lawlessness, terrorism and confusion have been increasing in our public life since 1980s. This state of confused political situation has discouraged women from taking active role in politics.

• ***Minimum representation of women in lok sabha:*** The representation of women in Lok Sabha has been very poor since 1962 elections. **For ex:** there were only 33 elected women members in the third Lok Sabha [out of 494 members] after the 1962 elections. In the 6th Lok Sabha out of 544 elected members there were only 19 women members and their percentage was only 3.4. In the 10th Lok Sabha [1991 Elections] there were 39 elected women members and their percentage was 7.4.

• ***In the 1996 elections for the 11th lok sabha*** though the total number of women voters increased to 28.24 crores [47%], only 477 women candidates as against 14,250 men candidates contested for 543 seats. [In the 1991 Elections for the 10th Lok Sabha 325 women candidates contested as against 8,374 men candidates for 521 seats]. These figures reveal that only a small number of women are interested in political life.

• ***In the 1999 general elections for the 13th lok sabha*** also women's participation was the poorest one. Though political parties were speaking vociferously in terms of 33% reservation for women in legislative bodies including the Parliament, no political party had given tickets to women in more than **10%**. In some parties, the percentage of women candidates was not even 2 to 3.

• ***Poor participation of women in the party politics*** : Not only in the legislative bodies but even within the framework of the political parties also the participation of women is very poor. Political parties are still male—dominated and unwilling to give sufficient representation to women. ***For example***, at present, [that is, in 2001] the Congress Party has only 3 women in its 20-member Working Committee. In the BJP Working Committee, out of **75** members there are only 8 women, and in its **650** member National Council, there are only **150** women. The Communist Party [Marxists] has only **12** women in its **150** member National Council, and **3** women in its **21** member National Executive. Though theoretically women's representation in politics is regarded as the first step towards women empowerment, the socio-political atmosphere has not yet become condusive for that.

EMPOWERMENT OF WOMEN

Meaning of the Concept of Empowerment of Women

The term '*empowerment of women*' has become popular especially after 1980s. It refers to the process of strengthening the hands of women who have been suffering from various disabilities, inequalities and gender discrimination.

• *The term "empowerment of women' refers to the process of providing power to woman to become free from the control of others, that is, to assume power to control her own life and to determine her own conditions.*

• *The term of "empowerment of women" could also be understood as the process of providing equal rights, opportunities, responsibilities and power positions to women so that they are able to play a role on par with men in society.*

The Background of the Emergence of the Concept

Historically, women have been regarded as constituting a weaker section. They have ofien been treated as "*second grade citizens*". They have been pictured and presented as "*home - makers*" who are good in household chores. This image of women has been changing every Where. Extension of the voting right to women in Britain and America in the beginning of the 20th century brought about a series of changes in the status of women especially in the western world. Many of their disabilities and inequalities came to an end in due course. The quest for equality was pursued consistently by the Western women.

On the contrary, women of Asia and Africa were not able to secure equal status and opportunities even after 1950s. Women continued to suffer from one or the other kind of disability. Their exploitation was also continued. They were given unequal treatment on the basis of sex. This development was termed as "*gender discrimination*". The United Nations also through its various meetings and pronouncements was giving call to its member-nations to remove as early as possible, the ugly practice of "*gender discrimination*".

Shift in the Emphasis from Women's "Welfare" to "Development"

Due to the efforts of the UNO the issue of empowerment of women became an international issue. The UN declared the **Year *1975 as the International Women's Year***. Further, the U.N. Declaration of 1975 compelled the national governments *to shift their emphasis on women's programmes from welfare to development*. The Declaration prescribed for the all-round development of women.

Women's World Congress Insistence on Empowerment of Women

In continuation of the UN Declaration of 1975, the "***Third Women's World Congress***" [or conference] was held at **Nairobi** [Kenya] in 1985. A document released on this occasion recommended efforts towards empowerment of women. "*In this document, the question of women political participation was highlighted and it was recommended that 35% of the total seats should be reserved for women. It was also recommended that some posts should be reserved for women at the block and village level bureaucracy. On the economic front, a number of income generating schemes were introduced for women. In addition to that provisions were also made to certain proportion of women as beneficiaries in all the developmental schemes like the IRDP, JRX TRYCEM, and so on.*"[41].

The Fourth World Conference on Women was held in **Beijing** [China] in 1995 in which representatives from 189 nations including India had taken part. The Conference recognised some 12 serious areas such as - *women and poverty, health, economic position, media and rights, environment, girl child, human rights and women, institutional arrangement for women s development, women in decision - taking process, education and training for job, etc. in order to strengthen women. The Conference unanimously passed a resolution on "gender equality".*

[41] S.L. Doshi and P.C. Jain in *Rural Sociology*, p. 341.

• ***Special Session of the United Nations General Assembly*** was also convened in the year 2000 in New York to assess the progress of the programmes held in the direction of establishing gender equality. The topic of the conference was "*Women 2000 : Equality, Development and Peace for the 21 st Century.*" Only the NGOs, [Non-Governmental Organisations] had to take part in it. The basic purpose of the conference was to convince the member nations regarding the need for empowering women and to take appropriate steps in that direction.

The Indian Response towards the Conference Issue

On the basis of the proceedings of the world conference on women, the Government of India prepared a *National Document* concerning the development of women. The document lays down various strategies for women's development. The Government also declared the year **2001 as the "*Year of Women's Empowerment*"**.

STRATEGIES FOR WOMEN'S DEVEIOPMENT

The *national document* which the Government of India had prepared with the intention of promoting women's development, highlights the importance of three strategies which are mentioned below.

(i) Obtaining greater political participation of women : The document recommends that 33% of the seats should be reserved for women in order to get the effective participation of women in politics. It was also recommended that some power positions [posts] should be reserved for women at the block and village level bureaucracy.

(ii) Income generating schemes for women : On the economic front, a number of income- generating schemes were to be introduced to women as per the provisions of this document. It was insisted that sufficient provisions were to be made in all the rural developmental programmes [such as, IRDP: *Integrated Rural Developmental Programme*; JRY *: Jawahar Rozgar Yojana;* TRYSEM: *Training of Rural Youth and Self-Employment,* etc.] enabling a certain proportion of women to become their beneficiaries.

(iii) Increasing female literacy level : On the social front, it was recommended to obtain proper co-ordination between governmental and non-government institutions to increase considerably the literacy level of women. It was hoped that with the help of literacy, women would be able to lead a life of self-reliance.

Empowerment of Women and "The 73 Constitution Amendment Act, 1993"

'*The 73 Constitution Amendment Act 1993*' was undertaken mainly to give constitutional status to the "*The Panchayat Raj System* " and to introduce it in India on a uniform basis. Another purpose behind the Act was to *assure the empowerment of women.*

The framers of the *73rd Constitution Amendment Act believed that "social and economic status of women could not be improved much without political power The females in the village need to be given some political power They should have their share in the decisions made about the development of their villages. The new Panchayat Raj is a part of the effort to empower the women at least at the village level*" [42]

One-Third Reservation of Seats For Women

The 73rd Constitution Amendment Act has made an effort to give some special powers to women in all the three tiers of Panchayat Raj. As per this Act, 1/3 of the seats are reserved for women in addition to the reservation for SCs and STs. It was, indeed, a very bold step towards the empowerment of women. Rural women who have been working as farm labourers, cleaning the utensils, washing clothes, sweeping the court-yard, fetching drinking water from a distance, cooking food and serving the same to all, labouring in the fields, etc., are now able to exercise some amount of political power on par with men. They now have the role to play in matters of decision making that affect village affairs. "*The provisions of Act for the women are in no way less than a revolution.*" [**Doshi** and **Jain**]

A Brief Assessment of 73rd Constitution Amendment Act

The 73rd Constitution Amendment Act came into force in April 1993. The Act has not brought about miraculous changes as expected. Though it has created some awareness among women it suffers from many drawbacks. Some of them may be noted as below.

1. ***Illiteracy*** : Since female literacy rate is very poor in our villages, female members at different tiers of *Panchayat Raj* are not able to assert themselves. On the contrary, they are forced to work according to the wishes of the male members.

[42] S.L. Doshi and P.O. Jain in their *Rural Sociology*, p. 338.

2. ***Non-availability of women*** : It is very difficult to find out adequate number of females to work as members of the *Panchayat Raj* Committee. Either we will have to make a compromise with less qualified and totally ignorant women or be content with inadequate number of women.
3. ***Corrupt leadership and bureaucracy*** : Our leadership is highly selfish and our bureaucracy is totally corrupt. In this situation, it is very difficult for the women to work and to achieve progress.
4. ***Bias towards elites and middle class*** : The Act focuses its attention on women and weaker sections of the society no doubt. Women who are better off in one way or another alone can take the proper benefit of this Act. It means the creamy layer of the disadvantaged groups would corner most of the benefits of the Act. As a result, the weakest of the weak, the poorest of the poor would continue to suffer in the pattern of the *Panchayat Raj* also.

Factors Facilitating Empowerment Of Women

A big nation like India which consists of more than 50 crores women cannot afford to ignore the role of women in the national development. It is in this context the process of empowerment of women has assumed importance.

Women cannot be empowered in a magical manner. It is not an automatic or a spontaneous process but requires deliberate and consistent efforts. It is through the combined and co-ordinated efforts of the Government, people and the women the task can be fulfilled. Women cannot be effectively empowered by statutory provisions or governmental efforts alone. "*Women are empowered through — women emancipation movement, education, communication, media, political parties and general awakening*." - [**Doshi** and **Jain**]

Various socio-economic and political factors facilitate the empowerment of women. Among them the following may be noted.

1. ***Acknowledging women's rights*** : Society should recognise that like men, women are also entitled to equal rights.
2. ***Freedom to take decisions and make choices*** : Women should have freedom to decide whether to marry or not to marry; and after marriage, the freedom to decide as to how many children that they should have, and so on.
3. ***Access to education and employment*** : Women can become stronger only with educational and economic power. Mere expectations cannot help. Conditions must be created in such a way that women get easy access to education and later on become employed. Sufficient economic freedom is a must for women to lessen their dependence on men.
4. ***Opportunities for political participation*** : If women's voice is to carry more weight they must be given political power. They must be free to take part in the administrative process.

The process of empowerment of women belonging to weaker sections will definitely have multiplying effects on society. ***For example***, when a woman in the village gets elected as member of the Gram Panchayat Samithi, she becomes automatically powerful in the family, kin group and village. She is listened to by the people for she has the power to take a decision and she can do and undo certain things in the village, and so on. ***For example***, she can expand the facilities of the village school and raise it to higher standard; she can get a borewell and a water tank for the village, she may fetch for the village a community hall, a, reading room, and so on. She is not, of course, everything. But by becoming the member of the *Gram Samithi*, she can definitely influence the decisions of the *Samithi*.

Reasons behind the Need for Empowerment

In a nation like India the need for the empowerment of women is justified on account of the factors like the following.

1. ***Education or literacy*** : Among other countries of the world, India has the highest number of illiterate people. As per the 2001 Census report, 75% men are literate while only 54. 16% women are found to be so. In the rural areas, the level of illiteracy is still higher. [*For example*, the female literacy rate in rural Rajasthan was only 12%, while it stood at still a lower level, that is 10%, in rural Bihar in l991.] Illiteracy is the biggest weakness of women. *Giving them education means empowering them to enjoy the benefits of development* which in turn enables them to contribute further to the national progress.
2. ***Health problem of women*** : Poor health on the part of women has also added to their weakness. Women consume less food and work more. They are shy of complaining about their ill health. They prefer to suffer silently than to approach a medical practitioner for obtaining medical assistance. This is mostly true in the case of a large majority of rural women. Surveys and studies have revealed that traditional importance shown towards the male children is also one of the reasons for neglecting the health of female children. Women are found to be maintaining relatively good health in the regions wherever the rate of female literacy is higher. Kerala provides here the best example. *Thus, from the health point of view also,' womenfolk who are found to be weaker. are to be made stronger*.

3. ***Economic exigencies of women*** : Indian women are economically weak in two respects: (*i*) The per capita income of the Indians is quite low and a large number of families are under the tight grip of poverty. This economic distress naturally affects women who are a part and parcel of the family; (*ii*) Since property laws in this country were not in favour of women for hundreds of years, women do not seem to be possessing property of their own. Even the working women who get some income give it to the custody of their menfolk who take decisions to spend it. Economic dependence of women on men still continues. This dependence weakens them economically. *Thus, women require economic power to stand on their own legs on par with men.*

4. ***Atrocities against women*** : Women constitute the weaker sex. This fact is also borne by the number of crimes and atrocities committed against them. There are cases of rape, kidnapping of girls, dowry harassments, molestation, sexual harassments, abuse of women, incestuous sex relations and so on. Women in all walks of life are discriminated against by men. They become the victims of atrocities in a number of ways. *They require empowerment of all kinds in order to protect themselves against all types of atrocities and to preserve their purity and dignity.*

HUMAN RIGHTS AND WOMEN

The Concept of Human Rights

The concept of "human rights" did not exist the way it does, until recently. The "*human rights*" refer to all those rights which are common to all human beings. These rights were slowly incorporated into society, in different parts of the world. In the West, the British political thinker **John Locke** gave birth to the concept of "*human rights*" in the 17th century in his book "*The Second Treatise of the Government*". But the idea of human rights assumed the form of an international movement only in the second half of the 20th century. The human rights movement gained momentum in the decades of 1950, 1960 and 1970. It was during this period that human rights became a major political issue. The UNO took the issue of "human rights" as an article of faith and insisted on all its member countries to make provision for human rights in their respective territories. The UN General Assembly adopted the *Universal Declaration of Human Rights* [UDHR] a statement of universal goals concerning human rights and freedom Although it is not legally binding, its content has been incorporated into many national constitutions including ours. People are slowly becoming aware of the human rights. Hence, they have increasingly refused to accept regimes that do not provide for the perfection of human rights.

Meaning and Definition of Human Rights

The concept of 'human rights' does not have one single explanation or definition for it includes a multiplicity of factors that are interlinked. For the purpose of our study we may consider a few of the simple definitions of the concept.

• "*Human rights are literally the rights that one has simply because one is a human being*". - **Jack Donnelly**, *a leading human rights activist.*

• "*Human rights are those basic rights which everyone inherits the moment one is conceived in the mother': womb.*"

• In simple words, it could be said that "*human rights are those basic standards without which men cannot live in dignity*".

The Main Human Rights

The above definitions or explanations make it clear that human rights are a part and parcel of human life. People, thus, cannot lose their human rights, no matter what they do. These rights constitute the basic requirements of dignified life. Hence, they form a basic framework for the administration of society and political organisation. All civilised societies are expected to protect and ensure these human rights.

Human rights include the following rights -

- The right to life
- The right to food
- The right to shelter and necessities
- The right to health
- The right to education
- The right to dignity and liberty, and
- The right to be free.

Main Characteristics of the 'Human Rights'

The 'human rights' mentioned above reveal certain characteristics which may be mentioned below:

1. Human rights are **natural** rights that all human beings possess simply by virtue of being human.

2. Human rights are held by all persons **equally** and **universally**.
3. Human rights are **irrevocable** - they cannot be revoked or suspended for political expediency.
4. Human rights are **inalienable** - one cannot lose these rights any more than one can cease being a human being.
5. Human rights are **indivisible** - one cannot be denied a right because it is '*less important*' or '*non- essential*'.
6. Human rights are **interdependent** — all human rights are part of a complementary framework ***For example***, the ability to participate in government is directly affected by the right to express, to get some education, and even to obtain the necessities of life.

Human Rights and Women

"Human rights" - as the very term indicates represent the rights of all human beings of both the sex, men and women. Individuals of both the sex are born with these rights. Human rights are God given or Nature given rights. Both men and women have equal access to these rights. No discrimination is allowed or imposed in the exercise of these rights.

It is a fact of history that women have been denied equal rights for centuries. The "*philosophy of human rights*" became popular only during the second half of the 20th century and the issue of "*gender equality*" and "*equal rights*" for women assumed importance only after 1970's.[43]

Women's Rights and the Declaration of Human Rights

The "*Universal Declaration of Human Rights*" by the UNO on 10th December 1948 both directly and indirectly influenced its member nations to extend these rights to women also. India which joined the UNO after its independence paid sufficient importance to the human rights by incorporating many of these in its constitution. India which adopted a Constitution of its own in 1949 contains several Articles mandating equality and non-discrimination on the ground of sex.

RIGHTS AND PROTECTION GIVEN TO WOMEN BY THE CONSTITUTION OF INDIA

The Constitution of India in its attempts to provide equal rights and opportunities to women, and to ensure protection and justice has made the following provisions.

1. Constitution assures equality to all its citizens including women. [Article - I4].
2. Ensures that no discrimination be made against its citizens on the basis of caste, class, creed, race, sex, place of birth or region [Article - 15(1)].
3. Does not deny or impose sanctions or conditions on its citizens to make use of any public place or institutions on the basis of sex, race, caste, religion, etc., [Article 15 (2)]
4. Recommends the State to make certain special arrangements in order to provide protection to women and children and to promote their welfare [Article - 15(3)]
5. No discrimination be made by the State against its citizens including women while providing jobs. [Article - 16].
6. To pursue a policy of providing the minimum necessities of life to the citizen without discriminating between men and women [Article 39(a)]
7. Fixing "equal remuneration for equal work" without discriminating between men and women.
8. To provide human conditions for -the citizens to fulfil their occupational obligations. The state shall take it as its responsibility to provide maternity benefits for its women employees [Article - 42].
9. Promoting harmony and fraternity among people and doing away with all the humiliating customs in respect of women [Article 51 (A) and (e)]
10. *1/3 Reservation For Women in the Panchayats* : Reserving not less than 1/3 of the total number of seats for women in the Panchayats [including the women belonging to the SCs and STs] for which direct elections are held. These reserved seats in the range of the Panchayats are to be kept on rotation basis. [Article - 243 D (3)].
11. *1/3 of Reservation for women in the Presidential Posts of the Panchayats* : Reserving not less than 1/3 of the total number of the presidential posts at all the levels of the Panchayat [Gram Panchayat, Thaluk Panchayat and Zilla Panchayat] systems [Article 243 D (4)]
12. *1/3 of the Reservation for Women in the Municipalities* : Reserving not less than 1/3 of the total number of seats for women in the town municipalities [including the women belonging to the SCs and STs] for which direct elections are held. These reserved seats in the range of the town municipalities are to be kept on rotation basis [Article 243 (T) 3.]

[43] However. the *Women's Suffrage Movement* demanding the right to vote during the first phase of the 20th century, proved to be the beginning of women's rights as "human rights".

13. *Reservation for Women in the Presidential Posts of the Town Municipalities* : While reserving the presidential posts of the town municipalities for women and also for the SCs and the STs, the relevant law framed by the state legislative body is to be followed.

STRATEGIES FOR THE PROTECTION OF WOMEN'S RIGHTS AND REHABILITATION OF WOMEN

The independent Indian Government has undertaken a number of measures with a view to promote the development and welfare of women. Some of them may be briefly mentioned here.

1. Welfare of Women Through Legislations

To ensure equal rights and opportunities for women and to provide for them '*justice*', the government undertook several legislative measures. ***Examples*** : (*i*) *The Hindu Marriage Act, 1955*; (*ii*) *The Hindu Succession Act, 1956*," (*iii*) *The Hindu Adoption and Maintenance Act, 1956*; (*iv*) *The Suppression of Immoral Traffic of Women and Girls' Act, 1956*; (*v*) *The Dowry Prohibition Act, 1961*; (*vi*) *The Equal Remuneration Act, 1976*: (*vii*) *The Factories Amendment Act, 1976*; (*viii*) *The Family Court Act, 1984*," (*ix*) *Medical Termination of Pregnancy Act, 1971*; (*x*) *The Muslim Women's Protection of Rights on Divorce Act, 1986. and lddat.*

2. Legal Assistance to Assure Justice to Women

The government established a special '*Cell*' [attached to labour department] in 1976 with a view to provide due assistance to women in distress. The responsibility of this cell is entrusted to the '*Commissioner of Police*'. The central government has also established a separate ministry with a cabinet rank to deal with the issues and problems concerned with women. To assist judiciary in its task of ensuring judicial protection to women "*social vigilance groups*" are established. Family Courts established according to "*the Family Court Act, 1984* ", are giving legal protection to women. The Social Welfare Department has established "*Women's Bureau*" in order to look into the problems of women and to find solutions for the same.

3. Establishment of National Commission for Women

The Central Government established "*the National Commission For Women*" [**NCW**] in 1992 in order to check incidents of violence against women and to promote social, legal and economic equality of women. The Commission has a Chairman, 5 members, and a Member Secretary, all nominated by the Central Government. The Commission continues to pursue its mandatory activities, namely, review of legislations, interventions in specific individual complaints of atrocities and remedial action to safeguard the interests of women. The Commission has accorded highest priority to securing speedy justice to women. In addition to the NCW, several states of India established "*State Women's Commissions*" [SWC]. By 2001, there were SWCs in as many as l7 states.

The main function of these Commissions is to inquire into the "*unfair practice*" meted out to women which includes "*mental and physical torture*". Its other functions include studying inadequacies in laws, monitoring enforcement of laws, inspecting prisons, police stations, lock-ups, refuges for women victims of violence, etc. It makes recommendations for prosecution in individual cases. **Smt. Girija Vyas** is its present [2005] national level President.

4. Relief and Rehabilitation

As per ***The Scheduled Castes and Scheduled Tribes [Prevention of Atrocities] Rules, 1989***, compensation is to be paid to members of those communities who have suffered abuses. This compensation includes ₹50,000, to a woman who has had her modesty "outraged" or been sexually exploited, and **₹2 lakh** to a woman who has been raped. But it has been observed that proper economic and social rehabilitative facilities are not provided to the victims though such legal provisions are there.

5. Government's Concern for Women Through the Observance of Women's Day Programmes

The Government's concern for women has been expressed by means of its observance of "*Women's Day Programmes*". ***For Example***:-

(*i*) The *year 1975* was observed as "***International Year of Women***" as per the call of the UNO. From 1975 onwards, the ***8th Day of March*** is being observed as "***International Women's Day***".

(*ii*) The year 1990 was observed as "***The SAARC year of the Girl Child***".

(*iii*) The Decade between 1991-2000 AD was observed as "***The SAARC Decade of the Girl Child***".

(*iv*) The year ***2001*** was observed as the "***Year of Women's Empowerment***".

6. Social and Economic Programmes For the Benefit of Women

In order to protect the social and economic interests of women, the Government has undertaken a variety of programmes among which the following may be mentioned:

(*a*) ***Educational development plan for women*** - through women study Centres, Human Resources Department, the UNICEF, NCERT, Ford Foundations, and so on.

(*b*) ***Programmes for improving women 's health*** - through Indian Council of Medical Research Ministry of Health and Family Welfare, Central Govt. Health Services Scheme, and so on.

(*c*) ***Economic development programmes for women*** - Through various schemes such as - Institute for providing vocational training for women, Women's National Training Institute,

Working Women's Hostels, the National Committee for Women Welfare, Social Assistance Schemes, The Scheme of Training, - Employment Cum Production Centres, Rastriya Mahila, Kosh (1992); Mahila Samriddhi Yoj ana, Indira Mahila Yoj ana (1995), Women's Development Corporation [WDC - 1986-87], Welfare and Support Services, and so on.

(a) Educational Development Plan for Women

The University Grants Commission had stressed as early as in 1948 the essential need for the education of women. *The Central Education Department*, the [NCERT] *National Council of Educational Research and Training*, the [NAEP] *National Adult Education Programme* and other institutions have evinced greater interest in providing educational facilities for women.

• ***Women Study Centres*** have been established with the assistance of [UGC] University Grants Commission to study the status of women and problems and issues concerned with women.

• ***Other institutions:*** Institutions such as - (*i*) **UNICEF:** *United Nations' International Children's Educational Fund*; (*ii*) **ICSSR:** *Indian Council of Social Science Research*," (*iii*) **UNESCO**: *United Nations Educational Scientific and Cultural Organisation; (iv) CSIR: Council of Scientific and Industrial Research*," (*v*) *Ford Foundation*, etc. have shown a special interest in studying women's problems.

(b) Programmes for Improving Women's Health

Various organisations, independent surveys and studies conducted by prominent individuals and private institutions brought to the notice of the Central Government at different times between 1975-85 the urgent need for improving Women's health. Various governmental agencies such as "*Indian Council of Medical Research, Ministry of Health and Family Welfare, Central Government Health Services Scheme* [*CGHS*] etc. have been paying much attention to promote women's health.

• ***In rural areas*** institutional systems such as rural *Primary Health Centres* and *Family Welfare Centres* are trying to promote women's health. *World Health Organisation*, *World Bank* and *Ford Foundation* are also showing concern in providing medical protection to women and children.

(c) Economic Development Programme for Women

The Five Year Plans launched by the Government have paid due attention to enable women to attain greater economic participation. In some of the areas such as *factories, offices, mining, clerical posts, teaching, nursing, banking, tea and coffee plantations*, etc. women employees are found in a large number. To protect the economic interests of the employed women various legislations such as *Minimum Wages Act, 1948, Equal Wages Act, 1976; the Factories Amendment Act, 1976*; etc. have been undertaken. The Karnataka and Andhra Governments have reserved some jobs for women in government sector.

• ***Employment and training of women*** : The *Programme of Support to Training-cum- Employment for Women* [STEP] was launched in 1987 to strengthen and improve the skills for employment opportunities for women below poverty line in traditional sectors of agriculture, small scale industries, animal husbandry, handlooms, handicrafts, cottage and village industries, sericulture, etc. where women are employed on a large scale.

The scheme of *Condensed Courses of Education and Vocational Training* [CCE & VT] for adult women started in 1958, is implemented by the ***Central Social Welfare Board***. It aims at providing new vistas of employment through continuing education and vocational training to women and girls, particularly to school drop-outs. During the years 1997-1999, as many as 1,000 courses were sanctioned to benefit about 50,000 Women and girls.

• ***Institutes for providing vocational training for women*** have been established at various places and in 1984 there were about 125 such institutes throughout the nation.

• ***Women's national training institute*** was started in 1977 and its regional units in places such as Bombay, Bangalore, Thiruvananthapuram, Hissar, Calcutta were also opened. The *Regional Training Institute* at Bangalore gives "*basic*" and also modern training to about 1,426 girls and part-time training to about 141 girls every year.

• ***Socio-economic programme*** **:** Under this programme, the Central Social Welfare Board gives financial assistance to the voluntary organisations for undertaking a wide variety of income–generating activities, which include the production of central components in ancillary units, handlooms, handicrafis, agro based activities such as animal husbandry, sericulture, and fisheries, and self employment ventures like vegetables or fish-vending, etc.

• ***The dairy scheme*** focuses exclusively on women's organisations having at least 20 women members, including *Mahila Mandals, Indira Mahila Kendras, Self Help Groups*[44] and organisations already assisted under STEP scheme. The benefits of the scheme are meant for women whose families are below the poverty line.

• ***Mahila samriddhi yojana*** **:** This scheme was launched on 2nd Oct. 1993, through a network of 1.32 lakh rural Post Offices to promote thrift among rural women and to empower them with greater control over their household sources. After the completion of 2 years of implementation of this Yojana it was decided to launch a new scheme which would cover approximately 885 blocks in which about 20 lakh women would be benefited.

• ***Rashtriya mahila kosh*** **[RMK] :** The national credit fund for women called *The Rashtriya Mahila Kosh* was set up in 1992-93 with a corpus fund of ₹31 crores with a major objective of meeting the credit needs of poor women, particularly in the informal sector. The Minister of State for Women and Child Development is the Chairperson of this *Kosh*. The Rh/ [K has sanctioned up to 31st March 1998, loans of ₹47.85 crores to benefit 2.50 lakh women through 256 NGOs.

• ***Working women's hostels*** have been established in towns and cities mainly to provide board and lodging facilities to rural women who move on to urban centres to obtain jobs. Governmental and private agencies are taking initiative in opening such hostels. In some hostels, day-care centres for children of these women are also attached. During 1992-93 as many as 23 additional hostels were sanctioned to provide accommodation to 2,269 working women. This brought the total number of hostels to over 811 [by 1999] benefiting over 56,974 working women.

• ***The national committee for women welfare*** is instituted for framing appropriate policies for women welfare to suit to the changing needs of time.

• ***Indira mahila yojana*** **[IMY] :** The *Indira Mahila Yojana* that aims at organising women at the grass root level to facilitate their participation in decision making and empowerment, was launched on 20th August 1995, in 200 *Integrated Child Development Services* [ICDS] blocks. The strength of the scheme lies in the strength of group dynamics. The objectives of the scheme are – *awareness generation among the women from rural areas and urban slums and economic empowerment of women*.

7. The Central Social Welfare Board

The Central Social Welfare Board **[CSWB]** was set up in 1953 with the objective of promoting social welfare activities and implementing welfare programmes for women, children and the handicapped through voluntary organisations. The CSWB is unique in the sense that it was the first organisation in post independent era to achieve people's participation for implementation of welfare programmes for women and children through the Non-Government Organisations [NGOs].

The CSWB established by the *Planning Commission*, has its own women welfare programmes such as *providing housing protection to weak and helpless women, fallen women, helpless widows; creating centres of social education for women and adult education centres, condensed courses of education and vocational training courses for women and girls, awareness generation projects for rural and poor women, family counselling centres, holiday camps for children, welfare extension projects in border areas, opening centres for giving healthy entertainment to the women, giving assistance to creche: and hostels for working women*, etc. The Board gives financial subsidy of ₹50,000/- annually to those private agencies [NGOs] which provide good service to the women. Presently, more than 18,000 NGOs are receiving financial assistance and guidance from the Board.

• ***Voluntary organisation in the service of women:*** (*i*) *Mobile Creches* for working mother's children aged upto 12 years; (*ii*) "*Annapoorna*" women's co-operative Society to provide mid-day meal to working women; (*iii*) *Self-Employed Women Association*, a registered trade union to organise women rag-pickers, head-loaders, junksmith, fish vendors, bamboo-workers, beedi workers, block-printers, used garment dealers has come into being to get a fair deal for women workers.

---

[44] Stree Shakti Scheme Self-Help Groups - SGHs] to Empower Women Economically : Karnataka Model: In order to empower rural women economically, the Karntaka Govemment [under the Chief Ministership of S.M. Krishna] launched the '*Stree Shakti Scheme*' to forge "*Self-help* Groups" among women. ***Purposes***: (*i*) To strengthen the process of economic development of women. (*ii*) To establish at **least one lakh** SIIGs during 2000-2001. (*iii*) To enhance financial stability in rural women by involving them in income generating activities such as producing - detergent powder, cleaning powder, bleaching powder, candle making, coirs, mat-making, toy-making, agarbatti making, etc. This scheme was intended to empower at least two million rural women in Karnataka by the end of the year 2002. These SGHs seem to be functioning comparatively well in many of the rural areas of Karnataka at present [2005].

Conclusion: It is true that the Central and the State governments have undertaken various legislative and other measures for promoting the welfare of women. We cannot, however, say that the intended purpose of the Governments is fulfilled and the targeted persons have received all the benefits. The educated, middle class and upper caste women of towns and cities have taken relatively greater advantage of these measures, whereas the vast mass of uneducated, lower class and lower caste women of the rural areas are not even aware of most of these welfare measures. The deficiencies involved in these measures and the inefficient implementation of the developmental programmes by the indifferent bureaucrats have come in the way of the success of these measures. In spite of these shortcomings, the awareness of women regarding these measures is slowly growing. After the lapse of a few centuries, the society is becoming slowly aware of the historic necessity of providing women a respectable position in society and paying special attention to the problems haunting them.

THE POSITION AND THE PROBLEMS OF INDIAN WOMEN: FUTURE PROSPECTS

The discussion regarding the status of Indian women has been there since decades. It is an acknowledged fact that though the Indian women are given importance in society, their status is not equal to that of men. Indian women are not able to lead a free and independent life as their counterpart do in the West. Still it is astonishing to observe that Indian women who suffered from various problems and setbacks for more than 2000 years, have been trying to come out of their traditional shells and getting themselves ready to make the best use of the opportunities offered to them.

What will happen to the status of Indian women in the near future? Will they become free from the problems with which they suffered for centuries ? Can we expect better status and brighter prospects for our women in the years to come? Will they be able to lead a free and independent life as their counterparts do in the West ? Or, whether their status is going to deteriorate further in future? Will they attain equality with their menfolk ? These are some of the questions currently being discussed in connection with the status of Indian women. On the basis of the existing state of affairs some observations and broad generalisations could be made regarding this issue.

1. ***New problems in place of old ones*** **:** The age-old problems of Indian women such as *child marriage, sati system, prohibition on widow remarriage, purdah system, devadasi system* etc. have almost disappeared. They have disappeared only to give room for some other problems of modem times such as *atrocities against women, rape, dowry harassments and deaths, immoral trafic of women, oppression and exploitation of 'dalit' and minority women, torture and harassment of women undertrials, sexual harassment of employed women* etc. These problems have made it difficult for women to lead an equal life with men.
2. ***Continued dominance of male supremacy*** **:** The Indian society continues to be a male dominated society. Though sex equality has been achieved by law, it is difficult to practise it socially. The belief that the biological and cultural roles of men and women are different, is very strong in India. As long as this belief persists, and the value of male dominance prevails, male-female equality cannot be achieved in the Indian context.
3. ***Regional, caste and class differences*** **:** As **Andre Beteille** has observed that there is a close link between the statuses and problems of Women on the one band and the region, religion, caste and class to which they belong, on the other. These differences may continue in the coming years also. These differences are putting some hurdles on the way of Indian women developing some "*common interests*".
4. **Relaxed control over women :** As **S.C. Dube** has pointed out there are three principal areas in which controls are exercised on women:[45]-(*i*) *Women's sexuality" is controlled much more strictly than men's* (*ii*) *There are restrictions on women 's movements and contacts*; (*iii*) *Women's resources* [*labour and skills*] *need regulation and control*. On these three issues modern Indian women are more free, no doubt; but they are not equal to men. Most of them do not bother about attaining equality with men in these areas.
5. ***Women exploiting women*** **:** In the Indian context, we also find social situations in which women themselves are exploiting women in one way or another. **Examples:** '*Gharwalis*' or '*lady bosses* ' in the brothel homes exploiting prostitutes, mothers-in-law harassing and torturing daughters- in-law. Situation is improving in this field for the educated women are becoming quite conscious of their rights.
6. ***Lack of powerful women organisations and movements*** **:** Indian women are forging ahead in the fields of education and employment. But they have not developed powerful women organisations nor movements to safeguard their interests. Neither at the national level nor at the state' level, is such a strong women"s organisation found. This situation has further added to the exploitation of women.

[45] S.C. Dube in his *Indian Society*, p. 95

7. ***Is there not a need for women's liberation movement in india* ? :** On the basis of the existing social situations, it can be said that there is no possibility of a ***feminist movement*** or a women's liberation movement emerging out in India to assert the rights of women. Since Indian women give due importance to motherhood, rearing of children and household work which they consider as "*women's tasks*"; they do not appreciate "*women's liberation movement*" of the western type which fights for equality with men in all respects. As **Romila Thapar** has observed, "*women's liberation does not have any immediate relevance to the Indian social situation.*"[46]
8. ***No protection to the interests of lower class and lower caste women* :** In all discussions and debates relating to the status of Indian women, much is said about middle and upper class women and upper caste educated women. The statuses and problems of lower class and lower caste women who constitute the majority of womenfolk, are not given due importance. This only shows that our discussions are misleading, one-sided, partial and even prejudiced. Majority of Indian women who are illiterate and ignorant are not capable of changing their life-styles, beliefs and values overnight. They take time to change themselves. Hence, no revolutionary change can be witnessed in the overall social position of Indian women at least in the immediate future.
9. ***Indifferent attitude the governments and political leaders* :** The measures taken and the programmes implemented by the Central and State governments so far in the direction of raising the status of Indian women and protecting their interests, are neither promising nor adequate. Laws and legislations alone cannot bring about desired changes in the society. Consistent and honest efforts on the part of people's representatives and social leaders are required to persuade people to accept new situations and challenges. Such efforts are conspicuously absent in India.

Conclusion : Women in India are not yet equal to men. There is no legal or constitutional barrier to equality. There is only the social barrier. Women in India are more after a "*respectable*" and "*meaningful*" social status which is free from all sorts of exploitation. There is no urge in them to outsmart men. They want their interests to be protected and problems solved. As long as the problems of women remain as "*women's problems*" and not as "*societal problems*", so long, attempts at the solution of these problems do not get the required speed.

Indian women are not very much after equality with men. But they expect a change in the attitude of men towards them and their status. On the contrary, *they expect greater freedom, better education, self-dependence, decent jobs, a proper treatment of women by menfolk, and a socio-economic environment free from all types of exploitation.* Our attempts to provide such a type of socio-economic environment to women will definitely influence their social status and the socio-economic conditions in the days to come.

INDIAN WOMEN ON THE PATH OF EXCELLENCE.....

• During the recent years Indian women have been forging ahead as a powerful force of social change. This fact is home out by their exceptionally impressive achievements in certain fields. Some examples:

• So far 4 Indian women have secured "Bharata Ratna". The highest national award. The recipients of the award are : (*i*) **Indira Gandhi** [1917-1984] awarded in 1971; (*ii*) **Mother Teresa** [Mary Teresa Bojaxhiu [1910-1997] awarded in 1980; (*iii*) **Aruna Asaf Ali** [1909-1996] awarded posthumously in 1997; and (*iv*) **Lata Mangeshkar** [Sushri Lara Dinanatha Mangeshkar - [1929 ...] awarded in 2001.

• Indira Gandhi could rise to the level of Prime Minister and rule India for 10-11 years, while more than 11 other women could excel themselves as Chief Ministers.

• ***Women as IAS, IFS and IPS Officers*** : In 1948, there was not a single woman in these posts. In 1951, one woman was recruited to the post of I.A.S., it increased to 18 between 1951 and 1960, and then to 339 in 1987 [By then, women IAS officials constituted 7.45% of the total 4548 posts]. By 1993, 17 women IAS officers were working as Deputy Commissioners and around S7 women officers were working in different departments of the Central Government.

• ***Women in IFS and IPS* :** Up to 1993, around 409 people were selected IFS officers out of whom 40 were women. Of these 40 officers, only 6 were selected as Indian ambassadors in foreign countries.

• **Dr. Kiran Bedi** and **Kanchan C. Bhattacharya** have made name as IPS officers. [**Achievement of Dr. Kiran Bedi as IPS Officer** : Dr. Kiran Bedi was the first police officer [in the Cadre of [PS] in the world to enter the police service. When she was posted as the Inspector General of Prisons at the biggest national level jail, namely, **Tihar**, at New Delhi, she resorted to some innovative ways of reforming the jail and its conditions. She sought to breakdown adversarial relations between the police and the community of prisoners. She tried "*to replace the hard hand of punishment with the soft one of correction and rehabilitation*". In recognition of her yeomen service she was awarded in 1994 "*Ramon Magrayray Award*"

[46] Romila Thapar in her article Looking Back in History *in Indian Women, pp.* 5-6.

which is popularly known as the "*Asian Nobel Prize*". **Kanchan C. Bhattacharya** has been the first to become the woman DGP [Deputy General of Police] and is currently [2005] serving the State of Uttaranchal.]

• ***Women in the Field of Judiciary*** : At present, there are about 19 women judges out of a sanctioned strength of 647 judges in 21 high courts. **Fathima Bibi** of Kerala became the first woman judge in the Supreme Court.

• ***Women in the Educational Field*** : The literacy level of women has risen from 39.29% in 1991 " to 54% in 2001. As per the latest information. 1.25 lakh women graduate as doctors every year. This is 50% of the total number. Further, 21% of India's software professionals and 25% of science and engineering graduates are women. More than 50% of the students who pass out every year with a bachelor's degree in humanities are girls. **[*Source of these Vital Statistics*** : "*India Today*", April 4, 2005, Page : 32.] women are also not lagging behind in the fields such as art. literature and sports. Some have reached great heights in these fields.

REVIEW QUESTIONS

1. Write an essay on sexual inequality and sexual discrimination in society.
2. Throw light on the traditional bases of sexual identity.
3. Write the differences between the sexes based on the kinds of evidences.
4. Write a brief note on the gender-based division of labour in society.
5. Are women exceptionally delicate and weak? comment
6. Who is more important to society man or woman? Examine.
7. What is the role of women in society? Explain.
8. Explain the role of various agencies in the process of sex-role socialisation.
9. Discuss the theories of sex-role differentiation.
10. Explain the concept of sexism. Discuss the consequences of sexism.
11. Explain the concept of feminism. Discuss the growth of feminism.
12. Discuss the features of feminist movement.
13. Discuss the changes the occurred in the status of women in Indian society after independence.
14. Explain the problems of women in modern India.
15. Discuss the concept of empowerment of women. Highlight the strategies of the Government of India for women's development.
16. Discuss in detail about the schemes and strategies for women empowerment in India.
17. Explain the concept of human rights. What are the main human rights? Write their characteristic features.
18. What are the strategies of the Government of India for the protection of Women's rights and their rehabilitation? Explain.
19. Throw light on the future prospects of the position and problems of Indian women.

⌘⌘⌘⌘⌘⌘⌘⌘⌘⌘⌘

17

CULTURE AND CIVILISATION

CHAPTER OUTLINE

- Meaning of Culture
- Culture Contents
- Sub-culture
- Culture Growth: Cultural Diffusion, Invention and Discovery
- Cultural Systems and Sub-Systems
- Civilisation
- Interdependence of and Interrelationship between Culture and Civilisation.
- Characteristics of Culture
- Functions of Culture
- Development of Culture
- Elements of Culture
- Cultural Change
- Distinction between Culture and Civilisation

MEANING OF CULTURE

'Culture' is one of the most important concepts in social science. It is commonly used in Psychology, Political Science and Economics. It is the main concept in Anthropology and a fundamental one in Sociology. The study of human society immediately and necessarily leads us to the study of its culture. The study of society or any aspect of it becomes incomplete without a proper understanding of the culture of that society. Culture and society go together. They are inseparable.

Culture is Unique to Man

Culture is a unique possession of man. It is one of the distinguishing traits of human society. Culture does not exist at the sub-human level. Only man is born and brought up in a cultural environ- ment. Other animals live in a natural environment. Every man is born into a society is the same as saying that every man is born into a culture. The dictum *Man is a social being* can thus be redefined as '*man is a cultural being*'. Every man can be regarded as a representative of his culture. Culture is the unique quality of man which separates him from the lower animals.

Culture is a very broad term that includes in itself all our walks of life, our modes of behaviour, our philosophies and ethics, our morals and manners, our customs and traditions, our religious, political, economic and other types of activities. Culture includes all that man has acquired in his individual and social life. In the words of *MacIver* and *Page*, culture is "the realm of styles, of values, of emotional attachments, of intellectual adventures". It is the entire '*social heritage*' which the individual receives from the group.

What Culture is Not

The term '*culture*' is given a wide variety of meanings and interpretations. Some of them are purely non-sociological if not completely wrong. People often speak of culture as synonymous with education. Accordingly, they apply the term '*cultured*' to an educated person or group and '*uncultured*' to one lacking in or devoid of education. Difference between

'Cultured' and 'Uncultured' may have something to do with personal refinement also. Possession of it indicates that one knows how to conduct himself in all the social situations to which he is likely to be exposed. The man of culture has good manners and good tastes. Further, one may be inclined to believe that a bachelor of arts degree possesses '*better*' culture than others. In sociology 'culture' does not mean personal refinement. The sociological meaning of the word is quite different.

Historians use the word 'culture' in yet another way to refer to the so-called 'higher' achievements of group lite or of a period of history. By 'higher' achievements they mean achievements in art, music, literature, philosophy, religion and science. Thus, a cultural history of India would be an account of historical achievements in these fields. The adjective 'cultural' would differentiate this kind of history from political history, industrial history, military history, etc. Here again, sociologists never use the term culture to mean the so called 'higher' achievements of group life–art, religion, philosophy, etc. They use culture to mean '*all*' the achievements of group life. Further, culture and nationality are not necessarily synonymous. But in the modern world the nation state has become the strongest unifying force in social organisation. Social scientists treat modern nations as if they were cultural entities. But in reality people of the same nationality may have dissimilar cultural features too as it is in India.

DEFINITION OF CULTURE

1. *B. Malinowski* has defined culture as the 'cumulative creation of man'. He also regards culture as the handiwork of man and the medium through which he achieves his ends.
2. *Graham Wallas*, an English sociologist has defined culture as an accumulation of thoughts, values and objects; it is the social heritage acquired by us from preceding generations through learning, as distinguished from the biological heritage which is passed on to us automatically through the genes.
3. *CC. North* is of the opinion that culture 'consists in the instruments constituted by man tc assist him in satisfying his wants.'
4. *Robert Biersteat* is of the opinion that 'culture is the complex whole that consists of all the ways we think and do and everything we have as members of society'.
5. *E. V. de Roberty* regards culture as 'the body of thoughts and knowledge, both theoretical and practical, which only man can possess.'
6. *Edward B. Tylor*, a famous English anthropologist, has defined culture as 'that complex whole which includes knowledge, belief, art, morals, law, custom, and any other capabilities and habits acquired by man as a member of society'. Tylor's definition is widely quoted and used today.

CHARACTERISTICS OF CULTURE

The definitions cited above reveal some of the characteristics of culture. For a clear under standing of the concept of culture, it is necessary for us to know its main features.

1. ***Culture is learnt:*** Culture is not inherited biologically, but learnt socially by man. It is not an inborn tendency. There is no cultural instinct as such. Culture is often called '*learned ways of behaviour*'. Unlearned behaviour, such as closing the eyes while sleeping, the eye blinking reflex and so on. are purely physiological and not cultural. Shaking hands or saying '*namaskar*' or '*thanks*' and shaving and dressing, on the other hand, are cultural. Similarly, wearing clothes, combing the hair, wearing ornaments, cooking the food, drinking from a glass, eating from a plate or a leaf, reading a newspaper, driving a car, enacting a role in a drama, singing, worshipping, etc., are all ways of behaviour learnt by man culturally.
2. ***Culture is social***: Culture does not exist in isolation. Neither is it an individual phenomenon. It is a product of society. It originates and develops through social interactions. It is shared by the members of society. No man can acquire culture without association with other human beings. Man becomes man only among men. It is the culture which helps man to develop human qualities in a human environment. Deprivation of company or association of other individuals to an individual is nothing but depriva- tion of human qualities.
3. ***Culture is shared***: Culture in the sociological sense, is something shared. It is not something that at individual alone can possess. For example, customs, traditions, beliefs, ideas, values, morals, etc., are all shared by people of a group or society. The inventions of Arya Bhatta or Albert Einstein, 'Charaka' or Charles Darwin; the literary works of Kalidasa or Keats, Dandi or Dante; the philosophical works of Confucius or Lao Tse, Shankaracharya or Swami Vivekananda; the artistic works of Ravi Verma or Raphael, etc., are all shared by a large number of people.

'*Culture is something adopted, used, believed, practised, or possessed by more than one person. It depends upon group life for its existence*'. (*Robert Bierstedt*).

4. ***Culture is transmissive***: Culture is capable of being transmitted from one generation to the next. Parents pass on culture traits to their children and they in turn to their children, and so on. Culture is transmitted not through genes but by means of language. Language is the main vehicle of culture. Language in its different forms like reading, writing and speaking makes it possible for the present generation to understand the achievements of earlier generations. But language itself is a part of culture. Once language is acquired, it unfolds to the individual its wide field. Transmission of culture may take place by imitation as well as by instruction.
5. ***Culture is continuous and cumulative***: Culture exists as a continuous process. In its historical growth it tends to become cumulative. Culture is a '*growing whole*' which includes in itself, the achievements of the past and the present and makes provision for the future achievements of mankind. "Culture may thus be conceived of as a kind of stream flowing down through the centuries from one generation to another". Hence some sociologists like *Linton* called culture '*the social heritage*' of man. As *Robert Bierstedt* writes, culture is '*the memory of the human race*'. It becomes difficult for us to imagine what society would be like without this accumulation of culture, what our lives would be without it.
6. ***Culture is consistent and integrated***: Culture, in its development has revealed a tendency to be consistent. At the same time different parts of culture are interconnected. For example, the value system of a society is closely connected with its other aspects such as morality, religion, customs, traditions, beliefs, and so on.
7. ***Culture is dynamic and adaptive***: Though culture is relatively stable it is not altogether static. It is subject to slow but constant changes. Change and growth are latent in culture. We find amazing growth in the present Indian culture when we compare it with the culture of the Vedic times. Culture is hence dynamic.

   Culture is *responsive* to the changing conditions of the physical world. It is *adaptive*. It also intervenes in the natural environment and helps man in his process of adjustment. Just as our houses shelter us from the storm, so also does our culture help us from natural dangers and assist us to survive. Few of us, indeed, could survive without culture.
8. ***Culture is gratifying***: Culture provides proper opportunities and prescribes means for the satisfaction of our needs and desires. These needs may be biological or social in nature. Our need for food, shelter, and clothing on the one hand, and our desire for status, name, fame, money, mates, etc., are all, for example, fulfilled according to the cultural ways. Culture determines and guides the varied activities of man. In fact, culture is defined as the process through which human beings satisfy their wants.
9. ***Culture varies from society to society***: Every society has a culture of its own. It differs from society to society. Culture of every society is unique to itself. Cultures are not uniform. Cultural elements such as customs, traditions, morals, ideals, values, ideologies, beliefs, practices, philosophies, institutions, etc., are not uniform everywhere. Ways of eating, speaking, greeting, dressing, entertaining, living, etc., of different societies differ significantly. Culture varies from time to time also. No culture ever remains constant or changeless. If Manu were to come back to see the Indian society today he would be bewildered to witness the vast changes that have taken place in our culture.
10. ***Culture is superorganic and ideational***: Culture is sometimes called 'the *superorganic*'. By 'superorganic' *Herbert Spencer* meant that culture is neither organic nor inorganic in nature but above these two. The term implies the social meaning of physical objects and physiological acts. The social meaning may be independent of physiological and physical properties and characteristics. For example, the social meaning of a national flag is not just 'a piece of coloured cloth'. The flag represents a nation. Similarly, priests and prisoners, professors and professionals, players, engineers and doctors, farmers and soldiers, and others are not just biological beings. They are viewed in their society differently. Their social status and role can be understood only through culture.

Further, every society considers its culture as an *ideal*. It is regarded as an end in itself. It is intrinsically valuable. The people are also aware of their culture as an ideal one. They are proud of their cultural heritage.

CULTURE AND SOCIETY

Culture and society are not one and the same. A culture is a system of behaviour shared by the members of a society. A society is a group of people who share a common culture. As *Lalph Linton puts it, 'A society is an organised group of individuals. A Culture is an organised group of learned responses characteristic of a particular society*'.

A society is composed of people who are interacting on the basis of shared beliefs, customs, values, and activities. The common patterns which govern their interaction make up the culture of the society. As *Gillin* and *Gillin* have pointed out, '*culture is the cement binding together into a society its component individuals human society is people interacting; culture is the patterning of their behaviour ...*'

CULTURE CONTENTS

Every society has a culture of its own. Thus people in different societies all over the world have different cultures. These cultures are not only diverse but also unequal. Along with cultural diversities and disparities that are found in societies. throughout the world, we observe certain cultural similarities. People may worship different gods in different ways, but they all have a religion. They may pursue various occupations, but they all earn a living. Details of their rituals, ceremonies, customs, etc., may differ, but they all neverthless have some ritual, ceremonies, customs, etc. Every culture consists of such non-material things. Similarly, people of every society possess material things of different kinds. These material things may be primitive or modem and simple or complex in nature. These material and non-material components of culture are often referred to as "*the content of culture*".

A number of sociologists have classified the content of culture into large components '*material culture*' and '*non-material culture*'. *Ogburn* has even used this distinction as the basis for 'a theory of cultural change. As *Robert Bierstedt* has pointed out, the concept of 'material culture' is relatively more precise and less ambiguous. But the concept of non-material culture is more ambiguous and less clear. It may be used as a '*residual category*' that is to mean '*Everything that is not material*'.

Material Culture

Material culture consists of man-made objects such as tools, implements, furniture, automo- biles, buildings, dams, roads, bridges, and in fact, the physical substance which has been changed and used by man. It is concerned with the external, mechanical and utilitarian objects. It includes technical and material equipments like a printing press, a locomotive, a telephone, a television, a tractor, a machine gun, etc. It includes our banks, parliaments, insurance schemes, currency systems, etc. It is referred to as *civilisation*.

Non-Material Culture

The term '*culture*' when used in the ordinary sense, means 'non-material culture'. It is some- thing internal and intrinsically-valuable, reflects the inward nature of man. Non-material culture consists of the words the people use or the language they speak, the beliefs they hold, values and virtues they cherish, habits they follow, rituals and practices that they do and the ceremonies they observe. It also includes our customs and tastes, attitudes and outlook, in brief, our ways of acting, feeling and thinking.

FUNCTIONS OF CULTURE

Man is not only a social animal but also a cultural being. Man's social life has been made possible because of culture. Culture is something that has elevated him from the level of animal to the heights of man. Man cannot survive as man without culture. It represents the entire achievements of mankind. Culture has been fulfilling a number of functions among which the following may be noted.

1. ***Culture is the treasury of knowledge:*** Culture provides knowledge which is essential for the physical, social and intellectual existence of man. Birds and animals behave instinctively. With the help of instincts they try to adapt themselves with the environment. But man has greater intelligence and learning capacity. With the help of these he has been able to adapt himself with the environment or modify it to suit his convenience. Culture has made such an adaptation and modification possible and easier by providing man the necessary skills and knowledge. Culture preserves knowledge and helps its transmission from generation to generation through its element, that is, language. Language helps not only the transmission of knowledge but also its preservation, accumulation and diffusion. On the contrary, animals do not have this advantage. Because, culture does not exist at sub-human level.
2. ***Culture defines situations:*** Culture defines social situations for us. It not only defines but also conditions and determines–what we eat and drink, what we wear, when to laugh, weep, sleep, love, to make friends with, what work we do, what God we worship, what knowledge we rely upon, What poetry we recite and so on.
3. ***Culture defines attitudes, values and goals:*** Attitudes refer to the tendency to feel and act in certain ways. Values are the measure of goodness or desirability; Goals refer to the attainments which our values define as worthy. It is the culture which conditions our attitude towards various issues such as religion, morality, marriage, science,

family planning, prostitution and so on. Our values concerning private property, fundamental rights, representative government, romantic love, etc., are influenced by our culture. Our goals of winning the race, understanding others, attaining salvation, being obedient to elders and teachers, being loyal to husband, being patriotic, etc., are all set forth by our culture. We are being socialised on these models.

4. ***Culture decides our career:*** Whether we should become a politician, a social worker, a doctor, an engineer, a soldier, a farmer, a professor, an industrialist, a religious leader, and so on is decided by our culture. What career we are likely to pursue is largely decided by our culture. Culture sets limitations on our choice to select different careers. Individuals may develop, modify or oppose the trends of their culture but they always live within its framework. Only a few can find outlet in the culture.
5. ***Culture provides behaviour pattern:*** Culture directs and confines the behaviour of an individual. Culture assigns goals and provides means for achieving them. It rewards his noble works and punishes the ignoble ones. It assigns him statuses and roles. We see, dream, aspire, work, strive, marry, enjoy according to the cultural expectation. Culture not only controls but also liberates human energy and activities. Man, indeed, is a prisoner of his culture.
6. ***Culture moulds personality:*** Culture exercises a great influence on the development of personality. No child can develop human qualities in the absence of a cultural environment. Culture prepares man for group life and provides him the design of living. It is the culture that provides opportunities for the development of personality and sets limits on its growth. As *Ruth Benedict* has pointed out, every culture will produce its special type or types of personality. This fact has been stressed by her in her "*Patterns of Culture*"–an analysis of the culture of three primitive societies. Yet another American anthropologist by name *Margaret Mead* has stated that "a culture shapes the character and behaviour of individuals living in it This fact she has established in her "*Sex and Temperament in Three Primitive Societies*"–a study of New Guinea tribal life.

It is true 'that the individual is exposed to and moulded by the culture of the group into which he is born. But the culture provides not only for '*universals*' but also for '*alternatives*'. There is not only conformity in cultural learning but also variations. Still no individual is completely culturally determined. Every individual is unique in any culture. The uniqueness may be based on individual differences in ability, aptitude and learning. The impact of culture on the individual is not always identical in every case. Every individual is sooner or later exposed to influences which are not completely predetermined by culture. He meets other people outside the culture. Travelling, books, radio, cinema, television, theatre, newspapers expose an individual to many influences outside the culture. Various biological and social factors bring about the uniqueness of the individuals in any culture.

SUB-CULTURE

Meaning of Sub-Culture

The term '*Culture*' is used in various ways to mean various things. When used in a broad sense, it represents human life and portrays human achievements. In this sense the term culture is understood as the great social heritage of entire mankind. It is sometimes used in a limited sense to mean a "*national culture*", that is, to refer to the culture of a nation. A nation consists of a number of groups and subgroups. Each such group may have a way of life of its own. In other words, each such group has a culture of its own. Cultures of such groups are known as 'sub-cultures'. These groups and sub-groups that are found within a national society differ from one another not just with regard to one or the other cultural trait, but in many respects. They ...."constitute relatively cohesive cultural systems. They are world within the larger world of our national culture". They are sub-cultures.

As *Duncan Mitchell* has pointed out, "*a sub-culture is generally taken to mean a section of a national culture*".

Culture is not a uniform pattern that impresses alike upon all who are exposed to it. It is important to keep in mind that a person's exposure is not to "*culture in general*" but to the cultures of the particular groups in which he lives. It is so because in large societies, each person's groups are multiple. *For example*, we are members of Indian society and, therefore, share in Indian culture. But we are also members of smaller population segment within the larger society. Regional groups, religious groups, nationality groups, racial groups, occupational groups, class groups, caste groups, urban groups, rural groups, etc., represent such population segments. Each such group has a culture of its own. Such a culture is known as "*sub-culture*". These sub-cultures are parts of a national culture. According to *Sutherland*, *Woodward* and *Maxwell*, the main sub-cultures are–*regional sub-culture, ethnic or nationality sub-cultures, urban and rural sub-cultures, class sub-culture, occupational sub-culture, and the religious sub-culture*.

Sub-Cultures within Sub-Cultures

We have not only sub-cultures in our society, but we can identify sub-cultures within sub-cultures. Caste, for example, as a sub-culture has many small sub-cultures within itself in the form of sub-castes. Similarly, a district as a regional sub-culture may have many Thaluk sub-cultures, and so on. Thus, in a very restricted sense, each family may stand as an example of a small sub-culture.

Sub-Cultural Influence

The sub-cultures exercise a great influence upon the individual members. Not all of the children in the same society confront the same culture because of the many sub-cultures that every complex society contains. Greater the complexity of the society larger will be the number of such sub-cultures. Each sub-culture may have its own folkways, customs, etiquettes, mores, beliefs, practices, rites, rituals, ceremonies, dress styles, conversational styles, entertainment means, and so on. Thus they exert a wide influence upon the members.

As *Sutherland, Woodward* and *Maxwell* have pointed out that "*any one person experiences his several sub-cultures as a unit*". *Example*: A lower class Brahmin of Karnataka is not actually a member of three separate sub-cultures: lower class, *Brahmin*, and *Karnataka*. But he is a *Karnataka-Lower-Class-Brahmin*. He lives in a group of persons like himself and his personality has upon it the stamp of their common "*Karnataka-Lower-Class Brahmin Sub-Culture*". So it is with each person: his subcultural exposure is an integrated one. This fact does not undermine the importance of the various sub-cultures. But it only stresses the unified and integrated Way in which a particular person meets the sub-cultural influences. This influence contributes to an important difference in his personality.

DEVELOPMENT OF CULTURE

Man is the only animal who possesses *culture*. It is a unique possession of man. Culture is associated with the species known as '*Homo Sapiens*', the final product of organic evolution. When exactly the Homo Sapiens emerged and how exactly they developed 'culture'–their unique quality? What biological or other factors and forces have enabled or compelled man who belongs to the species Homo Sapiens, to become distinct from other animals by the possession of culture? These and such other questions are very much relevant in any discussion of the origin and development of culture. For want of space we are only making a brief reference to the development of culture.

The distinctive human way of life that we call culture did not have a single definite beginning in time. This is obvious because men never suddenly appeared simultaneously on all parts of earth at a single time. Culture evolved slowly just as some anthropoids gradually took on more human form.

Culture is often understood as anything that is created and cultivated by man. Man's culture in a way has begun with man's capacity to use and to create or produce tools and techniques. The earliest tools used by man cannot be dated exactly. *Australopithecus* may have used stones as long as 5 million years ago. The Australopithecus walked erect, lived on the ground and probably used stones as weapons. (Before these, a man–like primate called *Ramapithecus* lived about 14 million years ago). Stones that have been used as weapons do not differ systematically from other stones. However, nothing can be said with certainty about this early period. But we have evidence to say that the first stones shaped as tools were used some 5 to 6 million years ago.

The use of fire can be dated from 2 to 3 million years ago. Tools of bone have come into existence by one million B.C., that is, *Age of Neanderthal* man. The Neanderthals also apparently had some form of language and buried their dead with an elaborateness that indicates the possibility of religious ceremonies.

"*Cro-Magnon* dating from 25,000 years ago was a superior biological specimen, and he had correspondingly a more elaborate culture. Cro-Magnon's brain averaged 1650 c.c. even larger than that of modern man. His cave-paintings are also well known. He also made jewellery of shells and teeth, and he carved statuettes of women that emphasised pregnancy, and fertility. He made weapons of bone, horn, and ivory, and he used needles in the fabrication of garments".–*Leslie, Lorman* and *Gorman*.

Thus, we find a striking parallel between the biological evolution of man and the development of culture. But the parallel cannot be drawn in minute details. Because all our inferences relating to the period before the beginning of history must be made on the basis of the remains of the material artifacts that are collected. These do not tell us much about the total way of life of people who used. them. Further, the parallel between biological and cultural evolution should not be overdrawn.

CULTURE GROWTH

As it is stated already we do not know when exactly the human culture began. Any attempt to fix an exact date for the beginning of culture would be an extremely arbitrary one. One way of representing the growth of culture over time is to select an arbitrary starting date and to divide man's experience from that point into "*life-times*". *Alvin Toffler*, for example, in his "*Future Shock*", has made such an attempt. He divided the last 50,000 years of experience into 62 years 'life-times' placing man currently in his 800th life-time.

"According to this chronology, 650 life-times were spent in caves. Written language has existed only for the last 70 life-times, and the printed world has been widely available only for the last 6 life–times. The electric motor has existed for only 2 life-times. Television, airplanes, automobiles, and nuclear weapons all developed within the 800th lifetime and 90% of all the scientists who have ever existed are alive during this lifetime. All of modem technology has developed in less than l/25,000th of the total time it has taken for human culture to reach its present level of development". [*Leslie, Lorntan* and *Gorman*].

The above description reveals that in the beginning, "the growth of culture was exceedingly slow and only recently has culture begun to change rapidly. The explanation for this situation is to be found in the fact that culture grows in *two ways*: through (*i*) *invention of new traits within the culture* or through (*ii*) *diffusion of new traits from outside the culture*.

1. Cultural Diffusion

The process of diffusion involves the spread of cultural elements–both material artifacts and ideas–from one culture to another. *George Murdock* has estimated that about 90% of the contents of every culture have been acquired from other societies. Some social scientists and anthropologists like, for example, *Kroeber*, consider diffusion as the main source of cultural and social change.

The term '*diffusion*' which means "*the borrowing of cultural elements from another society*" is in contrast to the term '*invention*' which means finding out the new uses of existing knowledge by recombining the existing cultural elements.

Anthropologist Linton's classic illustration can be cited here to make *it clear* to what extent cultural borrowings–that is, '*diffusion*' takes place in every society. *Linton* writes, "*our solid American citizen awakens in a bed built on a pattern which originated in the New East but which was modified in North Europe before it was transmitted to America. He throws back the covers made from cotton domesticated in India. or linen domesticated in the Near East, or silk, the use of which was discovered in China. All of these materials have been spun and woven by processes invented in the Near East. He takes off his paijamas, a garment invented in India,"and washes with soap, invented by the ancient Gauls. He then shaves, a masochistic rite, which seems to have been derived from either Sumer; or ancient Egypt...*"

The illustration further continues. The hypothetical American citizen puts on shoes made from skins tanned by a process invented in Egypt. He glances through the window, made of glass invented in Egypt. He takes an umbrella invented in Southeastern Asia. The paper he uses was originally an ancient Lydian invention. Steel knife he uses for cutting his bread, is an alloy that was first made in South India. In his another hand he holds a fork which was a medieval Italian product. The spoon he uses was originally a Roman invention. The coffee that he sips with pleasure everyday is a product of coffee plant which was in the beginning an Abyssinian monopoly. He smokes cigars or cigarettes. This smoking habit he has borrowed from the American Indians. Similarly, the American uses or is benefited by many more such things, practices and habits which he has borrowed from other peoples and cultures long back.

Diffusion is one of the main sources of cultural and social change. "The most outstanding contemporary social change - the spread of the modernisation process around the world–represents the diffusion of industrialism from the advanced to the less developed societies". Each culture accepts elements from other cultures selectively. Material artifacts that prove useful are more readily accepted than new norms, values and beliefs. Innovations must also be compatible with the culture of the society into which they diffuse. For these reasons, white settlers in America accepted the Red Indian's tobacco and not their religion.

2. Invention

An invention refers to "a new combination of or a new use of existing knowledge" — *Horton* and *Hunt*

"An invention is the combination or new use of existing knowledge to produce something that did not exist before" —*Ian Robertson*

"An invention is any recombination of existing cultural elements in such a fashion as to produce something new" — *Leslie. Lorman* and *Gorman.*

Inventions may be either material (bow and arrow, gun, spacecraft, computer) or social or nonmaterial (constitutional government, corporations, alphabet, dance, drama, literature). All inventions are based on previous knowledge, discoveries, and inventions. Hence, the nature and rate of inventions in a particular society depends on its existing store of knowledge. For the cave-dweller the stored knowledge was, for example, very much limited. The production of bow and arrow was thus a great intellectual achievement of cave dwellers. We, the modem people, are not exceedingly cleverer than the "primitive" ancestors, because we have enough of stored knowledge to make achievements. As *Ralph Linton remarked, "If Einstein had been born into a primitive tribe which was unable to count beyond three, lifelong application to mathematics probably would not have carried him beyond the development of a decimal system based on fingers and toes*".

Ian Robertson writes, "Leonardo da Vinci, working in the 15th century, produced plans for many machines that were workable in principle, including helicopters, submarines, machine guns, air-conditioning units, aerial bombs, and hydraulic pumps, but his society lacked the technology necessary to build them".

It could be said that "*the more inventions that exist in a culture, the more rapidly further inventions can be made*". The already existing cultural store of knowledge always promotes new inventions. Ogburn listed 150 inventions that were made almost simultaneously by different scientists living in the same or similar cultures. This fact explains as to why the modernisation process spreads far more widely and rapidly in societies in which inventions are taking place at a fast rate than in those societies which merely adopt the inventions of others.

3. Discovery

'*Discovery*'–can also be stated here as the third source of socio-cultural change. *Horton* and *Hunt* have said that "*A discovery is a shared human perception of an aspect of reality which already exists*". The principle of the level [relating to water], a new continent, the composition of the atmosphere, the power of steam, the circulation of the blood, etc., were already there before their discovery. A new discovery becomes an addition to society's culture, only if it is shared within the society. It becomes a factor or source of socio-cultural change only when it is put to use. For example, the ancient Greeks had discovered the principle of steam power long back. In fact, a steam engine was built as a toy in Alexandria around 100 AD. But the principle was not put to use for nearby 1700-years after it was discovered.

ELEMENTS OF CULTURE

According to H.M. Johnson, the main elements of culture are as follows: — Cognitive elements, beliefs, values and norms, signs, and non-normative ways of behaving.

1. ***Cognitive elements:*** Cultures of all societies whether pre-literate or literate include a vast amount of knowledge about the physical and social world. The possession of this knowledge is referred to as the *cognitive element*. Even the most primitive or pre-literate peoples such as the Andaman and Trobriand Islanders must know about many things in order to survive. Their knowledge is practical knowledge and never "knowledge for its own sake". Knowledge, relating to how to get food, how to build shelter, how to travel and transport, how to protect themselves against storms, wild animals, and hostile people is nothing but practical knowledge. Such knowledge is carefully taught to each generation. In modern advanced societies knowledge is so vast, deep and complex that no single person can hope to master the whole of it. Further, every society has in its culture many ideas about its own social organisation and how it works.

2. ***Beliefs:*** Beliefs constitute another element of culture. Beliefs in empirical terms are neither true nor false. *Examples*: (*i*) The Eskimo shaman uses fetishes and goes into a loud trance in order to drive out the evil spirits from the body of a sick person. (*ii*) The Christian missionary who gives medicine to and advises the patient to take sufficient rest also utters a silent prayer for the speedy recovery of the patient. Such actions imply some kind of beliefs. The belief behind these actions cannot be confirmed or rejected on the basis of empirical evidence. For example, if the patient dies in spite of the efforts, of Shaman, he will have some "explanation" that will make him to stick on to the belief in evil spirits. Civilised men too create similar beliefs and pass them on to the succeeding generations.

   Tested empirical knowledge and untestable beliefs are "*elements*" *of culture*. Because, they are often mixed together in the same concrete acts. Only through an intellectual analysis the different elements could be separated from one another. For example, the missionary says a silent prayer and at the same time administers modern medical tests to the patient.

3. ***Values and norms:*** It is very difficult to enlist values and norms for they are so numerous and diverse. They are inseparable from attitudes, except perhaps, analytically.

Values may be defined as measures of goodness or desirability. They are the group conceptions of relative desirability of things. In sociology we are most concerned with values that are directly or indirectly involved in social relationships; moral, and religious values that have been to some extent institutionalised.

One way of understanding the values and their interconnections is to approach them through the four functional subsystems of society. These subsystems are: *government, family, economy* and *religion*. The function or the social activities that these four interconnected subsystems perform are to a great extent shaped by values. But these four subsystems are not equally stressed as equally important in all societies. The values most characteristic of one (or two) subsystem normally predominate in any society. It means political values, or family values, or economic values or religious values normally predominate. Example: In his study *Bellah* has shown that in Japan during the Tokugawa period (16th to 19th century A.D.) 'Political Values' were the most dominant ones. The emperor was at the top of hierarchy and enjoyed great power and respect. Merchants who pursued economic activities were given comparatively a low status. Even in the family loyalty to the nation and to the emperor was stressed as a great value. Japanese religion also stressed the dominance of political values. In Japan filial loyalty or piety which was equally both a religious and a social value, was subordinated to the loyalty of the state. Shintoism and Zen-Buddhism, the two main religions of Japan stressed much the value of loyalty to the nation. Here "*Other-worldly*" religious doctrine and practice were subordinated to political values. In the same manner, in India religious values dominated Indian social system for hundreds of years. Even now it is quite dominant.

But how can we know what values are dominant in society? Sociologist *Williams* has suggested the following criterion of dominant values: (*i*) *Extensiveness of the value in the total activity of the system*, (*ii*) *Duration of the value, that is how persistently it has been important over a period of time*, (*iii*) *Intensity with which the value is sought or maintained*, (*iv*) *Prestige of the value carriers — that is, of persons, objects, or organisations considered to be bearers of the value*.

Further, every society has secondary values in addition to its dominant values. For example, in Japan, "*aesthetic-emotional*" values are secondary for there is a considerable stress on them. In India, political values have secondary place.

Norms are closely associated with values. They are the group-shared standards of behaviour. Norms impose restrictions on our behaviour. They are model practices. they determine, control and guide our behaviour. In fact, values are cherished only through the observance of norms. Norms are established on the basis of values. Hence norms and values go together. For *H.M. Johnson*, "*Values are general standards, and may be regarded as higher order norms*". Norms and values together constitute an important element in culture.

4. ***Signs:*** Signs include signals and symbols. "*A signal* (also means sign) *indicates the existence-past, present, or future–of a thing, event, or conditions*" *Example*: A heap of half burnt particles of a house signalise that the house was caught by fire sometimes earlier. Similarly, wet streets are a signal that it has rained. Soldiers going to parade ground with uniform signal that they are going to have their parade. Thus, signal and its objects are both parts of a more complex event or unit. A number of invented or artificial symbols are used in social life which assume importance. *Example*: A shot may mean the beginning of a running race, the sighting of danger, the commencement of a parade, the starting of war, the killing of a wild animal, a terrorist activity, and so on.

Signals and symbols are slightly different. A placard bearing the words "*No Parking*" is a signal. It indicates the presence of a place where one is not supposed to park one's vehicles. But the words in the placard represent symbols. Like a signal, a symbol means something to the interpretant. But it serves to bring a concept of something to his mind rather than to announce the presence of the thing itself. For example, 'deer' or 'dove' indicates such a concept. 'Deer' or 'dove' indicates an animal or a bird of a particular kind. Thus, "*a signal is involved in a three-term relationship* (*interpretant, signal, object*) *while a symbol is involved in a four-term relationship* (*interpretant. symbol, concept, object*)". Signals are involved in all our practical activities. Symbols are important in many kinds of communication and expression, including religion and art.

In all societies language is an important symbol system. At the level of 'pre-literate' people language is entirely oral. Written records have helped people as symbol system to depend upon the memories, of the aged, and knowledge of the past. Because of his inability to make use of symbols of written records, the mental horizon of the preliterate man is likely to be very low. The languages (such as English, Spanish, French and German) which have a vast collection, of books on a wide variety of subjects or topics have the key to an extremely rich culture. Speech, an aspect of language system consists of vocal and other kinds of gestures–bowing, shaking hands, saluting, kissing. blushing, etc. These gestures too have symbolic meanings which are mostly cultural. For example, one smiles at known persons, weeps when confronted with grief, laughs when happy, and so on. In such instances, the gestures are interpreted correctly as signals based on internalised symbols. But all the gestures are not necessarily connected intrinsically with the feeling it connotes, For example, one must smile at acquaintances whether one is really glad to see them or not. Jesus kissed Judas who betrayed him. In the shared common system of symbols in addition to speech and gestures another factor is important and, that is, 'intentions' of the participants in any stabilised social interaction. It could be said that "Any object or aspect of objects that is involved in a stabilised social relationship may acquire a cultural symbolic meaning for the interacting participants".

Many material products or things are primarily symbol vehicles. Flags, pictures and statues serve here as examples. Similarly, a building or a camp, or a ship, or a tomb, or an idol, or physical place, etc., signifies a symbolic form, the meaning of which is cultural.

5. ***Non-normative ways of behaving:*** Certain ways of behaving are not compulsory and are often unconscious. Such patterns do exist. Non-normative behaviour shades over into normative behaviour and symbolic behaviour. For example, the Jewish gestures largely involve the hands, they tend to symbolise the subtle evolution of an argument, a train of thought. The Italian gestures involve the whole arm and they tend to express emotions. Both these symbol systems have tended to disappear in the second and later generations of the Jews and Italians in the United States.

CULTURAL SYSTEMS AND SUB-SYSTEMS

Culture which consists of different elements and items tends to form systems of its own. As *H.M. Johnson* has said these systems may have varying degrees of coherence or integration. For example, a well developed branch of science, such as physics, consists of logically coherent concepts, propositions and principles. Hence we would say that physics is a cultural system. Similarly, every language is a highly worked out system in the sense, it has its own rules regarding pronunciation, construction of sentences, combination of sounds in meaningful units, semantic rules, etc. Hence language is a complex cultural system. These are only sub-systems in a wider cultural system which is called a national culture.

The Wider cultural system which can be referred to as '*whole*' culture or '*total*' culture, represents virtually a national culture. Examples, Indian culture, Japanese culture, French culture, etc. The wider cultural system such as Indian culture, for example, consists of many smaller cultural sub-systems which are heterogeneous. Sciences and technologies, several dialects, several forms of religion, ideologies, kinship patterns, economic institutions, – these and many other components are found 'in the Indian culture. To what extent all these and various other components make up the Indian cultural system is a pertinent question here.

One thing is certain that such components of a culture do not form as coherent a system. as we find it in the case of physics, or in any established language. "The coherence of a culture is '*never*' complete and it cannot be analysed apart from the interaction system".

Incompatible values and beliefs do co-exist peacefully in the same society. According to *H.M. Johnson*, several factors are responsible for that. Among them, the following may be noted.

1. The potentially conflicting values are often reconciled through. What is known as "*hierarchisation*"? It means people tend to place values in the form of hierarchy in which 'dominant' values take precedence over secondary values in normal situations.
2. Most of the societies have '*safety-values*' in the form of secondary institutions which help them to get released their anxiety in more or less a controlled manner. Secondary institutions often shade over into near deviant patterns. The practice of prostitution is an example here.
3. Incompatible values and beliefs can exist peacefully by means of *insulation* also. Insulation is a technique which makes it possible to apply different values and beliefs to different times and situations. Or, a given actor may carry out different social roles to express different values and beliefs to avoid conflicts.
4. It is true that different religious groups within the society hold mutually incompatible beliefs or values. For example, Hindus consider cow as sacred animal and worship it whereas Muslims, and Christians practice beef-eating. Hindus are idol-worshippers and Muslims dislike and condemn idolatry, and so on. In spite of this incompatibility such religious groups hold some values–such as religious tolerance, human welfare, etc., which permit them to get along

with each other. Such values even help them to cooperate among themselves within limits.

5. Cultural '*middlemen*' may help reduce incompatibility of values. Some persons, or so-called 'middlemen' who hold different values and beliefs and whose cultural equipment or outlook is more flexible, may help to mediate the contacts between the incompatible groups.

It is to be noted that '*coherence*' and '*system*' are relative concepts. What appears to be coherent at one time turns out to be incoherent at another time in the same system. Further, the factor that helps 'coherence' or 'compatibility' in one system may hinder the same in another. Similarly, it is not only possible for social arrangements to mitigate cultural diversity, but also possible to intensify it. The British in India for example, followed the policy of 'divide and rule' to intensify the incompatibility between the Hindus and Muslims.

Further, it would be wrong to assure that *any* element of culture can cohere provided social arrangements are made for that. We observe, for example, the coexistence of two religions (for example Hinduism and Islam) at best creates a problem of integration. Moreover, the different parts of culture (such as religion and science, science and politics, economy and education, religion and political institution, etc.) are interrelated on the purely cultural level. It means they are interrelated at the level of ideas and values, each part influencing the other, some helping and some others hindering. Culture is dynamic by itself. It undergoes change relating to the changing needs and experiences of successive generations. In fact, no element of culture is transmitted with absolutely no change from a parent to a child. Hence a number of changes take place from one generation to the next. The integration of a culture is not necessarily affected by the historical origin of its various items.

CULTURAL CHANGE

According to *Kingsley Davis*, the cultural change "*embraces all changes occurring in any branch of culture including art, science, technology, philosophy, etc., as well as changes in the forms and rules of social organisation*".

According to *David Dressler* and *Donald Carns*, "*Cultural change is the modification or dis- continuance of existing 'tried' and 'tested' procedures transmitted to us from the culture of the past, as well as the introduction of new procedures.*

In brief, any change that takes place in the realm of culture can be called cultural change. Culture is not static but *dynamic*. It also undergoes change. *For example*, invention and popularisation of the automobile, the addition of new words to our language, changing concepts of property and morality, new forms of music, art or dance, new styles in architecture and sculpture, new rules of grammar or meter, the general trend towards sex equality, etc., all represent cultural changes. Nearly all important changes involve both social and cultural, material and non-material aspects.

All cultures change, although they do so in different ways and at different rates. Culture is normally regarded as conservative, especially in its non-material aspects. For example, people are reluctant to give up old values, customs and beliefs in favour of new ones. Changes in one area of culture affect in some way or the other, some other parts of culture. This is so because culture is strongly integrated. Further, one change may lead to another. Some of the basic changes, for example, the ways in which a society earns its living or conducts its economic activity and exploits the environment, can affect almost all the other cultural elements.

Causes of Cultural Changes

David Dressler and *Donald Carns* have made the following observations with regard to the causes of cultural change.

1. Sometimes members of a society are often confronted by customs that differ from those which they have learnt to accept. In such a situation they adopt some of the new customs, reject others, and follow modified versions of still others. This might be called cultural eclecticism.
2. New customs and practices are likely to be more readily adopted under two conditions: (*i*) if they represent what is viewed as socially desirable and useful and (*ii*) if they do not clash with pre-existed and still valued customs and practices.
3. It is widely observed that even if the people accept the new customs and practices, they do not completely abandon their traditional culture.
4. Changes in culture are always superimposed on existing culture especially during culture- contact.
5. Changes in culture are always relative. We do not have a "changed" culture but only a "changing culture", strictly speaking. Cultural changes normally emerge gradually but continuously. Hence we find a co-existence of old and new customs in the same society.

6. All the cultural changes are not equally important. Some changes are introduced to culture because they are considered necessary for human survival. Some other changes are accepted in order to satisfy socially acquired needs not essential for survival.
7. Still it could be observed that some cultural changes originally meet neither a "survival need" nor an "acquired need" of a people. Example: New ways of disposing of the dead.
8. It is a fact of common observation that crisis tends to produce or accelerate cultural change. If the changes are accepted once due to the crisis, they tend to persist. Example: Women were accepted in defence industry during the Second World War, and even now they continue to be there.
9. Cultural change is cumulative in its total effect. Much is added and little is lost. Its growth is like the growth of a tree that ever expands but only loses its leaves, sometimes its limbs from time to time, as long as it survives.
10. Cultural change leads to chain reaction. "Whenever a change is incorporated into the culture and becomes defined as a 'social necessity', new needs emerge, generating the desire for still further changes to complement or supplement the original change.

CIVILISATION

The term '*Civilisation*' is derived from the Latin word '*Civitas*' which means a city. Hence the term refers to all the attainments characteristic of human life in an organised city. Since cities appeared relatively at a later stage in human history, '*Civilisation*' indicates a particular stage in the evolution of man. In contrast with this, culture represents the group life of man at all the stages of his social development. The term civilisation is also used to cover all the social organisations and other attainments of man which mark him off from other animals.

Definition of Civilisation

1. *Goldenweiser* used the term 'Civilisation' identically with culture to refer to all the human achievements.
2. *Kant* used the term civilisation to mean outward behaviour of man.
3. According to *Gillin* and *Gillin* civilisation is a more complex and evolved form of culture.
4. *Ogburn* and *Nimkoff* conceived of civilisation as the latter phase of the superorganic culture.

According to *MacIver* and *Page civilisation* is the whole apparatus of life.

Civilisation refers to those devices and instruments by which nature is controlled. It includes technical and material equipments like a printing press, a locomotive, a tractor, a radio, television, teleprinter, typewriter, aeroplane, machine gun, etc. It also includes the whole apparatus of economic and political organisations like our schools, colleges, currency systems, banking system, parliament, insurance schemes, etc.

Civilisation is thus *external*, mechanical, *utilitarian*, and concerned with the *means*. We need the products of civilisation not for their own sake but for the satisfaction of our wants. For example, we need a car, a scooter, bus, a locomotive for travelling, we Want radio, television, wireless, post and telegraph, for communication, we want banks and currency systems for trade and commerce and so on. Definitely, we are not possessing these things just for the sake of possession.

DISTINCTION BETWEEN CULTURE AND CIVILISATION

The terms '*Culture*' and '*Civilisation*' are often distinguished on various grounds. Both represent two broad fields of human activity and experience. Some significant points of difference between them may be noted here.

1. ***Civilisation has a precise standard of measurement but not culture:*** The products of civilisation are such that they can be measured quantitatively on grounds of efficiency. We can easily say that a motor car is superior to a hand plough or the currency and the banking system are superior to the primitive barter system.

   But we cannot measure the cultural products. We can only assess the cultural products by our personal judgement; but we cannot measure or quantify them. If somebody were to say that the literary works of Kalidasa are better than those of Shakespeare, we cannot prove or disprove it, but we can only agree or disagree with that statement. Cultural things such as values, opinions, ideas, ideologies, morals, customs, beliefs, fashions, etc., are beyond measurement. Different ages and different groups have their own standards of judgements with regard to these cultural things.
2. ***Civilisation is always advancing but not culture:*** According to *MacIver* and *Page*, civilisation always marches on if there is no break of social continuity. It always shows a persistent already stored upward trend. Every generation adds its own achievements to the already stored up energy and intelligence. Thus every technical achievement is an improvement on the past. Once our instrument is discovered man goes on improving it. Change from mud road

to tar road and then to cement concrete road, from bow and arrow to the machine gun and then to atom bomb — indicate improvement. The progress of civilisation is assured.

Progress in the case of culture is *not assured.* Culture is not always advancing. The height reached by Gautama Buddha, Shankaracharya and Swami Vivekananda in the field of religion and spirituality had not been reached by their followers. In the same way Kalidasa, Bharavi and Bhasa of the Sanskrit literature still maintain their supremacy. But in the field of civilisation, what Newton or Edison discovered became the basis for further discovery. We cannot, however, say that culture is changeless. There is development in culture though it may not always indicate progress.

3. ***The products of civilisation are more easily communicated than those of culture:*** The products of civilisation are open to all. Knowledge regarding civilisation can be passed on very easily and without much effort. The work of an engineer or mechanic is not just for other engineers or mechanics. We can enjoy the products of civilisation without sharing the capacity which creates them. Millions may use radio, television, telephone, camera, etc., without understanding their techniques and mechanism.

   Products of culture, on the other hand, can be communicated only between like-minded. Those who have poetic talent can alone appreciate poetry. The work of an artist is only for a man with artistic appreciation.

4. ***Civilisation is borrowed without loss or change but not culture:*** People can borrow the products of civilisation very easily. Technical devices and plants can easily be borrowed or transferred. It will be easy for an Indian to borrow a scientific technique invented in the West, but it will be difficult for a foreigner to borrow the Indian cultural elements. Hence civilisation is far more Widespread than culture. Different groups may make use of similar products and yet may possess different cultures. Many of the Eastern countries have borrowed Western technology but all of them have retained their original cultures. Though there may be some "*cultural-borrowings*" (Example: dress styles, speaking styles, fashions, fads, food habits, entertainment, etc.). They are insignificant compared to the borrowing of civilisation.

5. ***Civilisation is external, but culture is internal:*** Civilisation is *external*, *mechanical* and *utilitarian* in character. It caters to the external needs of man. Civilisation is a means. In a way it reflects the material wealth of mankind. Culture is something internal. It refers to the intrinsic values. It is the expression of our modes of living and of thinking, in behaving and in acting, in art and literature, in philosophy, and religion, in morality, in recreation and enjoyment, in dance, drama and music. As philosopher Kant has pointed out, civilisation is a matter of outward behaviour whereas culture requires morality as an inward state of man. As *MacIver* and *Page* have said "*Civilisation is what we have, culture is what we are.*"

6. ***Finally, the products of culture reveal the nature of an individual or a social group or a nation but not the products of civilisation:*** In the realm of culture, an artist or a poet, or a painter can express his love of beauty, his admiration for literature, his fascination towards an by means of his artistic, literary or painting works. On the other hand, an engineer cannot express his personality, his love of beauty, his likes and dislikes, his morals and values by means of his machines, discoveries or inventions.

INTERDEPENDENCE OF AND INTERRELATIONSHIP BETWEEN CULTURE AND CIVILISATION

Civilisation and culture do not reveal two independent and separate systems. The distinction between them is only relative and not absolute. They are not only interdependent but also interactive. Both are man-made. One is for his comfort and luxury and the other for his satisfaction and happiness. One is as important as the other.

The '*Order*' of civilisation influences the '*order*' of culture. The articles of civilisation called "*artifacts*" are influenced by culture called "*mentifacts*". Culture is also influenced by the articles of civilisation. Cultural character is generally added to the utilitarian order. We want fashions and styles and show it in our automobiles, buildings, etc. Similarly, our philosophies, literatures and learning have been much influenced by the printing press.

Some objects of civilisation or some utilitarian things when become old acquire cultural character. The tools and implements of the primitive communities are also the symbols of culture. Various articles such as pots, vessels, ornaments, coins, weapons, tools, etc., found in excavations reveal the culture of the ancient people.

An environment of civilisation can affect our thoughts, values, morals, aims, objectives, ideals, ideologies, etc. The machine has brought new habits and enjoyments, new philosophy and ethics. Our world outlook has been changed due to the progress of science and technology.

The cultural order also affects civilisation. Every people, every age has its own way of life. We look at the new inventions and techniques in the light of our way of life and our values. New aspira- tions and values may bring about a new civilisation.

Culture is the breeding ground of civilisation. Civilisation gives strength and stamina for the wheels of society to march on. According to *Ogburn*, civilisation represents "*material culture*" and culture implies "*non-material culture*". If civilisation is like a body, culture is its" soul.

MacIver and Page have clearly stated the interrelationship between culture and civilisation. They say that civilisation is a ship "which can set sail to various ports. The port we sail to remains a cultural choice. Without the ship we could not sail at all; according to the character of the ship we sail fast or slow, take longer or shorter voyages. But the direction in which we travel is not predestinated by the design of the ship. The more efficient it is, the more ports lie within the range of our choosing". *In short, civilisation is the driving force of society. Culture is its steering wheel.*

REVIEW QUESTIONS

1. What do you mean by culture? Bring out its characteristic features.
2. Define culture. Culture is unique to man, discuss.
3. Assess the relation between culture and society.
4. Give the classification of the content of culture. Discuss each in component brief.
5. What are the functions of culture? Discuss its development and growth.
6. Give an account of various elements of culture.
7. Write the meaning of sub-culture. Discuss the main divisions of sub-culture.
8. Define cultural change. Explain its causes.
9. Highlight the features of culture and civilisation.
10. Define civilisation. How does it differ from culture?
11. "Civilisation is external but culture is internal". Examine.
12. Assess the interrelationship between culture and civilisation.
13. Explain the concept of cultural lag.
14. Write short nots on the following:
    (a) Cultural diffusion
    (b) Cultural systems and sub-systems
    (c) Cultural lag

⌘⌘⌘⌘⌘⌘⌘⌘⌘⌘⌘

18

SOCIALISATION AND CULTURE

CHAPTER OUTLINE

- Concept of Socialisation
- Process of Socialisation
- Internalisation of Social Norms
- Types of Socialisation
- Conditions of Learning
- lnternalised Objects
- Theories of Socialisation: C.H. Cooley's Theory of 'Looking-Glass Self' G.H. Mead's Theory of 'Self' Freud and his Concept of the Human Mind, W.I. Thomas' Theory of the 'Definition of the Socialisation
- Durkheim's Theory of Collective Representations
- Stages of Socialisation
- Adult Socialisation
- Agents of Socialisation
- Culture, Socialisation and Personality
- Socialisation and Cultural Differences
- Can Culture Determine Personality?
- Importance of Socialisation
- Failures of the Socialisation Process and the Problems of Faulty Socialisation.

Man is not only social but also cultural. It is the culture that provides opportunities for man to develop the personality. Development of personality is not an automatic process. Every society prescribes its own ways and means of giving social training to its new born members so that they may develop their own personality. This social training is called '*Socialisation*'.

The process of socialisation is conditioned by culture. Since every society has its own culture the ways of the process of socialisation also differ from society to society. Further, the same culture and the same ways of socialisation may have diverse effects on the development of the personality of the members of the same society. Thus, a culture need not necessarily produce stereotype personalities. There is scope for individuality in the process of socialisation. But the fact the culture puts limitations on the development of personality cannot be ignored. The mutual interplay of culture and socialisation in conditioning human personality with special emphasis on the phenomenon of socialisation, is briefly examined in this Chapter.

CONCEPT OF SOCIALISATION

Little of man's behaviour is instinctive. Rather, man's behaviour is 'learnt' behaviour. The human child comes into the world as a biological organism with animal needs. He is gradually moulded in society into a social being and learns social ways of acting and feeling. The continued existence of society becomes impossible without this process. No individual could become the person and no culture could exist without it. This process of moulding and shaping the personality of the human infant is called '*socialisation*'.

Man is Not Born Social

At birth the human child possesses the potentialities of becoming human. The child becomes a man or a person through a variety of experiences. He becomes then what the sociologist calls '*socialised*'. Socialisation means the process whereby an individual becomes a functioning member of the society. The individual becomes socialised by learning the rules and practices of social groups. By this process the individual develops a personality of his own.

Man is man because he shares with others a common culture. Culture includes not only its living members but also members of past generations and those as yet unborn. Sociologists have given more importance to socialisation because man is a cultural being. Socialisation is often referred to as the '*transmission of culture*', the process' whereby men learn the rules and practices of social groups. Socialisation is an aspect of all activity within all human societies. Just as we learn a game by playing it, so we learn life by engaging in it. We are socialised in the course of the activities themselves. For example, if we do not know correct manners, we learn them through the mistakes that we make and the disapproval that others exhibit. We may learn the ways of behaviour through imitation and purposeful training. Education–purposeful instruction–is thus only a *part* of the socialisation process. It is not, and can never be, the whole of that process.

Definition of Socialisation

1. *Bogardus*: Socialisation is the "process of working together, of developing group responsi- bility, or being guided by the welfare needs of others".
2. *W.F. Ogburn*: "Socialisation is the process by which the individual learns to conform to the norms of the group".
3. *Peter Worsley* explains socialisation as the process of "transmission of culture, the process whereby men learn the rules and practices of social groups".
4. *Harry M. Johnson* understands socialisation as "learning that enables the learner to perform social roles". He further says that it is a "process by which individuals acquire the already existing culture of groups they come into".
5. *Lundberg* says that socialisation consists of the "complex processes of interaction through which the individual learns the habits, beliefs, skills and standards of judgement that arc necessary for his effective participation in social groups and communities".

PROCESS OF SOCIALISATION

Every man tries to adjust himself to the conditions of his social environment. This process of adjustment is itself socialisation. The social order is maintained largely by socialisation. Individuals learn to conform to the norms of the group. This helps the group to maintain its order. Socialisation is a process of transforming the human animal into a human being, of converting the biological being into a social being. '*No one understands the process thoroughly*'–as *Kingsley Davis* remarks. It is still as mysterious as photosynthesis or organic ageing. It is true that direct socialisation begins only after birth. Man, as an organism, has some internal factors or forces which limit or help his socialisation. These internal forces relevant to the process of socialisation are: (*i*) *reflexes*, (*ii*) *instincts*, (*iii*) *urges*, (*iv*) *capacities*, and (*v*) *comprehension and educability*. We shall now examine the phenomenon of socialisation as such.

Socialisation is a Continuous Process

Socialisation is a process of *inducting* the individual into the social world. It consists in teaching culture which he must acquire and share. *Socialisation is social learning*. This learning is not intermittent but *continuous*. The more we try to learn the more remains to be learnt. Perfection in social learning is rarely achieved. The process of socialisation is something that continues through- out life. We must not think that there is a stage in learning at which a man has learnt everything about his group and that there after, he ceases to learn.

Man belongs to different groups at different stages of his life. As these groups change, so we must learn new rules, new patterns of behaviour. Moreover, we do not remain within the same role. Eventhough, we are members of family all our life, we are constantly changing our roles within it, acquiring new roles, dropping or modifying old ones. We begin as children, pass through adolescence into adulthood, marry, become parents, enter middle age, retire and grow old. With each role come new patterns of behaviour that we must learn. Thus, throughout our life, we are involved in the socialisation process. Even at the door of death we are being socialised. The staffs of hospitals, for example, have a conception of what is a '*good*' way to die. They try to socialise their dying patients into the ways of dying in a '*proper*' manner.

Timing

Timing is important in socialisation. Physical maturity by itself cannot produce perfect human adults without socialisation. Socialisation and maturation may proceed together in the early years of the life cycle. Our attempts to teach the child will have varying effects depending upon the point reached in the maturation of the child. For example, we cannot expect the child to be quiet before he is capable of sustained inhibition.

Socialisation and Development of the 'Self'

The heart of the process of socialisation is the emergence and gradual development of the '*self*' or '*ego*'. It is in terms of the self that personality takes shape and mind comes to function. The notion of self begins to arise as the child learns something of the world of sensations about him.

Everyone who is alive, in any society, has a consciousness of self. When a child is born it has no consciousness of itself or of others. He does not possess those behaviour mechanisms which make an individual a part and member of any group. The child at birth is not conscious of any of the self and other relationships. These relationships the child learns through the process of socialisation.

The 'Self' is Social. The term 'self' is often used to mean '*self-image.*' Some writers like *G. Murphy* view the self simply as the person's conception of himself as a totality. But *G.H. Mead* would rather regard self as purely '*social*' in nature. It is true that the self develops out of the child's communicative contact with others. The idea of self develops in conjunction with the idea of other things. He learns that they are distinct beings and that he too has individuality. Acquaintance with his name and use of pronouns such as '*I*', '*Me*', '*Myself*', etc. help the process of self discovery. Little children's answers to such questions as '*What is your name*?' and '*Whose boy are you?*' etc., would emphasise the idea of self in relation to others.

INTERNALISATION OF SOCIAL NORMS

Socialisation is often described as the process whereby an individual *internalises* the norms of the group. As a result of this a distinct '*self*' emerges unique to the individual. In the process of socialisation, the individual learns culturally approved habits, ideas and attitudes. He is fitted into the social group by being taught the rights and duties of his position. His drives are guided into approved channels of expression. The cultural rules and restrictions are so internalised that they become part of his personality.

Thus, *Internalisation of norms' refers* to the process in which the norms become a part of the personality. To begin with, the human child does not have the sense of right and wrong, desirable and undesirable, moral and immoral, acceptable and unacceptable, good and bad, justifiable and unjustifiable and so on. By trial and error and by direct or indirect observation and experience the child slowly learns the approved way of behaving. He learns to distinguish between the right and wrong. Parents and other members also help the child to learn the norms of the groups. They reinforce the child's learning by rewards and punishments or by means of approval and disapproval. The repeated experiences of the child help him to internalise the norms in his personality.

Internalised Norms and the Daily Life. In our daily life we interact with many people and do many tasks. We do not think about what we are going to do when we get up from our bed, go out from the home, enter a shop, get into a bus, classroom, cafeteria, and meet a friend, a clerk, a teacher or a traffic police and so on. Because the norms, which we have internalised, help us to decide what to do and what not to do under different social situations.

The development of 'self' is closely associated with the internalisation of norms. As and when the child grows he learns to enact various roles, the role of a child, a son, a brother, a playmate of the neighbouring child, a student in a school and so on. Every role is woven around a set of norms. Whether directly or indirectly, consciously or unconsciously these norms are learnt by the child. This process of learning the norms proceeds to such an extent that they become internalised in his personality.

Internalisation of Norms Helps Self—Control. Internalisation of norms is an important aspect of socialisation. It lessens the problems of social control for society. Ultimately, *social control is achieved when self-control is mastered.* The individual is able to exercise discipline by himself over his own actions and behaviour. More than the enforced means of social control such as customs and traditions or laws and legislations, the internalised norms are more effective. They have an enduring effect on the personality of the child. Internalised norms provide the best explanation to certain widely accepted and obeyed social taboos such as the '*incest*'. No son wants to have sex relations with the mother and no father with the daughter or the brother with the sister. The incest taboos that prohibit the sex relations between the so called blood relatives, have become so much internalised that no one ever thinks of having sex relations with his closest relatives.

Internalisation of Norms Due to Indoctrination. It is wrong to assume that hope of reward and fear of punishment are the only reasons as to why people conform to the norms. People conform to the norms because they are *indoctrinated* to do so. Indoctrination refers to the process of injecting into the personality of the child the group norms. Sometimes even prejudices, fears, superstitious beliefs, strong likes and dislikes are also injected into the mind of the child. This may have an adverse effect on the personality development. Indoctrination provides an answer for class or caste hatreds, racial prejudices, religious intolerance, ideological commitments, etc. Further, people conform to the norms because they become *habituated* to them. They also realise that norms are useful and serve some purpose. Conformity to the norms is a means of *group identification.*

Internalisation of Norms and the Development of Individuality. It is wrong to suppose that internalisation of norms provides no scope for the development of individuality. The individual is not only socialised, he also influences others and socialises them. He participates in the society both by being influenced by others and by influencing them. The individual has a self which is unique to itself. Hence the same socialisation process may have different effects on different individuals de- pending upon their potentialities and peculiarities. Socialisation provides enough opportunities to display individual peculiarities.

TYPES OF SOCIALISATION

Ian Robertson in his book *Sociology* (1977), has mentioned four types of socialisation. According to him, the socialisation that a person undergoes in the course of his lifetime may be one or more of four different types: 1. *Primary socialisation,* 2. *anticipatory socialisation,* 3. *developmental socialisation* and *re-socialisation.*

1. ***Primary socialisation:*** This is the most essential and basic type of socialisation. It takes place in the early years of life of the newborn individual. It concentrates on the teaching of language and cognitive skills, the internalisation of cultural norms and values, establishment of emotional ties, and the appreciation of other roles and perspectives. 'Internalisation of norms' is the most important aspect of primary socialisation. Internalisation of norms refers to the process in which the norms of society become a part of the personality of the individual. The human child does not have a sense of right and wrong, desirable and undesirable, moral and immoral. By trial and error, by direct and indirect observation, and experience, the child gradually learns the norms relating to right and wrong behaviour. The socialising agents reinforce the child's learning by rewards and punishments or by means of approval and disapproval.
2. ***Anticipatory socialisation:*** Men not only learn the culture of the group of which they are immediate members. They may also learn the culture of groups to which they do not belong. Such a process whereby men socialise themselves into the culture of a group with the anticipation of joining that group, is referred to by socialogists like *Merton* as '*anticipatory socialisation*'. A person who intends to join the army may start doing physical exercises to toughen his body and learning the manners of army personnel to become one with them later. People may be socialised into groups of which they are already members or into groups to which they wish to become attached. Socialisation is not a process that takes place merely in early childhood. On the other hand, it takes place at different times and places throughout life.
3. ***Developmental socialisation:*** This kind of learning is based on the achievements of primary socialisation. "It builds on already acquired skills and knowledge as the adult progresses through new situations such as marriage or new jobs. These require new expectations, obligations, and roles. New learning is added to and blended with old in a relatively smooth and continuous process of development".–*Ian Robertson*
4. ***Re-socialisation:*** Not only do individuals change roles within groups, but they also change membership-groups. In some instances, '*resocialisation*'–"the stripping away of learned patterns and substitution of new ones for them"–must occur. Such re-socialisation takes place mostly when a social role is radically changed. It may also happen in periods of rapid social mobility. For example, a newly wedded housewife may be forced to become aprostitute in a brothel. In this instance the social role of the individual got changed radically.

CONDITIONS OF LEARNING

From the point of view of socialisation, some learning is regarded as '*good*' or '*successful*', and some learning as '*bad*' or '*unsuccessful*'. Socialisation, as a kind of learning, contributes to one's ability to perform social roles. From the stand point of any particular social system, it is desirable and desired learning. Hence it is quite appropriate to discuss the conditions under which 'successful' learning takes place. *H.M. Johnson* mentions three such conditions: 1. *discrimination,* 2. *reward and punishment*, and 3. *control of the effects of frustration.*

1. ***Discrimination:*** The person to be socialised must be enabled to distinguish between the new objects and the behaviour patterns which are already known to him. This is essential for the successful internalisation of new objects or behaviour patterns. The socialising agent must provide some '*cues*' or '*hints*' which help the learner to learn new things. If the learner has to react appropriately, he must know what he is acting to. Hence it is necessary to define the situation correctly, for often the same manner of behaving, is appropriate in some situations but inappropriate in others.
2. ***Reward and punishment:*** Another condition that favours successful learning is with regard to reward and punishment. The socialising agent must give reward for the child for '*correct*' performances, and either withhold reward or punish for "*incorrect*" performances. Reward and punishment are said to "*reinforce*" the desired behaviour patterns. Sometimes, a mere smile is more effective than a chocolate as a reward. Similarly, a mere staring is more effective as a punishment than beating.

   As *Johnson* has stated, the effectiveness of reinforcement of desired behaviour patterns increases under certain conditions. That is (*i*) *When the correct behaviour is rewarded very often*; (*ii*) *when such a behaviour is more consistently rewarded* (*iii*) *when there is greater difference between the satisfaction coming from the correct behaviour and the dissatisfaction resulting from incorrect behaviour in the same situation*; and (*iv*) *when the reward comes soon after the correct behaviour*.

   Various studies have revealed that both reward and punishment are effective in training. Still some societies depend more on one than on the other. Are they equally effective? It is known that reward is quite effective and is less likely than punishment to produce undesirable side effects on the personality. Punishment, if exceeded, may bring about deep frustration. It has some dangerous effects also. It may produce hatred for the socialising agent. It may make the learner to become less sensitive to the disapproval of others, or may induce him to disobey or retaliate the socialising agent. Another danger is, it may make the person to "*over-learn*". This 'over-learning' may develop undue anxiety which may inhibit his normal and desirable behaviour patterns. Punishment for aggressive behaviour may produce anxiety about normal expression. Still it could be said that we have no good reasons to give up punishment completely in socialisation. It is better to train by punishment than to leave the child with its own tendencies.

3. ***Control of the effects of frustration:*** This is yet another condition of learning. Any learner has to face the problem of frustration in socialisation. The feeling of frustration is an unpleasant response. Due to frustration one may feel that he is thwarted in some activity, deprived of some— thing that others are enjoying, refused something that one wished to have.'Frustration is likely to be relatively severe during the early years for two reasons: (*i*) *The young child cannot understand the 'reasons' as to why others are frustrating him.* (*ii*) *Secondly, the child is yet to know clearly his own feelings and to cope with them.* Hence he may feel that the socialising agents are unjustly and arbitrarily thwarting, depriving and refusing him whatever is due to him. Whatever be the causes of frustration, frustration tends to produce aggressive feelings and sometimes indignation. Due to the feelings of aggression, indignation and anxiety the child is not able to give attention to the 'task' of learning. He may even fail to make the necessary discrimination. He may even refuse to cooperate. Hence it is necessary for the socialising agent to do something to counteract the effects of frustation. The child must be taken into confidence and reward be given whenever it is required. As it is noted, same amount of frustration is bound to be there in socialisation. But the amount of frustration the child must undergo in socialisation varies considerably from one society to another. It all depends upon the practices of society and its value systems.

INTERNALISED OBJECTS

No infant possesses a personality at birth. Because personality depends upon a consciousness of 'self' as against the external world of animate and inanimate objects. But the child is not born with a 'self' it only develops one. As *H.M. Johnson* has remarked, for the newborn child there is no objective reality, no space, no time, and no casualty. The child does not distinguish between his own perceiving and the things that are perceived. For example, the mother's breast, a bottle, a toy, etc., by themselves are not things which are independent of child's existence. For the child they are some sensory images but not distinguished from the acts of sucking, seeing, hearing, touching. Since the child has no self-consciousness, he acts as though the entire world is a part of himself.

According to *Piaget*, the child goes through some six stages before he is able to understand that there are external objects with an existence, of their own. It is only during the, 6th stage (15th to 19th month) that the child "constructs" the objects in the mind so that he can imagine their existance even when they are not present. At this stage only the child-reveals its ability to have "internalised objects" in relation to the external objects as they are perceived by adults. Till the 15th month the child only tries to learn in a gradual manner that there are such things as external objects.

What then is an internalised object? It refers to the objects that the child 'constructs' in his own mind so that he can, imagine it even in its absence. On the physiological level, it may be understood as a group of cell assemblies in the brain. Psychologically, it has two aspects: 1. *the cognitive aspect* and 2. *the motivational aspect.—H.M Johnson.*

1. ***The congnitive aspect:*** The cognitive aspect actually refers to the development of congnitive abilities which is one of the most important achievements of socialisation. The cognitive abilities refer to – the intellectual capacities such as reasoning, remembering, perceiving, calculating and believing. Our knowledge of this process is based largely on the work of *Jean Piaget*. He emphasises the internal processes of the mind as it matures through interaction with the social environment. He sees the individual as actively trying to make sense of the world rather than being passively conditioned by it. He is of the opinion that the cognitive abilities are developed slowly and gradually by children. The cognitive aspect refers to a '*cognitive map*' of external objects. It refers to the cognition that the object itself is 'external' and has an objective existence, and is not a product of imagination. Like any ordinary map, the cognitive map indicates that the internalised object is a *symbol* of something else. *For example*, the map of India 'represents' or 'symbolises' various rivers, cities, mountains, forests, etc. By looking at the map of a city one can imagine a number of buildings, places, parks, entertainment centres, etc. In the same manner, the internalised objects would help the person to make 'predictions' with some accuracy. It would help him to predict what would happen if he goes around the object, speaks to it, touches it, manipulates it, and so on.
2. ***The motivational aspect:*** The internalised object has a motivational aspect also. It is not emotionally a natural concept. The internalised object as a system of cell assemblies, carries a great motivational energy, a set of positive and negative charges. This energy has some direction of flow. It may motivate the persons to '*approach*' or '*avoid*' the external object, or *change* it, or to *influence* in some way or the other. It means, the internalised object is not

just the 'cognitive map' but it is charged with 'meaning' in "*the emotional life of the personality*" with whom it is related. *For example*, the person thinks of Mr. Sham whom he admires, loves and whose approval he always seeks to have. But his '*cognitive map*' of Sham reveals to him that his particular behaviour is disapproved by Sham. Now some amount of motivational energy is directed towards changing Sham's attitude. As a result, the person's '*internalised object*' gets changed a little for it includes a "*region*" which indicates Sham's approval of him and his behaviour.

Internalised objects are built up gradually in the course of interaction with the environment. This is especially so when the internalised objects are "*social objects*", that is, persons. The internalised objects are built by direct or indirect experience or interaction; that is, *directly* when the 'social object' such as Sham is present; and *indirectly* when Sham is not physically present but one hears of him or reads about him, or gets sources of information about him.

From the *sociological* point of view, the two main internalised objects are: 1. *self*, and 2. *social roles*.

1. ***The self and its origin:*** The heart of the process of socialisation is the emergence and the gradual development of "*self*". The infant at birth has no self-consciousness. No child is born with a 'self' as such. The child has no consciousness of itself or of others at birth. But the child gradually makes an attempt to build up internalised objects corresponding to other people, things and finally a concept of himself as an object. In this way, as *Johnson* has stated, "*the 'self' might be regarded as the internalised object representing one's own personality*". The notion of 'self' begins to arise as the child learns something of the world of sensations about him. Thus, the 'self' as an internalised object, includes one's own conception of one's abilities and characteristics, and an evaluation of both. The person due to this evaluation develops certain feelings of pride, shame, and self-respect. The construction of the self and the construction of other internalised objects go on together. Because, if one cannot distinguish one's own being as a separate entity, one cannot distinguish other beings or other things as separate entities.

   The term 'self' is often used to mean 'self-image'. Some writers like *G. Murphy* are of the view that the 'self' implies a person's conception of himself as a totality. But one's conception of oneself one gets only through others. Hence many writers like *Cooley, G. H. Mead*, and others have stated that self-arises only in interaction with the social and non-social environment. The self develops out of child's communicative contact with others. The child learns that others are distinct beings and that he too has an individuality distinct from others. Acquaintance with his name and use of pronouns such as 'I', 'Me', 'Myself', etc., help the process of self-discovery. Little children's answers to such questions as "*what is your name*?" and "*whose boy are you*?" etc., would emphasise the idea of self in relation to others. Social psychologists like *C.H. Cooley* and *G.H. Mead* have established their own theories, relating to the origin and development of 'self' which we shall discuss a little later.

2. ***Social roles:*** From the stand point of sociology, as *Johnson* opines "social roles are among the most important objects that are internalised in the course of socialisation." An internalised role is a little different from the role itself. Internalised roles are similar to all the other internalised objects. A role is a part of personality and is composed of norms. An internalised role is invested with some personal meaning. The nature of role is "partly determined by the place it has in the personality and partly by the place among other interalised roles, persons and things." Motivation behind the roles in a particular personality is also not the same among similar roles in other personalities. For example the role of merchant in a particular society is part of the culture of that society. But the role object internalised by any particular merchant is influenced by the culture of his group and also his experience. Similarly, many may be the residents of the same village but the village object internalised by each inhabitant is unique in the sense he has his own personal meaning of that.

THEORIES OF SOCIALISATION

C.H. Cooley's Theory of 'Looking-Glass Self'

The 'self' might be regarded as the *internalised* object representing one's own personality. Where does this selfarise? Are we born with it? Is it something we have to learn to recognise and to know? Is it something that the individual brings with him as we confront society? or Is it some-thing that he receives from society as a gift of the confrontation? A brilliant American social psychologist *Charles Horton Cooley* made some sustained attempts to find answers to these questions.

C.H. Cooley has placed before us two primary propositions–(*i*) *The mind is social*, and (*ii*) *Society is mental*. Of the two, the first one has impressed a good number of sociologists. He wrote in his *Social Organisation*, that "self and society are twin-born, we know one as immediately as we know the other, and the notion of a separate and independent ego is an illusion". Observing his own children, he concluded that the very idea of '*self* or '*ego*'–of *I*–can arise only in relationship with other people.

Three Main Elements of 'Looking-Glass Self'

Cooley held that self and social are two sides of the same coin. Our ideas, loyalties, attitudes, and points of view are derived from others. One means of their transmission Cooley called the '*looking-glass self*'. According to him, self-ideas or self-attitudes develop by a process of imagining what others think of us by a kind of 'looking-glass' process. A self-idea of this sort seems to have three main elements:

1. The imagination of our appearance to the other person.
2. The imagination of his judgement of that (imagined) appearance.
3. Some kind of self-feeling such as pride or mortification.

As Cooley has stated in his '*Human Nature and the Social Order*', the individual develops the idea of self through contact with the primary group, particularly with the members of the family. This he does by becoming conscious of their attitudes towards him. In other words, the child gets his conception of his self, and later of the kind of person he is, by means of what he imagines others take him to be. Cooley, therefore, called the child's idea of himself the '*looking-glass self*'. The child conceives of himself as better or worse in varying degrees, depending upon the attitudes of others towards him. Thus, the child's view of himself may be affected by the kind of name given by his family or friends. A child called '*angel*' by his mother gets a notion of himself which differs from that of a child called '*rascal*'.

The 'looking-glass self' assures the child which aspects of the assumed roles will bring him praise, which blame; which ones are acceptable to others, which ones unacceptable. People normally have their own attitudes towards social roles and adopt the same. The child first tries out these on others and in turn adopts towards his self. The self thus arises when the person becomes an '*object*' to himself. He is now capable of taking the same view of himself that he infers others do. The moral order which governs the human society, in large measure, depends upon the "looking-glass self '.

Thus it is clear that we are prone to look at ourselves through *other's eyes*. Depending upon the character and weight of that '*other*' [in whose mind we see ourselves] we develop different feelings. We are ashamed to seem evasive in the presence of a straightforward man; cowardly in the presence of a brave man, indecent in the presence of a refined man, greedy in the presence of a generous man and so on. We may boast to one person of an action but we may feel ashamed to express it to another. The way we imagine ourselves to appear to another person is an essential element in our conception of ourselves. Thus, '*I am not what I think I am and I am not what you think I am. I am what I think you think I am*'. Cooley concludes that "the self is social and that self-consciousness would not exist in the absence of society". The 'looking-glass self' affects the daily life of all individuals.

George Herbert Mead's Theory of 'Self'

G.H. Mead, the famous philosopher and psychologist at the University of Chicago, also held the opinion like that of Cooley that the society is the determining factor in the socialisation of the individual. He agreed with Cooley that the '*Self* is social. Mead has stated, 'the individual, largely through interaction, becomes aware of himself'. It means the individual comes to know about him- self by what is known as '*role playing*'.

'Role-playing'

Mead has said that the individual in order to get a picture of himself plays the roles of others. *In seeing himself as others see him, the individual is actually putting himself in the place of others, and imagining what their response might be*. This is 'role-playing'. The 'others' may be his parents, close associates, and finally, society as a whole. As the child gets older, he can be observed to act towards his dolls or toys as the mother or other members of the family have acted towards him. The child, in his play, is taking the role of another person. Through '*role-playing*', that is, by playing the role of the mother, father or other persons, the child is enabled to see himself objectively through the eyes of others. Of these '*others*' some are more "*significant*".

Significant others: The new-born infant has needs like those for food, clothing that press for satisfaction. The mother satisfies these needs and the child comes to depend upon her and '*identifies himself*' with her emotionally. But in course of time, the child differentiates himself from his mother and comes to know that he has a sub-ordinate role to the superior role of the mother. Then the child understands the role of the father. He differentiates his father from his mother and then integrates him into the social system. In this way, the number of the '*significant others*' increase for the child.

Generalised others: The child not only differentiates itself from others but also begins to act towards himself from the viewpoint of the Whole group. The child tries to understand the relative roles of various individu- als involved in the same social context. The child begins to anticipate the behaviour of all the mem- bers of a group in a particular context. In other words, the child generalises the roles of others. For example, if the child is playing the role of a '*bridegroom*' in its game of marriage, he must know not only the role of the bridegroom but also that of the bride, the father-in-law, priest, relatives, etc.

In the above example, the child plays a number of roles simultaneously, *a generalised role of a number of people*. The roles, moreover, are built around the rules of the game. According to the rule, the child generalises his behaviour. He plays the role of what Mead calls 'the generalised other'. The team of children with its rules is thus a carbon copy of the organised community. The whole community is '*generalised other*' with which the child becomes identified. '*Self*' and '*society*', in the child's experience; are the two sides of the same coin. This is exactly like a situation in which every one of us may say, or more likely think,— '*what will people think if I do this, or that*' ? The '*people*' in this expression are not any particular persons, but rather, *generalised persons*, or *generalised others*. This 'generalised others' may include the associates of our community. In this way the social explanation of the self is complete.

It is clear from the above description that the self is not something that exists first and then into relationship with others. The '*self*' is a product of social interaction. '*It arises in social experience*'. "It is something that develops out of social interaction and is constantly changing and adjusting as new situations and conflicts arise... " *The self develops and grows in a social context*.

Freud and His Concept of the Human Mind

Sigmund Freud was an Austrian Psychiatrist and the founder of Psychoanalysis. Much of the works of Freud centre around the '*Human Mind*' rather than the process of socialisation. Though Freud has not established any theory concerning socialisation as such his ideas have contributed much towards the *clarification* of that process. This can be ascertained by an understanding of his analysis of the human mind.

Freud has divided human mind into three compartments. They are as follows:

1. ***Id:*** The '*id*' is concerned only with satisfying the animal impulses of man.
2. ***Ego:*** The '*ego*' serves as the mediator between desire and action. It represses the urges of the '*id*' when necessary.
3. ***Super ego:*** The '*super ego*' always holds up the behaviour norms of society. It provides the 'ego ' the idea of moral and immoral and this in turn intervenes with the *id*.

In the Freudian analysis of the human mind the concept of '*super ego*' is of great sociological importance. It is significant in the study of socialisation also. According to Freud, the individual's *super ego* is a reflection of his parents' standards of right and wrong. The individual imbibes these into his own personality by identifying himself with his parents. The parents' standards are no other than the society's or one of its sub-group's in which the individual happens to live. Thus, logically the child, in its socialisation process adopts the norms of conduct of the society through the super ego.

W.I. Thomas Theory of the 'Definition of the Situation'

The views of *W.I. Thomas* concerning the process of socialisation can be understood by an analysis of his theory of "*the definition of the situation*". According to Thomas, the situation in which the child finds himself has already been defined for him. The rules according to which he must behave are determined by the group into which he is born. The child cannot behave according to his own whims and fancies. He must act according to the expectations of the group and compromise his wishes with those of the group. The wishes and the expectations of the group always call for restraint, order, discipline and self-sacrifice in the child. A kind of conflict may take place between the wishes of the child and those of the group. Though not always, the group usually wins out in such a conflict. Thomas has described this situation graphically in his "*The Unadjusted Girl*".

Thus, according to Thomas any deliberate action calls for an appraisal of the situation within which the person finds himself. Once the situation is defined for him, he can act appropriately in it in the normal course of life. His role also becomes apparent. Thomas has pointed out, that in infancy situations are defined for the infant by the mother and other members. The parents define the situa- tion through speech and other signs and pressures. The parents may give instructions to their child to correct his behaviour. Thus, they may instruct: "*Be quiet*", "*Sit up straight*", "*Blow your nose*", "*Wash your face*", "*Mind your mother*", "*Be kind to sister*", "*Pray God*", and so on. The child's wishes and activities are inhibited by these instructions or definitions. Thomas has argued that by definitions within the family, by playmates, in the school, by formal instruction, and by signs of approval and disapproval, the child, that is, the growing member, learns the norms of his society.

Durkheim's Theory of 'Collective Representations'

Durkheim's theory of '*Collective representations*' throws some light on the study of the process of socialisation. In his theory of socialisation Durkheim has asserted that the individual becomes socialised by adopting the behaviour of his group. By '*collective representations*' he meant *the body of experiences, ideas and ideals of a group upon which the individual unconsciously depends for his ideas' attitudes and behaviour*. To Durkheim, collective representations are objects or factors of social value. These objects are symbol-products and are mutually owned and mutually proclaimed.

Durkheim has stated that the 'collective representations' *have a great force* because they are collectively created and developed. It means, collective representations or social values are the product of collective action. Hence they are *imperative* and *compulsive*. For *example*, the flag is a political representation; sacred writings are religious representation and so on. Durkheim has said that these collective representations or social values directly or indirectly mould the character and the behaviour of the new born child.

According to Durkheim, the individual mends his ways in accordance with the group standards. The accumulated group experience provides the individuals the necessary guidance in learning the appropriate behaviour. It is in this respect

Durkheim's 'collective representations' resemble Sumner's concept of *folkways and mores*. Durkheim believed that the 'collective representations' have an autonomous existence, completely independent of individuals. He advocated a theory of "*Collective Consciousness*" and "*group mind*", which he believed, exist independent of individual consciousness. This part of Durkheim's doctrine has been severely criticised and is, at present, rejected by many of the American sociologists.

STAGES OF SOCIALISATION

Socialisation is a gradual process of learning. The new born child is not taught all the things about social life at once. It proceeds from simplicity to complexity. During the early stages of life (infancy and childhood) socialisation takes place within the 'simple', limited social world. Gradually this social world becomes broader and broader and the child is confronted with several things to learn and to adjust.

Socialisation means the child's learning to participate in social roles. Hence the main objects to be internalised by the child are the social roles themselves. In order to perform any social role adequately, one must '*know*' the other social roles in the same social system. Hence the child must internalise the roles that he is expected to perform by himself and also the roles of the other persons with whom he interacts. In fact, the internalisation of roles is almost the same thing as the growth of personality. At each stage of socialisation the child internalises a '*system*' of roles, not just one role.

Socialisation consists of four stages from infancy to adulthood. They are– 1. *the oral stage*, 2. *the anal stage*, 3. *the oedipal stage*, and 4. *the stage of adolescence*.

1. ***The oral stage:*** This stage begins with the birth of the child and continues upto the completion of one year. Before birth the child in the mother's womb is in the foetal form and is warm and comfortable. At birth the little infant must breathe, must exert himself, to be fed and he must be protected from cold, wet and other discomforts. For everything the child cries a great deal. By means of crying the child establishes its *oral dependency*. The child here develops some definite expectations about the feeding time. The child also learns to give signals for his felt needs. In this stage the child is involved in himself and his mother. For the other members of the family, the child is little more than a 'possession'. If the father or some other person is providing the proper care for the child, that person will also be performing the role of 'mother'.

   It is difficult to say whether the child internalises two roles–the role of the mother and his own role–at this stage. *Freud* called this stage–the stage of "*primary identification*". It means the child merges his identity with that of the mother. The child only tries to establish some control over the hunger drive.

2. ***The anal stage:*** The second stage normally begins soon after the first year and is completed during the third year. It is here that the child learns that he cannot depend entirely on the mother and that he has to take some degree of care for himself. "*Toilet training*" is the main focus of new concern. The child is taught to do some tasks such as toileting, keeping clothes clean, etc.

   The child in this stage internalises two separate roles–his own role and that of his mother. The child receives '*care*' and also '*love*' from the mother and learns to give love in return. The child is enabled to distinguish between correct and incorrect actions. The correct action is rewarded and the incorrect action is not rewarded but punished.

   In this second stage the socialising agent, that is, the mother plays the dual role. She participates in the interaction system with the child in a limited context and she also participates in the larger system that is the family. The dual role of the mother helps the child to participate in a more complex social system. Thus the mother '*represents*' the larger social system in relation to the smaller. Further the mother as a socialising agent mediates between the sub-system and the larger system sometimes yielding to the child's demands and some other times resisting its tendencies.

3. ***The oedipal stage:*** This stage mostly starts from the fourth year of the child and extends upto puberty (the age of 12 or 13 years). It is in this stage the child becomes the member of the family as a whole. It is here the child has to identify himself with the social role ascribed to him on the basis of his sex.

   According to *Freud*, the boy develops the '*Oedipus complex*"–the feeling of jealousy towards father and love towards mother. In the same way, the girl develops the "*Electra Complex*"–the feeling of jealousy towards the mother and love towards the father. Freud believed that the feelings are mainly sexual. But most of the writers do not subscribe to this opinion. They say that the child of four, five, or six rarely has a clear knowledge of sex or sexual function.

   In this stage sufficient social pressures are brought on the child to identify with the right sex. Boys begin to be rewarded, for behaving like boys and girls are rewarded for acting like girls. After the age of six the child is able to understand the sexual difference. The boy tries to identify himself with the father and the girl with the mother. When the children go to the school or mix with other children they prefer to join their respective playgroups. In this period interest in the opposite sex tends to be suppressed for the boy or girl is busy with learning various skills.

   In this stage the boy makes three kinds of identification (*i*) *He identifies with his father and brothers* (sex–role identification) (*ii*) *He identifies with all his siblings* (role of child in the family); and (*iii*) *He identifies with the whole family as a member*. Thus, in this stage the child internalises clearly his role–the role of the father, mother and siblings of each sex (brother and sister). It is here he realises that the father has a dominant role in the family, more dominant than that of the mother. The parents help the children to make proper sex identification. The father helps the son by showing him, how to do things. *For example*, the Eskimo father shows the boy how to shoot. In Bali Island the father helps the boy to learn the art of dancing. When once the boy has learned the goal of being like men, he will tend to imitate men especially the father and so is the case with the girl who will tend to imitate the mother.

4. ***The stage of adolescence:*** The fourth stage starts with the period of adolescence. Due to the physiological and the psychological changes that take place within the individual this stage assumes importance. During this stage the boys and girls try to become free from parental control. At the same time they cannot completely escape from their dependence on their parents. Hence they may experience a kind of strain or conflict in themselves. They want to be free in doing various activities. But the parents continue to control many of their activities. This is particularly true of sexual activity.

In the modern society the parents intend to give more freedom to the boys and girls to do some of their activities independently. The parents try to lessen the open expression of their emotional attachment towards the adolescent children. They encourage them to select their line of education, their occupation and their life partners. They expect the adolescent children to accept responsibility and learn new roles assigned to them. The adolescents thus learn new roles and new behaviour patterns and internalise new social norms associated with them. Hence in the modem society the transition from the adolescent stage to the adult stage is more difficult than in the traditional societies. In the traditional societies, all such "*life decisions*" are mostly made by the parents.

ADULT SOCIALISATION

It is wrong to presume that the process of socialisation comes to an end when once the individual reaches the adulthood from that of the adolescent stage. In fact, socialisation is a lifelong process. At no point in the life of a man it comes to an end. Even at the door of death one has something to learn. Naturally, the adult individuals who are to undertake major responsibilities in life have many things to learn in the course of their adulthood. In the modern society adulthood is considered to be attained when a person can support himself or herself entirely independent of the parental family. Full adulthood also implies the ability to form a family of one's own.

The socialisation of adults is relatively easier than the socialisation of children for three reasons: (*i*) *The adult is normally motivated to work towards a goal which he has already picked up.* (*ii*) '*The new role that he is trying to internalise has many similarities to the roles which he has already internalised.* (*iii*) *Finally, the socialising agent can communicate with him easily through speech.*

Still the socialisation of adults can be a prolonged and a tough process. This is particularly so when the skills to be learnt are complex and the responsibilities of the role are heavy. It becomes still more difficult when the new role requires the internalisation of norms and attitudes that are almost the opposite of those which are established in his personality. *For example*, a rural youth who comes from a male-dominated family may have to face difficulties when required to work under a female boss in a city office.

As a part of the preparation for many adult roles the adolescents are not only given training in necessary skills but are also instilled with proper motivation and values. Thus, most of the adoles- cents want to become parents, workers, citizens, etc. They try to play these roles well when the time comes for that. Learning of these roles becomes easier if it is preceded by *anticipatory socialisation*.

Sometimes, adult socialisation is affected by early socialisation. **Freud** has thrown light on the fact that the childhood events have long range effects upon personality. *For example*, children who are allowed to eat freely whatever they want may find it difficult in later life to have control over their tongue. Similarly, the highly talkative children will face difficulties in exercising constraint over their talk in adult life.

Even in the case of adults educational institutions, the mass media and peer groups continue to serve as agencies of socialisation. They are often supplemented by the complex organisations. These agencies help the new comer to get attuned to the established routines and also to develop values and loyalties relevant to the new roles.

Differences between Adult Socialisation and Child Socialisation

According to *Orville G.Brim Jr*, adult socialisation differs from child socialisation in five main ways.

1. "*Adult socialisation is more likely to change overt behaviour whereas child socialisation moulds basic values*". *Example*: Adults can take on the roles of parents but their basic views on love, sharing, understanding, cooperation, etc., were formed in childhood. Similarly, values also change in adulthood when, for example, religious conversions take place. Still, the basic temperamental traits developed in child socialisation may continue.

2. "*Adult socialisation stresses the informal nature of social positions, whereas child socialisation highlights the formal aspects*". *Example*: Young children tend to see teachers as authority figures, while adults would look-beyond their social positions and see them as individuals.
3. "*Adults realise that there is difference between ideal behaviour and what can reasonably be expected. Children take ideal expectations seriously*" *Example*: If the children are told, even if it is through stories, about the good qualities of a teacher who loves the students very much, they start expecting the same thing from their teachers. As they mature, children learn the distinction between the ideal things and what is really expected of them and of others.
4. "*Adult socialisation often involves juggling the conflicting demands of various roles. Childhood socialisation, however, stresses conformity to rules and to one source of authority*". *Example*: Many employed women face the conflict between their commitment to their family as Wives and mothers, and their commitment to their office or place of work as employees. But children are comparatively free from such conflicts. At home, they are trained to accept and submit to the authority of the parents and elders, and in schools of the teachers.
5. "*Adult socialisation is designed to help the person gain specific skills whereas childhood socialisation is more generalised*". *Example*: Adults are socialised to do specific jobs. Children are socialised to do things like sex–appropriate behaviour and adherence to the values of their class, caste, ethnic or religious group.

AGENTS OF SOCIALISATION

Personalities do not come ready-made. They are moulded or shaped through the process of socialisation. The process of socialisation is operative not only in childhood but throughout life. It is a process which begins at birth and continues till the death of the individual. It is an endless process. From the societal point of view, the child is valued more for '*what he will be*' than for '*what he is*'. Socialisation helps the child to become a useful member of the society. It gives him social maturity. Hence it is quite natural that the child's socialisation has not been left to mere accident. Rather, it has been given an institutional framework and controlled through institutional channels. The following are the agencies that have been established by culture which socialise the new born child.

1. ***Family and parents:*** The process of socialisation begins for every one of us in the family. Here, the parental and particularly the maternal influence on the child is very great. The intimate relationship between the mother and the child has a great impact on the shaping of child's abilities and capacities. The parents are the first persons to introduce to the child the culture of his group. The child receives additional communications from his older siblings, *i.e.* brothers and sisters, who have gone through the same process–with certain differences due to birth order and to the number and sex of the siblings.
2. ***Peers or agemates:*** 'Peer groups' means those groups made up of the contemporaries of the child, his associates in school, in playground and in street. He learns from these children, facts and facets of culture that they have previously learnt at different times from their parents. The members of peer groups have other sources of information about the culture their peers in still other peer groups–and thus the acquisition of culture goes on.

   As time passes by, of course, the peer group surpasses the parental and family groups in importance. It is true that the '*peer culture*' becomes more important and effective than the '*parental culture*' in the adolescent years of the child. The advice of one's agemates whether overtly or co- vertly communicated. sets the standards in almost every aspect of conduct. However, we should not assume that the socialisation process is completed by the time the teen ages are reached. On the other hand, this is the time when pressures for conformity are perhaps, at their heights.
3. ***Teachers:*** The teachers also play their role in socialisation when the child enters the school. It is in the school that the culture is formally transmitted and acquired, in which the lore and the learning, the science and art, of one generation is passed on to the next. It is not only the formal knowledge of the culture that is transmitted there but most of its premises as well – its ethical sentiments, its political attitudes, its customs and taboos. The children in the earlier school may uncritically absorb the culture to which their teachers give expression. They may in the high school respond with increasing scepticism. But wherever they are, and at whatever age, the communications they receive from their teachers help to socialise them and to make them finally mature members of their societies.
4. ***Literature and mass media of communication:*** There is another source of socialisation. This is, of course, found only in literate societies and that is the *literature*. The civilisation that we share is constructed of words or literature. "Words rush at us in torrent and cascade; they leap into our vision, as in billboard and newspaper, magazine and textbook; and assault our ears. as in radio and television". The media of mass communication give us their messages. These messages too contain in capsule form, the premises of our culture, its attitudes and ideologies. The words are always written by someone and these people too–authors and editors and advertisers–'join the teachers, the peers and the parents in the socialisation process. In individual cases, of course, some of these influences are more important than others. The responses can also differ. "Some of us respect tradition; others fear the opinions of their peers,

and still others prefer to listen to the '*thousand tongues of conscience*". But all three modes of socialisation result in conformity of a kind and all three thus contribute to the transmission of a culture by some and its acquisition by others.

Who Socialises the Child?

Is a question that can be answered in another way also. *Kingsley Davis* says that there are two categories of persons from whom the child acquires the sentiments, beliefs, and knowledge of his culture. The *first* includes those who have *authority over him*. Persons having authority over the child are generally older than he and command obedience. They are the parents. Socialisation must naturally proceed from those who have more of the culture to those who have less, front the mature to the immature. Since the infant has no juniors and no capacity for associating with equals, the parents play an important role at this stage.

The *second* category includes those persons who have *equality with him*. Persons sharing equality with the child, whether kin or not, are apt to be of the same age. The child maintains equalitarian relations with those who are of the same age, sex and rank. It is through the agemates or peers that one learns some of the more informed aspects of culture such as folkways, manners, style, shades of meanings, fads, fashions, crazes, habits, secret modes of gratification and forbidden knowledge. Some such things are often socially necessary and yet socially tabooed. *Example*: knowledge of sex relations.

ROLE OF CULTURE IN SOCIALISATION

Socialisation is Culture Learning

Socialisation is mainly a matter of social learning or cultural learning. Cultural learning is the process by which the individual learns the fundamental culture patterns of the society in which he will live. Through cultural conditioning one learns to walk, talk, wear dress, greet friends, handle social obligations, develop the attitudes approved in his society. Still cultural learning does not completely determine socialisation. In learning to live in society, an individual gets some experiences which influence his personality but which do not teach him the culture he will share. Those experiences may be his unique experiences. They are not cultural but personal.

Culture defines situations: Culture defines social situations for us. It not only defines but also conditions and determines – what we eat and drink, what we wear, when to laugh, weep, sleep, love, to make friends with, what work we do, what God we worship, what knowledge we rely upon, what poetry we recite and so on.

Culture defines attitudes, values and goals: Attitudes refer to the tendency to feel and act in certain ways. Values are the measure of goodness or desirability. Goals refer to the attainments which our values define as worthy. It is the culture which conditions our attitudes towards various issues such as religion, morality, marriage, science, family planning, prostitution and so on. Our values concerning private property, fundamental rights, representative government, romantic love, etc., are influenced by our culture. Our goals of winning the race, understanding others, attaining salvation, being obedient to elders and teachers, being loyal to husband, being patriotic, etc., are all set forth by our culture. We are being socialised on these models.

Culture decides our career: Whether we should become a politician, a social worker, a doctor, an engineer, a soldier, a farmer, a professor, an industrialist, a religious leader, and so on is decided by our culture. What career we are likely to pursue is largely decided by our culture. Culture sets limitations on our choice to select different careers. Individuals may develop, modify or oppose the trends of their culture but they always live within its framework. Only a few can find an outlet in the culture.

Culture provides behaviour patterns: Culture directs and confines the behaviour of an individual. Culture assigns goals and provides means for achieving them. It rewards his noble work and punishes the ignoble ones. It assigns him statuses and roles. We see, dream, aspire, work, strive, marry, enjoy according to the cultural expectations. Culture not only controls but also liberates human energy and activities. Man, indeed, is a prisoner of his culture.

No individual is completely culturally defined. Every individual is unique in any culture. The uniqueness may be based on individual differences in ability, aptitude, and learning. The impact of culture on the individual is not always identical in every case. Every individual is sooner or later exposed to influences which are not completely predetermined by culture. He meets other people outside the culture. Travelling, books, radio, cinema, television, theatre, newspapers expose an individual to many influences outside the culture. Various biological and social factors bring about the uniqueness of the individuals in any culture.

CULTURE, SOCIALISATION AND PERSONALITY

Culture and socialisation are very much interrelated. Culture refers to the social heritage of it group of people. It consists of the shared behaviour, beliefs, and material objects belonging to a society or part of a society. It is the more or less organised and persistent patterns of habits, attitudes and values which are transmitted from generation to generation. Every human infant is not only exposed to a culture, but assimilates it and in its turn transmits it.

Socialisation can be understood as all experiences by which the newly arrived young members learn the culture of the society. Culture not only conditions the process of socialisation but also has an impact on the formation of personality. In fact, it is mainly through the process of socialisation that a child develops a personality in a cultural context. It is interesting to note that different cultures provide for different ways of socialisation. These ways of socialisation have their own impact in the formation of personality.

Meaning of Personality

Personality is the product of culture It is through the process of socialisation that the child develops a personality according to the cultural expectations of his society. According to the social psychologist *G.M. Allport*, personality is–a person's pattern of habits, attitudes, and traits which determine his adjustment to his environment. According to the sociologist *Kimball Young, personality "consists of habits, attitudes, and ideas which are built up around both people and things*". No man is born with a personality but everyone develops it through socialisation.

Individuals everywhere will react to and be influenced by their culture in different ways and degrees. Culture provides the limits within which personality will develop, through socialisation each culture places its distinctive work on human personality. The more homogeneous the culture the more likely it is to produce a characteristic type of person who reflects the dominant ethos or culture theme.

Ruth Benedict's Classification of Cultures

An American anthropologist Ruth Benedict in her "*Patterns of Culture*" published in 1935 has classified cultures into two broad types on the basis of their 'ethos' or distinctive feeling tones. [*Sumner* defines 'ethos' as the totality of characteristic traits by which a group *i.e.*, a society is individualised and differentiated from others]. She has made a comparison of three tribal cultures–the Zuni, the Dobuan and the Kwakiuti Indian – and shown how each has its own unique impact on personality. The two types of cultures which she has mentioned are:

(*i*) *The Apollonian Culture*, and

(*ii*) *The Dionysian Culture*.

(*i*) *The Apollonian Culture* is characterised by qualities such as self-control, even-temperedness, moderation, mutual understanding, mutual assistance and co-operativeness. (*ii*) On the other hand the Dionysian Culture is marked by high emotionalism, aggressiveness, individualism, superficiality, prestige and competitiveness. As Ruth Benedict has pointed out the *Zuni tribe* of the South Western U.S.A. represents the Apollonian Culture whereas the *Dobuans* of Melanesia and the *Kwakiuti Indians* represent the Dionysian Culture.

In the *Zuni* tribe or society which represents the Apollonian Culture, the members reveal char- acteristics which are peculiar to their culture. The Zuni people dislike individualism, violence and power. They respect moderation and modesty, co-operation and mutual understanding. They are emotionally undisturbed. The spirit of competition is virtually absent in them. The mountain dwellers of New Guinea, called *Arapesh* who are mild, gentle, calm and quiet also represent the Apollonian Culture.

In the *Dobuan* and *Kwakiuti* societies, which are *Dionysian* in character, members exhibit traits common on their culture. The Dobuans make virtues of ill-will and treachery. They fight against one another for the possession of good things in life. Suspicion, cruelty, animosity, and malignancy are traits of almost all Dobuans. The *Kwakiuti* Indians of the Pacific Northwest Coast define everything that happens in terms of triumph or shame. For them, life is a constant struggle to put one's rivals to shame. They destory the material possessions of the defeated. The defeated resort to sulking or to acts of desperation.

In her study Benedict has tried to show that it is possible to identify the influence of the total culture on personality. She has tried to establish that each culture will produce its special type or types of personality. It is true that her study reveals the mutual interplay of culture and socialisation in conditioning personality. Culture provides for the way in which personality is to be developed. But personality as such is developed through the process of socialisation. It may also be argued that different ways and means of socialisation may produce different personalities. Individuals try to develop their personalities in accordance with their cultural ideals and expectations. If the people of three tribal communities develop different types of personality it is because their cultural ideals, values and expectations differ significantly.

SOCIALISATION AND CULTURAL DIFFERENCES

Cultures of different societies are-not uniform. They differ in various respects. Socialisation is one of the factors that contribute to cultural differences. Different ways of socialising the children in different societies have contributed to the continuity of differences in cultures. It is even argued that cultures not only produce distinctive types of personalities but also shape the character and behaviour of individuals living in them. A study conducted by Margaret Mead is supportive to this argument.

Study of Margaret Mead

Margaret Mead, a famous anthropologist, in her "*Sex and Temperament in Three Primitive Societies*", has shown how sex has to do with personality. She has tried to prove that some traits which we call '*masculine*' and some other '*feminine*' do not necessarily go with the biological fact of sex. These differences are matter of cultural definitions. Three New Guinea Tribes which she has studied, reveal three different kinds of personalities.

1. Mead has found that the **Arapesh**, the mountain dwellers of New Guinea are gentle, mild, maternal and affectionate. Both men and women act in a fashion which we would call '*feminine*'.
2. **The Mundugumor.** Tribals of New Guinea are cannibalistic. Both men and women act in ways which we would call predominantly "*masculine*". Both are expected to be violent, competitive, aggressively sexed, jealous and rough. Here every man is pitted against every other, including his brothers and father. Their world is charged with hostility and conflict.
3. But in the **Tchambuli** tribe male and female roles are defined in a way that is quite con- trary to our modern way. Here women are more dominant than men. Men gossip, wear curls, and go shopping, are emotionally dependent upon, and less responsible than women. The people live chiefly for art. Women manage and do major tasks of the family.

The above examples make it clear that such differences are not inborn. Each of these societies has chosen one type of temperament and built its culture upon it, expecting all its members to conform to it. Needless to say, the basic training is given and the proper atmosphere is created for the children in these societies to develop their cultural requirements. Children in these societies have been socialised according to their respective cultural ideals. It becomes unfair, then, to judge or evaluate the life of one community or society from the cultural viewpoint of another. Normality, then, is a matter of cultural definition. The ideal person of one society is misfit of another. Thus, the gentle Arapesh would be sconed by the Mundugumor. The violent Mundugumor would be a puzzle to the gentle Arapesh.

CAN CULTURE DETERMINE PERSONALITY?

Some writers have popularised the idea that personality and culture are two sides of the same coin, and that culture determines personality. The studies of *Margaret Mead* and *Ruth Benedict* are almost illustrative of this idea. But most of the writers believe that this idea is only a half truth. Anthropologists and sociologists are very careful now in using the term "*representative personality*" or "*basic personality*" or "*distinctive personality*", or "*model personality*" for they have observed Wide variation in personalities within cultures. *Ralph Linton* has pointed out that personality traits differ within any culture. Hence within the same culture some are found to be more aggressive than others, *some* are more submissive, kind, benevolent, competitive and so forth. It is because culture is *only one* determinant of personality among others.

It is true that cultures emphasise certain practices, motivations and values. Majority of the people embody in their personalities the dominant action patterns and thought ways. Culture exerts a powerful and consistent pressure on the individual to develop his personality, the common and socially approved traits and values. Hence a large number of them develop personalities which may most fully express the spirit or ethos of their culture. Still, we cannot say that culture and personality always coincide exactly. When we say that the *Dobuans* and *Kwakiuti Indians* are highly competitive, aggressive and known for ill-will, treachery, etc., it should not be taken to mean that all the *Dobuans* and *Kwakiuti Indians* are like that. Similarly, when we say that modern. Americans give utmost importance for "*individual success*", we do not mean that all the Americans cherish that value equally. Some may *cherish* competition to achieve individual success, while some others may be *indifferent* towards it. Still others *renounce* personal success altogether condemning it as a devil's work. There are also some monks who dedicate their lives to poverty and mystic contemplation. Personality is *not totally* determined by culture, even though no personality escapes its influence.

Causes for the Differences in Personality within the Culture

In our common observation we note that in certain respects we are like other people, in certain respects like some other people, and in still others like no one except ourselves. On the basis of this observation we can infer that not all those who are exposed to the same culture are alike. Wide differences in human personalities are found within the same culture. It is difficult to explain how each human personality could be unique. However, the following factors throw some light on the differences in human personalities within the same culture.

1. ***Sub-cultural influence:*** Culture of any society consists of many sub-cultures. Shared behaviours which are common to a regional, racial, religious, rural, urban, ethnic, class, caste, occupational and other kinds of sub-culture. Each sub-culture has its own impact on the members. All the children of the same society do not confront the same culture because of these sub-cultures that it consists of. Thus culture is not a monolithic entity, a hardened mould into which each individual is poured at birth. "*Culture is not a uniform that all must wear*"—*Robert Bierstedt.*

2. ***Cultural alternatives:*** As *Ralph Linton* has pointed out every culture offers for its people not only '*universals*' but also "*alternatives*". 'Universals' are those core features of a culture which are widely accepted and required by the society. They are learnt behaviours widely shared by them. *For example*, the language spoken in the society, deep-seated moral and social values such as humanitarianism, patriotism, monogamous marriage, sacrifice, sexual fidelity, respect for fundamental rights, religiosity, etc. represent the cultural universals of Indian society.

   "*Cultural alternatives*" represent those activities in which individuals are allowed a choice. *For example*, a cultural universal demands legalised marriage. But the individuals who want to marry are allowed alternative lines of action which are equally acceptable. They may be married at home, in a temple or church, or at the community hall or in the registrar's office. Similarly, the babies may be breast-fed or bottle-fed and both procedures are allowed. Thus, the alternatives are different activities allowed and accepted for achieving the same end. The effect of these on personality is found to be different.

3. ***Biological factor:*** The inherent organic differences in individuals also contribute to the differences in their personalities. No two newly born babies are exactly alike in every talent, attribute, and trait. The biological differences that are genetic and hereditary in character make every human infant different from every other. Hence each infant may respond to the same or similar cultural stimuli in its own way.

4. ***Situational differences:*** Social situation in which the infant finds himself also has an effect upon the development of personality. *For example*, the social situation in which the parents possess the only child differs from the one in which the parents have two children–or three or five or ten. A child who has brothers only is in a different social situation from the one who has only sisters. Further the child's sex is an additional variable in the situation. Birth order is still another factor that can affect the personality. Similarly, the age of parents is another variable in the situation. The child of young parents may have better chance to learn than the child of older parents.

5. ***Differences in the transmission of culture:*** Socialisation is understood as the process of cultural transmission in which the rules and practices of the group are learnt. But culture does not transmit itself. It is transmitted only by individuals who have absorbed some aspects of culture to which they were initially exposed. Hence different parents will transmit to their children different cultural items and traits even though they belong to the same race, religion, region and social class.

6. ***Changes in culture:*** Variety is endless in human life. Changes in culture may also add to it. Culture is neither uniform nor static. It is dynamic. In complex societies culture is changing all the times. In every passing period it presents new facets and elements. Hence its influence on the developing personality cannot be uniform.

7. ***Culture encourages individuality:*** Culture places emphasis not only upon conformity but also upon individuality. Culture provides for '*alternatives*' as well as '*specifications*'. Initiative, inventiveness, originality, adaptability to new situations, etc., are values that are cherished and encouraged in some cultures. In some respects, culture even encourages idiosyncrasy.

Conclusion

It is clear from the above that personality is not a "*cultural mould*". It is not a passive creation of culture. Individuals react in different ways to these cultural pressures and impressions. As *Gardner Murphy* suggests, "one child is easily moulded with regard to food but fights constantly against socialisation of his aggressive impulses; the reverse may be true of another child". All cultures produce variety as well as uniformity of personality. Every socialised individual has a personality of his own. Personality is the organisation of a person's habits, attitudes and traits. It arises from the inter-play of biological, social and cultural factors. Personality is never determined by culture entirely. Still no one can ignore the influence of culture as such.

IMPORTANCE OF SOCIALISATION

Is socialisation necessary ? Does it really help the individual to become a person and to express himself more fully and effectively as a person? Is it essential to ensure stability, conformity and continuity in society? Or, does it hinder the expression of individuality? Will it not hamper the expression of free will of the individual and reduce him to the level of the small fragment of the charmless societal uniformity? Will it not make his life more miserable? These are some of the questions relevant to our discussion of the importance of socialisation.

In Europe, a few centuries ago, there was a widespread belief that civilisation corrupted man's basic good nature, so that only the primitives remained as "*pure*" human beings. A number of novels appeared on "*noble savage*" and read by people who had never seen one. For example, in his book '*Emile*' (1762) J.J. Rousseau urged that children be reared out in forests so that society would not spoil their natural goodness.

Most sociologists do not agree that socialisation necessarily brings misery. "It is true as Freud suggested that we must renounce the gratification of many impulses, but we learn to channel others into directions that can be gratified within our own society". As *Metta Spencer* and *Alex Inkeles* have noted, "*without experience in society a human being would become, not a "noble Savage" but an unlovely brute, insensitive to the minds and feelings of others*".

Society can grant people some amount of freedom of impulses, but never total freedom. Freud was right then. "*Civilisation itself requires some self-denial for the sake of beauty, cleanliness, and social order*". We do not face a choice between whether to socialise our children or not, but only how to do it. Social research can shed light on many factors relevant to that issue. No research can, of course, provide a foolproof formula for child-rearing. No form of upbringing will fix a person's character so firmly that he can never change.

The importance of socialisation in our life can hardly be exaggerated. The following descrip- tion makes it very clear.

1. ***Socialisation converts man, the biological being into man, the social being:*** Man is not born social. He becomes social by virtue of the process of socialisation. Various instances like that of *Kaspar Hauser, Anna*, the '*wolf children*' of India and others have made it very clear that only through constant training the new born child becomes social in nature.
2. ***Socialisation contributes to the development of personality:*** Personality is a product of society. In the absence of groups or society no man can develop a personality of his own. But socialisation is a process through which the personality of the new born child is shaped and moulded. The process of socialisation prepares the child to lead an approved way of social life. At the same time, it also provides enough scope for the individual to develop his individuality.
3. ***Helps to become disciplined:*** Socialisation is social learning. Social learning is essentially the learning of rules of social behaviour. It is through socialisation that the child learns not only rules of social behaviour but also the values, ideals, aims and objectives of life and the means of attaining them. Socialisation disciplines an individual and helps him to live according to the social expectations.
4. ***Helps to enact different roles:*** Every individual has to enact different roles in his life. Every role is woven around norms and is associated with different attitudes. The process of socialisation assists an individual not only to learn the norms associated with roles but also to develop appropriate attitudes to enact those roles.
5. ***Provides the knowledge of skills:*** Socialisation is a way of training the new born individual in certain skills which are required to lead a normal social life. These skills help the individual to play economic, professional, educational, religious and political roles in his later life. In primitive societies for example, imparting skills to the younger generation in specific occupations was an important aspect of socialisation.
6. ***Helps to develop right aspiration in life:*** Every individual may have his own aspirations, ambitions and desires in life. All these aspirations may not always be in consonance with the social interests. Some of them may even be opposed to the communal interests. But through the process of socialisation an individual learns to develop those aspirations which are complementary to the interests of society. Socialisation helps him to direct or channelise his whole energy for the realisation of those aspirations.
7. ***Contributes to the stability of the social order:*** It is through the process of socialisation that every new generation is trained according to the cultural goals, ideals, and expectations of a society. It assures the cultural continuity of the society. At the same time it provides enough scope for variety and new achievements. Every new generation need not start its social life afresh. It can conveniently rely on the earlier generation and follow its cultural traditions. In this regard, socialisation contributes to the stability of the social order.
8. ***Helps to reduce social distance:*** Socialisation reduces social distance and brings people together if proper attention is given to it. By giving proper training and guidance to the children during their early years, it is possible to reduce the social distance between people of different castes, 'aces, regions, religions and professions.
9. ***Provides scope for building the bright future:*** Socialisation is one of the powerful instruments of changing the destiny of mankind. It is through the process of socialisation that a society can produce a generation of its expectations. By giving appropriate training to the new born children the coming generation can be altered significantly. "*The improvement of socialisation offers one of the greatest possibilities for the future alteration of human nature and human society*".
— Kingsley Davis
10. ***Helps the transmission of culture:*** By transmitting the contents of culture such as ideas, beliefs, language, skills, etc., from one generation to the other, socialisation contributes to the continuity of culture also.

FAILURES OF THE SOCIALISATION PROCESS AND THE PROBLEMS OF FAULTY SOCIALISATION

It is true that socialisation is a powerful factor that helps to bring about social conformity. It is equally true that socialisation is an effective instrument of creating a new generation of our expectations. Still, like any other social mechanism it has its own limitations. Socialisation is not an all-out cure for all problems of personality. Neither we can assure that socialisation would be a success always, with all the equipments and techniques of modern civilisation and with all the knowledge of human psychology, socialisation often results in failure. Failures of socialisation on the one hand. and inappropriate or wrong way of socialisation on the other, often lead to serious consequences including problems of personality.

1. ***Culture cannot be understood completely:*** 'Socialisation' is said to be the process in which the culture of the group is introduced to the new individual. But *no individual can internalise the total culture of the society*. No person can internalise all the ways of creating works of art, using mechanical equipment, interpreting language, etc. Further, no individual can know and put into practice all the norms of the group or society. The expected results of socialisation is no doubt conformity. But some deviation from what is considered proper behaviour is always found everywhere. In fact, some amount of deviation is allowed everywhere due to inevitability.

2. ***Damage to the self-image:*** Development of proper self-image is vital to successful socialisation. Personal self-image is a highly active factor in behaviour. Various research studies have revealed that self—image affects vitally task performance. *Coleman's* famous study of '*Equality of Economic Opportunities 1966*', has revealed that the child's self-concept and sense of control over the environment have a great bearing on the child's performance at school. Effective teaching in school rests upon building the learner's self-confidence. Conversely, the lack of self-image always cripples learning or task performance. *For example*, some years ago, it was found that in schools the *black* children had lower self-esteem than white children and this was reflected in the poorer performance of black children, Recent studies, however, no longer, find lower levels of self-esteem among the black children. It would appear that '*black-life*' and '*black-consciousness*' have changed enough in recent years so that black children no longer see themselves as inferior.

   Failure in socialisation would damage the self-image of the child. An unsatisfactory self-image often leads to unpleasant anti-social or delinquent behaviour. "In fact, a great deal of behaviour ranging from mildly annoying habits to serious neuroses and delinquencies can be viewed as desperate attempts to repair an intolerable image of 'self' as incompetent, unworthy, or unimportant. The ultimate response to feelings of unworthiness is suicide. Truly, the image of self lies at the core of behaviour". — *Horton* and *Hunt*

3. ***Failure of socialisation and mental illness:*** Several sociologists have studied the relations between socialisation and mental illness. Some such studies have revealed that communication problems between the child and parents, and the child and others often lead to mental illness on the part of the child. Sociologist *Lennard* has found that among families with schizophrenic children worst type of communication prevails between the parents and children.

   Wrong parenting is often the cause of mental illness of children, Due to '*communication block*' parents do not allow children to identify and control their own reality. "Children need to develop such control if they are to reject false labels that others may apply to them and to their feelings. Children must learn how to use anger, joy and sorrow to deal with tension" [Smelser]. In this way they will be able to manage both the internal world and the external one. Schizophrenic children do not gain this ability.

   Further, lower–class parents also do not stress self-control and autonomy as much as middle class parents do. Schizophrenia is more common among the lower class people. This fact suggests a link between socialisation methods or ways and mental illness.

4. ***Resistance to excessive control:*** Successful socialisation requires the parents to be support- ive to their children and at the same time *controlling* also. It has been observed that teenagers who recalled their parents' child caring method as both "*supportive and controlling*" were more committed to traditional religious beliefs and norms in general. Teenagers who got little support but a great deal of control were often found to be non-conformists particularly in religious matters. Many children rebelled by adopting values that were opposed to those of their parents and the larger society.

5. ***Failure to prepare children to face the challenges of "life-cycle":*** Socialisation in complex, modern societies is not a simple process. It often fails to prepare people for the challenges of '*life cycle*'. In most of the civilised societies it does not equip people properly for the challenges of adolescence. The media, for example, glorify the virtues of sexual satisfaction and the value of money. But adolescents are usually *denied full access to either* even though they have physical maturity to do both Adolescence, thus, in modem society, is often experienced as a stage of confusion and personality crisis.

6. ***Confusions of mature adults:*** Mature adulthood in some societies also brings its problems particularly in the middle-years of the forties and fifties. The Western "women are socialised to value their youth, their beauty and their roles as mothers. When their youthfulness fades, and their children leave home, they may become disappointed and feel desolate and purposeless." [*Ian Robertson*]. In the same manner, "the western men are socialised to value occupational and financial success. But a man who has not achieved these goals by the early forties must face an uncomfortable situation. His self-concept may suffer very badly.

7. ***Inability to equip people to face old age and death:*** The greatest failure of the process of socialisation is, perhaps, its inability to equip people sufficiently to face old age and death. The old have very little role to play and fewer links with society. They are often treated as a '*burden*' by their own children. Hence they may suffer severe personality disorganisation resulting from feelings of isolation and rejection rather than from the ageing process itself.

   Further, *socialisalion for death* is also not there in the modem societies. In preindustrial societies deaths used to take place at home only, that is, in family and young people were getting a close understanding of its experience. But in modern societies old people and also severely diseased people die in formal organisation such as hospitals, old-age homes, etc. The young do not get a first hand experience of it. When someone is dying, many times, the relatives and medical personnel hide the fact from the dying person as if like a conspiracy. "Recent research into the sociology of death and dying, however, has produced an impressive and growing body of evidence to suggest that people die far more happily–even contentedly–if death is openly and honestly discussed with them beforehand".

   — *Ian Robertson*

8. ***Inconsistency in the ways of socialisation:*** Socialisation of different socialising agents may also produce confusion and conflict for the child. When there is conflict between the ideas, examples and skills transmitted in the home and those transmitted by the child's peers, teachers at school, the socialisation of the child suffers very badly. Rate of speed of learning comes down and uncertainty and confusion will prevail. *Example:* Parents may teach a child in a rural context that formal schooling serves no useful purpose; teachers tell him that it is essential to his well being, that is, to lead a happy and a successful life–which of the two he should accept? The child is at a confusion, nay, at a conflict. It could thus be generalised that "*the more in agreement the socialising agencies are, the more securely and rapidly socialisation of the individual takes place*". (*David Dressler and Donald Cams*).

The child may resist and alter the process of socialisation at many points in his or her development. Parents, attempt to impose their wishes, plans and ambitions upon their children are also often resisted by them. Socialisation sometimes fails from the stand point of society, that is, in so far as the child develops "non-conformity, rebelliousness, and counter-cultural tendencies". Such failures "may often serve as the basis of social change in larger generations". —*Smelser*

REVIEW QUESTIONS

1. Give the meaning of socialisation. Describe the agents of socialisation.
2. Explain the term 'socialisation'. Discuss the process and types of socialisation.
3. What do you know about internalisation of social norms? Discuss.
4. Highlight the conditions of learning.
5. What are internalised objects? Write in brief about internalised objects.
6. Throw light on the theories and stages of socialisation.
7. What do you mean by adult socialisation? How does it differ from child socialisation?
8. Assess the role of culture in socialisation.
9. Analyse the interrelationship between culture, socialisation and personality.
10. Examine the importance of socialisation.
11. Discuss the factors that throw light on the differences in human personalities within the same culture.
12. Can culture determine personality? Examine.
13. Man is not born social. Prove.
14. Discuss the various agencies of socialization.
15. Explain the need for socialisation and bring out its stages and process.
16. Write short notes on the following:
    (a) Concept of socialisation
    (b) Socialisation and cultural differences
    (c) Failures of the socialisation process
    (d) Problems of faulty socialisation

⌘⌘⌘⌘⌘⌘⌘⌘⌘⌘⌘

19

SOCIAL GROUPS

CHAPTER OUTLINE

- Man is a Social Animal
- The Factors of Group Life
- Classification of Social Groups
- Primary Groups Meaning, Characteristics and Importance
- Differences between Primary Groups and Secondary Groups
- Crowd and Public as Unorganised Groups
- Differences Between the Organised and Unorganised Groups
- Definition and Characteristics of Social Group
- Importance of Social Groups
- Summar's classification of Social Groups: In-Groups & Out Groups
- Primary Groups and Secondary Groups
- Secondary Groups Meaning, Characteristics and Importance
- Organised and Unorganised Groups
- Differences Between the Crowd and the Public
- Reference Groups

Society consists of groups. Society starts with an aggregate of people. But the mere congregation of people in a physical area does not make them a social group. A social group exists when two or more people are in direct or indirect *Contact* and *Communication*. The members of the group stimulate and respond to one another in some meaningful way. *This mutual stimulation and response of individuals and groups is social interaction*. Society is rooted in social interaction. It represents the conditioned behaviour of persons and groups. "Both society and culture are the products of social interaction". Social interaction is the most elemental social phenomenon from which spring all other social phenomena. When interaction recurs often enough so that we can perceive a pattern of behaviour, a *social relation* exists. Social relations may be friendly or unfriendly, intimate or non-intimate, inclusive or non-inclusive, specialised or non-specialised in character. The nature and character of social relationships underlie different forms of social groups such *as primary* and *secondary groups*, *in-groups* and *out-groups*, *organised* and *unorganised* groups, *formal* and *informal groups* or *organisations* and so on.

MAN IS A SOCIAL ANIMAL

No man normally lives alone. Man does not live in isolation for a long time. He is basically a social creature. The great Greek Philosopher–*Aristotle* said long back that man is a social animal [*Zoon, Politikon*]. He further remarked that he who does not live in society is either a beast or an angel. With the exception of hermits, shepherds, light house keepers, prisoners in solitary confinement and possibly a few others, all human beings live in groups. Men everywhere live in groups. Man's life is to an enormous extent a group life. A completely separated or isolated individual is purely hypothetical. On the contrary, man's daily life is made up largely of participating in groups. Not only our life becomes boring and unbearable without fellow human beings but also our very survival becomes problematic. Total ostracism from one's group is probably the cruelest punishment – short of only death–that men are ever called upon to endure.

THE TERM 'GROUP' LACKS PRECISION

'*Group*' is one of those terms which in common usage lack exactness. We use the word 'group' to mean such groups as family group, kin group, racial group, church group, religious group, occupational group, age group, sex group, vast community group, abstract group, statistical group, collectivity and so on. Even in sociology the word group is not always consistently used by the sociologists. The word 'group' is very loosely used. Sometimes, the word 'group' is used to refer to entire human group. Sometimes, it is used to mean a small group which consists of two (dyad) or more individuals. The term 'group' is not used with any specifications. Hence, it is difficult to give a single satisfactory definition to the concept of group.

DEFINITION AND CHARACTERISTICS OF SOCIAL GROUP

Definition of Social Group

1. *Harry M Johnson* says that 'A social group is a system of social interaction.'
2. *Marshal Jones* is of the opinion that a social group is 'two or more people between whom there is an established pattern of interaction.
3. *R.M MacIver* and *Page* define social group as 'any collection of human beings who are brought into human relationships with one another.
4. *Ogburn* and *Nimkojf*: "Whenever two or more individuals come together and influence one another, they may be said to constitute a social group."
5. *Emory S. Bogardus* defines social group as 'a number of persons, two or more, who have common objects of attention, who are stimulating to each other, who have common loyalty and participate in similar activities.'

Characteristics of Social Group

The main characteristics of social groups are as follows:

1. ***Collection of individuals:*** Social group consists of people. Without individuals there can be no group. Just as we cannot have a college or a university without students and teachers we cannot have a group in the absence of people.
2. ***Interaction among members:*** Social interaction is the very basis of group life. Hence mere collection of individuals does not make a group. The members must have interaction. A social group, is in fact a system of social interaction. The limits of social groups are marked by the limits of social interaction.
3. ***Mutual awareness:*** Group life involves mutual awareness. Group members are aware of one another and their behaviour is determined by this mutual recognition. This may be due to what *Giddings* calls '*the consciousness of kind*'.
4. ***'We-feeling':*** 'We-feeling' refers to the tendency on the part of the members to identify themselves with the groups. It represents group unity.' 'We-feeling' creates sympathy in and fosters co-operation among members. It helps group members to defend their interests collectively,
5. ***Group unity and solidarity:*** Group members are tied by a sense of unity. The solidarity or integration of a group is largely dependent upon the *frequency*, the *variety*, and the *emotional quality* of the interactions of its members. A family or a friends' group, or a religious group is highly united and integrated, because its members are related by several common interests and have frequent social contacts with one another and express a high degree of morale and of loyalty. Unity is maintained more often by conscious effort.
6. ***Common interests:*** The interests and ideals of group are common. Groups are mostly formed or established for the fulfilment of certain interests. In fact, men not only join groups but also form group for the realisation of their objectives or interests. Form of the groups differs depending upon the common interests of the group. Hence, there are political groups, religious groups, economic" groups, educational groups, racial groups, national groups and so on.
7. ***Similar behaviour:*** The members of group behave in more or less similar way for the pursuit of common interests. Social groups represent collective behaviour.
8. ***Group norms:*** Every group has its own rules or norms which the members are supposed to follow. These norms may be in the form of customs, folkways, mores, traditions, conventions, laws, etc. They may be written or unwritten norms or standards. Every group has its own ways and means of punishing or correcting those who go against the rules. The continued group-life of man practically becomes impossible without some norms.
9. ***Size of the group:*** Every group involves an idea of size. Social groups vary in size. A group may be as small as that of dyad [two members' group *e.g.*, husband-and-wife-family] or as big as that of a political party having lakhs of members. Size will have its own impact on the character of the group.
10. ***Groups are dynamic:*** Social groups are not static but dynamic. They are subject to changes whether slow or rapid. Old members die and new members are born. Whether due to internal or external pressures or forces, groups undergo changes.
11. ***Stability:*** Groups are stable or unstable; permanent or temporary in character. Some groups like, the crowd, mob, audience, spectators' group etc., are temporary and unstable. But many groups are relatively permanent and stable in character.

12. ***Influence on personality:*** Social groups directly or indirectly shape the personality of their members. They also provide opportunities for the expression of individuality

SOCIAL BONDS: GROUP LIFE

Man Becomes Man Only Among Men!

It is true that man everywhere lives in groups. Group life is almost inevitable for him. Man fails to develop human qualities in the absence of a human environment. Man can become man only among men. The one who fails to live in human groups fails to develop human traits. One or two instances may corroborate this point.

1. ***The Case of the Wolf Children:*** In 1920, two Hindu children were traced out in a wolf den, one at the age of eight and the other under two. The younger child died within a few months of discovery. But the elder one called *Kamala* survived until 1929. Kamala had developed no human qualities when she was discovered. She could walk only on '*fours*', possessed no language and was shy to meet or face people. After some sympathetic training she was taught basic social habits. Before her death she had slowly learned some simple speech, human eating and dressing habits and the like. This wolf child had no '*sense of human selfhood*', when she was discovered, but it emerged gradually. The emergence of individuality was altogether dependent upon her membership in human group or society.
2. ***The Case of Anna:*** Another such example is that of Anna, an illegitimate American child who had been placed in a room at the age of six months. She was isolated there until her discovery five years later in 1938. During her confinement Anna was fed but received no training and had no contacts with other human beings. After five years of this cruel social isolation Anna was allowed to go out. But she could not walk or speak. She was completely indifferent to people around her. As in the case of Kamala, Anna was given some training to which she responded. She became '*humanised*' much more rapidly before she died in 1942. Here improvement showed that socialisation could do a great deal towards making her a '*person*'. Not only these two, but many other instances have convincingly proved that man becomes social only in social groups.

Factors of Group Life

Various forces are at work to make man social. Particularly, the psychological, biological, kinship and physical factors have enforced man to lead group life. These factors can be called *social bonds.*

1. ***Psychological Factors:*** The psychological bond that promotes group life is what *Prof. Giddings calls "the consciousness of kind*". It means the recognition of similarities. It compels men to come together and live in groups. Further, man is psychologically equipped to live together. Solitary life is unbearable for him. Groups provide opportunities not only for the development of man's personality but also for the expression of his individuality. It is in an environment of groups only that man discovers his capacities, learn new ideas and new habits and new attitudes.

   Reaction to fear is another psychological force that drives man to lead a group life. Solitary life brings man not only boredom but also fear. As *Herbert Spencer* has pointed out, *the fear of the living produced the state* [a political group], *and the fear of the dead created religion.*
2. ***Biological Factor:*** Unlike other animals, human beings are susceptible to sexual pressures throughout their life. *Sex desire* on the one hand, and the *desire for progeny* on the other, have drawn nearer men and women into group called *family*. Thus, strong sexual impulse, the natural biological processes of procreation and upbringing of children have made family almost universal and inevitable. *The prolonged human infancy* coupled with the *helplessness of the newborn baby* have further added to this inevitability. Human beings at birth possess the '*biological potentially*' of being converted into social animals.
3. ***Kinship Bond:*** Kinship is popularly known as '*blood relationship*'. Kinsmen are regarded as people who are related by '*blood*' through descent from some human or mythical ancestor. Kinsmen are better united and have a sense of identity. In primitive societies the element of kinship is more effective in bringing people together than in the civilised societies. But still, the social bond of racial kinship also promotes group life. However, in modern times, the influence and the hold of the kinship factor are declining due to urbanisation, industrialisation and other processes.
4. ***Geographic Factor:*** The geographic factors such as climate, soil, natural resources, rivers, mountains, play their role in helping people to have social relations with others. The fact of living in a particular physical area has made possible for people to have regular contacts. These contacts are the basic requirements of social group. Good and conducive geographic environment attracts people to live together than the unfavourable one. Ancient civilisations, for example, flourished on the banks of the rivers while dense forests, barren lands, dry deserts are uninhabited by the people even today. Groups are rarely founded in such places.

5. ***Cultural Factors:*** A common cultural outlook and group interests together have long constituted a significant element in promoting group life. Common language, common historic traditions, common literature, common faith, beliefs, values, attitudes, customs, traditional and educational heritage have all served to bring people together and cement them into groups.
6. ***Economic Factors:*** Experience has taught man that his basic economic needs–the need for food, clothing and shelter–can better be fulfilled by being in groups than alone. The major economic processes of production, distribution and exchange take place primarily in groups. Economic groupings have become more prominent especially after Industrial Revolution of the 19th century.
7. ***Religious Factors:*** Man is a religious or spiritual being also. His soul craves for religious experience. Worshipping, meditation, prayer, singing songs in praise of God. etc., are the essence of religious experience. These are commonly observed. Religion brings people together into religious groups in the name of God or some supernatural force. A sense of belonging to a religion holds people together into groups.
8. ***Political Factors:*** The need for safety, security of life, liberty and property and pursuit of happiness has brought people together into political groups. Particularly, the modern democratic set up encourages people to have their own political groups. State, the basic political group, has become today the most powerful of all the groups.

Other Factors: In addition to the above, other factors such as common occupations or professions, common language, common historic traditions, common educational heritage, common faith, belief, values, attitudes and outlook etc., also have made people to form groups or to join groups.

IMPORTANCE OF SOCIAL GROUPS

The study of human society is essentially the study of human groups. Society consists of groups of innumerable kinds and variety. No man exists without a society and no society exists without groups. Groups have become a part and parcel of our life. Out of necessity and inevitability human beings are made to live in groups. Knowingly or unknowingly or unwillingly, with pleasure or contempt, people live in groups and societies. Man's life is to an enormous extent lived and controlled by groups of different kinds.

Survival Becomes Problematic without Groups

Groups have become so necessary that our very survival becomes problematic and doubtful in their absence. Groups are complementary to the development of human faculties, traits and human nature. Man by birth itself has the biological potentiality of becoming man–the social being.

Man Becomes Man Only Among Men

Man becomes man only among men. Various studies have convincingly proved that man fails to develop human qualities in the absence of human envi- ronment. The famous case of *Kasper Hauser*, a youth who was bereft of human contacts because of political mechanisation, the most interesting feral case of the two Hindu female children *Kamala* and her sister found in an wolf's den and the pitiable case of *Anna*, an illegitimate American child which was kept away from human contacts for more than five years and several other instances have proved beyond doubts that only a human environment makes a man; a *biological animal*,- a human being. The biological potentiality of man to become a '*person*' does not happen on its own automatically, even in the absence of a human environment. The biological potentiality blossoms only in social situation, to be more precise, only in the context of groups. Added to this, the prolonged human infancy and the helplessness of new born baby have almost made it a prisoner of the most elementary social group, that is family.

Groups Help Social Survival Also

Not only from the point of view of survival but also from the viewpoint of leading a successful life man depends on groups. By engaging himself in constant relations with others he learns things and mends his ways. He keeps his eyes wide open, lends his ears to what others say, tries to keep his memory ever fresh to remember the good things of the past and to refrain from repeating the blunders of the past. In brief, from birth to death, man is engaged in the process of socialisation. Socialisation or the process of humanisation helps man to develop a personality of his own.

Groups Contribute to the Development of Personality

Personality is the product of the group life. The '*self*' that every individual develops, though unique, is itself a product of the group. No '*self* ' *arises in isolation*. Groups provide scope for the individuals to *express* their real nature, their talents and abilities. Hidden potentialities can find their expression only in the context of social groups. What is latent in man becomes manifest only in groups. The groups shape man's attributes, his beliefs, his morals and his ideals. Emotional development, intellectual maturity, satisfaction of physical and social needs are unthinkable without groups. Group is a part of our mental equipment and we are a part of group.

CLASSIFICATION OF SOCIAL GROUPS

Social groups are not only innumerable but also diverse. It is not possible to study all the groups. A systematic study of groups demands a scientific classification. But such a classification is difficult to be made because of the very complex nature of the group. Sociologists have not been successful in providing a satisfactory classification of groups. We have not one but several classifications. Some thinkers have given simple classification while others have given an elaborate classificatory scheme.

Criteria of Classification

Classification of any kind in any field is always made on some basis. But social groups are classified not on the basis of any one factor, but on several factors. Different sociologists have classified social groups on the basis of different criteria. Groups have been classified variously on the basis of factors such as — *racial features, religious beliefs, territory, nature of government, size, caste, sex, age, class, occupation, blood relationships, degree of organisation, nature of social interaction, range of group interests, permanent or temporary nature, degree of mobility* and so on. A single criterion may be taken or a combination of some factors may be preferred for a classification. The following are some of the main classifications. Of course, they are not mutually exclusive and they do overlap.

THE CLASSIFICATIONS

1. ***'In-groups' and 'out-group':*** *W. G. Sumner* in his '*Folkways*' differentiates between 'in-groups' and 'out-groups'. An '*In-Group*' is simply the *We-group*, an '*Out-Group*' the '*They group*'. This classification is more subjective, in the sense, it depends on the tendency on the part of an individual to identify himself with a particular group in a particular situation for a particular reason. For example, for a Hindu, all the other Hindus constitute his '*in-group*' and members of other religious groups, '*out-group*'. For a Lingayat, the other Lingayats may constitute his 'in-group', and other people, his '*out-group*' and so on.
2. ***Involuntary and voluntary groups, institutional and non-institutional groups and temporary and permanent groups:*** *Charles A. Ellwood* in his '*Psychology of Human Society*' has mentioned these three categories. Involuntary groups include the groups such as family, city, the state, community, caste, race etc., and the voluntary groups include political parties, trade unions, youth associations, religious associations, cultural associations and so on. *Institutional* groups are mostly permanent in nature and include church, state, caste, the school and so on while the *non-institutional* groups are temporary in nature and include groups such as crowds, mobs, public, audience and so on.
3. ***Horizontal groups and vertical groups:*** *P.A. Sorokin* has divided groups into two major types–the horizontal and the vertical. The former are large, inclusive groups; such as nations, religious organisations and political parties. The latter are smaller divisions, such as economic classes which give the individual his status in society.
4. ***Territorial groups and non-territorial groups:*** *Park* and *Burgess* have distinguished between territorial groups [*e.g.*, communities and states] and non-territorial groups [*e.g.*, classes, castes, crowds and public].
5. ***Crowds, groups and collectivities:*** Leopold Von Wiese and Howard Becker classified human groups into three categories: (1) *Crowds*, which are described as 'loose-textured and transitory', (2) *Groups*, aggregations of long duration, and (3) *abstract collectivities* such as a state or a church.
6. ***Primary groups and secondary-groups:*** On the basis of *nature* and *quality of social interaction* groups have been classified into *primary* and *secondary*. The name of C.H. Cooley is very much associated with this classification though in actuality, he has not made any such classification. Cooley introduced the term 'primary group' and spoke nothing about 'secondary group'. The secondary groups are regarded as a '*residual*' category.
7. ***Social groups, social category and statistical aggregate:*** A distinction is also made between social groups, social categories and statistical aggregate. (*i*) Social groups arc those which are characterised by some established pattern of interaction. *Example*: Peer groups, classroom groups, family, political party etc. (*ii*) *A social category* refers to the people who share a common status. *Example:* Bank officials, soldiers, teachers, farmers, women etc. (*iii*) *A statistical aggregate* include people who share similar interests. *Example:* Cricket fans, subscribers of a magazine.
8. ***Genetic groups and congregate group:*** *F. Q. Giddings* has introduced this classification. Genetic groups are involuntary in nature and the individuals are born in them. Congregate groups are voluntary in nature and the individuals are at liberty to join them or not. Family groups, racial groups, ethnic groups are genetic groups, political parties, trade unions, etc. are congregate groups.
9. ***Tonnies' classification of communities (or groups):*** A German Sociologist *Ferdinand* Tonnies has classified communities into "*Gemeinschaft*" and "*Gesellschaft*". These two terms have been translated into English as

"*Community*" and "*Association*" respectively. Tonnies made the distinction between 'Community' and 'Association' at two levels. The distinction was applied to both: (*i*) *to the social groups within a society*, and (*ii*) *to the societies themselves*.

(*i*) **Gemeinschaft (Community).** The '*Gemeinschaft*' is characterised by "*intimate, private, and exclusive living together*." It represents a community or social groups in which individuals are involved in the process of interaction as '*persons*'. They feel that they can satisfy all or most of a wide range of purposes in the group. The family, kin group, the neighbourhood, the rural village, the friends group represent the Gemeinschatt. In such groups intimate, friendly and personal relations are found among the members.

(*ii*) **Gesellschaft (Association).** The *Gesellschaft* is defined as "*public life*", as something which is purposefully entered upon. Tonnies says that these associations largely represent group with *economic interests*. The Gesellschaft or the '*association*' represents relationships that are specific, partial, and utilitarian. Business contract, legal pacts between individuals represent the Gesellschaft relationships. Business Companies, Corporations, Cities, Towns etc. represent 'Gesellschaft' type groups. In these groups the individuals are not wholly involved in the group life. They look to the group for the satisfaction of some specific and partial ends.

Thus, Gemeinschaft or the Community is united by kind of feeling or sentiment between individuals. It acts as a cementing factor. On the other hand, Gesellschaft or the Association is united by a *rational agreement of interests*. This classification of communities made by Tonnies is very much akin to the classification of groups into '*primary groups*' and '*secondary groups*.

10. ***Small groups and large groups:*** *George Simmel* introduced this classification. *Size* is the basis of this classification. Small groups include 'dyad', 'triad' and other small groups. Large groups represent racial groups, political groups, nation and other big collectivities.

Other Classifications

In addition to the above, there are also other classifications such as the following:

1. Organised groups and Unorganised groups
2. Congregated groups and Dispersed groups
3. Majority groups and Minority groups
4. Open groups and Closed groups
5. Independent groups and Dependent groups
6. Formal groups and Informal groups

SUMMER'S CLASSIFICATION OF SOCIAL GROUPS IN-GROUPS AND OUT-GROUPS

American sociologist **W.G. Summer** in his book "*Folkways*" has classified groups into "*in groups*" and "*out-groups*". This classification depends more on the psychological factors rather than on the external physical factors. The group which an individual belongs [or feels that he belongs] is an "*in-group*" and the rest of the groups are "*out-groups*". *Example: One's own family, peer group, friendship group, religious group, caste group, linguistic group, occupational group etc*., are "*in groups*", and other groups, are "*out-groups*".

The explanation of what constitutes an '*in-group*' and an '*out-group*' is very much personal. *Horton* and *Hunt write*: "*Three are some groups to which I belong — my family, my church, my clique, my profession, my race, my sex, my nation — any group which I precede with the pronoun, "**my**". These are "in-groups", because I feel 1 belong to them. There are other groups to which I do not belong — other families, cliques, occupations, races, nationalities, religious, the other sex —These are "out-groups", for I am outside them.* "[1]

Two Aspects of This Classification

This classification hinges on **two** important factors: **Firstly**, an individual's *mental preparedness or readiness to identify himself with a group or a set of groups and to separate himself from the father' groups,* **Secondly**, *the classification depends on an attempt to identify the boundaries of group which serve as "in-groups" Ian Rebertson too has pointed out "All groups, however, tend to maintain their boundaries by developing a strong sense of the distinction between the "we" of the group and the "they" who are outside the group.*"

In-group and Out-group Relationships are Overlapping

In the simple tribal societies 'in- and out-group' relationships are very simple and direct. All those who belong to the same class or totemic group, or kingroup are identified as members of 'in-groups', and others out-siders.

1 *Horton and Hunt in their Sociology, p. 190.*

In modern society, people belong to so many groups that a number of their in-group and out- group relationships may overlap. *For example*, a person in the urban neighbourhood may consider all the people [who belong to different social classes, caste groups, religious groups, political groups, linguistic groups, etc.] living in his neighbourhood as members of his '*in-group*' for some limited purposes, When the question of his caste interest or linguistic interest or religious interest arises the same person may consider people who belong to his own caste or linguistic or religious group as members of his in-group and others are outsiders.

Relative Influence of In-groups and Out-groups

In-group and out-group relations lead to some consequences. Members tend to regard their own group, the in-group, as being *something special, more worthy, more intimate, helpful, dependable* and so on. On the contrary, an out-group to which other people belong, is considered *less worthy, less intimate, not dependable, and it may even be viewed with hostility*.

Exclusion from an in-group can be a brutal process. Most primitive societies treated outsiders with hostility. The word '*stranger*' meant for them nothing but "*enemy*" [Even the Nazis during Hilter's regime treated Jews with utmost hostility and animosity].

In-groups and Out-groups affect Behaviour

In-groups and out-groups are important because, they affect behaviour. From fellow members of an in-group we expect recognition, loyalty and helpfulness. From *outsiders* our expectation varies with the kind of out-group. We expect hostility from some out-groups, a more or less friendly competition from some others; from still a few others, total indifference.

As far as **ingroups** are concerned, *they draw the members together and increase the solidarity and cohesion of the group*. In the presence of a common enemy, real or imaginary, in-group plays a vital role in uniting people against the *common* '*danger*'.

In-group and Out-groups and Social Distance

People keep different social distances[2] between different in-groups and out-groups. People are not equally involved in all of their in-groups. One might, *for example*, be a radent admirer of a political party and be a rather indifferent Rotarian. Nor do the people feel equally distant from all their out-groups. *For example*, member of the Bharathiya Janata Party will feel ideologically closer to the Congress (I) party than to the communists.

Sumner also stressed upon the fact that strong in-group solidarity and identity often lead to the development of ethnocentric[3] attitudes. Strong sense of in-group loyalty may induce the members to judge other people's behaviour from the standards of the in-group. Because of the ethnocentric attitude, "*out-groups are often shown in stereotyped ways which emphasise their imperfections*." —Horton and Hunt, p. 193

PRIMARY GROUPS AND SECONDARY GROUPS

The classification of social groups into '*primary*' and '*secondary*' has become very popular today. An American social psychologist *Charles Horton Cooley* has introduced the term '*primary group*' in his book '*Social Organisation*'. He has given a detailed analysis of the concept of primary group and has not even mentioned the term '*secondary group*' in his book. Sociologists like *Kingsley Davis*, *Ogburn, MacIver* and others have popularised the concept of secondary group. According to them, groups other than those of primary ones can be called '*secondary*'. Hence, the secondary groups are treated as a '*residual category*'. This classification of groups into primary and secondary is, however, made on the basis of the nature and character of social interaction. It means, it depends on the nature of social contact and the degree of intimacy among the members concerned. Primary groups are also called '*face-to-face*' groups and secondary groups, the '*derivative group*'.

The classification of social groups into '*Primary*' and '*Secondary*' resembles *Summer's* classification of '*In-groups*' and '*Out-groups*' and *Ferdinand Tonnies*' classification of groups into the '*Gemeinschaft*' [community] and the '*Gesellschaft*' [society]. But the distinction between primary groups and secondary groups is only relative but not absolute. Both the kinds of groups are in away '*ideal types*'. In the actual world the groups may not possess such distinct characteristics and satisfy all the conditions. The groups that we call '*primary*' are those in which we find the dominance of primary relations and in the same way, the '*secondary*' groups exhibit the dominance of secondary relations. It is relevant here to make a distinction between two types of social contacts namely: '*sympathetic contact*' and '*categorical contact*', which play an important role in the analysis of '*primary groups*' and '*secondary groups*'.

---

[2] Bogardus developed the concept of 'social distance' to measure the degree of closeness or acceptance we feel towards other groups.

[3] "Ethnocentrism" refers to the "tendency to judge other cultures by the standards of one's own," Ian Robertson, p. 64.

Sympathetic Contact and Categorical Contact

It is on the basis of the nature of social contacts and social relations that the groups can be classified into *"primary"* and *"secondary"*, *'in-groups'*, and *'out-groups'*, and so on. The social contacts are of two types: 1. *sympathetic contact* and 2. *categorical contact*.

1. ***Sympathetic Contact:*** Sympathetic Contact is a kind of contact between two or more persons characterised by some degree of mutual understanding and interest in the whole personality of the other. It represents one's personal involvement in the affairs of another. *Example*: Contacts between the mother and the child, parents and children, close relatives, close friends etc. represent sympathetic contacts, Individuals among whom such type of contacts exist, are mutually helpful, co-operative, sympathetic and merciful. The primary groups are characterised by sympathetic contact.
2. ***Categorical Contact:*** A categorical contact is a contact between two people whose interaction is governed by the positions which they occupy. The interaction is limited to what is appropriate to these positions. *Example*: Contacts between lawyer and client, store-keeper and customer, doctor and patient, bank officer and the peon, teacher and student and so on. Such a contact may be bereft of intimacy, friendliness, sympathy and mutual helpfulness. It does not indicate one's personal interest in the other person. In the secondary groups the categorical contacts are predominantly found.

The Primary Groups

Meaning of Primary Groups

The concept of *'primary groups'* is a significant contribution of C.H. Cooley to the social thought. Primary groups are found in all the societies. The primary group is the nucleus of all social organisations. It is a small group in which a few persons come into direct contact with one another. These persons meet face to face for mutual help, companionship and discussion of common questions.

Cooley used the term 'primary groups' to mean *a social group characterised by 'face-to-face' relationship, mutual aid and companionship*. By primary groups, Cooley meant the intimate, personal 'face-to-face' groups in which we find our companions and comrades as the members of our family and our daily associates. These are the people with whom we enjoy the more intimate kinds of social relations. The primary groups can be referred to as the 'We' groups. Cooley explained that a primary group *involves the sort of sympathy and mutual identification for which 'We' is the natural expression*.

Cooley writes–"By primary groups I means those characterised by intimate face-to-face association and co-operation. They are primary in several senses, but chiefly in that they are fundamental in forming the social nature and ideals of the individual ......"

Primary groups are universal groups functioning in all states of cultural development. They are the chief basis of what is universal in human nature and human ideals. The 'self' is developed and moulded by the primary group relations. Primary groups socialise the individuals. As *MacIver* says they are *'the breeding ground of our mores and the nurse of our loyalties.'* In primitive culture, and even in advance cultures before the growth of cities, the majority of associations occur in primary groups. *Example for primary groups*: family, neighbourhood, children's playground, local brotherhood, friends' club, peer group etc.

Chief Characteristics of Primary Groups

The characteristic features described below throw more light on the nature and character of primary groups.

1. ***Dominance of face-to-face relations:*** Primary groups are characterised by close and inti- mate relationships. There exists a fact-to-face relationship among the members. In primary groups everyone knows everyone else; one's name and fame, one's status, wealth, occupation, level of education etc. Close contact between them increases intimacy among the members. Face-to-face relations are commonly observed in small groups like family, children's playgroup, neighbourhood and so on.

Character of Primary Relations:

(a) ***Identity of ends:*** Members of the primary groups have more or less identical desires and attitudes. They work together for the attainment of their common ends without disagreement. They look at the world through the same eyes. Every member of the group pursues, as one of his ends, the welfare of the other. The identification of ends is connected with the fusion of personalities within the group.

(b) ***The relationship is an end in itself:*** The primary relationship is regarded as an end in itself, but not a means to an end. It is neither utilitarian nor motivated by any economic gain. It is intrinsically enjoyable. True love between husband and Wife or genuine friendship between two individuals is for example, beyond the consideration of any selfish motive.

(c) ***The relationship is personal:*** In the primary group the interest of each is centered in others as persons. The relationship disappears if the particular person disappears from it. As *Kingsley Davis* says, '*the primary relationship is a matter of persons, it exists because of the person, not despite him*'. The relationship is non–transferable and irreplaceable. For example the relationship between the husband and wife is such that no third person can replace any one of the two.

(d) ***The relationship is inclusive:*** The individual in a personal relationship is not an abstraction. Individuals are treated as complete human beings. All persons of the group are fused together completely. Individuals know each other very well. Different sides of member's personality are known to all the other members.

(e) ***The relationship is spontaneous:*** A purely primary relationship is voluntary. It is *not planned.* It is not based on any contract. Relationships develop between members naturally and spontaneously. The relationships that develop between the mother and the child, friend and a friend, husband and wife, child and a child are, for example, purely voluntary, and spontaneous.

2. ***Small-size:*** Primary Groups are smaller is size. Effective participation of the members is possible only when the group is of a small size. Other factors being equal, the smaller the group the more intimate it is. The character of the group tends to change with its size. The increase in the size of the group will have a negative effect on the intimacy of the members.
3. ***Physical proximity or nearness:*** Face-to-face relations can be found only when members reside in a particular area more or less permanently. Seeing and talking with each other facilitates the exchange of ideas, opinions and sentiments. It makes possible the '*conversation of gestures*' of which *Mead* speaks. Caressing, kissing, eating and dwelling together, playing, travelling, studying together–all tend to be regarded as external symbols of close solidarity. Physical proximity provides an opportunity for the very development of primary groups.
4. ***Stability of the group:*** A primary group is relatively a permanent group. Other things being equal, the longer the group remains together, the more numerous and deeper are the contacts between its members. Social ties deepen in time. Although a husband and wife may have quarreled for ten years, the very fact that they have lived together for that long, makes it hard for them to do without each other.
5. ***Similarity of background:*** The members of a primary group must have more or less the same background. There must be some approximations in their levels of experience. Each must have something to contribute, to give as well as to take. The person "who is too far above or below it, disturbs the process of group participation". This is essential even for the easy interplay of personalities in the family, the play group, the gang etc.
6. ***Limited self-interest:*** Members of the primary group subordinate their personal interests to the interests of the group. The common interest of the group is strong enough to control individual interest. The commonness of interests provides mental pleasure and contentment to the members.
7. ***Intensity of shared interest:*** The shared interests of the group also hold them together. The interest which is shared acquires a new significance, a new emphasis; a new valuation. It has a breadth of support. The group is relatively durable because of these shared interests. The primary group *sustains the interest of living itself.*
8. ***Communication:*** Communication in the case of primary group like family or children's play group, for example, is very quick and effective. Direct or face-to-face contact helps easy communication between the members.
9. ***Unspecialised character of the primary group:*** A primary group is not deliberately created nor is it specialised in character. It has not come into being for the pursuit of any particular interest of the people. On the other hand, the interests of primary groups are always comprehensive. Hence, the group is unspecialised in character.
10. ***Direct cooperation:*** Members work directly and in cooperation with each other to achieve their common interests. They do not act independently nor even interdependently, but all participate in the same process. Division of labour as it is understood in a complex industrial society, does not exist in a primary group. Work is essentially '*a mode of sharing a common experience*'. The group is '*a unity* in the performance of its function'.

Importance of Primary Groups

Primary groups are of great individual as well as social importance. They are the medium through which we learn our culture. They prepare the individuals to lead a successful social life. They socialise individuals and give proper shape to their personality. Some of the primary groups may secure certain external advantages such as better wages, production efficiency, workers' morale, counselling and guidance and so on.

1. ***Primary group–A great humanising agent:*** The primary group enacts the role of a humanising agency. Family is the immediate primary group in which a child finds itself as soon as it is born. The family, peer groups and the neighbourhood play an important role in socialising or humanising the child. Primary groups teach the child the

social norms, standards, morals, beliefs, values and ideas of the society. They introduce to the child the culture of the society. They emotionally condition the child's personality. The animal drives of man become human only through constant training. The primary groups; as *MacIver* says, are '*the nursery of human nature*.'

2. ***Development of personality:*** C.H. Cooley is of the opinion that the primary group, particularly the family, is the chief moulder of the human personality. The primary group is the source of '*our notions of love, freedom, justice and the like*'. The qualities of behaviour that a child picks up during the early years in primary groups find their expression in his adult life. Fair play, equality, free expression, submission to the will of the group and willingness to sacrifice for it are characteristics of family groups. These have a great impact on the personality development of the individuals. Primary groups mould our opinions, guide our affections, influence our actions, and in large measure determine our loyalties. These are not the groups in which we merely work or play. These are the groups in which *we live* and *have our being*.
3. ***Satisfaction of psychological needs:*** Primary groups satisfy many psychological needs of the individuals. Individuals get mental happiness, contentment and security from the primary groups. They get the advantages of companionship, sympathy and exchange of thoughts and feelings. They reduce mental tensions and emotional stresses and strains. An individual finds his nearest and the dearest companions in the primary groups. He also realises from his experiences that the primary group is his noble centre of human affection, love and sympathy.
4. ***Provision of stimulus:*** The primary group not only provides satisfaction and happiness to the individuals, but it also provides a stimulus to pursue their interests. With confidence and courage the individual members work, strive and struggle to achieve their goals. Everyone feels that he is not alone pursuing the interest but there are others who along with him are devoted to same pursuit. This feeling stimulates him to keener efforts.
5. ***United in process:*** The primary group is a cohesive group. Direct cooperation characterises the face-to-face group. Hence the members participate in the same group process. The group is essentially a "*mode of sharing a common experience*". There is a unity in the performance of its function. Hence it meets the physical as well as psychological needs of its members. It is better equipped to face crisis also.
6. ***Strengthens the democratic spirit:*** The primary group serves the needs of society also. Primary groups help the individual to acquire basic attitudes towards people, social institutions and the world around him. The attitudes of kindness, sympathy, love, tolerance, mutual help and sacrifice which provide the cementing force to social structure are developed in the primary groups. From such experiences and attitudes spring the desire for democracy and freedom. The very democratic spirit is developed and reinforced in primary groups.
7. ***Acts as an agent of social control:*** From the point of view of society the primary group acts as an agency of social control. Primary groups not only provide security to the members but also control their behaviour and regulate their relations. For example, family, neighbourhood, peer group or friends' group control much of the activities of their members.

Secondary Groups

An understanding of the modern industrial society requires an understanding of the secondary groups. The secondary groups are almost the opposite of primary groups. The social groups other than those of primary groups may be termed as 'secondary groups'. They are a *residual category*. They are often called '*special interest groups*'. *MacIver* and *Page* refer to them as '*great associations*'. They are of the opinion that secondary groups have become almost inevitable today. Their appearance is mainly due to the growing cultural complexity.

Primary groups are found predominantly in societies where life is relatively simple. With the expansion in population and territory of a society, however, interests become diversified and other types of relationships, which can be called '*secondary*' or *impersonal*, become necessary. Interests become differentiated. The service of experts is required. Techniques are elaborated, and the aver- age member has neither the time nor the energy nor the skill to attend to them. The new range of the interests demands a complex organisation. The members are numerous and too scattered to conduct their business through face-to-face relationships. Specially selected persons must act on behalf of all and hence, arises a hierarchy of officials called '*bureaucracy*'. These features characterise the rise of the modern state, the great corporation, the large church, the factory, the army, the labour union, a university, a nationwide political party and so on. These are secondary groups.

Meaning of Secondary Groups

Ogburn and *Nimkoff* say that the '*groups which provide experience lacking in intimacy*' *can be called secondary groups*.

Frank D. Watson writes, 'the secondary group is larger and more formal, is specialised and direct in its contacts and relies more for unity and continuance upon the stability of its social organisation than does the primary group'.

Characteristics of Secondary Groups

1. ***Dominance of secondary relations:*** Secondary groups are characterised by indirect, impersonal, contractual and non-inclusive relations. Relations are *indirect* because secondary groups are bigger in size and the members may

not stay together. Relations are *contractual* in the sense, they are oriented towards certain interests or desires. Further, members are bound to one another by mutual rights, duties and obligations for the realisation of their objectives or interests. Relations are *impersonal*, because members are not very much interested in other members as '*persons*'. They are more concerned with their self-centered interests than with other persons. Relations are *non-inclusive*, because they are partial and have limited range. These kinds of relations among people can be found in big factories, business corporations, governmental offices, banks, universities, political parties, trade unions, international associations etc.

2. ***Largeness of the size:*** Secondary groups are relatively larger in size. City, nation. political parties, trade unions, corporations, international associations, such as the Rotary Club, Lions Club, Vishwa Hindu Parishad, Society of Jesus, etc., are, for example, bigger in size. They may have thousands and lakhs of members. There may not be any limit to the membership in the case of some secondary groups.
3. ***Membership:*** Membership in the case of secondary groups is mainly voluntary. Individuals are at liberty to join or to go away from the groups. For example, they are at liberty to join political parties, international associations like the Rotary Club, Lions Club, business corporations and so on. However, there are some secondary groups like the state whose membership is almost involuntary.
4. ***No physical basis:*** Secondary groups are not characterised by physical proximity. Many secondary groups are not limited to any definite area. There are some secondary groups like the \ Rotary Club and the Lions Club which are almost international in character. The members of such groups are scattered over a vast area.
5. ***Specific ends or interests:*** Secondary groups are formed for the realisation of some spe- cific interests or ends. They are called '*special interest groups*' Members are interested in the groups because they have specific ends to aim at.
6. ***Indirect communication:*** Contacts and communications in the ease of secondary groups are mostly indirect. *Mass media of communication* such as radio, telephone, television, newspapers, movies, magazines, post and telegraph etc., are resorted to by the members to have communication. Communication may not be quick and effective even. Impersonal nature of social relationships in secondary groups is both the cause and the effect of indirect communication.
7. ***Nature of group control:*** Informal means of social control are less effective in regulating the relations of members. Moral control is only secondary. *Formal means of social control such* as law, legislation, police, court etc., are made use of to control the behaviour of members. The behaviour of the people is largely influenced and controlled by public opinion, propaganda, rule of law and political ideologies.
8. ***Group structure:*** The secondary group has a *formal* structure. A formal authority is set up with designated powers and a clear cut division of labour in which the function of each is specified in relation to the function of all. Secondary groups are mostly *organised groups*. Different statuses and roles that the members assume are specified. Distinctions based on caste, colour religion or region, class, language etc., are less rigid and there is greater tolerance towards other people and groups.
9. ***Limited influence on personality:*** Secondary groups are specialised in character. People's involvement in them is also of limited significance. Members' attachment to them is also very much limited. Further, people spend most of their time in primary groups than in secondary groups. Hence secondary groups have very *limited influence on the personality* of the members. *MacIver* is of the opinion that the specialised character of the secondary group is an obstacle to the realisation of the individual's fuller life and the development of his humane impulses.

Importance of Secondary Groups

The secondary groups are playing a very important role in the modern civilised and industrialised societies. For a long time the primary groups could meet the essential requirements of people. Due to the *growth of cities* and *population*, *complexity of social structure* and *differentiation of interests*, secondary groups have become a necessity. Particularly, the processes of *Industrialisation* and *urbanisation* have added to the unprecedented expansion and growth of society. As a result, the simple face-to-face groups could no longer serve the basic needs of the people. Secondary groups have replaced the earlier primary groups in many fields.

The Industrial Revolution, modern science and technology on the one hand, and the new political and religious outlook and ideologies on the other, have changed the very character of the modern society. There has been a radical change in the attitudes and outlook, interests and tastes, needs and necessities, ideas and ideologies of the people. Secondary groups of innumerable kind have come into being in order to cater to the needs and demands of the modern society. Not only the number but even the *variety* of the secondary groups is increasing. People are becoming more and more dependent on these groups now.

Our life is, today, to a great extent, *lived* and *controlled* by large number of secondary groups. Our social set up is such that we are often inevitably dragged into one kind of secondary group or another. For example, a labourer working in a factory is forced to join a trade union whether he wants it or not. It becomes almost a necessity for the labourer to join one union or the other to protect his rights and fulfil his interests. Secondary groups have entered almost all the fields–political, economic, commercial, industrial, religious, educational, cultural etc.

More than the primary group the secondary groups are *dominanting* our life. Much of our activities and achievements are carried on through secondary groups. They *provide opportunities* for us to develop our faculties and express our talents. They *liberate* and *limit* our energy. Much of our attitudes and outlook, ideas and ideologies are shaped and moulded by them. The modern civilised life is such that men have started establishing primary groups within the broader secondary groups. Small '*cliques*', '*gangs*', '*unions*' consisting of a few may be found in the form of *informal groups* within the larger secondary groups.

Men have started showing their loyalties towards their larger groups. The spirit of sacrifice, helpfulness, service, cooperation, dedication, sympathy, fair play etc., which we consider to be the characteristic qualities of primary group are also often found to a very great extent in secondary groups. Commitment to a political party or religious association, loyalty to the nation, sense of duty towards society, identification with a trade union, allegiance to the army etc., are qualities which are found commonly in many secondary groups.

Differences between Primary Groups and Secondary Groups

The classification of social groups into '*primary groups*' and '*secondary groups*' is not rigid. These groups are not watertight compartments. The groups having preponderance of primary or 'face-to-face' relations are primary groups. And the groups other than those of the primary groups are secondary groups. They constitute a *residual category*. Differences between the two are relative but not absolute. Even in secondary groups we find some elements of primary relations. Secondary groups too possess to some extent some attitudes of loyalty, devotion, faith, cooperation, sympathy, kindness etc., without which they cannot function. Members of primary groups such as family, neighbourhood are also members of political patties, trade unions, religious associations and so on. Still these two types of groups can be distinguished on some grounds. The following table makes evident the difference between the two.

	Primary Groups	*Secondary Groups*
1.	**Meaning:** Groups which are characterised by 'face-to-face' relations, mutual aid and companionship are primary groups. *Ex*: family, neighbourhood, community, children's playgroup, local brotherhood.	Groups which provide experience lacking in intimacy are secondary groups. Ex: Political parties, trade unions, religious associations, the state, city, corporation, factory, Rotary Club, Lions Club, etc.
2.	**Nature of Social Relations:** Social relations are 'face-to-face, direct intimate, personal, contractual, non-specialised, non-partisan and non-economic in character.	Social relations are indirect, impersonal, non-intimate, contractual, specialised, partisan, and more economic in-nature.
3.	**Size:** Primary groups are smaller in size. They are localised or limited to a definite area.	Secondary groups are relatively bigger in size. They are not necessarily restricted to a small area.
4.	**Physical Proximity:** Groups are confined to a small geographical area.	Groups are not characterised by a physical area.
5.	**Communication:** Since members stay together communication is not only direct but also quick and effective.	Since members are spread over a vast area direct communication is difficult. It is mostly indirect in nature.
6.	**Group Interests:** Interests of the members are not specific but general. Everyone is interested in the welfare of everyone else.	Interest of the members is more specific. Hence groups are often called 'special interested groups'.
7.	**Nature of Cooperation:** Cooperation is direct. Members work together, play together, enjoy together and in times of crisis struggle together. Cooperation is natural and spontaneous.	Cooperation is mostly indirect. Cooperation is an intended act to serve a particular need. It is limited to that purpose only. It is not spontaneous but deliberate and cultivated.
8.	**Group structure:** Group structure is very **informal**. Members are not particular about their rights and powers or statuses and prestige. No formal or detailed rules are drafted as guide lines. The group is not very much '**organised**' in the modern sense.	Group structure is **formal**. The group is regulated by a set of formal rules. Statuses and roles, rights and powers of the members are well defined. The **organisation** of the group is carefully planned and worked out.

(*Contd.*)

	Primary Groups	Secondary Groups
9.	**Durability:** Groups are relatively durable.	Groups may be **temporary** or **permanent**.
10.	**Effects on Personality:** The group has a long lasting influence upon the personality development of the members.	The impact of the group on the personality of the members is rather limited.
11.	**Nature of Group Control:** Primary groups control the behaviour of the members to a great extent. Informal means of social control are enough to regulate the relations.	Secondary groups have limited control over the behaviour of the members. Informal means are not enough and hence formal means of social correct are resorted to for maintaining the group control.

ORGANISED GROUPS AND UNORGANISED GROUPS

Social groups have been classified on the basis of their degree of organisation into *organised groups* and *unorganised groups*. Some social groups have well-built organisations while others do not have any organisational basis at all. The former ones are organised groups while the latter can be regarded as unorganised groups.

Organised Groups

Organised groups are often called *associational groups*. These groups come to be through a formally articulated process known as 'organisation'. Here, the word 'organisation' does not refer to social organisation nor does it specifically mean '*bureaucracy*'. It only means the organisation of associations. Organisation is an important phenomenon of modern complex societies.

1. ***Element of organisation:*** In modern complex societies a very large number of social relations and social interactions among people are conducted in organised groups. As *Ogburn* and *Nimkoff* have said, an organisation is *an active group device for getting something done*. It helps us to interact with others for the pursuit of a common goal. It assigns us statuses and roles. It *regulates our relations* and controls our behaviour. It decides who shall command and who shall obey in a group. It adds to the *stability* of the group and makes *it durable*. It is the factor of organisation that makes our life livable in innumerable groups.
2. ***Size of the groups:*** Organised groups may be as *small* as the family, the neighbourhood, children's play group, or as *big* as political parties, trade unions, international associations and so on. Organised groups may be *locally limited* or they may be *spread over a vast area*.
3. ***Nature of social relations:*** The *social relations* in the case of the organised groups may be personal or impersonal, intimate or non-intimate, direct or indirect, specialised or non-specialised, contractual or non-contractual, economic or non-economic in nature, in this sense, all the *primary groups* and majority of the *secondary groups* come under the category of organised groups.
4. ***Durability of the group:*** Organised groups are comparatively durable. They are not impermanent nor are they transitory. The durability of the group helps the members to pursue their specific interest. Members *cooperate* among themselves to a great extent for the realisation of their ends. Identity of interests may also contribute to a *feeling of unity* or to a sense of belonging.
5. ***Group structure:*** The *structure* of the organised groups may be *simple* as it is in the case of family or it may be complex as in the case of the modern business corporations or industries. Organised groups may be *formal* or *informal* in nature. The social relations among the members may be formal and specialised as it is in the case of trade unions or political parties, or the relations may be highly informal and unspecialised as it is in the case of friends' clubs, children's play groups, peer groups, 'cliques' and so on.
6. Further, organised groups may be found in the *institutional* and *non-institutional, territorial* and *non-territorial, voluntary and involuntary*, '*in-group*' and '*out-group*' and other forms or types. Modern civilised societies consist of a number of such organised groups.

Unorganised Groups

Social groups that conspicuously lack the attribute of organisation can be called unorganised groups. They are unorganised in the sense, they do not have any well defined pattern of social interaction. Social interaction in the case of unorganised groups is characterised by indefiniteness, uncertainty, irregularity and unpredictability. These groups are not deliberately created or established. They are not born out of a careful planning and systematic work. On the other hand, they may come into being suddenly or spontaneously. They are purely temporary in character. They are not centred around any commonly felt need or carefully planned objective or end. *Crowd, mass, mob, public* are some of the examples of unorganised groups.

Though the unorganised groups are temporary in character, sociologists have evinced great interest in them for they appear and disappear in society every now and then. Through them are often expressed, some of man's keenest and his most deeply seated attitudes. Moreover, the unanticipated, irrational and often undesired behaviour of these groups reflects, in a large degree, the particular characteristics of the community organisation, the institutional arrangements, the mores and the social cleavages of a given time and place. The unorganised groups have become an object of interest not only for the sociologists but also for the political scientists and social psychologists. The nature of unorganised groups can be better understood by an analysis of the characteristic of '*crowd*' and the '*public*', the two main examples of unorganised groups.

Crowd: As an Unorganised Group

The crowd represents an unorganised group. Crowd is a collectivity of substantial number of individuals responding within a limited space to some object of attention. It is a temporary, or a transitory and an unstable group. The main characteristics of crowd are as follows:

Characteristics: 1. *Crowd consists of people*. Individuals are physically present in a particular place reacting or responding to a particular object of attention. *Examples*: People thronging near a theatre to get tickets, people gathering in a big number in a fish market, people gathering in a big number near the road to witness a circus or to listen to a speech. 2. A crowd is *spontaneously formed* and is temporary in its nature. *Examples:* people who gather to witness the roadside circus, disperse the moment the circus is over. 3. A crowd has no *definite leader*, *objective*, *social norms*, *plan of actions, purposes*. The interaction among the individuals is unsystematic. 4. The people who constitute a crowd are together *by accident*. A road accident, the sight of an immoral act, a fire alarm, a clash between two or more individuals, a house amidst fire etc., may be their objects of attention. These common objects provide common orientation to the people. 5. The individuals in a crowd act in an *impulsive way*. They are highly *emotional* and *suggestible*.

The Psychology of the Crowd Behaviour: It is interesting to note that an individual behaves differently in a crowd than when he is alone. Psychologists like *Le Bon* have tried to explain crowd behaviour by means of the '*group mind*' or '*crowd mind*'. 1. An individual in a crowd is *susceptible to the interstimulation of suggestions*. There exist heightened emotions and intense excitements. Drums, trumpets, flags, banners, placards, slogans and songs may be used to make people to become emotional and to get excited. 2. The size of the crowd also influences the conduct of its members. Individuals behave in an irresponsible way. There is a loss of personal identity in a crowd. 3. A crowd is more emotional, highly suggestible and *impulsive*. It is credulous, brutal, irrational, instinctive, uncritical and an impulsive social phenomenon. It is more destructive than constructive. It lacks *self-consciousness*. It is *spontaneous* and uncontrollable. It is *temporary* and has no culture or tradition of its own. Still, the crowd is not always evil or cruel.

Public

The public represents another kind of unorganised group. According to *Ginsberg*, the word '*public*' refers to an unorganised aggregation of persons "*who are bound together by common opinions, desires, but are too numerous for each to maintain personal relations with others*". It does not depend upon physical contact. In a public, there occurs '*contagion without contact.*' What exactly constitutes a '*public*' in any context depends upon the issue that we have in our mind. If the issue is election, the public consists of registered voters. Thus, for a religious leader, public may mean all devotees, for an industrialist, all the consumers of his product, and so on. Thus, *public is a social area of interaction with non-intimate group making interests*. These social areas of interaction may be occupational, recreational, political, economic, educational, religious, artistic, and literary in nature.

Characteristics

1. The public is a *dispersed group*. Physical proximity is not found here. 2. The relationship among the individuals is *indirect, non-intimate* and *impersonal.* 3. Indirect or *mass media of communications* such as radio, television, post and telegraph, telephone, newspapers and journals, movies and platform speeches are made use of to keep in contact with the members. 4. The public, at least in theory, is based upon a *rational difference of opinion*. It is a *discussion group for excellence*. 'Here, there is scope for discussion, debate, disagreement, disapproval, criticism and condemnation. The decisions are marked by rational calculations. However, it is possible to heighten the degree of suggestibility of the group by means of the mass media of communication.

DIFFERENCES BETWEEN PUBLIC AND THE CROWD

	Public	*Crowd*
1.	The public is not based on physical proximity.	The crowd is based on physical proximity.
2.	One can be a member of several publics simultaneously.	One can belong to only one crowd at a time.
3.	Ideas cannot be communicated quickly.	Ideas can be communicated very quickly.

(*Contd.*)

	Public	Crowd
4.	There is less suggestibility and more rationality. There is scope for debate and discussion and disagreement.	The crowd is highly suggestible, emotional, rational and impulsive. There is no scope for discussion.
5.	The public is bound by norms. It forms various organisations. Hence the behaviour of people is more regular and predictable.	The crowd is bound by no norms. It behaves impulsively. Hence people's behaviours is irregular and unpredictable. It may even become violent.

DIFFERENCES BETWEEN ORGANISED GROUPS AND UNORGANISED GROUPS

	Organised Group	Unorganised Groups
1.	Organised groups possess the attribute of organisation. Ex. Trade unions, political parties, religious organisation etc.	Unorganised groups do not possess organisation. *Ex.* crowd, mob, audience, public etc.
2.	They are established purposefully for the fulfilment of some specific interests.	Unorganised groups are not established deliberately. They are mostly spontaneous in their formation.
3.	Here the social interaction among the members is systematic, orderly and patterned. Hence the behaviour is predictable.	Social interaction is not systmatised. Behaviour is unpredictable especially in crowds and mobs.
4.	Groups have their own definite social norms.	Definite social norms may not be observed.
5.	Groups possess definite structure. They may be simple or complex and formal or informal in nature.	Groups may not have any definite structure. Even the structure of the public is vague.
6.	Members have understanding and may work and cooperate together for the realisation of their specific interests.	Since the members do not have any specific interest as such the question of working together does not rise.
7	Groups are relatively more durable.	Groups like crowd, mob and purely temporary.
8.	Some groups may cover the entire range of one's life. Their impact on personality is considerable, because they have definite membership.	Groups rarely covers the entire life of the members. Their impact on personality is negligible, they do not have any specific membership as such.

REFERENCE GROUPS

The term '*reference group*' was introduced into the literature on small groups by *Muzafer Sherif* in his text book "*An Outline of Social Psychology*"—1948. He used the term in contrast to the term membership group. Membership group refers to a group to which a person belongs, while the 'reference group' refers to a group that affects his behaviour. The two, of course, may coincide.

According to *Ogburn* and *Nimkoff* "groups which serve as points of comparison are known as reference groups". They have further added that the reference groups are those groups from which "we get our values, or whose approval we seek".

As *Horton* and *Hunt* have pointed out "A reference group is any group to which we refer when making judgements–any group whose value-judgements become our value-judgements". They have further said, "groups which are important as models for one's ideas and conduct norms...." can be called reference groups.

The concept of "reference group" arises essentially from the fact that any person acting in any situation may be influenced not only by his membership groups but also by his conception of *other groups* of which he is not a member. These other groups exert their influence as reference groups in a purely passive or silent way, that is, simply by being thought of. They do not, of course, entirely exist as reference groups, but they are called so only from the point of view of their capacity in exerting influence. The young child in the family is interested in the reactions of everyone in the family with whom it is in contact. The family is both a membership group and a reference group for the child. But when the child becomes mature he selects particular groups which are understood here as reference groups whose approval or disapproval he especially desires.

The concept, reference groups, as distinct from membership groups, has particular relevance for modern complex, heterogeneous society with its high rates of physical and occupational mobility. In such a complex society a person may be a member of one group but prefer membership or aspire for membership in another. In a small folk society, the distinction between membership group and reference groups is less common and may be nonexistent.

Only under certain circumstances a group may become reference group for the members of a particular social group. H.M Johnson has mentioned four such circumstances.

1. When some or all the members of a particular group aspire to membership in the reference group. *Example*, the ambitious upper-middle class people are always interested in joining the rank of upper-class people. In order to get an admission into upper-class, they may show their prejudice and even aggressiveness towards low-ranking groups.
2. When the members of the particular group struggle to imitate the members of reference group, or try to make their group just like the reference group at least in some respects. *Example*: The lower caste people in India who suffer from a sense of inferiority are found to be emulating some of the styles and practices of Brahmins to feel equal to them at least in some respects. Similarly, members of the minority groups may try to incorporate in their personality dominant-group standards to help better their relationship with the dominant majority group.
3. When the members of the particular group derive some satisfaction from being *distinctive* and *unlike* the members of reference group in some aspects. Further, they may try to maintain the difference between the two groups or between themselves and the members of the reference group. *Example:* If Whites as a status group are a reference group for Negroes, so are Negroes a reference group for Whites because both want to retain their difference. Whites want to remain *unlike* the *Negroes* and so is the case with *Negroes*. Similarly, Muslims may be interested in maintaining their difference with the majority community, especially in the Indian context.
4. When the members of a particular group consider the reference group *or* its members as a standard for comparison. *Example*: The teachers of a city college may always make references to the most prestigious college of the city as a measuring rod to assess their position, service condition, performance and so on. Such contemplation of reference groups may have some consequences for the moral of the group.

REVIEW QUESTIONS

1. Man is a social animal. Give reasons in support of your answer.
2. Define social groups. Bring out the characteristic features of social group.
3. Define social groups. Discuss its types.
4. What are social bonds? Elaborate.
5. Give the classification of social groups. Examine the importance of social groups.
6. Discuss the characteristic features of primary and secondary groups.
7. Write a detailed note on the importance of primary and secondary groups.
8. What are the differences between organised and unorganised groups?
9. Clarify the concept of social group and discuss the primary group as a type of social group.
10. Define social group. Discuss the features and importance of primary and secondary groups.
11. Analyse the role of primary group and secondary group in the development of individual.
12. Explain the concept of social structure. Describe its major elements.
13. Write short notes on the following:
    (a) Organised and unorganised groups
    (b) Reference groups
    (c) Public and crowd

⌘⌘⌘⌘⌘⌘⌘⌘⌘⌘⌘

20

SOCIAL PROCESSES

CHAPTER OUTLINE

- THE SOCIAL PROCESSES
- THE CONCEPT OF SOCIAL PROCESS
- MEANING OF SOCIAL INTERACTION
- KINDS OF SOCIAL INTERACTION
- CO-OPERATION
- COMPETITION
- CONFLICT
- ACCOMMODATION AND ASSIMILATION.

Society is not only a system of moral norms and defined statuses which embody those norms, it is also a system in action. As individuals and groups meet, as they strive, as they attempt to solve problems, their statuses and even their moral norms are to some extent changed. Thus, moral norms and statuses comprise the static element in society; social interaction, the dynamic element. Social interaction discloses the concrete results of striving behaviour upon roles, statuses, and moral norms. Social interaction represents the social dynamics. People are always engaged in action. People in action with others mean interaction in some measure and form. Social processes are merely the characteristic ways in which interaction occurs. Interaction is always subtle, complex and dynamic. It can never be totally identified with one social process to the exclusion of all the others. Any concrete situation always contains more than one process. The different social processes depend upon the most inclusive social process, *i.e.*, social interaction.

SOCIAL PROCESSES

The Concept of Social Process

Society is a system of social relationships. The term social relationship refers to the relationship that exists among people. We may witness such relationships between father and son, employer and employee, teacher and student, merchant and customer, leader and follower, or between friends and enemies, between children, etc. Such relationships are among the most obvious features of society. Sociology must analyse and classify social relationships because they represent social facts and social data.

Social relationships represent the functional aspects of society. Analysing the classifying social relationships is a difficult talk. Social relationships involve *reciprocal obligations*, *reciprocal statuses, and reciprocal ends and, means* as between two or more actors in mutual contact. They refer to a *pattern of interaction* between these individuals [and this is why the school of sociology which has attempted to systematise its thought in relationship terms has been called the '*formal school*'. Simmel, Von wise, Park, Burgess, Becker belong to this school.] Thus social relationships may be studied by the *kind* or *mode of interaction* they exhibit. These kinds or modes of interaction are called *social processes*. *Social processes are the fundamental ways in which men interact and establish relationships*.

Definition of Social Process

1. *MacIver*: "Social process is the manner in which the relations of the members of a group, once brought together, acquire a distinctive character".
2. *A. W Green*: The "Social processes are merely the characteristic ways in which interaction occurs".
3. *Ginsberg*: "Social processes mean the various modes of interaction between individuals or groups including

cooperation and conflict, social differentiation and integration, development, arrest and decay".

4. *Horton* and *Hunt*: The term social processes refer to the "repetitive forms of behaviour which are commonly found in social life."

Forms of Social Processes

The society contains hundreds and perhaps thousands of socially defined relationships. These relationships are beyond measurement. It is humanly impossible for any individual to make a detailed study of each and every social relationship. Instead they must be classified and dealt with as '*general types*'. For this reason social relationships have been classified and discussed in terms of the '*kinds of interaction*' they manifest. These kinds of interaction or '*patterns of interaction*' are called social processes. The kinds of interaction or social processes include–*cooperation, competition, conflict, contravention, accommodation, assimilation, accumulation, isolation, differentiation, disintegration* etc.

SOCIAL INTERACTION

Meaning of Social Interaction

Social interaction is the foundation of society. It is the very essence of social life. Hence, the concept is crucial to any study of the dynamics of society and culture. Without interaction there would be no group life. Mere presence of individuals in a place does not weld them into a social unit or group. It is when persons or groups of persons do such things as work or play or talk together with common end, or when they compete or quarrel with each other that group life, properly speaking, exists. Thus, it can be said that *interaction is the basic social process, the broadest term for describing dynamic social relationships*. Social interaction is the dynamic element in society, while statuses and norms represent its static element. It is true that life is stable, confined and defined by traditional systems, norms and patterned ways. It is also true that life is fast-moving, dynamic and changing, breaking out at the weak point [or where conflict is greatest]. People are on the move. They are striving, competing, conflicting, cooperating, appeasing, adjusting, reconciling and then challenging again. This action element or functional element itself represents social interaction.

Definition Social interaction

1. *Eldredge* and *Merrill*: 'Social interaction is the general process whereby two or more persons are in meaningful contact as a result of which their behaviour is modified however slightly.'
2. *Drawson* and *Gettys*: 'Social interaction is a process whereby men interpenetrate the minds of each other'.
3. *Gish, N.P.*: 'Social interaction is the reciprocal influence human beings exert on each other through interstimulation and response'.

Two Conditions of Social Interaction

Park and *Burgess* are of the opinion that contact and communication are the two main conditions of social interaction.

1. ***Contact:*** Contact is the first stage of interaction. Contact means simply a coming together of independent social units [individuals]. It involves a *mutual response*, *an inner adjustment of behaviour to the actions of others*. The two kinds of contact are: (*i*) *contact in time* and (*ii*) *contact in space*. The first one refers to contact of group with the earlier generations through customs, traditions, folkways, morals, etc. The second one refers to the relationship between contemporary individuals and groups within a particular area. The contacts may be primary and personal or secondary and impersonal in nature.
2. ***Communication:*** Communication is the medium of interaction. In communication one person infers from the behaviour of another the idea or feeling of the other person. It may take place at three levels–through *the senses*, *the emotions* and *the sentiments* and *ideas*. The first two are called 'the natural forms of communication'. They are common to man and the animals. On the sensory level, seeing, hearing, smelling, and touching all, plays a role in evoking responses. On the emotional level, such thing as facial expression, blushing and laughing arouse responses. Communication on the third level, taking place, through the intellect, is, strictly limited to man. Here speech and language play an important role. Language helps man to transmit abstract ideas to his fellow beings. It facilitates the transmission of cultural heritage.

Direct and Symbolic Interaction

Interaction may be direct or symbolic. Direct interaction refers to the activities of a person which may be seen in such conduct as pushing, fighting, pulling, embracing, dashing, or in other forms of bodily contact with other individuals. Symbolic interaction consists of vocal or other gestures and language, spoken or written. *A symbol is a summary of experience*. It may represent an object, act, quality, value, idea or any expected response. Language is the rich store-house of such symbols.

Interstimulation and Response

The central nature of interaction is *interstimulation* and *response*. One stimulates the actions, thought or emotions of another person/s and responds to the similar behaviour of the others. Interaction increases mental activity, fosters comparison of ideas, sets new tasks, accelerates and discovers the potentialities of the individual.

Importance of Social Interaction

Social interaction is the basic condition of our social existence. It is the most inclusive group process. It is a context in which the personality grows. Man cannot be called man outside the range of human interaction. Groups develop through interaction with other groups and disintegrate without some stimulation from outside. Society exists only when a large number of persons are interacting. Human interaction takes place in the context of social expectations, rules and norms. Social interaction is the basic process through which human nature and social structure develop and are changed.

Kinds of Social Interaction

The kinds of social interaction include cooperation, competition, cooperative and competitive societies, conflict, accommodation, assimilation, etc. These are discussed below.

COOPERATION

Meaning of Cooperation

'*Cooperation*' is one of most basic, pervasive and continuous. social processes. It is the very basis of social existence. Cooperation generally means working together for the pursuit of a common goal. The term 'Cooperation' is derived from the two Latin words: '*Co*' meaning together and '*operari*' meaning to work. Literally, cooperation means *joint work or working together for common rewards*.

Definition of Cooperation

1. ***Merrill and Eldredge:*** 'Cooperation is a form of social interaction wherein two or more persons work together to gain a common end.'
2. ***A. W Green:*** 'Cooperation is the continuous and common endeavour of two or more persons to perform a task or to reach a goal that is commonly cherished.'
3. ***Fairchild:*** 'Cooperation is the process by which the individuals or groups combine their effort, in a more or less organised way for the attainment of common objective.'
4. Cooperation is 'joint activity in pursuit of common goals or shared rewards'. Thus, cooperation is mutual working together for the attainment of a common goal. It implies a regard for the wishes, needs and aspirations of other people. It is often considered to be unselfish. But men may also find that their selfish goals are best served by working together with their fellows. Cooperation may be found in groups as small as the dyad [group of two persons — Ex: husband and wife] and as large as the modern countries. *People may cooperate for self-centred gain or for self-protection, or to do good to others*. Groups may cooperate for self-advancement as in the case of a monopoly, for mutual protection, or for the welfare of all groups.

Cooperation requires *sympathy* and *identification*. We cannot have cooperation without the development of sympathy. Sympathy depends upon the capacity of an individual to imagine himself in the place of another, particularly when the other person is in difficulties. *Mutual aid* is another name for cooperation. Cooperation is possible only when there is like-mindedness, similarity of purpose, mutual awareness, mutual understanding, mutual helpfulness and selfless attitude.

Types of Cooperation

Cooperation may be direct, or indirect, or it may be primary, secondary and tertiary in character.

1. ***Direct cooperation:*** Here, the individuals involved do the identical function. Ex; Playing together, worshipping together, tilling the field together, taking out a cart from the mud, etc. People do work *in company* with other members. Performance of a common task with joint efforts brings them social satisfaction.
2. ***Indirect cooperation:*** In this case, people work individually for the attainment of a common end. People here do unlike tasks towards a similar end. This is based on the principle of division of labour and specialisation. For example, farmers, spinners, weavers, dyers, tailors are different people engaged in different activities. But their end remains the same, that of producing clothes. The modern technological age requires specialisation of skills and functions. Hence it depends on co-operation.
3. ***Primary cooperation:*** Primary cooperation is found in primary groups such as family, neighbourhood, friends' group, children's play group and so on. Here there is an *identity of ends*. Every member works for the betterment of all. There is an interlocking identification of individuals, groups, and the task performed. The group contains all

or nearly all, of each individual's life. The rewards for which everyone works are *shared*, or meant to be shared, with every other member in the group. Means and goals become one, for cooperation itself is a highly prized value.

4. ***Secondary cooperation:*** Secondary cooperation is the characteristic feature of the modem civilised society and is found mainly in secondary groups. It is highly *formalised* and *specialised*. Cooperation is not itself a value; attitudes are more likely to be individualistic and calculating. Most members of the group feel some loyalty toward the group, but the welfare of the group is not their first consideration. Each performs his task, and thus helps others to perform their tasks, so that he can *separately* enjoy the fruits of his cooperation. Each may work in cooperation with others for his own wages, salaries, promotions, profits and in some cases power and prestige. Such kind of Co-operation may be witnessed in political, economic, religious, commercial, educational and other groups.
5. ***Tertiary cooperation:*** Cooperation may be found between bigger groups also. It may be found between two or more political parties, castes, tribes, religious groups' and so on. It is often called *accommodation*. The two groups may cooperate and work together for *antagonistic goals*. Two political parties may work together in an attempt to defeat a third party. Still, one pasty may intend to seize power while the other to get sufficient public support. Similarly, the labour and management may work together for different ends.

Role of Cooperation in Social Life

Cooperation as a form of social process is universal and continuous. It has made our social life possible and livable. It surrounds us on all sides. It is both a psychological and a biological necessity and a social condition of man's continued existence. As *MacIver* and *Page* say, "Man cannot associate without cooperating, without working together in the pursuit of like or common interests". *C.H. Cooley* says that cooperation arises only when men realise that they have a common interest. They cooperate because they have sufficient time, intelligence and self-control to seek this interest through united action.

Cooperation takes place under some conditions. As *Young* and *Mack* have said, cooperation requires *first* of all a motivation to seek a goal. *Secondly*, people must have some knowledge of the benefit of cooperative activity. This requires some kind of education, for cooperation is not an inborn tendency. *Thirdly,* people must have a favourable attitude towards sharing both the work and the rewards involved. *Finally*, they need to equip themselves with the skills necessary to make the cooperative plan work.

Cooperation is so important in the life of an individual that according to *Prince Kropotkin* it is difficult for man to survive without it. He calls it *mutual* aid. In rearing of progeny and in the provision of protection and food cooperation is inevitable. The continuation of the human race requires the cooperation of male and female for reproduction and upbringing of children. *Cooperation has its origin in the biological level*. The principle of struggle for existence and survival is essentially the principle of cooperation.

Cooperation *helps society to progress*. Progress can better be achieved through united action. Progress in science and technology, agriculture and industry, transport and communication, etc., would not have been possible without cooperation. Persons who cooperate *may generate unbounded enthusiasm*. It is the main spring of our collective life. It gives strength in union. It builds, it conserves. In democratic countries, cooperation has become a necessary condition of people's collective life and activities. The growth of the role of cooperation is seen in the increase in the size of communities.

Cooperation is an urgent need of the present-day world. It is needed not only among the individuals, associations, groups and communities but also among the nations. *It provides solution for many international problems and disputes*. Since interdependence is widespread in all walks of life, cooperation is all the more needed. Society advances through cooperation and declines in its absence.

COMPETITION

Oppositional Processes: Competition and Conflict

Opposition and cooperation occur in every society although their form and direction are culturally conditioned. Opposition may be defined as a struggle *against* another or others for a commodity, goal or value. Cooperation is a joint venture *with* another or others for a commodity, goal or value. Opposition may be divided into *competition* and *conflict*. *Competition* is a less violent form of opposition in which two or more persons or groups struggle for some end or goal. Attention is focussed on the reward or the goal rather than on the competitor. In *conflict*, the person or group thwarts, injures, or destroys the opponent in order to secure a goal or a reward. As competition becomes more personal, it shades into conflict–the more disruptive, disjunctive social process.

Meaning of Competition

Competition is the most fundamental form of social struggle. It is a natural result of the universal struggle for existence. It is based on the fact that all people can never satisfy all their desires. Competition takes place whenever there is an insufficient supply of things that human beings commonly desire. *Whenever and wherever commodities which people want are available in a limited supply, there is competition.*

Definition of Competition

1. *Park* and *Burgess*: "Competition is an interaction without social contact".
2. *Biesanz*: "Competition is the striving of two or more persons for the same goal which is limited so that all cannot share."
3. *Horton* and *Hunt*: "Competition is the struggle for possession of rewards which are limited in supply, goods, status, power, love–anything."
4. Competition may also be defined as *"the process of seeking to monopolise a reward by surpassing all rivals."*

Nature and Characteristics of Competition

1. ***Scarcity as a condition of competition:*** Wherever there are commonly desired goods and services, there is competition. In fact, economics starts with its fundamental proposition that while human wants are unlimited the resources that can satisfy these wants are strictly limited. Hence people compete for the possession of these limited resources. As *Hamilton* has pointed out competition is necessitated by *"a population of insatiable wants and a world of stubborn and inadequate resources."*
2. ***Competition and affluence:*** Competition may be found even in circumstances of abundance or affluence. In a time of full employment competition may take place for the status of the top class. There is competition not only for food, shelter and other basic needs, but also for luxuries, power, name, fame, social position, mates and so on.
3. ***Competition is continuous:*** Competition is continuous. It is found virtually in every area of social activity and social interaction. Particularly, competition for status, wealth and fame is always present in almost all societies.
4. ***Competition is universal:*** Modern civilised society is marked by the phenomenon of competition. Competition is covering almost all the areas of our social living. Business people compete for customers, lawyers 'for clients, doctors for patients, students for ranks or distinctions, athletes and sportsmen for trophies, political parties for power, young men and women for mates and so on. Still no society can be said to be exclusively competitive or cooperative.
5. ***Competition is dynamic:*** It stimulates achievement and contributes to social change. It lifts the level of aspiration from lower level to a higher level. A college student who competes with others to get selected to the college cricket team, after becoming successful may later struggle to get selected to the university cricket team, to the state team, to the national team and so on.
6. ***Competition–A cause of social change:*** Competition is a *cause* of social change in that, it causes persons to adopt new forms of behaviour in order to attain desired ends. New forms of behaviour involve inventions and innovations which naturally bring about social change. It is an *effect* of social change also, because a changing society has more goals to open than a relatively static society.
7. ***Competition may be personal or impersonal:*** Competition is normally directed towards a goal and not against any individual. Sometimes, it takes place without the actual knowledge of other's existence. It is *impersonal* as in the case of civil service examination in which the contestants are not even aware of one another's identity. Competition may also be personal as when two individuals contest for election to an office. As competition becomes more personal it leads to *rivalry* and shades into conflict. Competition in the social world is largely impersonal. The individual may be vaguely aware of, but has no personal contact with other competitors.
8. ***Competition may be constructive or destructive:*** Competitions may be *healthy* or *unhealthy*. If one of the two or more competitors tries to win *only* at the expense of the others, it is destructive. Sometimes, big industrialists or capitalists resort to such a kind of competition and make the small petty businessmen to become virtually bankrupt. But constructive competition is mutually stimulating and helpful. It contributes to the welfare of all at large. For example, farmers may compete to raise the best crops, workers in a factory to maximise production, students in a college to get distinctions and so on.
9. ***Competition is always governed by norms:*** Competition is not limitless nor is it unregulated. There is no such thing as '*unrestricted competition*'. Such a phrase is contradiction in terms. Moral norms or legal rules always govern and control competition. Competitors are expected to use '*fair tactics*' and not '*cut-throat devices*'.
10. ***Competition may be unconscious also:*** Competition may take place on an unconscious level. Many times individuals who are engaged in competition may become oblivious of the fact that they are in a competitive race. Rarely do they know about other competitors.

Forms or Types of Competition

Bernard mentions three broad types of competition: *Social, Economic* and *Political* competition.

1. ***Social competition:*** People always compete to get into higher status and position. Competition of this kind is mostly observed in '*open*' societies. Wherever individual ability, merit, talent and capacities are recognised, competition

for status is acute. Democratic nations encourage such competitions.

2. ***Economic competition:*** The most important and at the same time the most vigorous form of competition is the economic competition. It is witnessed in the processes of production, distribution and consumption of goods. Men compete for jobs, customers, clients, patients, profits, wages, salaries, increments and promotions, money, wealth, property, etc. Man always struggles for higher standard of living. Economic competition can be observed at the individual as well as group level.
3. ***Political competition:*** In the modem world competition for political power is always present. Political parties are always engaged in competition to secure power. Such a competition becomes apparent especially during elections. Similarly, on the international level, there is a keen competition between nations. Nations like Russia and America which are wedded to different political ideologies, are always at a competition for one thing or the other.
4. ***Cultural competition:*** Some sociologists have also spoken of cultural competition. It may take place between two or more cultural groups. Human history provides examples of such a competition. For example, there has always been a keen competition between the culture of the natives and that of the invaders. Ex: competition that prevailed between the Sumerians and Akkadians, Aryans and Dravidians, the British and the Indians.

Competition may also take place between *racial groups* such as the Negroes and the Whites, *religious groups* such as the Protestants and the Catholics, Hindus and Muslims, Muslims and the Christians and so on.

Role of Competition in Social Life

Competition plays an important role in our social life. Competition performs a number of useful functions in society. Some of them may be noted here.

Social Functions of Competition

1. ***Assigns statuses to the individuals:*** Competition assigns individuals their respective place in the social system. Social status and competition are always associated. Some people compete with others to retain their status, others compete to *enhance* their status.
2. ***Source of motivation:*** Competition is a source of motivation for the individuals. It makes the individual to show his ability and express the talents. It *increases individual efficiency*.
3. ***Provides for social mobility:*** As far as the individual is concerned competition implies mobility and freedom. The spirit of competition helps the individual to improve his social status.
4. ***Competition contributes to Socio-economic progress:*** Fair competition is conducive to economic as well as social progress. It even *contributes to general welfare* because it spurs individuals and groups on to exert their best efforts. When the competition is directed to promote the general interests of the community as a whole, it can bring about miraculous results.
5. ***Provides for new experiences:*** As *Ogburn* and *Nimkoff* have pointed out, competition provides the individuals better opportunities to satisfy their desire for new experiences and recognition. As far as the group is concerned, competition means experimental charge.

G. R. Madan in his "*The Theoretical Society*" Vol. III mentions three major functions of competition. They are as follows — (*i*) Competition *serves to satisfy some desire* of the competing individuals or groups. (*ii*) Competition *focuses attention on alternatives*. New inventions and discoveries; innovations in behaviour, variant philosophies, and systems of beliefs, etc., provide the rich menu from which may be satisfied the wants of the society. (*iii*) The competition provides the mechanism by which *well qualified, and competent persons can be selected to perform special junctions of the group*. When there is free play of competition, it becomes easier to select men of ability from groups such as occupational, religious, artistic, recreational, reformist, political, economic, etc., to carry on special responsibilities.

Competition is beneficial only when it is constructive. It must function within limits. Uncontrolled competition is always dangerous. As *Park* and *Burgess* have pointed out *unrestrained competition is neither desirable nor even possible*. Limitless and unhealthy competitions may even cause disorder in society. Hence, rules and regulations are framed everywhere to regulate and to channelise the competitive spirit of the individuals.

DIFFERENCES BETWEEN COOPERATION AND COMPETITION

	Cooperation	*Competition*
1.	Cooperation refers to a form of social interaction wherein two or more persons work together *to gain a common end.*	Competition is a form of social interaction wherein the individuals try to *monopolise rewards* by surpassing all the rivals.

(*Contd.*)

	Cooperation	Competition
2.	Cooperation is always based on the combined or the *joint efforts* of the people.	Competition can take place at the level of the group and also at the level of the individual.
3.	Cooperation normally brings about *positive results*. It rarely causes losses to the individuals involved in it.	Though competition can bring about *positive* results, it can *cause damages* or losses to the parties and persons involved.
4.	Cooperation is *boundless*. It has no limitations. One can go to any extent to help others.	Competition has its own *limitations*. It is bound by norms. Limitless or unregulated competition can cause much harm.
5.	As C.H. Cooley has pointed out Cooperation requires qualities such as *kindness, sympathy, concern for others, mutual understanding* and some amount of readiness to help others.	Competition requires qualities such as –*strong aspirations, self-confidence, the desire to earn name and fame in society, the spirit of adventure and the readiness to suffer and to struggle*.
6.	Cooperation brings people *satisfaction and contentment.*	But competition may cause satisfaction as well as dissatisfaction, anxiety, indefiniteness and uncertainties.

COOPERATIVE AND COMPETITIVE SOCIETIES

Cooperation and Competition as two forms of social processes are universal in nature. They are fundamental for the social existence of man. Both play an important role in the smooth functioning of the society. They exist side by side. Still, no society can be regarded as *exclusively* cooperative or competitive. Societies are not equally cooperative or competitive in every phase of life. In spite of this fact, some societies are regarded as more cooperative and some others, as more competitive. From the sociological point of view, there can be no exclusively cooperative or competitive societies.

Societies vary a great deal in the degree to which they are competitive. This is true of primitive as well as of civilised societies. Studies have revealed that some of the primitive tribes such as the *Zuni Indians* and the *Arapesh* are more cooperative than *Kwakiuti Indian* and the *Dobuans*.

Some civilised societies are found to be more cooperative and less competitive than others. In *democratic societies* competition in the social and economic spheres is generally stronger than in the *authoritarian societies*. This may be due to the greater freedom of initiative in the former than in the latter.

Some societies are more cooperative in some fields and less competitive in some others. *For example*: *in the political sphere*, England is said to be less competitive than France. The U.S.A. and Canada may also be said to be politically less competitive than the Latin American countries. On the other hand, in the *social and economic spheres*, America and Canada are more competitive than the Latin American countries. Soviet Union may be said to be more cooperative than the Capitalist countries, particularly in the economic sphere. In U.S.A. competition in economic and social fields, is perhaps, greater than in any other Western country.

It is difficult to determine the factors that are likely to make the societies to become largely competitive or cooperative. According to *Gillins*, two factors are significant here: 1. *the system of values in a society*, and 2. *the social structure*. Competition will be greater when the system of values is such that success is measured in terms of individual efforts and achievements. In such a society competition will be upheld as a great ideal. People of such a society may believe in the idea that "*God helps him who helps himself*". On the other hand, in societies where the individual can realise his basic desires by cooperating with others, competition will be weak.

According to *Ross*, *the form of social stratification and the nature of the political system* also influence the relative cooperativeness and competitiveness of the societies. As Ross has pointed out, competition is most intense in an open-class and rapidly changing society. But it is less intense in a closed-class and a slowly changing society. *For example*, in a rapidly changing society such as America, competition is stronger, and in a slowly changing caste-ridden society such as India, competition is weaker. Similarly, democratic political system encourages competition more than the totalitarian system.

Advantages of Cooperative and Competitive Societies

Cooperation and competition have become an essential aspect of the modem industrialised and urbanised societies. Hence they have become almost universal. Societies that are based on the principles of cooperation and competition have their own advantages. Some of the advantages of such societies may be mentioned here.

	Advantages of Cooperative Society	Advantages of Competitive Society
1.	A cooperative society offers for its people opportunities to satisfy their desires by collective efforts.	A competitive society offers for its people opportunities to fulfil their aspirations by *individual* efforts.
2.	As *Ogburn* and *Nimkoff* have pointed out a cooperative society provides the individuals a better chance to achieve *security* and social *prestige*.	Ogburn and Nimkoff have opined that a competitive society provides for the individuals new experience and recognition. It helps them to *achieve name and fame.*

(*Contd.*)

	Advantages of Cooperative Society	Advantages of Competitive Society
3.	A cooperative society provides *social stability and persistence.*	A competitive society provides for *social stability and social change.*
4.	A cooperative society is better equipped to make provision for *social equality.*	A competitive society is better suited to *achieve economic and technological progress.*
5.	It minimises the tensions and conflicts for an individual in reaching his goals.	Healthy competition helps not only the individuals but also the society to move towards greater perfection.
6.	A cooperative society helps to establish better understanding and develop the spirit of mutual assistance and helpfulness among the people.	A competitive society can keep the people always active and ever ready to face challenges of life.
7.	Cooperative society helps its members to settle their internal group conflicts peacefully by a spirit of give and take.	A competitive society inspires its members to concentrate their efforts in making new researches, investigations and achievements.

CONFLICT

Definition of Conflict

Conflict is an ever-present process in human relations. It is one of the forms of struggle between individuals or groups. Conflict takes place whenever a person or group seeks to gain a reward not by surpassing other competitors but by preventing them from effectively competing.

1. *Horton and Hunt:* Conflict may be defined as a process of seeking to monopolise rewards by eliminating or weakening the competitors.
2. *A.W. Green*: "Conflict is the deliberate attempt to oppose, resist, or coerce the will of another or others."
3. *Young and Mack*: "Conflict takes the form of emotionalised and violent opposition, in which the major concern is to overcome the opponent as a means of securing a given goal or reward."
4. *Gillin* and *Gillin*: "Conflict is the social process in which individuals or groups seek their ends by directly challenging the antagonist by violence or threat of violence."

Nature and Characteristics of Conflict

1. ***Conflict is universal:*** Conflict or clash of interests is universal in nature. It is present in almost all the societies. In some societies conflict may be very acute and vigorous while in some others it may be very mild. *Karl Marx, Frederich Engels, Saint Simon, Gumplowicz* and others have emphasised the role of conflict as a fundamental factor in the social life of man. *Karl Marx*, the architect of communism, has said *that the history of the hitherto existing human society is nothing but the history of the class struggle*. He has mentioned the capitalists and the labourers as belonging to two distinct social classes which have mutually opposite interests.
2. ***Conflict is a conscious action:*** Individuals and groups who are involved "in conflict are aware of the fact that they are conflicting. As *Park* and *Burgess* have pointed out conflict is always *conscious and evokes the deepest emotions and strongest passions*.
3. ***Conflict is personal:*** When competition is *personalised* it leads to conflict. In the struggle to overcome the other person or group, the goal is temporarily relagated to a level of secondary importance.
4. ***Conflict is not continuous but intermittent:*** Conflict never takes place continuously. It takes place occasionally. No society can sustain itself in a state of continuous conflict.
5. ***Conflict defines issues about which individuals differ a lot:*** A great part of human history consists of information about conflicts of one sort or the other. These conflicts may be between social classes, religious groups, social groups, political groups and nations. The pattern of struggle or conflict always changes as a result of changes in values, ideals, goals, religious notions, attitudes, ideologies, national interests, and so on.
6. ***Conflict is conditioned by culture:*** Conflict is affected by the nature of the group and its particular culture. *The objects of conflicts may be property, power and status, freedom of action and thought, or any other highly desired value*. When the stability of a political order is threatened, political conflict may be the result. If sectarianism is rife, we may expect conflict to occur in region. The culturally determined values of a society will set the stage for its struggles.

7. ***Conflicts and norms:*** Not only culture modifies conflict and its forms but also *controls and governs* it. When conflict is infrequent and when no adequate techniques have been worked out, more violent and unpredictable sorts of conflict such as race riots arise.
8. ***Conflict may be personal or impersonal:*** Conflict may assume a variety of forms. We may observe conflicts between two individuals, families, classes, races, nations and groups of nations. It may take place between smaller or larger groups.
9. ***Ways of resolving conflict:*** Conflict can be resolved in two main ways: (*a*) *accommodation*, and (*b*) *assimilation*. *Accommodation* refers to the adjustment of hostile individuals or groups. It is a temporary solution to the conflict. It either suspends, stops or postpones the conflicts for some time. It may assume various forms such as — coercion, compromise, arbitration and conciliation, toleration, rationalisation, sublimation and conversion. *Assimilation* is "a process whereby individuals or groups once dissimilar become similar, and identified in their interests and outlook." It is a permanent way of settling conflicts.
10. ***Frustration and insecurity promote conflicts:*** Sometimes, factors like frustration and insecurity promote conflicts within the same society. Individuals feel frustrated if they are thoroughly disturbed in their attempts to reach their goals. These goals may be desire for power, position, prestige, status, wealth, money, etc. Insecurities like economic crisis, unemployment, the fear of deprivation of love and affection may add to the frustration. In extreme cases of this sort one may even lose mental balance or even commit suicide. *A society marked by widespread insecurity is one in which conflict is potential.*

Forms or Types of Conflict

George Simmel has distinguished between four types of conflict: 1. war, 2. feud or factional strife, 3. litigation, and 4. conflict of impersonal ideals.

1. **War**, according to *Simmel*, represent, a deep seated antagonistic impulse in man. But to bring out this impulse into action some definite objective is needed. The objective may be the desire to gain material interests.
2. **Feud** is an intra-group conflict. It may arise because of injustice alleged to have been done by one group to another
3. **Litigation** is a judicial struggle by an individual or group to protect right to possessions. This kind of conflict is more objective in nature.
4. **Conflict of impersonal ideas** is a conflict carried on by the individuals not for them- selves but for an ideal. In such a conflict each party attempts to justify truthfulness of its own ideals. For example, the communists and the capitalists carry on conflict to prove that their own system can bring in a better world order.

Apart from *simmel's* typology the following forms of conflict may generally be observed in our social life:

1. ***Corporate and personal conflict:*** Corporate conflict occurs among the groups within a society or between two societies. When one group tries to impose its will on the other conflict takes place. Ex: race riots, communal upheavals, religious persecutions, labour-management conflict and war between nations, etc.

   Personal conflict takes place *within* the groups. It is more severely restricted and disapproved than the conflict between the groups. The group as a whole has nothing to gain from internal conflict. Personal conflicts arise on account of various motives, envy, hostility, betrayal of trust and so on. Violence occurs much less often though not always, in personal conflict than in corporate conflict. Husband may quarrel with the wife, student with the teacher, friend with the friend, but they may not start fighting.
2. ***Latent and overt conflict:*** Conflict may be overt or latent. In most cases, long before conflict erupts in hostile action, it has existed in latent form in social tension and dissatisfaction. Latent conflict becomes overt conflict when an issue is declared and when hostile action is taken. The over conflict takes place when one side or the other feels strong and wishes to take advantage of this fact. For example, the latent conflict between democratic and communist countries may become oven at the time of war between them.
3. ***Class conflict:*** It arises between social classes which have mutually hostile or opposite interests. Karl Marx has spoken much about the conflict between the social classes: *the rich and the poor* or the *capitalists* and the *proletariats*.
4. ***Racial conflict:*** Racial conflict is mostly due to the physiological differences which are apparently seen among people. One race may claim superiority over the other and start suppressing the other resulting in conflicts. *Ex*: conflicts between Whites and Negroes.
5. ***Caste conflict:*** A sense of '*highness*' and '*lowness*', of '*superiority*' and '*inferiority*', of '*holy*' and '*unholy*' which some caste groups have developed have been responsible for caste conflicts. The so-called upper-caste or 'Savarna Hindus' conflicting with the so-called 'Harijans' or lower castes ['untouchables'] has become a common feature in India.
6. ***Group conflict:*** Group conflict is found between two or more groups of any kind–political, social, economic, religious or otherwise.

7. ***International conflict:*** It refers to conflict between two or more nations or groups of nations. It may take place for political, religious, economic, imperialistic, or ideological or for any other such reasons.

Role of Conflict

Conflict is a fundamental social trait. According to *Gumplowicz*, the development of society has been marked by a ceaseless struggle. *Karl Marx* has explained this struggle as class struggle. George simmel has maintained that a conflict-free harmonious group is practically an impossibility. Society requires for its formation and growth both harmony and disharmony, association and disso- ciation. Conflict may have positive as well as negative results. The negative and the positive effects of conflict may be briefly examined here.

Negative Effects of Conflict

Conflict has its own negative effects. Conflict is the most vigorous form of social interaction and evokes the deepest passions and strongest emotions. It *disrupts social unity*. It is a *costly* way of settling disputes. The results of intragroup conflict are largely negative in that such a struggle *lowers the morale* and *weakens the solidarity* of the group.

Conflict causes *social disorder, chaos* and *confusion*. War as a form of conflict may destroy the lives and properties of countless individuals. It may bring incalculable damage and immeasurable suffering to a number of people. Human history is a monumental evidence in this regard. The modern mode of warfare which can destroy millions of people and vast amount of properties within a few minutes, has brought new fears and anxieties for the mankind.

Conflict does a lot of psychological and moral damage also. It spoils the mental peace of man. Conflicts may even make the people to become inhuman. Lovers of conflict have scant respect for human and moral values. Conflicts between the labour and the management have resulted in material losses. Due to the labour strikes productivity decreases and men and machines become idle.

Positive Effects of Conflict

It is wrong to assume that conflict has only the negative side and does always disservices. Thinkers like *Ratzenhofer* and *Gumplowicz* have said that society overcomes its problems and regis- ters progress through ceaseless conflicts and endless struggles.

1. A limited amount of *internal conflict* may indirectly contribute to group stability. An occasional conflict within the group may keep its leadership alert and its policies up-to-date. If there is no scope for occasional expression, of conflict, and if it is deliberately suppressed, the accumulated discontent may explode and cause irreparable loss.
2. *External Conflict* brings about social unity and oneness among the members. During the Indo-Pak War, all the political parties joined together forgetting their differences and supported the Government of India in facing 'the challenge.
3. *Personal Conflicts* also have their advantages. It is through constant struggling only that individuals can rise to a higher level. The opposition of one individual by the other is the only way in which the continued relationship can be made personally tolerable. *A.W. Green writes*: "..... The verbal conflicts of friends, lovers and married couples, provided they stop short of personal abuse and are restricted to specific issues; often clear the air and permit once again the acceptance of relationship,"

Like competition, conflict is a fundamental human and social trait. *Simmel* maintained that a completely conflict-free, harmonious group is an impossibility. *C.H. Cooley* writes, "it seems that there must always be an element of conflict in our relations with others as well as one of mutual aid: the whole plan of life calls for it and love and strife sit side by side upon the brow of man." He further says that the forms of opposition may change, but its amount is subjected to no general law of diminution.

The positive effects of conflict can be summed up in the following words: "Conflict of some sort is the life of society, the progress emerges from a struggle in which each individual, class or institution seeks to realise its own ideals of good. The intensity of this struggle varies with the vigour of the people, and its cessation, if conceivable would be death."

DIFFERENCES BETWEEN COMPETITION AND CONFLICT

	Competition	*Conflict*
1.	Competition is a process of seeking to monopolise a reward by overtaking all rivals.	Conflict is a process of seeking to possess a reward by weakening or eliminating all rivals.
2.	Competition may be conscious or unconscious.	Conflict is always a conscious activity.
3.	Competition is universal as Well as continuous.	Conflict is 'universal but not continuous. It is intermittent.
4.	Here, the attention of an individual is concentrated on the object or the goal. It is mostly impersonal in nature.	Here, the concentration is on the person rather than the object. Hence it is mostly personal in nature.

(*Contd.*)

5. Competition may lead to positive as Well as negative results. Healthy competition even contributes to progress.	Conflict mostly brings negative results. Its negative results outweigh its positive results.
6. Competition when becomes rigorous. results in conflict.	Competition when becomes personalised, leads to conflicts.

DIFFERENCES BETWEEN COOPERATION AND CONFLICT

Cooperation	*Conflict*
1. Cooperation refers to "joint activity in pur- suit of common goals or shared rewards."	Conflict is a process of seeking to monopolise a reward by weakening or destroying the other competitiors.
2. 'Cooperation may be conscious or uncon- scious. It may not be deliberate act always.	Conflict is mostly conscious in nature. It is mostly a delib- erate act.
3. Cooperation requires sympathy and identification, kindness and consideration for others.	But conflict is always associated with the deepest emotion and the strongest senti- ments. In it, there is no regard for others.
4. Cooperation is universal and continuous in nature.	Conflict is universal no doubt. But it is not continuous, it is intermittent.
5. Cooperation brings mostly positive results. It builds, conserves, and leads to progress.	Conflict brings mostly negative results. It harms, destroys and retards progress.
6. Cooperation is basic to group life. There can be no society without cooperation.	Conflict is not fundamental to the group life of man. Society can persist without it.
7. Cooperation assumes different forms–primary, secondary and tertiary cooperation, direct and indirect cooperation.	We may speak of class conflict, personal conflict, group conflict, international conflict, conflict of impersonal ideas, religious, cultural, racial and caste conflicts.

ACCOMMODATION

Meaning of Accommodation

Accommodation is one of the principal types of social processes. It is through this process that social order arises. *Park* and *Burgess* have said that human social organisation is fundamentally the result of an accommodation of conflicting elements. Throughout his life man has to face a number of conflicting situations. Since conflict cannot continue indefinitely and man does not cherish the prospects of conflict, adjustments are always made. Such adjustments that man does continuously to pull on with other people and situations can be called '*accommodation*'. Accommodation is the process of getting along in spite of differences. It is a way of inventing social arrangements which help people to work together whether they like it or not.

"Life is a series of interruptions and recoveries." Thus, conflicts are bound to be there in life. Still the conflicting individuals and groups sooner or later are forced to find a way to reconcile their differences. *Examples*: Husband and wife may quarrel for some petty or serious things at one time or another but most of the times they live together with mutual love and affection. Workers may go on strike today for some reason but they are bound to come back to work tomorrow after some settlement with the management. Students may boycott their classes in the morning to register their protest against a particular policy of the college authority, but they may reconcile with the situation and return to the classes in the afternoon. Similarly, war is followed by peace. It is in this sense of compromise or agreement reached by the conflicting individuals and parties that the sociologists have used the concept of accommodation.

Definition of Accommodation

1. The famous psychologist *I.M. Baldwin* was the first to use the concept of accommodation. According to him, the term denotes acquired changes in the behaviour of individuals which help them to adjust to their environment.
2. *MacIver* says that "the term accommodation refers particularly to the process in which man attains a sense of harmony with his environment."
3. *Lundberg* is of the opinion that "the word accommodation has been used to designate the adjustments which people in groups make to relieve the fatigue and tensions of competition and conflict."

4. According to *Ogburn* and *Nimkoff* "Accommodation is a term used by the sociologists to describe the adjustment of hostile individuals or groups."

Characteristics of Accommodation

1. ***Accommodation is the natural result of conflict:*** Since conflicts cannot take place continuously they make room for accommodation. When parties or individuals involved in conflict do not relish the scene of conflict they sit down for its settlement. Such settlements, temporary or permanent, may be called 'accommodation'. In the absence of conflicts the question of arriving at accommodation does not arise.
2. ***Accommodation may be a conscious or an unconscious activity:*** Man's adjustment with the social environment is mostly *unconscious*. From birth to burial man has to behave in conformity with the normative order. The new born individual learns to accommodate himself with the social order which is dictated by various norms such as customs, morals, traditions, etc. He would not become a full-fledged member of the group if he failed to adjust himself to the social environment. Thus, unconsciously the new born individual accommodates himself with his family, caste or race, neighbourhood, play-group, school, church, place of work, in brief, with the total environment. Life is full of such unconscious accommodative activities.

   Accommodation becomes *conscious* when the conflicting individuals and groups make a deliberate and an open attempt to stop fighting and start working together. *Example*: warring nations entering into pacts to stop wars. Striking workers stopping strike after having an understanding with the management, etc.
3. ***Accommodation is universal:*** Accommodation as a '*condition*' and as a '*process*' is universal. Human society is composed of antagonistic elements and hence conflicts are inevitable. Since no society can function smoothly in a state of perpetual conflict, accommodation becomes necessary. Thus accommodation is found in all societies and in all fields of social life.
4. ***Accommodation is continuous:*** The process of accommodation is not confined to any particular stage in the life of an individual. It is not limited to any fixed social situation also. On the contrary, throughout the life one has to accommodate oneself with various situations. Further, as and when conflicts take place sooner or later accommodation would follow. Not only the individuals but also the groups within the society are obliged to accommodate among themselves.
5. ***The effects of accommodation may vary with the circumstances:*** It may act to *reduce the conflict* between persons or groups as an initial step towards assimilation. It may serve to *postpone outright conflict* for a specific period of time, as in a treaty between nations or labour-management agreement. It may *permit groups marked by sharp socio-psychological distance to get along together*. It may prove to be beneficial for the parties involved in it. Sometimes it may help the superior or more powerful party to impose its will on the weaker party.

Forms or Methods of Accommodation

Accommodative arrangements between groups or individuals take a variety of forms. *Gillin* and *Gillin* have mentioned of seven methods of adjustment. They are: 1. Yielding to coercion, 2. compromise, 3. arbitration and conciliation, 4. toleration, 5. conversion, 6. sublimation, and 7. rationalisation. But these are not mutually exclusive and are very often found in combination.

1. ***Yielding to coercion:*** Coercion involves the use of force or the threat of force for making the weaker party to accept the conditions of agreement. This can take place when the parties are of unequal strength. It implies the existence of the weak and the strong in any conflict. *For example*, slavery is an arrangement in which the master dominates the servant. Similarly, in wars the victorious nation imposes its will on the vanquished. Various political dictatorships are also instances of coercive accommodation in which a strong minority, group which seizes political power imposes its will on the masses.
2. ***Compromise:*** When the contending parties are almost equal in power they attain accommo- dation by means of compromise. In compromise each party to the dispute makes some concessions and yields to some demand of the other. The "*all or nothing*" attitude gives way to a willingness to give up certain points in order to gain others. Certain international agreements and management- labour agreements on wages, hours of work, are examples of compromise.
3. ***Role of third party in compromise. arbitration, mediation and conciliation:***

   (*a*) **Arbitration.** When the contending parties themselves are not able to resolve their differ- ences they may resort to arbitration. Arbitration is a device for bringing about compromise in which a third party (who may be chosen by both the sides) tries to bring about an end to the conflict. Here the *decision of the third party is binding on both the parties*. Labour-management disputes, some political disputes are often resolved in this way.

(*b*) **Mediation.** Mediation is more akin to arbitration. This involves the introduction into the conflict of a neutral agent whose efforts are directed towards bringing about a peaceful settlement. But the mediator has *no power to settle the conflict as such for his decisions are not binding on the parties*. His function is advisory only. In religious and industrial disputes mediators and arbitrators are commonly used.

(*c*) **Conciliation.** Closely related to compromise is conciliation. This is *an attempt to persuade the disputants to develop friendship and to come to an agreement*. Conciliation has been used in industrial, racial and religious struggles. Conciliation implies a milder response to an opponent than coercion. In the end, conciliation, like toleration opens the door to assimilation.

4. ***Toleration:*** Toleration is another form of accommodation in which the *conflicts are avoided* rather than settled or resolved. Toleration or tolerant participation is an outgrowth of the "*live-and- let-live*" policy. It is a form of accommodation without formal agreement. Here there is no settlement of difference but there is only the avoidance of overt conflict. Each group tries to bear with the other. The groups realise that their differences are irreconcilable. Hence they decide to coexist with their differences. Racial groups, caste groups, political groups wedded to mutually opposite ideologies for example, resort to toleration.

5. ***Conversion:*** This form of accommodation involves a *sudden rejection of one's beliefs, convictions and loyalties, and the adoption of others*. This term is ordinarily used in the religious context to refer to one's conversion into some other religion. The concept is now used in the literary, artistic, economic, political and other fields. In the political fields, in India now the change of party affiliation and ideological conviction has become very common.

6. ***Sublimation:*** Adjustment by means of sublimation involves *the substitution of non-aggressive attitudes and activities for aggressive ones*. It may take place at the individual as well as at the group level. The method suggested by Jesus Christ, Gandhiji and most of the religious prophets to conquer violence and hatred by love and compassion, is that of sublimation.

7. ***Rationalisation:*** This involves plausible *excuses or explanations for one's behaviour*. One is not prepared to acknowledge one's failures or defects for it may indicate guilt or the need for change. Hence one blames others for one's own fault. By ascribing one's failures to others instead of accept- ing one's own defects, one can retain self-respect. Thus a student who fails in the examination for his negligence of studies may put the blame on teachers or valuators of answer papers. Even groups also try to justify their action on purely imaginary grounds. *For example*, Nazi Germany which initiated the Second World War dubbed the Allies as aggressors and held them responsible for the war. In the same way, United States justified its participation in the First World War under the pretext of "Saving the World for Democracy".

Need for Accommodation

It is clear from the above that accommodation assumes various forms. Without accommodation social life could hardly go on. Since conflict disturbs social integration, disrupts social order and damages social stability, in all societies efforts are made to resolve them at the earliest. Accommodation checks conflicts and helps persons and groups to maintain cooperation. It enables persons and groups to adjust themselves to changed functions and statutes which are brought about by changed conditions. It helps them to carry on their life activities together even with conflicting interests. It is a means of resolving conflict without the complete destruction of the opponent. It makes possible cooperation between antagonistic or conflicting elements or parties. Hence it is often called "*antagonistic cooperation*". Thus two or more conflicting political parties may come together to forge a union to defend a third party. Accommodation may take place at personal or social level.

ASSIMILATION

Meaning of Assimilation

Assimilation is one of the types of interaction. Like accommodation it is also a form of social adjustment. But it is more permanent than accommodation. If person-to-person, person-to-group, or group-to-group relations were to remain at the level of accommodation only, there would not have been any fusion of groups and their cultures. Assimilation is concerned with the absorption and incorporation of the culture by another. Hence assimilation requires more fundamental changes than accommodation. When the process of assimilation takes place, the people in two distinct groups do not just compromise with each other, they become almost indistinguishable.

Definition of Assimilation

1. According to *Young* and *Mack*. "Assimilation is the fusion or blending of two previously distinct groups into one".
2. *Bogardus*: Assimilation is the "social process whereby attitudes of many persons are united, and thus develop into a united group"
3. *Biesanz*: Assimilation is the "social process whereby individuals or groups come to share the same sentiments and goals".
4. *Ogburn* and *Nimkoff*. "Assimilation is the process whereby individuals or groups once dis- similar become similar and identified in their interest and outlook".
5. *Samuel Koenig* writes; Assimilation is "the process whereby persons and groups acquire the culture of another group..."

Characteristics of Assimilation

1. *Assimilation is not confined to single field only:* The term assimilation is generally applied to explain the fusion of two distinct cultural groups. But this process is by no means limited to any single field. *For example*, children are gradually assimilated into adult society. Husband and wife who start their marital life with their dissimilar family backgrounds normally develop a surprising unity of interest and purpose. In the religious field, assimilation may take place when an individual or a group of individuals of a particular religious background get converted into some other religious sect or group. As a group process assimilation encompasses life in general.
2. *Assimilation is a slow and gradual process:* Assimilation cannot take place all of a sudden. It takes time. Fusion of personalities and groups usually takes time. It occurs only when there is relatively continuous and direct contact. The speed of the process of assimilation depends on the nature of contacts. If the contacts are primary assimilation occurs naturally and rapidly. On the contrary, if the contacts are secondary and, superficial, assimilation takes place very slowly. The assimilation of the Anglo-Saxon and Norman cultures has taken more than two centuries in Britain. The formation of American culture due to the assimilation of British, Scottish, German and other European cultures also has taken several decades and centuries.
3. *Assimilation is an unconscious process:* In the process of assimilation the individual or group is usually unconscious of what is taking place: Mostly in an unconscious manner individuals and groups discard their original cultural heritage and substitute it with the new one.
4. *Assimilation is a two-way process:* Assimilation involves the principle of give and take. It is normally preceded by another process called '*acculturation*'. Acculturation is a preliminary and necessary step towards assimilation. It takes place when one cultural group which is in contact with another borrows from it certain cultural elements and incorporates them into its own culture. Contact between two groups essentially affects both. Usually, the culturally '*weaker*' group borrows most of the traits from the culturally '*stronger*' group. *Examples*: The American Indians adopted cultural elements of the Whites with whom they came into contact. The Whites also borrowed some of the cultural traits (for instance, food items) from the native Indians. In the same way, immigrants to America adopted American customs and ways and in turn, the native Americans borrowed many of the cultural traits which the immigrants had brought along with them. Such exchanges of cultural traits also have taken place between Aryans and Dravidians. The adoption of some traits of the 'dominant' culture by another 'weaker' cultural group paves the way for the total merger of the latter with the former.

Factors Favouring Assimilation

1. ***Toleration:*** Assimilation is possible only when individuals and groups are tolerant towards the cultural differences of others. Tolerance helps people to come together, to develop contacts and to participate in common social and cultural activities. When the majority group or the dominant group itself is secure, hospitable and tolerant toward differences, the immigrant groups or minority groups have a greater opportunity to join and to participate in the total community life.
2. ***Intimate social relationships:*** Assimilation is the final product of social contacts. The relative speed in which it is achieved depends on the nature of the contacts. It takes place naturally and quickly in primary groups such as family and friendship groups. On the contrary, where contacts are secondary, that is, indirect, impersonal and superficial assimilation is slow to take place.

3. ***Amalgamation or intermarriage:*** A factor which helps complete assimilation is amalgamation which refers to the intermarriage of different groups. Without biological amalgamation complete assimilation is not possible. Mere intermixture of the groups to a limited degree does not guarantee assimilation. But inter marriage or amalgamation must be accepted in the mores and become a part of the institutional structure, before assimilation exists.
4. ***Cultural similarity:*** If there are striking similarities between the main constituents of culture of groups assimilation is quick to take place. In America, *for example*, English-speaking Protestants are assimilated with greater speed than non-Christians who do not speak English.
5. ***Education:*** Education is another conducive factor for assimilation. For immigrant people public education has played a prominent role in providing culture contact. Maurice R. Davis has pointed out in his "*World Immigration*" that in America the public school has been playing the vital role in the process of Americanising the children of foreign-born parents.
6. ***Equal social and economic opportunity:*** Public education alone is not enough. People of all groups must have equal access to socio-economic opportunities. Only then, they can come closer and establish relations among themselves with mutual trust. As it has been observed in the case of America full assimilation is possible only when full participation in social, cultural and economic life is allowed.

Factors Retarding or Hindering Assimilation

1. ***Isolation:*** Assimilation is possible only when the groups and individuals are in continuous contact with others. Hence isolation is a negation of assimilation. Not only physical isolation but even mental isolation retards assimilation.
2. ***Physical or racial differences:*** Differences in physical appearance are often used as a means of discrimination. It is easy to keep some people apart on the basis of their skin colour or other physical features. *For example*, we can see widespread discrimination between the Whites and the Negroes in almost all the places in the world.
3. ***Cultural differences:*** If there are no common elements in the two cultures, the groups may remain apart socially even though they happen to stay together physically. They may even struggle for supremacy in their intermittent conflicts. Thus wide cultural differences between groups in customs, religious beliefs, morals, values, languages come in the way of assimilation.
4. ***Prejudice as a barrier to assimilation:*** Prejudice is the attitude on which segregation depends for its success. As long as the dominant group is prejudiced against a particular group which is kept apart assimilation cannot take place. Prejudice also hampers assimilation between constituent elements within a given society. Prejudice within a community, within a family, or within any group can only contribute to disunity and not to unity.
5. ***Dominance and subordination:*** Dominance and subordination often come in the way of close and intimate contact between groups. If the dominant group does not provide equal chances and opportunities for the minority or immigrant groups, assimilation is very slow to take place. Further, complete assimilation may not take place. Strong feeling of superiority and inferiority associated with dominance and subordination also retard the rate of assimilation.

DIFFERENCE BETWEEN ACCOMMODATION AND ASSIMILATION

	Accommodation	*Assimilation*
1.	Accommodation may take place suddenly and in a radical manner. *Example*: Workers after having talks with the management may decide to stop their month-long strike all on a sudden.	Assimilation is a slow and a gradual process. It takes time. *For example*, immigrants take time to get assimilated with the majority group.
2.	It may or may not provide permanent solution to group differences and disputes. It may only provide a temporary solution.	Assimilation normally provides a permanent solution to inter-group disputes and differences.
3.	It may be both conscious and unconscious a process. In most of the instances it takes place consciously. *Example*: Labour leaders who come for talks are sufficiently aware of the fact that they are purposefully seeking out a solution to their dispute.	It is mostly an unconscious process. Individuals and groups involved in it are often not aware of what actually happens within themselves or in their group.

REVIEW QUESTIONS

1. Explain the concept of social process and describe the various forms of social processes.
2. Give the meaning of social interaction. Discuss its various kinds.
3. What do you mean by cooperation? Throw light on the types of cooperation.
4. Assess the role of cooperation in social life.
5. Give the meaning of competition. Discuss the nature, characteristics and forms of competition.
6. Evaluate the role of competition in social life.
7. What are the differences between cooperation and competition?
8. Define conflict. Describe its various forms.
9. Throw light on the negative and positive effects of conflict.
10. Bring out the differences between competition and conflict.
11. Define accommodation. Discuss its various forms and characteristic features.
12. What do you mean by assimilation? Describe its characteristic features.
13. Explain the factors which retard or hinder assimilation.
14. Explain the dissociative types of social processes with examples.
15. Write short notes on the following:
    (a) Cooperative and competitive societies
    (b) Role of conflict
    (c) Accommodation and assimilation.

⌘⌘⌘⌘⌘⌘⌘⌘⌘⌘⌘

21

ORGANISATION AND INDIVIDUAL

CHAPTER OUTLINE

- Concept of Organisation
- Some Salient Aspects of Social Organisation
- Meaning and Characteristics of Formal and Informal Organisations
- Interrelationship and Differences between Formal and Informal Organisations
- Role of Individual in Organisations
- Nature and Characteristics of Organisations
- Formal and Informal Organisations
- Formal Organisation and Bureaucracy

CONCEPT OF ORGANISATION

The modem civilised society is characterised by a large number of organisations. Our society in a way is an organisational society. We not only live in, belong to and work through organisations but satisfy most of our desires and fulfil our aspirations through organisations. The term '*organisation*' is used in different ways to mean different things. The term is generally used to mean an 'association' or an '*associational group*'. In a restricted sense, it refers to *one of the attributes* of an association [to mean an arrangement of statuses and roles]. In a specific sense, it represents 'bureaucracy' like that of a business corporation, government or industry. Sometimes, it is used in a broad sense to mean the '*social organisation*' itself. The term 'organisation' when used liberally may mean *any organised* group in contrast with an unorganised group.

Views of Early Sociologists about Social Organisation

Early sociologists and social philosophers used the term 'social organisation' in a broad sense to refer to societies'. *Auguste Comte* defined social organisation as "*general social agreement*" or "*social consensus*". He agreed that government is powerless without the support of social agreement. 'Social agreement' refers to people's agreement or consensus. *Herbert Spencer* used 'social organisation' to refer to *interrelations* of the economic, political and other divisions of society. *Emile Durkheim* used the term to refer mostly to *social integration* and individual regulation through consensus about morals and values. Durkheim was of the opinion that social integration or social equilibrium would prevail as long as morals and values maintained their hold over individual behaviour. *C.H. Cooley* used the term social organisation to refer to the "*differentiated unity of mental or social life*", According to Cooley, social organisation is the result of "the shared activities and understandings" of the people.

Current Use of the Term 'Social Organisation'

At present the term "*social organisation*" is used to refer to the interdependence of parts in groups. These groups may vary in size and nature from small cliques of workers, to hospitals and factories. Today very rarely sociologists use the term 'social organisation' in a comprehensive way. Many sociologists prefer to use the term "*social system*" to refer to the society as such rather than "*social organisation*". *Talcott Parsons, G.H. Homans, R.K. Merton* and others use the term 'social system' in place of social organisation to refer to society.

The term is used in sociological studies and researches today to stress the importance of arrangement of parts and their interdependence in groups and in societies. The concept is of help in understanding the way in which the parts of society are related to each other and how each is related to the whole society. It is now widely recognised that social organisation is required for the survival and the effective functioning of groups and societies. Hence, implicit or explicit reference to the concept is to be found in almost all sociological research and all sociological theory.

Definition of Social Organisation

1. *According* to *Duncan Mitchell*, social organisation means "the interdependence of parts, which is an essential characteristic of all enduring collective entities: groups, communities and societies.
2. *Ogburn* and *Nimkoff* An organisation is an articulation of different parts which, perform various functions, it is an active group device for getting something done.
3. *Leonard Broom* and *Philip Selznick* have defined social organisation as "the patterned relations of individuals and groups". (According to them, it is one of the sources of order in social life).
4. *Louise Weston* and *Others* have said that "social organisation can be thought of as the pattern and processes of relations among individuals and among groups".
5. *According to H.M. Johnson*, "Organisation refers to an aspect of interaction systems".
6. *Elliott* and *Merrill* have said, "Social Organisation is a state of being, a condition in which the various institutions in a society are functioning in accordance with their recognised or implied purposes'.

Organisation: The Need of the Day

Organisation appears in society simply because many of the things we do could not be done without it and many other things we do can be done much better because of it. No game involving more than one player would be possible if it were not for organisation. There would be no such things as *a college, a university, a store, an industry, a church, a court of law, a government or a state* without organisation. Organisation makes possible the complex activities in which the members of a complex society participate. Thus, a football team of eleven members well organised, can defeat an unorganised group of eleven men under any circumstances. A very small body of organised police can control a very large crowd. A small number of men, constituting themselves as a government, can rule a nation. A small board of trustees can operate the enterprise of a university. All this is possible because of organisation. What then do we mean by an organisation?

Innumerable Organisations

Sometimes the word '*organisation*' is used to refer to the *associational groups*. It includes corporations, armies, schools, churches, banks, prisons etc. The society consists of many such organisations. A state is frequently called a political organisation. A factory is called an economic organisation. A church is a religious organisation. A bank is a financial organisation. A school may represent an educational organisation and so on. They are all social organisations *i.e.,* organisations of society. Here *Ogburn* and *Nimkoff* do not make a clear distinction between organisation and social organisation as such. As they say, the entire 'society' represents a wider organisation, a social organisation. They write: '*But society is also quite generally an organised group of interacting individuals*.' Society indeed, consists of innumerable organisations.

NATURE AND CHARACTERISTICS OF ORGANISATION

1. ***A definite purpose:*** An organisation has its own definite purpose or purposes. Without any purpose or goal individuals rarely come together and establish among themselves a definite pattern or system of interaction. *For example*, the bank as an organisation has a definite purpose of facilitating the financial transactions. A College or a University has the aim of promoting education, and so on.
2. ***Unanimity or consensus among the members:*** The smooth running of an organisation depends much on the mutual understanding, cooperation and consensus among its members. *The family* as an organisation, *for example*, can run smoothly only when its members like the father, mother and the children, have mutual understanding, cooperation and consensus among themselves. Similarly, political parties, trade unions, business houses. corporations etc., can successfully work only when their members have mutual faith and consensus.
3. ***Harmony between statuses and roles:*** An organisation is understood as a mechanism that brings different people together into a network of interaction to perform different functions. The organisation assigns statuses and roles to the individuals and makes them to assume statuses and enact roles. The 'status' and roles are conditioned by many

factors such as birth, sex, age, race, caste, achievements, physical and mutual abilities, skill, intelligence, etc. The organisation can function without any problem if there prevails harmony between the acceptance of the statuses by the members and their enactment of the related roles. The College, *for example*, as an organisation can function well when its principal, teachers, office staff, students, peons and such other members understand the statuses assigned to them and enact their definite roles in an appropriate manner.

4. ***Control of the organisation on the behaviour of the individuals:*** Organisation maintains its control over the behaviour of its members and regulates their activities. It makes use of various formal as well as informal means of social control for this purpose. The failure of social organisation to maintain its hold over the behaviour of the members may contribute to the process of disorganisation.

SOME SALIENT ASPECTS OF SOCIAL ORGANISATION

According to *Ogburn* and *Nimkoff,* social organisations reveal the following aspects:

1. *Social Organisations are not functioning in the same way in all societies.* Monkeys and apes do not have much social organisation. Pre-literate human groups in the hunting and food-gathering stages of culture have social organisations in the form of families, hunting panics, clans, age societies, ceremonial organisation in religion, etc.
2. *Social Organisations are not found in equal number everywhere.* Their number differs with the size of population; the larger the population the more organisations there are, In small communities we may find one or two organisations with several functions and not several organisations with one function each.
3. *Social Organisation differs with the extent of accumulation of culture*. Tribals, *for example*, do not have sophisticated organisations such as a bank, court, a flying club. etc. The Eskimos, for example, do not have chess clubs or flying club, or Rotary Club or Lions Club, because their culture has not accumulated to that extent.
4. *Social organisation is also a function of the division of labour that is, of specialised activities*. Greater division of labour and specialisation are to be found in more complex societies. The need for social organisation is greater in complex societies than in simple societies.
5. *When the number of social organisations increases more and more single purpose organisations come to be established. Example:* Chess club, flying club, philatelic club, etc. Further, due to social changes, an organisation having many functions may lose or transfer some of them to other multi purpose organisations. *For example*, family has almost lost its economic function and has transferred educational and recreational functions to other organisations such as school, college on the one hand, and cinema house, sports club, entertainment club, etc., on the other.
6. *Of the various social organisations some are not only multipurpose in nature but also almost universal in nature*. They have existed over hundreds of thousands of years and in many different cultures. They are expressed in institutions such as - the family, religion and government. They have more than one function. Family, *for example*, performs functions such as procreation, education and regulation of sex relations.
7. *Social Organisations found in the form of associations have a shorter history and are less widely distributed.* They often have only one function or very few functions. *Examples:* A parent teacher association, an athletic club, or a secret fraternal society.
8. *There are minor social organisations which function as the subdivisions of associations and institutions. Example*: Individual business, committees or social clubs. These are more short-lived, less widespread and more specialised.
9. *Further, social organisations may be formal or informal in nature*. Organisations characterised by a specific function, division of labour, a hierarchy of authority, and formal relations are formal organisations. *Example*: Bank, hospital, army, court, corporation, government departments, political party, etc.

Some organisations are '*informal*' in nature. They are smaller in size and are based on informal relations. These develop to supply needs neglected or not fully met by the formal organisations. *Example:* clique, friendship groups, gangs, bands, etc. These organisations normally develop within the formal organisation. The formal organisations in their efforts at fulfilling some established purpose or interest with efficiency many neglect or sacrifice some human values. To achieve these personal values, informal organisations may develop within the formal organisation. *For example*: for the sake of friendship and fellowship, cliques or gangs may develop within a bank or a factory.

FORMAL AND INFORMAL ORGANISATIONS

In order to fulfil the basic needs, satisfy the multi-faceted desires and promote the diverse interests of men, a large number of organisations have come into being in the *modern complex societies*. These organisations are of two kinds; (*i*) *The formal organisations*, and (*ii*) *the informal organisations*.

Formal Organisations

The modern industrialised, urbanised and civilised societies of the world consist of a large number of formal organisations. Due to the complexity in the growth of societies, the number and size of the formal organisations have increased. They are found in the economic, political, educational, industrial and other fields.

Meaning of Formal Organisation

Formal Organisations represent those organisations which are characterised by a specific function, division of labour, a hierarchy of authority, rationality and a proper arrangement of statuses and role. They are carefully planned and systematically worked out. *Examples*: Banks, Colleges, Universities, Factories, Corporations, Government, Political Parties, Trade Unions, Courts,

Libraries, Police, Army, Government Offices, Life Insurance Corporations, Religious, Cultural and other organisations.

Characteristics of Formal Organisations

It was *Max Weber* who for the first time made a sociological analysis of formal organisation. In his "Bureaucracy "*Organisation*", "*Theory of Social and Economic Organisation*", Max Weber has provided his conception of formal organisation, particularly of bureaucracy.

The main characteristics of formal organisations are as follows:

1. ***A specific function:*** Formal Organisation has its own specific function or functions. A university, for example, has the main function of promoting education. But it may also promote the specific artistic, literary, athletic and other interests of the members. The principal function of the church is religion. But it may also promote charitable, ethical, athletic, recreational, educational, missionary and other activities. Thus, the formal organisation may have its '*latent*' as well as '*manifest*' functions.
2. ***Norms:*** The formal Organisation has its own norms or rules of social behaviour. Certain conduct is appropriate in a university classroom, a factory, an office, a department store, a hospital, a government bureau, a military unit, and so on. Students and teachers, foremen and workers, vice-presidents and secretaries, managers and clerks, doctors and nurses and similar other members observe norms in their interaction. Formal Organisation lays down *procedure* to be followed by the members.
3. ***Formal organisation implies statuses and division of labour:*** Members of an organisation have different statuses. A bank, for example, may have manager, a public relations officer, a field officer, a cashier, a few clerks, a few peons, and so on. These statuses determine one's social relations with other members. *Statuses imply division of labour*. The division of labour is characteristic of all organisations, and in a sense, organisation is synonymous with the division of labour. Organised actions in 'a formal organisation are possible because of division of labour. It contributes to the efficiency of the organisation. Division of labour leads to specialisation. The modem hospital for example, may consist of a number of specialists like the gynaecologists, pediatricians, surgeons, anaesthetists, heart specialists, urologists, neurologists, psychiatrists and others working together, each one complementing the knowledge and skill of the others.
4. ***Authority:*** The formal organisation creates authority. Where there is no organisation there is no authority, where there is no authority there is no organisaton. Authority is one of the most significant criterion of organisation. Authority refers to the presence of one or more power centres which control the concerted efforts of the organisation and direct them towards its goals. These power centres also must review continuously the organisation's performance and re-pattern its structure where necessary, to increase its efficiency.
5. ***Bureaucracy:*** Bureaucracy refers to the administrative aspect of the formal organisation. It refers to the arrangement

of the organisation designed to carry out its day-to-day business. It is represented by a hierarchy of officials who are assigned different responsibilities and provided with different statuses and roles. Here, the roles are official roles. The role is enacted according to its corresponding official status. Status implies authority. Authority resides with the offices and not with the persons.

6. ***Rationality:*** The formal organisation is based on rationality. The rationality of formal organisations has two sources: (*i*) " *the predominance of rules that have been devised to help achieve definite results*", and (*ii*) "*the systematic reliance on knowledge in the operation of the organisation*". "*Knowledge*" here means something more than the knowledge of the bureaucratic rules. *For example*, business firms depends upon the '*professional*' knowledge of a good number of technical experts such as lawyers, accountants, advertisers, scientists, engineers. Similarly, hospitals depend upon medical doctors, nurses, pharmacists and many technicians.
7. ***Relative permanence:*** The formal organisations are relatively permanent. Some organisations last for longer time while others perish within a short period of time. Relatively few organisations survive for generations such as The Roman Catholic Church, The Society of Jesus, The Bank of France, The Oxford University which have survived for generations. Comparatively the business organisations are more flexible. Some organisations continue to function by aiming at the fulfilment of new goals even though their initial goals are fulfilled.
8. ***Tests of membership:*** It is easy to join some formal organisations and difficult to join others. All organisations require certain qualifications. All formal organisations without exception, in fact, are relatively closed. All of them have tests of membership. It is easy to join political party or an industry, but it is difficult to get into the army, the Bar Council, the Cabinet of the ruling party. Membership in an organisation is almost always an achieved status, seldommerely an ascribed status.
9. ***Substitution of personnel:*** The unsatisfactory persons of the formal organisation can be removed and others assigned their tasks. The formal organisation can also recombine its personnel through transfer and promotion.
10. ***A name and other identifying symbols:*** Well established formal organisations have their own names and also symbols. The symbols of identification may be mottoes, slogans, songs, colours, ribbons, seals, trademarks and so on. These are sometimes called '*symbolic culture traits*', and they serve to distinguish one from the other.

Formal Organisation and Bureaucracy

The earliest use of the term '*bureaucracy*' was made by the economist *Vincent De Gournay*. Due to the efforts of Max Weber the term assumed its sociological importance in the beginning of the 20th century. Sociologists are using this term in two ways: (*i*) According to *Talcott Parsons* '*bureaucracy*', represents one of the most salient structural characteristics of the modern Western Society. In a loose sense, the relatively large-scale organisations with specialised functions can be called bureaucracies. (*ii*) According to *W.R. Scoot, RM. Blau* the term bureaucracy has a restricted meaning. They have stated in their "*Formal Organisations*" that the term bureaucracy must be "*used neutrally to refer to the administrative aspects of organisations*."

Characteristics of Bureaucracy

Max weber's "*Wirtschaft Und Gesellschaft*", "*The Theory of Social and Economic Organisation*", "*Bureaucracy*", "*Organisation*" and other writings provide us more details regarding bureaucracy and its characteristics. It was he who for the first time made a sociological analysis of bureaucracy. According to him, bureaucracy reveals the following characteristics:

Bureaucracies have: 1. fixed areas of official, jurisdiction governed by laws and regulations, 2. offices organised on the basis of a clear hierarchy of authority, 3. administration based on written documents and conducted according to procedures for which special training is required, 4. personally free officials appointed on the basis of technical qualifications, 5. officials who are employed on fulltime basis and subject to strict discipline, 6. the officials who are employed must know the distinction between their private affairs and public affairs. The misappropriation of the office or that of the means of administration is disapproved and forbidden, 7. the official of the bureaucracy has a career in which the promotion is governed by seniority or merit, 8. the officials are also paid a fixed salary, according to their ranks. Generally, they are paid pensions,

9. the officials maintain contact and communications among themselves in a particular way. Orders and communications among them always proceed through "*proper channels*." 10. bureaucracy normally has an office of its own and all the documents pertaining to its business are maintained in files.

Criticism of Max Weber's Theory of Bureaucracy

Max Weber has made use of historical data in order to establish his propositions about the characteristics of "*bureaucracy*' He tries to describe a so-called '*pure*' or '*ideal*' type of bureaucracy, the characteristics of which are functionally connected with the rationality or efficiency of organisation. It means, his '*pure*' type of bureaucracy seems to be a set of hypotheses concerning the institutional characteristics of the most efficient kind of organisation. Many of Weber's propositions have been accepted by the critics, but some have been criticised. Some of the main criticisms are as follows:

1. Weber failed to distinguish markedly different types and sub-types of highly rationalised bureaucracy. 2. Even those of his hypotheses that are considered to be more reasonable, need much more empirical verification and specification before they can be accepted as scientifically established. 3. Weber neglected the dysfunctional or the negative aspects of certain features of modem organisations.

Informal Organisations

In no society only the formal organisations are found. No society can maintain its existence based solely on the formal organisations. It is difficult to imagine that the members of bureaucracy or any other formal organisation always behave in the manner that is required by the formal organisation. Informal relations are bound to develop among the members. These informal relations provide the basis for the formation of informal organisations.

Meaning of Informal Organisation

'*Informal Organisation*' refers to a small group the members of which are tied to one another as persons. The group is characterised by informal and face-to-face relations, mutual aid, cooperation and companionship. The members of informal organisations work together not in their official capacities, but as persons. They share their hopes and fears, their joys and sorrows. Examples: Groups such as–'*Gangs*', '*cliques*', '*friendship groups*', '*peer groups*', '*Bands*', *etc*., represent the informal organisations.

People are not only the members of formal organisations but also are connected with informal organisations. Members of the formal organisations such as banks, colleges, universities, business houses, hospitals, army, etc., are likely to develop informal relations among themselves. These informal relations contribute to the development of informal organisations. But the same kind of informal relationship may not be formed among all. *Example:* A formal organisation such as a college may consist of hundreds of members. All these members do not have among themselves the same kind of relationship. We may find among them several small groups, cliques, bands, friendship groups, peer groups, each consisting of a limited few. The members of each such group may always move together, play together, study together, see movies together, sit together, study together inside the class rooms and so on. Their tastes, interests and attitudes may also be more or less similar. These groups represent informal organisations. These informal organisations may be formed on the basis of ethnic groups, religious, caste and linguistic groups, regional origins, schools or colleges from which they have passed or fraternitites to which they belong.

A formal organisation may consist of a number of informal organisations. The informal organisations consist of only rules and not statuses. Here there is no authority but only leadership. Esteem is awarded to persons independently of the statuses they occupy. Their membership is limited. Still they are relatively permanent. Informal relations of the members last for a longer time. Informal organisations have their own unwritten norms of behaviour. They have their own ways of correcting and punishing the violators of the norms. Though they are smaller in size they give strength to the formal organisations to function effectively. These informal organisations resemble *Cooley's* '*Primary Groups*' and *Sumners* '*In-groups*'.

Replacement of Formal Organisation by Informal Organisation

The line between formal and informal organisation is not always clear. Sometimes, the formal organisation may be replaced by the informal organisation. If the formal organisation breaks down at some point, it may be replaced by informal organisation. An example may be cited here in order to clarify this point.

Example. In an electrical equipment company, the president, who was about to retire, paid less and less attention to company affairs. Informally, his duties were gradually taken over by the treasurer. This new arrangement was an informal one. It was also latent, in the sense that the new allocation of authority and responsibilities in the company was not fully recognised by all personnel. Just as there may be latent functions, so there may be latent structure. In small informal groups, latent structure is common and probably works well. But in predominantly formal organisations there is usually some advantage in having the lines of authority fairly well recognised. In the electrical equipment company, failure to make the new lines of authority explicit caused a certain amount of bad feeling, or low morale.

Interrelationship between Formal and Informal Organisations

The formal and the informal organisations are very much interrelated. They are *not mutually exclusive*. We find many informal organisations existing simultaneously with the formal organisations A single formal organisation like the state, the university, the industry, the church, etc., may consist of several informal organisations in the form of '*chiques*', *gangs*, *friendship groups*, *etc*. The line separating formal and informal organisations is not always clear.

It is observed that no formal organisation by itself is sufficient to achieve its goals. *Any formal organisation functions best when the informal organisation supports it*. The most orderly and efficient structure does not automatically produce a successful organisational administration if the members have no goodwill towards one another and have only personal hostilities. The exercise of authority in such situations brings nothing but resentment, which makes the orderly intercourse of people difficult, [if not impossible].

On the contrary, the best goodwill in the world will be insufficient for the successful pursuit of an organisational activity if the formal organisation is deficient. Two good friends placed in a top position in an organisation may very quickly become enemies because of conflict between them. Further, if the formal organisation breaks down at some point, it may be replaced by informal organisation. "The most efficient and satisfactory organisation is the one in which formal organisation is supported by the informal organisation". When the discrepancy between the two becomes too great the organisation.... is in danger of dissolution.

The relationships between the formal and informal organisations are 'always subtle, always complicated, and always interesting. And it is in this area, particularly with respect to the political organisation of society, that sociology and political science meet on common ground'-*Robert Bierstedt*

Sociologist *Charles H. Page* has opined that the continuous interaction and association among the members of formal organisation result in the emergence of informal structure of roles and relationships. He calls such informal structure consisting of primary group relations, friendships and cliques, ties of mutual obligations of aid and assistance, – '*bureaucracy's other face.*'

According to *Charles Bernard*, the informal organisations are necessary "*to the operation of formal organisations as a means of communication, of cohesion, and of protecting the integrity of the individual.*" *The experiments of George Elton Mayo conducted in Hawthorne Works in Chicago of the Western Electric Company* have proved convincingly that the informal organisations are important and without them no large-scale system could ever be stable and efficient.

DIFFERENCES BETWEEN FORMAL AND INFORMAL ORGANISATION

Formal Organisations	*Informal Organisations*
1. The formal organisation consists of the formally recognised and established statuses of the members. The relationship between the members is more a status relationship than a personal relationship.	The informal organisation consists of role rather than statuses. The relationship between the members is more a personal relationship or role relationship than the status relationship.

(*Contd.*)

	Formal Organisations	Informal Organisations
2.	In the formal organisation statuses have differential prestige in independence of the persons who occupy them. In brief, here we find prestige which is attached to the status.	In the informal organisation social relations occur on the basis of the esteem that the members have for one another in independence of their statuses. Here we witness esteem which is associated with the persons.
3.	There is authority in formal organisation. Hence there is super ordination and sub-ordination. Individuals are extrinsically valuable because of their status and prestige.	There is leadership in informal organisation. Hence we find dominance and submission. Individuals are intrinsically valuable because of their roles and esteem
4.	The norms of formal organisation differ. They are found in the form of written rules, regulations, laws contracts or constitutions.	The norms are more subtle. They are also informal. They may be found in the form of customs, morals, folkways, belief etc. They are not written.
5.	Formal organisations may have a long history of their own. The state, the Rotary Club, for example, have a long history. They are relatively permanent and stable.	Informal organisations are not very permanent. Informal organisations may, in course of time, develop into formal organisations.
6.	Interaction and communication in the formal organisation are Indirect, non-intimate and goal-oriented to an end. Formal organisations resemble the secondary groups.	Interaction and communication in formal organisations are direct, face-to-face and intimate. Interaction is an end in itself. In this respect, informal organisations are akin to primary groups.
7.	Formal organisations are comparatively more inflexible. it is not easy to bring change in them. *For example*, it is not easy for the state to change or amend its constitution.	Informal organisations are more flexible. There is no rigidity here. Changes can be brought forth easily. It requires only the change in attitudes of the members.
8.	Formal organisations are bigger in size and more complex in their structural arrangement.	Informal organisations are smaller in size. Their structural arrangement is less complex.

ROLE OF INDIVIDUAL IN ORGANISATIONS

We are living in a world of organisations. Our society is an organisational society. "We are born in organisations, educated by organisations, and most of us spend much of our lives working for organisations. We spend much of our leisure time paying, playing and praying in organisations. Most of us will die in an organisation, and when the time comes for burial, the largest organisation of all–the state–must grant official permission writes *Amitai Etzioni* in the '*Modern Organisations*."

Modern civilisation depends largely on organisations as the most rational and efficient form of social grouping. The organisation creates a powerful social instrument by coordinating a large number of human actions. It combines its personnel with its resources, weaving together leaders, experts, workers, machines and raw materials. At the same time, it evaluates its performance and orients its efforts to achieve its goals. Organisations serve the various needs of society and its citizens more efficiently than smaller and more natural human groupings, such as families, friendship groups and communities. Still, organisations are not a modern invention. "The pharaohs used organisations to build the pyramids. The emperors of China used organisations a thousand years ago to construct great irrigation systems. And the first Pope created a universal church to serve a world religion". Modern society has more organisations and these fulfil a great variety of societal and personal needs. These organisations involve a great proportion of citizens, and affect a large segment of their lives.

Organisation Goals and Individual Motives

Organisations have their own goals. There is a close relationship between organisation goals and individuals motives. But some writers are of the opinion that the organisations do not have any goals and only the individuals possess them. It is true that the participants in an organisation have a variety of personal goals. It is also true that their conceptions of the group goals or organisation goals may not be exactly alike. Still, the concept of organisation becomes meaningless unless there is a significant amount of agreement about the "*common objectives*" of cooperation. Unless the participants in an organisation are convinced of its purpose or objectives or goals, they cannot work for it collectively.

The term '*organisation*' implies some coordination of activities. "Coordination" means orientation to common goals and specialisation of contributions to the common effort. As long as the individuals are bound by the rules and regulations of, and work according to the ways of the organisation in cooperation with others, so long the organisation can be said to have its own goals or purposes. Thus, it is not by a chance that the unskilled and skilled workers, the technicians and the mechanics, the supervisors and the engineers, the clerks and the accountants and others work together in an iron and steel industry.

Every organisation has its own specific goals or purposes. The organisation is carefully worked out and designed for the realisation of its goals. *Example*: The *University* as an organisation, has the goals of promoting education, spreading knowledge, conducting researches and so on. *Army* as an orgnisation, has goals such as the nation and fighting against the enemies in wars. It must be noted that all the members of the organisation may not have the same conception regarding its goals. *For example*, the army officials may not have a total conception of the goal of the army. Their conceptions of the comprehensive goal of the army may be simply '*winning*' something–a hill, a battle, a bridge, a victory and so on. We must, however, remember that the attainment of group goals is almost always a matter of degree.

Organisation and Individual Motives

The individual motives play an important role in the functioning of the organisation. As *Harry M. Johnson* has pointed out "*the members of an organisation must be induced, coerced, or forced to participate in it.* "Some of the motives for participating in an organisation are similar to the motives for economic activity. People participate in organisations when they are going to gain something out of them. *For example*, the desire for remuneration in cash or kind, prestige, the desire to show the skills already acquired, the desire to have good connections with men of prestige, etc., represent some of the motives of the people in participating in organisations.

People tend to *identify* themselves with the organisation in which they participate. There is a close affinity between people's motives on the one hand, and their identification with the organisation on the other. The degree of their identification with the organisation depends on the nature and intensity of the motives for participating in them. The following factors are significant in understanding an individual's strong or weak identification with an organisation:

The individual's identification with the organisation is stronger if–(*i*) a number of individual needs are satisfied in it, (*ii*) the organisation goals are perceived as shared, (*iii*) the prestige of the organisation is perceived to be the greater, (*iv*) there is a greater frequency of interaction in the organisation, and (*v*) there is less competition within the organisation.

The individual motives play an important role in the fulfilment of organisation goals. People cannot work in organisation without any motives, purposes or thinking. They do not work in it automatically or mechanically or in an impulsive manner. It is wrong to presume that in an organisation like *hospital*, the doctors, nurses, servants, and other assistants, work in without any motive, intention or purpose. it is not by accident that they are made to work together in one place. These people may work together in the hospital for various purposes. The intentions or motives of looking after the patients, serving the people, earning money, securing name, fame and recognition, etc., make them to work together. In order to accomplish its goals an organisation such as the hospital has to inspire, motivate and provide incentives to its members. It can do so by highlighting the importance of medical service, elevating the status of the doctors, providing attractive working conditions and facilities, and paying handsome salaries and so on.

Organisation Equilibrium

The success of an organisation depends not only on the proper coordination and cooperation of its members but also on the cooperation of '*others*'. The '*others*' must also be made to contribute to the smooth functioning of the organisation. *For example*, success of an industry depends not only on the employees and the employers but also on 'others' such as the customers of its finished products. Similarly, the library depends on its readers; the army, on the people for whose sake it fights battles; the college, on the parents of the students, and so on.

An organisation can be said to have attained "*equilibrium*" when it is able to maintain the continued contributions of all its participants–members and others, by providing them various kinds of inducements to work for its success. Equilibrium, in this sense, may be achieved at various levels. Further, the state of equilibrium may change over time. The scope of an organisation's activities may remain roughly constant or may grow or diminish at another level.

REVIEW QUESTIONS

1. Explain the concept of organisation. Discuss the views of early sociologists about social organisation.
2. Throw light on the nature and characteristics of organisation.
3. Define social organisation. Write its salient features.
4. Discuss the characteristics of formal and informal organisations.
5. Bring out the interrelationships between formal organisation and bureaucracy.
6. Throw light on the replacement of formal organisation by informal organisation.
7. Explain the interrelationship between formal and informal organisations.
8. Assess the role of individual in organisations.
9. Write short notes on the following:
   (a) Weber's theory of bureaucracy
   (b) Characteristics of bureaucracy
   (c) Informal organisations

⌘⌘⌘⌘⌘⌘⌘⌘⌘⌘⌘

PART FOUR

SOCIAL INEQUALITY

[illegible] all societies [illegible]
[illegible] a [illegible] study [illegible]
[illegible] history [illegible]
[illegible] relation [illegible]
men. Socially [illegible]
Russia which [illegible]
people according [illegible]
different [illegible]
societies [illegible]
[illegible]
[illegible] and [illegible]
the society [illegible]

SOCIAL DIFFERENTIATION

[illegible]

[illegible] *Differences*

[illegible]
[illegible] very [illegible]
[illegible] characteristics
[illegible] men [illegible] old men. Masters
and servants [illegible] and the poor, [illegible] and the illiterate,
engineers and [illegible] equal, there [illegible]
equalitarian [illegible] societies may only differ in the degree of
differentiation [illegible]

Differences in Different Ranks

Some type of [illegible] society. It is clearly related to the
rise and operation of social classes [illegible] is found in the different roles of entrepreneur,

22

Social Differentiation and Social Stratification

Chapter Outline

In all societies there is differentiation of the population by age, sex, and personal characteristics. The roles and privileges of children differ from those of adults; and those of good hunters or warriors differ from those of the rank and file. It is not customary to speak of a society as stratified if every individual in it has an equal chance to succeed to whatever statuses are open. Strictly speaking, there are no purely equalitarian societies, only societies differing in degree of stratification. Even Russia which dreamt of a 'classless society', could not, any more than any other society escape the necessity of ranking people according to their functions. The criteria of rank have changed along with values of society. "*Unstratified society with real equality of its members, is a myth that has never been realised in the history of mankind* — [*P.A. Sorokin*]. All societies exhibit some system of hierarchy whereby its members are placed in positions that are higher or lower, superior or 'inferior, in relation to each other. The concept of '*social stratification*' is made use of to refer to such classification or gradation and placement of people in society. Through this process of stratification people are *fixed* in the social structure of the society. Stratification assumes three main forms: caste, *estates and class*.

SOCIAL DIFFERENTIATION

Meaning and Causes of Social Differentiation

Society Rests on Differences

Everywhere individuals and societies differ. In no society people are absolutely equal in all respects. Differentiation is the keynote of human society. Society rests on the principle of difference. Differences are inherent in the very nature of the society. In all societies there is social differentiation of the population by *age, sex, occupation and personal characteristics*. There are the major factors of social differentiation Men and women, teenagers and adults, children and old men, masters and servants, managers and attendants, rulers and ruled, teachers and he taught, rich and the poor, literate and the illiterate, engineers and doctors, teachers and advocates, shopkeepers and hotel-owners are not always adjudged as equal. There are no equalitarian societies in the world. Societies are marked by differentiation. Societies may only differ in the *degree* of differentiation and '*nature* of stratification.

Differences in Different Fields

Some type of differentiation or specialisation of role is found in practically every society. It is clearly related to the rise and operation of social classes. In the *economic order*, differentiation is found in the different roles of entrepreneur, manager, and skilled and unskilled labourers. It is evident in the *professions*; in the *political order* as witnessed in the varying roles of public administrators, legislators, and judges; in *education* as between teachers and administrators; and in *religion*, as in the distinct roles of prophet, seer and priest. In reality, some form of specialisation of the role is found in every association of men.

Causes of Differentiation

Talcott Parsons mentions three causal factors of social differentiation — (*i*) *possession*, (*ii*) *qualities*, and (*iii*) *performance*. These three are, however, interrelated.

Possession refers to mainly material possessions, such as money, wealth, property, and all the other valuable, utilitarian material objects. People do not have equal access to these possessions. The unequal distribution of these material possessions has contributed to inequality and differentiation.

Qualities refers to the intrinsic capacities or abilities of people to undertake or to do a task. These qualities are also not equally distributed. For example, physical strength, intelligence, 'beauty', courage, loyalty to a cause, moral courage, industriousness, selflessness, sacrifice and other internal qualities are not equally distributed. People are ranked differently depending upon the degree of possession of these qualities.

Performance refers to the execution of a task in a given time under a given situation. Performances are always judged *first* according to their products or results. *Secondly*, they are judged according to the manner and style of the performing. Performances are always subject to regulatory norms, When the norms are violated, performances are often disvalued, regardless of their results.

Possessions, qualities and performances are closely related. Material possessions like wealth may help a man to develop his qualities which may better his performance. Similarly qualities may help a man to make possessions or to acquire material possessions. We should note that a person's qualities, possessions and performances are usually judged in relation to his age and with references to a particular social role. Not only persons but also groups are ranked according to the merit of their imputed qualities and performances. The term '*prestige*' is used to refer to the approval, respect, admiration, or deference a person or group is able to command by virtue of his or its imputed qualities or performances. The term '*ranking*' is generally used to refer to the degree of prestige. The term '*stratification*' denotes the process or condition in which layers [strata] of persons or groups are ranked differently. Any one stratum contains many persons or groups of roughly the same rank. Standards of evaluation vary from one social system to another, and from one situation to another within the same social system.

DISTRIBUTION OF DIFFERENCES IN SOCIETY ON THE BASIS OF AGE, SEX AND OCCUPATION

Differentiation Based on Sex

Differentiation based on Sex Differentiation based on sex is one of the most fundamental features of human society. There are only *two sexes*, *male* and *female*–not one, not three–and this is one of the brute facts of the universe. The existence of two sexes, a biological differentiation results in what is also one of the most important kinds of social differentiation. In no society males and females do the same things, occupy the same statuses, share identical interests, conform to the same norms, or aspire to the same kinds of achievement. All societies canalise the conduct of the sexes in different directions, just as they signalise the difference by the distinction in dress. No society treats its men and its women exactly alike. In all societies they think differently, and do different kinds of work. Some writers have even spoken of 'male culture' and 'female culture' to denote their diverse way of life. In any event, it is certain that the biological fact of sexual differentiations has manifold social consequences.

Sexual Differentiation is Cultural Also. It is wrong to presume that sexual differentiation is basically a biological and not a cultural one. It is cultural also. The male is not the dominant sex everywhere. There are communities wherein female is the dominant sex. In such communities women initiate sexual behaviour. They are the aggressors in courtship and they only make the marital decisions. In such communities prostitution is a male and not a female institution. If we are male, our society bends our conduct in one way; if we are female, in another. How much of this difference is due to nature, how much to culture? This question is answered differently by different thinkers.

Women: The Weaker Sex? The general belief everywhere is that man is the *dominant sex* and the woman is the *weaker sex*. The woman is called the *second sex*. The philosopher *Nietzsche* regarded women as the *'God's second mistake'*. *Robert Bierstedt writes*: 'In all societies it is woman who has been subject and slave; man who has been ruler and master. Woman is vessal, receptacle, utensil. She is conquered, subdued, vanquished, in sexual encounter as in life. Man takes, woman gives; man acts, woman waits'. *Plato* thanked God for he had been born free and not a slave and that he was a man and not a woman. *St. Paul* concluded that "*the man is not of the woman; but the woman of the man. Neither was the man created for the woman: but the woman for the man*".

It is significant to note that *women have greater immunity to diseases than men*. The rate of infant mortality is comparatively less in women than in men. In a way, man is a weaker sex. The general belief is that men are more intelligent and do greater achievements than women. *Robert Bierstedt writes that 'men of genuine distinction appear in positive profusion in comparison with women of distinction*'. *Margaret Mead* writes: 'A woman's life is punctuated by a series of specific events: the beginning of physical maturity the end of virginity, pregnancy and birth, and finally, the menopause... Sex in its whole meaning, from courtship through parenthood, means more to women than it does to men'. 'Indeed, a woman is always reminded that 'A woman can never forget her sex'.

Age Differentiation

All societies differentiate their members on the ground of age also. In no society the same norms govern the behaviour of the very young, the very old and the adult members in the same way. Age, as a biological factor contributes to social differentiation. *It distributes privileges and responsibilities, rights and duties*, in term of separate statuses. Age statuses, like sex statuses, are ascribed and not achieved. In almost all the societies the following age groups are recognised: 1. *Infancy*, 2. *Childhood*, 3. *Adolescence*, 4. *Adulthood*, and 5. *Old Age*. In some societies, the *unborn* and the *dead individuals* are also given some importance.

Age Grading. *Age stratification or age grading* is here in all the societies. Thus one has to attain a certain age in order to go to school, to join a church, to be considered responsible (or a 'major') in a court of law, to sign a valid contract, to be guilty of a crime, to vote, to marry, to earn a commission in the armed services, to sit in the Parliament, and so on through an entire roster of abilities and disabilities. We expect people to conform to the norms attached to their age statuses. We become surprised and sometimes shocked when deviations take place from this. When an old man marries a young woman, for example, or vice versa, we tend to respond with some discomfort. It becomes the 'new', it may become even scandal.

Age and Social Expectations. Further, our social expectations are also woven around different ages. We do not expect college students to be in their fifties, their professors in their teens. Workers may not like to have a 'boss' who is considerably younger to them. Definitely, certain ages are right for certain activities and wrong for others. We expect people to occupy certain statuses at definite stages in their lives. Seniority is a factor in all associational life, whether in business, the army, the university, or elsewhere.

Finally, people who associate with one another informally also tend to segregate themselves in terms of age. For the very young, a difference of a year to two is a very large difference. In a college a final year student, *i.e.*, a senior student may not like to have close friendship with the fresh students. Later on, differences in age often years or more may seem very little. Outside of families, intimacies rarely develop among people of different generations. The factor of age is rarely neglected in social intercourse. Neither can it be ignored in sociology. '*Like sex differentiation, it* (*age*) *is one of the ties that bind people together as well as one of the barriers that keep them apart'.–Robert Bierstedt.*

Occupational Differentiation

Age and sex differences are no doubt obvious foundations of specialisation everywhere. So *too different occupations create conditions for variation in roles and statuses*. At the same time, they foster *interdependence* also. An occupation is more than simply a way of earning money. It is an *index* and *symbol of the style* that people live and the *level of prestige* that is accorded to them by others. The concept of '*occupation*' is more or less appropriate for most modern industrialised societies. But it is less appropriate in many primitive and traditionalistic societies. In every society there is some degree for role differentiation according to function, whether this differentiation is 'occupational' or not. It is significant to note that occupation is the most used measure of class system.

Occupational Ranking. One of the best-known attempts to rank occupations in the U.S.A. was made by *P.K. Hatt* and *C. C. North*. In this test a nationwide sample of adults was asked to rate ninety occupations in accordance with prestige [associated with each occupation]. Thus, '*physician*' with the highest prestige occupation, and '*shoe shiner*' was the lowest. In between these came the other professional occupations, clerical and sales occupations, skilled and unskilled workers, etc.

Occupation and Prestige. There is no doubt that *occupations are related to social status* in advanced industrial societies. People in those societies perceive the prestige differences between occupations. Two factors seem to account for greater prestige of some occupations: (*i*) *The functional importance of an occupation to the social system in which it is rated: and* (*ii*) *the scarcity of personnel for the occupation relative to demand*. For example, the occupation of physicians is associated with higher prestige in many societies because of its importance and the scarcity of the physicians to meet societies' actual needs.

Income. Income is a factor in occupational prestige but it is not only factor. One of the tests conducted in U.S.A. has revealed that the majority of people rate occupational prestige not on the basis of money but on something else. It is found that factors such as *responsibility for public welfare and highly specialised training* influence the prestige of an occupation to a great extent.

Costumes. Occupational statuses are often symbolised by various kinds of *costume*. These vary all the way from the complete uniform to a distinctive kind of cap or hat. Policemen, priests and soldiers are, for example, easily distinguishable by differences in dress. In hospitals the white uniforms of the doctors and nurses prevent them from being mistaken for patients and visitors. Briefcases are status symbols for sales representatives, diplomats, professors and attorneys. Rank within an occupation, moreover, may also be designated by differences in dress and *badges* [as it is in the case of the army].

In the modem industrial societies the occupational roles are more complex and the functional expectations are more specifically stated. Occupations or jobs are ranked in terms of number of criteria such as *education qualifications, higher intelligence and skill, experience and difficulty of performance*.

SOCIAL STRATIFICATION

Meaning and Characteristics of Social Stratification

Differentiation is the law of nature. True, it is in the case of human society. Human society is not homogeneous but heterogeneous. Men differ from one other, in 'many respects. Human beings are equal so far as their bodily structure is concerned. But the physical appearance of individuals, their intellectual, moral, philosophical, mental, economic, religious, political and other aspects are different. *No two individuals are exactly alike*. Diversity and inequality are inherent in society. Hence, human society is everywhere stratified.

All societies arrange their members in terms of *superiority, inferiority*, and *equality*. *The vertical scale of evaluation, this placing of people in strata, or layers, is called stratification*. Those in the top stratum have more power, privilege and prestige than those below.

Society Compares and Ranks Individuals and Groups. Members of a group compare different individuals, as when selecting a mate, or employing a worker, or dealing with a neighbour, or developing friendship with an individual. They also compare groups such as castes, races, colleges, cities, athletic teams. These comparisons are valuations, and when members of a group agree, these judgements are *social evaluations*.

All societies differentiate members in terms of roles and all societies evaluate roles differently. Some roles are regarded as more important or socially more valuable than others. The persons who perform the more highly esteemed roles are rewarded more highly. Thus *stratification is simply a process of interaction of differentiation whereby some people come to rank higher than others*.

Definition of Social Stratification

1. *Ogburn and Nimkoff*: "The process by which individuals and groups are ranked in a more or less enduring hierarchy of status is known as stratification."
2. *Gisbert*: "Social stratification is the division of society into permanent groups of categories linked with each other by the relationship of superiority and subordination."
3. *Melvin M. Tumin*: Social stratification refers to "arrangement of any social group or society into a hierarchy of positions that are unequal with regard to power, property, social evaluation, and/ or psychic gratification."
4. *Lundberg*: "A stratified society is one marked by inequality, by differences among people that are evaluated by them as being lower' and 'higher"
5. *Raymond W. Murry*: "Social stratification is a horizontal division of society into 'high' and 'lower' social units".

The Universality of Social Stratification

Social stratification is ubiquitous. In all societies there is social differentiation of the population by age, sex, and personal characteristics. The roles and privileges of children differ from those of adults; and those of good hunters or Warriors differ from those of the rank and file. It is not customary to speak of a society as stratified if every individual in it has an equal chance to succeed to whatever statuses are open. Strictly speaking, there are no purely equalitarian societies, only societies differing in degree of stratification. Even Russia which dreamt of a 'classless society' could not, any more than any other society, escape the necessity of ranking people according to their functions. The criterion of rank have changed along with values of society. *P.A. Sorokin wrote in his 'Social Mobility' that 'Unstratified society with real equality of its members, is a myth which has never been realised in the history of mankind.'*

Social Differentiation and Stratification

As it is clear from the above, all societies exhibit some system of hierarchy whereby its members are placed in positions that are higher or lower, superior or inferior, in relation to each other. The two concepts–'*social differentiation*' and '*social stratification*'–are made use of to refer to such classification or gradation and placement of people in society. In **differentiation** society bases status on a certain kind of trait which may be (*i*) *physical* or *biological* such as skin-colour, physical appearance, age, sex, (*ii*) *social* and *cultural* such as differences in etiquettes, manners, values, ideals, ideologies, etc. Thus, differentiation serves as a sorting process according to which the people are graded on the basis of roles and status.

Stratification tends to *perpetuate* these differences in status. Hence, through this process people are fixed in the structure of the society. In some cases, [as it is in the case of caste] status may become hereditary. Differentiation may be considered the *first stage* preceding stratification in society, sorted and classified into groups. It does not, however, mean that all differentiation leads to stratification in society.

Characteristics of Social Stratification

According to *MM. Tumin* the main attributes of stratification are as follows:

1. ***It is social:*** Stratification is social in the sense, it *does not represent biologically caused inequalities*. It is true that such factors as strength, intelligence, age and sex can often serve as the basis on which statuses or strata are distinguished. But such differences by themselves are not sufficient to explain why some statuses receive more power, property, and prestige than others. Biological traits do not determine social superiority and inferiority until they are socially recognised and given importance. *For example*, the manager of an industry attains a dominant position not by his physical strength, nor by his age, but by having the socially defined traits. His education, training skills, experience, personality, character, etc. are found to be more important than his biological equalities.

   Further, as *Tumin* has pointed out, the stratification system is - (*i*) governed by social norm is and sanctions, (*ii*) is likely to be unstable because it may be disturbed by different factors, and (*iii*) is intimately connected with the other systems of society such as the political, family, religious, economic, educational and other institutions.

2. ***It is ancient:*** The stratification system is quite old. According to historical and archaeologi- cal records, stratification was present even in the small wandering bands. Age and sex were the main criterion of stratification then. '*Women and children last*' was probably the dominant rule of order. Difference between the rich and poor, powerful and humble, freemen and slaves was there in almost all the ancient civilisations. Ever since the time of *Plato* and *Kautilya* social philosophers have been deeply concerned with economic, social and political inequalities.
3. ***It is universal:*** The stratification system is a worldwide phenomenon. Difference between the rich and the poor or the 'haves' and the 'have nots' is evident everywhere. Even in the 'nonliterate', societies stratification is very much present. As *Sorokin* has said, all permanently organised groups are stratified.
4. ***It is in diverse forms:*** The stratification system has never been uniform in all the societies. The *ancient Roman society* was stratified into two strata: the patricians and the plebians, the *ancient Aryan society* into four Varnas: the Brahmins, Kshatriyas, Vaishyas and the Shudras, the ancient Greek Society into freemen and slaves; the *ancient Chinese society* into the mandarins, merchants, farmers and the soldiers and so on. Class, caste and estate seem to be the general forms of stratification to be found in the modem world. But stratification system seems to be much more complex in the civilised societies.
5. ***It is consequential:*** The stratification system has its own consequences. The most important, most desired, and often the scarcest things in human life are distributed unequally because of stratification. The system leads to two main kinds of consequences: (*i*) '*life chances*' and (*ii*) '*life- styles*'. '*Life-chances*' refer to such things as infant mortality, longevity, physical and mental illness, childlessness, marital conflict, separation and divorce. 'Life-styles' include such matters as–the mode of housing, residential area, one's education, means of recreation, relationships between the parents and children, the kind of books, magazines and TV shows to which one is exposed, one's mode of conveyance and so on. Life-chances are more involuntary, while life-styles reflect differences in preferences, tastes and values.

Origin of Social Stratification

There are two main theories concerning the origin of "social stratification": 1. *theory of economic determinism of Karl Marx, which is often referred to as the conflict theory, and* 2. *the functionalist theory*.

1. Theory of Economic Determinism or the Conflict Theory

According to *Marx*, economic factors are responsible for the emergence of different social strata or social classes. Therefore, social classes are defined by their relation to the means of production (*i.e.*, by their ownership or non-ownership). Thus, there are, in every society two mutually conflicting classes—the *class of the capitalists* and the *class of the workers* or *the rich and the poor*. Since these 'two classes have mutually opposite interests, conflicts between the two are inevitable–Marx maintained.

Gumplowicz and *Oppenheimer* and others have argued that the origin of social stratification is to be found *in the conquest of one group by another*. The conquering group normally dominates the conquered. The conquered group is forced to accept the lower status and lower class life. C. C. North also has expressed more or less the same opinion.

2. Functionalist Theory

Kingsley Davis, P.A. Sorokin, MacIver and others have rejected the conflict theory of Marx. Soronkin maintained that conflict may facilitate stratification but has never originated it. He attributed social stratification mainly to *inherited individual differences in environmental conditions*.

Kingsley Davis has stated that the stratification system is universal. According to him, it has come into being due to *the functional necessity of the social system*. The main functional necessity is "*the requirement faced by any society of placing and motivating individuals in the social structure....*" Social stratification is an unconsciously evolved device by which societies ensure that the most important positions are conscientiously filled by the most qualified persons.

The *Conflict Theory of Marx* emphasises conflict between large and stable groups, with strong community sentiments, while the *Functional Theory* emphasises the integrating function of social stratification based upon individual merit and reward. Both have their own merits and demerits.

Social Stratification and Social Mobility

Meaning of Social Mobility

Individuals are normally recognised through the statuses they occupy and the roles they enact. Not only the society is dynamic but also the individuals are dynamic. Men are normally engaged in endless endeavour to enhance their statuses in society, move from lower position to higher position, secure superior job from an inferior one. For various reasons people of higher status and position may also be forced to come down to a lower status and position. *Thus, people in society continue to move up down the status scale*. This movement is called '*social mobility*'.

'*Social mobility*' may be understood as the movement of people or groups from one social status or position to another status or position. *For example*, the poor people may become rich, the bank peons may become bank officers, farmers may become ministers, a petty businessman may become a big industrialist and so on. At the same time a big businessman may become a bankrupt and the ruling class may be turned out of office, and so on.

Kinds of Social Mobility

Social mobility is of two types: 1. *Vertical Social Mobility*, and 2. *Horizontal Social Mobility*.

1. **Vertical Mobility** refers to the movement of people of groups from one status to another. It involves change in class, *occupation or power*. *For example*, the movement of people from the poor class to the middle class, from the occupation of the labourers to that of the bank clerks, from the power position of the opposition to that of the ruling class.

2. **Horizontal Mobility** is a change in position without the change in status. It indicates a *change in position, within the range of the status*. For example, an engineer working in a factory may resign from his job and join another factory as an engineer and may work in more or less the same capacity. Similarly, a teacher may leave one school to join another as a teacher.

Social Mobility and Social Stratification

The nature, form, intensity and magnitude of social mobility depend on the nature and the type of social stratification. *Class* and *Caste* are the two main types of stratification. In both the systems same kinds of opportunities are not provided for social mobility. Because, in both the societies the factors that determine the statuses of the individuals differ radically. There is a close link between the way in which individuals obtain their statuses and the nature of social mobility. In the **caste system**, the status is determined by birth. Since birth cannot be changed, the status which is deter- mined on the basis of birth cannot be changed. For example, a Harijan cannot attain the status of a Vokkaliga, or Lingayat or Brahmin. Similarly, a Brahmin, born as a Brahmin, dies as a Brahmin. Caste-statuses cannot be changed. Hence, the caste as a form of social stratification does not facilitate vertical social mobility. It is for this reason the caste system is called a '*closed system*', and the caste-ridden Society, the '*immobile*' society.

In a **class system** opportunities are provided for social mobility. Here, the status is determined mainly by the talents, intelligence, wealth and achievements of the persons. The status is not ascribed by birth but '*achieved*' by individual attempts. *For example*, by his endless efforts and struggles a labourer may become the owner of a factory, a salesman of a business house, the owner of a business firm, and so on. There is scope for the improvement of the social status in the class system. Hence, the class system is called an '*open system*', and the open-class society, the '*mobile' society*.

As and when the society becomes more and more complex, and the life of its members improves, individuals may find better opportunities for the expression of their abilities and talents. But in no society all the deserving individuals can obtain statuses of their liking, desires and expectations. As *Sorokin* has pointed out in his "*Social Mobility*", only in an '*ideal*' society all the individuals get employments and statuses in accordance with their capacities. At the same time, it is not possible to make people to confine to their status when once they occupy or assume a status without going away from it, or changing it in any manner. *For example*, even in the so called '*immobile*' society like India, though a Harijan cannot change his caste-status, he can change his educational, economic, employment and political status. In this sense, there are no completely '*open*' and mobile societies and completely '*closed*' and '*immobile*' societies.

Principal Types of Social Stratification: Caste–Estates–Social Class

Sociologists have recognised three major types of social stratification: Caste, estates and social class. Of these, caste system with all its peculiar features is to be found in India only. Estate system as a kind of stratification system existed in Europe during the medieval period. But social classes are almost universal in nature. They are found in all the civilised, industrialised and literate societies of the world. These stratification systems decide largely the position that a man occupies in society. The extent of social mobility is mostly conditioned by them. The range of one's social contacts is almost fixed by one's caste or estate or class. They influence and condition the way of life of people or their 'life-styles' to a very great extent.

Functions of Social Stratification

The glimpse of the cultures of the world reveals that no society is '*classless*', that is, unstratified. All the known established societies of the world are stratified in one way or the other. According to *Wilbert Moore* and *Kingsley Davis*, stratification system came to be evolved in all the societies due *to the functional necessity*. As they have pointed out the main functional necessity of the system is: "*..... the requirement faced by any society of placing and motivating individuals in the social structure........ Social inequality is thus an unconsciously evolved device by which societies ensure that the most important positions are conscientiously filled by the most qualified persons*". As analysed by H.M. Johnson certain things here can be noted about the "functional necessity" of class stratification system.

1. ***Encourages hard work:*** One of the main functions of class stratification is to induce people- to work hard to live up to values. Those who best fulfil the values of a particular society are normally rewarded with greater prestige and social acceptance by others. It is known that occupations are ranked high if their functions are highly important and the required personnel is very scarce. Hard work, prolonged training and heavy burden of responsibility are associated with such occupational positions. People undertaking such works are rewarded with money, prestige, comforts, etc. Still we cannot say that all those positions which are regarded as important are adequately compensated for.
2. ***Ensures circulation of elites:*** To some extent class stratification helps to ensure what is often called "the circulation of the elite". When a high degree of prestige, comforts and other re- wards are offered for certain positions, there will be some competition for them. This process of competition helps to ensure that the more efficient people are able to rise to the top, where their ability can best be used.
3. ***Serves an economic function:*** The competitive aspect has a kind of economic function in that it helps to ensure the rational use of available talent. It is also functionally necessary to offer differential rewards if the positions at the top are largely ascribed as it is in the case of caste system. Even in caste system the people at the top can lose their prestige if they fail to maintain certain standards. Hence differential rewards provide the incentives for the upper classes to work at maintaining their positions.
4. ***Prevents waste of resources:*** The stratification system prevents the waste of scarce resources. The men in the elite class actually possess scarce and socially valued abilities and qualities, whether these are inherited or acquired. Because of their possession of these qualities their enjoyment of some privileges such as extra comfort and immunity from doing menial work, are functionally justified. It becomes functionally beneficial for the society to make use of their talents without being wasted. *For Example*, it would be a waste to pour the resources of society into the training of doctors and engineers, and then making them to work as peons and attendants. When once certain individuals are chosen and are trained for certain difficult positions it would be dysfunctional to waste their time and energy on tasks for which there is enough manpower.
5. ***Stabilises and reinforces the attitudes and skills:*** Members of a class normally try to limit their relations to their own class. More intimate relationships are mostly found between fellow class- members. Even this tendency has its own function. It tends to stabilise and reinforce the attitudes and skills that may be the basis of upper-class position. Those who have similar values and interests tend to associate comfortably with one another. Their frequent association itself confirms their common values and interests.

6. ***Helps to pursue different professions or jobs:*** The values, attitudes and qualities of different classes do differ. This difference is also functional for society to some extent. Because society needs manual as well as non manual workers. Many jobs are not attractive to highly trained or 'refined' people for they are socialised to aspire for certain other jobs. Because of the early influence of family and socialisation the individuals imbibe in them certain values, attitudes and qualities relevant to the social class to which they belong. This will influence their selection of jobs.
7. ***Social Control:*** Further, to the extent that 'lower class' cultural characteristics are essential to society, the classes are, of course, functional. In fact, certain amount of mutual antagonism between social classes is also functional. To some extent, upper-class and lower-class groups can act as negative reference groups for each other. Thus they act as a means of social control also.
8. ***Controlling effect on the 'shady' world:*** Class stratification has another social control function. Even in the 'shady' world of gamblers and in the underworld of lower criminals, black-marketeers, racketeers. smugglers, etc. the legitimate class structure has got respectability. They know that money is not a substitute for prestige but only a compensation for renouncing it. Hence instead of continuing in a profitable shady career, such people want to gain respectability for their money and for their children. They try to enter ligitimate fields and become philanthropists and patrons of the arts. Thus the legitimate class structure continues to attract the shady classes and the underworld. This attraction exerts a social control function.

SOME PRELIMINARY CONCEPTS: EQUALITY, INEQUALITY, HIERARCHY, EXCLUSION, POVERTY AND DEPRIVATION

Equality and Inequality

The study of social stratification is invariably associated with the concepts of *equality* and *inequality*, which in sociological context mean "*social equality*" and "*social inequality*". Both these concepts seem to be as old as social thought for they are inextricably linked with our value system. Human history is marked by endless efforts of a large number of social leaders and reformers who toiled and struggled to establish equality in society and to remove, or at least, reduce inequality. Despite their efforts, inequality still persists and establishment of equality remains an unfulfilled dream.

Concept Of Equality

"Equality" has been one of the cherished values of the people since times immemorial. Though some religious doctrines hold the view that all people are in some sense equal at birth, people have never been equal anywhere at any time in human history. Because, social inequality has been the fact of human group life. **J.J. Rousseau**, one of the intellectual brains behind the French Revolution of 1789, had recognized this fact when he said that "*men are born free and equal but everywhere they are in chains*." The quest for equality and the struggle against inequality and injustice continue even today.

Meaning of Equality

- *The term equality refers to "the state of being equal in some respect*"[1]
- *Equality or social equality refers to a condition in which members of a group or society have equal access to, or amounts of wealth, prestige, or power.*
- *Social equality exists when all people have equal access to, or share power*; *wealth* or *prestige*. Though the term 'equality' has political, legal and philosophical overtones, most of the sociological discussions have focused on equality as an aspect of social context. The lack of equality — that is, inequality — is 'a vital element in the discussions of social stratification and in any of its forms- caste, class, or estates system.

Greater Emphasis on Political Equality: Ever since the time of the French Revolution and the growth of liberal democracies in Europe, equality has usually been interpreted mostly as political equality. *For example*, liberal democracy assumes that equality means equality between individuals as citizens. Here, equality includes constitutional rights, that is, the right to a fair trial, the right to hold political office, the right to exercise all civic rights, etc.

Social Equality Emphasises the Fair Distribution of Income and Wealth: The liberal democratic concern with individual equality does not give prominence for equality of income and wealth. The critics have argued that the unequal distribution of income and wealth undermine all the other attempts at equality. Because, the holders of material wealth or

[1] Jary and Jary in *Collins Dictionary of Sociology*, p. 201.

resources, always have an advantage over other citizens. Sociologists have demonstrated how material resources affect people's life chances. For example, they have shown how material resources have been affecting child's progress in the educational system. Such an access to material resources also affects one's access to legal representation.

Five Different Models of Equality

Britain, which claims itself to be a welfare state, has been promoting equality by means of its social policies which have been considered to be equalitarian. **Le Grande** (1982) suggests five different models of equality in the context of social policies.[2] They are as follows.

1. ***Equality of public expenditure:*** Here, everyone receives the same amount of help and support from the public.
2. ***Equality of final income:*** Public resources are directed at those whose needs are found to be greater.
3. ***Equality of use:*** In this model, every one receives the same service irrespective of the expenses involved in providing such a service.
4. ***Equality of opportunity:*** This model refers to the idea that all per sons, regardless of class, age, race or gender should have equal rights to compete for all the desirable positions in society. The idea of equality of opportunity is the legacy of the French Revolution and strongly supported by liberalists.
5. ***Equality of outcome:*** Here, resources are provided so that everyone is equal after a service has been given. This notion of equality has been particularly developed in socialist political ideologies.

Equalitarian Objectives of Welfare Still Remain Unfulfilled

Various empirical researches have clearly shown that attempts to provide various social services to the needy people particularly in the fields of education, housing, health care, income maintenance, etc. inequalities have persisted and in some cases, actually increased. It is surprising to note that the western experience with the liberal democracies has revealed that the equalitarian objectives of welfare are not acceptable to the majority. In fact, that in many of the nations of the west such as U.I. (and U.S.A., "*governments holding the belief that the egalitarian objectives of welfare are wasteful and unfair*"[3] have been elected to power between 1970s and 1980s.

Concept of Social Inquality

Social inequality is as old as society and throughout history it has been a constant source of tension, conflict, violence, injustice, and oppression. In most societies, social inequality is built into the social structure in such a way that it is passed down from generation to generation. It is due to this fact whole categories of a population are denied a fair share of their society's resources right from the moment of their birth. Hence, fight fork equality and struggle against inequality have been the two important characteristic features of the social history of almost all societies.

Meaning of Inequality

- *Social inequality* refers to the " ....existence of unequal opportunities and rewards for different social positions or statuses within a group or society"[4]
- "*Social inequality exists when some people have a greater share of power, wealth or prestige than others*". — Ian Robertson, p. 213
- "*Social inequality exists when people have different access to social rewards such as money influence, or respect because of their personal or group characteristics*".

Some Salient Features of Social Inequality

1. ***Social inequality is the result of differentiation:*** All societies differentiate among their members. Some people who have certain characteristics are treated differently from other people. Every society for that matter differentiates between the old and the young and between males and females. Society treats its members in different ways on various grounds such as *skin colour; religion, physical strength, or educational achievement.* The result of this differentiation is nothing but inequality.

[2] Views of Le Grande as quoted in *Collins Dictionary of Sociology*, p. 202.
[3] *Collins Dictionary of Sociology*. p. 202.
[4] William P. Scott in *Dictionary of Sociology*, p. 201.

2. ***Social inequality is Universal:*** In no society of the world all people have equal recognition. It is in this simple sense, inequality is universal in human societies. Thus, in all societies known to us, large or small, modern or extinct, there have been distinct differences in the statuses of the individual members. Social inequality is apparent when a society values males over females, the rich over the poor, Christians over Muslims, or Brahmins over the Dalits or Whites over Blacks, and so on. It goes without telling that those with the higher status have a superior access to whatever rewards the society offers. At the same time, those with the lower status are deprived of these advantages.
3. ***Social inequality is normally built into the social structure:*** In all the modem societies, social inequality takes a much elaborate and structured form in which different categories of people have different statuses. In these societies, inequality is built into the social structure, and unequal statuses are passed down from generation to generation. Like the layers of rock, people in these societies are grouped into "strata". People in any one stratum have a different access to social rewards than people in any other stratum, so the society as a whole is said to be stratified.
4. ***Social inequality is a source of social conflict and social change:*** Inequality is one of the most pressing social problems of the present day society as it has been so right from the beginning of history. Throughout history, social inequality has been a source of tensions, revolutions and social change. It has generated bloody conflict between slave and master, peasant and noble, worker and capitalist, poor and rich. Ever since Karl Marx brought the issue of social inequality to the fore front of political debate with his Communist Manifesto in 1848, these tensions and conflicts have assumed I global importance. Social inequality is strongly related to various other problems of our society such as – social instability, economic ups and downs, political conflicts, potential violence, status insecurities, fear and uncertainties, and so on.
5. ***Social inequalities are normally sustained by the power of ideas:*** It is significant to note that "*social inequalities are rarely maintained primarily through force. Instead, they are sustained by the power of ideas. Members of both the dominant and sub-ordinate groups are inclined to accept unquestioningly the ideologies, or sets of ideas that justify the inequalities and make them seem "natural" and even moral*"[5] For example, the sex roles in our society show how traditional roles have ensured the dominance of men over women. Similarly, the caste roles in India reveal that normally the upper castes tend to dominate the lower castes by virtue of their traditionally ascribed superior status.
6. ***Social inequalities are not necessarily based on natural or biological inequalities:*** Many stratification systems are accompanied by beliefs which state social inequalities are biologically based. *For example*, Whites claim biological superiority over Blacks, and see this as the basis for their dominance. Similarly, followers of Adolf Hitler in Germany believed in the inborn superiority of the people of Aryan race. In India also, the higher castes claimed biological superiority over the untouchable castes. "*The question of the relationship between biologically based and socially created inequality has proved extremely difficult to answer. ...*" "Rousseau *believed that biologically based inequalities between men were small and relatively unimportant whereas socially created inequalities provide the major basis for systems of social stratification. Most sociologists would support this view.*" [6]

The beliefs that social inequalities are caused by natural or biological inequalities seem to serve as rationalizations to justify the stratification system. The beliefs serve to make social inequality appear rational and reasonable.

Currently, the existence of inequality, its causes and consequences as related to social class, genders, ethnicity, and even region or locality, continues to assume sociological prominence.

Concept Of Hierarchy

The term "**hierarchy**" refers to a gradational or a ranking system. This term is very commonly used in the discussions of social stratification for it signifies that individuals and groups in any society are not socially treated equally but graded differently. The concept of hierarchy denotes that people in a society are graded or ranked differently depending upon the type of the statuses that they occupy.

- Hierarchy refers to "*Any relationship of individuals, groups, or classes involving a system of ranking*".
- Hierarchy refers to "*ranking of statuses within an organization according to some criterion of evaluation accepted as relevant within the system*". — W.P. Scott, p. 186

[5] Ian Robertson in *Sociology*, p. 213.
[6] M. Haralambos and R.M Heald, p. 27.

Usage of the Concept of Hierarchy in the Analysis of Social Stratification

Any system, social or otherwise, is said to be hierarchical or gradational in nature if it consists of different strata or layers one on top of another. The more hierarchical a system is, the greater the number of layers and, generally, the greater the distance between the top and bottom are found.

Hierarchy is an important concept because, by making use of the hierarchical principle it is comparatively easier to trace out the relative status or position of an individual or group in a particular society. Thus, it is through the principle of hierarchy, we can say, that in a caste system, the Brahmins as a caste group occupy the top-most position enjoying the privileges associated with it, while the untouchable castes occupy the bottom most position suffering from all the disabilities related with it. A large number castes, often referred to as '*intermediary castes*' occupy different positions which lie in between these two extreme positions. Similarly, class system, is also hierarchical in which the capitalists and the rich occupy the top position in the hierarchy while the workers and the poor occupy the bottom most position. The position in between these two is occupied by the middle class. Sociologists have also spoken of a six-fold division of class hierarchy.

Hierarchy and its Relations with Power and Authority

The principle of hierarchy is also important in the area of operation of power and authority. Normally, power and authority flow from higher level to lower level as we witness it in all types of bureaucracies. The exercise of power and authority and the control of people and resources become organized in a hierarchical way. The higher the position of an individual in the hierarchy, the greater the power and control of resources that he has access to and vice versa. This kind of hierarchical principle can be seen in virtually every area of social life, from politics and economics to religion and education.

Concept of Social Exclusion

- Social exclusion refers to – "*A process by which individuals or households experience deprivation, either of resources such as income, or of social links to the wider community or society*" — Oxford Dictionary of Sociology, p. 212.
- "*Social exclusion refers to the ways in which individuals may become cut off" from full involvement in the wider community.*"

During the 1980s, the concept of social exclusion came to be used increasingly along with that of poverty especially in the discussion of social policy in Europe. It is commonly used to refer to some cluster of social problems associated with unemployment, low income, poor housing, deficient health, or social isolation.

Nature of Social Exclusion

Social exclusion indicates deprivation of opportunities: The concept focuses attention on a broad range of factors that prevent individuals or groups from having opportunities open to majority of the population. It indicates that some are denied of having access to essential goods and services such as education, health, transportation, insurance, social security, banking and even access to the police or judiciary. It is not enough if individuals are just provided with food, clothing and shelter. A fuller and an active involvement in life demands greater freedom and better access to all the essentials of civilized life on par with all the others in the society.

Social exclusion is not accidental: Social exclusion in most of the cases, is found to be an in-built mechanism to deprive a few of their social rights. It is the result of the structural features of society. The 'untouchables' in India, were excluded from doing many things, for example, entering temples, sharing food along with higher caste people, drawing water from public wells, receiving education on par with others, etc. as a matter of caste rule.

Social exclusion is involuntary: Social exclusion is practiced regardless of the wishes of those who are excluded. In the case of the untouchables of India, for example, it is thrusted upon them. They are prevented from having access to something desirable, say for example, having access to education, or entering religious institutions, etc.

Prolonged exclusion leading to a reaction against inclusion: Prolonged experience of discrimination and insult underwent by an excluded group often compels it to develop a reaction against inclusion. As a result, it may stop making attempts for inclusion. For example, the denial of temple entry for the *dalits* in India for decades together by the upper castes, may ultimately compel the *dalits* to build their own temple, or to convert to another religion like Buddhism, Christianity, or Islam. When once they start doing it, they may no longer desire to be included in the Hindu temple or religious events. [However, it cannot be concluded that all the excluded would think and act on the same line.] Instances of this kind point out that social exclusion occurs regardless of the wishes of the excluded.

Three Broad Overlapping Usages of the Concept

1. ***Social exclusion in relation to social rights:*** This usage refers to the context in which people are prevented from exercising their rights due to certain barriers or processes.
2. ***Social exclusion in relation to social isolation:*** This usage throws light on the context in which some people or some section of the population is kept away or distanced from others in most of the social dealings. Example: Practices of social discrimination and exclusion during the British rule in South Africa which led to the social isolation of the natives.
3. ***Social exclusion in relation to marginalisation:*** This usage refers to the social exclusion of the extreme kind in which some are denied of opportunities and avenues under the pretext of educational credentials, party membership, skin colour, religious identity, proper manners and style of life, social origins, etc.

Exclusion is not Always Deprivation and Inclusion is not Always Justice

It is a common practice to equate exclusion with inequality, deprivation, unfairness and injustice; and inclusion with equality, fairness and justice. In our practical life this is not necessarily so. There are situations in which even inclusion would lead to painful experiences. For example, after successfully fighting against exclusions and discriminations, some women members may be recruited as employees to a men-dominated company. After getting included or recruited also these women may find it highly embarrassing to work in the company which is dominated by men who are not that co-operative.

Concept Of Poverty

Poverty is a social problem and it is one of the manifestations of inequality. The study of poverty is central to any examination of social equality, including an analysis of who is poor and the reasons for their poverty.

- Poverty refers to "*A low standard of living that lasts long enough to undermine the health, morale, and self-respect of an individual or group of individuals*". **W.P. Scott** - Page: 307.
- Poverty refers to "*A state in which resources, usually material but sometimes cultural, are lacking*" – "*Oxford Dictionary of Sociology*" – 516.
- "*Poverty is insufficient supply of those things which are requisite for an individual to maintain himself and those dependent upon him in health and vigour*"- **Goddard**.

Absolute Poverty and Relative Poverty

The term poverty is relative to the general standard of living in the society, the distribution of wealth, the status system, and social expectations. It is common to distinguish between absolute and relative definitions of poverty.

1. ***Absolute poverty*:** Poverty defined in absolute terms refers to a state in *which the individual lacks the resources necessary for subsistence.*
2. ***Relative poverty*:** Relative definitions of poverty, frequently favoured by sociologists, refers to t*he individual's or group is lack of resources when compared with that of other members of the society – in other words, their relative standard of living.*

Absolute poverty is often known as "subsistence poverty" for it is based on assessment of minimum subsistence requirements such as food, clothing, shelter, health care, etc. … Subsistence definitions of poverty [or definitions of absolute poverty] are of considerable value in examining, Third World poverty. International studies show that the overall level of poverty measured in subsistence terms is very high. Some studies suggest that almost half of those in low-income countries live in absolute poverty. Even in India, poverty is still posing a challenge. As per poverty projection made for the year 2007 by the Planning Commission of India, 220 million people [that is, 19.3% of the population] live below the poverty line. [For more details on Poverty, please read Chapter on "The Problem of Poverty."]

Concept Of Deprivation

"**Deprivation**" is one of the concepts closely associated with the discussions of social inequality. Sociological analysis defines deprivation broadly as inequality of access to social goods. It includes poverty and wider forms of disadvantage.

- "*In general, deprivation refers to a condition in which people lack what they need.*" — **The Blackwell Dictionary of Sociology** - Page - 77.

- Deprivation refers to " .... *the lack of economic and emotional supports generally accepted as basic essentials of human experience. These include income and housing, and parental care for children.*" - **Collins Dictionary of Sociology** – 159.

The above mentioned definitions make it clear that some human needs [such as income, care, shelter and security] are very basic and their fulfilment leads to fuller and more comfortable life experience. Satisfactory fulfilment of these needs is believed to contribute to more complete development of the individual's potential.

Absolute Deprivation and Relative Deprivation

Like the notion of poverty, deprivation can be viewed in absolute or relative terms.

- ***Absolute deprivation*** refers to the lack of life necessities such as food, water, shelter and fuel. It means the loss or absence of the means to satisfy the basic needs for survival— food, clothing and shelter.
- ***Relative deprivation*** refers to deprivations experienced when individuals compare themselves with others. In this case, individuals who lack something compare themselves with those who have it, and in so doing feel a sense of deprivation. Consequently, relative deprivation not only involves comparison, it is also usually defined in subjective terms. The concept is intimately linked with that of "reference group" – the group with whom the individual or set of individuals compare themselves.

Deprivation disadvantage is measured not by objective standards but by comparison with the relatively superior advantages of others, such as members of reference group with whom one desires to emulate. Thus, the mere millionaire can feel relatively disadvantaged among his multi-millionaire friends.

The concept of relative deprivation has been used in the study of social movements and revolutions, where it is argued that relative, not absolute deprivation is most likely to lead to pressure for change. The term "relative deprivation" was originally used by **Samuel A. Stouffer** in the classic socio-psychological study "*The American Soldier*" [1950].

REVIEW QUESTIONS

1. What is social differentiation? Write its causes.
2. Define social stratification and write its characteristic features. What are the principal types of social stratification?
3. Throw light on the origin of social stratification. Discuss the theories concerning the origin of social stratification.
4. Analyse the functions of social stratification.
5. Define social mobility. Discuss the kinds of social mobility.
6. Write short notes on the following:
   (a) Differentiation in society
   (b) Causes of differentiation
   (c) Social differentiation and stratification
   (d) Social mobility and social stratification
   (e) Principal types of social stratification
   (f) Occupational differentiation
7. Give the meaning of equality. Discuss its different models.
8. Define social inequality. Highlight the salient features of social inequality.
9. What is hierarchy? Assess its relation with power and authority.
10. Explain the concept of social exclusion. Discuss the nature and usages of social exclusion.
11. What do you mean by poverty? Differentiate between absolute poverty and relative poverty.
12. Give the definition of deprivation. How does absolute deprivation differ from relative deprication?
13. Write a short note on subsistence poverty.

⌘⌘⌘⌘⌘⌘⌘⌘⌘⌘⌘⌘

23

CASTE—ESTATES—CLASS

CHAPTER OUTLINE

- Caste System
- Meaning and Characteristics
- Changes in Caste System During the British Rule
- Caste in Independent India
- Merits and Demerits of Caste
- Merits and Demerits of Caste System
- Estates System
- Social Class: Nature and Characteristics
- Criterion of Class
- Differences between Caste and Class
- Marxian Analysis of Class

Caste and class are the two main forms of *social stratification*. Both are the agencies of social mobility and selection. They decide largely the position that a man occupies in society. The range of one's social contracts is almost fixed by one's status in society. One's status is recognised mainly through one's caste or class. If the caste system is unique to India the class system is universal in nature. Both of them influence and condition the way of life or the '*life-styles*' of people to a very large extent. The caste system is the basis of stratification in India whereas the class system constitutes the basis of the stratification system in the western society.

CASTE SYSTEM

Caste System is Unique to India

The caste system, the joint family system and the village system of life — are often regarded as the three basic pillars of the Indian social system. The caste system as a form of social stratification is peculiar to India. The caste is an inseparable aspect of the Indian society. It is peculiarly Indian in origin and development. There is no comparable institution elsewhere in the world for the caste system. Still traces of caste were found in Ancient Egypt, Japan, Rome, Burma and Persia. It is said that even the ancient Persians, Siberians, Etruscans, Mexicans, Peruvians and Spartans had their own type of caste system. Some systems resembling caste are found at present in Burma, Polynesia, Massai and Somali of East Horn. But the caste system which we understand today with all its peculiarities is found in India alone.

Caste is Embedded in the Indian Social Structure

Caste is closely connected with the Hindu philosophy and religion, customs and tradition, marriage and family, morals and manners, food and dress habits, occupations and hobbies. The caste system is believed to have had a *divine origin* and *sanction*. It is endlessly supported by rituals and ceremonies. It is a deep-rooted and a long-lasting social institution of India. India is a classical land of the caste. It is here, in India, we find more than 2800 castes and sub-castes with all their peculiarities. Of these, the major caste (previously known as varnas) such as Brahmins, Kshatriyas, Vaishyas and Shudras (or depressed caste) are found in almost all the states. But none of these castes is numerically dominant in any of the states of India.

Origin of the Word 'Caste'

The term '*caste*' is derived from the Spanish (also Portuguese) word '*caste*' meaning '*breed*' or '*lineage*'. The Protuguese used the term '*caste*' first to denote the divisions in the Indian caste system. The word '*caste*' also signifies '*race*' or '*kind*'. The Sanskrit word for caste is '*Varna*' which means '*colour*'. Races and colour seem to be the bases of Indian caste in addition to the division of labour and occupation. The popular equivalent of caste is '*Jati*'.

Origin of Caste System

The caste stratification of the Indian Society has had its origin in the '*Chaturvarna*' system. According to the Chaturvaena doctrine, the Hindu society was divided into four main varnas namely: the Brahmins, the *Kashtriyas*, the *Vaishyas*, and the *Shudras*. The Varna system which was prevalent during the Vedic period was mainly based on the *division of labour and occupation*. The Caste system owes its origin to the Varna system. The present caste system can be said to be the degenerated form of the origional Varna system. Varnas which were four in number and castes which are found in hundreds and thousands are not one and the same.

Factors Which Facilitated the Growth of Caste System in India

Among the factors that have facilitated the continued existence and growth of the caste system, the following are the most important:

1. The *geographic isolation* of the Indian Peninsula for a long time made the people to foster old customs, mores, traditions and superstitious beliefs which in turn encouraged the caste system to grow.
2. The *influence of religion* is one of the main factors that caused the continuation of the caste system. The Hindu Caste system is looked upon as a divine ordained institution. Beliefs in reincarnation and the doctrine of Karma also further strengthened the caste system.
3. The existence of *many races* in the country led to the formulation of many strict laws concerning discrimination since each race endeavoured to maintain its purity.
4. The *rural social structure* has its own impact on the caste. The unchanging, static rural social structure of India favoured the growth of caste system.
5. The *unwillingness of rulers* to enforce a uniform standard of law and custom and their readiness to recongnise the varying customs of different groups as valid, also facilitated the growth of caste system.
6. *Lack of education* has contributed in no small measure to the growth of caste system. Illiteracy and ignorance have made the people to become orthodox and to implicitly accept the caste rules and restrictions;
7. Further, factors such as the *hereditary occupations: the desire of the Brahmins to keep themselves pure: ideas of exclusive family, ancestor worship, the sacramental meal, the deliberate economic and administrative policies followed by the various conquerors, particularly the British, clash of races, colour prejudices and conquest*, etc., also have contributed to the growth of caste system in India.

DEFINITION AND CHARACTERISTICS OF CASTE

Definition of Caste

'Caste' is so complex a phenomenon which is difficult to define. Writers and thinkers are not unanimous in their opinion regarding caste, its definition and characteristics. Hence caste has been defined variously.

1. *Sir Herbert Risely*: Caste is a "collection of families, bearing a common name, claiming a common descent, from a mythical ancestor, human and divine, professing to follow the same hereditary calling and regarded by those who are competent to give an opinion as forming a single homogeneous community."
2. *MacIver* and *Page*: "When status is wholly predetermined so that men are born to their lot without any hope of changing it, then the class takes the extreme form of caste."
3. *C.H. Cooley*: "When a class is somewhat strictly hereditary, we may call it a caste."
4. *A. W. Green*: "Caste is a system of stratification in which mobility up and down the status ladder, at least ideally may not occur".
5. *Ketkar*: "A caste is a group having two characteristics; (*i*) membership is confined to those who are born of members and includes all persons so born, (*ii*) the members are forbidden by an inexorable social law to marry outside the group."
6. *D.N. Majumdar* and *T.N. Madan* have said that caste is a 'closed group'.

Characteristics of Caste

The caste system is highly complex in nature. As *Dr. G.S. Ghurye* says, any attempt to define caste is 'bound to fail because of the complexity of the phenomenon.' He describes the characteristics of caste in his '*Caste and Class in India*' 1950-56 [also in his *Caste, Class and Occuption-1961 and Caste and Race in India-1970*]. The following have been the main traditional features of the caste system.

1. ***Caste: As a hierachical division of society:*** The Hindu society is gradational one. It is divided into several small groups called castes and subcastes. A sense of 'highness' and 'lowness' or 'superiority' and 'inferiority' is associated with this gradation or ranking. The Brahmins are placed at the top of the hierarchy and are regarded as '*pure*', supreme or superior. The degraded caste or the so called '*untouchables*' [Harijans] have occupied the other end of the hierarchy. All over India neither the supremacy of the Brahmins nor the degraded position of the Harijans or 'outcastes' has been questioned. It is taken for granted, but regarding the exact position of the intermediary castes there are disputes on the part of the members.

2. ***Caste:*** As a Segmental Division of Society. The Hindu society is a caste-ridden society. It is divided into a number of segments called 'castes'. It is not a homogeneous society. Castes are groups with defined boundary of their own. The status of an individual is determined by his birth and not by selection nor by accomplishments. No amount of power, prestige and pelf can change the position of man. The membership of the caste is hence *unchangeable, unacquirable, inalienable, unattainable* and *nontransferable*. Further, each caste in a way, has its own way of life. Each caste has its own customs, traditions, practices and rituals. It has its own informal rules, regulations and procedures. There were caste councils or '*caste panchayats*' to regulate the conduct of members also. The caste used to help its members when they were found in distress. Indeed, '*the caste was its own ruler*'.

   Caste Panchayat: During the early days in every village every caste used to have its own caste *Panchayat*. It consisted of five chosen members who enjoyed much social privilege and respect. The caste panchayat used to perform a number of *functions*. It used to make the members comply with caste rules and regulations. Settling caste disputes and giving its final verdict on the issues referred to it, were also its other functions. It was giving punishments to those who violated caste rules and obligations. Matters such as–breaking the marriage promise, refusal on the part of the husband to take the wife to his house, cruelty to wife, adultery on the part of wife, killing the cows, insulting the Brahmins, having illicit sex relations with other caste people, etc., were dealt with by the panchayat. It was giving *punishments* such as—arranging dinner party for the fellow caste-men, imposing fine, purification, pilgrimage, outcasting etc., for the offenders. The caste panchayat was also striving to promote the welfare of the caste members. Safeguarding the interests of the caste members was yet another function of the panchayat. These caste panchayats have become weak and ineffective now-a-days.

   The castes and subcastes together make up the Hindu social system. Still in some respects each is isolated from the other. It is in a way *semisovereign*. The castes are a '*complete world*' in themselves for their members. The members are expected to be loyal to the caste. Caste feeling is hence very strong. It is very much stronger in rural areas than in the urban area. It is because of this the amount of community-feeling is restricted.

3. ***Restrictions on food habits:*** The caste system has imposed certain restrictions on the food habits of the members, they differ from caste to caste. *Who* should accept *what* kind of food and from *whom*?–is often decided by the caste. For example, in North India, a Brahmin would accept '*pakka*' food [cooked in ghee] only from some castes lower than his own. But he would accept '*kachcha*' food {prepared with the use of water] at the hands of no other caste except his own. As a matter of rule and practice, no individual would accept '*kachcha*' food prepared by an inferior caste man. Generally, any kind of food that is prepared by the Brahmins is acceptable to all the caste people. This factor explains as to why the Brahmins dominated the hotel industry for a long time. Further, restrictions are also there still on the use of certain vegetables for certain castes. Even today, some traditional Brahmins do not consume onions, garlic, cabbage, carrot, beatroot, etc. Eating beef is not allowed except for the Harijans.

4. ***Restrictions on social relations:*** The caste system puts restrictions on the range of social relations also. The idea of '*pollution*' makes this point clear. It means a *touch of a lower caste man* (*particularly Harijan*) *would pollute or defile a man of higher caste*. Even his shadow is considered enough to pollute a higher caste man. In Kerala for a long time, a Nayar could approach a *Nambudari* Brahamin but would not touch him. Further, a *Tiyan* was expected to keep himself at a distance of 36 steps from the Brahmin and a pulaya at a distance of 96 paces. In Tamilnadu the *Shanar* toddy tapper was expected to keep a distance of 24 paces while approaching a Brahmin. This has resulted in the *practice of untouchability*. This practice has made the lower caste people to be segregated completely from the higher caste.

5. ***Social and religious disabilities of certain castes:*** In the traditional caste society some lower caste people [particularly, the Harijans] suffered from certain civil or social and religious disabilities. Generally, the *impure* castes are made to live on the outskirts of the city or the village. In south India, certain parts of the towns or the villages are not accessible to the Harijans. It is recorded that during the *Peshwa rule* in Maharashtra the *Mahars* and *Mangs* were not allowed within the gates of Poona before 9.00 A.M. and after 3.00 P.M. The reason was during that time their bodies would cast too long shadows which, if they were to fall on the Brahmins, would defile them.
   Socially, Harijans or the so called 'untouchables' are separated from other members. Even today, in many places they are not allowed to draw water from the public wells. During the early days, public places like hotels, hostels, public lecture halls, schools, temples, theatres were not kept open for the lower caste people. Entrance to temples and other places of religious importance was forbidden for them. Educational facilities, legal rights and political representation were denied to them for a long time. In South India, restrictions were placed on the mode of constructing houses of the lower caste people, and their types of dresses and patterns of ornamentation. The toddy-tappers of Malabar were not allowed to carry umbrellas, to wear shoes or golden ornaments and to milk cows. They were forbidden to cover the upper part of their body.
6. ***The civil and religious privileges of certain castes:*** If the lower caste people suffer from certain disabilities, some higher caste people like the Brahmins enjoy certain privileges. Nowhere the Brahmins suffered from the disabilities cited above. They are given more liberty, because they are believed to be born '*pure*' and '*superior*'. The Brahmins never saluted others, but they always had the privilege of being saluted by others. They never even bowed to the idols of the lower caste people. Education and teaching were almost the monopoly of the higher caste people. Chanting the Vedic Mantras was great privilege of the Brahmins. The upper caste people in general, enjoyed social, political, legal and religious privileges.
7. ***Restrictions on occupational choice:*** In the caste-ridden society there is a *gradation of occupations* also. Some occupations are considered to be *superior* and *sacred* while certain others *degrading* and *inferior*. For a long time, occupations were very much associated with the caste system. Each caste had its own specific occupation. The caste members were expected to continue the same occupations. Occupations were almost *hereditary*.
   Weaving, shoe-making, oil-grinding, sweeping, scavenging, curing, hides tanning, washing clothes, barbering, pottery, etc., were considered to be somewhat '*degrading*'. Learning, priesthood, teaching were the prestigious professions which mostly the Brahmins pursued. Individual talents, aptitudes, interests, enterprise, abilities, and achievements were neglected. But agriculture, trade and labouring in the field were thrown open to all the castes. At the same time, no caste would allow its members to take up to any profession which was either degrading or impure.
8. ***Restrictions on marriage:*** The caste system imposes restrictions on marriage also. *Caste is an endogamous group.* Endogamy is a rule of marriage according to which an individual has to marry within his or her group. Each caste is subdivided into several subcastes, which are again endogamous. *For example*, Iyers, Iyengars, Smarthas, Madhvas, Having Brahmins, Kota, Shivalli, Kandavara Brahmins, etc., are all Brahmin subcastes which are endogamous. Similarly, the Vokkaliga caste consists of Morasu, Hallikar, Nonaba, Gangadiga and other subcastes. According to the rule of endogamy a Shivalli Brahmin, for example, has to marry a Shivalli girl, an Iyengar; an Iyengar girl and so on. Intercaste marriages were strictly forbidden then. Even at present, intercaste marriages have not become popular. Violation of the rule of endogamy was strictly dealt with during the early days. This rule of endogamy has resulted in close in-breeding. Some writers like *Hutton* have re- garded endogamy as the very essence of the caste system. Exception to this rule of endogamy is seen in places like the hill parts of Punjab and also in Malabar. The Caste provides for some kind of exogamous marriages also. They can be briefly examined here.

Sapinda and Sagotra Exogamy: Sapinda and Sagotra marriages have been generally forbidden by the upper castes and Sapinda and Sagotra exogamous marriages have been insisted upon.

Sapinda Exogamy: In Hindu society marriage within the '*Pinda*' is prohibited. Pinda means common parentage. According to *Brahaspathi*, offsprings from five maternal generations and *seven* paternal generations are '*Sapinda*' and they cannot intermarry. This opinion, however, is not universally accepted. Though certain exceptions are there in South India, in North India, generally, Sapinda marriages do not take place. But Sapinda exogamy, that is, marrying outside one's pinda is commonly found.

Sagotra Exogamy: Sagotra exogamy, that is, marrying outside one's own '*gotra*' is very much prevalent among the upper caste such as Brahmins and Kshatriyas. Marriage within the gotra is prohibited. This restriction has been imposed since people of one gotra are believed to have similar blood. Similarly, *Sapravara* marriages are also forbidden especially for the Brahmins. Persons be- longing to the same pravara cannot intermarry. People who utter the name of a common saint at religious functions are believed to belong to the same pravara. The pravara is a kind of religious and spiritual bond. *Sapravara exogamy*, that is, marrying outside one's own pravara, has been imposed as a rule for the upper castes, especially for the Brahmins.

CHANGES IN THE CASTE SYSTEM

The caste system which is an integral part of the Indian system, has a long standing history or its own. To understand how the system has come to be what it is today, one has to go back through the pages of history to trace its origin, evolution and growth. It is not easy to say precisely when, how and under what circumstances and pressures the system took its birth and developed. The task of tracing the evolution and growth of this system in precise and unambiguous terms is equally problematic. For the purpose of study three main stages in the evolution of caste may be identified. They are mentioned below:

1. ***Caste in ancient age*** [The period upto 1100 A.D. which is inclusive of Vedic Age, Post- Vedic Age and Puranic Age].
2. ***Caste in medieval age*** [The period between 1100 A.D. and 1757 A.D. which includes mainly the age of Muslim Rule in India].
3. ***Caste in modern age*** [The period after 1757 A.D. which includes the Pre-Independent British period and the period after Independence].

It is not within the framework of this book to discuss in detail the developments which took place in the caste system during the first two major periods. Hence the description is confined to the 'third stage, that is, Caste in Modern Age.

CASTE IN MODERN AGE [AFTER 1757 A.D.]

The modern period in which some major developments took place in caste system can be divided into two stages namely: 1. Caste during British rule, and 2. Caste in Independent India.

Changes in Caste System During the British Rule

Prior to the coming of the British, caste had grown into a powerful social institution, with the dominance of Brahmins at the top of its hierarchy. The Hindu kings also upheld this institution with the help of their civil power. With the advent of the British as the political head of the society, the traditional form of the caste started taking a different shape.

The British Intention was to Rule and Not to Initiate Reformative Chances

The British brought with them their own traditional form of government which was quite different from that of the indian monarchical system. But as Christians the British "*...could not have much sympathy with the institutions of the Hindus*" - [*Ghurye*: Page - 270]. As prudent foreigners they were more interested in consolidating their power over a strange land and people rather than initiating reformative changes in its peculiar institutions such as "caste". They introduced a system of education which did not demand of the learners any change of caste or religion. *The policy of comparative non-interference* followed by the British made the lower castes revolt against the Brahmin spremacy. *Growth of modern industrial organisation and the rapid spread of urbanisation* further altered the social situation. This situation made it inevitable for people of different castes, classes and religions to live in close congregations in cities. With this background the changes in the caste system during the British rule can be studied in two stages: (*A*) *Pre-Industrial British Period 1757-1918 A.D., and* (*B*) *Pre-Independent Industrial Period - 1918-1947 A.D.*

Pre-Industrial British Period [from 1757 to 1918 A.D.]

The *East India Company* of the British obtained from the Moghal rulers some commercial privileges in the beginning of the l7th century. It tightened its political hold over the Whole of India within 7 to 8 decades. The appointment of *Warren Hastings* in 1774 as the first Governor General of India, marked the beginning of the British Age in India.

1. ***Declining hold of the caste panchayats:*** After consolidating their power the British introduced throughout India *uniform legal, legislative and judicial systems*. The British transferred the judicial powers of the caste councils to the civil and criminal courts which affected the authority which the Panchayats had held over the members. Questions of assault, adultery, rape and the like were taken before the British Courts for decision. In civil matters such as marriage, divorce, caste-based occupational disputes, disputes between husband and wife, parents and children etc., the intention of the British was to be guided by the caste customs. But in actual practice various decisions of the High Courts virtually set aside the authority of the caste.
2. ***Influence of social legislation on caste:*** Some of the legitations which the british introduced shook the integrity of the caste system. Specific mention can be made of a few of the legislatons such as the following:
   (*i*) ***The Caste Disabilities Removal Act of 1850*** [which served to remove some of the disabilities associated with caste including the practice of untouchability].

(ii) ***The Special Marriage Act of 1872*** [which legalised inter-caste and inter-religious marriages].

(iii) ***The Hindu Widows Remarriage Act of 1856*** [which gave legal permission for widows to remarry].

These and many other socio-legal measures of the British government gave a severe blow to the integrity of the caste system. But as *Prof. Ghurye* has pointed out, all these measures were taken by the British Government *purely for administrative convenience and it had no desire to reduce the rigidity of caste.*

3. ***Impact of social reform movements:*** Some of the social reform movements launched by social reformers during the British rule also attacked the caste system and its inequalities.

   (i) *The Brahma Samaj* founded by *Raja Ram Mohan Roy* in 1820 and developed by Devendranath Tagore and Keshav Chandra Sen condemned the barriers of caste divisions, idol worship, human and animal sacrifies. It advocated universal brotherhood of men.'

   (ii) *The Prarthana Samaj* launched by *Justice Ranade* devoted its attention to social reforms such as interdining, intercaste marriage, remarriage of widows, etc.

   (iii) *The Arya Samaj founded by Swami Dayanand saraswathi* in 1875 repudiated the caste restrictions, protested against prohibition of sea-voyages and insisted that even the shudras could study the Vedas. It tried to remodel the Hindu society on the basis of the Vedic ideals. It functioned as a militant force to protect the Hindu society from the "*onslaughts of Western rationalisation*". It started the "*Shuddhi*" (purification) movement to re-Hinduise the converts, the fallen, the outcastes and other externals.

   (iv) *The Ramakrishna Mission* started by *Swami Vivekananda*, a great disciple of Sri Ramakrishna Paramhamsa, in 1897 represents the *synthesis of the ancient or oriental and the modern* or western culture. Vivekananda who had imbibed in himself Raja Ram's rationalism and Dayananda Saraswathi's spirituality, was pragmatic in his approach. He condemned caste inequalities, exploitation of lower castes and women. He stressed on education, self-reliance and freedom of women. He even predicted that the Shudras ["Shramiks" or "labourers"] would dominate in the years to come.

   (v) *Other reform Movements*: Other social movements such as – (*i*) Jyotirao Phooley's (1873) "Satyashodak Samaj" ; (*ii*) Annie Besant's "*Theosophical society*"; (*iii*) Maharishi Arvind Ghosh's "*Divine Life Society*"–also served to loosen the hold of caste restrictions.

What is to be noted is that these reform movements "*did not succeed in removing the rigidity of the caste system in this period...*" -[*Ram Ahuja* - Page: 277]. However, they could only affect some of the structural features of caste.

4. ***Spread of english education and influence of the western ideas:*** Spread of English education exposed Indians for the first time to the Western World. The popular Western. ideas and values such as - "*liberty, equality* and *fraternity*", democracy, rationalism, individualism, women's liberation, secularism, humanitarianism etc. made their inroads into India. These ideas had deeply influenced the Western educated Indians. People who had hitherto been the targets of atrocities, deprivation, exploitation and humiliation could now voice their protest by asserting their rights. Increasing influence of science and technology added greater strength to the growing awareness of the masses.

5. ***Birth of the backward castes movement:*** Movements of a more militant nature against caste started with the founding of *Satyashodhak Samaj* in 1873 by *Jyotirao Phooley* of Poona, a man of *Mali caste*. The main purpose of this Samaj was to assert the worth of man irrespective of caste. Through his writings and practices he led a revolt against the tyranny of the caste system and the hegemony of the Brahmins. He appealed to the non-Brahmin castes not to engage any Brahmin priest to conduct their marriage ritual. He tried to reduce the enormous ritual system into a simple procedure. He perceived the necessity of educating the lower-caste people. He could translate his vision into practice when he opened a primary school for the so called untouchables in Poona [the very centre of orthodoxy] as early as in 1851.

Phooley's was not just a revolt against caste to cast off the domination of the Brahmins. In his writings he demanded representation for all classes of the Hindus in all the local bodies, the services and the institutions. Phooley's struggles marked the beginning of the non-Brahmin movement.

Pre-Independent Industrial Period [1919-1947]

The caste system underwent a-few more significant changes when India stepped into the 20th century. The role of three factors in bringing about such changes is worth mentioning here.

1. ***Influence of industrialisation: decline of caste-based occupational system:*** The advent of Industrial Revolution

also affected Indian socio-economic conditions. The British brought modern machineries and introduced factory system of production. New industries, occupations, employment opportunities, salary-based service system came to be established. The growth of industries destroyed the old crafts and household industries and provided for countless ways earning livelihood. Introduction of railways, telegraph and laying of roads helped trade and commerce. People of all castes started making use of the new economic Opportunities.

Industrialisation also resulted in occupational and geographic mobility. Movement of people from the compact ancestral village to the towns and cities started breaking down many of the caste norms. Crowded trains and buses could bring together lakhs of people of all castes and left little room for the niceties of ceremonial purity. Taboos against some foods and accepting food and water from persons of other castes also started weakening. Hotel system of food and hostel system of residence served to bring together people of different castes. The "*jajmani*"[1] system of economy which had made *economic 'interdependence of different castes, started declining. It slowly gave place to the capitalist system of economy*. These industrial and their concomitant developments made caste-members to come out of the hold of caste-based occupations and to resort to the new occupational avenues based purely on personal preferences and choices.

Influence of industrialisation was, no doubt, widespread. But its impact was not uniform and absolute on all the basic features of caste. *For example*, its impact on the endogamous nature of marriage and various marriage practices, rules and beliefs was almost negligible. Rapid industrialisation never led to the automatic dissolution of the caste system and its progressive replacement by a class system as it was believed by some Western scholars. *The economic aspects of caste underwent swift changes where as its socio-cultural aspects never got changed with equal speed.*

2. ***Impact of urbanisation:*** 'In order to reap the benefits of new educational and occupational opportunities people started moving towards towns and cities in large number. The necessities of city life relaxed the commensal taboos imposed by caste and lessened the dominance of Brahmins. As *Srinivas* has pointed out, the non-brahmins refused to show the same respect to the Brahmins which they used to show earlier. The growth of city life with its-migratory population brought about changes in the rigidity of the caste system [*Ghurye* - Page: 262]. *Kingsley Davis also "held that the anonymity, congestion, mobility, secularism and changeability of the city make the operation of caste virtually impossible*" [*Prof. Ram Ahuja - Page: 280*].

3. ***Influence of freedom movement and the role of gandhiji:*** Indian freedom struggle also altered the character of caste to some extent. The freedom struggle organised by the Indian National Congress brought together people of different castes, classes, religions and regions under one banner. The Congress led by Gandhiji launched a campaign against untouchability and roused the conscience of the people against its practice. Participation of the lower castes in the freedom struggle boosted their image'.

At the fag end of the British rule, though the traditional influence of caste started declining, its organisational strength was increasing. As Ghurye observed, "At about the end of the British rule in India, caste-society presented the spectacle of self-centered groups more or less in conflict with one another". [Ghurye - Page: 303]

Caste in Independent India [After 1947]

The political independence of the country, besides the process of industrialisation, urbanisation, secularisation etc. brought in a series of changes in the caste system. These changes can be classified into two categories: 1. *Changes in the traditional features of caste*; 2. *Changes in the role for functioning of the caste*.

Changes in the Traditional Features of Caste

Caste has assumed a different form in the modem times. Some of the traditional features [de- scribed earlier] have been radically altered. Here is a brief survey of the changes that have taken place in caste system after Independence.

1. *The religious basis of the caste has been attacked.* Caste is no more believed to be divinely ordained. It is being given more a social and secular meaning than a religious interpretation.
2. *Restrictions on food habits have been relaxed.* Distinction between '*pakka*' food and '*kachcha*' *food* has almost

[1] Jajmani system: This rcfers to a system of distribution whereby high caste landowning families [called "***jajmans***"] are provided services and products by various lower castes such as carpenters [***Badagi***], barbers [***Nai***], porters [*Kumbars*], blackmiths [*Kammars*] washerman [*Dhobis*], etc. The servicing people called "Kamins" are paid in cash or in kind [grains, fodder, clothes, animal products like milk, butter, etc.] It is a system governed by relationship based on reciprocity in intercaste relations in villages. *Ref:* Ram Ahuja's *Indian Social System*, p. 322

vanished. Food habits have become more a matter of personal choice than a caste rule. Still commensal taboos are not completely ignored especially in the rural areas. Interdining has not become the order of the day.

3. *Caste is not very much associated with hereditary occupations*. Caste no longer determines the occupational career of an individual. Occupations are becoming more and more "*caste-free*". Even Brahmins arc found driving taxis, dealing with foot-wears and running non-vegetarian hotels and bars and so on.
4. Endogamy, which is often called the very essence of the caste system, still prevails. Intercaste marriages though legally permitted, have not become the order of the day. As *KM Kapadia says, "there is an indifference to the intercaste marriages if not tacit acceptance by the society*".
5. The special civil and religious privileges which the Brahmins enjoyed are *no more being enjoyed by them*. The Constitution of India has removed all such privileges and made all castes equal.

   Most of the legal, political, educational, economic and other disabilities from which the lowest caste people had suffered, have been removed by the constitutional provisions. They are given spe- cial protection also. *Adult franchise* and "*reservation*" have given them a strong weapon to protect their interests.
6. *Caste continues to be a segmental division of Hindu society*. Caste with its hierarchical system continues to ascribe statuses to the individuals. But the twin processes of *Sanskritisation* and *Westernisation* have made possible mobility both within and outside the framework of caste.
7. *Caste panchayats, which used to control the behaviour of caste-members, have either become very weak or disappeared*. Though they are often found here and there in the village areas, they are almost non-existent in the urban areas.
8. *Restrictions imposed by the caste on social intercourse are very much relaxed*. Distinction between '*touchable*' and '*untouchable*' is not much felt especially in the community of literate people. However, instances of untouchability are heard in the rural areas.
9. *Other Important Changes*
   - (*i*) Though the dominance of caste is still found in villages it no *longer depends upon its ritual status*.
   - (*ii*) Casteism which is associated with caste, instead of disappearing in the wake of modernism, has become *still stronger*.
   - (*iii*) The '*jajmani*' system which used to govern the inter-caste relations especially in the villages has become very weak. In many places it has vanished. In place of intercaste dependence, intercaste strifes are found.
   - (*iv*) *Caste has lost much of its hold over the social usages and customs* practised by its members.
   - (*v*) *Caste today does not dictate individual's life* nor does it restrict newly valued individual freedom. Hence it no longer acts as a barrier to the progress of an individual.

Changes in the Role of Caste

The caste system in its attempts to adjust itself to the changed conditions of life has assumed new roles. Besides industrialisation and urbanisation, other factors such as Westernisation, Sanskritisation, reorganisation of Indian states, spread of education, socio-religious reforms, spatial and occupational mobility and growth of market economy have greatly affected the caste system. Changes in the role of caste must also be understood in the light of the influence of these factors.

1. ***Increase in the organisational power of caste:*** Education makes people liberal, broad-minded, rationale and democratic. Educated people are believed to be less conservative and superstitious. Hence it was expected that with the growth of literacy in India, caste-mindedness and casteism would come down. On the *contrary, caste-consciousness of the members has been increasing. Every caste wants to safeguard its interests. For fulfilling this purpose castes are getting themselves organised on the model of labour unions*.

   Today every caste 'wants to organised itself. Such caste organisations are on the increase. Mainly to cater to the educational, medical and religious needs of their members, these organisations are running hostels and hospitals, schools and colleges, reading-rooms and libraries, dharmashalas and temples and so on. These caste-based organisations are also *trying to project the leadership* of some of their members to serve as their spokesmen.
2. ***Political role of caste:*** Caste and politics have come to affect each other now. Caste has become an inseparable aspect of our politics. In fact, it is tightening its hold on politics. Elections are fought more often on the basis of caste. Selection of candidates, voting analysis, selection of legislative party leaders, distribution of ministerial portfolios etc., are very much based on caste. Even the communist parties which project the ideal of a casteles

and classless society are also not an exception to this. Politics of each state, as *M.N. Srinivas* says, is virtually the politics of confrontation of its "*dominant castes*". Thus, unless one knows the political confrontation between the dominant castes such as Ligayats and Vokkaligas in Kamataka and Reddys and Kammas in Andhra Pradesh, one cannot understand the politics of these two states. *M.N. Srinivas* also makes a distinction between *caste at the ritual level* and *caste at the political level*. Caste at the ritual level is smaller unit than the caste at the political level.

3. ***Protection for scheduled castes and other backward classes:*** The constitution of India has made enough provisions to protect the interests of Scheduled Castes and Tribes. They are offered more political, educational and service opportunities through the reservation policy. Seats are reserved for them from Mandal panchayat to Parliament and in all government departments. Though the reservation policy is against the declared goal of establishment of a casteless society, all political parties have supported it mostly, for political purposes. According to *M.N. Srinivas*, "*The provision of constitutional safeguards to....Scheduled Castes and Tribes has given a new lease of life to caste*." These provisions have made some of them develop vested interests to reap permanently the benefits of reservation. They are also tempting many other Castes to bring pressure on the government to declare them as belonging to the category of Scheduled castes.

4. ***Sanskritisation and westernisation:*** As *M.N. Srinivas* has pointed out, two important trends are witnessed in caste—*the process of Sanskritisation and that of Westernisation*. The former refers to a process in which the lower castes tend to imitate the values, practices and other life-styles of some dominant upper castes. The letter denotes a process in which the upper-caste people tend to mould their life-styles on the model of Westerners.

5. ***Backward classes movement:*** The non-Brahmin castes today are getting themselves more and more organised to challenge the supermacy of the Brahmins and to assert their rights. The establishment of "*Satyashodhak Samaj*" by *Jyotirao Phooley* in Poona in 1873 marked the beginning of such a non-Brahmin movement. This movement against the Brahmin supermacy by the lower castes came to be known as *Backward Classes Movement*. In the beginning, the main aim of this movement was to limit the Brahmin monopoly in the two fields such as *education* and *appointment to government posts*.

   The Backward Classes Movement has become a vital political force today. Its influence has changed the political scenario of the country. This movement has made the Brahmins politically weak and insignificant especially in Kerala and Tamilnadu. This movement has also brought pressure on different political parties to create special opportunities for the lowest caste people enabling them to come up to the level of other higher castes. Due to this pressure, *Backward Classes Commissions* were established at Central and State levels which recommended "*reservation*" for backward castes/classes.

6. ***Competitive role of castes:*** Mutual interdependence of castes which existed for centuries and was reinforced by the institutional system of "*jajmani*", is not found today. As MN. Srinivas points out, the "*vertical solidarity*" of castes has been replaced by "*horizontal solidarity*". "*Live and let live*" policy which was once associated with the caste makes no sense today. On the contrary, each caste looks at the other with suspicision, contempt, and jelousy and finds in it a challenger, a competitor. Excessive *caste-mindedness* and *caste-patriotism* have added to this competition. The economic base of a caste and its hold over the political power virtually determine the intensity of this competitiveness; This competitive spirit further strengthens caste-mindedness.

7. ***New attempts to strengthen caste-loyalty, caste-identity, caste-patriotism and caste mindedness:*** Today caste organisations are increasing and are making every attempt to obtain the loyality of their members and to strengthen their *caste-identity* and *solidarity*. Some such attempts can be cited here.

   (*i*) *Though Caste Panchayats are dwindling, caste organisations are on the increase*. Some of these organisations have their own written constitutions and managing committees through which they try to preserve some of the caste rules and practices.

   (*ii*) *Caste organisations run their own papers, bulletins, periodicals, monthlies etc.*, through which they regularly feed information to the members regarding the activities of caste organisations and achievements of caste-members.[2]

   (*iii*) Attempts are also made to increase caste integration through the *establishment of caste based trusts and trust-*

---

[2] As Ghurye has stated [pp. 443-44] between 1950-60, there were about 913 papers in Hindi, Gujarati and Marathi speaking areas out of which at least 85 were caste-based.

units.[3] These trusts arrange annual gatherings, get-togethers, annual dinners, occasional festival celebrations. they provide shelter to the needy members of the caste. They offer scholarships to the poor students of the caste. Some of them run schools, colleges, hostels, maternity-homes for caste members and so on.

(*iv*) The occupational castes are making determined efforts to improve the economic conditions of caste members by establishing *cooperative credit and industrial societies*.

(*v*) Caste organisations collect regular subscription from the members, arrange annual confer- ences, discuss matters and issues affecting caste interests and caste solidarity and organise agitations and protest meetings against the governmental policies if they were to damage caste interests. In states like Bihar, some upper and lower castes have formed their own '*senas*' [militant groups] to protect their interests.

CAUSES FOR THE CHANGES IN CASTE SYSTEM

The caste system has undergone vast changes in modem times. Factors that contributed to the changes in the caste system are briefly examined here.

1. ***Uniform legal system:*** The uniform legal system introduced by the British made the Indians feel that "*all men are equal before the law*". A number of legislations which the British introduced also struck at the root of the caste system. Independent India followed the same legal system. The Constitution of India has not only assured equality to all but also declared the practice of untouchability unlawful [Articles l5and 16]. Articles 16, 164, 225, 330, 332, 334, 335, 338 and the 5th and 6th Schedules of the Constitution provide for some special privileges to the Scheduled Castes and Scheduled Tribes to enable them to come up to the level of other upper castes.
2. ***Impact of modern education:*** The British introduced the modem secular education in a uniform way through out India. In independent India educational facilities are extended to all the caste people. The lowest caste people are also entitled to avail themselves of these facilities. Modern education has given a blow to the intellectual monopoly of a few upper castes. It has created an awareness among people and weakened the hold of caste over the members. It does not, however, mean that the modern educated people are completely free from the hold of the caste.
3. ***Industrialisation, urbanisation and westernisation:*** Due to the process of *industrialisation*, number of non-agricultural job opportunities were created. This new economic opportunity weak- ened the hold of the upper castes people who owned vast lands. People of different castes, classes, and religions started working together in factories, offices, workshops etc. This was unthinkable two centuries ago. *Growth of cities* has drawn people of all castes together and made them to stay to gether ignoring many of their caste restictions. The upper caste people started looking to the West for modifying their life-style on the model of the West. Thus they became more and more westernised without bothering much about caste inhibitions.
4. ***Influence of modern transport and communication:*** Modern means of transport such as train, bus, ship, aeroplane, trucks etc. have been of great help for the movement of men and materials. Caste rules relating to the practice of purity and pollution and untouchability could no longer be observed. Modern means of communication, such as, newspapers, post, telegraph, telephone, radio, television etc., have helped people to come out of the narrow world of caste.
5. ***Freedom struggle and the establishment of democracy:*** The freedom struggle waged against the British brought all the caste people together to fight for a common cause. Establishment of democratic type of government soon after Independence gave yet another blow to the caste by extending equal socio-economic opportunities to all without any discrimination.
6. ***Rise of non-brahmin movement:*** A movement against the Brahmin supermacy was launched by *Jyothirao Pooley* in 1873. This movement became popular in course of time particularly in the South. It created an awareness among the lower castes and instilled in them the feeling of "*self-respect*". This movement which became a great political force, brought pressure upon the government to establish Backward Classes Commissions at Central and State levels. The recommendations made by these commissions and their implementation provided vast scope for the lower castes to achieve progress.
7. ***Other Important Causes:***

(*i*) **Social Legislations.** A series of social legislations introduced by the British as well as by the Indian governments

---

[3] Ghurye has stated that he himself counted not less than 1700 caste-based trust-units in Bombay and Greater Bombay Suburban District in the published report of the Charity Commissioner of Maharashtra in 1954.

[such as the *Caste Disabilities Removal Act* 1872, *The Hindu Marriage Act of* 1955, *The Untouchability Offences Act of* 1956 etc.] directly and indirectly altered the nature of the caste system.

(*ii*) **Social Reform Movements.** Various social reform movements [such as *Satyashadhak Samaj, Brahma Samaj, Arya Samaj, Sri Ramakrishna Mission* etc.] launched during the second half of the 19th and the beginning of the 20th centuries have been able to remove the rigidity and some of the evil practices associated with the caste system.

(*iii*) **Impact of the West.** Influence of the Western thought and particularly the ideas of — rationalism, liberalism, humanitarianism, egalitarianism etc., made the educated Indians to come out of the clutches of the caste.

(*iv*) **Threat of Conversion.** Social disabilities imposed on the lower castes made some of them to get themselves converted to either Christianity or Islam. Pressure tactics and temptations further added to this conversion process. The threat of conversion compelled the upper castes to relax many of the caste rigidities so that they could hold back the lower caste people who were getting ready for conversion.

(*iv*) **Improvement in the Status of Women, Evolution of New Social Classes.** [working class, middle class and capitalist class] and radical changes in the system of division of labour especially in the rural areas have further loosened the roots of caste system.

MERITS AND DEMERITS OF CASTE SYSTEM

The Indian caste system has its own merits and demerits. Some of its merits and demerits may be mentioned here.

Merits of Caste

1. Caste represents a harmonious division of society based mainly on division of labour and occupation.
2. Caste promotes the spirit of cooperation and fellow-feeling at least within its range. It helps the poor, the needy and strengthens group sentiment.
3. Caste is a source of social stability. It has given strength to the Indian society to withstand the "shocks of politics and the cataclysms of nature".
4. The caste functions as the constitution of the Hindu society. It rendered most important services in the past and continues to sustain the social order and its solidarity,
5. The caste preserves the racial purity by prohibiting inter-marriages and by imposing endogamy on its members.
6. It defines the economic pursuits and provides professional career to each individual. It provides for cultural diffusion within the group. The 'caste culture' is passed on from one generation to the next, very systematically. As *Hutton says*, the caste canalises an individual's choice in marriage, "acts as his trade union, his friendly or benefit society, his state club and his orphanage: it takes care for him of health, insurance and if need be provides for funeral."

Demerits of Caste

1. The caste system has unwarrantedly divided the Hindu society into mutually hostile and conflicting groups and sub-groups. It has given scope to the inhuman practice of untouchability. It has cut across the social solidarity.
2. As *Gandhiji* has said, untouchability is "the hatefullest expression of the caste."
3. It has hindered the growth of a strong national unity. The spirit of 'caste-patriotism', endangers the growth of national consciousness.
4. The excessive caste loyality has brought political disunity. It has wrecked the successful working of the multi-party system.
5. It has prevented the proper growth of democracy. Strictly speaking, democracy and caste cannot go together. The caste engenders inequality while democracy assures equality.
6. It has retarded progress. The caste is more conservative, reactionary and orthodox. It is for the *status quo*.
7. It has hindered mobility; it has made our society more static than dynamic.
8. It has lowered the status of women. In a caste-ridden society women have only a subordinate role to play.
9. It has given scope for religious conversions. The lower caste people are getting converted into Islam and Christianity due to the tyranny of the upper castes

ESTATE SYSTEM

Meaning and Nature of Estates

The term '*Estates*' represents a type of stratification that existed in Europe during the Middle Ages. Estates system has a long history. The system emerged in the ancient Roman Empire, and existed in Europe until very recent times. The estates system consisted of three main divisions—*the clergy, the nobility*, and *the commoners or the ordinary people*. In England and France, *for example,* these three divisions were found. In some parts of Europe, *for example*, Sweden, almost upto 1866 there were four estate divisions; Nobles, Clergy, Citizens and Peasants.

These historical estates were akin to social classes in at least two respects. (*i*) *Each estate, was to some extent characterised by a distinctive style of life*. (*ii*) *The three estates could be thought of as representing a hierarchy*. In this hierarchy the clergy were at the top and the commoners at the bottom. The intermediary position was occupied by the nobles. It should be noted that the clergy was called the First Estate only in consonance with the medieval idea that the Church is supreme and the state is subordinated to it. Hence, in reality there were three classes, but with the nobility (including royalty) at the top.

Characteristics of Estates

T.B. *Bottomore* has mentioned about three important characteristics of the feudal estates of medieval Europe. They are as follows:

1. ***Legal basis of estates:*** Estates were legally defined. Each estate had a '*status*' of its own. More precisely in a legal sense the status was associated with rights and duties, privileges and obligations. As it has been said, "to know a person's real position "it was first of all necessary to know" the law by which he lived". In comparison with the first two estates—the clergy and nobility—the third estate consisting of the serfs or commoners suffered from many legal disabilities. *For example, the serfs had the inability to appeal to the king for justice. They had no rights over their chattels or properties and holdings*. They had the *liability of paying the fines* of '*merchet*' and '*heriot*'. (*i.e.*, a fine paid to a lord for the marriage of a daughter, and a fine paid to the lord on the death of a tenant). Even different penalities were imposed on them for similar offences.
2. ***Estates representing division of labour:*** The estates represented a broad division of labour. They had some definite functions. According to the law of the day, *the nobility were to fight and defend all, the clergy were to pray and the commoners were to pay* or provide food for all.
3. ***Estates as political groups:*** The feudal estates were political groups. An assembly of estates possessed political power. From this point of view the serfs did not constitute an estate until the l2th Century A.D, The decline of Education feudalism after the 12th Century is associated with the rise of a third estate. The third estate behaved for a long period *within* the feudal system as a *distinctive group* before they overthrew it.

Thus the three estates—clergy, nobility and the commoners functioned like three political groups. As far as participation in government was concerned, the clergy used to stand by the nobility. In France, the political position was more rigid. This system of three estates remained there until 1789, that is, till the outbreak of the Revolution. In the French Parliament called '*States-General*', these estates used to sit separately and not together. That differentiation within the estates prevailed for a long time. The political movement of the French Revolution brought about some radical changes in France.

THE CASTE SYSTEM AND THE ESTATES SYSTEM

The Caste System of India and the Estates of Medieval Europe are not one and the same. The differences and the similarities between the two systems may be noted here:

1. A pure caste system is rooted in the *religious order* whereas the estates system is rooted in the *legal order*. Divisions within the caste system are an interpretation of the laws of religious ritual, the divisions of estates system are defined by the laws of man. Hence it is not necessary in the estates system to know a man's place in a ritual order. But it is significant to know the man-made law by which he lives. These laws were somewhat complicated. Still their universal characteristic was that they defined not only the rights but also the duties and obligations of the members of estates. These could be enforced either in the courts or by military strength.

2. Unlike the caste system the estates system has no "out-castes". Because, at least in theory, all the estates of the system enjoyed their own rights, duties and obligations. All could establish some claim on the established social order. Here in the caste system; the outcastes suffered from all kinds of social, political, religious, legal and other disabilities.
3. Difference between these two systems could be observed with regard to *the nature of social mobility*. Both, of course, had institutionalised barriers for social mobility. The barriers in the caste system are based on ritual impurity whereas the barriers of the estate system are legal. Since these legal barriers are manmade they can be modified in particular circumstances. *For example*, in the religious sphere, anyone belonging to any section of the community was recruited into the church. At least in theory, anyone could attain any high place in it. Promotion within the Church indicated some kind of social mobility. In the secular sphere, however, the king could provide a distinguished servant a noble position. In both these circumstances, changes of social position were essentially inherited.

The caste system, on the other hand, suffers from irreparable inequality created by divinity as it is believed. Hence, *no caste member could rise or improve upon his position* in the caste system even as an exceptional case.

SOCIAL CLASS

'Social Class' is a principal type of social stratification found especially in the modem civilised countries. If the caste system is found to be unique to India, the class system is universal in nature. Sometimes, the word 'class' is used to represent groups of professors, artists, engineers, doctors, Students, etc. The word 'class' is also used to refer the quality of the things whether good, better, best and so on. But the concept of 'social class' is more used in sociology representing a kind of social Stratification than anything else.

Definition of Social Class

1. *P. Gisbert*: A social class is 'a category or group of persons having a definite status in society which permanently determines their relation to other groups'.
2. *Ogburn and Nimkoff:* 'A social class is the aggregate of persons having essentially the same social status in a given society'
3. *MacIver and Page*: 'A social class is any portion of the community marked off from the rest by social status'.
4. *Max Weber*: social classes are aggregates of individuals 'who have the same Opportunities of acquiring goods, the same exhibited standard of living'.
5. *Lapire*: 'A social class is culturally defined group that is accorded a particular position of status within the population as a whole'.

Thus, it is clear that *social class is a segment of society with all the members of all ages and both the sexes who share the same general status*. As *MacIver* says, whenever social intercourse is limited by the consideration of social status by distinctions between *higher* and *lower*, there exists a social class.

NATURE AND CHARACTERISTICS OF SOCIAL CLASS

1. ***Class: A status group:*** A social class is essentially a status group. Class is related to status. Different statuses arise in a society as people do different things, *engage* in different activities and pursue different vocations. The consideration of the class as a status group makes it possible to apply it to any society which has many strata. The idea of social status separates the individuals not only physically sometimes even mentally.
2. ***Achieved status and not ascribed status:*** Status in the case of class system is achieved and not ascribed. Birth is not the criterion of status. Achievements of an individual mostly decide his status. Class system provides scope for changing or improving one's status. Factors like income, occupation, wealth, education, 'life-styles', etc. decide the status of an individual.
3. ***The class system is universal:*** Class is almost a universal phenomenon. The class system appears in all the modern complex societies of the world. It is a phenomenon that is absent only in the smallest, the simplest, and the most primitive of societies. All other societies of any size have a class structure.

4. ***Mode of feeling:*** In a class system we may observe three modes of feelings. (*i*) There is a *feeling of equality* in relation to the members of one's own class (*ii*) There *is feeling of inferiority* in relation to those who occupy the higher status in the socio-economic hierarchy. *(iii)* There is a feeling of superiority in relation to those who occupy the lower status in the hierarchy. This kind of feeling develops into class-consciousness and finally results in class solidarity.
5. ***Element of prestige:*** Each social class has its own status in society. Status is associated with *prestige*. The relative position of the class in the social set up arises from the degree of prestige attached to the status. Thus, the status and the prestige enjoyed by the ruling classes or rich classes in every society is superior to that of the class of commoners or the poor people. The prestige which a class enjoys depends upon our *evaluations*. In many societies *knowledge*, *purity of race* or *descent*, *religion, wealth, heroism, bravery* and similar other qualities confer a high degree of prestige on the persons possessing them. These qualities on which our evaluations are based vary considerably in different societies, and in the course of time, within the same society.
6. ***Element of stability:*** A social class is relatively a stable group. It is not transistory nor unstable like a crowd or a mob. Though status in the case of class is subject to change, it is to some extent stable. Status in the case of class may undergo radical changes in extraordinary circumstances *i.e.*, in times of wars, revolutions, economic, political and social crisis and so on.
7. ***Mode of living:*** A social class is distinguished from other classes by its customary modes of behaviour or mode of behaving. This is often referred to as the '*life-styles*' of a particular class. 'Life-styles' or the modes of living include such matters as the mode of dress, the kind of house and neighbourhood one lives in, the means of recreation one resorts to, the cultural products one is able to enjoy, the relationship between parents and children, the kinds of books, magazines and TV shows to which one is exposed, one's friends, one's mode of conveyance and communication, one's way of spending money and so on. 'Life-styles' reflect the speciality in preferences, tastes, and values of a class
8. ***Social class: An open group:*** Social classes are '*open groups*'. They represent an '*open*' social system. An open class system is one in which vertical social mobility is possible. This means there are no restrictions, or at the most only very mild restrictions are imposed on the upward and downward movement of individuals in the social hierarchy. However, a completely open class system and a completely closed class system are only hypothetical.
9. ***Social class: An economic group:*** The basis of social classes is mostly economic, but they are not mere economic groups or divisions. *Subjective criteria* such as class-consciousness, class solidarity and class identification on the one hand, and the *objective criteria* such as wealth, property, income, education, occupation, etc., on the other, are equally important in the class system. Classes, thus, are not merely economic groups, they are something more than these.
10. ***Classification of social classes:*** Sociologists have given three-fold classification of classes which consists of (*i*) *Upper Class* (*ii*) *Middle Class*, and (*iii*) *Lower Class*. *Warner* and *Lunt* in their study of a New England town [their book being '*The Social Life of a Modern Community*], have divided each of the traditional classes into two sub-classes. They have given a six-fold classifi- cation consisting of (*i*) *The Upper-Upper Class* (*ii*) *The Lower-Upper Class*, (*iii*) *The Upper-Middle Class*, (*iv*) *The Lower-Middle Class*, (*v*) *The Upper-Lower Class*, and (*vi*) *The Lower-Lower Class*. *Karl Marx*, the champion of the theory of social class and class conflicts, has spoken of only two major social classes, the '*haves*' and the '*have nots*' or the rich and the poor, or the capitalists and the workers, or the Bourgeosie and the *Proletariat*. *Sorokin* has spoken of three major types of class stratification. They are *economic*, *political*, and *occupational* classes.
11. ***Class consciousness:*** Class system is associated with class consciousness. Class consciousness is "*the sentiment that characterises the relations of men towards the members of their own and other classes*." It "consists in the realisation of a similarity of attitude and behaviour with members of other classes." Class consciousness is the means by which the integration of persons possessing a similarity of social position and of life-chances is transformed into a common group activity.

Conditions of Class Consciousness. *Ginsberg* has mentioned three conditions of class consciousness. First is the ease and amount of social mobility. If *movement up* and *down* is easy and rapid, differences in mode of life disappear; if it is possible but not easy, the consciousness of differences is increased. The *second* condition of class consciousness is *rivalry* and *conflict*. When the members of a class realise their common interests, then they may think of defending their interests against the common enemy. The *third* factor is the growth of a *common tradition* embodying common standards of value and common experiences. When the people come to possess common traditions and common experiences, they may develop class consciousness.

Class Consciousness and Class Struggle. *Karl Marx*, who championed the cause of workers, laid great emphasis on 'class consciousness' among the working classes. According to Marx, the rise of class consciousness among the workers leads to their *class identification, class solidarity* and finally to *class struggle*. Hence he gave a clarion call to the workers in his *Manifesto of the Communist Party* of 1848 that "*Workers of the world unite, you have nothing to lose, but your chains, you have a world to win*". Class consciousness can be transformed into same group activity with the help of some organ or instrument. *Political party* is such an organ. Hence, *Lenin* added the idea of a party in Marxism to prepare the workers for class struggle.

CRITERION OF CLASS

It is true that society has been divided into different classes at different times. Classification of social classes has been made on the basis of objective criterion or subjective criterion or both.

1. **Subjective Criteria** may include the class *consciousness, class solidarity* and *class identi- fication*. the subjective criteria are essentially psychological. Members who have common interests and attributes have a sense of in-group solidarity. They feel that their socio-economic opportunities are almost equal. *Warner and Lunt* in their study of the American class system have observed the importance of subjective factors in determining a class. According to them, (*i*) *belonging to the 'right family'*, (*ii*) *doing the 'right things'*. (*iii*) *knowing how to 'act right'* (*iv*) *associating with the 'right people'* , (*v*) *living in the 'right' section of the town*, (*vi*) *one's feelings and beliefs concerning certain things*—all have their impact on the status of individuals according to which their class is determined. 'Wealth' *alone* is not a sufficient qualification for being admitted to the upper-class-they maintained.

Objective Criteria. Objective criteria include those factors with the help of which one's status may be determined. They may include—(*i*) *wealth*, *property* or *income*, (*ii*) *family* or *kinship*, (*iii*) *location of residence*, (*iv*) *occupation*, (*v*) *level of education*, (*vi*) *physical marks of difference such as skin colour*, etc. Some sociologists have given more importance to the objective factors.

It may be noted that the criteria upon which class is determined vary from time to time and place to place. *For example*, in *pre-Nazi Germany*, the combination of old aristocratic family line and high rank in the army put one in the top position. In *Russia*, during the *Czarist regime*, nobility with a military career represented the top class position. In the *Soviet Russia* today, a high position in the communist party is a basis to become a member of the top-class position. In the *U.S.A.*, today, the combination of high level business, high political status, wealth, education and old family descent represent a man's high status in the society.

Karl Marx on the contrary, has placed premium on the objective factors particularly the economic ones. According to him, social classes originate only from economic struggle. He neglected other subjective factors. his theory of social class is, hence, regarded as one-sided, misleading and deterministic.

MARXIAN ANALYSIS OF CLASS

Marx defined a social class as all those people who share a common relationship to the means of economic production. Those who own and control the means of production (slave owners, feudal landowners or owners of property such as factories and capital) are the dominant class. They exercise power because of their ownership of means of production. In an industrial society the means of production include the factories, and the machinery and raw materials used for manufacturing goods. Marx called them the class of '*Bourgeoisie*' or capitalists or owners of property.

All those who work for dominant class are — slaves, peasants, or industrial labourers. They constitute the subordinate class. *Marx* called this class — the '*proletariat*' or the labour class or working class or poor class. Members of the proletariat own only their labour which they hire out to the owners of industry in return for wages.

The relationship between these two classes is not only one of dominance and subordination but also of '*exploitation*'. The workers produce more wealth in the form of food, manufactured products and services than is necessary to meet their basic needs. It means they produce 'surplus wealth'. But they do not enjoy the use of the surplus they have created. On the contrary, those who own the means of production are able to grab this surplus wealth as '*profit*' for their own use. The capitalists are a non-producing class. They do not actually produce anything. Still much of the wealth produced by the proletariats is taken away by the capitalists. According to *Marx*, this kind of exploitation has been the main source of conflict between the two classes throughout history.

Marx believed that the economic base of society influences the general character of all other aspects of culture and social structure, such as law, religion, education, and government,. The dominant class is able to control all of those institutions and to ensure that they protect its own interests. "*The laws. therefore, protect the rich, not poor. The established religion supports the social order as it is, not as it might be. Education teaches the virtues of the existing system, not its vices. Government upholds the status quo rather than undermines it.*"*–Ian Robertson*

Marx was of the opinion that as a result of the exploitation of workers by the capitalists the gap between the two goes on widening. Thus the rich become richer and the poor become poorer. This results in an imbalance in the production and distribution. Goods will be produced and flooded in the market in abundant quantity and there will be only a handful of people to purchase them. Majority of the people in society who mostly belong to the working class cannot purchase the goods due to their poop purchasing capacity. *Marx* calls this situation '*the anarchic character of production*'. Hence capitalism suffers from its own internal contradictions. "*The seed of destruction of capitalism is ripening in the very womb of capitalism*"—Marx said. He has foretold that capitalism would end in failure. "*The prophecy of capitalism is a prophecy of doom*"—Marx stated emphatically.

Marx believed that the members of the proletariat would eventually realise that they were being exploited and oppressed. They would then join together to overthrow the bourgeoisie either by force or by voting their own representatives into the government. As a champion of the cause of the workers Marx called upon the workers to hasten the process of the destruction of the capitalist system. Marx and Engles made a fervant appeal to the working class in their *Manifesto of the communist Party of 1848* in the following Way: "*Let the ruling classes tremble at a communist revolution. The proletarians have nothing to lose but their Chains. They have a world to win. Working men of all countries unite*". Marx has even predicted that a historic revolution would mark the end of capitalism and lead to a classless society. After their successful revolution the workers would set up a communist society which means that the forces of production would be communally owned, that is jointly owned by all members of society. Goods produced would be equally shared and everyone would work for him and for the benefit of society as a whole.

Criticism

Marx's views on class are part of his more general theory of the history of society. Some sociologists agree that they are more appropriate to 19th century Europe and have little relevance today.

Marxian definition of class and its interpretation can be misleading in many marginal cases. When Marx wrote, industry was owned and controlled primarily by individual capitalists. But this is no longer the case today. Most industry is now run by large corporations, which are owned by thousands of stockholders but controlled by salary managers. As a result the *ownership* and *control* of the means of production have been largely separated. Executives, technicians, scientists, and other professionals may control the means of production, but they do not own it. They are on the payroll like any other workers. Marx's definition in this way does not help very much in determining their social class.

Further, Marxian definition of social class does not answer a few of the questions such as- "*What is the social class of a dropout, who does not own or control the means of production but does not work either? What is the social class of an impoverished member of the European aristocracy, who enjoys high social prestige because of ancestry rather than any relationship to the means of production? What is the class of a wealthy black surgeon who suffers racial prejudices and discrimination almost every day of his or her life*? .... .." (Ian Robertson). The Marxian explanation does not handle these ambiguous cases very satisfactorily.

Differences between Caste and Class

Caste and class represent two main forms of social stratification. They can be distinguished on the following grounds.

Cast	*Class*
1. *Particular:* The system with all its pecularities is unique to India. It is peculiar to India and hence it is not universal.	*Universal:* The class system is universal in nature. It is found in almost all the modern complex societies.
2. *Ascribed Status:* Status is ascribed to the individuals by birth. Birth is the criterion of status and not achievement. Status can neither be changed for be improved.	*Achieved Status:* Status is achieved by the individuals. There is scope for achievement. Hence, status can be changed or improved.
3. *Closed system:* Caste is a closed system. It restricts social mobility; *i.e.*, the movement of people from one social status to that of the other.	*Open system:* Class is an open system. It provides for social mobility. Individuals can move from the lower class to the upper class.
4. *Divine Origin:* The caste system is believed to have had a divine origin. It is closely associated with Hindu tradition.	*Secular:* The class system is secular. It has nothing to do with religion. It has been given no religious explanation.
5. *Purity and Impurity*: The idea of purity and impurity is associated with the caste. some castes are called '*pure*' while others are regarded as '*impure*'. '*Impure*' castes are regarded as '*untouchables*'.	*Feeling of Disparity:* There is a feeling of disparity on the part of the members of a class. The question of purity and impurity does not arise. Hence there is no practice of untouchability.
6. *Regulation of relations:* The caste system controls the activities and regulates the relations of its members to a great extent. As MacIver says, it fixes the role of a man in society. It regulates even the routine activities of the members.	*Limits Relations:* The class system, on the other hand, limits the range of contacts and communications of its members. Individuals are more free in a class. It does regulate the daily tasks of its members.
7. *Greater Social Distance:* There is comparatively a greater distance being kept between different castes.	*Less Social Distance:* There is less social distance between different classes. Members are more tolerant than others.
8. *Conservative:* The caste ridden system tends to become conservative, orthodox and reactionary. Castes become in course of time, water-tight compartments.	*Progressive:* The class-laden system is regarded as more progressive. Classes give more freedom to the members. It permits greater social mobility.
9. *Endogamous Group:* Caste is an endogamous social unit. Accordingly, every caste member has to marry within the group selecting the life partner from his or her own caste. Intercaste marriages are not allowed.	*Not endogamous:* A class is not an endogamous unit. The members are free to select his or her life partner from any of the classes. The class system never imposes restrictions on marriage.
10. *Complexity:* The caste system is a complex system. The very fact that more than 2800 castes and subcastes are found in India, makes it evident how complex it is.	*Simplicity:* The class system is known for its simplicity. Broadly speaking, there are only three classes — the upper, middle, and the lower — and hence the network of relations is also simple.
11. *Caste-consciousness:* Caste consciousness is more dangerous to democracy. Democracy and caste strictly speaking, cannot go together, because caste is based on inequality. Caste-feeling may also endanger the growth of national 'sentiments and unity'. Caste restricts the amount of community feeling. Casteism has been a great hinderance to the national integration in India.	*Class-consciousness*: Class-consciousness is not inimical to democracy. Class and democracy go together. Class on the other hand, does not restrict the amount of community feeling. In spite of the Communist influence to internationalise, the class system never disturbs the growth of national sentiments.

REVIEW QUESTIONS

1. Discuss the origin of the caste system. Give an account of the factors which facilitated the growth of caste system in India.
2. Describe the origin of the word 'caste'. Write its definition and characteristic features.
3. Analyse the changes in the caste system during the British rule and in independent India.
4. Throw light on the changes in the role of the caste system.
5. Explain the causes for the changes in the caste system.
6. Assess the merits and demerits of the caste system.
7. What do you mean by estates? Describe the nature and characteristic features of estates.
8. Define social class. Explain its nature and characteristic features.
9. Write a detailed note on the criteria of class.
10. What is the difference between caste and class?
11. Write about the major charges that took place in the caste system.
12. Write short notes on the following:
    (a) Caste panchayat
    (b) Social movements and the caste system
    (c) Estate systems
    (d) Caste and class
    (e) Marxian analysis of class

⌘⌘⌘⌘⌘⌘⌘⌘⌘⌘⌘⌘

24

Race and Ethnic Relations

Chapter Outline

- Racial Groups and Ethnic Groups : Meaning and Definition of Race
- Race is not a Biological Concept
- Rejection of the Conventional Three Fold Classification of Races
- Concept of Pure Race is a Myth
- Meaning and Definition of Ethnic Groups
- Racial and Ethnic Groups
- Meaning and Definition of Ethnic Groups
- Racial and Ethnic Groups: Main Differences
- Minority Groups: Meaning and Definition of Minority
- Characteristics of minority Groups
- Racism and Its Nature Ethnocentric Attitudes at the Root of Racism?
- Causes of Racism
- Ideology of Racism
- Patterns of Race and Ethnic Relations: Assimilation, Cultural Pluralism, Legal Protection of Minorities, Population Transfer or Relocation, Continued subjugation, Extermination or Genocide
- Minorities As a problem
- Main Problems of the Minorities
- The Problem of Preserving the Distinct Social and Cultural Life
- The Problem of Prejudice and Discrimination
- Minorities as Targets of Discrimination
- Institutionalised Discrimination
- Prejudice and Discrimination are Interrelated
- Causes and consequences of Prejudice and Discrimination
- Problems of Religious Minorities in India: Welfare of Minorities
- National Commission for Minorities
- National Minorities Development and Finance Corporation.

Of the millions of species of animals on earth, the *Homo sapiens* is the most widespread. For the past ten thousand years we have been spreading northward and southward and across the oceans to every corner of the globe. But we have not done this as one single people; on the contrary, throughout our history we have been divided into innumerable societies. Each of these societies maintains its own culture and thinks of itself as *"we"* and looks upon all others as *"they"*. One of the most fascinating aspects of our species, is the extra-ordinary physical and cultural diversity of its members throughout these 10,000 years of warfare, migration and expansion, we have been conflicting, competing and learning to co-operate and co-exist. The realisation that we are all one great people despite our immense diversity has been slow to evolve. The diversity that is found among the people serves as a source of conflict and inequality. Because, human relationships are all too often conducted on the basis of the differences rather than the similarities between groups. These differences are either physical or cultural in nature. The arbitrary human divisions made on the basis of the physical characteristics or cultural traits are often termed as *'racial* and *ethnic groups.'*

"Race and ethnic relations are the patterns of interaction among groups whose members share distinctive physical characteristics or cultural traits."[1] It could be said that those people who share similar physical characteristics are socially defined as a ***"race"***; and those who share similar cultural traits are socially defined as an ***"ethnic group"***.

[1] Ian Robertson in *Sociology,* p. 261.

It is a fact of history that relationships between racial and ethnic groups have been marked by prejudice, antagonism, warfare and social inequality. Even in the course of the recent one or two decades, hundreds of thousands of people have been slaughtered and millions more subjected to cruelty and injustice for no apparent reason other than their membership in some hated group.

This chapter explores the ideas of *race, ethnicity, prejudice* and *discrimination*. The purpose here is to understand better why racial and ethnic groups sometimes live and thrive in harmony and sometimes kill and die in discard. An attempt is made here to examine the nature and character of race and to understand the problem of minority groups.

RACIAL GROUPS AND ETHNIC GROUPS

The terms *'racial groups'* and *'ethnicity'* or *"ethnic groups"* are being used in a confusing manner. Sociologists are also not using these terms in a consistent manner. Hence, it is necessary to clarify the difference in the meanings of these terms. The term ***"race"*** *refers to the genetically transmitted physical characteristics of different human groups*, and the term **"ethnicity"** *refers to culturally acquired differences.* Both the words are often misused in ordinary speech, and we must examine their meaning more closely.

Racial Groups

What is Race?

As it is already mentioned, the term "race" is a controversial concept, for it is understood differently by different people. In the popular usage, *"race"* may mean all of humanity [the *"human race"*], a nationality (for example, the *'German race'*) or even a group which is mixed in nearly all respects but socially designated as different (for example, the *'Jewish race'*). Almost any kind of category of people may be called a *"race"*.

Race is not a biological concept **:** The word *'race'* as a biological concept is almost meaningless today. There are over **6** billion people in the world, and they display a wide variety of skin colours, hair textures, limb-to-trunk ratios and other characteristics such as distinctive nose, lip, eyelid forms and so on. Some have defined a race as a group of people separated from other groups by a distinctive combination of physical characteristics. Such a definition invites problems, because of intermixing, overlapping and the gradual shading of physical characteristics. Thus, a *"race"* is not a biologically distinct grouping of people.

Race is a social creation **:** Social scientists recognise that there is no such thing as a race based *purely* on objective biological differences. On the contrary, *races are regarded as social creations*. They result from the attribution of biological characteristics - real or imagined - to a group, which is then treated as different from other groups. Race is a socially significant reality.

Definition of Race

1. **Horton and Hunt :** *"A race is a group of people somewhat different from other groups in its combination of inherited physical characteristics, but race is also substantially determined by popular social definition."* [2]
2. **Richard T. Schaefer :** *"The term racial group is used to describe a group which is set apart from others because of obvious physical differences."* ***For example***, whites, blacks, and Asian Americans are all considered racial groups within the United States" [3]
3. **N.J. Smelser :** *"Racial group is a kind of ethnic group, one that is set apart from others by some combination of inherited biological traits such as - skin colour, facial features and stature."* [4]

Rejection of the Conventional Three-Fold Classification of Races

Though at present, race is more regarded in social terms than biological, for decades together it was regarded as a human category based on biological qualities. Until very recently, many scholars particularly anthropologists and text-book writers grouped human beings into three major races namely:

---

[2] Horton and Hunt in *Sociology,* p. 389.

[3] Richard T. Schaefer in *Sociology - International Edition,* pp. 238-239.

[4] Milton Yinger in the words of N.J. Smelser in *Sociology,* Fourth Edition, p. 186.

(*i*) ***The caucasoid race*** : which included most people of Europe, the Middle East, and India as well.

(*ii*) ***The mongoloid race*** : which included most Japanese, Chinese, Nepalese, Koreans, Vietnamese

(*iii*) ***The negroid race*** : which included black African people, and the American Negroes and their descendants.

This kind of classification system grew out of 19th century theories that attributed not only specific physical traits but also certain moral and mental traits to each *"race"*. Thus most of the human group could be placed in one of these three categories.

No Fixed Set of Physical Traits to Classify Races

Classification schemes of this sort have been discredited and rejected today. No set of physical traits serves to define any *"race"*, moreover, there is too wide a range in any given trait for it to serve as a basis for classifying people into one or the other race. The racial placement of some groups is uncertain because their characteristics overlap. ***Examples*** : (*i*) *Asian Indians* have Mongoloid skin colour but Caucasoid facial features; (*ii*) Some dark-skinned Africans have straight hair, narrow noses, and thin lips; (*iii*) Some light-skinned Europeans have wolly hair, wide noses, and thick lips; (*iv*) *The Ainu of northern Japan* have Caucasoid skin colour and hair but Mogoloid facial features.

Interbreeding has Blurred the Physical Traits

The above examples make it evident that it is difficult to establish race as a biological category. One major difficulty in this regard is that over the centuries inbreeding among peoples has blurred the physical traits. Thus physical lines of differences cannot help to demarcate races. Nearly all racial groups are considered intermixed. The Jews of Israel provide the best example in this regard. The complexions of Jews who have migrated to their homeland are as diverse as those in the various countries from which they have come. The Jews, in the light of this fact cannot be stated as constituting a biological race.

Physical Differences are Often Due to Adaptations

Physical differences also cannot decide race: These physical differences have resulted from the adaptations that human groups have made to the environments in which they lived. For ***example***, population in tropical and subtropical areas tend to have dark skin, which protects them against harmful rays from the sun. Populations in high altitudes tend to have large lung capacity, which makes breathing easier for them. Populations in very cold climates tend to have relatively short limbs, which enable them to conserve body heat. Further, there is no convincing evidence that different groups inherit different psychological characteristics, whether these be general traits such as intelligence, or more specific ones such as artistic ability.

The Concept of 'Pure Race' is a Myth.

All existing sociological and biological evidences point to the conclusion that there is no such thing as a *"pure race"*. Different population groups have been inbreeding for tens of thousands of years, and categories of *"race"* are only a creation of observer, not of nature. As it is stated, there is a great deal of overlap among the so called races in the distribution of the physical traits such as skin colour, hair texture, blood type, nose shape, facial features, and so on. *"Human groups have exchanged their genes through mating to such an extent that any attempt to identify 'pure races' is bound to be fruitless"* [5]

Race Assumes Importance Because it is a Social Fact, and Not Because, it is a Biological Fact

All races are approximately alike in every important physical characteristic. The physical differences within the human species are very modest compared with the differences within many species-dogs or horses, for example. Many anthropologists have now abandoned the attempt to classify human species into races and consider the term *"race"* to have no scientific meaning at all.

It is true that physical differences between human groups constitute a biological fact. As such, they are of no particular interest to the sociologist. *The sociologist is interested in race because race assumes importance as a social fact.* It means, people attach meanings to the physical differences, real or imagined, between human groups. If people believe that a certain group forms a biological unity, they will act on the basis of that belief. The members of such group tend to develop in-group feelings and a common loyalty and decide to intermarry with another. They also tend to develop *"they"* - feelings towards other groups, and may regard them as *"different."*

What is important here is that the question, whether social beliefs about race have any biological basis or not, is

[5] Views of Alland (1973), Dobzhansky (1962), and Gould (1981) - as mentioned by Kornblum in his *Sociology—In a Changing World,* p. 291.

irrelevant. *Because, race does not have any biological basis.* However, people's *beliefs about race influence race relations, for better or worse*. Many people, for ***example***, consider the Jews, a race. From the biological point of view, this idea is baseless. Jews who were scattered over several nations have always interbred to some extent with their host populations and that the so called *'original'* or *'pure'* Jewish race is not found anywhere. Yet when any group is arbitrarily defined as a race, as Jews were in Germany, important consequences may follow.

Ethnic Groups

Unlike the term race, the term *"ethnic group"* has a cultural meaning. It is regarded as a human group which has its national origin or distinctive cultural patterns. The term ethnic group or ethnicity signifies cultural features which may include - *language, religion, national origin, dietary practices, a sense of common historical heritage, or other distinctive cultural traits.*

According to **Milton Gordon**, the word *ethnicity* comes from the Greek *"ethnos"*, which mean *people* or *nation*. Thus, an ***ethnic group*** thinks of itself as a people or nation or is viewed by others as culturally different. ***Ethnicity** is a sense of peoplehood or nationhood.* The members of an ethnic group feel themselves set apart from other groups by a sense of belonging together, usually due to shared customs, beliefs, language or religion.

Definition of Ethnic Group

1. **Horton** and **Hunt:** The term ethnic group could be used to refer to - *"any kind of group, racial or otherwise, which is socially identified as different and has developed its own subculture."*
2. **Richard T. Schaefer:** *"An ethnic group is set apart from others primarily because of its national origin or distinctive cultural patterns."*
3. **David Popenoe:** An ethnic group is defined as *"a group that is socially differentiated, has developed its own subculture, and has 'a shared feeling of peoplehood.'"*
4. **J. Milton Yinger:** *"An ethnic group is a segment of a large society whose members are thought, by themselves or others, to have a shared culture."*

Essential Aspects of Ethnic Groups

J.M. Yinger's definition, in particular, point out at three important elements of ethnic groups

1. *Outsiders view of the group*: An ethnic group is seen by others as a distinctive group on the basis of the following aspects: *language, religion, race and country of origin.* ***For example***, the Palestinian Arabs living in Israel constitute an ethnic group. Because, unlike the Israelis, they speak Arabic and not Hebrew, they are Muslims and not Jews. Like all other Israelis, however, they are identified as Semitic peoples. They claim that the land of Israel was originally Palestine and it has been taken from them illegally.

2. *Insiders view of themselves* : People who belong, or feel belong to the group, consider themselves different from the society at large. In the above mentioned example, the Palestinian Arab's differentiate themselves sharply from the Israel population.

3. *Participation in common activities* : Members of an ethnic group take part together in activities that are centred in their shared traits and background activities. ***Example***, people visiting *"their own kind", celebrating holidays special to them.*

Other Aspects of the Ethnic Group

***Membership through biological continuity* :** Membership in an ethnic group is believed to be passed on from generation to generation, from parent to child. It is through this hereditary membership that the biological continuity assumes importance as an element in the definition of an ethnic group.

***Maintenance of a sense of peoplehood* :** Ethnic groups have a sense of *"peoplehood"* that is maintained within a larger society. The members of ethnic groups usually have migrated to a new nation or have been conquered by an invading population.

Race and Ethnic Groups: Main Differences

1. ***'Race'*** as a concept refers only to physical characteristics, but the concept of ***ethnicity*** refers to cultural features which include *religion, language, national origin*, etc.

2. Unlike racial characteristics *ethnic differences are culturally learnt,* and not genetically inherited.
3. *Racial characteristics are mostly inherited.* But no ethnic group has any inborn cultural traits; It acquires them from its environment. For ***example***, the Tamilians of India and the Srilankan Tamilians ancestry share the same genetic heritage, yet they display very different cultural norms and values.

MINORITY GROUPS

Human life in pre-industrial societies was different from what it is today. The nature of the pre-industrial society in the past was such that it was simple, small and homogeneous. People in such societies used to share the same values, speak the same language, worship the same goals; and had very similar characteristics.

Societies in the modern world are large and heterogeneous. As a result of colonisation, missionary work, migration, and the movement of the refugees due to famine, poverty persecution, etc., these societies frequently contain minorities. The physical appearance and cultural practices of these minorities are different from those of the dominant group. Wide differences are hence seen between these so called *"minorities"* and the *"dominant group"*. This often makes the dominant group in these societies to differentiate between its members and the minority. Very often unequal treatment is meted out to the members of the minority group denying them equal access to power, wealth and prestige.

Who constitute the minority then, and how to define it ? The concept of *'minority group'* is an important one in sociology, and it is used in a specific manner. Let us now try to understand its nature.

Meaning and Definition of Minority Group

1. **The Dictionary Meaning** [*Chambers Dictionary*] of the word minority is - *"less than half'"*, *"the smaller number, "the condition or fact of being little or less."*
2. **The New Encyclopaedia Britanica** [Vol. 27. Page: 356] : 'The most common general description of a minority group used, is of - *an aggregate of people who are distinct in religion, language, or nationality from other members of the society in which they live and who think of themselves, and are thought of by others, as being separate and distinct."*
3. **N. J. Smelser**: A minority group may be defined as *"a group of people who, because of their physical or cultural characteristics, are singled out from the others in the society in which they live for differential and unequal treatment and who, therefore, regard themselves as objects of collective discrimination* (**Wirth**, 1945, Page: 347.)
4. **Wallace and Wallace**: *"A minority group is one which has less power and influence than the dominant group."*
5. **Richard T. Schaefer :** *"A minority group is a sub-ordinate group whose members have significantly less control or power over their own lives than the members of a dominant group have over theirs."*

Characteristics of Minority Groups

Sociologists[6] have identified five basic properties of a minority group such as - *physical or cultural traits, unequal treatment, ascribed status, solidarity, and in-group marriage.*

1. Physically and/Or Socially Visible Group Characteristics

Members of a minority group share physical or cultural characteristics that distinguish them from the dominant group. The characteristics and boundaries of a minority group are socially defined on arbitrary grounds. Thus, for example, all people sharing some visible or noticeable [physical or non-physical] characteristics, such as skin colour, religion or language are grouped together into a single category. What particular characteristic is used to make this differentiation matters very little, but it is believed to be of great social importance. Further, individual characteristics of a minority group member are regarded as less important than the branded or assumed characteristics of the group to which the individual belongs.

2. Self-Conscious Group With a Strong Sense of Oneness

Minority group members have a strong sense of group solidarity. Members of a minority, such as Jews in America, Muslims in India, Tamilians in Srilanka, Blacks in America, Palestinians in Middle East tend to feel a strong affinity with one another. Their sense of common identity or *"consciousness of kind"*, is often so strong that differences within the group are neglected and a common loyalty to the group is developed. The minority group's shared experience of suffering heightens

[6] Wagley and Harries, 1964; Williams, 1964; and Vander Zanden, 1972 as referred to by Ian Robertson in *Sociology*, p. 266.

these feelings. When a group is the object of long term prejudice and discrimination, the feelings of group solidarity are likely to become more intense.

3. Minority Group Suffers from Unequal Treatment

Members of a minority group experience unequal treatment and have less power over their lives than members of a dominant group have over theirs. They suffer disadvantages at the hands of another group. The minority is denied equal access to power, wealth and prestige. What is more significant here is that - *the minority's disadvantage itself is an important source of the dominant group's advantage.* The dominant group exploits the minority relegating its members to low status positions in society. Social inequality is meted out to the minority group, they are exploited, and are made to become the victims of prejudice, discrimination, abuse, and humiliation. They are also considered by deeply held social beliefs as somewhat *"inferior"*

4. Membership in Minority Group is Not Voluntary

Membership in a dominant or a minority group *is not voluntary, people are born into the group*. Thus, race and ethnicity are considered as *"ascribed"* statuses. Common ancestry and common tradition often lead to a sense of common identity. It is often difficult for a member of a minority group to leave the group, for the reason that dominant group regards any one with minority group ancestry as a permanent member of that minority. In America, for example, a person with one black parent, or even a person with white parents and only one black grandparent - is still regarded as black rather than white.

5. Minority People Marry Within the Group

Members of a minority generally get married from the same group *by choice or necessity*. This practice of *endogamy* may be encouraged by the dominant group, or by the minority group, or by both. A member of a dominant group is often unwilling to join a supposedly inferior minority by marrying one of its members. In addition, the minority group's sense of solidarity encourages marriages within the group and discourages marriages outside.

In addition to the above explained five characteristics of the minority group, we may add a sixth one. It is stated below.

6. Minority Status Does Not Always Depend Upon Numerical Strength

In some peculiar circumstances, a minority group can sometimes be a numerical majority. Minority group status is not always a matter of numbers, on the contrary, it is determined by the presence of the distinguishing features explained above. The situation in which a community which has numerical majority assuming a minority status is rather very strange and rare. But such situations do exist in our practical life. ***Example:*** (*i*) In the African country of the **Burundi,** the small **Tutsi** tribe dominates the large **Hutu** tribe. (*ii*) In South Africa, the small White population dominates the much larger Black population.

RACISM AND ITS NATURE

Modern societies consist of people who belong to different racial and ethnic groups. Some of these racial and ethnic groups are able to live together in harmony and mutual respect, but others are in a state of constant antagonism and conflict. The dominant race tries to impose its will on the weaker ones. This domination of one race over another leads to suppression and exploitation also. This phenomenon is often interpreted as *"racism"*.

1. ***Collin's Dictionary of Sociology*** : *"Racism or racialism is a set of beliefs, ideologies and social processes that discriminate against others on the basis of their supposed membership of a racial group"*.

2. **N.J. Smelser :** *"Identifying a group as belonging to a different race and subjecting its members to discrimination, exploitation, or violent oppression is known as racism."*

3. **Blauner :** *Racism is a phenomenon in which a group that is seen as inferior or different is exploited and oppressed by a dominant group.*

Examples **:** Among the most notorious examples of racism, the following may be noted. 1. The domination of the non-western world by the European powers during the late 20th century. 2. The partial extermination and subsequent segregation of native Americans; 3. The oppression of Black Americans first as slaves and then as exploited minority; 4. The genocide of an estimated 6 million Jews by Nazi Germany after *the World War I.*

Ethnocentric Attitudes at the Root of Racism

Extreme ethnocentric attitudes are found to be at the root of racism. Ethnocentrism[7] seems to be common to most of the human groups. To most people, it is self-evident that their own norms, religion, attitudes, values and cultural practices are right and proper, while those of other groups are peculiar, stupid and even immoral. A certain amount of ethnocentrism seems to be inevitable and even functional also. But the problem is the ethnocentric attitudes that are functional for one group may prove to be highly dysfunctional for another group. Under certain conditions, ethnocentric attitudes can take an extreme and aggressive form and can be used to justify the oppressive treatment of other racial or ethnic groups. This leads to what is known as ***racism.*** It should not be generalised that contact among different groups inevitably leads to racism. Further, ethnocentrism also develops into racism only under some conditions, and not always. Sociological studies have tried to reveal some of these conditions leading to racism.

The Causes of Racism

The perspective of the conflict theory is of great help in understanding the problem of racism. Three basic conditions are necessary for racism to develop according to **Noel** and **Vander Zanden**. They are stated below.

1. ***Visible physical or cultural characteristics:*** The phenomenon of racism presupposes the existence of two or more social groups, identifiable by their visible physical characteristics or cultural practices. People should be aware of differences between the groups and should be able to identify themselves as belonging to one group rather than another. Only then, racism can develop.
2. ***Competition between the groups:*** It is necessary for the groups to have competition between themselves for valued resources, such as power, land, or jobs. In this condition of extreme competition, members of one group will be inclined to secure their own interests by denying members of other group full access to these resources.
3. ***Presence of groups with unequal power:*** Another condition of racism is that the group must be unequal in power. In such a condition, one of them is able to make good its claim over scarce resources at the expense of the other group or groups. At this point, inequalities become structured into the society.

The conditions stated above, provide a favourable atmosphere for racism to thrive. Extreme competition between groups for example, make them to develop negative attitude towards each other. The dominant group develops racist views about the supposed inferiority of the minority group or groups. The dominant group uses these views to justify its continued supremacy. Any attempt made by the minority group to assert its own interests is likely to be regarded as threatening by the dominant group and as a result, further repression may follow.

The conflict theorists are of the opinion that economic inequalities underlie racism. They are of the view that disputes between groups are not so much about racial or ethnic distinctions as about the use of supposed distinctions to preserve an unequal society.

Marxian conflict theories trace the origins of racial and ethnic inequality to the conflict between classes in capitalist societies. Marx believed, for example, that American wage earners were unlikely to become highly class conscious because ethnic and racial divisions continually set them against one another and the resulting strife could be manipulated by the capitalist class. To forge class solidarity it would be necessary for workers to renounce their smaller group loyalties, including their loyalty to a particular ethnic or racial group.[8]

The Ideology of Racism

Racism is used as an ideology by a dominant group to legitimate its interests. An ideology or set of beliefs defines the existing system as just and moral. *"Racism is an ideology based on the belief that an observable, supposedly inherited trait, such as skin colour, is a mark of inferiority that justifies the discriminatory treatment of people with that trait".*[9]

No group can systematically exploit and debase another group without using some values of ideology to justify this behaviour. The ideology of racism serves to legitimate the social inequalities between groups by making them *"natural"*,

[7] Ethnocentrism refers to the tendency to judge other cultures by the standards of one's own."—Ian Robertson in his *Sociology,* p. 64

[8] Kornblum in his *Sociology,* pp. 309-310.

[9] Ibid, p. 292.

or *"right"*. The racial ideologists, for example, by making use of the people's beliefs and sayings such as *"slaves are happy"*; *"the only good Indian is a dead Indian"*, etc., intend to make *"Slavery and slaughter"* more acceptable policies.

Racial Ideology Supporting the 'Self-Fulfilling Prophecy'

The ideology of racism also supports the existing inequalities by the social process of the *"self-fulfilling prophecy"* [**Merton**, 1968]. American sociologist **W.I. Thomas** explained this idea in the form of a simple statement which is popularly known as *"Thomas Theorem"*. *"If men define situation as real, they are real in their consequences"*. This is made clear by Merton by means of an ***example*** **:** *If people wrongly believe that a bank will go bankrupt, they will rush to withdraw their money with the result that the bank will go bankrupt.* The self-fulfilling prophecy is a false definition of a situation, but the definition leads to behaviour that makes the prediction come true. The actual course of events then seems to justify and confirm the original prophecy.

This *self-fulfilling prophecy* also works in the case of race relations. The racist ideology of the dominant group defines the minority as inferior. Since the minority group is branded as inferior, they are considered as unfit for higher - status jobs, higher education and responsible positions in society. Hence, they are denied these opportunities. As a result, they are forced to stick to low - status jobs, and are poorly educated. This situation makes the minority group inferior, and the racist ideology is confirmed.

Four Beliefs at the Root of Racism

Simpson and **Yinger** in their classic text on racial and cultural minorities highlighted four beliefs at the root of racism. They are as follows:

(*i*) The first one is *the doctrine of "biologically superior and inferior races*[10]

(*ii*) *Members of different races have different personalities;*

(*iii*) *That there are identifiable "racial cultures", and*

(*iv*) *That ethical standards differ from one race to another.*

Social scientists have rejected all these doctrines or beliefs which are at the root of racism as baseless through their studies over the past 6-7 decades. But eventhough these doctrines have been discredited they continue to play a major role in intergroup relations in many nations. And this tendency to denigrate or degrade socially defined racial groups extends to members of particular ethnic groups as well.

PATTERNS OF RACE AND ETHNIC RELATIONS

What type of relations prevail between different racial and ethnic groups - ? and majority and minority groups - ? This is an important question in the study of race and ethnic relations. It is observed that race and ethnic relations and majority and minority relations range from harmonious co-existence to outright conflict. According to **Simpson** and **Yinger** (1972), six basic patterns of intergroup hostility or co-operation are identifiable. This typology covers virtually all the possible patterns of race and ethnic relations, and each pattern exists or has existed in some part of the world. This typology includes: 1. *Assimilation*, 2. *Pluralism*, 3. *Legal Protection of Minorities*, 4. *Population Transfer*, 5. *Continued Subjugation*, and 6. *Extermination*.

1. Assimilation

Assimilation involves outright elimination of the minority group as a minority. In some cases, a minority group is simply eliminated by being assimilated into the dominant group. *"Assimilation is the pattern of intergroup relations in which a minority group either is forced or encouraged or voluntarily seeks to blend into the majority population and eventually disappears as a distinct people within the larger society"*[11]

The process of assimilation, may involve cultural assimilation, racial assimilation, or both. Cultural assimilation occurs when the minority group gives up its distinctive cultural traits and adopts those of the dominant culture. Racial assimilation

---

[10] For example, before World War I, most of the social thinkers in the Western world firmly believed that Whites were genetically superior to Blacks in intelligence. However, the conduct of IQ tests particularly after 1930s revealed that performance on such test was linked to social class background rather than to race.

[11] Kornblum in *Sociology*, p. 299.

takes place when the physical differences between the groups disappear as a result of inbreeding. Many Latin American societies offer examples of peaceful, long-term assimilation of various racial and ethnic groups. Brazil is a good example of a country following the policy of assimilation. In Brazil, the various racial, ethnic groups within the society, with the exception of some isolated Indian groups, interbreed more or less freely. There are some places in Brazil in which there is discrimination against Blacks, but these are the exception rather than the rule. Similarly, Portugal attempted a policy of assimilation in the African colonies that it ruled in the mid-seventies. For most ethnic minorities in the United States, assimilation has been both forced and peaceful.

2. Cultural Pluralism

The recognition that ethnic groups maintain their own communities and subcultures even while some of their members are assimilated into the larger society, gave support to the concept of cultural pluralism. *"A pluralist society is one in which different ethnic and racial groups are able to maintain their own cultures and life-styles even as they gain equality in the institutions of the larger society."*[12]

Pluralism involves a commitment on the part of the dominant group to maintain diversity among minority groups. It also involves a willingness to permit the diversity. Hence, it may encourage cultural variation within the broader confines of national unity. ***Example*** **:** Switzerland is the most outstanding example of pluralism. In Switzerland four ethnic groups speaking German, French, Italian and Romanche, retain a sense of group identity while living together amicably in the society as a whole. (*ii*) In **Tanzania** also Africans, Europeans and middle Eastern peoples participate with relative equality in the public life of their society while retaining distinctive languages and customs. No group dominates the others.

3. Legal Protection of Minorities

In some societies, significant sections of the dominant group may have hostile attitudes towards the minority groups. But such minorities may enjoy the protection of the government. This is a kind of *"official"* pluralism in that it involves legal protection of differences and a guarantee of autonomy for minority groups. The government may even take necessary legal measures to protect the interests and rights of the minorities. ***Example*** **:** (*i*) The Indian Government has declared in the preamble of the Constitution itself that all its citizens are assured of liberty, equality and justice. *Article*s 29 and 30 of the Indian Constitution protect the religious, educational, linguistic, literary and other interests of the minorities. (*ii*) In Britain, *the Race Relations Act of 1965* makes it illegal to discriminate against any person on racial grounds in employment or housing. (*iii*) In America also, the constitution underwent the 13th, 14th and the 15th Amendments in order to empower it to protect the rights of the minorities.

4. Population Transfer or Relocation

Population relocation or transfer occurs when the minority group relocates either outside the territory or in a particular part of the territory. In some situations of intense hostility between groups, the problem is *"solved"* by removing the minority from the scene altogether. Population relocation can be either forced or voluntary, for ***example,*** during 1970s General Idi Amin of Uganda sought to relieve ethnic tensions by ordering all Asians to leave Uganda. He wanted native Ugandans to occupy the business and trade positions vacated by Asians.

Sometimes relocation creates an entirely new nation, as when India was divided into India and Pakistan in order to create separate states for Hindu and Muslim citizens. There are signs that Cyprus is becoming permanently divided into Greek and Turkish territories, and Lebanon into Muslim and Christian Territories. Voluntary and forced population transfers have been taking place in both territories.

5. Continued Subjugation

In some cases, the dominant group has every intention of maintaining its privilege over the minority group indefinitely. It may be ready to use force to achieve this objective, and it may even physically segregate the members of the various groups. Historically, continued subjugation has been a very common policy. Subjugation usually takes the form of racism as we witnessed it in an extreme form in the policy of apartheid. The white minority proposed to keep its power over the Black majority for ever and openly declared this goal.

[12] *Ibid*, pp. 302-303.

As a result of the apartheid policy, the Whites controlled the government and owned all farm land, factories and natural resources. Non-Whites, that is, the Blacks and others were concentrated in the lowest-paid, lowest-status jobs and had only limited access to schools, housing, and medical care. Until recently, most attempts by non-Whites to resist this system were violently suppressed by the White government.

6. Extermination or Genocide

An extreme form of subjugation is genocide, the murder of a race. This has been attempted and even achieved in several parts of the world. The methods of genocide include systematic slaughter by force of arms and the deliberate spreading of infectious diseases, particularly small pox, to peoples who have no natural immunity to them. ***Examples*** : (*i*) The notorious example is the attempted extermination of **Jews** by the Nazis during the World War II. More than 6 million Jews were slaughtered by various means. (*ii*) Dutch settlers in South Africa entirely exterminated the **Hottentots**. They almost came to exterminate the **San**, who in the South African history were actually classified as *"vermin"*; (*iii*) In the 1890's and in 1915, the **Turks** massacred Armenians in thousands, (*iv*) The capitalists with vested economic interests in possessing land slaughtered the Indian occupants of the land with the secret support of the Brazilian government. There are many such examples of genocide. The Spanish conquerors exterminated some of the native populations of Central and South America during the 16th and 19th centuries. (*v*) The European settlers in North America, aided by the army in many cases exterminated tribes of native Americans. (*vi*) Examples of massacres include the slaughter of Protestants in Catholic Countries and of Catholics in Protestant countries during the 16th and 17th centuries; (*vii*) A more recent example of attempted genocide occurred in the African state of Burundi in 1972, when the dominant **Tutsi** tribe massacred nearly one lakh members of the **Hutu** tribe. (*vii*) More recently the Paraguayan Government systematically attempted to destroy the primitive **"Ache Indians"** [Arens - 1976.][13] (*ix*) Even India is experiencing the pinch of it at the hands of Pakistani infiltrators in Kashmir. Continuous attacks on and the murder of Hindus in Kashmir reveal that Pakistan has the hidden agenda of making Kashmir a totally Muslim inhabited state so that it could grab it one day. As per one estimate as many as 75000 civilians mostly Hindus and army and paramilitary personnel have been killed in Kashmir by the Pakistan terrorists in the past 10 years.

Simpson and **Yinger** point out that these types of relationships among majority and minority groups are not mutually exclusive. A society can adopt more than one of them at the same time. They can range from official government policies to completely informal, day by day responses of individuals. The United States at some point in its history made use of every single one of these strategies. **Banton** (1977) has suggested several typical sequences of racial and ethnic relations. For example, the relations among Europeans and Africans during the colonial and post-colonial period could be described as an initial period of contact, followed by a period of paternalism and domination of the Africans and then, in the post-colonial period, by the integration of two groups.

MINORITIES AS A PROBLEM

"Minorities" or *"Minority Groups"* - as such have started emerging as a social as well as a national problem especially after the First World War. Due to the historico-political changes that took place in the beginning of the 20th century, many nations started taking their birth from the remnants of the medieval imperialism. Communities of people which once constituted majority communities got reduced to the status of *'minorities'*. ***For example,*** Germans in Poland and Austrians in Czechoslovakia, suddenly became *"minorities"*. To ensure international peace in the midst of these developments, and to protect the interests of the minority groups *"project Guarantee Treaties"* were also held between nations. As per these treaties, it was decided that the newly formed minority communities should be loyal to their new states and their Governments; and these Governments in turn, would consider these peoples as their new national citizens and not as enemies, and would give them all the needed protection.

Dimensions of the Minority Problems

For the past one hundred years, the problems of minorities have been assuming extra-ordinary importance in the day to day politics of many nations. Many of these problems are still alive. In the Western nations, in Asia and Africa this problem is cropping up every now and then. ***For example,*** racial conflicts and riots are still taking place in England and America.

[13] Quoted by Wallace and Wallace, p. 314.

In Russia, the Armenians and Azerbaizanions have fought bloody wars. The Serbs and Croats in Yugoslavia have fought each other in order to go apart.

Many developing nations in the Third World are also caught by the problems associated with the minorities. In many of these nations, racial tensions, communal riots; ethnic clashes have become almost the daily political news. In Srilanka, conflicts are still going on between the Buddhists and the Tamil ethnic groups. The position of India is also very precarious. The communal riots which have a history of more than 100 years costed India very heavily in 1947, when it was divided into two separate nations purely on communal lines.

MAIN PROBLEMS OF THE MINORITIES

Minorities of ethnic, religious, racial or linguistic character of different nations of the world are facing two important problems: (*i*) *the problem of prejudice and discrimination,* and (*ii*) *the problem of preserving their distinct social and cultural life.*

Problem of Prejudice and Discrimination

Prejudice and discrimination are found in any situation of hostility between racial and ethnic groups and divergent religious communities. The two terms are often used interchangeably in ordinary speech, but in fact, they refer to two different, but related phenomena.

The phenomenon of Prejudice

Prejudice refers to a *"pre-judged" attitude towards members of another group.* These groups are regarded with hostility simply because they belong to a particular group, and they are assumed to have the undesirable qualities that are supposed to be characteristic of the group as a whole.

False definitions of individuals and groups are perpetuated by prejudice. Prejudice is a *negative attitude towards a category of people* often an ethnic or racial community. It is *a judgement based on group membership or racial status."* [**Wallace and Wallace**].

Prejudice implies a negative or an unfavourable attitude: Prejudice, in normal usage means preconceived opinion or bias against or in favour of a person or thing. Biases could be positive as well as negative. But the term *'prejudice'* most commonly refers to a negative or unfavourable attitude towards a group or its individual members. Prejudice is characterised by stereotyped beliefs that are not tested against reality, but rather have to do with a person's own feelings and attitudes.

As **Gordon Allport** writes in his classic book *"The Nature of Prejudice" - (1954) - "prejudice is an antipathy based upon a faulty and inflexible generalisation."*[14] Prejudice may be felt or expressed. It may be directed towards a group as a whole, or towards an individual member of that group. Some people are more prone to have prejudiced outlooks than others.

Prejudice violates social norms and sense of justice: Sociological definitions of the term tend to stipulate that prejudice violates some social norms such as rationality, justice, or tolerance. It violates rational thought. As far as its net effect is concerned , - it places the individual or group at some disadvantage that is not merited. Prejudice is inherently unjust. It involves intolerance and even the violation of human dignity.

Prejudice works on the "in-group and out-group" principle: Prejudice is both a consequence of and *a reinforcement for the existence of in-groups and out-groups,* which embody the distinction between *'them'* and *'us'*. In-group and out-group attitudes are intrinsically related, because in-group feeling results in out-group sentiment, and vice versa. It could almost be claimed that one side derives its identity from the fact of its opposition to the other. In this sense, the out-group is necessary for the cohesion and emotional security of the in-group, and an out-group might need to be invented, if one does not already exist.

"Prejudice, by magnifying the vices of the enemy, ensures that norms of justice and tolerance no longer apply. Prejudice does not always result in any hostile action, but when prejudice is made manifest it can range from (at minimum) avoidance or discrimination, through to mass extermination, as in the Holocaust."[15]

Prejudice may lead to social oppression: Sociologically speaking, the social consequences of prejudice focusing on

[14] *Oxford Dictionary of Sociology*, p. 522.

[15] Gordon Marshall in *Oxford Dictionary of Sociology*, p. 523.

race, or gender or on ethnic and other minorities are very significant. Technically, for example, any prejudice with a racial basis constitutes racism, just as any based on *sex is sexism and any based on ethnicity is ethnicism. This means that prejudice directed against men is sexist, just as the prejudice directed by the Blacks against the Whites is racist. One objection to this view is that the consequences of prejudice aimed at the minorities are very different from the prejudice aimed at the dominant groups by the minorities, usually in self-defence. The former supports and perpetuates social oppression. The latter, however, has relatively trivial consequences for members of the dominant groups since they are unlikely even to be aware of them.*[16] Further, prejudice is sociologically important because it underlies discrimination, the unequal treatment of people who happen to belong to a particular group or category.

The Phenomenon of Discrimination and Its Consequences

Discrimination refers to *action against other people on the grounds of their group membership.* It involves the refusal to grant members of another group the opportunities that would be granted to similarly qualified members of one's own group.

- *"Discrimination involves treating someone differently because of his or her group membership or social status."*[17]
- *"Discrimination refers to the "process by which a member, or members, of a socially defined group is, or are, treated differently, that is, unfairly, because of his/her/their membership of that group."*[18] A social group to be selected for less favourable treatment may be a racial group, ethnic group, gender group, or religious or linguistic group.

Minority Groups as the Target of Discrimination

The essential feature of a minority group is that its members are subject to **discrimination,** or unequal treatment because of *"bad"* traits.

***The dominant group claiming social advantage at the expense of the minority groups*:** Discrimination takes place when the dominant group regards itself as entitled to social advantages and uses its power to secure those advantages at the expense of the minority groups. These advantages may be of many different kinds. The dominant group may, for example, reserve positions of political power for itself; it may establish a claim over desirable residential areas; it may demand the exclusive use of certain recreational facilities and schools; it may claim right to high-status jobs. In extreme cases, it may even enforce the physical segregation of the minority group from the rest of society.[19]

***Prevalence of discriminatory practices*:** Discriminatory practices often become embedded in society's laws. A few years ago, for example, it was illegal in many southern states of USA for the Blacks to vote, to ride anywhere except in the rear of buses, or to eat in the same restaurants and use the same toilet facilities as the Whites. Discrimination has an informal side also. This is also illustrated by the traditional Southern USA, where it was expected that a Black person would step off and make the way for an approaching White. In fact, similar, and even more severe discriminatory practices against the Blacks prevailed in South Africa during the British rule against which Mahatma Gandhiji waged a successful and an untring non-violent battle.[20]

***Institutionalised discrimination*:** The concept of *"institutionalised discrimination"* reveals that *"discrimination against some groups in a society can result from the majority simply adhering, unthinkingly to the existing organisational and institutional rules or norms"*[21] Institutionalised sexism and institutionalised racism are most common manifestations of this phenomenon. Institutionalised discrimination invariably leads to unequal treatment. When unequal treatment takes the form of systematic abuse, exploitation, and injustice, it becomes social oppression.

Institutionalised discrimination prevails in many areas of society*:** This could be observed in the United States where discrimination is still practised in their race relations. ***For example, informal barriers to residential integration have resulted in a pattern of urban racial segregation. As a result, the Whites and the Blacks tend to use segregated schools and other

---

[16] Allan G. Hohnson *The Blackwell Dictionary of Sociology,* p. 213.

[17] Wallace and Wallace, p. 311.

[18] *Collin's Dictionary of Sociology*, p. 169.

[19] Ian Robertson in his *Sociology*, p. 277.

[20] However, in the U.K., at present, there are laws that deal with both sex and race discrimination: *The Sex Discrimination Act,* (1975) and *The Race Relations Act*, (1976). In both Acts, direct discrimination is made illegal, in that a person may not be treated less favourably than another on the grounds of gender, colour, ethnicity or race."—*Collins Dictionary of Sociology,* p. 169.

[21] *Oxford Dictionary of Sociology*, p. 318.

facilities. Similarly, there is a strong tendency towards discrimination in hiring practices, so that the Blacks have much higher unemployment rates and consistently earn less than the similarly qualified Whites. The Blacks are underrepresented in all the high-status positions in society – ***for example***, in Congress, in the judiciary, or at the upper levels of military and corporate power. In the same way, there is institutionalized discrimination within the legal system: the Blacks are likely to receive more severe sentences than the Whites convicted of the same crimes.

Prejudice and Discrimination are Interrelated

Prejudice and discrimination are closely linked, but they may exist separately. Prejudice is a judgement whereas discrimination is the actual practice of treating people or groups unfairly. A person may hold a prejudice without discriminating. He may, indeed, hold hundreds of prejudices against different groups but may not act upon them. Also, some people may discriminate without feeling any prejudice. ***For example,*** a business person might refuse to serve people of a particular minority group on the grounds that serving them would cause other customers to stay away, although he does not feel prejudiced against the minority group. Four variations of these qualities have been suggested by **Simpson** and **Yinger**. They are stated below.

1. *There can be prejudice without discrimination;*
2. *There can be discrimination without prejudice;*
3. *Prejudice can be among the causes of discrimination; and*
4. *Probably, most frequently, prejudice and discrimination are mutually re-inforcing*

Robert K. Merton (1949) has introduced a typology consisting of four distinct persons and their characteristic responses relating to prejudice and discrimination. The typology is stated below.

1. ***The unprejudiced nondiscriminator*:** Some do not have any prejudice and do not engage in discriminatory practices. *The unprejudiced nondiscriminator* adheres to the ideal of equality in both theory and practice. Such a person is not prejudiced and does not discriminate against others on racial or ethnic grounds.
2. ***The unprejudiced discriminator*:** Some may indulge in discriminatory practices but may not have prejudices. *The unprejudiced discriminator* has not personal prejudices, but may discriminate when it is convenient to do so. ***For example,*** *an employer may have no personal hostility towards members of another group, but may not hire their services for fear of offending customers.*
3. ***The prejudiced non-discriminator*:** Some may have prejudice but may not practice discrimination. *The prejudiced non-discriminator* is a *"timid"* person who is prejudiced against other groups but does not have the courage to translate attitudes into action.
4. ***The prejudiced discriminator*** does not genuinely believe in the values of freedom or equality and discriminates on the basis of prejudiced attitudes.

CAUSES AND CONSEQUENCES OF PREJUDICE AND DISCRIMINATION

Prejudices and discriminatory practices play a vital role in determining ethnic and race relations and also majority and minority relations. An analysis of these relations has to address a few basic questions. *What actually contribute to the attitude formation ? What factors influence individuals' and groups' toleration towards the minority groups ? Why do some people look at the minorities with malice, while a few others make friendship with them ?*

Of the various factors that contribute to prejudices and discrimination, the following are important.

1. Learnt Behaviour

As the psychologist **Gordon Allport** has pointed out both prejudice and discrimination are learnt. Attitudes are taught to children by adults and peers through direct statements [***Example*:** *Don't play with unclean caste people.*] and indirect messages [***Example*:** *"Thank God, no Black has become so far the president of USA.*] Children receive hints or clues from such statements and messages. Their mind become conditioned. Unknowingly, they start disliking or hating or keeping themselves away from such people.

2. Stereotype

The culture of a group defines whom to hate and why hate them. Sometimes, it may even describe the minority members in terms of a stereotype [22]

- *Stereotype is a set of inaccurate simplistic generalisations about a group of individuals.....*
- *"A stereotype is a rigid, over simplified, often exaggerated belief that is applied both to an entire category of people and to each individual within it."* [23]
- *"A stereotype is an exaggerated belief associated with a category."* [24]

The main function of a stereotype is to justify or rationalise one's conduct in relation to that category. ***Examples*** : (*i*) *The belief that people who depend upon public assistance are lazy — is a stereotype.* (*ii*) *The belief that man cannot take care of children like women – is also stereotype.* (*iii*) *In America, the Blacks have been stereotyped as lazy, superstitious, ignorant, musical and happy-go-lucky,* (*iv*) *Jews have been depicted as clannish, financially shrewed and pushy.* (*v*) *In India, the Hindus are often stereotyped as cowards, the Muslims as fanatics, Christians as converters, and so on.*

Stereotypes of racial, social class, caste, religious and gender groups are commonly held and they often lead to the treatment of individuals according to unjustified preconceptions. Stereotypes are important because they form the basis of prejudice which in turn, is used to justify discrimination and both positive and negative attitudes. Though stereotypes can be positive also, their negative aspect is more often stressed. Stereotypes are regarded as undesirable because of the prominent role they play in social oppression based on characteristics such as race, gender, ethnicity, etc.

Like ethnocentrism, stereotyped thinking is an almost unavoidable feature of social life. The essence of the prejudiced thinking is that the stereotype is not checked against reality. It is not modified by experiences that contradict the rigid image. If a prejudiced person finds that an individual member of a group does not conform to the stereotype for the group as a whole, this evidence is simply taken as *"the exception that proves the race"* and not as grounds for questioning the original belief.

3. Impact of Socialisation

Because of continuous contact, intergroup relations assume a particular pattern. They get established to become a part of culture. When they become a part of culture, attitudes relating to these intergroup relations are taught to younger generation through socialisation. Thus, an individual's degree of tolerance or intolerance is at first usually a reflection of the culture and of socialisation. Where intergroup relations are strained and unequal, prejudice and discriminatory behaviour will probably exist. As the culture changes, individual attitudes change as well.

4. Self-Fulfilling Prophecy

Prejudice and discrimination are often reinforced by what **Robert K Merton** has called the *"self-fulfilling prophecy"* (1968). ***For example,*** the Blacks in North America were initially defined by the slave traders as sub-human and not capable of any high achievement. This assumption became a kind of prophecy. For more than three centuries, the policy of discrimination continued in America under the pretext of this policy. As a result, only a few Blacks in America have attained high positions. The original prophecy is thus fulfilled by its own consequences: The Whites were continuously told that the Blacks were inferior and hence they were treated as such. It often happens, too, that the minority group [Blacks in the cited example,] shares the beliefs that the dominant group [the whites] holds about them for it is quite common for an oppressed group to accept the ideology that justifies their oppression.

5. The Authoritarian Personality

Psychologists have attempted to determine whether certain types of people are more likely to be prejudiced than others. **Theodore Adorno** and his co-workers [1950] developed a model of a prejudiced individual which they call the *"authoritarian personality"*. Adorno was among the first to suggest a link between an "authoritarian personality" and prejudicial attitude.

Adorno concluded that some people have a distinct set of personality traits which together make up what he called the

[22] In fact, the word "stereotype" is borrowed from the printing process in which one impression is used to stamp out many exact copies.

[23] *The Blackwell Dictionary of Sociology*, P. 282.

[24] Wallace and Wallace, p. 318.

authoritarian personality. People who have this personality pattern are intolerant, insecure, highly conformist, submissive to superiors, and bullying to inferiors. They tend to have anti-intellectual and antiscientific attitudes; they are disturbed by any ambiguity in sexual or religious affairs; and they see the world in very rigid and stereotyped terms. The authoritarian personality, Adorno claimed, was primarily a product of a family environment in which the parents were cold, aloof, disciplinarian, and themselves bigoted.

People who are prejudiced against one group tend to be prejudiced against others as well. [**Hartley** -1946]. When surveyed, many prejudiced persons even indicated prejudice against fictitious minority groups [which were mixed in with the real ones] and endorsed expulsion from the United States of such non-existent minority groups as the *Danireans, Wallonians and Pireneans*. These three so called human groups do not exist, and never existed in the past. Their names were concocted by **Hartley** to see if people who were prejudiced against existing groups would also be prejudiced against groups they could never have met or even heard of. His study suggests that prejudice is learnt not through contact with the groups against whom prejudice is directed but through contact with other prejudiced people.

6. Scapegoating

"A scapegoat is an individual, group, or category of people used as an object of blame in a social system" [25]

Scapegoating typically occurs when the members of one group feel threatened but are unable to retaliate against the real source of the threat. Scapegoating provides a mechanism for venting rage, frustration, resentment, fear and other emotions. It is a mechanism for placing or putting the blame for one's troubles on some individual or group incapable of offering resistance. Hence, in scapegoating, people vent their frustrations on some weak and despised group. Immigrants and minorities are often used as scapegoats during the times of economic hardship and blamed as the cause of unemployment and other social problems. ***For example***, the low-status White may resent their low-social and economic status, but they cannot strike at the source of the problem - the *'employer'* or the *"system"*. Instead, they direct their hostility at the members of minority group normally, the Blacks, whom they believe to be competing for jobs at the same level. The best example of the scapegoating group were the Jews of Nazi Germany. The Jews in Germany were conveniently blamed for Germany's economic hardships after World War I.

PROBLEMS OF RELIGIOUS MINORITIES IN INDIA

India is a multi-lingual and a multi-religious country. Indian society is pluralistic in character from the religious and other points of view. Since a very long time people belonging to various religious communities have been living together in this country. Though the majority of the people living in this land are **Hindus** [82.41%], people belonging to other religious communities such as **Muslims** [11.67%], **Christians** [2.32%], **Sikhs** [2%], **Buddhists** [0.77%], **Jains** [0.41%] and **others** [0.43%][26] are also living along with the Hindus by enjoying on par similar rights and opportunities. By virtue of their numerical strength, the Hindus constitute the majority while the rest of the religious communities come under what is known as ***"religious minorities"***.

Regarding the concept of *"minority"* in the Indian context, it can be said that the term has not been properly defined anywhere in the Indian Constitution. But *"minority status"* has been conferred on many groups.

- According to the ***Article 29*** of the Constitution, *any group living within the jurisdiction of India is entitled to preserve and promote its own language, script or literature, and culture.*
- ***Article 30*** states that a minority group *"whether based on religion or language shall have the right to establish and administer educational institution of their choice."*

Problems of Religious Minorities

Racial, religious, ethnic, linguistic and other minorities are subject to some or the other problems everywhere. The two main problems which they normally face are: (*i*) *the problem of prejudice and discrimination, and* (*ii*) *the problem of preserving their distinct social and cultural life.*

[25] *The Blackwell Dictionary of Sociology*, p. 244.

[26] Statistics as per 1991 Census Report, *India Year Book*, 1999, p. 16

1. ***Problem of prejudice and discrimination:*** In the Indian context, ***discrimination*** *especially in providing opportunities to people of different religious communities* ***is, not at all in practice.*** The Preamble of the Constitution itself declares that all people irrespective of their caste, class, colour, creed, sex, region or religion will be provided with equal rights and opportunities. *Articles 15(1) and 15(2)* prohibit discrimination on grounds of religion. *Article 25* promises the right to profess, propagate and practise religion. It is clear that there is no legal bar on any religious community in India to make use of the opportunities [educational, economic, etc.] extended to the people. It is true that some religious communities [for example, Muslims] have not been able to avail themselves of the opportunities on par with other communities. This situation does not reflect any discrimination. It only reveals that such communities have been lagging behind in the competitive race, mainly because of the lack of educational qualification.

   As far as ***prejudices*** are concerned, prejudices and stereotyped[27] thinking are common features of a complex society. India is not an exception to this. Commonly used statements such as – *"Hindus are cowards and Muslims are rowdies; Sikhs are dullards and Christians are converters"*, etc. – reflect the prevalent religious prejudices. Such prejudices further widen the social distance among the religious communities. This problem still persists in India. Except in some sensitive areas this problem of prejudice is not disturbing the routine life of different communities, including that of the minorities.

2. ***Problem of preserving distinct social and cultural life:*** India is one among the very few nations which have given equal freedom to all the religious communities to pursue and practise their religion. *Article 25 of the Constitution* provides for such a right. Added to this, *Article 3D*(1) *states all minorities whether based on religion or language shall have the right to establish and administer educational institutions of their choice.* They are given the right to preserve their socio-cultural characteristics. It has set up a *"Minorities Commission"* to help the minorities in seeking justice. No minority community can have a grievance against any government particularly in this matter.

Some of the Problems of Minorities in India

In spite of the provisions of the constitutional equality, religious minorities in India, often experience some problems among which the following may be noted.

1. ***Problem of providing protection*:** Need for security and protection is very often felt by the minorities. Especially in times of communal violence, caste conflicts, observance of festivals and religious functions on a mass scale, minority groups often seek police protection. Government in power also finds it difficult to provide such a protection to all the members of the minorities. It is highly expensive also. State governments which fail to provide such protection are always criticised. ***For example,*** (*i*) the Rajiv Gandhi Government was severely criticised for its failure to give protection to the Sikh community in the Union Territory of Delhi on the eve of the communal violence that broke out there soon after the assassination of Indira Gandhi in 1984. (*ii*) The Gujarat State Government was criticised for its inability to provide protection to the Muslim minorities in the recent [Feb. Mar. - 2002] communal violence that burst out. (*iii*) Similarly, the Government of Jammu-Kashmir's inefficiency in providing adequate security to the Hindu and Sikh minorities in that State against the atrocities of Muslim extremists, is also widely condemned.
2. ***Problem of communal tensions and riots*:** Communal tensions and riots have been incessantly increasing since independence. Whenever the communal tensions and riots take place for whatever reason, minority interests get threatened; fears and anxieties become widespread. It becomes a tough task for the government in power to restore the confidence in them.
3. ***Problem of lack of representation in civil service and politics*:** Though the Constitution provides for equality and equal opportunities to all its citizens including the religious minorities, the biggest minority community, that is, Muslims in particular, have not availed themselves of these facilities. There is a feeling among them that they are neglected. However, such a feeling does not seem to exist among the other religious minority communities such as the Christians, Sikhs, Jains and Buddhists, for they seem to be economically and educationally better than the majority community.

[27] *Stereotypes:* "Prejudiced thought always involves the use of a rigid mental image that summarises whatever is believed to be typical about a group. This kind of image is called a *stereotype.*"—Ian Robertson in his book *Sociology.* p., 275.

4. ***Problem of separatism***: Some of the demands put forward by some religious communities in some areas are not acceptable to others. This has widened the gap between them and others. ***Examples***: The separatist tendency present among some Muslim extremists in Kashmir and their demand for the establishment of Independent Kashmir is not acceptable to others. Such a demand is regarded as anti-national. Similarly, some of the Christian extremists in Nagaland and Mizoram are demanding separate statehood for their provinces. Both these demands are supportive of *"separatism"* and hence cannot be accepted. Supporters of such demands have been causing lot of disturbances and creating law and order problems in the respective states.
5. ***Failure to stick on strictly to secularism***: India has declared itself as a *"secular"* country. The very spirit of our Constitution is secular. Almost all political parties including the Muslim League claim themselves to be secular. But in actual practice, no party is honest in its commitment to secularism. Purely religious issues are often politicised by these parties. Similarly, secular issues and purely law and order problems are given religious colours. These parties are always waiting for an opportunity to politicalise communal issues and take political advantage out of it. Hence, the credibility of these parties in their commitment to secularism is lost. This has created suspicion and feeling of insecurity in the minds of minorities.
6. ***Problem relating to the introduction of common civil code***: Another major hurdle that we find in the relation between the majority and the minority is relating to the failure of Governments which have assumed power so far, *in the introduction of a common civil code.* It is argued that social equality is possible only when a common civil code is enforced throughout the nation. Some communities, particularly the Muslims oppose it. They argue that the imposition of a common civil code, as it is opposed to the *"Shariat"* will take away their religious freedom. This issue has become controversial today. It has further widened the gap between the religious communities.

It is true that communal disturbances, religious conflicts, group clashes are taking place frequently in India. In spite of these disturbances the nation has maintained its secular character for the past 55 years. Further, the government has been making special efforts to safeguard the interests of the religious minorities. Some of the governmental efforts in promoting the welfare of the minorities are mentioned below.

WELFARE OF MINORITIES

Government of India has notified **5** communities, viz. *Muslims, Sikhs, Buddhists, Christians* and *Zoroastrians* as religious minorities at the national level. As per the Census of 1991, population of the minority groups constitutes 17.17% of the total population of the country. The Constitution of India protects the interests of the minority and recognises their rights to conserve their languages, scripts or culture and establish and administer educational institutions of their choice.

1. Constitutional Provisions for the Protection of Minorities

Constitutional provisions that are made for protecting the interests of the minorities can be classified into two groups: (*a*) *General provisions*, and (*b*) *Specific provisions.*

(*a*) ***General provisions***: The Constitution of India treats the minorities on par with the other people. *Article 14* of the Constitution assures them equality before law, *Article 15* prohibits discriminatory treatment, *Article 16* provides for equal employment opportunities in the public sector, *Article 29(2)* provides for equality of educational opportunities, *Article 325* and *326* provide for right to universal adult franchise to all, including the minorities and *Article 44* maks provision for common civil code.

(*b*) ***Specific provisions*** : *Articles 29 and 30* of the Constitution provide protection to the linguistic, educational and cultural rights of the minorities. ***Article 29*** states that any community in India is entitled to have and preserve its own specific language, script or culture ***Article 30*** declares (*a*) that all minorities in India are having constitutional right to establish and run their own educational institutions. (*b*) it also states that the State while giving grants shall not discriminate against any institution just because it belongs to a linguistic or religious minority. (*c*) *Articles 331 and 333* also make provisions to give protection to the interests of the Anglo-Indian communities.

2. Fifteen Point Programme For the Welfare of the Minorities

In 1985, the then Government of India, under the directions of the Prime Minister Smt. Indira Gandhi, framed a 15 point programme to promote the welfare of the minorities. The programme consists of the following recommendations and activities.

(a) Protection against communal riots

1. In areas identified as sensitive from the religious point of view, very efficient, honest and strict police officers known for their secular outlook should be appointed so that better protection could be given to the minorities.
2. Police officers and district collectors who render an impartial and an efficient service in controlling communal riots must be felicitated.
3. Stringent legal action must be taken against those who instigate communal riots and violence.
4. Separate courts to be established to investigate into the criminal cases connected with communal riots.
5. Immediate legal steps to be taken to give reliefs to those affected by communal riots, they must also be rehabilitated at the earliest.
6. Mass media such as radio and T.V. etc., must assist the establishment in reviving communal harmony, peace and mutual understanding in the riot-hit areas.
7. News papers and periodicals are specifically requested not to disturb the communal harmony of an area through their prejudiced articles.

(b) Appointment in state and central services

8. The States are to be instructed to take extra care regarding the minorities in making appointments for the police department.
9. The Central Govt. must also have the same stand while making appointments to Central Reserve Police-force.
10. The railways, nationalised banks and industries in the public sector do provide employment opportunities to a large number people. These establishments should pay proper attention to the employment needs of the minorities.
11. Special training classes should be held in the minority institutions to the candidates belonging to the minority communities, so that they improve their qualities in competing for competitive examinations. Such a training may help them to become successful in getting jobs.[28]
12. Special encouragement must be given to open technical institutions such as ITI, polytechnics and engineering colleges in the areas in which the minorities are found in a large number.

(c) Other programmes

13. In the various developmental programmes and projects of the Government including the 20 point programme, care should be taken to see that the minority people are also able to obtain their due share in these programmes.
14. In addition to the above mentioned general matters, many local issues such as Wakfs properties, cremation ground encroachment disputes, conversion cases, etc. may create lot of tensions. If these are not settled immediately and amicably they may turn out to be big problems tomorrow. Local administrations must pay proper attention to these.
15. Problems confronting the minority groups must be frequently dealt with and settled to their satisfaction. This may help them to develop confidence in the establishment. A separate wing in the Home Department could be created to look into the grievances of the minority groups.

The Central and the State Governments frequently meet to discuss the various aspects of the above mentioned 15 point programme. They also take suitable decisions to assure better protection to the minorities. The Central Cabinet Committee which met on Jan. 30th 1990 decided to take some short-term measures to promote the welfare of the minorities. Some of these decisions are as follows.

---

[28] For improving the employability of minorities in public employment and increasing their intake in professional courses, a pre-examination coaching scheme is being implemented by the *Ministry of Social Justice and Empowerment* since 1992-93. During the Eighth Five Year Plan period (1992-93 to 1996-97) ₹3.65 crore has been sanctioned for training 9,480 candidates of the weaker sections among minorities and SEBCs. [that is, socially and economically backward communities During the year (1997-98), an amount of ₹82 crore has been released benefiting 1,360 candidates. The overall success rate under the scheme is 21.7 percent.—*India Year Book,* 1999, p. 201.

(a) The Cabinet Committee decided to establish special courts in the areas which are susceptible to frequent communal riots, to look into criminal cases and settle them at the earliest. It also decided to establish such courts in Delhi and Meerut.

(b) The Committee decided to increase the compensation amount payable to the victims of communal riots from ₹20,000 to 50,000 in case of death or permanent disability.

(c) It was also decided to pay a monthly allowance of ₹500/- to the riot-hit widows with the lowest income.

3. National Commission for Minorities

The Govt. of India, that is, the first non-Congress Government had set up a *"Minorities Commission for Minorities"* in January 1978 to evaluate the working of the various safeguards in the Constitution for the protection of religious minorities and to make recommendations to ensure effective implementation of enforcement of all the safeguards and laws. It appointed M.R. Masani as its president and justice M.R.A. Ansari and Prof. V.N. John as its members. The Commission was assigned the following tasks.

1. The commission was expected to assess the implementation of the various laws, policies and programmes of the Union and the State Governments towards minority. It was also asked to report on the working of the various provisions of the Constitution towards the welfare of the minorities.
2. It was asked to give suggestions regarding the effective implementation of the protective measures.
3. The Commission was assigned the task of reviewing the Central and State Governments' policies towards the minorities.
4. To review the complaints lodged with it relating to the abridgement of the rights and protection of the minorities.
5. To conduct studies, and make analysis and researches relating to the issues of discrimination against the minorities.
6. To give regular reports to the Government on the working of the Commission.

The National Commission for minorities was not having any statutory status. It came into being only because of the Governmental decision. Due to its weak legal position, the Government was also not serious about its reports and recommendations. Hence, the Commission itself had requested the Govt. in its 3rd annual report that it should be provided with a statutory status with greater power and authority. The Govt. accordingly introduced the *National Commission for Minorities Act. in 1992.*

The national commission for minorities act, 1992 was passed by the Parliament with the main intention of providing protection to the minority community. Under this Act, the National Commission for Minorities was constituted on 17th May 1993, with a statutory status replacing the previous Commission. The Commission has a Chairperson, a Vice Chairperson and five members to be nominated by the Central Government. The National Commission was reconstituted with effect from 21st January 2000.

The commissioner for linguistic minorities appointed under the *Article 350-B* of the Constitution investigates all matters relating to the safeguards provided for the linguistic minorities. He looks into representations and complaints received from various associations and individuals belonging to the linguistic minorities. The Commissioner has his headquarters at Allahabad, with regional offices at Calcutta, Belgaum and Chennai. So far [upto 2001], 35 reports have been laid before the Parliament.

Pre-examination coaching scheme for minorities: For improving the employability of the minorities in the public employment and increasing their intake in the professional courses, a pre-examination coaching scheme is being implemented by the *Ministry of Social Justice and Empowerment,* since 1992-93. During the Ninth Plan, provision of ₹12 crore was made of which ₹5.51 crores was released for training 13,150 candidates of the weaker sections among minorities upto March 2000. The Government has approved area-based approach for socio-economic development of the minority concentration areas. In the first phase, 41 districts identified on the basis of 1971 census would be taken up.

4. National Minorities Development and Finance Corporation

The Government has set up a *National Minorities Development and Finance Corporation* with an authorised share capital of ₹500 crores. The Corporation would provide economic and developmental activities for the benefit of the backward sections among the minorities. Preference is given to the occupational groups and women among minorities. The Govt. of India has raised the level of contribution from ₹125 crore to 300 crore subject to pro-rata contribution from the State

Governments and Union Territories towards the share capital of the Corporation. During 1999-2000, Corporation disbursed ₹60.78 crore as loan covering 22,510 beneficiaries. The cumulative assistance provided by the Corporation since 1994-95 amounts to ₹224.34 crore for 66,891 beneficiaries.[29]

5. Administration of Wakfs to Promote Muslim Interests

The Ministry of Welfare of the Central Government takes upon itself the responsibility of administering the Wakfs, the institutions meant for the protection and promotion of the Muslim interest. *"Wakfs are permanent dedication of movable or immovable properties for purposes recognised by the Muslim Law as religious, pious or charitable. Better management of these institutions and fuller realisation of their objectives contribute to development and progress of the society."*[30]

The wakfs act, 1995 : In order to further strengthen administration of Wakfs a legislation known as *"The Wakfs Act 1995"* was passed in 1995. This legislation came to be enforced from 1st Jan. 1996. This Act which repeals the previous ones [of 1954 and 1984] extends to the whole of the country except the State of Jammu and Kashmir. It envisages a decentralised set up and also provides for democratisation of Wakfs Boards. As per this Act, the manager of each individual Wakf who is known as *"Mutawali"*, retains his autonomy in the discharge of his responsibilities. This Act, however, states that the general superintendence of all 'wakfs in a State vests in the Wakf Board, set up by each State Government. The Board has to ensure that the Wakfs are properly maintained and administered and that their income is duly spent on objectives for which such Wakfs were created. The Board has its own office and staff. The overall supervision of the Wakfs Boards rests in the State Government concerned which appoints the Chief Executive Officer or the Secretary of the Board and audits its accounts. The Central Government has the power to co-ordinate the functions of the Central Wakfs Council and the State Wakfs Boards. The Central Wakfs Council was reconstituted on 26th June 1997 under the provisions of the Wakfs Act, 1995.

6. Maulana Azad Education Foundation

The Maulana Azad Education Foundation was established by the Central Wakf Council to promote education amongst minorities and backward classes in particular. It has now been delinked from the Council. The foundation was registered as a Society under the *Societies Registration Act, on 6th July 1989.* The Govt. of India provides grants-in-aid to the Foundation to achieve its aims and objectives. During 1994-95, a sum of ₹25.01 crore was released and it was increased to ₹40.00 crore during 1997-98.

7. National Foundation For Communal Harmony

The Central Govt. recently established the "National Foundation For Communal harmony" as an autonomous body under the purview of the Home Department, to work for the rehabilitation of children who become victims of communal riots and terrorist violence. Children and women normally become the sufferers of the group riots. The above mentioned is established especially to make proper provision for the future of the riots hit children.

REVIEW QUESTIONS

1. Give the meaning and definition of race. What are the major groups of human races?
2. Define the term 'racial group'. Write its characteristic features.
3. Define the term 'ethnic group'. What are the essential aspects of the ethnic groups? Explain.
4. Give the meaning and definition of minority group. Highlight the characteristic features of the minority groups.
5. What do you mean by racism? Highlight its nature.
6. Discuss the causes and ideology of racism.
7. Describe the patterns of the race and ethnic relations.
8. Throw light on the main problems of the minorities.
9. Discuss the causes and consequences of prejudice and discrimination.
10. Write an essay on the problems of the religious minorities in India.
11. What are the various schemes and programmes of the Government of India for the welfare of the minorities? Elaborate.

⌘⌘⌘⌘⌘⌘⌘⌘⌘⌘

29 *India Year Book,* 1999 and 2000.

30 *Idid.,* p. 202.

25

Social Mobility

Chapter Outline

- Meaning of Social Mobility
- Definition of Social Mobility
- Forms of Vertical Social Mobility
- Causes of Vertical Mobility
- Social Mobility and Social Stratification: Interrelationship
- Channels or Factors that Promote Social Mobility
- Determinants of Social Mobility
- Mobility of Women
- Consequences and Importance of Social Mobility
- Education and Social Mobility

MEANING OF SOCIAL MOBILITY

Individuals are normally recognised in society through the statuses they occupy and the roles they enact. Not only the society is dynamic but also the individuals are dynamic. Men are normally engaged in endless endeavour to enhance their statuses in society, move from lower position to higher position, secure superior job from an inferior one. For various reasons people of higher status and position may also be forced to come down to a lower status and position. *Thus people in society continue to move up and down the status scale.* This movement is called *'social mobility'*.

The study of social mobility is an important aspect of social stratification. In fact, it is an inseparable aspect of social stratification system because, the nature, form, range and degree of social mobility depend on the very nature of stratification system. *Stratification system refers to the process of placing people in different layers or strata.* A discussion of social mobility probes into the process of placement of individuals in different strata. It seeks to answer questions such as - *Is the placement of individuals permanent and unalterable ? Is there any scope for individuals to change or modify it? If so, what factors contribute to the changes in the statuses of the individuals and what are its consequences for the society?* A series of questions like these is tackled in our analysis of social mobility.

DEFINITION OF SOCIAL MOBILITY

1. ***Wallace and Wallace:*** *"Social mobility is the movement of a person or persons from one social status to another"*[1]
2. ***W.P. Scott:*** Social mobility refers to *"the movement of an individual or group from one social class or social stratum to another"*[2]
3. ***N. Abercrombie and Others:*** Social mobility refers to *"the movement of individuals between different levels of the social hierarchy, usually defined occupationally"* [in *"The Penguin Dictionary of Sociology"*. Page: 227].

Thus, it is clear, *"social mobility"* may be understood as the movement of an individual or group from one social status or position to another. *For example,* the poor people may become rich, the bank peons may become bank officers, farmers may become ministers, a petty businessman may become a bankrupt and the ruling class may be turned out of office, and so on.

---

[1] Wallace and Wallace in *Sociology*, p. 275.

[2] W.P. Scott in *Dictionary of Sociology*, p. 260.

Individual and Group Mobility

Mobility can take place at the individual as well as group level. It may take place at the level of the individuals, families, groups or even societies.

Individual mobility*:** When individuals get into seats of political position; acquire money and exert influence over others because of their new status, they are said to have achieved *individual mobility*. ***For example, (*i*) Uma Bharathi who was born in an ordinary family has now attained the status of the Chief Minister of Madhya Pradesh by leading her party [Bharateeya Janatha Party] to victory during recent [2003 Nov.] Assembly Elections. (*ii*) Smt. Rabri Devi who had hardly obtained any formal education, has now become the Chief Minister of Bihar, (*iii*) Jimmy Carter, a ground-nut growing farmer became the President of America, (*iv*) Similarly, Sri Narayana Swamy of Karnataka who was born in poor circumstances has now become the architect of an internationally reputed Computer Software Company, namely: Infosys. Since such individuals are members of family, individual mobility influences family mobility also.

Group mobility*:** Like the individuals even groups also attain high social mobility. The **Jews** as a community in America and **Parsis** as a group in India, for ***example, have been able to attain a relatively high position in their respective societies.

The two kinds of mobility very often go together. A disadvantaged group [such as scheduled castes and tribes in India.] may produce an occasional celebrity, but the higher the status of the group, the greater the number of high achievers.

TYPES OF SOCIAL MOBILITY

The Russian born American sociologist of great reputation ***P.A. Sorokin,*** has distinguished between two types of social mobility namely: 1. *Vertical Social Mobility*, and 2. *Horizontal Social Mobility.* This typology is normally followed by the other sociologists also.

1. ***Vertical social mobility:*** Vertical social mobility refers to the movement of an individual or people or groups from one status to another. It involves change in class, occupation or power positions. It involves a change within the lifetime of an individual to a higher or lower status than the person had to begin with. Example: (*i*) Movement from the status of plumber to that of a corporation president, or vice versa, is an example of vertical mobility. (*ii*) Movement of people from the poor class to the middle class, from the occupation of labourers to that of bank clerks, from the position of the opposition to that of the ruling class, etc.
2. ***Horizontal social mobility:*** *"Horizontal mobility" is a change in position without the change in status.* It indicates a change in position within the range of the same status. It is *"movement from one status to its equivalent"* [*David Popenoe* - 244]. *Example*: (*i*) A college graduate with a degree in chemistry planned to work in the research department of a large chemical company, but after a year he finds that the work seems dull and repetitive, with no improvement in sight. He quits that job and instead becomes a professor of chemistry at a nearby university. Because the two occupations are at roughly the same level *his mobility involved no essential change of status; it was simply a move to a more satisfying job.* (*ii*) An engineer working in a factory may resign his job and join another factory as an engineer and may work in more or less the same capacity, or join an engineering college and start working as a professor. In this example also, though there is change of workplace and work, the general status of the person does not change much.

Horizontal mobility can cause disruptions in family life and community ties. Some of the recent studies suggest that people are becoming more aware of these disruptions and increasingly resistant to unwanted job changes. Most Indians typically cling on to jobs whenever they get into them. They are normally not prepared to take a risk to change their job.

FORMS OF VERTICAL SOCIAL MOBILITY

Vertical social mobility assumes different forms among which the following may be noted. 1. *upward mobility,* 2. *downward mobility,* 3. *Intergenerational mobility,* 4. *intra-generational mobility,* and 5. *structural mobility.*

1. ***Upward mobility:*** Upward mobility, as the term indicates, refers to social ascendance or upward movement of the individuals or groups in the status scale. It denotes the said movement from a lower social position or status to a higher social position or status. It reflects social improvement, an onward march. ***Example:*** 1 A retail businessman who earns lot of profit may become a wholesale businessman. In the same manner, the son of a mason through educational attainments may become a university professor. Both of these examples of upward mobility indicate an improvement or ascendance in the status of the concerned persons.
2. ***Downward mobility:*** This type of mobility denotes *"social descendance"* or *"social failure"* on the part of the individual or group. In spite of their attempts to go up some individuals go down in the status scale. Sometimes individuals who fail to maintain their social, political or economic positions, lose their statuses. It means, individuals'

attempt to go up in society is not destined to be a successful one. Often they stand to lose their positions. *Example*: (*i*) Big businessmen who have invested huge money in business may often incur heavy loss and even become pauper. (*ii*) People in high offices might be demoted due to their corrupt practices, and so on.

3. ***Inter-generational social mobility:*** Time factor is an important element in social mobility. On the basis of the time factor involved in social mobility some have spoken of a third type of social mobility namely; *"Inter-generational mobility"*.

   Inter-generational social mobility is a change in status from that which a child began within the parents, household to that of the child upon reaching adulthood. In simple words, it refers to a change in the status of family members from one generation to the next. *Example*: A plumber's son becoming the president of the city corporation, or bus conductor's son becoming the chief minister of a state.

   Inter-generational mobility is important because the amount of this mobility in a society tells us to what extent inequalities are passed on from one generation to the next. If there is very little intergenerational mobility, inequality is clearly deeply built into the society, for people's life-chances are being determined at the moment of birth. If there is a good deal of intergenerational mobility, people are clearly able to achieve new statuses through their own efforts, regardless of the circumstances of their birth.

4. ***Intra-generational mobility:*** Mobility taking place in personal terms within the life-span of the same person is called *"intra-generational mobility"*. It refers to the advancement in one's social level during the course of one's lifetime. It may also be understood as *"a change in social status which occurs within a person's adult career"* [Wallace and Wallace]. *Example*: (*i*) A lecturer in a preuniversity college becoming a professor at the university centre after doing his doctoral degree. (*ii*) A person working as a supervisor in a factory becoming its assistant manager after getting promotion.

5. ***Structural mobility:*** Stratum or Structural Mobility is a kind of vertical mobility. *"Structural mobility refers to mobility which is brought about by changes in stratification hierarchy itself."*[3]

The term structural mobility refers to *"the vertical movement of a specific group, class, or occupation relative to others in the stratification system."*[4]

Structural mobility is a type of forced mobility for it takes place because of the structural changes and not very much because of individual attempts. For ***example***, historical circumstances or labour market changes may lead to the rise of decline of an occupational group within the social hierarchy. (*i*) Military officers are likely to be regarded highly in times of war. (*ii*) These are the days of computers and information technology. Hence, computer engineers and technicians and information technologists receive greater respect which was previously reserved for scientists and advocates. (*iii*) An influx of immigrants may also alter class alignments - especially if the new arrivals are disproportionately highly skilled or unskilled.

Thomas Fox and **S.M. Miller** who sought to identify the *determinants* of upward mobility in different nations have found out two important conditions: (*i*) *advanced stage of development of an industrial economy,* and (*ii*) *a large educational enrollment.* As societies become more and more industrialised, the unskilled, low-salaried jobs at the bottom of the occupational status - ranking are slowly eliminated. Because, these jobs are now more easily and profitably performed by machines. Simultaneously, more jobs are added at the middle and upper levels to manipulate and control the flow of machine produced goods. *The vertical mobility resulting from such system changes-rather than individual achievement is called **structural mobility**.*[5] What is to be remembered here is that the higher ranking job opportunities will not be fully utilised unless the parents of lower-level parents are given the knowledge and training necessary to achieve them. Compulsory public education also becomes another necessity to achieve it.

CAUSES OF VERTICAL MOBILITY

Vertical mobility is present in some form or other in all societies whether they are relatively *'closed'* or *'open'*. In fact, mobility seems to be an inherent trait of all stratified societies. There are some obvious causes for it. Some of these causes are mentioned below.

1. ***The necessity of filling in emptied or vacant positions:*** In most of the societies some upper positions are filled in for a fixed period by some persons. On the expiry of their term, they will have to be replaced by some new persons.

---

[3] Wallace and Wallace, p. 274.

[4] Richerd T. Schaefer, p. 229.

[5] David Popenoe in *Sociology*, p. 242.

It means, the inevitable social conditions help the new persons to be elevated to high positions. If these new persons are chosen from all the strata of society, it provides a chance to the substantial number of people of different strata to achieve upward vertical mobility or social ascendance.

2. ***Obtaining eligibility by imitating the life-styles of the upper strata:*** There are various criteria by which the social status of the people is evaluated. 'Life-styles' represent one such criterion. Hence, people in the lower strata always try to emulate or acquire the ways of life, manners and life-styles of those who belong to the upper strata. In course of time, it may become possible for the people of the lower strata to qualify for membership of the upper strata. *Example*: People belonging to the lower castes in the Indian society are trying to acquire higher prestige, and social recognition by imitating the life-styles of the upper caste people. This process is known as *"Sanskritisation"*.
3. ***To fill in the social vacuum created:*** Because of a lower birth rate within the upper strata, a social vacuum is created. This can be filled in by persons recruited from the lower layers. *Example,* If the owners or founder directors or general managers of the private companies or industries are not having children, or if they are too young to assume high offices, then, the relatively efficient individuals occupying lower positions get a chance to assume high posts.
4. ***Inability to perform the tasks assigned:*** The unfitness of many individuals to perform the proper functions relevant to their stratum often causes vertical mobility. This unfitness may be caused because of various factors. ***For example,*** owing to physical or mental sickness, accidents, old age, family problems and such other factors, some people occupying high positions may find it difficult to carry on the functions assigned. Under such circumstances the need arises for replacing these persons with different ones.
5. ***Effect of widespread changes in the social - cultural and political environment:*** When widespread changes take place in the socio-cultural environment of groups and their members, vertical social mobility may be caused. As *Sorokin* has pointed out; *"A whimsical change in public taste makes millionaires out of Sinatras and beggars out of many old fashioned singers"*[6] In the same manner, *"rich deposits of oil, iron ore, etc., among a population that is aware of their industrial and economic uses serve to enrich the owners of such land and elevate them in social hierarchy"* [Parimal B. Kar. Page: 145.]
6. ***Readiness for mobility:*** Providing opportunities for mobility alone is not sufficient. The concerned individuals must have the mental willingness and the physical preparedness for mobility. All the people are not equally interested in availing of opportunities for mobility. Some are not ready to leave their family and their birth place even if attractive avenues are offered to them. Rural people, illiterate and less literate people, are said to be less prepared for mobility than the urbanites and the more literate people. Further, people who have been living in a particular place permanently show less interest in mobility than those who are forced to migrate to faraway places.

SOCIAL MOBILITY AND SOCIAL STRATIFICATION: INTERRELATIONSHIP

The nature, form, intensity and magnitude of social mobility depend on the nature and the type of social stratification. *Class* and *Caste* are the two main types of stratification. In both the systems same kind of opportunities are not provided for social mobility. Because, in both the societies, the factors that determine the statuses of the individuals differ radically. There is a close link between the way in which individuals obtain their statuses and the nature and type of social mobility. In the **caste system**, the status which is determined on the basis of birth cannot be changed. *For example,* a *Harijan* or *dalit* cannot attain the status of a Vokkaliga, or Lingayat or Brahmin in the caste hierarchy. Similarly, a Brahmin, who is born as a Brahmin, would die as a Brahmin. Caste-statuses cannot be changed. Hence, the caste as a form of social stratification does not facilitate vertical social mobility. It is for this reason the caste system is called a *'closed system'*, and the caste-ridden society, the *'immobile'* society.

In a **class system,** opportunities are provided for social mobility. Here, the status is determined mainly by the talents, intelligence, wealth and achievements of the persons. The status is not ascribed by birth but *'achieved'* by individual attempts. *For example,* by his endless efforts and struggles a labourer may become the owner of a factory, a salesman of a business house, the owner of a business firm, and so on. There is scope for the improvement of the social status in the class system. Hence, the class system is called an *'open system'*, and the *'open-class'* society, the *'mobile'* society.

As and when the society becomes more and more complex, and the life of its members improves, individuals may find better opportunities for the expression of their abilities and talents. But in no society all the deserving individuals can obtain statutes of their likings, desires and expectations. As *Sorokin* has pointed out in his *"Social Mobility"*, only in an *'ideal'* society all the individuals get employments and statuses in accordance with their capacities. At the same time, it

[6] Sorokin P.A.—As quoted by Parimal B. Kar in *Sociology — The Discipline and Its Dimensions*, p. 145C.

is not possible to make people to confine to their status when they occupy or assume a status without going away from it, or changing it in any manner. ***For example,*** even in the so called *'immobile'* society like India, though a Harijan cannot change his caste-status, he can change his educational, economic, employment and political status. In this sense, there are *no* completely *'open'* and '*mobile'* societies and completely *'closed'* and *'immobile'* societies.

"Open" and "Closed" Societies

Open societies based on achieved statuses: Societies or social stratification systems are said to be *"open"* or *"closed"* systems only in a relative sense and not in an absolute sense. A completely *"open"* society, which exists only in theory, would be one in which all individuals could achieve the status for which their natural talents, abilities, inclinations and training best suited them. Here, the statuses are **"achieved"** because, individuals obtain them through direct efforts or through competition. Most occupational positions in the modern societies are achieved statuses.

An "open society" would not be a society of equals; because, there would be still inequality stemming from unequal achieved social positions. But these social positions would be gained solely by personal achievement and merit.

'Closed societies' based on ascribed statuses: Just as totally open societies would never exist, completely "closed societies could be found nowhere in the world. A closed society is said to be one in which all individuals were assigned a status at birth or at a certain stage, which could never be changed either for better or worse. Such statuses are called **ascribed statuses.** Parentage, that is, children inheriting the social position of their parents is the usual position for the ascribed status. But various factors [personal qualities, political and economic conditions, etc.,] from time to time may influence such statuses. In a completely closed society, no individual action, no outstanding merit, or notorious misconduct, could alter one's ascribed status.

In actuality, all societies fall between these two extremes of 'open' and 'closed', they contain both achieved and ascribed statuses in varying proportions. India itself is a good example in this regard. Caste based Indian society was regarded as rigidly stratified and relatively closed society for a very long time, even up to the first half of the 20th century. Yet, the caste-ridden society too afforded some chance for social mobility. Talented individuals could occasionally marry into a higher caste; or acquire patronage and the means of education and a better occupation from members of a higher caste. Such individuals and certainly their children, would eventually be able to move into that higher caste.

CHANNELS OR FACTORS THAT PROMOTE SOCIAL MOBILITY

Though all the societies permit some amount of mobility for their individual members, no society provides equal chances for all the members to achieve social mobility. Even in a relatively *'open class society'* upward mobility is not open equally to everyone. For example, middle class children typically have learning experiences which are more helpful in gaining upward mobility than the experiences of lower-class children. Overt discrimination against racial and ethnic minorities, lower-class and lower-caste persons seriously limit upward mobility and protect the children of the upper classes and castes from downward mobility.

Structural Aids and Individual Factor of Mobility

There are some structural aids to mobility. Antidiscrimination legislation is an important factor in this regard. In the same way, publicly financed job training programmes leading to marked increase in employment opportunities and modest gains in income for many lower-class and caste people, are factors helping mobility.

In addition to the structural factors, which determine the proportion of high-status, well-paid positions in society, there are certain individual factors that greatly influence as to which persons get those high-status positions. Other things being equal. the talented usually earn more than the untalented. The problem here is that we do not know about the ability of all the individuals. *How to measure ability ?* and *how much of mobility can be attributed to ability differences ?* These questions cannot be answered easily. Yet, it is a fact that not all people are equally talented. While it is impossible to measure individual ability differences satisfactorily, we assume that they are important factors in life success and mobility. Some such factors may be briefly examined here.

1. ***Education***: Education is an important mobility ladder. It is only through education that the *'social graces'* are acquired. It makes possible the upward movement in the social structure. Today, white-collar jobs are increasing in a larger number than the manual jobs. This means that more people are profiting from the kind of education that will fit them for these jobs. Education is not equally important for all careers. College and professional degrees are essential for careers as doctors, engineers, chartered accountants, advocates, professors, etc. These degrees are helpful but not essential in business ownership and operation. There is a general belief that education has a magical

power of radically improving the positions of individuals in society. Hence there is a mad rush towards college admission and to obtain university degrees. As *Peter Worsley* has pointed out of the students studying in the British Universities more than 25% belong to the lower-class. In the case of India, bigger number of students belong to the category of lower-class, lower-caste, lower-middle class, etc.

2. ***Occupation and economic activities***:

   (a) ***Occupation***: Mobility can take place through a change in occupation from father to son. This is a function of economic opportunities. Where the opportunities are boundless, the trend is for a son to try his career in another and more highly paid occupation carrying a higher status. This is the most significant trend today. Mobility takes place through a change from one occupation to another involving a change in status.

   Mobility may also take place *through a change from one occupation to another* involving a change in status. For example, a skilled manual worker might just with some retraining fit himself for another occupation.

   Further, mobility may also take place *through promotion within the same occupational group.* Though always possible, this is open only to a few. Among manual workers, it is virtually ruled out. In the professions where promotions are very less, chances for this type of mobility are comparatively less.

   Through achieving seniority within a given occupation, this type of mobility could be achieved. But this is not applicable to manual workers. In the professional field, for example, a junior partner in a law firm can look forward to the prospect of becoming a senior partner with the consequent higher status and bigger income that seniority carries.

   (b) ***Economic activities***: Economic activities also provide opportunities of social mobility. Agriculture, business, mining, fishing, hotel industry, film industry, etc., for example, represent income fetching economic activities. The quantum of income, amount of property and the available avenues of making money normally influence the rate of social mobility, its magnitude and its effects. Even amongst a few tribals money and wealth often function as the criteria for deciding the leadership. Throughout human history, the propertied class of the aristocrats had enjoyed a relatively higher status in the society. Incidentally, they had greater chances for mobility than the ordinary classes. However, we cannot generalise like Marx and his followers, that the amount of wealth and the nature of economic activity always and invariably decide the nature of social mobility, its range and its rate.

3. ***Religious institutions***: Religious institutions also provide opportunities for vertical mobility. Religions such as Christianity, Islam, Buddhism and Hinduism have paid attention to this aspect. After obtaining the state recognition during the rule of the Roman emperor Constantine, the Christian church played an important role in helping many individuals of the lower class to achieve social ascendance. It had selected a few capable slaves, semi-serfs and commoners to become church officials. Pope Gregory VII, himself, for example, was the son of an ordinary carpenter.

   Even in India, social reformers and reformation movements launched by them, helped many people belonging to lower classes and castes to achieve social ascendance. The religious conversion process has often helped a few to achieve social ascendance.

4. ***Political institutions***: Political institutions also provide opportunities for social mobility, if not for all, at least for a few. *Example:* Those who enter government service at an young age, would often assume a very high office over the years either through seniority or through selection. The reservation policy of the Indian Government too has provided lot of opportunities for the scheduled caste and scheduled tribe people to achieve social ascendance. Even during the period of feudalism good number of efficient serfs and semi-serfs could obtain relatively prestigious positions due to the political opportunities provided for them by the feudal lords. In the same manner, soldiers occupying almost the lowest position in the army were commissioned as higher ranking officials in recognition of their heroism and good performance in the battles. In the case of Indian history, two slave leaders namely Qutub-ud-din Aibak and Iltumish themselves emerged as famous slave-kings [of the Slave Dynasty].

   Political opportunities often make ordinary people big leaders and national level administrators. *Examples*: (*i*) Pandit Nehru's personal secretary namely, Lal Bahadur Shastri could become the Prime Minister of India. (*ii*) H.D. Deve Gowda, son of an ordinary farmer, could become the Prime Minister. (*iii*) K. Gundu Rao, who was working in an ordinary transport company could become the Chief Minister of Karnataka, and so on.

5. ***Family and marriage***:

   (a) Family: Family also assumes importance in the study of social mobility. As *Peter Worsley* has pointed out, studies of social mobility have considered family as one of the influential agents contributing to vertical mobility. It is quite common to observe in India, that some times, the entire family lends its helping hand to the daughter or the son to achieve success in his educational or business endeavours. According to *J.H. Abraham*, a person's decision to achieve social mobility is *"bound to be affected by what his wife feels and thinks, by the size and age-range of his family"*[7]

(b) Marriage*:* Sometimes marriage becomes a determining factor in social mobility. *Example*: Hypergamous[8] marriages are helpful for unmarried women to attain personal ascendance in the status scale. On the contrary, a girl practising hypogamy[9] would lose her status and suffer the risk of social descendance. In early Rome, Egypt, Greece and other countries a free woman marrying a slave was not only losing her status and reputation but also her freedom. In societies, where marriage enjoys more social importance [for example, India], individuals often improve their social status by means of their marriage.

6. ***Windfall or the luck factor:*** Many people who really work hard and follow all the rules fail to succeed, while success sometimes seems to fall into others. Anyone who tries to prove that life is always fair has assumed a difficult task. But for some, success hinges just on the factor of *"luck"*. A large part of "luck" probably consists of working in a favourable sector of the economy. Some sectors of the economy are fast expanding [for example, computer software industry], while some others are declining [example, the decline of real estate business in India especially after 1996]. The young worker who finds a position in an expanding industry has excellent chances for lifetime job security with pleasant retirement on a good pension. Those who pick a declining industry may find themselves in their later middle age with no job and no pension. Engineering graduates had very poor mobility prospects in India during 1970-1985. After 1990s they have again wonderful prospects. The luck factor, however, is impossible to measure and is a handy excuse for failure, yet it is undeniably a factor in mobility.

DETERMINANTS OF SOCIAL MOBILITY

An important consideration in our discussion of social mobility is the range or extent of social mobility and the factors that determine it. The two main determinants of social mobility are 1. *the amount of mobility,* and 2. *conditions of mobility.*

Amount of Mobility

The amount or the extent of mobility which a society can support depends on how many different statuses there are in the society. If more statuses exist, then, greater opportunities are available for the people to avail them of. In ***traditional agricultural*** *societies,* for example, a very limited number of statuses [say, of the skilled workers, owners of the landed property, aristocrats, and so on.], were in existence. If the eldest son inherited the property and also of the high status of the father, the younger sons had to seek their fortunes elsewhere, may be in the military or in the Church. Or, if the property of the father was evenly divided among the children, each was left with a low status than the father enjoyed. In these societies there were very few high statuses for people of low status to move into. Hence, upward mobility was virtually absent.

Industrial societies, on the contrary, offer greater opportunities for mobility. The level of economic development and condition of the economy influence the range of social mobility in these societies.

(i) The example of a rapidly expanding economy: In such an economy, new high-status positions are constantly available. The demand for workers to fill these positions causes a general trend towards social mobility.

(ii) The example of an economy in a condition of depression: In such an economy, the proportion of high-status positions decreases and the proportion of lower-status positions increases. This results in a downward trend in mobility. People here tend to lose their jobs and the new entrants to labour market are not able to get jobs.

Conditions of Mobility

The conditions under which the people allowed to be mobile also influence social mobility. It has been observed that some societies impose greater restrictions on changes in status than other societies do. In *pre-industrial societies,* there was very little upward mobility, because of the prevalent restrictions a peasant could hardly become a member of the land owning class: once a peasant, always a peasant. On the contrary, in *industrial societies,* which place high value on individual merit, the rate of mobility is very much greater. 'In these societies, some categories of people suffer from some disabilities which stem out of ascribed status. For example, the mobility of women is relatively lower than that of men. In a country

[7] J.H. Abraham in *Sociology - Teach Yourself Books*, 1973, p. 193.

[8] Hypergamy [*Anuloma*] refers to the marriage of a lower class or lower caste woman with a man of upper class or upper caste.

[9] Hypogamy [*Pratiloma*] refers to a marital practice in which a higher class, or caste woman marries a lower class or caste man.

like India, some lowest caste people still suffer from disabilities, while in America and South Africa, the Blacks are found in that condition.

MOBILITY OF WOMEN

Societies are not equally mobile. Similarly men and women who build societies are also not equally mobile. For centuries, only men took the lead in mobility and most of the women simply followed them. Women have traditionally achieved mobility mainly through marriage. Married women could work in *"suitable"* occupations but the occupational statuses of these women were not too far beneath the occupational statuses of their husbands. But only an insignificant number of women gained social status through occupation. In the Indian context, women very rarely entered the occupational fields up to the beginning of the 20th century.

Today, things have changed. Women are now claiming equal occupational opportunity. Occupations do provide women with a mobility ladder apart from marriage. Women are showing dramatic increases in their presence in the professions not only in the West but even in the developing countries like India. Women students were found in an incredibly smaller number in the professional courses such as law, engineering, medicine, pharmacy, polytechnics etc., some 30-35 years ago in India. Today, they are found pursuing these courses in an almost equal number on par with men students.

In most of the industrialised and urbanised countries, career and mobility patterns for men and women are growing almost equally. Even then, differences remain. Majority of working wives still judge their class position by their husband's occupations. At the same time, there is a growing number of working wives using both their own and their husbands occupations in judging their class. An experience felt everywhere is that the career mobility of married women is still greatly handicapped by household duties and child-bearing with its career interruptions. *"True equality in career mobility will demand fundamental changes in both our familial and our politco-economic institutions."*[10]

CONSEQUENCES AND IMPORTANCE OF SOCIAL MOBILITY

Social mobility is the manifestation of the dynamic nature of society. Societies are not static but changeful. Individuals who constitute the basic social units of society are also moving up and down in the status hierarchy. They also move from one place to another and from one occupation to another. Not only are individuals mobile but even the groups are subject to mobility. Social mobility leads to some consequences or effects. Some of these consequences or effects are positive in nature while some others are negative. They may be briefly examined here:

Positive Consequences, or Importance or Gains of Social Mobility

Social importance of mobility consists of its positive consequences. They are also referred to as the *"gains of mobility"* or *"benefits of mobility."* The so called gains of mobility may be briefly examined here.

1. ***Social mobility provides opportunity for the expression of individual talents:*** As *P.M. Blau* and *O.D. Duncan* have pointed out social mobility makes it evident that a talented individual is bound to achieve "social ascendance" by means of his talents and efforts irrespective of the stratum to which he belongs. According to them, social mobility becomes inevitable if the most important functions of the society are to be performed by the most capable persons.
2. ***Acts as a safety-valve:*** According to *S.M. Lipset* and *R. Bendix,* providing opportunity for social mobility virtually means creating a 'safety-valve' to escape from the dangers. Since the lower classes are provided with an open chance to enhance their social statuses or to enter into the status-positions of other upper class people by means of their performances; they do not normally organise themselves to dislodge the upper-class people of their statuses. Social mobility becomes inevitable and essential from this point of view.
3. ***Social justice:*** *D.V. Glass* and others have felt that providing equal chances or opportunities for social mobility for all social classes is a democratic commitment. According to them, a democratic society has to depend upon *"an eagalitarian opportunity structure"*.
4. ***Job satisfaction:*** Social mobility is inclusive of occupational mobility also. Most of the instances of social mobility are occupational in character. In the traditional societies [for example, traditional caste society] occupations are normally hereditary in character and hence children are obliged to follow the occupations of their parents whether they have a liking for it or not. Now in modern industrial society things are different. People need not stick on to their parental occupations. They have a vast opportunity and freedom to change their occupations. This opportunity for job selection or change has contributed to their job satisfaction.

---

[10] Horton and Hunt, p. 380.

5. ***Improvements in the life-styles:*** A person who gets into an occupation or profession as per his capacities and expectations is likely to be more satisfied with it. For the very same reason, he may work sincerely, put in more efforts and earn good income also. This higher income or economic rewards help him to improve his "life-styles". For example, a lower-class man after obtaining the middle-class status, will definitely pay attention to improve his style of life. He may purchase a vehicle, wear relatively costly dresses, get better education for his children, construct his own house, and so on. Social mobility, many times helps economic improvement.
6. ***Opportunity for competition:*** Social mobility is of great importance in helping individuals to improve their capacity and work-efficiency. It provides motivations for progress and higher attainments. It makes individuals active, alert and dynamic. It keeps the individuals fit to life in a competitive society. It is important to note here that the societies that provide greater opportunities for social mobility are also those that entertain and encourage competitive values.
7. ***Reposes confidence in the established system:*** Average individuals of all types of societies expect some chances or the other to improve their positions. People in the higher strata also expect still better opportunities. Individuals who feel that their social system is providing them opportunities to grow well, are the ones who toil and struggle for improvement. They do not lose faith in the system. They believe that their hard work would yield them due rewards, if not immediately, at least, in the near future. Because of this faith, they would remain as the supporters of the system even if their actual mobility involves difficulties and challenges.

Negative Consequences or Costs of Mobility

It is normally believed that social mobility is good and supportive of democratic ethos. Supporters of democracy and social equality strongly advocate that opportunities for social mobility must be provided for all. A closed class system which thwarts the fulfilment of individual personality is criticised because such a system deprives society of the contributions of talented people.

Social mobility, no doubt, permits a society to fill its occupational positions with the most able people and offers the individual a chance to attain his or her life goal. But such a provision which society makes, *involves certain costs.* Some of them may be noted below.

1. ***Rising expectation leading to dissatisfaction and frustration:*** Upward mobility is not always advantageous for a society. A mobile society arouses expectations which are not always fulfilled, thereby creating dissatisfaction and unhappiness. Even in societies where upward mobility is both valued and highly visible, expectations may be over aroused. Although many want to be upwardly mobile, not everyone can succeed. A traditional society in which one is born into one's appointed place, may not arouse many hopes. Hence, possibilities of one getting disappointed or frustrated are also fewer as long as the traditional social structure remains in tact. *The benefits of social mobility are inseparable from its costs*.
2. ***An open class society or A mobile society may impose penalties also:*** An open class society may be desirable from the viewpoint of both society and the individual, but it still may impose some penalties. These penalties may include - *"the fear of falling in status as in downward mobility; the strain of new role learnings in occupational promotions; the disruption of primary group relationships as one moves upward and onward."*[11] One who moves higher and higher in social status as a result of promotion may feel less and less secure. Since terrorism of different type is becoming widespread now a days, people in top positions [in politics, business or administration] seek the support of security guards for they feel that they may be attacked at any time. Thus, one who is passed over for promotion to a higher position may envy the security of a less mobile society. Social attitudes of such persons change to such an extent that their own parents, friends and relatives may appear to be strangers. High Court and Supreme Court judges in India, for ***example,*** are expected as a matter of legal norms, to minimise their social contacts with the people.
3. ***Social mobility often demands geographic mobility:*** People are often made to move from one geographic area to another if they are to accept new prospects in life. This results in *"a painful loss of treasured social ties."* Further, new physical and social set up demands new adjustments. These adjustments may often bring in new fears and anxieties. Such anxieties and tensions are bound to be very high especially at present when the whole world is experiencing the complex process of globalisation.
4. ***High rate of mental illness is associated with mobility:*** An offer of promotion is normally associated with the burden of new responsibilities. One who is ready to accept such offers must be mentally ready to shoulder new responsibilities, face new challenges, and compromise with new situations. Any failure in these areas, brings

[11] Horton and Hunt in *Sociology*, p. 372.

tensions, anxieties, mental worries. Even marriages may be threatened when spouses are not equally interested in mobility. One mate resents the implied position of being neglected by the other; while the other resents the mate's lack of co-operation in social climbing. Upward mobility puts a great strain on the relationship between parents and children. Upward mobility is linked with upwardly mobile person who exhibits more prejudice against low-status people than do non-mobile individuals at the same level. Some studies have even found that a high rate of mental illness may accompany either upward or downward mobility.

Downward mobility also creates mental disturbances: Mental anxiety and tension also goes with downward mobility. In fact, a number of studies have reported that downward mobility is associated with many unpleasant accompaniments, *such as poor health, marital discord and feelings of alienation and social distance*. But these studies have not properly identified the cause and effect relationship. Such unpleasant developments could be either a cause or an effect of downward mobility. The cost and benefits of mobility to the individual and the society in an open class society are open to debate.

EDUCATION AND SOCIAL MOBILITY

(***Note:*** For an explanation about *Education and Social Mobility,* kindly refer to Chapter entitled "The Educational System")

REVIEW QUESTIONS

1. Define social mobility. Describe with illustrations the types of social mobility.
2. Give the meaning of social mobility. Explain the general characteristics of social mobility.
3. Point out the characteristic features of social mobility.
4. What are various forms of vertical social mobility? Discuss the various causes of social mobility.
5. Assess the interrelationship between social mobility and social stratification.
6. What are the factors that promote social mobility? Discuss in detail.
7. Write a detailed note on the factors that determine social mobility.
8. Give an account of the consequences and importance of social mobility.
9. Analyse the impact of social mobility.
10. Write short notes on the following:
    (a) Individual and group mobility
    (b) Horizontal mobility
    (c) Determinants of social mobility
    (d) Mobility of women
    (e) Amount of mobility

⌘⌘⌘⌘⌘⌘⌘⌘⌘⌘⌘

26

SOME ASPECTS OF SOCIAL MOBILITY

(SANSKRITISATION–WESTERNISATION–MODERNISATION)

CHAPTER OUTLINE

- Meaning and Definition of Sanskritisation
- An Analysis of the Process of Sanskritisation
- Westernisation Definition of the Term
- Westernisation: Some Comments
- Definition of Modernisation
- Characteristics of Modernisation
- Problems of Modernisation
- Westernisation and Modernisation: Comparative Views.
- Sanskritisation and Brahminisation
- Sonskritisation: Some Comments
- Main Features of Westernisation
- Modernisation. Meaning of Modernisation
- Process of Modernisation
- Process of Modernisation in India
- Sanskritisation and Westernisation Comparative Views

Though the Indian society which is based on the caste system is often regarded as a "*closed society*", it is not altogether changeless. Within the framework of the caste itself some kind of mobility is observed. Lower castes have often tried to claim higher status by imitating the life-styles of upper-castes particularly of Brahmins and Kshatriyas. *M.N. Srinivas* used the term '*Sanskritisation*' to denote such a type of process. The upper castes including Brahmins, on the contrary, have started orienting their life-styles on the model of the Westerners. The term '*Westernisation*' introduced by *M.N. Srinivas* describes this process. Today not only the upper class and middle class people including upper caste and intermediatry caste people are trying to orient their behaviour, attitudes, beliefs and life-styles towards those of developed societies; but also the entire mass of people are involved in this process. *Daniel Lerner* calls this process '*modernisation*'. It denotes a process of social change whereby "*less developed societies acquire the characteristics common to more developed societies*".

Here is an attempt to understand the socio-cultural changes that have been taking place in India in terms of these processes namely: *Sanskritisation*, *Westernisation* and *Modernisation*. These three processes reflect an attempt on the part of the Indian masses to achieve some amount of mobility both within and outside the framework of the caste system.

SANSKRITISATION

Meaning of Sanskritisation

The term "*Sanskritisation*" was introduced into Indian Sociology by Prof. *M.N. Srinivas*. The term refers to a process whereby people of lower castes collectively try to adopt upper caste practices and beliefs, as a preliminary step to acquire higher status. Thus it indicates a process of cultural mobility that is taking place in the traditional social system of India.

M.N. Srinivas in his study of the Coorg in Karnataka, found that lower castes, in order to raise their position in the caste hierarchy, adopted some customs and practices of the Brahmins, and gave up some of their own which were considered to be "*impure*" by the higher castes. *For example*, they gave up meat-eating, drinking liquor and animal sacrifice to their deities. They imitated Brahmins in matters of dress, food and rituals. By doing this, within a generation or so they could claim higher positions in the hierarchy of castes. In the beginning, *M.N. Srinivas* used the term "*Brahminisation*" (in his book "*Religion and Society Among the Coorgs*"—1971) to denote this process. Later on, he replaced it by "Sanskritisation".

Definition of Sanskritisation

M.N. Srinivas, in fact, has been broadening his definition of the term 'Sanskritisation' from time to time. Initially, he described it as—"*the process of mobility of lower castes by adopting vegetarianism and teetotalism to move in the caste hierarchy in a generation or two*" (1962). Later on, he redefined it as "*a process by which a low caste or a tribe or other group changes its customs, rituals, ideology, and way of life in the direction of a high and frequently, twice—born caste*"— (*M.N. Srinivas in his "Social Change in Modern India*–1971). The second definition is much broader for it includes ideologies also (which include ideas such as '*Karma*' '*dharma*', '*papa*' (sin), '*punya*' '*moksha*' etc.).

Sanskritisation and Brahminisation

Sanskritisation is a much broader concept than Brahminisation. *M.N. Srinivas* preferred it to Brahminisation for some reasons:

(*i*) *Sanskritisation is a broader term and it can subsume in itself the narrower process of Brahminisation*: For instance, today, though by and large, Brahmins are vegetarians and teetotalers, some of them such as Kashmiris, Bengalis and saraswath Brahmins eat non-vegetarian food. Had the term 'Brahminisation' been used, it would have become necessary to specify which particular Brahmin group was meant.

(*ii*) Further, *the reference groups of Sanskritisation are not always Brahmins*. The process of imitation need not necessarily take place on the model of Brahmins. Srinivas himself has given the example of the low castes of Mysore who adopted the way of life of Lingayats, who are not Brahmins but who claim equality with Brahmins. Similarly, the smiths (one of the lower castes) of Mysore call themselves *Vishwakarma Brahmins* and wear sacred threads and have sanskritised some of their rituals. (Still, some of them eat meat and drink liquor. For the very same reason, many castes, including some untouchable castes do not accept food or water from their hands).

The lower castes imitated not only Brahmins but also Kshatriyas, Vaishyas, Jats, Shudras, etc. in different parts of the country. Hence the term Brahminisation does not completely explain this process. MN Srinivas himself acknowledged this fact and wrote: "*I now realise that, I emphasised unduly the Brahminical model of Saskritisation and ignored the other models Kshalriya, Vaishyaand Shudra...*" ("Social Change in Modern India — 1971 Page - 7)

An Analysis of the Process of Sanskritisation

An Analysis of the process of 'Sanskritisation' would reveal to us the following facts:

1. 'Sanskritisation' denotes the process in which the *lower castes try to imitate the life-styles of upper castes in their attempt to raise their social status*. The process seems to be associated with the role of local "*dominant caste*". Though for some time, the lower castes imitated Brahmins they soon shifted it towards the local dominant caste which in most cases a non-Brahmin dominant caste.
2. *Sanskritisation denotes the process of upward mobility*. In this process, a caste is trying to increase its position in the caste hierarchy not at once, but over a period of time. It would take, sometimes, a period of one or two generations.
3. Mobility that is involved in the process of Sanskritisation *results only in 'positional changes*" for particular castes or sections of castes, and *need not necessarily lead to a "structural change*", It means, while individual castes move up or down, the structure as such remains the same.
4. *Sanskritisation is not a new phenomenon as such. MN. Srinivas* writes: "Sanskritisation has been a major process of cultural change in Indian history, and it has occurred in every part of the Indian sub-continent. It may have been more active at some periods than at others, and some parts of India are more sanskritised than others; but there is no doubt that the process has been universal" (*Social Change in Modern India* — 1971 *Page* - 23).
5. *The castes which enjoyed higher economic and political power but rated relatively low in ritual ranking went after Sanskritisation for they felt that their claim to a higher position was not fully effective*. The three main aspects of power in the caste system are the *ritual, the economic and the political ones*. The possession of power in any one sphere usually leads to the acquisition of power in the other two. But Srinivas opines that inconsistencies do occur.

6. "*Economic betterment is not a necessary pre-condition to Sanskritisation, nor economic development must necessarily lead to Sanskritisation*. However, sometimes a group (caste, tribe) may start by acquiring, political power and this may lead to economic development and Sanskritisation. Economic betterment, the acquisition of political power, education, leadership, and a desire to move up in the hierarchy, are all relevant factors in Sanskritisation, and each case of Sanskritisation may show all or some of these factors mixed up in different measures"— (*Ram Ahuja*-in "*Indian Social System*" 4 Page: 355).
7. *Sanskritisation is not necessarily confined to the castes within the Hindu community, it is found in tribal communities also. Example, The Bhils* of Western India, the *Gonds* and *Oraons* of Middle India, and the *Pahadiyas* of Himalayan region have come under the influence of Sanskritisation. These tribal communities are now claiming themselves to be Hindus for their communities represent some caste groups within the fold of Hinduism. (It should be noted that in the traditional system, a group could be called 'Hindu' only if it was regarded as a caste group).
8. *The process of Sanskritisation serves as a "reference group"*. It is through this process, a caste group tries to orient its beliefs, practices, values, attitudes and "life-styles" in terms of another superior or dominant group, so that it can also get some recognition. Since this term was made applicable by M.N. Srinivas even to Kshatriya, Vaishya and Shudra models (in addition to Brahmana model), it has greater relevance to function as a "*reference group*'.
9. *Sanskritisation does not take place in the same manner in all the places*. Studies have revealed that in most of the cases the lower castes tend to imitate the upper castes particularly the Kshatriya and Brahmin castes. There are instances of upper castes imitating some of the practices of lower castes, and sometimes of even tribal groups. *For example*, a Brahmin may make a blood sacrifice to one of the local deities through the medium of a non-Brahmin friend. The Muslim cultural ways have imposed some limitations in the imitation process of some upper and lower castes. This is very much in evidence in Punjab. Thus, it can be generalised that *Sankritisation is not a one-way process; it is a two-way process*. Not always one caste "*takes*" from the higher caste, sometimes, it also '*gives*' in return.
10. *The British rule in India provided a favourable atmosphere for Sanksritisation to take place*. Political independence has weakened the trend towards this change. Now the emphasis is on vertical social mobility and not on the horizontal mobility. In this process of mobility the basic unit remains the group only and not the individual or family.
11. *The process of Sanskritisation does not automatically result in the achievement of a higher status for the group*. People will have to wait for a period of a generation or two before their claim can be accepted. Further, it may so happen that a claim which may not succeed in a particular area or period of time, may succeed in another.
12. *Significant developments in the realm of material culture have accelerated the process of Sanskritisation*. Industrialisation, occupational mobility, mass media of communication, spread of literacy, advent of Western technology, improvement in the transportation system, etc., have speeded up the process of Sanskritisation. Introduction of parliamentary system of democracy and universal suffrage have also contributed to the increased Sanskritisation.
13. As *M.N. Srinivas* has pointed out, *Sanskritisation serves to reduce or remove the gap between the ritual and secular ranking*. It is, indeed, one of its main functions. *For example*, if a caste, or its segment gains secular, that is, political power, it immediately starts imitating the so called "*status-symbols*" of the customs, rituals, ideals, beliefs, values, life-styles, etc. of the upper caste communities. The lower caste group which successfully gets into the seat of secular power also tries to avail of the services of Brahmins especially at the time of observing some rituals, worshipping and offering things to the God in the Centres of pilgrimage, celebrating important Hindu festivals, fixing "*muhurtam*" (auspicious time for doing good works or starting ventures) for some important occasions and programmes, and so on.
14. *Sanskritisation has often been construed as a kind of protest against the traditional caste system*. Sanskritisation is a type of protest against the caste system in which the status is ascribed or predetermined. Lower castes which are disillusioned with their predetermined statuses and impressed by the higher statuses accorded to the upper castes, naturally desire to go up in the status hierarchy. This desire is virtually against the traditional hierarchical principle of the caste system. Making an attempt through Sanskritisation to move up in the status hierarchy setting aside the hierarchical principle of caste, amounts to a protest against the caste system itself.

15. *Sankritisation*, as *M.N. Srinivas* himself has said, *does not denote a basic change in the structure of the Hindu society*. It should not be construed that through this process any kind of social change can be brought about in the caste—ridden society. Since caste is a '*closed*' society in which the membership is based on the unchangeable factor of birth, no one can become a member of the "*reference group*" as such (Reference group in this context may be an upper caste Brahmin or non- Brahmin caste group which is locally dominant and influential). However, an individual or a group may improve his or its social position within the range of one's own Varna group. *Srinivas* further observes that *the process of Sanskritisation can only support the existing system but can never remove it*. Hence the changes that are effected through Sanskritisation though cannot be neglected, *have only limited significance*.

Sanskritisation: Some Comments

Though the concept 'Sanskritisation' introduced by *Prof M.N. Srinivas* has been regarded as a significant contribution to the sociological literature, it is not free from criticisms. Number of comments have been made about the term by the scholars. Some of them may be cited here:

1. According to *J.F. Stall*, "Sanskritisation as used by Srinivas and other anthropologists is a complex concept or a class of concepts. The term itself seems to be misleading, since its relationship to the term Sanskrit is extremely complicated". — (quoted by Yogendra Singh in his "*Modernisation of Indian Tradition*", p. 10).
2. *Yogendra Singh* comments: Though "Sanksritisation and Westernisation, in logical sense, are "*Truth asserting*" *concepts*.,. They "fail to lead to a consistent theory, of cultural change. Such consistency is far from realisation...". The concepts "*contain no hypotheses*", and in *Zetterbergs* words, "*Cannot be true or false. They can be clumsy or elegant, appropriate or inappropriate, effective or worthless but never true or false*".
3. *Yogendra Singh* also opines that "*Sanskritisation fails to account for many aspects of cultural change in past and contemprorary India as it neglects the non-Sanskritic traditions*". *Mckim Marriot* has observed that truism of Yogendra Singh's comments in one of his studies in a village. M. Marriot observes, we cannot establish that the process of Sanskritisation always takes place by replacing or removing the non-Sanskritic rituals. "*Sanskritic rites are often added on to non-Sanskritic rites without replacing them" Mckim Marriot*.
4. It is also commented that much against the assumption of *M.N. Srinivas*, the "*Sanskritic influence has not been universal to all parts of country. In most of northern India, especially in Punjab, it was the Islamic tradition which provided a basis for cultural imitation*". In Punjab, writes *Chanana*, "Culturally Sankritic influence has been but one of the trends, and at times, it could not have been the main trend. For a few centuries, until the third quarter of the 19th century Persian influence had been the dominating one in this area" (as quoted by Prof. Yogendra Singh, pp. 11-12).
5. "*As suggested by Harold A. Gould, often the motive force behind Sanskritisation is not of cultural imitation per se but an expression of challenge and revolt against the socio-economic dep- rivations*". *Yogendra Singh* writes; "Sankritisation is thus a cultural camouflage for latent interclass and intercaste compeititon for economic and social power, typical of a tradition bound society where traditionally the privileged upper castes hold monopoly to power and social status. When the impact of the external forces like political democratisation, land reforms and other social reforms break, this monopoly of the upper castes, the cultural camouflage of Sankritisation is thrown away, in favour of an open conflict with the privileged classes based on nativistic solidarity" — (*ibid.*, pp. 12).
6. *Dr. D.N. Majumdar comments that it is wrong to assume the process of Sanskritisation as universal process to be observed throughout India*. In his study of *Mohan village* in Uttar Pradesh he observed a strong exception to this assumption. In this village, as he observed, the lower caste people do not have any urge or inclination to imitate the 'life-styles' of Brahmins or any other dominant higher caste of that region. If a cobbler wears tilak, (or Vibhuti) dhoti and the sacred thread and follows some of the customs of higher castes, nobody recognises him as an upper caste man "*If Sanskritisation is really a universal process, where exactly it stops and why*? *Dr. Majumdar* questions.
7. *M.N. Srinivas has been changing the definition of the term* "*Sanskritisation*" *from* '*time to time* and *this adds to the problem of understanding its meaning and range of operations in clear terms*. First, *Dr. Srinivas* used the term to mean Brahminisation. Later on, he extended its meaning. He used it to mean a process in which a lower caste, a tribal group or any other group attempts to imitate the 'life-styles' of a locally dominant upper caste, mostly a twice-born' caste. As per his recent interpretation, the process includes the imitation of ideas, values and ideologies. Here also it becomes difficult to ascertain the real meaning of the term "*ideology*".

8. *When we try to interpret certain changes that have taken place in the field of social mobility in the light of Sanksritisation, we face certain paradoxes. According to Dr. Srinivas*, political and economic forces are normally favourable for Sanskritisation. But the '*policy of reservation*' a politico- constitutional attempt to elevate the status of lower caste, and class people, presents here a different picture. Theoretically, the policy of reservation must be supportive of Sanskritisation. But paradoxi- cally it goes against it. Those who avail of the 'reservation' benefits have developed a vested interest in calling themselves 'dalits' or Scheduled Caste people. They want to be called 'dalits' or people of Scheduled Caste category so that they can permanently avail of the benefits of reservation.

Finally, it can be said that the twin concepts of Sanskritisation and Westernisation introduced by M.N. Srinivas in explaining the cultural changes that are taking place in India, do have their own importance. But the basic question in this: Do these twin concepts explain cultural change with all its ramifications ? Are they inclusive and universal enough to provide a satisfactory explanation to all the major cultural changes that have taken place throughout the country? According to Yogendra Singh, the concept of "*Modernisation*" can only provide a satisfactory answer to these questions.

WESTERNISATION

The role '*Westernisation*' has been very significant in understanding the socio-cultural changes of modern India. British rule produced radical and lasting changes in the Indian society and culture. The British brought with them, (unlike the previous invaders) new technology, institutions, knowledge, beliefs, and values. *These have become the main source of social mobility for individuals as well as groups*. It is in this context, *M.N. Srinivas*, a renowned sociologist of India, 'introduced the term' '*Westernisation*' mainly to explain the changes that have taken place in the Indian society and culture due to the Western contact through the British rule.

Definition of the Term "Westernisation"

According to *M.N. Srinivas*, "Westernisation" refers to "*the changes brought about in Indian society and culture as a result of over 150 years of British rule and the term subsumes changes occurring at different levels —'technology, institutions, ideology, values* (*Ref:* "*Social Change in Modern India*" By **M.N. Srinivas**, p. 47).

M.N. Srinivas criticises *Lerner's* concept of '*modernisation*' on the ground that it is a *value- loaded term*. According to him, "Modernisation" is normally used in the sense that it is good. He, therefore, prefers to use the term '*Westernisation*'. He describes the technological changes, establishment of educational institutions, rise of nationalism and new political culture, etc. as almost the bye- products of Westernisation or the British rule of two hundred years in India. Thus, by Westernisation, *Srinivas* primarily meant the British impact.

"During the 19th century the British slowly laid the foundations of a modem state by surveying land, settling the revenue, creating a modern bureaucracy, army and police, instituting law courts, codifying the law, developing communications–railways, post and telegraph, roads and canals— establishing schools and colleges, and so on " (Srinivas). The British brought with them the printing press which led to many-sided changes. Books and journals made possible the transmission of modern as well as traditional knowledge to large number of Indians. Newspapers helped the people living in the remote corners of the country to realise their common bonds and to understand the events happening in the world outside.

More than any other thing the Western education had an impact on the style of living of the people. They gave up their inhibition towards meat-eating and consumption of alcohol. They also adopted Western style of dressing and dining. As Gandhiji wrote in his "Autobiography", educated Indians undertook the task of "*becoming English gentlemen in their dress, manners, habits, choices. preferences, etc.*" It included even learning to appreciate Western music and participating in ball dancing. Western education resulted in a big change in the outlook of those educated.

M.N. Srinivas says that it is necessary "to distinguish conceptually between Westernisation and two other processes usually concouilait with it. —Industrialisation and Urbanisation." He gives two reasons for this: "(*i*) Urbanisation is not a simple function of "industrialisation" and there were cities in Pre-industrial world" also. "(*ii*) There are cases of rural people who are more urbanised than urban people".

Main Features of Westernisation

1. *In comparison with Sanskritisation, Westernisation is a simpler concept*. As it is already made clear, it explains the impact of Western contact (particularly of British rule) on the Indian society and culture. *M.N. Srinivas* defends the uses of the term when he says that there is "*need for such a term when analysing the changes that a non-Western country undergoes as a result of prolonged contact with a Western one*".

2. Westernisation implies, according to Srinivas, "*certain value preferences*". The most important value, which in turn subsumes several other values, is "*humanitarianism*". It implies "*an active concern for the welfare of all human beings irrespective of caste, economic position, religion, age and sex*". He further observes that equalitarianism and secularisation are both included in humanitarianism. Humanitarianism underlay many of the reforms introduced by the British in the first half of the l9th century. As British rule progressed "*rationality* and *humanitarianism became broader, deeper and more powerful...*"

   The humanitarian outlook among the Westernised elite led first to social reform movement and later on to the independence movement. They were actually aware of existing social evils like child marriage, taboos against widow remarriage, seclusion of Women, hostility to women's education, tabooes against intercaste marriages, intercaste dining, untouchability etc. Social reform movements started with the efforts of Raja Ram Mohan Roy who founded the "*Brahma Samaj*". *Arya Samaj, Prarthana Samaj, Sri Ramakrishna Mission and such other movements that followed later, too had imbibed in them the humanitarian values.*

3. *Westernisation not only includes the introduction of new institutions (for example, newspapers, elections, Christian missionaries) but also fundamental changes in old institutions. For example*, India had schools long before the arrival of the British. But they were different from the British- introduced schools in that they had been restricted to upper caste children and transmitted mostly traditional knowledge. Other institutions such as the army, civil service and law courts were also similarly affected.

4. *The form and pace of Westernisation of India varied from region to region and from one section of population to another*. (Srinivas 1985). *For example*, one group of people became Westernised in their dress, diet, manners, speech, sports and in the gadgets they used. While another absorbed Western science, knowledge and literature, remaining relatively free from certain other aspects Westernisation. *For example*, Brahmins accepted the Western dress habits and educational systems and also used gadgets such as radio, television, car, telephone etc. But they did not accept the British diet, dancing, hunting and such other habits, This distinction is, however, only relative and not absolute.

5. *According to Srinivas, Westernisation pervades political and cultural fields also*. He writes: "In the political and cultural fields, Westernisation has given birth not only to nationalism but also to revivalism communalism, 'casteism', heightened linguistic consciousness, and regionalism. To make matters even more bewildering, revivalist movements have used Western type schools and colleges, and books, pamphlets and journals to propagate their ideas"— (pp. 55-56).

6. As *M.N. Srinivas* claims, "*The term Westernisation unlike 'Modernisation' is ethically neutral. Its use does not carry the implication that it is good or bad, whereas modernisation is normally used in the sense that it is good.*"

7. According to *Srinivas*, "*the increase in Westernisation does not retard the process of Sanskritisation*. Both go on simultaneously, and to some extent, increase in Westemisation accelerates the process of Sanskritisation. *For example*, the postal facilities, railways, buses and newspaper media, which are the fruits of Western impact on India render more organised religious pilgrimages, meetings, caste solidarities, etc., possible now than in the past"— (*Ref*.: **Yogendra Singh** in "*Modernisation of Indian Tradition*", p. 9).

8. *The term Westernisation is preferable to* '*Modernisation*', M.N. Srinivas asserts. "He contends that modernisation presupposes '*rationality of goals*' which in the ultimate analysis could not be taken for granted since human ends are based on value preferences and "*rationality could only be predicted of the means not of the ends of social action*". He considers the term "*Modernisation*" *as subjective and the term 'Westernisation' as more objective*. (Whereas writers such as Daniel Lerner, Harold gould, Milton Singer and Yogendra Singh consider the term 'Modernisation as more preferable in place of Westernisation).

Westernisation: Some Comments

Most of the scholars have recognised the importance of the twin concepts of '*Westernisatio*n' and '*Sanskritisation*' introduced by *M.N. Srinivas* in explaining the social and cultural changes taking place in the Indian society. *Westernisation can be considered an agent of Sanskritisation* in so far as it promotes the spread of cultural ideas and values among the lower castes. The process of *Sanskritisation implies mobility within the framework of caste, while westernisation implies mobility outside the framework of caste*.

As *M.N. Srinivas* has pointed out "*One of the many interesting contradictions of modern Hindu social life is that while the Brahmins are becoming more and more Westernised, the other castes are becoming more and more Sanskritised. In the lower reaches of the hierarchy, castes are taking up customs which the Brahmins are busy discarding*"— (M.N. Srinivas in his "*Caste in Modern India and other Essays:* Pages 54-55). It is also true that with the Westernisation of Indian society, caste becomes more or less secular due to the new ideas introduced by the West. Westernisation as a social process has influenced the various aspects of social life of the Indian community.

Scholars like *Bernard Cohn* and *Milton Singer* have supported the validity of the concept of Sanskritisation on the basis of their empirical studies. They observed that "*while upper caste was West arising its style of life and religious beliefs, the lower caste was Sanskritising and assuming more traditional forms of ritual, practice and belief.*

Scholars have also criticised the concept 'Westernisation'. Some such criticisms can be recalled here.

1. The concepts of Sanskritisation and Westernisation primarily analyse social change in 'cultural' and not in 'structural' terms. This denoted that *these terms have limited range of application and use.*
2. "*Srinivas's model explains the process of social change only in India which is based on the caste system. It is not useful for other societies*" — Prof. Ram Ahuja, p. 360
3. *Zetterberg* (1965) has stated that the twin concepts of *Srinivas* are "*Truth asserting*" concepts. *Yogendra Singh* also endorses this opinion in his own way: "*Obviously, Sanskritisation and Westernisation are, theoretically loose terms ; but as Truth-asserting' concepts they have great appropriateness and viability*". This connotation is often vague especially regarding Sanskritisation. Because, *Srinivas himself has said Sanskritisation is an extremely complex and heterogenous concept.*
4. *Though Srinivas claimed that the concept of Westernisation is "ethically neutral*", it is not *really so*. He himself says that it implies "*certain value preferences*" such as *humanitarianism*, *equalitarianism*, *secularisation*, and a degree of *rationalism*. A reference to these values definitely implies that Westernisation is, in general, good and desirable.
5. It is also commented that the *Western model which Srinivas has eulogised has its own contradiction*. The Western model sometimes conveys values that are contrary to the ones mentioned above. In this context, mention can be made of the facts of Western life such as racial prejudice, colour segregation and exploitative nature of the Western economy, etc. These facts contradict humanitarian ideals or rational outlook on life.
6. The concept has its own limitation in yet another sense. *The concept will be of little use in explaining the nature of social change taking place in post-Independent India*. Professor Srinivas is aware of this limitation when he say: "*I am using it deliberately in spite of its vagueness and omnibus character*".
7. *Daniel Lerner* has raised some objections to the use of Westernisation as conceived by Srinivas: (*i*) *It is too local a label* and the model which is imitated may not be a Western country, but Russia; (*ii*) "One of the results...of prolonged contact with the West is the rise of an elite class whose attitude to the West is ambivalent". It is not invariably positive. In this context, Lerner refers to the appeal of Communism in non-Western countries; (*iii*) Westernisation in one area or level of behaviour does not result in Westernisation in another related area or level. The two remain discrete; (*iv*) 'While there are certain common elements in Westernisation, each European country along with the U.S.A., Canada, Australia, and New Zealand, represents a particular variant of a common culture and significant difference exist between one country and another".

MODERNISATION

Meaning of Modernisation

The term modernisation "*does not denote any philosophy or movement, but it only symbolises a process of change. In fact, "Modernisation" is understood as a process which indicates the adoption of the modern ways of life and values*". The term was being used previously to refer only "*to change in economy and its related effect on social values and practices*". It was also described as a process that changed the society, from primarily agricultural to primarily industrial economy. As a result of the change in the economy, the society itself underwent changes in values, beliefs and norms. But, *today, the term is given a broader meaning.*

Today, the term, '*Modernisation*' is understood as an attempt, on the part of the people, particularly those who are custom-bound, to adopt themselves to the present time, conditions, styles, and ways in general. It indicates a change in people's food habits, dress habits, speaking styles, tastes, choices, preferences, ideas, values, recreational facilities and so on. It is also described as "*social change involving the elements of science and technology*". The scientific and technological inventions have brought about remarkable changes in the whole system of social relationship and installed new ideologies in the place of traditional ones.

M.N. Srinivas, however, criticises the concept of Modernisation. according to him, it is a *value- loaded term*. He says that "*Modernisation is normally used in the sense that it is good. He, therefore, prefer to use the term "Westernisation which characterises the changes brought about in Indian society and culture as a result of over 150 years of British rule*".

Yogendra Singh, on the other hand, defends the concept of modernisation. According to him, it is broader than the two processes of Sanskritisation and Westernisation. *It is, indeed a 'cultural universal' and not necessarily confined to any single society*. Like science, modernity is not an exclusive possession of any one ethnic or cultural group. It belongs to the humanity as a whole. This does not mean that everywhere it should reveal the same pattern. *It need not always take place on the model of England, Germany, France or America*. It can take place on the model of Russia, India, Japan, Australia, or any other country for that matter. What is essential to modernisation is this — a commitment to "*scientific world view*" *and a belief in the humanistic and philosophical viewpoint of science on contemporary problems*.

Definition of "Modernisation"

1. *Daniel Lerner*. Daniel Learner who introduced the term "*Modernisation*" for the first time in his study of the middle-Eastern societies—uses it to refer to the changes brought about in a non- Western country by contract, direct or indirect with a Western country. To quote his own words: "*Modernisation is the current term for an old process of social change whereby less developed societies acquire the characteristics common to more developed societies*".
2. *Smelser*. Modernisation refers to "*a complex set of changes that take place almost in every part of society as it attempts to be industrialised. Modernisation involves ongoing change in a society's economy, politics, education, traditions, and religion*".
3. *Alatas*. "*Modernisation is a process by which modern scientific knowledge is introduced in the society with the ultimate purpose of achieving a better and a more satisfactory life in the broadest sense of the term as accepted by the society concerned*".
4. *Rutow and Ward (1964)* have said that *the basic process in Modernisation is the application of modern science to human affairs*.
5. *Eisenstadt* says that Modernisation refers to both (*a*) *structural aspects of social organisation*, and (*b*) *socio-demographic aspects of societies*.

Process of Modernisation

The key to understanding Modernisation lies in thinking of it as a set of change that affect the whole society. These changes are many and complex. Each is linked to the others. Moreover, the process is different in each country, depending on its history.

Modernisation involves a transformation of social, political and economic organisations. "This includes the transformation indicated by *Durkeim*, from "*mechanical solidarity*" to "*organic solidar- ity*"; that indicated by *Becker*, the transformation from the "*change-resistant sacred outlook*" to the "*change-ready secular-outlook*"; the transformation indicated by *Weber*, from "*personal bonds*" to "*impersonal relation*" with bureaucracy; and the transformation from '*status-based*' *relations to* '*contract-based*' *relation*" *as indicated by Maine*, long ago. It applies .to the individualist forms of organisation of the Western model, the Communist form of organisation of the Russian or Chinese model as well as to the socialistic pattern of the Indian model" (*Ref*.: **B. Kuppu Swamy** in his "*Social Change in Modern India*", 1972, pp. 54-55).

Students of Modernisation have identified many dimensions of this process. The process has its economic, political, educational, technological, military, administrative, cultural and other faces. The concept has been used in a very diffused manner. Still, some of the patterns that are common to most modern countries have been identified. *Smelser* makes a reference to them in the following way.

1. It involves a change from simple, traditional techniques such as hand-weaving toward the use of scientific knowledge and technology, *for example*, powerlooms.
2. Agricultural shifts from subsistence farming to commercial farming on a larger scale. This means growing cash crops, buying non-agricultural products in the markets on a large quantity and often hiring people to do farm work.

3. "In industry there is a movement away from the use of human and animal power and towards the use of machinery driven by non-human power". *For example*, ploughs pulled by oxen are replaced by tractors driven by hired hands.
4. The society changes from the farm and the village centred one to that of the industry and city centred one (Ref: "*Sociology*" by *N.J. Smelser* — 4th Edition, 1993 - Page: 395).

In addition to the four major patterns, other patterns of change have been observed in modernising social structure. Traditional religious systems tend to lose influence. *Powerful non-religious ideologies such as patriotism, nationalism, democracy, secularism, etc. arise*. The family changes in many ways, both in terms of its structure and functions. Its economic, educational, recreational and other functions tend to diminish. Its size gets smaller and smaller. Extended families and kingroups break up into smaller units. Personal choice becomes the basis of marriage rather than parental arrangements.

In *education*, the literacy rate increases greatly and formal educational institutions become widespread. Mass media also serves the purpose of educational resource and information channel. New form of administrative organisation such as bureaucracies develop in the political, economic, educational and other fields.

In addition to these changes in the social structure, some psychological changes do take place in the society's members. Studies of *Alex Inkeles* and *David H. Smith* (1974) have revealed that the modem man has become an informed participant citizen. He is highly independent and takes independent decisions relating to his personal affairs such as education, marriage, occupation, etc. He is not much carried away by the traditional influence. He is ready for new experiences and ideas. He is relatively open-minded and cognitively flexible.

Thus, the process of modernisation includes in itself the gradual development of a vast new system of social structures and psychological traits. "*As a society becomes more productive and prosperious, it also becomes more complex in social and cultural terms*."

Characteristics of Modernisation

As it has already been mentioned, the process of modernisation has different dimensions. The spirit of modernisation is expressed in different areas such as — *social organisation, culture, political field, economy, education, etc. in different ways*. Broadly speaking, the process of modernisation reveals the following important characteristics:

'Modernisation includes–"*a temple of science, reason and rationalism, secularism, high aspiration and achievement orientation, overall transformation of attitudes norms and values, creation of new fuctional institutions, investment in human resources, a growth oriented economy, a national interest rather than kin, caste, religion, region or language oriented interests, an open society, and a mobile person*"–(*Ram Ahuja* in his "*Indian Social System*"). According to *B. Kuppuswamy*, "*the main feature of Modernisation is the building up of an "open society" in which individuals of talent, enterprise and training can find places in the society appropriate to their achievement. The process of Modernisation involves an increase in social unrest till the social* '*system is responsive to the new aspirations built up by the Modernisation process*". It should, however, be noted that the same process of modernisation institutes appropriate change in the social system to meet the rising expectations of the people.

Criteria of Modernity or Measures of Modernisation

Modernisation has been referred to as a process whereby less developed societies acquire characteristics common to more developed societies. Now our task is to identify the characteristics that are common to more developed societies,— that is, to identify the criteria of modernity.

Sociologists have not yet found out an efficient method of measuring modernisation. Because, there is no consensus among them regarding the criteria of modernity. Still, there has been some broad agreement among scholars on certain key points concerning Modernisation.

Rustow and *Ward* (1964) have mentioned some measures of modernisation. They include such specific aspects of changes as:

1. Industrialisation of economy and adopting a scientific technology in industry, agriculture, dairy farming, etc., to make them highly productive;
2. Secularisation of ideas — that is, a diffusion of secular — rational norms in culture;
3. A remarkable increase in geographic and social mobility which includes occupational mobility also;
4. A spread of scientific and technical education;

5. A transition from ascribed to achieved status;
6. An increase in material standard of living;
7. High proportion of working force employed in secondary and tertiary rather than primary production, that is, manufacturing and services as opposed to agriculture and fishing ;
8. An increment of mobility in the society, understood in terms of urbanisation, spread of literacy and media participation ;
9. High expectancy of life at birth ;
10. Relatively greater measure of public participation in the polity — or at least democratic representation in defining and choosing policy alternatives.

While discussing the criteria of modernity *Daniel Lerner* observes: "*According to this typology the modern person is an urban literate who participates fully in the public forum, market place, political arena*".

Causes of Modernisation

What factors condition modernisation? What conditions lead to modernisation? What conditions hinder it ? In exploring suitable answers to these questions sociologists look within the society to discover the various factors, groups, people and agencies and instruments that contribute to modernisation. Modernisation is not caused by any single factor. It is the net result of a number of factors. Myron Weiner speaks of five main instruments which make modernisation possible: *education, mass communication, ideology based on nationalism, charismatic leadership and coercive governmental authority.*

1. Education

Education, that too higher education, pertaining to the fields of science and technology, provides the basis of modernisation. Education involves a sense of national loyality and creates skills and attitudes essential for technological innovation. *Edward Shils* has also emphasised the role of education in the process of modernisation. Still people like *Arnold Anderson* feel that formal education is not sufficient for teaching skills. University education may increase the number of students with degrees without an increase in the number of people with modern skills and attitudes. By this we cannot underscore the importance of education in national development which is believed to be associated with modernisation. "*National development depends upon a change in knowledge – what people know, skills — what people can do, and attitudes e what people can aspire and hope to get*". This is the reason why in the recent decades education including mass communication is given utmost importance.

2. Mass Communication

The process of modernisation hinges on the phenomenon of mass communication. The development of mass communication (including newspapers, periodicals and magazines, T.V., radio telephone, movies, etc.) is an important means of spreading modern ideas at a faster rate. The function of mass media is to open up to the large masses in society, new information, new thought, new attitude and new aspirations which lead them to new achievement. "*The mass media is the device that can spread the requisite knowledge and attitudes quickly and widely*". The only danger with the mass media is that if these are controlled by the government, they will spread only one-sided view that suits their political ideology. But in democracies, however, the press is often given sufficient independence to express its views.

3. Ideology Based on Nationalism

Nationalism and democracy are very much linked with modernisation. Nationalism is connected with national awareness and political consensus. As far as the West is concerned, the democratic system came to be strengthened along with the development of nationalism. The nationalistic ideologies serve as unifying influence in bridging social clevages within plural societies. They also help the political elite in changing the behaviour of masses of people. Mass media plays a vital role in democratic societies to spread modern views, ideas, values, etc., by persuading the masses. But it is argued out that even though the political elite have modern ideology. Their mere possession of it does not guarantee development from the modern perspective.

4. Charismatic Leadership

A Charismatic leader is in a better position to impress upon the people to adopt modern beliefs, values, practices and behaviour patterns. But the danger involved here is that this popular leader may take the undue advantage of his position and use modern values, ideas etc., for his personal glorification rather than for the national development.

5. Coercive Governmental Authority

A strong and stable government may adopt coercive measures to compel people to accept the modern values and ways of life. It may also bring pressures on other governments and people to follow the same. The Government of America under the presidentship of George Bush (The previous President of U.S.A.) made use of various tactics and strategies to bring pressure on the underdeveloped and developing countries to follow the modern ways and practices.

6. Other Factors

To the list of factors explained above, we may add two other factors: (*a*) urbanisation and industrialisation; and (*b*) universal legal system.

(a) Urbanisation and Industrialisation: Urbanisation and industrialisation are the two interrelated processes that are assumed to be invariably linked up with modernisation. These two processes can also be understood as two factors that accelerate the tempo of modernisation. '*Urbanisation*' *refers to the process of growth and expansion of cities*. Most of the modernised countries are either dominated by the cities or under the grip of the process of urbanisation. "*Industrialisation*" *refers to the unprecedented growth and expansion of industries*. It has become virtually the sine quo non of economic and technological development.

(b) Universal Legal System: In a traditional society bound by traditional values and customs the rate of change is relatively slow. But a society that functions on the basis of the universally accepted legal system is bound to be more '*open*'. The "*rule of law*" is indeed, one of the prerequisites of Modernisation. The present legal system places premium on the individual protecting his rights and assuring his freedom. This role of the legal system supports the cause of "*Individualism*". The modern legal system has contributed a great deal to the scientific management of the industries.

Process of Modernisation in India

Modernisation in India started mainly with the Western contact, especially through the establishment of the British rule. This contact brought about many far reaching changes in culture and social structure of Indian society. *Not all these changes could be called modernising*. The basic direction of this contact was towards modernisation, but in the process, good number of traditional institutions got strengthened.

There was, however, one important feature of Indian modernisation during the British period. *The growth of this process was very much selective and partial*. It never encompassed the micro- structures of Indian society such as—family, caste, kin group and village community. British people intelligently followed the policy of "*least interference*" especially at these micro-levels.

But at the macro-level, the components of modernisation such as a universalistic legal system, expansion of Western form of education, urbanisation and industrialisation, spread of new means of communication and transport and social reforms—led the way in the transformation of Indian society. Along with these, *aspects of structural modernisation* such as — rational bureaucratic systems of administration and judiciary, army and industrial bureaucracy, new classes of business elite and entrepreneurs—came into being. There was the emergence of political elite and a nationalist leadership. These modernising structures had a uniform character throughout the country.

After Independence, modernisation process in India has undergone a basic change from its colonial pattern. Discontinuity in modernisation between macro-structures and micro-structures slowly disappeared. Introduction of adult franchise and federal parliamentary form of political structure have carried new political values to all the sections of the population. Planned legal reforms in Hindu marriage and inheritance laws have tremendously influenced the Hindu family system. Community development projects and the Panchayat Raj System created political awareness and participation in local level management and administration of justice. Caste too has undergone radical transformation making lot of compromises with the changed conditions.

In spite of the British contact Indian society at the time of Independence has deep-rooted traditions. Still it decided to go in the direction of modernity. There were people to support the cause of modernism and there were also people to cling on to the traditional way of life. We had to strike out a balance between the two. Thus people had to tolerate the coexistence of tradition with modernism. But, coexistence cannot last long in all the areas. Because, many a time, traditional ethos and values become irreconcilable. We were thus confronted with the practical problem of either sticking on to tradition or to go on the path of modernisation.

We decided to modernise our society at various levels. "*What aspects of life were sought to be modernised and in what manner*?" Prof. *Ram Ahuja* replies to this question in the following way— "At the *social level*, we Wanted social relations to be based on concepts like equality, human dignity, and social values which would ensure social mobility, removal of caste disabilities, amelioration of the conditions of women, and so forth. At the *economic level*, we wanted technological growth and distributive justice. At the *cultural level* we wanted secularism, rationalism, and liberalism. At the *political level*, we desired representative government, democratic institutions, achievement — oriented power-structure, and a greater voice and participation for Indians in the governance of the country. The *means* for *agents* selected for modernising the society were—*planning, education, legislation, assistance from foreign countries, adopting the policy of liberalisation, and the like*"— (*Ref: Ram Ahuja in his "Indian Social System*" — Page: 427).

Problems of Modernisation

Prof. Ram Ahuja speaks of five main problems of modernisation. They can be briefly stated below:

1. Modernisation demands that society must change in all ways at once. 'But such a regular and co-ordinated pattern of growth cannot be planned and materialised. *Some amount of social interest, hence, is bound to be there*. *Example*. Discrepancy between mass education and employment opportunities.

2. *During the period of modernisation structural changes mostly remain uneven. Example*. Industries may be modernised but religious system, family system etc., remain conservative.

3. *Modernisation of social and economic institutions may create conflicts with the traditional ways of life. Example*, trained M.B.B.S. doctors may pose a threat to the traditional medical practitioners.

4. Another problem is that, *most often roles adopted by the people are modern, but their values continue to be traditional. Example*. New Business firms and industrial establishments and, shops etc., are either opened or inaugurated as per the dictates of the traditional "*Muhurtam*":

5. Yet another problem is that there is lack of cooperation among agencies which modernise and among those institutions and systems which are already modernised. This is more or less like the problem of "*cultural lag*",

6. Finally, *though modernisation raises the aspirations of people, the social system does not provide enough chances to materialise them*. This creates frustration, disappointment and social unrest.

Sanskritisation and Westernisation: Comparative Views

Sanskritisation and Westernisation help us as conceptual tools in understanding the nature of social and cultural changes that have been taking place in" the Indian society. Both have their own strengths and limitations. In some respects there are conflicts between the two also.

While Sanskritisation (more precisely here Brahminisation) puts a taboo on meat-eating and consumption of alcohol, Westernisation promoted meat-eating and consumption of alcohol. The highly Westernised Brahmins of Kashmir, Bengal and South Kerala (who consume meat and first) *for example*, shed their inhibitions about these two taboos.

As *B. Kuppu Swamy* has pointed out *there is conflict between the two processes with respect to marriage and divorce*. "Among the 'lower' castes there is no taboo against widowhood, divorce, and remarriage, nor does custom enjoin on the wife to look upon her husband as a '*deity*'. These customs are in line with Westernisation but were all tabooed by the Brahmins. The conflict among these groups between these two sets of processes has been removed after Independence by the promotion of equality of sexes and legislation providing for divorce, and remarriage"— (*Ref.*: *B. Kuppu Swamy* in his "*Social Change in India*"— Page: 60).

Further, while Sanskritisation process promoted the "*sacred*" outlook, Westernisation process promoted the '*secular*' outlook. Here also the conflict has been removed by the constitution which is secular in outlook and emphasis.

"The Brahmins looked up to the British, and rest of the people looked up to both the Brahmins and the British. The fact that some of the values and customs of the British were opposed to some Brahminical values made the situation confusing" — (Srinivas-62). But in spite of these contradictions between Brahminism and Westernism, a section of the Brahmins adopted Westernism because of the prestige that it entailed.

But the main task of the lower castes was to catch up with the Westernised Brahmins who were well educated and enjoyed prestige in society. They soon realised that "*mere Sankritisation was not enough*" for it could only help them to improve their status in the "*immutable*" varna system. Hence they decided to adopt Westernism which would help them to move up in the social scale Without the limitation of the Jati or Varna. They thus decided to obtain Western education which would fetch them the fruit which they wanted. This awareness among the lower castes; and the high caste dominance in education and in new occupations provided a strong basis for the Backward classes movement. The *lower castes, thus, chose Westernisation, that is, education through English medium, rather than Sankritisation, as the means to enable them to move up in status in the society*.

WESTERNISATION AND MODERNISATION: COMPARATIVE VIEWS

The two terms namely: *Sankritisation and 'Westernisation'*, introduced by *Prof. M.N. Srinivas*, and "*Modernisation*", introduced by *Daniel Lerner* must be understood as *conceptual tools* to understand the nature and character of social changes that have taken place in the developing countries.

1. *MN. Srinivas* Writes: "I have used...The term 'Westernisation' to characterise the changes brought about in the Indian society and culture as a result of over 150 years of British rule..." He also writes 1 "A popular term for the changes brought about in a non-Western country by contact, direct or indirect, with a Western country is "*Modernisation*"— (Srinivas in his "*Social Change in Modern India*" - Pages: 47 and 50). *Srinivas* finds the necessity of finding an appropriate term when analysing changes that a non-Western country undergoes as a result of prolonged contact with a "Western one". But Daniel Lemer, "after considering the suitability of 'Westernisation' as well as 'Modernisation' ", has opted for the latter. *M.N. Srinivas*, on the other hand, has criticised Lerner's concept of 'Modernisation' and felt that his term 'Westernisation' is more relevant in the context in which it is used. comparatively speaking, the term '*Modernisation ' is a broader one and has a wider range of application*. The term *'Westernisation'* as *M.N. Srinivas* himself has recognised "*...is too local a label...*" to have wider range of use.
2. In a broad way it may be said that the concept of Westernisation as used by Srinivas covers: (*a*) *the behavioural aspects like eating, drinking, dressing, dancing, etc*. (*b*) *the knowledge aspects like literature, science, etc*. (*c*) *the values aspects like humanitarianism, equalitarianism and secularism, etc*. (**B. Kuppu Swamy** - 72). The term 'Modernisation' "*involves a transformation of social; political and economic organisation*". As a concept it is greatly helpful to the sociologists and anthropologists who have been primarily concerned with the process of differentiation that characterised the modern societies. It helps them' to know the way in which new structures arise to assume new functions, how new occupations emerge, how new complex education institutions develop and so on.
3. It is said that '*Westernisation*' (*of the 19th century*) *is mostly a middle class phenomenon whereas Modernisation is a mass process involving mass media*. "Thus while the 19th century Westernisation process was essentially a middle class affair involving fashions in speech, clothing, food and drink habits, the modernisation process involves a fundamental, deep-seated and widespread change involving attitudes, the development of a rationalist and positivist spirit and the application of the new knowledge to the ways of living. It is essentially a mass affair ... *It involves a fundamental change in social structure from the "Immutable" Varna society which is a closed society to a casteless, classless, open society*" — (**B. Kuppuswamy**: 1972; Pages: 63-64).
4. *Lerner* emphasises that the modernisation process involves the replacement of sacred revelation by secular enlightenment in the guidance of human affairs. *He considers the term Westernisation as inadequate and parochial*. As he points out modernisation is essentially based on "a rationalist and positivist spirit". He writes while Westernisation "*once penetrated only the upper level affecting mainly leisure class fashions, modernisation today diffuses among a wider population and touch public institutions as well as private aspirations with its diquieting positivist spirit*".

Conclusion

In conclusion, as *B. Kuppuswamy* has said that "*The concepts* Sanskritisation and Westernisation help us only to analyse the superficial change processes which took place in the later half of the 19th century and the first two decades of 20th century. Neither Sanskritisation nor Westernisation affect the social structure, So they are entirely inadequate to help us to analyse the change processes which are currently taking place in the Indian society". Though one cannot say that the terms Westernisation and Sanskritisation are useless one can definitely assert that the term '*Modernisation*' is more appropriate and relevant in providing a satisfactory explanation of social change.

REVIEW QUESTIONS

1. What do you mean by sanskritisation? Give an analysis of the process of sanskritisation.
2. Write the comments of the scholars on sanskritisation.
3. Define westernisation. Bring out the main features of westernisation.
4. Write the comments of the scholars on westernisation.
5. Give the definition of modernisation. Explain its process and characteristics.
6. Bring out the characteristic features of modernisation. What are the criteria of modernity?
7. Examine the causes of modernisation.
8. Discuss in detail the process of modernisation in India.
9. Analyse the problems of modernisation.
10. Give a comparative account of sanskritisation and modernisation, and westernisation and modernisation.
11. Write a short note on sanskritisation and brahminisation.
12. Modernisation is more appropriate and relevant in providing a satisfactory explanation of social change. Comment.

⌘⌘⌘⌘⌘⌘⌘⌘⌘⌘⌘

PART FIVE

SOCIAL INSTITUTIONS

27

MARRIAGE

CHAPTER OUTLINE

- DEFINITION AND CHARACTERISTICS OF MARRIAGE
- FROM OF MARRIAGE: POLYGYNY, POLYANDRY MONOGAMY–GROUP MARRIAGE—ENDOGAMY–EXPGAMY
- FUNCTIONS AND IMPORTANCE OF MARRIAGE

Marriage is one of the universal social institutions. It is established by the human society to control and regulate the sex life of man. It is closely connected with the institution of family. In fact, family and marriage are complementary to each other. As *Gillin* and *Gillin* have said, "Marriage is a socially approved way of establishing a family of procreation". As *Westermarck* has remarked, "Marriage is rooted in the family rather than the family in the marriage". Marriage is an institution of society which can have very different implications in different cultures. Its purposes, functions and forms may differ from society to society, but it is present everywhere as an institution.

DEFINITION AND CHARACTERISTICS OF MARRIAGE

Definition of Marriage

There is no definition which adequately covers all types of human marriage. It has given a number of definitions and explanations among which the following may be noted.

1. *Edward Westermarck* in his "History of Human Marriage" defines marriage as "the more or less durable connection between male and female lasting beyond the mere act of propagation till after the birth of offspring".
2. *Malinowski* says that marriage is a "contract for the production and maintenance of children".
3. According to *Robert H. Lawie*, "Marriage is a relatively permanent bond between permissible mates".
4. Broadly speaking, however, marriage may be defined as "a socially sanctioned sex relationship involving two or more people of the opposite sex, whose relationship is expected to endure beyond the time required for gestation and the birth of children".—*Duncan Mitchell's* "A dictionary of Sociology".
5. *Alfred McClung Lee* writes, "Marriage is the public joining together, under socially specified regulations of a man and woman as husband and wife".

Characteristics of Marriage

1. ***Universality:*** Marriage is more or less a universal institution. It is found among the preliterate as well as literate peoples. It is enforced as a social rule in some of the societies. *Examples*: In Japan, celibacy is publicly condemned. In Korea, unmarried individuals are called 'half' persons. Among the Hindus, marriage is a sacrament which is regarded as more or less obligatory. The Todas of Nilagiri refuse to perform funeral rites for a girl if she dies before her marriage. But they do perform it after completing some sort of marriage ceremony for the corpse. According to the Chinese philosopher *Confucius*, an individual who remains unmarried throughout his life commits a great crime. As *Levi-Strauss* has observed that the unmarried primitives of Central Brazil are made to lead a miserable life.

2. ***Relationship between man and woman:*** Marriage is a union of man and woman. It indicates relationship between one or more men to one or more women. Who should marry whom? One should marry how many?–are the questions which represent social rules regarding marriage which differ significantly.
3. ***Marriage bond is enduring:*** Marriage indicates a long lasting bond between the husband and wife. Hence it is not coextensive with sex life. It excludes relationships with prostitutes or any other sexual relationship which is viewed as casual and not sanctioned by custom, law or church. Marital relationship between man and woman lasts even after the sexual satisfaction is obtained. The Hindus, for example, believe that marriage is a sacred bond between the husband and wife which even the death cannot break.
4. ***Marriage requires social approval:*** A union of man and woman becomes a marital bond only when the society gives its approval. When marriage is given the hallmark of social approval, it becomes a legal contract.
5. ***Marriage is associated with some civil or religious ceremony:*** Marriage gets its social recognition through some ceremony. This ceremony may have its own rites, rituals, customs, formalities, etc. It means marriage has to be concluded in a public and solemn manner. Sometimes it receives as a sacrament the blessings of religion. Marriage among the Hindus, for example, is regarded as a sacrament. It is connected with rituals such as–Homa, Saptapadi, Panigrahana, Mangalya Dharana, etc.
6. ***Marriage creates mutual obligations:*** Marriage imposes certain rights and duties on both the husband and wife. Both are required to support each other and their children.

FUNCTIONS AND IMPORTANCE OF MARRIAGE

The importance of marriage consists in the functions that it performs. The main functions of marriage are as follows:

1. ***Regulation of sex life:*** Marriage is the powerful instrument of regulating the sex life of man. Sexual impulse is powerful in man. He is exposed to its influence throughout his life. It is an urgent and an irresistible need of man. It has to be controlled and regulated in a proper manner to avoid chaos and confusion in society. Marriage has come to be such a regulative means. Hence marriage is often called the licence for sex life.

   Marriage regulates sex relations also. It prohibits sex relations between the closest relatives, that is, between father and daughter, mother and son, brother and sister, etc. Such a kind of prohibition is called "incest taboo". Marriage also puts restrictions on the premarital and extra marital sex relations.
2. ***Marriage leads to the establishment of the family:*** Sexual satisfaction offered by marriage results in self-perpetuation. It means marriage insists on the couple to establish a family of procreation. It is here the children are born and bred up. It is the marriage which determines the descent of the new born individual. Inheritance and succession follow the rule of descent.
3. ***Provides for economic cooperation:*** Marriage makes division of labour possible on the basis of sex. Partners of marriage distribute and divide work among themselves and perform them. In some of the primitive tribes we find a clear-cut division of work between the husband and wife. Even in the modern industrial societies, we find husband and wife working outside the family to get more income to elevate their economic status.
4. ***Marriage contributes to emotional and intellectual interstimulation of the partners:*** Marriage brings life-partners together and helps them to develop intense love and affection towards each other. It deepens the emotions and strengthens the companionship between the two. It also helps them to develop intellectual cooperation between them.
5. ***Marriage aims at social solidarity:*** Marriage not only brings two individuals of the opposite sex together but also their respective families, groups and kindreds. Friendship between groups is reinforced through marriage. It is often suggested that by encouraging marriage between different groups, castes, races, classes, religious, linguistic and other communities, it is possible to minimise the social distance between groups and strengthen their solidarity.

FORMS OF MARRIAGE

The main forms of marriage are: *Polygyny, Polyandry, Monogamy*, and *Group Marriage*. Each of these types may be analysed here.

Polygyny

Polygyny is a form of marriage in which one man marries more than one woman at a given time. Polygyny is more popular than polyandry but not as universal as monogamy. It was in practice in most of the ancient civilisations. It prevailed among the ancient Hebrews, Assyrians, Babylonians, Indians and others. At present, it is widespread among primitive tribes but it is often simply confined to the wealthier classes. Polygyny is in practice among the *Eskimo tribes, Crow Indians, Hidatsa of North America, African Negroes, the Nagas, Gonds and Baigas of India. However, it is permitted in Muslim Community.*

Types of Polygyny

Polygyny is of two types: 1. *Sororal Polygyny* and 1. *Non-Sororal Polygyny.*

1. *Sororal Polygyny is a type of marriage in which the wives are invariably the sisters*. It is often called 'sororate'. The Latin word 'Soror' stands for sister. When several sisters are simultaneously, or potentially the spouses of the same man, the practice is called 'sororate'. It is usually observed among the tribes which pay a high bride price. The death of the wife or her childlessness is compensated by supplying a new spouse who is generally the younger sister of the deceased woman.
2. *Non-Sororal Polygyny* as the term indicates, is a type of marriage in which the wives are not related as sisters. For social, economic, political and other reasons, both the types are practised by some people.

Causes of Polygyny

Sociologists and anthropologists have made several studies to find out the causes of polygyny. Some of the factors mentioned by them are as follows:

1. ***More women less men:*** Polygyny becomes a natural practice whenever there is an excess of females over males. Even though the balance of sex ratio is normally maintained, it is likely to be upset for some reason or the other. Such a situation makes the members to practise either polygyny or polyandry if they want to have legitimate sex life. *Plains Indians* and *Eskimos*, for example, practise polygyny due to the imbalance in the sex-ratio.
2. ***Economic advantage:*** Some of the African tribes (Ex: *Longos* and the *Thongas*) practise polygyny for economic reasons. In the tribes women contribute to the family income by various means. Sometimes the first wife compels the husband to go for second marriage so that she can reduce her load of work at home.
3. ***Women as badges of distinction:*** Among some tribals, a man's social status is often measured in terms of the number of wives that he has. Greater the number of women greater is the prestige. Early Kings used to many more women for this reason also.
4. ***Childlessness of the first wife:*** Barrenness on the part of the first wife is also the cause of polygyny. The childless Wife herself may insist on the husband to go for the second marriage.
5. ***Constancy of sex urge in man:*** Unlike the woman, man is susceptible to sex stimulation throughout the year. Polygyny provides him opportunity to enjoy sex life throughout the year.
6. ***Other factors:*** In addition to the above, the following factors also favour polygyny.
   (*i*) *Taste for variety*. Men go after several women for they have a taste for variety.
   (*ii*) *Enforced celibacy*. Sex relations with a woman during her menstrual, pregnancy and lacta- tion periods are tabooed. This enforced celibacy is a case in favour of polygyny.
   (*iii*) *Earlier ageing of the female*. Among some tribes men marry more women because, they believe that ageing is faster in women.
   (*iv*) *Desire for more children*. The desire for more children on the part of men also supports polygyny. The African 'Guni' and 'Hihi' tribals practise polygyny for this reason.
   (*v*) *Captured women* in wars and fights are normally taken and enjoyed by the victorious men as their additional wives.
   (*vi*) *Men* may also marry more women to establish their masculinity.

Polyandry

Polyandry is the marriage of one woman with several men. It is much less common than polygyny. It is practised among the *Tibetans, Marquesan Islanders of Polynesia, the Bahama of Africa*, the tribals of *Samoa* and others. In India, the tribes such as *Tiyan*, the *Toda*, the *Kata,* the *Khasa* and *Ladakhi Bota* also practise polyandry. The *Nairs* of Kerala were polyandrous previously.

Types of Polyandry

Polyandry is of two types. 1. *Fraternal Polyandry*, and 2. *Non-Fraternal Polyandry*.

1. ***Fraternal polyandry:*** When several brothers share the same wife, the practice can be called *alelphic or fraternal polyandry*. This practice of being mate, actual or potential, to one's husband's brothers is called "levirate." It is prevalent among the Todas.
2. ***Non-fraternal polyandry:*** In this type, the husbands need not have any close relationship prior to the marriage. The wife goes to spend some time with each husband. So long as a woman lives with one of her husbands, the others have no claim over her. Nair polyandry was of this type. Tibetans too have this type. Both these types of polyandry

must be distinguished from "*wife-sharing*" or '*wife-lending*', which is much more common among the primitives. But in all cases it is temporary.

Causes of Polyandry

No universal generalisations can be made with regards to the causes of polyandry. Still factors such as scarcity of women, the desire to keep the property intact, heavy bride price, poverty and the sterility of men, etc., are favourable to polyandry though not always.

The *Todas of India* used to practise female infanticide prior to the British influence. This led to a surplus of males and naturally to polyandry. For the same reason the *Marquesan Islanders* practise polyandry. Still, in Ladakh polyandry was practised even though women outnumbered men there.

Polyandry is often practised due to poverty and heavy bride price. Poor young men who are not capable of paying the bride price and maintaining the wife individually often marry a woman collectively. Still, in some instances, even the rich people practised polyandry.

Among the *Toda*, property considerations and sex-parity have also caused polyandry. The *Tibetans* practised polyandry in order to keep the joint property intact.

Social Implications of Polyandry

Polyandry has its own implications. It gives rise to the *problem of determining biological paternity of the child.* But the primitives have their own social methods of determining the father- hood of the child. Such kind of fatherhood is known as "*sociological fatherhood*".

Among the Polyandrian Todas, one of the husbands goes through what is called a "*bow-and- arrow*" ceremony with the woman and thereby becomes the legal father of her child. He continues to be called the father of the children born to her till the other husband(s) goes through the same ceremony.

Among the *Samoa*, the children after the first few years are given the liberty to choose their parents for their permanent stay. The selected parent becomes the actual father of the children. If they feel that they are not treated properly they may move on to others.

Polyandry is said to be an adjustment with poverty. It tends to keep the birth-rate at a low level even by providing sexual satisfaction to all. Hence, *it tends to have an adverse effect on the growth of population*. The practice of polyandry requires good understanding between the wife and the husbands on the one hand and among the husbands themselves. *It may also lead to extra-marital and pre-marital sex relations*. The polyandrous Khasa wife has to follow the norms of marriage. But her unmarried daughter can freely mix with visitors at home.

It is to be noted that polyandry is not the common practice even among the communities where it is permitted. On the contrary, monogamy is becoming popular everywhere. Polyandry is slowly disappearing.

Monogamy

Monogamy is the form of marriage in which one man marries one woman. This is the most widespread form of marriage found among the primitives as well as the civilised people. If it was very popular during the early times, it has almost become a universal practice at present. It is prac- tised among the tribals such as *Kadars, Santals, the Khasis, the Canella, the Hopi, the Iroquois, the Andaman Islanders, the Veddas of Ceylon, the Sevangas of Malaya* and others.

Monogamy has a long history of its own. *Westermarck* is of the opinion that monogamy is as old as humanity. Ancient Greek philosopher Aristotle had recommended only monogamous mar- riage. Ancient Romans and Spartans also had given recognition to it. Ancient Jews, Christians and Indians had given importance to it. Ancient Hindus regarded monogamy as the most ideal form ot marriage.

Advantages of Monogamy

Monogamy seems to be superior to other forms of marriage. It enjoys certain merits over other forms. Some of them- may be noted.

1. ***Universally practicable:*** Since there is one-to-one ratio (One-man-to-one-woman) in almost all the societies, only monogamy can provide marital opportunity and satisfaction to all the individuals. Neither polygyny nor polyandry can equally satisfy all,
2. ***Economically better suited:*** No man of ordinary income can think of practising polygyny. Only a rich man can maintain a couple of wives and their children. Only monogamy can adjust itself with poverty. *For example*, even though Koran permits a Muslim to have four wives at a time, no ordinary Muslim can think of marrying four wives for the simple reason that he cannot maintain them.

3. ***Promotes better understanding between husband and wife:*** Monogamy produces the highest type of love and affection between husband and wife. It contributes to family peace, solidarity and happiness. *Vatsayana*, an authority on "Kama Sutra" remarked, "At best a man can only please one woman physically, mentally and spiritually. Therefore, the man who enters into marriage relations with more than one woman, voluntarily courts unhappiness and misery".
4. ***Contributes to stable family and sex life:*** Monogamous family is more stable and long- lasting. It is free from conflicts that are commonly found in polyandrous and polygynous families. There is no scope for sexual jealousy also. Unlike polyandry and polygyny, it does not give opportunity for having extra-marital sex relationship because sex relations are more strictly regulated here. *Herbert Spencer* has said that monogamy is more stable and the consequent family bond is stronger.
5. ***Helps to better socialisation:*** Since husband and wife have better understanding, they can give greater attention to the socialisation of their children. Children are well looked after and the parents can give their special attention to them. Under polygyny, the husband cannot devote himself fully to each of his wives and children because they are too numerous.
6. ***Aged parents are not neglected:*** It is only in monogamy that old parents are protected and looked after properly. Under polygyny, old wives are often discarded and in their place younger wives are brought in.
7. ***Provides better status for women:*** Women are given only a very low position in polygyny. Their rights are never recognised. They can be divorced at will. But in monogamy, women enjoy better social status. In the modem societies they enjoy almost equal social status with men.

Group Marriage

Theoretically group marriage means the marriage of two or more women with two or more men. But this arrangement is practically rare. Here the husbands are common husbands and wives are common wives. Children are regarded as the children of the entire group as a whole. Children call men of such a group their fathers and all the women their mothers. Some of the tribals in Australia, India, Tibet and Ceylon are believed to have practised group marriage.

Some writers have said that group marriage is not in existence. If at all it is in practice, it is clubbed with polyandry. For example, two *Toda* brothers marry two women as their common wives.

It is also said that monogamous or polygynous or polyandrous marriage associated with the practice of concubinage, sexual hospitality or socially tolerated adultery, is mistaken to be group marriage. Many studies have revealed that the practice of group marriage is almost on the verge of extinction.

Marriage Restrictions or Rules of Marriage

No society gives absolute freedom for its members to select their life-partners. Even in societ- ies where 'free marital choice' is allowed, the selection is not absolute but relative. Rules regarding "*who should marry whom*" always govern such a selection. Endogamy and exogamy are the two main rules that condition marital choice.

Endogamy

Endogamy is a rule of marriage in which the life-partners are to be selected within the group. It is marriage within the group, and the group may be caste, class, tribe, race, village, religious group, etc. Thus, we have caste endogamy, class endogamy, subcaste endogamy, race endogamy, tribal endogamy and such other forms.

Example. In caste endogamy, marriage has to take place within the caste. Brahmin has to marry a Brahmin. In subcaste endogamy, it is limited to the subcaste groups. Here a Shivalli Brahmin has to marry within Shivalli subcaste, a Gangadiagar Vokkaliga has to marry within his sub-caste group, and so on. Endogamy prohibits marriage outside the group. Even today intercaste marriages are not encouraged:

Factors, such as–the policy of separation, virtual geographic separation of people, the desire to keep wealth Within the group, religious, racial and cultural differences between peoples, sense of superiority or inferiority, etc., are said to be the causes of endogamy.

Endogamy as a rule of marriage has its own *advantages*. It contributes to the group unity and solidarity. It keeps women happier within their group. It helps to preserve the property within the group. It also safeguards the purity of the group. Finally, it helps to keep under secret the strength and weakness and also the professional secrets of-the group.

Endogamy has its, *disadvantages* also. (*i*) By dividing the society into small endogamous units, it strikes at national unity. (*ii*) By limiting the choice of life-partners, it often gives scope for evil practices such as polygyny, dowry system, bride price, etc. (*iii*) It may also make its followers to develop hatred and contempt for other groups. (*iv*) It is also said that "close-in-breeding caused by endogamy may affect the biological potentiality of the offsprings. For these disadvantages, endogamy is condemned. The modern civilised people are more in favour of exogamy than end gamy.

Exogamy

Exogamy is almost the opposite of endogamy. *Exogamy is a rule of marriage in which an individual has to marry outside his own group*. It prohibits marrying within the group.

The rule of exogamy insists that the so-called blood relatives shall neither have marital connec- tions nor sexual contacts among themselves. Near relatives are not supposed to marry among them- selves. But the degree of nearness differs from community to community. In Malenesia and Austra- lia among some people, a son may marry his father's wife if she is not his direct mother. Similarly, marriage of cousins is allowed among Muslims.

Forms of Exogamy

Exogamy assumes various forms in India.

1. ***Gotra exogamy:*** The Hindu practice of one marrying outside one's own 'gotra' is gotra exogamy.
2. ***Pravara exogamy:*** Those who belong to the same pravara (uttering the name of a common saint at religious functions) cannot marry among themselves.
3. ***Village exogamy:*** Many Indian tribes (Example: Naga, Garo, Mundal have the practice of marrying outside their village.
4. ***Pinda exogamy:*** Those who belong to the same 'Pinda' (or sapinda) cannot marry Within themselves ('Pinda' means common parentage).

Causes of Exogamy

Various factors must have caused exogamous marriages.

1. The desire on the part of a few to show that they are distinct from others must have encour- aged exogamy.
2. Somepeople feel that they become very cheap and insignificant if they marry within the known circle of relatives and friends. Hence, they want to go out of the group to select their life-partners.
3. The practice of female infanticide must have compelled a few tribals to go out of the tribe to find out mates for them. Due to the shortage of girls they are forced to do this. Some used to kidnap girls belonging to other groups.
4. The belief that close in-breeding would affect the biological quality of the offsprings, has also added to the practice of exogamy.

It may be noted that endogamy and exogamy are not mutually exclusive. In some societies both the rules may coexist. For example, in India both are practised by the caste Hindus. Castes and subcastes are endogamous in nature. But 'Gotra'–a small unit of subcaste is exogamous. Such rules differ from society to society.

Today there is a greater trend towards exogamous marriages. Endogamy is said to be conservative. It is widely criticised. Exogamy is appreciated as progressive and more scientific. Exogamy has brought peoples of various castes, races, religious groups, tribals together. It can effectively reduce social distance among peoples and encourage and support social solidarity and communal unity.

REVIEW QUESTIONS

1. Write the definition and characteristics of marriage.
2. What are the functions of marriage? Examine its importance.
3. What are the various forms of marriage? Discuss each in detail.
4. Elaborate on the rules of marriage.
5. Define polygamy. Explain its types and causes.
6. What do you mean by polyandry? Discuss the types and causes of polyandry.
7. Give the definition of monogamy. What are its advantages?
8. Write a detailed note on endogamy.
9. Give the meaning of exogamy. What are its various forms?
10. Examine the causes of exogamy.
11. Write short notes on the following:
    (a) Social implications of polyandry
    (b) Group marriage
    (c) Marriage restrictions

⌘⌘⌘⌘⌘⌘⌘⌘⌘⌘⌘

28

MARRIAGE IN INDIA

CHAPTER OUTLINE

- HINDU MARRIAGE
- DOES THE HINDU MARRIAGE CONTINUE TO BE SACRED?
- FACTORS AFFECTING HINDU MARRIAGE
- CONDITIONS OF VOID OR INVALID MARRIAGE
- IMPORTANCE OF "IDDAT" IN MUSLIMS' DIVORCE
- HINDU MARRIAGE—A SACRAMENT
- RECENT TRENDS IN HINDU MARRIAGE
- MARRIAGE AMONG MUSLIMS IN INDIA
- DIVORCE AMONG THE MUSLIMS
- DIFFERENCE BETWEEN HINDU AND MUSLIM MARRIAGES

Marriage and family, the two social institutions with biological foundations, are complemen-tary to each other. Both have a long standing history of their own. In the Indian context also both the institutions have been in existence since time immemorial. Both have withstood the ravages of time and the shocks of centuries. They are the permanent elements in our social system.

In the Hindu social heritage marriage has never been looked at from the materialistic point of view. Marriage among the Hindus is a sacrament and not a contract. The Rig Veda itself [Rig Veda- X 85] speaks of the sanctity of the institution of marriage. The tie of marriage was regarded even at that stage also as a binding force all through life. Marriage was a ritual which enjoined the husband to regard his wife as a god-given gift. Centuries have rolled on since then. The Hindu marriage though it has undergone vast changes has not totally lost its sanctity.

With the marriage sacrament of '*vivah samskara*' men and women as husband and wife establish the family or the '*Griha*'. *Grihasthashrama* is not merely a biological necessity but is also a social ideal. In the "Indian social evolution the family has always meant the joint family". *Grihyasutras* have highlighted the importance of the Hindu family. The Hindu joint family is said to be the bed-rock on which Hindu values, beliefs and attitudes are built. The family is also a sacred institution for the Hindus deriving sanctions from religion and social traditions.

Here is a glance of these two social institutions with a special reference to their importance and the changes taking place in them. The chapter also makes a brief survey of the Muslim marriage in India.

HINDU MARRIAGE

The Hindus have been giving great importance for marriage since time immemorial. Marriage is almost obligatory and unavoidable for an average Indian. Life without marriage is almost unthink-able in this country and there is a sharp social stigma attached to those who remain unmarried for long. There is a deep-rooted, long standing and widespread tradition here in favour of marriage as a basic ritual. Hence *C.B. Mamoria* rightly commented that "*we are a much marrying people. We marry early and we marry in large number*."[1]

Hindu Marriage: A Religious Duty and Not a Contract

Marriage is a matter of religious duty for the Hindus. Every Hindu is committed to marriage for the regards it as a great *sacrament*. [*sacred Vivaha Samskara*]. For the Hindus, marriage is *not* a matter of "social contract", nor is it deemed as "a licence for sex life". In the Hindu scheme of the Ashramas, one can enter the much praised "*grihasthashrama*" only after the marriage. With the marriage sacrament, man and woman as husband and wife establish the family, the home or "*griha*".

[1] C.B. Mamoria in his *Social Problems and Social Disorganisation in India.*

HINDU MARRIAGE: A SACRAMENT

Among the Hindus, marriage is not a social contract; it is religious sacrament. Marriage to a Hindu is of great individual and social significance. It is a socially approved union of man and woman aiming at procreation, pleasure and observance of certain social obligations.

The Hindu ideal emphasises the individual as well as social aspects of marriage. *K.M. Kapadia* in his "*Marriage and Family in India*" has given much information in support of the view that Hindu marriage is a sacrament. His explanation can be analysed from three angles: 1. *aims of the Hindu Marriage*; 2. *Main rituals which are involved in the Hindu marriage*; and 3. *the basic beliefs and values underlying the Hindu marriage*.

Aims of Hindu Marriage

As *Kapadia* has pointed out, the main aims of the Hindu marriage are: '*dharma*', '*praja*' and '**rati**'. Of these *aims*, dharma is given the first place, '*rati*' or pleasure is given only the third place, and '*praja*' or progeny is given the second place.

(i) ***Dharma:*** The Hindu thinkers regarded Dharma as the first and the highest aim of the Hindu marriage. Marriage is desired not so much for sex or for children as for acquiring a partner for the fulfilment of one's religious duties.

On the marriage, the sacred fire is enkindled, and it is the duty of the householder to offer "*panchamahayajnas*" daily in the company of his wife. These obligations would cease to exist only on the death of the householder. They get disturbed on the death of the wife, and hence the house- holder could marry immediately a second wife. The basic aim of marriage is *Dharma* for it necessarily involves the fulfilment of a number of moral duties.

(ii) ***Praja [Progeny]:*** The desire to get issues or children is completely felt by all the people. Psychologists call it *parental instinct*. The desire for '*praja*' or progeny is regarded by the Hindu Shastrakaras as one of the sacred purposes of marriage. The Upanishads have also stressed the continuance of the line of progeny. Getting a son is essential for a Hindu, for it is believed that one can fulfil one's "*Pitri Rina*" [paternal obligations only by getting a son. It is "*Kutumba Dharma*"[family obligation] also. In one of the important marriage rituals called "*saptapadi*" also the husband prays to the wife to fetch children for the family.

(iii) ***Rati [Kama or Pleasure]:*** Though sex is one of the functions of marriage it is given the third place. It is least desirable aim of marriage. To stress the lower role of sex in marriage, the marriage of a, Shudra is said to be for pleasure only. The Brahmanic legislations enjoins that the Shudra wife would be taken only for pleasure. However, sex is never condemned or degraded. It is given the third place because dharma is more expected of '*vivaha*' than '*kama*'.

Important Rites Associated with Hindu Marriage

Among the Hindus there are certain rites which must be performed for marriage to be complete. The main rites are: *vagdana, kanyadaana, homa, panigrahana, saptapadi* and *mangalyadharana*. These rites and the importance attached to them have added to the sanctity of the Hindu marriage.

(i) ***Vagdana [oral promise]:*** In the presence of the people gathered for the marriage the *names, gotras* and *pravaras* of the bride and the bridegroom are announced along with the announcement that they are ready for the marriage. This ritual 'is known as "*Panigrahana sankalpa*" or *Vagdana*.

(ii) ***Homa:*** 'Homa' refers to the offering in the sacred fire. A number of 'homas' tor fire rituals are observed in the marriage of which "*Laja Homa*" is an important one. This 'homa' is symbolic of fecundity and prosperity. Fred grains dipped in ghee are offered to fire [that is to lord Agni] by the couple with a prayer to the God requesting him to bless them with progeny and prosperity.

(iii) ***Kanyadaana:*** This is the most important ceremony connected with marriage. It is the ceremony of giving away the bride as a gift to the bridegroom in the presence of the sacred fire and in the presence of the people gathered. The father of the bride gifts her away to the bridegroom with a promise on his part that he would not transgress her "*in the attainment of piety, wealth and desire*". The same promise is repeated thrice and the bridegroom affirms his promise thrice.

(iv) ***Panigrahana [holding the hand of the bride]:*** This ritual refers to taking the right hand of the bride with the words: "*I seize thy hand for the sake of happiness that you may live to old age with me...*" With this the bridegroom takes the responsibility of looking after the bride.

(*v*) ***Mangalaya dharana [tying of the tali or mangalasutra]:*** This involves the act of tying the tali or mangalasutra [which is regarded as the sign of longevity of the husband] round the neck of the bride by the bridegroom. This ritual for which there is no reference in the Dharmashastras is more in practice in South India than in the North. It has even influenced the Catholic Christians of the South. [In north India, particularly in Bengal, Bihar, U.P. and Orissa the binding part of the marriage ceremony is "*sindurdan*" or painting of the part of the hair on the bride's forehead with vermilion and putting lac bangles in her lands by the groom - **C.B. Mamoria** [Page: 221]

(*vi*) ***Saptapadi:*** This is the ritual in which the bride and the bridegroom go 'seven-steps' together. The husband makes the bride step forward in the northern direction seven steps with the words: "*one step for sap, two for juice, three for wealth, four for comfort, five for cattle, six for seasons, friend be with seven steps united to me*". This ritual is important from the legal point of view, for the Hindu marriage is regarded legally complete only after it is performed.

The rites cited above are performed by a Brahmin priest in the presence of the sacred fire and are accompained by the Vedic mantras. "*They are necessary for marriage to be complete, because when they or any of them are not properly performed, the marriage may be legally questioned. Hindu marriage is a sacrament. It is considered sacred because it is said to be complete only on the performance of the sacred rites accompanied by the sacred formulae*".[2]

Sacred Beliefs and Values involved in Hindu Marriage

The Hindu marriage is a sacrament from the point of view of the sacred beliefs and values involved in it.

(*i*) ***Indissoluble marital bond:*** According to the traditional Hindu belief, martial bond is said to be inseparable and irrevocable. The parties to the marriage cannot dissolve it at will. They are bound to each other until the death of either of them. The belief states that the wife is supposed to be bound to her husband even after his death.

This concept of marriage that is indissoluble, is itself a sublime one which makes the husband and the wife to adjust their tastes, tempers, ideals, interests, choices and preferences. It thus involves sacrifices on the part of both the husband and the wife for each is called upon to bear with the other. Each individuals is here called upon to make marriage a success by means of compromise and adjustment.

(*ii*) ***Belief that marriage is a social duty towards the family and the community:*** The question of conflict between the husband and the wife did not perhaps arise in the old days for it never involved purely individual interests. The husband never expected any intellectual co-operation from his wife. The wife was more of a passive partner in the performance of religious duties than an intellectually active participant in all his affairs. "*Marriage was a social "duty toward the family and the community and there was little idea of individual interest*" [**Kapadia** - Page: 169]. The social background provided by the authoritarian joint family and the semi-sovereign caste never gave any scope for the recognition of any personal factor, individual interests or aspirations, in the relations between the husband and the wife.

(*iii*) ***The ideal of 'Patirvratya' associated with marriage:*** As per the ideal 'Potirvratya' popularised by the *puranic* writers, the wife is expected to be devoted to her husband alone. It implies that fidelity and modest service to the husband are the sole duty and main purpose in her life. As a river merging itself in the ocean loses its identity so a wife is supposed to merge her individuality with that of her husband. Her only concern in life is to provide all services to the husband; for the satisfaction of her husband is her sole joy in life. The wife is expected to prove herself as a real "sati" with all dedication and reverence to the husband.

- **The glorification of 'Sati' System.** The ideal of 'Patirratya' was stretched too much. It made the wife to be not only attached to the husband as long as he lived, but even after his death, because a 'sati' could never conceive of a second marriage or a second husband. Hence on the death of the husband the wife had either to live chastely, renouncing all the joys of life, or to follow her husband by jumping into the funeral pyre. The ideal of patirvratya gave rise to and glorified the practice of '*sati*'[3] or self-immolation.

  With the passing of time, the ideal of Patirvratya became to deeprooted in the mind of the Hindu woman that immolation became not only customary but a woman's highest aspiration.

[2] K.M. Kapadia in his *Marriage and Family in India*, p. l68.
[3] "The practice of 'sari' seems to have been first recommended in *Vishnu Dharmasamhita* in the 2nd or 3rd century A.D., Kapadia, 170.

- **Marriage, the only sacrament for women.** The Hindu marriage is a sacrament in another sense also. A Hindu male goes through the performance of several sacraments during the course of his life. These begin with the laying of the foetus and end with the cremation of his body. For the Hindu woman marriage is said to be essential for it is *the only sacrament* that can be performed for her. The Hindu women normally prefer to marry and aspire to marry for they know that the unmarried women are always put to hardship in the Indian social set up.

DOES THE HINDU MARRIAGE CONTINUE TO BE SACRED?

The Hindu marriage has undergone changes in the last few decades. These changes have given rise to two questions: 1. *Does the Hindu marriage continue to be sacred* ?; 2. *Has it lost its sanctity, or is it to be treated as a contract*?

Three Significant Changes

Three significant changes in the Hindu marriage may be noted here.

1. The Hindu young men and women today marry not very much for performing religious duties but for *life long companionship*.
2. The martial relations are no longer treated as unbreakable, or irrevocable, as *divorce* is socially and legally permissible, and
3. The ideal of '*patirvratya*' has lost its significance for there is legal provision for widow remarriage and divorce.

Hindu Marriage Continues to be a Sacrament

The above cited changes in the Hindu marriage have not affected its main character. "Widow remarriages and divorces have not become the order of the day. Though they are legally permitted, they are still looked down upon socially. Mutual fidelity and devotion to the partner are still consid-ered to be an essence of marriage. "*So long marriage is not performed for sex gratification alone but for "living together" and "begetting children", marriage will continue to be a sacrament for Hindus. Freedom in marriage [mate selection, etc.] does not destroy but rather confirms the stability of marriage and purifies its practice.*"[4]

Changes are taking place in the Hindu marriage but they have not disturbed its universality and damaged its sanctity. As *Kapadia writes,"....marriage continues to be a sacrament; only it raised to an ethical plane. We rather go back to our Vedic ideal embodied in the 'saptapadi' formula: "I take thee to be my companion in life*." - [**Kapadia** - Page: 197].

RECENT TRENDS IN HINDU MARRIAGE

The Hindu marriage system has undergone radical changes especially after independence. Even though the basic religious beliefs associated with marriage have not crumbled down, many of its practices, customs and forms have changed. The recent trends in this regard may be briefly discussed here.

1. ***Changes in the form of marriage:*** The traditional forms of Hindu marriages [as described by Shastrakara Manu] such as - 1. *Brahma*, 2. *Daiva*, 3. *Arsha*, 4. *Prajapatya*, 5. *Asura*, 6. *Gandharva*, 7. *Rakshasa* and 8. *Paisacha* — are no more in practice. Polygamy, polyandry and even bigamy are also not found for they are legally prohibited. Only monogamous marriages are universally practised.
2. ***Change in the aim or purpose of marriage:*** The traditional Hindu marriage considers "*dharma*" as its primary object whereas the modern Hindus give more importance to "*life-long companionship*" between husband and wife. Marriage is taking place not very much for the performance of religious duties, but for obtaining "lifelong companionship" of the individuals of the opposite sex.
3. ***Change in the process of mate selection:*** In the three areas of mate selection we find significant changes today.
   (*i*) **Field of selection** has become very wide. It is wide enough to include inter subcaste and intercaste marriages.
   (*ii*) **Party to selection:** Parents do not take an active role in the selection of life-partners of their children. The practice of young men and women selecting their life-partners by themselves is becoming popular today.
   (*iii*) **Criteria of selection.** Much importance is given to individual interests, preferences and considerations rather than to family considerations. This trend is reflected in the increase in the instances of love marriages.
4. ***Change in the age at marriage:*** Child marriages [at least at the level of middle and upper class people and educated people] are virtually not found now. As per the present marriage Act [that is 1978 amendment to the *Child Marriage*

[4] Ram Ahuja in his *Indian Social System*, p. 121.

Restraint Act, 1929] a boy below 21 years and a girl below 18 years cannot marry. Pre-puberty marriages have thus given place to post-puberty marriages.

5. ***Change in the stability of marriage:*** Legislative provision for divorce has virtually affected the stability of the marriage. Hindu marriage is no more regarded as indissoluable. The legislative provisions for divorce and widow remarriage have undermined the importance of the value of "*patirratya*". The concept of equality of sex has also affected the value of '*patirratya*'.
6. ***Change in the economic aspect of marriage:*** The practice of paying dowry is associated with marriage. This practice has grown into a big social evil today. Bride's parents are compelled to pay a huge amount of money as dowry. This practice has made marriage a costly affair. Marriages are often settled only on considerations of dowry. Marriage ceremony is also becoming a costly affair since huge amount of money is lavishly spent on decorations, processions, band sets, video-shooting, music, orchestra and so on.
7. ***An increase in the instances of divorce and desertion:*** Though the Hindu marriage is regarded as a sacrament instances of divorce and desertion are on the increase.

Though these new trends are observed today the importance of marriage has not diminished. It is still universally practised. Though its sanctity is affected a little, it is not reduced to the level of a mere civil contract. Hindu men and women are still emotionally involved in their marriages. There is no apparent danger as such to the Hindu marriage at present.

FACTORS AFFECTING HINDU MARRIAGE

The Hindu marriage has undergone vast changes during the recent years. Traditional values of marriage, *the form of marriage, type of marriage ceremony, the way of selection of life-partners in marriage, age at marriage* - and in such other areas significant changes have occurred. These changes have been caused by a number of factors among which the following may he noted: *Industrialisation, urbanisation, education and legislation.*

1. Influence of Industrialisation

Industrialisation refers to the phenomenal growth of modern sophisticated industries and its consequent dominance over agriculture. "industrialisation is a term covering, in general terms, the growth in a society hitherto mainly agrarian, of modern industry with all its attendent circumstances and problems, economic and social." Industrialisation directly affected the institutions of family and marriage and brought about changes in both.

Modern industries have minimised economic functions of the family and reduced its size. Nuclear families have replaced joint families. People have started "going out of family" for Work, for eking out their livelihood. Women also have joined men in the process of finding out jobs and eaming money. This has boosted the self-respect and self-confidence of women. Men could no longer boss over women and suppress their attempt to become self-reliant. These developments have affected the institution of marriage.

Employed women today take an active role in the selection of their life-partners. They do not just leave it to the decision of their parents. In addition to a girl's beauty, family to which she belongs, education and character and such other considerations, due importance is given today to her job and the salary she gets before she is selected as a life-partner. Daughters", earnings in many instances have reduced the financial burdens of their parents in marriage. Daughter's job itself may function as a *substitute for dowry*. Parents who were searching a suitable match for their daughters within the narrow circle of relatives and friends are now ready to go beyond the borders of even the state, because they want to fix a suitable and a good life-partner for their daughters. Instances of young men and women working in the same industry or office falling in 'love with each other and getting married are also not uncommon today.

2. Impact of Urbanisation

Industrialisation and urbanisation normally go together. Industrialisation accelerates the process of urbanisation. "Urbanisation' refers to the phenomenal growth of towns and cities or urban centres. It "*denotes a diffusion of the influence of 'urban centres to a rural hinterland.*" It is "*a process of becoming urban. moving to cities, changing from agriculture to other pursuits, common to cities and corresponding change of behaviour patterns.*"[5]

[5] Duncan Mitchel in his *Dictionary of Sociology*.

Growth of cities and city environment has its impact on the institutions of family and marriage. Selection of life-partners, age at marriage, nature and type of marriage ceremony, expenses of marriage etc., are affected by the modem urban environment. Normally young men and women of cities want to select their life-partners on their own. Arranged marriages have become rarer in cities. In comparison with villagers, urban people delay their marriages. Child marriages normally do not take place in cities.

Marriage is often held in cities more as a social or a civil ceremony than a religious ceremony. Non-availability of seasoned priests, scarcity of and too expensive choultries or '*kalyana manap*', difficulties involved in collecting number of items necessary for the conduct of a traditional type of marriage–all must have added to this new trend in marriage. Hence marriage ceremony in cities is tending more towards modernity than to traditionality. Huge amount is spent [sometimes running to a couple of thousands, and even a few lakhs] on the ceremony to make it a 'grand gala'. Money is spent lavishly for decorating marriage manap, putting up pandals, arranging grand dinner, take- home sweets, music orchestra, video shooting, photography, marriage procession, etc. The duration of marriage ceremony is also cut short in city. Elaborate customs are either avoided or shortened. Then, the whole ceremony is over within a couple of hours. It is rarely stretched over for several days.

It is generally observed that in a city a bigger number of instances of divorce, desertion, sepa- ration etc. is found than in a village. There is greater scope for developing pre-marital and extra- marital sex relations in cities.

3. Role of Education

Modern education has played its role in initiating some changes in marriage. It is through modern education that some of the modern values and western ideologies such as rationalism, individualism, equality of sex, democracy, individual freedom, secularism, etc., have influenced the outlook of our educated young men and women. Hence, they want to take their independent decisions on the main events of their life such as line of education, job and marriage. Thus our educated youths have their own views and stand on matters like to marry or not to marry, when to marry, whom to marry, how to marry etc. They do not want their families to decide these matters.

Educated youths do not hesitate to go beyond the boundaries of family ties to select for them suitable life-partners. For this purpose they sometimes contact "*marriage bureaus*" and give adver-tisements in the matrimonial columns of the newspapers.

In the circle of the college educated young men and women marriage is becoming a simple ceremony losing many of its rigid traditional customs. They give more importance to personal preferences and choices in marriage rather than to the gotra rules, family traditions and rules of horoscope. Some of them are even ready for intercaste marriages and if necessary, even for registered marriages.

Modern education has influenced marriage in different ways. Parents cannot impose any unwanted marriage on their educated daughters in the name of "*family decision or prestige*". Well educated people are expected not to insist on dowry in marriage. In India paradoxically, higher educated modem men demand a higher dowry than the uneducated or less educated. Educated and employed women are also not able to resist such a demand. They normally yield to its pressure and some of them even become victims of dowry disasters. Instances of divorce, desertion and separation are found in a larger number in the circle of educated persons than in the midst of the uneducated.

4. Influences of Legislations on Marriage

Many of the beliefs, values, ideals and rules of marriage laid down by the *Hindu shastrakaras* have lost their original meaning and purpose now. As a result, the Hindu marriage has developed some defects. Attempts were also made by some of the social reformers to remove these defects and correct the system. During the British rule and also after independence legislations were passed in order to bring about desirable modifications in the Hindu marriage system.'

The laws enacted in India relate to: (*i*) *age at marriage*; (*ii*) *field of mate selection*; (*iii*) *number of spouses in marriage*; (*iv*) *breaking of marriage*; (*v*) *dowry to be given and taken and* (*v*) *remar-riage*. The most important legislations relating to these six aspects of marriage passed from time to time could be briefly explained here.

1. ***The Prevention of Sati Act, 1829:*** The glorification of the ideal of "*Patirvratya*" had led to the inhuman practice of "*Sati*". Widows were often forced to make a vow or "*sankalpa*" to die after their husbands. Some were forcibly pushed to their husbands' funeral pyres. Famous Brahmo Samajist, Sri Raja Ram Mohan Roy took up the cause of women and impressed upon Lord Bentick who was the then British Governor General of India to bring out a legislation prohibiting the practice of "*Sati*".

The Prevention of Sati Act, 1829 made the burning or burying alive of widows cupable homi- cide punishable with fine and /or imprisonment. This legislation could save the lives of a number of widows though it could not immediately stop the practice in total.

2. ***The Hindu Widow Remarriage Act, 1856:*** This legislation was complementary to the previous legislation, that is, '*Prevention of Sati Act of 1829*'. Though widows were saved from the jaws of death they were subject to exploitation and humilitation. To remove the deplorable condition of the Hindu widows, a leading social reformer of the day, *Pandit Ishwara Chandra Vidya Sagar* brought pressure on the British Government to make legal provision for widow marriages. *The Hindu Widow Remarriage Act of1856* was hence passed.
3. ***The Civil [or Special] Marriage Act, 1872:*** This legislation treated Hindu marriage as a "*civil marriage*" and provided legal permission for intercaste, inter-religious and even "registered" marriages. [This Act was repealed by the *Special Marriage Act of 1954*. According to this Act, the parties interested in registered marriage must notify the marriage officer at least one month before the date of the marriage. It insists on the presence of two witnesses for marriage].
4. ***The Child Marriage Restraint Act, 1929:*** This Act came into force on April l, 1930. The Act restrains the marriage of a child. According to this Act, marriage of boys under 18 and girls under 14 years of age was an offence.
    - **Latest Amendment.** The Act was amended in 1978 which further raised the age for boys to 21 years and for girls to 18 years. The violation of this Act prescribes penalty. It provides punishment [three months of simple imprisonment and a fine of upto ₹ 1000] for bridegroom, parent, guardian and the priest who are party to the marriage. No woman is, however, punishable with imprisonment under this Act.
5. ***The Hindu Marriage act, 1955:*** This Act which came into force from May 18, 1955 brought revolutionary changes not only in the martial relations but also in various other social aspects. This Act applies to the whole of India, except Jammu and Kashmir. The word "Hindu" in the Act includes Jains, Sikhs, Budhists and the Scheduled Castes.
    - **Conditions for valid marriage as provided in this Act.** (l) neither party has a spouse living; (2) neither party [bridegroom or bride] is an idiot or a lunatic; (3) the groom must have completed 21 years and the bride 18 years of age as per the 1978 Amendment brought to this Act; (4) the parties should not be 'sapindas' of each other unless the custom permits such a marriage.
    - **Conditions under which divorce is permitted as per this Act.** (*i*) The spouse must have been impotent at the time of marriage and continues to be so even afterwards; (*ii*) party to the marriage was an idiot or lunatic at the time of marriage; (*iii*) consent of the petitioner or of the guardian was obtained by force or fraud; (*v*) the wife was pregnant by some person other than the petititoner at the time of marriage.
    - **Other conditions providing for divorce.** The dissolution of marriage may be obtained on the grounds of adultery, conversion of religion, unsound mind, leprosy, venereal disease, renunciation, desertion for seven years and cohabitation not resumed after two years after judicial spearation.
    - **Other important aspects of marriage.** (*i*) *This Act gives permission for intercaste and inter-religions marriages*; (*ii*) *It provides for equality of sex*; (*iii*) *It provides equal rights for men and women in marriage, divorce or separation*; (*iv*) *Its 1986 amendment permits divorce on the ground of incompatibility and mutual consent*; (*v*) *During judicial separation and after divorce, both husband and wife have the right to claim maintenance allowance.*
6. ***The Dowry Prohibition Act, 1961:*** This Act which prohibits the practice of dowry was passed on May 20th 1961. The Act does not apply to Muslims. It permits exchange of gifts for not more than ₹ 2000. It prescribes the penalty of 6 months imprisonment or a fine upto ₹ 5,000 or both for its violation. This Act got amended in 1986 and thereafter its rules have become still more stringent.

The above mentioned legislations in addition to many other social legislations, have affected the Hindu marriage in several ways. These legislations, however, have not transformed it into a mere legal contract. The Hindu beliefs and values relating to marriage are still alive and legislations have only strengthened it by removing some of the anamolies associated with it.

MARRIAGE AMONG MUSLIMS IN INDIA

Marriage is Universal among the Muslims

In the Muslim community marriage is universal for it discourages celibacy. Islam has almost made it compulsory, Prophet Mohammad also stressed that married life is preferable to unmarried life. Both the main sects within Islam called "*Sunnis*" and "*Shias*" consider marriage almost obligatory.

Main Aims and Objects of Muslim Marriage

Muslims call their marriage '*nikah*'. Marriage among the Muslims is regarded not as a religious sacrament but as a *secular bond.* The important objectives of Muslim marriage are - *control over sex, ordering of domestic life, procreation of children and perceptual increase of family, and upbringing of children.*

- **Marriage as a Civil Contract.** According to *Roland Wilson* [1941], "*Muslim marriage is a contract for the purpose of legalising sexual intercourse and the procreation of children.*"
- **S. C. Sarkar** [1948] has also said that "*marriage among Muslims is not a sacrament but purely a civil contract.*"
- **Marriage is a Religious Duty Also**. On the basis of the above statement it should not be concluded that the Muslim marriage does not have any religious significance. Marriage in the Muslim society is a religious duty also. It is a devotion and an act of "*ibadat*" [or religious duty]. It is believed that a person who does comply with it is rewarded in the next world, and he who does not, commits a sin. Hence, *Jang* [1953] has maintained that 'nikah', though essentially a contract, is also a *devotional act.*

Characteristic Features or Pre-conditions of Muslim Marriage

The important pre-conditions or characteristics of valid Muslim marriage called "*Nikah*" are as follows:

1. ***Marriage proposal and its acceptance - Ijab and Qubul:*** As marriage is a civil contract in Islam, a proposal for the marriage and the acceptance of the proposal are essential. The bride-groom makes a proposal to the bride just before the wedding ceremony in the presence of two witnesses and a "*mauvli*" or *kazi* [Muslim priest]. The proposal is called '*ijab*' and its acceptance is called '*Qubul*'. These two Words must be uttered clearly before the assembled persons by the bride and the bridegroom or by their agents of sound mind. It is necessary that both the proposal and its acceptance must take place at the same meeting to make it a "*sahi nikah*" [or "regular marriage"].
2. ***Capacity of a person to contract marriage:*** This is the second condition of marriage according to which only adult persons of sound mind can enter into a marriage contract. Child marriages and marriages of people of unsound mind are not recognised. However, the marriage of a minor could be contracted by his or her guardians.
3. ***Observance of the doctrine of equality:*** It is a matter of tradition among the Muslims to have marriage among equals. Though there is no legal prohibition to contract marriage with a person of low status, such marriages are looked down upon. The run-away marriages called '*kifa*' [girls running away with boys and marrying them on their own choice] are not recognised. Marrying idolators and slaves is also not approved. [Among the sunnis, social inferiority on the part of bride-groom could be a ground for cancellation of marriage but not among the Shias].
4. ***Preference system in the male selection:*** There is traditional insistence on the preferential system in mate selection. *For example*, a person is expected to give preferences to his cousins and of the cousins, first preference to parallel cousins [*chachera cousins* or father's brother's daughter] and next to the 'cross cousins' [*mamera cousins* or mother's brother's daughter'. But these days no such preferences are given to cousin marriages. A person can prefer to marry his deceased or divorced *wife's sister*. But a widow cannot give, preference to marry her deceased husband's brother.
5. ***Marriage should be free from legal complications:*** Muslim marriage can be called "sahi nikah" [valid marriage] only if it is not against 'shariah'.

CONDITIONS OF VOID OR INVALID MARRIAGE

Muslim marriage held according to the stipulated Islamic rules is called '*sahi nikah*' or regular marriage or valid marriage. Marriage which is held contrary to the islamic rules is called '*batil*' or *invalid marriage* or *void marriage*. Some of the conditions of invalid marriage are mentioned below:

1. ***Polygamy:*** A woman cannot marry second time as long as she has a living husband who has not divorced her. A man also cannot marry the fifth woman as long as the first four are alive and not divorced.
2. ***Marriage within the circle of close relatives:*** Marriage with relatively close kins such as–*mother, mother's mother, sister, sister's daughter, mother's sister, father's sister, daughter wife's mother, wife's daughter born to the first husband, son's* wife – is not allowed.
3. ***Marriage with idolators:*** Islam opposes idolatory. Hence marriage with idolators is not permitted. However, a man can marry a non-Muslim girl if he believes that her idolatory is only nominal. The purpose is to keep idolatory out of the islamic body politic, but a Muslim woman under no circumstances is permitted to marry non-muslims.

4. ***Marriage with people of prematured age and unsound mind:*** Marriage with a man of unsound mind is regarded as invalid. Marriage of immatured persons without the prior consent of their parents is also treated as invalid marriage.
5. ***Sisters becoming co-wives:*** As per the Islamic rule sorrate is not allowed. Sisters cannot be married simultaneously by the same person. However, one can marry one's wife's sister only after the death of the wife or only after giving divorce to the wife.
6. ***Marrying a woman during her 'Iddat' period:*** No Muslim woman is allowed to marry a man as long as she is undergoing "*iddat*".

Difference between Irregular Marriage and Invalid Marriage: 'Fasid' and 'Batil'

Muslims distinguish between two types of unacceptable marriages called "*irregular marriage* "and "*invalid marriage*", specifically known as '*fasid*' and '*batil*'. Main differences between the two can be mentioned here.

'***Fasid***' or irregular marriage, is one which could be converted into '*sahi marriage*' or 'nikah' by removing its impediments or irregularities. '*Batil*' marriages. on the contrary, cannot be converted to 'sahi' marriages.

(i) Examples for Fasid: (*i*) Absence of witnesses at the time of making or accepting the pro- posal; (*ii*) Muslim man marrying the fifth woman; (*iii*) marriage with a woman who is undergoing '*iddat*', etc. These *irregularities* could be corrected.

(ii) Example For Batil (*i*) Marriage within the close circle of relatives; (*ii*) Muslim woman marrying an idolator; (*iii*) Muslim man marrying two-three women who are sisters, etc. These ir- regularities cannot be corrected and hence such marriages become invalid.

Importance of Mehr or Dower in Muslim Marriage

Mehr or dower is a practice associated with Muslim marriage. "***Dower** is the sum of money or other property which a wife is entitled to get from her husband in consideration of the marriage.*"

***Purpose of Mehr*:** As per the muslim law, dower is an obligation imposed upon a husband as a mark of respect for wife. Its main purposes are - (*i*) *to put a check on the husband to divorce wife* (*ii*) *to enable a woman to look after herself after her husband 's death or divorce.*

***Proposal of Mehr before the marriage*:** Marriage proposals and Mehr discussions normally go together. The bride's relative called **'wali'** plays an important role in the discussion. He only keeps the account of "Mehr". Normally, a part of 'Mehr' [in majority of the instances 1/3 of the amount agreed upon] is paid by the bridegroom to **"wali"** [an elderly relative of the wife who may be her own father or any other such responsible person] on the third day of the marriage. The balance is generally paid when the husband dies or divorces the wife. It is her right to claim the *Mehr* from her husband. She may even refuse to acompany him if the agreed-upon-instalment of *Mehr* is not paid.

***Mehr is different from bride-price*:** Mehr is not bride-price for the wife is not purchased just by throwing some money as it was the case centuries ago. In the modem Islamic societies the bride's consent **[qubul]** has become pre-requisite for marriage. As it is made clear the main purpose of mehr is to give financial security to the woman and to create responsibility in man.

***Determinants of Mehr*:** The Muslim law does not fix the amount of mehr. The husband 15 obliged to pay some amount as *mehr*. The amount to be paid as mehr is normally decided before or after or at the time of the marriage ceremony. The amount of mehr, depends upon the *social position. descent, age, intelligence, beauty and other qualities of the bride.*

The amount of mehr cannot be reduced but it can be increased at husband's will. A wife can voluntarily agree to reduce the amount or make a gift of whole of it to her husband or to his heirs. The amount of Mehr varies from one **'dinar'** upwards. There is no maximum limit for that.

***Muslim wife's right over Mehr*:** As per the Islamic law, the wife has absolute right over the mehr amount. A widow's claim for *mehr* is normally regarded as her claim over her husband's property. She can retain the property till her *mehr* is paid. She need not wait for the consent of heirs for the possession of her husband's property. In case the divorce takes place through mutual agreement or by *wife's* initiative, her right to *mehr* gets extinguished.

***Specified Mehr and proper Mehr*:** When the amount of mehr is fixed between the two parties, it is called "**specified Mehr**". The minimum specified amount cannot be less than ten dinars. When the amount is not fixed but is given whatever is considered to be proper it is called "*proper Mehr*". The amount given here normally depends upon the financial position of the husband.

***Prompt Mehr and deferred Mehr*:** The amount which is payable on demand is called 'prompt Mehr'. Mehr which is payable on the dissolution of marriage [that is, after husband's death or di- vorce] is called '*deferred mehr*'.

DIVORCE AMONG THE MUSLIMS

Muslim marriage which is treated as a contract can be dissolved in the following ways.

1. Divorce as per the Muslim law but without the intervention of the court;
2. Divorce as per the Shariah Act, 1937
3. Divorce as per the Muslim Marriage Dissolution Act, 1959, that is, as per the court's intervention.

Divorce According to Muslim Law: Khula/Mubarat and Talaq

According to 'the traditional Muslim law, divorce can be obtained directly in two ways without the intervention of the civil court. They are: (1) *Khula/Mubarat* and (2) *Talaq*.

(1) Khula or Kohl and Mubarat: Husband and wife can obtain divorce by mutual consent either by '*Khula*' or by '*Mubarat*'. Difference between *Khula* and *Mubarat* is simple: In *Khula* divorce is initiated atithe instance of the wife. In *Mubarat*, since both the parties desire separation, the initiative may come either from the wife or from the husband.

(2) Talaq: *Talaq* represents one of the ways according to which a Muslim husband can give divorce to his wife as per the Muslim law without intervention of the court. In *talaq*, the husband has the right to dismiss his wife by repeating the dismissal formula thrice. The talaq may be affected either orally by making some pronouncements or in writing by presenting '*talaqnama*'. *Talaq* may be given in any one of the following three ways:

(*i*) *Talaq-e-Ahsan*. This involves a single pronouncement of *talaq* followed by a period of conjugal abstinence till the completion of '*iddat*'.

(*ii*) *Talaq-e-Hasan*. This consists of three pronouncements of '*Talaq*' made during three - successive menstrual periods and no sexual contact has taken place between the spouses during these months.

(*iii*) *Talaq-ul-Bidat*. Here, talaq, pronouncement takes place in any one of the following ways. (*a*) in a single sentence, for example, "*I divorce thee thrice*" or in three separate sentences: "*I divorce thee*, "*I divorce thee, I divorce thee*" (*b*) in a single but clear pronouncement such as, "*I divorce thee irrevocably*".

In the first two types cited above, there is a chance for re-establishing the martial ties but not in the third form.

Divorce as Recognised by Shariah Act, 1937

The Shariah Act, 1937 provides for three forms of divorce. They are mentioned below.

(*i*) *Illa*. If the husband swears by God to abstain from sexual relations with his wife for a period of four months or more, or for a specified period, he is said to make *illa*. If he sticks on to his words, then marriage gets dissolved.

(*ii*) *Zihar*. In this type the husband of sound mind declared in the presence of two witnesses that his wife is like the back of his mother to him. Though marriage is not dissolved with this, it gives scope for the wife to go to court on this ground.

(*iii*) *Lian*. In this type the husband accuses his wife of being guilty of adultery. This, however, gives an opportunity for the wife to go to court insisting on her husband either to withdraw such an allegation or prove the same.

Provisions for Divorce as per the Dissolution of Muslim Marriage Act, 1939

The Dissolution of Muslim Marriage Act, 1939 passed during the British period entitled a Muslim woman to seek the dissolution of her marriage on the following grounds:

(*i*) whereabouts of husband not known for 4 years.

(*ii*) failure of husband to provide for her maintenance for 2 years.

(*iii*) imprisonment of husband for 7 years or more.

(*iv*) impotency of husband since the time of marriage.

(*v*) failure of husband to fulfil martial obligations for 3 years.

(*vi*) insanity of husband for a period 2 years and husband's incurable diseases like leprosy, venereal diseases, etc.

(*vii*) husband's physical and mental cruelty.

(*viii*) marriage being thursted upon her before she attained 15 years, [but in this, the wife has to seek divorce before she completes 18th year].

(*ix*) any other valid ground which the muslim law' permits.

IMPORTANCE OF "IDDAT" IN MUSLIMS' DIVORCE

"*Iddat*" plays an important role in Muslim divorce cases. "*Iddat" denotes a period of awaiting.*

- **Iddat** refers to a period of seclusion for three menstrual periods for a woman after the death of or divorce by her husband to ascertain Whether she was pregnant.
- "*Iddat*" "....implies the period of waiting incumbent on a woman between disolution of one marriage and the contracting of another."[6] it is important to note that in this period of waiting [for three consenutive menstrual periods] husband and wife are not supposed to have sexual contact.

Legal and Social Effects of Iddat

Legal effects: (*i*) In a divorce case the wife involved is bound to wait for "iddat" period. (*ii*) During the period of "iddat" the husband is obliged to provide for her maintenance. (*iii*) the wife is not supposed to give her consent for another marriage till the iddat period is completed. (*iv*) On the completion of 'iddat' period, the wife can legitimately demand the "*deferred mehr*".

Social effects: '*Iddat*' serves as a restraining influence on inconsiderate haste on the part of the husband and on the tempo of divorce. It gives time for the husband to think and act. The husband may simply take back the wife during the period of *iddat* and suspend the divorce. (*ii*) *Iddat* makes it clear whether the wife is pregnant or not. The fact of pregnancy sometimes brings reconciliation between them. (*iii*) It it becomes apparent during '*iddat*' that the divorced wife is pregnant, the husband is recommended to take her back and treat her with consideration till the child is born. The child belongs to the husband if it is not born out of adultery. 'The wife also cannot marry any one else until her delivery. (*iv*) The iddat period is normally **three** months. In the case of a widow the duration is 4 months 10 days.

It may be noted that according to the **Muslim Women's Protection of Rights on Divorce Act 1986** and **Iddat**. a wife can demand from her husband her maintenance during the Iddat.

DIFFERENCE BETWEEN HINDU AND MUSLIM MARRIAGES

Main difference between the Hindu and Muslim marriages may be noted here.

Hindu Marriage	Muslim Marriage
1. *Aims and Ideals:* Main aims of Hindu marriage are: *dharma, praja* and *rati*. Hindu marriage is a matter of religious duty. For performing *panchamahayajnas* and getting a son to fulfil '*pitri-rina*', a Hindu is obliged to marry. It is hence sacred for him.	Muslim marriage is regarded more as a con- tract than as an important sacred rite. The main purpose is to obtain *sexual satisfaction* and along with it, *children*. Religious senti-ments do not characterise such a marriage.
2. *Relative Performance of Marital Bond:* As per the Hindu belief the *marital bond* is *in-separable*. It cannot be dissolved, according to the tradition. Hindu males cannot indiscriminately divorce their wives. Hindus can break the marriage only through the court.	Muslims do not consider marital contract as irrevocable. Here marital ties can be dissolved at the whims of the males. Muslim males can divorce their wives without the interven-tion of the court. Only men have such right.
3. *Remarriages and Widow Remarriages:* Since the Hin-dus consider marriage sacred, they are generally not prepared for remar- riage or Widow remarriage even though there is legal provision for that. Instances of such marriages are comparatively less.	Among the Muslims' there is scope. for remarriage and widow remarriage. *There is no blemish attached for that.* One contract can be broken to enter into another contract. After completing the "*Iddat*" a divorced woman can offer herself as a life-partner for another.
4. *No Scope for Polygamy:* There is no scope for the prac-tice of polygamy among the Hindus as per the existing marriage rules. Hindus have been cherishing the ideal of monogamy right from the times of Ramayana.	Muslims have been observing polygamy since a long time. Even now it is in practice. There is scope for polygamy as per the Koranic rules. Koran, however, restricts the number of wives to 'four'.

(*Contd.*)

[6] Ref: Quoted by C.B. Mamoria in his *Social Problems and Social Disorganisation in India*, p. 224.

Hindu Marriage	Muslim Marriage
5. *Mehr and Dowry:* Among the Hindus there is the practice of bridegrooms faking dowry. But the practice is neither obligatory nor universal. The practice of taking dowry has developed into a social evil now. It flourishes even though it is prohibited by legislation.	Among the Muslims, bridegroom gives some amount as mehr to the bride at the time of or after the marriage. The Muslim wife has the right to demand for it if she is being divorced by her husband. It is an obligatory practice. It is not considered a social evil.
6. *The question of temporary marriage* does not arise among the Hindus. Marriage as per the Hindu traditional belief, is permanent and irrevocable. There is no "*void marriage*" also.	Among the Muslims, at one time there was the practice of temporary marriage called "*Muta Marriage*". it could be contracted even for a day. Among the Sunnis its practice has disappeared.
7. *Legislations Affecting Marriage:* Hindu marriage in its history right from the British period till today has witnessed a number of legisations affecting its nature, form, practice etc.	Muslim marriage, especially in India has not been affected much by the legislative factors,. It has undergone just two or three legislations.

REVIEW QUESTIONS

1. Throw light on the Hindu marriage. Write its aims.
2. What are the important rites associated with the Hindu marriage?
3. Write an essay on the sacred beliefs and values involved in the Hindu marriage.
4. Discuss the factors that affect Hindu marriage.
5. Elucidate the recent trends that take place in the Hindu marriage.
6. Write a detailed note on Muslim marriage in India.
7. Discuss the characteristic features of Muslim marriage.
8. Assess the importance of 'Iddat' in Muslims' divorce. Discuss its local and social effects.
9. Differentiate between Hindu marriage and Muslim marriage.
10. Write short notes on the following:
    (a) Legislations related with marriage
    (b) Conditions of void or invalid marriage
    (c) Importance of 'Mehr' in Muslim marriage
    (d) Divorce among the Muslims
11. The Hindu marriage is a sacrament. Comment.

⌘⌘⌘⌘⌘⌘⌘⌘⌘⌘⌘

29

THE FAMILY

CHAPTER OUTLINE

The family is the most important primary group in society. It is the simplest and the most elementary form of society. It is the most basic of all social groupings. It is the first and the most immediate social environment to which a child is exposed. It is an outstanding primary group, be- cause, it is in the family that the child develops its basic attitudes.

Further, of all the groups that affect the lives of individuals in society none touches them so intimately or so continuously as does the family. From the moment of birth to the moment of death the family exerts a constant influence. The family is the first group in which we find ourselves. It provides for the most enduring relationship in one form or other. Every one of us grows up in a family and every one of us too will be a member of one family or other.

"The family, almost without question, is the most important of any of the group that human experience offers. Other groups we join for longer or shorter periods of time for the satisfaction of this interest or that. The family, on the contrary, is with us always. Or rather more precisely, we are with it."

— *Robert Bierstedt*

The family, as an institution is *universal*. It is the most permanent and the most pervasive of all social institutions. All societies both large and small, primitive and civilised, ancient and modern, have some form of family or the other. No one knows, or can know, how or when the family began. It is safe to surmise that the family in some form will always be with us. With regards to the future as the mind can imagine, the family will continue to be a central and indeed a nuclear component of society. "There may be no families in Utopia, and none in paradise, but the planet we know best will probably always contain them".

— *Robert Bierstedt*

It may be noted that our purpose here, is not to give counsels on family relations but lo acquire sociological knowledge regarding family. The family is a small group consisting ordinarily of father, mother, one or more children and sometimes near or distant relatives. It should be noted that it is not our purpose here to offer advice on the age at which people should marry, on how to choose a husband or a wife, how to get along with a difficult mate, how many children to beget, what to do about a mother-in-law problem, how to avoid divorce, and so on. Our study is confined to the family as a social phenomenon. *Our approach is sociological.* We are interested in the family both as an association and as an institution, but We give no counsel or advice as to how to be happy though married.

MEANING AND DEFINITION OF FAMILY

The word '*Family*' has been taken over from Latin word '*Famulus*' which means a servant. In Roman Law the word denoted a group of producers and slaves and other servants as well as members connected by common descent or marriage. Thus, 'originally, family, consisted of a man and woman with a child or children and servants. The meaning of family can be explained better by the following definitions:

1. *M.F. Nimkoff* says that "Family is a more or less durable association of husband and wife with or without child, or of a man or woman alone, with children".
2. *Burgess* and *Locke*. "Family is a group of persons united by ties of marriage, blood or adoption constituting a single household interacting and intercommunicating with each other in their respective social roles of husband and wife, father and mother, son and daughter, brother and sister, creating a common culture".
3. *Eliot and Merrill*: Family is "The biological social unit composed of husband, wife and children".
4. *MacIver*: Family is "*a group defined by sex relationship sufficiently precise and enduring to provide for the procreation and upbringing of children*"

GENERAL CHARACTERISTICS OF FAMILY

1. ***A mating relationship:*** A family comes into existence when a man and woman establish mating relation between them.
2. ***Selection of mates:*** Wife or husband may be selected by parents or by the elders, or the choice may be left to the wishes of the individuals concerned. Various rules govern this selection.
3. ***A form of marriage:*** The mating relationship is established through the institution of marriage. Marriage is an institutional arrangement made by the society according to which the individuals establish marital relationships among themselves. Marriage may assume any one of the forms-monogamy, polygamy, polyandry or group marriage.
4. ***A system of nomenclature:*** Every family is known or recognised by a distinctive name.
5. ***A way of tracing the descent:*** Every family has its own mode of tracing the descent. *Descent refers to the social recognition of biological relationship between individuals*. Descent may be traced through the male line (*Patrilineal Descent*) or through the female line (*Matrilineal Descent*) or through both the lines (*Bilateral Descent*).
6. ***A common residence:*** Family requires a home or a household to live in. After the marriage the wife may reside in husband's parental home (*Patrilocal or Virilocal Residence*) or she may stay in her parental home to which the husband pays occasional visits (*Matrilocal or Uxorilocal Residence*) or both of them may establish a separate home of their own (*Neolocal Residence*).
7. ***An economic provision:*** Family provides for the satisfaction of the economic needs of its members.

DISTINCTIVE FEATURES OF FAMILY

The family is an organisation *par excellence*. Of all the social organisations, large or small, family is of the greatest sociological significance. It occupies the central position in our social struc- ture. The family, unlike other institutions, enjoys a unique position in society. Its distinctive features may be noted here.

1. ***Universality:*** After having made an analysis of more than 250 societies, *Murdock* concludes that the family is universal. There is no human society in which some form of the family does not appear nor has there ever been such a society. *B. Malinowski* writes: "The typical family, a group consisting of mother, father, and their progeny, is found in all communities, savage, barbarians, and civilised". *The irresistible sex need, the urge for reproduction and the common economic needs* have contributed to this universality.
2. ***Emotional basis:*** The family is grounded in emotions and sentiments. It is based on our impulses of mating, procreation, maternal devotion, fraternal love and parental care. It is built upon sentiments of love, affection, sympathy, co-operation and friendship.
3. ***Limited size:*** The family is smaller in size. As a primary group its size is necessarily limited. It seems to be the smallest social unit. The biological conditions have also contributed to its small size.
4. ***Formative influence:*** The family is the earliest social environment which surrounds, trains and educates the child. It shapes the personality and moulds the character of its members. It emotionally conditions the child. It is the '*nursery of human nature*', *and the* '*breeding ground of our mores and the nurse of our loyalties*'.

5. ***Nuclear position in the social structure:*** The family is the nucleus of all other social organisations. The whole social structure is built of family units. It influences the whole life of society.
6. ***Responsibility of the members:*** The member of the family has certain responsibilities, duties and obligations. The smooth running of family depends on how best the members discharge their responsibilities in co-ordination with the other individuals of the family. As *MacIver* points out, "*In times of crisis men may work and fight and die for their country, but they toil for their families all their lives*".
7. ***Social regulation:*** The family is peculiarly guarded both by social taboos and by legal regulations. The society takes precaution to safeguard this organisation from any possible break- down: by divorce, desertion or separation.
8. ***The permanent and temporary nature of the family:*** The family as an *institution* is perma- nent. Since it is based on the organic and emotional nature of man, it continues to exist. But family as an *association* may be temporary in character. These characteristics indeed reveal the *sociological significance* of the family.

FUNCTIONS OF FAMILY

The family as a social institution performs several functions. Various opinions have been expressed regarding the functions of family. *Kingsley Davis* speaks of four main functions of the family: (*i*) *Reproduction*, (*ii*) *Maintenance*, (*iii*) *Placement*, and (*iv*) *Socialisation*.

Ogburn and Nimkoff have mentioned six major functions of family: (*i*) *Affectional*, (*ii*) *Economic*, (*iii*) *Recreational*, (*iv*) *Protective*, (*v*) *Religious*, and (*vi*) *Educational*. *Reed* has described four functions of the family: (*i*) *Race perpetuation*, (*ii*) *Socialisation*, (*iii*) *Regulation and satisfaction of sex needs*, and (*iv*) *Economic functions*.

Primary and Secondary or Essential and Non-essential Functions

MacIver classifies the functions of family into two types: *Essential* and *Non-essential* functions. According to him, the essential functions include (*i*) the stable satisfaction of sex need, (*ii*) production and rearing of children, and (*iii*) provision of a home. Under the non-essential functions he includes, religious, educational. economic, health and recreation, and other functions.

PRIMARY FUNCTIONS OF FAMILY

Some of the functions of family are basic to its continued existence. They are referred to as *essential* functions by MacIver. They may also be regarded as *Primary* functions of family. They are explained below.

1. ***Stable satisfaction of sex need:*** Sex drive is powerful in human beings. Man is susceptible to sexual stimulation throughout his life. The sex need is irresistible also. It motivates man to seek an established basis of its satisfaction. Family regulates the sexual behaviour of man by its agent, the marriage. Thus it provides for the satisfaction of the sex need for man. Even Manu, the Hindu Law- giver and Vatsyayana, the author of *Kamasutra*, have stated that sexual satisfaction is one of the main aims of family life.
2. ***Reproduction or procreation:*** Reproductive activity is carried on by all lower and higher animals. But it is an activity that needs control or regulation. The result of sexual satisfaction is reproduction. The process of reproduction is institutionalised in the family. Hence it assumes a regularity and a stability that all societies recognise as desirable. Thus family introduces a legitimacy into the act of reproduction. All societies surround this function with norms and support them with strong sanctions. By fulfilling its reproductive function family has made it possible to have the propagation of species and the perpetuation of the human race.
3. ***Production and rearing of the child:*** The family gives the individual his life and a chance to survive. We owe our life to the family. The human infancy is a prolonged one. The child which is helpless at the time of birth is given the needed protection of the family. Further, family is an institution *par excellence*, for the production and rearing of children. No other institution can as efficiently bring up the child as can the family. This can be referred to as the function of *'maintenance'* also.
4. ***Provision of home:*** Family provides the home for its members. The desire for home is strongly felt in men and women. Children are born and brought up in homes only. Though, often children are born in hospitals, clinics, maternity homes, etc., they are nursed and nourished in the homes only. Even the parents who work outside are dependent on home for comfort, protection and peace. Home remains still the *'sweet'* home.

5. ***Family–an instrument of culture transmission and an agent of socialisation:*** The family serves as an *instrument of culture transmission*. The family guarantees not only the biological continuity of the human race but also the cultural continuity of the society of which it is a part. It transmits ideas and ideologies, folkways and mores, customs and traditions, beliefs and values from one generation to the next.

   The family is *an agent of socialisation* also. Socialisation is its service to the individual. Socialisation is the process whereby one internalises the norms of one's groups so that a distinct '*self*' emerges unique to the individual. The family indoctrinates the child with the values, the morals, beliefs, and ideals of the society. It prepares its children for participation in larger world and acquaints them with a larger culture. It is a chief agency which prepares the new generation for life in community. It emotionally conditions the child. It lays down the basic plan of the personality. Indeed, it *shapes the personality* of the child. Family is a mechanism for disciplining the child in terms of cultural goals. In short, it transforms the infant barbarian into the civilised adult.

6. ***Status ascribing function:*** The family also performs a pair of functions–(*i*) *status ascription for the individual*, and (*ii*) *societal identification for the individual*. Statuses are of two kinds: *Ascribed* and *achieved*. The family provides the ascribed statuses. Two of these, age and sex are biological ascriptions. Others, however, are social ascriptions. It is the family that serves almost exclusively as the conferring agency or institution.

   People recognise us by our names, and *our names are given to us by our family*. Here, the family is the source of our societal identification. Various statuses are initially ascribed by our families. Our *ethnic* status, our *nationality* status, our *religious status*, or *residential* status, or *class* status–sometimes our *political* status and our *educational* status as well–are all conferred upon us by our families. Of course, these may be changed later. Wherever statuses are inherited as in the case of royalty and nobility it is the family that serves as the controlling mechanism. Status ascription and societal identification are two faces of the same process. The importance of family in this regard can hardly be exaggerated.

7. ***Affectional function:*** Man has his physical, as well as mental needs. He requires the fulfilment of both of these needs. Family is an institution which provides the mental or the emotional satisfaction and security to its individual members. It is the family which provides the most intimate and the dearest relationship for all its members. The individual first experiences affection in his parental family as parents and siblings offer him love, sympathy and affection. Lack of affection actually damages an infant's ability to thrive. *A person who has never been loved is seldom happy*.

Secondary Functions of Family

In addition to the above described essential or primary functions the family performs some secondary or non-essential functions in some way or the other. Of these, the following may be noted.

1. ***Economic functions:*** The family fulfils the economic needs of its members. This has been the traditional function of family. Previously, the family was an economic unit. Goods were produced in the family. Men used to work in family or in farms for the production of goods. Family members used to work together for this purpose. It was to a great extent self-sufficient. A clear cut division of labour between sexes, that is, between men and women, was evident. But today, the situation has changed. The family members do not work together at home. They are engaged in different economic activities outside the home. They are no longer held together by division of labour.

   The economic role of modem family is considerably modified. The process of industrialisation has affected family. The centre of production has moved from home to the factory. The factory is giving job only to the individual worker and not to the entire family. The factory is producing goods which are consumed within the family. Thus, family has become more a consuming unit than a producing one. Its members are busy with "earning wages" rather than with "making a living". Family is thus slowly transferring its economic functions to the external agencies. Still, the institution of property is embedded with the family.

2. ***Educational functions:*** The family provides the basis for the child's formal learning. In spite of great changes, the family still gives the child his basic training in the social attitudes and habits important to adult participation in social life. "The manner in which he learns how to get along with his family will be carried over to his interactions with school authorities, religious leaders, the police and other agents of social control". When the child grows up, he learns to manage situations outside the home and family. He extends his interests to other groups. With all this his intelligence, his emotions, and his social habits develop until he weans himself from the original dependence on the mother, father and other family members.

3. ***Religious functions:*** The family is a centre for the religious training of the children. The children learn from their parents various religious virtues. Previously, the homes were also centres of religious quest. The family used to teach the children the religious values, moral precepts, way to worshipping God, etc. Even today, it is in the family that the foundations are laid down for the moral standards that are to guide the children throughout their life. *The family meets the spiritual needs of its members*. It is through the family that the religious inheritance is passed on to the next generation.
4. ***The Recreational Functions:*** At one time, recreation was largely family based. It fostered a close solidarity. Reading aloud, visiting relatives, family reunions, church socials, singing, danc- ing, playing indoor games, etc., brought together the entire family. Elders would organise social gathering among themselves in each other's homes. Children would organise their own recreations among themselves or together with other children. Often parents and children would join together in the same recreational activities. The effect of this on- the cohesion of the family was considerable.

Recreation is now increasingly organised outside the family. Modern recreation is not de-signed for family-wide participation. Whether in the form of movies, sports events, plays, cricket, 'kabaddi', tennis, dinner parties, or 'yakshagana', it is designed for the couple or individual participation.

The Changing Family Patterns

The family as a basic social institution has been undergoing change. The modern family radically differs from that of the traditional one. The family has never been at rest. Both in its structure and functions changes have taken place. Some of these changes may be examined here.

Changes in Functions of Family

Some of the functions of family have radically changed today while some others have received more attention of the public. A glance at these changes would clarify this point.

1. *The Sexual Regulation Function* of the family has not changed much. The family through its agent, marriage, still regulates the sexual impulse of the people. Illicit sexual behaviour is fairly uncommon. But it is true that in the Western societies pre-marital and extra-marital sex relations are on the increase.
2. *The Reproductive Function* of the family has *suffered* particularly in the Western societies. In the Western societies, it is said, parents no longer desire more children. Absence of children has become the most glaring feature of the Western families. However, it is impossible to take away this reproductive function of the family. The very survival of the human race is based on reproduction.
3. In the past fifty years the *Parental* and *the Educational Functions* of the family have been *shifted* to certain external agencies like hospitals, out-patient clinics for mothers, maternity homes, the baby clinics, nurseries, kindergartens, etc. "The modern home is not equipped to train children for their adult careers, because the specialised division of labour requires specialised training, which only the specialised agency of the school can supply".–*A.W. Green*
4. *The Protective Functions* of the family have declined particularly in the West. Families are no more the place of protection for the physically handicapped, mentally retarded, aged, diseased, infirm and insane people. Other agencies have taken over this function. But, for the young children it continues to provide physical and emotional protection.
5. *The Economic Function* of the family has been disturbed a great deal. The family is no longer the economic unit, neither is it self-sufficient. It is no longer united by shared work, for its members work separately. It is more a consuming unit than a producing centre. However, the family is not completely losing this function, but it is *transforming* this function to some external agencies.
6. It seems that the *Socialisation Function* of the family is gaining increased attention particularly in the Western society. An earlier generation knew little about the *personality development*. We know something today of the role of emotional development, school progress, career success, physical well-being, and practically all other aspects of the good life.
7. *The Status-Ascription Function* has been weakened since in modern society much emphasis is laid on achieved status. Still, the ethnic, religious, class, residential, nationality and other kinds of statuses are ascribed by the family to the individual at least in the initial stages in some way or other.

8. *The Recreational Function* of the family is losing importance. External agencies have taken away this function. Modern recreation is highly commercialised. Movies, dance halls, night clubs, gambling centres have come into being. People leave home to seek these commercialised recreations. But they tend to leave home as single adults or married couples, as adolescents or children, *rather than as a family unit*. This has affected the cohesion of family.

Functions Lost or Modified?

In spite of the changes that have overtaken the family, its traditional functions have been more modified than lost. If all of the functions described above were in fact *totally* provided outside the home, it is doubtful that the family could survive. But, certain unique functions remain solely within the family. The "primary universal function of the family is the creation of new members of society-their reproduction, maintenance, status ascription, and socialisation. As always, reproduction remains, and maintenance and socialisation are still carried on chiefly within the family" —A. W. Green

Some writers have expressed the opinion that at the present rate of change the family may lose its functional importance very shortly. Such a fear is unfounded because, that stage may never be reached. "Over the centuries, no permanent direction of change has ever been maintained. At some time in the future, the present forces of change may reach out in an unforeseen direction permitting family to regain its old strength and renew its old functions." —A.W. Green

Summary

From our discussion of the family and its functions it is possible to draw at least three conclusions: (*i*) The family still enjoys importance as a biological group for procreation and for the physical care of the children, (*ii*) There is the considerable decline in what Ogburn calls the "*institutional functions*' of the family, economic, recreational, protective and educational, (*iii*) the '*personality function*' (the socialisation function) of the family "that is, those which provide for the mutual adjustments among husbands, wives, parents and children and for the adaptation of each member of the family to the outside world" —have assumed importance.

TYPES OR FORMS OF FAMILY

Sociologists have spoken of different forms or types of family. They have taken into consideration different factors as the basis for the classification of the family. A few classifications can be mentioned.

(*i*) On the basis of *marriage* family has been classified into three major types: (*i*) Polygamous or Polygynous Family. (*ii*) Polyandrous Family, and (*iii*) Monogamous Family.

(*ii*) On the basis of the nature of *residence* family can be classified into three main forms: (*i*) Family of Matrilocal Residence, (*ii*) Family of Patrilocal Residence, and (*iii*) Family of Changing Residence.

(*iii*) On the basis of *ancestry* or *descent* family can be classified into two main types: (*i*) Matrilineal Family, and (*ii*) Pratrilineal Family.

(*iv*) On the basis of the nature of *authority* family can be classified into two main types. (*i*) Matriarchal Family, and (*ii*) Patriarchal Family.

(*v*) On the basis of *size* or *structure* and the depth of generations family can be classified into two main types: (*i*) the Nuclear or the Single Unit Family, and (*ii*) The Joint or the Undivided Family.

(*vi*) On the basis of the *Nature of Relations* among the family members the family can be classified into two main types: (*i*) The Conjugal Family which consists of adult members among whom there exists sex relationship, and (*ii*) Consanguine Family which consists of members among whom there exists what is known as "*blood relationship*"—brother and sister, father and son, etc.

MATRIARCHAL FAMILY

The matriarchal family is also known as the mother-centred or mother-dominated family. Here, the mother or the woman is the head of the family and she exercises authority. She is the owner of the property and the manager of the household. All the other members are subordinated to her. *L.H. Morgan*, *Bachopen*, *Tylor, Briffault* and others are of the opinion that matriarchal family has been the earliest type of family. But some have expressed their doubts regarding their very existence. Such controversial opinions still prevail. On the basis of some studies now it is known that matriarchal families are found among the *Eskimos*, *Malay Islanders*, *Odama Indians, Labradar Indians, Trobsiand Islanders, the American Iroquois, the Khasi tribals of India* and others.

Characteristics of Matriarchal Family

1. ***Descent, inheritance and succession:*** Here the descent is traced through the mother. Hence it is matrilineal in descent. Daughters inherit the property of the mother. They succeed their mother and the sons. The status of the children is mostly decided by the status of the mother.
2. ***Matrilocal residence:*** Matriarchal family is *matrilocal in residence*. After the marriage the wife stays back in her mother's house. The husband who normally stays in his sister's house, pays occasional visits to the wife's house. He is treated as a '*privileged visitor*'. But he is given only secondary position. Sex relations between husband and wife tend to be very loose and both may often develop extra-marital sex-relations.
3. ***Exercise of power:*** In theory, the mother exercises authority and power in the matriarchal family. She is the head of the family and her decisions are final. But in practice, some relative of the mother, mostly her brother, exercises authority in the family and looks after property. *Ex.*: Among the *Malay* people the wife's brother exercises authority in the family and among the Labradar Indians the wife's father manages the household.
4. ***Structure of the family:*** The maternal family brings together the kinsmen- (the wife, her mother and grandmother, her children and brothers, etc.) and welds them together into a powerful group. This type of family is normally associated with exogamy.

PATRIARCHAL FAMILY

The patriarchal family is also known as *father-centred* or *father-dominated* family. Here, the father or the eldest man is the head of the family and he exercises authority. He is the owner and administrator of the family property. On all family matters his is the final voice and opinion.

Characteristics of Patriarchal Family

1. ***Descent, inheritance and succession:*** These are recognised through the male line. Patriar- chal families are *partilineal* in character, because the descent is traced through the male line. Here, only the male children inherit the property of the father. In some instances, the eldest son enjoys some special rights. Her normally succeeds the father after his death. Children are recognised as the children of the father and the mother is practically ignored.
2. ***Residence:*** Patriarchal family is *Patrilocal* in residence. Sons continue to stay with the fa- ther in his own house even after their marriages. Only the wives come and join them. Women have secondary position in these families for they have to be at the mercy of their menfolk. Children are brought up in their father's, family.
3. ***Authority:*** Here the father or the eldest male member of the family is the dominant person. He is all in all. All the members are subordinated to him. He dictates terms for other members. All the major decisions pertaining to the family affairs are taken by him only. Nobody has the authority to question him. He is the owner and the manager of the family property. During the early days, the patriarch had absolute authority over all the members of the family. The patriarch could sell his sons and wife or even kill them. In religious matters also he was the head.

Some Examples of Patriarchal Families

The typical patriarchal families are not found today in the modern industrial societies. But they prevailed among the ancient *Hebrews*, *Greeks*, *Romans*, and the *Aryans of India*. The *Roman* patriarch had "*the Patria Potestas*" (the power of the father) which gave the head of the family an unlimited authority over all the other members. There was no legal jurisdiction to challenge the authority of the patriarch. In ancient *Palestine* the father could sell his daughter into servitude. In the same manner the *Hebrew* patriarch exercised despotic power over all his dependants. In *India* also during the Vedic period woman was subject to three kinds of successive obediences–to her father before her marriage, to her husband after the marriage and to her son during her widowhood or old age. In ancient *Athens,* women were not given an opportunity to lead public life. On the other hand, wife and daughters were kept in secluded "*women's apartment*".

At present, both matriarchal and patriarchal families have diminished. In their place *egalitarian* or *equalitarian* families in which father and mother enjoy equal status and opportunities, have emerged. Most of the families in the industrial societies are equalitarian families. They are often called '*modern families*', and also '*nuclear families*'.

NUCLEAR FAMILY

The individual nuclear family is a universal social phenomenon. It can be defined as "*a small group composed of husband and wife and immature children which constitutes a unit apart from the rest of the community*."–(Duncan Mitchell in his "Dictionary of Sociology').

In simple words, a nuclear family is one which consists of the husband, wife and their children. Soon after their marriage, the children leave their parental home and establish their separate household. Hence, a nuclear family is an autonomous unit free from the control of the elders. Since there is physical distance between parents and their married children, there is minimum interdepen- dence between them. Thus, a nuclear family is mostly independent. The American family is a typical example of the modern independent nuclear family.

The nuclear family is a characteristic of all the modern industrial societies. As *Lowie* writes: "It does not matter whether marital relations are permanent or temporary ; whether there is polygyny or polyandry or sexual licence;.....the one fact stands out beyond all others that everywhere the husband, wife and immature children constitute a unit apart from the remainder of the community".

According to *TB. Bottomore*, the universality of the nuclear family can be accounted for by the important functions that it has been performing. The nuclear family has been performing the sexual, the economic, the reproductive, and the educational functions. According to him, the indispensability of these and a few other functions has contributed to its universality. Anthropologists too have consistently emphasised the economic functions of the family in primitive societies. A major factor in maintaining the nuclear family is economic co-operation based upon division of labour between sexes. *Levi Strauss* has said much about the miserable situation of unmarried individuals in most of the primitive societies.

Structure of Nuclear Family

The nuclear family depends very much on incest taboos. The members of the family cannot have marriage from among themselves. Hence it is confined to two generations only. A third generation can be established by the formation of new families. This can be done by an exchange of males and females between existing nuclear families. It means daughters can be given in marriage to other nuclear families and girls of the other nuclear families can be taken in as spouses to the sons. This gives rise to two kinds of nuclear families: (*a*) *the family of orientation*, and (*b*) *the family of procreation*.

Every normal, adult in every human society belongs to two nuclear families. The first is *the family of orientation* in which the person was born and brought up, and which includes his father, mother, brothers and sisters. The second is the *family of procreation* which the person establishes by his marriage and which includes the husband or wife, the sons and daughters.

The structure of the nuclear family is not the same everywhere. *Bottomore* makes a distinction between two kinds of family system; (*i*) the family systems in which the nuclear *family is relatively independent*, and (*ii*) systems in which *the nuclear family is incorporated in, or subordinated to, a larger group, that is to the polygamous or the extended family*. The independent nuclear family is more often incorporated in some larger composite family structure.

The independent nuclear family which is dominant in modern industrial societies has emerged mainly due to the growth of individualism and intense geographic and social mobility. The social welfare functions of the modern state have also affected it. The state now comes to the help of the individual to face misfortunes. Hence he is no longer dependent on his family in times of distress.

The modern nuclear family is mostly found in the advanced societies of the West and in the U.S.A. Its solidarity largely depends on sexual attractions and the companionship between husband and wife and between parents and children. But the family bonds tend to weaken as the children grow up.

Recent Trends in Modern Nuclear Family

The family has undergone some radical changes in the past half a century. Its structure has changed, its functions have been altered and its nature has been affected. Various factors—social, economic, educational, legal, cultural, scientific, technological, etc. have been responsible for this. It is, indeed, difficult to analyse the recent trends in the family and to account for its causes. Still, a few significant trends may be noted:

1. ***Industrialisation:*** The Industrial Revolution of the 18th century and the consequent birth of the factory system of production affected the economic functions of the family. Family transferred its economic functions to the factory and became more a *consumption unit* than a productive centre.
2. ***Urbanisation:*** Industrialisation and urbanisation very often go together. Cities are growing in size and in number. Family is cut to size. Families are now the smallest, and home ties are the weakest. Trends towards disorgarnisation are set in motion.

3. ***Democratic ideals:*** Democratic ideals and values are in currency today. Democracy assures equality and provides liberty to all, to women too! Women now play not only domestic roles but also economic and political roles. They have now become property owners and business managers. They have the voting power and with it, they have entered politics. The world has already witnessed four women prime ministers.
4. ***The decline of the influence of mares and the religious beliefs, and the spread of secular attitude:*** Morality and religion are slowly losing grounds. Family members have become more secu- lar in outlook. The religious functions of the family have diminished. Religious sentiments, beliefs and attitudes have come to be dissociated with the family.
5. ***The spirit of individualism and romantic love:*** Today individualism and romanticism are widespread. Their very spirit has destroyed the authority of the family over the individual members Individualism has affected love-making and marriage. Romanticism has encouraged the idea of free choice of mates on the basis of love. Marriage has become as easily dissolvable as it is entered into by a mutual consent of the partners.
6. ***Economic independence of women:*** Employment opportunities are thrown open for women also. The woman has become now the earning member. She now works in offices, factories, banks, schools, colleges, hospitals, administrative offices, ministries, etc. The economic independence has increased her status, but affected her attitude. The age-old doctrine *men for the field and women for the kitchen*—is exploded.
7. ***Emancipation of women:*** Women are now liberated from the chains of traditionalism They stand on an equal footing with men. Aggressive leaders of the *Woman's Liberation Movement* have attacked the double standard of morality. They are demanding more rights and liberty for women.
8. ***Decline in birth rate:*** The size of the family is becoming smaller. Joint family is fairly uncommon. The birth rate is adversely affected. Absence of children is a glaring feature of the Western families.
9. ***Divorce:*** Today, more stress is laid on romantic love. "Love is no more sacramental" now. In the West, *Love at first sight and divorce at next* is quite common. Instances of divorce, desertion and separation are mounting in the West. Marriage has become a civil contract only.
10. ***Parent-youth conflict:*** Inter-personal conflicts in the family are increasing. An unusual amount of conflicts between parents and their adolescent children is taking place. This is often denoted in terms of the *generation gap. Kingsley Davis* says that "The stress and strain in our culture is symptomatic of the functionless instability of the modem small family".

Many sociologists have expressed their grave concern regarding the rapid changes that are taking place in it. Some have said that "family has gone to the dogs" while some others lamented that family is *heading towards disorganisation*. But it would be more appropriate to say that "it (family) is merely seeking to adopt itself to changed conditions".

Functions of Modern Nuclear Family

The modem nuclear family continues to stay because of the essential functions that it performs even today. Those essential functions are explained below.

1. ***Stable satisfaction of sex need:*** The modern nuclear family continues to be the executive means of providing sexual satisfaction to its members. No other agency has been able to take up this task to the satisfaction of the members. The family does this task through its agents the marriage. Though pre-marital sex relations are on the increase especially in the West, they are still treated as 'deviant trends' or stray instances.
2. ***Procreation and upbringing of children:*** The modern family still fulfils the functions of procreating and upbringing of children. The family is regarded as the "proper" authority to produce children and to bring them up. Even today most of the children are born and brought up in the family only. Family alone is well equipped to produce and bring up children. This function has been asso- ciated with family since centuries. It continues to be the biological group for procreation and for the physical care of the children.
3. ***Socialisation of children:*** The modern family still remains as the main architect of socialising the new born child. The child develops a 'self' and a personality of its own mainly in its family. Most of the social norms, values and ideals are picked up by the child in the family only. Parents are showing more interest now-a-days giving proper social training to their children.

4. ***Provision of home:*** The modern family provides for its members house to live in. Due to economic, and other exigencies, family members may go out for some time but they spend much of their time in 'the home itself. It is a happy place to live in both for parents and their children. It still continues to be the noblest centre of human affection, love and sympathy. Other agencies such as hotels, hostels, lodging houses, etc., may provide shelter to the members, but not the needed love and affection. Only the home can provide permanent homely atmosphere for its members.

The general view of the modern nuclear family is that it is not a highly ritualised and institutionalised entity. It is rather what *Burgess* has called "*a unit of interacting personalities, set in a cultural framework, responsible for a limited number of social functions and for a biological function*". It is held together by internal cohesion rather than external pressure. It is more unstable than what it was in the past. Still it is more free to fit the variations in human personality.

JOINT FAMILY (A STUDY OF JOINT FAMILY WITH REFERENCE TO INDIA)

The joint family is also known as '*undivided family*' and sometimes as '*extended family*'. It normally consists of members who at least belong to three generations: husband and wife, their married and unmarried children; and their married as well as unmarried grandchildren. The joint family system constituted the basic social institution in many traditional societies, particularly in the Eastern-societies. In India, this system prevailed among the Hindus as Well as non-Hindus.

Joint Family in India

The joint family, the caste system and the village system are often regarded as the pillars on. which the whole Hindu social edifice is built. The joint family is the bedrock, on which Hindu values and attitudes are built. It is found in almost all the part of India. Family for at Hindu is a sacred institution deriving sanction from religion and social traditions with myths and legends. Hence this form of family is still found in India. It is deeply rooted in the traditional Hindu culture. It is an age system having a long history of its own

Definition of Joint Family

1. The joint family is a mode of combining smaller families into larger family units through the extension of three or more generations including at least grandparents, parents and children.
2. The joint family is one which consists of members related through blood and spread over several generations living together under a common roof and work under a common head.
3. The definition given by *Smt. Iravati Karve* seems to be more satisfactory. According to her, the joint family may be defined as "*a group of people who generally live under one roof who eat food cooked at one hearth, who hold property in common, and who participate in common family worship and are related to each other as some particular type of kindred*"

Types of Joint Family

The joint family may assume two forms: 1. *Patriarchal joint family*; and 2. *Matriarchal joint family*. Both the forms are found in India. The patriarchal joint family is father-centred and the matriarchal joint family is mother-dominated. *Examples*: The patriarchal joint families are found among the *Nambudaris* of Malabar, the *Mundas* of Chhotanagpur and the *Angami Nagas* of Assam. The Nambudari joint family is generally described as "*Illom*". The matriarchal joint families are found among the *Nairs* of Malabar, the *Khasis* and *Garos* living on the Garo hills of Assam. The Nair joint family is popularly known as "*Tarawad*".

Characteristics of Joint Family

1. ***Depth of generations:*** The joint family consists of people of three or more generations including at least grandparents, parents and children. Sometimes, other kith and kin such as uncles, aunts, cousins and great grandsons also live in the joint family itself.
2. ***Common roof:*** Members of the joint family normally reside together under the same household. Due to the scarcity

of accommodation or due to educational and employment problems, members of the joint family may reside separately. Still, they try to retain regular contacts and the feeling of belonging to the same family.

3. ***Common kitchen:*** Members eat the food prepared jointly at the common kitchen. Normally, the eldest female member of the family supervises the work at the kitchen. In the patriarchal joint families, women serve the food to men at first and take their meals afterwards.

4. ***Common worship:*** The Hindu joint family derives its strength from religion. Hence, it is associated with various religious rituals and practices. Every family may have its own deity of 'Kula devata' and its own religious tradition. Members of the family take part in common Worship, rites and ceremonies.

5. ***Common property:*** The members hold a common property. As *Melley* writes: the joint family "is a co-operative institution similar to a joint stock company in which there is a joint property". The head of the family manages the family property like a trustee. The total earnings of the members are pooled into a family treasury and family expenses are met without of that.

6. ***Exercise of authority:*** In the patriarchal joint family usually the eldest male member exercises authority The super-ordination of the eldest member and the subordination of all the other members to him is a keynote of the joint family. His commands are normally obeyed by others. As opposed to it, in the matriarchal joint family the eldest female member in theory exercises the supreme authority.

7. ***Arranged marriages:*** In the joint family, the head considers it as his privilege to arrange the marriages of the members. The individual's right to select his/her life-partner is undermined. The younger members rarely challenge their decisions and arrangements. But now-a-days, the feelings of younger ones are being given due weightage.

8. ***Procreation:*** The size of the joint family is by nature bigger. It is found to be associated with higher rate of production. It is so because in the past procreation was regarded as a religious duty. Member's rarely practised birth control measures. But today the situation has changed.

9. ***Identification with obligations towards the family:*** The members tend to identify themselves with their family. Every member has his own duties and obligations towards the family. The family in turn, protects the interests and promotes the welfare of all. The senior-most member of the family acts as the guide for other members.

10. ***Self-sufficiency:*** There was a time when the joint family was mostly self-sufficient. It used to meet the economic, recreational, medical, educational and other needs of the members. The rural agricultural joint families were mostly self-reliant. But they can hardly depend on themselves today. No type of family is self-reliant that way to day.

Merits and Demerits of Joint Family

The joint family claims certain merits and suffers from certain defects. Some of them may be mentioned here.

Merits of Joint Family

1. ***Stable and durable:*** The joint family is more stable and durable than the single unit family or the nuclear family. Individuals may come and go but the family as a unit stands. It contributes much to the continuation of the cultural tradition.

2. ***Ensures economic progress:*** The joint family meets the basic needs of its members—food, clothing and shelter–a first condition of economic progress.

   Further, it provides larger labour force especially for the agricultural communities. It prevents the sub-divisions and fragmentation of land-holdings and helps scientific farming.

3. ***Ensures economy of expenditure:*** Savings are possible here since the household purchases are done jointly. No single member has an absolute right in family property. Everyone is bound to become spendthrift. The head of the family does not permit the members to become extravagant.

4. ***Secures the advantage of division of labour:*** Here the work is distributed among the members on the basis of age and sex. Members co-operate with one another since they hold the property in common. Especially for agricultural

tasks, the joint family is better fitted. As *K.M. Kapaziia* has pointed out: "The Indian farmer used to be producer, seller, labourer and investor combined. Each of these functions can be perfomed efficiently to the advantage of the family if it is a joint one."

5. ***Serves as a social insurance company:*** For the people such as orphans, widows, the de- serted, divorced, separated and the neglected, the joint family serves as a social insurance company. It gives them food, shelter and protection.
6. ***Provides social security:*** The joint family gives social security to the weak, aged, sick, infirm, the unabled, the disabled and such other needy persons. An individual's life from cradle to cremation is looked after by the joint family. In times of accidents, crises and emergencies, one can rely on one's joint family for the needed help.
7. ***Provides leisure:*** Since the work is shared by all the members on the basis of age, sex and experience, they get more leisure time. More hands at home can finish off the work with minimum time and provide enough leisure to the members to relax. Here women are the main beneficiaries of leisure.
8. ***Provides recreation also:*** The joint family is an ideal place of recreation for all the members. Childish play between the too aged and the little babies, the funny talks of the old, the broken language of the younger ones, the expression of sisterly, brotherly and motherly love and the like make the joint family life a pleasureable one. Social and religious ceremonies that take place at the family bring even the relatives together and tigthen the ties.
9. ***Helps social control:*** The joint family by exercising control over the behaviour of its members acts as an agency of social control. The individuals are taught to subordinate their individual interests to the group interests.
10. ***Provides psychological security:*** The joint family provides psychological security to its members. By creating a harmonious atmosphere in the family, it contributes to the development of social solidarity. It prevents the growth of excessive individuation inside the family.
11. ***Promotes co-operative virtues:*** Joint family is said to be the breeding ground of love, self-help, co-operation, tolerance, discipline, loyalty, generosity, sacrifice, service-mindedness and obedience and such other virtues. It instils the socialistic spirit among the members. "*Work according to one's ability and obtain according to one's needs", and "all for one and one for all*",–are said to be the mottos of a joint family.

Demerits of Joint Family

1. ***Retards the development of personality:*** The joint family does not provide enough scope for the members to develop qualities of adventure, self-determination, industriousness, etc. The elder ones take up too many responsibilities and the younger ones are overprotected.
2. ***Damages individual initiative and enterprise:*** The joint family does not provide proper opportunities for the members to develop their talents. Any new enterprise or adventure on the part of the young people is discouraged by the head of the family. This adversely affects the individual- ity, originality and creativity of the young members.
3. ***Narrows down loyalties:*** Joint family makes the members to develop narrow-mindedness. It is said that a member is more likely to develop a sense of loyalty to the family rather than to the larger society. These family units develop strong opposite principles which result in disintegration and division within the society at large.
4. ***Promotes idleness:*** The joint family is said to be the home of idlers and drones. Since all the members are assured of their basic necessities of life, no one takes much interest in the produc- tive activities. Further, all the relatives may flock to the joint family with their idle habits and may become life-long parasites.
5. ***Not favourable for saving and investment:*** The need for saving does not arise here because all are assured of their basic needs. There is no inspiration for the accumulation of capital and invest- ment. Saving is not possible also for one has to share one's income with the large family.
6. ***The centre of quarrels:*** The joint family is said to be the hotbed of quarrels and bickerings especially among the womenfolk. Since women come to the family (after the marriage) from diverse socio-economic and religious backgrounds, they may find it difficult to adjust themselves properly. Quarrels very often take place between the elder and the younger members of the family.

7. ***Denies privacy:*** Since the joint family is always overcrowded, privacy is denied to the newly wedded couple. They cannot express openly their love and affection for the invariable pres- ence of other members causes embarrassment for them. They rarely get opportunity to talk about their personal matters. Hence they fail to develop intimacy.
8. ***Affects socialisation of children:*** Due to the lack of intimacy and privacy between the husband and wife, the socialisation of children is affected very badly. The parents cannot always give personal attention to the upbringing of their children. The children become more attached to their grandparents and often they pick up the idle habits and age-old ideas.
9. ***Undermines the status of women:*** In patriarchal joint families, women have only secondary role. They are not given sufficient freedom to express and to develop their personality. Their inner feelings are never recognised. They are made to work like servants. Women are treated as non- entities here. They can hardly resist their elders even for just causes because obedience is enforced upon them. In such families sons are preferred to the daughters.
10. ***Encourages litigation:*** The joint family encourages litigation. Normally disputes over the common property crop up at the time of partition. Such disputes are taken to the courts which are dragged on for years leading to the waste of time, energy, money and more than that, loss of mental peace.
11. ***Favours uncontrolled reproduction:*** The joint family is found to be associated with higher birth rate. Members do not feel the need to adopt birth-control measures. Since the joint family takes up directly the responsibility of feeding, rearing and educating the children, the married members do not experience the urgency and necessity of restricting the number of issues.
12. ***Limits social mobility:*** The joint family is said to be more conservative in nature. Since it is dominated by tradition, it is slow to respond to the modern trends. It does not encourage its members to go after change. Members are more concerned with safeguarding their statuses rather than with changing them. Hence social mobility is very much limited here.
13. ***Encourages nepotism:*** Some are of the opinion that the joint family system is the root cause of nepotism and discrimination. It is said that the public servants and officials belonging to one or the other family are more likely to favour their own kith and kin on public issues or in matters of providing job even at the cost of merit.

Causes for the Changes in the Joint Family System

The traditional joint system of India has undergone vast changes. These changes have not destroyed the system as such. They have definitely affected its structure and functions and also its stability. **Milton Singer** [1968] has identified five factors which have affected the family most. These are: *education, industrialisation, urbanisation, change in the institution of marriage*, specially in the age of marriage and the legislative measures.

1. Influence of Education

Modem system of education introduced by the British Government affected joint family in several ways. It has brought about a change in the attitudes, beliefs, values and ideologies of the people. Education which is spreading even amongst the females has created and aroused the individualistic feelings. While the male literacy level has increased from 9.8% in 1901 to 55.7% in 1991, among the females it has increased from 0.6% to 30.09% during the same period.

The increasing education not only brings changes in the philosophy of life of men and women, but also provides new avenues of employment to the latter. After becoming economically indepen- dent, women demand more freedom in family affairs. They refuse to accept anybody's dominance over them. Education in this way *brings changes in relations in the family*. As the level of education rises, the percentage of those in favour of nuclear families increases and the percentage of those supporting joint family living, decreases.

2. Impact of Industrialisation

Factory system of production, new system of organisation and management and new style of life have also affected the joint family. It has made young men and women leave their joint family to far away places in search of better prospects and employment. It has resulted in the breakdown of the link between the kinship and the occupational structure. Many of the traditional skills, crafts and household industries associated with the joint family have declined because of the onslaught of factory system of production.

Some important effects of industrialisation on joint family system may be noted here.

(*i*) The family which was a principal unit of production has been transformed into a *consumption unit*. Instead of all family members working together in an integrated economic enterprise, a few male members *go out of the home* to earn the family's living. This affected *family relations*.

(*ii*) Factory employment has *freed young adults from direct dependence upon their families*. This financial independence of the youngesters has *weakened the authority of the head* of the house- hold over those earning members. In many cities even women too joined men in working outside the families on salary basis.

(*iii*) In the changed social situation *children have ceased to be economic assets* and *have become liabilities*. Children's educational requirements have increased. They are to be supported for a very long time till they get into some good job.

(*iv*) Industrialisation *separated the home from the work*. This has made the working members to bear themselves all the burden and headache connected with their job. Their families can hardly lend support in this regard.

3. Influence of Urbanisation

The phenomenon of urbanisation has become now widespread. Urban population is increasing steadily. In the mid-eighteenth century, around 10% of the population in India were urban residents. Their percentage increased to 36.19% in 1991. The studies made by **Aileen Ross, M.S. Gore, Milton Singer** and others have revealed that the *city life is more favourable lo small nuclear families than to big joint families*.

On the basis of the studies made, it could be said that the *urban living weakens joint family pattern and Strengthens nuclear family patterns*. Educated persons in urban areas are less in favour of joint family norms. Cities provide opportunities to women also for gainful employment and when woman starts earning, she seeks freedom in many spheres. She tries to break away more and more from her husband's family of orientation. Urban residence thus seems to introduce a certain measure of variation in family pattern in our society.

4. Change in Marriage System

Change *in the age at marriage, freedom in mate-selection and change in the attitude towards marriage* have also affected our family system. Modem young men and women not only marry at a late age but also take personal decision in this matter. They do not wait for parental permission. Parents' role in mate-selection has diminished. Marriage is not very much considered a religious affair but only a social ceremony. Modern marriage does not symbolise the superior authority of the family head over other members.

5. Legislative Measures

The impact of legislative measures on the family system cannot be ignored. Prohibition of early marriages and fixing the minimum age of marriage by the *Child Marriage Restraint Act, 1929 and the Hindu Marriage Act, 1955*, have lengthened the period of education. The freedom of mate-selection and marriage in any caste and religion without the parents consent after certain age permitted through by the *Special Marriage Act, 1954*, gave a blow to the parental authority to decide their children's marriage. Other legislations such as the *Widow Remarriage Act, 1856* which gives sanction for widow remarriage, the *Hindu Marriage Act*, 1955 which permits divorce and the *Hindu Succession Act, 1956* which gives share to daughters in parental property - all have modified *inter- personal relations within the family, the composition of the family and the stability of the joint family*.

6. Other Causes

(*i*) ***Influence of western values:*** The western values relating *to modern science, rationalism, individualism, equality, free life, democracy, freedom of women etc*. have exerted a tremendous influence on the Hindu family system. The modern educated youths who came under the influence of these values took the earliest opportunity to become free from the tight grip of the joint family.

(*ii*) ***Awareness among women:*** Increasing female education, widened freedom and employment opportunities for women created awareness among women particularly in the middle and upper class. They also sought chances of becoming "*free*" from the authoritarian hold of the joint family.

Is the Hindu Joint Family Disintegrating?

Scholars have been discussing since several years the question of the disintegration of the Hindu joint family in India. No social institution can withstand change for long. The Indian family system including the traditional Hindu family system, too has undergone changes. The question that is debated is whether these changes are causing the disintegration of the family or not. There are three views among the scholars relating to this question. They are mentioned below.

1. ***The joint family system is not only changing fast, but also tending towards disintegration:*** K.T. Merchant [1935], A.M. Shaw [1955-58], Aileen Ross [1961], William Goode [1963], Prameel Kapoor[1970], B.R. Ghosh [1974]-and others supported this view on the basis of their field studies.
2. ***Joint families are successfully continuing in India withstanding all the disintegrating forces:*** This view has been held by the scholars-K.M. Kapadia [1956], I.P. Desai [1964], B.R. Agarwala, M.S. Gore [1968] and others on the basis of their field studies conducted at Surat, Navsari, Baroda, Poona, Kheda, Delhi, Rohtak and other places.
3. ***Joint families though are changing fast they continue to stay with relatively smaller size*:** Dr. Iravathi Karve, David G. Mandelbaum and others strongly held this opinion.

Joint family is facing changes. It is true that joint family system is undergoing fast changes. Some of these changes have disintegrating influence also. This disintegration is more evident in big cities and in industrial centres than in rural areas. But the disintegrating rate is slow and not fast. If some forces are at Work towards the breaking up of the joint family system, some other forces are striving for maintaining its existence.

Forces of Chang are not destroying the system as such. Since India is a land of villages, the joint family system has still scope for its continuation in the villages. The forces of mechanisation, industrialisation, urbanisation, education, etc. have not taken place to the extent of destroying all the prevailing joint families.

Joint family is not dying out. As **K.M. Kapadia** has pointed out, "*the general assumption that the joint family is dying out is invalid.*" The rural people who desert their joint families and move to the cities due to some economic and other exigencies still want to have their connection with their parental joint families. They want to visit their native families at least at the time of marriages, festivals and such other family rites and ceremonies. Educated Indians still feel morally obliged to retain their links with the traditional joint families. They consider it their moral duty to bring up their younger brothers and sisters in the lines of education and employment. The *sentiment of jointness is very much alive* in them and they cherish it as a cultural objective. Hence joint families do not dwindle away so easily. On the contrary they are making enough compromises with the modern trends for their survival.

REVIEW QUESTIONS

1. Give the meaning of family. What are its general characteristics?
2. Define family. Explain the characteristics of family as a social institution.
3. Explain the distinctive features of family.
4. What are the functions of family?
5. Throw light on the changing patterns of family.
6. Define family. Discuss the main features of the various types of family.
7. What do you mean by matriarchal family? Write its characteristic features.
8. What do you know about patriarchal family? Write its characteristics. Give some examples of the typical patriarchal families.

9. Define nuclear family. Discuss the structure of nuclear family.
10. Elucidate the recent trends that take place in the modern nuclear family.
11. Describe the functions of modern nuclear family.
12. Define joint family. Write its types and characteristic features.
13. Discuss the merits and demerits of joint family.
14. Analyse the causes that change the joint family system.
15. Write short notes on the following:
    (a) Joint family
    (b) Nuclear family
    (c) Modern nuclear family
16. Is the Hindu joint family disintegrating? Examine.
17. Joint family is not dying out. Comment.
18. What are the reasons behind the breakdown of joint family?

⌘⌘⌘⌘⌘⌘⌘⌘⌘⌘

30

KINSHIP SYSTEM

CHAPTER OUTLINE

- DEFINITION OF KINSHIP
- KINSHIP: A SIGNIFICANT CONCEPT IN ANTHROPOLOGY
- STRUCTURAL PRINCIPLES OF KINSHIP
- RULE OF DESCENT: IMPORTANCE OF THE RULES OF DESCENT
- PRIMARY, SECONDARY AND TERTIARY KINS
- UNILINEAL OR UNILATERAL GROUPS
- KINSHIP USAGES: RULE OF AVOIDANCE — JOKING RELATIONSHIP — TEKNONYMY — AVUNCULATE — AMITATE — COUVADE

Kinship system represents one of the basic social institutions. Kinship is universal and in most societies plays a significant role in the socialisation of individuals and the maintenance of group solidary. It is supremely important in the primitive societies and extends its influence on almost all their activities - social, economic, political, religious, etc.

DEFINITION OF KINSHIP

1. ***Robin Fox:*** "*Kinship is simply the relations between 'kin' that is persons related by real, putative or fictive consanguinity*"[1]
2. ***Aberchrombie and others:*** "*The social relationships deriving from blood ties (real and supposed) and marriage are collectively referred to as kinship*".[2]
3. ***A.R. Radcliffe Brown:*** Kinship is "*a system of dynamic relations between person and person in a community, the behaviour of any two persons in any of these relations being regulated in some way, and to a greater or less extent by social usage*".[3]
4. In simple Words, "*The bond of blood or marriage which binds people together in group is called kinship*".

KINSHIP: A SIGNIFICANT CONCEPT IN ANTHROPOLOGY

The concept of "kinship" is vitally important in Anthropology. In simple societies, the kinship relations are so extensive, fundamental and influential that in effect they in themselves constitute the 'social system'. But in more complex societies kinship normally forms a fairly small part of the totality of the social relation which make up the social system. Sociologists do not attach much importance for it except in their study of the sociology of family. Anthropologists, on the contrary, give more importance to this concept because kinship and family constitute the focal points in athropological studies.

STRUCTURAL PRINCIPLES OF KINSHIP

The kinship system is governed by some basic principles which can be called the "facts of life". Robin Fox speaks of four such basic principles which are mentioned below:

Principle 1: The women have the children

---

[1] Robin Fox is his *Kinship and Marriage*, p. 39

[2] Aberchrombie and others in *The Penguin Dictionary of Sociology*, p. 131.

[3] A.R. Rudclifle Brown in *Structure and Function in Primitive Society.*

Principle 2: The men impregnate the women

Principle 3: The men usually exercise control

Principle 4: Primary kin do not mate with each other.

These principles emphasise the basic biological fact on which kinship system depends. Men and women indulge in sexual interaction and as a result women bear children. This leads to blood ties between the individuals and the special terms are used to recognise this relationship: mother, child, father. The relationship based on blood ties is called "*consanguineous kinship*", and the relatives of this kind are called '*consanguineous kin*'.

The desire for reproduction gives rise to another kind of binding relationship. "*This kind of bond, which arises out of a socially or legally defined marital relationship, is called affinal relationship*", and the relatives so related are called '*affinal kin*'. The affinal kins [husband and wife] are not related to one another through blood.

RULE OF DESCENT

'**Descent**' refers to the social recognition of the biological relationship that exists between the individuals. The '*rule of descent*' refers to a set of principles by which an individual traces his descent. There are three basic rules of descent: *patrilineal descent, matrilineal descent* and *bilateral descent.*

1. ***Patrilineal descent:*** According to this rule, descent is traced through the father's or male line. Here the descent criterion is restricted to males, and only descendants of a common ancestor in the male line will be recognised as kin. These are known as agnatic or patrilineal kin.
2. ***Matrilineal descent:*** Here the descent of the individual is traced through the mother or female exclusively. The descendants are called here uterine or matrilineal kin.

   These two modes of tracing the descent are called "*unilineal*", that, they select one "*line*" only either the male or female. These principles or rules are not necessarily mutually exclusive within a society.
3. ***Bilateral descent:*** This is a rule in which the descent is traced through both the lines, the female line and also the male line for some or the other purpose.

What is important here is that almost all kinship systems recognise 'bilateral' relationships, that is, relationships to both maternal and paternal kins. *Ex:* Some societies such as the "**Yako**" of Nigeria, utilise matrilineal descent for some purposes and prilineal descent for others. Here there exists a system of '*double unilineal descent*' which is normally known as "*double descent*".

Importance of the Rule of Descent

The rule of descent is very important for two main reasons:

1. *Rule of descent establishes for every individual a network of social positions in which he participates. He comes to know about his obligations and rights.*
2. *Rule of descent invariably defines some rights of inheritance. Inheritance and succession would go normally along the line of descent.*

PRIMARY, SECONDARY AND TERTIARY KINS

Kinship has got various ramifications. On the basis of nearness or distance, kins are classified into 1. *primary kins*, 2. *secondary kins*, and 3. *tertiary kins*.

1. ***Primary kins:*** Every individual who belongs to a nuclear family finds his primary kins within the family. There are 8 primary kins: *husband-wife, father-son, mother-son, father-daughter, mother-daughter, younger brother-elder brother, younger sister-elder sister, and brother-sister*.
2. ***Secondary kins:*** Outside the nuclear family the individual can have 33 types of secondary relatives: *Example*: *Mother's brother, brother's wife, sister's husband, father's brother, etc....*
3. ***Tertiary kins:*** Tertiary kins refer to the secondary kins of our primary kins. *Example*: *wife's brother's son, sister's husband's brother, and so on. Anthropologists have spoken of 151 tertiary kins.*

UNILINEAL OR UNILATERAL GROUPS

Lineage

"*A lineage is a unilineal descent group in which membership may rest either on patrilineal descent [patrilineage] or an matrilineal descent [matrilineage]*". A lineage thus consists of descendants in only one line, either the father's or the mother's. These descendants know their exact genealogical relationship and who recognise obligations to one another. A lineage is thus smaller and more localised than the broader category of kinship grouping.

Clan or Sib

"*A clan is a unilineal descent group, the members of which may claim either patrilineal descent (patrician) or matrilineal descent (matrician) from a founder, but do not know the genealogicalities with the ancestor / ancestress*". [**Abercrombie** and mother's - page: 66]

"*A clan is a named unilineal descent group: that is, a body of persons claiming common descent from an ancestor (often mythical) and recruiting the children of either male or female members, but not both* ".[4]

The ancestor or mythical ancestor through whom the descent is claimed, may be human, human - like, animal, plant or even inanimate object. The "**gotra**" group of the Hindus represents a clan. These clans are larger groups and are geographically more dispersed. The clans may have a common totemic name and common ritual taboos against eating the flesh of the totemic animal.

Phratry

"*A Phratry is a grouping of clans which are related by traditions of common descent*". [**Abercrombie** and others - page: 219]. Mythical ancestors are common in clans and phratries. The Phratry is larger than the clan and includes people scattered over relatively large areas among whom it is not possible to trace relationship without bringing in a mythical common ancestor.

Moieties

"*Where the descent groups of a society are organised into two main divisions, these are known as moieties* [*halves*] [**Abercrombie**-page: 66]

The term "*moiety*" refers to the bisection of a tribe into two complementary social groups. Some writers would restrict the term 'moiety' to '*exogamous*' social divisions, while others use the term to mean any dualorganisation, exogamous or not.

KINSHIP USAGES

Kinship usagers or the rules of kinship are significant in understanding kinship system as such. Kinship usagers serve two main purposes:

1. Firstly, they create groups or special groupings or kin. *Example*: Family, extended family, clan etc.
2. Secondly, the kinship rules govern the role of relationships among the kins. Kinship usage provides guidelines for interaction among persons in these social groupings. It defines proper and acceptable role relationships. Thus it acts as a regulator of social life.

The kinship relations are regulated according to usages prevalent in the society. Some of these relationships are: *avoidance*, *teknonymy*, *avunculate*, *amitate*, *couvade* and *joking relationship*.

Rule of Avoidance

Avoidance means that two kins normally of opposite sex should avoid each other. "*In almost all societies avoidance rules prescribe that men and women must maintain certain amount of modesty in dress, speech, gait and gesture in a mixed company*".

Example, the father-in-law should avoid daughter-in-law. The bride must also avoid mother- in-law's brothers. The son-in-law must also avoid his mother-in-law and other female relatives of his wife. [mostly mother-in-law's sisters]. (*i*) Amongst the **Yukafir**, the son-in-law is not supposed to see the faces of his mother-in-law and father-in-law. (*ii*) Amongst the **Ostiyak**, the married man is not supposed to see the face of his mother-in-law atleast till he gets a child. (*iii*) Amongst the **Aruntas**, if the mother-in-law enters or approaches the hut of her son-in-law she would be excommunicated. (*iv*) Amongst the **Veddas** of Ceylone elder brother and sisters are not supposed to live in the same house and even eat together.

In some societies, even the husband and wife are not supposed to touch each other or show affection in the presence of others. Calling of the personal name is also tabooed. *Example*: The Hindu wife is not supposed to call her husband by his name.

The rule of avoidance is believed to serve two purposes:

1. Avoidance rules serve to stop the development of complications in the relations between the parties concerned. It is said it seeks to minimise the chance of the development of open hostility in the relations between the parties.
2. According to the Murdock G.P., rules of avoidance exists because they reinforce incest taboos.

Joking Relationships

"*A joking relationship involves a particular combination of friendliness and antagonism be- tween individuals and groups in certain social situations. In these situations one individual or group is allowed to mock or ridicule the other without offence being taken*". **Duncan Mitchell** (page: 103).

---

[4] Duncan Mitchell in *A Dictionary of Sociology*, p. 30.

The usage of the joking relationship permits to tease and make fun of the other. Such relation- ships prevail between a grandson or grand-daughter on the one hand, his or her grand-father and grand-mother, on the other. *Example:* (i) Amongst the **Oraons** of Orissa and the **Baigas** of Madhya Pradesh such relationships prevail between the grandfather and grandmother and their grand chil- dren. Majumdar and Madan have cited the example of a case in which a grandfather had married his grand-daughter and got a child in her.

(*ii*) Amongst the *Crow-Indians* such relationships may prevail between a man and his wife's sisters. They could be very friendly and even talk freely about sex matters.

(*iii*) Amongst the original inhabitants of **Fiji** island a son-in-law could be very friendly with his father-in-law and could ask for anything in his house and he may even spoil a few articles just for fun. The father-in-law is expected to bear with that and not to react harshly.

A.R. Radcliffe Brown in his book "*Structure and Function in Primitive Society*", 1952 has thrown much light on this type of relationship. The origins and causes of joking relationships are not clearly known. Some enthropologists say this kind of relationship acts as a "*safety valve*" for giving expression or release to the pent up feelings and emotions. As *Chapple* and *Coon* have said these relationships help the individuals to develop intimacy and closeness among themselves.

Teknonymy

According to this usage, *a kin is not referred to directly but is referred to through another kin. Examples*: (*i*) In a traditional Hindu family, wife does not directly utter the name of her husband but refers to her husband as the father of so and so, say, Deepti or Swathi, or Vikram or Varun, (*ii*) amongst the **Hopi**, a woman refers to her mother-in-law as the grand-mother of so and so.

James Frazer has said this kind of a usage is found amongst people in many places such as Australia, New Guinea, China, North Siberia, Africa, British Columbia, Andaman Island, and so on.

Avunculate [Avunciate]

This refers to "*the special relationship that persists in some societies between a man and his mother's brother*"

This term, from the Latin "*avunculus*" [mother's brother] is sometimes used to describe the authority of the mother's brother over his sister's children in a matrilineal society. This usage is found in a matriarchal system in which prominence is given to the maternal uncle in the life of his nephews and nieces.

Amitate

Amitate is a usage which gives special role to the father's sister. Here the father's sister is given more respect than the mother. *Examples*: This usage is more prevalent amongst the **Kongs** of Polynesia, **Thodas** of Nilgiri, and amongst the **Crow-Indians**. Amongst the Thodas, the child gets its name not through its parents but through the father's sister. Because, naming the child is her privilege. This usage is normally prevalent in patrilineal systems.

Couvade

This kinship usage involves only husband and wife. According to this usage, the husband is made to lead the life of an invalid along with his wife whenever she gives birth to a child. He is then not supposed to engage himself in hardwork but expected to observe dieting and certain other taboos.

Anthropologists have observed the practice of this usage amongst the **Khasis** and **Thodas** of India, the **Karibs** of South Africa.

According to Malinowski, the usage of couvade contributes to a strong marital bond between the husband and wife. Some have given a phychoanalytical explanation to this practice. "*They have attributed this usage to the husband's desire to lighten the wife's discomfort; by a process of participation through identification*". **[Parimal B Kar.** Page 222].

REVIEW QUESTIONS

1. Define kinship. Discuss the structural principles of kinship.
2. Explain the rule of descent. Assess its importance.
3. Give the classification of kins. What are the usages of kinship?
4. What are unilineal or unilateral groups? Discuss.
5. Write an essay on the kinship relationships.
6. Explain the terms 'clan', 'phratry' and 'moiety'.
7. Write short notes on the following:
   (a) Concept of kinship
   (b) Joking relationships

⌘⌘⌘⌘⌘⌘⌘⌘⌘⌘⌘⌘

31

THE EDUCATIONAL SYSTEM

CHAPTER OUTLINE

- MEANING OF EDUCATION
- DEFINTION OF EDUCATION
- EDUCATION AS A SOCIAL PROCESS
- SOCIAL FUNCTIONS OF EDUCATION
- OTHER FUNCTIONS OF EDUCATION
- EDUCATION AND SOCIAL CHANGE
- EDUCATION: SOCIAL STRATIFICATION AND SOCIAL MOBILITY
- EDUCATION AND SOCIAL STRATIFICATION
- EDUCATION AND SOCIAL MOBILITY
- EQUALITY OF EDUCATIONAL OPPORTUNITIES
- EDUCATION AND MODERNISATION

MEANING OF EDUCATION

Education is one of the basic activities of people in all human societies. The continued existence of society depends upon the transmission of culture to the young. It is essential that every new generation must be given training in the ways of the group so that the same tradition will continue. Every society has its own ways and means of fulfilling this need. 'Education' has come to be one of the ways of fulfilling this need.

The term *education* is derived from the Latin *educare* which literally means to '*bring up*', and is connected with the verb '*educare*' which means to '*bring forth*'. The idea of education is not merely to impart knowledge to the pupil in some subjects but to develop in him those habits and attitudes with which he may successfully face the future. The Latin author *Varro* wrote. '*The mid-wife brings forth, the nurse brings up, the tutor trains and the master teaches*'. Plato was of the opinion that the end of education was '*to develop in the body and in the soul* (*of the pupil*) *all the beauty and all the perfection of which they are capable*'. It means, in short, '*a sound mind in a sound body* (*mens sana in corpore sano*). According to the Aristotelian conception, the aim of education is "to develop man's faculties, especially, his mind, so that he may be able to enjoy the contemplation of the supreme truth, goodness and beauty in which perfect happiness essentially consists".

As *Peter Worsely* says, "A large part of our social and technical skills are acquired through deliberate instruction which we call education. It is the main waking activity of children from the ages of five to fifteen and often beyond..." A large part of the budget of many developed and developing countries is set apart for education. Education employs a large army of people. Sociologists are becoming more and more aware of the importance and role of educational institutions in the modern industrialised societies. In recent years education has become the major interest of some sociologists. As a result a new branch of sociology called *Sociology of Education* has become established.

DEFINITION OF EDUCATION

1. *Durkheim* conceives of education as "the socialisation of the younger generation". He further states that it is "a continuous effort to impose on the child ways of seeing, feeling and acting which he could not have arrived at spontaneously".
2. *Sumner* defined education as the attempt to transmit to the child the mores of the group, so that he can learn "what conduct is approved and what disapproved....how he ought to behave in all kinds of cases: what he ought to believe and reject".
3. *F. J. Brown* and *J.S. Roucek* say that education is "the sum total of the experience which moulds the attitudes and determines the conduct of both the child and the adult".
4. *James Welton* in Encyclopaedia Britannica (11th Edition) writes that education consists in "an attempt on the part of the adult members of human society to shape the development of the coming generation with its own ideals of life".
5. *A. W. Green writes*: "Historically, it (education) has meant the conscious training of the young for the later adoption of adult roles. By modern convention, however, education has come to mean formal training by specialists within the formal organisation of the school."
6. *Samuel Koenig*: "Education may also be defined as the process whereby the social heritage of a group is passed on from one generation to another as well as the process whereby the child becomes socialised, *i.e.*, learns the rules of behaviour of the group into which he is born".

EDUCATION AS A SOCIAL PROCESS

Education stands for deliberate instruction or training. Man does not behave in society impulsively or instinctively. He behaves in a way according to which he is trained. Some thinkers have equated it with *socialisation*. A few others regard education *as an attempt to transmit the cultural norms of the group to its younger members*. It is also understood as a continuous effort on the part of the individuals to *acquire more* and *more knowledge*. All these *three* interpretations of education stress upon education *as a process* or *a continuous entity*. The word *process* stresses continuity.

Firstly, education, viewed as *socialisation*, is continuous. Socialisation is social learning. This social learning is not intermittent but continuous. Perfection in social learning is rarely achieved. The more we try to learn about our own society and fellow beings the more remains to be learned. Social learning begins at birth and ends only at death. It continues throughout our life. There is no point or state in our life at which we have learnt everything about one group or society and beyond that nothing remains to be studied. We belong to different groups at different stages of our life. As these groups change we must learn new rules and new patterns of behaviour. Furthermore we do not always remain within the same role. We begin as children, pass through adolescence into adulthood, marry, become parents, enter middle age, retire, grow old and finally die. With each role, comes pattern of behaviour that we must learn and, thus, throughout our life, we are involved in the socialisation process. Even at the door of death we are being socialised.

Secondly, education, viewed as *an agent of cultural transmission, is also continuous*. Culture is a *growing whole*. There can be no break in the continuity of culture. If at all there is a break, it only indicates the end of a particular human group. The cultural elements are passed on from generation to generation. The family, school, and various other associations act as the agents of cultural transmission. Education in its formal or informal pattern, has been performing this role since time immemorial. Education can be looked upon as process from this point of view also.

Thirdly, education, implied as an *attempt to acquire knowledge*, is also continuous. Knowledge is like an ocean, boundless or limitless. No one has mastered it or exhausted it. No one can claim to do so. There is a limit to the human genius or the human grasp of the things. The moral man can hardly know anything and everything about nature which is immoral. The universe is a miraculous entity. The more one tries to know of it, the more it becomes mysterious. Not only the Natural Universe but also the Social Universe is complex. The human experience is limited to have a thorough knowledge of this universe. Hence, man since time immemorial, has been engaged in this endless endeavour of acquiring more and more knowledge about the Universe with all its complexity. Education, thus, is a continuous endeavour, a process.

SOCIAL FUNCTIONS OF EDUCATION

'Education, as a social institution has a great social importance especially in the modern, complex industrialised societies. Philosophers of all periods, beginning with ancient sages, devoted to it a great deal of attention. Accordingly, various theories regarding its nature and objectives have come into being. Let us now examine some of the significant functions of education.

1. ***To complete the socialisation process:*** The main social objective of education is to *complete the socialisation process*. The family gets the child, but the modern family tends to leave much undone in the socialisation process. The school and other institutions have come into being in place of family to complete the socialisation process. Now, the people feel that it is "the school's business to train the whole child even to the extent of teaching him honesty, fair play, consideration for others and a sense of right and wrong". The school devotes much of its time and energy to the matter such as co-operation, good citizenship, doing one's duty, and upholding the law. Directly through textbooks, and indirectly through celebration of programmes patriotic sentiments are instilled. The nation's past is glorified, its legendary heroes respected, and its military ventures justified.
2. ***To transmit the central heritage:*** All societies maintain themselves by the exploitation of a culture. Culture here refers to a set of beliefs and skills, art, literature, philosophy, religion, music, etc. that are not carried through the mechanism of heredity. They must be learned. This social heritage (culture) must be transmitted through social organisations. Education has this function of cultural transmission in all societies. It is only at the upper levels of the school that any serious attempt has been, or now is, made to deal with this area.
3. ***For the formation of social personality:*** Individuals must have personalities shaped or fashioned in ways that fit into the culture. Education, everywhere, has the function of *the formation of social personalities*. Education helps in transmitting culture through proper moulding of social personalities. In this way, it contributes to the integration of society. It helps men to adapt themselves to their environment, to survive, and to reproduce themselves.
4. ***Reformation of attitudes:*** Education aims at the reformation of attitudes wrongly developed by the children already. For various reasons the child may have absorbed a host of attitudes, beliefs and disbeliefs, loyalties and prejudices, jealousy and hatred, etc. These are to be reformed. It is the function of education to see that unfounded beliefs, illogical prejudices and unreasoned loyalties are removed from the child's mind. Though the school has its own limitations in this regard, it is expected to continue its efforts in reforming the attitudes of the child.
5. ***Education for occupational placement–An instrument of livelihood:*** Education has a practical end also. It should help the adolescent for earning his livelihood. Education has come to be today as nothing more than an instrument of livelihood. It should enable the student to eke out his livelihood. Education must prepare the student for *future occupational positions*. The youth should be enabled to play a productive role in society. Accordingly, great emphasis has been placed on vocational training.
6. ***Conferring of status:*** Conferring of status is one of the most important functions of education. The amount of education one has, is correlated with his class position. This is true in U.S.A., U.S.S.R., Japan, Germany and some other societies. Education is related to one's position in the stratification structure in two ways: (1) An evaluation of one's status is partially decided by *what kind of education* one has received and (2) many of the other important criteria of class position such as occupation, income, and style of life, are partially the results of the type and *amount of education* one has had. Men who finish college, for example, earn two and a half times as much as those who have only a grammar school education.
7. ***Education encourages the spirit of competition:*** The school instills co-operative values through civic and patriotic exhortation or advice. Yet the school's main emphasis is upon personal competition. For each subject studied the child is compared with the companions by percentage of marks or rankings. The teacher admires and praises those who do well and frowns upon those who fail to do well. The school's ranking system serves to prepare for a later ranking system. Many of those who are emotionally disappointed by low ranking in the school are thereby prepared to accept limited achievement in the larger world outside the school.

OTHER FUNCTIONS OF EDUCATION

Peter Worsley has spoken of a few more functions of education. Some of them may be noted:

1. ***Education trains in skills that are required by the economy:*** The relation between the economy and education can be an exact one. For example, the number and productive capacity of engineering firms are limited by the number of engineers produced by education. In planned economy, normally, it is planned years in advance to produce a definite number of doctors, engineers, teachers, technicians, scientists, etc. to meet the social and economic needs of the society.
2. ***Fosters participant democracy:*** Education fosters participant democracy. Participant democracy in any large and complex society depends on literacy. Literacy allows full participation of the people in democratic processes and effective voting. Literacy is a product of education. Educational system has thus economic as well as political significance.
3. ***Education imports values:*** The curriculum of a school, its "extra-curricular" activities and the informal relationships amongst students and 'teachers communicate social skills and values. Through various activities a school imparts values such as 'co-operation' or team-spirit, obedience, 'fair play'. This is also done through curriculum, that is, through lessons in history, literature, etc.
4. ***Education acts as an integrative force:*** Education acts as an integrative force in society by communicating values that unite different sections of society. The family may fail to provide the child the essential knowledge of the social skills, and values of the wider society. The school or the educational institutions can help the child to learn new skills and learn to interact with people of different social backgrounds.
5. ***Values and orientations which are specific to certain occupations are also provided by education:*** For example, the medical students are socialised and educated in a particular way in medical college. This may help them to become proper medical practitioners. Other values and orientations relevant to the functioning of industrial society are also provided by education.

EDUCATION AND SOCIAL CHANGE

The role of education as an agent or instrument of social change and social development is widely recognised today. Social change may take place (*i*) *When human needs change*, (*ii*) *When the existing social system or network of social institutions fail to meet the existing human needs, and* (*iii*) *When new materials suggest better ways of meeting human needs*.–Social changes do not take place automatically or by themselves. As MacIver says, social change takes place as a *response to many types of changes* that take place in the social and non-social environment. Education can initiate social changes by bringing about a change in outlook and attitude of man. It can bring about a change in the pattern of social relationships and thereby it may cause social changes.

There was a time when educational institutions and teachers were engaged in *transmitting a way of life* to the students. During those days, education was more *a means of social control than an instrument of social change*. Modern schools, colleges and universities do not place much emphasis upon transmitting a way of life to the students. The traditional education was meant for an unchanging, static society, not marked by rapid changes. But today, education aims at imparting empirical knowledge that is, knowledge about science, technology and other type of specialised knowledge.

Education was associated with religion. It has, however, become secular today. It is an independent institution now. Education today has been chiefly instrumental in preparing the way for the development of science and technology.

Education has brought about phenomenal changes in every aspect of man's life. *Francis J. Brown* remarks that education is a process which *brings about changes in the behaviour of society*. It is a process which enables every individual to effectively participate in the activities of society, and to make positive contribution to the progress of society. (For more details please see the chapter on "Social Change".

EDUCATION: SOCIAL STRATIFICATION AND SOCIAL MOBILITY

"***Social Stratification***" which is necessitated by the phenomenon of social differentiation refers to "*a process of placing people in different strata or layers*". It is an ubiquitous phenomenon of human society. All the existing societies are stratified.

The essence of social stratification is social inequality which manifests in various forms. It may involve the differential allocation of income, status, privileges, and opportunities. A stratified society represents a ladder of hierarchy in which its population is distributed. People who occupy the higher place in this hierarchy or ladder enjoy higher status, opportunities and privileges and the people who occupy lower positions have limited access to the same.

"*Social Mobility*" refers to the movement of an individual or group from one social position or status to that of another. People who occupy different status or places in the above said hierarchy may often change their places depending upon the opportunities made available to them.

Based on this movement of people from statum to stratum which is called "*social mobility*" two systems of social stratification are distinguished:

1. ***The open society*** or the *fluid system of stratification* in which there is greater scope for movement up and down the hierarchy. The Western society with its class system of stratification is very often cited as the typical illustration of this.
2. ***The closed society*** or the *rigid system of stratification* is the second one in which the boundaries of various strata are very rigid and movement between the strata is extremely difficult, if not impossible. The Indian caste is very often mentioned here as the typical example of this. It may, however, be noted that as two broad types they are not found in pure form in any society of the world. Existing socieities, however, lean towards one or the other depending upon certain economic and cultural conditions.

Education: As a Powerful Correlate of Social Stratification and Social Mobility

There are various correlates of social stratification and mobility. These correlates vary from society to society depending upon the level of their socio-economic and technological development. In general, in urban - industrial societies - education, occupation, income and wealth-have been found to be the main correlates of social stratification and also of mobility.

EDUCATION AND SOCIAL STRATIFICATION

Education: As a Criterion of Social Stratification

In technologically advanced countries education has become the most important criterion of social stratification. In such societies occupation is the determinant of income. It is also found that recruitment to various occupations in these societies is determined by the education levels of individuals.

Education: As a Determinant of Social Placement and Social Stratification

In the technologically advanced countries normally the status gradation is defined by the occupational and educational levels of education. "*Briefly, in view of the close relationship between education and occupation, and to the extent that occupation is an important, if not the only avenue, for income and social status, education acquires significance as a determinant of social placement and social stratification*".[1]

It is noticeable that in the industrial societies the most prestigious jobs tend to be not only those that yield the highest incomes but also the ones that require the longest education. The more education people have, the more likely they are to obtain good jobs and to enjoy high incomes.

The Complex Relationship between Education and Social Stratification

Though education acts as a generator of upward mobility it does not invariably do that. Empirical evidences suggest that in the reciprocal relationship between education and social stratification it is stratification that affects education primarily. This effect is greater than the effect of education on stratification.

In many societies the facilities for education leading to higher levels of occupations and professions like medicine, engineering, management, etc., are limited. But the number of aspirants to make use of such facilities is very high. Since the cost of higher education is very high and several constraints govern admission to such education courses, only a select section of the society can manage to enter such courses. This section is normally the privileged section of the society,

[1] N. Jayaram in *Sociology of Education in India,* 1990, Rawat Publications, Delhi, p. 42.

which occupies a top position in the stratification system. Such a system of higher education with all its constraints etc., is often defended on *meritocratic grounds*. *Thus education instead of being a generator of upward social mobility is forced to function as an agency of stratification, to function as an agency of 'status retention'*.[2]

Social Stratification Affecting Lower Levels of Education

Social Stratification affects lower levels of education especially in the rural areas. In many of the developing countries wastage and stagnation in school education is found to be very high. This problem seems to exist even in the advanced countries to a certain extent. It is found that generally students belonging to the lower stratum background drop out of the school in a large number. Even though education is provided free and additional incentives are given, the situation does not seem to improve much.

It is clear from the above that the relationship between education arid social stratification is more complex than what it appears to be. It is true that education has enough potentiality for changing the system of stratification. But this potentiality itself seems 'to be governed by the existing system of stratification.

In conclusion, it can be said that from the point of view of an educational system those who are already at the upper strata of the society are likely to gain more. They have higher achievement motivation and their environment helps them. If we wish to provide equality of educational opportunities we will have to keep this aspect in mind.

EDUCATION AND SOCIAL MOBILITY

Education as a Promoter of Upward Mobility

In the context urban-industrial society education functions as a promoter of upward social mobility. In such societies occupations the principal channel of social mobility. Occupations that help social mobility require certain educational qualifications. It is in this context education acquires significance as a promoter of upward social mobility. Sociologist **Reid** Writes: "*The functions of the educational system are to provide people with the qualifications and aspirations to meet society 's occupational needs. Built into the system is that assumptions that people will or should want to be upwardly mobile. Underlying such reasoning is, then, the belief that social mobility is a desirable characteristic of that society and that the education system exists to promote and facilitate it*" - [Quoted by **N. Jayaram** - Page: 121]

Peter Blau and **Otis Duncan** (1967), in their study of social mobility in America, found that the important factor affecting whether a son moved to a higher social status than his father's was the amount of education the son received. *A high level of education is a scarce and valued resource*, and one for which people compete vigorously.

Due to the increased awareness regarding the importance of college-level education, large number of persons are trying to avail of the same to increase their social standing. As a result, the number of new college graduates is now far greater than the number of 'college-level' jobs available to them. "*Infact, it has been calculated that only 15% of the increase in educational requirements for jobs during the course of this century can be attributed to the replacement of low-skill jobs by new jobs requiring greater expertise* [Collins - 1971]". *What has actually happened is that the "educational threshold" has risen: people need higher qualifications to get jobs that previously required much lower educational credentials*".[3]

Lack of Educational Qualification Restricts Social Mobility

In developed nations people want to attain higher level of education to equip themselves to obtain more prestigious jobs. What is observed is that people want to receive extra years of education even if it is not necessary for some of the jobs or occupations that they are seeking for. There is evidence that educational achievement has no consistent relationship to later job performance and productivity. What is significant, however, is that *the lack of educational qualifications restricts social mobility of those people* who for one reason or another, have been unable to obtain them.

Education as a Solvent of Inequalities?

Education serves as a solvent of inequalities to certain extent especially in societies where the traditional systems of stratification did not permit large scale social mobility. Here the introduction of formal education [as was done by the British

[2] Dr. N. Jayaram in *Sociology of Education in India*, p. 43.

[3] Ian Robertson, p. 354.

in India] gave an opportunity for people who were hitherto confined to lower or intermediary statuses in the traditional system of stratification [say caste] to try for attaining a higher status in the changed situation. That is what the scheduled caste and the scheduled tribe people and the people belonging to the backward classes have done and are doing. Thus, education under conditions has the potentiality of radically altering the previous system of stratification. Thus education has often been hailed as a solvent of inequalities.

Education and Internal and External Constraints on Mobility

There are a number of factors which impede mobility of the individuals in a social structure. They are referred to here as constraints on mobility. These constraints may be internal or external. The internal constraints are *values, aspirations and personality patterns of the individuals*. The external constraints are the *opportunity structure of a society* with which the individual is influenced.

1. ***System of beliefs and values:*** The major constraints in the upward mobility are a system of beliefs and values prevailing in social structure. *H. H. Hyman* in his study regarding[4] class differences in educational values, motivations for economic advancement and perceptions of the opportunity structure found that the lower socio-economic groups place less emphasis upon college education as necessary for advancement, and are less likely to desire college education for their children. This holds true in the Indian situation also.

   Further, *opportunities for education to the lower classes are very limited, particularly in the rural areas*. Thus the prevalent value system governs their aspirations and actions. Hence they may lag behind the upper classes in this regard.

2. ***Family influence:*** Upward mobility is also restricted due to the family influences. In a study made by **Stephenson**[5] it was found that both occupational plans and aspirations are positively associated with the prestige ranking of father's occupation. If the family itself lacks initiative it is reflected in the child's desire for not moving out of the family bonds. The child develops a tendency to take up a job which the parent wants him to take up in his hierarchical set up. The child also does not show much interest in education because the parents are least concerned about it. This influence is very much visible in joint families.

3. ***Factors in individual personality:*** Individual's personality structure may also contribute to his immobility. It has been found in a number of studies that achievement motivation, intelligence, aspirations and values are related with mobility. In one study[6] it was found that I.Q (Intelligence Quotient] plays an important role in the school performance in the early years of an individual's life. But as the person grows older he begins to shape his performance according to certain values that he learns from his family and friends. Here desire to go to the college is taken as an aspect of mobility. One who performs well is expected to go to college and thus is mobile in upward direction.

In the above mentioned study it was found that upper-status boys learn that good performance in school is necessary, and that they are expected to do well enough in secondary school to get admitted to college. On the other hand, a *boy from a lower status home is taught that college is either not meant for him or at best a matter of indifference to his parents*. The boy's friends are not interested in college nor in high school. Consequently, even a bright boy among them gets discouraged.

Various findings have revealed that *the strength of the achievement motive is clearly related to upward mobility*. It seems that youth from upper strata of society may not need strong personal motivation for mobility. Such youth get good advice, they live in such environment where '*looking up*' is encouraged and where they are provided with wise decisions for setting up their careers. This is not the case of lower class youth. They have to learn a great deal to make these decisions.

EQUALITY OF EDUCATIONAL OPPORTUNITIES

It is an accepted working policy of all the democratic nations to make provision for equal opportunities. As **Dr. Radhakrishnan** had pointed out long back "*Democracy only provides that all men should have equal opportunities for the development of their unequal talents*". The Indian Constitution also as per the articles l5, 16, 17, 38 and 48, guarantee

[4] H.H. Hyman's Study: "The Value System of Different Classes: A Social Psychological Contribution to the Analysis of Stratification.

[5] Richard M. Stephenson: *Mobility Orientation and Stratification*: *A Study of One Thousand Nineth Graders*, Unpublished doctoral dissertation, Columbia University, New York - as quoted by *Dr. S. S. Mathur* in *A Sociological Approach to Indian Education,* 1975, p. 260.

[6] Study of Joseph A. Kahl: *The American Class Structure*, Holt, N.Y. 1960, as quoted by Dr. S. S. Mathur, p. 261.

that the State shall not discriminate between persons on account of their religion or region and caste or class. The Preamble of the Constitution also assures equality to all the citizens. It means that our Constitution is committed to the principle of equality and accepted it as an article of faith.

It is in tune with this spirit of the constitution the *Education Commission* has observed thus: "*One of the important social objectives of education is to equalise opportunity, enabling the back- ward or underprivileged classes and individuals to use education as a lever for the improvement of their condition. Every society that values social justice and is anxious to improve the lot of the common man and cultivate all available talent, must ensure progressive equality of opportunity to all sections of the population. This is the only guarantee for the building up of an egalitarian and human society by which the exploitation of the weak will be minimised.*"[7]

Need for Equalisation of Educational Opportunities

The equalisation of educational opportunities is essentially linked with the equality notions in the social system. The social system which intends to provide equal opportunities for the advancement of all has to make provision for equal educational opportunities also. The need for emphasising the equality of opportunity in the education arises for various reasons. They may be cited here.

1. Equality of educational opportunities is needed for the establishment of egalitarian society based on social equality and justice;
2. It contributes to the search for talents among all the people of a nation;
3. It is essential to ensure rapid advancement of a nation;
4. It is needed for the successful functioning of a democracy. Educated and enlightened people alone can ensure a meaningful democracy, and
5. It helps to develop a closer link between manpower needs of a society and the availability of the skilled personnel.

Problems Concerning Equality of Opportunities in Education

Education is of great help in establishing equality and ensuring social justice no doubt. But the system of education itself can add to the existing inequalities, or at least perpetuate the same. This has been the major problem in providing equal educational opportunity for all. Inequalities of educational opportunities arise for the following reasons.

Causes for the Inequalities of Educational Opportunities

1. Inequalities of educational opportunity occurs due to the poverty of a large number of people. The poor cannot afford to meet the expenses of education.
2. Children in rural areas studying in poorly equipped schools have to compete with the children in urban areas where there are well-equipped schools. The poor exposure of rural children may lead to their poor performance.
3. In the places where no primary, secondary or collegiate educational institutions exist, children do not get the same opportunity as those who have all these in their neighbourhood.
4. Wide inequalities also arise from differences in home environments. A child from a rural household or slum does not have the same opportunity as a child from an upper class home with educated parents.
5. There is wide sex disparity in India. Hence, girls' education is not given the same encouragement as boys.
6. Education of backward classes including scheduled castes and tribes and economically backward sections is not at par with that of forward communities or classes.

Suggestions for Reorganising Educational System for Providing Equality of Educational opportunity in India

The Government of India has been striving to achieve the target of providing equal educational opportunities to all the people. Some suggestions could be cited in this regard. These suggestions may be of some help in reaching the target.

[7] Report of the Education Commission, 1964-66, Govt. of India, Ministry of Education, New Delhi, 1966, as quoted by Dr. S.S. Mathur, p. 267.

1. In order to reap the fruits of education and also to remove the prejudices and biases, adult illiteracy has to be removed by launching appropriate programmes.
2. By following a "*policy of protective discrimination*" all efforts must be made to increase the opportunities for education to all the weaker sections of the society like the scheduled castes, scheduled tribes, backward communities and even women.
3. Honest attempts be made to provide compulsory education to all the children at least upto 14 years. No one should be made to suffer for want of educational opportunity and facilities.
4. The higher educational chances should be extended to all on merit.
5. Education Commission suggests that for equalisation of educational opportunity the following measures may be adopted:
   (*a*) Education should be made tuition free for all immediately at the primary and secondary levels and in course of time, at the university level at least for the needy deserving students;
   (*b*) Free textbooks and writing materials should be supplied at the primary stage;
   (*c*) Transport facilities should be provided to reduce cost on hostels and scholarships;
   (*d*) Facilities for the students to earn a part of their educational expenses, that is, "*earn while you learn*" schemes should be developed;
   (*e*) There should be liberal schemes for scholarships;
   (*f*) Wide differences that are found in the educational development in different states and districts must be minimised to a desirable extent.

In the industrialised countries the idea of equality of opportunity is very firmly rooted. *Halsey believes that the principle of equality has a powerful and a persistent appeal. He further points out that "its influence is reinforced in advanced society by the impersonal demands of the economy for efficiency, for a fluid labour force, and for rational allocation of jobs by tests of fitness to fill them.*[8]

EDUCATION AND MODERNISATION

Education has become today an essential aspect of the modern industrial society. It is more regarded as an agent of social change than an instrument of social control. It has become increasingly secular. All the nations of the world are investing huge amount of money on education for it has become an essential condition of advancement.

Education, modernisation, advancement in science, technology and industry normally go together. Formal professional education has become an absolute necessity today. Education is needed just to read, write and do simple 'calculations but, it is essential to cam one's living. It is the main source of supply of trained and technical persons to industry. The job that one gets today depends largely on the type of education that one has secured.

Modern schools, colleges and universities do not give much emphasis upon transmitting a way of life to the students as was given by the earlier forms of education. This is due to the fact that traditional education was meant for an unchanging and static society, a society not marked by rapid changes associated with industrialisation. Modern society, on the other hand, is a changing society. In such a society education aims at communicating empirical knowledge, that is, knowledge about science, technology and other types of specialised knowledge. A transformation in the contents and methods of education has taken place to meet the demands of the changing society. This transformation has led to some far-reaching consequences, some of them are mentioned below:

1. ***Heavy study materials:*** Modern education includes heavy study materials on modern science and technology into the syllabus. Due to this inclusion and over emphasis on this, courses of study on classical language and literature had to be abridged or altogether dropped. This has prevented the modern learners from knowing their own past traditions and cultural heritage. "*It is argued that in such circumstances an individual would*

[8] H. H. Halsey in *The Sociology of Education in Sociology*, 1967, p. 434, as quoted. by Dr. S. S. Mathur, p. 273.

be cut off from his 'roots' and his creative faculties, particularly his emotional and spiritual talents, would languish for want of nourishment."[9]

2. ***Values losing their importance:*** Due to the impact of modern science and technology many of the cherished values of the past have lost their previous importance. There is no attempt to persuade people of the younger generation to accept these values uncritically. At the same time, new set of values have not been developed to occupy the place of the old ones. This situation has created confusion both to the individual and to the society. In the absence of meaningful human values the life of modern educated man has become more mechanical and materialistic. In the absence of consensus regarding some basic questions as to what is right and what is wrong, what is desirable and what is not - the society has to face conflicts.

3. ***The dangerous face of science and technology:*** Science and technology are growing today at a fast rate. Modern education has accelerated this growth. The uncontrolled growth of technology and the directionless development in science have today added much to human tension, anxiety and misery. *Francis Bacon* at one stage had said that "*knowledge is power*". But today many eminent scientists have reluctantly come to the view that "*knowledge is unfortunately power*". The manufacturer of deadly war weapons has created fear in the minds of people about science and technology. This only calls for rethinking and reappraisal in the field of educational planning as part of modernisation.

REVIEW QUESTIONS

1. Define education. Discuss its importance as a social process.
2. Write the social functions of education.
3. Assess the role of education as an agent of social change and social development.
4. Education is a criterion of social stratification. Discuss.
5. Evaluate the role of education as a determinant of social placement and social stratification.
6. Education is a powerful correlate of social stratification and social mobility. Analyse.
7. Discuss the role of education as a promoter of upward mobility.
8. Bring out the relation between education and social mobility.
9. Write an essay on equality of educational opportunities.
10. Today education has become an essential aspect of the modern society. Discuss.
11. Write short notes on the following:
    (a) Need for equalisation of educational opportunities
    (b) Problems concerning equality of opportunities in education
    (c) Education and modernisation

⌘⌘⌘⌘⌘⌘⌘⌘⌘⌘⌘

[9] Parimal B. Kar in Sociology — *The Discipline and Its Dimensions*, p. 284.

32

THE ECONOMIC SYSTEM

CHAPTER OUTLINE

CONCEPT OF ECONOMIC SYSTEM

Man is not only a social animal; he is also an economic being. He is incessantly engaged in what are known as economic pursuits or activities. These economic activities are so multifaceted, varied and complex that they constitute what is known as an *economy*. The economy may be treated as a system or a *sub-system*. It is a sub-system in the wider social system. It is possible to view the economy as the parent system, and analyse its constituent clusters of activities–production, investment, innovation, and so on–as themselves constituting sub-system. Then, within the econmy, we could take a more concrete structure, such as a bank, or a corporation and analyse it in terms of the basic functional necessities of social systems.

IMPORTANCE OF WORK AND OCCUPATION IN MODERN SOCIETY

Concept of Work

The term 'work' would seem to have a perfect unambiguous meaning in our modern society. But some difficulties arise in defining the concept.

1. The *Concise Oxford Dictionary* defines work as an "expenditure of energy, striving application of effort to some purpose".
2. The economists speak of work as "one of the major factors of production consisting of manual or mental exertion for which wages, salaries or professional fees are received".
3. The famous anthropologist Raymond Firth defines work as "an income producing activity" or as "a purposeful activity entailing expenditure of energy at some sacrifice of pleasure or leisure".
4. R.B. Lal in his *The Art of Working* refers to work as "the fundamental law of creation. Labour is essential for the preservation of life".

5. Henri Arvon describes it as "a muscular effort inducing fatigue and exhaustion" or "a spontaneous, conscious and deliberate effort".
6. Peter Worsely refers to it as "a specialised undertaking, clearly marked of from other activities in time and space"

Work–Play, Recreation or Art

It is necessary at this stage to make a distinction between work on the one hand and play, recreation or art, on the other. All the human activities that involve '*expenditure of energy*' cannot be treated as work. The activity peculiar to work is essentially central on the object. Work, therefore, is a human activity directed to an *object*—as the making of furniture, the taking of a photo, the building of a house, the repairing of a motor car, or simply running with a special object in view whether the activity is useful, pleasurable, painful or implies expenditure of energy or not, is quite *immaterial*.

Play and recreation or art are of a different nature. They are not addressed to an external object. But in these activities the individual himself plays to take recreation. Playing activity, recreational activity and artistic activity may assume the character of work when they become addressed to an external object, say, the acquisition of material or monetary reward. Thus, the activities of a woman who engages herself in household tasks, an artist who paints the images, a musician who plays on violin, can be regarded as work when these activities are intended to obtain some material benefits.

However, it would be desirable that the working activity could be exercised as an art or recreation. But this ideal cannot be perfectly attained as long as work is just 'work'. Work is *civilisational* as being a *means* for attaining something else, while art and recreation are *cultural* as having value in themselves and existing for their *own sake*. Work may be also free or servile: not so art or recreation which are essentially free. These may, indeed be practised for the sake of gain or some other external interest, but in this case they are combined with work. In fact, a branch of sociology, called *Sociology of Work* has emerged recently in order to examine the social implications of work. It also deals with the economic, and the psychological aspects of work.

CONCEPT OF OCCUPATION

The words 'work' and 'occupation' are often used interchangeably. In fact, occupation is essentially a kind of work. But the word 'Occupation' is used mostly to refer to the specialised and established kind of work. It refers to some kind of work with which an individual becomes completely engaged, It denotes the habitual employment, profession, craft or trade of an individual. It takes up much of his time and attention. In modern connotations it means an instrument of livelihood. It is usually associated with one or the other kind of organisation; agriculture, industry, governmental organisation, etc. People pursue one occupation or other in order to eke out their livelihood. It has become an essential feature of the modern economic life. Life without occupation or profession of any kind is simply inconceivable today. The importance of occupations is recognised by the sociologist and accordingly a branch of sociology has emerged to deal with the phenomenon of occupation, the *Sociology of Occupations*.

Classification of Occupation

Peter Berger has suggested a threefold classification of occupation.

Firstly, there are those occupations which provide some kind of *Self-identification* and *satisfaction*, *Ex*: Professions like teaching, contracting, business, agriculture and craft or artistic occupations.

Secondly, there are tasks which are almost the exact opposite. They are seen as a direct threat to person's identity, reducing him to the status of "*an appendage to a machine*". Example: The poorly paid occupations of labourers who work in big factories, industries, business firms, mining concerns, agricultural fields, coffee, tea, rubber and such other estates, etc., represent such occupations.

Thirdly, there are occupations regarded as neutral, that is, they are neither a direct threat to one's personal identity nor a major source of identity. Such occupations are neither very hateful nor very pleasurable. Example: The occupations of bankers, life insurance employees, high level government executives, clerks, accountants, etc., which are prosaic and monotonous but fetching handsome salary, represent such *neutral* occupations.

Berger argues that the first two types have declined in modern society. It is also because, working for large bureaucratic organisations results in a loss of personal freedom, and secondly many unpleasant and routine tasks have been eliminated in modern industry.

It is to be noted that occupations have become very much diversified and complex today. The nature and type of occupations go on changing in accordance with the change in the industrial advancement. The modern industrial system has evolved through different stages like–(1) the family economy, (2) the guild or handicraft system, (3) domestic industry, and (4) the modern industrial or factory system (Capitalist or industrial economy). In all these stages occupations differ significantly.

SOCIAL IMPORTANCE OF WORK AND OCCUPATIONS

Work and occupation have assumed utmost social importance today. They have not only social importance but also have economic, psychological and human significance.

1. ***They satisfy the material needs of man:*** Work and occupations are a fundamental necessity in life. Society depends upon the production of food, machine, various utensils and articles of daily use, newsprint, etc. The very existence of man depends upon the production of necessities of life. Work and Occupations are the means of producing them.
2. ***They satisfy man's social and psychological needs also:*** Work is not the same thing as physical effort or the expenditure of energy. What is and what is not work is *socially defined*. It is not a quality inherent in any particular act. It is true that without the achievement of certain level of production, society could not survive. However, there are also the *leisure classes,* the non-working people. In reality, even the leisure classes do some kind of work. Those who are able to live without work normally do work, because, *work gives them a valued status*, in society in other people's eyes, and therefore, in their eyes. Work and occupations meet certain obligations, to *be seen as significant people, and to feel significant to themselves*. Much work, however, is far removed from food production, or even from direct production of commodities at all. "With the growth of service industries in the modern economy, fewer and fewer people work at producing material objects and more and more work at manipulating paper and people"—*Peter Worsley*. Thus, people work more today to satisfy social and psychological needs.
3. ***People work not just for money:*** It is wrong to assume that man always works or is in some occupation or the other, just for money. It is true that in a subsistence economy money, or its equivalent economic reward is of paramount importance—life in fact, depends on it. In this case money is a key motivating factor. But when the situation improves and money becomes sufficient or abundant, it loses its importance. Security, good working conditions, opportunity for promotion, mental satisfaction, status, etc., usually become more important. As Gisbert writes: "Money, or the economic factor while remaining always a reason, may not act at all in particular circumstance, either as a motive or as an incentive".
4. ***Work-occupation and mental health:*** Work and occupations have great therapeutic qualities for mental illness. Men have often resorted to external occupations in order to keep the mind healthy and free from mischief. Dr. H. Simon, the Director of Gutersloh Mental Hospital in Germany, recommended as a remedy for mental patients meaningful work in order to link them with their community and break the isolation both internal and external, with which the mental patients are threatened. He stresses in particular–"The necessity of finding an occupation especially suited to the patient as an individual."

   Among other qualities of work, "it may also be stressed that it is not only a bond or social union, but *also an important requisite for mental health*. It has been proved to be one of the best remedies to break the mental isolation of the patient by renewing the social contacts with his fellow-men."
   — J. Gisbert
5. ***Work in industrial society is a major key to social placement and evaluation:*** When we ask the question–what is he ?–the kind of answer we normally expect may be—*He is an engineer or He is an advocate*, or *He is a professor*. Such answers reveal not only the kind of technical function a person fulfils in society, but they also indicate the social *placement* or *status* of an individual. Hence in most studies of social stratifications *Occupation is used as a criterion of social class or status*. People do, in fact, use occupation as a means of classifying or ranking people. *Thus a man's work may affect his social standing*.
6. ***Work has become 'central' to the life of man today:*** Work is central to the life of man in that it gives the worker a sense of identity, *not just in the eyes of others but in his own eyes*. Work may be a source of satisfaction *to the individual* even where it is not necessarily recognised by others as *important*, *valuable* or *desirable*. *Marx* said that work should always be an expression of personality and never become just an instrument of livelihood. Workers should never be made to feel themselves to be *mere cogs in a complicated machine*, performing unsatisfying tasks. He forewarned that man would become *dehumanised* if inhuman conditions are thrust upon his work and work-place. If a man has to work under such conditions, it may be just a *means to an end*. If a person loses occupations or becomes unemployed, he loses not only money but, more than that, *self-respect* and *the respect of others*.
7. ***Moral evaluation of work:*** The concept of work is invested with varying degrees of moral evaluation. *Jean Calvin*, the founder of *Calvinism*, emphasised that work is not only an economic need but also a moral necessity. *Calvin* said that man, in order to prove worthy of God's Creation, was morally obliged to work; that is, to work for the production of wealth. Wealth, he asserted, was not for enjoyment but for the investment, that is, for further production of wealth. *Accordingly idleness* and its synonyms are not merely the state of non-working but are, in fact, also redolent with *moral disapproval*. The *Marxists* have also stressed that "Work is the basis of social life, a co-operative and creative activity that lifts man above the animals."

8. ***Social evaluation of work:*** It must be admitted that different *kinds* of work are valued differently by different people. Within a single society there is no general agreement as to what constitutes real work and who are the real workers. Some kinds of work are regarded as more *fulfilling* or *more dignified*. Thus the terms *vocation*, *career* or *profession*, or occupation, all carry slightly higher prestige than the word *job*. The clerks may show their distaste towards *mere physical toil*, (that is, manual labour) in terms of Plebian resentment of *obligatory back breaking labour*. Similarly, the manual workers may have their resentment against clerical workers.
9. ***Work and unemployment:*** The role that work plays in the life of many may easily be seen in case of unemployment. "*Men dread unemployment, not merely because it means loss of money, but mostly because it means loss of life*. To find oneself without work in society, without the social connections and hopes rooted in work, is like experiencing the withering away of one's very life."– P. Gisbert. Loss of work is acknowledged by modern psychologists as a *toxic condition* which demands for its rehabilitation special remedies social as well as psychological. *Permanent unemployment is a real threat to mental health*. The popular saying an idle mind is a devil's workshop is meaningful in this context. Probably it is because of this, time of retirement is looked upon with so much dread by ageing men. For some of them the shock is such that they never recover from it in their lives. The abnormally high rate of death within the first year of retirement in many nations is a clear proof of this fact.

Summary

Thus, it is clear that work is universal and natural to men. Man wants to be in some occupation or other whether or not he really loves it, or likes it. But, as a rule, men like work, as constant experience shows. Even a common man feels that it is better to be in some filthy job or occupation than not to be employed anywhere in any profession. In spite of the existence of work *avoidence* the fact is that man likes work. *The idea of hating it never conquered any society*. This is confirmed by the various inquiries conducted in various parts including India. *Work* now is universally recognised as a *necessary condition of civilised life*. This fact has its own political implications. It has now become obligatory for all the responsible governments to provide opportunities for their citizens to work. In Communist countries *right to work* has been accepted as a fundamental right and incorporated in their constitutions. Even in India, there is a demand to include the right to work in the list of fundamental rights by making the relevant amendments to the constitution. The unemployed people are given maintenance allowance in many countries. That shows importance of the work.

MECHANISATION OF WORK AND DECLINE OF TRADITIONAL SKILLS: EFFECTS OF MECHANISATION AND INDUSTRIALISATION

Mechanisation: A Great Event of History

There has been a revolutionary change in the nature of work since the beginning of the 18th century. This is due to the *Industrial Revolution*, an event of great historical importance. *Industry* may be defined as the invention and use of tools in order to achieve material ends. Industry in this sense is as old as man himself, as he has always been a user of tools. Industry may be *simple* when very simple tools like the bow and arrow, or hoe are used; and *complex* when the instruments used are more sophisticated. The *former* is represented by the family economy, the guild system, the domestic system while the latter by the modern industrial or factory system. The Industrial Revolution of the 18th century, more than any other event of the age, profoundly affected every aspect of human life. It changed the direction of civilisation. It destroyed, or radically altered, the medieval customs, beliefs and ideals. The simple rural life and small-scale home or cottage industry were replaced by complex urban life and mass production of goods. It made the traditional values of life and the knowledge of crafts superfluous. It made thousands of people to flock to cities to work in factories and disappear into the urban jungle. The factory system of production began and along with it the process of *mechanisation*. The process of mechanisation refers to the application of machines or mechanised power for the production of goods which have economic value.

Domination of Machines

As a result of the Industrial Revolution, everything was dominated by the machine in the industrial field. It has been well said that, "the most novel and pervasive phenomenon of our age is not capitalism but mechanisation, of which modern capitalism may be merely a by-product." Steel and steam revolutionalised life by taking machine, and power everywhere. Standardisation of goods has made possible not only cheap production of goods but highly organised, efficient, mass distribution of goods. Increased productive efficiency in industry released a considerable proportion of the population for service functions. A large body of men such as engineers, book-keepers, technicians, planners, repairers, builders, buyers of raw materials and sellers of finished products, not actually engaged in the process of production grew. The application of science to industry, agriculture and health gave rise to a host of new service activities. When once the use of machines was learnt, it was sooner or later applied to meet needs of all kinds. Industry, not agriculture or commerce became the chief source of wealth. Heavy machinery and complex methods of running it demanded courage, cleverness and capital. This necessitated the emergence of joint-stock companies. The rise of cities and factories destroyed the guilds and the feudal order. Men became workers in factories. The machine, the tool of man to begin with, became the master of mankind.

Concentration of Productive Process and Wealth

The modern industrial system or the factory system of production reveals three things:

1. Concentration of the productive process in large factories or places located near the sources of power, raw materials or markets;
2. Application of mechanical power which replaced sheer manpower as well as animal power.
3. Concentration of wealth: The factory system could not have been possible without accumulation of wealth especially in the form of capital in the hands of the entrepreneur. The entrepreneur or the organiser was able to combine the four *Ms*: *men*, *money*, *materials* and *machines* in the most productive way. The system became more effective as *Max Weber* observed when the market mechanism diversified into a *consumer market*, *a labour market* and *money market*.

Decline of Traditional Skills

Prior to the Industrial Revolution there were handicraft industries in India and abroad. These had their own guild organisations. Even during the Vedic period in India there was a clear cut division of labour. There were rules to regulate wages and working hours, and sanctions in the form of fines to be imposed on those who violated the rules. Even during the Mughal period Indian skills and handicrafts were well appreciated. India was called *The workshop of the world*. Indian textile fabrics, cotton, silk, and other industrial goods like saltpetre and indigo were exported to Europe and other parts of the world. The cottage industries served local needs and produced goods such as coarse cloth, baskets, earthenware, etc. In England Indian fabrics and muslins were described as light *as women and as slight as cobwebs*.

The fall of the Mughal Empire and later the advent of industrialisation almost put an end to the guild system and the traditional skills of the Indian artisans. Indian cotton, silk and calicos could not be sold in England due to the competition from the factory-made goods. The British tariff policy was also against the Indian interests. Indian markets became flooded with cheaper British goods. Indian hand-made goods lost the markets in the competitive economic race. By 1880 the decline of handi-crafts was an accomplished fact. Many artisans had to find an alternative means of livelihood. They were forced to become agriculturists or to sell their skills as labourers in the new industries, railways or mines started by the British capital. India had been reduced to a *colonial agrarian appendage* of British. Not only in India, in other countries also wherever industrialism spread, traditional skills declined.

Radical Transformation of Economy

The mechanisation of production brought about a radical transformation in capital economy. The rise of cities and factories, the increase in population and production, the emergence of new classes called the *Capitalists* (the rich class) and the *Proletarians* (the working class) were some of the results of Industrial Revolution. It brought about changes in agricultural methods and led to a large-scale increase in production. Large estates, fenced and fertilised, were filled and cultivated on scientific lines under a system of rotating the crops. These maximised production. This increased production helped the growing population to maintain the standard of living in Europe. Bigger and better markets emerged in urban areas and ports and the marketing system also improved.

Misery of Workers

The Industrial Revolution deprived the people of their traditional roles and skills. They fled to cities and became workers in factories. The gulf between the capitalist with his money and the skill to organise production and distribution, and the worker, gradually increased. The capitalists aimed at more production and profits. They recruited men, women and children, made them to work long hours, under filthy and insanitary conditions. Under these conditions, labour was put entirely at the mercy of the machine and its owner. The machinery had set into motion a vicious circle for the worker. Mechanisation was carried to the extremes and resulted in technological unemployment also. The workers had no security of job. The worker's anxiety to secure work in order to survive, led to a steep fall in Wages. Industrialism compelled the man, the woman and the child to work in industries to balance the family budget. "The horrid scenes of women and children at work, tired and emaciated by overwork and strain, some of them even dying away while working, would send a cold shiver through the spine of the stoniest of men". It wrecked family system and put "an end to the old rustic joy and peace". In his *Deserted Village, Oliver Goldsmith* describes the condition of the deserted village and the sufferings of the poor under the factory system. So also, *Carlyle, Dickens* and *Ruskin* poured forth their wrath against the evils that the Industrial Revolution had brought in its train.

The 'Haves' and 'Have-Nots'

The industrialism widened the gap between the rich and poor or the *Haves* and *Have-Nots*. The industrialists or the capitalists became the *exploiting* class. As a result of the exploitation the rich became richer and the poor, the poorer. Karl Marx championed the cause of the workers and gave birth to ideology of *Communism* which in course of time, became the ruling ideology in many nations. Intellectuals attacked the brutality of the factory system in general. Industrialism wrecked the social harmony and contributed to class-conflicts. It altered the basic structure of society even. In course of time, it gave rise to capitalism, colonialism and imperialism. "Industrialism dealt a poor hand to labour under crushing power of which labour had to organise itself into an international force of exceptional potency. Industrialism has led the world to internationalism as a result of imperialism and economic exploitation."

PROPERTY

Concept of Property

Property is one of the basic institutions of society. In everyday speech we think of "*property*" as referring to an object or objects. Strictly speaking, however, property refers not to an object but to the rights that the owner of the object has in relation to others who are not owners of the object Property rights are backed by the state and enforced through its legal institutions.

Definitions of Property

- "Property may be described as the set of rights and obligations which define the relations between individuals or groups in respect of their control over material things or persons treated as things" — **Morris Ginsberg**
- "Property consists of goods and services that society gives an individual or group of individuals with the exclusive right to possess, use and dispose of" — **Anderson and Parker**
- "Property consists of the rights and duties of one person or group (the owner) as against all other persons and groups with respect to some scarce good. It is thus exclusive, for it sets off what is mine from what is thine; but it is also social, being rooted in custom and protected; by law". — **Kingsley Davis**

The definitions stated above make it clear that the whole pattern of rights have obligations with respect to the possession, use, acquisition and disposal of scarce valuable things.

Nature and Characteristics of Property

1. ***Transferability:*** Property can be transferred by its owner by way of sale, exchange or gift. For example, one can sell one's house, or vehicle or ornaments to another, or exchange it for another, or give away as gift to another.
2. ***Ownership and possession of property:*** From the legal point of view a distinction can be made between the ownership of property and the possession of the same. Property rights do not guarantee that the actual owner always enjoys his properties. Property rights and the actual use of the property do not always go together. For example, one may have the ownership of a landed property, but in actuality, the tenant who has its possession may have the direct access to its regular use and enjoyment.
3. ***Property rights are not absolute but only relative:*** Property not only confers rights on the owner it may impose duties as well. Further, no society permits unrestricted rights over property. For example, if one has some land in a thick populated residential area of a city, one cannot build a factory or a poultry farm or pig farm on it.
4. ***Property and scarcity:*** Property exists because resources are very scarce. If resources were to be as unlimited and inexhaustible as the air, nobody would want to claim ownership.
5. ***Property and power:*** The possession of property may mean possession of power over others. The ownership and possession of property help an individual to exert influence or exercise control over those persons who do not have it. As Kingsley Davis has pointed out, "The possession of exclusive rights to something that is scarce and valuable necessarily implies the possession of power over others who also desire the scarce and valuable things... The amount of power which property gives to the owner depends not only upon the definition of his rights but also on the intensity of others' needs for that which is owned."[1]

[1] Kingsley Davis in his *Human Society*, p. 454.

6. ***Tangible and intangible nature of property:*** The things in which an individual may hold property rights may be both tangible and intangible. For example, the forms of property such as automobiles, houses, ornaments and the like, are tangible in nature, whereas copy rights of books or goodwill of a business are intangible.
7. ***Property and social norms:*** The institution of property like all other institutions, is governed by the normative system that regulates the relations between individuals and/or groups. Thus, property owners are under the obligation to use property according to social norms. In the same way, those who do not possess a particular property right are under the general obligation not to infringe upon the right of the possessor.

Ownership of Property

Ownership of property may assume one of the following three forms:

1. ***Communal ownership of property:*** Communal ownership virtually refers to the community ownership. This kind of property exists when property belongs to the community as a whole and may be used but not owned by any member of the community. Communal ownership of land is frequently found in small pre-industrial societies.**2.** ***Private ownership of property***: Private ownership normally refers to the ownership of property by one or a few specific individuals. Private property is recognised in all the societies throughout the world. In some societies it is restricted to a few household possessions while in others it includes various objects of property worth crores of rupees.
3. ***Public ownership of property:*** This type of ownership of property exists when property as such belongs to the state or some other recognised political authority that claims the property on behalf of the people as a whole. In Industrial societies vast amount or size of property is publicly owned.

ADVANTAGES OF PRIVATE PROPERTY

1. ***Contributes to progress:*** Majority of the people of the world support private property. It has contributed a lot to the march of civilisation. Private property guarantees the person, the benefit of his hard labour. The acts of acquiring private property, developing it and preserving the same are protected by law.
2. ***Provides incentives to work hard:*** Private property always recognises hard work and rewards it. The reward system contributes to efficiency and progress.
3. ***Ensures security:*** Private property instils in the minds of the individuals a sense of security. It encourages a person to take risk and serves as an insurance against odds and tough times. The hungry men and the insecure persons yield to exploitation and not the propertied people.
4. ***Generates social virtues:*** Private property gives scope for the individuals to develop certain social virtues such as - generosity, hospitality, family commitments, social service, sacrifice, charity and so on.
5. ***Satisfies man's inherent need for the possession of things:*** It is said that man has an instinctive desire for possessing things. The institution of private property provides scope for fulfilling the desire.

DISADVANTAGES OF PRIVATE PROPERTY

1. ***Private property breeds inequality:*** Since property is scarce, all the people cannot possess it to the extent, which they wish to possess. Further, private property by nature cannot be equally shared or distributed amongst people. Those with better life chances begin well and acquire more property in comparison to those who do not have. It is said that inequality perpetuates inequality.
2. ***Leads to exploitation:*** Private property which causes inequality leads to exploitation. It tempts the rich to become richer at the cost of the poor. According to the communists, this is the way in which capitalism grows. They oppose private property for this reason.
3. ***Private property contributes to greediness and corruption:*** Private property is said to be the root cause of greediness and corruption. Greediness makes man to earn money or wealth by any means. He neglects morality and resorts even to immoral or illegal way of maximising property.
4. ***Damages human values:*** Private property makes man to become more and more selfish. It promotes materialistic outlook. In a private property system things are measured in terms of money. In private property system, values of human life are sacrificed at the alter of money.

DIVISION OF LABOUR AS A SOCIO-ECONOMIC SYSTEM

Division of labour is one of the basic socio-economic institutions of human society. It is as old as human groups or human society. Division of labour and specialisation are the hallmarks of modern complex society.

Division of labour involves the assignment to each unit or group a specific share of a common task. For Example, the principal, the teachers, attenders, office clerks, librarian and other employees of a college do the specific tasks assigned to them and yet contribute to the fulfilment of the common purpose of running a college to promote education.

Every human society, however, large or small, establishes some division of labour among its members. People are expected to specialise, at least to some extent, in particular economic activities. In family, for example, work is divided and shared by the father, mother and children. The father looks after the outdoor work, the wife and children remain at home and do the household work.

The division of labour occurs in all societies, because it is highly functional. It ensures that particular categories of people have specific jobs to do. It helps them to become experts in their assigned activities. Division of labour in this way contributes to the efficiency of economic life, but it may have other far-reaching effects also.

Increased Specialisation

Division of labour leads to specialisation. Specification refers to the art and science of knowing more and more about the smaller units or objects. There has been a general historical trend towards increased specialisation in economic activities. This trend has reached its climax in modern industrial society.

In small hunting and food gathering societies there is little division of labour except on grounds of age and sex. With the expansion of the economy division of labour also becomes more complex. An elaborate system of division of labour persists in the industrial societies today.

Modern industrialisation breeds on entirely new form of division of labour: "The high degree of specialisation found in factories, offices, and other formal organisations, where each individual contributes only a minute part to the final product. The worker no longer creates a total product but is instead merely a minor component in an elaborate mechanised or bureaucratised process".

— Ian Robertson, p. 410.

Socio-Economic Dimensions of Division of Labour

The socio-economic dimensions of division of labour can be understood by an analysis of the merits and demerits of division of labour.

Relative Merits of Division of Labour

Merits

1. ***Fits in the right man for the right task:*** Under division of labour tasks can be distributed among the workers in such a way that each worker is placed in the right place.
2. ***Large-scale productions:*** When there is division of labour the worker becomes more efficient in his work. This helps the industries to increase production on a large scale by installing sophisticated machines.
3. ***Improved quality of product at low cost:*** Under division of labour the quality of the product is improved and the cost of production of the same reduced.
4. ***Helps mobility of labour:*** Division of labour facilitates the opening of a large number of big and small industries which facilitates the use of more and more machines. It in turn enables the easy mobility of labour from one industry to another industry.
5. ***Improves skill:*** Division of labour helps the workers to become experts in their fields by making them to do the same work over and again.
6. ***Less physical and mental strain:*** As the worker is asked to do a small part of the work continuously for a long period, he becomes accustomed to it. This reduces his physical and mental strains.
7. ***Other advantages:***
   (*i*) Division of labour increases the number and variety of jobs.
   (*ii*) It helps the introduction of sophisticated machines for facilitating production.
   (*iii*) It saves the time and energy of the worker who every time does the same work.

Demerits

1. ***Monotony in work:*** Under the division of labour, a worker works on the same kind of job over and over again, the job becomes monotonous and highly boring.
2. ***Dependence on others:*** Here the work of one worker is dependent on the work of other workers in the process of production.

3. ***Unemployment:*** The introduction of new machinery often leads to the displacement of labour and creates unemployment.
4. ***Loss of skills and retards development of personality:*** Since the worker does only a part of the job, it reduces the skill of the worker. Further, when the worker does the same operation again and again, his muscles and mind move in the same direction. As a result of this repetitive movement of mind, his intelligence gets blunted and outlook narrowed. This retards human development.
5. ***Loss of responsibility and pride in work:*** Here an article is not entirely made or produced by a single worker. Each individual worker's contribution to the final product is very less. Hence he loses the sense of responsibility and pride in his work.
6. ***Other disadvantages:***
   (*i*) It may contribute to the problem of over production.
   (*ii*) Employment of large number of workers in a single firm or industry may lead to the ex-ploitation of the workers and then to worker's unity and class conflict.
   (*iii*) Mobility of workers get disturbed.

SOCIAL CONSEQUENCES OF DIVISION OF LABOUR

Durkheim's Functionalist Perspective

It was Durkheim who developed his theory of "*division of labour*" from a functional point of view. In his famous book "*Division of Labour in society*" Durkheim tried to determine the social consequences of the division of labour especially in modern societies. Durkheim has stressed in all his major works the importance of shared social norms and values in maintaining social cohesion and solidarity. He agreed that *the nature of this social solidarity depends on the extent of the division of labour.*

Distinction between Two Types of Solidarity

Durkheim made a fundamental difference between pre-industrial and industrial societies and in tune with that also made a difference between two types of solidarity namely, 'mechanical solidarity' and 'organic solidarity'.

1. ***Mechanical solidarity:*** According to Durkheim, 'mechanical solidarity' prevails in the simpler folk societies, where the division of labour is restricted to family, to the village or small region. Here the individuals do not differ much from one another. Here everyone does much the same work, the members are all socialised in the same pattern, share the experiences, and hold common values. These values, which are mainly religious in nature, form a "*collective consciousness*" for the community, a set of norms, beliefs, etc. shared by one and all. There is little scope for individuality here. The society is harmonious and coherent because there is little social differentiation and division of labour is unspecialised.
2. ***Organic solidarity:*** According to Drukhiem, the modern societies are held together by a much looser bond which he calls "*organic solidarity*". Here, the individuals who are the members of the same collectivity are not similar, but different. Because these societies are large and people engage in a variety of economic activities, the members have quite different experiences. They hold different values and socialise their children in many varying patterns. Here people think of themselves as individuals first and as members of a kinship or wider social groups second. "The basis for social solidarity and cohesion is no longer the similarity of the members but rather their differences".

— Ian Robertson, p. 412

In the modern industrial society all parts are held together by an interdependence which is imposed by an elaborate division of labour and specialisation. Here co-operation among all individuals and groups is necessitated by interdependence.

Division of Labour and Anomie

According to Durkheim, the conditions of the modern society compel division of labour to reach its logical extreme. This extreme form of division of labour leads inevitably to feelings of individualism. The feelings of individualism are developed only at the cost of shared sentiments or beliefs. The result, according to Durkheim, is 'anomie'.

- "Anomie" according to Durkheim, refers to a state of normlessness in both the society and the individual.
- Anomie is "a social condition characterised by the breakdown of norms governing social interaction."[2]

---

[2] Duncan Mitchel (Editor) in *A Dictionary of Sociology*, p. 7.

- "Any state where there are unclear, conflicting or unintegrated norms, in which the individual had no morally significant relations with others or on which there were no limits set to the attainment of pleasure was a state of anomie."[3]

According to Durkheim, 'anomie' indicates a condition in which social norms become con- fused or breakdown, and people feel detached from their fellows. Having little commitment to shared norms, people lack social guidelines for personal conduct. They are inclined to pursue their private interests without regard for the interests of society as a whole. Social control of individual behaviour becomes ineffective, and the society is threatened with disorganisation or disintegration as a result.

The word 'anomie' has emerged from the Greek word "anomia" which simply means lawless- ness, worse than anarchy. Anarchy means a society in which there is no ruler but in that society the anarchists hope, the natural order prevails.

Durkheim uses the word 'anomie' in the sense that people have a sense of '*normlessness*', the term has been applied to the *state of mind* of individuals regardless of the state of society. Anomie is not the same thing as the absence of norms. In the condition called anomie norms are present. They are comparatively clear also. People, in general, are oriented to them. But this orientation on the part of many, is ambivalent. It either leads towards conformity, but with suspicion, or lean towards deviation but with suspicion.

Durkheim, during his time, was probably right in his view that the division of labour and the resulting growth of individualism would breakdown shared with commitment to social norms. But today that there is no widespread anomie in modern societies. Modern societies do retain some broad consensus on norms and values, as we can readily see when we compare one society with another; say, India with Pakistan. There is no doubt that this consensus seems much weaker than it was in preindustrial societies. It is probably still strong enough to guide most individual behaviour and to avert the social breakdown that Durkheim feared.

"Durkheim's analysis remains highly valuable however, for his acute insights into the farranging effects that the division of labour has on social and personal life".

— Ian Robertson, p. 414

Merton's View of Anomie

Durkheim's concept of 'anomie' has been enlarged by *R.K. Merton* (1957) into a *general theory of deviant behaviour*. Merton distinguishes culturally defined goals and institutional means of achieving those goals. Societies vary in the degree to which they stress one or the other. Those societies which lay great emphasis on goals but little on means make or tempt individuals to adopt technically most efficient means to reach the goals even if these are illegitimate. Merton cites American society as an example of such an anomic society. Crime may be normal in certain groups because, in those groups there is widespread emphasis on the importance of worldly success, particularly in terms of wealth. But in these groups equal importance is not given for insisting on the right means to reach goal. The result is, people tend to follow the deviant methods. Thus, according to Merton, anomie arises out of "the seeming contradictions between cultural goals and socially restricted access to these goals."

WORK AND ALIENATION

Work has become an inseparable part of our life. It is not only a means of making a living but a way of acquiring our social status in society. Work helps to define the respective social roles of both the sexes. Though work has assumed importance in our social life it cannot be generalised all that we do as work is satisfying. When work becomes an enforced activity and not a creative one, it may bring us dissatisfaction. This situation is very much aggaravated in capitalist economies and also in societies where technology has advanced very much. One of the effects of advanced technology or capitalist economy is that the labourer or the worker suffers from the process of what Marx calls "*alienation*".

The concept of 'alienation' was introduced to modern sociology by Karl Marx. It is defined in the following way. "*Essentially, alienation refers to the sense of powerlessness, isolation and meaninglessness experienced by human beings when they are confronted with social institutions and conditions that they cannot control and consider oppressive*". Seeman, 1959 as quoted by Ian Robertson.

Three Elements of Alienation

Seeman speaks of three important elements of alienation. Alienation consists of:

1. ***A feeling of powerlessness:*** The workers do not own the tools they use, buy the resources they use, or sell the products they make.
2. ***A feeling that work lacks meaning:*** The workers contribute only one bit, such as checking the speedometer of a car to the final product, and may lack contact with other workers; and

[3] N. Abercrombie, S. Hill and B. Turner in their *The Penguin Dictionary of Sociology*.

3. ***Estrangement from the job:*** Many jobs do not provide opportunities for promotion or advancement, a chance to spend time with friendly workmates or a chance to create a product with pride and satisfaction.

Sources of Alienation

Marx has spoken of three important sources of alienation. They are as follows:

1. According to Marx, alienation results from the lack of a sense of control over the social world. The social world confront, people as a hostile thing making them 'alien' in the very social environment that they have created.
2. Another important sources of alienation which Marx speaks of is the extreme division of labour in modern societies. Here each worker has a specific, restricted, and limited role to play. He or she no longer applies his or her total capacity for work. The worker here is reduced to the level of a "mere cog in a machine".
3. Marx predicted that the situation of 'alienation' would ultimately ripen the mood of the workers for an outright conflict with the capitalists.

CAPITALISM AND SOCIALISM AS TWO MAIN FORMS OF ECONOMY

Capitalism and socialism represent two basic ways in which an industrial society can produce and distribute goods and services. There are strong ideological differences between countries adopting either strategy. In general, the *American economy* is a model of '*capitalism*' and the *Soviet economy* is generally regarded as a model of '*socialism*'. Still, it would be inappropriate to regard either all capitalist or all socialist societies as being fundamentally identical.

Capitalism

Capitalism is an economy in which the means of producing are largely in private hands and the main incentive for economic activity is the accumulation of profits.[4] In practice, capitalist systems vary in the degree to which private ownership and economic activity are regulated by government.

Two Essential Qualities of Capitalism

An ideal form of capitalism contains the following two essential qualities or ingredients:

1. ***Personal profits:*** As Max Weber remarked, the outstanding characteristic of capitalism is production "for the pursuit of profit and ever renewed profit". Seeking self-interest or profit is considered here as normal, morally acceptable, and socially desirable. But this notion of profit was unknown when exchange was affected by barter or by various forms of gifts.
2. ***Free competition:*** Competition is regarded as necessary if the capitalist system is to work effectively. John D Rockefeller, a multi-millionaire of America had said that competition "is not an evil tendency in business. It is merely a working out of law of nature and a law of God".

Why the pursuit of profit in an atmosphere of unrestricted competition is necessary for capitalism? The Answer is simple. Adam Smith had said in 1776 itself that under these two conditions – the forces of supply and demand will ensure the production of the best possible products at the lowest possible prices.

Competition among capitalists will give the public the opportunity to compare the quality and prices of goods. Through this competition producers who are inefficient or who charge excessive prices will be put out of business.

In capitalism efficient producers are rewarded with profits and consumers get quality products at competitive prices. It is also essential that for this system to work in an ideal manner, there should be minimum of government interference in economic life. The government is expected to follow a policy of '*laissez-faire*' or ["leave at alone"] or *the policy of non-interference*. This pure form of capitalism does not exist anywhere now although it did exist in somewhat that way in the early phase of industrial development. Today the modern governments consider it necessary to regulate the economy to put necessary restrictions on its activities.

A typical capitalist country like America too has realised the necessity of governmental intervention in certain fields of its economic activity. *For example*, the American government supervises the economic activities. It supports the price of some commodities and puts ceilings on the prices of others. It intervenes in international trade, protects some natural resources and encourages the exploitation of others. It sets minimum wage standards and provides for unemployment benefits and so on.

Demerits or Limitations of Capitalism

1. Capitalism overemphasises profits and neglects group interests and social functions.
2. It provides no guarantee that profits will correspond to service and that economic activities will further the interests of the community.

---

[4] D. Rosenberg's definition as quoted by Richard T. Schaefer in *Sociology-International Edition*, 1989, p. 413.

3. Capitalism inevitably leads to labour exploitation. This contributes to the misery of the workers.
4. Capitalism necessitates the birth of labour unions which very often fights against management for securing justice to the workers. Labour unions disturb the development of harmonious relationship between labour and management.
5. Capitalism does not give scope for the customers to develop contacts or communication with the owners particularly when business houses are owned by a large number of shareholders. Ownership becomes somewhat anonymous here.
6. Minute division of labour and specialisation lead to adverse consequence and particularly to the alienation of workers.

Socialism

Socialism is a type of economy in which the means of production and distribution in a society are collectively rather than privately owned.

Here the basic objective of the economic system is to meet people's needs rather than to maximise profits. It also believes that competition between different firms producing similar products is a waste of resources. The pursuit of private profit is regarded as fundamentally immoral because one person's profit is another person's loss. Production should not be done for profit; it should be designed to serve social goals. Since private owners exploit both workers and customers and will not produce unprofitable goods and services, it is necessary for the means of production to be taken into public ownership and run in the best interests of society as a whole. The aims of a socialist economy are the efficient production of needed goods and services and the achievement of social equality by preventing the accumulation of private wealth. Soviet Union conforms in some respects to this classic model.

Important Characteristics

1. In a socialist economy there is a common ownership of the means of production and distribution.
2. Here the economic activities are planned by the state and the market plays virtually no role in the allocation of resources.
3. Since there is no scope for private property social classes with wide economic dispairty do not appear.
4. Since the legal system here is primarily concerned with administration, it involves important changes in criminal and property law.
5. 'The structural changes mentioned above, contribute to the insignificant role of religion. It may even disappear, or its disappearance may be hastened.
6. Since private property has no scope here, human alienation will not be found.

Three Main Advantages of Socialism over Capitalism

Socialist economy claims superiority over capitalism in three respects:

1. Socialist economies are more efficient economically. Because there is less scope for waste [Example: unemployment, over production, idle machinery, inflation, etc.] which is normally associated with capitalism.
2. Socialist economies do not have colonical markets. Because they do not require an outlet for capital or commodities.
3. Socialist economies are more democratic than capitalist societies. Because, decisions about the satisfaction of human needs are taken collectively and publicly.

Limitations or Demerits of Socialist Economies

1. Socialist economies have not proved more economically efficient and dynamic than the capitalist societies. The Western societies such as USA, UK, France with capitalism have established their lead in economic, scientific and technological fields.
2. Socialist societies are not democratic, because major decisions are taken by the ruling communist party and not by the people or public in general.
3. Socialist societies have also proved to be imperialist. In order to satisfy the requirements of rapid industrialisation, they are also forced to exploit their indigenious workers or the farmers of the underdeveloped nations.
4. Though private property is abolished here social stratification persists in the form of income inequality, differences in prestige, and inequalities of power.
5. In a socialist society, inequality is determined not by the market but by the party and its bureaucratic apparatus which enjoys autocratic power.

6. In actuality, operation of economic markets cannot be completely removed. Hence the black market serves to reinforce social inequalities.
7. The party which rules derives strength from the socialist ideology. In other words, the socialist ideology is made use of for legitimating the party power.

MULTINATIONAL CORPORATIONS AND THEIR IMPACT ON WORLD ORDER

The third type of the economy which is growing at a fast rate [almost at an annual rate of 10%], in the world today is no other than the "*multinational corporations*" or "*companies*". They are potentially the most influential and are perhaps the most controvertial economic units in the world today.

"A multinational corporation is simply one which owns or manages businesses in two or more countries."[5]

Normally, in their pure forms the multinationals manufacture various goods in many countries, sell to World markets, draw management from several nations, and are owned by shareholders around the world. *Examples*: Shell, Unilever, I.B.M., Nestle, Coco Cola, ITT [International Telephone and Telegraph]. At present, multinational company is likely to be centered in one home country.

Mighty Economic Forces

Multinationals have emerged as very powerful economic forces. *For example*: The ITT which has diversified into hundreds of industries, now employs 400,000 workers in 68 countries.

Many multinational corporations are wealthier than some of the countries in which they operate. Already, they account for more than 1/4 of the total economic production. This share is likely to rise over one-half in the next 25 years.

They Represent a New Independent Politico-Economic Force

It is difficult to deny the fact that multinationals constitute a major new and independent force in the world politico-economic scene. By crossing the national boundaries, these multinational corporations gain independence. *For example*: Nestle company of Switzerland [which is one of the world's thirty largest corporations, does 98% of its business outside of Switzerland. Hence the Switzerland Government can hardly exercise control and authority over this company.

Criticisms Levelled Against Functioning of Multinational Companies

1. ***Political interference:*** Multinational Companies have drawn criticism during the recent years. To safeguard their interests they have started interfering in the internal political affairs of the countries in which they have their business activities. *For example*: (*i*) The ITT attempted to sabotage 1970 Chilean Presidential election to protect its 160 million dollars investment in that country. (*ii*) It is said, that the Fire Store Company, United Fruit Company, and the Royal Dutch Shell Company had instigated internal conflicts in Liberia, Latin American countries and Sumatra respectively leading to the establishment of military governments. (*iii*) It is also reported that the American intelligence agency called the CIA had made use of the multinational companies to create political anarchy in nations such as Namibia, Philippines, Nigeria and Morocco.
2. ***Encourage corruption:*** The multinational companies are prepared to spend any amount to pay towards bribe to protect their interests. *For example*: "the ITT secretly requested the Nixon administration to overthrow the government of Chile, offering upto ₹One million dollars to the federal government as a contribution towards the expenses involved".

   — Sampson[6]
3. ***Cause unemployment:*** Conflict theorists have branded multinationals as irresponsible exploiters who export jobs from the home country to the poor countries, where they can exploit the unorganised labour of the people. *For example*, the Wimco company manufacturing match boxes made 55,000 families in Shivakashi and other places in Tamil Nadu to lose their jobs.
4. ***Consumerism and cultural invasion:*** These companies have made people to become crazy after new things. They manufacture certain luxurious commodities such as chewing gums, soft drinks, cleaning synthetics, face cream, shampoo, hair oil, lip stick etc., and through attractive advertisements bring heavy mental compulsions on people to purchase these. This tendency has led to unwanted consumerism. Further, by introducing Western styles, practices, values, etc., wherever they do their business, they have virtually launched a type of cultural invasion against the local cultures.

---

[5] Wallac and Wallance in their *Sociology*, p. 510.

[6] Ian Robertson in his *Sociology*, p. 427.

5. ***Danger of aid and death trap:*** The multinational companies are making huge profits. They are trying to trap the poor countries by giving them financial and other types of aid. They now represent a disturbing concentration of unscrutinised political and economic power that they may have adverse social impact,

JAJMANI SYSTEM AND ITS IMPORTANCE

The "Jajmani System" represents one of the types of exchange that prevailed in India for a long time. As Prof. Yogendra Singh has said "The jajmani system is a system governed by relationships based on reciprocity in intercaste relations in village."

The term 'jajmani' is derived from the Vedic term "Yajman" who in Vedic times conducted '*Yajna*' or fire sacrifice to appease the Gods. The term denotes a significant person and in the village context, a landowner. The people who rendered services to him, the priest, the carpenter, ironsmith, Washerman, barber, potter, were collectively known as "*praja*", (and in due course as "*Kamins*"]. Generally, the uppercastes such as Brahmins and Rajputs, remained as jajmans. For their services rendered to the Yajmans the praja or the 'Kamins' received payment in kind (grains, cloth, fodder, buttermilk, ghee, etc.), which provided economic security.

Some Characteristics of Jajmani System

1. ***Jajmani system implies traditional occupational obligations between castes:*** It forges interdependence of castes. The servicing castes called "Kamins" and the recipients of the services called '*jajmans*' are dependent on each other for the fulfilment of their economic needs.
2. ***Jajmani system establishes closer family links:*** The jajmani links are to be found between families rather than between jatis. For example, a farmer's family gets its wooden agricultural tools from a particular carpenter family, and in return, the carpenter gets a share of the farmer's crop at harvest.
3. ***Jajmani relationships are durable:*** Here the link is inherited on both the sides. Thus the carpenter serves the same farmer family, that his father and grandfathers served. In the same manner, the farmer family gets its tools made and repaired by the descendants of the carpenters family whose members made tools for their forefathers.
4. ***Jajmani relationships are exclusive:*** For example, the farmer family is supposed to carry on transactions with a particular carpenter family only. Reciprocally these carpenters are supposed to make tools for their own 'yajman' families only. However they are free to make some tools for sale in the market.
5. ***Jajmani relationships are multiple:*** This relationship is not restricted to economic exchange alone. Economic exchange is only one facet of the jajmani relations. As Mandelbaum has pointed out "a family of cultivators expects help on its ceremonial occasions from most of the associated families. There is also an expectation of mutual personal support in family emergencies or fractional quarrels. Sometimes the specialist families are pressurised to support the jati of their patrons when that whole jati is embattled."
6. ***Jajmani system adds to the village solidarity:*** According to *M.N. Srinivas*, jajmani system which is based on the interdependence of castes is one of the main factors that add to the village solidarity. Indian village is based on caste system. Different castes are brought together and welded into a unity by this system. This system contributes to the *vertical solidarity of the caste system*. Vertical solidarity of the caste system refers to the unity existing among different caste groups in a village. Vertical solidarity of the caste thus contributes to the village solidarity.
7. ***Coercion and consensus in jajmani relations:*** Some writers have strongly criticised the jajmani relations as "exploitative." According to them, the jajmani relationships are "the means by which the rich and powerful exploit the poor and coerce the workers into sustaining the power of those who have the upper hand and the higher rank."

Some other writers have argued that in spite of the coercive element in the jajmani relations, such exchanges "bring solidarity and mutual benefits." They have said that each jati system tries to maximise its gain and exercise as much power as it can in the matter of jajmani transactions. As M.S.A. Rao has pointed out criticism of jajmani transactions "as brutally exploitative is too sweeping and obfuscating a generalisation."[7]

Decline of Jajmani System

At present, in most of the villages in India, the jajmani arrangements are not seen in the village economy. In fact, in over all terms this system declined after the introduction of British rule in India. By now the jajmani relationship has been largely supplanted in many villages. In some of the villages, it has completely disappeared. Still, it persists in some way

[7] M.S.A. Rao, "The Jajmani System", *The Economic Weekly,* 1961, as quoted by Parimal B. Kar, p. 229.

in some parts of North India. "We may further note that jajmani relationship is now increasingly being supplanted mainly because more money is new used in village economy and also because modern transport makes market transac- tions more feasible."

— Parimal B. Kar, p. 230

SOCIAL DETERMINANTS OF ECONOMIC DEVELOPMENT

It is now increasingly being recognised that economic development of any country is influenced and sometimes determined by a large number of social factors. It is in this connection economists have sought the help of sociology in understanding the social factors that have contributed to the economic backwardness of a few countries. Economists have now realised the importance and practical helpfulness of sociological knowledge in analysing the economic growth or economic affairs of a country.

Economic development is very much influenced by various social factors. But it should be noted that the social factors or forces causing underdevelopment vary from country to country. It follows, then that the remedies for the problems of underdevelopment must also vary.

1. ***Role of people's ability, experience and knowledge:*** Economic development of any country hinges on the efficient employment of factors of production (such as, land, labour, capital and organisation). The employment of a factor of production is not just a matter of choice but is very much conditioned by cultural and social factors. The people must have the required ability, experience and knowledge to make the best use of the facilities that are made available. Economic development is, therefore, not a function of economic resources alone, but of social and cultural factors as Well.
2. ***Adoption of technology:*** Adoption of technology is not just governed by simple mechanical considerations. Technology can yield results only when appropriate social conditions are present. All types of technology are not suitable to all types of societies. A particular type of technology (say, introduction of computers) that serves a purpose in a few societies may prove to be meaningless or dysfunctional in some others–(say, tribal societies or underdeveloped societies). Labour-saving machines are more ideally suited to the more advanced Western societies. They may be dysfunctional for societies wherein large number of unemployed and unskilled workers are ready to work for very low wages.
3. ***Innovative personality:*** Economic development requires innovative personality. Early socialisation and the nature and contents of education to which the child is exposed decide largely the emergence of innovative personality. In some societies a child is taught to solve problems inde- pendently and encouraged to be creative. In traditional societies on the other hand, more importance is given to *confirmity*. Here the children are encouraged to accept uncritically the lore and practices handed down from the previous generations. In such traditional societies innovative personalities do not grow easily. Hence economic development in these societies would be very slow and gradual.
4. ***Time gap between the introduction of technology and cultural support for the same:*** For its fast growth technology requires a favourable cultural support. Adoption of technology in a meaningful manner naturally involves a preparatory stage. There is bound to be a time gap between preparation for its technology and its adoption. The Western societies have developed over decades the cultural traits and social conditions appropriate to technology. As a result, they could get the cultural support when they started technological inventions and introducing sophisticated technology.

   The underdeveloped countries do not have this advantage of the Western societies. As R. T. Gill has pointed out "In underdeveloped countries, however, the problem is to accomplish simultaneously both the industrial revolution and the preparation for such a revolution.[8]

   In such countries the mass media of communication carry advertisements of products produced by the Western industries. Due to these advertisements people may develop craziness towards these products. Hence, in these underdeveloped countries there arises a need for what is known as "*a revolution in the expectations of the people*". The elected "government cannot ignore the rising expectations of the people and it is obliged to go in for sophisticated technology in the absence of appropriate cultural and social support. This creates complications for smooth economic development".

   — Parimal B.Kar, p. 251
5. ***Explosive growth of population:*** The biggest social impediment for economic growth is the explosive growth of the population that we see in countries such as India, Bangladesh, Pakistan, China, etc. The Third World countries are all experiencing this problem. Explosive population growth is dysfunctional to the economic growth. Professor

[8] R.T. Gill as quoted by Parimul B. Kar in *Sociology—The Discipline and its Dimensions*, 1990, p. 251.

Gill writes in this connection thus: "Population growth is not a stimulant to development, but a depressant. Because of the lack of industrial capital the growing labour force cannot find jobs in the city and therefore adds itself to the already congested rural area. Rapid population growth in such "labour surplus" economies may mean that despise the attempts to increase industrial employment. the absorption rate is sufficient and that open and disguised unemployment increases as a percentage of the labour force - the reverse of successfull development? [9]

REVIEW QUESTIONS

1. Explain the concept of economic system. Assess the importance of work and occupation in modern society.
2. Discuss the concept of occupation. Give the classification of occupation.
3. Elucidate the social importance of work and occupation.
4. Describe the effects of mechanisation and industrialisation on the economy of India.
5. Explain the concept of property. Describe the nature and characteristics of property.
6. What is division of labour? Discuss its merits and demerits.
7. Write an essay on social consequences of division of labour.
8. What is alienation? Discuss the elements and sources of alienation.
9. Define capitalism. Discuss its essential qualities and limitations.
10. Give the definition of socialism. Bring out its characteristic the features.
11. What are multinational corporations? Assess their impact on world order.
12. Write a detailed note on the jajmani system. Write its importance and assess the causes of the decline of the jajmani system.
13. What are the social determinants of economic development? Discuss.
14. Write short notes on the following:
    (a) Mechanisation
    (b) Socialist economies
    (c) Industrial Revolution

⌘⌘⌘⌘⌘⌘⌘⌘⌘⌘⌘⌘

[9] T.N. Gill in *Economic Development: Past and Present*, 1970, p. 186.

33

THE POLITICAL SYSTEM

CHAPTER OUTLINE

THE UBIQUITY OF POLITICS

"Whether he likes it or not, virtually no one is completely beyond the reach of some kind of political system. A citizen encounters politics in the Government of a country, town school, Church, business firm, trade union, club, political party, civic associations—*Politics is one of the unavoidable facts of human existence. Everyone is involved in some fashion at sometime in some kind of political system*."

— *Robert A. Dahl.*

Politics is essentially an ancient and universal experience. The art and science of political analysis have developed over several thousand years throughout many parts of the world. In particular, political analysis has thrived in all cultures that have inherited the rich legacy of the ancient people like ancient Greeks, Romans and the Indians. Like many other arts and sciences political analysis achieved an extraordinary degree of sophistication among the Greeks some 25 centuries ago under the leadership of Socrates, Plato and Aristotle. Since their time every age produced a few great students of politics who have contributed much to the development of the discipline, *i.e., political science*.

DEMOCRACY AND TOTALITARIANISM

Classification of Political Systems

Thinkers distinguish between different kinds of political systems. Long back Aristotle introduced a six–fold classification of political system: *Kingship* (Monarchy) and *Tyranny* (rule by one); *Aristocracy* and *Oligarchy* (rule by a few) and *Polity* and *Democracy* (rule by many).

Max: Weber was of the opinion that the type of the political system depends upon the nature of its legitimacy. Legitimacy rests on three factors: (*i*) *Tradition*, (*ii*) *Exceptional Personal Qualities or Charismatic Personality*, and (*iii*) *Legality.*

T.B. Bottomore makes a distinction between three kinds of political systems: (*i*) Political system of tribal societies which are slowly getting modernised and industrialised. *Ex*: African Societies (*ii*) Political systems in *non-industrial Countries* of ancient civilizations which are being industrialised after emancipation from colonial and autocratic rule. *Ex*: Countries of Asia, Middle East, some Latin American Countries. (*iii*) Political systems of the *industrial societies*. Here two major types of political systems can be witnessed: (*a*) *The Democratic-Capitalist or Democratic-Socialist*, and (*b*) The *Communist-Totalitarian* including other kinds of totalitarianism.

Democracy as a Political System

Democracy as a political system, *i.e.*, as a form of government, has become politically the most fashionable one today. It is often said to be the best and the most civilised form of political system. Still, as Burns says, "*Democracy is a word with many meanings and some emotional colour*." He further says, "Few words have been more loosely and variously defined than democracy. *It has almost literally meant all things to all men*."

Definition of Democracy

The term *democracy* is derived from two Greek words demos which means the *people* and *kratia* which means the *power*. "*Literally*, therefore, democracy is regarded as that government where the power is vested in the people".

1. *Gettell* defines democracy as–"that form of government in which the mass of the population possesses the right to share in the exercise of sovereign power".
2. *MacIver writes*: "Democracy is, not a way of governing whether by majority or otherwise but primarily a way of determining who shall govern and broadly, to what ends".
3. *Sardar Panikkar*, a noted Indian Historian writes: "Democracy is in fact, not merely a form of government, it is a complex of social, economic and political factors, affecting the relationship of the state of the individual, guaranteeing essential freedoms, personal liberty, freedom of expression of organisation and of governing activities".
4. *Abraham Lincoln* has said that democracy is a "*government of the people by the people and for the people*".
5. For *Aristotle* democracy was "a perverted form of popular rule".

Basic Principles of Democracy

The basic principles of democracy can be listed here–(1) Democracy guarantees all individuals the right to speak, criticise and disagree with others. (2) It stands on the spirit of tolerance and allows people to have diverse views, ideas and ideologies. (3) It believes in the methods of persuasion and peace. (4) It is opposed to the use of coercive methods or to the threat of power. (5) It upholds the dignity of the human personality. (6) It guarantees fundamental rights to its citizens like the right to freedom of speech, press, peaceful assembly, to contest the elections, constitutional remedies, etc. (7) It is built on the foundations *of Liberty, Equality and Fraternity*. (8) In democracy sovereignty rests with the people. (9) It is a rule by the majority with full safeguards for the right of the minorities. (10) It is a government by the representatives of the people who are elected on the basis of universal adult franchise. (11) It functions strictly according to the provision of the constitution, written or unwritten, which has been accepted by the people. (12) It gives adequate opportunities to all and assures every one full justice. (13) Though it is a rule by majority, it aims at the welfare of all. (14) It provides for a change in government according to constitutional provision.

Essential Conditions of Democracy

There are certain conditions which must be fulfilled if democracy is to become successful. Some of them are as follows: (1) Democracy requires some amount of political maturity and education on the part of its people. (2) Eternal vigilance is the price of democracy. People must be alert to protect it at all costs. (3) It requires an efficient and elaborate system of self-governing institutions like *Village Panchayats*, Municipalities, Taluk Boards, District Boards, etc. (4) Democracy survives only if people have a strong desire for democracy. (5) Democracy is a government by debate, discussion and criticism and consensus. Hence it requires the *spirit of toleration*. (6) It requires well-organised party system. (7) It Works well if it has a strong, Well-organised, ever-vigilant opposition. (8) In a representative democracy, the majority party forms the government. (9) For its undisturbed functioning it requires a peaceful atmosphere in its jurisdiction. (10) Proper leadership is indispensable for the smooth working of democracy. (11) Free and independent press is the watchdog of democracy. (12) It requires non-corruptible citizens or citizens of a high moral character. (13) It provides enough opportunities for political participation for all the citizens. (14) It requires a strong sense of solidarity and feeling of unity on the part of the people. (15) It requires social as well as economic equality for its success. There can be no political equality in the absence of socio-economic equality. (16) It requires a sound constitution and an independent judiciary. (17) The wheel of democracy marches on with the help of a body of efficient and honest civil servants. (18) For the success of democracy it is essential that the army is sub-ordinated to civil authority.

Forms of Democracy

Democracy is of two types: 1. *Direct* and 2. *Indirect*. This is determined by the nature of relationship between people and the government. When they coincide democracy is direct; when they differ democracy is indirect.

1. ***Direct democracy:*** Direct democracy is also known as *pure* democracy and *simple* democracy. A direct democracy is one in which the people themselves take direct part in the affairs of the state, in passing laws and in executing them. Here, people exercise power directly. This kind of democracy can exist and function only in small states with limited population, where all the people can conveniently assemble at a given place and pass laws. This kind of democracy existed in the ancient city-states of Greece. But it survives in some of the small *Cantons* in Switzerland. It cannot be put into practice in the modern complex societies.
2. ***Indirect or representative democracy:*** Modern states, are generally very large in size and population. Hence direct democracy cannot function in these states. Modern democracy is mostly indirect or a representative democracy. In an indirect democracy the government is run by the representatives who are elected periodically by the people. *J.S. Mill* defines indirect democracy as one in which "the whole people or some numerous portion of them, exercise the governing power through deputies periodically elected by themselves." The people judge the representatives by their deeds. If they are found to be efficient they are re-elected, otherwise, new members are elected. Still, the people do not have direct control over the representatives, when once they are elected. They may fail to perform their duties properly. Some states have introduced various 'direct democratic checks' like *Referendum, Recall*, etc. In India, U.S.A., U.K., France, Japan, Austria there is indirect democracy.

Democracy as an Order of Society

"A democratic society is one in which the spirit of equality and fraternity prevails. Such a society does not necessarily imply a democratic state or democratic government." As *Burns* observes, "democracy as an ideal is a society of equals in the sense that each is an integral and irreplaceable part of the Whole". "A democratic society is a society of free, equal, active and intelligent citizens, each man choosing his own way of life himself and willing that others should theirs".

Political Parties and Voting

Political parties are an inseparable part of the democratic system. Elections and voting are also invariably associated with the democratic political process.

POLITICAL PARTIES

Meaning of 'Political Parties'

1. According to **MacIver**, "A political party is an association organised in support of some principle or policy which by constitutional means it endeavours to make the determinant of government."
2. According to *Ian Robertson*, "*Political parties are collectivities of people organised for the specific purpose of joining legitimate control of government.*"

Essentials of Political Parties

1. A group of people to constitute a political party, must be organised for a political purpose.
2. There should be similarity of principles helping to unite people.
3. The political parties should have the main aim of attaining political power.
4. The parties should use peaceful and legitimate means for attaining political power.
5. It becomes necessary for a political party to pronounce its main principles in public and make equally known to the electorate its plans, programmes and the course of action which it is going to follow.
6. The political parties which are found within the framework of the national boundaries are expected to protect and promote the national interests.

Main Functions

Political parties are expected to perform two main functions. They are the following:

1. Political parties have the basic task of propagating their ideals, policies and programmes.
2. The second main task is to contest and win elections.

The political parties normally follow four main ways for attaining success in their attempt at obtaining political power.

(*a*) *Firstly*, every political party strengthens its organisation by holding regular meeting, rallies, training camps, orientation courses for the workers, etc.

(*b*) *Secondly*, every political party tries its level best to increase its membership.

(*c*) *Thirdly*, political parties encourage the electorate and supporters through speeches, programmes and other means, and

(*d*) *Finally*, political parties also impart political education to the voters.

Bi-Party or Two-Party System

The two-party system refers to a political system in which two major parties are engaged in political rivalry to get into power. Even if a few more political parties exist in such a political system, they do not play any decisive role for they are politically insignificant. For example, there are more than two political parties in England, namely, (*i*) *Conservative Parry*, (*ii*) *Labour Party*, Fascist *Party, Communist Party, Liberal Party* and so on. Of these, the first two are the main parties and the remaining ones have only limited significance. Similarly, in America the two main political parties are: (*i*) the *Republican Party* and (*ii*) the *Democratic Party*.

Advantages of Two-Party System

1. Under two-party system the government becomes more stable.
2. Formation of the government, the cabinet, allotment of portfolios become less complicated
3. It ensures a strong government and continuity of policy.
4. Here the responsibility for the failure and shortcomings of the government can easily be located in this system.
5. This system makes the opposition party to indulge in constructive criticism of the government and its policies, programmes and performances.

Disadvantages of Two-Party System

1. In the two party system the choice before the voters become very much limited.
2. There is the possibility of the majority party to conduct itself in a dictatorial manner especially when it obtains a landslide victory in elections.
3. It is said that in a bi-party system the prestige of the legislature gets lowered particularly when the cabinet functions in a dictatorial manner.
4. The two party system cannot provide sufficient opportunity for all shades of opinion to be represented in the legislature.

Multiple Party System

Multiple Party System refers to a political system in which more than two political parties are functioning. *Example*, India, France, Itlay, West Germany, Sweden, Denmark and Switzerland have such a type of party system.

Advantages of Multiple Party System

1. It provides an opportunity for all shades of opinion to be reflected in the legislative house.
2. This system does not make the Parliament to become a puppet in the hands of the cabinet.
3. It provides a wider choice for the electorate and the nation is not divided into two camps.
4. It provides little or no opportunity for the cabinet to become dictatorial in its attitude and functioning.

Demerits of Multiple Party System

1. Since multiple party system leads to the establishment of coalition government; it remains very weak and ineffective.
2. It is said the position of the Prime Minister in a coalition government is very weak.
3. Since the governments are subject to frequent changes, it is difficult to maintain the continuity in policies. Further, indefiniteness characterises the governmental policies.
4. In this system, there is a lack of administrative efficiency, because the governments change very often.
5. This system encourages political defections and trading in votes. Hence it undermines the political morality.

Multiple Party System in the Indian Context

India has accepted the multiple party system. For about 40 years after Independence this system functioned successfully in India. Among all the parties, the Congress party held a dominant position and provided a stable government. The defects of this system came to limelight especially after 1990s. In a brief spell of 8 to 9 years India witnessed the rise and fall of about six Prime Ministers. At present (1998-99), there is the central rule of the coalition government headed by Shri Atal Bihari Vajpayee of the Bharatiya Janata Party. In the absence of a clear majority Vajpayee's party is forced to forge an alliance with many national as well as regional parties, very often doubts are raised about the stability of the present government.

Party system has undergone several changes in India. The domination of the Congress Party is more found now. No single party has been able to capture clear majority during the 11th and 12th parliamentary elections. Due to the practice of personality cult, patty splits and defections party polarisation has not taken place. Attempts at polarisation are very often spoiled by the personal ambitions and temperamental differences of the leaders.

VOTING BEHAVIOUR

Elections and voting are an indispensable pan of the democratic political system. One of the major tasks of the political parties is to contest elections. They select such candidates who have greater chances of winning. Candidates who have greater influence on voters and who have greater vote-catching capacity are an asset to any political party.

Voting refers to the political process of electing representatives to a legislative body. The elected representatives would play an important role in decision-making process.

Modern democracies have introduced universal adult franchise. The right to vote has been conferred on all the citizens without any kind of discrimination. In India also all the citizens irrespec- tive of their difference of colour, class, caste, creed, religion, region, race or sex are given the right to vote. The right to vote is a fundamental right guaranteed by the constitutional law of the country. In India, every man or woman of 18 years of age is entitled to enrol himself or herself as a voter and to vote in the public elections.

Voting Behaviour: Some Observations

Voting behaviour of the people is not uniform. It differs from place to place, culture to culture and time to time. It is very difficult to make generalisations about the way in which people vote in the elections.

The social scientific analysis of voting behaviour in Britain and America has been studied by various scholars. The studies revealed some of the facts about the voting behaviour of the people.

1. The voting behaviour in Britain and America, has since the 1950s, rested heavily on what is known as "*the party identification model.*" People tended to vote parties with which they had a long-term association and identification.
2. After the Second World War, for about 30 years in the Western nations the main influence on voting appears to have been the *family*. People tended to vote like their parents due to the impact of "*political socialisation in the home.*"
3. The *factor of social class* was associated with voting. For example, in Britain, in the post-war period about 2/3 of the manual working class voted for the Labour Party and 4/5 of the non-manual middle class voted for the Conservative Party.
4. The other important influence on the voting behaviour has been the "*community*". For example, the middle-class voters living in predominantly working class communities ar more likely to vote Labour Party than if they lived in a middle-class area. In the same way, working class voters living in middle-class areas show some tendency to vote the Conservative Party.

Studies have also revealed that since the mid l970s voting has radically changed. Factors such as - *mass media, the type of electioneering campaign, party performance, efficiency of the candidates*, etc. - also have their own impact on the voting behaviour of the people.

Voting Behaviour in the Indian Context

In India also the voting behaviour of the people has undergone a tremendous change. It is observed: "*Given the level of literacy in India, political consciousness is remarkably high. Since independence, levels of political awareness and participation have risen among all segments of the population...*" Political awareness is increasing even among the rural poor and illiterate populations. There is an increase in the identification with political parties and leaders. Since the voting age is reduced to 18 years, even the college-going students get an opportunity to exercise their vote. With each election, millions of new voters enter the political arena as active participants.

Voting behaviour is influenced in the Indian context by various factors such as *religion, caste, community, language, class, money, personal charisma of the leaders* and also by certain unforeseen or accidental factors.

Though majority of Indian voters are found to be illiterate and ignorant, they are politically more alert than the educated persons. They take an active role in voting. They have shown on some occasions appreciable political maturity in unseating some of the inefficient state governments. It is because of their faith in the democratic processes, interest in elections and active participation in voting, India continues to be the largest democracy in the world with 50 years of history.

PRESSURE GROUPS

Groups also play a direct role in political life. People organise social movements, interest groups, and pressure groups in order to influence the governments. Ethnic groups, racial groups, religious and linguistic minority groups have also acted collectively to influence governmental decisions.

Thus, a pressure group refers to an interest group which tries to safeguard and promote the interests of its members. It is not a political group seeking to capture political power, though it may have a political character of its own. *A pressure group can be understood as an association of persons with a common economic interest who try to influence government judicial decisions. For example*, The Trade Unions, Dalit Sangharsha Samithis, Kissan Sabhas, Mahila Samajs, Minority Groups, etc. function as pressure groups.

These "pressure groups", which are also known as '*interest groups*', pursue their political goals through **lobbying** - "*the process by which individuals and groups communicate with public officials in order to influence decisions of government. They also distribute presuasive literature and launch public campaigns to build grass root support for their political objectives*."

The pressure groups attempt to force their will on a resistant public. **In the view of functionalists**, such groups play a constructive role in decision-making. They prepare the ground for The orderly political participation. They also provide legislators with a useful flow of information. They also provide legislators with a useful flow of information.

Conflict theorists, on the other hand, argue that although a few organisations work on behalf of the poor and disadvantaged, most of the pressure groups represent the vested interests of the business leaders, the lobbies of multinational companies, rich professionals and disgruntled political leaders. The conflict theorists further assert that these powerful lobbies discourage political participation by the individual citizens. The enormous lobbying work of the pressure group raises serious questions about who actually rules a democratic nation.

The pressure groups play a greater role in a democracy than in a totalitarian state. The party in power in a totalitarian state does not recognize the existence of such pressure groups and does not tolerate them also.

In a democratic system, the role of the pressure groups becomes conspicuous especially at the time of elections. The different levels of electoral process such as filing of nomination or fielding of the candidates, canvassing and campaigning, financing the parties, etc. These groups bring heavy pressures to win favours to their side. In spite of their limitations and defects, they have become an essential pan of the modern democratic process

THE TOTALITARIAN SYSTEM

The totalitarian system is one of the rivals of the democratic system. It is a system in which the total power is vested in one individual or party. It is popularly known as *dictatorship*. It is opposite to democracy. While democracy upholds liberty, dictatorship suppresses it. As *F. Neumann* says: "*By dictatorship we understand the rule of a person or a group of persons who arrogate to themselves and monopolise power in the state, exercising it without restraint.*" A dictator dictates terms, *i.e.*, he orders and rules as he pleases. He passes laws to strengthen his own hands. There are no restraints on his own hands. There are no restraints on his authority. He ruthlessly suppresses opposition. If democracy is based on consent, dictatorship is based on *force*.

The Ways of Dictatorship or Totalitarianism

Dictatorship makes its sheer will the sole justification of its authority. Its own being is the only answer it permits. It ignores community. It has no abiding rules, no fundamental laws. Its own law is always that of the hour. There is no law or basis of law beneath it. No law has any higher status than his mere decree. There is no social ground on which his pronouncement of justice rests. *Dictatorship comes into being when the social order is shaken or broken, in the time of crisis when men for sake their traditions*. It comes in the time of desperate conflict when men are willing to sacrifice if only the strong man restores to them assurance and order. In such times they abandon the accepted standards of legality. The anti-thesis between dictatorship and legality has been recognised since the days of the Greek city-states.

The coming of dictatorship is usually *abrupt*. It represents a sharp break from tradition. A crisis occurs. The old legality cannot be restored and the people are unready for the alternative of democracy. Because, it requires a process of maturation. The contentions between the classes or between ethic, religious, or other groups may be too irreconcilable for orderly settlement, Such a situation sows the seeds of dictatorship. During one crisis in England, when a severe break with the tradition occurred, there appeared its only dictator, *Oliver Cromwell*. In France, during the historic Revolution there came the dictatorship of Robespiere and soon after the Revolution, of *Napoleon Bonaparte*. Nepoleon, of course, constitutionalised his dictatorial power.

Every dictatorship maintains power by unconstitutional means. It elevates the executive above the legislative, it makes its decree, its law; it insists on political orthodoxy, it suppresses unfavourable opinions. It exalts the state. It builds its own organisations which markedly differ from those of the community associations. It can invent no constitutional device for succession to dictatorial power.

Types of Dictatorship

Modern dictatorship can be classified into three main types: (*i*) *The Fascist and the Nazi Dictatorship*, *e.g.*, Italy and Germany–before World War II, (*ii*) *Communist Dictatorship e.g., Soviet Russia* and *China*, and (*iii*) *Military Dictatorship*, *e.g.*, Indonesia, Pakistan, Egypt, Bangladesh, Iran, Iraq. Between 1919–1939 dictatorship rose in Italy, Germany, Spain, Turkey, Soviet Russia and other countries. After the end of World War II, it rose in China, Indonesia, Pakistan, Burma, Sudan, Egypt, Iraq and other countries.

ESSENTIAL FEATURES OF MODERN DICTATORSHIP OR TOTALITARIANISM

1. ***Totalitarian power:*** In a totalitarian system the government assumes complete power and covers all aspects of the individual's life. The state is glorified. Mussolini of Italy said: "All within the state, none outside the state, and none against the state".
2. ***One man rule:*** One man or a minority group assumes supreme authority. This person or group is not responsible "*to the people over whom control is exercised*".
3. ***One party rule:*** The party to which the dictator belongs exercises ruthless control over the state. Opposition is simply crushed. In Russia, for example, there is only one party–The Communist Party.
4. ***No civil, political and economic liberty:*** The totalitarian denies individual liberty, it abridges or abrogates fundamental rights. Virtually, people become the slaves of the state. Individual becomes the means and the state, the end.
5. ***Based on fear and force:*** Since the dictator is always doubtful about his position, he adopts violent and coercive methods to suppress opposition. He deals with the opposition with an iron hand.
6. ***Militant nationalism:*** The totalitarianism often stands for the *purity* of race, language, literature and culture. It often breeds militant or aggressive nationalism.
7. ***Absence of free and independent press:*** In a totalitarian system free expression of public opinion is crushed. It controls in countless ways the mass media of propaganda, including the radio and the Press. The Press cannot be free, frank, and independent.
8. ***No distinction between the state and government:*** In a totalitarian system the state and government are not distinguished. The dictator himself represents both. He is all in all, and the state is omnipresent and omnipotent. The state is deified. An individual must be ready to sacrifice himself for the sake of the state. *Hitler* said the functions of the citizens were, *duty, discipline and sacrifice*.
9. ***Hostile to internationalism:*** Dictators are opposed to internationalism. They follow the policy of personal glorification.

DISTINCTION BETWEEN DEMOCRACY AND TOTALITARIANISM

	Democracy	*Totalitarianism*
1.	Democracy gives importance to the indi- vidual. *Individual* is an end and the state is a means.	Totalitarianism glorifies the state. *The state is the end* and the individual is means.
2.	Power is *decentralised* and distributed.	Power is *centralised* and monopolised.
3.	Distinguishes between society and the state and the government.	No clear distinction between the state and society and government.

(*Contd.*)

	Democracy	Totalitarianism
4.	It ensures *equality and liberty and stresses* duty.	Liberty and equality *are not* guaranteed. Duty, discipline and sacrifice are emphasised.
5.	Stands for peace at home and abroad. It believes in friendly relations between men and nations.	Glorifies war. War is openly preached. Hitler said, "In Internal warfare mankind has become great; in eternal peace it will be ruined". Peace is regarded "the humanitarian weakness of democracy".
6.	Assures fundamental rights: The right to speak, associate, own property, marry, worship etc.	Fundamental rights are abridged or abolished. *Mussolini* said: "People do not want liberty but they want law and order." He also said: "Liberty is a dead carcass. I kick it".
7.	Makes provisions for *plurality* of political parties.	Believes in a *single* party. All the other political organisations are banned.
8.	It is based on the *principle of reason.*	It is based on the *unquestioned obedience* to the law of the state.
9.	Believes in *self-government*. Hence the slogan; "good government is no substitute for self–government".	Never believes in self-government. It is the *antithesis of self-government.*
10.	Believes in tolerance and gives opportunities to *all.*	Totalitarianism is *opposed* to such things.
11.	Upholds the intrinsic worth of dignity and man. Encourages the development of personality.	Suppresses the development of personality. Scant respect is shown to the intrinsic worth of man. Individuality is snubbed.
12.	It is a *costly* government and administration is more expensive.	Expenses of administration are *very much limited.*
13.	The government is *complex* and *complicated.*	The government is known for its *simplicity.*
14.	Makes provision for an orderly change in government and avoids revolutions and bloodshed.	Revolutions and bloodshed are common events in changing the governments.
15.	It is comparatively *slow* in arriving at decisions. It finds it difficult to face emergencies.	Decisions are arrived at *quickly*. It can meet the emergencies quickly and effectively.
16.	It is a government *responsible* to the governed.	It is a government responsible to *none* except the dictator.
17.	It is away of life and a *spirit of mind*, more than being a form of government.	It is only *a form of government* and can never be a way of life.
18.	Aims at the welfare *of all.*	Aims at the welfare *of a few* in the name of all.

MERITS AND DEMERITS OF DEMOCRACY

	Merits or Advantages of Democracy	Demerits or Disadvantages of Democracy
1.	Democracy gives importance to human liberty and equality. It protects the fundamental rights of the people and safeguards their life. Democracy treats all the citizens as equal before the law.	Though democracy assures equality to all, it ignores the natural and inborn inequalities. Providing equal opportunities to unequal people can only perpetuate inequalities.
2.	Democratic government is a responsible government. The party which is in power has the fear of the opposition parties and hence is very careful in its functioning.	There is no guarantee that a democratic government works efficiently. The possibility of a democratic government being dominated by unscrupulous and dishonest legislators cannot be ruled out.
3.	Here, due weightage is given to the opinions and valuable suggestions of intellectuals, statesmen, scholars, etc.	Democracy gives more importance to quantity rather than to the quality. Sometimes the ruling party rejects the valuable suggestions of the opposition by its brute majority.
4.	The Democratic government gives political education to the people through the political parties. The political parties hence play a vital role in democracy.	The political parties instead of serving the people become tyrannical in the nature. They may give wrong versions of the issues and confuse and mislead the people. They may politicalise even the non-political issues.

(*Contd.*)

	Merits or Advantages of Democracy	Demerits or Disadvantages of Democracy
5.	Democracy provides for peaceful change. Elections are held periodically and people can vote to power the party which they like. Government can be changed through the constitutional methods in a peaceful manner. It averts bloodshed, wars and revolutions.	Democracy is criticised as a coslty govern-ment. It results in high expenses and wastes in the form of salaries and allowances to the legislators and ministers and also in the form of elections.
6.	Democracy is a government by consent and criti-cism, debates and discussions. Hence policies and programmes are undertaken only after obtaining the consent and cooperation of the people or their repre-sentatives.	Democracy is a slow and a time-consuming process. Hence it becomes difficult for the government to deal effectively with emergencies and crises. Democracy nece-ssarily entails delay.
7.	Democracy is not based on force or violence, it believes in peaceful methods, in non-violence, co-operation and persuasion.	Democracy is often denounced as inefficient and corrupt. Money plays a vital role here. In a democratic nation like India votes are purchased and legislators bribed,
8.	In democracy, people are supreme and the rulers are only their elected represen- tatives. Hence the rulers are responsible and answerable to the governed.	Democracy gives scope for politicians to become prosper-ous. As *Lord Bryce* has pointed out, it contributes to "the tendency to make politics a gainful profession".
9.	Democracy requires the active participation of the peo-ple. Hence, people will be alert regarding the political actions of their rulers.	Democracy is a rule by the majority. With a brute majority in the Parliament it may ignore and even suppress the interests of the minority.
10.	Democracy strengthens nationalism and fosters pat-riotism.	Democracy indicates the existence of party system. Parties may often mislead and confuse the people.

MERITS AND DEMERITS OF DICTATORSHIP OR TOTALITARIANISM

	Merits or Advantages of Dictatorship	Demerits or Disadvantages of Dictatorship
1.	Dictatorships are often claimed as regimes of "strong men who get things done". They are regarded as more efficient and strong.	The greatest demerit of dictatorship is that it does not grant freedom and fundamental rights to the people.
2.	The dictatorship brings unity. One man rule or one party rule does not give room for divergent views. On the other hand it wields people together as one unit.	Dictatorship is based on force and fear. Dictators create terror and horror in the minds of the people. Hitler and Mussolini, for example, terrorised people into submission.
3.	Dictatorship is known for its simplicity. Decisions are taken promptly and immediately and unnecessary delay is avoided.	Dictatorship makes the people its slaves. It buries their sense of self-prestige and self respect.
4.	Dictatorship is economical also. It avoids wastes and unnecessary expenses.	A government which is based on force cannot last long. Hence, dictatorship may not last for a long time.
5.	Dictatorship as a form of government is stable also. Since it suppresses all opposition it is easy for the government to function without disturbances.	The dictatorial government suppresses the freedom of the people. This may damage the creativity and adventurous spirit of the people.
6.	Dictatorship is better suited to meet emer-gencies. It can effectively and efficiently meet with and face any crisis or challenge.	Dictatorship glorifies the state and goes to the extent of sacrificing the interests of the individual in the name of the state.
7.	A dictatorial government can achieve progress in a short period. Progress, here means the material pro-gress. Communist China and Russia, for example, have achieved progress in a relatively short period.	Dictatorship does not prescribe peaceful means of changing the government. In it, ambitious men and groups will be preparing grounds to seize the reins of administration into their hands by violent methods.

(*Contd.*)

	Merits or Advantages of Dictatorship	Demerits or Disadvantages of Dictatorship
8.	A dictatorial government gives importance to army. Hence it builds up military strength to meet any challenge or threat from outside.	Dictatorship is opposed to world peace, because, dictators believe that wars are necessary for the nations. It builds its military strength more for waging wars than for self-reliance.
9.	Dictatorship can effectively put an end to corruption, tax evasion, work avoidance, nepotism and other evil practices.	Dictatorship strikes at the very root of the self-reliance of the people. It makes the people to become dependants on the state.
10.	Dictatorship is well suited to bring about strict discipline in the country. Disobedients, indisciplined and unscnipulous individuals are dealt with by iron hand.	Finally, by imposing unwanted and unwarranted discipline at the gun point, dictatorship causes incalculable damage to growth of personality of its own subjects.

THE WELFARE STATE

There is a growing tendency on the part of the modem states to claim themselves to be 'welfare states'. Writers and thinkers differ in their opinions regarding the definition and functions of the welfare state. Still, a welfare state is commonly understood as *an agency of social service than as an instrument of power*.

Definition of Welfare State

1. *D.L. Hobman* in his *The Welfare State*, defines welfare state as "a compromise between the two extremes of communism on the one hand and unbridled individualism on the other".
2. *Herbert H. Lehman opines that* "the welfare state is simply a state in which people are free to develop their individual capacities, to receive just awards for their talents, and to engage in the pursuit of happiness, unburdened by fear of actual hunger, actual homelessness or oppression by reason of race, creed or colour."
3. *G. D. H. Cole* says, "The welfare state is a society in which an assured minimum standard of living and opportunity becomes the possession of every citizen."
4. *Arthur Schlesinger* says, "The welfare state is a system where in government agrees to underwrite certain levels of employment, income, education, medical aid, social security, and housing for all its citizens."

It is clear from the definitions cited above that *the welfare state is one, which is wedded to the principle of promoting the general happiness and welfare of all the people*. As *P. Gisbert* says, the welfare state is one which takes upon itself the responsibility "to provide social services for the nation to bring under public ownership important industries or enterprises placing certain controls on private enterprise, and to organise democratic planning on a national scale." The objective of the welfare state lies mostly in the economic field. It consists in the readjustment of incomes to provide for the less privileged citizen. The state reduces inequalities of income through taxation and strives to increase national production.

Functions of the Welfare State

The concept of the *Welfare State* is of tremendous significance all over the world. Irrespective of the type of the government, whether democratic or totalitarian, communist or socialist, monarchic or oligarchic, all the modem states call themselves *welfare states*. The so-called modem welfare states perform certain functions to promote the well-being of the people. The type of their welfare activities and the manner in which they under take them depend upon the nature of their political systems; whether democratic or totalitarian. However, the main functions which a welfare state normally performs may be explained here.

1. ***Maintenance of peace and order:*** The welfare state ensures internal peace and order and provides security to its citizens. It efficiently guards its territory against external aggressions or threats. It maintains law and order and establishes political stability. This reduces constant tension and anxiety for its people.
2. ***Protects people's rights and provides justice:*** The welfare state assures for its people the inalienable fundamental rights. It assures right to *life, liberty, and pursuit of happiness*, equality, property, freedom of thought and expression. It provides justice to all irrespective of class, colour, creed, caste, religion or region.

3. ***Conservation of natural resources:*** In the general interest of the community the welfare state tries to conserve its natural resources *against the competitive private interests*. It prevents the wasteful consumption of the community's resources, its forests, fisheries, wild life, minerals, art treasures, etc.
4. ***Provision of education:*** The welfare state gives high priority for education. It creates opportunities for the individuals to develop their personality. It encourages more the weaker sections of the society to come up educationally and economically. Some states like India have introduced free but compulsory education at primary and secondary levels. The welfare state on its own provides for primary and secondary schools, colleges, universities, research centres, libraries, art classes, technical schools and institutes, medical and agricultural institutes, etc.
5. ***Arrangement of public utility Services:*** The modern welfare states construct roads, railways and provide for irrigation, water-supply and electric works. It provides for post and telegraph, radio, television, telephone and other services. It makes arrangement for transport such as buses, railways, aeroplanes and ships.
6. ***Encouragement of trade, industry, commerce and agriculture:*** The welfare state on its own establishes some big industries to promote industrial advancement and also to avoid exploitation. Iron and steel, locomotives, aircraft and other heavy industries, big dams, multi-purpose projects, major transport and communication lines, etc., are often controlled by the states. Certain industries are nationalised in the interests of the people. Still the welfare state gives enough scope for the private parties and individuals to establish factories and start business to promote industrial growth. The state also encourages cottage or household industries and agriculture.
7. ***Organisation of labour:*** The welfare state gives special attention to needs of the working class. It makes appropriate labour legislations and prevents their exploitation. It promotes their welfare in various ways. It gives them freedom to organise labour unions to protect their rights. It tries to better the living conditions of the people also.
8. ***Protection of old, poor and the handicapped:*** The modern welfare states have taken it for granted as their main canon to protect the interests of the old, poor, and the invalid. The old and the retired people are given pension, the unemployed and the handicapped are given maintenance allowance. Various social security measures are undertaken in order to give the needed protection to all the needy people of the state.
9. ***Maintenance of public health:*** The welfare state provides many preventive and curative medical facilities to safeguard the public health. It makes provision for sanitation, hospitals, free medicine, vaccination and essential energising foods for the poor and so on. It arranges to control deadly diseases like malaria, cholera, small pox, plague, T.B., venereal diseases, skin-diseases, leprosy, etc. It runs medical colleges, research centres, training schools for nurses, etc.
10. ***Arrangement of recreation:*** The state provides for various means of recreation to its citizens, like films, drama, music, exhibitions, fairs, etc. It also establishes public parks, museums, libraries, playgrounds, conducts competitions to encourage merit, gives awards to the talented persons.
11. ***Maintains social harmony:*** The welfare state lays down laws against evil and harmful customs and practices. By various means it tries to bring people with different socio-religious background nearer. It strives to promote social harmony by creating better understanding among people.
12. ***Prevents disorganisation:*** The welfare state also tries to prevent or check the process of socio-economic disorganisation. By making use of various means it tries to solve such socio-economic problems like crime, juvenile delinquency, prostitution, untouchability, population problem, poverty, beggary and so on. The efficiency of a welfare state can be measured by its successful attempts in removing these problems.

Thus, it is clear now that the function of the welfare state is not merely administration, but an integral welfare and development of its subjects. In fact, there is no limit to what the welfare state can do for the service of the community. The popular statement *state help kills self-help* is not always true. Still. *the Welfare State is not all in all*. The state *cannot interfere* in all kinds of human activities in the name of welfare. It cannot prescribe morality, cannot dictate opinion, cannot proclaim new customs and fashions, cannot create a new culture and also cannot advocate new religious doctrines of universal application. The state should know its limitations. It should not venture to do a task for which it is unqualified. Too much interference of the state in the life of the people would destroy the very spirit of freedom. It was the veteran Indian Sarvodaya leader *Late Sri Jayaprakash Narayan*, who said in unmistakable terms that "in the present world the state, not only in its totalitarian form but also in its welfare variety, is assuming larger and larger power and responsibility. The welfare state in the name of welfare threatens as much to enslave man to the state as the totalitarian. The people must cry halt to this creeping paralysis..."

REVIEW QUESTIONS

1. Write a note on the ubiquity of politics.
2. Classify political systems. Discuss the relationship between democracy and totalitarianism.
3. Define democracy. Write its basic principles essential conditions and forms.
4. What are the merits and demerits of democracy?
5. What are political parties? Discuss the characteristic features, functions, advantages and disadvantages of political parties.
6. Write a detailed note on the voting behaviour.
7. Write an essay on the totalitarian system.
8. What is dictatorship? Discuss its types.
9. Write the essential features of modern dictatorship.
10. Differentiate between democracy and totalitarianism.
11. What do you mean by the welfare state? Write its functions.
12. Write short notes on the following:
    (a) Democracy as a political system
    (b) Pressure groups
    (c) Welfare state

⌘⌘⌘⌘⌘⌘⌘⌘⌘⌘⌘

34

RELIGION—MORALITY—MAGIC

CHAPTER OUTLINE

- Man is a Spiritual Being
- Definition of Religion
- Basic Components of Religion
- Religion as a System of Belief and Ritual
- The Sacred and the Profane
- Theories of Origin of Religion: Fetishism — Animism—Totemism — The Fear Theory — The Functional Theory — The Theory of the Aleatory Element
- Structural Aspects of Religion
- Religious Roles
- Functions of Religion
- Dysfunctions of Religion
- Morality: Meaning of Morality
- Differences Between Religion and Morality
- Religion and Science
- Recent Trends in Religion
- Magic: Definition — Types: White and Black Magic
- Differences Between Religion and Magic
- Magic and Science
- Secularisation

MAN IS A SPIRITUAL BEING

Man, the social animal, is also a religious or spiritual being. Religion is a major concern of man. It is one of the earliest and the deepest interests of the human beings. Religion is universal, permanent, pervasive and perennial interests of man. Man not only, has biological, economic and social needs, but also, what is known as a religious need. He has *religious quest* which makes him to become restless even beyond the satisfaction of his basic physical needs. Hence the Biblical saying, *Man cannot live by bread alone*. It is also said that man from the earliest times has been *incurably religious*.

Religion is not a phenomenon of recent emergence. Its beginning is unknown. It is dateless. Some artifacts and evidences of the burial practices of Neanderthal man indicate that human being was a religious creature long before history began. The institution of religion is *universal*. It is found in all the societies, past and present. Religious beliefs and practices are, however, far from being uniform. Laws, customs, conventions and fashions, etc., are not the only means of social control. Overriding them all, are *religion* and *morality* which formulate and shape all of them. They are not only the most influential forces of social control, but also *the most effective guides of human behaviour*. The social life of man in addition to its economic, political, philosophical, scientific and other aspects, has also the *religious* aspect. Not only religion has been in existence from the beginning but also it has been exerting a tremendous influence upon other institutions. Religious dogmas have influenced and conditioned economic endeavours, political movements, property dealings, educational tasks, ideological fervours, scientific inventions and artistic developments. Religion, which is based on the cultural needs of men, has added new dimension to human life and human development.

Religion revolves round man's faith in the supernatural forces. Religion is a concrete experience which is associated with emotions, especially with fear, awe, or reverence. Many societies have a wide range of institutions connected with religion and a body of special officials, with forms of worship, ceremonies, sacred objects, tithes, pilgrimages, and the like.

In modern civilised societies, religious leaders have developed elaborate theories or theologies to explain man's place in the universe. Religion is closely associated with morality and has elaborate rules of conduct. Further, the World religions–Hinduism, Buddhism, Confucianism, Judaism, Christianity, and Islam–are really centres of elaborate cultural systems that have dominated 'whole' societies for centuries.

DEFINITIONS OF RELIGION

Though religion is a universal phenomenon it is understood differently by different people. On religion, opinions differ from the great religious leader down to an ordinary man. There is no consensus about the nature of religion. Sociologists are yet to find a satisfactory explanation of religion. Writers have defined religion in various ways. A few definitions may be mentioned here.

1. *Durkheim* in his book *The Elementary Forms of the Religious Life* defines religion as a "unified system of beliefs and practices relative to sacred things, that is to say, things set apart and forbidden."
2. *James G. Frazer*, in his *The Golden Bough* considered religion a belief in "powers superior to man which are believed to direct and control the course of nature and of human life."
3. *Edward Sapir*, an American anthropologist, says that "the essence of religion consists in man's never-ceasing attempt to discover a road to spiritual serenity across the perplexities and dangers of daily life".
4. *MacIver* and *Page* have defined, "*Religion as we understand the term, implies a relationship not merely between man and man but also between man and some higher power*."
5. According to Ogburn, "*Religion is an attitude towards superhuman powers*."
6. *Max Muller* defines religion as "a mental faculty or disposition which enables man to appre- hend the infinite".
7. *Thomas F. O'Dea*, a functional theorist, defines religion as "the manipulation of non-empirical or supra-empirical means for non-empirical or supra-empirical ends". He further adds, "Religion offers what is felt to be a way of entering into a relationship with the supra-empirical aspects of reality, be they conceived as God, gods, or otherwise".

BASIC COMPONENTS OF RELIGION

1. ***Belief in supernatural forces:*** Religion is a matter of belief. It is a belief in supernatural or superhuman forces. Some people believe in several kinds of forces and accordingly worship them all. They are called polytheists. Some others believe in only one force, or the God or the Almighty. He is formless and shapeless. They consider Him omnipresent, omniscient and omnipotent. They worship Him in different ways. They are called *monotheists*.
2. ***Man's adjustment with the supernatural forces:*** Man believes that he is at the mercy of the supernatural forces. He expresses his subordination to them by means of prayers, hymns, and other acts. Worship is the essence of religion. Man believes that his disrespect to and negligence of them would bring him disaster. He is, hence, engaged in endless endeavour to adjust himself with the divinity or the supernatural. His adjustment is onesided.
3. ***Acts, defined as righteous and sinful or sacred and the profane:*** Religion considers some acts as righteous and sacred and encourages such acts. It regards some other acts as sinful and profane and denounces such acts. Behaving in accordance with the religious code or standards is righteous; going against them is sinful. The good or the righteous acts are believed to bring man good results, while the sinful acts result in disaster. As *Durkheim* says, a distinction between the sacred and the profane is made in all the societies. The conceptions of heaven and hell are woven around the righteous and the sinful acts.
4. ***Some methods of salvation:*** Every religion has its own explanation regarding *salvation*. It is regarded as ultimate aim of a devotee. The Buddhists called it *Nirvana*, a process of becoming one with the God. The Hindus termed *Mukti* or *Moksha*–release from the chain of birth and death. They have prescribed four. paths for its attainment–the Yoga Marga, the Jnana Marga, the Bhakti Marga and the Karma Marga.

RELIGION AS A SYSTEM OF BELIEF AND RITUAL

Religion is a matter of belief. It is nothing but man's belief in supernatural or superhuman forces. As *Durkheim* has said the concepts of *sacred* or holy and *profane* or unholy are central to religion. What makes a thing holy or unholy is our attitude, an aspect of our mind. It is a quality which we attribute to the thing. It is not inherent in the thing. It is an *attitude* packed with emotion and *sentiment* that makes us feel that *certain things are above and apart from the ordinary matters of everyday life*. In the light of this subjective attitude two different aspects of the *holy* can be recognised. They are: *belief* and *ritual*.

Religion as a System of Belief

All religious organisations depend upon beliefs, knowledge, and training to exercise influence upon their members. Religious belief is the cognitive aspect of religion. It tries to explain the nature and origin of sacred things. It assumes that the sacred things do exist. It tells us what this world is like, what kind of creatures inhabit it, and what their past history and present interests are. It gives us information about the universe, creation, life and death, future of the world and such other deep but subtle matters. This is the information that belief gives about the superempirical world. It also tells us how the world is related to the one we actually live in. It tells us what the nature of sacred objects is and how these objects relate to the superempirical world. This is the knowledge that belief gives us about the so called sacred objects and their links with the superempirical world. But in both the cases belief rests upon an attitude, not upon observation. "*It is belief based on faith rather than upon evidence; it is in Biblical language the substance of things hoped for, the evidence of things not seen*." The sacred character is not observable to the sense. Hence, even a visible and touchable sacred object would be just an ordinary object if it were not for the belief. For example, there is nothing to distinguish a sacred cow from any other animal except the faith of the Hindus who regard the cow as sacred.

Religion as a System of Ritual

Religious ritual is the practical side of religion. As *M. Douglas in his Purity and Danger, 1966, says ritual refers to symbolic actions concerning the sacred. Kingsley Davis says that ritual is behaviour with reference to superempirical entities and sacred objects*. Like the belief itself, it has a sacred character. "It expresses in internal attitude symbolic of the unseen powers. "It can include any kind of behaviour known, such as the wearing of special clothing, the recitation of hymns or special formulas, and the immersion in certain rivers. It can also include singing, dancing, weeping, bowing, prostrating, crawling, feasting, reading, etc. The religious character of the behaviour does not come from the behaviour itself, but from the attitude taken towards it. The same actions, the same motions or the same behaviour may be holy in one context but ordinary or unholy in another.

Ritual is a means to remind the individual of the holy world. It strengthens and supports his faith in this world. It helps him to give expression to his religious sentiments and emotions. This brings him emotional ecstasy. Ritual when performed together (as when the Muslims do Namaz together in a Mosque and Christians their Prayers in a Church, and Hindus their Bhajanas in a Temple) by several individuals, becomes effective as a unifying factor. This collective aspect of religion was very much stressed by *Durkheim*. He said that "The function of religious rituals is to affirm the moral superiority of the society over its individual members and thus to *maintain the solidarity of the society*". "The god of the clan can be nothing but the clan itself."

Religion as a social system can be understood only if both belief and ritual are understood. The early thinkers gave more importance to the intellectual aspects of religion and ignored the ritual aspect. They were more busy in discussing whether or not religious beliefs are true; if not true, how they came to be established. This question is only secondary for us. We are more interested in the social function of religious beliefs and rituals. Religious beliefs may not be scientific even. Their non-scientific character by no means lessens their social relevance and human significance.

THE SACRED AND THE PROFANE

The concepts of '*sacred and profane*' are central to Durkheim's theory of religion. According to him, all aspects of human experience can be divided into two radically and diametrically opposed categories: the *sacred* and the *profane*.

What is the Nature of the Sacred?

Durkheim says that the sacred is ideal and transcends 'everyday existence; it is extra-ordinary, potentially dangerous, awe-inspiring, fear-inducing. The sacred, for Durkheim, refers to things set apart by man, including religious beliefs, rites, duties, or anything socially defined as requiring special religious treatment. The sacred has extra-ordinary, supernatural, and often dangerous qualities and can usually be approached only through some form of ritual, such as prayer, incantation, or ceremonial cleansing. Almost anything can be sacred: a god, a rock, a cross, the moon, the earth, a king, a tree, an animal or bird, or a symbol, such as swastik. These are sacred only because some community has marked them as sacred. Once established as 'sacred', however, they become symbols of religious beliefs, sentiments and practices.

What is the Profane?

The profane is mundane, that is, anything ordinary. It is a part of the ordinary realm rather than the supernatural world. The profane or ordinary or '*unholy*' embraces "*those ideas, persons, practices, and things that are regarded with an everday attitude of commonness, utility and familiarity*". It is that which is not supposed to come into contact with or take precedence over the sacred. The 'unholy' or the 'profane' is also believed to contaminate the 'holy' or 'sacred'. "It is the denial or subordination of the holy in some way. The attitudes and behaviour toward it are charged with negative emotions and hedged about by strong taboos"—(*Kingsley Davis*.) A rock, the moon, a king, a tree or a symbol may also be considered profane. It means something becomes sacred or profane only when it is *socially defined* as such by a community of believers.

The sacred and the profane are closely related because of the highly emotional attitude towards them. The distinction between the two is not very much clear, but ambiguous. As *Durkheim* has pointed out, "The circle of sacred objects cannot be determined, then, once and for all. Its extent varies indefinitely according to different religions". The significance of the sacred lies in the fact of its distinction from the profane: "The sacred thing is par excellence that which profane should not touch and cannot touch with impurity". Man always draws this distinction of the two orders in different times and places. Participation in the sacred order, for example, in rituals and ceremonies, gives a special social prestige, which actually reveals one of the social functions of religion. "Mecha- nisms are established by all religions for keeping these two worlds (sacred and profane) from communication with one another. One result of this segregation is that the sacred cannot be questioned or challenged by the profane. The sacred can remain fixed or stable to the degree that it succeeds in insulating itself from the secular or profane. Breaches of this segregation are treated as sacriligious or heretical and may be dealt with by a wide range of sanctions"–*Bernard S. Philips* writes in his book, '*Sociology—Social Structure and Change*'.

Nature and Qualities of the Sacred

Metta Spencer and *Alex Inkeles* have enlisted seven qualities of the sacred as described by Durkheim. They are:

1. The sacred is recognised as a power or force,
2. It is characterised by ambiguity in that, it is both physical and moral, human and cosmic, positive and negative, attractive and repugnant, helpful and dangerous to men,
3. It is non-utilitarian,
4. It is non-empirical
5. It does not involve knowledge of any rational or scientific character,
6. It strengthens and supports worshippers, and
7. It makes moral demand on the believer and worshipper.

The sacred quality is not intrinsic to objects but is conferred on them by religious thought and feeling. "The sacred does not help one to manipulate natural forces and is useless in practical sense. It is not even an experience based on knowledge and the senses, but involves a definite break with the everyday world".

God as Sacred

The sacred may be a supernatural being, that is, god. Those who believe in one god are *monotheists*. More than 985 million Christians, 14.5 million Jews and 471 million Muslims are monotheists. Those who worship more than one god are *polytheists*, say, the Hindus, whose number exceeds 472 millions.

Ghost as Sacred

Gods are not alone among the sacred. Many worship the sacred ghost or ancestor spirit. Such spirits are also believed to possess superhuman qualities. But they are of human origin rather than of divine. Shintoism, for example, with its more than 60 million followers (mostly found in Japan) is based on reverence towards family ancestors.

Moral or Philosophical Principle as Sacred

A moral or philosophical principle can also be sacred. For example, the Asian religions such as Buddhism, Confucianism, and Taoism-all stress the importance of certain ethical and spiritual ideals. Buddhism is more concerned with Buddha's message of "*four noble truths*" than with him as the god. Similarly, more importance is laid on the '*Eight-fold path*' to attain '*nirvana*' a state of spiritual detachment.

Totem as the Sacred

Totems are another example of Durkheim's "*sacred things*". The totemic object–an animal or plant–is worshipped by primitive people all over the world. The totem is a symbol, a treasury of deep group-based sentiments and feelings. It is worshipped as a god or as an ancestor, or both, and it generally possesses some special quality or significance for the religious community.

Supernatural Force as Sacred

A supernatural force is still another example of a sacred thing although it has no shape of its own. *Example*: On certain islands of Oceania, a warrior successful in battle while using a particular spear will attribute his victory to '*mana*'–a supernatural force that entered his spear. The supernatural force, on the whole, may be good or bad.

Thus, whether be it a force, or a god, a ghost, a moral principle, or a totemic object–all are elements of Durkheim's definition of religion. All are forms of the sacred and all bear witness to the existence of religious behaviour.

"*To what do the sacred symbols of religious belief and practice refer*?" —Durkheim asks. Durkheim is of the opinion that "they cannot refer to the external environment or to individual human nature but only to the moral reality of society. The source and object of religion are the collective life; the sacred is at bottom society personified" — *Dr. Timasheff*

Thus, according to Durkheim, man's attitudes towards God and society are more or less similar. Both "inspire the sensation of divinity, both possess moral authority and stimulate devotion, self-sacrifice and exceptional individual behaviour. The individual who feels dependent on some external moral power is not, therefore, a victim of hallucination but a member of and responding to society itself. Durkheim concludes that the substantial function of religion is the creation, reinforcement and maintenance of social solidarity. So long as society persists so will religion" — *Dr. Timasheff*

THEORIES OF ORIGIN OF RELIGION

The origin of religion is hidden in the unfathomable past. When exactly, how exactly and in which form religion came into being we do not know. Its origin in a way is mysterious. Still sociologists, social anthropologists, and social scientists in general have made lot of efforts to explain the origin of religion. In their attempts to do so they have given birth to a number of theories some of which are more plausible than scientific. Some are not susceptible of any scientific proof, while some others remain either as only logical assumptions or as figment of imaginations. Hence there is a great deal of disagreement among the thinkers regarding the origin of religion. But they do agree that religion, like other social institutions arose in responses to certain felt needs of man. Let us briefly discuss a few theories of origin of religion.

1. Fetishism

Fetishism has been defined both as religion and as magic. In origin, it is the most primitive form of religion. It endows objects with supernatural or mystical powers for good or evil. The person who possesses the fetish can ward off bad luck and will have good fortunes. Hence, fetishism is nothing but the adoration of material things because of their mysterious power.

Though the Portuguese explorers used the term '*fetishes*' to refer to the wooden images of the west African Negroes, the term is not necessarily restricted to denote artificial things.

A leaf, a feather, a horn, a stone or any such thing with unusual shape is adored in the same manner as a carved figure. "Most fetishes are inanimate objects whose alleged powers are based on the naive belief, or superstition, that events that happen together or sequentially, are causally related and will continue to happen together". [*Leslie*, *Larson* and *Gorman*] Further, one of the two elements, cause or effect, is believed to have special power.

The mysterious power that is attributed to inanimate objects has been called by some primitives "mana The Melanesians and Maoris, for example, employed the term 'mana' to signify such a power. The term 'mana' was first used by the anthropologist R.H. *Codrington*. The belief in 'mana' has been referred to by *R.R. Marett* as '*animatism*'. Hence this theory is also known as "*Animatistic theory* The belief in '*mana*' or some fetish is found to be universal among primitive people. Anthropologist *Lowie* described the mysterious power as kind of "*electric fluid that could charge persons and things and be diverted from one to another*"

Fetishism or animatism is a very personal form of religion compared to most other belief systems that are group forms. Fetishism locates power in inanimate objects whereas most other religions locate it in animate ones. (The Americans who attach special power to a rabbit's foot which is believed to bring good luck, is an example of fetishism).

2. Animism

The theory of '*animism*' is the work of *E.B. Tylor* and may be found in his "*Primitive Culture*" first published in 1871. *Sir John Lubbock* and *Herbert Spencer* too could be considered as the other chief exponents of this theory. According to *Tylor*, animism is essentially a belief in the spirit of the dead. Tylor argued that early men had a need to explain dreams, shadows, hallucinations, sleep, and death. The need to understand such phenomenon led to the belief in the existence of the soul or an indwelling personality.

Animism is essentially a belief in the existence of some supra-physical being within the body of every living being. This super-natural being survives even after the collapse of the physical body in which it is contained. After the death of a person this so-called super-natural being is freed from the physical limitations and can wander anywhere without being restricted by time and space.

Tylor considered the belief in spirit or invisible soul or 'self' as almost an inevitable result of a universal phenomenon such as dreams. Very commonly the view is held that spirit visits a man in sleep, that too when he is experiencing dreams. Tylor asserted that the primitive man could hardly explain a dream in which he had certain "*actual*" experiences. For example, he dreamt of a hunting adventure which resulted in his 'taking home the hunted animal and enjoying fine dinner. After waking up from the sleep, he found, in reality that he had not left his cave. How could he explain this? The primitive man hence believed in a spiritual self which was separable from his bodily self and which could lead an independent existence. When once he got this idea, he gradually started extending the same to regard other animate beings and inanimate objects, as possessing a spirit. In this way, the primitive man was led to animism. Tylor is of the opinion that animism lies at the very basis of all religions.

Herbert Spencer did not completely accept Tylor's theory of animism. In his "*Principles of Sociology*" he has stated that religion originated mainly in ghost-fear. The ancestral ghosts which were endowed with superhuman powers, were believed to manipulate human affairs and natural forces. Hence the primitive men had to keep the ancestral ghosts in good humour if they were to act in his behalf. Spencer, further said that the deceased tribal leaders of great power came to be eventually worshipped as gods. The belief in gods originated in this way. In congruence with Spencer's 'ghost-theory' the Hindus still believe in the spirits or ghosts of ancestors and observe annually '*shraddha*' to offer some food or '*pinda*' to them to keep them happy.

Most of the anthropologists believe that the concepts of animism and animatism are fundamental to all religions. One is not believed to precede the other for both coexist and underlie all religions. Hence, Marett's assertion that animatism precedes animism has not been accepted by many others.

3. Totemism

Totemism is an extension of fetishism. "A totem is a species of animal or plant; or part of an animal or plant; or a natural object or phenomenon or the symbol of any of these which signifies distinguishing features of a human group vis-a-vis other groups, similarly represented, in the same society"–*H.D. Munro* in '*Dictionary* of Sociology'.

In the words of *J. G. Frazer*, a totem is a class of material objects which a savage regards with superstitious respect believing that there exists between him and every member of the clan an inti- mate and altogether a special relation. A totem is generally an animal, rarely a plant which gives its names to clan or may be otherwise associated with it.

The concept of totemism has not been satisfactorily defined. However, it could be said that according to the theory of 'totemism', a tribe is supposed to be related to an object–mainly animal or plant towards which they behave in a reverent manner by adopting its name and offering sacrifices or adoring it. The totems usually belong to the animal world–real or imaginary–and a few belong to the vegetable world. *Durkheim* found 460 of 500 totemic names in South Eastern Australia to be names for animals and plants. Only 40 were for inanimate objects such as the moon, sun, stars, fire, smoke and water.

Members of the tribal group affiliate themselves with the totem. The totem is a collective religious object having supernatural or mysterious powers for the group. Totem is associated with tribal organisation, and it becomes the name of the tribe, an image of the totemic spirit, and animal or plant with which the tribe identifies. The tribe–the spirit and the animal–are united in a trinity which cannot be separated into parts.

Totemism appeared to be important to those societies in which it was found, by observers. It seemed to be associated with the rule of exogamy between totemic groups. The relation that exists between the totem and the people is sometimes taken to be one of blood relationship. Hence the totem has to be crossed in marriage. The killing or eating the groups totem or insulting it, or using it for some purpose other than worshipping is tabooed. The totemic emblems are evoked at with religious attitude and the descent is traced through the totemic line. Totem may be a wolf, bear, turtle, hawk, fox, etc. It has to be admitted that none of the traits mentioned above are invariable features of totemic societies. Though totemism is universally found it exhibits considerable variations. It is not found among *Veddas of Ceylon, Punnan of Borneo, the Andaman Islanders, Pygmies of Congo, the Bushmen of South Africa*.

4. The Fear Theory

Fear, a psychological phenomenon is often said to be the cause for the emergence of religion. This view is quite old, as old as the ancient Greeks and Romans. Ancient Roman philosopher and poet *Lucretius* contended that the belief in the gods was based on an illusion and that fear was at the root of religion.

David Hume, a British philosopher of the 18th Century, in his "*Natural History of Religion*" pointed out that a fear of natural forces led man to believe in gods who manipulated nature. Hence man felt and believed that gods would intervene in his behalf if he tried to please them. German scholar *Max Muller* also supported this theory. 'According to him, the basis of religion is to be found in man's awe in the presence of extraordinary and terrifying natural phenomenon. According to *Prof Giddings*, the awe and fear of the "*Great Dreadful*" and of the mysterious forces, have been responsible for the genesis of religion.

5. The Functional Theory

Modern sociologists have been making scientific efforts to understand and explain the non-scientific social phenomenon that consist of beliefs and practices. In their attempts to do so, they have laid the foundations of some social theories of religion. The functional theory of religion is basically a sociological theory which has been developed by thinkers such as—*William Robertson Smith, Emile Durkheim, A.R. Radcliffe-Brown, B. Malinowski, Max Weber, Talcott Parsons*, and their followers. The basic assumption of the functionalist approach to religion is that religion is universally found because it has a vital function in maintaining the social system as a whole. The main social requirement that religion is deemed to fulfil has been "*the necessity of ideological and sentimental cohesion, or solidarity*".

How does religion serve to achieve social solidarity? *Kingsley Davis*, one of the champions of functionalist approach, says that religion does this in two ways: *Firstly*, "Religion is a part of society. It is common to the group; its beliefs and practices are acquired by each individual as a member of the group.... The worship of gods is a public matter supported by the community and performed for communal purposes. ..".

Secondly, the "common beliefs through common ritual seems to enhance the individual's devotion to group ends. It strengthens his determination to observe the group norms and to rise above purely private interests. It reinforces his identification with his fellows. . . ".

W. Robertson Smith seems to be the earliest exponent of this theory. In his book "*The Religion of Semites 1894* "*he concluded that "ancient religions consisted primarily of institutions and practices that is, of rites and ceremonies, and that myths, that is, beliefs and creeds, were an outgrowth of these*". In fact, Smith's ideas later contributed to the formulation of the sociological theory of religion.

Emile Durkheim, one of the earliest functionalist theorists, was the first sociologist to apply the functional approach to religion in a systematic way. His theory of religion got its proper form in his famous book "*The Elementary Forms of Religious Life, 1912*".

Durkheim in his study stressed the social role or functions of the most simple form of religion called totemism of Australian Aborigines. The totem, as it is noted already, denotes a common object such as an animal, or a plant, and a symbol representing that it is sacred. Each tribal clan is organised around totem. The totem, then, is sacred but is also the symbol of society itself From this fact Durkheim concluded that when people worship religion, they are really worshipping nothing more than their own society: "*divinity is merely society transformed and symbolically conceived*"

What happens, Durkheim argued, is that the members of the clan gather periodically. They participate in some group functions with emotional excitement and feel great ecstacy and elation of a kind which they would never feel alone. Now, the "*Men know well that they are acted upon, but they do not know by whom*". They pick on some nearby item such as a plant or animal, and make this the symbol of both their clan gathering (or society) and their experience of fervour and ecstacy (or religion). Their shared religious belief arises from the society and, in turn, it helps to hold the society together."—*Ian Robertson*.

The unity and solidarity of the community is further increased by the rituals that are enacted on religious occasions. These rituals also have the capacity of bringing people together and reaffirming the values and beliefs of the group. They also help to transmit the cultural heritage from one generation to the next. The rituals maintain taboos and prohibitions and those who violate them are punished. The disobedients or violators of norms may even be required to undergo ritual punishment or purification. The rituals have another function also. In times of individual distress or group crisis the rituals provide help and comfort. "*The social function of shared religious beliefs and the rituals that go with them is so important, Durkheim argued, that every society needs a religion or at least some belief system that serves the same function*"—*Ian Robertson*.

According to Durkheim, much of the social disorder in modem times is due to the fact that people no longer believe deeply in religion and that they have found no satisfying substitute for that. Lacking commitment to a shared belief system, people tend to pursue their private interests without regard for their fellows.

It is true that much of Durkheim's work on religion was purely speculative. His account of the origins of religion would not be accepted by most of the modern sociologists. *Goldenweiser*, for example, criticised Durkheim's theory as one-sided and psychologically untenable. He argued that a "*society possessing the religious sentiment is capable of accomplishing unusual things, but it can hardly produce that sentiment out of itself*. Some others have stated that "by making the social mind, or 'collective representations' the sole source of religion, Durkheim resorted to something quite mysterious in itself and, hence failed to give a satisfactory explanation". But the real merit of his analysis is his recognition of the vital social functions that religion plays in society.

6. The Theory of the Aleatory Element

Sumner and *Keller* in their book "*The Science of Society*" have stated that the ever present element of chance or what they call "*The aleatory element*" has been the main factor for the rise of religion. According to them, the primitive man is very much perturbed about the problem of bad luck. He is always concerned with the question of avoiding the misfortunes and securing good luck. In his attempts to find out an explanation for the occurrence of fortunes and misfortunes, the primitive man has pictured this 'aleatory element' as being controlled and manipulated by supernatural forces. Hence the primitive focuses his attention on winning the favours of such forces so that he gets only fortunes and not misfortunes. He is also very much bothered to avoid bad luck. Hence, Sumner and Keller have argued that human beings at all times attempted to devise means of insuring themselves against misfortune. They thus stressed the fact that "*religion arose in response to a definite need-adjustment to the supernatural or imaginary environment*" which has the capacity of causing fortunes or misfortunes.

STRUCTURAL ASPECTS OF RELIGION

Religion as a social institution has two aspects; *structural and functional*. The structure of religion includes theologies, creeds, practices, rituals, sects and symbols.

1. ***Theologies and creeds:*** Theology is the systematic explanation which religious leaders work out to show man's relation to his God and to the Universe. Almost all religions have their bodies of ideas, beliefs, doctrines, dogmas, articles of faith, ideals and ideologies. These things are systematized and rationalised in the form of theologies and creeds. Often this includes some account of the origin of the world, and of man, like the stories of Creation in the Bible. The Hindu concept of the Trinity, that is, God described in three forms–Brahma, the Creator; Vishnu, the Preserver; and Shiva, the Destroyer, explains the creation, the preservation and the destruction of the world. Theology represents the creed, or body of beliefs and doctrines of the Church or the Temple. The written words become the sacred scriptures.
2. ***Ceremony and ritual:*** Ceremony or ritual is a standardised and accepted action directed towards some specific end. Ritual refers to "*symbolic actions concerning the sacred.* " Every religion has its own practices and techniques or rituals and ceremonies in order to communicate with the supernatural. Ritual expresses awe and reverence, obedience and homage to the God. Sacrifices, sacred music, drama, dances, hymns, prayers, feasting, fasting, reading scriptures, writing, festivals, etc. represent various forms of rituals. They are found in all religions but in different ways. These bring emotional unity among people and secure for them some kind of security. These rituals are relatively simple in some religions but complex and elaborate in some others. However, rituals and ceremonies are not confined to religion alone.
3. ***Symbolism "Throughout religion symbolism is important:*** Symbols are substitutes for or representation of objects or situations. They may be verbal or tangible. A religious symbol enables an individual to identify himself with his fellow-beings. It thus promotes a sense of social solidarity. A symbol may often come to represent not the particular object or situation to which it was originally attached, but the entire group and its culture. For example, the cross stands for Christianity, the Crescent for Islam, the Swasthik for Hinduism. Normally these symbols are emotion-charged.
4. ***Religious codes:*** 'Religious Code' refers to a body of rules prescribed by a particular religion for its followers to observe and follow. The code prescribes desirable conduct and prescribes undesirable behaviour. The desirable behaviour brings rewards while the undesirable one brings punishment to the individual. In religious terminology there is a close connection between one's behaviour and the probability of one's attaining Heaven or going to Hell after one's death. The religious code defines the way in which one has to maintain one's relation with the Supernatural and also with the fellow-beings. Buddhism thus places emphasis on "*Ashta Marg* (Eight-Fold Path), Jainism on "*Triratnas*" (Three- Jewelled Path), Islam on "*Shariat*" (Muslim Personal Law), Hinduism on "*Manu Smriti*", Christianity on 'Ten commandments' and so on.
5. ***Sects:*** A sect is a body of believers with similar religious attitudes and interests. The group of believers may hold a common body of beliefs, values and objectives. Certain persons, often only a few in the beginning, begin to disagree about more or less important points in the main ceremonials and doctrine of the parent organisation. In course of time, they may go out of the organised Church, or they may be expelled by the Church itself. Now they formulate

their own creed, their own official hierarchy, and take on a distinctive name and become a new "*denomination*". Today's sect is quite likely to become tomorrow's Church. In time, a sect makes its peace with the wider society and becomes a Church itself. Later, a new generation of people may break away from it and form another sect. Christianity has two main sects like Catholicism, and Protestantism and several other smaller sects like *Puritanism, Presbyterianism, Lutheranism, Calvinism*, etc. Similarly, Buddhism has *Mahayanism* and *Hinayanism*, Jainism has the *Svetambarus* and the *Digambaras*, Islam has the *Sunnis and the Shias*; Hinduism has the sects like *Shaivites*, the *Vaishnavites* and the *Shaktheyas* on the one hand; and *David, Advaita* and the *Vishishtadvaita* on the other.

6. ***Festivals:*** Every religion has its own festivals. A religious festival is a kind of social get together wherein people observe some rituals collectively. It may consist of prayers, processions, feasting or fasting, chanting of hymns and singing devotional songs, etc. Festivals reaffirm the faith and fidelity of the people into the principles and practices of religion. Festivals promote emotional integration and social harmony. A common feature of the festival is that people clean their homes, wear ceremonial dresses and ornaments. Feasts and parties are often arranged and there is an exchange of greetings, sweets and presents. Some popular festivals of the Hindus are–Yugadi, Sankranthi, Navaratri, Vijaya Dashami, Ramanavami, Krishna Jayanthi, Deepavali, Ganesh-Chaturthi, Naga Panchami, Gauri Pooja, Rishi-Panchami, Guru-Purnima, Rakshabandhan, Shivaratri and Holi.

7. ***Sacred literature:*** The theological explanation of a religion when it takes the written form becomes the sacred literature. In other words, the sacred scriptures of a religion represent its sacred literature. Every religion has its own sacred literature. The essential principles, and theological ex- planations of a religion, in general, are incorporated in its sacred literature. This literature has a great survival value.

   The *Vedas*, or '*Srutis*', *Upanishads* or '*Smritis*', Bhagavad Gita and the *Epic* are the sacred scriptures of Hinduism. '*Bible*' is the main religious authority on Christianity and similarly, '*Quran*' on Islam; '*Tripziakas*"–(Sutta Pitaka, Vinaya Pitaka and Abhidhamma Pitaka) on Buddhism; "*Agama Siddhanta*" on Jainism; '*Jend Avestu*' on Zoroastrianism; The Old Testament of the Jewish Bible" and '*Talmud*' on Judaism and so on.

8. ***Myth:*** Myth refers to "an ancient traditional story of Gods or heroes, especially, the one offering an explanation of some fact or phenomenon"—(*Chamber's Dictionary*). It has been said that myth "is primitive philosophy, the Simplest presentational form of thought, a series of attempts to understand the world, to explain life and death, fate and nature, gods and cults"–(*E.Bethe*). As *Malinowski* says myths are "statements of reality, products of a living faith, intimately connected with word and deed."

   Myth is also a complex kind of human assertion. it is a dramatic assertion, not simply a rational statement. It is a dramatic assertion in which the thoughts and feelings, attitudes and sentiments, are involved. It is the emotion-laden assertion of man's place in a world that is meaningful to him, and of his solidarity with it. It makes past and future immediately present; it expresses man's solidarity with his world, and reasserts that solidarity in the face of human doubt. "Through it (Myth) men are related to their environment, to their ancestors, to their descendants, to the beyond which is the ground of all existence, to what is permanent beyond all flux."–(*Thomas.F.O' Dea*).

9. ***Mysticism:*** '*Mysticism*' refers to the habit or tendency of religious thought and feeling of those who seek direct communion with God or the divine. In mysticism, religious life for some people becomes "*transformed into a purely personal and inward experience*". Hence, a '*Mystic*' is one who seeks or attains direct relationship with the God in elevated religious feeling or ecstacy. He seeks to rise above all forms of the world–both those of the natural and societal environment and those of formalised cult as well. The mystic response is found in all the world religions; in Christianity, Buddhism, Hinduism, Judaism and even in Islam. Mysticism attracts varied types of people, but especially the intellectual and cultured groups. It is often an expression of protest in a subtle way. It expresses a desire to break out of established forms of worship and often of ideas. Like the protest response, however, it can also be reincorporated into the Church. It contributes considerable enrich- ment to their subjective religious life. The l4th century saw the development of crisis in the Church, the beginning of scientific and positive thought. and a great increase in mysticism.

RELIGIOUS ROLES

Religious norms and practices give rise to different social roles, someone has to carry on. It is said that "*Gods die if there are no priests to keep them alive*". Social roles in religion are of two main categories: 1. The *religious thinkers and mystics*; and 2. *The executives or operators of the formal structure of the Church or The Temple*. The first category includes the *Prophets*, and the *messiahs*. The second category consists of the *priests* or *pastors*, *formal teachers, missionaries*, and various *administrators*.

1. (*a*) The **Mystic** plays an important part in the growth of religion. He identifies himself or comes into union with the God or the Absolute. The mystics believe that, through their dreams, visions, and other unique mental experiences, they come into personal communication with divine powers. Mystics are likely to be innovators and disturbers of the established order (*b*) The **Prophet** is an important religious leader. He may be a priest or a mystic. He serves as a spokesman for some divine power, issuing warnings, giving commands, and revealing the course of future events. The role of the prophet is set by the culture. The disruption in the established Church hierarchy may give rise to the emergence of mystics and prophets (*c*) The **Messiah** is the divine leader or prophet who is recognised as having supernatural attributes. He often assumes the role of final judge. The messiah comes from among the people themselves, who at a time of crisis look to him to save their society from disaster. Jesus Christ, Moses, Prophet Mohammed, for example, were regarded as the messiahs or redeemers.
2. The *religious executives* include the priests, teachers and the missionaries. (*a*) The *Priest* or *Pastor* carries on the religious rituals and expounds or explains the theology. He officiates at the Church ceremonies and cares for both spiritual and temporal or worldly affairs— (*b*) Religious Teachers or *Philosophers* have played a significant role in the history of the great world religions. Jesus Christ, St. Paul, Mohammed, the Buddha, Mahavira, Shankaracharya, Basavanna are all well known instances (*c*) The *Missionary* is a special teacher whose task is to carry the message, rituals and symbolism of an established religion to non-believers—(*d*) The *Religious Executive* may be, like St. Paul, Shankaracharya, Allammaprabhu, both missionaries and organisers. Sometimes these executives may undertake the priestly work as well as social-service work and management.

The mystics and the religious thinkers are likely to be innovators and disturbers of the established order. On the other hand, the religious executives are generally conservative, who always prefer the old to the new. There is, in fact, a sort of continuous struggle in religious organisations between these two kinds of persons. "Some would confine religious expression within rather definite limits set by symbols, rites, traditions, and established theology. Other would not unduly hamper religious experience by such established patterns of thought and action but would leave much to the individual's unique experience."— *Young* and *Mack*.

FUNCTIONS OF RELIGION

The universal existence of religion shows that religion has a great survival value. "The universality of religion is not based upon the forms of belief and practice, but upon the social functions which religion universally fulfils". These functions are of great individual as well as social significance.

1. ***Religion provides religious experience:*** This is the basic function of religion. *Prayer, worship* and *meditation* are the summary of religious experience. Through these means man expresses awe, reverence, gratitude and allegiance to the Almighty or the God, or the Supernatural Force. When an individual comes into contact with the supernatural he undergoes some sort of peculiar, inexplicable experience. He converses with the divine through prayers. He forgets the worldly life and its problems. This religious experience ennobles the human desires, ideals and values. It facilitates the development of personality, sociability and creativeness.
2. ***Religion provides peace of mind:*** Religion provides for the individual the most desired peace of mind. At every crisis, personal or collective, religion is called in for consolation and peace of mind. It promotes goodness and helps the development of character. In a world full of uncertain- ties, indefiniteness, dangers, insecurities and unhappiness, the need for safety and security is really great. Religion here acts as the healer of the ills of life. it reduces one's grievances to some extent. It gives the individuals emotional support in the face of uncertainty. It consoles them when they are disappointed. It reconciles them when they are estranged from the goals and norms of society. In doing this it supports established values and goals and reinforces the morale. It offers man inspiration, hope, faith, optimism and courage.
3. ***Religion promotes social solidarity, unity and identity:*** Religion upholds and validates the traditional ways of the life. More than that it unites people. It is known that a common faith., common value-judgements, common sentiments, common worship are significant factors in unifying people. By their participation in religious rituals and worship, people try to identify themselves as having something in common. Religion affects an individual's understanding of *who they are* (*people*) *and what they are*. As *Davis* points out, "Religion gives the individual a sense of identity with the distant past and the limitless future." As *Thomas F. O' Dea says, "In periods of rapid social change and large scale social mobility, the contribution of religion to identify may become greatly enhanced.*" "As A.W. Green has pointed out religion is "the supremely integrating and unifying force in human society."

4. ***Religion conserves the value of life:*** Religion is an effective means of presenting the values of life. Religion defines and redefines the values. Moral, spiritual and social values are greatly supported by religion. It exercises a tremendous influence over the younger ones and their behaviour. Through such agencies like the family and the Church, religion inculcates the values of life in the minds of the growing children. Further, as *Thomas F.O'Dea* says, "*religion sacralises the norms and values of established society*". It maintains the dominance of group goals over individual impulses."
5. ***Religion–As an agent of social control:*** Religion is one of the forms of informal means of social control. It regulates the activities of people in its own way. It prescribes rules of conduct for people to follow. The conceptions of spirits, ghosts, taboos, souls, commandments, sermons, etc., control human action and enforce discipline. Ideas of hell and heaven have strong effect on the behaviour of people. Thus, religion has a great disciplinary value.

   Religion has its own methods to deal with those individuals who violate its norms. *It has its own ways to reintegrate the disobedient into the social group*. Further religious sanctions are widely made use of to support the ethical codes and moral practices among many peoples.
6. ***Priestly function of religion:*** By performing its priestly function religion contributes to the *stability* and order *of the society*. Religion offers a kind of relationship with the beyond through different kinds of worship and beliefs. By this it provides the emotional ground for a new security. Through its authoritative teaching of beliefs and values, it provides similar points of opinion and avoids conflicts. It contributes to the *maintenance of the status quo*.
7. ***Religion promotes welfare:*** Religion renders service to the people and promotes their welfare. It appeals to the people to be Sympathetic, merciful and co-operative. It rouses in them the spirit of mutual help and co-operation. It awakens the philanthropic attitude of the people. It reinforces the sense of belonging to the group. It promotes art, culture and provides means for the development of character on the right lines. Various religious organisations like the Vishwa Hindu Parishad, Hindu Seva Pratishthana, Ramakrishna Mission, Arya Samaj, Brahma Samaj, The Society of Jesus, etc., are engaged in various social, educational, aesthetic, cultural, civic, medical, and other activities.
8. ***Religion provides recreation:*** Religion promotes recreation through religious lectures, Kirtanas, dramas, dance, music, *bhajanas*, *puranas*, *harikathas*, fairs, festivals, musical concerts, art exhibitions and so on. It tries to make men sorrowless and fearless. Various religious festivals and rituals can provide relief to the disturbed mind.
9. ***Religion explains individual suffering and helps to integrate personality:*** Man has never lived by knowledge alone. Man is a rational as well as an emotional creature. The things for which men strive in this world are in some measure denied to them. If the aim is to Propagate a faith, persecution may bring failure. If the aim is to achieve fame, a mediocre career may bring disillusionment. If the aim is to become rich in business, heavy loss in it may bring disheartenment. With a multiplicity of goals no individual can escape frustration. But the culture provides him with goals that anybody can reach. These are goals that *transcend* the world of actual experience, with the consequence that no evidence of failure to attain them can be conclusive. If the individual believes that he has gained them, that is sufficient. All he needs is sufficient faith. The greater his disappointment in this life, the greater his faith in the next. *Religion tries to give release from the very thing it instils, guilt*. Ritual means are freely provided for wiping away guilt, so that one can count on divine grace.
10. ***Religion enhances self-importance:*** Religion expands the *self* to infinite proportions. Religious belief relates the self to the *infinite* or *Cosmic Design*. Through unity with the infinite the self is ennobled, made majestic. Man considers himself the noblest work of God with whom he shall be united. His self thus becomes grand and elevated.

Conclusion

It is true, that the rapid developments in the field of civilisation, in physical and biological sciences, have affected the functions, of religion to a great extent. Some of the age old religious beliefs have been exploded by the scientific investigations. Science has often shaken the religious faith. The growing secular and the rationalist attitude has posed a challenge, a serious question—*Can the society rely on the acceptance of certain ethical and moral priniciples without believing in the existence of a spiritual or superempirical world*?—Still, it is understandable that the institution of religion is so deep-rooted and long lasting that it will continue to function in the near future withstanding the dangers of changes and the ravages of time.

DYSFUNCTIONS OF RELIGION

Religion as a basic social institution of human society has been fulfilling certain positive functions no doubt. Its role in promoting social solidarity, as Durkheim has pointed out, and its need in providing inner individual peace and solace as

Edward Sapir has pointed out cannot be undermined. By looking at these manifest positive functions of religion one should not jump to the conclusion that religion brings man only advantages. Religion, on the contrary, has its own dysfunctional aspect also. It does certain disservices also. Sumner and *Keller, Benjamin Kidd, Gillin, Karl Marx, Thomas F. O'dea* and others have pin pointed the negative side of the functions or the dysfunctions of religion also.

According to *Thomas F. O'Dea*, one of the functionalists, the main dysfunctions of religion are as follows.

1. ***Religion inhibits protests and impedes social changes:*** Religion provides man emotional consolation and helps him to reconciliate himself with situations. In doing so, *T.F.O'Dea* remarks, religion inhibits protests and impedes social changes which may even prove to be beneficial to the welfare of the society. All protests and conflicts are not always negative. Protests and conflicts often become necessary for bringing out changes. Some changes would certainly lead to positive reforms. By inhibiting protests and preventing changes religion may postpone reforms. This effect of religion can contribute to the build up of explosive resentments which eventually result in revolution and in most costly and destructive changes. In fact, "In Europe and America the vigorous conflict of classes and other groups led to a better distribution of the national product, a more harmonious relationship of classes, a better control of the society over its environment, and a more stable and orderly society." Religion often played a role in that history, to some extent inhibiting such conflict.
2. ***Hampers the adaptation of society to changed condition:*** A religion can make norms of behaviour and can also sacralise the norms and values of society. Some of the norm's which lose their appropriateness under changed conditions may also be imposed by religion. This can "impede a more functionally appropriate adaptation of society to changing conditions." *Example*: During the Medieval Period in Europe, the "Church refused to grant the ethical legitimacy of money-lending at interest, despite the great functional need of this activity in a situation of developing capitalism". Even today, traditional Muslims face religio-ethical problems concerning interest-taking. Similar social conflict is evident in the case of birth control measures including abortion, in the Catholic world.
3. ***Religion increases conflict and makes the evolution of realistic solutions more difficult:*** By performing its prophetic function religion may "provide standards of value in terms of which institutionalised norms may be critically examined and found seriously wanting". But this function can also have its dysfunctional consequences. Religious criticism of the existing norms and values may become so unrealistic that it beclouds genuine issues. The religious "demands for reform may become so utopian that they constitute an obstacle in the working out of more practical action". Religion may also set up standards that are untimely. Religion always seeks to see its demands as the will of God, and in that, it may impart an extremism to the conflict that renders compromise impossible. *Example*: Because of religious convictions, the left-wing Protestant sects of the Reformation period became the victims of intolerance. Due to this intolerance some of these Protestants took some extreme positions that any compromise between them and the general society was actually impossible.
4. ***Impedes the development of new identities:*** "In fulfilling its identity function religion may foster certain loyalties which may actually impede the development of new identities which are more appropriate to new situations." Religious identification may prove to be divisive to societies. Religion builds deeply into the personality structures of people a strong animosity that makes them to oppose their opponents tooth and nail. In the religious wars that followed Reformation this animo sity (which was the result of religious identifications) was very much evident. *Like the ideology of communism and nationalism, religion too provides for an element of identity which promotes inter-group conflicts by dividing people along religious lines.*
5. ***Religion may foster dependence and irresponsibility:*** Religion often makes its followers to become dependents on religious institutions and leaders instead of developing in them an ability to assume individual responsibility and self-direction. It is quite common to observe in India that a good number of people prefer to take the advices of priests and religious leaders before starting some great ventures instead of taking the suggestion of those who are competent in the field. However, it is difficult to assess the exact role of religion in hampering the sense of responsibility and self' dependence of an individual, without an appeal to his own values. Still it could be said that religion's role with respect to individual development and maturation, is highly problematic.

OTHER DYSFUNCTIONS

1. ***Conservative and retards progress:*** Religion is said to be conservative. It is regarded as retrogressive and not progressive. Religion upholds traditionalism and supports the *status quo*. It is not readily amenable to change.

2. ***Promotes evil practices:*** Religion in its course of development, has at times, supported evil practices such as–cannibalism, suicide, slavery, incest, killing of the aged, untouchability, human and animal sacrifice, etc. "*There is hardly a vice which religion has not at one time or another actively supported.*"
3. ***Creates confusions, contradictions and conflicts:*** Religion consists of some of inconsisten- cies. It has supported war and peace, wealth and poverty, hard work and idleness, virginity and prostitution. Religion has not offered any absolute standard of morality.
4. ***Contributes to inequalities and exploitation:*** Religion perpetuates the distance between rich and the poor, the propertied class and property less class. More than that, as *Marx* said, religion has often been used as an instrument of exploiting the poor and the depressed class. Hence *Marx* calls religion as "the opium of the masses."
5. ***Promotes superstitious beliefs:*** Superstition is closely related to religion. Religion has pro- moted superstitious beliefs which have caused man more harm than good. *Ex*: the belief that evil spirits and ghosts cause diseases, the belief that God is responsible for the birth of children.
6. ***Religion causes wastes:*** *Sumner and Keller* are of the opinion that religion often causes economic wastes. *Ex*.: Investing huge sums of money on building temples, churches, mosques, etc., spending much on religious fairs, festivals and ceremonies, spoiling huge quantity of food articles, material things, etc., in the name of offerings. It leads to waste of human labour, energy and time.
7. ***Religion wrecks unity:*** Religion creates vast diversities among people. Religion not only brings people together but also keeps them at a distance. Wars and battles have been fought in the name of religion. Loot, plundering, mass killing, rape, arson and such other cruel treatments have been meted out to some people in the name of God and religion.
8. ***Religion undermine human potentiality:*** Religion by placing high premium on divine power and divine grace has made people to become fatalistic. By tracing the cause of all the phenomenon to some divine power, religion has undermined human power, potentiality. This adversely affected the creativity of man.
9. ***Religion retards scientific Achievements:*** Science is often regarded as a challenge to religion. Religion has time and again tried to prevent the attempts of scientists from revealing newly discovered facts. It made *Galileo* to renounce his painstakingly established doctrines. Similarly, it tried to suppress the doctrines of *Darwin*, *Huxley* and others. Thus religion has interfered with the free inquiry of scholars. Further, it has suppressed the democratic aspirations of the people.
10. ***Religion promotes fanaticism:*** Faith without reasoning is blind. Religion has often made people to become blind, dumb and deaf to the reality. On the contrary, it has often made people to become bigots and fanatics. Bigotry and fanaticism have led to persecution, inhuman treatment and misery in the past.

It is clear from the above description that religion has its bright as well as the dark side on positive and negative functions. Religion as a social mechanism or phenomenon has been subject to human use and abuse in the past. Religion has been used to serve humanity and also abused to exploit people.

"Religion can sacralise finite ideas and provincial attitudes to an extent which inhibits further progress in the society's knowledge of its environment and in man's efforts to control nature." The long conflict between science and religion is quite known in history.

MORALITY

Morality is one of the fundamental social institutions. Religion and morality are usually recognised as among the most effective guides of human behaviour. Both formulate rules of conduct in society. Each is having its own code of conduct as such. Religious ideas are embodied in the religious code and the moral ideas are embodied in moral code. Both act as powerful means of social control.

Strictly speaking, morality deals with the rules of conduct. It prescribes good behaviour and prohibits undesirable one. Moral values are an important element in our normative pattern. Moral values are the most dynamic, creative and important driving force behind human actions and endeavours. Such concepts as–justice, honesty, fairness, righteousness, conscientiousness, disinterestedness, prudence, incorruptibility, freedom, mercy, etc., are purely moral concepts because they represent the moral values. They are capable of deeply influencing and also changing the course of society. Political and social movements normally hinge upon the values of this kind. What then do we mean by morality?

Meaning of Morality

'Morality' which is often equated with '*moral code*' is sometimes taken for those rules of behaviour which are admitted at large in society. In this sense, it is equivalent to "*mores*" and mostly coincides with customs, conventions, fashions, etiquettes, folkways, etc. But actually, in sociology, we make a distinction between moral rules or code and other kinds of social rules.

As *Gisbert* has pointed out, in a strict and more accurate sense, the moral code is "*that body of rules or principles concerned with the good and evil as manifested to us by conscience*". This body of rules is admitted at large by the society.

P. Gisbert is of the opinion that, "*the moral good is essentially different from the utilitarian and sectional good*". When we speak of Mr. Sharma as being good at business or in public speaking, we ordinarily mean his ability in that particular field. But when we apply the term '*good*' to man in the *moral sense*, we mean that he is living upto the moral code, and that he is trustworthy, helpful, sympathetic, and humble towards his fellowmen, faithful to his wife and children, honest in bussiness, loyal to the nation, and possesses similar other qualities. This "goodness" is not utilitarian, nor sectional, but integral.

Moral principles, ideas and notions are crystallised in the form of an institution called 'morality'. Morality has been a vital factor in all the societies of the world, including the uncivilised, in affecting and controlling the social behaviour of man. Moral rules which prescribe the wrong, are the very basis of our collective life. Hence the evolution of the group life of man is connected with the evolution of his notions. Moral notions are at the back of the give-and-take policy without which group life is difficult. Because of moral force an individual tries to suppress his impulsive behaviour and individualistic tendencies. Moral principles get the sanction of society and strongly support the general system of values. Since moral ideas are inculcated into the personalities of the children from the very beginning they become habituated to honour them and obey them. Much of the moral norms are internalised by the individuals during the period of socialisation and hence they obey them due to some internal pressure. The pressure is sometimes so strong that some individuals even in critical situations may not be prepared to go against it. They are more powerful than laws and legislations. Sometimes the people who are prepared to break the laws on some grounds are not ready to go against the dominant moral values.

Differences between Religion and Morality

Both religion and morality prescribe and control human behaviour. The prescribed form of behaviour is obeyed by internal urges or pressures. In religion, this internal pressure is '*fear of God*' and in morality, it is the '*pressure of conscience*'.

The sanction and authority behind each one of them are also different. Behind the religious standards there is *divine authority* and the *sanction of God*. Disobedience of religious standard is believed to result in incurring the displeasure of God. Hence the violation of laws of religion is considered a '*sin*'.

But the authority and sanction behind morality is *society* itself. It is not divine. Morality defines our conduct towards fellow beings and not towards the God. Morality does not require any external sanction. Its sanction is *internal*. Its disobedience incurs the displeasure of the society and not that of the God.

Interrelationship between Religion and Morality

However, religion and morality are closely interrelated. Religion prescribes rules of conduct and in so doing it tends to identify these with moral conduct. In fact, each religion has a code of conduct of its own which is very often based on moral values. Many times, moral standards draw their support from religion itself. The moral and the religious standards are interlinked. If the moral standards are addressed to man directly the religious standards are addressed to him indirectly. The violation of moral codes will have direct consequences to man whereas the disobedience of the religious code or standards will have indirect consequences, in the sense it is believed to incur the wrath of God. The disobedience of the moral code results in societal disapproval. *Benjamin Kidd* and *C. S. Lewis* have remarked that the moral standards cannot have any meaning without the support of religion. In the words of *Mathew Arnold*, "*Religion is morality touched with emotion*". *F.H. Bradley* writes. "*It is a moral duty not be immoral and that is the duty to be religious*".

RELIGION AND SCIENCE

"Religion versus science"–issue occupied a prominent place in the ideological discussions of the 19th century but now it has lost much of its vigour. The topic of discussion was whether the discoveries of science had disproved the concept of religion and whether science alone would be sufficient to explain all the riddles and mysteries of the universe. In simple words, the debate was on the compatibility or incompatibility of religion with science.

There are two major opinions regarding the relationship between science and religion: 1. Religion and Science are mutually conflicting, and 2. Science and religion are not mutually opposing.

The View that Religion and Science are Mutually Conflicting

In some circles, there is the opinion that science should clash with religion because religion is incompatible with science. Some reasons are attributed for this conflict.

(*i*) ***Religion is based on faith and rituals whereas science depends on observations, experiments, verifications, proofs and facts.*** Religion is more than a body of dogma, faith and ritual in connection with unseen forces. It is also an explanation of the universe and a way of interpreting the natural order.

The outlook of science is one of observation and test and verification. By studying only that which can be observed and tested by means of various scientific techniques science has struck at the root of man's conception of the super-natural realm. The following examples clarify this point. *Examples*: (*i*) Plague, proved to be transmitted by infected rats, no longer remains as an evidence of God's wrath. In the same way, the serum which stops the plague cannot be interpreted as God's blessing, since men devised it and men administer it; (*ii*) In the same manner, from the scientific point of view a successful crop cannot be attributed to God' boon; (*iii*) As per the scientific view, a hysterical man is no longer "possessed by the devil", an earthquake cannot be explained as the consequence of man's failure to obey the "*Ten Commandments*" and so on.

(*ii*) ***Ritualism, religious fundamentalism and fanaticism rooted in religion are very much opposed to science.*** Religion does not always remain at the theoretical plane. Religious beliefs are expressed in human actions and practices called rituals. In the practice of rituals, normally the original belief is either forgotten or ignored and only the external usages come to be called the real practice of religion. *This is nothing but ritualism.* Ritualism devoid of the original religious beliefs definitely opposed to science. For example, the ritualisic practice of human and animal sacrifice, is definitely opposed to science.

Religious fanaticism and fundamentalism are also opposed to science. As *H.E. Barnes* has pointed out fundamentalist religion and modern science are definitely at a conflict. It is on record that dogmatic religion opposed science and interfered with its development by every means possible. Dr. William Harvey's Blood Circulation Theory, Galileo's Theory of the Planetary System and Giordano Bruno's repeated advocacy of a 'sun-centred universe', etc., had to meet with religious opposition. Even now religion hardly encourages free inquiry. *Sumner* and *Keller* writes, "*It is difficult to find any type of religion which has welcomed free inquiry*"

Causes for the Conflict between Science and Religion: Views of Kingsley Davis

According to *Kingsley Davis*, there are two important causes for the conflict between religion and science. They are stated below.

(*i*) ***Science deals with the 'known' or the empirical world. Religion is concerned with the 'unknown' or supernatural world.*** *As Kingsley Davis* point out, "*The boundary between the unknown and the known is a shifting one*". What was unknown yesterday is known today. Science could not give an account of the origin of man then. Religious belief filled in the gap by giving its own account of that. Later with its progress science too could give a satisfactory explanation of that. Here arose the conflict between the two. Because the scientist could not accept the religious account as true even though he lived among the people who believed in religious explanation. This situation created tension between him and the ordinary people or the religious leader. *Thus, Davis writes, "So long as the frontier between the known and unknown is a shifting one, so long as science is expanding, there will be conflict between religion and science.*" Still in this battle neither one will be vanquished. When religion loses, it merely retreats to higher levels. The religious ideology becomes more philosophical "*It changes from fundamentalist to liberal, from dogma to philosophy*".

(*ii*) ***The second cause of conflict is that science believes in empirical truth whereas religion pursues the non-empirical truth*:** As *Davis* writes, "*The scientific pursuit of empirical truth as the highest goal is exactly the opposite of religious pursuit of non-empirical truth.*" Thus the scientist develops his scepticism about religious beliefs and explanations concerning creation, heaven, hell, life after death, miracles, etc. The sharpest conflict between the two comes when religion itself is subjected to scientific analysis.

The View that Science and Religion are not Mutually Opposing

Some writers hold the view that science and religion have no need to be at conflict. *C.E.M. Joad* writes: "*I have sought to establish the commonplace proposition that there is no conflict between science and religion.....*"

Viewed analytically, however, science and religion need not be at conflict. Science deals with what is known. It is potential knowledge based on sensory evidences. Religious beliefs refer to the world beyond the senses. *If they cannot be proved by the methods of science, they cannot be disproved also. As A. W. Green* has pointed out, "*anything which lies outside the narrow area of investigation that science has marked out is not and cannot be proved nonexistent*." Any claim to the contrary would be itself unscientific.

Science Cannot be Opposed to Religion

It is wrong to say that religion is based on emotion; and science, on thought. In fact, both are based on thought though this is applied to different types of reality. But here is always "*the danger of disagreement when the temporal is taken as eternal and the doubtful as certain; or when the scientist tends to interpret every advance of science as a defeat of religion*."

True religion and true science cannot clash. *K. Davis* has pointed out it is possible for a scientist to have belief in God and still work as a good biologist or a physicist. "His and his behaviour in church appropriate to religious situation, with no feeling of incongruity." *Prof. Culson* has said that "true religion and "*true science, lead to the same end*."

Scientists are not always hostile towards religion. Even the attitude of scientist towards religion has not been that of a hostile one. A large number of scientists such as Newton, Descartes, Pasteur, Lister, Kepler, Galileo, Copernicus, Euler, Franklin, Boyle, Mariette, Haller, Linneo, Galvani, Cuvier, Ampere, Volta and others were either sincere believers, or at least were not opposed to religion.

Religion is not unscientific, it is only non-scientific. Scientific truth is that which is known by the evidence of the senses. Religious truth is that which is known by revelations, by faith. An attempt to "reconcile" the two can promote mutual respect across the barrier. Any reconciliation which attempts to combine them can only undermine both. *A.W. Green* writes: "*Religion is not unscientific. it is only non-scientific.*"

Relationship between Religion and Science: Concluding Remarks

Religion is a social reality. "*The persistence of religion throughout the ages very much im- pressed* **Sumner** and **Keller** *as proof of its* "survival value."[1] It has rendered undeniable services to the humanity and is still sewing. Scientific investigators agree that religion like other institutions, *has its roots in certain human needs. Hence, it was felt to be a necessity and continues to be a necessary thing.*

What type of religion we should have? What type of worshipping is acceptable? What type of ritual system must be accepted? What type of religion, in brief is worth building and preserving?– These questions are more philosophical than sociological. They are value-based questions. Even if one attempts to answer them, the answers become subjective. Hence, sociologists don't suggest any answers for them. Sociologists can only suggest that any religion for that matter should adjust itself to changes in life conditions. *The more it is adapted to existing conditions and knowledge, the greater the chance of its being effective as an institution.*

Is Religion Compatible with Science?

Our answer to this question depends upon the kind of religion that we have in our mind. If religion is construed as nothing but belief in superhuman force or power, it remains incompatible with science. If, on the other hand, it is understood as a kind of "*ethical philosophy*", serving the cause of humanity, then the two are compatible. According to *H.E. Barnes*, fundamentalist religion and modern science are always conflicting, but *no conflict exists between modern science and the latest trend in religion called* **"*humanism*"**.

It should be noted that religion in its real sense is not conflicting with science. It is only the dogma or theology or the distorted version of religion, that conflicts with science. Champions of humanism, like *H.E. Barnes* and others who have tried to give a new interpretation to religion have said that religion should be based "*upon the service of man rather than the worship of God*". If the sole purpose of religion, is, "*service to mankind*", then, it can never clash with science. Humanism, a new trend in religion, represents such kind of service-oriented religion. *MacIver* and *Page*, *Barnes*, *Albert Einstein*, *Gandhiji* and many others have strongly supported humanism.

The discussion of the relationship between science and religion can be concluded in this way: *If religion respects and accepts the values of science and if science recognises and accepts the reality and necessity of religion (of course, with is own limitations) then, there could be no conflict between religion and science.*

RECENT TRENDS IN RELIGION

"Recently religion in the Western world has tended to place less emphasis on dogma and more on social values. It has also tried to reconcile its doctrines with scientific knowledge."–*Samuel Koenig*.

[1] Samuel Koeing in his *Sociology*, p. 126.

A more radical group is represented by the *Humanists*. They have rejected all connections with conventional Christianity. To quote Barnes they have attempted to construct a religion based entirely, "*upon the service of man rather than the worship of God*."

John H. Dietrich, one of the chief exponents of Humanism points out that "Humanism believes in the supreme worth of human life and that man must therefore be treated as an end, *not as a means* to some other end..... Humanism is the effort to enrich human experience by means of human inquiry It has no blind faith in the perfectibility of man, but it believes that his present condition can be immeasurably improved..... Humanism accepts the responsibility for the conditions of human life and relies entirely upon human effort for their improvement. The humanist makes no attempt to shove the responsibility for the miserable conditions of human life onto some God or some cosmic order. He fully realises that the situation is in our own hands, and that practically all the evils of the world have been brought up by men by themselves".

Humanism, it may be said, represents an attempt to divorce religion from supernaturalism. It tries to secularise and socialise it completely. Humanism actually is not at all different from other idealistic social reform movements. Many will doubt whether it can be called a religion. The trend towards the socialisation and secularisation of religion is there no doubt. Religious leaders are advo- cating greater participation by the Church in meeting social problems and concentration upon the ethical rather than the dogmatic content of religion. As *MacIver* has pointed out if religion emerges as a social force above tribal and national egoisms, with the help of science, it will become consistent with a purely moral code and this be brought into harmony with the needs of life.

As *Barnes* has pointed out religion adapted to our changed conditions of life is worth preserving and it must seek to organise the masses and guide their activities for the benefit of society rather than for the purpose of pleasing the God. It is doubtful whether an institution which has been de- voted to the supernatural can be changed into one dedicated to furthering the welfare and happiness of mankind here on earth. It is highly questionable, wrote *Barnes*, that a religion with a mass appeal can exist without elements of mystery and fear dominating. It is equally doubtful whether a religion exists without dogma and ritual.

MAGIC

Meaning of Magic

The phenomenon of magic is closely associated with religion. Magic is often regarded as a form of religion. Magic and religion are however different. They represent two aspects of the same non-empirical power. Of the two, religion is more widespread whereas magic is very much limited.

Definition of Magic

1. As *H.M. Johnson* has pointed out "when the goal of action is empirical and the means are supernatural, we call the action magic."
2. *Max Weber* used the term "magic" "to refer to religious action believed to be automatically effective, whether the goal is empirical or non-empirical."
3. *B. Malinowski* defines 'magic' as "the use of supernatural means to try to obtain empirical ends." He, however, distinguished magic from religion.
4. In simple words, magic can be understood as the use of some supernatural power to obtain the desired ends.

British anthropologist *James Frazer* in his '*Golden Bough*' has spoken of two aspects of magic: (*i*) *magic by imitation*, and (*ii*) *magic by contagion*. (*i*) **In magic by Imitation** an individual imitates what he wants or expects to happen. *Example*: If an individual wants rainfall to take place, he may fill his mouth with water and squirt it around in different directions. Similarly, to finish off an enemy, a wax or wooden image of him may be made and pierced with a needle or chisel. (*ii*) **Magic** by **Contagion** is based on the belief that whatever would come into contact with the supernatural power, will be swayed by it. Thus the forehead of a person may be rubbed off with some ashes so that he may be free from headaches. Further, it is because of this belief the survivors of the deceased person used to bury or burn along with his dead body all his articles, (dress, walking stick, foot wear, bed, mat, etc.) to keep themselves free from his bad influence.

Types of Magic

Sociologists have spoken of two types of magic. (*i*) *White magic*, and (*ii*) *Black magic*. The distinction between the two does not always correspond to the distinction between "*approved*" and "*disapproved*" or between "*legitimate*" and "*illegitimate*." White magic is normally approved of; but black magic is sometimes approved of, while some other times disapproved of.

1. White Magic

White magic is that kind of magic which is never used to do harm within the magician's own society. *Example*: Magic to restore health is "*white*". Similarly, magic to ensure victory in war is 'white' even though it may harm the enemy.

White magic is perhaps most commonly practised in fields such as agriculture, hunting, war- fare, and health. The magic rite or spell may be used for an individual's benefit or for the benefit of some larger group, upto the whole society. *Example*: The *Navaho singer*, by various supernatural means such as singing, chanting and making sand paintings, tries to restore people to health. He is a specialist, and gets fees for his services.

We may expect magic under two conditions; that is, (*i*) *when there is emotional involvement in the outcome of action*, and (*ii*) *when there is no adequate rational control over the outcome*. Magical ritual is not used as a *substitute* for rational techniques for magic is only a *supplement*. By performing magic, men assure themselves that they are doing everything possible to produce a favourable outcome. Through magic they try to express their strong wishes symbolically and renew their confidence. *Ex*: Trobriand Islanders consider magic as inevitable for deep sea fishing which involves risk. But they do not use magic in their fresh-water fishing, which involves no risk.

2. Black Magic

Black magic consists of sorcery and witchcraft. *Sorcery* consists of rites and spells, the efficacy of which does not depend upon the supernatural power vested in the magician himself. Hence sorcery can be learnt and practised with efficacy by any one. It only requires that the ritual is correctly performed and that the victim or his protector does not use counter magic of greater power. *Witchcraft*, on the other hand, is black magic that is thought to depend upon the supernatural power of the magician. Thus it cannot be transmitted, except possibly by heredity. *Ex*: Among the *Dobuans* of the Western Pacific, black magic is used to protect property right and hence to punish theft. The *Maori* Chieftains in New Zealand try to reinforce their authority by their control of black magic. Among the *Pondo* of South Africa, mothers-in-law and daughters-in-law most frequently accuse each other of being witches. The use of black magic on a large scale in some societies such as those of Dobuans, is an indication of strains and tensions in the social structure of a society.

Difference between Religion and Magic

Magic and religion are closely linked. According to some writers magic is also a kind of religion, while some others never consider it so. What they have in common is the reference to a supernatural realm. According to *Kingsley Davis*, magic and religion could be distinguished on the basis of the following: (*i*) *the kind of ends pursued*, (*ii*) *the types of attitudes involved*, (*iii*) *the particular kind of supernaturalism required*, and (*iv*) *the pattern of behaviour exhibited*. These may be explained in the following way.

1. ***The kinds of ends pursued:*** The magic implies that a definite end is being pursued. This end is immediate, practical, and usually private. *Ex*: Among the Northern Chins, a sick man may offer a young foul or small dog to the angry deity (who he thinks is responsible for the disease) in sacrifice to satisfy his deity so that he gets cured of his disease.

   But religion has no definite end. It is not used as means but stands as an end in itself. Even when the religious behaviour and holy objects are used to attain an end; the end is either ultimate or public in nature. Thus a man may pray God for his salvation or for group welfare.

2. ***The types of attitudes involved:*** In religion, emphasis is laid on the subjective attitude of the participants. For example, feelings of awe, reverence, elevation, sublimation, and inspiration are experienced by the individuals with regard to the holy. But in magic the attitude is more materialistic. The attitude is more a matter of fact. It is similar to the attitude which one holds. when using any ordinary technological instrument. Most of the magical spells are spoken in normal, matter-of-fact voices. If a magician wants a medicine to bring the immediate effect of a cure, he says so.

3. ***The particular kind of supernaturalism required:*** Religion brings into play the entire supernatural world with all its creatures capable of responding to human wishes and sorrows. On the other hand, magic accomplishes its effect simply by automatic action. In magic, the supernatural agency may be nothing more than an imaginary force or principle attributed to some objects. *Ex*: In order to secure long life which lasts longer resisting the fire.

   Thus, the intellectual content of magic is very narrow for it is mainly utilitarian in purpose. But the intellectual content of religion is relatively wider. It includes various aspects such as myths relating to the origin of man and his major institutions, accounts of gods and their power, elaborate rituals, ceremonies, etc.

4. ***The Pattern of behaviour exhibited:*** A magical behaviour is mostly a commercial transaction in which trickery and deceit become possible. But religion establishes a bond between man and God, and such a bond is absent in magic.

Magic diverges most from religion when it is used to accomplish aims not sanctioned by the group. It may be employed to achieve vengeance, to acquire property illegally, to steal another man's wife, to, commit murder, etc. In such cases it is carried out in secret. Hence members of the group fear black magic. For the same reason "Magic is now, and for a long time has been regarded with some moral reprobation..."

Magic and Science

Magic is often called a type of primitive science. This view is based on some analogies. *Ex*: Magic, like science, pursues practical ends, conceives that certain effects follow certain causes, takes an impersonal attitude towards causation, and has little to do with morality. In spite of these analogies, magic is in many ways the opposite of science. Because, unlike science, magic relies on supernatural causation. Magic unscientifically believes that some effect is produced because of the mystical power associated with the spell, rite or object. In magic, the facts are not used to test the theory as in science. On the other hand, the theory that is, the magical procedure is always assumed to be right. Here the elements of faith and wishful thinking enter. A failure in magical performances is therefore attributed to a failure to carry out the procedure correctly, and *not to the procedure* itself. The function of magic is to give confidence and a sense of security. For this reason the individual must have a non-rational faith in its adequacy. Hence it can exist side by side with perfectly good scientific and technological practices. During the World War II the pilots used to carry in their planes some animals, articles of clothing, mystic numbers, etc., that were believed to give them luck. Magic deals in absolutes whereas science deals in probabilities. Science is tentative and partial and it cannot give the confidence in the way in which magic gives. As *K. Davis* says magic may become less important, but it is not going to disappear as technology and science advance.

SECULARISATION

It is generally felt that the growth of modernism and modern civilisation has affected religion, its functions and the religiosity of the people. Developments in the fields-of science, technology and education have also adversely affected religion and its traditional functions. There is a growing trend towards secularism and secularisation today.

Meaning of Secularism

- 'Secularism is a system of social or political philosophy that rejects all forms of religious faiths' - *Random House Dictionary*.
- '*Secularism*.....,means liberation of politics from the hegemony of religion' - *Sri Asghar Ali Engineer, Indian Express, dated 30-4-1991*.
- *Secularism*: "Belief that morality, education, etc. should not be based on religion" - *Oxford Advanced Learner's Dictionary*.

Meaning of Secularisation

- "The term 'secularisation' implies that what was previously regarded as religious is now ceasing to be such, and it also implies a process of differentiation which results in the various aspects of society, economic, political, legal and moral, becoming increasingly discrete in relation to each other". *M.N. Srinivas* in "*Social Change in Modern India*"
- "*Secularisation is the process by which traditional religious beliefs and institutions lose their influence in society*"
  —*Ian Robertson* in *Sociology*, p. 384

As industrialisation advances, the general historical tendency is for societies to become increasingly secular, or worldly, in their values, beliefs and institutions.

The principal cause of secularisation is to be found in the complexity of modern urbanised industrialised society. In simple societies, religion extends to every aspect of experience. In a complex society many new specialised institutions arise, As a result, religion becomes a separate and a distinct institution with a limited field of influence, and may find itself in competition with other institutions such as science or government. Religious belief is no longer self-evidently true. Religion loses its monopoly of faith and has to compete with alternative belief systems, including even atheism, Religious commitment tends to become part time rather than full time.

1. *Differentiation is one of the salient features of Secularisation*. The ethical, political and economic issues are separated from each other. For example, the economic issues are decided on the basis of economic principles only in a true secular state.

2. *Rationality, scientific attitude, and humanistic outlook - are some other characteristics of secularisation*. Modern education lays stress upon scientific attitude towards human problems. It has also contributed to the development of humanitarian outlook.
3. *Development in the means of transport and communication, urbanisation, legislation, social and reformative movements* - all these have added to the secular thinking.

Measures of the Process of Secularisation

The process of secularisation may be measured in several ways. *Ian Robertson* has mentioned the following measures [Page: 385]:

1. *The establishment of religion as a separate and distinct institution with a limited role in society*–is a true measure of secularisation. The process is occurring in all industrial societies.
2. A second measure of secularisation is *the extent to which the religious institutions such as churches, temples, mosques, etc. which have modified their teachings and rituals in order to come to terms with secular society*. "As *Peter Berger* [1970] suggests, the churches and secular society are engaged in a bargaining process, but the compromise inevitably favours the stronger party, secular society. The churches may thus become more concerned with preserving themselves than with their original mission". — Ian Robertson - 385
3. A third measure of secularisation is the *declining membership of the churches and the decreasing attendance at worship and other rituals*. This process is in fact very difficult to measure. How many people are going to the church or temple or mosque regularly? How many are going there with real religious commitment? These questions cannot be answered satisfactorily. However, the evidence from all industrial societies points to a steady decline in church membership and attendance.

REVIEW QUESTIONS

1. Give the definitions of religion. Indicate its basic components.
2. Assess the importance of religion as a system of belief and ritual.
3. Man is a spiritual being. Discuss.
4. Explain the concepts of sacred and profane. Discuss the nature and qualities of sacred and profane.
5. The sacred and profane are closely related. Analyse.
6. Elaborate on the theories of the origin of religion.
7. Comment on the structural aspects of religion.
8. Describe the functions and dysfunctions of religion.
9. Throw light on the religious roles.
10. Explain the meaning of mortality. Differentiate between religion and mortality.
11. Analyse the interrelationship between religion and mortality.
12. How is science related to religion? Discuss.
13. Define magic. Discuss the types of magic.
14. Differentiate between religion and magic, and magic and science.
15. What do you mean by secularisation? Discuss the measures of the process of securatisation.
16. Write short notes on the following:
    (a) Fetishism
    (b) Animism
    (c) Totemism
    (d) Recent trends in religion

⌘⌘⌘⌘⌘⌘⌘⌘⌘⌘⌘

PART SIX

SOCIAL CONTROL

35

Meaning and Nature of Social Control

Chapter Outline

- Meaning, Definition and Nature of Social Control
- Purposes of Social Control
- Types of Social Control: Formal and Informal Control
- Agencies of Social Control: — Control By Law — Control By Education — Control By Public Opinion — Control By Propaganda — Control By Coercion — Control By Customs — Control By Folkways and Mores — Control By Religion and Morality — Control By Sanctions — Control By Fashions, Rites, Rituals and Ceremonies, Etiquettes.

Rousseau's book "*Social Contract*" begins with a famous sentence: "*Man is born free, and everywhere he is in chains*". It is true that man cannot be absolutely free in society. The collective life of man is possible only in the context of social constraints. The sustained social experience of man has revealed to him that in his own interest and in the interest of others he must subject himself to some kind of control which is over and above him. Attainment of individual happiness is the main aim of social life. The happiness can be attained not with unbounded freedom for action but with restrained behaviour. Man has given to society the power of exercising its control over his behaviour. The control which the society exercises over the behaviour of its members through various mechanisms can be referred to as '*social control*'.

MEANING OF SOCIAL CONTROL

The survival and smooth functioning of the society is possible only when there exist in it social harmony, social solidarity and social order. Social harmony or solidarity is not an automatic devel- opment. Individual members of the society must strive and struggle to bring it out. Members of the society are able to bring about social harmony or order only when they conform to certain accepted standards of behaviour or norms. Conformity to norms must prevail over the self-seeking impulses of the people. Group welfare or societal welfare must take precedence over individual pleasures. Individual by himself cannot do this. Hence society exercises its force or control over the individual members. *Thus social control refers to the control of society over the individual*. Social control implies a system of device through which society controls the activities of individual members.

E.A. Ross was the first American sociologist to deal with this concept of social control in his famous book "*Social Control*" published in 1901. In fact, it was he who first used the concept of '*social control*' in sociological discussion. Since then the concept has become quite popular. According to Ross, the individual has deeprooted sentiments that help him to cooperate with other fellow members to work for social welfare. These sentiments are *sympathy, sociability* and a *sense of justice*. But these sentiments by themselves are not enough to suppress the self-seeking impulses of the individual. Society has to make use of its mechanisms to accomplish the necessary order and discipline. Ross has stressed upon the roles of *public opinion, law, belief, suggestion, religion, ideols, ceremony*, etc. in establishing social control.

DEFINITION OF SOCIAL CONTROL

1. *Fairchild.* "Social Control is the sum total of the processes where by society, or any sub group within society, secures conformity to expectation on the pan of its constituent units, individuals and groups".
2. *E. A. Ross*. "Social Control refers to the "system of devices whereby society brings its members into conformity with the accepted standards of behaviour".
3. *Manheim*. "Social Control is the sum of those methods by which a society tries to influence human behaviour to maintain a given order."
4. *Ogburn* and *Nimkoff* have said that social control refers to "the patterns of pressure which a society exerts to maintain order and established rules."
5. *J.S. Roucek.* 'Social Control' is a collective term used to refer to "those processes planned or unplanned, by which individuals are taught, persuaded or compelled to conform to the usages and life-values of groups".
6. *G.A. Lundberg* and others have said that social control designates "those social behaviours which influence individuals or groups toward conformity to established or desired norms".

Nature of Social Control

The above-mentioned definitions suggest that social control consists of the following essential aspects:

1. ***Social control denotes some kind of influence:*** The influence may be exercised in various ways by means of public opinion, coercion, religion, morality, ideology, leadership, etc.
2. ***The influence is essentially exerted by the society or community:*** The influence is exerted at various levels. It may indicate the entire society's influence over all the innumerable smaller groups, sub-groups and individuals. It may denote the influence of a dominant group over several smaller groups. It may signify the group's dominance over the individual members. It may reflect in some cases the influence of a few extra-ordinary individuals over other ordinary individuals.
3. ***The influence is exercised for promoting the welfare of all the individuals or of the group as a whole:*** Social Control is not aimless. It is there to serve the general interests of all and to curb the dangerous selfish interests of those who try to satisfy them.
4. ***The influence of the society has been there since times immemorial:*** Social Control is as old as human society. It is an essential condition of the human society. In the absence of social control no society can ever hold together its members for any length of time.
5. ***The influence is universal:*** Where there is society there is social control. It is there even in the so-called uncivilised, barbaric and cannibalistic societies.

PURPOSES OF SOCIAL CONTROL

The purpose of 'social control' as the very term indicates, is to exercise control over people in an effective manner. Why the control is needed? According to *Kimball Young*, it is necessary "*to bring about conformity, solidarity, and continuity of a particular group or society*". The three purposes of social control mentioned by Kimball Young — conformity, solidarity and continuity of the group — may be described below.

1. ***Social control brings about social conformity:*** This is the main purpose of social control. Since the modern complex society is a multigroup society differential norms will have to co-exist. As a result, behavioural patterns of different groups differ significantly. But these differences should not be allowed to exceed the limits of tolerance. People must be made to feel the need for security. For the sake of security they are obliged, to accept conformity. Social Control thus provides for conformity.
2. ***Social control brings about solidarity:*** The second main purpose of social control is to create in the minds of people *the feeling of identity and of solidarity*. For the proper and smooth functioning of the society the different organisations and institutions of the social system must be properly integrated. Otherwise, in this competitive world the weaker group may be completely exploited by the stronger one, or equally powerful groups may clash among themselves and spoil peace and order. Some groups may even develop anti-societal attitudes and pose permanent danger to the organisation of the society. It becomes necessary for the society to establish a reasonable balance or

equilibrium between different groups and institutions. This would repose confidence among people. Society does this through various means of social control.

3. ***Social control assures the continuity of social group or society:*** Societies not only struggle for stability and solidarity but also for their own survival or continuity. Continuity is the bed-rock on which the future of the society depends. Society maintains its continuity by controlling effectively its people and their groups. Due to this continuity the means of social control become in course of time a pan of culture. As a part of culture they are transmitted from one generation to another. Thus, various means of social control function endlessly to maintain the continuity of the society.

TYPES OF SOCIAL CONTROL

Society makes use of various means of social control depending upon the time and social situation for the realisation of its purposes. It is left to the discretion of the group to decide what means must be used at what time and in what social situation. In some primitive communities magic and superstitious beliefs are enough to exercise control. In a rural society means such as folkways, mores, customs, traditions, beliefs are enough to act as social pressures on individual behaviour. 'But in the modem urban society, radio, television, newspapers, schools and colleges, police force, etc., may be used for enforcing conformity. In fact, societies have developed consciously or unconsciously various devices for the purpose of controlling the behaviour of their members. *Formal* and *informal control* represent two kinds of devices.

Formal and Informal Control

Social Control can be classified into two major types on the basis of the means of social control that are employed. They are: 1. *Formal control*, and 2. *Informal control*.

1. Formal Control

The state makes use of *law, legislation, military force, police force, administrative devices*, etc., for the purpose of social control. Similarly, different political, religious, economic, cultural and other associations and institutions also institute formal control over the behaviour of the members. Formal control is deliberately created. Various rules are laid down to make it specific. The necessity of following formal control or rules is clearly stated by associations and institutions. Violators of formal control are given punishments depending upon the nature and type of violation. The organisation that makes use of formal control may even create a body of officials vested with power to enforce control as we find it in the case of state which has established the police, military force, etc. In brief, an association, whether it is a state or a bank, or an army, or a factory or anything has its own norms through which it controls the behaviour of the members. All these come under formal control. Formal control has become a necessity in the modern complex societies in which interaction is mostly impersonal in nature.

2. Informal Control

Informal Control includes *gossip, slander, resentment, public opinion. sympathy, sense of justice, folkways, mores, customs, religion, morality* and such other agents. These are not purposefully created. Nothing could be said with certainty regarding their origin. They arise on their own way and in course of time gain currency and popularity. They become deep-rooted with people in their practices. No specific punishment would be given to the violators of informal control. Still they are more effective than the formal control. They do not require any extra staff to enforce them as it is so in the case of formal control. They do not have the physical force to enforce conformity to them. Hence, people may not observe them or go against them without being physically punished for the same. Faith in religion, moral convictions, public opinion, artistic standard, and the general state of enlightenment are found to be more important in informal control.

Informal control is more effective in primary social groups such as family, neighbourhood, tribe, rural community where interaction takes place on a personal basis. Whenever the group or the society becomes larger (in terms of population) and more complex, the informal devices of control become less effective. Simple gossip and slander and censure can correct an erring ruralite but not an urban citizen. The anonymity of city life which has added to the confidence of the individual that he could commit an offence without being noticed or caught by others who are mostly engaged in their own business, contributes to the non-effectiveness of informal control. Hence informal methods have given place to the formal ones such as law, education, coercion and codes, though less effective informal control also functions along with formal control in urban areas in regulating people's activities.

AGENCIES OF SOCIAL CONTROL

Society or group maintains social control by creating its own agencies which may enforce formal or informal control. Agencies such as law, education, physical coercion and codes on the one hand, folkways, mores, customs, convention, tradition, religion, etc., on the other, have been used by the society for this purpose. The number and variety of devices and agencies employed depend on the degree of complexity of life in a society. The role of some of these agencies may be briefly discussed here.

1. Control by Law

Law is the most powerful formal means of social control in the modern society. Laws appear only in societies with a political organisation, that is a government. The term '*Law*' has been defined in various ways. *J.S. Roucek* opines that "*Laws are a form of social rule emanating from political agencies*". *Roscoe Pound* says that "law is an authoritative canon of value laid down by the force of politically organised society".

The main characteristics of law are — (1) Laws are the general conditions of human activity prescribed by the state for its members. (2) Law is called law, only if enacted by a proper law-making authority. It is a product of conscious thought, deliberate attempts and careful planning. (3) Law is definite, clear and precise. (4) Law applies equally to all without exception in identical circumstances. (5) Violation of law is followed by penalties and punishments determined by the authority of the state. (6) Laws are always written down and recorded in some fashion. Hence they cannot appear in non-literate society. (7) Laws are not the result of voluntary consent of persons against whom they are directed.

Law is derived from various sources. As *J. S. Roucek* has pointed out. "All social rules including political rules, or laws, originated first in custom or folkways of long standing and are based upon existing conceptions of justice and right in a given community". It is true that "*in all societies law is based upon moral notions*". Laws are made and legislations are enacted on the basis of social doctrines, ideals and mores. It does not mean that the domains of law and morals are co-extensive. Still it can be said that "*the maintenance of legal order depends upon the moral climate of a society*". (*Bottomore*). The effectiveness of legal regulation never rests solely upon the threat of physical sanctions. It very much depends upon a *general attitude of respect for law, and for a particular legal order*. This attitude itself is determined by moral approval of law as containing social justice.

Law requires enforcing agencies. Laws are enforced with the help of the police, the court, and sometimes the armed forces. Administrative machinery of the state is the main law-enforcing agency. Increasing complexity of the modern industrial society has necessitated enormous growth of administrative agencies. Law is, in fact the control of administrative power which is vested in the government officials. Law as an instrument of control performs two functions: (*i*) *It eliminates and suppresses the homicidal activities of individuals*. (*ii*) *Law persuades individuals to pay attention to the rights of others as well as to act in co-operation with others*. In this way law tries to protect the individuals and society and promotes social welfare.

It is almost impossible now-a-days to conceive of a society of any degree of complexity in which social behaviour would be completely regulated by moral sanctions. Law has thus become inevitably a pervasive phenomenon. Contemporary international relations would reveal the importance of law in social control it may be true that the moral unity of the mankind is now greater than ever before. But moral sentiments alone are not enough today to regulate relations. They are by necessity supplemented by the law.

2. Control by Education

Education may be defined as a process whereby the social heritage of a group is passed on from one generation to another. It is in this sense, *Durkheim* conceived of education as "*the socialisation of the younger generation*". He also stated, "It is actually a continuous effort to impose on the child ways of seeing, feeling and acting which he could not have arrived at spontaneously". *Brown* and *Roucek* have said that education is "the sum total of the experience which moulds the attitudes and determines the conduct of both the child and the adult". Education is every experience, trifling or profound, which durably modifies, thought, feeling or action.

Education is not just concerned with transmitting a way of life. In the modern times it is largely devoted to the communication of empirical knowledge. It is required today to prepare individuals for a changing rather than a static world. Formal education has been communicating ideas and values which play a part in regulating behaviour. In modern society science and technology are the basis of a general rational approach to nature and social life. The whole rationalisation of the modern world is connected with the development of science. The chief instrument of this development is educational system. In this way, formal education can be viewed as a type of social control. Education has contributed to the regulation of conduct in the early socialisation of the child. Educational reformers such as *Montessori* and *Froebel* have brought about great changes in the education of young children. These reforms reveal the moral notions external to the educational system. But they have been influential in changing moral ideas in society at large.

Some educators have suggested that education must be used for making a "*good society*". Education is not primarily an attempt to stuff the mind with information, but train people to think to distinguish between truth and error to arrive at reality. In this regard, the school is taken to mean a "*community of experience*" rather than as a "*series of planned lessons*". *George S. Counts* has remarked that "*Education, emptied of all social control and considered solely as method, points no-where and can arrive nowhere... .*" Today people send their children to the schools to be taught properly. "To be taught properly means, of course, to be taught in accordance with the wishes of the community". The community is most sensitive, in particular, to those aspects of teaching that have social and moral significance. Hence much attention is paid to select right persons for the teaching profession.

Education from infancy to adulthood is a vital means of social control. Through education new generation learns the social norms and the penalties for violating them. Theoretical education, that is reading and writing, serves to form the intellectual basis and with practical education one learns to put this into practice. Without proper education the harmony of the individual and society is not merely difficult but also impossible. Education makes social control quite normal. *It converts social control into self-control*. In the absence of a well organised educational system, social control would remain merely as an arbitrary pressure which may not last long. Hence, education is a necessary condition for the proper exercise of social control.

Control by Public Opinion

Public Opinion is an important agency of social control. As *K. Young* has said, "*Public Opinion consists of the opinion held by a public at a certain time*". According to *V. V. Akolkar*, "Public opinion simply refers to that mass of ideas which people have to express on a given issue". Public opinion may be said to be the collective opinion of majority of members of a group.

Public opinion is of great significance especially in democratic societies. Through public opinion the knowledge of the needs, ideas, beliefs, and values of people can be ascertained. It influences the social behaviour of people, Behaviour of the people is influenced by ideas, attitudes and desires which are reflected by public opinion. People get recognition and respectability when they behave according to accepted social expectations. Public opinion helps us to know what type of behaviour is acceptable and what is not.

There are various agencies for the formulation and expression of public opinion. The press, radio, movies and legislatures are the main controlling agencies of public opinion.

The **'press'** includes newspapers, magazines and journals of various kinds. The newspaper provides the stuff of opinion for it covers everyday events and policies. Many decisions of the people are influenced by information available through the press. As an agency of social control the press seeks to influence the tastes, ideas, attitudes and preferences of the readers. It affects their ideology also. It enforces morality by exposing the moral lapses of the leaders.

Radio is another agency of public opinion that influences behaviour. It influences our language, customs and institutions. It is through the radio that human voice can reach millions of people at the same time. It can dramatise and popularise events and ideas. In the same way, television has also been influencing people's behaviour.

Movies or motion pictures exert great influence on public opinion. They have effectively changed the attitudes and behaviour of the people. Movie-goers are relaxed and unaware of the fact that they are being affected by ideas and values. They identify themselves with the leading characters and unconsciously accept the attitudes, values, etc., implicit in the role. Some emotionally disturbed people often search solutions for their problems through, movies. Through films it is possible to improve people's tastes, ideas and attitudes to some extent.

Legislature at present is the most effective agency for the formulation and expression of public opinion. The debates in the legislatures influence public opinion particularly in democratic system. It makes laws that control people's life and activities. It should be noted that legislature itself is subject to the influence of the people.

Control by Propaganda

"*Propaganda is an organised or systematic attempt made by a person or a group to influence public opinion and attitudes in any sphere*"–*Akolkar*. It refers to the techniques of influencing human action by the manipulation of representations. It is a means of influencing others, often towards a' desirable end.

Propaganda can affect people's faith, ideology, attitude and behaviour. It can also be used to replace old beliefs and practices with the new ones. Propaganda may bring about positive as well as negative results. Governmental departments such as medical department, planning department, cooperative department, customs department, income tax department, etc. make propaganda to help people to mend their ways and also to develop right habits, practices and approaches. Every government maintains a department to influence people in the direction of accepted patterns. This department is called the department of '*public relation*' or "*publicity*". The health department may make use of various devices and techniques of propaganda to impress upon people to take precautions to control contagious diseases. The planning department may try to appeal to the people through effective propaganda the necessity of controlling birth rate. The income tax department may try to create fear in the minds of tax payers of the consequences of evading taxes through propaganda.

Propaganda plays a vital role in both democratic and dictatorial countries. In democratic countries propaganda is mainly used to persuade people to accept some opinions or reject some others or to follow some new practices or drop out some old ones. But in dictatorial countries it is used by the government mainly to suppress public opinion or to make people to believe what it wants them to believe. Mass media of communication are used for this purpose. Propaganda by itself is neither good nor bad. It depends on the purpose for which it is used and how it is used.

To make propaganda very effective the propagandists repeat them regularly and systematically. They present only one side of the question and furnish vast evidences in support of it. They condemn their opponents and resort to self-praise in an intelligent way. To get enduring effects they concentrate on children and try to '*brainwash*' them. Totalitarian states normally try to do this. They even make education an instrument of propaganda.

Control by Coercion

Coercion, that is, the use of physical force is one of the forms of social control; Coercion refers to the use of physical force to stop or control a work or an action. Whenever people are refrained from doing a particular work or whenever some limits are put deliberately on the range of their choice through the use of force, or through the threat of its consequences, they may be said to be under coercion.

Coercion is an extreme form of violence. State is the only association which is empowered to use coercion in social control. No other association is vested with this power. It becomes necessary for the state to resort to coercion to suppress anti-social trends and activities, Otherwise there would be no security for social life. It is necessary to keep within limits the self-interest, the greed, the lawlessness, and the intolerance ever ready to assert its will over others. It is necessary to protect the interests of the weaker groups, minorities, servants, slaves, poor and the like. Safeguarding the political and social order is the main service of force.

Force *alone* cannot protect the social order, but without force the order could never be secure. "Without force law is in danger of being dethroned, though force alone can, never keep law in its throne".

Though force is essential, it has its own limitations. The intervention of force substitutes a mechanical for a social relationship. The use of force indicates the denial of the possibility of co- operation. It treats the human being as though he were merely a physical object. Force is the end of mutuality. Force by itself admits no expression of human impulses against whom it is wielded. Further, the exercise of power is a wasteful operation. It checks all the ordinary processes of life, all the give-and-take of common living. The more it is used the more it breeds resistance, thus necessi- tating still more enforcement.

Human experience has revealed that coercion or force is necessary as the guarantee of political laws. Its service is best rendered when it is used to the minimum. Where a common rule is consid- ered necessary or beneficial for the common good, some degree of compulsion is involved. Hence force becomes necessary to enforce the common rule. But only when the use of force is limited it becomes the servant of fundamental liberties of people. Only then the harmony of individuality and society could be most fully achieved.

Control by Customs

'*Customs*' represent a kind of informal social control. "*The socially accredited ways of acting are the customs of society*".—*MacIver* and *Page*. Many of our daily activities are regulated by customs. Our ways of dressing, speaking, eating, working, worshipping, training the young, celebrating festivals, etc., are all controlled by customs. They are self-accepted rules of social life. Individuals can hardly escape their hold.

All normal people prefer to live according to the customs for *they save much of our energy and time*. They save us from the objections and ridicule of the society. Customs give guidance for people in every activity. One need not have to resort to original thinking on every aspect. The role played by customs in life is comparable to the role of instincts in animals. Customs enlighten man in his social life.

Customs are conformed mostly *unconsciously*. Man learns them from his very childhood and goes on obeying them. Customs are very rarely opposed. Even the harmful customs are also obeyed by most of the people because they do not consider them harmful. While those who consider them harmful lack the courage to oppose them, only some exceptional individuals have the courage of going against them or carrying on protest against them.

Customs are *basic* to our collective life. They are found everywhere. They are more influential and dominant in the primitive society than in the modern society. In the tribal societies they act as the "*King of Man*". In the modern complex society custom is slowly losing its hold over people, and giving place to law.

Control by Folkways and Mores

Folkways and mores represent two important types of informal control.

Control by Folkways

'*Folkways*' refer to the ways of the people. They are "*the repetitive petty acts of the people*". Folkways are the norms to which people conform because it is expected of them. Confor- mity to the folkways is neither required by law nor enforced by any special agency of society. For example, there is no law that compels us to wash clothes, to take bath, to brush teeth, to greet friends, to give respect to elders, etc. Still we do many such activities without thinking over them. It is a matter of usage. They are our folkways.

Folkways are not as compulsive and obligatory as laws or morals. Those who violate folkways are not punished by formal means. But the violators are put to gossip, slander and ridicule. One can ignore a few of the folkways but no one can neglect or violate all of them. They constitute an important part of the social structure. They contribute to the order and stability of social relations. Human infants learn them through their elders through socialisation. They learn different folk-ways at different stages relevant to their class, caste, ethnic, religious, occupational, marital and other statuses. We are made to follow them because they are binding. They become with us a matter of habit.

Control by Mores

'*Mores*' or '*Morals*' represent another category of norms. *When 'folkways' act as regulators of behaviour then they become 'mores'*. Mores are considered to be essential for group welfare. The *positive mores* prescribe behaviour patterns while the *negative mores* or *taboos* prescribe or prohibit behaviour patterns. Mores for example, instruct people to love their country, to look after their wives and children, to tell the truth, to be helpful to others, etc. They also insist on people not to become unpatriotic, not to show disrespect to the god, not to steal, cheat, etc.

Mores represent the living character of the group. They are always considered as '*right*' by the people who share them. They are morally right and their violation morally wrong. Hence they are more compulsive in nature. Mores contribute to the solidarity and harmony of the group. They help the individuals to identify themselves with the group. Every group has its own mores. There are mores for each sex, for all ages, for all classes, for all families and so on.

Mores help the individuals to realise that community living or collective life is possible only when one conforms to the norms. Mores weld the individual with the group or the society without damaging his personal liberty. Individual learns through mores that the society is not against him. They differ from place to place and time to time. They become in course of time the basis of law. Laws are often called "*codified mores*".

Control by Religion and Morality

Religion and morality are the most effective means of informal social control in both modern and primitive societies

Control by Religion

Religion refers to man's faith or belief in some supernatural power or force. As *MacIver* and *Page* have said, religion "*implies a relationship not merely between man and man but also between man and some higher power*". Religious concept is thus linked with man's relationship with God. The behaviour which is in conformity with this relationship is religious behaviour. The norms concerned with religious behaviour constitute the religious code. The main purpose of religious code is to insist on religious conformity. Religious conformity in most of the cases will be in consonance with social conformity. Because, the main intention of the religious code is to make man basically good, obedient and helpful to others.

Religion regulates the activities of people in its own way. It regulates human conduct, through religious code. The conceptions of spirits, ghosts, taboos, soul, divine commandments, sermon, etc., control human actions and enforce discipline. Ideas of hell and heaven too have great effects on the behaviour of people. It has a great disciplinary value.

Man as a religious being tries to adjust, or restrain or mend his behaviour to secure the blessings of the divinity. He is afraid of going against the divine will or the divine rule. Religion has a '*supra- social sanction*' to enforce obedience to the religious code. Religion demands total surrender to the divine force or power. Man by surrendering himself to the divine force tries to suppress his own impulses and selfish desires.

In yet another way also religion serves as a means of social control. Religion *conserves the norms and values of life*. Religion defines and redefines values. Moral, spiritual and social values are strongly supported by religion. Through the agencies such as family, church, school, religion inculcates the values of life in the minds of growing children. As *Thomas F. O'Dea* has pointed out, "*religion sacralises the norms and values of established society*". It "*maintains the dominance of group goals over individual impulses*".

Religion has its own methods to deal with those individuals who violate religious code or norms. Various religious agencies such as temples, churches, mutts, monasteries created by religion also help to control and humble the disobedients. Religion has its own ways and means to re–integrate the disobedients into the social group. Further, religious sanctions are widely made use of to support the ethical codes and moral practices.

Control by Morality

Morality is an institution that is closely related to religion. Morality is concerned with the conceptions of goodness and evil. It refers to "*that body of rules and principles concerned with good and evil as manifested to as by conscience*". These rules are admitted at large by the community. Honesty, faithfulness, fairness, service-mindedness, truthfulness, conscientiousness, kindness, sacrifice, incorruptibility, etc., represent some of the moral concepts. People who are morally good are also socially good.

Morality always helps to make a distinction between right and wrong or good and bad. Hence morality acts as a guide of human behaviour. Moral rules are obeyed because of internal pressure. This pressure refers to *the pressure of conscience*. But in the case of religion, man obeys religious rule because of his fear towards God. In morality, man is not very much afraid of God, but he is afraid of society. Morality is based on rational judgement or rationality whereas religion is based on faith and emotions.

Religion and morality are mutually complementary and supportive. What is morally good is in most of the cases good spiritually also. The fulfilment of God's will and the performance of moral actions are, therefore, two aspects of the same process. Both are concerned with the '*higher law*' which stands over and above the sphere of the state and outside state control. Though not always morality supports religious beliefs and considers religiosity as a moral virtue. In the same way, religion reinforces morality with its super-natural sanctions. Both jointly command and control human conduct. *Mathew Arnold* says that "*Religion is morality touched with emotions*". *F. H. Bradley* opines, "it is a moral duty not to be immoral and that is the duty to be religious".

Control by Sanctions

Sanctions are the supporters of norms. '*Sanctions*' *refer to* "*the rewards or punishments used to establish social control, that is, to enforce the norms in a society*". The basic purpose of sanction is to bring about conformity. They are used to force or persuade an individual or group to conform to social expectations.

Sanctions may be applied in various ways, ranging from the use of physical force to symbolic means, such as flattery. *Negatively*, they may be anything from a raised eyebrow to the death sentence. *Positively*, they range from a smile to an honorary degree.

Sanctions are applied in various ways. The type of sanctions also vary with the groups and situations. They may be positive or negative. Those sanctions which inflict pain or threaten to do so are *negative*. Those which elicit and facilitate response by rewards are *positive*. Both positive and negative sanctions may apply a wide variety of means. *Positive sanctions* include verbal methods such as praise, flattery, suggestion, persuasion, some of education, indoctrination, advertising, propaganda, slogans, giving rewards, medals, badges, uniforms, titles, etc. *Negative means* include-gossip, slander, satire, laughing at others, name-calling, threats, commands, censorship, and finally oven action. The method of overt action is the final sanction when no other way remains open. In this method pain, suffering and even death is included. Overt action also includes fines, imprisonment, whipping, mutilation, torture, banishment, ostracism and death. Extreme negative sanctions are applied only by the state.

Control by Miscellaneous Norms

Control by Fashion

Fashion may be defined as *permitted range of variation around a norm*. People want to be like their associates and friends and also want to be different from them. Fashion is a device beautifully suited to reconcile these opposing tendencies. Fashion permits and regulates variety and thereby avoids a dull and deadening uniformity. They help us to express our individuality without going against norms. In conforming to fashion we imitate our contemporaries. Sanctions that support conformity to fashion in dress are very powerful. Thus no woman wants to attend a dinner party in a night dress. *Superficial or trivial changes in fashions are called* '*fads*'. People follow both and try to conform to their requirements. Fashion has become all pervasive. People want to eat fashionable foods, wear fashionable dresses, read fashionable books, enjoy fashionable amusements, etc.

Control by Ceremonies, Rites, Rituals and Etiquette

Rites, rituals and ceremonies add dignity and a kind of special significance to various events of social life. They mark some occasions with solemnity and introduce enjoyment to others. More than that they serve to identify the individual with his groups, his community, and his nation.

Ceremonies are observed everywhere. The birth of a baby, confirmation, graduation, the death of an old man, the inauguration of a new factory, a promotion, the publication of a book, a new record in athletics, etc., are all events that draw special attention. Ceremony confers public recognition to them. Ceremony regularises or standardises situations which people confront for which they may not otherwise find a guide for action. *For example*, the funeral ceremony helps the survivors to meet the crisis of death.

'Rite' also refers to a ceremony. It sometimes conveys a sense of secrecy, of a ceremony known only to the initiated. All secret societies have their rites and also people with high qualifications have them. *Example*: An oral examination for the degree of doctor of philosophy. Through this the candidate joins the limited and selected few.

Ritual is also a ceremony but it is characterised by repetition. It is periodically or repeatedly performed. Ex. Republic Day, Independence Day, Wedding Anniversary, New Year's Day, Martyrs' Day, May Day, etc. Ritual introduces temporal regularity and a precision of detail into many of the events that characterise our social life. Ritual also induces a sense of identification with the group.

Etiquette: Etiquette is a code of precise procedures that governs the social interaction of people. It contains the notion of propriety. *Example*: To give some gifts to the host, to place a guest of honour at appropriate seat at a formal dinner, to present some gift to the bride, etc., Sociologically speaking, etiquette serves three functions. (*i*) It prescribes standard procedures to be followed on specific occasions. (*ii*) It indicates membership in a certain social class, and (*iii*) It serves to maintain social distance where intimacy or familiarity is not required. Etiquette repels unwanted approaches at specific occasions.

REVIEW QUESTIONS

1. What do you mean by social control? Discuss its nature, purpose and types.
2. Bring out the importance of social control.
3. Give the definitions of social control.
4. Describe the formal and informal means of social control.
5. Elucidate the role of various agencies in social control.
6. Give the classification of social control. Discuss each type in detail.
7. Assess the impact of religion on social control.
8. Folkways and mores represent two important types of informal control. Discuss.
9. Critically analyse the role of miscellaneous norms in social control.

⌘⌘⌘⌘⌘⌘⌘⌘⌘⌘⌘

36

FOLKWAYS – MORES – CUSTOMS – SANCTIONS

CHAPTER OUTLINE

- FOLKWAYS: DEFINITION — NATURE AND SOCIAL IMPORTANCE OF FOLKWAYS
- MORES: MEANING — DEFINITION — TYPES — NATURE — CHARACTERISTICS AND FUNCTIONS OF MORES
- DIFFERENCES BETWEEN FOLKWAYS AND MORES
- CUSTOMS: DEFINITION — NATURE AND SOCIAL IMPORTANCE OF CUSTOMS
- CUSTOMS AND HABITS
- SANCTIONS: INFORMAL AND FORMAL SANCTIONS — POWER AS THE BASIS OF SANCTION — TYPE OF SANCTIONS: POSITIVE AND NEGATIVE SANCTIONS

'*Folkways*', '*mores*', and '*customs*' represent different kinds of social norms. 'Social norms' refer to the group shared standards of behaviour. A social norm is a pattern setting limits on individual behaviour Norms are the 'blueprints' for behaviour. They are the rules for social living or for social being. They determine, guide, control and also predict human behaviour.

Human society assumes and enjoys remarkable order and stability. It tries to with stand disorder and instability. By the mechanism of social norms it is able to preserve itself. Social norms help society to maintain the unity of social life. Hence, they are called the 'sustaining forces' of a society.

Social norms are numerous and varied. They assume different forms. In terms of severity and durability they differ. Their influence and effect on the individual and society have not been uniform. Norms are not systematically classified by any sociologist. But broadly, they are grouped into—folkways, mores, customs, fashions, rites, rituals, ceremonies, taboos, traditions, conventions, statutes, laws, etiquettes and the like. We shall now discuss the nature of 'folkways', 'mores' and 'customs'.

FOLKWAYS

The term 'folkways' was introduced into sociological literature by *W. G. Sumner* in a book with the title 'Folkways' published in 1906. The word means literally "the ways of the folk". 'Folk' means people and 'Ways' refers to their behavioural habits. 'Folkways' are norms to which we conform because it is customary to do so in our society.

Folkways are the accepted ways of behaviour. According to *Summer*, folkways represent man's unique means of adapting himself to the environment. The term is often broadly used to include customs, conventions, usages, etiquettes, etc. It includes several modes of behaviour which men have evolved to meet the needs of their social life.

Definition of Folkways

1. *Gillin* and *Gillin* say that "Folkways are behaviour patterns of everyday life which generally arise unconsciously in a group".
2. *A. W. Green opines*, "Those ways of acting that are common to a society or a group and that are handed down from one generation to the next are known as folkways."

3. *Lundberg* has said that "Folkways are the typical or habitual beliefs, attitudes and styles of conduct observed within a group or community".
4. *Merill* says that folkways "are literally the ways of the folk, that is, social habits or group expectations that have arisen in the daily life of the group".
5. In simple words, 'folkways' can be understood as "repetitive petty acts of the people".

Examples of Folkways

The ways of eating, talking, dressing, playing, walking, working, greeting, conversing, expressing love and affection, etc., represent folkways. Taking three meals a day, walking on the right side of the road, driving on the left, wearing different kinds of dresses at different times, regular brushing of the teeth, washing of the clothes, taking bath regularly, respecting the elders, showering love and affection on the younger ones, wife and husband expressing mutual love, etc., represent different kinds of folkways.

Nature of Folkways

1. ***Social in nature:*** Folkways are the products of man's group life. They are created by the groups for their sustenance and maintenance. Individuals get social recognition by conforming to the folkways.
2. ***Repetitive in character:*** A social practice becomes a folkway when majority of people observe it constantly and regularly. The oft-repeated practices of the majority normally become the folkways, because such practices become standardized practices by constant repetition. In this sense also folkways represent the mass phenomena and not the individual peculiarity.
3. ***Unplanned origin:*** The origins of folkways are very obscure. Sumner believed that they arise automatically and unconsciously. They are not the result of any advance planning. Someone in the group starts a new way (may be a hairstyle, a dress style, a conversational style) and in course of time it becomes popular and a good number of people may start following it. But by the time it becomes the folkway, neither the originator nor the time of origin can be traced. For example, we cannot name the person who invented the greeting style or the hairstyle. Neither can we fix precisely the date of its origin.
4. ***Informal enforcement:*** Folkways constitute one of the types of informal means of social control. Folkways are not as compulsive and obligatory as that of laws or morals. Conformity to the folkways is neither required by law nor enforced by any special agency of the society. Those who violate folkways are not punished by formal means. They are not absolutely obligatory though they are considered as necessary. *For example*, one who does not brush his teeth regularly, take bath daily, and wash his clothes regularly and properly, is not going to be punished by law. But such an individual is put to gossip and ridicule. One can neglect and violate one or a few of the folkways but no sane person can neglect and violate *all* of them.
5. ***Folkways differ a lot:*** Folkways differ from group to group and society to society. They may also undergo changes in course of time within the same group or society. It is customary in India for women to keep their hair long while their counterpart in the West normally keep it short. Table meals are common in the West whereas majority of the Indians squat on the floor and take their meals with hands. But now changes have occurred.

   Further, *folkways vary with age* and *sex* in almost all the places. They vary according to the social class status. They differ according to region, ethnic group, racial group, caste, class and occupation.
6. ***Folkways are numerous:*** It is not possible for anyone to enlist all the folkways. No encyclopaedia could contain all of the folkways observed by all of the peoples of history. They are so diverse and numerous. Folkways touch upon even the titbits of our social behaviour. No social act of man can escape from its boundary. They range from most of the trivial acts and behaviour patterns to the most serious ones.
7. ***Folkways are subject to change:*** Folkways change with changing social conditions. Still changes are often resisted. Some folkways undergo relatively rapid change. *Summer* called them 'fashions'. Fashions relating to dress, hairstyle, architectural designs, etc., have undergone rapid Change. Folkways associated with beliefs and practices regarding the family, property, etc., resist change very often.

Social Importance of Folkways

The Folkways are the foundation of every culture. When fully assimilated they become personal habits. They save much of our energy and time. They are generally observed by the people. Hence all are free to solve problems and strive towards individual and collective goals. They have reduced much of our mental strain and nervous tension by helping us to handle social relations in a comfortable way. Sumner believed that "the life of society consists in making folkways and applying them. The science of society must be construed as the study of them". This is, of course, an exaggerated view.

Folkways have become a universal characteristic of human societies. No society docs or could exist without them. Hence they constitute an important part of the social structure. They contribute to the order and stability of social relations. Human infants learn the folkways through the elders as naturally as they grow older. They become a part and parcel of the personality of the infants through the process of socialization. They learn different folkways at different stages relevant to their class, caste, racial, ethnic and other statuses. Much role-playing in occupational statuses has almost become part of the folkways. We are made to follow them because they are binding. They become with us a matter of habit. They come to form the unstated premises in our mental life. They provide predictability to both of our behaviour and that of others. As one of the types of informal means of social control, folkways have assumed importance in the study of social control.

MORES

The '*mores*' represent yet another category of norms. 'Mores' is a term used to denote behaviour patterns which are not only accepted but are prescribed.

All the folkways are not equally important. Some of them become more compulsive and regulative in character. These folkways which become regulators of behaviour are normally referred to as 'mores'. *Sumner* applied the term 'mores' (singular '*more*') to those folkways which are considered by the group to be essential for its welfare and existence. "When the elements of truth and right are developed into doctrines of welfare, the folkways are raised to another plane"— to the plane of mores.

Definition of Mores

1. According to *R.M. MacIver* and *C.H. Page*, "When the folkways have added to them conceptions of group welfare, standards of right and wrong, they are converted into mores".
2. *Gillin* and *Gillin* say that "Mores are those customs and group routines which are thought by the members of the society to be necessary to the group's continued existence".
3. As *Edward Sapir* has pointed out, "The term 'mores' is best reserved for those customs which connote fairly strong feelings of the rightness or wrongness of mode of behaviour".
4. In simple words, we can say when the folkways clearly represent the group standards, the group sense of what is fitting, right and conducive to well-being, then they become mores.

Types of Mores

A distinction is made between two kinds of mores: 1. 'positive mores', and 2. 'negative mores'.

1. ***Positive mores:*** Positive mores always 'prescribe' behaviour patterns. They represent the 'do's'. They give instructions and provide guidance for the people to behave in a particular way. Examples: respecting elders, protecting children, taking care of the diseased and the aged people. loving one's country, doing service to the society, worshipping God, speaking the truth, leading a righteous life, etc.
2. ***Negative mores:*** Negative mores 'prescribe' behaviour patterns. They represent the 'don'ts'. They are often called 'taboos'. Taboos forbid or prohibit certain behaviour patterns. Taboos put severe restrictions on the range of one's behaviour. *Examples*: Don't appear before the people without dress, don't be cruel to the wife and children, don't steal, don't commit adultery, don't tell lies, don't be irreligious, don't disrespect the God, don't be unpatriotic, etc.

Nature and Characteristics of Mores

1. ***Mores are the regulators of our social life:*** Mores represent the living character of the group or community. They are always considered as right by the people who share them. They are morally right and their violation morally wrong. Hence, they are more compulsive in nature. They put restrictions on our behaviour.
2. ***Mores are relatively more persistent:*** Mores are relatively long lasting than ordinary folk- ways. In fact, they even become conservative elements in society. They also put up resistance to changes. For example, people at one

time resisted the efforts of the law-makers to abolish the so- called morals such as slavery, child marriage, human sacrifice, practice of 'sati', etc. Still it is wrong to conclude that mores are fixed things that do not change. They change subtly from age to age. In the examples cited above considerable changes have taken place now.

3. ***Mores vary from group to group:*** Mores have not always been uniform. What is prescribed in one group is prohibited in another. *Eskimos*, for example, often practise female infanticide, whereas such a practice is strictly forbidden in the modern societies. The Mundugumor tribals of New Guinea practise cannibalism, even today, whereas such a practice is beyond our comprehension in the modern society. Similarly, some practise strictly monogamy, whereas others practise polygamy, and so on. Further, what is right at one time may be wrong at another and vice versa. The practice of 'sati' was 'moral' then but not now. Slavery was regarded as 'right' then and not now.
4. ***Mores are backed by values and religion:*** Mores normally receive the sanction and backing of values and religion. When this occurs they become still more powerful and binding. Mores backed by religious sanctions are strongly justified by people. Ten commandments, for example, are considered to be important and essential for the Christians, because they are backed by their religion.

Social Importance or Functions of Mores

MacIver and *Page* have mentioned the following social functions of mores.

1. ***Mores determine much of our individual behaviour:*** Mores always bring direct pressure on our behaviour. They mould our character and restrain our tendencies. They act as powerful instruments of social control. Mores are indoctrinated into the personalities of the individuals from the beginning and hence they help them to exercise constraints over their own behaviour.
2. ***Mores identify the individual with the group:*** Mores are the means by which the individual gains identification with his fellows. As a result of that, he maintains social relations with others that are clearly essential for satisfactory living.
3. ***Mores are the guardians of social solidarity:*** Mores bring the people together and weld them into one strong cohesive group. Those who share common mores also share many other patterns of behaviour. Every group or society has its own mores. There are mores for each sex, for all ages, for all classes, for all groups from the family to the nation. The mores of each of these help to maintain the solidarity of the group.

With the evolution of society, the mores have become more 'specialized'. Their control on the civilized and the advanced people is also diminishing. Hence, they are supplemented with laws and legislations.

Differences between Folkways and Mores

Folkways and mores can be distinguished in the following manner.

1. Mores are relatively wider and more general in character than the folkways.
2. Mores imply a value—judgement about the folkways.
3. Out of the mores comes our profound conviction of right and wrong and not out of the folkways.
4. An individual may disobey the ordinary folkways without incurring any severe punishment. But violation of the mores brings him strong disapproval and severe punishment.
5. Mores are more compulsive, regulative and rigid than the folkways. Hence, mores are more effective and influential in moulding our character and restricting our tendencies.
6. As *Sumner* has suggested when the folkways take on a philosophy of right living and a life policy of welfare, folkways become mores. Hence the mores always contain a welfare element in them.
7. Folkways are less deeply rooted in society and change more rapidly. On the other hand, mores are deeply rooted in society and change less frequently. Folkways may change with one's social status and occupational position. But mores do not change in that manner for they are permanent standards of right conduct.

From the above description, we may feel that the line dividing the folkways from mores is clear and definite. But it is not so always. Differentiating one from the other becomes extremely difficult especially in the marginal cases. For example, drinking liquor is regarded by some as simply bad and must be avoided. But some others may condemn it as highly immoral a practice.

As *Sumner* has remarked our conceptions of right and wrong, proper and improper are mostly determined by the folkways and mores. They can make anything right and anything wrong. Of the two, mores are more dominant than the folkways. Even the laws are often called the 'codified mores'.

CUSTOMS

Like folkways and mores, 'customs' also represent one of the types of informal means of social control. They are as universal and pervasive as those of folkways and mores. Customs are the socially accepted ways in which people do things together in personal contacts.

As *MacIver* and *Page* have pointed out, groups, institutions and associations sustain their formal order by means of an intricate complex of usages or practices. Such accepted procedures or practices of eating, conversing, meeting people, training the young, caring for the aged, playing, working, etc., can be called *customs*.

Definition of Customs

1. According to *MacIver* and *Page*, "The socially accredited ways of acting are the customs of society",
2. According to *Kingsley Davis*, "Custom refers primary to practices that have often been repeated by a multitude of generations, practices that tend to be followed simply because that they have been followed in the past".
3. *Duncan Mitchell* in his 'Dictionary of Sociology' writes: "The term 'customs' refers to established modes of thought and action."
4. *Lundberg* says that customs are those "folkways that persist over relatively long periods of time so as to attain a degree of formal recognition and so as to be passed down from one generation to another".
5. In simple words, customs are the long established habits and usages of the people.

Nature of Customs

1. *Custom is a social phenomenon.* Customs are the oft-repeated practices of the people, They represent the routine acts of daily life of the people. Customs are created by the groups, associations, communities and institutions. Customs are considered to be conducive to the good of the society. They enjoy the social sanction.
2. *Customs are followed by people mostly unconsciously*. As MacIver and Page have pointed out, "We conform to the customs of our own society, in a sense, 'unconsciously'? Because they are a strongly imbedded part of our group life. We are trained from our infancy itself to behave in a customary way. Human infants learn the customs by imitation or by direct instruction. In course of time, they become a part of the personality of the children.
3. *Customs are varied in nature*. Though customs are universal in nature they differ from community to community and society to society. Examples: The customary dressing at occasions such as marriage and funeral ceremonies differs from group to group. Similarly, eating behaviour, worshipping behaviour, etc., differ a lot. Among the Christians, the husband and wife exchange their rings on the occasion of their marriage. Among the Hindus the husband ties the 'tali' around the neck of the wife at the time of marriage. Among the Maoreies of New Zealand people rub each other's nose in order to express their love and affection.
4. *The origin of custom is obscure.* It is difficult to ascertain the exact way in which customs emerged. As McDougall writes, "The ends and purposes of many customs are lost in the midst of antiquity". No single theory or explanation can be offered about the origin of custom. Numerous customs have arisen in different ways to satisfy the varied needs of man.
5. *Customs are relatively durable*. In comparison with the folkways, fashions and fads, customs are more durable. Customs evolve gradually and hence they are obeyed mostly in a spontaneous manner. When once the customs are established they gain grounds to become firm. They are implicitly obeyed with least resistance by the majority of the people. The sole justification for following the custom is that it has been in existence since a long time.
6. *All customs are not irrational*. It is wrong to assume that all customs are irrational and meaningless. Still a good number of customs are found to be illogical, meaningless, non-utilitarian and unethical in character. In modern times, much stress is laid on following the rational, useful and meaningful customs.

Customs and Habits

Customs and habits are very closely related. "Habit means an acquired facility to act in a certain manner without resort to deliberation and thought"—*MacIver* and *Page*. Persons tend to react in the manner to which they have become accustomed. Example: smoking, drinking coffee or tea regularly, reading newspaper daily, drinking liquors, morning exercises, shaving daily in the morning, etc.

Habit is a "second nature" with us. When once they are developed they tend to become permanent. Then it becomes difficult for us to act in a way different from the habitual ways. It is the strongly established and deeply rooted mode of response. As *MacIver* and *Page* have pointed out "habit is the instrument of life, it economises energy, reduces drudgery and saves the needless expenditure of thought". *William James* has pointed out habit is "the enormous fly–wheel of society, and its most precious conservative agent".

Differences between Customs and Habits

1. Custom is a social phenomenon whereas habit is an individual phenomenon.
2. Custom is socially recognised. Habit does not require such recognition.
3. Custom is normative in nature. It has the sanction of the society. Habit is not normative and requires no external sanction.
4. Custom contributes to the stability of social order. Hence it is of great social importance. Habit can only facilitate individual activity. It has prominence only for the individual who is accustomed to it.
5. Customs are socially inherited, whereas habits are learnt individually.

Social Importance of Customs

1. ***Customs regulate our social life:*** Customs act as the effective means of social control. Individuals can hardly escape their grip. They are the self-accepted rules of social life. They bind people together, assimilate their actions to the accepted standards and control their purely egoistic impulses. They are found among the preliterate as well as the literate people. They are the strongest ties in building up a social order.
2. ***Customs constitute the treasury of our social heritage:*** Customs preserve our culture and transmit it to the succeeding generations. They have added stability and certainty to our social life. They bring people together and develop social relationships among them. They provide for a feeling of security in human society. People normally obey them for their violation is always condemned and resisted. The children learn the language spoken, and the occupation followed by their parents through the customs. The imprint of custom can be found on various activities of the members of society.
3. ***Customs are basic to our collective life:*** Customs are found in all the communities of the world. They are more influential and dominant in the primitive society than in the modern industrial society. Still no society can do without them. Customs are mercilessly imposed on the people in the primitive societies. As *Malinowski* writes in the context of the study of *Trobriand Islanders* that "a strict adherence to customs....is the main rule of conduct among our natives...". In the traditional societies customs are like sacred objects and their violation cannot be thought of.

   Customs are so dominant and powerful that they can be called the "King of man". *Shakespeare* called it a "tyrant". *Bacon* considered it "the principal magistrate of man's life". People follow customs not just because they are traditionally enforced but very much because they are mixed with people's sentiments, feelings and personal obligations.
4. ***Customs support law:*** Customs also provide the solid ground for the formulation and establishment of law. Customs become laws when the state enforces them as rules binding on citizens. Law divorced from custom is bound to become artificial. Such laws may often end in failures, as it has happened in the case of 'prohibition' in U.S.A. Customs consolidate law and facilitate its practice. If the laws are not supported by customs, they cannot succeed. It is to be noted that in the modern complex society customs are not enough to control the behaviour of the people. Hence they are supplemented with various formal means of social control.

SANCTIONS

'Sanctions' represent a means of maintaining social control. As *Robert Bierstedt has pointed Out "Sanctions are the supporters of the norms, the punishments applied to those who do not conform and the rewards given to those who do*".

According to *Duncan Mitchell*, "*A sanction is a means of enforcing a rule or law and may be positive or negative, i.e., it may take the form of o reward or a punishment*". As applied to a group or society the prefix 'social' is commonly used.

Young and *Mack* opine that "*sanctions are the rewards or punishments used to establish social control — that is, to enforce the norms in a society*".

Sanctions are applied for the purpose of maintaining social control, that is, to bring about conformity. They are used to force or persuade an individual or group to conform to social expectations. Sanctions may be applied in various ways, from the use of physical force to symbolic means, such as flattery. *Negatively* they may be anything from a raised eyebrow to the death sentence. *Positively*, they range from a smile to an honorary degree.

Informal and Formal Sanctions

In primary groups and in small, simple societies sanctions are informal in nature. Informal sanctions are illustrated by customs, mores, and public opinion. In mass societies with many second- ary groups, some sanctions are necessarily formal. The formal sanctions are those worked out by the state through law and administrative devices, and those consciously developed within organisations for their own regulation.

As societies and their cultures become heterogeneous and as secondary groups arise, the whole problem of social control changes. It is our necessity that the formal sanctions are developed and applied to compensate the deficiency of informal sanctions. Still, the formal and informal aspects of control are interlinked. In the more loosely organised areas of community life we find the dominance of informal sanctions, whereas in the more highly institutionalized groups we find major controls flow through formal sanctions.

Power as the Basis of Sanctions

The application of regulatory or controlling devices of any kind implies the use of power. The form and intensity of power may vary greatly. "*Power' means the possession of some influence or force which may be used to oblige another to conform to some expectation*". — *Young and Mack*. The sanctions through which power is exercised may be formal or informal, and they may be either physical or psychological. As the basis of sanctions power has to be understood in relation to its four aspects. They are:—(*i*) *The amount or quantity of power*, (*ii*) *the distribution of power among individuals and groups*, (*iii*) *the purposes for which power is used, and* (*iv*) *the means by which it is applied.*

Aims of Sanctions

The primary aims of sanctions are to bring about conformity, solidarity, and continuity of a particular group, community, or larger society. These aims could be achieved by maintaining a balance of power among the contending social units. Sanctions of any type are applied to prevent individual or group disorganisation. Sanctions are also concerned with the *control of deviant individuals who* threaten solidarity and continuity.

To control behaviour means to bring about regular and recurrent actions of responses. Such regulation makes possible the prediction of behaviour. By discouraging deviance and by encouraging conformity sanctions can foster solidarity and integration. They make possible the continuity of social order. The sanctions constitute a part of culture which is passed along from generation to generation. Each generation gets a pattern of control which keeps the social order running smoothly.

Types of Sanctions

Sanctions are applied in various ways. The types of sanctions also vary with the groups and situations. Sanctions are broadly of two types: (*i*) Positive, and (*ii*) Negative.

1. ***Positive sanctions:*** As *Young* and *Mack* have said those sanctions which elicit and facilitate response by rewards are positive in nature. They include various means such as praise, flattery, suggestion, persuasion, some amount of education, indoctrination, advertising, propaganda, slogans, giving rewards, medals, badges, titles, uniforms etc. *Praise* is a reward in words. *Flattery* is undue, exaggerated, and somewhat false praise usually made for some ulterior purpose. *Indoctrination, advertising* and *propaganda*–all condition persons to act in lines which they like or believe that they like. Persuasion is a form of suggestion which is vital to above three and some other situations. Slogans help to define situations and direct behaviour in the desired lines. *Rewards* are unexpected benefits normally accorded to some exemplary behaviour. Medals are granted for meritorious action, Uniforms also represent such material symbols.

2. ***Negative sanctions:*** Those sanctions which inflict pain or threaten to do so are negative in charactor. As *Young* and *Mack* have suggested, they include various means such as—gossip, slander, satire, laughing at others, name-calling, threats, commands, censorship and even overt action. *Gossip* as a means of social control is largely critical in tone. It helps in moulding public opinion against violating norms. *Satire* is the method of exposing the foibles and weaknesses of persons through verbal lashes. *Laughing at others* has been an age-old method of isolating the person of its target from his fellows and putting him to shame. *Name-Calling* means labelling persons and groups with debasing names. It is a common device in propaganda. Here the targets of attack are branded, for example, as 'communist', 'fascist, 'reactionary, 'communalist' and so on. *Commands* represent direct power. They are a direct verbal form of ordering. *Threats* are the most severe form of verbal sanctions. They become very effective when supported by physical force. *Censorship* is complementary to propaganda. It is restraint on the expression of opinion. The method of *over action* is the final sanction when no other way remains open. In this method, pain, suffering and even death may be inflicted on the person. It includes fines, imprisonment, whipping, mutilation, torture, banishment, ostracism and even death. Extreme negative sanctions are applied only by the state.

REVIEW QUESTIONS

1. Define the term 'folkways.' Discuss the nature and importance of folkways.
2. Give the definition of the term 'mores'. Describe the types and nature of mores.
3. Highlight the characteristic features of mores. Assess the social importance of mores.
4. Differentiate between folkways and mores.
5. Define customs. Discuss the nature of customs.
6. Customs and habits are closely related. Critically analyse.
7. Explain the social importance of customs.
8. What are sanctions? Describe the types and aims of sanctions.
9. Write short notes on the following:
   (a) Mores
   (b) Customs and habits
   (c) Informal and formal sanctions
   (d) Types of sanctions
10. Sanctions represent a means of maintaining social control. Critically analyse.

⌘⌘⌘⌘⌘⌘⌘⌘⌘⌘⌘

37

SOCIAL NORMS AND SOCIAL VALUES

CHAPTER OUTLINE

SOCIAL NORMS

The concept of 'social norms' is of special interest for sociology because they constitute the very foundation of the social structure. The primary task of sociology is to discover the source of 'order' that society exhibits. Norms here, represent such a source of social order. No society and no social group can exist without Norms. Norms have made it possible the orderly social intercourse of people in societies. Hence, everywhere they serve the individual as guides to conduct. They are generally known as "*standards of group behaviour*".

The term 'social norms' is relatively a newcomer to the dictionary of sociology. *M. Sherif* in '*The Psychology of Social Norms*", 1936, used the term for the first time to describe the common standards or ideas which guide members' responses in all established groups. Today, the word norm is very often used as a genetic term to represent folkways, mores, laws, customs, etc., If, today, some action is called a norm or normative it only emphasises that it conforms to community expectations of behaviour. The degrees of conformity may, however, vary very much."

MEANING AND DEFINITION OF NORMS

Meaning of Norm

"Social norms" refer to the group—shared standards of behaviour. Norms represent "*standardized generalization*" concerning expected modes of behaviour. They are based on social values. A norm is a pattern setting limits on individual behaviour. Norms are the 'blueprints' for behaviour. They determine, guide, control and also predict human behaviour.

Norms are group-shared expectations. Such expectations are reflected in statements such as– "A good citizen always respects laws", "A gentleman pays his debts", "Younger one must always respect elderly people", "One is supposed to be quiet and respectful, and not to disturb others in a place of worship", "A lawyer must not produce damaging evidence in the court against his own client", "A scientist must be a restless searcher of truth and free from prejudices", "Any occupant of any profession must follow the professional ethics associated with it", "He should not have done that." Countless such norms govern our social life in all situations.

Definition of Norms

1. According to *Young* and *Mack*, 'norms' refer to the "*group-shared expectations*".
2. According to *H.M. Johnson*, "A norm is an abstract pattern held in the mind, that sets certain limits for behaviour".
3. Norms refer to "the rules that guide behaviour in everyday situations and are derived from the value"–*Donald Light Jr*. and *Suzanne Keller*.
4. As *Robert Bierstedt* has pointed out, "A norm is a rule or standard that governs our conduct in the social situations in which we participate." He further writes that a norm can be treated as "a cultural specification that guides our conduct in society."
5. "Social norms are rules developed by a group of people that specify how people must, should, may, should not and must not behave in various situations."–*G.R. Leslie, R.F. Larson and B.L. Gorman*.

It is clear from the above definition that norms can be understood as rules and regulations that groups live by. Norms are the means through which values are expressed in behaviour.

Personal or Private Norms and Social Norms

We can make a distinction between personal or private norms and social norms. Private norms are purely individual in character and they reside with individuals only. They may influence only the behaviour of the individual concerned. *For example*, an individual may make some individual resolutions on the New Year's Day and decide to comply with them. Similarly, one may impose on oneself the norm of doing routine things on time schedule. As such, the sociologists are least interested in these personal or private norms.

Sociologists are more interested in '*operative*' social norms. Operative social norms are always backed by *sanctions*. Because of sanctions, the violators of norms suffer some penalties in the group, while those who conform are rewarded. Sociology studies in detail the types of social norms, the manner in which they are implemented, the way in which they differ from society to society, the way in which they are backed by sanctions, the functions they perform and so on.

Norms and Values

'*Values*' may be defined as measures of goodness or desirability. They provide general guide- lines for conduct. In this sense they are often referred to as "*higher order norms*". But norms are given much more specific meaning. They define appropriate and acceptable behaviour in particular situations. Values are cherished only through the observance of norms. The relationship between the two can be made clear by the following example.

Example. A society may cherish the value of "*privacy*". This value provides only a general guide to behaviour. Norms define how the value of 'privacy' is translated into action in particular situations and circumstances. For instance, norms relating to privacy may insist that person's mail must not be opened by other people. Similarly, an individual's house must not be entered without his permission, etc. A person's private life or individual life is his own concern and others must not poke their nose into the personal affairs. In this way a series of norms direct how people should behave in terms of the value of 'privacy'.

CHARACTERISTICS OF SOCIAL NORMS

1. ***Social norms are universal:*** Social norms are the very basis of social order. No society can function smoothly in the absence of norms. In fact, the concept of society pre-supposes the presence of norms. Even in the uncivilized and barbaric societies also we find some norms
2. ***Norms are related to the factual order:*** In every society we find two types of order—(*i*) *the normative order* that insists how the individuals should or ought to behave, and (*ii*) *the factual order* that is related to and based on the actual behaviour of the people. It is through the normative order or system that society regulates the behaviour of its members. But this normative order should be related to the events in the real world for it is meant to achieve result in the factual world. The factual order also exercises an influence on the normative system. *For example*, a rule requiring all men to have three wives would be valueless if the sex ratio did not permit it. Similarly, a rule requiring everybody to bathe in salt water in order to prevent tuberculosis would be valueless if bathing in salt water had nothing to do with curbing the disease. Thus norms in order to become effective must represent correctly the relations between real events. They must take into account the factual situation.
3. ***Norms incorporate value judgements:*** A norm is a standard or behavioural expectation shared by group members. They represent "*standardized generalization*" concerning expected modes of behaviour. As standardized generalizations, they are concepts which have been evaluated by the group and they incorporate value judgements. It is in terms of norms that we judge whether some action is right or wrong, good or bad, wanted or unwanted,

expected or unexpected. *Norms are normally based on values*. Norms do not refer to an average tendency of man. But they denote expected behaviour or even ideal behaviour.

4. ***Norms are relative to situations and groups:*** Norms vary from society to society. Sometimes, within the same society they differ from group to group. Each group in a society, to a certain extent at least, has its own norms. There is no social group without norms. Within the same society they differ with age, sex, occupation and social status of the individuals. Some norms do not govern the behaviour of all the people always. Norms of behaviour meant for old people are not applicable to the children. What is 'alright' for a man is not 'alright' for a woman. Norms meant for soldiers and policemen are different from those of teachers and advocates. Behaviour patterns meant for married people cannot be followed by unmarried people. Especially in a multigroup society or a complex society such wide variation in norms is found. But in primitive societies, in general, single set of religious beliefs, practices and norms is found, because their culture exhibits high degree of integration.
5. ***Norms are not always obeyed by all:*** It is wrong to assume that people in a society obey all the norms always. Some obey some norms at some times and disobey or ignore some others at some other times. Even those who normally respect and obey norms may go against some norms in some particular situations. This we can observe in some big political and religious gatherings when highly religious and law abiding people break laws and "behave in a frenzy mood when they are provocated. If everyone always did the 'right' things at the 'right' time and place, there would be no need to have rules or laws.
6. ***Norms vary with sanctions:*** Norms also vary in the kinds of sanctions that are attached to the violation of norms. Norm's and sanctions go hand in hand. Norms are the group's rules of proper behaviour; sanctions are the group's punishments for violation of the norms. *Sanctions are the reward: or punishment used to enforce the norms in a society*. In addition to being punished for violation of norms, people tend to be rewarded for the proper observance of them. Sanctions may be applied in various ways, ranging from the use of physical force to symbolic means such as flattery. They are used to enforce or persuade an individual or group to conform to social expectations. Rewards may include smiles, approval, praise, appreciation, money, prestige, etc. Conformity to social norms is secured through both rewards and punishments in most of the instances.
7. ***Norms are normally internalised by the people:*** People in most of the instances accept norms and follow them or obey them. They do not question most of the norms and accept them implicitly. It is because norms become the part and parcel of personality of the individual through the process of *socialization*. In fact, socialization is often described as the process whereby an individual internalises the norms of the group. The cultural rules and restrictions or norms are internalised by the new born individuals through socialization and hence, in most of the times they tend to honour and obey them implicitly.

According to *H.M. Johnson*, a social norm would state the following: *Who is expected, by whom, to do what, or refrain from, doing what, and in what circumstances*. Further, it would specify what *penalties* will be imposed if the norm is violated, or what *rewards* will be conferred if it is conformed to. It would decide *who will administer* the penalties or give the rewards. It would also specify under what *circumstances* a violation of norm will be regarded as unimportant or ignorable.

CONFORMITY TO AND VIOLATION OF NORMS

Conformity to Norms

Society exerts its pressure upon people to conform to the norms. A norm by definition implies a sense of obligation. It lays down a standard of behaviour which everyone ought to follow. Conformity to norms is normal. The sanctions behind the mores make us to follow them. But hope of reward and fear of punishment are not the only reasons for conformity to the norms of our society. There are other bases for conformity. Some are mentioned below:

1. *Indoctrination*. We conform to the norms because we have been indoctrinated to do so from our very childhood.
2. *Habituation*. We conform to them because we become habituated to them.
3. *Utility*. We appreciate the utility of the norms and hence we conform to them.
4. *Group Identification*. By conforming to the norms we gain identification with the group. Hence we prefer to conform to them.

Violation of Norms

Society functions in orderly fashion most of the times because most people conform to the norms of their group unthinkingly. Thus, ordinarily people wear what is expected of them, eat what is expected of them, do what is expected of them, talk what is expected of them, and even think what is expected of them. And so long as this occurs the society functions smoothly.

But this is not the whole story. People not only conform to the norms automatically but also violate the normative expectations with more or less the same frequency. The violation of the norms is often called "*deviance*". The violation of norms may be traced to at least three sources:

1. ***Simple violations of norms:*** Some norms which are not strongly enforced are often violated. Government officials may often use their official vehicles for personal purposes. Some may force their entry into the bus without observing the rule of queue, etc.
2. ***Norm conflict:*** Complex societies have multiple, and sometimes conflicting value systems. It follows then, that norms frequently are in conflict. *Example*: American sex norms. In America, there are some groups which condemn and disapprove of pre-marital and extra-marital sex relations and some others that approve of such relations. Normative conflict is deeply involved in the process of social change.
3. ***Existence of systematic norms evasion:*** Sometimes norms are systematically or cleverly evaded on certain occasions. *For example*, forbidden drugs are sold and used in festivals, causal gathering places, university campuses in an illegal way. Law enforcement officials also fail to take actions on some such occasions. Some of the norms are carefully evaded permanently. Tax payers often evade taxes in such a way.

FUNCTIONAL IMPORTANCE OF SOCIAL NORMS

1. ***Norms assist survival:*** The human beings would not have survived in the absence of proper norms concerning courtship, marriage, childbearing and childcare, etc. Hence the first function of norm is that of *ensuring survival* itself. Unlike the young ones of other species, human infants must be cared and instructed for at least some years. *For example*, if the young matured girls are not protected by proper norms they would be subject to sexual exploitation which would lead to serious, consequences.
2. ***A normless society is an impossibility:*** Norms constitute an important element of society. Norms and society go together. Without norms social interaction would be dangerous, difficult and chaotic. The normative order of the society makes the factual order of society possible. Man cannot live alone. He depends upon society for his existence. Living together in society is made possible because of norms. Man's dependence on society is ultimately a dependence upon a normative order.
3. ***Norms guide behaviour:*** Norms guide behaviour in all aspects of social life. There are norms of dress which define the type of clothing appropriate for members of each age, sex and social situation. There are norms governing behaviour with family, friends, neighbours and strangers. There are norms which define acceptable behaviour in the home, in the classroom, working place, worshipping place, at a party, wedding and funeral, in a cinema, market place, doctor's waiting room, etc.
4. ***Norms permit efficient functioning:*** Norms provide for the routinisation of behaviour so that complex learnt tasks come to be performed efficiently and automatically. Most of our responses to most of the situations must be habitual ones; norms ensure such habitual responses. If we had to think about what we are going to do when we enter a shop, a showroom, a classroom, a cafeteria, or meet a bank clerk, an advocate, an insurance agent, a ticket seller, we should be able to do only a few tasks in the course of a day. But *norms reduce the necessity for decision* in the innumerable social situations which we face and in which we participate. Without them we would be faced with the problem of almost intolerable burden of decision. *Norms thus provide practical solutions to everyday problems*. Even cooking becomes problematic if cooking norms are not known. Social life would be much less efficient if the methods of doing had to be constantly reinvented by trial and error.
5. ***Norms help the maintenance of social order:*** The social order is developed and maintained through social norms. Groups are able to function because human behaviour is generally predictable. If this were not so chaos would result. Thus, a classroom would be chaotic in which teachers and students fail to establish a set of rules for conducting lessons. Drivers of vehicles are bound to meet with accidents if they fail to conform to traffic rules in a busy street.

   Human culture can be understood as vast integrated normative system. That system serves for man the functions of controlling and other animals through instincts. *Normative system permit more variability and flexibility of behaviour* than biological structure does. Hence human societies have achieved wonderful complexity. Social norms provide the primary mechanism through which that complexity is achieved and maintained.
6. ***Norms give cohesion to society:*** A society without norms would be, as *Hobbes* pointed out, '*solitary, poor, nasty, brutish and short.*" The collective and co-operative life of people is made possible because of norms. The *normative system gives to society an internal cohesion* without which social life is not possible. This cohesion or unity contributes to co-operation and mutual helpfulness.
7. ***Norms help self-control:*** Norms not only lessen the problems of social control but also help individuals to have self-control. In fact, social control is achieved when self-control is mastered. Because of the pressure of norms the

individual is able to exercise discipline by himself over his own actions and behaviour. Norms in this way influence an individual's attitude and his motives and impulses. They determine and guide his intuitive judgements of others and his intuitive judgements of himself. *They lead to the phenomena of conscience, of guilt feelings, of striving, of elation and depression.* They are deeper than consciousness. Through internalisation they become an inseparable part of the personality of the individual.

INSTITUTIONALIZATION

The concept of "*institutionalization*" actually refers to the process of institutionalization of norms. To understand this concept the meaning of the terms-norms and institution must be known. The term '*Norm* 'refers to "*an abstract pattern held in the mind, that sets certain limits for behaviour*". The term '*institution*' refers to "*recognised normative pattern*" of a society or part of a society. The concept of '*institutionalization*' *refers to the process in which norms become institutionalized, that is, when they are sanctioned by the group or its part and accepted and internalised by a large number of members*.

Institutions emerge mostly as unplanned products of social living. People search for practical ways of meeting their needs. In their attempts they find some workable patterns which become standardized in course of time through constant repetition. As time passes they acquire a body of supporting sanctions. People tend to orient their behaviour in accordance with these standardized practices. They may also define and redefine these practices in tune with the changes that take place in their environment. This is how institutions normally arise.

'Institutionalization' consists of the establishment of definite norms which assign status positions and role functions in connection with such behaviour. A norm is a group expectation of behaviour. *Institutionalization involves replacement of spontaneous or experimental behaviour with behaviour which is expected, patterned, regular, and predictable*"—*Horton and Hunt*.

Social norms are ever operative in society. But these operative norms differ from one social system to another. *For example*, Muslim societies permit polygyny, but the Hindu and Christian Societies have not permitted it. Hindus have tabooed beef-eating, Muslims the pork-eating, but both are permitted in the Christian society. As *H.M. Johnson* has pointed out, a social norm can be said to be institutionalized in a particular social system when the following three conditions are met:-

1. *When a large number of the members of the social system accept the norm.*
2. *When the norm is taken seriously and internalised by a sizeable number of people who accept it.*
3. *When the norm is sanctioned, that is, when certain members of the system are expected to be guided by the norm in appropriate circumstances.*

Example:- Dating in America has been institutionalized. Most of the Americans have accepted it as a necessary and proper activity through which young people mature emotionally and eventually find agreeable partners. In the same way, a few societies have institutionalized premarital sexual intercourse, making it a normal and expected part of the activities leading to marriage. Though this practice has not become institutionalized in America the present trends there, for example, providing contraceptives to the unmarried, and allowing them to have all-night visitations, etc., reveal that it may become institutionalized very shortly providing for an accepted and safeguarded pattern of behaviour. But in the traditional Hindu society both the practices of dating and premarital sexual intercourse are abhorred.

Other Aspects of Institutionalization

1. Institutionalized norms apply to members of the social system according to their social positions within the system. *For example*, in family, father, mother, son, daughter all are bound by some family norms which do not apply equally to all. The rights and obligations of the mother are different from those of the mother and children and they are not the same between parents and children. Still all the members know and support the entire normative pattern of the family because it has become a part of their common culture.
2. The internalisation of a norm by an 'average' member of a social system is a matter of degree. The given norm may be internalised by the people in different degrees or different norms may be internalised in different degrees. *For example*, the obligation of parents to protect their child is normally deeply internalised. The obligation to vote in elections according to the dictates of conscience is not that deeply internalised.
3. Further, 'widespread' acceptance of a norm in a social system is also a matter of degree. There is no specification as to the exact proportion of the members of a social system who must know about and accept norms before the norm can be said to be institutionalized. The necessary proportion varies from case and the complexity of the social system. In a large-scale social system, it is impossible for us to expect all the members to know and accept all the operative norms.

4. *Finally*, even the beliefs and patterns of overt behaviour may become institutionalized. *For example*, a dogma is a religious belief that, members of a particular religious group 'must' accept. Similarly, members of a political party are expected to accept its political ideology.

SOCIAL NORMS AND THE INDIVIDUAL

Norms govern the behaviour of individuals and facilitate interaction to take place between them. They add some amount of regularity and predictability to our behaviour. They act as our guides. They help to mend our ways. More than that they regulate our daily life. No individual can ignore social norms without incurring the displeasure of others.

Norms are an indispensable part of our life. In our daily life we do a lot of work and interact with a number of people without much thinking. It is not possible for us to think over each and every act that we do. As philosopher *Alfred North Whitehead* once remarked, "*the more things we can do without thinking, the better off we are*" Thus, if we had to think about what we are going to do when we get up from our bed, go out of home, enter a hotel or a shop, get into a bus, enter a bank, or a government office, and meet a friend, a relative, a banker, a policeman, an advocate, a professor, etc.,–we should be able to do only a few limited things in the course of a single day. Here the norms come to the help of the individual. They reduce the necessity for decision in most of the situations in which he participates.

Without the norms the individual would be faced with the burden of taking decisions at every moment. The following example reveals how norms can ease our daily work: *Ex*: A college going student gets up early in the morning, brushes his teeth and takes his bath, eats his breakfast, wears college going dress, rides the vehicle to the college, greets friends and wishes lecturers, attends to class-room lectures, makes reference study in library during free hours, plays cricket in ground with other friends, returns home early in the evening, studies his daily lessons during the night, and so on. The hypothetical student may not find it difficult or problematic to do all these activities, because each of these activities is governed by norms. The student's knowledge of these norms has eased his work.

Without social norms our social relations become haphazard, chaotic and even dangerous. Norms give order, stability, and predictability to social life. In the absence of norms, a state of 'anomie' would prevail as *Durkheim* spoke of it. Anomie is the contradiction of society. Where there are no norms, there is also no society.

ASSOCIATIONAL NORMS

Modern civilized society consists of a large number of organized as well as unorganized groups. All organized groups have their own rules and regulations. These formal rules or norms define the mutual rights and obligations of the members including their obligation towards the association or group. Such norms are called "*associational norms*" The nature of these norms can be better under- stood by contrasting them with the norms of the state technically known as 'laws'. According to *Robert-Bierstedt*, associational norms differ from state laws in three main ways.

Norms of the State vs Associational Norms

1. ***Universal state laws vs limited range of associational norms:*** Though the state is often called an association it is not like others. It is larger, more pervasive, more comprehensive and more compulsive. It has a special set of norms called 'laws'. The laws are *applicable to all the inhabitants* who live in its jurisdiction. Associational norms are in a way different from those of state laws. They have limited range of influence. They are applicable only to their respective members. For example, political parties have rules for their party members, trade unions have norms for union members, college hostels have rules for hosteliers, and so on. Only the concerned members are bound by them. Students are expected to be punctual to their classes, as a matter of college rule. Similarly, a ladies hostel may insist on its inmates to return to the hostel before 6.30 PM. in the evening. A policeman who represents the state is not bothered about these rules for *they are purely meant for a few who* happen to be the members of the related associations.
2. ***The sanctions behind state laws and associational norms also differ.*** Associations may have their own positive and negative types of sanctions for enforcing compliance. Some members may be honoured with titles, medals and gifts for their exemplary work, while a few others may be suspended or dismissed from their membership in organisation for their neglection of associational norms or anti-associational activity. Thus, the hostel warden may suspend a hostel inmate who always returns late and dismiss another for regularly violating hostel norms. The member of a Rotary club may lose his membership if he continuously absents himself for three consecutive meetings without providing any explanation for his absence. The Indian Bar Association may suspend from membership an advocate who is guilty of violating its norms. Many such examples could be given. But no association can legitimately apply physical force for making its members to comply with norms. It is the privilege of the state to use force in a legitimate manner to ensure conformity to its laws. It can even go to the extent of killing those who violate its rules, if need arises.

3. ***Sometimes associational norms may come in conflict with the laws of the state:*** Criminal gangs, gambling syndicates, secret associations of black-marketers, dacoit groups may have their own norms which may come into clash with state norms. *Example*: These associational groups may insist on their members to use physical force in a surreptitious manner if need arises, to serve their purpose of making money, The state may consider this as anti-societal and anti-national and may take relevant steps to suppress such a trend. The relationship between the laws of the state and associational norms has become particularly complex in the modern complex societies.

RELATIONSHIPS BETWEEN NORMS

Though we make a distinction between formal rules and informal rules it is not easy to ascertain the exact nature of relationships that prevail between these two types of rules. Similarly, the precise nature of relationship between different types of informal norms or rules is also very difficult to understand. For example, the relationships between folkways, mores, customs on the one hand, and laws on the other: and similarly, relationship between customs, folkways and mores themselves cannot be easily perceived. *Robert Bierstedt's* attempt to make a study of the relationship between different types of norms can throw some light on some interesting facts.

It is generally believed that mores are more compulsive than folkways, and the laws are more coercive than the mores. In practice, is it invariably so? Does the greater severity of norms necessarily ensure greater conformity? An example may be mentioned as an answer to these questions. *Example*, we do not consider paying fine to the Electricity Board *or* Municipal Corporation for having not paid the bill amount well in time, as more severe a sanction than facing a 'ridicule' for having worn a shabby dress in a marriage ceremony. In the same manner, a man who deals with illicit trade by violating state laws and who maintains a mistress in addition to the wife by violating mores, may, in practice, be afraid of ridicule. To avoid ridicule, he may dress always in the most conservative manner and conform to all the norms of fashion and etiquette. These examples reveal greater severity of norms does not necessarily ensure greater conformity.

A nation like India which is characterised by diversity has a multiplicity of laws and it is not possible for even the most law-abiding citizen to conform to all of them. If it is a crime to violate a law we are all criminals. We may not pay all kinds of taxes well in time always, we may force our entry into bus or train without waiting for our turn in queue, or we may exceed the speed limit while driving a vehicle, or throw some dirt on the public road at some time or the other, and so on. We violate many such laws with impunity largely because everyone else does so.

Though we do not hesitate to violate some laws without fear of punishment, we are not prepared to go against certain folkways or mores or customs. *For example*, we do not eat peas with knife. No woman is ready to attend a marriage party with a night dress. No organiser of a public programme can ignore to thank the president of the function. No law compels us to observe these practices. Thus, it could be said that the laws are not necessarily more effective instruments of social control than the folkways, mores and customs.

In primitive societies the institution of government is not found and hence they have no law. Still they have folkways and mores. They are found in all societies without exception. The laws that are found in complex societies are to some extent formed on the basis of the mores and customs present in them. In such societies mores gain formal recognition in the laws. The mores get the additional sanction–that is, the physical force to enforce compliance to them, Sometimes, *mores may change while the laws remain in force*. Hence the law may fail to keep pace with the mores. Sometimes the converse may be true, that is, *laws may be enacted before their provisions have the support of the community*.

Folkways, in comparison with laws, *are more changeable*. Folkways associated with fads and fashions are so dynamic they often get changed from year to year and even from month to month. Most of the folkways do not require any formal legal recognition too. But the laws are more important, stable, and comprehensive. They are so complex in modern societies that some specialists such as lawyers, judges, legislators are professionally concerned with them.

Sometimes, laws and mores may come into a conflict because of some disparity between them. As societies become more and more complex such disparities are unavoidable. If, in an extreme conflict of this kind, one has to 'give' place to another, it is the law that has to make way for mores. Hence the Roman historian *Tacitus* exclaimed: "*What are laws without mores*?" To stress the supremacy of mores someone has spoken of the following principle: "*When the mores are adequate, laws are unnecessary; and when the mores are inadequate, laws are useless*" This principle though sounds interesting is not true. It is not out of place to discuss here the relative validity of this principle. Let us consider *Robert Bierstedt*'s analysis of this principle in the present context.

The first half of the statement that is—'*When the mores are adequate, laws are unnecessary*'—is not true in all situations. In small primitive societies where the institution of government is not there, laws do not exist, they have only mores. They do not require laws also. But they cannot dispense with mores. In fact, they are necessary even for the civilized societies. Further, the civilized societies can hardly maintain their social order without laws. In these societies mores alone cannot operate by themselves to ensure obedience, because their sanctions are not effective all the times. *For example,* in modern societies, some are not going to pay the tax if it is legally alright. Still it is known to us that paying the tax is morally obligatory for us. Here, the mores alone cannot ensure obedience. Thus tax evaders who are not going to be penalised for their tax evasion are actually violating the mores with least hesitation. Tax evader's offences are not going to be discovered and hence his associates cannot bring on him any moral pressure. Thus law is essential in modern society.

Moreover, law in a complex society is a necessity from another point of view. Modern society consists of number of groups and sub-groups as such with its own set of formal and informal rule. When these rules or norms of groups clash among themselves law is needed to adjudicate between them. Law does this function. In this way, the first half of the principle is not correct.

The second half of the principle–"*When the mores are inadequate, laws, are useless*"—is mostly true. It is true that no law could be passed without the support of mores. When the mores of the majority are strongly opposed to the laws, the laws are bound to give place for mores. A legislation introduced in U.S.A. relating to prohibition had; to be withdrawn within a short time because it was opposed to the mores of the majority. In India too legislation relating to smoking has been an utter failure because it could not get the support of the mores of the people.

Sometimes what the rules cannot accomplish at all, the folkways, customs and mores can accomplish with ease. *For Example*, people avoid illicit sex relations not much because it is illegal, but very much because it is immoral. No law can control our dress habits but folkways and fashions can comfortably do that. No law can prescribe our religious behaviour but customs can, to some extent, do so. We respect authority more as customary rather than as a rule.

The question whether law should be used to enforce morality is often debated. Most people believe that these two–law anu mores–should control two different aspects or areas of human life in their own way. If law should deal with crime mores should deal with *indecency* (or sin). From this point of view, the law for example, should not bother about sexual behaviour between freely con- senting adults who are not husband and wife when conducted in private. Because it is not the task of law to enforce morality. Even if it tries to do this function it cannot succeed. Though it is important both for the intellectual and social order to make a clear distinction between what is illegal and what is immoral, it is not easy to do so. Because some instances or issues such as 'bigamy' or 'abortion' could be listed on either sides.

Thus it is clear from our discussion that norms differ a lot depending upon the nature of sanction behind them. The laws are not necessarily more coercive than the folkways, mores and customs in all instances. When the laws are obsolete, some folkways, or mores may prove to be stronger than them. Laws become useless when the mores are inadequate. Thus Aristotle was right when he said that "*a law derives all its strength from custom*".

DIFFERENTIAL NORMS IN A MULTI-GROUP SOCIETY

Modern complex societies have a multiplicity of groups each with its own norms. Members of up may be bothered about conforming to their group norms only. Sometimes as *R. Bierstedt's* out, they have to face problems in conforming to their group norms for two reasons: (*i*) *The is of some groups do not harmonise with the norms of some other groups* (*ii*) *An individual may be same time be a member of a few such groups with contradictory norms*. The following exes may reveal this fact.

Beef-eating is tabooed for traditional Hindus whereas Christians and Muslims may like it more. eating is tabooed for Muslims whereas Hindus and Christians have no such taboos. Traditional JS and Catholics consider abortion as sinful whereas Protestants do not find any sin in that. vegetarian food is tabooed for traditional Brahmins and not for most of the other caste people. Differences in the norms of multi-group society have some important implications. Some of may be noted.

Firstly, a multigroup society with divergent norms does not exhibit a single homogeneous, but reflects a many-faceted culture. Diversity of group norms found in the modern complex societies sets them off from the primitive societies. The primitives have a simple normative system. They have less number of groups. Political parties, trade unions, youth organisations, business groups, commercial organisations, etc., that we find in modem societies are virtually absent in them. Their culture reveals a high degree of integration. Hence, they have almost single set of norms. But in modern complex societies we find a wide variety of groups which have their own norms that demand conformity on the part of their members. What is conformity in one group may be deviance in another. Idol worship is accepted among the Hindus, but the Muslims condemn it. If the members of the ruling party are obliged to welcome and support government policies even if they are against personal views, the opposition party members consider it as a privilege to oppose them. Thus the communists and democrats, theists and atheists, Hindus, Muslims and Christians, Whites and Negroes, modernists and traditionalists, materialists, and idealists, conservatives and progressivists and an infinite variety of such people representing different groups which work on different norms are found in our modern society. Obviously, the modern society reflects a multifaceted culture.

Secondly, wide variety of norms is in a multigroup society leads to conflicting situations. Individuals are faced with them and spend much of their lives trying to adjust to conflicting obligations. Too many groups that are found have too many contradictory norms. Individuals, are at a conflict in conforming to them. *For example*, business norms clash with religious norms, political norms conflict with ethical norms, family norms tussle with occupational norms and so on. Thus it is difficult to be a good husband and good doctor at the same time. It is difficult to be a good housewife and a good social worker at the same time. It is not easy to be a good parent and a good neighbour at the same time, and so on. These examples reveal how individuals are made to face conflicting situations in conforming to all the norms.

Thirdly, vast differences in norms may undermine social understanding and spoil social unity. It is true that norms are necessary for social interaction. Indeed a normless situation is a situation of anomie which represents chaos, confusion and disorderliness. But contradictory norms can also place a barrier on interaction and create a wide gap between groups. *For example*, the upper-caste people are opposed to the policy of reservation of the government which has made special provisions for the Scheduled castes and tribes for they consider it as a blatant violation of the principle of equality and justice. The scheduled castes and tribes consider the policy as highly legitimate and just. Similarly, some of the non-Muslim communities in India are highly critical of the exceptions made to the Muslims in the Indian civil code. Some may be even opposed to the minority rights. Some communities want the religious conversions to be banned while others want to have a provision for that. Thus different feelings, sentiments and ideas associated with these divergent norms of multigroup society may put obstacles for free interaction. It is unavoidable in a multigroup society.

SOCIAL NORMS AND ANOMIE

Meaning of Anomie

The French sociologist *Emile Durkheim* used the term '*anomie*' for the first time in his book "*The Division of Labour in Society*" (1893), and again in his sociological study of *suicide rates* (1897). According to Durkheim, 'anomie' refers to "*Any state where there are unclear, conflicting or unintegrated norms, in which the individual had no morally significant relations with others or in which there were no limits set to the attainment of pleasure...* ".

'Anomie' literally means normlessness. It signifies a state of normlessness in both the society and the individual. In such a state social norms become confused or breakdown and people feel detached from their own fellows. Having little commitment to shared norms, people lack social guidelines for personal conduct. They are inclined to pursue their private interests without regard for the interests of society as a whole. Social control of individual behaviour becomes ineffective. Hence, the society is threatened with or even disorganisation.

Durkheimian Concept of Anomie

Durkheim's viewpoint is that the traditional societies are held together by what he calls "*chanical solidarity*". These societies are small and everyone does much the same work. The members are socialized in the same way, share the same experiences, and hold common values. There is little individuality for the society itself consists of a collection of kinship groups which are strongly welded together.

Modern societies, according to Durkheim, are held together by "*Organic solidarity"* If mechanical solidarity denotes a strong bond, 'organic solidarity' indicates a mush looser bond. Here, societies are larger, the members have quite different experiences, hold different values, and socialize their children in different ways. The '*Collective consciousness*' has much less binding power on the community. People think of themselves as individuals first and only then as members of wider social group. The basis for social solidarity and cohesion is no longer the similarity of the members but rather their differences. People are now interdependent. They must depend on one another if their society is to function effectively.

According to *Durkheim*, the main problem in modern society is that, the division of labour leads inevitably to feelings of individualism. This individualism can be achieved only at the cost of shared sentiments, or beliefs. Hence the result is '*anomie*' — a state of normlessness in both the society and the individual.

Durkheim's views seem to be reasonable. It is true that the division of labour and the resulting growth of individualism would breakdown shared commitment to social norms. We do notice that there is widespread anomie in modern societies. Still it is wrong to conclude that modern societies with very high degree of division of labour are heading towards 'disintegration' or breakdown. Because even these societies do retain some broad consensus on norms and values. Durkheim's analysis is significant for it throws light on the far-ranging effects that the division of labour has no social and personal life.

Anomie and Social Deviance

R.K. Merton in his book "*Social Structure and Anomie*" (*1938*) has thrown much light on the relationship between anomie and social deviance. In fact, he uses the term anomie to refer to "*a state in which socially prescribed goals and the norms governing their attainment are incompatible*".

According to *Merton*, anomie is not the same thing as the absence of norms. He even states that it does not indicate "the lack of clarity in norms". If there are no norms, there could be no deviation. If norms are not clear, it becomes then difficult and even embarrassing to call any specific action 'deviant'.

Thus, "In the condition called anomie, norms are present, they are clear enough, and the actors in the social system are to some extent oriented to them. But this orientation, on the part of many, is ambivalent; it either leans towards conformity, but with misgivings, or leans towards deviation, but with misgivings. Further more, anomie is not any condition whatever in which there is a high rate of deviation from a social norm or from a system of norms..." — *H.M. Johnson*

Causes of Anomie

R.K. Merton stresses upon two factors that produce anomie condition: 1. *role conflict or conflict of norms, and* 2. *incompatibility between goals and means.*

1. ***Role conflict or conflict of norms:*** Role Conflict refers to the conflict experienced by the individual at the time of role-playing. An ambivalent attitude on the part of an individual towards norms also contributes to role conflict and then to deviation. The following example may clarify this point.

   Example. In India, we may witness conflict between universalistic and particularistic standards in the treatment of Harijans. The anomie character of this conflict becomes evident when we observe the Brahmins and other upper caste people's treatment of Harijans in some areas. All the upper-caste people *feel* the moral obligation to be fair in their treatment of Harijans (even though no consensus is there regarding what is meant by fair treatment). The Brahmins and other upper-caste people have a sort of sentimental commitment to their castes and the so called caste norms and values which keep them at a distance from the Harijans. This state of affairs may lead to role conflict. It may also lead to the neglection and disregard of norms of fair play as far as Harijans are concerned. This condition is 'anomie' because the norms have not disappeared. Brahmins and other upper-caste people are very much aware of them but they are troubled by them.

2. ***Incompatibility between goals and means:*** According to *Merton*, anomie would be the result in "*a situation in which many persons in a social system are required to strive for some goal but are not provided with adequate legitimate means to reach it* ...." Merton has given in this regard an example that is quite relevant to American society. It is given below.

   Example. 'The goal of competitive occupational success' is a preferred goal in America. The American ideology of individual success provides at least theoretically equality of opportunity to all. This ideology poses a problem of self-esteem for virtually every man in the American society. "*Success*" is a relative goal. The belief that any common man can rise to the top and attain 'success' is quite pervasive in America. In actuality, this belief leads to an anomie situation, because, the goal of moving from an ordinary position to a white-collar position seems to be *frustratingly difficult to lower-class boys*" who are not doing well in school, have no money, and are bogged down by various internal and external conditions.

This is an example of an ideology that to some extent indirectly encourages deviant behaviour. The source of anomie as identified by *Merton* may be traced to "*a frustrating gap between a culturally favoured goal and the actual possibility of attaining it*". Even though all adults know about the culturally favoured goal, all of them never strive to reach it. Further, the institutionally permitted means for achieving it are not distributed evenly throughout the social structure. *Merton* has also pointed out that the anomie widespread in American society, and particularly, in the lower classes, does not exist "where there is no great gap between what people are expected to do and what they can do legitimately".

SOCIAL VALUES

The term '*value*' has different meanings in economics, philosophy and sociology. In *economics*, 'value' means 'price'. The "theory of value" is almost co-terminous with "the theory of price". The philosophical treatment of "values" is part of ethics, political philosophy and aesthetics. In sociology, the term 'values' represents constituent parts of social structure.

MEANING AND DEFINITION OF SOCIAL VALUES

Meaning of Social Values

'Social Values' form an important part of the culture of a society. Social values, norms and institutions explain the way in which social processes operate in a given society. They are the social sources of patterned interaction. Values account for the stability of the social order. They provide the general guidelines for conduct. In doing so, they facilitate social control. Values are the criteria people use in assessing their daily lives, arranging their priorities, measuring their pleasures and pains, choosing between alternative courses of action.

Definition of Social Values

1. "Values are group conceptions of the relative desirability of things"

   —*G.R. Leslie, R.F. Larson, H.L. Gorman.*

2. According to *H.M. Johnson*, "Values are general standards and may be regarded as higher order norms".
3. "Values are assumptions, largely unconscious, of what is right and important"

— *Young* and *Mack*.

4. "A value is a belief that something is good and worthwhile. It defines what is worth having and worth striving for".

— *Michael Haralambos*.

5. "Values are general conceptions of "the good", ideas about the kind of ends that people should pursue throughout their lives and throughout the many different activities in which they engage" — *Peter Worsley*.
6. *In simple words*, values may be defined as measure of goodness or desirability.

Thus, it is clear from the above definitions that values represent wide range of ideas about the ends that men should pursue in their life. The values of a society provide goals or ends for its members to aim for. These goals or ends are to be pursued in different contexts and situations. If the dominant value is "*success*" then, it expects all the individuals to become successful at school, in work, at sports and in life, in general. *Values provide the general guidelines for the behaviour of the people*. Thus, values such as respect for human dignity, fundamental rights, private property, patriotism, fidelity to wife or to the husband, religiosity, sacrifice, helpfulness, co-operation, individual enterprise, free marital selection, individuality, social equality, privacy, democracy, etc., guide our behaviour in various ways.

FUNCTIONS OF VALUES

1. As it is already made clear, *values provide goals or ends for the members* to aim for.
2. *Values provide for stabilities and uniformities in group interaction*. They hold the society together because they are shared in common. Some sociologists argue that shared values form the basis for social unity or social solidarity. Since they share the same values with others, the members of a society are likely to see others as "*people like themselves*". They will, therefore, have a sense of belonging to a social group. They will feel a part of the wider society.
3. *Values bring legitimacy to the rules that govern specific activities*. The rules are accepted as rules and followed mainly because they embody the values that most people accept. The Americans for example, believe that the capitalist organisation is the best one because it allows people to seek success in life.
4. *Values help to bring about some kind of adjustment between different sets of rules*. The people seek the same kinds of ends or goals in different fields of their life. Hence it is possible for them to modify the rules to help the pursuit of this end. *For example*, if the Indian people cherish the value of "*the principle of equality*", then they will have to modify the rules governing the interpersonal relationship of husband and wife; and man and woman. As and when new activities emerge, people create rules in the light of their beliefs about what is 'good' and 'right'.

FOUR ASPECTS OF VALUES

1. General and Specific Values

(*a*) **General Values.** Values such as democracy, freedom, the right to dissent, respect for fun- damental rights and dignity of labour, etc., for example, are very general in character. These values are abstract in nature and they pervade many aspects of life. A large proportion of values are found to be very general in nature. Sociologically, these are more significant.

(*b*) **Specific Values.** Values are often stated in specific terms. *For example*, we may value physical health or affluence. More specifically, we may value silk over nylon or the writing of a particular novelist over that of another. Values normally range from highly abstract to specific levels.

2. Values are Hierarchically Arranged

All the values are not equally significant. We can make a distinction between—'*Means Values*', '*Ends Values*', '*Dominant Values*' and '*Ultimate Values*. **(*a*) 'Means Values'** are instrumental values. They are sought as part of the effort to achieve other values, **(*b*) 'Ends Values'** are more general and more important from the point of view of the groups who are doing the valuing work. *For example*, if health is the value, then the maintenance of good nutrition, securing proper rest, avoidance of alcoholic drinks and drug addictions, doing proper exercises regularly, etc., become means to that end. This difference is based on contexts and situations. But it helps us to understand how the values are patterned and how one is related to another.

(*c*) **'Dominant Values'** are those values which influence and condition the behaviour of the people to a great extent. Sociologist Williams has suggested the following criteria for dominant values:

(*i*) *Extensiveness*. Whether the value is extensively found in the total activity of the people?

(*ii*) *Duration*. Whether the value has been durable and observed over a long period of time?

(*iii*) *Intensity*. With what intensity the value is pursued or maintained by the people?

(*iv*) *Prestige of Value Carriers*: To what extent the value carriers such as persons, objects, or organisations enjoy prestige in the society? *For example*, 'sacrifice' and 'service' are the two among many dominant values of the Indian society. Similarly, 'individual enterprise' and 'success in life' represent two dominant values of American society.

(*d*) The 'Ultimate Values' refer to those values of the group that give meaning, substance and direction to the lives of people. *Example*: If we take the above-mentioned example of the physical health we may say, that it is required for longevity. Longevity or longer life span can be justified in terms of 'ultimate value' to do service to the humanity and to be worthy of God's creation. There can be no higher or more ultimate value than this.

3. Explicit and Implicit Values

Most of the social values are clearly stated and explicitly held. They are deliberately taught to the children. Through official, governmental and other organisational means they are reinforced to the adults. They are also promoted through mass media. *Example*: democracy, freedom, fundamental rights, social equality, etc. These values are explicitly held and cherished.

Some of the values are **implicitly** held by the people. Public leaders, spokesmen for the society and even religious leaders may not stress upon these much. They may even ignore them. For example, respect for elders and conformity, taking care of old parents, respect for authority are values implicitly held in our society.

4. Values may Conflict with One Another

Values may often conflict with one another. In complex societies we generally observe not just one value system but more than one. We find multiple, overlapping and sometimes even opposing value systems in the same society. *For example*, the right to dissent, conformity, respect for authority, respect for elders–are values that are in conflict.

Some of the values are potentially conflicting. When they are pervasive, it becomes impossible for us to pursue some of them without violating others. *For example*, we value religious worship for personal gratification. At the same time we equally value achievement of status, accumulation of wealth, etc. Here, the first one may clash with the latter.

Normally, in modern complex society, we find conflict between groups that hold mutually opposite values. *For example*, some may value patriotism, respect for authority and disapprove of dissent. Some others, may give high importance to the value of establishment of peace. For them, establishment of peace is more important than submitting to or accepting of the war policies of their national leaders. No wonder, if, at times, the first group clashes with the second. In the same manner, during the British rule in India, while some of the Indian nationals preferred to cherish the values of "*respect for authority*" and "*obedience to the master*"; some others dedicated themselves to uphold the values of '*independence*' and '*fundamental liberties*'.

It seems reasonable to assume that there are less value conflicts in small homogeneous societies than in large heterogeneous ones.

REVIEW QUESTIONS

1. Explain the concept of social norms. Highlight the characteristic features of social norms.
2. Examine the functional importance of social norms.
3. What is the concept of institutionalization? Highlight its various aspects.
4. How do social and associational norms are interrelated? Critically analyse.
5. Comment on the relationships between norms.
6. What do you mean by anomie? Discuss the causes of anomie.
7. What are social values? Discuss the functions and various aspects of values.
8. Write short notes on the following:
   (a) Private and social norms
   (b) Norms and values
   (c) Differential norms
   (d) Social norms and anomie

⌘⌘⌘⌘⌘⌘⌘⌘⌘⌘⌘

38

Social Conformity and Deviance

Chapter Outline

The society maintains its order by means of Normative system. Normative system refers to the system of rules which the people are expected to accept, obey and appreciate. Most of the people follow most of the rules. But some may go against or violate some of the rules. When the people act in consonance with the norms they become '*Conformists*.' But when they go against them, they become '*deviants*'. '*Conformity*' and '*deviance*' go hand in hand.

SOCIAL CONFORMITY

Meaning of Social Conformity

"Conformity" is action that is (*i*) *oriented to a social norm or norms* and (*ii*) *falls within the range of behaviour permitted by the norm*. When a person accepts both goal and means, the result is generally "conformity". Thus, a student who values higher education and thinks that the college rules are necessary for earning a degree, always tries to conform to the rules to get the degree. His is the typical, normal, conventional attitude and behaviour.

'Conformity' thus implies behaving in accordance with the norms. It is not limited to the external behaviour alone. It implies that the individual consciously approves of a particular behaviour and is prepared to follow the same. It does not mean that the norms must always be present in his mind. On the contrary, we do a lot of activities in accordance with the norms without being sufficiently aware of the norms. *Example*: Walking on the right side of the road and riding on its left side, showing respect to the national flag when it is hoisted in a programme, respecting elders, dressing in a modest way, etc. Our behaviour is in conformity with the rules that we know. But we are not sure that in our behaviour the norms are always alive at the level of our consciousness.

Causes of Conformity

Harry M. Johnson has spoken of a few causes of conformity to the social norms. Some of them may be briefed here.

1. ***Socialisation:*** It is through the process of socialisation that social norms are internalised by the individuals. Hence norms become an inseparable part of their personality. Proper social training always supports conformity.
2. ***Insulation:*** Role conflict and conflict in the norms that apply to the same actor may contribute to deviance. But some built-in-arrangements may serve to reduce normative conflict and thereby contribute to conformity. (*i*) One such arrangement is that the norms that might conflict are prevented from doing so by applying to different times

and places. (*ii*) Another kind of insulation is that a given actor carries out the activities of his various roles with, or face-to-face with different role-sets. *For example*, a bank manager may learn music through his own sub-ordinate during non-official working hours accepting him as his own teacher. He may give rewards and show respect to his sub-ordinate in this regard. But during the working hours the sub-ordinate will have to accept his inferior status and obey the commands of the manager. Thus, even though the individuals remain the same in both the contexts their roles and role-expectations differ markedly. The clarity with regard to the role expectations helps to reduce uncertainty and conflict and support conformity.

3. ***Hierarchy of norms:*** Norms that apply to the same actor are found to be in the form of a hierarchy. It means the norms are ranked in order of precedence. Hence if role-expectations conflict with one another the actor has grounds for making a choice. The hierarchy of norms as well as their time and place aspect is part of culture. *For example*, a soldier may be put to such a conflicting situation in which either lie will have to attend to the needs of the ailing mother who is on the deathbed or rush to the battle-ground to attend to the urgent call of the army. The hierarchy of values and norms of his society help the soldier to take the appropriate decision. It is through socialisation the hierarchical aspects of the norms are learnt. If the different aspects of a cultural system are properly integrated and if socialisation helps the individual to understand this integration he will have no difficulty in following the expected forms of behaviour. The integration of the cultural system serves as a guide for the individual behaviour.
4. ***Social control:*** Various formal as well as informal means of social control help the socialised actor to imagine and anticipate what would happen to him if he violated the norms. Thus sanctions lead the conformity even though they are not actually applied.
5. ***Ideology:*** People's conformity to group norms depends to some extent upon the ideas and ideology that they hold. The norms partly express broader values that are more purely and precisely emphasised in ideology. Ideology strengthens faith in the existing system. Ideology adds to the norms themselves a kind of an "intellectual" support. Hence it helps to motivate people to conform to its norms.
6. ***Vested interest:*** Conformity to social norms does not always depend upon idealistic motives alone. Sometimes, due to vested interest or self-interest also people conform to them. Norms define rights as well as obligations. They protect our rights also. Some of the rights protect the exclusion of other members. Those who enjoy such advantages are likely to be satisfied, with the norms that protect them. Hence they support these norms with a greater sense of conviction than the disadvantaged persons. Property rights are a good example in this regard.

The term 'vested interest' is used here in a *neutral* sense. Hence it may represent one's genuine interests or purely selfish interests. Thus landlord's rents are vested interests for they are legitimate. Illicit liquor makers support prohibition laws with a vested interest that it would help them to make money.

Other Causes

Robert Bierstedt gives four causes for the question–'*why we conform to the norms*'. They may be briefly discussed here.

1. ***Indoctrination:*** We conform to the norms simply because we have been indoctrinated to do so. Indoctrination refers to the process of injecting into the personality of the child the group norms. We are taught, for example, to take our bath at certain times, to wash our clothes, to respect our elders, to avoid vulgarity, to walk on the right side of the road, and so on. The norms are indoctrinated through the process of socialisation. As a result, they become a part and parcel of the personality of the individual. Conformity to the norms becomes very natural because of indoctrination.
2. ***Habituation:*** We conform to the norms because we become habituated to them. What is customary is likely to become in many cases habitual. Some of the norms are indoctrinated in the beginning, but they become habitual practices afterwards. We are taught to wash our hands and mouth after the meal but after a while it becomes a matter of habit. Repetition makes a practice a habit and most of the folkways come to be rooted in the individual in this way. When one is habituated to a practice, one observes it automatically, without thinking or putting forth deliberate attempts. Habituation reinforces the norms and guarantees the regularity of conformity.
3. ***Utility:*** We appreciate the unity of norms and hence we conform to them. Norms help us to interact with others with much comfort and ease. *For example* (*i*) we are asked to sell the tickets of a drama show for which only a limited number of seats are available. Then we prefer to sell them to those who come first to purchase them. We justify

our action with an expression "*first come first served*" (*ii*) Similarly, we recognise that the flow of traffic at busy intersections is smoother and less dangerous when signal lights are installed. Thus, we stop at red light and start at green one. We find it reasonable to obey the traffic rule for it has the slogan "*the life you save may be your own*". In many social situations we realised the utility of the norms to which we conform.

4. ***Group identification:*** We conform to the norms of our own social groups rather than to those of groups to which we do not belong. We thus conform to the norms because conformity is a means of group identification. By conformity to the norms we express our identification with the groups. Sometimes, we even conform to some irrational folkways because they are our own and they identify us with our own society and our own social groups. *For example*, a particular student tries to bring home prepared lunch to the college to eat during the lunch interval (even though it is very difficult for him to bring it because of particular domestic situation) just to be in the company of his fellow-members of the 'clique'.

In some situations we may try to conform to the norms of the group to which we would like to belong and to identify ourselves. Such groups are called by Merton '*reference groups*'. *For example*, a medical student or a law graduate may begin to observe and to conform to the norms of doctors or lawyers. Even in this case group identification is significant.

Social Control and Conformity

'*Social control*' refers to various ways and means by which a group or society attempts to achieve social order. Social Order could be achieved by making the people to accept and follow the group norms. Behaving in accordance with norms or rules can be referred to as conformity. Thus, one of the main purposes of social control is conformity. Social control also involves the processes and means whereby deviations from social norms are limited by the group.

Conformity to institutionalised norms is, of course, '*normal*'. The individual having internalised the norms, feels something like a need to conform. The '*conscience*' that he has developed will not allow him in ordinary circumstances to break the norms or to go against them. Further, irrespective of his own attitude, the group or the other people will disapprove of him if he violates the established pattern. Both internalised "need" and external sanctions are effective in bringing about conformity. Conformity is achieved by two different ways:—(*i*) *Immediate conformity* which is the result of social pressure or control; and (*ii*) *Long-term result of conform which is the product of socialisation*. Only the former kind is at discussion here.

When we conform to the will or opinions of the majority, even though, we know the majority is wrong, social control is manifested in its purest form. Various experiments were held to find out the extent to which the individuals normally yield to group pressures. *Ogburn* and *Nimkoff* have stated that independence of or yielding to group pressure depends on–(*i*) "*the clarity of the stimulus, with the majority effect increasing as the clarity of the stimulus decreases*; (*ii*) *social structure with the majority effect proportional to the size of the majority, and* (*iii*) *the character of the individual, whether he is selfconfident or dislikes to appear different*.

Social factors constrain the individual to follow the group pattern. The appropriation of property from a group associate, for example, is usually condemned everywhere. This is in tune with the commandment, "thou shalt not steal". But the appropriation of property from strangers or from the enemy may be permitted and even lauded. In this case, it is not defined as stealing. The reason is that we greatly value group life because the group provides us many advantages and satisfaction. Hence the group is, therefore, a kind of defence against the more assertive and pugnacious and irregular members.

Like the taboo against stealing, innumerable group norms serve as integrating factors if there is conformity. Non-conformity threatens the integration of the group, hence the group acts to bring non-conformists into line.

The idea that the group shapes the conduct of its members carries with it the implication of group pressure. The group not only moulds behaviour, but also, restrains and disciplines. Durkheim has made it clear that the group exercises constraint or coercive power upon the individuals. It thus acts as a conservative force that limits variations. There is considerable evidence that social pressure operates to reduce variations from the average.

It is observed that if the members of the group hold decided views on the question and these views were known, then the effect is to encourage conformity to the group opinion. Sociologist *Moore* in one of his studies asked 95 subjects "to make judgements in the fields of morals by indicating which of the two ethical choices they regard as less offensive; for example, *disloyalty to friends* or *cheating on examinations*, when all the replies were in, the subjects were informed of the majority opinion, then retested. There was a swing away from the original answers. The effect of announcing the majority opinion was to bring about a greater degree of conformity to it....". It is thus concluded that *the influence of the group makes for conventional or conservative behaviour on the part of the individual*.

The social control towards conformity is always in terms of the prevailing norms. Some such norms such as taboos against stealing, killing, within the group become highly stable. They are essential to organised group life.

The goal of social control is no doubt overt conformity. Many people who are not individually agreeable to certain norms accept and conform to them outwardly. Those who are not convinced of them lack the power to resist them successfully. Thus, in conformity we find two factors which may or may not be consistent: *compliance* and *conviction*. Most compliance is associated with conviction, since members of a group are generally persuaded of the rightness of their way of doing things. But there is a good deal of overt conformity without conviction, especially on the part of new comers to a group. The saying "*Be a Roman when you are in Rome*" is reflection of this fact. "Conformity without conviction occurs when the individual cannot withdraw from the group, or values much his membership in the group, and does not wish to offend, or is afraid of the consequences of non-conformity".

Group norms are actually group standards which the members are encouraged to imitate or follow. But some deviation is bound to be there in every group even in the so called utopias. If the deviation is of very mild nature the controlling agency of the group may ignore it. *For example*, in spite of the well established moral rule, "*Thou shalt not steal*", it is generally known that in all societies stealing takes place. In modern societies cheating in the matter of paying income tax is practised by even the most educated and learned people. If such cases are traced out and the guilty is found to pay only a marginal amount as income tax, he may be cautioned to pay that with some amount of fine. But if the amounts unreported are large, and there is proof of intention to defraud, the penalty is likely to be more severe, including a jail sentence. Thus, "*As the deviation from the norm becomes greater, the more serious becomes the offence in the eyes of the group and the more severe becomes the penalty*", But the seriousness of the offence is always culturally defined. Hence members of a society may have in their mind an idea of the hierarchy of offences defined in terms of their seriousness.

SOCIAL DEVIANCE

It is true that the social order is mainly maintained by means of social control and socialisation. It is equally true that most of the people follow or conform to most of the norms most of the times. But all the people or even most of people do not conform to all the norms always. As *Young* and *Mack* have pointed out, "*No norm is always obeyed*; *no individual always conforms to every set of expectations*". Hence, deviance, that is, the act of going against the rules or norms is there everywhere. Deviant behaviours such as knavery, cheating, adultery, unfairness, crime, malingering, immorality, dishonesty, betrayal, burglary, corruption, cunningness, sneakiness, wickedness, gambling, drunkenness etc., go along with conformity. Deviance in one shape or another is found everywhere.

Definition of Deviance or Deviancy

1. *Horton* and *Hunt*: "The term deviation is given to any failure to conform to customary norms".
2. *Orville G. Brim Jr*: "Deviance can be defined as failure to conform to the expectations of other persons".
3. *Louise Weston*: "Deviance can be defined as behaviour that is contrary to the standards of conduct or social expectations of a given group or society'.
4. *M.B. Clinard* suggests that the term deviance should be reserved for "those situations in which behaviour is in a disapproved direction, and of sufficient degree to exceed the tolerance limit of society".
5. In simple words. deviance many be defined as *the act of going against the group-shared expectations and norms*.

Types or Deviance

Deviance may assume different forms. Some of them may be noted here.

1. ***Innovation:*** Society sets forth goals for the individuals to aim at and also lay down means to achieve them. When a person accepts both goals and means the result is generally "*conformity*" Sometimes, a person may accept the goal but not the means. He may innovate or create his own means for achieving the goals and in this sense, he becomes a deviant. If this innovated means brings positive results it poses no problem for the social order and if it brings negative results it may pose a danger to the society. Example: Some poor people and pleasure-seekers may be forced to 'innovate' or resort to illegitimate, "dishonest" means to get money. Such 'innovators' are problematic deviants.

2. ***Ritualism:*** Sometimes a person gives up important social values yet does lip service to them by carefully observing related norms of behaviour. They are *ritualists*. They abandon the pursuit of success as fruitless and yet strictly adhere to the prescribed means. They regard rules as sacred. They tend to lower their aspirations and never expect success. Because they find themselves unable to break out of their commitment to the rules.

   Ritualists are also deviants because such persons refuse to take courageous and possibly dangerous action demanded by true adherence to values. On the other hand, they take refuge in neutral but safe behaviour which looks like decent conformity. *Example*: A person stabbed to death within the sight of a number of neighbours who refuse to get themselves involved in the case. This kind of behaviour is ritualistic. It is difficult to criticise such behaviour harshly. It is also a form of deviance because norms exist or should exist to serve values. They should not eclipse values or transcend them.

3. ***Retreatism:*** The rejection of both values and norms is '*retreatism*'. It is in one way or another of '*dropping out*' of society. The person who drops out '*resigns*' so to speak. Those who 'retreat' from the society refuse to pursue wealth either by legal or illegal means. They also refuse to lead a '*conventional*' life. They are unable to get success 'honestly'. They are not able to break the conventional procedure because of the strongly internalised norm. The best solution to their dilemma is to 'drop out' of society. Hence 'retreatism' is a kind of passive rejection of the goal of success and of respectable occupational activities. According to *Merton*, in this category fall "*some of the adaptive activities of psychotics, autists, pariahs, outcastes, vagrants, vagabonds, tramps, chronic drunkards and drug addicts*". Such people receive strong disapproval because they care little of the values most people live by.

4. ***Rebellion:*** Rebellion is another response open to those who reject both ends and means. Some people reject the prevailing order and engage in efforts to replace that order. They try to substitute new ends and means for those that exist. They are called '*rebels*'. Rebellion is produced by alienation from both values and norms. Instead of 'retreating' the rebel gives active support and loyalty to an incompatible set of values and norms. He feels that they are superior to those of conventional society. He seeks some reconstruction, some change in the existing order. He may even attempt at the complete destruction of that order or struggle to replace it with another order. Rebellion may vary from small-scale to that of greater scale. *Example*: A student giving up education in the name of doing greater things is an example of small-scale rebellion. A law-abiding young man going away from society to form a criminal gang to take revenge upon some authority is an example of greater-scale rebellion. Political and religious revolutions that were initiated by one or the other individual also come under this category.

FACTORS FACILITATING DEVIANCE

Social deviance refers to the non-conformity to or violating of the norms of the group. The violation of norms is not evenly spread in a population. In the same way, all the norms are not violated. What we normally observe in society is that some particular norm is violated or some particular persons violate a given norm, or both. *H.M. Johnson* had listed a few factors that facilitate deviance among which the following may be noted:

1. ***Faulty socialisation:*** Socialisation is the process by which the individual learns to conform to the norms of the group. When he fails to conform to the norms systematically he becomes a social deviant. Socialising agents often fail to inculcate in the new born person the strong morals. Sometimes socialising agents themselves may directly or indirectly, overtly or covertly, consciously or half-consciously encourage such deviant behaviour of the new members. *Parsons* has pointed out that deviance proneness is more potential in the lower classes mainly because of failure in socialisation.

2. ***Weak sanctions:*** Sanctions refer to the rewards or punishments used to establish social control or to enforce norms in a society. If the positive sanctions (rewards) for conformity and the negative sanctions (punishments) for deviance are weak, the individual may simply neglect them.

3. ***Poor enforcement:*** Even though the sanctions are stronger they are often not enforced effectively due to the too small enforcement staff. Because of this the validity of the norm is weakened. *For example*, it is not possible for a handful of traffic police staff to enforce traffic rules on all vehicle riders. The result is, many ignore and some even openly violate traffic rules.

4. ***Ease of rationalisation:*** The violators of norms try to soothe or satisfy their conscience by inventing some plausible rationalisations. Such people have constructed an intricate system of '*ego defense*' which they use to brush aside the reactions and comments of other people. "*They are picking on me; I could not help myself; I did not do it for*

myself; They asked for it; It is a deal; It is all a matter of buck"–These expressions or slogans reflect the attitudes of such violators. *Example*: Police constables may rationalise their regular habit of taking ('*mamul*') bribes by saying that they are paid very low salary. Jobs are often secured with bribes under the pretext of inevitability. During the Second World War some women offered themselves as bedmates to the soldiers with the '*belief*' that the young men going off to war and possibly to death deserved the comfort of sexual relations.

5. ***Unjust or corrupt enforcement:*** People may lose respect for law and norms when they have no faith in law enforcement agency or authority. It is known that police corruption and illegal violence damage very much respect for the law in the areas affected by such practices. It is also observed that in some instances police maintain '*informal relations*' or *secret understandings* with the violators. As a result, such relations condone the activities which the police are supposed to suppress.
6. ***Ambivalence of the agents of social control:*** Ambivalence refers to the co-existence in one person of opposing emotional attitudes towards the same object. *For example*, a person may consider woman not only as an object of respect, but also as an object of love, particularly of sexual love. A doctor with such ambivalent attitude may inflict sexual crime on young and beautiful female patients. Policemen, teachers, parents, business superiors, all may have such complex personalities with unconscious deviant tendencies. These tendencies may lead them unconsciously to encourage certain kinds of deviation rather than to counteract it.
7. ***Subcultural support of deviance:*** Different groups have different ideas of permissible behaviour. The range of acts that would be approved by the working class people differs from that which would be approved by the middle class people. What is non-conforming in the outside world becomes conforming in the group. *For example*, the frustrated children of the working class flock together in little gangs. The subculture of this gang may emphasise malice and negativism. The gang may even reward delinquent behaviour for it represents an attack on the values of the respectable middle class.
8. ***Sentiments of loyalty to deviant groups:*** When once a person is involved in a deviant group he is obliged to co-operate with other members. He will find it difficult to '*betray*' his co-members and suffer their disapproval and rejection. He is forced to approve of the behaviour even if he no longer believes in their activities. As *Parsons* has remarked, deviant groups deal harshly with disloyal members. Because, such members not only pose a threat of exposure to enforcement agencies but also a threat to the stability of the group. The defection of one member may tempt other members to go away from the group. Defection destroys the very solidarity that made the deviant group strong and satisfying in the beginning.
9. ***Indefinite range of norms:*** Some norms relating to some values are not probably specified. *For example*, the scope of patriotism and freedom (political values) is not clearly defined. Hence, some even defend their deviant behaviour in the name of patriotism and freedom. Thus, one may use harsh language against another in the name of freedom.
10. ***Secrecy of violations:*** Some susceptible persons are more prone to commit deviant acts if they are assured that such acts are not going to be made public. *For example*, sex crimes and illegal abortions very often take place because of the confidence on the part of the actors that their behaviour would remain secret.

Social Significance of Deviant Behaviour

Deviance and Disorganisation

Deviance poses a danger to the stability of the social order. It may be destructive of organisation in at least three ways.

1. *Deviance is more or less a less or defect of a critical part in a complicated mechanism*. An organised social activity is possible only when the different members perform their respective functions in accordance with the expectations. If some members fail to do their duties the continued functioning of the larger activity is endangered. *For example*, if the commanding officer of a military unit defects in the middle of the War, the army as such suffers a terrible setback.
2. *Deviance may undermine organisation by destroying people's willingness to play their parts*. Deviance offends people's sense of justice and makes uneven the ratio between effort and reward. 'Idlers', 'fakers', 'chiselers', 'sneaks', 'smugglers', 'blackmarketeers', 'gangsters', 'cheats', and the like offend and threaten the interests of the virtuous. Because, they take away share in rewards sometimes disproportionately without undergoing the sacrifices, sufferings, struggles and disciplines of the virtuous. Deviance may also provoke bitterness and resentment. It may

also damage one's determination to play one's role according to the rules.

3. *The most destructive impact of deviance on organisation is through its impact an trust, on confidence that others will, by and large, play by the rules.* Each participant to the collective enter- prise suppresses some of his impulses, makes some sacrifice of time, money and labour, rejects illegal temptations. He does this on the assumption that, if he plays by the rules, so will other. "Distrust, even if it is unfounded, weakens organisation by undermining motivation; to distrust others is to see one's effort as pointless, wasted, and foolish, and the future as hazardous and uncertain." –(*A.K. Cohen*).

Deviance in Support of Organisation

It is wrong to believe that deviance is always destructive of organisation. On the other hand, deviance, in some circumstances, may make positive contributions to the stability and vitality of social organisation. Albert K. Cohen mentions the following functions of deviance in support of organisation.

1. ***Deviance versus 'Red tape' or official delay:*** Sometimes deviance provides solutions to some typical, recurrent problems. For example, a military unit may face an unanticipated situation in which it needs immediate supply of some articles in a quantity in excess of its normal quota. If the suppliers conform to the rules delay would be the result. The delay may even damage the interests of the military unit. In this example, if the organisational interest is to be safeguarded somebody must violate the rules. Here, deviance stems from one's strong *identification* and *concern* with the interests of the large organisation.
2. ***Deviance as a 'safety valve':*** A certain amount of deviance may perform a '*safety valve*' function by preventing excessive accumulation of discontent. It may also reduce some amount of strain of the legitimate order. From this point of view, it may be said that prostitution serves such a 'safety valve' function. It provides some satisfaction to some unsatisfied needs without necessarily endangering the institution of the family.
3. ***Deviance may clarify the rules:*** Social norms reduce some of the anxiety and uncertainty of social interaction by specifying rights and duties, and the 'dos' and 'don'ts'. To do this task norms must be clear to all the participants. But some norms are often found to be vague and ambiguous. "*Don't take what is not yours*", "*Do your own work*", "*Friends should stand by one another*" — and such other normative statements do not make clear the real meaning and expectation of the norms. One comes to know the range or the boundaries of norms only when deviance takes place. Thus, the deviant one renders an important service to the other members by providing an occasion for the clarification of a rule. *Due to deviance people come to know more clearly than before what they may and may not legitimately do*.
4. ***Deviance helps the unity of the group (Against the deviant):*** It is often said that a common enemy unites the members of a group. The deviant acts as a common enemy against whom the people get organised to revive and revitalise the weakening solidarity. The deviant, thus, functions as a 'built-in' out-group, and contributes to the integration of the group.
5. ***Deviance also helps to unite the group on behalf of the deviant:*** Deviants are not external enemies. They are the people estranged from the norms. They are to be set right. They cannot be destroyed or banished from the society. Because they perform a variety of functions for the group. Majority of the people try to keep the deviants within the group by helping them tic come back to the conventional life. They try to protect the deviant from the consequences of his own deviance. The group shows its limitless patience and kindness in the face of provocation from the deviant member.
6. ***The contrary effect: Increasing conformity:*** "*The good deed shines brightest in a naughty world*," said Shakespeare. In the face of deviance even average conformity is appreciated. For ex- ample, the conductor who issues tickets to the passengers, or the police who refuses to accept the offer of bribe becomes a '*model*'. The deviants provide the contrast effect that makes conformity something "special" and a source of satisfaction.
7. ***A warning signal:*** Deviance may also function as a signal light or warning. It invites attention to defects of organisation. *For example*, increases in absenteeism from work, 'drop outs' from primary schools, failures in college examinations, runaways from rehabilitation centres, deliberate defects of workmanship, etc., may compel re-examination of existing procedures. Such instances lead to changes that contribute to efficiency and morale.

Conclusion

Deviant behaviour is one way of adapting a culture to a social change. Deviant behaviour thus often represents tomorrow's adaptations in their beginnings. Without any deviant behaviour, it would be difficult to adopt a culture to changing needs and circumstances. A changing society therefore needs deviant behaviour. But *how much and what kinds*—are the debatable questions. Still it can be said that much deviation is destructive in nature. Only some deviation is socially useful for they help us to forecast tomorrow's norms.

REVIEW QUESTIONS

1. Define social conformity. Discuss its various causes.
2. How do social control and conformity are interrelated? Critically examine.
3. What is social deviance? Describe its types.
4. Examine the factors that facilitate deviance.
5. Write a detailed note on the social significance of deviant behaviour.
6. Write short notes on the following:
   (a) Social conformity
   (b) Indoctrination
   (c) Social deviance
7. Deviant behaviour is one way of adapting a culture to a social change. Examine.

⌘⌘⌘⌘⌘⌘⌘⌘⌘⌘⌘

PART SEVEN

SOCIAL CHANGE

39

MEANING AND NATURE OF SOCIAL CHANGE

CHAPTER OUTLINE

- Meaning and Definition of Social Change
- Nature and Characteristics of Social Change
- Social Change and Cultural Change
- Causes of Social Change
- Source of Social Change
- Resistance to Social Change
- The Role of Values in Social Change
- The Role of Great Men in Social Change
- Social Evolution
- Social Progress

Change is an ever present phenomenon everywhere. An ancient Greek Philosopher *Heraclitus* in an emphatic way hinted at this fact when he said that *it is impossible for a man to step into the same river twice*. It is impossible, because in the interval of time between the first and the second stepping both the river and the man have changed. *Neither remains the same*. "This is the central theme of the Heraclitean philosophy – *the reality of change, the impermanence of being, the inconstancy of everything but change itself*". The order that is society, is after all the changing order. Ever since Comte, sociologists have faced two large social questions – *the question of social statics and the question of social dynamics, what is and how it changes*. The sociologist is not satisfied when he has outlined the structure of society. He seeks to know its causes also. Thus, the Roman poet *Lucretius* remarks, "*Happy is he who can know the causes of things*". The casual curiosity of a sociologist never rests; nothing stills his desire to know and to understand. He is engaged in an endless endeavour to unravel the mystery of social change. Social change is indeed a perplexing problem. *Nothing social remains the same, nothing social abides*.

CHANGE IS THE LAW OF NATURE

The nature is never at rest. It is changeful. Change is ever present in the world, because change is the Law of Nature. Similarly, society is not at all a static phenomenon, but it is a dynamic entity. It is an "*on-going process*". Society is subject to constant changes. Social change has occurred in all societies and at all times. Of all the objects we study, none changes before our very eyes as the society itself. Every society and culture, no matter how traditional and conservative, is constantly undergoing change. Society changes in ceaseless flux and flow.

Incessant changeability is the very inherent nature of the human society. Individuals may strive for security and stability; societies may foster an illusion of permanence and the belief in eternity may persist unshaken. Yet the fact remains true that society like all other phenomenon changes inevitably. Society is influenced by many forces and factors that irresistibly cause changes. India of today is different from the India of yesterday; what it is going to be tomorrow is hence, difficult to predict. In course of a decade or two, significant changes can and do occur in human society. The territory which the sociologist explores, changes even as he explores it. This fact has an important bearing both on his methods and on his results. Here at least we can seek the principles of eternal change. What then, do we mean by change? and social change?

MEANING AND DEFINITION OF SOCIAL CHANGE

Any alteration, difference or modification that takes place in a situation or in an object through time can be called change. The term '*social change*' is used to indicate the changes that take place in human interactions and interrelations. Society is a "web of social relationships" and hence '*social change*' *obviously means a change in the system of social relationships*. Social relationships are understood in terms of social processes and social interactions and social organisation. Thus the term 'social change' is used to desirable variations in social interaction, social processes and social organisation. It includes alterations in the structure and functions of the society.

Definition of Social Change

1. *M.E. Jones*: "Social change is a term used to describe variations in, or modifications of, any aspect of social processes, social patterns, social interaction or social organisation".
2. *Kingsley Davis*: "By social change is meant only such alterations as occur in social organisation, that is, structure and functions of society".
3. *Majumdar, H. T.* "Social change may be defined as a new fashion or mode, either modifying or replacing the old, in the life of a people – or in the operation of society."
4. *MacIver and Page*: "Social change refers to 'a process' responsive to many types of changes; to changes in the manmade conditions of life; to changes in the attitudes and beliefs of men, and to the changes that go beyond the human control to the biological and the physical nature of things".
5. *MacIver* (in some other context) also refers to social change as simply a change in the human relationships.

Social Change: A Complex Phenomenon

"The fact of social change has fascinated the keenest minds and still poses some of the great unsolved problems in social science." The phenomenon of social change is not simple but complex. It is difficult to understand this phenomenon in its entirety. The unsolved problems are always pes- tering and pressurising us to find an appropriate answer. Some such problems are as follows — What is the direction of social change? What is the form of social change? What is the source of social change? What are its *causes*? Its *consequences*? What are its *conditions and limitations*? What is the rate of change? Whether the changes are due to human engineering or the uncontrollable cosmic design? Is it necessary to *control* social change? Can man, regulate it to suit his conveniences? Can he regulate and decide the direction of social change to satisfy his desires? These are some of the tantalising questions — tantalising not only because of their complexity but also because of their human significance.

NATURE AND CHARACTERISTICS OF SOCIAL CHANGE

1. ***Social change is continuous:*** Society is undergoing endless changes. These changes can- not be stopped. Society cannot be preserved in a museum to save it from the ravages of time. From the dawn of history, down to this day society has been in continuous flux.
2. ***Social change is temporal:*** Change happens through time. Social change is temporal in the sense it denotes the time-sequence. In fact, society exists only as a time-sequence. As *MacIver* says, "*it is a becoming, not a being; a process, not a product*". Innovation of new things, modification and renovation of the existing behaviour and the discarding of the old behaviour patterns take time. But the mere passage of time does not cause change as in the biological process of ageing.
3. ***Social change is environmental:*** It must take place within a geographic or physical and cultural context. Both these contexts have impact on human behaviour and in turn man changes them. Social changes never takes place in vacuum.
4. ***Social change is human change:*** The sociological significance of the change consists in the fact that it involves the human aspect. The composition of society is not constant, but changing. The fact that people effect change and are themselves affected by it makes change extremely important.
5. ***Social change results from interaction of a number of factors:*** A single factor may trigger a particular change, but it is always associated with other factors. The physical, biological, technological, cultural and other factors may, together bring about social change. This is due to the mutual interdependence of social phenomenon.
6. ***Social change may create chain reaction:*** Change in one aspect of life may lead to a series of changes in its other aspects. For example, change in rights, privileges, and status of women has resulted in a series of changes in home, family relationships and structure, the economic and to some extent, the political pattern of both rural and urban society.
7. ***Social change involves tempo (or rate) and direction of change:*** In most discussions of social change some direction is assumed. This direction is most necessarily inevitable. Some- times, the direction is determined ideally. Change towards such a destination is more appropriately regarded as *progress*. In actuality, social change may tend towards

any direction. The tempo or the rate of change is also not governed by any universal laws. The rate of change varies considerably from time to time and society to society depending upon its nature and character—open and closed, rural and urban and others.

8. ***Social change may be planned or unplanned:*** The direction and tempo of social change are often conditioned by human engineering. Plans, programmes and projects may be launched by man in order to determine and control the rate and direction of social change. Unplanned change refers to change resulting from natural calamities such as famines and floods, earthquakes, volcanic eruptions, etc.

9. ***Short versus long-run changes:*** Some social changes may bring about immediate results while some others may take years and decades to produce results. This distinction is significant, because a change which appears to be very vital today may be nothing more than a temporary oscillation having nothing to do with the essential trends of life, some years later. This is what historians mean when they say that time alone can place the events of the day in their true perspective.

10. ***Social change is an objective term:*** The term social change describes one of the categorical processes. It has no value-judgements attached to it. To the sociologist social change as a phenomenon is neither moral nor immoral, it is amoral. It means the study of social change involves no-value-judgement. It is ethically neutral. One can study change even within the value system without being for against the change.

SOCIAL CHANGE AND CULTURAL CHANGE

The difference between social change and cultural change has a great sociological importance. By '*social change*' is meant only such alterations as occur in social organisation, that is, structure and functions of society. Social change, in this sense, is only a part of what is essentially a broader category called "*cultural change*". The term "cultural change", according to *Kingsley Davis*, "em- braces all changes occurring in any branch of culture including art, science, technology, philosophy, etc., as well as changes in the forms and rules of social organisation." As he says, *cultural change is broader than social change*, and social change is only a part of it.

All social changes are cultural changes, but all cultural changes need not necessarily be 'the social changes also. Cultural changes can be called social changes only when they affect human relations and the social organisation and cause some variation in them. *Ex*. Changes in the musical styles, painting styles, rules of writing poetry and drama, pronunciation of words, etc., represent cultural changes. They are purely cultural changes. They cannot be called social changes, because, they do not in any way affect the existing pattern of human interactions, social system antisocial organisation.

On the other hand, the rise of organised labour in the capitalistic society and the introduction of communism in the place of democracy, represent social change. These two changes may cause a series of changes in human relations and social organisation. They represent a basic alteration in the relation of employer and employee, rulers and the ruled. They may contribute to the changes in the economic organisation, methods of administration, legislations, economic policies and programmes, and so on. These may, in course of time affect the way of life of people. Hence, they can also be called cultural changes.

Cultural change, is thus much broader than the social change. No part of culture is totally unrelated to the social order, but it remains true that changes sometimes occur in these branches without noticeably affecting the social system. Sociologically, therefore, we are interested in cultural change only to the extent that it arises from or has an effect on social organisation.

CAUSES OF SOCIAL CHANGE

Social change is a complex phenomenon in which the cause and effect relationship is not always clear. No single cause produces a single effect in the social world. There is always the *plurality* of *causation*. Several factors or causes operate together to produce the same results.

According to *Harry M. Johnson* the causes of social change are of three types: *Firstly*, the causes of social change are inherent either in social system in general or in particular kinds of social system. *Secondly*, the change may be due to some impact from the social environment of the social system of reference. *Finally*, change may also be due to some impact from the non-social environment. He is of the opinion that these are combined in various ways. One change may lead to a series of changes. The component parts of the social system are so interrelated that any change in one causes adjustive changes in the others.

Internal Causes of Social Change

1. ***Strain and conflict:*** Conflict of interests is always present to some extent in all the social systems. It is more evident in the political field. The concept of power virtually implies the idea of conflicting purposes. In the stable social systems conflicts of interest are settled largely within institutionalised rules. No society is free from conflicts. Any

attempt to resolve the conflict would lead to some kind of change or the other. A latent conflict is always present at all times between those whom the existing system is benefiting more and those whom it is benefiting less. This conflict will become manifest if the disadvantages are made to feel that the existing order is not the only realistically possible order.

2. ***Social problems:*** Problems such as caste prejudices, prostitution, juvenile delinquency, over 'population, unemployment, poverty, beggary, the need for slum clearance, etc., involve a good deal of social conflict, in the course of which social change occurs. These are social problems. They arise mainly due to some internal deficiencies. Therefore, if they are to be solved or reduced, the existing social order will have to be changed to some extent. Thus, an attempt to tackle social problem may contribute to social change. *For example*, in order to reduce the size of the growing population in India, people may have to be convinced of the importance of following birth control measures, family planning, etc. This may affect the value system, marriage and family system and moral system of India.
3. ***Revolutions and upheavals:*** The most intense conflict in a society is found during a revolution. Various internal factors may contribute to it. *For example*, the American Revolution, the French Revolution and the Russian, Revolution took place due to several factors such as - exploitation, suppression of liberty, hunger, tyranny, bad roads, commercial restrictions, corruption, military or diplomatic defeat, famine, high prices, low wages, unemployment, and so on. These revolutions brought about far-reaching changes.
4. ***Cultural change:*** Cultural innovation also contributes to social change. *An innovation is a new combination of old elements* which may come from the innovator's own society or from some other. The diffusion of culture within society and from one society to another has been a great source of social and cultural change in every society.

The Impact of the Social and Nonsocial Environment

The environment, whether social or nonsocial, has its own influence on social structure. As far as social change is concerned, the impact of the social environment is more important than the impact of the nonsocial environment.

The **impact of the non-social environment** on the social structure is relatively slight under normal conditions. Changes in the non-social environment (which are due to human engineering) such as — soil erosion, deforestation, exhaustion of mineral resources, etc., may bring about some social changes. Changes in the nonsocial environment due to nature itself such as–floods and famines, earthquakes and volcanic eruptions, cyclones and hurricanes, etc., may sometimes cause adoptive social changes.

The **influence of the social environment** is more significant in bringing about social changes. Shifts of political alliances, military invasions, peaceful immigration, trade shifts, etc., can present difficult problems of adjustment to the social system. Any one of these changes is likely to affect some parts of the social structure first and then have effects in other parts later.

SOURCES OF SOCIAL CHANGE

Sociologists have been debating and discussing the question of the sources of social change. Cultural anthropologists are more interested in this topic. There are two groups among them (1) the *diffusionists*, and (2) *inventionists*.

1. According to the *diffusionists*, social or cultural change takes place due to cultural diffusion. Diffusion refers to the introduction of a behaviour modification from another culture. *It denotes the spread of elements of culture, either singly or in a complex, from one local group to another local group. It is less frequently used to refer to dissemination within a group*. The argument of the diffusionists is that since inventions do not take place all the time and in all the societies in the same manner, every society borrows the cultural elements of another society for its progress directly or indirectly. They have cited the example of several tribes who could achieve progress by borrowing the cultural elements from the other groups. It takes very long time for a society to achieve progress if it fails to get profited by the achievements of others. *For example, the Maori people* of New Zealand became civilised within one hundred years by borrowing many cultural elements from others. Thus, according to the diffusionists, the source of social change is to be found in cultural diffusion.
2. According to the *inventionists*, the source of social change is to be found in the inherent capacity of the people to make inventions. They have said that inventions constitute the major source of social change. Invention, whether in the field of social organisation or the cultural framework, refers to the *rearrangement of known traits into new patterns or configurations*. These inventions, whether material or non-material, have led to profound social changes. The invention of electricity, for example, has led to astounding changes in the fields of industry, agriculture, communication, transport and so on. Inventionists have argued that it is wrong to assume that social change always takes place due to cultural diffusion. They have criticised the argument of diffusionists that many of the elements of South American culture have been borrowed from India, Egypt, Jawa Polynesia and other places. They have contended that people are capable of initiating changes on their own.

Conclusion

The arguments of diffusionists as well as inventionists involve in themselves some amount, of truth. Both can neither be completely accepted nor rejected. The source; of social change is to be found in both diffusion and inventional. Sometimes, it becomes difficult for us to say with certainty when, where, how and from whom the inventions took place. Further, some inventions take place in two or three places simultaneously. The invented thing may undergo change while getting diffused to other places. A single invention may cause several other inventions also.

Internal invention and *external diffusion* are two originating sources that have cumulative mutual influence on change. An internally inventive society also seeks knowledge through contact with other societies. In a sense, *every social change is strange and foreign whether it originates at home or comes from abroad.*

RESISTANCE TO SOCIAL CHANGE

Though social change is universal, societies and cultures are relatively permanent. The social and cultural functions do not change 'overnight' even in the most dynamic populations. Certain resistance to change is there everywhere. In no society all the changes are welcomed by the people without questioning and resistance. To some extent the removal of the evil practices such as child marriage, human sacrifice, animal sacrifice, untouchability, taboos on intercaste marriages, etc., could be achieved after a long struggle in India. The opposition to woman suffrage in the United States lasted for more than *fifty* years, and the opposition to the abolition of slavery was accomplished only after a prolonged civil war. It was only in the beginning of 20th century that women were given voting right in Britain after much opposition. It took centuries for some major reforms to take place in Christianity. In the midst of strong opposition and violence communism was introduced in Russia. *Ogburn* and *Nimkoff* wrote: "*It is a curious phenomenon that some of the greatest blessings of the human race should have been bitterly resisted, at times with the spilling of blood before humanity was allowed to profit by them...* "

Reasons for the Opposition to Social Change

The main reasons for the opposition to social change are as follows:

1. ***Lack of new inventions:*** Social changes depend on the invention of new objects, techniques, thoughts, devices and plans to a great extent. Changes will take place without much opposition if the people have the strong craving for new things. Lack of interest in inventions and lack of inventions as such, do not provide a favourable atmosphere for change.

2. ***Rejection or non-acceptance of new inventions:*** No change is possible if people go on rejecting the new inventions. New inventions have been more resisted than welcomed by the people. *Dr. William Harvey's Blood Circulation Theory and Galileo's theory concerning the planetary system and the movement of earth*, were opposed in the beginning. Opposition came in the British Parliament for the use of steam energy in British Naval Ships. Several such instances can be quoted from history.

3. ***Imperfections of new inventions:*** In the beginning inventions are generally subject to imperfections, such as inadequate performance, easy breakage and difficulty of repair. Social inventions also have imperfections in the beginning. People may oppose them for their inadequacies.

4. ***Fear towards the new:*** Man has not only *love for the past but also fear towards the new*. People express their fear towards the new while making use of the new objects, listening to the new thoughts and following a new practice. Indians have shown in the beginning their fear and suspicion while accepting the British medicine, undergoing English education-and undertaking sea voyages.

5. ***Tradition and reverence for the past:*** People are traditional in their attitude. The old and the traditional practices and things and ideas are upheld by the people. People are emotionally and sentimentally bound by them. Sometimes, people cling themselves tenaciously to the harmful, out- dated and inefficient practices. Thus, the traditional attitude of the people will not allow them to accept new things.

6. ***Ignorance:*** Due to ignorance people often oppose new inventions or changes. It usually takes time for a new discovery, tool or technique to be understood. Thus for a long time, the germ theory of disease was rejected. The iron plough was not accepted easily in America. It took several years to find acceptance with the farmers. Opposition to technical or material invention can be removed in course of time by demonstrating its effective workability. But the social invention may be opposed by the people for an indefinite time, because its concrete *demonstration is difficult*.

7. ***Habit:*** Habit is another obstacle to social change. Individuals are very much influenced by habits and customs. People dislike or fear the unfamiliar. They are not ready to give up a practice to which they have been habituated to and adopt a new one. Hence the new practice is looked down upon or rejected.

8. ***Economic disparity and difficulty:*** Wide gap between the rich and poor, and extreme economic distress also come in the way of social change. People who are suffering from various economic problems are not prepared to accept changes, for they are either sceptical about it or they are economically incapable of accepting a new change.
9. ***Intellectual laziness and administrative defects:*** In order to give up the old ideas and accept the new ones, people require some amount of creativity, dynamism and rationality. If these qualities are *lacking* among people they may fail to realise the importance and usefulness of the new ideas and things. Further inefficient and corrupt administrative machinery also provides obstacles to change. The bureaucratic element of the administration has been said to be conservative in nature and a stumbling block on the path of change and progress.
10. ***The power of vested interests:*** The vested interests constitute yet another source of opposition to innovations. Individuals who feel that social change endangers their interests are likely to oppose it. They therefore fight every proposal in this direction. Such persons may organise them- selves as opposition groups when their "*rights*" *are threatened*. Similarly, people oppose changes if their *self-interests are endangered*. The capitalists have been opposing the progressive labour legislations for this reason. The social reforms have been opposed by the so called traditionalist section of the Indian Society.

All Resistances are Not Harmful

We cannot say that all the resistances are harmful. In some instances, opposition to social change is justifiable. Some innovations or changes will prove to be harmful when they are judged from the point of view of a certain standard of values. The proposal that a totalitarian type of government be substituted for the democratic system is an instance of a reform that is considered definitely harmful. Opposition to technological inventions is justifiable, if they are unworkable or impractical, or if their disadvantages outweigh their advantages. *Resistance to change has its positive side also*. All the innovations and changes cannot be welcomed as worthwhile and beneficial.

ROLE OF VALUES IN SOCIAL CHANGE

The most important kind of structural change is change in the comprehensive standards that are called "*values*". Values refer to the constituent facts of social structure. The values we have in mind here are, of course, values that directly affect the content of social roles and social interaction. They are not purely cultural values, such as classicism in art.

Values constitute one of the elements of culture. Like culture, values also undergo changes. Values normally undergo changes slowly and gradually. In fact, values are often regarded as the static element of society. In a highly industrialised and urbanised society values undergo change comparatively at a greater speed. In a highly tradition-bound society values undergo change slowly. Scientific and technological innovations, political and economic changes, widespread education, high rate of urbanisation and industrialisation, etc., have caused changes in values.

Social values not only undergo changes, but also contribute to social change. Social values and moral norms greatly affect the rate and direction of social change. In comparative terms, preliterates resist all changes while members of modern Western society welcome almost all of them. The direction of change is also in large measure controlled by these subjective aspects of society. Modern Americans hail new gadgets and mechanical devices with an almost religious zeal. But they resist changes in politico-economic ideology. They abhor the term '*socialism*' and resist all '*socialist*' trends in administration. The democratic values are so deep-rooted in them that they hate and protest state intervention in many social matters.

Ideological values resist and limit social changes. Ideological values themselves, however, differ in the degree to which they resist change. The American ideological values of race relations, education and religion have been less resistive to change than those connected with the politico- economic field. On the contrary, the Indian values pertaining to caste relations, education, religious institution are more resistive to change than those connected with their politico-economic field.

ROLE OF GREAT MEN IN SOCIAL CHANGE

Great men and their leadership constitute an important source of social change. Great men of genius, revolutionary thoughts, extraordinary talents, powerful expression, ability and efficiency, may sometimes bring about revolutionary and also longlasting changes in society. Human history provides innumerable examples of such men and women, who brought about far-reaching changes.

The political interpretation of social change, leads quickly and easily into the so called "*great-man*" *theory of history*. According to this theory, human history is the serialised biographies of great men. It is to be understood not in terms, of the movements of nameless masses but in terms of the achievements of elites. It is here, we are faced with some of the intriguing questions: *Do men make history or does history make the man ? Do they (great men), and to what extent do they, make social change*" ? Or, are they puppets of '*social forces*' that are operating beyond their control?

Sociological theory, as opposed to the interpretations of most Historians, has stressed the role of '*social forces*' in bringing social change. It has been noted for example, that the greatest American Presidents–Washington and Lincoln have been war presidents and the question arises whether they would have been equally great if they had lived in different times and circumstances. On the same plane, it can be said that the name of Gandhiji would have been simply insignificant had there not been the British rule in India. It is relevant to quote *Tolstoy* in this connection. Tolstoy writes in his "*War and Peace*": "*The higher a man stands on the social ladder, the more people he is connected with and the more power, he has over others". He further writes: "In historic events, the so-called great men are labels giving names to events, and like labels they have but the smallest connection with the event itself*"

No one, of course, has any idea how to weigh and to estimate the influence of single individuals in the process of social change. Sociologists are more inclined to agree with Tolstoy and to be extremely cautious about attributing major influence to the great personalities of men and women. "Personality itself is seen to be shaped and formed by patterns of culture and of historical circumstance..." Hence, sociologists tend "to interpret changes in societies in terms of deeper lying phenomenon, of which great men are only the surface representations."

There is no doubt that all social changes occur because of the actions of men and women. "*Culture is not self-innovating. ideas are not self-creating, and technology is not self-inventing*." Somehow, somewhere, in a society, a man breaks however slightly, from tradition. He does something in a different way. He finds a short cut. He has a new idea or makes a new discovery. "When that happens whether he is a "*great man*" or not, he has disturbed the stream of culture and, like a stone. tossed into the waters, its ripples may go on forever. It may affect, after a while, all the compartments of culture and all the sectors of society."–*Robert Bierstedt*.

Great men like the Buddha, Mahavira, Shankaracharya, Basaveshwara, Jesus Christ, Zoroaster, Prophet Mohammed, Confucius and others introduced revolutionary changes in the realm of religion. Napoleon Bonaparte, Washington, Lincoln, Karl Marx, Lenin, Mao Tse Tung, Kemal Pasha, Mahatma Gandhiji, Hitler, Mussolini, Indira Gandhi, Khomeini and others have caused revolutionary changes in the political field. Similarly, writers, scientists, philosophers have also contributed to social changes.

SOCIAL EVOLUTION

Meaning of 'Evolution'

The term '*evolution*' comes from the Latin word '*evoluere*' which means '*to develop*' or to '*unfold*'. It closely corresponds to the Sanskrit word 'Vikas'. Evolution literally means gradually '*unfolding*' or '*unrolling*'. It indicates changes from '*within*' and not from *without*'; it is spontaneous, but not automatic. It must take place on its own accord. It implies continuous change that takes place especially in some structure. The concept of evolution applies more precisely to the internal growth of an organism.

Meaning of Social Evolution

The term '*evolution*' is borrowed from biological science to sociology. The term '*organic evolution*' is replaced by '*Social Evolution*' in sociology. Whereas the term 'organic evolution' is used to denote the evolution of organism, the expression 'social evolution' is used to explain the evolution of human society. Here the term implies the evolution of man's social relations. It was hoped that the theory of social evolution would explain the origin and development of man. Anthropologists and sociologists wanted to find a satisfactory and significant explanation of how our society evolved. They wanted an explanation in this regard rather than a description. They were impressed by the idea of organic evolution which could convincingly explain how one species evolves into another, and wanted to apply the same to the social world. Hence the concept of social evolution is quite popular in sociological discussion.

The Concept of Social Evolution

Our explanation of the concept of social evolution revolves round two questions: (*i*) *How does society evolve* ? (*ii*) *How did our civilisation come to be what it is today*?

The common assumption is that society evolved because of man, who made society evolved. Accordingly, men who had not evolved too far, would have a crude culture while men who are more evolved would have an advanced society. Society is understood here in terms of social behaviour, and behaviour is a function of biological structure. Men with superior and more evolved biological structure, thus, could give rise to a more complex society.

When we consider the factors that explain social evolution we are confronted with another question, i.e., "*what is that evolving in the social world*?". The answer is usually '*society*'. As far as society is concerned, something other than the biological element in it is undergoing the change. To the anthropologists like *R.H. Lowie* and *A. Kroeber* and others that element is '*culture*'. Social evolution then becomes '*cultural evolution*' and evolution of groups from times immemorial becomes a part of the evolution of culture. "*What then are the factors that have caused the great evolution of our culture from crude and simple beginnings to the magnificence, it has now attained*?". The answer lies in four factors: *accumulation, invention, diffusion*, and *adjustment*.

Use of the of Social Evolution Concept to Understand Social Change

The concept of social evolution is highly useful in explaining the changes in and growth of society for the following reasons:

1. The nature of any system can be better understood if we look at it as it "*unfolds*" itself. Evolution is a principle of internal growth. It shows not merely what happens to a thing but also what happens within it. *What is latent becomes manifest in it, and what is potential is made actual*. The concept thus helps us to know what actually happens within the society in its structure, that is, in the social roles, positions and relations of people.
2. The evolutionary clue helps us to arrange *a multitude of facts in a significant order*; that is; in accordance with time succession giving them the coherence of successive stages. Example: It helps us to explain how the functions of modern family in course of time, have become more limited to those that arise out of their foundations in sex. Such an explanation may reveal a significant time succession
3. The evolutionary principle *provides a simple means of classifying* and *characterising the most diverse social systems*. Societies could be classified on the basis of their degree and mode of differentiation as revealed by customs, creeds, techniques devices, thoughts, etc.
4. Finally, the evolutionary clue *helps us to know the direction of change*. The direction of change is always the result of some persistent forces that are at work. If the forces at work are known through them, the direction can be ascertained.

Social Evolution vs Organic Evolution

The source of and the inspiration behind the use of the expression '*social evolution*' has been the biological concept of '*organic evolution*' introduced by Charles Darwin. But to equate the phrase 'social evolution' with 'organic evolution is incorrect since we find some basic differences between the two. A few of these differences may be noted here.

1. Organic evolution implies the *differentiation in the bodily structure* which is generally in the form of new organ to use for different purpose accompanied by a knowledge to use that. Man, who is at the centre of the theory of social evolution, need not have to develop new organ in order to adjust himself with the changed conditions of life. Because man has the capacity of inventing tools, making instruments and devising techniques to control the forces of nature and to adjust himself with the natural conditions.
2. *In the case of organic evolution only the descending generation is affected* by the structural alternations. But in the case of social evolution even the old as well as the new generations are affected by it. For example, invention of new techniques and devices is influencing the present as well as the future generations.
3. The change is transmitted in different ways in the two kinds of evolution. In the case of organic evolution the *transmission of qualities takes place through biological heredity*, that is, through genes. Social evolution takes place through idea, discoveries, inventions and experience. Here the changes are mostly initiated through the mental ability or genius of man.
4. The *organic evolution is continuous* and there can be no break in it. It is continuous because of the irresistible pressure within the organisation and of environment and natural forces. But such a continuity may not be observed in the case of social evolution, there may even be breaks. It is subject to disruption.

Application of the Concept of Social Evolution in Sociological Studies

The concept of 'social evolution' basically involves the notion that all societies pass through certain definite stages in a passage from a simple to complex form. All those who made use of this concept essentially meant the same. Some have stressed the analogy between the growth of an organism and the growth of human society. The concept has also been extended to include the process of gradual change taking place in all societies.

Saint Simon, for example, agreed that there was an evolutionary sequence through which all mankind must pass. He distinguished three stages of mental activity; the conjectural, the miconjectural and the positive.

Auguste Comte synthesised the works of his prodecessors and developed his own theory in which he asserted that all societies must pass through three stages: the theological, meta-physical and the positive or scientific. *Comte* saw society as a social organism possessing a harmony of structure and function.

Herbert Spencer in his 'Principles of Sociology' developed many of Comte's ideas even though he did not acknowledge this fact. Spencer presupposed rather than tried to prove the evolutionary hypothesis. "He felt that there was in social life a change from simple to complex forms–from the homogeneous to the heterogeneous and that there was with society an integration of the 'whole' and a differentiation of parts".

Other 19th century scholars were concerned with different aspects of social evolution. (*i*) *Sir Henry Maine* in his *Ancient Law*, 1861 argued that "societies developed from organisational forms where relationships were based on status to those based upon contract. (*ii*) *L.H. Morgan* in his "*Ancient Society*"—1878 "established an elaborate sequence of family forms from primordial promiscuity to monogamy through which he thought societies must pass. (*iii*) *E.B. Tylor* in his famous work "*Primitive Culture*"—1871, linked his observations covering a large number of societies to the evolutionary framework. In particular, he tried to establish a sequential development of religious forms. This particular work had great impact on Sir James Frazer and Emile Durkheim.

"The evolutionary doctrine provided a broad general framework through which the whole progress of human society could be conceptualised." This doctrine was, however, rejected in the early 20th century. This vacuum could only gradually be filled with the development of the structural system of analysis. This later development is more clearly witnessed in the field of social anthropology. In the field of sociology, the structural-functionalists have again renewed its usage by making a number of modifications so as to make it more scientific and less imaginary.

CONCEPT OF PROGRESS

Human society has evolved into a demonstrable certainty. But we cannot demonstrate with no less certainty that society has progressed? We may only believe in progress, but we cannot show it to others unless they first accept our evaluations. People may look on the same social changes and to some they spell progress, to others decadence. In early modern times one of the most widely accepted notions of social change was that of continuous progress. This view reflects man's growing confidence in himself and his conviction that he is a master of his own destiny. Then what do we mean by progress?

Definition of Social Progress

1. According to *Ogburn* progress "is a movement towards an objective thought to be desirable by the general group for the visible future".
2. *MacIver* writes: "By progress we imply not merely direction, but direction towards some final goal, some destination determined ideally not simply by the objective consideration at work".
3. *Ginsberg* defines progress as "a development of evolution in a direction which satisfies rational criterion of value".
4. In simple words, it may be said that social progress, indicates a change or *an advance towards a desirable end.*

Thus, the concept of social progress definitely involves and implies value-judgements. Whenever the change is for the better for an upward trend, there is progress. Because, social progress connotes improvement, betterment, going up from a lower position. When we speak of progress we imply not merely direction, but direction towards some final goal, some destination determined ideally. Progress always refers to the change that leads to human happiness.

Nature of Social Progress

Our concept of social progress involves the following attributes.

1. ***There is change in progress:*** The idea of social progress presupposes the presence of change. There can be no progress without some or the other change.
2. ***Change is towards some desired goal:*** Not all changes imply progress. A change can be called progress only when it fulfils or on the process of fulfilling the desired end. The "*desired end*" is deemed to be beneficial to and supportive of human welfare.
3. ***Progress is communal:*** Progress from the sociological point of view is communal in nature. Here the progress or the welfare of the entire group or society in the desired direction is taken into consideration and not the happiness of an individual.
4. ***Progress is defined in terms of values:*** It is on the basis of our value system that we always decide whether a particular change implies progress or not. Our own values would tell us whether a change is taking us towards the goal fixed ideally or towards the desirable end or not.
5. ***Progress does not have a definite measuring rod:*** The idea of progress is more subjective than objective. Because we do not have any objective means of measuring it. It even differs with people. What sounds as progress to one may appear to be decadence to another. Further, the same person's notion of progress may undergo change with the lapse of time.
6. ***Concept of progress is subject to diverse interpretations:*** Since the system of values differs from society to society and time to time within the same society, the interpretation of progress also differs accordingly. Goals and ideals change from time to time and place to place and along with them the idea of progress also changes.

According to Haridas T and *Majumdar*, the idea of social progress must at least contain some or all of the following points: (l) *Enhancement of dignity of man*, (2) *Respect for each human personality*, (3) *Ever increasing freedom for spiritual quest and for investigation of truth* (4) *Freedom for creativity and aesthetic enjoyment*, (5) *A social order that promotes the first four values, and* (6) *Promotion of life, liberty and pursuit of happiness with justice and equality to all.*

Development of the Concept of Progress

Historically speaking, as early as in the 17th century, *Francis Bacon* defended the concept of change as continuous progress. In 18th Century, the French thinkers Turgot and Condorcet maintained that human society was gradually but constantly advancing towards desirability.

Auguste Comte believed that the positive attitude to life itself was progressive. *Herbert Spencer* maintained that human society had been gradually progressing towards a better state. But he regarded it as an automatic process beyond the human control. He identified social progress with social evolution and said that the human society was inevitably moving towards ever greater heights of perfection. According to him, progress could not be affected by human engineering for it was determined by the cosmic forces.

The concept of progress was given greater importance during and after the Renaissance. After the American Revolution ushered in a new epoch of progress, the French Encyclopaedists began to preach the doctrine of progress and of human perfectibility. American sociologist *Lester F. Ward* (1841-1915) was a strong believer and an advocate of social progress. His doctrine of *Teleology* or *Telesis* was not just philosophical, he related it to society — *Social Telesis*.

The modern writers today speak of social progress though they do not have a single satisfactory explanation of the concept. They do not, of course, subscribe to the view that society gradually and inevitably moves to an ever higher state of perfection. They have almost abandoned the idea that society evolves in a linear fashion and in the direction of improvement.

'*Social Progress*' is no doubt an abstract term. We may or may not agree that there is progress, but we cannot prove it. Progress is a reality which is immeasurable and undemonstrable. Anything that cannot be demonstrated and measured scientifically cannot be rejected socially. It is especially true in the case of social progress.

REVIEW QUESTIONS

1. Change is the law of nature. Examine.
2. What do you understand by social changes? Explain its nature and characteristic features.
3. Differentiate between social change and cultural change.
4. Elaborate on the causes of social change.
5. What are the various sources of social change? Discuss in brief.
6. Mention the reasons for the opposition to social change.
7. Elucidate the role of values in social change.
8. Great men and their leadership constitute an important source of social change. Analyse.
9. Define the term 'evolution'. Explain the concept of social evolution.
10. Assess the role of social evolution in understanding social change.
11. What is the application of social evolution in sociological studies? Describe.
12. Write short notes on the following:
    (a) Resistance to social change
    (b) Social evolution
13. Define progress. Elucidate its nature and development.
14. Social change is a complex phenomenon. Examine.

⌘⌘⌘⌘⌘⌘⌘⌘⌘⌘⌘

40

THEORIES AND FACTORS OF SOCIAL CHANGE

CHAPTER OUTLINE

- THEORIES OF SOCIAL CHANGE: EVOLUTIONARY THEORIES
- CYCLICAL THEORIES
- FUNCTIONALIST OR DYNAMIC THEORIES
- CONFLICT THEORIES
- FACTORS OF SOCIAL CHANGE: GEOGRAPHIC FACTORS
- BIOLOGICAL FACTORS
- CULTURAL FACTORS
- TECHNOLOGICAL FACTORS
- SOCIAL LEGISLATION AND SOCIAL CHANGE
- EDUCATION AND SOCIAL CHANGE.

THEORIES OF SOCIAL CHANGE

Sociologists, historians and social anthropologists have proposed a number of general theories of social change. These theories may conveniently be grouped into four main categories: *evolutionary, cyclical, conflict theories* and *functional theories*. The following explanation provides a glimpse of these theories:

Evolutionary Theories

Evolutionary theories are based on the assumption that societies gradually change from simple beginnings into even more complex forms. Early sociologists, beginning with *Auguste Comte* believed that human societies evolve in a unilinear way that is, in one line of development. According to them, social change meant "*progress*" toward something better. They saw change as positive and beneficial. To them, the evolutionary process implied that societies would necessarily reach new and higher levels of civilisation.

During the 19th Century due to colonial expansion soldiers, missionaries, merchants and adventurers came in touch with distant lands whose peoples had been almost unknown in Europe. Most of these peoples happened to be '*primitives*'. Early anthropologists made some attempts to study such primitives and their societies. Based on their limited observations, inaccurate and unconfirmed information and unqualified imagination they argued that there was a universal evolutionary process. They claimed that all societies passed through a number of stages beginning in primitive origins and culminating in civilisation of the Western type. *L.H. Morgan, for example*, believed that there were three basic stages in the process: *savagery*, *barbarism* and *civilisation*. Even *Auguste Comte 's* ideas relating to the three stages in the development of human thought and also of society namely — the *theological*, the *metaphysical* and the *positive*–in a way, represent the three basic stages of social change.

This evolutionary view of social change was highly influenced by Charles Drawin's theory of '*Organic Evolution*'. Those who were fascinated by this theory applied it to the human society and argued that societies must have evolved from the too simple and primitive to that of too complex and advanced such as the western society. *Herbert Spencer*, a British sociologist, carried this analogy to its extremity. He argued that society itself is an organism. He even applied Darwin's principle of "*the survival of the fittest*" to human societies. He said that society has been gradually progressing, towards a better state. He argued that it has evolved from military society to the industrial society. He claimed that Western races, classes or societies had survived and evolved because they were better adapted to face the conditions of life. This view, known as *Social Darwinism*, got widespread popularity in the late 19th Century. It survived even during the first phase of the 20th Century.

Emile Durkheim identified the cause of societal evolution as a society's increasing "*moral density*". "Durkheim viewed societies as changing in the direction of greater differentiation, interdependence and formal control under the pressure, of increasing moral density". He advocated that societies have evolved from a relatively undifferentiated social structure with minimum of division of labour and with a kind of solidarity called '*mechanical solidarity*' to a more differentiated social structure with maximum division of labour giving rise to a kind of solidarity called '*Organic Solidarity*'.

Evaluation of the Evolutionary Theory

The early evolutionary doctrines were readily accepted because they served the colonial interests of Europeans. This theory provided a convenient justification for colonial rule over primitive peoples. "The enforced spread of western culture was conveniently thought of as "*the white man's burden*' — the thankless but noble task of bringing "*higher*" forms of civilisation to "*inferior*" peoples". Those who supported this theory had no concept of cultural relativity and hence judged other cultures purely in terms of their own culture's standards.

The unilinear evolutionary theories described but *did not explain* social change. They have not given any convincing explanation of *how or why societies should evolve* toward the western pattern.

The theories were based on the faulty interpretations of the data. "Different theorists grouped vastly different cultures into misleading categories so that they would fit into the various 'stages' of evolution". — *Ian Robertson*

The theorists in an *ethnocentric* way treated the trends in western civilisation as "*progress*". They largely stressed the importance of economic and technological changes in development and neglected other aspects. Thus, the non-westerners may regard western cultures as technologically more advanced, yet morally backward.

Further, the recent ethnographic data from primitive societies have proved that the *societies need not follow* the same step by step evolutionary sequence. In fact, societies have developed in different ways, often by borrowing ideas and innovations from other societies. *Ex*: The Bushmen of the Kalahari and the aborigines of Australia are being introduced directly to industrial society. Hence they are skipping the 'stage' which the theorists have spoken of.

The modern anthropologists have tended to support the theory of multilinear evolution rather than the unilinear one. Modern anthropologists like *Steward* agree that this evolutionary process is multilinear. It can take place in many different ways and change need not necessarily follow the same pattern everywhere. They do not press the analogy between societies and living organisms. They do not equate change with progress. They do not assume that greater social complexity produces greater human happiness. This theory is becoming relatively more popular in social anthropological circles today.

Cyclical Theories

"Cyclical theories of social change focus on the rise and fall of civilisations attempting to discover and account for these patterns of growth and decay"–(*Ian Robertson*). *Spengler*, *Toynbee* and *Sorokin* can be regarded as the Champions of this theory. Their ideas may be briefed here.

(a) Spengler: 'The Destiny of Civilisations'

Oswald Spengler, a German school teacher, in his book "*The Decline of the West*"–1918, pointed out that the fate of civilisations was a matter of "*destiny*". Each civilisation is like a biological organism and has a similar life-cycle; birth, maturity, old age and death. After making a study of eight major civilisations, including the West, he said that the modern Western Society is in the last stage. i.e. old age. He concluded that the Western Societies were entering a period of decay–as evidenced by wars, conflicts, and social breakdown that heralded their doom. This theory is almost out of fashion today. His idea of '*destiny*' is hardly an adequate explanation of social change. His biological analogy is also too unrealistic and his work is too mystical and speculative.

(b) Toynbee: 'Challenge and Response'

Arnold Toynbee, a British historian with enough sociological insight has offered a somewhat more promising a theory of social change. His famous book "*A Study of History*"—*1946*, a multivolume work, draws on materials from 24 civilisations. The key – concepts in *Toynbee's* theory are those of "*challenge and response*". "Every society faces challenges–at first, challenges posed by the environment; later challenges from internal and external enemies. The nature of the responses determines the society's fate. The achievements of a civilisation consist of its successful responses to challenges; if it cannot mount an effective response, it dies".–(*Ian Robertson*).

"Toynbee's views are more optimistic than those of *Spengler's*, for he does not believe that all civilisations will inevitably decay. He has pointed out that history is a series of cycles of decay and growth. But each new civilisation is able to learn from the mistakes and to borrow from cultures of others. It is, therefore, possible for each new cycle to offer higher levels of achievement. Still he has not explained *why* some societies are able to offer effective responses to their challenges while others do not, or *why* a society should overcome one challenge but become a victim of another.

(c) Sorokin: 'Sensate' and 'Ideational' Culture

The Russian-American sociologist, *Pitirim A Sorokin*, in his book "*Social and Culture Dynamics*"–1938, has offered another explanation of social change. His work has had a more lasting impact on sociological thinking. Instead of viewing civilisations into terms of development and decline he proposed that they alternate or fluctuate between two cultural extremes: The "*sensate*" and the "*ideational*". The *sensate culture* stresses those things which can be perceived directly by the senses. It is practical, hedonistic, sensual, and materialistic. *Ideational Culture* emphasises those things which can be perceived only by the mind. It is abstract, religious, concerned with faith and ultimate truth. It is the opposite of the sensate culture. Both represent '*pure*' types of culture. Hence no society ever fully conforms to either type. Without mentioning the causes, he said that as the culture of a society develops towards one pure type, it is countered by the opposing cultural force. Cultural development is then reversed moving towards the opposite type of culture. In brief, too much emphasis on one type of culture leads to a reaction towards the other. "Societies contain both these impulses in varying degrees and the tension between them creates long-term instability". Between these types, of course, there lies 9 third type '*ideastic*' culture. This is a happy and a desirable blend of the other two, but no society ever seems to have achieved it as a stable condition.

Sorokin's theory has not been accepted by the sociologists for it portrays his prejudices and probably his disgust with the modern society. His concepts of '*sensate*' and '*ideational*' are purely *subjective*. His theory is in a way *speculative* and *descriptive*. It does not provide an explanation as to why social change should take this form. Thus, the cyclical theories, in general are not satisfactory.

Functionalists or Dynamic Theories or Equilibrium Theories

In the middle decades of the 20th century a number of American sociologists shifted their attention from social dynamics to social statics or from social change to social stability. *Talcott Parsons* and his followers have been the main advocates of this theory. Parsons stressed the importance of cultural patterns in controlling the stability of a society. According to him, society has the ability to absorb disruptive forces while maintaining overall stability. Because it is "*constantly straining for equilibrium or balance*". The conservative forces of society such as shared norms and values resist radical changes and serve to hold the society together.

Between 1940-50s Parsons' Theory of social order or stability, gained wide acceptance especially in America. But critics began to doubt Parsons' assumptions during 1960s. Critics like *C. Wright Mills* and *Lockwood* questioned whether a theory of equilibrium and stability was relevant to societies that were in a state of conflict and constant change. Hence, Parsons, tried to include social change (1961-1966) in his functionalist model.

Parsons' Theory of Social Change

Parsons considers change "not as something that disturbs the social equilibrium, but as some- thing that alters the state of the equilibrium so that a qualitatively new equilibrium results". He has stated that changes may arise from two sources. They may come from *outside the society*, through contact with other societies. They may also come from *inside the society*, through adjustments that must be made to resolve strains within the system.

Persons speakes of two processes that are at work in social change. In simple societies, institu- tions are *undifferentiated*, that is, a single institution serves many functions. The family *for example*, performs reproductive, educational, socialising, economic, recreational and other functions. A process of *differentiation* takes place when the society becomes more and more complex. Different institutions such as school, factory, etc., may take over some of the functions of the family. The new institutions must be linked together in a proper way by the process of *integration*. New norms, *for example*, must be established in order to govern the relationship between the school and the home. Further, "*bridging institutions*", such as law courts must resolve conflicts between other components in the system.

Evaluation: The equilibrium theory is an ambitious attempt to explain both social statics and social dynamics. Still, greater stress is laid on the former. *Parsons*, as an advocate of this theory, concentrated more on institutional changes. Other functionalists such as *R.K. Merton* and others tried to overcome this limitation. *Merton* writes, "The strain. tension, contradiction and discrepancy be- tween the component parts of social structure" may lead to changes. Thus, in order to accommodate the concept of change within the functional model, he has borrowed concepts from conflict theories of change.

Conflict Theories

Whereas the equilibrium theories emphasise the stabilising processes at work in social sys-tems, the so-called conflict theories highlight the forces producing instability, struggle, and social disorganisation. *Ralf Dahrendorf* a German sociologist, says that the conflict theories assume that–(l) *every society is subjected at every moment to change, hence social change is ubiquitous.* (2) *Every society experiences at every moment social conflict, hence social conflict is ubiquitous;* (3) *Every element in society contributes to change; (4) Every society rests on constraint of some of its members by others.*

Karl Marx: Change Through Class Conflict

The most famous and influential of the conflict theories, is the one put forward by *Karl Marx*, a famous German social thinker and philosopher. "*All history is the history of class conflict*"— wrote *Marx* and *Engels* in the '*Communist Manifesto*' (1848). "*Violence is the midwife of history*"- Marx declared. Individuals and groups with opposing interests are bound to be at conflict — Marx asserted. Since the two major social classes, that is, the rich and poor, or capitalists and labourers have mutually hostile interests they are at conflict. History is actually the story of conflict between the *exploiting* (the rich) and the *exploited* (the poor) *classes*. This conflict repeats itself off and on until capitalism is overthrown by the workers and a socialist state is created. What is to be stressed here is that Marx and other conflict theorists deem society as basically dynamic and not static. They consider conflict as a normal, not an abnormal process. They also believe that "*the existing conditions in any society contain the seeds of future social changes*".

Like *Karl Marx*, another German Sociologist, *George Simmel* too stressed the importance of conflict in social change. According to him, conflict is a permanent feature of society and not just a temporary event. It is a process that binds people together in interaction. Further, conflict encour- ages people of similar interests to unite together to achieve their objectives. Continuous conflict in this way keeps society dynamic and ever changing, Simmel maintained.

Conflict theory is quite impressive and influential, no doubt. But it does not account for all forms of social change. It only gives us a means of analysing some of the most significant changes in history and present-day society. Still it is not a comprehensive theory of social change. *It cannot tell us much about the direction of social change.* Even the predictions of Marx have gone wrong. [*Note:* For more details about the Conflict Theory of Marx, Please see Chapter on "Karl Marx and his Thoughts.]

FACTORS OF SOCIAL CHANGE

Society is in continuous flux. Various forces and factors internal as well as external, are at work to make society changeful. The *physical, biological, cultural* and the *technological* factors have been generally regarded as the potential factors of social change. As Lapiere has pointed out these factors must be understood as '*intervening variables*' that condition social change rather than as '*determining*' or '*casual*' factors.

Geographic or the Physical Factors of Social Change

The physical factors consist of the surface of the earth, climate, rainfall, rivers, mountains, natural vegetation, forests, animal life, minerals, etc. They have a profound influence upon the human society Social change is, to some extent, *conditioned*, by the physical or the geographic factors. *Rate* and *direction* of social change are governed by the physical environment. At the polar regions, and in the deserts there can be no cities and almost changeless stabilities are maintained. The surface of the earth is never at rest. Slow geographic changes as well as the occasional convulsions in the form of storms, famines and floods, cyclones and hurricanes and earthquakes do take place. They may bring about social change. But these changes in nature are usually unaffected by the human activity. Here, *the causation is onesided.* The great volcanic eruption of Yokohama in 1923 was responsible for the new kind of architecture in Japan. It is said that the ancient civilisations of Egypt, Mesopotamia and Indus valley withered away due to bad climate. However, certain changes in the environment may be attributed to human activity. *For example*, soil impoverishment has taken place in South Italy, Greece, Palestine, Egypt and Morocco. The desert wastes of North Africa were once green and well populated. Man has disturbed the ecological balance by exhausting the minerals, destroying the forests and devastating the land and by the mass killing of the wild life.

The modes of culture, and the whole system of social institutions have undergone modifications. Consequently, *the centres of population, the routes of trade, the seats of empire and the systems of structures of societies* have been vastly affected.

Some social geographers and social ecologists have attributed too much importance to geographic factors in bringing about social change. The influences that geographic factors exert upon human societies are neither decisive nor negligible, they are *limiting* but not *determining*. Man is capable of modifying the 'natural landscape' into a cultural landscape. "*Geographic factors account for what can be and for what cannot be in human societies, but they do not account for what is*"—*Robert Bierstedt*. Geography *alone cannot* explain the rise and fall of civilisations. "For no period of human history do we have information of a geographic character that will adequately account for the social changes that occurred." As human societies grow incomplexity and as culture accumulates, geographic factors steadily decrease in sociological significance. "*Geography, in short governs the possible, not the actual. History is not a simple function of habital, nor culture of climate; neither mistral nor monsoon determines morality, nor soil society*."

— *Robert Bierstedt*

Biological Factors of Social Change

Biological factors, too, set limits to the social possibilities of human societies. In certain ways they *help to determine the form and structure* of these societies. Plants and animals form a part of man's non-human environment. Man is influenced by non-human biological factors. He modifies them to serve his purposes creating interaction between biological and cultural factors. Man, *for example*, has always utilised plant and animal life to meet his basic needs for food, clothing and shelter. The *biological factors influence the numbers, the composition, the birth rate, the death rate, the fertility rate and the hereditary quality of the successive generations*. Heredity, *for example*, is one of the important agencies of variation. It contributes to vast amount of diversity between the parents and the children. Therefore, no new generation can be an exact copy of the old. *Every life is a different distribution of qualities and potentialities*.

The biological factors like the *size* and *composition of population*, produce social changes. The *phenomenal growth of population* in the 19th century has led to vast social changes and brought problems. Food problem, housing problem, unemployment, poor health, poverty, low standard of living and the problems are its direct outcome. But there are also countries where there is the problem of *under-population*. The falling rate of population has posed a serious problem for countries like U.S.A., U.S.S.R. and Sweden, It is said that such countries are facing the threat of "*race suicide*". It has its own political implications also. Further, the proportion of younger people is decreasing in few countries like U.K., U.S.A., Sweden, etc. *The death rate has fallen* and hence the number of the old is increasing. It has its social implications. Some social arrangement such as *taboos on inter-marriage, customs respecting the age at marriage, persecution of the minorities, war*, etc. tend to lower the biological quality of the population. Hence the increase and decrease in population, a change in the ratio of men and women, changes in rates of birth and death are likely to affect our social system. The relations of man and his society to the biological environment are more *dynamic* than those of man and his society to the physical environment. The latter submits to his use and abuse. But the biological environment which is inherently unstable *responds* rather than submits to man's uses and abuses. It is more *sensitive*. Hence man has to fight against the diseases, harmful bacterias, Weeds, wild beasts constantly.

Cultural Factors of Social Change

Cultural factors constitute yet another source of social change. Cultural factors consist of our values, and beliefs, ideas and ideologies, morals and manners, customs and traditions and various institutions. Not only social values direct social changes but they themselves are subject to change. Ideas and ideals, ideologies and philosophies are inherently changeful. They change with time, and in turn, initiate change in the social order. In some periods ideas of liberty, equality and democracy may be found, in some others, ideas of strict discipline and centralised order may be observed, and still in some other periods religious orthodoxy or religious non-conformity may prevail. There is an intimate connection between our beliefs and institutions, our valuations and social relationships. Certainly cultural change involves social change (in so far as it affects human relations) as the social and cultural changes are closely related.

"*What people think, in short, determines in every measure...what they do and what they want*"

— *Robert Bierstedt.*

Culture gives speed and direction to the social change. Actually, the field of social change is limited in comparison with the field of cultural change. Our ways of behaving, living, thinking and acting are very much influenced by the changes in social values. These changes in social values are no doubt influenced, if not determined by the technological factors.

Culture is not something static. No culture ever remains constant. It may undergo change due to immigration, foreign invasion, international trade and contacts, exchange of cultural delegations, conquest of one nation by another, foreign rule, etc. Further changeability is inherent in culture. Culture not merely responds to the outside influences, but it itself is a force directing social change. It creates itself or develops by itself. It is men who plan, strive and act. Culture gives cues and directions to social behaviour. Men are beset with stresses and strains for which the past offers no guidelines. New ideologies cause significant changes in the models of group life. It is said that '*ideologies rule the world*'. The social philosophy of Marxism, *for example* has swept one-third of the world. Hinduism, Buddhism and Christianity, too wielded great influence on the social institutions. 'No culture ever remains constant and no culture ever develops in isolation.'

Cultural Factor influences the Direction and Character of Technological Change

Culture not only influences our social relationships, it also influences the direction and charac- ter of technological change. It is not only that our beliefs and social institutions must correspond to the changes in technology, 'but *our beliefs and social institutions determine the use to which the technological inventions will be put*. The tools and techniques of technology are indifferent to the use we make of them. *For example*, the atomic energy can be used for the production of deadly war weapons or for the production of economic goods that satisfy the basic needs of man. The factories can produce the armaments or necessaries of life. Steel and iron can be used for building warships or tractors. It is the culture that decides the purpose to which a technical invention must be put.

Although technology has advanced geometrically in the recent past, technology alone does not cause social change. It does not by itself even cause further advances in technology. Social values play a dominant role here. In one time and place, why are further technological advances welcomed? In other time and place, why are they resisted or rejected? India opposed technological innovations and refused to accept and use many of the technological products during the early stages of the British rule. On the other hand, America welcomed almost all kinds of technical inventions during the 18th and 19th centuries. Only the cultural factors can provide a satisfactory explanation for these phenomena. *The complex combination of technology and social values produce conditions that encourage further technological change. For example*, the belief or the idea that human life must not be sacrificed for want of medical treatment, contributed to the advancement in medical technology.

Max Weber in his "*The Protestant Ethic and the Spirit of Capitalism*" has made a classical attempt to establish a correlation between the changes in the religious outlook, beliefs and practices of the people on the one hand, and their economic behaviour, on the other. He has observed that capitalism could grow in the Western societies to very great extent and not in the Eastern countries like India and China. He has concluded that Protestantism with its practical ethics encouraged capitalism to grow in the West and hence industrial and economic advancement took place there. In the East, Hinduism, Buddhism, Judaism and Islam, on the other hand, did not encourage capitalism.

Thus, cultural factors play a *positive* as well as *negative* role in bringing about technological change. Cultural factors such as habits, customs, traditions, conservatism, traditional values, etc., may *resist* the technological inventions. On the other hand, factors such as breakdown in the unity of social values, the diversification of social institutions (that is, institutions such as family, religion, state, etc., becoming relatively independent) craving for the new thoughts, values, etc., may *contribute* to technological inventions.

Technological changes do not take place on their own. They are engineered by men only. Technology is the creation of man. Men are always moved by ideas, thoughts, values, beliefs, morals, philosophies, etc. These are the elements of culture. These sometimes decide or influence the direction in which technology undergoes change. Men are becoming more and more materialistic in their attitude. They are after pleasure. Hedonic or pleasure philosophy has become a practical ethic and is in currency especially in the West today. This change in the attitude and outlook is reflected in the technological field. Thus, in order to lead a pleasurely and a leisurely life and to minimise the manual labour and maximise merriment, man has started inventing new techniques, machines, instruments and devices. Various electrical equipments such as electric heater, boiler, electric iron, refrigerator, grinder, tape-recorder, fan, etc., have come into being to ease the routine tasks of the people and to provide them great pleasure.

Technological Factors

The technological factors represent the conditions created by man which have a profound influence on his life. In the attempt to satisfy his wants, fulfil his needs and to make his life more comfortable, man builds civilisation. Technology is a product of civilization. *When the scientific knowledge is applied to the problems of life, it becomes technology*. Technology is a systematic knowledge which is put into practice, that is, to use tools and run machines to serve human purposes. Science and technology go together. Technology is fast growing. The modern Age is often called the *Technological Age* or the Mechanical Era. In utilising the products of technology man provokes social changes. The social effects of technology are far-reaching. According to *Karl Marx*, even the formation of social relations and mental conceptions and attitudes are dependent upon technology. *Karl Marx*, *Veblen* and a few others have regarded technology as the *sole explanation* of social change. *W.F. Ogburn* says, '*technology changes society by changing our environments to which we in turn adapt. This change is usually in the material environment and the adjustment that we make with these changes often modifies customs and social institutions*'. A single invention may have innumerable social effects. Radio, *for example*, has influenced our entertainment, education, politics, sports, literature, attitudes, knowledge and so on. *Ogburn* and *Nimkoff* have given a list consisting of 150 effects of the radio in the U.S.A.

IMPACT OF TECHNOLOGICAL CHANGE ON SOCIAL ORDER

The development in the field of technology culminated in the great event of Industrial Revolution. The Industrial Revolution of the 18th century and the various developments woven around it, revolutionalised human life in several respects. The tempo of the technological changes has not vanished. Technology and technological changes continue to affect the human life and social order. The impact of technological change on the social order may be discussed here.

Effect of Technology

1. Industrialisation (The Birth of the Factory System of Production)

Technology has contributed to the growth of industries or to the process of industrialisation. '*Industrialisation*' is a term covering in general terms the growth in a society hitherto mainly agrarian of modern industry with all its attendant circumstances and problems, economic and social. It describes in general terms, the growth of a society in which a major role is played by manufacturing industry of the modern type. The industry is characterised by heavy, fixed-capital investment in plant and building, by the application of science to industrial techniques, and by mainly large-scale standardised production. Some writers hold that "*the best general test of the industrialisation of a nation's life under modern conditions is the rate and character of the growth of its industries*."

The Industrial Revolution that took place in England during the 18th century contributed to the unprecedented growth of industries. Industrialisation is associated with the factory system or production. Today, goods are produced in factories and not in homes. The family has lost its economic importance. The factories have brought down the prices of commodities, improved their quality and maximised their output. The whole process of production is mechanised. Consequently, the traditional skills have declined and a good number of artisans have lost their work. Huge factories could provide employment opportunities to thousands of people. Hence men have become workers in factories in a very big number. The process of industrialisation has affected the nature, character and the growth of economy. It has contributed to the growth of cities or to the process of urbanisation.

2. Urbanisation

In many countries, the growth of industries (industrialisation) has contributed to the growth of cities (urbanisation). *Urbanisation denotes a diffusion of the influence of urban centres to a rural hinterland. Mitchell* refers to urbanisation as being the process of becoming urban, moving to cities, changing from agriculture to other pursuits common to cities, and corresponding change of behaviour patterns. Hence only when a large proportion of inhabitants in an area come to cities urbanisation is said to occur.

Urbanisation has become a world phenomenon today. In 1800 (*i.e.*, before the Industrial Revolution) there were only 21 cities in the world each with a population of 100,000 or over, and all these were in Europe. By 1950 there were 858 such cities in the world (364 of them in the European continent) with a combined population of over 313,000,000. An unprecedented growth has taken place not only in the number of great cities but also in their size. England, where the Industrial Revolution took place first, became urbanised at a relatively faster rate. England, America, Germany and Israel are the most urbanised countries of the world where more than 75% of the people live in towns and cities.

As a result of industrialisation people have started moving towards the industrial areas in search of employment. Due to this the industrial areas developed into towns and cities. A number of such *industrial cities* are there in the world now. *Bangalore, Durgapur, Kanpur, Bombay, Calcutta* of India, *Manchester, Lancashire* of England, *Chicago* and *Detroit* of America can be mentioned here as examples.

The growth of cities or urbanisation has resulted in urban concentration and rural depopulation. The unregulated growth of cities has caused problems such as–overcrowding, congestion, insanitation, inadequate water and electricity supply; lack of privacy and intimacy, etc. The cities have also become the centres of various socio-economic problems such as crime, juvenile delinquency, gambling, prostitution, etc.

3. Modernisation

"*Modernisation*" *is a process which indicates the adoption of the modern ways of life and values*. It refers to an attempt on the part of the people, particularly those who are custom-bound, to adapt themselves to the present time, conditions, needs, styles, and ways in general. It indicates a change in people's food habits, dress habits, speaking styles, tastes, choices, preferences, ideas, values, recreational activities, and so on. People, in the process of getting themselves modernised give more importance to science and technology. The scientific and technological inventions have modernised societies in various countries. They have brought about remarkable changes in the whole system of social relationship and installed new ideologies in the place of traditional ones.

In the process of modernisation some typical forms of changes occur in the social structure of society. Changes in social structure involve role differentiations in almost all aspects of life. Growth of science and technology adds impetus to this process and finally accelerates the movement or the rate of change.

4. Development of the Means of Transport and Communication

Development of transport and communication has led to the national and international trade on a large scale. The road transport, the train service, the ships and the aeroplanes have eased the movement of men and material goods. Post and telegraph, radio and television, newspapers and magazines, telephone and wireless and the like, have developed a great deal. The space research and the launching of the satellites for communication purposes have further added to these developments. They have helped the people belonging to different corners of the nation or me world to have regular contacts. The nations have come nearer today. The world has shrunk in size. The intermixing of the people has led to the removal of prejudices and misunderstandings.

5. Transformation in the Economy and the Evolution of the New Social Classes

The introduction of the factory system of production has turned the agricultural economy into *industrial economy*. The industrial economy is popularly known as the *capitalist economy*. This transformation in the economy has divided the social organisation into two predominant classes–the *Capitalist Class* and the *Working Class*. These two classes, according to *Marx*, are always at conflict because both have mutually opposite interests. In course of time an intermediary class called '*the Middle Class*' has evolved. This class which consists of the so-called '*white collar*' people, is playing an important role in the society.

6. Unemployment

The problem of unemployment is a concomitant feature of the rapid technological advancement. Machines not only provide employment opportunities for men but they also take away the jobs of men through labour-saving devices. This results in what is known as technological unemployment.

7. Technology and War

The highly dangerous effect of technology is evident through the modern mode of warfare. Today, not men, but guns, not hands, but bombs fight the battle. The atom bomb and the hydrogen bomb have brought new fears and anxieties for mankind. The atomic and the bacteriological wars that can destroy the entire human race reveal how technology could be misused. Thus, the greater the technological advancement, the more ingenious is the devilish wholesale murder. However, tech- nology could be used for constructive purposes also.

8. Changes in Values

Industrialisation, urbanisation, development in the means of transport and communication, the progress of democracy, introduction of secular education, birth of new organisations political and economic, etc., have had profound effects on the beliefs, ideals, tendencies and thoughts of the people. This has led to a vast transformation in the values of life.

Industrialisation and mechanisation have brought new values and philosophies. The traditional values have changed. Things are measured more in pecuniary terms. *Men are devoted more to quantity than to quality, to measurement than to appreciation*. Human beings by the use of machines have become, less human, more passive and more mechanical. As *MacIver* and *Page* have said from the mechanistic point of view, "*all things are means to means and to no final end, functions to functions and of no values beyond*."

Technological invention and industrial expansion have very directly promoted hedonism. People want to have '*good time*' always. They have become pleasure-seekers. They want to maximise their pleasure by putting forth minimum, or no efforts. Mounting production has provided them with sufficient money and also leisure to play and to enjoy. More importance is given to pomp and show than to contemplation and thought. Human relations are becoming impersonal and secondary. On all sides one is confronted with "*human machines*" which possess motion but not sincerity, life but not emotion, heart but not feelings.

There has been a movement towards individualism. Individuals are moving away from their family and community loyalty and responsibility. Individualism has intensified social and psychological uprootedness. Technology has substituted the '*hand*' *work* with the '*head*' *work*. This kind of work requires manipulation of people instead of things. "*Manipulating others and being manipulated by others enhance individuation, the sense of being alone and operating alone*",

9. Changes in Social Institutions

Technology has profoundly altered our modes of life and also thought. Technology has not spared the social institutions of its effects. The institutions of family, religion, morality, marriage, state, property, etc., have been altered.

Modern technology, in taking away industry from the household, has radically changed the *family* organisation. Many functions of the family have been taken away by other agencies. Women are enjoying more leisure at home. Much of their work is done by modern household electric appli- ances. Due to the invention of birth control techniques the size of the family is reduced. *Marriage has lost its sanctity*. It is treated more as a civil contract than a sacred bond. Marriages are becoming more and more unstable. Instances of divorce, desertion and separation are increasing. Technology has elevated the status of Women no doubt, but it has also contributed to the stresses and strains in the relations between men and women at home.

Religion is losing its hold over the members. People are becoming more secular, rational and scientific, but less religious in their, outlook. Though religion has not been directly affected by the modern technology, inventions and discoveries in science have shaken the foundations of religion. They have changed attitudes towards religious rituals and creeds.

The *function of the state* or the field of state activity has been widened. The modern states call themselves '*welfare*' states. They have become secular in nature. Modern inventions have made the states to perform such functions as – the protection of the aged, the weaker section and the minorities, making provision for the schools, colleges, universities, child labour laws, health measures, juvenile courts, etc. Transportation and communication inventions are leading to a shift of functions from local government to the central government of the whole state. The modern inventions have also strengthened nationalism. The modern governments which rule through the *bureaucracy* have further impersonalised the human relations.

Perhaps, the most striking change in modern times is the change in *economic organisation*. Industry has been taken away from the household and new types of economic organisations have been set up, such as, factories, stores, banks, joint stock companies, corporations, amalgamations, etc. Introduction of factories changes the character of relations between the employer and the employees.

Conclusion

It is clear from the above explanation that technology is capable of bringing about vast changes in society. But technology should not be considered a '*determining*' factor of social life. Man is a master as well as a servant of the machine. He has the ability to alter the circumstances which have been the creation of his own technology. He is indeed, a creature as Well as a critic of the circumstances.

The Hypothesis of Cultural Lag

William F. Ogburn, in his famous book '*Social Change*', has formulated the hypothesis of '*cultural lag*'. *Ogburn* has divided culture into two parts namely: material and non-material culture. By material culture he means civilisation which includes tools, utensils, machines, dwellings, science, means of transport and technology, in brief, 'the whole apparatus of life'. By *non-material culture* he means just 'culture' in its ordinary sense which includes beliefs, practices, customs, traditions, morals, values, and institutions like family, morality, religion, education, etc. '*Cultural lag*', according to him, refers to the *imbalance in the rate and speed of change between these two parts of culture*. The word '*lag*' denotes crippled movement. Hence culture means the faltering of one aspect of culture behind another.

According to *Ogburn*, changes are quick to take place in the material culture. These in turn stimulate changes in the non-material culture. But the non-material culture may be slow to respond, giving rise to a gap or a lag between the material and the non-material cultures. This lag is called the cultural lag. *For example*, the development in the field of industry requires a corresponding change in the system of education. The failure of education to cater to the needs of modern industrial development leads to the cultural lag. Similarly, the forests of the country may be destroyed because the art of conservation docs not keep pace with industrial or agricultural development. Thus *Ogburn Writes, "the strain that exists between two correlated parts of culture that change at unequal rates of speed may be interpreted as a lag in the part that is changing at the slower rate for the one lag behind the other"*. If the society is to maintain its equilibrium it has to seek ways and means of bridging this gap. *Ogburn* has, therefore, concluded that *"the problem of adjustment in modern life is chiefly one of enabling the non-material aspects of culture to catch up, as it were, with the material aspects"*.

SOCIAL LEGISLATION AND SOCIAL CHANGE

"Laws are a form of social rule emanating from political agencies". Laws become legislations when they are made and put into force by law-making body or authority. Legislations, particularly social legislations have played an important role in bringing about social change.

There are two opinions about the functions of law. The function of law, according to one view, is to *establish and maintain social control*. Hence the major problem of law is to design legal sanctions to minimise deviance and to maintain social solidarity and social order.

Another view stresses the dynamic role of law. It states that the function of laws is not just to maintain social order through social control. It insists that *law must bring about social change* by influencing people's behaviour, beliefs and values. We shall now analyse the role of law or legislation in bringing about social change.

A careful analysis of the role of legislation in social change would reveal two things. (*i*) *Through legislations the state and society try to bring the legal norms in line with the existing social norms*. (*ii*) *Legislations are also used to improve social norms on the basis of new legal norms*.

Social legislation can be an effective means of social change only when the existing social norm is given a legal sanction. No legislation by itself can substitute one norm with another. It can hardly change norms. *Unaided social legislation can hardly bring about social change*. But with the support of the public opinion it can initiate a change in social norm and thus a change in social behaviour. Some examples of social legislations made in India will help us to understand this point.

A number of social legislations were made in India both before and after independence with a view to bring about social change. Some of these could achieve success while a few others still remain as dead letters. The legislations that secured public support and the support of social norms could become a great success. *For example, the Hindu Marriage Act* was passed in 1955 enforcing monogamy and permitting judicial separation and divorce. Though polygamy was permitted among the Hindus, majority of the people practised monogamy only. Public opinion was in favour of monogamy. For a long time social reformers agitated that Hindu marriage should be monogamous. The Hindu women also resented the second marriage by a man when the first one was alive. Those who opposed monogamy were branded as conservative, orthodox and selfish. When the Hindu Marriage Act was passed in 1955 it could get the support of the people and the opposition gradually died down.

The Hindu Marriage Act of 1955 could bring about a number of social changes. The Act abolished all caste restrictions as a necessary requirement for marriage. The Hindus of all castes have the same rights with respect to marriage. Intercaste marriages are now allowed. The Act provides for a secular outlook with respect to marriage and enables the registration of marriage. It enforces monogamy making both the sexes equal in marital affairs. It provides equal rights for both to get judicial separation and divorce on legal grounds. It treats various sects of people such as Jains, Buddhists, Sikhs, Veera Shaivas, Harijans, Girijans and many others as 'Hindus'. Thus, it paved the way for bringing about a uniform Civil Code for all the citizens of India.

In the same way, *the Hindu Succession Act of 1956* could attain success. The Act confers for the first time absolute rights over the property possessed by a Hindu woman. Both sons and daughters get the right of inheritance of property because of this Act. The Act removes the prejudice against women getting the property of the father. Since public opinion is in favour of women enjoying equal rights and opportunities, the Act could be enforced easily.

The *Hindu Adoption and Maintenance Act of 1956* has been a step toward the upliftment of the status of women. It permits the adoption of a son or a daughter. It makes the consent of the wife necessary for adopting a child. It has also given the right to the widows to adopt.

The Legislative Acts mentioned above could bring about changes in some areas of our life because they are backed by public opinion and current social norms and values. *Whenever the social norms are ahead of the legal codes, it becomes necessary to bring the legal code into conformity with the prevalent social values*. Sometimes dominant minority groups may cherish some 'advanced' values and may bring pressure upon the legislative bodies to make legislations to enforce such values on masses. Such legislations become an active social force only when they are internalised by the people.

In pre-Independent India, social legislations such as - *The Hindu Widow Remarriage Act of 1856, Female Infanticide Prevention Act of 1870, the Special Marriage Act of 1872* (Which made marriage a civil marriage free from religious barriers), *Child Marriage Restraint Act of 1929*, etc., could attain success and pave the way for changes in society because they were in tune with the trends and tides of the time.

On the contrary, *those social legislations that are far ahead of the social norms and values and those that lack popular support and public opinion are bound to be a failure*. They may become only dead letters. Some of them may bring about changes very gradually in the long run. Some others may be simply ignored or even resisted.

The *Untouchability Offences Act of 1955* was passed by the Parliament in accordance with the provisions of Article 35 of the Indian Constitution. It made the practice of untouchability a cognisable offence punishable under law. (This Act was, however, substituted by the *Protection of Civil Rights Act in 1976*). All the social disabilities from which the Harijans suffered have been removed legally and constitutionally. But in reality, Harijans suffer from many kinds of social disabilities especially in rural areas even today. Here the law is ahead of the social norm particularly in the villages where untouchability is still in practice. The institutionalisation of this new rule has not affected people's ways of life. Because the majority of the village people have not yet internalised this norm. It makes clear that passing an Act is not enough to alter the social practice. A social movement educating the public through propaganda, is necessary to make effective such social legislations.

Law relating to prohibition was also a grand failure for want of public support. Gandhiji launched a crusade against drunkenness. He even tried to persuade Congressmen to work for total removal of alcoholism. But right from 1937 there has been a strong opposition against prohibition. Not all the Congressmen supported it. Those who were used to liquor consumption carried on a silent wave against prohibition. All the provinces never legislated laws in favour of prohibition. Some states kept neutral while a few states enacted legislations against taking alcoholic drinks. In such states illicit distillation started as kind of "cottage industry". Public opinion was not properly mobilised in favour of it. Hence it failed. In America also law relating to prohibition was a grand failure and hence it was withdrawn.

For the same reasons as mentioned above the *Hyderabad Beggary Act of 1940* passed in order to prevent the beggars from begging, failed. Some other states such as Bengal, Bombay, Karnataka also made legislations for the prevention of beggary. Nevertheless, beggary continued to be practised by beggars in all these states. In the same way, the *Dowry Prohibition Act of 1961* which made the giver as well as receiver of dowry punishable also has become ineffective. The social norms, in other words, have not been affected by this law, and hence the society follows the social norms rather than legal norms in these fields. Mere threat of punishment will not be effective. Such a situation produces what *Festinger* calls '*forced compliance*". So long as behaviour involves forced compliance, there is no internalisation of the new values and so there will be disobedience of the law. Forced compliance can only create a discrepancy between public behaviour and private belief.

Unintended Consequences of Legislations

As *Richard T. Lapiere* has pointed out, one of the major tasks of the governments is to produce desired changes through legislative enactments. Hence legislations may be enacted for slum clearance, for providing assistance for the poor to construct low-cost houses, for providing social security to the labourers, handicapped persons, for providing protection to women, children, weaker section, minorities, etc. But sometimes such legislations may produce unintended consequences in society.

For example, the Government of Napoleon in its efforts to keep France agriculturally self- sufficient, established subsidies for the production of sugar beets. No one anticipated or could have anticipated that this legislation would in the course of time help to make France the heaviest per capita consumer of alcoholic beverages in the whole world.

In the same way, a legislation in America also brought about an unintended result. The New Deal ideologists wanted to save the small single family agricultural units from the economic crisis of 1930s. Hence they designed the agricultural parity price system to help such small growers. The ideologists could hardly foresee that the long-run effects of such a legislation would be to speed up the growth of large-scale industrial agriculture and to hasten the doom of the small-scale agriculturists.

Legislation or any other governmental agency has its own inability to pre-determine the consequences of politically sponsored changes. Legislation has its own limitations in inducing significant qualitative changes by coercion. Of course, men may be deterred by coercion from doing something that they might like to do. They may be encouraged by the government to work at their trade, pursue their scientific investigations, treat sick patients, etc.

People cannot, however, in the same ways be induced either to want to be creative or to act for long in ways that are contrary to their established cultural attributes. It is for this reason the governmental efforts to increase national birth-rates through legal means have failed. Its efforts to establish racial equality through legislation have failed. Similarly, no legislation can be made to make a people religious or to deprive them of an established religion; to change their sex morals, to improve domestic harmony, to substitute one custom with another, and so on. Legislations can be made by governments to sanction changes that have already occurred. In fact, in the long run, legislations are made for sanctioning changes. But legislations cannot be made in the social field directly. They cannot fix the course of social changes in a predetermined fashion.

EDUCATION AND SOCIAL CHANGE

'Education' is one of the intervening variables in the phenomenon of social change. '*Durkheim*' conceives of education as "*the socialisation of the younger generation*". According to *James Welton*, education consists in "an attempt on the part of the adult members of human society to shape the development of the coming generation with its own ideals of life." As *Samuel Koenig* has pointed out, it is a "process whereby the social heritage of a group is passed on from generation to another .... ..".

Education can also be understood *as a factor of social change*. The role of education as an agent or instrument of social change and development is widely recognised today. Education can initiate social change by bringing about a change in the outlook and attitudes of man. It can bring about a change in the pattern of social relationship and thereby it may cause social changes. One of the purposes of education is to change man and his life and living style. *To change man is to change society only*.

There was a time when educational institutions and teachers were engaged in *transmitting a way of life to the students*. During those days, education was more *a means of social control than an instrument of social change*. Modern schools, colleges and universities do not place much emphasis upon transmitting a way of life to the students. The traditional education was meant for an unchanging, static society, not marked by rapid changes. But today, education aims at imparting empirical knowledge, that is, knowledge, about science, technology and other type of specialised knowledge. Education was associated with religion. It has, however, become secular today. It is an independent institution now. Education today has been chiefly instrumental in preparing the way for the development of science and technology.

Education has brought about phenomenal changes in every aspect of man's life. *Francis J. Brown* remarks that education is a process which *brings about changes in the behaviour of society*. It is a process which enables every individual to effectively participate in the activities of society, and to make positive contribution to the progress of society. As *Drucker* has stated that the "highly educated man has become the central resource of today's society and the supply of such men is the true measure of its economic, military and even its political potential."

Modern education has changed our attitude and outlook. It has affected our customs and traditions, manners and morals, religious beliefs and philosophical principles. It has removed to a great extent the superstitious beliefs and unreasoned fears about the supernatural beings. It has widened our vision and removed our narrow ideals, prejudices and misunderstandings. Higher education has brought about more refined behaviour.

Education has contributed to a radical *improvement in the status of women*. Educated modern women no more tolerate the double standard of morality. It has helped them to seek employment outside the family. Particularly, mass education in civilised societies has fostered the sense and the feeling of equality.

Referring to the relation between education and social change and development, *Peter Worsely* points out "that education reflects society, and educational change follows social change". Though education *conditions* development it itself is a product of prior social and economic changes in society. Further, education is an independent factor in social and economic development producing intended and unintended consequences and conflicts of values and goals.

Education is *an important means of attaining social and economic rewards of society*. It has become essential for the economy. Education has now become a large-scale and a highly visible organisation. Education is now controlled by the dominant groups of society so as to meet their definition of society's needs. Changes in the educational system condition social and economic changes, greater social mobility and more skilled man-power for technologically based industry. Planned educational innovations, policies and programmes may contribute to the social integration and a more highly educated labour force and electorate.

Education has been playing a great role in getting occupations which are key determiners of general social status. Thus the schools are agents in realising the desire for upward social mobility. In many highly industrialised societies the proportion of people in the manual working class has steadily declined. It is so in the case of America, Britain, France, etc. The schools have been instru- mental in transforming the occupational structure and modifying the class structure as well. In most developing countries education is regarded as "*the gateway to an improved social position*." Hence one may find an unsatisfied demand for education in such countries. This is especially true in the case of a developing nation like India. Educational change in these countries can effectively proceed only if corresponding changes take place in the other aspects of their social structure.

Where education is a condition of social and economic change, it is more likely to produce intended consequences. This happens because educational change is following other changes in society. The social context is thus favourable to particular change. *For example*, educational reforms, designed to raise educational standards among low-income people have become more successful in Cuba than in Guatemala. This has been so, because, in Cuba, more than in Guatemala, educational change has followed social and economic changes enabling the low-income people to take an active participation in the development of national society. As far as India is concerned, there is no proper coordination between educational changes and socioeconomic needs.

Education increases political awareness among poor people also. This would bring about wider political changes with the increasingly organised participation of people in national politics. Modern states, particularly the totalitarian ones, have made education an instrument for establishing their regime. Under authoritarian principles, the control of the school touches every aspect of education, The teachers are carefully chosen and supervised, and deviations from the *party line* are severely punished. Students of all ages must be given nothing but the truth as the ruling elite see it. The principal of a school in Moscow once said: "*the prime duty of the Soviet teacher is to train our younger generation for the work of building communism*". On the contrary, in the democratic countries there is the belief that "*The State is for man, not man for the State*". *Education is made* free and open. Here, education makes a man to become more conscious of his rights and also of his duty *to* provide and guard similar rights for others.

Education is expected to contribute to 'progress', to modify the cultural heritage as well as to preserve and transmit it. In modern industrial societies *educational organisations have become innovators*. They are gathering and storing new knowledge and are promoting change in the process of transmitting that knowledge.

It is now widely held that educational system should dedicate itself to the task of bringing about desirable changes. The emphasis upon research in universities reflects the judgment that discovery itself is good. For the first time in history, societies are marshalling their huge resources and talents to make advances in knowledge through educational organisations.

Changes do not take place with equal rate of speed in all areas of life. Generally, there is more enthusiasm for change in areas of material culture than in non-material culture. Through educational researches any kind of innovation can be made to maximise production and minimise cost. When education challenges cherished traditions, it becomes the object of some hostility. Education cannot be used as an instrument to bring about any kind of change. Because education operates in the context of other institutions and is constrained by them.

As *Alex Inkeles* has pointed out, different levels of education have different levels of effects. In the developing countries primary school education is enabling whole population to do things they would never have been able to do before. Literacy helps them to read labels on cans, bottles, tins, to read sign boards, newspapers, birth-control leaflets, to move around the strange city, etc. These events are social changes. In the developing countries primary school education is more important than higher education.

Even though widespread primary education can have a great impact upon people in the devel- oping countries the *ideological content of primary school education remains almost conservative*. Because, governments organise school systems in a stereotyped way. There is less or no scope for the teachers to make researches or to become revolutionary leaders.

It can be said that basic literacy brings a society into the modern world. But only higher education provokes persons to question the values of everyday life. The high school or primary school teacher is not as free to speak critically as the university professor is. At elementary level of education students normally live with their parents at home and hence not free to entertain ideas which their parents may dislike. On the other hand, at the university level, the intellectual work requires students to do more critical thinking than they might do at a lower level.

University student movements have often been the major force demanding social change in many societies. A decade between 1960 and 1970 witnessed a large number of student upsurges resulting in social and political changes. *For example*, in China, India, Japan, America, Germany, France, Italy, England, Indonesia and in many other countries students agitated for various reasons causing vast changes. In some cases, the student movements stood with the establishment and in majority of the cases they tried to discredit, transform or topple governments. The students are today a new social force of incalculable significance. But student movements have been far less active in the late 1970s than a decade ago. It is true that college educated persons are still the most progressive group in society whether they are quiet or vocal in calling for social reform or change. More and more persons are receiving higher education. Majority will attain a degree. If that is so, it means that society will contain a "*built in*" engine for social change. As long as universities continue to occupy an increasingly important place in society, so long changes are bound to be initiated through education in some way or the other.

REVIEW QUESTIONS

1. Examine the theories of social change.
2. Discuss the various factors which read to social change.
3. Briefly explain the social and economic factors of social change.
4. Assess the impact of technological change on social order.
5. Evaluate the role of technology in social change.
6. Explain the hypothesis of cultural lag.
7. Bring out the relation between social legislation and social change.
8. Write short notes on the following:
   (a) Evolutionary theories
   (b) Cyclical theories
   (c) Conflict theories
   (d) Factors of social change
   (e) Parsons' theory of social change
   (f) Education and social change
9. Cultural factor influences the direction and character of technological change. Comment.

⌘⌘⌘⌘⌘⌘⌘⌘⌘⌘⌘⌘

PART EIGHT

COLLECTIVE BEHAVIOUR AND SOCIAL MOVEMENTS

41

COLLECTIVE BEHAVIOUR

CHAPTER OUTLINE

- Definition and Characteristics of Collective Behaviour
- Collective Behaviour and Social Movements
- Difficulties Involved in the Study of Collective Behaviour
- A Theory of Collective Behaviour
- Some Forms of Mass Behaviour: The Concept of Mass and Mass Behaviour
- Some Basic Forms of Mass Behaviour: Rumours, Parties, Mass Hysteria
- Fashions and Fads
- Crowd Behaviour: Characteristics of Crowd
- Types of Crowd
- Theories of Crowd Behaviour: The Contagion Theory and the 'Emergent Norms' Theory
- Mobs and Riots as Forms of Crowd Behaviour': Audience as a Crowd with a Difference
- Publics and Public Opinion
- Propaganda and its Techniques
- Limitations of Propaganda

THE CONCEPT OF "COLLECTIVE BEHAVIOUR"

The term "*collective behaviour*" is used by the sociologists to refer to group behaviour that is apparently not guided by the usual norms of conduct. Though in most group situations peoples' behaviour is governed by clearly defined norms, in some circumstances, they just do not bother about the norms and behave in their own way. The term '*collective behaviour*' may be used to denoted such a kind of behaviour.

DEFINITION OF COLLECTIVE BEHAVIOUR

1. *Ian Robertson*. "*Collective behaviour refers to relatively spontaneous and unstructured ways of thinking, feeling and acting on the part of a large number of people*".
2. *N.J. Smelser*. Collective behaviour may be defined as "*The relatively unorganised patterns of social interaction in human groups*".

AN ILLUSTRATIVE EXAMPLE FOR COLLECTIVE BEHAVIOUR

As it is mentioned above, most social behaviour follows a regular, patterned and predictable course. Most of the people play their roles obliging the norms that are woven around the roles. This is true of a normal class-room situation in a college. Students arrive more of less on time, they seat themselves in an orderly way, they listen to lectures, take notes, ask question at appropriate points, and finally they leave the classroom when the lecture is over and the lecturer goes out. There is a good ideal of other things that a group of students would do in a room, but in practice everyone behaves mostly in a predictable fashion.

But suppose a fire suddenly breaks out in the class room. Confusion prevails everywhere. The normal pattern of behaviour gets immediately disrupted. The norms that pevailed a few moments before, are suspended, and *social behaviour becomes 'unstructured'* and '*unpredictable*' virtuality, there are no norms to govern this unanticipated situation. It is possible, though not inevitable, that a panic will result. If panic pervades, cooperative behaviour will also break down. There will be disorderly rush to the exits, even though this will actually reduce people's chances of escape. Students may shout, cry, and move hither and thither in a panic.

It is also possible that there will be little panic, particularly if leaders emerge who take charge of the situation, supervise an orderly exit and attempt to put off the fire. But whether the student crowd becomes panicky or not, its behaviour is no longer guided by everyday norms. Sociologists use the term "*collective behaviour*" to refer to such a type of behaviour.

CHARACTERISTICS OF COLLECTIVE BEHAVIOUR

1. Collective behaviour normally *centres around a phenomenon which is essentially temprorary in nature*. Further, it is entirely an unplanned one;
2. This type of behaviour is *not regulated by any set of rules or procedures*;
3. Since this behaviour is not bound by any defined norms, it *becomes unpredictable also*;
4. People who are attracted by an accident, riot, street fight, fire casualty or any such event gather at the spot *without any prior planning*. They do not even know one another. This *anonymity encourages them to behave in an irresponsible manner*;
5. The event that cause the people to gather in a spot is *not an usual event*. It is generally unusual. Communal riots, street fight, fire accidents, etc., are not the usual or routine events ;
6. *Rumours and misinformation normally run rampant during the course of collective behaviour*. Nobody knows exactly the cause of such a behaviour and everybody reacts in his own way contributing to the confusion or the disorderliness that is already there in behaviour;
7. This kind of behaviour is triggered not only by rumours but also *guided by beliefs, hopes, fears, enmity and hatreds*.
8. *Collective behaviour, may, in certain respects have a close relationship with the broad cultural pattern of the community. For example*. Muslims may react more sharply to the issues when the religious matters are involved in them, than to the business or political matters. Similarly, Hindus may respond much quickly when the caste matters are involved, and so on.

COLLECTIVE BEHAVIOUR AND SOCIAL MOVEMENTS

'*Social movement*' represents another form of social behaviour that has similarities to the kind of collective action which we have discussed above. "*A social movement consists of a large number of people who have joined together to bring about or resist social or cultural change*".

— Ian Robertson

Example. Women's *liberation movement, the Ayodhya movement, Naxalite movement*, "*Save the environment*" *movement, Trade union movement, student movement, tribal movement, etc*.

According to some sociologists social movements also constitute one form of collective behaviour but according to some others, they represent a separate, though related phenomenon. Sometimes it becomes difficult to point out the differences between the two in precise terms. Some, such as the "*hippie*" countercultures of sixties, seem to fit the definition of collective behaviour. Such movements are very '*unstructured*' *and not organised*. On the other hand, we have movements, such as "*human rights*" movement, "*Right to life*" movements the *Ayodhya movement*, etc. which are highly organised. Some movements such as those of environmental preservation, seem fall between these two extremes.

A sociologist is interested in the study of both collective behaviour and social movements not just because such a study is highly fascinating. Their significance lies in the fact they constitute an important element in social change. "*They can serve as the source of new values and norms and even of sweeping changes in human history*" (**Robertson**). But it must be admitted that we have to go a long way to understand their real nature and their implications on our social life. The study of social movements and collective behaviour is still in its infancy.

DIFFICULTIES INVOLVED IN THE STUDY OF COLLECTIVE BEHAVIOUR

Though the study of collective behaviour assumes great importance, it involves some practical difficulties.

1. The first problem is that *collective behaviour* is *unstructured*. Hence it is highly challenging to find underlying regularities, or to make generalisations on the basis of one or the other study.
2. The second problem is that *collective behaviour often occurs as a spontaneous outburst*. It cannot be artificially created or reproduced for the convenience of the sociologist. He is obliged to make a study of them as and when

they occur, whether it is a road accident, fire accident, bomb blast, ship wreckage, plane crash, or anything. Hence, *firsthand studies of collective behaviour are therefore, difficult to conduct*. He may have to depend on so many untrained observers or on-goers who happened to be there at the time of the occurrence of the event.

3. The third problem of the study is that the concept of "*Collective behaviour*" has a very wide range of meaning. It includes in itself — fashions, feuds, riots, mass hysteria, mob, and many such things between which we find lot of variance. Each such a thing or component will have to be understood in its own way. In spite of these limitations, however, sociologists have made some inroads into the study of this complex phenomenon of collective behaviour.

A THEORY OF COLLECTIVE BEHAVIOUR

Sociologists have been trying to provide a satisfactory explanation for the phenomenon of collective behaviour. Why people often exhibit such a peculiar kind of behaviour? This is a challenging question to answer. One of the most promising attempts to provide a comprehensive theory of collective behaviour has been made by *Neil Smelser* (1962).

Smelser argues that collective behaviour is essentially an attempt by people to alter their environment particularly when they are under conditions of uncertainty, threat or strain. These conditions may involve factors such as fear, tension, anxiety, boredom, feeling of exploitation, etc. People find these conditions as highly stressful and they want to change them. The form that their collective behaviour actually takes depends largely on how they define the situation that is bothering them.

Smelser speaks of six basic conditions that provide the "*necessary and sufficient*" grounds for collective behaviour to occur, Those six conditions can be briefly explained here.

1. ***Structural conduciveness:*** This refers to the structured elements within the society that make a particular form of collective behaviour possible. In other words, the structure of the society may encourage or discourage collective behaviour. Simple, traditional societies such as the tribal or rural societies are less prone to collective behaviour than are the modern, complex urban societies.
2. ***Structural strains:*** Situations such as poverty, conflict, discrimination, uncertainty about the future, deprivation and fears of deprivation etc., lie at the base of much of collective behaviour. Feelings of injustice and exploitation prompt many to extreme action. Such situations encourage people to make a collective effort to relieve the problem. Exploited classes, humiliated castes, oppressed racial groups, insecure minorities — are potential groups for collective behaviour.
3. ***Growth and spread of generalised belief:*** Structural conduciveness and strains alone cannot lead to collective behaviour. Before any collective action, people must develop some general belief about the situation. The belief may help them "*to identify the source of the threat, the route of escape, or the adventure of fulfillment*". The belief may crystalise into an ideology. The ideology identifies the causes and nature of the problem and is used to justify collective action for social changes.
4. ***Precipitating factors:*** All of a sudden, collective behaviour does not take place, Some dramatic event or rumour sets the stage for action. A "*cry of police high handedness*", rumour that a mosque is destroyed, a newspaper that some lower caste woman is tripped of her clothes in public by some upper caste gangmen, etc., may suddenly spark of the event. As a result, a panic is created. Such precipitating events serve to confirm people's suspicion and uneasiness that already exist. In many cases, violence is also caused.
5. ***Mobilisation for action:*** The precipitating factors make the people to get involved and encourage them to organise themselves for action. The mere lush of people towards some spot and the very fact of their physical closeness make them to have interaction and some group cohesion. If leaders emerge and encourage others to take some action, collective behaviour will probably follow.
6. ***Operation of social control:*** When the conditions stated above are met, the outcome depends upon the success or failure of social control mechanisms, such as leadership, police power, mass media, governmental authority, and so on. Even if the above mentioned five conditions are met, the social control mechanisms may be strong enough to suppress collective behaviour. Or they may be too weak to prevent such a behaviour; or they may be counterproductive and may actually magnify the behaviour.

"Smelser's theory provides us a useful means of analysing Collective behaviour. Fads, fashions, and crazes, for example, can be interpreted as a response to the conditions of boredom ; panics as a response to conditions of threat; or riots as a response to conditions of strain and resentment"

— *Ian Robertson.*

"Smelser's formulation has stimulated a good deal of criticism and experimentation; ...*yet it remains perhaps the most widely used theoretical approach in the study of collective behaviour today*" — *Horton* and *Hunt*.

SOME FORMS OF MASS BEHAVIOUR

Crowd Behaviour and Mass Behaviour

Collective behaviour that describes "the actions, thoughts and feelings of a relatively temporary and unstructured group of people"— can be separated into two categories; "*crowd behaviour*" and "*mass behaviour*".

A *crowd* is a set of people who are physically close together and share a common concern. Whereas "*mass behaviour involves action by people with common concerns who may or may not have met each other*" — Wallace and Wallace

The Concept of 'Mass' and 'Mass Behaviour'

"A mass is not the same as crowd. A group of spectators watching a cricket match constitute a '*crowd*'. But a large number of people who watch the same game at home on television constitute a "*Mass*"

Hoult defines mass as a "relatively large number of persons, spatially dispersed and anonymous, reacting to one or more of the some stimuli but acting individually without regard to one another".

Mass behaviour is the unorganised, unstructured, uncoordinated, individually chosen behaviour of masses. If the '*crowd behaviour*' is very brief and confined to an event at a particular spot and is acted out by people as a group ; '*mass behaviour*' is more enduring and arises from the sum total of many individual actions. If *in crowds people are gathered in a place* to provoke immediate interaction; in *masses, people are scattered over a vast area* and do not have any direct and continuous contact with one another. "*When many people, acting individually rather than as a group, move in the same direction, this is mass behaviour*". *Examples*: Refugees in search of security; the popularity of videogames ; fans of a film star celebrating the release of a new movie of their favourite actor in their own diverse ways, hundreds of people rushing to a new model vehicle because of an impressive newspaper and television advertisement in its favour, etc.

SOME BASIC FORMS OF MASS BEHAVIOUR

They are rumours, panics, mass hysteria, fashions and fads. They are discussed below.

Rumours

One aspect of public opinion which has become a focus of attention is the transmission of rumours. "*A rumour is a rapidly spreading report unsubstantiated by fact*"—*Horton* and *Hunt*.

- "*A rumour is information that is transmitted informally from anonymous sources*"

  — *Ian Robertson*

- Rumour refers to "*information which travels from person to person by word of mouth*"

  — *Wallace* and *Wallace*.

The *spreading of a rumour itself is a form of collective behaviour*. Hence rumours are an important element in virtually all forms of collective behaviour.

A rumour may be true, false, or a combination of truth and falsehood. Much or casual conversion consists of rumour mongering. From neighbours, narration of stories to the sate of a nation all topics attract interesting and disturbing rumours. Its origin is usually difficult to trace out and verify. Its method of transmission is also a curious one. Most of the times it is transmitted outside the formal communications system of TV, government announcements, radio, newspapers, and the like.

Rumours normally rise in situations *where people are deprived of information or where they do not trust the official information* they are given. Thus, a rumour can be regarded as a sussbtitute for hard news. People want information, and rumour fills their need if dependable information is lacking. Whenever there is social strain, rumours flourish. Further, rumours can ruin reputations, discredit causes and undermine the morale. Hence *the manipulation of rumour is a common practice in propaganda.*

Allport and *Postman* (1947) after a curious study of rumour have pointed out that a great deal of rumour mongering springs from nothing more than *the desire for interesting conversion of the enjoyment of salacious story.*

It is also observed that people are most likely to believe and spread rumour *if it will justify their dislikes or relieve their emotional tensions. For example*, people who dislike capitalists, hate Brahmins and condemn religious leaders — will listen, remember and repeat damaging rumour about these set of people.

The *rumour changes continuously as it spreads* for people unconsciously distort it. People uncritically accept and believe a rumour if it fits in with their pattern of beliefs, likes and dislikes. People support rumour if it provides an emotionally satisfying explanation of something.

When once they are spread, *rumours cannot easily be dispelled by truthful pronouncements*. As *Horton* and *Hunt* have said "*Rumours are believed and spread because people need and like them*". *Shibutani* (1966) says "*The process of rumour construction is terminated when the situation in which it arose is no longer problematic*". Rumours, *for example*, flourish where people feel that they cannot trust government officials to tell them the truth.

Rumours that are usually persistent often become legends. The legends are accepted by many people as. Some legends are there since generations.

FASHIONS AND FADS

Fashions and fads also represent two forms of collective behaviour. Both of them arise in most of the instances in a spontaneous manner and tend to disappear after some time. They may also become a permanent component of culture.

Meaning and Nature of Fashions

"*Fashions are the currently accepted styles of appearance and behaviour*"—*Ian Robertson*. When some style is termed as "*fashion*", it is taken for granted that it is temporary and will ultimately be replaced by a new style.

In simple, rural and tribal societies, fashions are not very much apparent. In many traditional societies they are virtually not found. In modern complex societies, fashions are not only rampant but also change very rapidly. Automobile paintings, college students' hair styles and dress styles, style of house construction etc., *for example*, change with the passage of time.

Why do the Fashions Arise and Spread?

1. In a modern complex society *novelty is considered desirable rather than threatening.* Hence people want to exhibit their likings towards novelty in all aspects — say, in their dressing, spoken style, habits, etc. Societies which are oriented more towards the future rather than the past, give lot of scope for fashions to arise and spread.
2. Fashion is often used as *a means of indicating one's social characteristics to others*. This is especially so in competitive and a status — conscious society. In such a society, people may try to appear more attractive, distinctive, or affluent, and a new fashion helps them to do so.
3. According to *Koeing* (1974), fashion *originates in the desire to decorate one's body for greater sexual attractiveness*.
4. It is *in the open class society with considerable mobility that fashion is important*. The middle class tending to move upwards is more fashion-conscious. Those who are already there in the upper class in a secured place can afford to ignore fashions.
5. *There is no rule as such that fashions always originate among the upper class or elite* and spread downwards to the middle and lower classes. They may originate at any class levels. *For example*, blue jeans are the traditional dresses of the working classes, but they are now highly acceptable for young men and women of the middle and upper classes.
6. *A new fashion is generally more likely to be accepted if it does not differ too much from existing fashions*. *For example*, "*Chudidar*" has become a popular dress style among the college going young girls throughout India. They do not mind minor changes introduced by their tailors in stiching such a type of dress.
7. *Fashions spread very fast among people who always wish to be up-to-date in all respects*. They are the people always on the lookout for a favourable selection from many competing models.
8. "*Fashion may involve almost any aspect of group life manners*, the arts, literature, philosophy, even the methodologies of Science". But fashion is most often seen in clothing and adornment.

Fashions are not entirely silly or whimsical. They reflect the dominant interests and values of a society at a particular time.

Fashion-changes often reflect changes in needs, attitudes and values. There was a time, when the use of dining table and chair for dining purpose was condemned , but it has become the order of the day especially among the urban middle and upper classes. Similarly, '*disco*' dances and '*break*' dances were not allowed in college day celebrations some time ago, but now, they have become fashionable.

The Fads

- "*A fad is a trivial, short-lived variation in speech, decoration, or behaviour*"

  — *Horton* and *Hunt*.
- "*A fad is a temporary form of conduct that is followed enthusiastically by a large numbers of people*" — *Ian Robertson*.

Fads differ from fashions in that they are more temporary and they are mildly scorned by the majority of the population. Those who take interest in them are called '*faddists*'. They are believed to follow a fad simply because they are "*caught by it*", and not because it has any intrinsic value. On the other hand, those who are "*fashionable*" are more positively regarded till at least the fashion lasts.

A fad often provides a means of asserting personal identity. It is a way of showing that one is worth noticing, and that one is a little different from everyone else. It is for this reason they appeal more to young people, who often have less stable identities than their elders. They have a greater appeal to the rich rather than to the poor, because the rich can afford to spend for the fads. When a fad becomes wide-spread, it loses its charm and gets abandoned quickly. In general, fashions and fads have a greater appeal for the young rather for the old, to the rich and middle class people, rather than to the working people.

Panics

- "*A Panic is a form of collective behaviour in which a group of people, faced with an immediate threat, engages in an uncoordinated and irrational response*" — *I. Robertson*
- "*Panic is an attempt to flee from an imagined or real threat*" — *Wallace* and *Wallace*.

In the event of panic, people's behaviour is uncoordinated, because co-operative social relations breakdown. The event may create new problems, fears and dangers. It is irrational, because, in a panic situation people's actions are not appropriate for the goals they wish to achieve.

What happens in a panic is this: A sudden crisis occurs. it may be a flood, cyclone, bomb blast, earthquake, military invasion, fire accident, ship wreckage, or any such event. Since people are unprepared to face it, they develop intense tension and experience great fear. The normal social expectations are disrupted. Each individual tries desperately to escape from the source of danger. mutual cooperation breaks down and hence the situation becomes even more threatening.

For example, when a bomb blast takes place in one of the floors of a multi-storied building , people staying in the building experience panic. They make quick efforts, to run away from the source of threat. But in doing so, they create only bottleneck at the exist for themselves and others. Awareness of the bottleneck further increases the panic. People may even go to the extent of dashing and fighting against others in a bid to escape. Not all panics are as short-lived as the onecited above. Panics relating to financial crises, and stock market situations may prevail for some time.

Mass Hysteria

- "*Mass hysteria is a form of collective behaviour involving widespread and contagious anxiety usually caused by some unfounded belief*" — *Ian Robertson.*
- "*Mass hysteria is some of irrational, compulsive belief or behaviour which spreads among people*" — *Horton* and *Hunt*.
- "*Mass hysteria is a generalised anxiety about some unknown situation*" — *Wallace* and *Wallace*.

Rumours play an important role in the development of hysteria and panic. Mass hysteria may extend beyond a single collection of people at a single moment in time. In extreme cases mass hysteria can result in panic. particularly if the source of anxiety is believed to be sufficiently close and threatening.

A Classical Example in the Study of Mass Hysteria

The Martian Invasion of Earth. In 1938, a dramatic radio broadcast of *H.G. Well's* novel "*War of the World*" produced amazing reaction among its listeners. Its main result was mass hysteria and even outright panic. Of the six million people who heard the broadcast as many as one million people got panicked, started going west with their cars. Their fear and anxiety produced panic action.

CROWD BEHAVIOUR

Crowd behaviour, as it is already mentioned, represents a form of collective behaviour. Crowd behaviour virtually stems from the crowd situations.

- "*A crowd is a set of people who are physically close together and share a common concern*" — *Wallace and Wallace.*
- "*A crowd is a temprorary collection of people reacting together to stimuli*" — *Horton and Hunt.*
- "*Crowd is a collectivity of substantial number of individuals responding within a limited space to some object of attention.*

Examples.

1. A group of bus passengers forming a crowd near a roadside canteen on the highway when the driver stops the bus for light refreshment.
2. A group of people gathered in a bus stand or railway station waiting for their relevant vehicles.
3. A group of people gathered in a fish market to sell or purchase fish; or in a spot near the road to witness roadside circus, etc.

Characteristics of Crowd

Crowds are loose textured groups. They are not just congregations of people. Here physical closeness leads to social interaction. Even if the members of the crowd actually try to avoid interper- sonal contact, they are compelled to be bound by it.

Crowds vary greatly in character and behaviour. It means, a crowd of one type, say, a crowd of cricket match spectators, differs from a crowd whose members are gathered in a bus stand to catch their bus. Most crowds, however, have certain characteristics in common. Four such characteristics may be noted.

1. ***Suggestibility:*** People in a crowd are said to be highly suggestible. An individual in a crowd is susceptible to the interstimulation of suggestions. There exist heightened emotions and intense excitements in a crowd. People are carried away by the opinions, feelings and actions of one another, Drums, trumpets, flags, banners, placards, slogans, and songs may be used to make people to become more emotional and to get excited. Emotions and excitements always add to the suggestibility.
2. ***Anonymity:*** The individuals in a crowd feel that their identities will remain anonymous. They also feel that they are relatively insignificant and they could remain unrecognised. This feeling of anonymity add to the irresponsible behaviour of its members.
3. ***Spontaneity:*** A crowd is spontaneously formed and is highly temporary in nature. Members of a crowd also tend to behave in a more spontaneous manner than they would on their own. They are more likely to be impulsive.
4. ***Invulnerability:*** A crowd lacks self-consciousness. Since their personal identities are not recognised they feel that they can behave freely and without any inhibitions. They do not just bother about the hold of social control mechanisms. [*Note: for some more details, please refer to the topics "Unorganised Groups" in Chapter on "Social Groups."*]

Types of Crowd

Herbert Blumer (1951) has spoken of four main types of crowd:

1. ***Casual crowds:*** The casual crowd gathers around a specific event, and its members have little interaction with one another. These are the most loosely structured of all crowds. The individual members here have the least emotional involvement in the crowd. Hence they can easily go away from it. *Example*. A group of people forming a crowd at the spot of car accident in a busy street.
2. ***Conventional crowds:*** These type of crowds are deliberately planned and relatively structured. It is called "*conventional*" because its behaviour follows the established social norms and conventions. *Example*. An audience filled with parents and grand parents at a graduation ceremony is a conventional crowd. A conventional crowd gathers for a socially sanctioned purpose.
3. ***Expressive crowds:*** An expressive crowd gathers specifically for the purpose of letting out emotions. They are usually organised to permit the personal gratification of their members. It is an activity viewed as an end in itself. *Example*. A college dance, 'Camp fire day' celebrations at the end of N.S.S. or N.C.C. Camps, a religious" revival meeting, the Holi festival celebrations of the Hindus, etc.
4. ***Acting Crowds:*** The acting crowd focuses its attention on a specific action or goal. They are the crowds in action-mobbing, rioting, or engaging in other extreme forms of behaviour. The members are generally angry at some force or person outside of the group and want to act against it. Comparatively it is least common one. But socially it is the most significant of the four basic crowd types.

THEORIES OF CROWD BEHAVIOUR

Crowd behaviour, particularly of the highly irrational and destructive behaviour of the acting crowds, has been a fascinating subject of study of a good number of sociologists. How can this type of unusual phenomenon be explained? Sociologists have developed number of theories in their attempt to explain it. Two major theories can be considered here for consideration.

The Contagion Theory

The earliest systematic interpretation of this theory was proposed by a French writer, Gustave *Le Bon* in 1895. *Le Bon* suggested that a "*Collective mind*" forms in a crowd and with this the conscious personality of the individual members almost disappear.

Le Bon believed that the members of a crowd are dominated by a single impulse and act almost identically. He felt that individuals become susceptible to "*suggestion*" in crowds. People actually "*melt into the group and become anonymous*". People are less capable of rational thought when once they are caught up in the frenzy of the crowd. Since nobody notices what anyone says or does in a crowd, one's personal beliefs become less important. The collective beliefs formed from the "*contagious growth of a belief that is suggested and spread throughout the crowd*". This happens more or less like the way in which contagious disease spreads.

Le Bon was an aristocrat and thoroughly disliked crowds drawn from the ranks of the ordinary classes. He had his own prejudices towards them. He was firmly convinced that a person in a crowd "*descends several rungs in the ladder of civilization. Isolated, he may be a cultivated individual; in a crowd, he is a barbarian ; that is, a creature acting by instinct*". (Ref.: Quoted by *I. Robertson*) '*In crowds' Le Bon wrote*, "*It is stupidity and not mother-wit that is accumulated*" (as quoted by Samuel Koenig). "*The great accomplishments of civilisation, however, he claimed, have been achieved by means of deliberate thought and by a small intellectual aristocracy, never by crowds. This led Le Bon to a certain mistrust of masses, whom he associated with crowd behaviour, and to dislike of what he called the philosophy of number*". — Koenig

Assessment of the Theory

Le Bon's theory of the crowd has exercised a tremendous influence on the sociological research of collective behaviour. There is no doubt that the members of the crowds are subject to certain amount of contagion from others. They are highly suggestible and look to others for cues and behave in a less critical and more irresponsible manner. These aspects of *Le Bon's* theory have been almost accepted.

But no one subscribes to the view that there is a separate mind called "*the group mind*" or "*collective mind*". There is no crowd mind with its independent existence. *Le Bon's* prejudices towards the lower classes are also not justifiable.

The "Emergent Norms" Theory

The most accepted theory of crowd today is the "*emergent norms*" theory of *Turner* and *Killian* (1972). Supporters of this theory have charged that the 'contagion theory' exaggerates the irrational and purposeless components of crowd behaviour. Crowds are never entirely like-minded, and contagion theory does not explain why the crowd takes one action rather than another. Turner argues there are considerable differences in the motives, and actions of crowd members. Some of the people present in the crowd may be more impulsive, while others are passive supporters. Again, some may take on the role of onlookers while some opportunistic individuals try to seek their own gratification from the crowd situation. *The unanimity of the crowd is only an illusion*. Even in the midst of a riot, some people may have very different motives and intentions. Some may even behave in an indifferent manner.

"*According to this theory, crowds are guided by norms, just as other groups in society are, but the norms are devised as the crowd goes along rather than assumed from the beginning as they are in most social situation*" — *Wallace and Wallace*

What happens in a crowd, according to turner is that — new norms emerge in the course of social interaction. These norms define appropriate behaviour in a crowd situation. These norms emerge from the visible actions of a few people. When utter confusion prevails in the crowd, these few activists, are able to define the norms — whether they are norms regarding applause, violence, clapping or anything else—for most of the members. Though good number of people do not accept the direction that is being given by these activists , they do not express any opposition, may be because of fear of ridicule, coercion, or even personal injury. Hence casual observers from outside believe that the crowd is unanimous. Crowd behaviour in this way can very much be explained in terms of norms. The only difference is that the *norms are improvised on the spot*. The crowd itself evolves the norms and then enforces them on it members.

MOBS AND RIOTS AS FORMS OF CROWD BEHAVIOUR

Mobs

Mob is an important form of the acting crowd. "*A mob is an emotionally aroused crowd bent on violent action*" — *I. Robertson*

Mobs have their own leaders and "*are single minded in their aggressive intent*". They impose strong conformity on their members. Like any other crowd mob is particularly temporary and unstable in character. The mob has its own limited but immediate objectives and concentrates on its realisation.

Two Types of Mob

The mobs are of two types:

1. ***The purposive and active mobs:*** These are deliberately planned by some interested parties to achieve their own predecided purpose. *Example*. Opponents of a political leader purposefully attacking a big rally; or leaders of the opposition and trade union leaders direct their followers to attack government offices, public properties, etc.
2. ***The confused and random mobs:*** These are not deliberately created, nor there is any attempt in them on the part of the leaders to give direction for their followers. Due to confusion a crowd may get converged into a mob. *Example*. (*i*) A ferocious bull may, all of a sudden, rush towards a big gathering of people who have assembled in a field to listen to a political speech. Due to fear and confusion people may become panicky. Some may consider it to be the handiwork of the political opponents and may resort to violence in a bid to register their protest against it ; (*ii*) Sudden outbursts of people and unanticipated communal disturbances, can also be cited here as examples.

Riots

The Riot is another important form of crowd behaviour. It is a violent and destructive collective outburst. "*A riot is the action of a violently aggressive, destructive crowd*" — *Harton* and *Hunt*

Rioting crowds differ from mobs in that their behaviour is less structured, purposive and unified. On the other hand, the mob usually has some specific target — lynching a victim, attacking a police vehicle, burning down a foreign embassy, ransacking the property of an anti-national smuggler. It could be said that riot involves behaviour which has the main objective of creating nothing but disorder.

AUDIENCE: AS A CROWD WITH A DIFFERENCE

"*An audience is a crowd with centred on stimuli outside themselves*" —*Horton* and *Hunt*. *Example*. People who gather in an auditorium to listen to a lecture, constitute an audience.

The first requirement of an audience is that people must assemble or gather at a particular place *to share some Common or similar interest*. The second requirement is that *the audience is expected to conform to the universally accepted code of conduct*. *For example*, people are not expected to talk aloud in the middle when the speaker is performing his task on the stage. People are expected to clap at appropriate times only and not whenever they want it, and so on. But this code differs with the type of audience.

With an audience there may be significant two-way stimulus and response even though the audience situation discourages communication. The most successful performers cultivate a two-way communication which seems to make the performer a part of the group. Members of the audience participate in communication particularly when they cheer, applaud, boo, whisper, mutter, doze or snore during the course of the performance of the performer. Social contagion still operates here; it may be very mild during a religious discourse and it may be highly expressive at a political rally or a sports event. Audiences may become unruly and may even becomes riotous.

Types of Audience

Kimbal Young makes a distinction between three kinds of audience: (*a*) **Information Seeking Audience**. 'Those who assemble in a lecture hall to listen to a scholarly lecture; (*b*) **Recreation Seeking Audience**. Those who go to the playground to watch a match, or to a theatre to witness a drama, and so on; (*c*) **Conversional Audience**. Those who go to attend some meetings wherein they can dispel some doubts they have regarding some beliefs or ideologies etc. This also includes those who attend religious discourses or political meetings to familiarise themselves with some ideas or ideologies which are normally propagated through such meetings.

PUBLICS AND PUBLIC OPINION

Most of the forms of collective behaviour involve some amount of direct contact and contagion among the participants. The study of public and public opinion presents a different picture as such . Here individuals are mostly dispersed and likely to have their own individual opinions and decisions.

Publics

- According to *Ginsberg*, the word '*public*' refers to an unorganised aggregation of persons "*who are bound together by common opinions, desires, but are too numerous for each to maintain personal relations with others*".
- "*A public is a substantial number of people with a shared interest in some issue on which there are differing opinions*" — *Ian Robertson*.

People sometimes use the word 'public' to mean an entire population. Actually, there is no issue for which the entire population is a public either because people are not interested in it, or because, they are ignorant of it. The public for any single issue such as *secularism, love marriage, reservation to Scheduled Castes and Tribes, India becoming a party to the GATT* ("General Agreement on Trade and Tariffs"— an international trade agreement signed by more than 110 countries at Morocco, including India, on April 1994) etc., may either expand or contract depending upon the number of people who get involved in the topic.

The members of a public are not gathered like the members of a crowd. *It is a dispersed group*. Here one can have communication with others not directly but indirectly through mass media. The activities of a public are more rational than those of the crowd. A public does not act together. But it does form opinions on the issue around which it is focussed.

Publics are created by cultural complexity. In a simple culture there would be few, if any, publics. A complex culture produces many interest groups. There could be as many publics as there are special interests or issue.

In a simple, stable culture, very few issues arise and most of these could be handled in a traditional way. But, in a complex, changing culture, issues are constantly arising. In many instances they cannot be handled by the traditional ways. Because the tradition gives no clear answer to them. In the modern culture, '*publics*' are formed on each specific activity, interest, or issue. As the members of the public consider the issue and form opinions regarding it, "*public opinion*" is developed. [*Note for some more details on 'public', please refer to the topic* "*Unorganized Groups*" *in Chapter on "Social Groups."*]

Public Opinion

- *Wallace* and *Wallace*. "*Public opinion consists of the views of the members of a public on a certain issue*".
- *Ian Robertson*. "Public opinion is the sum of the decisions of the members of a public on a particular issue".
- *Horton* and *Hunt*. "Public Opinion has two definitions: (*i*) *an opinion held by a substantial number of people*, (*ii*) *the dominant opinion among a population*" (According to the first usage, there can be many public opinions ; according to the second, public opinion refers to a public 'consensus' upon an issue. both usages are common in other literature).

Since people do not hold the same opinion always, there cannot be a permanent public opinion as such. People do change their opinions. Opinion on many issues is often in a state of flux. An assessment of public opinion is, therefore, valid for a particular time and place in which it was made.

In democratic societies like ours, public opinion plays a considerable role. Political parties, industrialists, businessmen and others always keep a watch on public opinions. As a result, a good deal of effort goes into finding out what the public thinks about particular issues. Efforts are also being made constantly to find out the factors that influence it. Huge amount of money is spent every year to make market surveys, to conduct public opinion polls and to develop favourable opinion through mass media. In fact, public opinion is a creation of the complex society and the mass media. Attempts are made in a systematic manner to build up public opinion through what is known as "*propaganda*".

Manipulation of public opinion is done through propaganda. Measurement of public opinion becomes essential to attempt at systematic propaganda. Public opinion generally becomes known through the reporting of the public opinion, polls such as the "*Gallop Polls*". Public opinion polls is a recent invention for finding out what people are thinking. A poll is simple in concept but difficult to carry out because the formation, expression and change of public opinion constitute a very complicated phenomenon. "*Because public opinion changes so rapidly, however, it has been suggested that public opinion polls may not actually report the trends in the society, as opinion pollers claim, but only how some people feel about one issue at one particular moment in time*". (Blumer's views in the words of **Wallace** and **Wallace**). Another criticism is that, instead of simply reporting opinions, they may help to form opinion and the behaviour that accompany it.

PROPAGANDA AND ITS TECHNIQUES

Public opinion researches normally stress upon the manipulation of public opinion through propaganda.

- Propaganda refers to the "*Techniques of influencing human action by the manipulation of representations*" — *Harold D. Lasswell*.
- "*Propaganda is the attempt to persuade people to a point of view upon issue...* "

  — *Clyde R. Miller*.
- "*Propaganda is the attempt to persuade people to a point of view upon issue...*"

  — *Horton* and *Hunt*.

Propaganda is very often thought of as an attempt to win people over to an unpopular cause or to influence them to follow a generally disapproved course of action. But actually, the purpose of propaganda can be quit varied. It can be generally understood as a means of influencing others, often towards a desirable end. Every public enterprise, on a governmental department has its own department which is presently called "*publicity*" department, "*advertising department*" or "*public relations*" department, instead of propaganda. Propaganda has become a science as well as an art. Individuals even specialise in it as a profession and represent the organisations or persons employing them. Propaganda is also used for educational and a public welfare purposes. Various means of mass media are applied for propaganda purposes.

Techniques of Propaganda

Propagandists can use several methods to persuade people to accept their views. These techniques have one element in common. They make an appeal to the values and attitudes of the people. *Alfred M. Lee* and *Elizabeth B. Lee* in their "*The Fine Art of Propganda*" — classified the techniques of propaganda into seven main categories. They are as follows:

1. ***"Name-calling"*** is a method used in negative propaganda. Attempts are made here to label the opponent as "communist", "*fascist*", "*anti-secular*", "*reactionary*" "*fifth columnist*", and so on. This is the way of discrediting the opponent.
2. ***"Glittering generalities"*** refers to the technique of using universally cherished sentiments such as "*social justice*", "*freedom of expression*", "*fundamental rights*", "*human rights*", "*patriotism*", "*secularism*", and the like. Manipulation of these sentiments is likely to evoke favourable response.
3. ***"Transfer"*** is a method of winning approval for something by associating it with something else that is known to be viewed favourably. *Example. Associating an idea with a revered person like Gandhi or an image or symbol like the Ayodhya Ram temple, or the Indian National Flag.*
4. ***"Testimonial"*** is a technique of using famous or respected people to make public statements favouring or opposing something. It is a common practice for advertisers to use sports heroes, film stars, freedom fighters to recommend their products on television and in magazines.
5. ***"Plain folks"*** is the technique of identifying the propgandist's ideas or product with "ordinary" people. Political and public leaders, *for example*, pose themselves to be very simple, generous, merciful, sympathetic, and so on. They often shake hands with very poor people, kiss little babies, visit the huts of the lowest caste people and pose themselves as very helpful and accommodative.
6. ***"Card stacking"*** is an argument in which the facts (or false-hoods) are arranged in such a manner that the only one conclusion seems to be logically possible. In this technique, the propagandist goes on mentioning the good points or virtues of one person, or ideology, or policy or any such thing in which he is interested. He carefully omits all its defects and exaggerates that it is better than all other alternatives. Industrialists make such advertisements in papers, televisions, etc.
7. ***"Band wagon"*** is a method to build support for a particular view point, idea, policy, or product by creating the impression that "*everyone is doing it*". Those who come under this kind of propganda are made to feel that they should also go with the "*same trend*" or else they will be "kept out". This is like the joining the "*camp of the winners*" or of those who are likely to get a victory.

The phenomenon of propganda is actually a wonderous one. Opinions are not formed in vacuum. They are made in the context of existing cultural values and personal preconceptions. Public opinion is often formed in a very informal manner and cannot be easily studied. People do not necessarily get their opinions directly from media sources. Opinions are often formed, or developed *through the influence of one's own primary group members, friends, workmates, neighbours* and so on. The public is also influenced by the prominent members of the community who act as "*opinion leaders*". These individuals are normally status people and have their own range of influence. Contagion may also play its role in the formation of public opinion through what is known as the "*band wagon*" effect. The modern means of mass communication—such as radio, television, newspapers, films etc., have been playing a vital role in the formation and spread of public opinion.

Limitations of Propaganda

The powers of the propaganda are not unlimited. Propaganda, however sophisticated it may be, has its own limitations. Some of the limits of propaganda are mentioned below.

1. ***Competing propagandas*** seem to be a great limiting factor. The mere existence of competing propagandas, particularly in a democratic set up, restrains the influence of the propagandists.
2. ***The credibility of the propagandists*** in the eyes of its receivers, is of great importance. It is indeed a limiting factor. If the propagandist has a vested interest, the credibility of his propaganda naturally gets reduced when the receivers discern it.

3. ***The sophistication of the receivers*** limits the effects of propaganda. It can be generalised, that more educated and informed people are less affected by propaganda than the uneducated and poorly informed people.
4. ***The beliefs and values of the recipients*** also place some limits on the effects of propaganda. People normally accept any kind of propaganda if it fits into their beliefs and values or attitudes and reject even uncritically if that propaganda conflicts with their beliefs.
5. ***Cultural drafts and trends*** will have their influence on propaganda. A cultural drift cannot easily be stopped by propaganda. However, it may speed up or weaken the cultural drift. It is doubtful whether the propaganda is capable of initiating or halting a cultural trend, destroy a well-established value or, instill a view for which the society is not looking for at the moment.

REVIEW QUESTIONS

1. Define collective behaviour. Give an example which illustrates collective behaviour.
2. Write the salient features of collective behaviour.
3. What is the relationship between collective behaviour and social movements? Examine.
4. Discuss the difficulties involved in the study of collective behaviour.
5. Explain the concepts of mass and mass behaviour. Describe the basic forms of mass behaviour.
6. Define panic and mass hysteria. Cite a classical example of mass hysteria.
7. Define crowd. Discuss its salient features and types.
8. Discuss the theories of crowd behaviour.
9. Define mob. Discuss its types.
10. Give the definition of audience. What are its types?
11. Who do you mean by publics and public opinion? Explain.
12. Define propaganda. Discuss the techniques of propaganda. What are limitations of propaganda?
13. Write short notes on the following:
    (a) Theory of collective behaviour
    (b) Crowd behaviour

⌘⌘⌘⌘⌘⌘⌘⌘⌘⌘⌘⌘

42

SOCIAL MOVEMENTS

CHAPTER OUTLINE

THE CONCEPT OF SOCIAL MOVEMENT

"Social movement"—is one of the major forms of collective behaviour. In the recent years the study of social movements has attracted the attention of a large number of sociologists not only in India, but also in the West. We hear of various kinds of social movements launched for one or the other purpose, There are movements to demand more and more reservation for the SCs and STs and other backward classes and there are counter movements demanding its cancellation or at least the status quo. There are movements to "*save environment*", to "*save wildlife*" and to "*save world peace*". There are movements for and against the construction of Sri Ram Temple at the disputed place of Ayodhya. There are Fascist Movements, Communist Movements, Naxalite Movements, Tribal Movements, Peasants' Movements, Women's Movements, Youth Movements, Labour Movements, Civil Rights Movements, Human Rights Movements, Aforestation Movements, and so on. What then do we mean by social movements?

Definition of Social Movement

- A social movement is formally defined as "*a collectively acting with some continuity to promote or resist change in the society or group of which it is a part*" — *Turner and Killian*.
- "*A social movement is a collective effort to promote or resist change*" — *Horton* and *Hunt*.
- Social movements can be defined as "*organised group effort to generate or resist social change*"

  — *Neil J. Smesler*.
- "*A social movement is a collective effort to transform established relations within a particular society*"

  — *Rudolf Herberle*

CHARACTERISTICS OF SOCIAL MOVEMENTS

M.S.A. Rao, one of the prominent Indian sociologists, has made a mention of the nature of social movements in the book "*Social Movements in India*", edited by him. According to him, social movement includes two characteristics about which there is considerable agreement among the sociologists. They are as follows:

1. ***Collective action:*** Social movement undoubtedly involves collective action. However, this collective action, takes the form of a movement only when it is *sustained for a long time*. This collective action need not be formally organised.

It could be an informal attempt also. But it should be able to create an interest and awakening in relatively large number of people.

2. ***Oriented towards social change:*** A Social movement is generally oriented towards bringing about social change. This change could either be partial or total. Though the movement is aimed at bringing about a change in the values, norms, ideologies of the existing system, efforts are also made by some other forces to resist the changes and to maintain the status quo. The counter attempts are normally *defensive and restorative rather than innovative and initiating change*. They are normally the organised efforts of an already established order to maintain itself.

As *M.S.A. Rao* points out, though sociologists are almost agreeable on the above mentioned two characteristics or social movement; they differ a lot regarding other criteria — such as *the presence of an ideology, method of organisation, and the nature of consequence*.

1. ***Ideology behind the movement:*** An important component of social movement that distin- guishes it from the general category of collective mobilisation, is the presence of an ideology. Example. A student strike involves collective mobilisation and is oriented towards change. But in the absence of an ideology a student strike becomes an isolated event and not a movement. On the contrary, if the strike is committed to an ideology, it may last for longer period and assume the form of a movement.
2. ***Organisational frame work:*** As *Paul Wilkinson* has pointed out that a social movement requires a minimum of organisational framework to achieve success or at least to maintain the tempo of the movement. *To make the distinction clear between the leaders and followers, to make clear the purposes of the movement, to persuade people to take part in it or to support it, to adopt different techniques to achieve the goals* — a social movement must have some amount of organisational framework.
3. ***The techniques and results:*** A social movement may adopt its own technique or method to achieve its goal. There is no certainty regarding it. It may follow *peaceful* or *conflicting, violent or non-violent, compulsive or persuasive, democratic or undemocratic* means or methods to reach its goal. The same thing is true of the results. It may become successful or *it may fail* ; it may become *partial success* or at least *it may create a general 'awakening'* in the public regarding an issue. The result of a movement has a close bearing on the ideology and the organisational framework.

THE FORMATION OF SOCIAL MOVEMENTS

Social movements do not emerge spontaneously as we observe it in the case of a crowd or mob. *Herbert Bhumer* (1951) has done much theoretical work in the field of social movements. According to him, social movement involves a few stages in its formation.

The Preliminary Stage

This stage can also be called *the unrest stage*". In this stage we find some confusion or discontentment among people. Hence they are restless. In fact, as *N.J. Smelser* has pointed out "*All social movements begin with some feeling of discontent with the existing social order*..." Discontent is always a product of a relationship between objective conditions and ideas about those conditions.

If all the members in a society feel satisfied about everything, there is no chance for any social movement to emerge. The very presence of a movement indicates that people are dissatisfied with something or the other. More *dissatisfaction* or *feeling of deprivation* or *restlessness* along does not lead to a movement. People should believe or should be made to believe that these *deprivations are man-made and they can be effectively tackled through collective actions. Only then, the stage is set for the emergence of a movement.*

The Popular Stage

In the popular stage the movement begins to rally around a figure or a leader who promises to alleviate the sufferings of the people. This leader may be a charismatic leader with some extraordinary qualities who is capable of giving a leadership to the movement. He may speak of reform, revolution, resistance or express himself in such a way that the followers are made to feel that *he will do something or the other to find solution to their problem*. If the message of the leader is appropriate and very much appealing people would definitely rally around him.

The Formalisation Stage (The Stage of Formal Organisation)

This is the stage in which programmes are developed, alliances are forged, and organisations and tactics are developed. In this stage, *a party, organisation, or group of individuals* may put forward an alternative vision, world-view or ideology, to understand, analyse and solve a prevailing crisis. Once the ideology gains acceptance among people, efforts must be made to translate it into a programme which calls for collective action. This leads to the birth of the movement.

Not all the times movements are launched by the charismatic leaders. Very often they are sponsored, supported or spearheaded by some organisations. The deprived collectivity may realise the necessity of forming an organisation to strengthen their position. The already existing organisation may also take up the cause of the masses and head the movement. The ideology is usually used to sustain the organisational set up. But the success of the movement demands the organisation to function more as a movement, and less as a rigid formal structure. For some reason or the other, people may lose faith in the charismatic leader and incline towards an organisational leader.

The Stage of Institutionalisation of the Movement

If the movement becomes successful, then it destroys itself in its last stage of development. When it becomes an institution. "*At this point, it is no longer collective behaviour, because it is organised; follows accepted norms of society, and has replaced its emotional base with the assumption that change will take time*" (**Wallace** and **Wallace**). When once, it assumes this stage the institution tries to bring down the wrath of the people and assures them that things would become normal in due course. With this, the active life of the movement may come to an end.

In the stage of institutionalisation, as *Horton* and *Hunt* have pointed out, the movement almost becomes routinised. They have said that in an institutionalisation stage, "*as organisations take over from early leaders, bureaucracy is entrenched, and ideology and programme become cystalised. It Often ending the active life of the movement*".

The Dissolution Stage

Horton and *Hunt* have 'spoken of the last stage of social movement namely, '*the dissolution stage*'. When the movement becomes an enduring organisation (like the Indian National Congress, or the Y.M.C.A.) or fades away, possibility to be revived sometimes later, it can be said to have entered this last stage of dissolution.

According to *Horton* and *Hunt*, this "*like-cycle fits poorly the expressive and migratory movements but is more applicable to the utopian, reform, revolutionary, and resistance movements*".

CONDITIONS OF A SUCCESSFUL SOCIAL MOVEMENT

All the social movements do not become successful in achieving the target. Sociologist Abel (1937) has spoken of some conditions which, if satisfied. would contribute to the success of the movement.

1. *Many individuals must experience the events which are perceived as a threat* ;
2. *The reaction to the events must be a strong and emotional dissatisfaction:*
3. *Personal values must be involved*;
4. *There must be some object which becomes the focus of dissatisfaction and opposition of the movement.*

TYPES OF SOCIAL MOVEMENTS

Sociologists classified social movements into different types on the basis of their objectives *Wallace* and *Wallace*, *Horton* and *Hunt*, *M.S. Rao*, and others have mentioned of three main types of movements:

1. Reform Movements

Reform movements are satisfied with the existing, social order but believe that certain reforms are necessary in some specific areas. The reformers endeavour to change elements of the system as it currently stands. *Example. The Civil Rights Movement, Women's Liberation Movement, Save the Environment Movement, the Arya Samaj Movement*, *Brahmo Samaj Movement*, *etc*.

2. Revolutionary Movements

The revolutionary movements deny that the system will even work. These movements are deeply dissatisfied with the social order and work for radical change. They advocate replacing the entire existing structure. Their objective is the reorganisation of society in accordance with their own ideological blueprint. Revolutionary movements generally prefer not to use violence although some of them do resort to violence. *Example. The Protestant Reformation Movement, the Socialist Movement, the Communist Revolution of Russia and also of China, the Indian National Freedom Movement*, and so on.

3. Reactionary or Revivalist Movement

Some movements are known as *reactionary or regressive movements*. These aim at "*putting the clock back*". Their members view certain social changes with suspicion and distaste and try to reverse the current trends. They highlight the importance and greatness of traditional values, ideologies and institutional arrangements. They strongly criticise the fast moving changes of the present.

Example. The Catholic Counter Reformation, The Brahma Samaj, Arya Samaj, The Sarvodaya Movement, "Khadi and Gramodyog Movement of Gandhiji; and the like.

In addition to the above, mentioned three main types of movements, we can add two other types of movements as suggested by *Horton* and *Hunt*.

4. Resistance Movements

These movements are formed to resist a change that is already taking place in society. The many social and cultural changes of recent decades have been profoundly disturbing to many of the Indians who feel that our national virtues, traditional values, and cultural greatness, are being eroded by Secularism, minority appeasement, sexual permissiveness, moral degradation, political corruption and sell-out of national interests for the partial political interests, and so on. Good number of contemporary resistance movements express their dismay at the directions in which our nation has been moving. *Example. Anti-Abortion Movement, Anti-Hindi Movement, Anti-Reservation Movement, the 'Swadeshi Movement against the movement towards Economic Liberalisation, the Movement towards indianising Indian Education, etc.* This type of movement is not very much revolutionary in character, but more resistant in nature.

5. Utopian Movements

These are attempts to take the society or at least a section of it towards a state of perfection. "*These are loosely structured collectivities that envision a radically changed and blissful state, either on a large scale at some time in the future, or on a smaller scale in the present. The utopian ideal and the means of it are often vague, but many utopian movements have quite specific programmes for social change*". (**I. Robertson**) *Examples*. The "*Hare Krishna Movement*" of the seventies, the movement towards the establishment of "*Rama Rajya*"— as envisioned by the B.J.P, and the "Sangh Parivar" (The community of the supporters of the R.S.S, School of Thought), the Communists' and Socialists pronouncement of a *movement towards the classless, casteless society* free from all kinds of exploitation, etc.

THEORIES OF SOCIAL MOVEMENTS

Why do people join these various types of social movements? Is it because, some people are highly vulnerable to such appeals due to their psychic make-up? Or, to ask in a crude way, does it mean that something is "*wrong*" with some people? If individuals are not causing it, then, is it the society that is at the root of the movement? Is it true, that when something goes "wrong" with the society people try to change it through social movements? Questions like these come to our mind when we ponder over the motivating factor behind social movement. But one thing is certain — that the reason for the emergence of a social movement need not be the same as the reason why people join it.

Social movements arise because, social conditions create dissatisfaction with the existing arrangements. People join specific social movements for an almost infinite variety of reasons — including idealism, altruism, compassion, political considerations, practical benefits, religious fervour, as well as neurotic frustration.

It is indeed true that one of the main issues in the study of any movement, concerns its emergence. This point leads to three basic questions? *What are structural conditions under which movements emerge ? What are the motivational forces ? What are the theories which conceptualise the beginning of a movement*?

According to *M.S.A Rao*, there are three main theories concerning the emergence of social movements. They are: 1. *The Relative Deprivation Theory*; 2. *The Strain Theory*, and 2. *The Revitalisation Theory*.

1. ***The relative deprivation theory:*** "*Relative Deprivation*" is a concept developed by Stouffer (1949). "It holds that one 'feels' deprived according to the gap between expectations and realisations. The person who wants little and has little, feels less deprived than the one who has much but expects still more" — *Harton* and *Hunt*, p. 501

   "*A point that is conceded by relative deprivation theorists is that a position of relative depri- vation alone will not generate a movement. The structural conditions of relative deprivation provide only the necessary conditions. Sufficient conditions are provided by the perception of a situation and by the estimate of capabilities by certain leaders that they can do something to remedy the situations*." — M.S.A. Roa

   Relative deprivation is increasing throughout most of the underdeveloped countries. A weakening of the traditional and tribal controls generally leads to an enormous increase in desires. People long for so many things, better living conditions, facilities, luxury goods (like phone, T.V., Vehicles, electrical appliances, etc.) without knowing the difficulties involved in producing them and supplying them to all the people. Hence the recently established independent governments of Third World Countries have no hopes of keeping up with their peoples' expectations. The clouds of mass movements and revolutions, seem to be widespread in these countries. "*Revolutions seem most likely to occur not when people are most miserable, but after things have begun to improve, setting off a round of — rising expectation*"

— Brinton

Though this theory seems to be more acceptable, it is yet to be proved beyond doubts. *Feelings of deprivation are easy to infer but difficult to measure*. It is still more difficult to measure it over a period of time. This factor could be taken as only one among the many factors in social movements.

2. ***The strain theory:*** The '*Strain Theory*' of social movement has been propounded by *Smelser* (1962). This theory considers structural strain as the underlying factor contributing to collective behaviour. Structural strain may occur at different levels such as norms, values, mobility, situational facilities, etc. Because of these structural strains some generalised belief that seeks to provide an explanation for the strain, may emerge. Both strain and generalised belief require precipitating factors to trigger off a movement.

   Smelser's analysis of the genesis of social movements is very much within the structural functional framework. Smelser considers strain as something that endangers the relationship among the parts of a system leading to its malfunctioning. It places stress on the feeling of deprivation also. On the contrary, the "relative deprivation theory", though emphasises the conflict element (which contributes to change) fails to consider it (conflict) as something that may contribute to the malfunctioning of the system.

3. ***The theory of revitalisation:*** The "*Relative Deprivation Theory*" and the '*Strain Theory*' — give us an impression that social movements necessarily arise out of negative conditions such as '*deprivations*' and '*strains*'. In this context, *Wallac* (1956) has asserted "*That social movements develop out of a deliberate. organised and conscious effort on the part of members of a society to construct a more satisfying culture for themselves*"

   — quoted by M.S.A. Rao

   Wallace who analysed the dynamics of revitalisation theory has mentioned about its four phases: "*period of cultural stability, period of increased individual stress, period of cultural distortion and consequent disillusionment and period of revitalisation*".

   The revitalisation theory suggests that adaptive processes are employed to establish equilibrium situation. Social movements no doubt develop a programme of action. But these movements tend to be like a double-edged sword. On the one hand, they express dissatisfaction, dissent, and protest against existing conditions, and, on the other, they offer a positive programme of action to remedy the situation.

The Theory of Relative Deprivation is More Acceptable: M.S.A. Rao

According to *M.S.A. Rao*, the relative deprivation theory offers a more satisfactory explanation of the emergence of social movement. Its merit is that *it is pivoted around conflict and cognitive change.* It is motivating and mobilising people around some issues and interests.

Its another merit is that "*it offers the best explanation for the change orientation of movements rather than looking at movements as adaptive mechanisms restoring functional unity and equilibrium*" — *M.S.A. Rao*

The theory of relative deprivation, as *M.S.A. Rao* opines requires refinement in two directions: **Firstly**, "*it is necessary to make the concept sociologically more relevant by eschewing individual and psychic deprivations*" such deprivation remain "*personal, arbitrary* and *even frivolous*" ; **Secondly**, in considering areas of deprivation, it is necessary to include the areas such as religion, caste, etc. The area of religion, though some sociologists (like Aberle, Glock and others) have not included in the purview of this theory, *M.S.A. Rao* feels, is as important as those of economics, education and politics.

SOCIAL MOVEMENTS AND SOCIAL PROBLEMS

Social movements play a very important role in highlighting some of the social problems. Some undesirable conditions can exist for years or even centuries before they are recognised as social problems. Slavery, the subordination of women, untouchability, racial discrimination, communalism, poverty, inequality, pollution etc., were all generally regarded as either as natural or inevitable, or, as less important, until social movements drew the attention of the public, mobilised public opinion and campaigned for change.

The degree of success of a social movement determines not only how the social problem is confronted but also what happens to the movement itself. The interplay of social problems and social movements poroduces a typical "*life cycle*" or "*natural history*" that often ends with the disappearance of the movement.

SOCIAL MOVEMENTS AND SOCIAL CHANGE

Social movements do not necessarily bring solutions to the social problems. They may champion the cause of social problems but cannot always promise a lasting solution. Social movements may promise to bring about social change and they do bring it. But it is not a one-way-process. Not only do social movements bring about change, but social change sometimes gives birth to movement.

Social change often breeds social movements, and movements, in turn, breed additional change. In fact, *Smelser* has defined a social movement, "*as an organised group effort to generate socio- cultural change*."

For nearly every social movement, there is a counter movement. The purpose of these counter movements is to oppose the original movement. Counter movements struggle to maintain the status quo. *For example*, some parties, organisations and leaders have started the "*pro-reservation movement*", while some others, have floated "*anti-reservation movement*", in India. Similarly, good number of leaders, organisations and parties supported the Ayodhya movement and insisted on the construction of Sri Ram Temple at the "disputed place" at Ayodhya. At the same time, a sizeable number of people and parties launched a counter movement against the pro-Ram Temple movement. In the very same manner, trade union movements generate capitalist counter movements that try to preserve the free enterprise system. Youth movements stiffen the resistance of older groups.

Society is not a static element. It is a complex system of movements and counter movements pulling it in different directions. When this tussle is finally in favour of the movement, it becomes part of the social structure. A successful movement may become a part of the social order. *Example*, a trade union movement or "save environment movement". The movement may disappear after achieving its goal as it has been in the case of "Indian freedom movement".

Finally, it can be said that the intricate relationship between social movements and social change cannot be completely understood. *Smelser's* remarks are worth noting at this stage; "*while there is much that we don' t understand about the interplay of social movements and social change, it is clear that the two are linked in an inricate pattern.*

REVIEW QUESTIONS

1. What do you mean by social movement? Throw light on the characteristic features of social movements.
2. Social movement involves a few stages in its formation. What are that stages? Explain.
3. Highlight the conditions of a successful social movement.
4. Discuss the types of social movements.
5. Explain the theories of social movements.
6. Assess the relation between social movements and social problems.
7. Bring out the relation between social movements and social change.
8. Write short notes on the following:
   (a) Social movements
   (b) Utopian movements
   (c) Relative deprivation
9. Social change often breeds social movements. Analyse.
10. Social movement is one of the major forms of collective behaviour. Examine.

⌘⌘⌘⌘⌘⌘⌘⌘⌘⌘⌘⌘

PART

NINE

SOCIAL DISORGANISATION AND SOCIAL PROBLEMS

43

SOCIAL DISORGANISATION

CHAPTER OUTLINE

- THE CONCEPT OF SOCIAL DISORGANISATION
- SOCIAL ORGANISATION VS. DISORGANISATION
- DEFINITION AND CHARACTERISTICS OF SOCIAL DISORGANISATION
- CAUSES OF SOCIAL DISORGANISATION AND REMEDIAL MEASURES.

THE CONCEPT OF SOCIAL DISORGANISATION

Like nature, the human society too has its own order. The orderliness of society depends on its internal strength to maintain its equilibrium. Society will be in a state of equilibrium as long as its various parts are properly adjusted and fulfil their functions. The orderliness or the equilibrium that is normally maintained in the natural world is often upset due to certain forces at work. In the same manner, the equilibrium in the social world is also often disturbed. Whenever the social equilibrium is severely disturbed 'social disorganisation' sets in. Thus 'social disorganisation' can be understood as nothing but the state of social disequilibrium, in which the smooth functioning of various parts of society gets disturbed.

The concept of 'disorganisation' occupies a prominent place in modern sociological literature. The concept was developed by *Thomas* and *Zananiecki* in their famous book "*The Polish Peasant in Europe and America*". According to them, the term 'social disorganisation' refers to *the decrease in the influence of the existing social rules of behaviour upon individual members*. As a result of this there develops individuation and lack of cohesion in society. It was explained by them as a process which will automatically and inevitably create social problems.

SOCIAL ORGANISATION VS SOCIAL DISORGANISATION

The term '*social disorganisation*' is often held in contrast with '*social organisation*'. As *Ogburn* and *Nimkoff* have pointed out that "an organisation is an orderly relationship of parts. But the significance of this orderly arrangement of parts lies in what it does". *For example*, a factory is an organisation for the purpose of production. A factory is composed of internal suborganisations such as sales department, accounting department, supply department, etc. The factory as a social system performs yet another function. It serves to maintain a balance among its suborganisations or parts. This equilibrium of parts means a synchronisation or integration of functions. Hence the functions of selling department, production department, buying departrment etc., must be properly articulated and coordinated. *"Disorganisation is a disturbance of the balance existing in the functioning of parts. The criterion of disorganisation is function, what is done or not done"... Thus, a typewriter may write well or badly or not at all, because of an imbalance in the functioning of its parts as, for instance, in the ribbon or keys".–Ogburn and Nimkoff.*

What is true of a factory is also true of a society. Society can be said to be in a state of organisation, when all its parts such as associations and institutions are properly integrated so that they fulfil their recognised or implied functions or purposes. Social disorganisation implies some break down in the social organisation. Due to this breakdown, the normal functioning of the parts of the society gets disturbed leading to some or the other kind of problems. Disorganisation will lead to functional imbalance between various elements of social structure.

The terms 'social organisation' and 'social disorganisation' are relative. They represent two aspects of the whole functioning of the social system. As there may be various degrees of social organisation, so is the case with social disorganisation. No society can be in a state of either perfect organisation or disorganisation.

As *S.A. Queen, WB. Bodenhofer* and *E.B. Harper* have said social disorganisation is a counter- part, of social organisation. "Just as social organisation provides the means by which a society maintains its unity and cohesion through effective control of its members, and hence, functions smoothly, social disorganisation causes a weakening of group solidarity, loss of control over its members, and, therefore, conflict and disintegration. Social organisation implies the existence of institutions, which meet the needs of the members of a society. Social disorganisation, on the other hand, means the malfunctioning of institutions, their failure to satisfy the needs of the people and the consequent frustration of their desires." Thus, "*if social organisation means the development of relationships which persons and groups find mutually satisfactory, then, disorganisation means their replacement by relationships which bring disappointment, thwarted wishes, irritation and unhappiness*".

DEFINITION OF SOCIAL DISORGANISATION

1. *Emile Durkheim* considers social disorganisation as "a state of disequilibrium and a lack of , social solidarity or consensus among the members of a society".
2. *Ogburn* and *Nimkoff* have said that "when the harmonious relationship between the various parts of culture is disturbed, social disorganisation ensues".
3. *Robert Eolofairs* states that "social disorganisation is a disturbance in the patterns and mechanism of human relations".
4. According to *Elliot* and *Merrill*, "Social disorganisation represents a breakdown in the equilibrium of forces, a decay in the social structure, so that old habits and forms of social control no longer function effectively".

Thus, social disorganisation implies a breakdown in the bonds of relationship, coordination, teamwork and morale among groups of interrelated persons so as to impair the functions of the society or smaller social organisation. "Social disorganisation implies relative disharmony between individual attitudes and social values, when common agreement breaks down, then, consensus is partially or wholly disturbed, and, when individuals view the major group interest in individual rather than in common terms, some degree of social disorganisation is present."

CHARACTERISTICS OF SOCIAL DISORGANISATION

Just as a disease is known by its symptoms the nature of social disorganisations can be under- stood by means of its characteristics

1. ***Conflict of mores and of institutions:*** Every society has its own mores and institutions which regulate the social life of its members. With the passage of time some of these mores and institutions may become obsolete. New ideals and new institutions may arise to suit new needs. The existing mores and institutions instead of giving place for the new ones may come in conflict with them. This conflict between the old and new may destroy the social consensus. With the destruction of consensus, the organisation is disrupted. *For example*, in India, such conflicts may be found very often with regard to social practices, ideals, and institutions relating to divorce, female education, joint family, family control, widow remarriage, intercaste marriage, dowry system, untouchability family planning, etc.
2. ***Transfer of functions from one group to another:*** In an organised society the functions of different groups are relatively well defined and almost predetermined. Due to the dynamic nature of society some of these functions either undergo radical change or get transferred to other groups or agencies. As a result of this, social disorganisation may set in even if it is for a temporary period. *For example*, the joint family in India is no more performing some of its traditional functions for these have been transferred to some external agencies. Hence the joint family system is facing a crisis now. Some say, it is in a state of severe disorganisation and this may even lead to its extinction as it is happening in big cities. Similarly, the functions of caste and religious organisations have been transferred to other organisations or agencies leading to crisis.
3. ***Individuation:*** The modern age places a high premium on individualism or individualistic tendencies. Now everyone is more prone to think of himself and in terms of his own pleasures and wishes and expectations. Important issues such as education, occupation, marriage, recreation morality, etc., have almost become matters of individual

decisions. Individuals often fail to think in terms of the expectations and wishes of the groups or organisations of which they are a part. This tendency is, of course, caused by the changing social values. But it may shatter the social organisation and may drive it towards a state of disorganisation.

4. ***Inconsistency between expectations and achievements:*** In a disorganised society considerable inconsistency is visible between the expectations embodied in the social role and the extent to which these expectations can be realised by most persons. When a large number of people in the society try to achieve goals in an anti-social manner there is a clear indication of the society being in a state of social disorganisation. For instance, if a large number of students take part regularly in strikes and indulge in violence and resort to malpractices in examination, we have no hesitation to say that the college education system has become a disorganised one.

   According to *Cottrell*, "In a disorganised society there is a considerable discrepancy between what is given verbally and which is demonstrated in practice. An organised society has greater congruity between expectation and realisation but such is not the case in a disorganised society where the expectations do not come upto their full realisation".

5. ***Inconsistency between status and rule:*** In an organised society the status and role of each individual are well defined and hence the possibility of a conflict taking place between the two is comparatively less. Changing social values and social conditions may bring about some conflicts between statuses of the individuals and their roles. Due to this disorganisation may set in. Thus, a disorganised society is characterised by an extreme uncertainty and ambiguity of social roles. *Example*: Due to the change in her status, a modern housewife in an advanced society is not sure whether she should play the role of mother, or an employee, or a light-hearted companion, a social leader, and so on. She may try to perform all roles assigned to her, but not successfully. Her failure to perform the roles successfully may lead to personal dissatisfaction, frustration and insecurity which may disrupt the family life.

Finally, it may be said that in any instance of social disorganisation the following conditions may be present in one way or another either individually or collectively. In most of the cases, they are found in a combined form. Those conditions are : (1) diversity of opinions; (2) heterogeneity of population; (3) mutual distrust; (4) uncertainty and insecurity; (5) individuality and variety in interests and attitudes; (6) emphasis on rights rather than on duties; (7) contradiction between status and function; (8) lack of clarity in status and roles; (9) conflict of mores and conflict between institutions; (10) absence of or decreased social control; (11) conflict between society and individual, and (12) disregard of values, norms and laws.

TYPES OF DISORGANISATION

Elliot and *Merrill* have spoken of three types of disorganisation which are, of course, interrelated. They are as follows :

(*i*) *Personal* or *Individual disorganisation* which includes crime, insanity, or mental derangement, prostitution, juvenile delinquency, alcoholism, drug addiction, gambling and suicide.

(*ii*) *Family Disorganisation* which consists of divorce, desertion, separation, broken home, unmarried mothers, illegitimate births and venereal disease.

(*iii*) *Community Disorganisation* which comprises of poverty, beggary, unemployment, overpopulation, lawlessness, political corruption, crime and so on.

CAUSES OF SOCIAL DISORGANISATION

A complex phenomenon such as social disorganisation is caused by a number of factors. These factors are so intermingled that it becomes difficult to say which of these are predominant. Different writers have highlighted the importance of different factors. *For example*, *Elliot* and *Merrill* have given four causes: (1) the social processes under the three main heads: cultural, political and economic, (2) cultural lag, (3) conflicting attitudes and values, and; (4) social crisis.

Sorokin is of the opinion that disorganisation is mainly due to cultural degeneration of values in various spheres such as art, science, philosophy, religion, law, politics, economics, family, etc. In brief, change from the "*idealistic*", and "*ideational*" culture to "*sensate culture*" is the main cause of social disorganisation.

G.R. Madan has listed a few factors that invite the problems of disorganisation. They may be briefly explained below:

1. ***Psychological factors:*** Sometimes, the cause of social disorganisation is to be found in the human psychology itself. Psychological factors contribute to disorganisation in two ways: (*i*) *Failure to maintain proper communication among fellow beings*, and (*ii*) *Failure to modify or change one 's attitudes in tune with the demands of time.*

   (*i*) *Communication* is an essential psychological process among human beings. It is maintained through the social processes such as imitation, cooperation, competition, suggestion, conflict, accommodation, asimilation, etc., which are also psychological in character. Common understanding and common consciousness help the people to maintain communication. Due to lack of common consensus regarding values and due to divergent attitudes people may fail to maintain proper communication among themselves. Words, ideas, phrases and symbols that they use in their communication may sound different things to them. Thus, lack of appropriate communication or its total failure may create ill-will, prejudice and lot of psychological distance among people.

(*ii*) *The problem of attitudes*. Human tendencies and attitudes are modified very slowly whereas culture is modified with comparative rapidity. The sociocultural environment may impose much requirements on individuals which they find it difficult to fulfil. *For example*, the modern industralised and urbanised society is so competitive that some find it extremely difficult to cope with. Similarly, the cultural conflict between the older and the younger generation may result in disorganisation of the adolescents, juvenile delinquency, and sometimes in family disorganisation. Conflicts of attitudes between the old and new values are always pregnant with trends of disorganisation.

2. ***Cultural lag:*** 'Cultural lag', the concept used by *W.E. Ogburn*, refers to the imbalance in the rate and speed of change between the material and non-material culture. Objects of material culture such as mode of housing, means of transport and communication, type of dresses, patterns of ornaments, technical and mechanical devices, instruments, etc., change very quickly. But ideas, beliefs, attitudes, tastes, philosophies, habits, ideologies, institutional structures and such other aspects of non-material culture change slowly and gradually. Hence a '*gap*' or a '*lag*' arises between the material and non-material culture. This lag, referred to as '*cultural lag*' invites the process of disorganisation to set in. *For example*, though a good number of Indians have adopted Western technology, they have not very much changed their traditional beliefs, attitudes and customs, etc. This quality has often led to some conflicts which have opened the doors for disorganisation.
3. ***Physical or geographic factors:*** The maladjustment of man and his culture to certain extra-ordinary physical or geographic conditions or situations may cause disorganisation in society. This is especially true in the case of natural calamities such as storms, cyclones, hurricanes, famines, floods, earthquakes, volcanoes, epidemics, etc., which upset the social balance and bring in social disorganisation.
4. ***Biological factor:*** Population explosion or extreme scarcity of population, the instances of racial intermixture, defective hereditary traits and such other biological factors may also cause disorganising effects upon society. *For example*, if overpopulation has caused the problems of poverty and unemployment in some countries, the fact of underpopulation has created a psychological crisis manifested in what is known as "*race extinction*".
5. ***Ecological factor:*** Social disorganisation is related to environment in terms of regions and neighbourhoods. *Professor Shaw* and his associates at the institute of *Juvenile Research in Chicago* found that the delinquency was unevenly distributed in the city of Chicago. They observed that the delinquents mostly concentrated in the areas of poor housing, overcrowding, and the areas in which cinema houses, hotels, night clubs, liquor shops, gambling centres were found in a large number. Some findings have revealed that per capita crime rate is relatively higher in larger cities than in smaller ones.
6. ***Social problems leading to social disorganisation:*** Social problems and forces such as – a revolution, a social upheaval, a class struggle, a financial or economic crisis, a war between nations, mental illness, political corruption, mounting unemployment and crime, etc., threaten the smooth working of society. The social problems are the diseases of the society and they threaten the welfare of the society. They may bring in disorganisation.
7. ***Degeneration of values:*** Social values are often regarded as the sustaining forces of society. They contribute to the strength and stability of social order. But due to rapid social change new values come up and some of the old values decline. At the same time, people are not in a position to reject the old completely and accept the new altogether. Here conflict between the old and the new is the inevitable result of which leads to the social disorganisation.

   Changes in social values necessitate new social institutions and associations. These come into conflict with the older existing ones. This creates disorder in society. The statuses and roles of people will have to change in accordance with the changes in social values. But they take time to adjust themselves to new situations. In this way, disorganisation spreads. According to *Sorakin,* the cause of social disorganisation is nothing but degeneration of values in various spheres such as art, science, philosophy, religion, law, politics, economics, family, etc., which has lead to more wars, criminality, revolution, suicide, mental diseases, etc.

8. ***Disintegration and confusion of roles*:** Members of society are expected to perform certain definite roles in accordance with their placements in society. Due to profound social changes these expectations also undergo a change. Consequently, people are confused with regard to their new roles. *Professor Faris* considers this as the most important cause of disorganisation. According to him, it is due to the transition from pre-industrial folk society to modern complex society. *For example*, children are to be cared for and essential cultural education be given to them by the family members. The economic order is assumed to provide for the production and distribution of goods and wealth. The religious institutions are expected to maintain the religious heritage and to pass on the same to succeeding generation. When any of these functions are not properly fulfilled, disorganisation may be the result.
9. ***Political subordination:*** Political subordination of one country to another leads to social disorganisation in the former. The vanquished country is not allowed to develop its economy and institution in its own Ways. It is made a means to serve the interests of the dominant country. India suffered under the British rule in the same manner. The dominant country may not even care for the basic needs such as — food, clothing, shelter, basic education, medical facility, etc., of the people of slave country. As a result, the slave country may have to face a number of socio-economic problems.

***Other Factors*:** In addition to the above, a few other factors may also cause disorganisation.

(*a*) *Conflict of goals and means.* Conflict of goals and the means for achieving them may also cause disorganisation. Most of the individuals share the dominant goals of the society and act accordingly. But lacking the means for achieving the goals by legitimate means, some may resort to illegitimate and illegal means resulting in vice, crime and other expression of social disorganisation.

(*b*) *Decline of social control.* The declining control of religion, morals, customs, traditions, and other institutions on the behaviour of men has also enhanced the process of disorganisation. Hence we witness an increase in interpersonal conflicts, crimes, tensions, divorce, delinquency, mental derangement, etc. In fact, according to Thomas and *Znaniecki*, the very "*decrease of the influence of existing rule of behaviour upon the individual members of the group*" itself indicates social disorganisation.

(*c*) *Extreme divisions of labour.* According to *Emile Durkhem*, social disorganisation is often brought about by extreme division of labour. In normal course, according to him, division of labour leads to social solidarity, but when it becomes extreme and very complex, solidarity may become disturbed.

(*d*) *Disruptive social change.* Society undergoes change mainly due to the operation of physical, biological, technological and cultural factors. Sudden and radical social changes may, sometimes, disrupt the stability and the organisation of the society. The result is social disorganisation.

REMEDIAL MEASURES

To face the challenges of social disorganisation it is necessary first of all to study the nature and gravity of social disorganisation. Depending on its nature steps should be taken to counteract its influence. In this connection we may suggest the following remedial measures:

1. Able and efficient administration to flight against the disruptive forces.
2. Proper and comprehensive social and economic planning and policies.
3. Proper implementation of the plans and policies.
4. Organised social work and social welfare activities and social security measures.
5. Appropriate steps to rehabilitate and reform the beggars, criminals, juvenile delinquents, prostitutes mentally and physically handicapped, the aged and the diseased persons,
6. Effective enforcement of land reforms and fixing a ceiling on urban property,
7. Making effective and attractive family planning and welfare programmes and projects,

9. Providing ample educational and employment opportunities especially for the spread of diseases;

10. To create a psychological atmosphere of security and confidence, assuring and providing social equality, justice, and liberty to all.
11. Taking steps to mobilise public opinion against the evil practices of bribery, corruption, casteism, communalism, racism, exploitation, etc.
12. Instilling in the minds of people sentiments of unity, solidarity, patriotism and nationalism by making use of mass media of communication in the best possible manner.

REVIEW QUESTIONS

1. Explain the concept of social disorganisation.
2. Differentiate between social organisation and social disorganisation.
3. Define social disorganisation. Bring out its characteristic features.
4. What is social disorganisation? Explain the types of social disorganisation.
5. Examine the causes of social disorganisation.
6. Discuss the various factors which led to social disorganisation.

⌘⌘⌘⌘⌘⌘⌘⌘⌘⌘⌘

44

JUVENILE DELINQUENCY, YOUTH UNREST AND PROBLEMS OF AGED

CHAPTER OUTLINE

- JUVENILE DELINQUENCY: MEANING — DEFINITION — CAUSES — REMEDIES
- YOUTH UNREST: CAUSES — TYPES — GROWTH OF YOUTH UNREST IN INDIA—STUDENT UNREST AND POLITICAL PARTIES — REMEDIES
- PROBLEMS OF AGED: PSYCHOLOGICAL AND SOCIOCULTURAL SIDES OF THE PROBLEM — REMEDIAL MEASURES

JUVENILE DELINQUENCY

Juvenile delinquency is one of the serious problems of the mess society. It is almost an outcome of rapid urbanisation and industrialisation of modern times. Social conditions associated with these two processes have affected the family pattern. This resulted in an atmosphere that is favourable to the growth of juvenile delinquency. A large number of children moving from rural areas to the cities or living in slums in cities are found to be highly vulnerable to this process. This has almost become a universal problem in most of the industrialised countries including India. *Mr. G.C. Dutt* observes, "*Juvenile delinquency is rapidly becoming a serious menace in India and with the progressive industrialisation of many parts of the country....... this problem will soon assume the same proportions as in many of the Western Countries*".

Meaning of Juvenile Delinquency

Delinquency is a kind of abnormality. When an individual deviates from the course of normal social life, his behaviour is called "*delinquency*". When a juvenile, below an age specified under a statute exhibits behaviour which may prove to be dangerous to society and/or to himself he may be called a '*Juvenile delinquent*'. Each state has its own precise definition of the age range covered by the word '*juvenile*'.

Definitions of Juvenile Delinquency

1. *Cyril Burt* defines delinquency as occurring in a child "When his antisocial tendencies appear so grave that he becomes or ought to become the subject of official action".
2. *Friedlander* says, "Delinquency is a juvenile misconduct that might be dealt with under the law".
3. *The Second United Nations Congress on the Prevention of Crime and Treatment of Offenders* (1960) states, "By juvenile delinquency should be understood the commission of an act which, if committed by an adult, would be considered a crime."

4. *C.B. Mamoria* writes, "The phrase 'juvenile delinquency' may be loosely used to cover any kind of deviant behaviour of children which violates normative rules, understanding or expectations "of social system".
5. In simple words, it can be said that *juvenile delinquency is a type of abnormal or antisocial behaviour by a juvenile who is below an age specified by statute.*

Who is a Juvenile Delinquent?

Juvenile delinquents are those offenders including boys and girls who are normally under 16 years of age. A juvenile delinquent is a young person incorrigible, or habitually disobedient. Acts of delinquency may include (1) running away from home without the permission of parents, (2) habitual truancy beyond the control of parents, (3) spending time idly beyond limits, (4) use of vulgar languages, (5) wandering about rail-roads, streets, market places, (6) visiting gambling centres, (7) committing sexual offences, (8) shop-lifting, (9) stealing etc. Juveniles may do such activities singly or through a gang.

Causes of Juvenile Delinquency

There is no single cause or simple explanation for the development of delinquent behaviour. According to *Healy* and *Bronner*, the causes of juvenile delinquency are: (l) Bad company, (2) adolescent instability and impulses, (3) early sex experience, (4) mental conflicts, (5) extreme social suggestibility, (6) love of adventure, (7) motion picture, (8) school dissatisfaction, (9) poor recreation, (l0) street life, (11) vocational dissatisfaction, (12) sudden impulse; and (13) physical conditions of all sorts.

The causes of juvenile delinquency may be classified under two major factors: (1) *Social factors*, and (2) *Personality factors*.

Social Factors Favouring Juvenile Delinquency

1. ***Broken homes:*** British and American investigations reveal that nearly 50% of the delinquents come from broken homes. In one of the studies conducted by *Uday Shankar* in India only 13.3% of the 140 delinquents that he studied came from broken homes — (1–34). This shows the cultural differences between Indian and the Western countries. Still it can be said that broken homes and families, lack of parental affection and security, absence of a loving mother in the childhood or an affectionate mother substitute, lack of family ties, parental irresponsibility and a steep rate in divorce, desertion and separation are all contributory factors to delinquency.

   The home may be broken up by death of one or both of the parents, or by prolonged illness or insanity, desertion or divorce. Interaction in home is a very important means for socialising the child. The mother plays vital role in this regard. If she divorces her husband or deserts him or dies, the growth of the child will be affected. Such a child loses not only mother's love but also parental control and becomes an easy victim to the outside anti-societal influence. It cannot, however, be said that broken home *invariably* leads to delinquent behaviour on the part of the children.
2. ***Poverty:*** A very large proportion of delinquent children come from poor homes. It is generally, although not unanimously, accepted by professional students of juvenile delinquency that the vast majority of delinquents come from the lower class. They commit their offences as member of gangs. *Uday Shankar's* study has revealed that as many as 83% of the children come from poor families. Still it cannot be generalised that the children of the poor homes *invariably* become delinquents.

   Poverty compels sometimes both of the parents to be outside the home for a very long period to earn their daily bread. The children will be uncared for. Such children may consciously or unconsciously join hands with gangsters and become delinquents. This mostly happens in slum areas and areas in which mostly working class people live.
3. ***Delinquency areas:*** It is said that some areas are highly vulnerable to delinquent/trends. Long ago *Burt* in his study showed that there are certain areas in London from which the majority of delinquent children come. The delinquents mostly come from the areas of poor housing, overcrowding and the areas in which cinema houses, hotels, night clubs, liquor shops are found in a large number. It is true that when a family is living in the heart of the town the chances are greater for the children of such families to pick up delinquent behaviour. It is to be noted that not all the children living in the delinquent areas are delinquents.
4. ***Companions and gangs:*** As the child grows older he goes into the neighbourhood and becomes a member of the playgroup or peer group. If by chance he joins the group or the gang that fosters delinquent attitudes he is also

likely to become a delinquent. In fact, much delinquency springs up from the prevalent attitudes in the groups within which the youth has immediate contacts. *Charles Shaw* has opined that "*delinquency is a product of community forces*"

In cities, in slum areas peculiar social groups called 'gangs' are found. Generally the gang starts as a playgroup. In the absence of playground facilities, the children will start playing in streets and finally organise themselves into gangs. The gang has all the qualities of an ingroup such as loyalty, cooperation, social solidarity and unity. These gangs are found to be associated with crime in all its aspects like delinquency, rioting, corrupt politics, and so on. Children coming from poor families and broken families easily become the victims of gangs.

Due to *bad companionship* also offences are committed by the adolescents. Studies have shown that delinquent acts are done in company. In his *Illinois Crime Survey of 1928 Shaw* analysed 6000 boys were involved in the crime. He found that in 90% of the cases two or more boys were involved in the crime. But in *Uday Shankar's* study in India only 23% of persons committed delinquent acts due to bad company. It cannot, however, be presumed that mere companionship by itself causes delinquency.

Beggary: Beggary is often the cause of juvenile delinquency. Child beggars mostly come from either very poor families or broken homes. These children are betrayed of the needed love and affection of the parents. They crave for the satisfaction of their inner impulses, desires and ambitions. They choose to become beggars for the same. As beggars they get annoyed to see others enjoying life. Some of them may even become rebels. They realise that only through deviant practices, they can satisfy their desires and meet their needs. They thus become delinquents.

Other Social or Environmental Factors

1. ***School dissatisfaction***: Some students get dissatisfied with school life. Parental irresponsibility, unmanageable student-teacher ratio, lack of entertainment and sports facilities in schools, indifference of the teachers may contribute to this. Such dissatisfied students become regular absentees in schools and start wandering in streets. They may even form gangs of their own and become gamblers, eve-teasers, pickpockets, drunkards, smokers and drug addicts.
2. ***Films and pornographic literature*** have also added to the magnitude of delinquency. Cinema, television and obscene literature may often provoke sexual and other impulses in adolescents. Hence they may start their 'adventure' in satisfying them in the process of which they commit crimes.
3. ***Deep-seated inner desires*** coupled with *outside pressures*, *compulsions* and *temptations* also contribute to juvenile delinquency. *For example*, on hearing the interesting narration of the illicit sex experiences or such other criminal experiences from one's gangmate, one may be tempted to follow the same.

Personal or Individual Factors

Personal factors such as mental deficiency and emotional disturbances may also contribute to juvenile delinquency.

1. ***Mental deficiency in delinquency.*** It has been observed that good number of delinquents are mentally deficient. Studies have revealed that there is larger proportion of mentally defectives in the juvenile delinquent group than among the normal children. The relationship between intelligence and delinquent behaviour has been studied carefully. The average intelligence in a normal group of children is 100 I.Q. (Intelligence Quotient). But *Burt* in his study in London reported that the average I.Q. of delinquent children is 85, and Uday Shankar found that it was 83. These and many other studies have revealed that the average intelligence of the juvenile delinquents is certainly lower than the average intelligence of the normal group of children of the same age.
   It is quite natural to assume that the dull and mentally handicapped or defective adolescents do not have the necessary insight to make distinctions between '*right*' and '*deviant*' methods and behaviour Such children are often used by the more intelligent children of the gang or the adults for their criminal purpose.
2. ***Emotional problems of the individual.*** Mental troubles and emotional maladjustments are strong factors in delinquency. Emotional problems of inferiority, jealousy and being thwarted are very common among the delinquent children. *Healy* and *Bronner* in their study of 143 delinquents found that 92% of them revealed emotional disturbances. It is reported that in America about two-thirds of juvenile delinquents suffer from emotional personality and mental deviations. Thus from the psychological point of view "*Delinquency is a rebellion and an expression of aggression which is aimed at destroying, breaking down or changing the environment"*. This rebellion is mostly against the social conditions which deny the individual his basic rights and the satisfaction of his fundamental needs. Thus,

delinquents are not born so, but they become so due to social circumstances and personal deficiencies. They are mostly maladjusted persons.

According to psychoanalytic view, the delinquent is an individual who is governed by the "*pleasure principle*" He wants to get immediate pleasure and immediate satisfaction for his needs. So he becomes a victim to his own impulses. He is neither able to control his impulses nor able to imagine to think the consequences of his actions. 'It is also said that delinquent breakdown is an escape from emotional situation for some particular individuals with peculiar individual and family background. Some emotionally maladjusted children become delinquents to get the attention of their parents or as a protest against their treatment.

Thus, it may be said that juvenile delinquency is the result of both social or environmental and personal or individual factors.

Remedies for Juvenile Delinquency

The problem of juvenile delinquency is one that has drawn the attention of society. It is known that the *delinquent child of today may turn out to be a chronic criminal tomorrow*. Discussions, debates and studies have been made at the national as well as international levels by scholars to seek out effective remedy for this problem. Two methods have been suggested to deal with this problem: (A) *Preventive method*, and (B) *rehabilitative or curative method*. In the former, factors leading to delinquency are to be tackled, and in the latter, those who have committed delinquent acts are to be helped to become normal citizens.

Preventive Measures

In order to prevent juvenile delinquency from taking place the following measures may be suggested:

1. Creating and inspiring a team of work of private and public agencies devoted to preventive work.
2. Giving proper training to the members and staff of all organisations concerned with delinquency control.
3. Establishing child guidance clinics to give appropriate treatment to the disturbed and maladjusted children.
4. Educating of the family so as to help the parents to realise the importance of giving proper attention to the needs of their young children.
5. Establishing wholesome recreational agencies to prevent young children from becoming the victims of illicit or unwholesome recreation.
6. Giving proper assistance to under-privileged children to build in them good character and law-abiding attitude.
7. Adopting various means of propaganda such as radio, movies, television, newspapers, magazines etc., to realise the importance of law-abidingness and how it is always appreciated and rewarded.
8. Improving the social environment— slum areas, busy market places, gambling centres etc., to prevent children to get polluted.
9. Spotting potential delinquents by predictive tests in schools and giving appropriated treatment to such children.
10. The problems of beggary and poverty are to be removed or controlled and the general economic standards of the people must be increased to prevent children from becoming delinquents due to economic exigencies.

Method of Rehabilitation

The main purpose of the method of rehabilitation is not to punish nor to take revenge upon the delinquent. The intention behind this method is to help the delinquent children to get proper guidance and training so that they become normal children and never repeat delinquent acts. The measures taken for the prevention and treatment of juvenile delinquency in India after 1850 may be briefly examined here:

1. *Legislative measures.* Various legislations have been made in India from time to time to deal with juvenile delinquency. Some of them may be briefed here.

(*a*) *Apprentices Act of 1850.* This Act has been the earliest step taken in the direction of preventing delinquency. The Act provides for the binding of children, both boys and girls, between the ages of 10 to 18 as apprentices. Orphans and poor children could take the benefit of this Act. Employers could take such children as apprentices with the intention of training them in some trade, craft or employment by which they gain a livelihood later. The father or guardian may bind a child above 10 and under 18 upto 21 years of age for a period not exceeding

7 years. A female child may be so bound until her marriage. The Act also dealt with children who committed petty offences.

(b) *Reformatory Schools Act of 1897.* This Act can be considered a landmark in the history of treatment of delinquency. This Act is in force in almost all the states of India. Under this Act courts were empowered to send for detention youthful male offenders to Reformatory School for a period of not more than three years. It could be extended to seven also. No person may be detained in it after he attains the 18th years. In conformity with this Act the State Governments may establish and maintain Reformatory Schools to help the delinquents to get speedy recovery. Every school must provide sanitary arrangements, water supply, food, clothing, bedding, industrial training and medical aid to the inmates. These Reformatory Schools are reported to have done useful work.

(c) *Provision in the Criminal Procedure Code.* Under Section 399 of the Indian Criminal Procedure Code (ICPC) convicted young offenders below the age of 15 could be sent to Reformatory Schools established by the State Government. Section 562 of the C.P.C. also permitted discharge of certain convicted offenders on probation. It also permitted their release with advice. Under Section 82 of the Indian Penal Code children under seven cannot be held responsible for their criminal acts. Section 83 of the same Code relaxes this age upto 12 under some conditions.

(d) *Children Acts.* Various provinces of India took interest in making some comprehensive laws in 1920 and afterwards to deal with delinquent children. Of these, Children Acts enacted by Madras in 1920 and followed by other States, are more important. The main provisions of Children Act are as follows:

(1) No child under 14 years of age can be imprisoned under any circumstances and no young person between 14-16 years of age can be imprisoned unless he is certified to be an unruly person.

(2) Except in the case of grave offences any person arrested on a charge and is below 16, is required to be released or bailed. In any case such persons could not be kept in Jails.

(3) The child or youthful offender cannot be sentenced to death or imprisonment except under extraordinary conditions. Persons below 12 are to be sent to Junior Certified Schools and 12 to 16 Senior Certified Schools.

(4) The court may discharge the person after due admonition, it may hand him over to his parents or guardians after taking a bond from them that they would be responsible for his good behaviour for 12 months.

(e) *Juvenile smoking acts.* Some Acts to deal with the specific pattern of antisocial behaviour among children have also been passed. Of these the Juvenile Smoking Acts are in force in most of the states. This Act prohibits the sale of tobacco by children below 16. Children below 16 are not supposed to smoke in public places according to this Act. (But these Acts were never enforced in any of the States).

(f) *Suppression of immoral traffic acts.* These Acts are passed in order to protect young girls and to suppress prostitution. The Acts prohibit certain practices connected with prostitution such as soliciting in public places, using residential premises for running brothels, forcibly detaining young women in brothels, etc. Provisions are also made to protect girls from brothels or from moral danger.

(g) *Probation of offenders act.* Under these Acts Juvenile Courts can place the youthful offenders under the supervision of probation officers.

(h) *Borstal schools acts for adolescents.* These acts were passed to give a special treatment for adolescent offenders, that is, offenders between l5 and 21 years of age. A Borstal School is a corrective institution and is one in which the offenders are subject to disciplinary and moral influences; These influences would help their reform.

Institutions to Rehabilitate Juvenile Delinquents

Preventive measures alone are not enough. Rehabilitative or reformative measures are also needed to solve juvenile delinquency. Some of the institutions aimed at rehabilitating the juvenile delinquents are there in India. They may be briefly examined here

1. ***Juvenile courts:*** Juvenile Courts are established in order to treat separately juvenile delinquents from other adult criminals. Juvenile Courts have their own building, judicial bench and other arrangements. Juvenile delinquents cannot be tried in ordinary courts. Whenever the juvenile courts are not there they could however be tried in other

courts but on a separate day and at a fixed time so as to keep them separately from other adult criminals. Juvenile offenders cannot be chained and they cannot be produced to the courts by the police in their uniform. No advocates are needed to plead for them. The main intention behind this special treatment is to create positive feelings in the minds of juveniles. As per the report of the Union Ministry of Education, in 1950 there were only 39 Juvenile Courts in India.

2. ***Remand homes:*** When a child is arrested under the Act, he is produced before the magistrate within 24 hours and kept in Remand Home till the case is investigated. The child is kept in Remand Home until the final disposal of the case. Sometimes persons convicted are sent to Remand Homes for a few days and released later. These homes are mostly managed by Private Welfare agencies with the governmental assistance. The precise number of such Remand Homes in India is not known.
3. ***Certified schools:*** Certified Schools are established mainly to give some general education and technical training to the children. Here the children are sent for long-term treatment. They are run by voluntary bodies or local authorities with the financial assistance of the government and the public. There are two types of schools: (*i*) *Junior Schools for boys under 12 and* (*ii*) *Senior Schools for boys under 16*. The children are confined here for about 2 to 3 years. The school authorities can also make early discharge. After their release they are put under the charge of a Welfare or Probation Officer who watches their activities.
4. ***Auxiliary homes:*** These Auxiliary Homes are attached to Certified Schools just like remand homes. Here the convicted delinquents are kept for some time and studied by a social worker. Later on they are sent to certified schools depending upon the nature and attitude of the young offender.
5. ***Foster homes:*** Foster Homes are mostly run by the voluntary agencies and the governments give grants to them. They are specially created for delinquent children under 19 who cannot be sent to approved or certified schools.
6. ***Reformatory schools:*** In states where there are no Children Acts, Reformatory Schools are established. They are meant for the education and vocational training of delinquent children. The young convicted offenders below 15 years are detained here for 3 to 7 years. The delinquents are removed from bad environments through these schools.
7. ***Borstal institutions:*** Under Borstal system special treatment is provided for adolescent offenders between the age of 15 to 21 years. Borstal institutions are of two types: (*i*) *open type* and (*ii*) *closed type*. 'Open' institution is a camp in the open country with no surrounding wall. Closed institution is a converted prison building in which maximum security is given to inmates. Though it is called 'Closed' institution most of its activities meant for children are carried on outside the building.

   Young offenders are very often sent to Borstal institution for rehabilitation rather than kept under imprisonment. The term of Borstal is 2 to 3 years and in any case it should not exceed 5 years. If the offenders are found to be unruly and incorrigible they are sent to jails. Separate arrangement is there to give training to boys and girls. The training, physical exercises and education that are given here are very tough so as to prevent the inmates from committing offences again.
8. ***Fit persons institutions and uncared children institutions***: These are the two non-government institutions managed by private bodies and philanthropists. These institutions give refuge and protection to the destitutes, neglected children, children in the pre-delinquent stage, and to the delinquent children. Such children and their activities are supervised by the appointed officers.

Conclusion

A grave problem such as juvenile delinquency cannot be solved by means of legislations and government efforts alone. As far as India is concerned in many of the states Children Acts have not been effectively enforced. Some of these Acts themselves have defects. Official machinery is not effectively used for controlling this problem. Governmental as well as private agencies must work hand in hand with all sincerity and seriousness to find an effective remedy for the problem of juvenile delinquency. The public attitude towards juvenile delinquents must also change. A juvenile delinquent is a product of unwholesome environment congenial for the development of his faculties in conformity with social expectations.

YOUTH UNREST

'*Youth unrest*' which is often described as '*student revolt*', '*student power*' and '*student activism*'–has become today an established fact, a reality. The last three decades have witnessed innumerable outbursts of student power in many nations of the world.

Youth Unrest: A World Phenomenon

The phenomenon of '*youth unrest*' has become worldwide. As *Gareth Stedman Jonse* has rightly observed: "From Berlin to Peking, from Tokyo to New York, in Paris and in Prague, the rise of these movements (student movements) has altered the nature of politics. Virtually, every government has some reason to fear its students, with good reason. From Cuba in 1958 to Czechoslovakia and France in 1968 students have played a crucial role in political change, again and again helping to discredit, transform or topple governments. Students have erupted in the world of politics with a suddenness no one could have foretold". The students are today a new social force of incalculable significance.

The student power seems to have an anti-establishment and a revolutionary tone. In **Germany**, the *Socialist Student Union* (S.D.S.) declared the students' lack of confidence in political parties and parliament and justified their "*taking democracy into the streets*". In **Italy**, student strikes accompanied by an 'anti university' stance marked the happening at Turia and other universities including those of Rome, Naples, Bologna, etc. In Feb. 1968, the disturbances in the Belgian University of Louviah contributed directly to the fall of the Belgian Government. In **Czechoslovakia**, in the movement towards liberalism the students and the youth union joined hands with the workers in "*heralding the democratic revolution*". In **America**, the anti-Vietnam and civil rights issues brought about confrontation between the students and authorities. The students were led by the S.D.S–*Students for a Democratic Society*. In May-June 1968, **France** saw battles between demonstrators and police and violent attack of students and workers. Students boycotted examinations in Sorbonne and occupied the buildings. When the crisis was over, the Minister of Education was no longer in the Government for he had to resign. It is said that this event accelerated the downfall of De Gaulle. In **England**, the London School of Economics was the scene of confrontation between the radicals and the authori- ties. In **Indonesia**, the partnership of the students and the army militated against Communism and brought about the fall of the Soekarno regime. Japan has witnessed the most massive demonstrations by students. In **Bangladesh**, the students played a key role in its liberation movement joining hands with the Mukti Bahini.

Youth Unrest in India

In **India** the student activism has erupted in different forms and for totally unconnected reasons in different parts of the country. A quarrel between the staff of the bus transport and a group of students in Jabalpur led to massive demonstrations and strikes in the whole of M.P. and U.P. some time ago. A change in the method of payment of examination fees resulted in total strike in Lucknow university. A demand for a steel plant brought the Andhra students on the street. Vietnam has always provided an early opportunity to the Calcutta students to agitate. Demand for an Agricultural University gave rise to a massive agitation in the Vidarbha regions of Maharashtra. A demand for reforms in the Agricultural University was the reason behind agitation in Jammu and Kashmir. A few rusticated student leaders aided by the 'disgruntled politicians' brought the closure of the Banaras Hindu University. A rivalry between student factions, one supporting the Vice-Chancellor and the other, Chief Minister of Andhra Pradesh in the Osmania University was said to be the real beginning of the Telengana agitation. Anti-Hindi agitation and the Expo–70 agitation resulted in the closure of all the Colleges in Karnataka. Semester system was the target of attack for the students of the Mysore University some years back. The '*Nav Nirman Andolan*' of Gujarat (which toppled down Chimanbhai Patel's Government ultimately gave birth to the *Chhatra Sangharsha Samities* guided, inspired and led by Late Sri Jayaprakash Narayan and the Assam agitation spearheaded by the *All Assam Students Union* (being supported by the Gana Sangrama Parishad) have been the recent examples of student agitation of semi-political nature. Barring a few successful agitations the student solidarity has failed to be peaceful in its agitations.

Causes of Youth Unrest

Student unrest in this country has earned a peculiar connotation because of the unprecedented social dimension achieved by the student leadership at least in some instances. *The unrest is there no doubt but the student movement is not in sight anywhere*. The leftist slogan of the sixties, '*Students today and workers tomorrow*' seems to have become hollow. The students are no more visualised as '*Vanguards in a revolution led by and controlled under the hegemony of the working class*'. The students do not constitute a 'revolutionary class' as such. 'The promise held out by the activism in the sixties was, however, belied by the apathy in the seventies'. The American strident activism has slowly evaporated. The Japanese student enthusiasm has gone dormant. The student energy in India is dissipated. Lack of proper leadership, absence of clear national goal, lack of guidance and inspiring model have all made the youth power in India become idle.

Youth Unrest: A Reflection of Society!

It is true that *social situation breeds frustration*. It is also true that there is no national goal beckoning the spirit of the youth. It is a fact that the present education has failed to give any direction or purpose to the life of the student. The student is always asked to behave without any guidance as to how he should behave. He has tremendous energy but there is no consciousness as to his rights and responsibilities. By and large, he is apathetic, drawn in struggle only when mass frenzy grips his mind. There is no connection between his struggle for survival and the education which is supposed to help him in the matter. He is not interested in knowledge in the abstract. He goes to the college because he has no alternative. He must get a degree if he has to 'make it'. He has no options. '*Therefore, his only aim is to get in, get out and get on with it*'. The university is no more an isolated community of scholars but is more community of young people. The reality of the world today involves serious problems and the universities just are not doing much about it.

Factors of Youth Unrest

Various factors have contributed to the problems of youth unrest. Some of them may be noted here.

1. ***Improper socialisation and family problems:*** The failure on the part of parents to bring up their children, in accordance with the culture expectations of the society has made the youth to go astray. The evil habits and bad qualities of the parents also have a harmful effect on the personality growth of the children. The family problems spoil the mental peace and the emotionality of the growing children.
2. ***Political, social and economic inequalities:*** The young people are more sensitive to the political, economic and social inequalities and exploitation. They have contempt for the existing 'system'. They are disillusioned with what they are having and are *pessimistic* about the future.
3. ***Defective educational system:*** The students do not have any respect for the present defective educational system. The outdated, uninspiring, unintegrated and irrelevant educational system cannot make the students to become disciplined and responsible.
4. ***Unemployment:*** The unemployment of the educated youths is on the increase. The education that they receive does not enable them to become economically self-reliant. On the other hand, the government is not in a position to provide employment to all the educated youth. As a result, the youth are losing confidence in themselves and are becoming more and more restless.
5. ***Corrupt and discredited authority:*** The youth are disappointed with the corrupt and discredited authority. Corruption, craziness for power, moral lapses, opportunism, nepotism, discrimination, etc., found among the political and social leaders has made the youth to have nothing but contempt for them. The leadership has failed to set a good model for the students to emulate.
6. ***Misuse of student power by the politicians:*** The corrupt and unscrupulous politicians who are making use of student power to further their partisan political interests, are also contributing to the problem. Students are becoming puppets in the hands of some disgruntled politicians to serve their selfish ends.
7. ***Administrative failures:*** Youth unrest is often caused by administrative errors and miscalculations. The indifference and lack of sympathy for the student demands on the part of the administrations (of the university as well as the government) many times force the students, to resort to strikes.
8. ***Communication gap:*** Lack of understanding and lack of proper communication between the students and teachers on the one hand, parents and children on the other, also cause youth unrest. The failure on the part of the parents to understand the aspirations of their young children also adds to the problem.
9. ***Value differences and conflict of values:*** The value differences in society, the changes and conflicts of values also contribute to youth unrest. (*i*) Some of the old values are at conflict now. The traditional beliefs, practices, ideas, ideals and values appear to be outmoded; unscientific, irrelevant and irrational for the modern youths. (*ii*) The youths are becoming more and more rationalistic. They are impressed by the modern values based on science and rationalism. Still, they are not in a position to give up the traditional values completely. They are in a state of confusion. They can neither accept the new completely nor do away with the old once and for all. This has made them to become restless. (*iii*) The youth are influenced by values of individualism and democracy. Hence they are revolting against the old traditional order. (*iv*) The youths feel they are also matured, responsible and sensible. They resent their elders treating them as '*immatured*' and '*irresponsible lot*'. They feel annoyed and embarrassed to find themselves in a helpless situation. They do not want to remain dumb witnesses to all the unfortunate and

unwanted events that happen in society, (v) Some of the youths are carried away by the hedonistic values or pleasure philosophy. They want to take the maximum benefit out of the disturbed social situations. They have no respect for any values for they have lost faith in them.

10. ***Lack of opportunities:*** The youths do not get proper opportunities, to express their talents, cultivate their interests and develop their personality. This has contributed to their dissatisfaction.
11. ***Gap between the aspirations and achievement:*** The youths are likely to have their own aspirations and ambitions. They will be dreaming about it all the while. But the reality of life makes them to become disgusted. The youths with unfulfilled desires and aspirations can hardly be at rest.
12. ***Lack of determination and self-responsibility:*** Some of the youths lack will power and self-determination. They depend more, on others rather than on their intrinsic abilities and talents. They apishly imitate others and fail to develop the spirit of self-reliance. They are hesitant to assume responsibilities. Such youths are highly vulnerable for any kind of use.
13. ***Influence of movies:*** The modern movies which mostly portray violence, arson, loot, rape, murder, immorality, crimes, etc. have a great demoralising effect on the modern youths. Students, in particular, imitate their pet film actors and actresses with all their frailties. Scant respect for their cultural values and the apish imitation of the Western tendencies have further contributed to the problem.

Types of Youth Unrest

The youth unrest has assumed different forms. In no country, the youth unrest takes place for the same reason and assumes the same form all the time. The nature of youth unrest is that it is unsteady, irregular and sometimes happens spontaneously. *Myron Weiner* has classified the student unrest into four types.

Myron Weiner's Classification of Youth Unrest

According to *Myron Weiner*, the so called student indiscipline or youth unrest assumes four forms. They are as follows:

1. ***Political activities and movements.*** In some instances, youth unrest is associated with the larger political movements. Students often take up political issues and join hands with other non-youth organisations and political parties and fight for them. Students have participated in various political movements launched for issues such as — border disputes, steel plant location, price rise, water dispute, anti-Hindi and anti-English agitations, emergency, postponement of elections, dismissal of ministers, etc. They have taken out processions, staged demonstrations, gheraoed ministers, resorted to violence and conflicted with police authorities.
2. ***Student agitations for educational causes.*** Students have agitated for educational causes also. Students have agitated demanding the appointment of lecturers, enough supply of laboratory equipments and library books, cancellation of donation and capitation fees, reforms in examination system and type of question papers, retainment of carry over system, recognition of the student union, participation of students in University administrative bodies such as senate, syndicate, academic councils, postponement of examination, etc.
3. ***Agitations against non-university authorities.*** Students have agitated for non-educational, and non-political causes also. *For example*, they have agitated demanding special concessions for travelling in buses and trains, concessions in commercial recreational centres.
4. ***Spontaneous student agitations.*** Sometimes, students do agitate suddenly in an unexpected manner. They may quarrel with bus conductors, auto-rickshaw drivers, hotel-owners, police and public servants, and may even go on strike against them. These agitations can be treated as spontaneous outbursts of youth force. If these agitations are not handled carefully they may be intensified and prolonged in still worse a way.

Growth of Youth Unrest in India

The youth unrest in India started in the beginning of the 20th Century. Unorganised youth movements were taking place here and there. Most of them were directed against the British rule in India. The youths joined hands with the people in launching protest movements against the British. They played an important role in the freedom struggle.

Role of Students in Indian National Movement

The students took part in the Indian freedom struggle on a very wide scale for the first time when Lord Curzon partitioned Bengal in 1905. Since then, the students have been taking part in all the major national struggles. The youths were mainly behind the Indian National Congress at that time. When the Congress was split into two groups of extremists and moderates in its *Lahore Session* in *1907*, the students also distributed between these groups. They rallied round the leadership of *Bal Gangadhar Tilak* and later on, *of Mahatma Gandhiji*. Under the leadership and guidance of Gandhiji the students became a formidable force in India.

Role of Gandhiji in Student Unrest

After his return from South Africa, Gandhiji entered politics, *i.e.*, the freedom struggle in 1919 on the advice of his "*political guru*" *Gopalakrishna Gokhale*. Gandhiji launched his campaign against *Rowlatt Act* (1919), the *Jallianwalla Bagh* atrocities in 1919 in which the students had taken part in a big number. Gandhiji called the nation to wage a passive resistance movement against the govern- ment; to boycott all things British, break links with the government, resign from posts, surrender titles and offices, and withdraw from schools and colleges. The nation responded promptly and the students in a very big number boycotted schools and colleges. For the first time, the student force was organised and immobilised against the British rule.

In 1920, the First *All-India Students' Conference* was held in Nagpur under the Presidentship of *Lala Lajpat Rai*. Students could now, get the support and guidance of leaders like *Pandit Nehru*, *Subhas Chandra Bose* and others. Students took an active role in various campaigns launched by Gandhiji against the British such as — the 'No Tax' Campaign 1921, the Civil Disobedience Movement, the Dandi Satyagraha of 1930, etc. They also took interest in Gandhiji's constructive programmes such as—removal of untouchability and casteism, adult education, popularising the 'Swadeshi' articles and the use of 'Khadii, cleaning of the villages, promotion of communal harmony, and so on.

In 1936, The *All-India Students 'Federation*, the first student organisation of India, was born in order to support the Indian National Congress in its struggles. The followers of Gandhiji and also the communists supported this organisation in the beginning. Due to the clash of personalities and differences of opinion regarding its-principles the Students' Federation was divided into two factions (in 1938) such as — the *All-Indian Youth Congress* and *All-India Students' Federation* (AISF). The Socialists within the Congress and the Gandhians supported the former, while the Communists who wanted to follow the violent methods took into their hands the latter. Since then, the AISF is in the hands of the Communists.

Role of Students in the Quit India Movement of 1942

The '*Quit India*' Movement launched by the Indian National Congress under the Leadership of Gandhiji, was an important event in the Indian Freedom Struggle. The students participation in the freedom struggle took a new dimension in this movement. It was almost the climax of the youth movement. Students in the nook and corner of India took part in it. They came out of the schools and colleges and universities and boycotted the educational institutions. They organised mass processions and rallies in the towns and cities. They educated the uneducated and ignorant masses to fight for the cause of the nation.

The students took to some violent actions to paralyse the British administration. They resorted to such methods as cutting telephone wires, blocking transport routes, destroying public property, disturbing postal, police, banking and other services. They ransacked government offices, burnt official documents and *gheraoed* police stations. They brought the government machinery to a stand still. They also kept in touch with the underground leaders and carried on the tempo of agitation. The British Government resorted to suppressive measures. The police lathicharged on student gatherings, arrested and imprisoned a number of them and gave physical harassment to many of them. Some of them were killed in police firings also. The students made considerable sacrifice in this movement and demonstrated that the youths of India never lagged behind in the national struggle. They continued their struggle with the same spirit even upto 1947, that is till India got the Independence.

It is true that student movement was very much associated with politics before independence. But the *student energy was spent for a national cause*. From the political point of view, the youth movement in India before independence, performed two important *Political Functions*: *Firstly*, the youths supported the national freedom struggle and joined hands particularly with the Congress to disrupt the British institutions and paralyse the government. *Secondly*, the youth organisations and movements served as recruitment centres for the political parties. The then existing political parties (such as the Congress, Muslim League, Hindu Mahasabha) were looking forward with eagerness to catch young and dynamic persons for their parties from these movements and organisations.

Students Unrest After Independence

After the Independence, the student unrest, student organisations and youth movements assumed different roles and different proportions. Before Independence, the students had before them one common national goal, and that was to secure for India, freedom. The student energy or power was mobilised and directed for the fulfilment of that goal. They had good leadership and secured noble guidance. But the national scene was changed after Independence. The Congress which was a national movement then, became the ruling party and a number of political parties were also born In the beginning, the political parties seemed to have neglected the student force. They were more busy with their power politics. But after 1960, the student force gained strength. The incidence of student unrest rose to unimaginable proportions in 1960's and 1970's.

Philip G. Altabch observes: "Student unrest has been one of the India's most serious educational and political problems. Student agitation in India has caused State Governments to fall and it has forced the Central Government to revise its language policies. Students have paralysed Colleges and Universities and have caused serious damage to public facilities as well as to educational institutions".

The Social Compositions of the Students After Independence

Soon after Independence the Government started giving more importance to education and hence vast educational opportunities were created for all the sections of the people, without any discrimination. Those sections of the people which had ignored education or were deprived of educational facilities during the British rule, started availing of the same after Independence. This resulted in a change in the social composition of the students. Students belonging to almost all the *castes, classes, religious groups, tribal groups, linguistic, ethnic* and *racial groups* are found studying in schools, colleges and universities. Education is no more the monopoly of the upperclasses and the upper castes. The *Harijans* and *Girijans, Hindus* and *Muslims*, *Christians* and *Anglo-Indians*, the rich and the poor, the so-called '*forward communities*' and '*backward communities*' go to the same educational institutions. Education has become completely secular today. The depressed classes and communities are provided with special facilities to avail of educational opportunities. The student mass is mostly *heterogeneous*, especially in the cities. This heterogeneity has also contributed to the growing unrest among the students.

Student Unrest and Political Parties

Student unrest has been closely associated with politics in India. It cannot be completely divorced from the political movements and machinations and manoeuverings. After the Independence no attempt has been made by any political party, including the ruling party, to depoliticalise the youths and to disaffiliate them from the political activities. There has been no attempt to make the students feel that Independence has been achieved and there is no need for political activities by the youths. On the contrary, the political parties have found that the student force constitutes one of the most powerful instruments to achieve their political ends.

The political parties have started taking more interest in student activism for their political gains. Political parties have started their own youth wings. Almost all the political parties have their own youth organisations now. *For example*, Congress (I) has its *National Students' Union of India* (NSUI), the Bharatiya Janata Party, has its *Janata Yuva Morcha*, the Communist Party of India (CPI) has its *All-India Students Federation* (AISF), the Communist Party of India, Marxist (CPM) has its Student Federation of India (SFI), the Janata Party has its *Yuva Janata*, the Indian Union Muslim League (IUML) has its *Muslim Students Union of India* and so on. Even the regional parties also have their own youth wings. In addition to these, the *Rashtreeya Swayam Sevak Sangha* (R.S.S.), which was started in 1925 and the *Akhil Bharatiya Vidyarthi Parishad* which originated in 1949 — the two other prominent organisations also have been attracting good number of youths. Of the non-political student organisations, the *Akhil Bharibia Vidyarthi Parishad* (ABVP) seems to be the largest one. It has more than one thousand branches spread over almost all the major States of India and its activities are found in more than one hundred universities. The ABVP claims itself to be a non-political nationalist student organisation committed to the cause of the unity and welfare of the educational community of India, The ABVP seems to have a great appeal for teachers also. It has gained ground in a number of universities.

The student unrest in India, has been in many instances *an expression of political unrest*. The politicians very often use the students for their political ends and cause student unrest. Hostilities between political leaders and parties and similarly political conflicts, rivalries and differences of opinion have often been expressed through student agitations. Political parties with ulterior motives often fabricate student problems and champion such causes. Educational and student problems are often taken in hand by the political parties to serve their political interests. Some instances may be cited here. The DMK and ADMK (the two prominent parties of Tamil Nadu) have been supporting the anti-Hindi agitation to stabilise themselves and to win students to their sides. The late Devraj Urs and his group supported the *Expo-70 agitation* in 1970's to topple *Virendra Patil's ministry* in Karnataka. Opposition parties supported the *Nav-Nirmana Kranti* of the students to topple *Chimanbhai Patel's ministry* in Gujarat. Similarly, the students with the help of the opposition parties brought down *Abdul Gaffor's ministry in Bihar*. The students took an active role in the J.P. movement which was supported by all the democratic parties to topple Mrs. Gandhi's Government just before the emergency.

The students are highly vulnerable to political influences. They are prepared to defy authority and to wage battles against the established order. As *Peter Worsley* has pointed out that students have few family or financial responsibilities. They risk less than other social groups in espousing causes hostile to the established interests of their society. "*Students have the time and the intellectual inclination 'to attend to the politics of their country. They are one of the few social groups available for political action*." *Peter Worsley writes*: "that in most of the countries of the world students regard themselves as the vanguard of political action, with a special responsibility for advocating the interests of social groups who are unable to protest. The growth of student protest movements is thus closely related to the emergency of political problems and cleavages within the existing political and economic order of society."

Remedies for Youth Unrest

The problem of the youth must be understood in connection with the relationships of the students with parents, teachers, politicians, police authorities, student union leaders, university authorities, and the values, traditions, needs, motivations and aspirations of the students. Patterns of these variables are found to be associated with the tension in the college-going youth. A few suggestions may be made here to minimise the youth unrest.

1. ***System of education***: A thorough overhauling for our education system is necessary to help the students to face the problems and challenges of life. No hotch-potch change in education would suffice. But education requires a comprehensive planning and an integral approach. This would bridge the gap between what the students actually experience and what is taught to them in schools and colleges. Colleges and universities should make proper provision for (*a*) adequate boarding and lodging facilities, (*b*) better libraries and reading rooms and laboratories, (*c*) enough facilities for recreation and extra-curricular activities (*d*) seminar and tutorial, system.
2. ***Employment opportunities:*** Efforts should be made to provide opportunities for the students to offer courses in agriculture, engineering, business management, commerce, medicine, etc. The spirit of self-reliance must be created and the students should be encouraged to set up business and cottage industries of their own.
3. ***Provision for leisure-time activities:*** Students should not be allowed to idle their time. Hobby clubs and workshops catering to painting, music, photography, stamp collection, swimming, etc. may be established in colleges. Indoor games, dramatic performances, excursions and picnics, functions catering to the interest of fine arts and literature must be encouraged among them.
4. ***Economic difficulties:*** Poor and the needy students should be given financial help through scholarships, freeships, loan scholarships, free hostel facilities, stipends, etc. so that they do not drop out of schools and colleges. The programme of '*earn while you learn*' needs to be well organised.
5. ***Discipline:*** Students should be assisted in developing self-discipline for it is long lasting than the imposed discipline. Acts of indiscipline should be dealt with sternly, but of course, humanistically. The teachers must play an important role in this respect.
6. ***Able leadership:*** Students very badly need able and efficient leadership. In any democratic set-up leadership is very important. Leadership training programmes under supervision should be introduced in colleges. Politicians must not be allowed to misguide the students.
7. ***Role of political parties:*** Political parties should be kept out of the college campuses. The students should have political awareness, but their active participation in politics would spoil the peaceful atmosphere of the campus. The student leaders, teachers and university authorities must make joint venture to save education and campus from power politics.
8. ***Students' participation:*** As Dr. V.K.R.V. Rao, Ex-Union Minister for Education has suggested (in his address to the Commonwealth Inter-University Conference in New Delhi, Jan. 1970) 'Students the world over have become restive and are demanding a Voice in the affairs of universities and a fair share in running the machine and in decision-taking. This demand cannot be evaded for long except at great peril'. In brief, the students should be given ample opportunities to take part in the administrative bodies of the university.

Proper communication between students and teachers: The communication gap between the students and teachers should be bridged. The teacher must not look at the students with suspicion. He must have confidence in them. He must act as their friend, guide and philosopher. The teacher-student ratio must be reduced. Every student must get due attention of the teacher. More than this, basically the teacher must change his attitude towards the students and the profession.

Conclusion

It is true that there is youth unrest. But it is a part of the national malady. The student as a class can play a vital role in any attempt to change the national scene. Student activism is positively anti-establishment. As *Pater Worsley* says, it is quite obvious. *If the establishment, by the same logic tends to be anti-student it will create an extremely unfortunate situation*. Asking the students to behave, without the authorities doing anything to solve their problems, is not only unjust .to the students but will further alienate them from the authorities. *The student is a force. He is not a citizen of tomorrow, but he is very much a citizen of today*. He has a participatory role to play in the task of nation-building. What he wants is not a doze of advice but he wants to see the models to be emulated by him. Events, crises and challenges of constructive activity have shown that he can rise to the occasion and meet the challenges of reconstruction. In the changing society where the authority stands discredited, the youth shall triumph and usher in an era of social change. The student power has shown that it is a potential factor that can bring about vast socio-political changes.

PROBLEMS OF AGED

A man's life is normally divided into five main stages namely: infancy, childhood, adolescence, adulthood and old age. In each of these stages an individual has to find himself in different situations and face different problems. Infancy and childhood are periods of dependence. One is normally at the mercy of one's parents. In the later stage of childhood and during the period of adolescence how circumstances make a few of them to become delinquents, we have already examined. It is during the adulthood that an individual has to bear the main brunt of life. Old age is not free from problems. Though from the point of view of wider society the problems of old age are comparatively less, from the standpoint of the individual the problems are not less significant. In old age physical strength deteriorates, mental stability diminishes, money power becomes bleak and eye-sight suffers a setback. It is only for a blessed few old age may prove to be a stage of contentment and satisfaction. But for a large number of people it may actually become a period of disappointment, dejection, disease, repentance, and loneliness. In order to find some solace for their distressed mind good number of people turn towards religion. They become more and more other-worldly in their attitude. Some seek to get satisfaction through the achievements of their children or grandchildren. Some old people cut off their relations with the external world and prefer to live in solitude. Only a few make compromises and try to equip themselves to sail along with the currents of life. Old age, thus, has its psychological and socio-cultural sides. An insight into these may help us to understand the problem better.

The Psychological Side of the Problem

The problem of senility or that of the aged has been a curse of the modern civilisation. The increasing proportion of older people in modern civilised societies has given rise to a great many psychological, social and medical problems. The growing incidence of mental disorders is very much associated with old age. *For example*, in America, in 1970 an estimated 7 lakh older persons were institutionalised for such mental disorders. This figure, of course, does not speak of those older people with less pronounced mental disorders who were being cared for or ignored in the community. Even the ancient Roman writer *Juvenal* was quite aware of the mental problems associated with old age. Hence he wrote: "But worse than any loss of limb is the failing mind, which forgets the names of slaves, and cannot recognise the face of the old friend who dined with him the last night, nor those of children whom he has forgotten and brought up".

More than the physical disability, the mental disability and disorders make the old people to suffer. Long-standing neurotic, alcoholic, or drug-dependent patterns may continue into old age, or may make their appearance during this life period for the first time. Older people are very much susceptible to psychotic depressions. The two major psychotic disorders of older people are–" **senile dementia** (associated with cerebral atrophy and degeneration) and psychosis with **cerebral arterio-sclerosis** (associated with either blocking or ruptures in the cerebral arteries)". It has been observed that these two disorders account for approximately 80% of the psychotic disorders among older people in the civilised societies.

1. ***Senile Dementia:*** Older people who suffer from senile dementia develop some symptoms such as the following–poor memory, intolerance of change, disorientation, restlessness, insomnia, failure of judgement, a gradual formation of delusions and hallucinations, extreme mental depression and agitatedness, severe mental clouding in which the individual becomes restless, combative, resistive and incoherent. In extreme cases, patients eventually become

oblivious of their surroundings, bedridden, and reduced to a vegetative existence. Resistance to disease is lowered and death usually results.

2. ***Psychosis with Cerebral Arteriosclerosis:*** This is accompanied by physiological symptoms such as acute indigestion, unsteadiness in gait, small strokes resulting in cumulative brain damage and gradual personality change, convulsive seizures are also relatively common. Some patients suffering from this will be, in confusional state and may even die without being cleared of from that state. This is also associated with symptoms such as weakness, fatigue, dizziness, headache, depression, memory defect, periods of confusion, lowered efficiency in work, heightened irritability accompanied by suspiciousness.

Sociocultural Factors of the Problem

Sociocultural factors relating to the problems of the aged are equally significant. Cultural peculiarities and rural and urban background of the old people for example, have a close bearing with this problem. In one interesting study, psychologist *Carothers* (1947) found a high rate of senile psychoses among natives in Kenya and Africa. It is also observed especially in United States that the senile psychotic cases reported and hospitalised in the urban set up were almost twice the number of cases reported in rural set up. It can only be generalised that the urban set up is more favourable to the development of mental disorders than the rural set up. In the rural areas the older person enjoys higher social status and is generally able to work productively for a longer period. He is much cared for and respected at home.

But in the urban industrial society the problems of the old age have gripped the people for they are unprepared to face them. Proper opportunities and suitable conditions are not created for utilising the experience and wisdom of our older people. We have not even provided conditions necessary for them to live in reasonably respected and useful positions. On the contrary, they are treated as though they are persons who have outlived their usefulness. This attitude of modern urban society may contribute to the incidence of old age psychoses.

It is true that the experience of an older person seems to have little relevance to the problems of younger generations. He is deprived of active participation and decision making in both occupational and family settings. As *J.C. Coleman* and *W.E. Broen Jr.*, have remarked, "Not infrequently children assume a patronising and protective attitude toward the aging parent, and in other ways tend to deprive him of dignity, responsibility, and a feeling of importance. Many parents are treated as unwanted burdens, and their children may secretly wish that they would die to relieve them of financial and other responsibilities".

"In a study of older people in France, *De Beauviour* (1970) has pointed out that when the French go away for vacations, they sometimes 'deposit' their aged parents in rest homes. Then on their return home, they "forget" to pick them up, abandoning them like dogs in a Kennel"–(*Coleman*). Most of the civilised societies have "*youth-oriented cultures*'. In the nuclear families in such cultures generally, there is no place for the grandparents unless they are self-sufficient. Even in the U.S.A. many older people are "deposited" in rest or nursing homes to die, even though they may be in relatively good health. The older people who have already developed some physiological problems feel extremely bad to know that they are cast aside simply for "being old". Such a treatment would have devastating effects upon them.

Reactions to aging and reaching the status of "*senior citizen*" — are quite subjective. How people react depends heavily on their personality make up and on the challenges and frustrations of their life situations. A sense of status, self-identity and meaning are very important in old age for they are most threatened at this stage.

The Actual Problems of Old People

Old age is subject to stresses and strains. In fact, certain special stresses are typically confronting the aged. Some of them are as follows.

(1) Retirement and reduced income which may create a feeling that one's usefulness is essentially over and activities are restricted.

(2) With the passage of years the adults become physically weaker and weaker day by day. Old age has its direct impact on physical strength and stamina. Some old people fail to reconcile the fact that their physical strength is fading away.

(3) Even though the old people become weaker physically they want to tighten their grip over the younger ones in the family and also over family matters and business issues. The younger ones in the family instead of developing a sympathetic attitude towards the old, start asserting their rights and power. This may create tension in the family

and conflict between the young and the old. Neither one 'is prepared to understand or cope with the other. This does happen due to what is known as 'generation gap', and 'communication gap'.

(4) Reduction in physical attractiveness: This is especially more stressful for persons whose feeling of feminity or masculinity depends on their attractiveness to the opposite sex.

(5) Failing health and invalidism, particularly when the hopes of recovery are very bleak.

(6) Isolation and lonliness which is usually caused by the loss of contemporaries and loved ones. The negligence and indifference of others also impair the feelings of the ego.

(7) The problem of meaning of life and death. This is more aggravated in the case of those who look back on their lives and say, "It all adds upto nothing".

(8) Social changes are taking place at faster rate than they were some years ago. While we young are prepared to welcome and accept these changes the old find it extremely difficult to adjust mentally to these changes. This failure to accommodate the new trends on the part of the old would further alienate them from the young.

Remedial Measures

The problem of the old has become more pronounced now than before. The advent of industrial revolution, advancement of science and technology and development of medical science have added new dimension to this problem. Prior to the industrial revolution the average '*life expectancy*' of man all over the world was very low. Now it has increased tremendously. In most of the European nations the average life span of people has crossed the mark of 65 years. In India, at the time of Independence, *i.e.*, around 1950's, the life span of an average Indian was about 28 years and now it has increased to 50 years. As a result of this the number of old people has increased in almost all the countries. The presence of a large number of old people has affected the composition of population especially in countries such as Russia, Britain, Norway, Swedan, Switzerland, France and so on.

Today, all the developed countries have undertaken various social legislative, reformative, and welfare measures to protect the interests of the old people. *Old age homes* are to be found in all these nations which give physical protection, medical aid, and economic security to the old. Due to the new trends that have gripped the modern nuclear families old people are often deserted by their own children. Such old people normally take shelter in these homes. Even in these homes old people, often suffer from emotional problems.

In most of the modern countries under various welfare schemes due protection is given to the old by means of old age allowance, pension after retirement, accident benefit, free medical aid for the old, etc. To ensure economic security for the salaried people who become old at the time of retirement various labour legislations and welfare schemes have been introduced» which include provident fund, gratuity, life insurance, etc. Measures are also undertaken to take the benefit of the experience of the old people. While some retired persons are given part-time job, some intelligent ones are again appointed as advisers, while a few others are accorded the status of guides or counsellors. The old people can render relatively good service to the society in areas which require more mental ability, skill and experience and involve less physical work.

Problems of old age are relatively less in societies where the family ties are very strong. In the Eastern societies, including India, family ties are comparatively stronger. In these societies old people are not neglected. In their own families they still command respect and get the feeling that they are still '*useful*' and hence wanted. They spend much of their time in the family and devote more of their energy in bringing up the younger ones. They even try to maintain emotional balance at home. But their Western counterparts are beset with various strains because their family ties are very weaker. They are wanted in the family as long as they are '*useful*'. When once the younger ones feel that the service of the old is not required, they are either ignored or deserted.

How to Deal with the Aged?

How to deal with the aged? and what to do to minimise their problems? Whether or not to hospitalise the aged persons particularly those who are mentally deranged, is often a problem. Some individuals who manifest such symptoms as confusion, violent and noisy behaviour, depression, anti-social behaviour, etc., normally require institutionalisation. But some investigations regard hospitalisation as a last resort. The decision to hospitalise is based primarily on the fact that no other community facilities rife available to assist the individual.

Effective treatment of the older people suffering from mental and other problems requires a comprehensive use of medical, psychological, and sociological procedures. The treatment has to be administered depending upon the needs of the individuals. Some may require just dietary measures while some other may need a surgical operation. Many reports have revealed that both individual and group psychotherapy would yield favourable results in treating mental disorders associated with old age.

Administration of group therapy or sociotherapy to older patients would mean the creating of a social environment in which the person can function successfully. In a hospital setting or nursing home sociotherapy would include the provisions of comfortable surroundings, together with stimulating activities that encourage the patient to utilise his capacities. It also includes working with the family in an attempt to help them understand the nature of the patient's disorder, to be supportive, and to show that they care.

Scientists in many areas of the biological and social sciences are investigating the pathological and the normal aspects of aging. They are also exploring the ways to minimise the aging process. Community centres and clinics for assisting older people with retirement and other problems are increasing. Although society can do much to improve the status of the older person, the individual also needs to prepare himself for the problems typical of old age. He needs to face realistically the fact that he is getting older, and plan ahead for an active and useful life in his later years — a life that will take full advantage of the opportunities afforded to him. Of course, it is true that many of the adjustments of old age are highly specific to the situations of the given individual and hence cannot be fully anticipated. But at any rate, it is important to maintain mental flexibility and adaptability and establish new and satisfying interpersonal relationships. As *Simmons* has pointed out, "The secret of success for any one facing a long life... is to find for himself a suitable place in his society in which to age with grace and usefulness, and to participate tactfully and fully upto the very end if at all possible". "Old age thus poses special problems, but it is by no means incompatible with meaning and self, fulfilment." — *Coleman*.

REVIEW QUESTIONS

1. What is juvenile delinquency? Give the definitions of juvenile delinquency.
2. Explain the causes of juvenile delinquency.
3. Define juvenile delinquency. Briefly explain the social, environmental and personal factors of juvenile delinquency.
4. What are the remedies of juvenile delinquency?
5. What is youth unrest? Discuss its types.
6. Elucidate the factors of youth unrest.
7. Explain the causes of youth unrest.
8. Write a detailed note on the growth of youth unrest in India.
9. Examine the role of students in the Quit India Movement, 1942.
10. Write an essay an students unrest after independence.
11. What are the remedies for youth unrest? Write in brief.
12. Discuss the problems of the aged. What are the ways to reduce elder abuse.
13. Write Short notes on the following:
    (a) Juvenile delinquency
    (b) Youth unrest in India
    (c) Problems of the aged

⌘⌘⌘⌘⌘⌘⌘⌘⌘⌘⌘

45

THE PROBLEM OF OVERPOPULATION IN INDIA

CHAPTER OUTLINE

Population of the world has been consistently increasing especially after the II world war. In demographic terms, the world is experiencing a period of population explosion. Even India also experienced unprecedented and accelerated growth of population. Its population has already crossed the alarming mark of one billion. Prior to 1921, the population growth in India was insignificant; between 1921 and 1951 it was rapid, and after 1951, it has become "***explosive***."

Population, itself is not a problem, qualitatively good population with a manageable size, represents the strength of a nation. But if the size becomes unmanageable, the same population invites unwanted problems. It not only halts economic progress but also poses innumerable challenges to the social system. India is unfortunately caught in such a precarious position.

No social problem is beyond human control and solution. A serious problem like "*the problem of overpopulation in India*" requires an immediate solution. Though it cannot be solved by an act of legislation or by the Presidential promulgation, it can very well be handled skillfully and efficiently. The Government must be sincere and efficient in tackling this problem. But more than the Government, people must be made to realise the need for controlling the size of their population. A strong "political will" on the one hand, and creation of "*general social awareness*" on the other, can alone provide a lasting solution to this problem. This chapter highlights the recent demographic situation in India.

GLOBAL POPULATION TRENDS

The world population is continuously increasing. Several nations of the world are gripped by the problem of overpopulation. Most of the developing countries are experiencing this problem. At the beginning of the Christian era, nearly 2,000 years ago, world population was estimated to 250 million. Subsequent estimates of the world population, and rates of increase are given in **Table 1**.

Table-1

World Population

Years	Population (million)	Average Annual Growth Rate (%)
1750	791	–
1800	978	0.4
1850	1262	0.5
1900	1650	0.6
1950	2526	1.1
1960	3037	1.79
1970	3696	1.92
1975	4066	1.89
1980	4432	1.72
1987	5000	1.63
1991	5385	1.7
1998	5884	1.6
2000	6054	1.4

Source: **Park's** *"Text Book of Preventive and Social Medicine."* Page - 325

It required all the human history upto the year 1800 for the world population to reach one billion. The second billion came in 130 years [around 1930] the third billon in 30 years [around 1960], the fourth billion came in 15 years [in 1974], the fifth billion in 13 years [in 1987], and the sixth billion in 12 years [1999]. On October 12th, 1999 world population became 6 billion. It is expressed to reach 8 billion by 2025.

Growth Rate is Faster in the Developing Countries

About three fourths of the world population lives in the developing countries. The UNO has estimated that world's population grew at an annual rate of 1.4% during 1990-2000. But China registered a much lower annual growth rate of population [that is, 1%] during 1999-2000, as compared to India [1.93%]. In fact, the growth rate of China is now very much comparable to that of USA [0.9%].

India, Indonesia and Bangladesh, the three countries of the South-East Asia Region [SEAR], are recognised among the most populous 10 countries of the world. According to UN projections, India's population will reach 1.53 billion by the year 2050, and that will be the highest population in the world. The trend of population increase in the SEAR countries is shown in **Table - 2.**

Table-2

Trends in Increase of Population of South East Asia Region (SEAR) Countries (In thousands)

Country	1985	2000	2005 (Projected)
India	797940	1008937	1082184
Bangladesh	99310	137439	139911
Bhutan	1451	2085	2313
DPR Korea	18942	22268	25416
Indonesia	167332	212092	226938
Maldives	184	291	355
Myanmar	37544	47749	53479
Nepal	16503	23043	27439
Sri Lanka	16060	18924	19858
Thailand	51128	62806	62612
Total	1176394	1535634	1640505

Source: WHO-World Health Report - 2001.

Growth Rate of World Population

The growth rate is not uniform in the world. There are many countries in the world [**Ex.** European countries] where the growth rate is less than 0.5 per cent per year. In developing countries, the growth rates are excessive - it is around 2.8 per cent in Africa, 1.5 per cent in Latin America, 0.5 in Europe and 1.9 per cent in Asia. A population growing at 0.5 per cent per year will double in about 140 years, a population growing at 3 per cent per year will double in 20-25 years. These differences in growth rates are largely the result of fertility and mortality patterns.

Salient Features of World Population Growth

The salient features of the world population growth at a glance are as follows :

(*i*) Approximately 95 per cent of this growth is occurring in developing countries.

(*ii*) Currently, one third of the world's population is under the age of l5 and will soon enter the reproductive bracket, giving more potential for population growth.

(*iii*) The UNFPA estimates that world population is most likely to nearly double to 10 billion people in 2050, peaking at 11.6 billion reaching 20.7 billion a century later.

(*iv*) The expected number of births per women, at current fertility rate, is : Africa 6.1; Asia, 3.2; Latin America 3.4; North America 2.0; Europe 1.6.

(*v*) World population is currently growing at 176 people per minute; 10,564 people per hour; 253,542 people per day; and 92,543,000 people per year.

The world population is indeed, increasing at an alarming rate. This speedy growth of population is one of the greatest obstacles to the economic and social advancement of the majority of people in the underdeveloped world.

IS INDIA OVER-POPULATED?

India has a vast population, that is, **121.02** crore in 2011. With a huge population of **121** crore [April lst 2011] India is the second most populous country in the world, next only to China, whereas seventh in land area. With only 2.4 per cent of the world's land area. India is supporting about l7.5 percent of the world's population. The population if India since 1901 is shown in ***Table*** - 3. In 2001, India accounted for 19.96% of the estimated population of developing countries.

Table-3

Growth of Population in India, [1901-2001]

Year	Total population (in million)	Average Annual exponential growth rate (%)	Decadal increase or decrease (in crores)	Increase in Population during the decade [in percentage]
1901	238.4		—	—
1911	252.1	0.56	+ 1.6	5.7%
1921	251.3	(–) 0.03	– 0.1	0.3%
1931	279.0	1.04	+ 2.8	11.0%
1941	318.7	1.33	+ 4.0	14.2%
1951	361.1	1.25	+ 4.2	13.3%
1961	439.2	1.96	+ 7.8	21.5%
1971	548.2	2.20	+ 10.9	24.8%
1981	683.3	2.22	+ 13.5	24.8%
1991	843.9	2.14	+ 16.1	23.5%
2001	1027.0	1.93	+ 18.4	21.34%
*2011	1210.02	1.76	+ 18.5 (crore)	17.64%

Source: Govt. of India-2001 Census of India 2001. Provisional population Totals, Paper 1 of 2001

*(As per the first set of data from the 2011 Census (as on March 31st).

Population Itself is not a Problem

Population, if manageable and efficient, is an asset to any country. It is the index of its inner strength. It leads to a better and fuller exploitation of its natural resources. But if it becomes unmanageable, it eats into the vitals of the nation and becomes an evil. A large size of population by itself must not be confused with overpopulation. A country is overpopulated or under-populated in relation to its *area, resources*, and *their utilisation*.

At the present stage of her economic development, there is little doubt that India is over-populated, India's population is about one-fifth of the total world population. Population has become a socio- economic problem for India. The following facts would fortify this.

Population Explosion in India!

India is the 2nd most populous country in the world. Its population has been steadily increasing since 1921. Having crossed the mark of **121.02 crore** in 2011 A.D., India's population is currently increasing at the rate of **18.15 million** each year and its annual growth rate is 1.76% as per 2011 census report. India's population is consistently increasing in all the States. State-wise break-up of India's population along with variation in sex-ratio is given in ***Table* - 4**.

Alarming growth of population has become one of the most formidable problems of India today. Massive population is seriously threatening our economic development. ***Tables* 3 - 4** make clear the abnormal growth of population which is, indeed, the population explosion.

India's population numbered 238 million in 1901, doubled in 60 years to 439 million [1961]; doubled again, this time in only 30 years to reach 846 million by 1991. India's population was projected to cross 1 billion mark on 11 May 2000, and to reach l.53 billion by the year 2050. This will then make India the most populous country in the world, surpassing China.

Some Important Aspects of the Growth of Indian Population

- As per the 1991 census, India's population was 844 million, and it increased to 1027 millions in 2001, and to 1070.3 million [107.3 crore] in 2004, and 121.02 crore in 2011.
- The land area of the country is only 2.4% of the total land area of the world. But its population is about 17.5% of the total population of the world as per 2011 census.
- At the present rate of growth, India is adding every 10 years a number of people more than double the total population of the U.K., or equal to the entire population of Pakistan or Brazil or more than the half the population of the USA or of the USSR.
- India is just two-fifth of the USA, but India's population is more than 2 and a half times the population of the USA and USSR put together.
- India's population is equal to the total population of 55 countries of Africa and Latin America. India's present population [121.02 crore] is equal to the combined population of USA, Indonesia, Japan, Brazil, Bangladesh and Pakistan.
- In India today, 30 babies are born every minute, 55,000 babies are born everyday and about 13 million babies are born every year as per 2001 census.
- India, it is remarked, adds one Australia [that is the population of Australia] to its population every year.

The Reality of Population Explosion

It is clear from ***Table* - 3** that the population of India has increased by 21.5% during the decade 1951-1961, by 24.8% during the decade 1961-1971, by 24.8% during the decade of 1971-1981, by 23.5% during the decade of 1981-1991, by 18.5% between 1991-2001 and by 17.64 in 2011.'Table-3 shows that the increase in population of India was rather slow upto 1921. The year 1921 is called "*the year of the great divide*" as the growth rate after this has been very sharp. After 1911-21, the decade between 2001-2011 is the first decade to witness a reduction in the rate of population growth. This reduction, however, is only marginal. Hence the rate of growth of population as well as the size of the population of India is definitely very high. On the basis of the rate of growth and the size of population, one can certainly say that there is population explosion in India.

Tests of Overpopulation

The following test makes it evident that India is over-populated:

1. The rate of population growth in India is abnormally high, that is 1.76% per annum according to 2011 census report.
2. The rapid increase in population is eating away the fruits of the Five-Year Plans.

3. Per capita income of India is extremely low in comparison with that of many other countries.
4. The country is not able to provide for the minimum requirements of its people for the population is too large and the production too less.
5. Population growth has created problems such as unemployment, illiteracy, poverty, beggary, housing problem, ill-health, etc., which are not met with.

CAUSES FOR THE RAPID GROWTH OF POPULATION IN INDIA

Various factors have contributed to the rapid growth of population in India among which the following can be noted:

(*i*) ***Peaceful conditions***: For nearly a century [1860-1960] India enjoyed comparative peace without involving herself in major inter-conflicts or wars especially after the establishment of British rule. Peaceful conditions provided an impetus for overpopulation.

(*ii*) ***Excess of birth over death***: Growth of population depends on the excess of births over deaths. Death rate has been declining rapidly in India. It was 42.6 per 1000 in 1911 and it decreased to 807 per 1000 in 2001. The birth rate is still high in India. It was 49.2 per 1000 in 1991 and it decreased to only 26.] per 1000 in 2001. The gap between birth rate and death rate has widened leading to an increase in the population. [The average annual rate of increase of population in India is 1.76% at present [2011] whereas it is only 1.2% in U.S.A., 0.4% in U.K., 1.1% in China, 0.4% in France and 0.3% in Japan.]

(*iii*) ***Progress in medical knowledge*** and its application has considerably reduced the death rate. It has helped us to control the spread of diseases like Malaria. T.B. Cholera, Plague, Influenza, Smallpox, etc., and protected the lives of people from the jaws of death. Positively, it has contributed to greater population, because, those persons saved from the death also produced children to add to the existing numbers.

(*iv*) ***Improvement in transport facilities*** has helped people to avail of medical and health facilities without much difficulty. These have saved countless lives and added to the size of the population.

(*v*) ***Improvements in the field of agriculture and industry*** also contributed to an increase in population. Uncertainties in the field of agriculture have largely been removed with the help of science and technology. Food production has considerably increased. Industries have been providing employment opportunities to thousands of persons. These developments have given people the confidence that they can afford to feed more people if they beget.

(*vi*) ***Certain social factors like universal marriage, child marriage, early marriage*** have also contributed to the problem. Indians consider marriage as a social obligation and almost all marriageable persons are in a married state. Life-long bachelorship is looked down upon. Particularly for women marriage is almost an inescapable obligation. Further, the number of children born per couple is also large.

(*vii*) ***Social attitudes of indians*** also favour an increase in population. Poverty, illiteracy, ignorance, absence of recreational facilities, attitudes of conservatism, orthodoxy, feeling of dependence on God, a sense of resignation towards life. looking upon children as old age pension, etc., are all responsible for the rapid growth of population.

Table-4

Population Size of States/UTs As Per 2001 Census

S. No.	India/State/Union Territories	Population			Population variation 1991-2001	Sex Ratio (Female per 1000 miles)	Population Share of some states in 2011 in %
		Persons	*Males*	*Females*			
	INDIA	**1,027,015,247**	**531,277,078**	**495,738,169**	**21.34**	933	
1.	Andaman & Nicobar is*	356.265	192,985	163,280	26.94	846	
2.	Andhra Pradesh	75.727,541	38,286,811	37,440,730	13.86	978	7
3.	Arunachal Pradesh	1,091,117	573,951	517,166	26.21	901	
4.	Assam	26,638,407	13,787,799	12,850,608	18.85	932	3
5.	Bihar	82,878,796	43,153,964	39,724,832	28.43	921	9
6.	Chandigarh*	900.914	508,224	392,690	40.33	773	
7.	Chhattisgarh	20,795,956	10,452,426	10,343,530	18.06	990	2
8.	Dadra & Nagar Haveli*	220,451	121,731	98,720	59.20	811	
9.	Daman & Diu*	158.059	92,478	65,581	55.59	709	

(*Contd.*)

10.	Delhi	13,782,976	7,570,890	6,212,086	46.31	821	1%
11.	Goa	1,343,998	685,617	658,381	14.89	960	
12.	Gujarat	50,596,992	26,344.053	24,252,939	22.48	921	5
13.	Haryana	21,082,989	11,327,658	9,755,331	28.06	861	2
14.	Himachal Pradesh	6,077,248	3,085,256	2,991,992	17.53	970	
15.	Jammu & Kashmir[2, 3]	10,069,917	5,300,574	4,769,343	29.04	900	1%
16.	Jharkhand	26,909,428	13,861.277	13,048,151	23.19	941	3
17.	Karnataka	52,733,958	26,856,343	25,877,615	17.25	964	5
18.	Kerala	31,838,619	15,468,664	16,369,955	9.42	1,058	3
19.	Lakshadweep*	60,595	31,118	29,477	17.19	947	
20.	Madhya Pradesh	60,385,118	31,456,873	28,928,245	24.34	920	6
21.	Maharashtra	96,752,247	50,334,270	46,417,977	22.57	922	9
22.	Manipur	2,388,634	1,207,338	1,181,296	30.02	978	
23.	Meghalaya	2,306,069	1,167,840	1,138,229	29.94	975	
24.	Mizoram	891,058	459.783	431.275	29.18	938	
25.	Nagaland	1,988,636	1,041,686	946,950	64.41	909	
26.	Orissa	36,706,920	18,612,340	18,094,580	15.94	972	3
27.	Pondichery*	973.829	486.705	487.124	20.56	1.001	
28.	Punjab	24,289,296	12,963,362	11,325,934	19.76	874	2
29.	Rajasthan	56.473.122	29,381,657	27,091,465	28.33	922	6
30.	Sikkim	540.493	288.217	252.276	32.98	875	
31.	Tamil Nadu	62,110,839	31,268,654	30,842,186	11.19	986	6
32.	Tripura	3,191,168	1,636,138	1,555,030	15.74	950	
33.	Uttar Pradesh	166,052,859	87,466,301	78,586,558	25.80	898	16
34.	Uttaranchal	8,479,562	4,316,401	4,163,161	19.20	964	16
35.	West Bengal	80,221,171	41,487,694	38,733.477	17.84	934	8
							Other states-2%

Notes: 1. The population of India includes the estimated population of the entire Kachchh district. Morvi, Matiya-Miyana, and Wankaner talukas of Rajkot district, Jodiya taluka of Jamnagar district in Gujarat and the entire Kinnaur district oi Himachal Pradesh where population enumeration of the Census of India 2001 could not be conducted due to natural calamity.

2. For working out density of India, the entire area and population of those portions of Jammu and Kashmir that are under occupation of Pakistan and China have not been taken into account.

(***Source: Provisional Population Totals : India.*** **Census of India, 2001, Paper 1 of 2001 as quoted by "India Book of the Year 2002"** published by *Encyclopedia Britannica* (*India*) *Pvt. Ltd.* 6 *The Hindu.* Page 253-254)

*As per the provisional data of 2011 census as published on 1st April 2011.

(*viii*) ***Lack of conscious family planning*** : There is the lack of conscious family planning on the part of the married people. The use of contraceptives is unknown to the illiterate masses. People feel that more children are wanted for economic purposes. Further, blind faith in fate and the existence of joint family system induce thoughtlessness in the matter of begetting children.

(*ix*) ***The climatic conditions of india*** are also very conducive to the growth of population. The tropical climate stimulates sex urge. **Montesquieu** said that people of warm land are more sex-indulgent. Further, girls become physically mature at an early age ranging from 11 to 15 years of age. Immediately after puberty they are pushed into marriage and they begin to bear children. Child-bearing capacity of women lasts in the tropical places.

(*x*) Added to this, during the earlier days the ***Government did not take much interest in introducing family planning*** to slow down the rapid growth of population. Though family planning programme was started under the Five Year Planning system, proper attention was not given to popularise it in the beginning. People also failed to recognise its importance. The result is the phenomenal growth of population.

(*xi*) ***Lack of entertainment facilities*** : It has been observed that people especially in the rural areas, have been forced to find *entertainment in the sex-play* in the absence of proper entertainment facilities. This has further aggravated the problem.

MAJOR DEMOGRAPHIC TRENDS IN INDIA

India, as it is made clear, is the second most populous country in the world. Its total population crossed the mark of 121.2 crore by March 2011. Its population is currently increasing at the rate of 18.15 million per year. The average annual exponential growth rate of India's population is 1.76% in 2011. The salient demographic features or trends of India's population may be noted below.

1. Growth Rate of Population

The population of India grew at a slow rate prior to 1921. But its population has started growing at a fantastic rate of speed particularly after 1931 . The population growth rates in India are presented in ***Table* - 3**. The average annual growth rate of India's population was 0.56% in 1911 and it reached the record height of 2.22% in 1981. However, it has come down to 1.9% in 2001, and further to 1.76% in 2011.

2. Uneven Distribution of Population

Population of India is not equally distributed among all the states. On the contrary, we find heavy concentration of people in some states rather than in others. ***Table* - 5** shows the ten most populous

Table - 5

Ranking of Most Populous States by Population size in 2001 and 2011

Rank	State	Population 1-3-2001 (Million)	Per cent to total population of India 1-3-2001	*Population March -2011 (Millions)	*Percent in to Total population of India
1.	Uttar Pradesh	(a) 166.05	(b) 16.17	(c) 200	(d) 16%
2.	Maharashtra	96.75	9.42	112	9%
3.	Bihar	82.87	8.07	103	9%
4.	West Bengal	80.22	7.81	91	8%
5.	Andhra Pradesh	75.72	7.37	84	7%
6.	Tamil Nadu	62.11	6.05		6%
7.	Madhya Pradesh	60.38	5.88		6%
8.	Rajasthan	56.47	5.50	611	6%
9.	Karnataka	52.73	5.14		5%
10.	Gujarat	50.59	4.93		5%

Source: Census of India 2001. Provisional Population Totals, Paper 1 of 2001.
*Provisional statistics Relating to 2011 censes.

states in the country by rank. As per 2011 Census, the state of Uttar Pradesh comes first with about 20.0 million people followed by Maharashtra with 112 million, Bihar with 103 million and so on. It is significant to note that these 10 states account for about 76.34% of the total population of India.

3. Age Composition

As per 2011 Census, the population of children [0-to-6 years] has declined by 5 million over the 2001 Census. In general, the proportion of population below 15-years is showing decline, whereas the proportion of elderly people in the country is increasing. This trend may continue in the time to come. The increase in the elderly population will impose a greater burden on the already outstretched health services in the country.

The age composition of India's population according to National Family Health Survey - 2 [NFHS-2] done in 1998-99 is shown in ***Table* - *6***. The age composition of people in any country is very much related to components of population change like *fertility*, *mortality*. *age at marriage*. *migration*, *etc*. Its distribution also has its important socio-economic effects. A large number of people under the age group of 14, that is, 37.3% in 2001 would lead to certain effects such as — allocation of large amount of fund to provide for health, medical and educational needs for children; more dependents on working people and low productivity of labour.

Table-6

Percent Distribution of Population by Age and Sex from the NFHS-2, India, 1998-99

Age	Male	Female
0-4	11.2	11.1
5-9	12.8	12.4
10-14	12.1	11.8
15-19	10.4	10.3
20-24	8.5	9.3
25-29	7.8	8.7
30-34	6.7	7.1
35-39	6.6	6.4
40-44	5.1	4.7
45-49	4.5	4.2
50-54	3.4	3.1
55-59	2.6	3.3
60-64	2.9	3.0
65-69	2.0	2.0
70+	33	28
Total	100.0	100.0

Source: Govt. of India [2000] Annual Report 1999-2000

Table 6(A)

Percentage Distribution of India's Population by Age Groups.

Year	Age Group		
	0.14	15-60	60 and above
1911	38.8	60.2	1.0
1921	39.2	59.6	1.2
1931	38.3	60.2	1.5
1951	37.4	57.1	5.5
1961	41.0	53.3	5.7
1971	41.4	53.4	5.2
1981	39.7	54.1	6.2
1991	36.5	57.1	6.4
2001	37.3	55.4	7.3

Source: IAMR, Fact Book on Manpower, Census of India 2001.

4. Sex Composition

A Sex ratio is one of the characteristics of the population. It has an important bearing upon marriage rate, death rate, birth rate and even migration rate. The sex ratio is defined as "*the number of females per 1,000 males.*" In any study of population, analysis of the sex composition or sex ratio plays a vital role. The major trends in the sex ratio in the country from 1901 onwards are represented in ***Table*** **- 7**. According to the 2001 census figures, there are 933 females per 1000 males in India. This sex ratio recorded a slight increase from 933 in 2001 to **940 in 2011**. There are various reasons for this imbalance in the sex ratio. Factors such as *female infanticide, neglect of female in fants, early marriage, bad treatment and hardwork of women, craving for male children, practice of dowry. dominant patriarchal values, etc*. have been instrumental in reducing the number of females in India. It is also significant to note that the sex ratio is higher in the urban areas and

1901-2011

Table-7

Sex Ratio in India

Year	Females per 1000 Males
1901	972
1911	964
1921	955
1931	950
1941	945
1951	946
1961	941
1971	930
1981	934
1991	927
2001	933
2011	940

Table-8

Density of Population in India 1901-2011

Year	per sq. km.
1901	77
1911	82
1921	81
1931	90
1941	103
1951	117
1961	142
1971	177
1981	216
1991	267
2001	324
2011	382

among the educated, than in the rural areas and among the uneducated. It is also observed that there are 13 States with sex ratio above the national level and 12 States with sex ratio lower than the national level. Kerala and Pondicheiy the only states wherein women outnumber men, and there are 1084 and 1038 women per 1000 men in 2011 in these states respectively.

5. Density of Population

Density is also a major factor in the study of population. In the Indian context, *density is defined as the average number of persons living per square kilometre*. The trends of the density of population in the country from 1901 onwards are shown in ***Table - 8***. The density of population was found to be 77 in 1901 and 324 in 2001 and it increased to the record mark of **382** in **2011**. Delhi with 11297 persons per sq. km in 2011 is the most densely populated state in India. Arunachal Pradesh with just 17 persons per sq. Km is the least densely populated state. Comparatively, China has a density of population of 135 persons. whereas Canada. Australia and America have 3, 2, and 31 persons respectively.

6. Life Expectancy

Life expectancy or expectation of life at a given age is the average number of years which a person of that age may expect to live, according to the mortality pattern prevalent in that country Demographers consider it as one of the best indicators of a country's level of development and the overall health status of its population.

Tables - 9 and 10 present life expectancy at birth in India and those in selected countries. Japan leads in life expectancy for both males and females, 77 and 83 years respectively for the year 1998.

Table-9

Expectation of Life at Birth-India

Year	Males	Females
1901	**23.63**	**23.96**
1911	22.59	23.31
1921	19.42	20.91
1931	26.91	26.56
1941	32.09	31.37
1951	32.45	31.66
1961	41.89	40.55
1971	46.40	44.70
1981	50.90	50.00
1991	58.10	59.10
2000	62.80	63.80

Source: **Park's** 'Text-book of *Preventive* and *Social Medicine*' [2002] Page-331

Table-9(A)

Rural and Urban Population 1901-2001

Census Year	Population (m.)		Percentage of (m.)	
	Rural	Urban	Rural	Urban
1901	213	26	89.2	10.8
1911	226	26	89.7	10.3
1921	223	28	88.8	11.2
1931	246	33	88.0	12.0
1941	275	44	86.1	13.9
1951	299	62	82.7	17.3
1961	360	79	82.0	18.0
1971	439	109	80.1	19.9
1981	524	159	76.7	23.3
1991	629	218	74.3	25.7
2001	741.7	285.4	72.22	27.78

Source: Census of India, 2001

Table-10

Expectation of Life at Birth in Selected Coutries-2000

Developing countries	2000		Developed countries	2000	
	Male	Female		Male	Female
Nepal	58.8	58.3	UK	75.2	80.2
Bangladesh	59.4	29.5	USA	74.1	79.9
Myanmar	53.7	28.5	Sweden	77.2	82.2
India	62.8	63.8	Switzerland	75.6	82.0
Sri Lanka	69.5	75.3	Russian Federation	61.0	73.0
Thailand	67.3	73.2	Japan	77.4	84.4

Source: **Park's** "Text-book of Preventive and Social Medicine" [2002] Page 331.

As far as India is concerned, in the year I901, the life expectancy of males and females at birth was found to be 23.63 years and 23.93 years, respectively. These figures have increased respectively to 62.80 years and 63.80 years in 2000.

Trends in life expectancy show that people are living longer and they have a right to a long life in good health, rather than one of pain and disability. Health policy makers need to recognise this changing demographic pattern, and plan for prevention and control of diseases associated with old age.

7. Dependency Ratio

The proportion of persons above 65 years of age and children below 15 years of age are considered *to be dependent* on the economically productive age group [15 - 64 years]. *The ratio of the combined age groups 0 - 14 years plus 65 years and above to the 15 - 65 years age group — is referred to as the total dependency ratio.* The dependency ratio reflects the need for a society to provide for their younger and older population groups.

Table - 11

Trends in Dependency Ratio in India (per 100)

Year	Total Dependency	Child Dependency	Old-age Dependency
1985	71.5	64.3	7.2
1995	65.5	57.8	7.6
2005 (projected)	55.5	47.2	8.3

Source: WHO [1999] Health Situation in the South East Asia Region 1994-97.

In terms of dependency ratio, we can also speak of *young age dependency ratio* [0 - 14 years]; and *old age dependency ratio* [65 years and more]. These ratios are, however, relatively crude, since they do not take into consideration elderly or young persons who are employed or working age persons who are unemployed. ***Table* - 11** shows the trends of dependency ratio in India.

8. Population and Urbanisation

Growth of population in most of the developing countries is closely associated with growing urbanisation. Urbanisation is taking place at a relatively greater speed in India. The proportion of urban population in India increased from 10.84% in 1901 to 17.3% in 1951, to 25.7% in 1991, and to 27.8% in 2001 and was projected to be 32% in the year 2011. In absolute terms, the urban population in India was 285 million in 2001 compared to 217.17 million in 1991. See ***Table* - 9(A)**.

The percentage of population residing in urban areas has increased marginally. The number of urban areas and towns increased from 3,378 in 1981 to 3,768 in 1991. In 2001, three major cities of India - Mumbai, Kolkata and Delhi - attained the status of **mega-cities** each with a population of more than 10 million. The pace of urbanisaion is relatively due to predominance of agriculture, slow rate of industrialisation, low rate of literacy, slow growth of towns and cities, slow rate of social and occupational mobility, shortage of capital, etc.

9. Birth and Death Rates

The birth and death rates are important components of population growth. The birth and death rates in India are shown in ***Table*** - 12. A look at ***Table*** - 12 shows that whereas the death rate considerably declined from 42.6 in 1911 to 8.7 per thousand population in 2001; and the birth rate declined niggardly from 49.2 in 1911 to 26.1 per thousand in 2001.

The birth rate in India was 26.1 per thousand in 2001 and the death rate was 8.7 per thousand for the same period. This widened the gap between the birth rate and the death rate. As a result, the net rate of increase of population in the country is 1.9%. This is the most significant factor behind the population explosion in India.

India like many other developing countries is faced with the problem of a high birth rate and a declining death rate. ***The causes of high birth rare are***–(*i*) universality of marriage, (*ii*) early marriage, (*iii*) early puberty, (*iv*) low standard of living, (*v*) low level of literacy, (*vi*) traditional customs and habits, (*vii*) absence of family planning habit, etc.

Declining death rate has been attributed to – (*i*) mass control of diseases such as smallpox, plague, cholera, malaria, etc. (*ii*) better health facilities, (*iii*) impact of national health programmes, (*iv*) absence of natural checks as found in the instances of famines, floods, large scale epidemics, etc., (*v*) improvements in food supply, (*vi*) international aid in different ways, (*vii*) development of social consciousness among the masses. The demographers are of the opinion that in future rapid decline in India's death rate may not be continued.

Table-12

Birth and Death Rates in India

Year	Birth Rate	Death Rate
1911	49.2	42.6
1941	39.9	27.4
1951	41.7	22.8
1961	41.2	19.0
1971	37.2	14.8
1981	33.9	12.5
1991	29.5	9.8
1995	28.3	9.0
1996	27.5	9.0
1997	27.2	8.9
1998	26.4	9.0
1999	26.1	8.7
2001	26.1	8.7

Source: Govt. of India [2002] Annual Report 2001-2002. Ministry of Health & Family welfare, New Delhi.

Table-12(A)

Birth and Death Rates in India

Census Year	Percentage of total Population		Urban-rural ratio
	Rural	Urban	
1901	89.0	11.0	1:8.1
1911	89.6	10.4	1:8.6
1921	88.7	11.3	1:7.8
1931	87.8	12.2	1:7.2
1941	85.9	14.1	1:6.1
1951	82.7	17.3	1:4.7
1961	82.0	18.0	1:4.5
1971	80.1	19.9	1:3.7
1981	76.7	23.3	1:2.9
1991	74.3	25.7	1:2.9
2001	72.2	27.8	1:2.6
2011	68.0	32.0	
2026	63.8	36.2	

Source: Register General, India.

10. Literacy Structure

As far as the literacy structure of the country is concerned, in 201 l, on an average, around **74.04%** people are found to be literate [**82.14%** males and **65.46%** females]. Kerala is a state wherein we find the highest literacy rate. that is **93.91%** and Bihar has the lowest one, that is, **63.82%**.

Table-13(A)

Literacy Rates in Major States of India—2001

States	Male	Female	Total
U.P.	71	44	58
Bihar/Jharkhand	62	35	49
Rajasthan	76	44	61
M.P.	77	51	64
Haryana	79	56	69
Assam	72	56	64
Gujarat	80	59	70
Orissa	76	51	61
Maharashtra	86	68	77
Punjab	76	64	70
West Bengal	78	60	69
Karnataka	76	56	67
A.P.	71	51	61
Tamil Nadu	82	65	73
Kerala	94	88	91
India	76	64	65.38

Source: Govt. of India [2001] Census of India 2001 Provisional Population Totals, Paper 1 of 2001.

Table-13(B)

Literacy Rates in India: 1951-2001

Year	Total Persons	Males	Females
1951	18.33	27.16	8.86
1961	28.30	40.40	15.35
1971	34.45	45.96	21.97
1981	43.57	56.38	29.76
1991	52.21	64.13	39.29
2001	65.38	75.85	54.16
*2011	74.04	82.14	65.46

Source: Census of India 2001.

* Provisional Statistics, census 2011

Of the total literate people in India in 1991 [8463 million], 56.7% had less than 3 years education, 23.8% 3-6 years education. 11% 7-11 years education, 6.8% 12-l4 years education and 1.7% more than 14 years education. It is evident that -we find a very limited number of people with college education. While the literacy rate for males rose from 75.26 to 82.l4% marking a rise of 6.9% it increased by **11.8%** for females to go from 53.67 to 65.46 per cent.

If we look at the State-wise break-up of the literacy rate , we find that Kerala continues to occupy the top rank in the country with about 93.91% literates (2011). Ten states and union territories. including -Kerala, Lakshdveep, Mizoram, Tripura, Goa, Damun and Diu, Puduchery, Chandigarh, Delhi, Andaman and Nicobar Inlands - have attained a literacy rate of above **85%**, one target set by the planning commission to be achieved by 2011-12.

Occupational Distribution of Population in India

Occupational distribution of population or occupational pattern in India refers to — *the proportion of total working population engaged in different broad sectors of the economy*. These broad sectors are– **1. *Primary sector*** which includes occupations like agriculture, mining, fishing, animal husbandry and forestry, **2. *Secondary sector*** which consists of occupations like manufacturing, construction, electricity, etc., and **3. *Tertiary sector*** which consists of occupations such as trade, transport, communications, banking, insurance, personal services, and both government and non-governmental services, etc. This sector is supposed to meet the needs of both primary and secondary sectors.

Table-14

Occupational Distribution of Working Population in India [in %]

Year	Primary Sector	Secondary Sector	Tertiary Sector
1901	72%	12%	16%
1951	72%	11%	17%
1971	72%	11%	17%
1981	68.7%	13.5%	17.8%
1991	65%	15.0%	20.0%
1999-2000	60.4%	15.8%	23.8%

Source: Census of India, 1981-1991. For 1999-2000, NSSO 55th Round

It is quite significant to note that the occupational distribution of population in the country remained almost constant over the last 90 years. ***Table*** **- 14** reveals the same. Even after the vigorous efforts by the Central and the State Governments to develop industries, trade, transport and communication, banking, insurance, etc. the majority of our working population are still dependent on agriculture for their livelihood. During the recent years, that is, after 1991 sizeable number of educated people have been able to get jobs with attractive salaries in the service sector.

The occupational distribution of population in India is imbalanced. It shows that India is still backward in the field of industries and depending too much on agriculture. Inadequate and lop sided growth of secondary and tertiary sectors is another fundamental cause for this imbalance in the occupational distribution. The performance of public sector industries is not that satisfactory, and the tertiary sector too has failed to absorb the excess population.

In order to forge a balance in the occupational distribution of the people. It is necessary for us to give more importance to industrial growth. Industry should be able to attract and accommodate a size able number of people from the rural areas to lessen their dependence upon agriculture. Further, the tertiary sector which consists of trade and commerce should be developed to absorb increasing number of unemployed youths.

EFFECTS OF OVERPOPULATION

If the size of population of the country reaches the optimum level, it will not pose any problem. If the growth exceeds the reasonable limits, problems will crop up and that has happened in India. It means population in excess of demand or need proves to be a great liability to the society. The unprecedented growth of population in India during the recent years, has brought about a series of serious consequences. Some of the main effects of population may be described here.

(*i*) ***Population and poverty:*** Poverty and population very often go hand in hand. In fact, poverty is both the cause and the effect of rapid growth of population. The mass poverty of our country is due to the rapid growth of population. It is estimated that about 26% [1999-2000] of the people of India still live below the poverty line. They are ill fed, ill clothed and ill housed. Thus, mass poverty is due to rapid growth of population.

(*ii*) ***Unemployment and under employment***: Not only new born individuals are to be fed and sheltered but they are also to be provided with jobs. New jobs are to be created for new hands. It is not easy to create jobs. There is already unemployment coupled with under employment. Every year more than 5 million people who attain the working age join the group of job seekers. Job opportunities that are created during the course of the Five Year Plans are not enough to meet the demand. For instance, the number of the unemployed increased from 12 million at the end of the Third Plan to 16 millions at the end of the Fourth Plan, and to 21 millions at the end of the Fifth Plan. The percentage of the people who did not get employed as per 1991 census was 42.3%. As per the figures for 2003, about 41.19 million individuals were waiting [for jobs] in the live registers of 945 employment exchanges scattered over the whole nation. [Bhagavati Committee estimate]. As per the estimates of the 8th and 9th Plan, there would be 106 million job-seekers in India by 2000 A.D.

(*iii*) ***Low per capita income***: During the past 50 years of planning, the national income of the country has increased by about 3.6% per annum. But the per capita income has increased only by 1.5% per annum. This low per capita income of the people in India is attributed to the rapid growth of population.

(*iv*) ***Shortage of food***: The rapidly growing population in India has led to the problem of shortage of food supply. In spite of the fact that more than two-mud of its population engaged in agriculture, people do not get even minimum necessary amount of food. Even though we have attained self-sufficiency in food production, due to improper distribution, all the people do not get sufficient food to sustain their health. As a result one out of every four is suffering from malnutrition and two out of every four get only half of the daily required quantum of energising food.

(*v*) ***Increased burden of social overheads***: When there is rapid growth of population in the country, the government is required to provide the minimum facilities for the people for their comfortable living. Hence it has to increase educational, housing, sanitation, public health, medical, transportation, communication and other facilities. This will increase the cost of the social overheads. Government finds it difficult to find sufficient funds to meet these "*unproductive expenses.*"

(*vi*) ***population and labour efficiency***: Since an increase in population reduces per capita income, the standard of living of the people deteriorates. This affects very badly the health and efficiency of the workers. The physical and the mental efficiency of the workers naturally comes down. Labour inefficiency reduces productivity and the nation at large loses very heavily.

(*vii*) ***Population and the standard of living***: The standard of living denotes the way in which people live. It reflects the quantity and the quality of the consumption of the people. Due to the rapid growth of population standard of living of the people has been adversely affected.

(*viii*) ***Population and pressure on land***: Overpopulation inevitably leads to heavy pressure on land. Since land is limited and fixed in supply, an increase in population can only bring more pressure on it. Hence the new born people will have to share the land with the existing people. With the exception of Rajasthan and Madhya Pradesh, in all the other states heavy density of the population is to be found. Further, the per head availability of the land for cultivation in the 1911 was 1.1 acres, and this has declined to 0.3 acres in 1992. On the contrary, the average size of the agricultural land that each person could get is 2.59 acres in Russia, and 2.68 acres in America.

(*ix*) ***Increased unproductive consumers***: When there is a rapid growth of population in a country like India, there will be large proportion of unproductive consumers. In fact, today about 51% of the total population of India is unproductive. Rapid increase in the population contributes to an increase in the dependency ratio. [See ***Table* - 11**].

(*x*) ***Slow economic development***: Economic development is bound to be slower in a country in which the population is growing at a very fast rate. Absence of savings results in low capital formation. The shortage of capital has restricted investments and contributed to the slow economic growth of the country.

(*xi*) ***Political unrest***: Unmanageable population size may contribute to political instability and unrest. The failure of the government to provide the basic minimum facilities to the people contributes to agitation and unrest among the masses.

It is true that India is gripped by the problem of overpopulation. It has shaken the stability; integrity and the security of the nation. The progress that has been made is being eaten up by the growing population. A careful study of the adverse effects of population leads us to realise the need to control it. We cannot destroy or remove our large population so as to bring it down to the optimum level. We can only control it. "*If population is not checked our progress would be like writing on sand with waves of population growth washing away what we have written.*"

NATIONAL POPULATION POLICY, 2000 [NPP-2000]

It is an undeniable fact that India is over-populated. How to face this problem of overpopulation? India must make planned efforts to control the growing population for which she should have a well thought out population policy. A more positive and more effective policy of population control is the need of the hour.

Population policy in general refers to the policy intended to *decrease the birth rate or the growth rate*. Statement of goals. Objectives and targets are inherent in the population policy.

India formed its first "*National Population Policy*" in April 1976. It called for an increase in the legal minimum age of marriage from l5 to 18 for females and from 18 to 21 years for males. The policy was, however, modified in 1977. The new policy statement emphasised the importance of the small family norm without compulsion and changed the programme title to–"*Family Welfare Programme.* "

National Population Policy 2000 **[NPP-2000]** is the latest in the series. It was announced on Feb.15th 2000 A.D. It reaffirms the commitment of the government towards target free approach in administering family planning services. The NPP-2000 is not just a matter of fertility and mortality rates. *It deals with women education; empowering women for improved health and nutrition; child survival and health; the unmet needs for family welfare services,'healthcare for the under-served population groups like urban slums, tribal community, hill area population and displaced and migrant population; adolescent's health and education; increased participation of men in planned parenthood; and collaboration with non-governmental organisations.*

The object of NPP-2000 is to bring the total fertility rate [TFR] to replacement levels by 2010. The long term objective is tu achieve requirements of suitable economic growth, social development and environment protection. it contains the goals and the target to be achieved by 2010. They can be briefed here.

1. Giving rewards to panchayats and Zilla Parishads for promoting small family norm.
2. Reduce infant mortality rate to below 30 per 100 live births.
3. Reduce maternal mortality ratio to below 100 per l lakh live births.
4. Achieve universal immunisation of children against all preventable diseases.
5. Achieve 80% institutional deliveries and 100% deliveries by trained persons.
6. Achieve 100% registration of births, deaths, marriage and pregnancy.
7. Prevent and control communicable diseases.
8. Promote vigorously the small family norm to achieve TFR.
9. Contain the spread of AIDS [Acquired Immune Deficiency Syndrome].
10. Address the unmet needs for basic reproductive and child health services. supplies and infrastructure. Strict enforcement of Child Marriage Restraint Act.
11. Make school education up to age 14 free and compulsory. and reduce drop-outs at primary and secondary school levels to below 20% to both boys and girls.
12. Health insurance cover of ₹5000 per couple below the poverty line with two living children, who undergo sterilisation.
13. Achieve universal access to information/counselling and services for fertility regulation and contraception.
14. To take appropriate steps to make family welfare programme a people-centred programme.
15. Setting up of a National Commission on Population, headed by the Prime Minister.

The planning of the population must also include the improvement of quality of population. Further, life expectation has to be increased. If the NPP-2000 is fully implemented, it is anticipated that in the year 2010 the population will be 1,107 million instead of 1,162 million projected by the Technical Group of Population Projections. Similarly, the anticipated crude birth rate will be 21 per thousand population, infânt mortality rate 30 per thousand live births and total fertility rate 2.1. The NPP-2000 is to be largely implemented and managed at *panchayat* and *nagurapaltka* levels in co-ordination with the concerned State/ Union Territory administration.

Ninth Five Year Plan Objectives

The planning commission observed that given the present demographic situation in the country, the achievements are lagging behind the proposed goals for the year 2002. Against this background fresh targets were formulated to be achieved by the end of the Ninth Five Year Plan. The goals are revised to slightly lower levels. These are as follows:

Infant Mortality rate per 100 live births	56-50
Crude birth rate per 1000 population	24/23
Crude death rate per 1000 population	9
Maternal mortality rate per 1000 live births	3
Life expectancy	
Male	62 [1996-2001]
Female	63 [1996-2001]
Couple protection rate (%)	51-60
Growth rate (%) annual	1.6/1.5
Total fertility rate	2.9/2.6
Immunization	Universal
Pregnant mothers receiving antenatal care (%)	90
Delivery by trained personnel (%)	45
Institutional deliveries (%)	35

MEASURES FOR CONTROLLING THE RAPID GROWTH OF POPULATION

Need for Controlling the Growth of Population

Overpopulation is, indeed a serious socio-economic problem of India. This problem has adversely affected the progress of the economy and the standard of the living of the people. The problem is an urgent one and needs immediate solution.

The problem of overpopulation is to be tackled immediately. There is an absolute need to contain the rapid growth of population. If this growth is not checked it is going to affect adversely the various aspects of our economy. It brings down per capita and national income, brings down standard of living of the people. It becomes difficult to face the challenges of poverty, unemployment and underemployment. Basic needs of the people cannot be met with, political unrest and immorality cannot be efficiently dealt with.

Overpopulation is related to *the size of the population and the utilisation of the countries resources.* The problem should be tackled from both the sides. *Firstly*, production should be increased to meet the needs of the people. *Secondly*, size of the population should be controlled and reduced.

Measure to Increase Production

Growing population of the country can be supported through increased production. Agricultural and industrial productions are to be increased for this purpose.

1. ***Increase in agricultural production***: It is necessary to resort to modern scientific cultivation in order to increase agricultural output. Use of irrigation, high yielding seeds, rotation of crops, utilisation of chemicals, fertilisers, manures and such other means are to be adopted for this purpose. *Production should keep pace with increasing population, if possible, should outstrip it.*
2. ***Increase in industrial production***: The process of industrialisation is to be accelerated. Modern sophisticated technology must be made use of for industrial production. The industrial strategy should be such that it should be able to increase production and at the same time provide job facilities to a sizeable number of people. Industries are to be established in different places by making use of the locally available raw materials and human resources.
3. ***Development of trade and commerce***: The development of trade and commerce will contribute to additional income and help the country to support the growing population.

Measures to Control and Reduce Population

The problem of overpopulation can be effectively dealt with only if the rapid growth rate of population is contained. Various measures are to be undertaken in this regard.

1. ***Family planning measures***: Family planning is nowadays considered an indispensable method of controlling population. The motto of family planning is — "*child by choice and not by chance*" or "child by desire not by accident." The size of the family must be limited voluntarily. It can be done in two ways : (*a*) *Birth control methods*, (*b*) *Other family planning methods*.

(a) *Birth control methods* include–use of rubber contraceptives by males, use of pills by females, use of loops by females, sterilisation for both males and females [that is, vasectomy for males and tubectomy for females], abortion, *i.e.*, medical termination of pregnancy.

(b) *Other family planning methods* include practice of celibacy [that is, practising brahmacharya or self-restraint], postponement of marriage [or resorting to late marriage], observance of moral or self-restraint.

2. ***Providing education facility to the people***: Illiteracy is one of the factors of overpopulation. It is to be countered in order to contain the population growth. Spread of education among illiterate masses is a significant step in reducing the birth rate. People must be educated regarding the benefits of small family and late marriage. Education helps to increase the earning capacity of males and females. It improves the status of women, it creates awareness regarding family planning.
3. ***Rise in the age of marriage***: In order to reduce the child-bearing period of women [reproductive span of women], it is necessary to rise the minimum age of marriage from 18 to 20 for females and from 21 to 24 for males. Child marriages should be strictly prohibited.
4. ***Improving status of women***: Experience in the West has shown that high status of women is closely associated with a low birth rate. The desire to rise in the social scale develops a strong feeling for a smaller family. The educated, employed urban women exhibit a desire for a small family. Efforts must be made to impress upon the rural women to go in the direction of a small family.
5. ***Propaganda in favour of small family***: Enough publicity is to be given in a country like India regarding the benefits of a small family to the general masses. Mass media of communication like the press, radio, television and movies are of great help in this regard.
6. ***Provision of incentives***: Incentives such as cash payments and promotion in jobs, free education, preference in admission to technical courses, etc. could be given to the people who accept and adopt family planning.
7. ***Increasing the standard of living of the masses***: People with higher standard of living normally opt for small family. Hence, it is necessary to increase the standard of living of the masses.
8. ***Providing enough recreational facilities***: It has been observed that lack of sufficient recreational facilities has often contributed to the problem of overpopulation. People must be provided with sufficient recreational facilities to relax and to refresh. This will prevent them from resorting to sex play whenever they feel like refreshing themselves.
9. ***Internal migration***: Unequal distribution of population in different parts of the nation can be dealt with if internal migration is allowed. It means people must be encouraged to move from the densely populated areas towards the thinly populated areas. This is not, however, easy. As **Adam Smith** observes, "*Of all sorts of luggage, man is the most difficult to be transported.*"
10. ***Provision of social security***: In the absence of comprehensive social security [especially, in old age, sickness, unemployment and accident] people have tended to depend on large families for security. The poor, in particular, consider children as their wealth. It is necessary to introduce various social insurance and social security schemes to help the poor to develop confidence to face the future.
11. ***Reduction in infant mortality***: By resorting to suitable medical steps the rate of infant mortality is to be reduced. If it is reduced, then parents will definitely feel that their children will survive and live long.
12. ***Changes in the tax structure***: **Dr. S. Chandrashekhar**, a noted Indian demographer, is of the opinion that by introducing a change in the taxation policy, especially that of income tax, the problem can be reduced a little. Instead of giving concessions to married people with more children, he has suggested. it is better to give such concessions to the unmarried, and also to those couples without children or with only one child.

FAMILY PLANNING

Meaning of Family Planning

Family planning basically means planning the number of children in the family. It is "*limiting the size of the family by conscious efforts*." The motto of family planning is "child by choice, and not by chance". Family planning can be defined as an instrument of social transformation which aims at creating better parents, heal their children and happier homes. It seeks to inject social responsibility into married life.

Family planning is described by an ***Expert Committee of the WHO*** in the following manner. "*Family planning refers to practices that help individuals or couples to attain certain objectives*:

(*a*) *to avoid unwanted births,*

(*b*) *to bring about wanted births,*

(*c*) *to regulate the intervals between pregnancies,*

(*d*) *to control the time at which births occur in relation to the ages of the parent; and*

(*e*) *to determine the number of children in the family.*

Family Planning as a Basic Human Right

The United Nations Conference on Human Rights at Tehran in 1968 recognised family planning as a basic human right. *The World Conference of the Women's Year in 1975* also declared — "*the right of women to decide freely and responsibly on the number and spacing of their children and to have access to the information and means to enable them to exercise that right*."

Scope of Family Planning Services

It is unfair to think that family planning is just equal to birth control. In fact. it is something more than mere birth control. WHO Expert Committee [1970] has stated that family planning includes in its purview the following aspects – 1. the proper spacing and limitation of births, 2. advice on sterility, 3. education for parenthood, 4. sex education. 5. genetic counselling, 6. premarital consultation and examination, 7. carrying out pregnancy tests, 8. marriage counselling, 9. preparation of couples for the arrival of their first child, 10. providing services for unmarried mothers, 11. teaching home economics and nutrition, 12. providing adoption services. These activities vary from country to country according to national objectives and policies with regard to family planning.

The Renaming of "Family Planning Programme" as "Family Welfare Programme"

The Government of India evinced greater interest in controlling population growth in 1976.'During the emergency [1976-78] compulsory sterilisation was carried on at great speed through coercive measures in various places in North India. For example, in 1976, more than 76 lakh sterilisations were carried out against a target of 43 lakh. Coercive methods adopted for the implementation of the programme during this period resulted in people's discontentment. 'Hence the Janata Government, which came to power soon after emergency, wanted to follow a soft policy. It announced a comprehensive population policy in that year. Family planning programme was renamed as "*Family Welfare Programme*." This welfare programme has experienced several ups and downs in its performance over time.

Achievements of Family Planning

Government's efforts at controlling population through family planning / welfare programme has not yielded consistent results. The programme has experienced several ups and downs in its performance over time. *For example*, the number of sterilisations increased from around 7000 on 1956 to 1.84 million in 1970-71. This figure increased to 2.19 million during 1971-72 but it came down to 0.94 million during 1973-74. This decline was particularly due to abandonment of camp approach. During the emergency period [1975-77] sterilisation performance of sterilisations was really good [about 8.26 million sterilisation cases in 1976-77 alone]. The performance of sterilisation came down particularly after emergency. But the trend nowadays is slowly changing in favour of family welfare programme. Particularly, in the nineties the total programme seems to have greater acceptance among the public.

The Central Government has been investing more and more money for the implementation of the family welfare programmes through its five year plans. The Government. for example, spent a meagre amount of ₹65 lakhs for this purpose in the First Five Year Plan. The Government however, started spending more and more money towards the programme in the other Plans. For example, it spent ₹27 crores in the Third Plan. ₹497 crores in the Filth Plan, ₹1,010 crores in the Sixth Plan, ₹3,221 crores in the Seventh Plan and ₹6,792 crores in the Eighth Plan. The Ninth Plan allocated ₹14,194 crores for this programme.

Uneven Response of the States for the Family Welfare Programme

A state-wise break-up of the figures indicates that while some states notably Punjab, Gujarat, Maharashtra, Karnataka, Haryana and Tamil Nadu are forging ahead in the direction of family planning, some other states such as Bihar, Uttar Pradesh, Assam, Rajasthan. West Bengal, Jammu Kashmir, etc. are lagging behind.

Difficulties Involved in the Implementation of the Family Planning

(*i*) Birth control is associated with a high standard of living, but in India it is very low.

(*ii*) The available contraceptives are not safe, cheap and easily available.

(*iii*) Due to administrative and organisational defects, the message of family planning programme has not reached properly the remotest comers of the country where it is all the more needed.

(*iv*) Illiterate and ignorant people have failed to understand the significance of the programme.

(*v*) Traditional-minded Indians look at the programme with disfavour and suspicion. This, they feel, strikes at the very root of their belief or faith in God.

(*vi*) The use of contraceptives requires privacy in the houses, which is not found in some large joint families.

(*vii*) Finally, the success of the programme depends upon the integrity, sincerity and honesty of the officials engaged in the programme. It is unfortunate, that these officials themselves are not much serious about it.

POPULATION BY RELIGION IN INDIA [1971-2001]

Religion group	1971		1981		1991		2001*	
	Number (million)	%age to total	Number (million)	%age to total	Number (million)	%age to total	Number (million)	%age to total
Hindus	453.4	82.7	549.7	82.6	672.6	82.4	827.50	80.5
Muslims	61.4	11.2	75.6	11.4	95.2	11.7	138.18	13.4
Christians	14.2	2.6	16.2	2.4	18.9	2.3	24.05	2.34
Sikhs	10.4	1.9	13.1	2.0	16.3	2.0	-	-
Buddhists	3.9	0.7	4.7	0.7	6.3	0.8	-	-
Jains	2.6	0.5	3.2	0.5	3.4	0.4	-	-
Other	2.2	0.4	2.8	0.4	3.5	0.4	-	-
Total	548.2	100.0	665.3	100.0	812.3	100.0		

Source: INDIA Year Book-1999. Page-16 * Census Report 2001

REVIEW QUESTIONS

1. What are the problems of overpopulation? Elaborate.
2. Throw light on the growth rate of world population.
3. Is India Overpopulated? Examine.
4. What are the causes for the rapid growth of population in India. Discuss.
5. Elaborate on the effects of overpopulation.
6. Bring out the features of National population policy, 2000.
7. What are the various measures for controlling the rapid growth of population
8. What do you mean by family planning? Discuss its achievements.
9. Write short notes on the following:
   (a) Problem of overpopulation in India
   (b) Population Explosion
   (c) Family planning
10. Highlight the recent demographic situation in India.

⌘⌘⌘⌘⌘⌘⌘⌘⌘⌘⌘

46

The Problem of Poverty

Chapter Outline

- Poverty As a Major Problem of India: Definition of Poverty
- Absolute Poverty and Relative Poverty
- Extent of Poverty in India
- Causes of Poverty
- Remedial Measures for Poverty: The Five Year Plans
- Nationalisation
- Twenty Point Programme
- Other Programmes for Employment Generation and Poverty Alleviation: JRY - PMRY - REGP - SGSY - PMGSY - PMGY - SGRY - VAMBAY - NFWP
- Rural Housing Scheme.

POVERTY AS A MAJOR PROBLEM OF INDIA

Poverty is one of the most widespread socio-economic problems of India. It is, indeed, a common problem being faced with most of the underdeveloped and the developing countries of the world. It is not only socio-economic but even emotional, cultural and political in nature. The developments that have been taking place in this land for the past six decades have not been able to wipe out poverty. Poverty has been the root cause of many of the problems.

The problem of poverty is very closely linked up with unemployment. Poverty and unemployment, the twin social problems are found throughout the length and breadth of this land. As **GR. Madan** points out, "*they have been in existence since the dawn of civilization and one method or the other was devised to help the poverty stricken, the dependent and the unemployed.*" These two problems are not peculiar to India for they are found in good number of Asiatic and African countries.

The study of poverty invites invariably a number of questions : *What is poverty ? What is the extent or magnitude of poverty/ What are the causes of poverty ? How to measure poverty ? What are the social effects of poverty ? What are its economic and social dimensions ? What are the effective solutions to poverty* ? etc. We shall try to find some satisfying answers for these questions.

Definition of Poverty

1. **Gillin** and **Gillin:** "*Poverty is that condition in which a person either because of inadequate income or unwise expenditures, does not maintain a scale of living high enough to provide for his physical and mental efficiency and to enable him and his natural dependents to function usefully according to the standards of the society of which he is a member.*"
2. **Adam Smith:** A person "*... is rich or poor according to the degree in which he can afford to enjoy the necessaries, the conveniences and the amusements of life.*" - [**Adam Smith** in his "*Wealth of Nations* "].

3. **Goddard:** "*Poverty is insufficient supply of those things which are requisite for an individual to maintain himself and those dependent upon him in his health and vigour*."

Explanation of Poverty in terms of "Poverty Line"

The first Director General of FAO [*Food and Agricultural Organization of the UNO*] was the first to explain poverty on the basis of 'starvation line' in 1945. According to him, an intake of less than 2300 calories of food per person per day, was considered the line of starvation and this has been transformed into "poverty line".

- The ***Indian Planning Commission*** defined "*poverty line*" on the basis of nutritional requirements of 2400 calories per person per day for rural areas and 2100 calories per person per day for urban areas.
- A group of Indian economists consisting of **Prof. Gadgil, Dr. V.K.R.V. Rao, Dr. Ganguli, Ashok Mitra** and **Dr. P.S. Lokanathan** worked out the poverty line in their own way. They recommended a standard of private consumption at ₹240 per capita per year at l 960-61 prices as the barest minimum.

ABSOLUTE POVERTY AND RELATIVE POVERTY

These two expressions, absolute poverty and relative poverty, are quite common in any in-depth study of poverty, What do we mean by them?

Absolute Poverty

Right from the 19th century, some researchers are trying to fix some yardstick for measuring poverty in precise terms. Ideally speaking such a yardstick would help us establish a fixed level of poverty, known as "poverty line" below which poverty begins and above which it ends. Such a yardstick is believed to be universal in character and would be applicable to all the societies. This concept of poverty is known as "*absolute poverty*".

Absolute poverty is often known as "*subsistence poverty*" for it is based on assessments of minimum subsistence requirements or basic "physical needs" such as food, clothing, shelter, health requirements etc. Some concepts of absolute poverty would even include the idea of "*basic cultural needs*" This broadens the idea of basic human needs beyond the level of physical survival. **Drewnowski** and **Scott** include education, security, leisure and recreation in their category of "*basic cultural needs*".

Criticisms : The concept of absolute poverty has been widely criticised. It is based on the assumption that there are minimum basic needs for all people in all societies. This is a difficult argument to defend even in regard to subsistence poverty measured in term of food, clothing and shelter. Such needs vary both between and within societies. It becomes still more difficult to defend the concept of absolute poverty when it is extended to include the idea of "basic cultural needs". Such "needs" vary from time to time and place to place and any attempt to establish absolute fixed standards is bound to fail.

Relative Poverty

The difficulties involved in the application of the concept of "absolute poverty", made some researchers to abandon the concept altogether. In place of absolute standards, they have developed the idea of relative standards that is, standards which are relative to particular time and place. In this way, the idea of absolute poverty has been replaced by the idea of relative poverty.

"*Relative poverty is measured in terms of judgements by members of a particular society of what is considered as reasonable and acceptable standard of living and styles of life according to the conventions of the day. Just as conventions change from time to time, and place to place, so will definitions of poverty* "[1]. In a rapidly changing world, definitions of poverty based on relative standards will be constantly changing. Hence, **Peter Townsend** has suggested that any definition of poverty must be "*related to the needs and demands of a changing society*."

Limitations of the Usage of this Concept

Even the concept of relative poverty presents certain problems. It cannot be assumed that there are universally accepted standards of reasonable and acceptable life-styles. Within a particular society, ethnicity, class, religion, region, age and a variety of other factors can vary judgements of reasonable living standards.

The concept of relative poverty poses problems for the comparison of the poor in the same society over time and

[1] M.H. Haralambos in "*Sociology Themes and Perspectives*", p. 142.

between societies. For example, it becomes difficult to make a comparison of the poor in present - day and 19th century India; or of present-day India and European countries or those of African countries.

EXTENT OF POVERTY IN INDIA

Though India is regarded as a developing country it is very badly facing the problem of poverty. We became independent six decades ago and still our society has not become tree from the stranglehold of the problems such as poverty, over-population, unemployment, illiteracy, etc. It is unfortunate that in India appropriate and reliable data for the direct estimation of poverty are not available. The government has not made any serious attempt in this direction. However, some private individuals and agencies have made their own attempts to estimate poverty.

(*i*) ***Estimates of Dandekar and Rath*** : As per the estimates of **Dandekar** and **Rath**, as early as in 1960-61 roughly 40% of the rural population and 50% of the urban population were living below poverty line.

(*ii*) ***Estimates of S.S. Minhas*** : The study of Dr. Minhas revealed that about 65% of population in 1956-57 and 50.6% of population in 1967-68 in rural India were living below the poverty line.

(*iii*) ***Planning Commission's estimates***: On the basis of a large sample survey data on consumer expenditure, conducted by the NSSO [National Sample Survey Organization], the Planning Commission estimated poverty in the country at the national and state level. These estimates made by the Commission at an interval of approximately five years, give us some picture about the extent of poverty in India uptil 1990-2000. The following *Table-1* throw some light on the extent of poverty in India. As the table reveals that in 1999-2000, 26.1% of the people, that is, 260.3 million people were living below the poverty line. As per the poverty projection made for the year 2007, the figures were likely to be at 19.3% and 220% million respectively.

Table 1 Estimates of incidence of Poverty in India

Year	Poverty ratio [percent]			Number of poor (million)		
	Rural	Urban	Combined	Rural	Urban	Combined
1977-78	53.1	45.2	51.3	264.3	64.6	328.90
1983	45.7	40.8	44.5	252.0	70.9	322.90
1987-94	39.1	38.2	38.9	231.9	75.2	307.10
1993-94	37.3	32.4	36.0	244.0	76.3	320.30
1999-00	27.1	23.6	26.1	193.2	67.1	260.30
2007*	21.1	15.1	19.3	170.5	49.6	220.10

*Poverty protection for 2007.

Source: Economic Survey, 2003-04.

Extent of Poverty in Different States

The level of poverty is not the same in all the states. Poverty was found to be highest in Orissa [47.15%] in 1999-2000 and Bihar [46.2%] respectively. in U.P., highest number of poor people [5.29 crore, or 31.5%] were found. The estimates reveal that in l999 – 2000, about **193.2** million poor people were living in rural areas and **67.1** million, in urban areas. In Karnataka, about 104.40 lakh [20.04%] people were living below the poverty line.

The following ***Table*** **2** reveals the number of persons living below poverty line in different states during 1999-2000.

Table 2 Percentage of Poor in Different States

States/U.T./s	No. of Persons [in lakhs]	% of Persons
Andhra Pradesh	119.01	15.77
Arunachal Pradesh	3.98	33.47
Assam	94.55	36.09
Bihar	425.64	42.60
Goa	0.70	4.40
Gujrat	67.89	14.07

(*Contd.*)

Haryana	17.34	8.74
Himachal Pradesh	5.12	7.63
Jammu & Kashmir	3.46	3.48
Karnataka	104.40	20.04
Kerala	41.04	12.72
Madhya Pradesh	298.54	37.43
Maharashtra	227.99	25.02
Manipur	7.19	28.54
Meghalaya	8.23	33.87
Mizoram	1.85	19.47
Nagaland	5.49	32.67
Orissa	169.09	47.15
Punjab	14.49	6.16
Rajasthan	81.83	15.28
Sikkim	2.05	36.55
Tamil Nadu	130.48	21.12
Tripura	13.02	34.44
Uttar Pradesh	529.89	31.15
West Bengal	213.49	27.02
A & N Island	0.82	20.99
Chandigarh	0.51	5.75
Dadra & Nagar Haveli	0.33	17.14
Daman & Diu	0.06	4.44
Delhi	11.49	8.23
Lakshadweep	0.11	15.60
Pondicherry	2.41	21.67

Source: Rajya Sabha, Unstarred question 807.

Estimates of Poverty. Based NSS Data—2004

The following ***Table*** 3 reveals yet another estimate of poverty for the latest period, that is 2004.

Table 3 Percentage of Poor and Total Number of Poor in India Since 1973

Year	Percentage of Poor (%)	Number of Poor (million)	Average Annual Rate of Decline
1973-74	54.9	321	0.59
1977-78	51.3	329	0.31
1983	44.5	323	0.31
1987-88	38.9	307	1.25
1993-94	36.0	320	0.70
1999-00	26.1	260	3.40
2004*	23.6	250	0.82

*Based on the estimated population of 2004 and poverty ratio calculated using latest NSS data in 2004.

Source: National institute of Rural Development [2004]; Rural Development Statistics [2002-03].

CAUSES OF POVERTY

The causes of poverty many sided. However, they may be discussed under the following heads: (*i*) *Individual incapacity,* (*ii*) *Economic factors*, (*iii*) *Social factors*. (*iv*) *Demographic factors, and* (*v*) *other factors*.

(i) Individual Incapacity and Other Deficiencies

From the view point of the ideology of individualism, the individual failure itself is responsible for poverty. Success or failure in life, according to this ideology, is entirely a personal matter. Hence, it is logical to conclude that if an individual fails to achieve success in life and suffers from poverty, he himself is to be blamed for his laziness, inactivity, lack of initiative, dullness and incapacities. The Protestant Ethic described by Max Weber also emphasizes this aspect.

What factors contribute to individual incapacity **?**: There are various causes for an individual's failure. Failure in life may be due to some inborn deficiencies such as physical or mental handicap, dumbness, deafness, blindness, feeblemindedness, deficient legs and hands, and so on. Some of the deficiencies might have been developed later in life. Since an individual does not have any control over many of these deficiencies, he is bound to yield to them and suffer from them. They make such an individual a parasite on society.

Some of the deficiencies which can be managed or overcome, are often neglected by some individuals and hence they fall a prey to the problem of poverty. We may include under this category, deficiencies such as illiteracy, laziness, extravagance, immorality, bad habits such as gambling, alcoholism, etc.

(ii) Economic Causes of Poverty

1. ***Inadequate economic development***: Our economic development since independence has been disappointing in certain respects. The rate of growth of our economy between 1951-91 has been just 3.5% which is negligible. During the year 2004-05, though this rate of growth increased to 5%, it was not enough to fight the challenges of poverty. Our per capita income is still very less. It was around ₹255/- in 1950-51, and it increased to ₹19,649/- [at 1990-00 prices] in 2004-05. In comparison with other advanced countries this is quite less.
2. ***Increasing unemployment***: Our economy has not provided enough employment opportunities for the people. Hence unemployment is mounting. In 1952, the number of registered unemployed persons was about 4.37 lakhs and it increased to 334 lakhs in 1990. By December 1991, the figure had swelled to 36.3 million. It further increased to 41.39 million by the end of December, 2003[2].
3. ***Unmanageable inflationary pressures***: Due to incessant inflation, the value of money has come down. It came down to 8.28 paise in 1990-91. The annual rate of inflation was estimated to be at 13.4% in 1991 and with great difficulty it was brought down to 7.3% in 1997. The value of rupee further decreased to 7.2 paise at 1960-61 prices. This uncontrolled inflation adversely affected the purchasing power of the common people.
4. ***Capital deficiency***: Industries require huge capital for their fast growth. But lack of enough capital has hampered the growth of our industries. The process of economic liberalization which has been let loose recently, has of course, started showing its positive results during these days. Time is not ripe to pass find judgements and its results.
5. ***Too much dependence on agriculture***: Our economy is primarily an agrarian economy. More than 65% of the people are still dependent on agriculture. Agriculture has its own limitations. In India, in particular, people are following the traditional method of cultivation and hence agricultural production is comparatively very less.

(iii) Demographic Factors

Population in India is growing at an alarming rate. Within 60 years [1921-1981] it had doubled. It has reached an incredible number of 122.3 crore in 2008. Hence, the little progress that is achieved in the economic sphere is being eaten away by the growing population. As per 1998-99 estimate, 8% of the people [9.60 crores] are above 60 years and their capacity to contribute to economic production is limited. About 35.7% of the people are below 14 years of age and hence are incapable of earning.

The size of the Indian family is relatively bigger. The average size of the Indian family is around 4.2. The growing size of the population has it adverse effects on people's health. A sizeable number of people are suffering from various diseases for which proper medical treatment is not available.

---

[2] As per the estimate of NSSO [National Sample Survey Organisation], by the end of 1999-2000, there were around 19.50 million unemployed people in rural India, and around 7.11 million in the urban sector.

(iv) Social Causes

(a) ***Traditionalism***: India is a land of traditionalism, communalism, casteism, linguism, parochialism, religious and linguistic prejudices and so on. These factors have a negative effect on country's progress by making people dogmatic in their approach and narrow — minded and selfish in outlook.

(b) ***Illiteracy and ignorance:*** Illiteracy and ignorance are supportive of poverty. By 2001, there were about 38 crore illiterates in the country. Further, our defective educational system is incapable of generating employment and there is no guarantee of job for the educated youths.

(c) ***Dominance of caste and joint families:*** Our caste system still has its hold on the caste members. The caste system compels its members to stick on to the traditional and hereditary occupations of the caste. It does not give encouragement to the caste members to take up to jobs of their choices. In the very same manner, the joint families which are still dominant in the rural areas do not allow young members to take initiative in making new adventures in the employment and economic spheres.

(v) Other Causes

1. ***Long period of foreign rule***: India was under foreign rule for a very long period. The British who ruled India ruthlessly, had systematically spoiled the basic economic structure of our land and destroyed the various arts, crafts, cottage and small scale industries which we had previously. They exploited Indian resources for the glory of Britain and made Indians parasites in several respects.
2. ***Climatic factors***: Climate can also be a cause of poverty. The hot climate of India reduces the capacity of the people to work, and hence, naturally, production cannot be increased in the desired quantity.
3. ***Wars and threats of war***: India had to spend huge amount of money on wars which she had fought with China and Pakistan. There is constant threat of war also. Hence huge amount of money is being spent on our defence industry. About 15% to 25% of national income was spent previously for defence purposes and it was reduced to 16.7% in 1989-90.
4. ***Defective political system and lack of political will:*** Indian political system is very often condemned as corrupt, inefficient and defective. Unhealthy competition among the political parties for power has many a times damaged our national interests. Our political leaders lack nationalistic fervour and will power to face the challenges that are confronting the nation.

REMEDIAL MEASURES FOR POVERTY

The British did not bother about the poor condition of Indians as long as they ruled over India. When India became independent in 1947, it started paying more attention to the problem of poverty and undertook many measures and launched many schemes, programmes and projects for the removal of poverty. Here is a brief survey of such measures.

1. The Five Year Plans

The Indian Government set up the Planning Commission in 1950 and started the Five Year Plans with a view to develop the country in a methodical manner.

The First Five Year Plan [1951-56] had spent about ₹2378 crores for various developmental. purposes and this amount had almost increased to 15.92 lakh crores in the 10th Five Year Plan, 2002-07. These Five Year Plans mainly aimed at–attaining self-reliance in agricultural production, the removal of unemployment; achieving desirable progress in industry, increasing standard of living, and finally, at wiping out poverty.

The progress achieved through these Plans, though not satisfactory cannot be neglected. In the time span of about 40 years after Independence we could achieve an annual economic growth of about 3% as against the world average of 4%. This annual growth rate, however, crossed 5.5% in the decade of 1980s, and the 10th Plan intended to achieve 8% growth of GDP. Between 1951-1991 , the number of people living below the line of poverty has been reduced by about 28%. The 10th Plan poised to reduce it to 21% by 2007. The government is hopeful of achieving considerable progress especially in the industrial sector by means of implementation of the policy of economic liberalization.

2. Nationalisation

With a view to facilitate economic growth, 14 banks were nationalized in 1962, when Indira Gandhi was the Prime Minister of India. Afterwards in 1972, coal mines were nationalized and that was followed by government taking control of big private iron and steel company and wholesale business in food grains. Nationalisation did not provide the expected benefits. Lack of efficiency, initiative and commitment to the cause, have been main casualities of the process of nationalization. Only in two areas, branch expansion and grant of loan to the weaker sections, the banks have achieved some progress. The overall performance of many of these banks is, far from satisfactory. The government now seems to have learnt that nationalization cannot be the panacea for problems and hence it is switching over to the opposite pole of privatization.

3. Twenty Point Programme

During the period of emergency (1975-78), Indira Gandhi, the then prime minister of India, introduced the much publicized 20-point programme with the main intention of removing poverty ("*Garibi Hatao*") and economic exploitation; and upliftment of weaker sections of the society.

Under this scheme, number of programmes were included: *development of S.C., S.T. and other backward classes: distribution of surplus land to the weaker sections, providing minimum wages to the landless workers, providing irrigational facilities to the rural people and expanding their employment opportunities, family planning, extension of primary health services, welfare of women, children and labourers, simplifications of industrial policy, extension of primary education facilities, providing drinking water to all villages, etc.*

Though many of the programmes included under the 20 point programme were laudable, they could not be effectively implemented for want of honesty and commitment on the part of the government officials and political leaders. The programme could only create awareness among the weaker sections, and in various other respects, it was a failure.

4. Other Programmes for Employment Generation and Poverty Alleviation

Among the other anti-poverty and employment generation programmes launched by the Government, the following ones deserve a special mention.

(i) The JRY: Jawahar Rozgar Yojana: The JRY [*Jawahar Rozgar Yojna*] was introduced in the month of April 1989 with the intention of helping at least one member of each poorest family by providing employment for about 50 to 100 days in a year at his own work place or residential area. About 30% of the jobs under this programme are reserved for women. The expenditure of this Yojna is to be shared by the Centre and State at 80:20 ratios respectively. About 80% of the funds obtained by the Centre and State are to be utilized through the Gram Panchayats for helping the targeted beneficiaries. The existing rural wage employment programmes such as NREP and RLEGP were merged into the JRY.

As per the provision of this Yojna, Panchayats with a population ranging between 4000 to 5000 persons are given an annual financial assistance from **₹0.80** lakh to **1** lakh. But 30% of the money goes only for women. In the year 1990-91, about ₹500 crore was spent under this Yojna. It covers about 46% of the population.

In the 8th Plan, about ₹30,000 crore was allotted for rural development out of which JRY got about ₹18,400 crores. Apart from this Central assistance, the JRY got the state assistance of about ₹400 crore. In the year 1998-99, ₹2095 crore was allotted for the implementation of this Yojna and by the end of 1998, around 190 million mandays of employment was created for the needy people. This scheme has been implemented in 2,20,000 villages all over the country. In April 1999, in place of JRY the Jawahar Gram Samriddhi Yojna came into being.

(ii) Prime Minister's Rozgar Yojana [PMRY] 1993: This scheme launched in 1995, has the objective of making available self-employment opportunities to the educated unemployed youth. The PMRY is meant for educated unemployed youth with family income up to ₹40,000 per annum, in both urban and rural areas, for engaging in any economically viable activity.

(iii) Rural Employment Generation Programme [REGP] 1995: With the objective of creating self-employment opportunities in the rural areas and small towns the REGP was launched in 1995. The scheme is being implemented by the KVIC, that is, *Khadi and Village Industries Commission*. A target of creating 25 lakh new jobs has been set for the REGP during the 10th Plan.

[It may be noted here that some of the schemes and programmes launched by the Government earlier were replaced by or got merged into the new ones. For example, the IRDP [Integrated Rural Development Programme] initiated in 1978–79 was replaced by the SGSY [Swarna Jayanthi Gram Swamzgar Yojna] in 1999; the NREP and RLEGP [National Rural Employment Programme and Rural Landless Employment Guarantee Programme] were merged into JRY that is Jawahar Rozgar Yojana in 1989; the EAS [Employment Assurance Scheme] got merged with the SGRY [Sampoorna Grameena Rozgar Yojana] and so on.]

(*iv*) ***Pradhan Mantri Gramodaya Yajana [PMGY] 2000***: The PMGY was launched in 2000-2001 in all the states with the objective of achieving sustainable human development at the village level. Initially, it had five components namely; *primary health, primary education, rural shelter, rural drinking water and nutrition, and rural electrification*. The Central Assistance for this yojna amounted to ₹2800 crores for the period 2003-05.

(*v*) ***Pradhan Mantri Gram Sadak Yojana [PMGSY] 2000:*** This scheme came into force in December 2000 to provide connectivity to 1.6 lakh unconnected habitations with population of 500 persons or more in the rural areas by the end of the 10th plan. The scheme estimate indicated a requirement of ₹60,000 crores in the beginning. The present estimates reveal that it requires at least. ₹1,130,000 crore for its achievement. It is being executed in all the States and Union Territories. The scheme is in force and about 88685 kms of rural roads have been taken up under this programmes.

(*vi*) ***Swarnajayanthi Gram Swarozgar Yojana [SGSY] 1999:*** The SGSY launched in April 1999 in place of the IRDP [Integrated Rural Development Programme], is the only self-employment programme currently being implemented. This scheme provides assistance to swarozgar is above the poverty line in the form of income-generating assets through bank credit and government subsidy. The scheme is being implemented on a 75:25 cost sharing between the Centre and the States. Since its inception, and up to April 2004, a total allocation of ₹6734 crore was made available for this scheme by the Centre and States.

(*vii*) ***Sampoorna Grameen Rozgar Yojana [SGRY] 2001***: This scheme came into force in Sept. 2001 by merging in it the on-going schemes of Jawahar Gram Samridhi Yojana [J GSY] and Employment Assurance Scheme [EAS]. This is open to all rural poor who are in need of wage employment and desire to do manual and unskilled work in and around the rural habitat. The programme is to be implemented through Panchayat Raj institutions. The cost-sharing of the scheme between the Centre and the States is in the ratio of 75:25. During the year 2003-04 alone an amount of ₹4,121 crore as cash component and about 50 lakh tones of food grains were released to the States/UTs.

(*viii*) ***Valmiki Ambedkar Awas Yojana [VAMBA Y] 2001***: The VAMBAY, launched in December 2001, intends to find remedy to the horrible conditions of the urban slum dwellers living below the poverty line without adequate shelter. The Centre provides 50% subsidy to the states to implement this scheme. Since its inception up to December 2004, the Central Govt. has released a total subsidy of ₹753 crore.

(*ix*) ***National Food for Work Programme [NFWP] 2004***: This programme was launched on November 14th 2004 in 150 most backward districts of the country. Its objective was to intensify the generation of supplementary wage employment. It is open to those rural poor who are in need of wage employment and desire to do manual unskilled work. This programme is 100% centrally sponsored one and the food grains are supplied to the states freely. Rupees 2020 crore had been allocated for the programme in the year 2004-05 in addition to 20 lakh tones of food grains.

(*x*) ***Rural Housing Schemes:*** The Government has also launched rural housing schemes such as *Indira Awas Yojana* [IAY] which intend to provide dwelling units, free of cost, to the poor families of the Scheduled Castes, Scheduled tribes, freed bonded-labourers and also to those who are below the poverty line in the rural areas. Since its inception up to June 2004, as many as 113.96 lakh houses have been constructed/upgraded by spending as much ₹19,869 crore.

Conclusion

It is an indisputable fact that India still remains a poor country in spite of our various developmental projects, plans and programmes. An all-pervading problem like poverty cannot be removed all on a sudden. Governmental agencies and instruments alone cannot fix a master solution for it. People's active involvement in various developmental programmes is equally important. Above all, we require committed civil servants, dedicated bureaucrats, strong political leaders committed to the cause of nation and a 'general will' on the part of people to march ahead, facing the challenges of poverty.

REVIEW QUESTIONS

1. Poverty is one of the most widespread socio-economic problems of India. Discuss.
2. Define poverty. Explain poverty in terms of poverty line.
3. Explain absolute poverty and relative poverty. What are the differences between these two.
4. Throw light on the extent of poverty in different states of India.
5. Analyse the causes of poverty.
6. What are the remedial measures of poverty? Explain.

⌘⌘⌘⌘⌘⌘⌘⌘⌘⌘⌘

47

UNEMPLOYMENT PROBLEM

CHAPTER OUTLINE

UNEMPLOYMENT – A GLOBAL PHENOMENON

Along with the problem of poverty, unemployment is also widespread in India. It is indeed, common to all the countries of the world whether they are industrially advanced or not. An international labour expert commented; (in September 1992) — "*About 400 million new workers are expected to enter the world's labour force this decade and prospects of finding jobs for all of them are gloomy*".

The Finnish directors of the *International Labour Organization's* (ILO) employment department, **Juhani Lonnroth**, has said in one of his speeches that "*the population of the working age in the world will grow by 700 million people in the 1990s. With the conserving assumption that 55% off " these people will seek employment, about 400 million jobs will have to be created to absorb the new entrants. Unfortunately, the prospects of achieving these rates of job creation are not yet very bright*". The problem is, of course, more acute for Asian countries rather than for the African and Latin American countries because of the serious population explosion in these countries. India with its huge population, thus cannot be an exception.

WHAT IS UNEMPLOYMENT?

- "*Unemployment is a state of worklessness for a man fit and willing to work, that is, it is a condition of involuntary and not voluntary idleness*."- **C.B. Mamoria**.
- Unemployment is defined as "*a condition in which an individual is not in a state of remunerative occupation despite his desire do so.* " - **D'Mello**.
- Unemployment is often described as a "condition of involuntary idleness"–**NAVA GOPAL DAS.**
- ***In simple words***, it could be said that *unemployment is largely concerned with those men and women who constitute the labour free of the country, who are able-bodied and willing to work but are not gainfully employed.*

MAGNITUDE OR ESTIMATES OF UNEMPLOYMENT IN INDIA

Though the problem of unemployment is growing in an unmanageable proportion we do not have authentic information regarding the exact number of unemployed persons in India. It is regrettable that institutions such as *Planning Commission*; *National Sample Survey*, and the, *Central Statistical Organization* (or the *Indian Statistical Institute*) have not made any systematic and satisfactory attempt to collect authentic information about unemployment.

We have, however, three sources to collect some statistics regarding the extent of unemployment in India. They are: (*i*) *The National Census* which is held once in ten years; (*ii*) *The National sample Survey*; and (*iii*) *The Employment Exchange Registrations*. Of these, the information collected through the National Sample Survey is being used widely. Neither *the Census Reports*, nor the *Directorate -General of Employment and Training* [D.G.E.T], nor the *Employment Exchanges* nor any other agency, could give any dependable quantitative estimate of the magnitude of the problem.

The statistics which we obtain through these three sources cannot be considered as highly authentic and foolproof. Many a times, they are to be treated only as approximations or rough estimates. These estimates very often take into consideration the number of persons registered in the employment exchange and these exchanges cover mainly the urban areas. Rural areas are not covered by them. Since registration with the employment exchange is voluntary, all the unemployed do not go for registration. Further, some people who are already in some ordinary jobs also go for registration for they intend to secure some good jobs. These exchanges may not supply full information about people who are "unemployed".

Some Estimates of Unemployment in India

(*i*) The number of unemployed persons in India registered in the employment exchanges in 1952 was 4.37 lakhs and it increased to 334 lakhs in 1990.[1]

(*ii*) Between 1952 and 1970, that is, within the time interval of 18 years, the number of registered unemployed persons had increased about 8 times; and between l971 and 1990 it got increased by 6.8 times. By the end of December 1991, the number of unemployed people had reached 36.3 million.[2]

(*iii*) ***Estimates of Bhagavathi committee:*** As per the estimates of this Committee, there were 18.7 million unemployed persons in the country in 1971 out of which 16.1 million were in rural areas and 2.6 million in urban areas. As per the figures for 2003, about **41.39** million individuals were waiting (for jobs) in the live registers of 945 employment exchanges scattered over the whole nation.

(*iv*) ***NSSO estimates*:** As per the 55th NASSO Round of reports (1990-2000), the absolute number of unemployed increased from 20 million in 1993-94 to 27 million in 1990-2000. Out of these 27 million unemployed individuals, 7.11 million were in urban areas and 19.50 million people were in rural areas.

(*v*) ***Planning Commission Estimates of 8th and 9th Plan*:** "*The total numbers of persons requiring employment during the 8th Plan (as per the estimates of Planning Commission) would be around 65 million. It is expected that during 1995-2000, labour force would increase by 41 million. Thus by the year 2000 A.D., the total number of job-seekers would be around 106 million.*"[3]

SOME SALIENT FEATURES OF UNEMPLOYMENT PROBLEM IN INDIA

We may identify the following as some special features of unemployment in India.

1. Unemployed people are not equally distributed in all the states of India. For example, more than half the total unemployed persons live in three states of northern India [as per the statistics of 1990s] that is, West Bengal, Bihar and U.P. and two states of South India, that is Kerala and Tamilnadu.
2. As per the Census report of 1991, excepting of 1991, excepting rural Kerala and urban Orissa in almost all other places, there has been an increase in the number of female employees. Of the total number of women of employable age, about 19.19% in the rural areas and about 8.63% in the urban areas were found to be full-fledged employees.
3. In spite of this increase in the number of female employees, unemployment rates for women are higher than those for men.
4. The incidence of unemployment is relatively lower in rural areas and higher in urban areas.
5. There is greater unemployment in agricultural sector than in industrial and other sectors.
6. The incidence of unemployment among the educated is much higher (about 12%) than overall unemployment that is found in the nation [that is 3.8%]

[1] *India Today*, May 31, 1991.

[2] *Manorama Year Book*—1993.

[3] Ruddar Datt and K.P.M. Sundharam in *Indian Economy* (2008 edition), p. 38.7

7. Finally, the growth of employment per annum is only about 2 per cent.

Table 1 Projection of Unemployment for 1990-200			
			Millions
1.	Backlog of unemployed in the beginning of 1990	-	28
2.	New entrants to the labour force during 1990-95		37
	Total unemployed for the 8th plan [1 + 2]		65
3.	New entrants to the labour force during 1995-2000		41
4.	Total unemployed for the 9th plan	-	106

***Source*:** Compiled from the Planning Commission.

TYPES OF UNEMPLOYMENT

We may speak of different types of unemployment such as the following : *seasonal unemployment, agricultural unemployment, frictional and technological unemployment, industrial unemployment, cyclical unemployment, educational unemployment, voluntary unemployment, involuntary unemployment or under—employment, open unemployment and disguised unemployment*.

Seasonal Unemployment

Seasonal unemployment is very much associated with agriculture. During the off- season many labourers will have to spend their time idly without having any work. In some industries such as sugar, woollen and ice factories, workers get jobs only for a certain period of the year or in a particular season. When the season is over, they don't get work in the factories and they will have to wait for the next season to come to find the same work. This type of unemployment may often make the labourers to become migratory in character.

Agricultural Unemployment

Agricultural unemployment is caused by a number of factors such as the very seasonal nature of agricultural work, the decay of cottage industries, lack of demand for homemade products, lack of alternative work in the rural areas, sub-division of land holdings, etc. **R.K. Mukherjee** has said in his "*Rural Economy of India*" that on an average a cultivator in north India does not remain busy for more than 200 days in a year.

Studies have revealed that "*of the total population in the rural areas, only 29.4% people are self supporting, 59.0% are non earning dependents, and I I . 6% are earning dependents. This means that 29.4% people not only support themselves but they also support the remaining 70.6% people as well*".[4]

Technological and Frictional Unemployment

Sometimes in the technological field '*friction*' is caused due to an imbalance between *the supply of labours and the demand for it*. This friction does not allow the potentialities of the labour to be tapped. Even though unemployed workers are there ready to work, they may not be fit for the work, or they may not have the required skill and qualification to do the work. Since the demand of the customers is constantly shifting from one product to another, it become difficult for workers to catch up with the tastes and choices of the workers. Such shifts in consumer demand may make certain factories to be closed down leaving behind a trail of unemployment.

Technological unemployment is caused mainly because of the introduction of labour-saving machines. It is caused due to the reduction of man power necessary to produce a finished article. The process of automation and mechanization have caused great anxieties and insecurities for worker: displacing good number of them from work. Introduction of computers in the beginning stages can be cited here as an example. Every advance in technology virtually means today, displacement of human labour to some or the other extent.

Industrial Unemployment

Industrial unemployment is caused in another manner. Due to high pressure of people on land, a large number of rural people are moving towards urban areas in search of jobs in some factories or the other, only to get disappointment in a short time. Slow growth of industries, competition with foreign industries, unplanned industrialization, defective industrial policies, labour strikes or employer's lock-out, rationalization, etc., may also cause industrial unemployment.

---

[4] Ram Ahuja in his *Social Problem in India*, p. 70

Cyclical Unemployment

Due to the "*trade cycles*"; booms, recessions and depressions are common in the business world. Such ups-and-downs in business influence the volume of unemployment which decreases when trade is good and increases when it is bad. If depression continues for a longer period (like the Great Depression of 1925-30) it adversely affects the labourers by turning them out of job or by providing no fresh job opportunities.

Educational Unemployment

There is a close link between the job opportunities and the system of education. In fact, in one of its annual report, the UGC (University Grants Commission) itself has commented that the present system of education is "*generating much waste and stagnation*". The ***Kothari Commission*** (1964-66) had admitted long back that there is a wide gulf between "*the contents of the present education and purposes and the concerns of national development*". Even after 1966, thorough overhauling of our educational system to make it relevant to the needs and demands of the time, has not been made. Hence, every year we are producing thousands of degree- holders only to join the rank of the educated unemployed youths. *For example*, in 1965 there were 9 lakh unemployed graduates in the country, and the number increased to 5.6 million in 1977. The figure of educated unemployed persons in the nation was 34,66,435 as on November 30th 1991. West Bengal has the largest number of educated unemployed persons (degree holders) in the country (27.21% of the total unemployed) followed by Bihar (24.85%), Kerala (21.10%) and Karnataka (18.49%).

Temporary Unemployment

Our young men and women who are capable of securing for themselves some jobs, do not get them soon after their education. Many of them are made to wait for some time during which they remain as unemployed. People often change their jobs, and in the interval of changing they may remain as unemployed for a short period.

Voluntary Unemployment

Voluntary unemployment is found when the worker voluntarily withdraws himself from the work. He may do so due to the quarrel with the employer, or he may have other sources of income. This condition is relatively rare and hence this type of unemployment is not given much importance.

Involuntary Unemployment or Under-employment

Lord Keynes uses the concept of involuntary unemployment for under-employment. It refers to a condition in which the self–employed working people are not working to their full capacity. People who are partially employed, or are doing inferior jobs while they could do better jobs are not adequately employed. It can be called a state of "*under-employment*".

Open Unemployment or Structural Unemployment

Open unemployment is also called "*structural unemployment*". It is the result of lack of complementary resources especially capital. *Open unemployment is a situation wherein a large labour force does not get work opportunities that may fetch them regular income*. Open unemployment is the result particularly when a large reserve army of labour exists which does not find any income- fetching job. Open unemployment emerges because the rate of capital accumulation lags behind the rate of population growth.

Disguised Unemployment

Disguised unemployment is that type of unemployment which cannot be seen or known from outside. It is concealed or hidden. It refers to a situation in which men or women work the whole day but fail to make any contribution to the total output. It is a state of affair in which a person's marginal productivity or contribution is close to zero. This type of unemployment is very much acute and apparent in the rural area. For example, of the **10** people who have been working in a piece of land, even if 3 persons migrate to cities, the productivity of the land does not get affected. This shows that the contribution of the 3 persons to productivity is virtually zero.

CAUSES OF UNEMPLOYMENT

The problem of unemployment is becoming a colossal one. Various factors, individual as well as social, have caused this problem. Here the causation is not one–sided. F or example, unemployment is often the cause of poverty and some other time, its consequence also. Hence, tracing the causes of unemployment is a difficult task.

C.B. Mamoria lists out the causes of unemployment in India in the following way:

(*i*) The policy of "*laissez-faire*" or free trade pursued by the British did not accelerate the process of industrialization in India. As a result, employment opportunities could not be generated on a large scale, during the British rule. This situation continued up to the end of their rule in India.

(*ii*) The unchecked growth of population from 1921 onwards posed the problems of finding job opportunities. *For example*, our population in 1921 was 251.3 millions and it increased to 361.0 millions in 1951. It has reached a record figure of 122.3 crore in 2008.

(*iii*) The decline of traditional skills and the decay of small scale and cottage industries led to a great pressure on land and this in turn resulted in the greater exodus of people from the rural to the urban areas. This added to urban unemployment.

(*iv*) The low level of investment and the neglect of industrial sector could not help the process of creating job opportunities.

GR. Madan speaks of two main types of causes of unemployment : (A) "*individual or personal factors* ", and (B) "*external factors*" or "*technological and economic factors*".

Individual or Personal Factors of Unemployment

(*i*) ***Age factor***: Age factor fixes limitations on the range of choice of job opportunities. Too young and too old people are not eligible for many of the jobs. Some young people due to their inexperience, and some old people due to their old age, fail to get some jobs. Young people do not get jobs soon after their studies. They will have to wait. People who are above 50 or 60 years are less adaptable and more prone to accidents. Their capacity to contribute to economic production is also relatively less.

(*ii*) ***Vocational unfitness:*** Many of our young people do not have a proper understanding of their own aptitudes, abilities and interests on the one hand, and the tasks or jobs or career they want to pursue, on the other. If willingness to do some job is not followed by the required abilities, one cannot find a job of one's selection. Employers are always looking forward to find persons who have the ability, experience, interest and physical fitness to work. Sometimes, there may be more men trained in a particular profession than required. The demand is less than the supply, and hence, unemployment.

(*iii*) ***Illness and/or physical disabilities or incapabilities***: Due to the inborn or acquired disabilities or deficiencies some remain as partially employed or totally unemployed throughout their life. Illness induced by industrial conditions and the fatal accidents that often take place during the work may render a few other people as unemployed.

External Factors or Technological and Economic Factors

(*i*) ***enormous increase in population***: The population in India is growing at an alarming rate. Every year India adds to her population 120 to 130 lakh people afresh. More than this, every year about 5 million people become eligible for securing jobs. All these people who are eligible to work are not getting the jobs. Hence, population explosion in India is making the problem of unemployment more and more dangerous.

(*ii*) ***Trade cycle***: Business field is subject to ups and downs due to the operation of trade cycle. Economic depression which we witness in trade cycle may induce some problematic or sick industries to be closed down compelling their employees to become unemployed. Fluctuations in international markets, heavy imposition of excise duties, business strains observed in the trade cycles adversely affect the security of jobs of some men.

(*iii*) ***Technological advance–mechanisation–automation***: Technological advancement undoubtedly contributes to economic development. But unplanned and uncontrolled growth of technology may have an adverse effect on job opportunities. Since industrialists are more interested in maximizing production and profit they prefer to introduce labour-saving machines. They always search for ways and means of reducing the cost of production and hence go after computerization, automation, etc. The result is technological unemployment. This state of affairs is very much in evidence in the Indian context today.

(*iv*) ***Strikes and lockouts***: Strikes and lockouts had been an inseparable aspect of the Indian industrial field. Due to strikes and lockouts production used to come down and industries were incurring heavy losses. Workers used to become unemployed for a temporary period and some were being thrown out of job. This state of affairs continued almost up to 1990s, that is, till the launching of the [NEP] *New Economic Policy*. This, prolonged period of four decades our industries received severe setbacks due to labour strikes which affected adversely industrial growth and industrial potential for fetching jobs. After 1990s, things however, have been changing and labour strikes are becoming comparatively rarer.

(*v*) ***Slow rtate of economic growth***: Job opportunities depend very much on economic growth. Since the rate of economic growth was very slow in the first 45 years after independence, the economy was not able to create enough job opportunities to the increasing number of job - seekers. For example, in 19805, the rate of growth of the number of job-seekers increased by 2.2%, while the rate of growth of the number of job opportunities was only 1.5%. This difference led to an enormous increase in the number of unemployed persons.

(*vi*) ***Backwardness of indian agriculture***: Age old mode of cultivation, too much dependence of too many people [more than 75%] on agriculture, widespread disguised unemployment, sentimental attachment towards land, etc., have adversely affected the–growth of Indian agriculture and its employment potential.

Other Causes of Unemployment

In addition to the two main types of the causes of unemployment as mentioned by G.R. Madan, we may add a few other factors causing the problem such as the following.

(*i*) ***Unpreparedness to accept socially degrading jobs:*** Some of our young men and women are not prepared to undertake jobs which are considered to be socially "*degrading*" or "*indecent*". *Example* : Auto rickshaw and taxi-driving, working as salesmen or sales girls in shops, doing waiter's work and clerical work in hotels, etc., could be mentioned here as examples. Since the spirit of the dignity of labour is not properly inculcated in them, they become the victims of "*false prestige*" and face the risk of unemployment.

(*ii*) ***Defects in our educational system***: Our system of education which appears like a remnant of the British colonial rule in India, has its own irreparable defects and its contribution to the problem of unemployment can hardly be exaggerated. There is no co-ordination between our industrial growth, agricultural development and our-educational system. Our education does not prepare the minds of our young men to become self-employed; on the contrary, it makes them to depend on government to find for them some jobs.

(*iii*) ***Geographic immobility of the workers***: Occupational mobility and geographic mobility on the part of the workers lessen the gravity of the problem of unemployment. But in the Indian context, workers are not adventurous enough to move from one physical area to another in search of jobs, or to change their jobs to brighten their economic prospects. They are either clinging on to their traditional profession or occupations especially in the rural area, or concentrated in one or the other urban centre, sometimes without any job.

(*iv*) ***Improper use of human resources***: Lack of planning for the efficient utilization of human resources for productive purposes has been one of the causes of unemployment in India. In fact, there has been no proper co-ordination between the availability of human resources and its utilization in the productive field. As a result, in some units, there is the dearth of qualified man power and in some other units; we find its excess.

(*v*) ***Lack of encouragement for self-employment***: Ever since the time of British, Indians have developed a tendency to give priority for salaried jobs rather than self-employment. Our education system has also been a failure in developing the spirit of self-employment among our youths. As a result, young people tend to wait for getting some salaried jobs in offices, factories or business firms and private or public firms and concerns. They often wait for such jobs for years together as unemployed or under-employed youths.

EFFECTS OR IMPACT OF UNEMPLOYMENT

The problem of unemployment is a serious one and it leads to a number of consequences. The evil of unemployment may be discussed under four heads; *personal disorganization, family disorganization, social disorganization* and *irreparable financial losses*.

Unemployment and Personal Disorganization

Unemployment is not only a social problem it is an individual problem also. An unemployed person loses self- respect and faces a discouraging and a disappointing outlook. "*Unsteady employment undermines the workers physique, deadens his mind, weakens his ambition, destroys his capacity for continuous sustained endeavour, induces a liking for idleness and self - indulgence, saps self- respect and the sense of responsibility, impairs technical skills, weakens nerve and will power, creates a tendency to blame others for failure, saps his courage, prevents thrift, and hope of family advancement, destroys a workman's feeling that he is taking care of his family, sends him to work worried, underfed, plunges him in debt*".[5]

Young persons who finish their education, find it very painful to join the army of unemployed persons. Many of them do not get any outlet for their creative energy, and their enthusiasm and vigor dies down as days pass on.

The pitiable position of the wage-earner who has lost his job for one reason or another, is equally unfortunate. The old and retired people who are still capable of working but unable to get suitable jobs suffer from bitterness, economic insecurity and loss of self-respect.

The deplorable position of the casual workers and the underemployed persons cannot be undetermined here. For them, life is full of uncertainties and insecurities. They struggle a lot to meet their minimum requirements of living.

Unemployment damages our physical, mental and moral health also. The unemployed persons may not get sufficient food and medical assistance to maintain good physical health. Mental worries, anxieties and tensions adversely affect the

[5] Mr. Lescohier in his book *Labour Market* as quoted by G.R. Madan in his *Social problems*, p. 250.

mental health of the unemployed persons. The age-old saying "*an idle mind is a devils workshop*"–speaks in volumes of the disastrous effect of unemployment on the moral health of the person.

Unemployment and Family Disorganization

Unemployment causes physical hardships and mental agony not only to the individual of the employable age, but also to his family members. If the bread-winner of the family loses the job, the entire family suffers. In the absence of regular income the family has to fall back upon its little savings; and when that is exhausted, it has to resort to borrowings. Valuable articles, golden ornaments, furniture, vessels and such other things are often sold or mortgaged to find money for immediate expenses. Families suffer starvation by resorting to unbelievable economies in food. Physical health of the family members gets damaged due to want of nutritious food and proper and timely medical care.

- ***Unemployment upsets the balance of the family life:*** Entire family faces uncertainty and indefiniteness. In desperation children may be asked to stop their education and join factories and such other business concerns at an early age. Even the wife may be compelled to go out of the household for work. This new role may make her to become highly irritable in temperament. Bickerings, simmerings and quarrels may become the order of the day. Since the parents are compelled to struggle a lot for the maintenance of the family, they do not get much time to give social training to their children. As a result, children may develop delinquent tendencies. This state of affairs may even lead to the breakdown of the family.

Unemployment and Social Disorganization

Unemployment, if not checked or controlled, may ultimately prepare the way for social disorganization. Due to unemployment, people fail to live up to the expectations of society. Some of them may even resort to anti-social activities. It tempts or provocates them to resort to begging, to indulge in criminal activities, to fall a prey to gambling, drug addiction, drunkenness, etc.

Unemployment is a social curse and it may even pollute the economic and political fields. It makes the non-corrupt persons to become dishonest, the responsible and dignified to become irresponsible and undignified, the active and creative persons to become idle and lethargic, and so on. The urge to do something in life, gets dried up.

Irreparable Economic Losses

Unemployment causes in calculable economic losses. Since the unemployed persons become parasites on society they pose a big economic burden. The failure to provide jobs to all those who have the willingness and the potentiality to work, inevitably brings down economic production. Low production would cause low per capita income. People will be compelled to share among themselves country's poverty and not its affluence. Unemployment adversely affects the standard of living of the people. In the long run this would bring down the labour–efficiency of the people.

Thus, unemployment as a socio-economic problem is capable of damaging the moral fibre of the individual and the social fabric of the society.

REMEDIAL MEASURES AND SUGGESTIONS

The problem of unemployment is growing day by day in India. It is becoming more and more complex also. Such a complex problem will have to be tackled in a planned manner. No single solution can be an effective remedy for this problem. Multi-pronged attempt is needed to face it in an effective manner. It is possible only with the combined efforts of the government and the public.

1. Population Control

The growing population in India is a major cause of many socio-economic problems. Our population is growing on an average at the rate of 2.48% per year. We are adding every year more than 120 lakh to 130 lakh people to our population. At the same time, about 5 million people attain the employable position every year. Job opportunities are not increasing at the same rate to accommodate the growing population. Hence the population growth has to be checked. Family planning programme has to be made more popular and other suitable steps are to be taken to minimize or neutralize its growth.

2. Promoting Economic Development

The main solution for the problem lies in achieving substantial economic development. This can be materialized, only if attention is paid equally to agriculture and industry.

(a) Promoting Agricultural Development

(*i*) ***Irrigation projects.*** The employment opportunities in the agricultural sector may be increased through the construction of major and minor irrigation projects, expansion and development of plantation, intensive agriculture and horticulture. Unutilised land may be brought under- cultivation.

(*ii*) ***Development of fisheries, forest and animal husbandry***: The development of forest and fisheries and encouragement of animal husbandry [dairy farming, poultry, piggery, etc.] is also a major step in the direction of improving agricultural production.

(*iii*) ***Encouragement of cottage and household industries***: In the Indian context, cottage and household industries which are often associated with agriculture play a vital role in the development of economy. Hence they should be given due encouragement. Basket making, brick-making, toy-making, beedi rolling, agarbati making, carpentry and furniture making, leather works, carving, smithery, and such other works are to be encouraged to keep our people engaged with work that fetch economic rewards.

(*iv*) ***Encouragement for growing commercial crops***: Commercial crops can make agricultural tasks economically attractive. Commercial crops such as areca, coffee, tea, pepper, ginger, cardamom, cashew, tobacco, ground nut, vegetables and fruits, etc., can bring good income to the farmers. Due encouragement is to be given to the farmers to grow such commercial crops.

(*v*) ***Attractive local programmes and projects***: Depending upon the local needs and feasibility new agricultural programmes and projects are to be launched so that the young people of the area get new opportunities to use their talents and energy for the developmental programmes. The U.P. Government, for example, introduced in 1990-91, a land army called "*Bhoomi Sena*". The *Bhoomi Sainiks* [young men of the local area] are given funds by the state government in the form of bank loans for the aforestation of land.

(b) Industrial Development

Planned development of industries is essential for creating more and more job opportunities. Development of industries may include: (*a*) *large-scale industries*, (*b*) *small scale industries*, and (*c*) *village and cottage industries including handicrafts*. Proper balance should be maintained between agricultural growth and industrial development, so that industry would not destroy handicrafts and household industries.

The *unchecked process of mechanization* and the *domination of multinational companies* are adversely affecting the creation of new job opportunities. In the name of industrial growth new labour–saving machine are installed which are taking away the jobs of men. Gandhiji had opposed the process of mechanization in this regard. Sufficient care should be taken to see no new machine takes away the jobs of existing workers.

The *process of economic liberalization* let loose by the central government recently has given new scope for die multinational companies to establish their domination over the indigenous industries. The governmental invitation for these companies may erode the job opportunities for millions of people.

3. Education Reforms

Education has much to do with employment and unemployment. Our education is not much job-oriented, it is degree-oriented. *It caters more to urban needs rather* than to rural requirements. It has not completely come out of the British colonial bias. Hence, it has failed to create an army of self-reliant, self-dignified young men and women. It very badly requires a thorough overhauling.

Throughout the country, primary education should be made more popular and effective. Much publicized slogan "*operation black-board*" must be transformed into reality. Our villages should become the centres of concentration in this regard. At the same time, some control has to be established over higher education. Long back in 1957, the then chairman of the UGC, **Sri C.D. Deshmukh**, had reiterated that *we shall have to restructure university education by and large ta the number of university educated men and women that the country will be needing from time to time.*

Due practical training should be given to our educated youths to help them to pursue one or the other vocation, and proper guidance and information should be given to them regarding new job opportunities. Employment guidance bureaus and employment exchange agencies can play a vital role in this regard.

4. Five-Year Plans

Almost all the Five-Year Plans have given utmost importance to generate as much employment opportunities as possible. They have given priority to agricultural growth, industrial development and creation of vast employment opportunities. Expansion of employment opportunities by making use of the available man power and natural resources was indeed, the main aim of the Third Five-Year Plan.

Though the Govt. had spent about ₹180 crores for creating employment opportunities in the First Five – Year Plan, there were about 5.3 million unemployed people at the end of the Plan period. From the beginning of the First Plan [1 951-56] till the completion of the 10th Plan in 2007 the number of the unemployed people went on increasing in spite of the efforts made by the planning system to provide maximum number of jobs. It was estimated that during the Tenth Plan [2002-07], the new entrants to the labour force would be around 35 million. Adding to this, the backlog of 35 million unemployed people, the job requirements of the Tenth Plan would be around 70 million. "*Since the economy at least would be able to create 50 million jobs, the backlog of 20 million will remain at the end of the Tenth Plan. But if proper policies are pursued, the rate of unemployment which was 9.21% in 2001-02 would decline at 5.11% in 2006-07*"[6].

Employment Requirements During the 11th Plan

On account of the increasing participation of females, the total increase in labour force will be around 65 million during the 11th Plan. To this may be added the present backlog of about 35 million. Thus, the total job requirements of the 11th Plan workout to be 100 million.

The planners intend to provide 65 million additional employment opportunities. Even then, the 11th Plan will not create full-employment, but it will at least ensure that the unemployment rate falls somewhat.

Promotion of Employment Generation in the 11th Plan

The 11th Plan intends to generate additional employment opportunities mainly in the services and manufacturing sector. Measures would need to be taken in the Plan to boost, in particular, labour intensive manufacturing sector such as food processing, leather products, footwear, textiles and service sectors such as tourism and construction.

The planners state. "Organised sector employment would double over the 11th Plan... but this would leave about 55 million new workers for the unorganized sector to absorb." "The 11th Plan aims to increase private organized sector employment ambitiously by at least 10 million. Along with the public sector, organized sector jobs would then expand by over 15 million, a growth rate of about 9% per annum. This would still leave nearly 50 million new workers to be absorbed in non-agricultural unorganized employment"[7]

Generation of Employment Opportunities by Information Technology [IT]

It is heartening to note that information technology [IT] has opened enormous opportunities for educated youth in the country. It is estimated that one segment of IT industry that is, computers which includes–both hardware and software, computer engineers and systems analysts is having a million jobs at present. In addition to this, the IT sector provided 2.2 million jobs to computer professionals and other related personnel engaged in IT sector. It is estimated [as per *NASSOM — McKinsey Report 1999*] that by the end of the year 2008, IT enabled services will provide 11 million jobs and generate a revenue of 17 to 18 billion U.S. dollars. In this sense, IT industry has great future in expanding employment opportunities.

What is disturbing in the present economic situation is that IT education is very costly and IT jobs are being grabbed by the relatively rich section of the society. The Government here has a major role to play in expanding computer education to rural areas in the country so that the capabilities of the people are developed to acquire better quality jobs in the IT sector.

To conclude, it could be said that the planning Commission has optimistic view of the economy's employment potential. As per its report, "*as against 3.9 million employment opportunities created during 1993 and 1999, additional employment generated during 1999 and 2002 averaged 8.4 million per year. There is need to increase it to 10 million per year.*"

Employment Guarantee Act-2005 [National Rural Employment Guarantee Act]

Under the *National Common Minimum Programme* of the UPA Government adopted in Sept 2004, and as per the advice of the National Advisory Council, the Govt. passed the *National Rural Employment Guarantee Act* in 2005. The main features of the Act are as follows:

1. Every household in rural India will have a right to at least 100 days of guaranteed employment every year for at least one adult member per family.
2. The employment will be in the form of casual manual labour at the legally fixed minimum wage that is, ₹60 per day.
3. Work should be provided in the local area, that is, within the radius of 5 K.M.
4. Work should be given within 15 days of demanding it.
5. For whatever reason, if work is not given, the person shall be paid a daily unemployment allowance. This allowance will be at least l/3 of the minimum wages.
6. For non-compliance with rules, strict penalties have been laid down.

[6] Ruddar Datt and Sundaram, p. 411

[7] Ruddar Datt and Sundaram, 2008, p. 414

7. The *gram sabha* will monitor the work of the *gram panchayat* by way of social audit.
8. The District Collector/Chief Executive officer will be responsible for the programme at the district level.

Probable Cost of this Employment Guarantee Programme.

It is estimated that employment Guarantee Programme will cost at least 1% of the GDP [Gross Domestic Product]. The calculations reveal that the said – programme will cost ₹100 per person per day at 2004-05 prices. This includes ₹ 60/- as wages and ₹40/- for the non-labour costs [including materials and administrative costs], Thus, the total cost for providing 100 days of employment in a year per person will be ₹10,000/-. As per 2001 Census, there were 20 crores of people, that is, 4 crore households, living below the poverty line. Thus. the programme per year will cost ₹40,000/- crores [₹10,000/- per person multiplied by 4 crore households]. As per this scheme, the Centre will bear 80% of the total cost [that is, 60% as wage component and 20% as share in materials component] and the State Govt. will share the remaining 20% of the total cost. The Centre, is however, conscious of the fact that once the programme gathers momentum, democratic pressures are bound to enlarge the programme to all unemployed and also to withdraw the limit of 100 days and make it a programme operative throughout the year.

Critical Remarks About the Programme

An important aspect of this *Employment Guarantee Act* is that, it gives a legal right to the people inforceable in court. This will increase the bargaining power of the people. It also makes administration accountable for if the jobs are not provided; unemployment allowance will have to be paid.

The critics have raised their own doubts about the practical benefits of this Act. The experience of Maharastra is also not encouraging. This programme has been implemented in Maharasthra for the past 30 years costing the State more than ₹9,000 crores and generating 370 crore mandays. But the programme has not produced adequate results other in terms of poverty reduction or reduction in unemployment. The programme still continues after 30 years without any decline in the demand for unskilled wage work under this scheme. No dramatic achievements have been made in poverty reduction or in unemployment reduction in the state. Critics also say that in fact, Maharasthra has done poorly as compared with other states.[8] Noted economist **Lord Meghanand Desai** considered this NREGA scheme as only a "*palliative*" a temporary measure and not a cure for the problem. **Dr. C. H. Hanumanth Rao** commented that the scheme was a failure in Maharasthra because it was not linked to the building up of rural infrastructure, such as rural irrigation, rural roads, etc.

REVIEW QUESTIONS

1. What is unemployment? Is unemployment a global phenomenon? Discuss.
2. Discuss the magnitude of unemployment in India.
3. Bring out the salient features of unemployment problem in India.
4. Discuss the types and causes of unemployment.
5. Assess the impact of unemployment.
6. What are the remedies of unemployment problem? Explain.
7. Elaborate on the features of the employment Guarantee Act, 2005

⌘⌘⌘⌘⌘⌘⌘⌘⌘⌘⌘⌘

[8] It may be noted that in view of the criticisms made against the proposed EGS Bill, the Govt made some amendments to it on 17th Aug. 2005 while getting the approved of the Parliament. For example, the scheme has been universalized to all persons living in the rural areas instead of its being available only to the families "below the poverty line". *Secondly*, there will be 1/3 preference for Women in areas where the number of 'applicants is very large. *Thirdly*, the scheme will be introduced in 200 districts in the beginning but later on it will be extended to the whole nation in five years. *Fourthly*, the Central Govt. will provide 90% of money for the scheme. *Fifthly*, the Govt. also promised to bring a similar scheme for the urban areas. Rudder Datt and Sundaram, p. 421.

48

Problems of the Under-Privileged (Scheduled Castes, Tribes and Other Backward Classes)

Chapter Outline

- A. The Scheduled Castes: Definition and Problems of the Scheduled Castes
- Untouchability
- Origin and Eradication of Untouchability
- Role of Gandhiji and Dr. Ambedkar in the Removal of Untouchability
- Measures for Welfare of SCs
- Harmful Effects of Untouchability
- Scheduled Tribes: Definition and Distribution of Scheduled Tribes
- Tribal Problems and Tribal Welfare
- The Backward Classes: Who Forms the Backward Classes? Definition and Description of Backward Classes
- The Backward Classes Movement.

As *Sorokin* has pointed out, all permanently organised societies are stratified. Most societies of the world have had their type of what *Ward* calls '*the lowly*'. The Romans had their *Plebians*, the Spartans their *heitos*, the British their villains, the Egyptians their slaves, the Americans their *Negroes*, and the Germans their Jews. So the Hindus have '*Untouchables*' and the *girijans*. Slavery, serfdom, villeinage have all vanished. But untouchability still exists. The practice of untouchability is the reflection of the state of affair of the unprivileged section of the country. Two-thirds or more of the population of India are very backward, being illiterate and living in utter poverty. Their disadvantage arises from the fact that their status is ascribed to them by *birth*. As members of *closed- status groups* with unequal ranks they suffer from various disabilities. *India is a class as well as caste-ridden* society. Hence these members suffer from economic as well as non-economic, that is, social, religious and educational disabilities. This unprivileged section, which is often treated as '*the backward classes*' in general consists of three main divisions: (*i*) *The Scheduled Tribes* (Girijans), (*ii*) The *Scheduled Castes* (Harijans), and (*iii*) *The Other Backward Classes. The first two groups are listed in the Constitution while the third group is unlisted and loosely defined; it is the least homogeneous*.

WHAT ARE THE SCHEDULED TRIBES AND CASTES

For ages certain groups of people in India's hill areas and villages have suffered isolation and disability. Geographic and social factors have added to their isolation. They have lived in a state of social and economic stagnation. These people belong to certain castes and tribes listed by the President of India in pursuance of the relevant provisions of the Constitution. Hence the name *Scheduled Tribes* and *Scheduled Castes*. These along with the '*denotified tribes*' and other economically backward groups, are sometimes referred to as '*backward classes*'. The Scheduled Castes and Tribes form roughly 22% of the total population.

THE SCHEDULED CASTES

The Scheduled Caste (SC) occupy the bottommost rung of the social ladder. They form a major part of the *Backward or Depressed Classes*. They are generally regarded as 'Untouchables' and popularly known as 'Harijans'. According to the Census Report of 1971 the Scheduled Castes constitute 15.04% of the total population, their total number being 8.25 crores. In Karnataka alone more than 38½ lakh Harijans are there. They are not in majority in any part of the country. They constitute more than 20% of the population, in more than 666 talukas. Hence they are scattered over the entire land. There is no district or taluk in India wherein the Scheduled Caste people are not found. Further, nowhere in India the Harijans or the Scheduled Caste people occupy the topmost position in the social, political and economic field. They are economically backward, socially depressed and educationally neglected section of the Indian population.

Early References to Harijans

The '*Harijans*' or the *Scheduled Caste* people were called by different names during the early days. For some time they were kept outside the Hindu social order and referred to as the fifth group (often as the fifth varna) or the "*Panchamas*". During the Vedic Period they were known as the '*Chandalas*'. The *Chandalas* were considered to be untouchables. The *chandalas* were the progeny of the most hated union of a Brahmin female with a Shudra male. In Vedic literature, we find the mention of chandalas as an ethnic group originating from inter-breeding of higher caste female and lower caste male. *Patanjali* considered chandalas as a variety of shudras. According to *Manu*, the chandalas were born out of the *Pratiloma marriages*. It is difficult to estimate the exact period in which the untouchables or chandalas originated. Still it can be said that they have existed in India since at least 2,000 years. Majority of the Scheduled Caste people have been regarded as "*untouchables*" at one time or the other. All the SCs are not regarded as untouchables in all the places of India.

British called the so-called '*untouchables*' the '*Exterior Castes*'. The term '*Untouchable Castes*' was made use of for the first time by the *Simon Commission* (1928). Under the *Government of India Act of I935* the untouchables are designated as '*Scheduled Castes*'. The Constitution of India (1950) has also referred to them as the "Scheduled Castes'. But Mahatma Gandhiji addressed them as "*Harijans*"—the people of the God.

Definition of Scheduled Castes

1. According to *Dr. D.N. Majumdar* the term '*Scheduled Castes*' refers to the '*Untouchable Castes*'. "The untouchable castes are those who suffer from various social and political disabilities many of which are traditionally prescribed and socially enforced by higher castes".
2. We can define the scheduled castes as those economically, socially, educationally and politically backward castes which are kept at a distance by the other castes as '*untouchables*'
3. Scheduled Castes are those untouchable castes which are subject to some disabilities in every walk of life—social, religious, educational, economic and political. *Examples*: Madiga Chalavadi gas, Billavas, Edigas, Korama, Machigars, Dhoras, Samagaras, Mahars, Mangs, Holeyas, Upparas, Ezhavas, Chamars.

The Scheduled Castes: An Integral Part of Village Life

The Scheduled Castes constitute an integral part of village life. According to the Census Report of 1971 the Harijans constitute 15.04% of the total population of India. More than 90% of them are living in the villages. Still they are not in majority in any part of India. About 75% of them are engaged in agriculture and large number of them are landless labourers. They are spread over the entire nation . In fact, there is no village in India in which the Harijans are not found. Even today, they continue to render some menial services to the other caste people. Most of them live below the line of poverty.

B. Kuppu Swamy in his "*Social Change in India*" states that for two reasons the Harijans were declared as '*impure*' castes or '*untouchables*' and were made to live outside the village. First, they were following the lowest kinds of occupations such as scavenging, leather work, removal of the carrion, etc. *Second*, they persisted in eating beef which was condemned as the most heinous crime by the caste Hindus.

Referring to the position and the role of Harijans, *M.N Srinivas* writes, "they are an integral part of the village life, they perform certain essential tasks in agriculture, they are often village servants, messengers and remove the leaves on which people have dined at community dinners".

Problems of the Scheduled Castes

The Varna System which existed during the Vedic period, in course of time degenerated into the caste system. Since then, the Scheduled Castes who are known as '*Untouchables*' have been suffering from various social, religious, legal, political, economic, educational, and other disabilities. For centuries they were denied political representation, legal rights, civic facilities, educational privileges and economic opportunities. During the British rule also nothing was done to uplift the Harijans and to relieve them from their bondages. Even today the Scheduled Castes are not free from problems.

(a) The Social Restrictions and Disabilities of the Scheduled Castes

The Scheduled Castes or the Harijans suffered for centuries from a number of social disabili- ties among which the following may be noted.

1. ***Lowest status in the hierarchy.*** In the Caste hierarchy the Scheduled Castes are ascribed the lowest status. They are considered to be '*unholy*', '*inferior*' and '*low*' and are looked down upon by the other castes. They have been suffering from the stigma of '*untouchability*'. Their very touch is considered to be polluting for the higher caste people. Hence they have been treated as the servants of the other caste people. The Scheduled Castes have always served the other castes, but the attitude of other castes is of total indifference and contempt. They were kept at a distance from other caste people. In some instances (in South India) even the exact distance which an upper caste man was expected to keep between himself and the Harijans was specified.
2. ***Education disabilities***. The Harijans were forbidden from taking up to education during the early days. Sanskrit education was denied for them. Public schools and other educational institutions were closed for them. Even today majority of them are illiterate and ignorant.
3. ***Civic disabilities. Prevention from the use of public places.*** For a long time the untouchable castes were not allowed to use public places and avail of civic facilities such as–village wells, ponds, temples, hostels, hotels, schools, hospitals, lecture halls, dharamashalas, choultries, etc. They were forced to live on the outskirts of the towns and villages during the early days. Even today they are segregated from others spatially. In South India, restrictions were imposed on the mode of construction of their houses, types of dresses and patterns of their ornamentation. Some lower caste people were not allowed to carry umbrellas, to wear shoes or golden ornaments and to milk cows. They were prohibited from covering the upper pan of their body. The services of barbers, washermen and tailors were refused to them.

(b) Religious Disabilities

The Harijans also suffer from religious disabilities even today. They are not allowed to enter temples in many places. The brahmins who offer their priestly services to some lower castes, are not prepared to officiate in the ceremonies of the 'untouchable' castes. They do not even bow down to the duties of these '*untouchable*' castes. The *Vedic mantras* which are considered to be more pure, could not be listened to and chanted by the Harijans because of the taboos. They were only permit- ted to make use of the *upanishadic mantras which are considered to be less pure. Burial grounds were also denied for them in many places*.

(c) Economic Disabilities

The Harijans are economically backward and have been suffering from various economic disabilities also.

1. ***No right of property ownership.*** For centuries the Harijans were not allowed to have land and business of their own. It is only recently their ownership to the property has become recognised. The propertied people are comparatively less in them. Majority of them depend upon agriculture but only a few of them own land.
2. ***Selection of occupations limited.*** The Caste system imposes restrictions on the occupa- tional choice of the members. The occupational choice was very much limited for the Harijans. They were not allowed to take up to occupations which were reserved for the upper caste people. They were forced to stick on to the traditional inferior occupations such as– curing hides, removing the human wastes, sweeping, scavenging, oil grinding, tanning, shoemaking, leather works, carrying the dead animals, etc. These occupations were regarded as '*degraded*' and '*inferior*'.
3. ***Landless labourers.*** Majority of the Harijans are today working as landless labourers. More than 90.1 of the agricultural labourers in India belong to the depressed classes which include the Scheduled Castes and Scheduled Tribes. More than 77.1% of the Scheduled Caste workers in rural areas are agricultural labourers. A large number of Harijan families are in debts. About 64.1% of the agricultural labour households of the Scheduled Castes were indebted during 1956-57 as against 45.1% in 1950-51. The average accumulated debt per household increased from ₹47 in 1950-51 to ₹88 in 1956-57. Their indebtedness is increasing day by day. The Harijans are economically exploited by the upper caste people. Even today they are the lowest paid workers, some of them continue to suffer as *bonded labourers* at the hands of the higher caste people.

(d) Political Disabilities

The untouchables hardly participated in the political matters. They were not given any place in the politics, administration and the general governance of India. they were not allowed to hold any public post. Political rights and representation were denied for them. Under the British rule, they were given the right to vote for the first time. After independence equal political opportunities and rights have been provided for the Harijans also. Politically, the Harijans are yet to become an organised force.

UNTOUCHABILITY

The practice of '*untouchability*' is a stigma attached to the Hindu society. It is an age-old one. It has its roots deep down in our social and religious system. Gandhiji regarded this practice as "*a leper wound in the whole body of Hindu politic*". He even considered it as "*the hatefullest expression of caste*."

It is very difficult to give a clear definition of untouchability. The word 'untouchable' applies to the despised and degraded section of the Hindu population. Untouchability is a *mass phenomenon of group prejudices and discrimination* affecting more than 80 million people of India. Untouchability refers to the *solid inhibition of touch emerging from the characteristics of the Indian caste system*. Ideas of occupational and ceremonial purity in the genesis of the caste system led to the practice of untouchability. Untouchability is a practice in which some lower caste people are kept at a distance and denied of social equality for their touch is considered to be polluting or contaminating the higher caste people.

Origin of Untouchability

There are different opinions regarding the origin of untouchability. According to Manu, the Hindu law giver, *practice of pratiloma marriage was the cause for the origin of untouchability*. Children born of such marriages were called '*chandalas*'. The chandalas were the progeny of the union of Brahmin female with a shudra male.

Hutton states, 'the origin of the position of the exterior castes' (untouchable) is partly racial, party religious and partly matter of social customs. *Dr. Majumdar, Sir Herbert Risley and Dr. Ghurye are in favour of the racial explanation of untouchability*. According to *Prof Ghurye*, "*Ideas of purity, whether occupational or ceremonial, which are found to have been a factor in the genesis of caste are the very soul of the idea and practice of untouchability*". *According to Dr. Majumdar. the disabilities of the so called "depressed castes" are not ceremonial, but are founded on racial and cultural differences*. According to Nesfield, association with dirty profession such as scavenging, sweeping public roads, curing the hides, tanning, leather works, carrying the dead animals, etc., gave rise to the feeling of untouchability.

Untouchability Offences

Article 17 of the Constitution of India states that "*untouchability is abolished and its practice in any form is for bidden. The enforcement of any disability arising out of untouchability shall be an offence punishable in accordance with law*". In pursuance of this provision, the Parliament passed the *Untouchability* (*Offences*) Act, 1955 (which was later substituted by the *Protection of Civil Rights Act*, 1978). According to this Act the offences of untouchability include the following :

(*i*) Committing any kind of social injustice, such as denying access to any shop, restaurant, public hospital, educational institution or any place of public entertainment.

(*ii*) Preventing a person, on the grounds of untouchability, from entering a place of worship and offering prayers or from drinking water from a public well or spring,

(*iii*) Refusal to sell goods or render services to a person on the grounds of untouchability is an offence punishable with imprisonment for six months or a fine upto ₹500 or both.

(*iv*) Enforcing occupational, professional, trade disabilities in the matter of enjoyment of any benefit under a charitable trust, etc.

Eradication of Untouchability

Ever since the time of the Buddha and Mahavira attempts have been made to remove the social disabilities of the degraded castes including untouchability. The Buddha and Mahavira said that caste is no bar to communion with God. In fact, the Buddhism and Jainism rose as a challenge to the rigid caste system with all its evils. Thinkers and reformers like Basavanna, Kabirdas, Santa Tukaram, Guru Nanak , Tulsidas, Ramdas Namadeva, Santa Jnaneshwar and a host of others have advocated the removal of caste distinctions, including untouchability for the good of humanity. The Bhakti Cult popularised by Purandara Das, Kanka Das, Vadiraj and others, and the Veershaivism established and propagated by Basavanna contributed a great deal to the removal of untouchability.

During the British rule in the 19th and 20th centuries, a number of social reformers tried to eradicate untouchability. They launched movements against untouchability and built organisations to reform the Hindu society. *Swami Vivekananda's* '*Sri Ramakrishna Mission*', Raja Ram Mohan Roy's '*Brahma Samaj*', Swami Dayananda Saraswati's '*Arya Samaj*', Atmaram Panduranga's 'Prarthana Samaj', Dr.. Anie Besant's, '*Theosophical Society*', Thakkar Bapa's '*Harijan Sevak Sangha*", Dr. Keshva Baliran Hedgewar's '*Rashtreeyu Swayam Sevak Sangha, the Indian National Congress* under the leadership of Mahatma Gandhiji, Dr. B.R. Ambedkar's *All-India Scheduled Caste Federation*, Sri. Naryana Guru and S.N.D.P. *Yogam* in Kerala the *Vishwa Hindu Parishad* and other organisations have played an important role in the removal of untouchability. Intellectuals like Keshabchandra Sen, Iswnra Chandra Vidya Sagar. Justice Ranade, Jyoti Rao Phule, Sri Narayana Guru. Gandhiji, Sri. Guruji Golwalkar, and others also tried to rouse the conscience of the people against the practice of untonchability. *The Harijan Sevak Sangha, Depressed Class Union, the Social Service League. Depressed Class League, the Scheduled Classes Federation etc. also tried to; remove the caste disabilities.*

Role of Dr. Ambedkar and Gandhiji in the Removal of Untouchability and Upliftment of Scheduled Castes

Role of Dr. Ambedkar

Dr. Bhim Rao Ambedkar [1891—19561 was a great modern social thinker, a born fighter, a famous advocate and a humanist. Dr. Ambedkar who was born in an "*untouchable*" or "*dalit*" community called "**Mahar**" in Maharashtra took a leading role in promoting the welfare of the untouchable castes and in elevating their status. Being the most highly educated untouchable in India Dr. Ambedkar became the undisputed spokesman of the untouchables. He took many steps to reform the ways of the untouchables. He fought against many of the injustices done to the untouchables by establishing a political party and a couple of organisations for the untouchables. **Pandit Nehru** rightly described him as the "*symbol of the great revolt against all the oppressive features of Hindu society*".

1. ***Dr. Ambedkar was the first man to make a scientific study of untouchability***: Even though Gandhiji had thought of the ways of removal of untouchability before the birth of Dr. Ambedkar, it was Ambedkar who drew the attention of the Congress Organisation and also of the entire nation towards the grave problems of the untouchables and their deplorable conditions. Ambedkar had made a detailed study of the problem of untouchability, its origin, development etc.
2. ***Self-respect movement***: Dr. Ambedkar had made it clear that his main aim in life was to remove the practice of untouchability and to 'take the so-called "*untouchable community*" towards socio–economic equality and justice. Through his social movement he wanted to instil in the minds of the untouchables the ideas of self–dignity, self-confidence and self-respect. Thus his movement is often called "*self-respect movement*." Ambedkar established an institution called "*Bahishkrita Hitakarini Sabha*" which added momentum to this movement.
3. ***Five-principles or "Pancha-Sutras" for the progress of 'dalits'***: Dr. Ambedkar wanted the untouchables or 'dalits' to follow some principles in life so that they could attain a respectable status by their own efforts as a community. He recommended "*Pancha-sutras*" for them. ***(i) Self -Improvement***: Making one's own efforts for one's improvement without expecting much from other; ***(ii) Self-Progress***: Making self-efforts for achieving progress in life; ***(iii) Self-Dependence***: Learning to lessen one's dependence on others and attaining finally self-reliance; ***(iv) Self-Respect***: Maintaining self-dignity and never sacrificing it for any reason. ***(v) Self-Confidence***: Developing confidence in oneself, in one's capacities and in one's efforts.
4. ***Call to reform the style of life***: Ambedkar made an appeal to his community to change its style of life to suit to the needs of time. "*He urged them to stop the dragging of dead cattle out of the village. He wanted them to give up eating carrion. alcoholic drinks and begging. He wanted them to become literates and send their children to schools. Finally, he wanted them to dress well and have self-respect for themselves. Thus, one of his chief aims was to bring about a revolution in the way of life of the untouchable and in their aspirations for themselves and for their children.*"[1]
5. ***Three principles of dalit movement***: "***Education, Agitation and Organisation***": Dr. Ambedkar suggested three principles to govern the "*dalit movement*". These principles are: "*education, agitation and organisation*".

   (i) Education is essential for helping the dalits to take out their mask of ignorance: ***(ii)* Agitation** becomes inevitable to fight against all the exploiters and cheats; ***(iii) Organisation*** is necessary to thrash out individual differences, to realise community interests and to fight for a common cause collectively. After the ***All-India Depressed Class Conference in Nagpur*** in 1942 Ambedkar declared, "*My final word of advice is to educate, agitate, organise and have faith in yourself It is a battle for the reclamation of human personality.*"

   Personal efforts to put the three principles into practice: Ambedkar himself worked to put these three principles into practice. Ambedkar encouraged the ***education*** of dalits through the organisations he established namely, "*Bahishkrita Hitakarini Sabha*", "*Independent Labour Party*" and "*Depressed Classes' Education Society*".

   Ambedkar organised ***agitations*** in the direction of reaching his goals. His own words reveal his faith in agitations. "*The direct action in respect of Chowder Tank in Mahad (of Kolaba District, Maharashtra), the Kalaram Temple at*

[1] B. Kuppu Swamy in his *Social Change in India*, p. 207.

Nasik and the Guruvayur temple in Malabar have clone in a few days what million days of preaching by reformers would never have done". He personally led the temple entry agitation at Nasik. In 1930, just 10 days before Gandhiji's "Dandi March", Ambedkar launched a big temple entry movement at Nasik before the Kalaram Temple in which more than 15000 volunteers including 500 women, had taken part. *The programme of temple entry was more for creating social consciousness than for asserting religious rights*.

Dr. Ambedkar realised the importance of "***Organisation***" and worked to build a few of them. Examples: "***Bahishkrita Hitakarini Sabha***" [1924], *Mahad Conference or Dasgaon, Dalit Conference*, [1927] **"*Independent Labour Party*"**. As early as in 1920 he had made attempts to organise all the untouchable castes and bring them under one banner. He had organised the first *All–India Conference of Untouchables* in May 1920 at Nagpur.

6. ***Call to destroy the caste system.*** Ambedkar in his efforts to raise the status of untouchables considered the caste system one of the great obstacles. He expressed his great disappointment with the caste as well as varna system. He even gave a call to destroy the caste system in his famous book called "*Annihilation of Caste*" [1936]. He wrote in "*Harijan*" in 1933 - "the Outcaste is a byproduct of the caste system". Nothing can emancipate the outcaste except the destruction of caste system." As an expression of his disillusionment with Hinduism, he rejected Hinduism and embraced Buddhism with his followers in 1956. [He, however, died in the very same year, that is on 6th December 1956].,

7. ***Political role of Ambedkar.*** Ambedkar made use of political instruments to achieve the purpose of protecting dalit interests.

   Demand for separate electorate for dalits. In the First Round Table Conference convened in London in November 1930 Dr. Ambedkar, who attended it on behalf of the depressed classes, spoke about the loathsome condition of the untouchables in India. He prepared a declaration of the fundamental rights of the depresssed classes and submitted it to the minorities sub-committee. He demanded the abolition of untochability and the establishment of equal citizenship. He *vehemently* demanded a separate electorate for the depressed classes. Gandhiji who boycotted the first Conference and participated in the Second Round Table Conference at London along with Ambedkar, Opposed the proposal. He said "*the political separation of the untouchables and the Hindus would be suicidal to the nation.*" He even said that he would resist such a proposal with his life. He declared his resolution of "*fast-unto-death*". The conflict between the two leaders was however, settled by the famous "Poona Pact" [1932][2]. Ambedkar was able to get some reasonable representation for the untouchables.

   Ambedkar who met Gandhiji in 1931 insisted on making the removal at untouchability a pre-condition for a person to become a member of the Congress. He supported the ***Anti-Untouchability League*** which launched a campaign all over the country to secure for the depressed classes enjoy- ment of their civil rights such as taking water from the village wells, admission of the children in village schools etc.

8. ***Ambedkar as the "Abhinava Manu".*** Ambedkar was invited by the Prime Minister Nehru to be the Law Minister in the First Cabinet of Independent India. Ambedkar accepted the offer. He was made the *Chairman* of the *Drafting Committee* to draft the Indian Constitution. Article 17 of the Constitution abolished untouchability. Ambedkar had once declared that he would burn "*Manu Smriti*" for its failure to provide justice to the dalits. The same Ambedkar now could get the opportunity and the honour of giving to the people of India their Constitution . He is rightly called the "*Abhinava Mann*" [or "*Modern Manu*"]. He was awarded the "*Bharata Rama*" title posthumously. Ambedkar's ideas, views and thoughts continue to influence and inspire a number of his followers who are spread over the entire nation.

Role of mahatma gandhi

Mahatma Gandhiji played a memorable role in uplifting the untouchables. Gandhiji popularised the word "**Harijan**"[3] meaning "*the people of God*"—a word which was first coined and used by a Gujarathi Brahmin saint by name *Narasimha*

---

[2] Through the "Poona Pact" Gandhi ensured that the election of the SC and ST representatives would be by all the voters in territorial constituencies allotted for the purposes: As there is no constituency in which SCs are in a majority, the Pact makes sure that the elected SC candidates are in practice acceptable to the other castes and communities in the area.

[3] Harijan-"was a word used by the great saint Narasinha Mehta, who by the by belonged to the Nagar Brahmanu Community and who defied the whole community by claiming the "untouchables" as his own. I am delighted to adopt the word which is sanctified by having been used by such a great saint, but it has for me a deeper meaning than you may imagine. The "untouchable", to me, is compared to us, really, a Harijan – a man of God, and we are "Dhurjan" [men of evil].

Source: M. K. Gandhi in "***The Removal of Untouchability***" - 1954, p. 14. Compiled and edited by Bharatan Kumarappa - Published by Navajivan Publishing House, Ahmedabad.

Mehta. According to Gandhiji, the practice of untouch- ability is "*a leper wound in the whole-body of Hindu politic*". He even regarded it as "*the hatefullest expression of caste*". He made it his life's mission to wipe out untouchability and to uplift the de- pressed and the downtrodden people. As a servant of mankind, he preached that all human beings are equal and hence the Harijans too have a right for social life along with other caste groups.

Gandhiji's appeal to the conscience of the people: Gandhiji believed in the four-fold division of the Hindu society into four varnas. He regarded untouchables as Shudras and *not as the Panchamas* or *fifth Varna* or *Avarna*. Hence he sincerely felt the need for bringing about a basic change in the caste structure by uplifting the untouchables and *not by abolishing the caste as such*. He appealed to the conscience of the people to realise the historical necessity of accommodating the "*Harijans*" by providing them a rightful place in the society.

Gandhiji had much compassion for the Harijans. He said : "*I do not want to be reborn. But if I am to be born, I would like to be born an untouchable, so that I may share their sorrows and sufferings." He was of the opinion that the practice of untouchability was a moral crime. He said that "if untouchability is not wrong, then nothing in the world is wrong.*" He believed that *a change of heart on the part of the Hindus was essential to enable the social and cultural assimilation of Harijans*. He was very much moved by their social distress and started a nationwide movement to remove their disabilities.

Gandhiji's campaign against untouchability: Gandhiji who regarded untouchability as a blot on Hinduism wanted to do away with it completely. He wrote in 1920 "... *Without the removal of the taint* [*of untouchability*], "*Swaraj*" *is a meaningless term*." He even felt that the foreign domination of our country was the result of our exploitation of almost one-sixth of our own people in the name of religion.

Gandhiji decided to stage a campaign against untouchability and was unprepared to make any compromise with it. He advocated positive means for the uplift of Harijans. He addressed various public meetings reposing doctrines of Harijan welfare. He led several processions of Harijans with other upper caste people and made them participate in "*poojas*, *bhajans*, *keerthans* and *puranas*". He believed that opportunities of *education* and *temple entry* would reduce social inequalities between Harijans and caste Hindus. He launched movements for cleaning Harijan residential areas, for digging wells for them and for similar other beneficial things.

Gandhiji wrote in "*Young India*" in April 1925. "*Temples, public wells and public schools must be open to the untouchables equally with caste Hindus*." He started two journals, 'Harijan' and 'Young India' through which he advocated his ideas. He started an ashram where people of all castes and creeds could come and stay without any differences.

Gandhiji served the "*Harijan Sevak Sangha*" started by the social reformer Takkar Bapa in the year 1932 for working out the religious and social welfare of the Harijans. The organisation opened schools and dispensaries in various places and arranged for free educational facilities and scholarships for Harijan children.

Political role of Gandhiji: As a much respected political leader of the masses, Gandhiji could never ignore the tasks of the removal of untouchability and upliftment of Harijans. Gandhiji entered the Indian freedom struggle in 1919. From 1920 onwards, under the leadership of Gandhiji the Indian National Congress became committed to get the independence on the one hand and to the removal of untouchability on the other. In 1920 itself, he declared that "*Untouchability cannot be given a secondary place in the programme*" of Congress.

Gandhiji's protest against the proposal of separate electorate for harijans. Gandhiji was very much against the British policy of "*divide and rule*". He condemned the British policy *of separating the Harijans from the rest of the Hindus*. Hence he protested against the proposal of creating separate electorate for the Harijans. He said to Ambedkar who was in favour of the proposal, that "*the political separation of the untouchables from the Hindus would be suicidal to the nation*."

Gandhiji declared at the *Minorities Committee of the Second Round Table Conference in London [1932] that "we do not want the untouchables to be classified as a separate class. Sikhs may remain such in perpetuity, so may Muslims and Christians. Will the untouchables remain untouchables in perpetuity? I would rather feel that Hinduism died than that untouchability lived. I will resist it with my life*."[4]

Impact of gandhiji's "fast-Unto-Death" Satyagraha. In spite of Gandhiji's protest, the British Prime Minister decided to grant separate seats for the depressed classes and the right of double vote in which they could elect their own representatives and also vote in which they could elect their own representatives and also vote in general elections. In protest against this "*communal award*" Gandhiji decided to stage the *fast unto death satyagraha*. This declaration of Gandhiji opened the eyes of the whole country towards the problem of untouchables.

[4] As quoted by B. Kuppu Swamy in *social Change in India*, p. 211.

In 1932 the *Harijan Sevak Sangh* was formed and its Conference at Bombay pledged that the right to use the public roads, wells etc. would be given statutory recognition when the Swaraj Parliament met. This pledge was stressed by Gandhiji in 1932 when he said, "*There could be no rest...until untouchability becomes a thing of the past.*" The Harijan movement gained strength throughout the country. Gandhi went on an all-India tour to collect huge sums of money for this programme.

Gandhiji commits congress for the removal of untouchability. At the behest of Gandhiji and the Congress, all the Congress candidates who contested elections in 1937 had pledged themselves to the removal of untouchability. An early as in 1931 itself at the *Karachi Session of the Congress* at the behest of Gandhiji, a resolution was adopted. It declared, "*all the citizens are equal before law irrespective of caste, creed or sex*." In 1938, *the Removal of the Civil Disabilities Act* was passed by the Madras Legislature which provided that no Harijan shall be disabled from any social or public amenity. In the same year, it also passed the Malabar Temple Entry Act which threw open the temples in Malabar. In 1939, the temple of Madurai was opened to the Harijans. Thus Gandhiji's fast and his Harijan movement released tremendous forces throughout the country, which led to the removal of some of the disabilities of the Harijans.

Gandhiji's personal involvement in the Harijan welfare activities. Gandhiji was not just a preacher. He practised what he preached. He could win the hearts of millions of Harijans because of his sincere approach to solve their problems. Gandhiji lived with the Harijans and shared their distress by indicating in them the ideas of better social adjustment with the rest of the Indian community. He advocated equal opportunities of education and intermingling of Harijan students with those of the upper castes. He fought for various legal protections against several kinds of injustices done to them. He adopted a Harijan child and set an example for others to emulate. As a result of his sincere efforts and strong recommendations, untouchability was declared illegal under the Indian Constitution. At his behest an opportunity was given to Dr. B.R. Ambedkar, leader of the depressed classes, to join the Central Cabinet and to be the chief architect of the Indian Constitution.

Gandhiji's proposals for harijan welfare: Gandhiji's proposals for Harijan welfare include the following:

1. Those who claim themselves to be the servants of Harijan must serve the Harijans with all the dedication.
2. Awareness must be created among the Harijans regarding cleanliness, sanitation and health.
3. The practice of carrying human waste on head must be stopped.
4. They should be persuaded to drop their habit of eating carrion and dead animals.
5. Practice of untouchability must be immediately stopped by all.
6. Harijans must be provided with drinking water facility.
7. Good houses at low cost but with enough provision for lighting and ventilation must be built for Harijans.
8. Harijan children must be made to go to school and even adult education programme should be introduced.
9. Harijans must be persuaded to drop their habit of drinking alcohol.
10. Harijans must be allowed to enter all the public places and to draw water from the wells.
11. There should be no bar for the entry of Harijans to temples.
12. "Harijan Day" should be observed by all at least one day in a year.

Ambedkar and Gandhiji who fought against the problem of untouchability and sewed to promote the welfare of "untouchables" are not alive today. Their followers are, however, continuing their work. Untouchability has not yet become "*the thing of the past*". The removal of untouchability requires a basic transformation in the general attitude towards it. Gandhiji was right when he wrote in his letter to Thakkar Bapa: "*The salvation of the depressed class will come only when the caste Hindu is made to think and is forced to feel that he must alter his ways. I want a revolution in the mentality of the caste Hindus*." The country is awaiting such a revolution.

Measures for the Welfare of Scheduled Castes

The Government of independent India has been trying to uplift the Scheduled Castes and Scheduled Tribes right from its very inception. The Governmental attempts to promote the welfare of the SCs and STs can be classified into two group. (*A*) *Constitutional and legislative measures and* (*B*) *Other welfare measures and programmes*.

The Constitutional and Legislative Measures

The Government of India has incorporated some special provisions in its Constitution for the removal of untouchability and to promote the welfare of SCs and STs. The Constitution ensures the protection and assures the promotion of interests of SCs, STs and other weaker sections of the population in the fields such as (1) *political representation*, (2) *representation in services*, (3) *economic development*, (4) *socio-cultural safeguards* and (5) *legal support*.

1. The Preamble of the Constitution of India declares that it assures equality, promotes fraternity, guarantees liberty and ensures justice to one and all.
2. Articles 15, 16, 17, 38 and 46 guarantee that the state shall not discriminate between persons on account of their religion or region and caste or class.
3. Article 15 prohibits discrimination on grounds of religion, caste, race, sex or place of birth.
4. Article 17 abolishes untouchability. It is further provided that the enforcement of any disability arising out of untouchability shall be an offence punishable in accordance with law.
5. Article 46 promotes educational and economic interests of Scheduled Castes, Scheduled Tribes and other weaker sections.
6. Article 330 reserves representation for Scheduled Castes and Scheduled Tribes in the House of the People.
7. Article 334 relates to reservation of seats and special representation to cease after fifty years (Originally reservation was made for ten years and it was extended four times, the present period of expiry being 2000 A.D.)
8. Article 335 mentions the claims of Scheduled Castes and Scheduled Tribes to services and posts.
9. Article 338 empowers the Central Govt. to appoint a National Commission for Scheduled Castes and Scheduled Tribes.
10. Article 339 empowers the President to appoint a Commission to report on the administration of the Scheduled Areas and the welfare of Scheduled Tribes in the States.
11. Article 341 empowers the President to specify the castes, races or tribes deemed as Scheduled Castes in a particular State or Union territory.
12. Article 342 empowers the President to specify the tribes or tribal communities deemed to be Scheduled Tribes in a particular State or Union territory.

- ***Legislative measures for the removal of untouchability:*** The Government has been taking up the required legislative measures for the removal of un- touchability. In pursuance of the provision of the Article 17 of the Constitution which declares the practice of untouchability a punishable offence, the Parliament passed the ***Untouchability Offences Act, 1955***. It was later substituted by **the Protection of Civil Rights Act, 1976.** According to this Act the offences of untouchability include the following.
- ***Offences of untouchability as per the "Protection of Civil Rights Act, 1976":***
  (*i*) Committing any kind of social injustice, such as denying access to any shop, restaurant, public hospital, educational institution or any place of public entertainment.
  (*ii*) Preventing a person, on the grounds of untouchability, from entering a place of worship and offering prayers, or from drinking-water from a public well or spring.
  (*iii*) Refusal to sell goods or render services to a person on the grounds of untouchability is an offence punishable with imprisonment for six months or a fine upto ₹500 or both.
  (*iv*) Enforcing occupational, professional, trade disabilities in the matter of enjoyment of any benefit under a charitable trust, etc.

Other Welfare Measures and Programmes for the Upliftment of Scheduled Castes

1. ***Appointment of a National Commission for the welfare of scheduled castes*:** A *National Commission for the Scheduled Castes and Scheduled Tribes* has been set up by the Central Government to safeguard the interests of the SCs and STs. It functions as an advisory body on issue and policies related to the development of the SCs and STs. The State Governments have separate departments to look after the welfare of the SCs and STs. Their administrative set up varies from state to state.
2. ***Educational opportunities:*** Due attention is paid to extend the educational opportunities of SCs and STs and hence special provisions have been made in this regard. Free education, free distribution of books, stationery, uniform etc. giving scholarships, banking loan facilities, providing mid-day meal, arranging for free boarding and lodging facilities, reserving seats for SCs and STs in all the government and government aided institutions, etc. are some of the concrete steps which the Government has taken in this regard.

- *Centrally Sponsored Schemes:* In addition to the above, there are some centrally sponsored schemes also for the educational benefit of both SCs and STs. (*i*) ***Free coaching*** and training for various competitive examinations [IAS, IPS, IFS, etc.] to increase their representation in various services. (*ii*) ***Past-matric scholarships*** for providing financial assistance for higher education. [Govt. spent 66.5 crore rupees for this purpose in the year 1993-94. The University Grants Commission [U.G.C.] and the Ministry of Education had earmarked 15% of their budget for this purpose during the 6th plan – 1980-85]. (*iii*) ***Construction of hostels*** for providing residential facilities to SCs and STs studying at college and university level. (*iv*) ***Financial assistance*** to those SC and ST students going to reputed research institutes for research work. (*v*) **Providing Text-books** to those studying in medical and engineering courses (*vi*) **Scholarships** and passage grants for higher education outside India.

3. ***Expansion of economic opportunities***: Government has taken up economic programmes also for the benefit of SCs and STs, *Examples*: Landless SC labourers are allotted land. Land reforms have been undertaken to bring benefits of land ownerships for them. Poor SC farmers are supplied with seeds, agriculture implements, fertilizers, pesticides, interest-free loans, pair of bullocks for ploughing, subsidy for developing dairy farming, poultry farming, poultry farming, piggery, animal husbandry, handicrafts, spinning and weaving. The "*loan-mela*" programme of Rajiv Gandhi Govt. [1984–89] also provided small loans for the poorer section to help them to earn money through some secondary sources such as toy-making, basket-making, agarbatti and beedi-rolling, tailoring, shoe-making, etc.
4. ***Expansion of employment opportunities and reservation***: In order to enhance the economic position of the SCs and STs the Constitution has provided *for the reservation in services*. Reservation of jobs operates in the all-India Services, Central Government, State Governments, and Government owned and managed public sector units and institutions. Reservation exists in all these for the SCs and STs to the tune of 15% and 7.5% respectively. Several State Governments have introduced reservation for OBC's (Other Backward Classes) also.

In government services, special quotas are also allotted to them. The reservations are also extended to promotions[5] to higher positions to facilitate their adequate representation. Concessions such *as relaxation in the standards of suitability, relaxation of the qualification and experience*, have also been provided to them.

5. ***Upliftment of scheduled castes through five-year plans***: The welfare of the Scheduled Castes (and STs) has been given special attention in the **Five-Year Plans**. The size of investment on the special programmes has been increasing from plan to plan The expenditure of ₹30.04 crore in the First Plan [1951-56] increased to ₹79.41 crore in the Second Plan [1956-61], ₹100.40 crore in the Third Plan [1961-66]. ₹172.70 crore in the Fourth Plan [1969-74], ₹296.19 crore in the Fifth Plan [1974-79], ₹1337.21 crores in the Sixth Plan [1980-85], and ₹1521.42 crore in the Seventh Plan [1985-90].[6] The State Governments have also been spending a sizeable amount on the welfare of these people.

- *Development Strategies in the Five-Year Plans:* The Central Government sponsored a comprehensive three-pronged strategy for the development of the SCs during the Sixth Five Year Plan [1980-85]. this consisted of three schemes. (*i*) *Special Component Plan* [*SCP*]. of the Central Ministeries and State Governments. (*ii*) Special Central Assistance [SCA] to SCPs for the Scheduled Castes of the States and (*iii*) Scheduled Caste Development Corporation [SCDCs] in the States.
  - **(*i*) *Special Component Plan [SCP]:*** The main objective of this plan is to assist the SC families to substantially improve their income. This plan envisages identification of schemes of development which would benefit SCs, quantification of funds from all programmes and determination of specific targets as to the number of families to be benefited from these programmes. During the Sixth Plan 1980-85] ₹4,481 crore were earmarked for the SCPs. Till the year 1990 only eight central ministeries had formulated the SCPs for the SCs.
  - **(*ii*) *Special Central Assistance [SCA]:*** The main purpose of this scheme is to provide additional assistance to the States from the Centre to help the economic advancement of the maximum possible number of Schedules Caste families living below the poverty line. This assistance is given through the SCP's. During the Sixth Plan ₹600 crore was earmarked for this purpose. Later, in 1993, in one year, about ₹273 crore was provided as SCA.
  - **(*iii*) *Scheduled Caste Development Corporation* [*SCDC*]:** The SCDCs have been set up in 18 states and 3 union territories. These SCDCs provide money and loan assistance to these families, thereby helping to increase the flow of funds from financial institutions to SC families. These Corporations established in the States are expected to interface between the SC families and financial institutions including banks. Both the Central and the State

[5] "The Supreme Court in its recent judgement on the reservation issue on Nov. 15th. 1992 adjudicated that there can be no reservations in promotions but the Central Government decided to continue them for some time. The Supreme Court also declared that reservation in certain technical posts like *scientific departments, super-specialities in medicine, engineering and defence research, professors in education, pilots in Indian Airlines/Air India, etc. is not advisable*."

[6] *Source of Statistics: Ram Ahuja's Indian Social System, p. 370.*

Governments, are contributing grants to these SCDCs. For example, the State Governments contribution in 1989-90 was ₹19 crore and the Central Government's ₹15 crore.

The Corporation also provides loan to the SC families upto ₹12,000. They not only arrange to provide financial assistance for occupations like agriculture, animal husbandry and household industry but also for small shops, industries, auto-rickshaws and many other trades and professions. Some corporations also arrange for irrigation facilities like digging wells and tubewells.

6. *Other Welfare Programmes*

(i) *Drinking water facility*. in SCs colonies and in the areas where they are found in large number, drinking water facility is provided through the construction of wells and borewells.

(ii) *Medical facility.* Free medical check-up facility is provided for the SCs. Those who undergo family planning operations are given financial assistance for purchasing required medicine and energising tonic.

(iii) *Janata houses:* In various States the SCs are given financial assistance to have their own houses. In States like Karnataka and Tamil Nadu low caste houses having all minimum required facilities, known as "janata" houses are built for them at State expenses.

(iv) *Liberation of bonded labourers*. A large number of bonded labourers particularly be- longing to the SCs have been liberated. As per the report of the 'labour Department of the Central Government in 1983 about 1.13 lakh bonded labourers [out of a total of 1.61 lakh] were liberated from their bondage with the Governmental assistance.

(v) *Sulab sauchalaya scheme.* This has been launched in several States for convening dry latrines into water-borne latrines in order to liberate SC scavengers and rehabilitate them in alternative occupations.

6. *Voluntary organisations.* In addition to the Governmental schemes and instruments, some of the voluntary organisations are also playing an important role in promoting the welfare of the SCs. *Examples* : (*i*) *Harijan Sevak Sangh* [New Delhi], (*ii*) *Indian Depressed Classes League* [New Delhi], (*iii*) *Hind Sweepers Sevak Sangh* [Delhi], (*iv*) *Servants of Indian Society* [Poona], (*v*) *Indian Red Cross Society* [New Delhi, "*Ishwara Sharana Ashrama*", Allahabad, (*vi*) *Sri Ramakrishna Mission* [Narendrapura, West Bengal]. The Central Government has been giving financial assistance to these organisations for their Harijan Welfare activities. In 1994, the Govt. spent about ₹6.5 crore for giving such an assistance.

Some other organisations which are not getting any financial help from the Government are also rendering Yeomen service to the Scheduled Castes. *Example*: "*Hindus Seva Prathisthana*", "*Vishwa Hindu Parishad*", *the service units of Rashtreeya Swayam Sevak Sangha*, "*Dalit Organisations*" and a number of *Christian Missionary Organisations*.

A Brief Evaluation of Welfare Schemes

Have these welfare measures really contributed to the upliftment of the SCs? The answer is somewhat disappointing.

- The Scheduled Castes spend their social energy in sanskritising themselves on the mode of the locally dominant castes. They do not gain much out of this. Their social mobility is very much limited. They continue to remain weak in the local power structure for asserting their rights. They still are economically insecure.
- Majority of the SCs are still illiterate and ignorant and hence they are *not able to make use of the constitutional provisions guaranteed to them*.
- The reports of the National Commission on Scheduled Castes and Scheduled Tribes reveal that *the crimes against SCs are increasing. Example*: The number of crimes against SCs recorded by the police in 1955 was 180; it increased to 13,884 in 1979 and to 19,342 in 1987.
- There has been a quality of *ritualistic formalism* about many welfare and development schemes formulated for the benefit of these people. *Lack of enthusiasm* and *sincerity* on the part of the Government officials and agencies have also been the cause of failure of many of the welfare schemes.
- The benefits of the SC welfare programmes have been availed of by *a few people belonging to Scheduled Castes*. This small minority has developed *vested interests* and contributes nothing for the benefit of the majority.
- The Scheduled Castes are largely concentrated in rural areas and 90% of them (including 35% agricultural labourers) derive their sustenance from agriculture. In most of the villages, they continue to suffer from residential segregation. Hence many of their disabilities still persist.
- The SCs are still *tradition-bound*. They suffer from a *sense of infertility* and this takes away their 'push' to develop further. They are not well-organised. Only in cities some "dalit organisations" are trying to fight for their rights.

Politically also they are not a single homogeneous entity. Hence their political bargaining power is comparatively less. However. their political consciousness is growing. The younger generation among them is becoming more assertive. There is a positive change in the attitude of the caste-Hindus towards the SCs. Hence the social distance between the two is gradually getting narrowed. The social position of the SCs is comparatively better in South India than in North India. In Kerala for example, the SCs do not suffer from the traditional type of disabilities. Greater changes are expected in their living styles in the years to come.

Harmful Effects of the Practice of Untouchability

The practice of untouchability gave rise not only to various kinds of disabilities but also caused damage to the Indian society, A few of such evil effects are mentioned below.

1. Untouchability ***divided the Hindu society into the 'touchable'*** and ***'untouchable'*** groups and served to develop mutual dislike, contempt and sometimes even enmity between the two. It damaged social harmony and created wide social distance between the two groups.
2. Since more than 1/6 of the total population of this land was labelled as "*untouchable*" its *socio-economic and educational progress was unwarrantedly halted for centuries*.
3. *Untouchability perpetuates inequality*. Hence it cannot support the development of healthy democratic traditions. It has affected our democratic system very badly.
4. *Untouchability provided scope for religious conversions*. Those untouchables who got disillusioned with the Hindu society got converted to other religions such as Christianity or Islam. Dr. Ambedkar himself had joined Buddhism at the fag end of his life in protest against the caste— conrolled Hinduism. [Such conversion of religion was reported in Meenakshipuram in Tamil Nadu in February l98l in which about 1000 Harijans were converted into Islam]
5. Untouchability led to *perennial conflicts between the upper castes and lower castes* for generations, sometimes resulting in loot, arson, murder, rape, molestation, burning of houses and crops and so on.
6. *Untouchability has damaged the self-image of the SCs*. It has developed in them a sense of inferiority and lack of confidence which damaged their personality development.
7. Due to the practice of untouchability, the nation was *deprived of the opportunity for making use of the talents, abilities and creative capacities* of a sizeable number of people for hundreds of years.
8. *The practice of untouchability is a black spot on the Hindu society.* It is an insult to the Hindu society. It has brought down the image of the Indians in the eyes of the foreigners.
9. Social reform movements and developmental activities could not take place in the Hindu society smoothly and effectively for it was divided vertically into "*touchable*" and "*untouchable*" castes. Even the great reformers such as Buddha, Mahaveera, Basavanna, Shankaracharya, Vivekananda, Dayananda Saraswathi, Gandhi, Ambedkar and a host of others could not attain complete success in their attempts to remove untouchability.

Untouchability has done enough damage to the Hindu society. As **Gandhiji** said *it should become the thing of the past*. It is slowly disappearing. The earlier it goes the better it will be for the nation.

THE SCHEDULED TRIBES

The second largest group of the backward classes of the unprivileged section consists of about 7.42 crores of *Scheduled Tribes* who constitute 8.8 % of the total population (1991 Census Report). The Scheduled Tribes, generally called tribal people, survived with their unchanging ways of life for centuries. The tribal people were the earliest among the present inhabitants of India. They are still in primitive stage and are far from the impact of modern civilization. They live in the forest areas, hilly regions, mountainous places and deep valleys. They are known by various names such as— *primitive tribes, animists, jungle people, 'adivasis'*, *aboriginals*, *original inhabitants of India* and so on. *Dr. Das* and *Das* have referred to them as "*submerged humanity*". *Gandhiji* called them '*Girijans*'. The Constitution of India has referred to them as the "*Scheduled Tribes*".

The Scheduled Tribes are in majority in more than 329 Talukas. On the basis of 50% of the Scheduled Tribes population, areas have been identified in the country. In such areas more than 65% of their total population lives. It means that the tribal people are the dominant groups in some areas. In Nagaland, Meghalaya, Arunachal Pradesh and Mizoram, majority of the population belongs to Scheduled Tribes. They are found in relatively a big number in Madhya Pradesh, Orissa, Bihar, Assam and Uttar Pradesh. In Madhya Pradesh alone more than one crore tribals are found. According to the Scheduled Tribe Lists Modification Order 1956, there are 414 different tribes in the various States of India.

Definition and Distribution of Scheduled Tribes

The term '*Tribe*' is nowhere defined in the Constitution and, in fact, there is no satisfactory definition for the same. 'To the ordinary man the word '*tribe*' suggests *simple folk* living in hills and forests; to people who are a little better informed, it signifies a *colourful people famous for their dance and song*; to an administrator it means *a group of citizens whose welfare is the special responsibility of the President of India*, to an anthropologist it indicates a *special field for study of a social phenomena*". In their own way all these impressions are meaningful. No standard explanation or definition has been accepted by all to denominate the people who are classified as the people of the tribal origin.

Reference in the Constitution

Though the Indian Constitution has not defined clearly the term '*tribe*', *Article 336 (25)* of the Constitution says that Scheduled Tribes are the tribes or tribal communities or parts of or groups within such tribes or tribal communities which the Indian President may specify by public notification under Article *342(1)*.

However, the term 'tribe' has been defined by various thinkers and writers in different ways. One or two definitions may be cited here.

1. *Dr. D.N. Majumdar*: A Scheduled Tribe refers to "a collection of families or groups of families, bearing a common name, members which occupy the same territory, speak the same language and observe certain taboos regarding marriage, profession or occupation and have developed as well as assessed system of reciprocity and mutuality of obligations".
2. *Imperial Gazetteer of India*: A tribe is a collection of families bearing a common name, speaking a common dialect, occupying or professing to occupy a common territory and is not usually endogamous, though originally it might have been so".
3. *Gillin* and *Gillin*: "A tribe is a group of local communities which lives in a common area, speaks a common dialect and follows a common culture".

The Distribution of the Tribes

The tribal population is divided into three zones, namely; North-Eastern Zone, the Central Zone and the Southern Zone.

1. ***North-eastern zone***: This zone consists of the sub-Himalayan region and the hills and mountain ranges of North-Eastern frontiers of India. The tribals of this zone mostly belong to the Mangoloid race and speak languages belonging to the Tibeto-Chinese family. This zone is inhabited by tribes such — *Gurung, Limbu, Lepcha, Aka, Mishmi, Mikir. Rabha, Kachari, Garb, Khasi, Chakma, Naga, Angami, Sema, Pham, Chang* and so on.
2. ***The central zone***: The tribal groups of this zone are scattered all over the mountain-belt between the rivers Narmada and Godawari. The main tribes of this area are the *Gonds, Munda, Kandh, Baiga, Bhil, Bhuiyari, Bhumji, Koli, Savara, Kharia, Oraon, Ho, Sanlal, Juortg*, and so on.
3. ***The southern zone***: This zone falls south of the river Krishna. The tribals of this zone are regarded as the most ancient inhabitants now living in India. This zone consists of the tribes like— *Chenchu, Kota, Kurumba, Badaga, Toda, Kadar, Malayan, Muthuvan, Urali, Koya, Soliga, Kanikkar, Paniyart, Yerava, etc.*

TRIBAL PROBLEMS

The tribals of India are faced with a number of problems among which the following may be noted.

1. The Problem of Geographic Separation

The tribals of India are in a way geographically separated from the rest of population. Some of them are living in the unapproachable physical areas such as deep valleys, dense forests, hills, mountains, etc. It is difficult for them to establish relations with others, and hence, socially they are far away from the civilised world. This kind of physical as well as social isolation or seclusion has contributed to various other problems.

2. Cultural Problems

The tribal culture is entirely different from the way of life of the civilized people. The tribals fail to understand the civilised people, their customs and practices, beliefs and attitudes and so on. They are suspicious towards the civilised people. They are clinging tenaciously to their customs and traditions. During the British rule some foreign Christian missionaries made an attempt to propagate their religion in some of the tribal areas, particularly in the North-Eastern provinces. They even try to impose their culture on them. Even today such an attempt is going on. On the other hand, the Ramakrishna Mission,

R.S.S, the Vishwa Hindu Parishad and other organisations are spreading the Hinduism in these areas. Some of the tribal leaders have now started popularising the tribal religion. These different propagandas have created a great confusion for them. The cultural gap between the civilised and the tribal people is coming in the way of the assimilation and integration of the tribal people into the mainstream of the national life of India.

3. Social Problems

The tribals have their own social problems also. They are traditional and custom-bound. They have become the victims of superstitious beliefs, outmoded and meaningless practices and harmful habits. Child marriage, infanticide, homicide, animal sacrifice, exchange of wives, black magic and other harmful practices are still found among them. They believe in ghosts and spirits. They have a keen desire to maintain all these practices in general, and their individual tribal character. Hence it is said that "*the tribals are the tribesmen first, the tribesmen last and the tribesmen all the time*".

4. Economic Problem

The tribal people are economically the poorest people of India. Majority of them live below the poverty line. The tribal economy is based on agriculture of the crudest type. The main economic problems of the tribals are explained below.

(i) ***Exploitation.*** The innocence, illiteracy and helplessness of the tribals are exploited by the outsiders. The British policy, in particular, had led to ruthless exploitation of the tribals in various ways as it favoured the zamindars, landlords, money-lenders, forest contractors and excise, revenue and police officials.

(ii) ***Unprofitable agriculture.*** About 90% of the tribals are engaged in cultivation and most of them are landless and practise shitting cultivation. They need to be helped in adopting new methods of cultivation. The tribals possess uneconomic holdings because of which their crop yield is very less. A very small percentage of the population participates in occupational activities in the secondary and tertiary sectors.

(iii) ***Problems of land ownership.*** A good portion of the land in the tribal areas has been legally transferred to non-tribals. Tribals demand that this land should be returned to them. In fact, the tribals had earlier enjoyed much freedom to use the forest and hunt their animals. They are emotionally attached to the forests for they believe that their gods, spirits live in forests. The tribals who are "*deprived*" of their rights to the land and forest have reacted sharply to the restrictions imposed by the government on their traditional rights.

(iv) ***Unemployment and underemployment.*** A large number of tribal young men and women are either unemployed or underemployed. They are unhappy for they are not able to get jobs that can keep them occupied throughout the year. They need to be helped in finding secondary source of income by developing animal husbandry, poultry farming, handicrafts, handloom weaving, etc.

(v) ***Non-availability of banking facilities.*** Banking facilities in the tribal areas are so inadequate that the tribals have mainly to depend on the money-lenders. The tribals, therefore, demand that "*Agricultural Indebtedness Relief Acts*" should be enacted so that they may get back their mortgaged land.

5. Educational Problems

Illiteracy is a major problem of the tribals. More than 80% of them are illiterate. Literacy among them has increased from 0.7% in 1931 to 11.30% in 1970 and to 16.35% in 1981. This shows more than 3/4 of the tribals are illiterate. They have no faith in formal educational organisation. Many of them do not know anything about education, schools, colleges, universities, degrees, etc. They feel no urge to educate their children. Since most of the tribals are poor, education appears to be a luxury for them. In the case of those people who are engaged in agriculture, their minor children are also engaged in it. The illiterate parents do not consider it as their primary responsibility to give education to their children.

- *The problem of language.* The medium of instruction is another hindrance to the promotion of education among the tribes. Most of the tribal languages do not have a script of their own. Hence the children are obliged to learn things in a language which is foreign to them. Even in tribal areas the number of tribal teachers is very less and hence communication problem always arises between the students and the teachers.
- *The curriculum of education is another main problem.* The existing curriculum, as experts rightly have pointed out, is not suited and has little relevance to the tribal people.

6. Problem of Health and Sanitation

Due to illiteracy and ignorance the tribals are not able to appreciate modern concept of health and sanitation. They do not take much care pertaining to their own health. They believe that diseases are caused by hostile spirits and ghosts. They have their own traditional means of diagnosis and cure. Good number of them fall a prey to the diseases such as skin disease, forest fever, typhoid, T.B., leprosy, malaria, veneral diseases, small pox, etc. Contact with outsiders further added to a few more diseases in the tribal areas. *Example: It is observed that the Thodas of Niligiri Hills have been suffering from some modern diseases like veneral diseases, diabetes, blood pressure, etc. after com- ing into touch with the British who made Niligiri Hills one of their summer resorts*. These diseases take a heavy toll of tribal life. Their suspicion and lack of faith in modern doctors have made them not to avail themselves of the modern medical facilities.

7. Problem of Separatism

The "*divide and rule*" policy adopted by the British did a lot of damage to the tribal community of India. The British had superimposed their own administrative patterns in tribal areas and deprived the tribals of their traditional methods of interacting with people. The "*Criminal Tribes Act*" which the British had introduced gave an impression that the tribals were either "*criminals*" or "anti-social beings". The tribal groups such as *Kolis, Mundas, Khasis, Santals, Naga*, etc, who fought against the British were branded as "*dacoits*" and "*robbers*". The British government which wanted to humble these tribals and "*correct*" them gave direct encouragement to the foreign Christian missionary activities especially in, the Central and the North-Eastern Zone. These activities which went on for more than 200 years, alienated many of the tribals and developed in them separatist tendencies.

- ***Tribal revolts and uprisings.*** Numerous revolts and uprisings of the tribals have taken place beginning with the one in Bihar in 1772, followed by many other revolts in Andhra Pradesh, Arunachal Pradesh, Assam, Mizoram and Nagaland. The important tribes involved in revolt in the 19th century were *Mizos*, [1810], *Kols* [1795 and 1831], *Mundas* [1389], *Daflas* [1875], *Khasi* and *Garo* [1829], *Kacharis* [1839], *Santhals* [1853], *Muria Gonds* [1886], *Nagas* [1844 and 1879], *Bhuiyas* [1868] and *Kondhs* [1817]. During the recent tribal uprisings the *Nagas*, *Mizos* and the *Bodos* took part in them in large number and created serious law and order problem.
- ***Smuggling, infiltration and drug addiction.*** The foreign infiltrators especially from Bangladesh, Pakistan, Burma and China are entering the borders of India through what are known as "*tribal belts*" Some of them take undue advantage of the tribals' innocence and ignorance for their *smuggling activities*. Prohibited drugs and unlicensed weapons are smuggled inside the land and beyond the borders of India through the tribal areas. Some of the tribal have been made the victims of drug addiction. Hence, tribal areas in the borders have become extremely sensitive areas.

Measures for the Upliftment of Scheduled Tribes

Independent India has been paying due attention to the problems of the scheduled tribes and attempts are being made to deal effectively with those problems. Before the independence, the British Government was only discussing the issues of tribal development and practically did nothing either to face them or to solve them. The only thing the British did was that, they kept the tribals away from the contact of the civilized people. Through their "*policy of indirect rule*" they wanted to protect them from the neighbouring dominant communities.

The British followed their so-called "*policy of giving special protection*" to the tribals till the *Government of India Act*, 1935 came into force. Afterwards, though the elected provincial legislative bodies were established, some tribal areas known as "*the excluded areas*" were brought under the direct control of the British Governor.

The British policy of separating the tribals from the rest of the people created suspicion in the minds of the nationalists. They severely criticised the British policy and charged the British with preventing a large section of our countrymen from joining the mainstream of national life. "*In practice what happened was that the tribes were isolated and then left to stagnate, halting the evolving process of cultural fusion.*" [S. C. Dube][7]

This brings us to the questions, *whether the tribals should be assimilated into the mainstream or whether they should be protected? And in what way they will benefit from the developments taking place in the country*? Let us consider the different approaches or viewpoints which the scholars have developed regarding the tribals and their development.

Three views to Solve Tribal Problems

Various solutions have been presented for dealing effectively with the tribal problems. The tribal problems have been approached from three viewpoints. They are as follows:

1. ***Assimilation.*** "Assimilation is the process whereby individuals or groups once dissimilar become similar and identified in their interests and outlook".–*Ogburn* and *Nimkoff.* Assimilation is one of the ways of dealing with the tribal problems. According to this solution advocated by the social reformers and voluntary organisations, assisting and encouraging the tribals to assimilate themselves with the mainstream of national life, can alone permanently solve the tribal problems. Thus, according to this approach, we cannot deal with tribal problems on the basis of

[7] S.C. Dube in *Encyclopedia of Social work in India*—Vol. III.

tribal culture and life but by changing them into the frame of new community. The Christian missionaries on the one hand, and the Hindu social reformers like Thakkar Bapa on the other, have been trying to assimilate them into Christian and Hindu community respectively. This approach has its own limitations. Complete assimilation is a difficult task. The tribals are not prepared to give up all of their traditional tribal beliefs, practices and ideas. Any attempt to impose the external cultural practices on them, creates in them guilt feelings, confusions and mental conflicts. This solution may even create economic, religious and moral degradation among them.

2. ***Isolation***: *Hutton*, who was a commissioner for census of 1931, and *Elwin* have suggested that the tribals must be kept at a distance from the rest of the society. Keeping them in isolation in some "*National Parks*" or "*reserved areas*" would solve two problems: (*a*) *the tribals would be in a position to maintain their independent identity,* (*b*) *they would be free from the exploitation of Outsiders*. The champions of this approach are of the view that sufficient time must be given to the tribals to assimilate themselves with the rest of the community. The limitation of this approach is that when once the tribals are kept in isolation they are likely to develop vested interests and keep themselves permanently away from others.

3. ***Integration***: The third view, which is actively followed in the recent years, is that of integration. The policy of isolation is neither possible nor desirable, and that of assimilation would mean imposition. Hence integration alone can make available to the tribes the benefits of modern society and yet retain their separate identity. This view recommends the rehabilitation of the tribals on the plains along with the civilised people, but away from their native places such as hills, mountains, forests, etc. This suggestion has also been criticised. It is said that this suggestion has been advocated to further the interests of industrialists and capitalists. This solution is not appreciated on the ground that it may create economic and moral decadence to those who are separated from their beloved land to plains. Still, the policy of integration which aims at developing a creative adjustment between tribes and non-tribes has been supported by thinkers and writers like Pandit Jawaharlal Nehru.

Conclusions

The solutions to the tribal problems mentioned above, have their own merits and demerits. Tribal problems are simple but very delicate to handle. No solution can be experimented with before winning the confidence of the tribals. The modern culture must not be imposed on them. It is essential to establish a harmonious compatibility between the tribal mode of living and the material advancement of culture. The integration of the tribal society into the Indian society takes time, and it has to be promoted while retaining the good points of the tribal culture. Only those elements of new culture which may vitalise them for material advancement, must be infused in them. *Pandit Nehru* observes that, "*Tribal people possess a variety of culture and they are in many ways certainly not backward. There is no point in trying to make them a second rate copy of ourselves*".

With regards to the tribal development and welfare Pandit Nehru observes that our duty which comes "First is to preserve, strengthen, and develop all that is best in tribal society, culture, art and language. In the second is to protect the tribal economic rights. The third is to unite and integrate the tribes in a true heart unity with India as a whole so that they may play a full part in their life. And the last is to develop welfare and educational facilities so that every tribesman may have an equal opportunity with the rest of the fellow citizens who work in the fields, factories, and workshops in the open country and the plains".

The Tribal 'Panchasheela'

Pandit Jawaharlal Nehru in 1957 in his foreword to *Verrier Elwin's* "*The Philosophy for NEFA* has laid down in five principles, that is, "*Panchasheela*", the policy of integration. The tribal "Panchasheela" as has been enunciated by him are as follows:

(*i*) Nothing should be imposed on the tribal people. They must be allowed to develop along the lines of their own genius. We should try to encourage in every way their own traditional arts and culture.

(*ii*) Tribal rights in land and forests should be respected.

(*iii*) Attempt must be made to train and build up a team of their own people to the work of administration and development. Some technical personnel from outside will be of great help for them in the beginning. But too many outsiders must not be sent to the tribal territory.

(*iv*) Over-administering the tribal areas or overwhelming them with too many schemes must be avoided. We should not work in rivalry to their own social and cultural institutions.

(*v*) The results of the work must be adjudged by the quality of the human character that is evolved and not by statistics or the amount of money spent.

The *Ministry of Home Affairs* and the *Ministry of Community Development* (under the *Article* 46 of the Constitution), set up 43 sub-multipurpose tribal blocks in the various States of India to promote the welfare and the integration of the tribals. Two Committees were set up one in May 1959 under the Chairmanship of the anthropologist *Verrier Elwin* and the other in April 1960 under the Presidentship of *Dhebar*, to examine the programmes and projects of these blocks. Both the Committees submitted their reports in 1960 and 1961 respectively. The reports have emphasised and amplified the five fundamental principles enunciated by Nehru in 1957.

Tribal Welfare Activities

The tribals constitute a sizeable proportion (8.8%) of the total population of India. The tribals are also the citizens of India and hence promotion of their welfare is of equal importance. Not only the Central and the State Governments have undertaken various steps in this regard, but also various voluntary organisations have evinced interest in this task. Organisations such as the *Bharatiya Adim Jati Sevak Sangh, the Bhil Seva Malndal, The Kasturba Gandhi National Memorial Trust, the Indian Red Cross Society, the Vishwa Hindu Parishad, The Ramakrishna Mission, The Rashtreeya Swayam Sevak Sangh*, etc., carry on welfare activities among the tribals. The Government through its *Department of Tribal Welfare* and through its Five-Year Plans has been trying to elevate the tribals from the state of ignorance, illiteracy and poverty. Some of the tribal welfare measures of the Government may be examined here.

1. Constitutional Safeguards

The Constitution of India has made various provisions to safeguard the interests of the tribals.

1. Article 15 of the Constitution provides equal rights and opportunities to all the citizens of India (including the tribals) without any discrimination.
2. Reservation in employment is made for the tribals under Article 16(4), 320(4) and 335.
3. Seats have been reserved for them in the legislatures (in Lok Sabha and State Vidhana Sabhas) under Articles 330, 332 and 334.
4. Under Article 19(5) the tribals can own property and enjoy it in any part of the country.
5. According to the Article 275 a large amount of money can be taken from the Consolidated Fund of India to be spent on tribal welfare activities.
6. Article 338 empowers the President of India to appoint a Commissioner to look after the tribal welfare activities.
7. Under Article 339(2) the Central Government can give directions to the States in the formulation and execution of tribal welfare plans, projects and programmes.
8. Under Article 275(i) the Centre is required to give grants-in-aid to the States for approved schemes of tribal welfare.
9. Article 164 empowers the State Governments to appoint a separate minister to look into the welfare of the tribals.
10. Article 46 consists of provisions that protect the economic and educational interests of the tribals.
11. Article 224 gives instructions to the administration to take special care to protect tribal interests in "*Scheduled Tracts*" or "*areas*".
12. Article 342 gives power to the President of India to declare on the recommendation of the Governor some groups or communities as "scheduled tribes". It also gives details on the basis of which new groups could be recommended as "scheduled tribes" entitling them for all the constitutional benefits.

- ***Committees and commissions***: In addition to the constitutional provisions mentioned above, the government appoints committees, commissions and study teams from time to time to look into the way in which the target groups are making use of the constitutional provisions, the problems faced by them and to suggest measures for further improvement. ***Examples of some commissions and Study Teams:*** *(i) Backward Classes Commission [1953-55], headed by Kuka Kalelkar; (ii) the Study Team of Social Welfare and Welfare of Backward Classes [1958-59] headed by Renuka Ray; (iii) The Scheduled Areas and Scheduled Tribes Commission – 1960-61 under the chairmanship of U.N. Dhebar; (iv) The Second Backward Classes Commission [1979-80] under the chairmanship of B.P. Mandal, etc.*]

2. Economic Programmes and Facilities

Majority of the tribals are extremely poor and economically backward. Various economic programmes and projects have been undertaken to improve their economic position.

(i) ***Development through five-year plans***: The Government spent ₹30 crores, ₹80 crores, ₹101 crores, ₹172 crores and ₹257 crores on tribal welfare activities during the 1st, 2nd, 3rd, 4th and 5th Five-Year Plans respectively. ***Integrated***

Tribal Development Projects [ITDPs] evolved for the tribal development during the 5th plan [1974-79] cover today 19 states/union territories and 374 lakh tribal population.

The amount allocated for the tribal sub-plans in the **5th plan** was ₹1100 crores, in the **6th plan** [1980-85] it was ₹5,535 crore and in the **7th Plan** [1985-90] it was ₹10,500 crore.

Specific objectives set forth under the tribal sub-plan strategy were: (*i*) raising production in the field of agriculture, small industries, horticulture and animal husbandry; (*ii*) elimination of exploitation of tribals in money lending, bondage, forest, liquor vending, etc; (*iii*) development of education and training programmes; (*iv*) development of tribal areas; (*v*) upgradation of environment of tribal areas.

(*ii*) ***Establishment of "LAMPS"***: *Large-sized Multi-Purpose Co-operative Societies*: These co-operative societies are established in the tribal areas for giving productive and unproductive loans, for sale of surplus produce and purchase of necessities of life to the tribal people. Through these societies the tribals are supplied with improved seeds. modern agricultural equipments, chemicals and fertilizers, pesticides, etc. These societies are striving to relieve the tribals from the exploitation of middlemen. contractors and money-lenders.

(*iii*) ***The 20-point programme focused*** its attention on the development of the scheduled tribes, including assisting the tribal families economically to enable them to cross the poverty line.

(*iv*) ***Encouragement to Crafts and Home Industries***: Encouragement is given to the existing crafts and home industries among the tribals and such new endeavours are also encouraged. Example: (*i*) In West Bengal, tribals are encouraged to develop silk industry. A training institute is established in Darjeeling to give proper training to those engaged in sericulture. (*ii*) in **Bihar, M.P., Orissa** and **West Bengal**: wax industry is encouraged among the tribals of these provinces. (*iii*) **Madhya Pradesh** Government is helping its tribals to prosper in their economic pursuit of collecting beedi leaves. (*iv*) **Bihar** Government has established a Woman's Co-operative Society for its tribal women to give encouragement to them to pursue their handicrafts.

(*v*) ***Agriculture made stable***: The tribals are persuaded to give up their system of "*shifting cultivation*" and to settle permanently in a place of their selection by making agriculture their profession. Thousands of tribals in Assam, Bihar, M.P., Orissa and Tripura, have been made to settle down permanently for agriculture. *Thodas of Niligiri Hills* and *Soligas of* Biligiri Rangana Hills in Mysore provide two other examples in this regard.

(*vi*) ***Promotion of labour interests of tribals engaged in mining industry and tea plantations***: Attempts have been made to protect the labour interests of the tribals in Bihar, West Bengal, Madhya Pradesh and Orissa who are engaged in mining industry and of the tribals such as Santals, Gonds, Khondas and others who are working in tea plantations of Assam.

3. Educational Facilities

Measures to provide educational facilities to the S.T. have been taken by the Government. Schools are established in some tribal areas. In the first Five-Year Plan itself about 4000 schools were opened in the tribal areas. Education upto 10th standard has been made completely free for them. The students belonging to S.T. are getting various concessions such as free tuition, stipends, scholarships, free supply of text books, stationery and other equipments. In some places mid–day meals are also supplied. Free boarding and lodging facilities are provided for them. For the S.T. and S.C., 20% of the seats are reserved in technical education and relaxation is made in respect of age limit and qualifying marks

- There are ***Ashroma Schools*** for providing basic education and vocation training for S.T. In these schools education and training is given in areas such as agriculture, forestry, animal husbandry, poultry, farming, bee keeping, handicrafts, etc. There are 600 Ashrama Schools of residential character situated in Andhra Pradesh, Gujarat, Himachal Pradesh, Chennai, Karnataka, Orissa, Rajasthan and Tripura.
- ***Pre-Examination Training Centres for S.C. and S.T.*** are established in some places to help them to appear for UPSC Examinations and for I.A.S. and I.P.S. Examinations. The I971 Census Report indicates that literacy has gone down in some tribal areas, while it has registered a slight progress in some other areas. Even in 1981 the literacy campaign could reach only 16.35% of the tribals. In some cases 100% of the expenses of the students may have to be met by the Government.

4. Medical Facilities

Various medical facilities have been provided for the tribals in the tribal areas. In some places, hospitals are established and in many places mobile hospital facilities have been provided. Many preventive and curative measures to combat the diseases like malaria, leprosy, forest fever, monkey fever, typhoid, small pox, skin diseases etc. are undertaken. Medical camps are organised in the tribal areas to enable the tribals to realise the importance of modern medical facilities.

5. Research Work into the Problems of the Tribals

Tribal Research Institutes, which undertake intensive studies of tribal arts, culture and customs and problems have been set up in Bihar, Madhya Pradesh, Orissa, Gujarat, Kerala, Maharashtra, Tamil Nadu, Andhra Pradesh, U.P., Rajasthan and West Bengal. The research work done in this field has thrown light on the tribal life and problems.

6. Role of Voluntary Organisations

The tribal welfare is not the concern of the government alone. Private organisations and individuals interested in the task of tribal upliftment must also be given due encouragement in this regard. **Takkar Bapu** and **Gandhiji** have shown that individuals and voluntary organisations with social commitment can do a lot for the welfare of tribals. Organisations such as — *Sri Ramakrishna Mission, Vanavasi Kalyanushrorna, the Rashtreeya Swayom Sevaka Songha and a number of Christian Missionary Organisations* are already working in the field. Such organisations can help the tribals to develop better interaction with the neighbouring people.

Conclusion

Though the Central and the State Governments have taken much interest in the tribal welfare programmes, projects and schemes, much remains to be done. The progress achieved in this field is far from satisfactory. The Sixth Plan document notes with concern that "*three decades of development have not had the desired impact on the socially, economically and educationally handicapped section*". The Welfare progammes have not been effective due to "inadequacies in the administrative machinery, lack of sensitive, trained management, lack of general preparedness for. large investments, deficiency in accounting systems, procedural delays and lack of proper monitoring and evaluation..." The plan document admits [in its clause 26-10] that "*no positive steps were taken to ensure that S. C. and S. T. obtained their share of the benefits of public distribution.*" Even after the completion of the 7th plan things have not radically improved. It is necessary that in the current plan and in the years to come, due attention is to be paid for the overall improvement of the tribals.

THE BACKWARD CLASSES

Who form the Backward Classes?

The term '*backward classes*' has not been defined properly either by the sociologists or by the constitution-makers. The backward classes are a large mixed category of persons with boundaries that are both unclear and elastic. They seem to comprise roughly one-third of the total population of the country. They consist of three main categories–the scheduled castes, the scheduled tribes and the '*other backward classes*'. The scheduled castes and scheduled tribes are comparatively better defined and form roughly 22% of the total population according to the 1971 Census. The "other backward classes" *is a residual category*. Their position is highly ambiguous and it is not possible to give an exact statement of their numbers.

'Other Backward Classes'

The third major group of '*backward classes*' consists of a big number of educationally and economically backward people. Though the term '*backward classes*' has not been defined by the Indian Constitution, the characteristics of backwardness are described here and there and also sometimes the categories are mentioned. *Article 15* (*4*) speaks of the socially and educationally backward. *Article 16* (*4*) uses the term 'backward class' and speaks of inadequate representation in services. *Article 45* mentions free and compulsory education. *Article 46* mentions the weaker sections of the people and includes the expression "the Scheduled Castes and Scheduled Tribes". *Article 340 em*powers the State to investigate the condition of the backward classes and to help them by grants, etc. Thus the Constitution has accepted the following elements of backwardness; *illiteracy and lack of education, poverty. exploitation of labour, non-representation in services and untouchability*.

Thus, the term '*backward classes*' is vague in the sense that it includes a wide variety of lower classes as well as castes consisting of millions of people. *Article 340* of the Constitution provide for the appointment of a commission to investigate the conditions of backward classes. Accordingly, the President (that is, the Union Govt.) had appointed on Ian. 29, 1953, **The Backward Classes Commission** under the chairmanship of *Kakasaheb Kalelkar*. The Commission prepared a list containing as many as 2,399 communities which were treated as socially and educationally backward. Out of these, 913 communities alone had an estimated population of 115 million. The commission adopted the following criteria for determining backwardness:

1. Low Social position in the traditional caste hierarchy of Hindu Society.
2. Lack of general advancement among the major section of a caste or community.
3. Inadequate or no representation in Government services.
4. Inadequate representation in the field of trade, commerce and industry.

Caste as the Basis to Determine Backwardness

It appears that after considering several criteria, the commission ultimately decided to treat the caste as an important factor for determining backward classes. The Commission made its list on the basis of caste. In fact, the chairman of the commission *Kalelkar* wanted to eschew the principle of caste for he saw dangers in suggesting remedies on caste basis. The Union Government, however, also felt the same. In addition to the above, several committees were appointed by the States and lists of backward communities were drawn up. The Havnoor Commission Report of Karnataka can be cited here as an example. Provision was made for reservations for these communities in educational institutions as well as in the state employment. It may be noted here that for the purposes of the Union of India at present there is no list of backward classes other than the Scheduled Castes and Scheduled Tribes and there are no reservations for them under the Union of India.

Definition of Backward Classes

Though the term "*Backward Classes*" is popularly used by sociologists it is not defined properly. Still for our purpose of study we may define it in the following way:

1. *Justice K. Subba Rao*, former Chief Justice of India, defined '*backward classes*' as—"an ascertainable and identifiable group of persons based on caste, religion, race, language, occupation and such others, with definite characteristics of backwardness in various aspects of human existence — social, cultural, economic, political and such others."
2. We can generally define '*backward classes*' as those social groups or classes or castes which are characterised by illiteracy and lack of education, poverty, exploitation of labour, non- representation in services and untouchability.
3. In simple words, the term '*backward classes*' can be defined as a social category which consists of all the socially, educationally, economically and politically backward groups, castes, and tribes.

Description of the Backward Classes

The *Backward Classes Commission* in its Report of 1956 described the Backward Classes as consisting of the following groups:

1. Those who suffer from the stigma of untouchability or near untouchability. These groups are classified as scheduled castes (SC).
2. Those tribes who are not yet sufficiently assimilated into the mainstream of the national life. These groups are classified as Scheduled Tribes (ST).
3. Those tribes who, due to long neglect, have been forced to commit crime. These tribes were previously known as criminal tribes (before 1953) and are presently called Denotified Tribes or Ex-Criminal Tribes.
4. 'Other Backward Classes' which consist of (*a*) those nomads who have no occupation of a fixed habitation and are given to mimicry, begging, jugglery, dancing, etc., (*b*) Communities consisting largely of agricultural or landless labourers, (*c*) Communities consisting largely of tenants without occupancy rights and those with insecure land tenure, (*d*) Communities consisting of a large percentage of small land owners with uneconomic holdings, (*e*) Communities engaged in cattle breeding, sheep breeding or fishing on small scale, (*f*) Artisan and occupational classes without security of employment and whose traditional occupations have ceased to be remunerative, (*g*) Communities, the majority of whose people, do not have sufficient education and therefore have not secured adequate representation in Government services, (*h*) Social groups from among Muslims, Christians and Sikhs who are still backward socially and educationally, and (*i*) Communities not occupying positions in social hierarchy.

The Backward Classes Movement

The *Backward Classes Movement* started in India in the early part of the 20th century. When the British introduced here English medium schools and colleges and the Western education, the upper castes like the Brahmins made use of them. As a result, they could easily get the jobs in the government services and increase their prestige. This further increased the cultural, social, and economic distance between them and the lower castes. Now the lower castes became more conscious of this situation. As *M.N. Srinivas* has said the lower castes realised that mere Sanskritisation was not enough. It did not provide them much scope for social mobility. They became more determined to obtain Western education in order to qualify themselves for the new jobs in administration and the new professions like law, medicine, engineering, etc. Higher caste dominance in education and in the new occupations thus provided the conditions for the Backward Classes Movement. As *M.N. Srinivas* has pointed out that such movement was inevitable in India where only one caste, the Brahmins, enjoyed a preponderance in higher education, in professions, and government employment. The cultural gulf between the Brahmins and others became very much pronounced now.

The characteristic feature of this movement is that it is *caste based*. In the Indian context, "backward classes" form an aggregate of '*closed*' status groups or castes. Caste associations came into existence in different parts of the country to press their claims for new designations and occupations. Many published journals devoted to caste welfare, collected funds for giving scholarships and building hostels for students from respective castes, and undertook reform of caste customs. The qualified youths of the lower castes soon realised that it was difficult to get admission in the professional courses and in the post-graduate courses. They could not compete with the upper caste youths such as Brahmins. They also failed to get jobs in the government services. They felt that they were discriminated against on the basis of caste. This led to anti-Brahmin feelings.

The desire for mobility among the backward caste came from the *census operations* also. The caste '*sabhas*' represented to the census authorities the demand of individual castes to belong to a particular '*varna*' and not to a lower one. For example, the two peasant castes of Tamil Nadu, the *Vellalas* and *Padaiyachis* wanted to be recorded as '*Vaishyas*' and '*Vaniya Kula Kshatriyas*' respectively, and not as '*Shudras*'. Many such claims were made in l931 census. The '*Sabhas*' also altered the styles of life of their castes in the direction of Sanskritisation. This included the giving up of forbidden meat (pork and canion beet) and liquor, and the donning of the sacred thread, the shortening of the mourning period like that of the Brahmins. In the case of very '*low-castes*' it included non-performance of a traditional degrading duty such as '*Carvee*' or other free labour or carrying palanquins, or beating the 'tom-tom' on ceremonial occasions. The upper caste people were mainly indifferent towards these trends. On some occasions, they used force to make the lower caste people to perform their traditional duties.

The partition of Bengal in 1905 led to the intensification of nationalism, and also to the rise of communalism, casteism, linguism and regionalism. The *Minto-Morley Reforms of 1909* conceded separate electorates to Muslims, Sikhs, Indian Christians, Anglo-Indians and Europeans. Now, the lower castes also demanded separate electorate. Dr. Ambedkar fought for it. *This made the backward class movement to become political*. In South India, in Madras Presidency the *Justice Party* was formed to protect the interests of the Non-Brahmins '*dominant castes*'. It started newspapers in English and other languages to educate and to represent the case of the Non-Brahmins. Similarly, many *periodicals* were started by caste organisations in different parts of India.

At the earlier stage '*Backward Classes Movement*' meant '*the non-Brahmin Movement*'. The non-Brahamin Movement had two aims: (*i*) demanding the sanction of more concessions and privileges (which would cause discrimination against the Brahmins) to surpass Brahmins in education and social status (*ii*) achieving "*Swayam Maryada*' or *self-respect. E. V. Ramaswamy Naicker* started the *Self-Respect Movement* in Tamil Nadu. This movement was *anti-Brahmin*, *anti-North*, *anti-Hindi*, *anti-Sanskrit* and finally *anti-God*. Ramaswamy Naicker founded the *Dravida Kazhagam*—D.K. (Dravidian Federation) in 1945. In 1949, his disciple **C. Annadurai** founded the Dravida Munnetra Kazhagam—D.M.K (Dravidian Progressive Federation) which completely wiped out the domination of the Brahmins in the politics of Tamil Nadu. The D.K. under the leadership of Naicker continued to pursue anti-Brahminism in social and cultural fields. The D.M.K. and the Anna D.M.K. (ADMK) continue their anti-Hindi and anti-Sanskrit attitude. But they are not very much anti-Brahmin now. The DMK penetrated the Tamil film industry also.

"Thus, the aim of the Backward Class Movement at this stage was to limit the Brahmin mo- nopoly in the two fields of education and appointment to government posts." This movement was by no means a mass movement. The opposition to Brahmin dominance did not come from the low and the oppressed castes but from the leaders of the powerful, rural dominant castes such as Reddis and *Kammas* in Andhra, V*okkaligas* and *Lingayats* in Karnataka, etc. These were high caste groups with a social position next to the Brahmins. They included not only the Hindus but also the Muslims, Christians and other communities who also suffered from the same social disabilities. Hence it is relevant to use the term "*Backward Classes*", and *not* '*Backward Castes*".

Role of the Dominant Castes

Some of the castes included among the '*Other Backward Classes*' are very powerful in the economic, social and political fields. They outnumber the Brahmins and own vast lands. They are not as well educated as the Brahmins; nor are they well represented in the government jobs. Being powerful land-owners and the traditional village headmen they are very powerful in the political field at the local, district and state levels. *M.N. Srinivas* refers to such castes as the '*dominant castes*'. *For example, Vokkaligas* and *Lingayats* of Karnataka. *Reddis* and *Kammas* of Andhra Pradesh, *Nairs* and *Ezhavas* of Kerala, *Vellals* and *Nadars* of Tamil Nadu, represent such '*dominant*' castes.

Some of the dominant castes are high-caste groups immediately below the Brahmins in status and have relatively high English education. These castes cannot be taken as the representatives of the Harijans and other low castes. In fact, at the village level they are, along with the Brahmins, the exploiters of Harijan labour. These castes have been able to utilise the funds provided by the Central and State Governments to further their interests. They are powerful in the legislatures also.

With independence and adult suffrage, the dominant peasant castes became so powerful that all political parties had to come to terms with them. They were well represented in the State legislatures and cabinets. The introduction of '*Panchayat Raj*' has made them to become powerful at the village, 'tehsil' and district levels. Political power enhances the status of the individual and his group. *Any political power can be translated into economic terms*. It can determine the future of young men and women by obtaining for them right careers and well paid and prestigious jobs.

Each state consists of more than one dominant caste. Hence conflicts between them for political power are quite natural. The Kammas and Reddis of Andhra, the Vokkaligas and Lingayats of Karnataka, for example, are at a conflict. From the point of view of the non-dominant castes, the 'dominant castes' have monopolised most of the benefits available in the new system. Hence, they feel frustrated. In Karnataka. such non-dominant castes, prefer to call themselves '*minor*' castes. They have been complaining about the "*ruthless manner*' in which the Lingayats and the Vokkaligas have grabbed the facilities and concessions provided for the backward classes. The dominant castes have developed a *vested interest* in remaining '*backward*' since it helps them to enjoy the benefits of education and employment. They protest all attempts to take them out of the "*other backward class*" lists. Hence various commissions (such as the *Nagan Gowda Committee* in Karnataka) have ventured to develop criteria to distinguish between "*backward castes*" and the "*more backward castes*".

Today new tensions are evidenced between the "*powerful backward castes*" and "*the weak backward castes*" as well as the *Scheduled Castes*. There are new signs of these two latter groups joining together to fight against the domination of the "*advanced backward castes*." Thus, a "*new backward classes movement*" is now emerging. During the first phase (say, from 1916 to 1969) the non-Brahmins together struggled to dislodge them from their advantageous position. In the second phase, the struggle of the "*more backward non-Brahmins*" is going on against the "*more advanced non-Brahmins*".

The Backward Classes Movement and Social Mobility

According to *M.N. Srinivas*, the Backward Classes Movement especially in South India, is fundamentally a *movement evolved to achieve mobility*. It was started by those groups which had lagged behind the Brahmins in Westernisation. Education, employment in the Government, and participation in the new political processes are essential for such mobility. Education is a necessary means for securing the other two involved in it. It has led to the "*Self-Respect Movement*". It has contributed to the widespread rivalry between castes which have shown eagerness to move-up. It has assaulted the Brahmins' cultural and social dominance and exclusiveness.

Increase in Horizontal Solidarity

In the process of participating in the modern political, educational, economic and other processes, the caste system has undergone a significant change. The caste has been made free from its traditional local and vertical matrix. Within the local area, the stress is laid on the interdependence of castes or local sections of castes. The coming into existence of new opportunities, educational, economic, and political, brought about an increase in *horizontal solidarity*. Internal differences of a caste are undermined now. "Different sections of a caste" are coming closer and getting united. Hence, the term '*Vokkaligas*' today includes the '*Nonaba, Hallikara, Halilmatha, Morasu, Kunchutiga*,' and such other different sections of Vokkaliga caste. The term '*Brahmins*' includes the *Smarthas, Madhvas, Iyers*, *Iyegngars* and other sub-sections.

It is difficult to say whether the increase in horizontal solidarity has occurred equally with all the castes. It is certainly taking place among the high castes. The Scheduled Castes have come together for political purposes. It is true that political forces have played a vital part in stimulating horizontal solidarity. Urbanisation has increased spatial mobility. Westernised style of life and modern ideology have also played an important part. The spread of equalitarian ideology, and increasing political and social mobilisation, reveal that a fundamental change is taking place. This does not mean that this movement cannot be described as a movement from a '*closed*' to an '*open*' system of social stratification.

REVIEW QUESTIONS

1. Give the definition of scheduled castes. Discuss their problems.
2. Define untouchability. Describe its origin and eradication.
3. Discuss the role of Ambedkar and Mahatma Gandhi in the removal of untouchability and upliftment of scheduled castes.
4. Throw light on the measures taken by the Government of India for the welfare of scheduled castes, scheduled tribes and backward classes.
5. What are the various programmes of the Government of India for the upliftment of scheduled castes, scheduled tribes and backward classes? Describe.
6. Define scheduled tribes. Discuss their problems.
7. Write an essay on tribal welfare activities.
8. Write a detailed note on the tribal welfare measures of the Government of India.
9. Give the definitions of backward classes and other backward classes. Write in brief about the backward classes movement.
10. Who form the backward and other backward classes? Explain.

⌘⌘⌘⌘⌘⌘⌘⌘⌘⌘⌘

49

CORRUPTION AND BLACK MONEY IN SOCIETY

CHAPTER OUTLINE

- CORRUPTION: DEFINITION OF CORRUPTION—CORRUPTION HAS BECOME PERVASIVE—CAUSES OF CORRUPTION—ORGANISED CRIME AND WHITE COLLAR CRIME: POLITICAL CORRUPTION AND ORGANISED CRIME
- WHITE-COLLAR CRIMES OR SOCIO-ECONOMIC CRIMES: DEFINITION AND NATURE OF SOCIO-ECONOMIC CRIMES—PREVENTION OF CORRUPTION
- PREVENTION OF CORRUPTION ACT, 1947
- BLACK MONEY: MEANING OF BLACK MONEY—CAUSES OF BLACK MONEY—THE EFFECTS OF BLACK MONEY—MEASURES TO CONTROL BLACK MONEY.

CORRUPTION

Corruption is one of the social evils found in all the societies of the World. In some societies, it is more rampant than some others. Unfortunately, India is regarded as one of the countries in which corruption has become very much widespread during the recent years. corruption is one of the factors that has contributed to the degradation of the Indian politics.

"*Power corrupts and absolute power corrupts absolutely*." That is what the events at the national political scene seem to suggest, at least, during the last couple of years. Practice of corruption at lower levels by some clerks, peons and attenders for some petty amount, is understandable and tolerable. They may practice it due to tough financial conditions, excessive demands from family, friends or society, health hazards, or some or other kinds of pressures. What is more disturbing and dangerous is corruption at higher levels. Corruption in various forms has become the mainstay of our national polity in the recent past. It is needless to say that the evil of corruption meaning bribery and graft, is not conducive to social stability and equilibrium. It invariably involves negation or betrayal of normative values of society, which are essential for the smooth functioning of society.

Definition of Corruption

1. **The dictionary** defines corruption as "*an inducement to wrong by bribery or other unlawful means: a departure from what is pure and correct.*"
2. **Bhargava** says that "*act of commission or omission by a public servant for securing pecuniary or other material advantage or indirectly for himself his family or friends, is corruption.*"[1]
3. **C.B. Mamoria** writes : *We may define corruption as an improper or selfish exercise of power and influence attached to a public office or to a special position in public life.*[2]

Corruption has Become Pervasive

Corruption has not only widespread everywhere, it has innumerable forms and dimensions. With the passage of time, corruption in India has become a '*convention*', a '*tradition*', '*psychological need*' and '*necessity*'. It is a regular practice,

---

[1] Bhargava G.S. in *India's Watergate: A Study in Political Corruption*, Amold Hienemann Publishers [India] Pvt. Ltd., New Delhi, 1974, p. 10.
[2] C.B. Mamoria in *Social Problems and social Disorganisation*, p. 839.

in business transaction or deal. It manifests itself in a variety of shapes varying in heinousness."

Corruption is there at the very root of our social life. **Suresh Kohli** points out in his "*Corruption in India*" [Page 32-33.]: "*There is not a single individual who has not been lured into corruption, if corruption is accepted in a wider perspective, exploitation of any kind is corruption; shirking work is corruption; waste of time, energy and money is corruption : deceiving or betraying is corruption," mismanaging of public or private funds is corruption; undue use of authority, force or power is corruption; smuggling is corruption....sex has become one of the biggest areas of corruption..... Corruption is the driving force and part of national character.*"

Most of the people are guilty of corruption in one way or another ; at one time or another, for one purpose or another. **G.S. Bhargava** observes [Page: 10]: "*Again the milk vendor, who adulterates milk; the sanitary inspector who connives at it; the grocer who uses false weights; the contractor who does a shady job of road building; the engineer who puts the seal of approval on it and the city father who has a 'cut' in the contractor's ill-gotten wealth, all these are corrupt. But there is an even more banal form of corruption when men who wear the purple of commerce control party machines and political power and those with political power trade it for money. This type of dishonesty is more dangerous because it sets in motion the machinery of corruption, eating into the very vitals of the society.*"

Corruption has been with the Indians since the mythological times and is found in every walk of life. "*The Far Eastern Economic Review" has called corruption.* " The Asian Lubricant". It says: Like the gods and goddesses who abound in Asia [of course in India too], each with many faces, many hands, and many names, corruption has diverse aspects and numerous ingenious ways of extorting an illegal "luck" ...... corruption in Indian public life is all pervasive..." [quoted by **C.B. Mamoria**, Page 842].

Causes of Corruption

Corruption is like blood cancer. It has taken deep-roots in the country. Corruption in Indian public life is "*all pervasive*" and that businessmen, bureaucrats, contractors, industrialists, entrepreneurs, journalists, vice-chancellors, teachers, doctors, nurses and the politicians all come under suspicion. As the time moves more and more people are being swept by the move of corruption.

Corruption is a complex phenomenon and various factors and forces have conspired to cause it and spread it everywhere. The causes responsible for corruption as enlisted by **C.B. Mamoria** [Page 844-847], may be discussed here.

1. ***Economic insecurity.*** This is regarded as the most important cause of corruption. The poor people become corrupt in the hope of becoming rich. The rich indulge in it for fear of losing what they have. The rich have craving for luxurious goods and imported commodities, such as – dresses, telephone receivers, calculators, cosmetics, transistors, air conditioners, T.V.s, wrist watches, etc. This encourages smuggling on a massive scale.
2. ***High rate of income tax.*** Since tax rates are comparatively high in India even the honest people are often tempted to escape from it by making false returns of their property and income. Many of the officers in the Income Tax Department are also equally corrupt and they thrive on bribery. Income tax officers, policemen, sales tax officers, excise inspectors and others started minting money not only from the black marketeers and tax evaders, but also from innocent people who gave bribes in order to avoid suffering and humiliation at the hands of these officials.
3. ***Meagre salary being paid to the government servants.*** Employees in some of the government departments are paid comparatively very less salary. This situation is said to be the cause of corruption in administration. Clerks in the court, peons and attenders in all government departments, police constables and such other employees draw poor salary. They expect tips and bribes even for doing their regular or routine duties. It has been estimated that 60% to 70% of the officers are corrupt in one form or the other. [C.B. Mamoria Page 845]
4. ***Emergence of new sources of wealth and power.*** The modern political economic set up provides a chance for the politicians in power to make money through illegal means. **As Lincoln Steffens** has said, "the politicians took bribes because business men gave them and businessmen gave them because they had to." This unholy understanding between the businessmen and the politicians always encourage corruption.
5. ***The system of democracy.*** The present style of functioning of democracy in India, also contributes to corruption. All parties, especially the ruling party spends crores of rupees on each election. This money comes from the big businessmen, industrialists and such other rich men who have their own vested interests in financing the elections. They supply money to the party elections in the form of "*black money*." This in turn, gives them licence, a '*moral*' justification for accumulating "*number-two*" money [unaccounted money] in different forms.
6. ***The very presence of black money.*** Existence of large amounts of unaccounted black money, is one of the main

sources of corruption. "*This money is obtained by various ways, namely, tax evasion, smuggling, speculation in immovable property and shares and stocks, receiving fees and remuneration partly or wholly in cash without showing them in the accounts, trading in licences and permits*, ... etc." [C.B. Mamoria Page 847]

7. ***Social and economic modernisation.*** It is said that modernisation breeds coruption in industrial society, which "*offers prizes for doing evil; money, position, power*", besides bringing about attitudinal changes in the system. New loyalties and new identifications emerge among individuals and groups. This contributes to an increase in the incidence of corruption. As **Huntington** said, "*corruption in a modernising society is in part not so much the result of deviance of behaviour from the accepted norms as it is the deviance of norms from the established patterns of behaviour*." More than any other thing "*the get-rich quick*" motivation inspires a large number of people both at the top and bottom of the society to become corrupt.

All the factors mentioned above have generated a favourable atmosphere for corruption.

Organised Crime

Corruption and organised crime very often go together. Corruption provides scope for organised crime. Organised crimes is different from the usual types of crimes such as murder, arson, loot, stealing, gang fight etc.

Organised crimes are normally committed by comparatively rich and statused people in society. They are often good family men who attend religious programmes and activities regularly and love their children. Some of them are in business and they are successful businessmen. But their business is crime and their business methods often include torture and murder. They are the leaders of organised crime.

"*Organised crime is distinguished from other types of crime by its hierarchical structure, monopolistic control and influence, dependence on violence for enforcement, immediately from the law through the corruption of police and judicial processes, and incredible financial success*." [3]

Traditionally, organised crime has been seen as a "*family*" affair led by some unscrupulous people with criminal tradition Today, however, organised crime is increasingly viewed as activity based on the same market processes as legal business, providing goods and services that are illegal.

Organised crime, thus can be viewed as "*the extension of legitimate market activities into areas normally proscribed, for the pursuit of profit and in response to latent illicit demand*."[4]

Since there is an unlimited demand for illicit goods and services many more suppliers are attracted to the field. As a result the traditional organised criminals are now being challenged by organisations which are capable of successfully organising any kind of crime.

Political Corruption and Organised Crime

Political corruption is the main motivating factor for organised crime in the modern societies. **Elliot** and **Merril** have rightly observed that "*political corruption and organised crime are so closely related that one cannot be considered without the other*." Another writer **Sullivan** has made more or less the same observation. He writes : "*Actually, organised crime could not exist if it were not fostered by corrupt politicians and corrupt police*." [Quoted by **Mamoria** - Page: 865]

There is an increase in the organised crime in India, that is, the development of large-scale organisations for criminal activities. The organised crime may take any one of these forms: racketeering, gambling, boot legging or smuggling, kidnapping, rape, etc. Organisers of these crimes indulge in anti-social activities — like carrying illegal prostitution in hotels, supplying liquors in prohibited areas, smuggling gold and other valuable goods, organising mafia gang to control various legitimate business activities [such as coal mines] and so on. The main purpose here is to get large profit in the form '***easy money***'. The activities of the organised criminals have a great disorganising effect on the community.

White-Collar Crimes or Socio-Economic Crimes

White-collar crimes account for enough violations of law. By comparison, the instances of white-collar crimes are more than the conventional types of crimes such as theft, burglary, arson, loot, murder, kidnapping, etc. The loss incurred through white-collar crimes is far higher than that of the conventional type. In the American context, it has been estimated that losses from such crime may be as high as 200 billion dollars every year. [as quoted by **Scarpitti** and **Anderson** - Page 49]. In India also, such types of crime are on the increase.

---

[3] F.R. Scarpitti and M.L. Anderson in their *Social Problems*, Harper and Row Publishers, New York, (1989), p. 48.

[4] Dwight Smith *as* quoted by Scarpitti and Anderson, p. 48.

Definition of White-Collar Crimes

1. According to **Sutherland**, "*White-collar crime is a crime committed by a person of respect- ability and high social status in course of his occupation.*"

   Examples of white-collar crimes as cited by sutherland: Illegal exploitation of employees, mislabelling of goods, violation of weights and measures statutes, selling adulterated goods, evading corporate taxes, manipulation in stock exchanges, commercial bribery, bribery of public officials directly or indirectly to secure favourable contracts and legislation, misgrading of commodities, tax frauds, illegal sale of alcohol and narcotics, performing illegal abortions, illegal services to criminals, infringements of patents, trademarks and copy rights and unfair labour practices.

2. According to **Sayre**, white-collar crimes can be called "*public welfare offences*". He has classified such offences into eight categories which may be noted here: (1) *illegal sale of intoxicating liquor*, (2) *sale of impure or adulterated food or drugs*, (3) *sale of misbranded articles*, (4) *violation of anti-narcotic acts*, (5) *criminal nuisances*, (6) *violation of traffic regulations*, (7) *violation of motor vehicles laws, and* (8) *violation of general regulations passed for safety, health or well-being of the community*.

3. At present, the term white-collar crime is used to mean "*socio-economic crimes*". According to *The* ***Santharam Committee***, such crimes include the following :
   (1) tax evasion and avoidance;
   (2) share pushing malpractices in share market and administration of companies;
   (3) monopolistic controls and usury;
   (4) under-invoicing or over-invoicing;
   (5) hoarding, profiteering and smuggling;
   (6) violation of foreign exchange regulations;
   (7) election offences and malpractices;
   (8) theft and misappropriation of public property and funds;
   (9) misuse of their positions by public servants in making contracts and disposal of public property;
   (10) offences relating to guest control orders and rationing;
   (11) violation of standards, weights and measure;
   (12) frauds in corporate bodies; and
   (13) professional misconduct.

Nature of Socio-Economic Crimes

White-collar or socio-economic crimes are radically different from ordinary or conventional type of crimes in several respects.

1. These crimes are committed by statused people in society such as — doctors, advocates, chartered accountants, government officials, repairers of mechanical goods [such as T.V.s, radios, refrigerators, etc.] and not the traditional criminals such as — robbers, thieves, dacoits, murderers, rapists, etc.
2. These crimes are normally committed by means of fraud, deceit, misappropriation, misrepresentation, adulteration, malpractices, irregularities and so on.
3. These crimes are committed by means of a deliberate and planned conspiracies without any feelings and sentiments.
4. When socio-economic crimes are committed people tend to tolerate them because they themselves indulge in them and they themselves often identify with those who do them.
5. Originally white-collar crime meant to describe middle and upper class business persons who committed crime in the normal course of their work. But now it refers to a wide variety of occupationally oriented violations committed by persons in any class.
6. The victim of socio-economic crimes is normally the entire community, society or even the entire nation besides the individuals.
7. These crimes do not involve or carry with them any stigma while the traditional crimes carry a stigma involving disgrace and immorality.
8. These crimes constitute a separate category because the control of such crimes "*involves the protection and*

preservation of the general health and economic system of the entire society against exploitation and waste..." [**Mamoria** - Page: 1025]

Prevention of Corruption

Corruption which has gone deep into our social life cannot be removed very easily. In fact, it can only be reduced or minimised, and can hardly be stopped altogether. No nation has become successful so far in this regard. Even for minimising this problem, both preventive and punitive measures will have to be taken. ***The Santharam Committee on the Prevention of Corruption***, instituted by the Central Government in 1964, observes, "*corruption cannot be eliminated or even satisfactorily reduced unless preventive measures are planned and implemented in a sustained and effective manner. Preventive action must include administrative, legal, social, economic and educative measures*". [as quoted by **C.B. Mamoria** - Page 865]

The Committee recommended the following measures:

1. A thorough study of the extent possible, scope and modes of corruption, should be undertaken regarding each department, undertaking or ministry. The study must also suggest preventive remedial measures for the same.
2. Administrative delays should be reduced to the minimum to avoid corrupt practices. For this purpose–
   (*a*) existing procedures and practices should be reviewed to avoid delays;
   (*b*) time-limits should be prescribed for dealing with receipts and should be strictly enforced; and
   (*c*) all notings at a lower level than that of undersecretary should be avoided.
3. Attempts should be made to educate citizens in regard to their rights, responsibilities and the procedures of the government.
4. Improvement must be made to increase the salary of the employers besides making necessary provisions for housing, medical facilities for the government employees, etc.
5. Informal codes of conduct for different categories of employees particularly belonging to the departments dealing with economic affairs must be evolved insisting on them not to avail themselves of entertainment and other facilities provided to them by those with whom they have official dealings.
6. Officials should not have any dealings with a person claiming to act on behalf of an industrial house unless he is properly authorised to do so.
7. Companies and businessmen should be obliged to keep detailed accounts of expenditure.
8. Officers for the administrative posts should be selected with great care. Only those whose integrity is tested to the fullest satisfaction must be appointed for the key posts.
9. There should be a complete ban against government servants accepting private commercial or industrial employment for two years after retirement.

Some Other Suggestions

In addition to the above recommendations made by The Santharam Committee, the following suggestions may be considered with a view to eradicate or minimise corruption:

(*a*) The taxation laws must be modified, licenses and permit system must be thoroughly reviewed.
(*b*) The law enforcing authorities must see that the laws are rigorously enforced without any fear or favour.
(*c*) Mass communication media must play a more positive role in encouraging honesty and discouraging and condemning dishonesty and corruption.
(*d*) The salaries of government officials and the ministers and legislators must be raised in tune with the price index.
(*e*) Bureaucratic corruption must be reduced by stringent enforcement of punitive measures against bribe-taking.
(*f*) Corruption trials should be given the widest possible publicity.

Prevention of Corruption Act, 1947

Certain sections of the IPC could be used for punishing those who are guilty of taking bribe. The Central Government introduced in 1947 "*The Prevention of Corruption Act*" for the more effective prevention of bribery and corruption. The Act, of course, has been a miserable failure in reaching its target. We know that corruption has increased out of all proportions.

BLACK MONEY

'Black Money' which is often referred to as "*parallel economy*" or "*unrecognised economy*" or "*unofficial economy*" is both an economic and a social problem. It has both social and economic consequences upon society. Black money is a problem with a difference. If the problem of poverty affects those who are poor, and if the problem of unemployment affects directly those who are unemployed, the problem of black money does not much affect those who have ample of black money, but it affects the common man and the society at large. Hence all the nations are concerned about checking or controlling the growth of black money.

Meaning of Black Money

- *Black money is that, which is earned or received in contravention of the prevailing Government acts and regulations, or money that has been retained without the payment of taxes which are due to the Government.*

Black money accrues everyday and everywhere and ranges from a few rupees to a few lakhs of rupees. **Example:** (*i*) It is black money when a minister or a parliament member or an official takes payment for giving a licence or a permit. (*ii*) It is black money when a cement or steel manufacturer or trader, sells the commodity at a price above the controlled rate without the money appearing in the official records. (*iii*) When a professor goes to another university to conduct an examination and travels in II class train while claiming I class fare, he also acquires money which is not white, but black. These examples could be multiplied.

The Origin of the Term 'Black Money'

"It was during the Second World War that the terms '*black market*' and '*black money*' came into vogue. Due to imposition of various controls on distribution and prices a clandestine market had sprung up in which things were still available, but at prices higher than the controlled ones. The term "black money" became current to describe the money received or paid in such 'black market' deals ...... with the passage of time, 'black money' acquired a wider connotation — wider than its association with black market transactions alone." [**Mamoria** - Page: 1036].

"*Today the term 'black money' is generally used to denote unaccounted money or concealed income and/or undisclosed with, as well as money involved in transactions wholly or partly sup- pressed.*" [**Mamoria** - 1034]

In simple words, it can be said that *black money is tax-evaded money*. This kind of money can be earned through either legal or illegal means.

(*i*) **Its legitimate source** is that when those who earn income through various ways do not reveal their entire income for tax purposes. **Examples:** (*i*) Teachers earning money through private tuition and book royalty not included it in their income tax returns. (*ii*) Music artists earning huge amount of money by giving programmes on contract basis and including only a part of it in their income tax returns and retaining with themselves a major portion of their earnings and so on.

(*ii*) **Its illegitimate sources** are many. **Examples:** Bribes, black marketing, smuggling, selling commodities at prices higher than the controlled prices, and so on.

Causes of Black Money

According to **Prof. Ram Ahuja**, several factors cause black money and he lists the following factors as important ones.[5]

1. ***High rate of tax***: An unrealistic and disproportionate increase in taxes and duties compel some people to evade tax and accumulate black money. As per the present rule [1998-99] the tax free income limit is fixed at ₹25,000/-. It is a known fact that no one can run his family smoothly in this age of inflation within this limit of ₹25,000/-. A mason, a carpenter, a plumber, a painter earns about ₹200/- to ₹250/- per day in a city. The yearly income of these people ranges between ₹60,000/– to ₹75,000/-. But they rarely file their income tax returns and pay their taxes, Similarly, doctors, advocates, charted accountants, who earn a few lakhs of rupees normally hide their real income to escape paying income tax between 50% to 70% of the total income. There is an argument that if income tax is reduced there is less likelihood of hiding the income and paying more tax.
2. ***Different rates of excise duty***: The Government has fixed different rates of excise duty. On the basis of the quality, the products [such as paints, pipes, textiles, electric wires, etc.] are classified into different grades, and tax duties are levied on the basis of the classification made by the manufacturer. Manufacturers, sometimes downgrade a product to pay. lower rates of excise, which will help generate black money.
3. ***Price-control policy of government***: The Government often regulates the prices of some commodities [such as sugar, cement, steel, paper, vanaspati, automobile tyres, fertilizers, etc.] by following what is known as "price-control policy". Since this policy is comparatively rigid it does not take into account the ups and downs in the market due

[5] Prof. Ram Ahuja in *Social Problem in India*, pp. 384-387.

to the interplay of demand and supply. The private manufacturer and merchants take undue advantage of this policy and resort to hoarding, fraud, artificial scarcity, etc., which will result in black money.

4. ***Inflation***: Inflationary situation is said to be one of the causes of black money. In this situation, the prices of certain commodities [like petrol] go up and moneyed people start spending their unaccounted money. They may also divert resources from production to speculation. This will cause inflation.

5. ***Quota system and scarcity***: The Government has fixed quota for import, export and foreign exchange. This quota system is misused to make black money.

   When there arises a **scarcity** of essential goods people are compiled to pay more for them than the controlled prices. This gives scope for black money. For example, people are paying now more money than what is fixed as its price for kerosene oil due to its scarcity. The extra payment made by the customer will add to the black money.

6. ***Elections in a democratic system***: Elections are a part of the democratic process. Electioneering has become a costly affair today. Hence the candidates contesting for elections are bound to spend more than what is legally permissible for them. These elections are generally financed by the black money holders. There is an unholy alliance between the political parties and the business tycoons. These business oriented black money holders expect political patronage and economic concessions. They obtain such concessions from the political leaders by paying them heavy donations through black money. The concessions will help them to generate more and more black money.

7. ***Real estate transactions***: People amass black money through real estate transactions. Purchasing a house and/ or land at a cheaper rate and selling it at a higher rate by manipulating to pay very less stamp duty has become a profitable business in all major towns and cities. This is also an important source of black money.

The Effects of Black Money

Generalisation of black money in society will have adverse economic as well as social consequences. Black money damages the economic development of the nation by hampering developmental programmes and plans. Due to tax evasion the exchequer loses huge amount of money which could have been used for developmental activities. It adds to inflation and the government loses its control over the economy. It contributes to economic instability.

The social consequences of black money are also severe. It increases social inequality, creates frustrations among honest people, increases crimes like smuggling, bribery, etc. The government may not get enough revenue to undertake social service programmes for the uplift of the poor and downtrodden. It leads to shifts in income and wealth. It is assumed that black money is mostly transferred from low income groups to the relatively large income groups. It appears that there would be a net loss of money to the poorer sections through black money. Needless to say it contributes to unemployment and poverty.

Measures to Control Black Money

The problem of 'black money' has to be tackled in a realistic and at the same time intelligent manner. Since it is not a problem with the poor but with the well-off people, it should be handled carefully. The following measures will be of some help in controlling, if not eliminating, this problem.

1. More than any other thing, the standards of public morality must be raised. In this regard, politicians, ministers, senior civil servants, intellectuals and the media people must play an impor- tant role. They must set up an example for others to emulate by paying taxes properly.
2. Public expenditure must come down and there must be stringent monitoring of expenditure, especially of public sector projects.
3. There must be much more effective supervision of private sector investment expenditures, particularly where there is greater reliance on development finance institutions and banks.
4. Tax system must be realistic. Unduly high rates of tax are counter-productive. It would lead to tax evasion — whether it is income tax, wealth tax, capital gains tax or transfer tax on real estate — and at a later stage creating black money.
5. Price controls should be done away with. Exchange rates should be realistic reflecting our comparative prices and competitive position in the world economy.
6. Tax collection machinery must be made more efficient than what it is now. Honest officials in this department must be profusely rewarded.
7. Attractive incentives must be given for voluntary disclosures of income [VDS].

8. A thorough overhauling of the economic intelligence unit must be made. Trusted officials must be recruited for this department.
9. Administrative corruption at different levels must be stopped.
10. Exempting tax on money spent on house construction may help mostly middle class salaried people who are normally made to pay taxes without fail.

With regard to this problem the harsh truth is that the government policies are the biggest sources of black money generation. Hence, the government must take extra-precaution in framing its policies to give no scope for black money.

REVIEW QUESTIONS

1. Define corruption. Discuss the causes of corruption.
2. What do you mean by organised crime and white-collar crime? Differentiate between these two.
3. Define white-collar crime. Explain its nature.
4. Discuss the measures for preventing corruption.
5. Define black money. Describe the origin of the term 'black money'.
6. Explain the causes of black money.
7. Assess the impact of black money on society.
8. Discuss the measures to control black money.
9. Write short notes on the following:
   (a) Meaning of corruption
   (b) White-collar crime
   (c) Prevention of Corruption Act, 1947

⌘⌘⌘⌘⌘⌘⌘⌘⌘⌘⌘

PART **TEN**

Applied Sociology

50

THE PROBLEM OF ORDER

CHAPTER OUTLINE

- THE CONCEPT OF SOCIAL ORDER
- ORDERLINESS IN HUMAN BEHAVIOUR
- DEFINITION AND NATURE OF SOCIAL ORDER
- THREE APPROACHES TO SOCIAL ORDER
- THE PROBLEM OF ORDER
- THE UNITY OF SOCIETY.

THE CONCEPT OF 'SOCIAL ORDER'

The term '*order*' refers to '*conditions of normal or due functioning*'. We say that there is order in nature. It means that nature maintains conditions for its normal functioning. The day and night, the sun and the moon, the seasons, the birth and death, plants and animals and their maintenance, the earth and its weather conditions and various other aspects of nature follow a regular order. The nature maintains its equilibrium or order even though it is likely to be upset now and then. Similarly, in the social world also we find an order. As Ogburn and Nimkoff have said, "*Indeed order is the rule in the social world as truly as it is in the physical world*". Hence sociologists call society the "*social order*".

ORDERLINESS IN HUMAN BEHAVIOUR

It is true that the 20th century has often been characterised as the age of speed. This statement stresses that individuals and things are moving fast, that changes are rapid. Newspaper, radio and television stress upon the changes, the unusual happenings and doings. Sometimes they give us an impression that nothing seems dependable in the modern world.

Radio and newspapers stress upon the exceptional occurrences and *not* the expected events and the routine happenings. We also tend to overlook the great regularities that actually underline most of the things that we do in course of our lives.

It is the overlooked regularities in social life, however, that are the most important from the point of view of understanding group behaviour. From the stand point of society the habitual things are most fundamental. In fact, it is the habitual and regular activity that dominates the lives of all individuals. Out of this regular and habitual activity '*order*' — that is, the condition of normal functioning — emerges.

If we analyse our daily life and activities from getting up from bed in the morning and going to bed in the night we come to know that in all of our daily activities we follow a routine order or a regular pattern. Day in and day out, our lives run the accustomed course prescribed by our social groups. Customs of education, customs of business, our part as citizens and voters, family customs, religious customs, social customs, and many others — to all of these we conform rigorously. No-where the things are haphazard; even the procedure in courtship is prescribed by rule and custom. Every aspect of life from birth to death is dominated by a formula of behaviour that demands compliance from us all. These ways of acting or doing things are not altogether our own, nor were they 'initiated by us. *They are group ways that we have acquired.* Thus we find, orderliness that pervades our behaviour. The term '*social order*' essentially refers to this orderliness that we find in social behaviour of man.

Orderliness in social behaviour is a universal characteristic. It is found in the most primitive societies as well as in the most advanced. The network of customs that holds modern society in check binds with equal strength the society of the Hottentot or Eskimos. Organised social life has been made possible because of that '*order*'. The conception of '*orderliness in behaviour*' can only explain the continued persistence of social organisation through the course of time.

DEFINITION AND NATURE OF SOCIAL ORDER

Definition of Social Order

Though the term "*social order*" is popularly used in sociological literature during the recent times, but it is not properly defined. It is given various interpretations. For our purpose of study we may consider here one or two definitions.

1. According to *Ogburn* and *Nimkoff,* "Order in society consists of the groupings of persons and the arrangements of their behaviour".

2. *P.B. Horton* and *C.L. Hunt* have said that social order refers to — "a system of people, relationships, and customs operating smoothly to accomplish the work of a society." It is clear from the above definitions that social order essentially refers to the orderliness in the behaviour and activities of people. The following example stresses the need for orderliness in behaviour — we find orderly arrangements in the midst of bustling confusions of a great city. Thousands of people take their places and perform their tasks with no apparent direction. Thousands of vehicles move their way avoiding accidents in most of the cases. Thousands of kinds of articles arrive at the expected places in the expected amounts at the expected times. Thousands of people labour their way so that meals will be ready when needed, drains will carry off wastes, moving vehicles will give place for pedestrians to pass, hospitals will give medical treatment to patients, banks will help financial transactions, police stations will offer protection to the needy and various conveniences will meet other needs. A hundred people may serve one within an hour, perhaps, without a word to any of them. This is what is meant by social order.

People cannot get the things done unless they know what they may expect from one another. No society, even the simplest, can function successfully unless the behaviour of most people can reliably be predicted most of the time. Unless we can depend upon police officer to protect us, workers to go on schedule, and motorists to stay on the left side of the road most of the time, there can be no social order. The orderliness of a society depends upon a network of roles according to which each person accepts certain duties toward others, and claims certain rights from others. An orderly society can operate only as long as most people reliably fulfil most of their duties toward others and are able successfully to claim most of the rights from others.

What makes the people to observe and maintain the network of reciprocal rights and duties? The mechanism of '*social control*' is the answer. Social Control includes all the means and processes whereby a group or society secures its members' conformity to its expectations. It is through social control that the activities of different individuals are brought together into stable and enduring patterns. It helps their activities to be fitted together so that the behaviour of one person produces appropriate responses in another.

Social Order Depends on Social Stability

Social system is subject to change. Indeed, it must change. But if it changes too rapidly, too completely or too constantly, there can be no system. *Order depends on certain amount of stability and continuity*. Societies must be stable enough so that their members have motivation to behave predictably. "*Only in this situation does yesterday's training and experience have relevance for today*".

Durkheim and *Parsons* have stressed upon the importance of stability of equilibrium in social order. Durkheim even believed the suicide rate in a society to be a function of the social order. He found higher suicide rates in developing countries than in the relatively stable societies. Though sociologists are divided on their emphasis upon consensus or conflict, they all recognise the crucial problem of social order. They also concede the fact that no order is possible without some stability or continuity through time. The basic source of stability of a society is its continuity of past with present.

Social Order Depends on Changes Also

Society is dynamic and not static. Nothing in this social world ever remains constant. Hence the concept of 'social order' presupposes the prevalence of change. The twin concepts '*order*' and '*change*' are not really contradictory. Rate of social change differs from society to society but change as such prevails over and pervades all the societies. If the change is too slow or inefficient, the social system will decay or be overwhelmed. If change is too rapid or uneven, the system may lose the thread of order that made it a system. Order and change at-tend one another in all social systems. Human affairs operate in the complex combination of the two. There is no point in trying to understand either without considering the other. Even in the midst of rapid changes if a society is able to retain some of its old ideas and operations it may survive. The society should not be too rigid nor too flexible as far as change is concerned.

Problems in the Maintenance of Social Order

According to *Talcott Parsons*, every society or organisation must solve four problems if order (more precisely, equilibrium) is to be maintained.

(*i*) ***Problem of adaptation:*** A society or social organisation has to successfully adapt itself to the extemal physical environment. With its system of *economy* society faces the problem of adaptation.

(*ii*) ***Development of goals:*** A society must develop a system of *manageable goals* and help people in mobilizing efforts to achieve them. The *political structure* of the society deals with the '*goals*'.

(*iii*) ***Development of social integration:*** Society must evolve the ways of handling the differences and conflicts that inevitably occur among members. This will lead to social integration. Through *legal system* society struggles to maintain integration.

(*iv*) ***Latent problems:*** The important set of problems is latent, that is, hidden. They are concerned with what Parsons calls "*pattern maintenance and tension management*". Through family, religion and education the society deals with latency and pattern management. Shared beliefs and values play a vital role in this respect.

THREE APPROACHES TO 'SOCIAL ORDER'

The concept of 'social order' has been explained and interpreted by different scholars in different ways. Three main approaches or explanations may be identified: (*a*) *the utilitarian approach,* (*b*) *the cultural approach, and* (*c*) *the compulsion approach*.

(*a*) ***The utilitarian approach*** suggests that it is in self-interest of all individuals to maintain social order. This is especially true in complex societies where division of labour is high and people are interdependent. Utilitatianism has more influence on economic theories rather than on sociological ones.

(*b*) ***The cultural approach*** stresses the role of shared norms and values. This approach is also known as "*value-consensus approach*". *Durkheim* and *Talcott Parsons* have been the influential sociological exponents of value-consensus approach. This approach states that the 'unity of society' or its 'order' arises naturally from the relations among men. These relations of the people are governed by sets of shared rules and values. A network of rules and values stabilizes peoples' relationships and contributes to the unity and solidarity of the group or society. The exercise of social control helps to sustain this solidarity.

(*c*) ***The compulsion approach*** or ***conflict View*** emphasises power and domination of various types — military, judicial, spiritual, economic. It also stresses the capacity of those who, dominate to enforce order. According to this approach, different people are placed in different positions in society. By virtue of these positions they develop different interests, different experiences and divergent outlooks on the world. These differences become so extreme that any action or policy intended for the benefit of one group or category may threaten the well-being of others. Hence the unity of any particular society is, therefore, to be seen as an outcome of the struggle by those who want to maintain status quo against the interests of those who want change. The exercise of social control here means the wish of one group to keep society in *status quo*, despite the desire of others for change. Among the sociological theorists, *Karl Marx* and *Max Weber* have been the chief exponents of this approach. But these theorists have not denied the contributory role of values.

THE PROBLEM OF ORDER

According to *Peter Worsley*, '*the problem of order*' is not a simple and a single one; it refers to a complex set of issues. If we try to delve deep into the issue of social order, its emergence, persistence, changes and conflicts in it, a number of questions would come to our mind. How social organisation is possible? How and why the persistence or organised social life comes about? Is it true to say that men are basically individualistic, and that society must have come into existence and is only maintained in existence, through being imposed upon man? Can society survive only through the constant suppression of these natural individualistic and anti-social inclinations? It is not easy to explain how societies do manage to "work", to remain in existence for any period of time. Societies are complex organisations of human activities, involving many different kinds of activities and kinds of persons. All these activities will have to be concerned and co-ordinated in delicate patterns of co-operation. The very existence of these different activities and different sets of people naturally makes for differences of interest. Still in all social organisations, there is some measure of stability and cohesion, the sources of which are not properly known. It is at this point that the problem of order arises; that is, the problem of explaining the integration and continuity of social structures.

As *Peter Worsley* has stated the problem of order centres round issues such as—"The co-ordination of activities, limitations upon the use of force; the containment of conflicts; and the unification of diverse activities". Three important problem-areas which involve different levels of analysis are as follows:

1. The Problem of Meaning

This refers to the "ways in which men came to experience the world as an orderly place and are able to communicate with others about it". People communicate among themselves and on that basis co-ordinate their activities. This co-ordination of activities and co-operation in actual work is possible because one tries to understand the intentions, desires, commands and refusals of another. A communication process, is, therefore, a precondition of cooperative and concerted social activity.

Here, the main emphasis is upon the way in which men try to understand their social world, and the connections between their understanding of the world and their mastery of it. Men "interpret the world and give it meaning so that they may act upon it, control their situation and destiny, and thereby achieve the ends that they desire". This does not mean that men often find their world as "meaningless" and "chaotic". It only means that even in situations of disaster when normal channels of communication breakdown, authority-structures collapse, a state of lawlessness prevails, "men immediately set out to discover sense and significance in them".

2. The Problem of Social Control

The problem of social control revolves round the following questions... "how are the activities of different individuals brought together into stable and enduring patterns? How can their activities be fitted together so that the behaviour of one person produces appropriate responses in another? How is it that when one individual initiates a particular line of action he finds that others respond to it in ways that he considers appropriate, act as he expects them to?"–*Peter Worsley*

The problem of meaning reveals as to how men transform their experience into a meaningful, orderly and predictable social world, and establish effective expectations about the behaviour of people who live in that world. The problem of social control reveals "how these expectations are effective, why the world behaves in accord, more or less, with our expectations". It studies as to how "Men do make decisions and choices and carry them out, not in a random and idiosyncratic way, however, but within the context of rules which they share with other individuals", Social control throws light on the fact that they act in terms of rules that makes men's conduct predictable. And it is a fact that these rules are shared that makes one man's conduct predictable to another.

3. The Problem of Unity of Social Life

Within the common social boundaries of society many different kinds of social groups are functioning pursuing a wide variety of activities. These groups may be mutually conflicting and their activities may be contradictory also. In the midst of these differences, divisions, conflicts and contradictions society strives and struggles to maintain stability and order. In their attempts to analyse the unity of society, that is, the integration of whole social life, social thinkers and sociologists have developed two theoretical models: (*i*) '*the value-consensus model*', and (*ii*) *the conflict model*. The former stresses the importance of shared values and rules in bringing about unity. It stresses that a network of rules and values stabilizes peoples' relationships which in turn contributes to the unity and solidarity of the society. The latter emphasises power and domination of various types–military, judicial, spiritual and economic. It also stresses the capacity of those who dominate to enforce order.

THE UNITY OF SOCIETY

As it has already been pointed out an analysis of the problem of the unity of society revolves round the discussion of two approaches or theories concerning the unity of social life or society. Those two approaches or theoretical models namely, *value-consensus theory* and *conflict theory*, as delineated by Peter Worsley, may be discussed at greater length here.

(i) The Consensus View Established

The consensus view stresses the social nature of man. It believes that the individual becomes truly human through socialization and through membership in society. *It stresses the co-operative nature of society itself.* Co-operation makes possible the completion of complex and elaborate tasks. Men appreciate the company of others, their approval, and want to participate with them on common enterprise. The unity of society arises "*naturally*" from the relations among men. It is through interaction that people develop sets of rules and values which they come to share with one another. *These shared rules and values stabilize their relationships. The unity of society emerges from commonly held beliefs and sentiments. The exercise of social control sustains the solidarity or unity of society* and maintains stability of relationships. Social control also indicates the response of the whole united group or society against the individual who violates its shared rules.

(ii) The Conflict View Established

The conflict model or view is also based on the belief that man is an essentially social creature. But it asserts that *not all societies are equally suited to "the realisation of man's human nature". Societies that are divided into exploiters and exploited do not allow a sizeable number of people to realise their human capacities, to the fullest extent.* They do not allow such people to derive full benefit from their membership in society. Co-operation, by itself is not virtuous. Even within the co-operative process some people may exploit an advantageous position at the expense of the others. "Differences of 'interest' are just as important as agreements upon rules and values". A given arrangement of relationships in such societies which benefits some will deprive and discomfort others. In such a society "any action or policy intended for the benefit of the group or category will threaten the well-being of others". It is quite natural that people who occupy different positions in such society have different interests, share different sets of rules and values, undergo different experiences and develop divergent outlook of the world. Thus, *Peter Worsley remarks: "The unity of any particular society is, therefore, to be seen as an outcome of the struggle by those with an interest in the status quo to maintain their advantage against those whose interests lead them to desire change*". The exercise of social control then, does not express the will of the whole community nor its moral unity. It only expresses the will of the group to keep society in status qua despite the desire of others, for change. The group with its interests in '*status quo*', that is, the dominant group may resort to the use of naked force to maintain their position.

Arguments in favour of both the theories

1. (*a*) *Consensus View: Reciprocity and Interdependence.* The consensus view of society places much emphasis on the reciprocity of relationships between one part of society and another. Society consists of various institutions, organisations and groups each specialising itself in some activity. Groups exchange the 'output' of their activities with one another. Each group depends upon other groups. The relationships between them are virtually the relations of interdependence.

(*b*) *Conflict View: Exploitation and Unilateral Relationship.* The conflict view recognises the fact of exchange and interdependence but it stresses that the parties involved in exchange are unequal. Hence there is '*exploitation*' in the relationship. As *Marx* said the labourer does not receive the full worth of his labour. He only receives such rewards as enable him to keep himself alive and at work and the remaining things are exploited by his employer. The relationship is unilateral because it is characterised by *one-sided dependence*. The subordinate party in this kind of relationship is dependent upon the dominant one for his livelihood, promotion, and increases in income. But this party has no control over other things, neither on the process of production nor on exchange.

2. The *consensus view* is more concerned with the society as a whole. Each society faces problems as a society. Each society for its existence has to meet certain requirements called "*functional prerequisites*". These ensure its survival. The society must 'produce members to fill the roles that are available within society; that is, to produce food, clothing and shelter, some kind of family system to produce and to socialize new members and so on.

The *conflict view* looks at the *ways* in which the functional prerequisites are met. It wants to know *how the benefits derived from a 'solution' are distributed.* It states that the same problem can be solved in many different ways and each solution has its own consequences for the people. A 'solution' which is in line with the interests of one group and satisfactory to the group's members may be thoroughly damaging to the interests of another group. The solutions arrived at are normally supportive to the interests of the ruling party.

3. From the standpoint of *consensus view*, the stratification system is essential for social organisation. It believes that inequalities of power and wealth are inevitable because they enhance the adaptive capacity of the society. Further, the system resolves the problem of *"role allocation"*, of getting people to fill available social roles. *The unequal distribution of rewards is essential because social roles are of differential importance and require, differential level of skill. Those who are allotted. 'Key roles' naturally must get higher rewards as an incentive.*

The supporters of *conflict view* do not consider the stratification system as very much inevi- table. They see it as *"one of the basic sources of division and conflict in society"*. This system always favours the ruling group or the dominant group for it secures the maximum rewards out of it. The disadvantaged group hence always demands and struggles for the redistribution of rewards in their favour. The true explanation for the power of ruling group is not to be found in its contribution which it makes to the well-being of the society, but it is to be found in their *monopolisation of power* itself.

4. The *consensus theorists* try to justify their power by making an appeal to beliefs and values about *what is 'right'*, and *'who is deserving'*. These beliefs and values are *shared in common* with these that they dominate. There would be no discontent and opposition in society if the power of the powerful is accepted as legitimate. Discontent occurs only when the actions of ruling groups go against the values and beliefs of those they dominate.

The *conflict theorists* though conceded the importance of shared rules and values, have, raised the doubts *whether such beliefs are 'really' shared.* "The dominant beliefs in society are those of the politically dominant group: they are expressed on behalf of that group by the major institutions of society..." Those who possess power over society also possess power over the machinery for the creation and dissemination of their ideas and values. Hence they are able to ensure that their own ideas and values are made acceptable to all the members of society. Thus the shared beliefs and values represent nothing but one more technique adopted by the ruling group to gain the implicit support to their own wishes and policies.

5. The *consensus theory* states that the political institutions "exercise power within society on the basis of the mandate from the members of society to implement the collective goals of the society". They "seek to realise the goals of all the members of society, acting within the broad framework of common values..." To organise activities in pursuit of these goals these institutions must command special use of some of the societies' resources — time, labour, wealth and so on. Power is to be found at all levels of society and is possessed by groups and institutions other than the political ones. *"Power, here, is a matter of degree: each group in society has power, but some have more and some less than others..."*.

The *conflict school* does not believe in the workings of democracy, and in the distribution of power. It says *that the political institutions always work for the ruling group*. They make legislations to further and protect the interests of the ruling group. Power can never flow directly from the large mass of the public, on the contrary, it is exercised by those who are in the commanding position. Even the 'public opinion' is not the spontaneous voice of the people themselves; it is to be seen as a product of the mass media and their opinion forming activities. *"Power, here, is conceived much more in terms of a division between the 'haves' and 'have nots'*. Power is limited in society and it is largely monopolised by elites. The existence of political parties and political competition is all a matter of formality. It only serves to mark the political realities and grant the people illusory share in power.

6. The *consensus view* admits that conflict will be there in every society. Because no real society can meet the conditions of the ideal model, and every existing society will be imperfectly integrated. But it is misleading to say that conflict is 'endemic' in society itself. *"Conflict is not rooted in the society but occurs because of 'readjustments'* which the society undergoes as a result of radical technical changes.

For the *conflict theorists* consensus is a temporary state, but *"conflict is endemic in society because of deep-rooted differences of interest among the various groups and because of the unequal distribution of resources*. The presence of consensus, if it is there, only indicates that the ruling group is successful in imposing its ideas on the ruled. The stresses and strains of social life cannot be ended by this.' Conflicts inherent in the social structure will rise to the surface again when time is ripe. *"Conflict will re-emerge, and eventually a revolution or internal war will lead to the establishment of a new balance of power and the emergence of a new ruling group"*.

7. The *consensus view* has been charged by the conflict theorists that it is incapable of explaining social change adequately. Still, the supporters of the consensus view have been trying to handle the issues of social change comfortably. They have argued that conflict and violence must be understood as a "response to disturbance in the society, disturbances created by the readjustment of relationships between family and economy. These conflicts, however, could be "handled and channelled by social control mechanism..." The consensus theorist can deal with the long-term trends but finds it difficult to explain the processes of radical and rapid or revolutionary change.

The *conflict model* can better handle the phenomenon of change; that is, change of both kinds; the gradual kind and of the rapid or revolutionary kind. It never assumes the consensus view that societies tend towards stability, but it begins with the idea that *society is inherently changeful*. It states that "*social structures are inherently unstable and will tend to change unless such tendencies can be stayed by the exercise of power*". It stresses "the role of conflict of groups struggling for advantage; and much social change is an outcome of shifts in the relationships between such groups. This theory is well equipped to explain those fundamental changes which involve the alteration of society's basic values". Consensus theory is not in a position to do so.

Conclusion

A glance at these two theories would make it clear that they occupy two extreme positions. As *Peter Worsley* has pointed out that these represent two "*visions*" of society. Each view tries to justify its own assumptions and is not prepared to look into evidence which contradicts them. But if we can consider them as two visions then we can understand them as two ways of looking at social organisation. Both the perspectives are equally important in getting a clear understanding of society.

Conflict theorists have not refused the existence of any consensus. They have recognised that some amount of consensus is necessary among group's members so that they can develop a sense of solidarity among themselves. Consensus is necessary for, the members of a class to realise its identical interests and to develop class-consciousness which is vital for them to have a common plan of action to realise their interests. This actually heightens the solidarity within classes. Thus, Marx who championed the theory of conflict, was vitally concerned with aspects of consensus also.

Conflict need not necessarily be disruptive. It can promote unity in the manner in which it contributes to class solidarity. it throws light on some open discontents and disagreements which are present now, but which have not previously been recognised and removed. Hence it may help to remove such relationships which have been a source of tension and lead to the formation of new relationships.

Consensus theorists do recognise that conflicts are bound to be there even in stable societies. But they assert that the promised proletarian revolution has not occurred. It means the social conflicts that take place in a basically stable society, can be treated as mild, insignificant, and of short duration. They may not produce change of any great importance. The theorists have stated that it is within the capacity of the developed societies to provide all their members with secure and decent lives. The

The Pluralist Model?

These two view points or perspectives are equally powerful. It is difficult to choose between these view points, for each can provide evidence to support its own case. "The fact that there is evidence for each view, but also evidence against it, shows that neither adequately accounts for the facts". One can recognise that both have their uses, that for some purposes it is best to use one perspective and for other purposes to use the other perspective. What is more important is that "*one should recognise that while both have their own virtues, neither has a monopoly of truth*". There is scope for a more comprehensive theory which will encompass both the phenomena of conflict and that of consensus. Hence this combination of conflict and consensus views would represent a third model—*The Pluralist model*.

It is true that in no social organisation individuals can carry on their everyday life activities without some measure of consensus. Without shared rules and values it would be impossible to concert and co-ordinate the actions of individual members. Society hence involves some moral order. "*But what is an open question is how much consensus is necessary for more complex forms of social life to operate*? — *Peter Worsley*.

The three models — the consensus model, conflict model and the pluralist model — are quite influential and impressive, no doubt. But no single of the first two models can account for all the facts about society. Still it can he stressed that each of them does have its uses and enables us to obtain some understandings of some problems. The third model which is having the least popularity cannot also said to be the most satisfactory theory.

REVIEW QUESTIONS

1. Explain the concept of social order.
2. Throw light on the concept of orderliness in human behaviour.
3. Define social order. Explain its nature.
4. Bring out the main features of social order.
5. What are the three approaches to social order? Discuss each in detail.
6. Write in detail about the problem of order.
7. Explain the various theories concerning the unity of society. Throw light on the arguments in favour of the theories.
8. Write short notes on the following.
   (a) Social order
   (b) Problems in the maintenance of social order
   (c) Pluralist model

⌘⌘⌘⌘⌘⌘⌘⌘⌘⌘⌘

51

Applied Sociology

Chapter Outline

- Pure Science and Applied Science
- What is Applied Sociology?
- Scope of Applied Sociology
- Role of a Sociologist in Applied Sociology
- Social Policy: What is Social Policy—Contribution of Sociology to Social Policy
- Social Planning: Definition of Social Planning— Objectives of Social Planning, The Pre-requisites to Effective Planning, Limittions of Social Planning, Obstacles of Social Planning, Application of Social Planning
- Sociology in Action

PURE SCIENCE AND APPLIED SCIENCE

A distinction is often made between 'pure' sciences and 'applied' sciences. The main aim of a pure science is the acquisition of knowledge and it is least concerned with the utility or usefulness of that knowledge. On the other hand, the aim of applied science is to apply the acquired knowledge into life and to put the same into some use. Each pure science may have its own applied field also. For example, physics is a pure science and engineering is its applied field. Similarly, the pure sciences such as economics, political science and history have their applied fields such as business, politics, and journalism respectively. Sociology as a pure science has its applied fields such as administration, diplomacy, social work, etc. Each pure science may have more than one application.

WHAT IS APPLIED SOCIOLOGY?

'Applied Sociology' is concerned with that part of sociological knowledge which is put to human use and human betterment. In fact, there is a controversy regarding the role being played by sociology in contributing practically to human betterment. There are some sociologists who advocated that sociology being a science should study only the society '*as it is*' and not "*as it ought to be*". It should not pronounce any judgements or suggest any solution for solving those problems. Sociologists should never determine questions of public policy and should not recommend legislations, what laws should be passed or repealed — they have argued. But majority of the sociologists do not agree with this point of view. In their opinion all social sciences are light bearing as well as fruit bearing sciences and it is quite justifiable for them to suggest ways and means to solve social problems and improve society. The aim of social sciences is and ought to be human betterment and applied sociology is concerned with human betterment.

Professor Davis observes, "we want to build the society for the better. There are certain citizens who may be contented and do not want to change but we must be careful not to give them undue weight. So long as there are people who feel that they are not receiving justice or fairplay to that extent, society needs reconstruction. It is the function of applied sociology to reconstruct that society. The objective is that in free society — (l) there should be variety of thinking, (2) equality of opportunity by eliminating inequalities — economic and educational, (3) there is no exploitation of special privileges by a particular group, and (4) social order in which social intelligence, social efficiency and voluntary co-operation produce the maximum good".

Professor Ford remarks, "the practical or 'applied sociology' may be designated as "applied social ethics" or "social policy". And the study of adaptation of social method of the achievement of moral purpose may be termed as applied social ethics". *Gillin* and *Gillin* have pointed out, "Some of the earliest sociologists ignored the pathological aspects of human association..." those who are interested in studying society as a dynamic rather than as a static phenomenon, are convinced that social pathology is as much a part of sociology as medical pathology is a part of scientific medicine".

Thus, it is clear that sociology has two parts, (l) *theoretical sociology*, and (2) *practical sociology*. Practical sociology itself is applied sociology. This second part is concerned with the getting of information upon problems of social experience and finding methods for their amelioration and, if possible, their solution.

Applied sociology is the search for ways of using scientific knowledge to solve practical problems. A sociologist making a study of "the social structure of a slum neighbourhood" is working as a pure scientist or theoretical sociologist. If this study is followed by a study of "how to prevent delinquency in a slum neighbourhood"— he would be acting as an applied sociologist also. Some people consider sociology as an entirely 'applied science' trying to solve problems, while many consider it is both.

Practical applications of sociological knowledge are not always appreciated by all. Only gradually, the services and advices of sociologists are sought. Some sociologists are employed by business corporations, government bureaus, hospitals, city municipal bodies, big factories, social welfare agencies, and sometimes in administration. They are engaged in planning, conducting community acting programmes, advising on public relations, employee relations, working on human relations and problems of many sorts. Sociologists are often consulted by legislative committees while planning new legislations. But the private citizens very rarely take decisions on the basis of knowledge supplied by sociologists.

On many social questions such as—the causes and treatment of crime and delinquency, drug and alcohol addiction, sex offences, the causes and consequences of racial discrimination, or the adjustment of the family to a changing society, etc.—there is considerable scientific sociological knowledge.

APPLIED SOCIOLOGY AND SOCIAL WORK

'Applied sociology' and 'social work' are not one and the same. Though sometimes these two terms are often used synonymously. The scope of both is in some sense, the same; but "in social work more emphasis is laid on rendering assistance through methods like social case—work, group work and community organisation". Further, applied sociology is treated as a branch of sociology also. On the contrary, social work is considered to be a profession.

SCOPE OF APPLIED SOCIOLOGY

According to *G.R. Madan*, the main task of applied sociology is to deal with social problems. From the point of view of applied sociology, social problems are divided into two categories that is—(*i*) problems of social disorganisation or social rehabilitation, and (*ii*) problems of social reconstruction. The first category includes problems of deviants, defectives and dependants, *e.g.* criminals, delinquents, orphans, mentally defectives, ills, blinds, etc. For the problems of this kind, measures are needed to cope with the evil. They are generally curative or rehabilitative in character. For example, something has to be done to help the poor, to educate the defectives, to reform the criminals, to prevent poverty, defectiveness and crime. In the second category such things as child welfare, women welfare, youth welfare, labour welfare, housing welfare, etc. are included. Here the preventive and constructive methods are more useful. *Example*: Education of the children is looked into so that they would not turn out to be either as child beggars or juvenile delinquents; but would be enabled to lead a normal life. Welfare of women is promoted so that they would not be either exploited or neglected.

According to *Groves* and *Moore*, applied sociology would include problems of poverty, crime, immigration, race, the family, the social hygiene, mental defects, housing, public opinion, and the organisations and practices of modern philanthropy.

ROLE OF A SOCIOLOGIST IN APPLIED SOCIOLOGY

An applied sociologist has been playing a vital role so as to fulfil four main tasks:

(*i*) He **conducts scientific researches** in various fields of human social life about which the existing knowledge is either scanty or erroneous. (*ii*) He **tries to correct popular nonsense** especially with regard to issues and problems such as — racial conflicts, communal tensions and riots, the myth of innate intelligence and inborn superiority of races, minorities, religious conversions, etc. (*iii*) He **tries to make sociological predictions.** ***Example*****:** (l) would the suppression of obscene literature help to reduce sex crimes and sex immorality? (Prediction: 'No'). (2) would low birth-rates and small family norm increase marital happiness? (Prediction 'Yes') (*iv*) He **works as a policy consultant**. An applied sociologist provides valuable suggestions to bodies with legislative power in framing suitable social policies. Sociological predictions can also help to estimate the probable effects of a social policy. Hence they can contribute to the selection of policies which achieve the intended purposes.

SOCIAL POLICY

What is Social Policy?

"The term 'social policy' is not used technically, but rather merely describes the policies of governments in respect to a range of social services. Thus matters pertaining to health, education, housing, social insurance and national assistance are to be included under this description".

—Duncan Mitchell

Since a very long time the social sciences in Britain have been oriented to discussion of social policies. During the recent years there has also been a development of thought about some aspects of the Welfare State. Attempts have been made to determine trends in social thought, to examine the implications of present policies for future policy-making, and to find out the issues involved in following given policies and their effects on social thought. *T.H. Marshall's* Social Policy' (1965), can be said to be a clear contribution to this field. In this work he has suggested that "the task of social policy is to determine the order or priority of claims against the national product".

Contribution of Sociology to Social Policy

Sociology has been helpful in making social policy a success. During the 19th century in France due to the writings of Comte, Saint and Simon and encyclopaedists, it was believed that sociology as a "positive science could establish universal laws of social behaviour by reference to which all disputes about social policy might be settled". But today it is well known that the socio-logical laws have their own limitations. Sociology cannot arbitrate all social disputes and settle all social controversies. In spite of this, no one can underestimate the practical help rendered by sociology to social policy.

1. Sociology has provided much exact and reliable information upon those matters of social policy with which politicians, administrators, and social reformers have to deal. The earliest socio- logical researches particularly in U.K., were the surveys of poverty and other problems of urban life. The surveys particularly those of *Booth* and *Rowntru* (1901) enabled to indicate some of the causes of extreme poverty, the lack of regular employment, and the accidents or illness suffered by wage- earners. These and similar researches have influenced social policy a great deal.

2. In a number of other fields sociologists have provided useful data for the formulation of rational social policies. *Example*: population studies, studies of social mobility, etc. Studies of social mobility, for instance, reveal the extent and forms of mobility in different societies. It also shows connections between mobility and such factors as family size, educational opportunity, and occupational structure.

3. "The contribution of descriptive sociology or sociological researches should not be limited to providing information which is useful at the stage of formulating and introducing new social policies; it is equally important in evaluating the operation and achievements of these policies.

4. Social sciences have begun to influence social policy in another way. They are also giving training to those who are concerned with the formation and execution of social policy. Thus sociology is giving training to social workers, industrial managers, personnel officers, teachers, and public officials responsible for the administration of social welfare services or of publicly owned enterprises.

5. It should be noted that not all social issues and policies are not without controversies. But where there is no agreement, sociologists can make a practical contribution by clarifying the points of controversy. It can do so by viewing alternative social policies in relation to the structure of society as a whole. Sociology attempts "to grasp every specific problem in its whole social context, and to conceive the alternative social policies which affect the entire life of society".—*Bottomore*.

6. "Sociology provides a framework of concepts, and a basis of exact knowledge, for the intel- ligent discussion of political issues". An example relating to educational policy may be considered here. As far as education is concerned, the recent sociological investigations show the connections between social class origin, educational opportunity, and achievement. An educational policy with an aim to establish equality of opportunity in education has to be pursued. Then, it is necessary to use the results of sociological research which show the sources and mechanisms of inequality.

7. Since the writings of sociologists are often read by the members of the industrial societies, a sociologist, more than a social anthropologist, often arouses, and expects to arouse, some response in some of the people he is studying and this influences his study.

The practical influence of sociology is quite wider. In addition to organisations and interested parties, even a larger section of the population may be influenced, through the media of mass communication about such problems in a more rational and dispassionate and objective way and to reject irrational opinions and policies.

"In this way, sociology has been successful in some extent to reducing racial prejudice and discrimination. "In these various ways—by the exact description of social problems, the search for causes and remedies, the training of social workers and administrators, the education of public opinion, the revelation of inequalities and privileges and of the political controversies to which they give rise, sociology has in fact contributed to the realisation of the ideal which was formulated... the participation of all men in the control of their conditions of life, a self-directing humanity"—*Bottomore*.

SOCIAL PLANNING

Social planning reveals a movement which has assumed tremendous significance nowadays. There is some degree of social planning in almost all modern societies. It was once felt that societies were at the mercy of impersonal cosmic forces and trends. It is now thought that man can to a great extent decide and plan the direction of social change. This change in attitude is because of the great advances in knowledge and technology, as well as existence of large and powerful organisations. Modern societies have now capacities to-make and implement collective social decisions. "*The new altitude towards 'social change reveals that people have chosen social planning' as a tool to help achieve common goals and values*". What then is meant by social planning.

Definition of Social Planning

l. *Kimball Young*: "Planning is a programme aimed at sociocultural change in a particular direction with a given aim or goal in mind".

2. *Sumner* and *Keller*: Social Planning "is the development of non-instinctive foresight that distinguishes the man".

3. *Merrill* and *Eldredge*: "Social planning is merely organised foresight aimed at accepted goals and based on existing knowledge of skills".

In the broadest sense, planning is one of the rational activities most characteristic of human beings. Individuals are forever planning their lives. Planning requires analysis, foresight, and a will- ingness to sub-ordinate the present to the future. It is the basis for social action in the alleviation of social problems. It differs from reform in various respects. "*While reform is remedial and corrective, planning is preventive and constructive. A plan is laid out as an achievement to be made in a certain length of time. The emphasis is on the practical side rather than an aspirations of the fantasy type*" —(*Ogburn and Nimkoff*). It is more so in the case of successful planning.

The idea of social planning is probably as old as *Plato* who had depicted an ideal society in which social planning was to be done by the greatest minds in the society. The idea of social planning has challenged men for centuries. "*Spencer* thought that the social heritage grows according to fixed, ineluctable laws and that interference usually makes things worse. *Comte*, on the contrary believed that man had the power to look ahead and to control his destiny. Later this idea was brilliantly developed by *L.F. Ward*, who used the phrase 'social telesis', meaning societal self-direction"–(*Ogburn*). Ward, was, of course, unduly impressed with man's intellectual power and exaggerated very much man's capacity to control things. Nevertheless he did perform a valuable service in stressing the possibility and importance of looking and planning ahead. In fact, *planning has the virtue of looking ahead*, which is essential in a changing society.

Efforts to direct social change through some type of coordinated planning have been quite numerous. Many of them have been quite successful too. Men have found that they could exercise some degree of rational control over such diverse developments as — *planning city recreational facilities, patterning residential zones, exploitation and conservation of wild life and natural resources, development of harbours, integration of school systems, setting new areas, rural improvement schemes, etc*. Indian and Russian Five Year Plans, are good examples here. Social planning in this sense is not only possible but practicable. But the controversy is with regard to the costs involved in it and ideological considerations.

Objectives of Social Planning

The general goal of all social planning is to "*improve*" *society*, but the definition of improvement differs, depending upon the underlying values of the social system. *Example*: (*i*) Assuring justice and providing equal socio-economic opportunities to all and achieving economic progress and political stability can be said to be the meaning of 'improvement' in the Indian context. (*ii*) Achieving increase in efficiency and widening democracy may mean improvement in the American context.

The short-range objective of social planning is to manipulate the social environment in some way that will enhance or change some designated value. Men can plan to change the structure of some important institutions. *Example*: a society can alter the bureaucratic system of the government so that it becomes more responsive to the needs and problems of the people. It may intend to make change in the laws governing marriage, property, divorce, punishment for crime, family planning, abortion, removal of untouchability, etc. Social planning may also try to manipulate the material goods of society. Thus, it may provide for housing on the basis of need rather than ability to pay, or by putting more desks in elementary schools. Social planning also increasingly deals with social as well as environmental concerns — poverty, education, family welfare and mental health.

Merril and *Eldredge* have prepared a list of values which the peoples of most of the societies respect and consider to be the objectives of social planning. They are as follows—

(*i*) *Physical Values* that consist of food, clothing, shelter, relaxation and sexual satisfaction.

(*ii*) *Cultural Values* that comprise of procreation, education, recreation, artistic development, technological development and satisfactory social change.

(*iii*) *Social Values* that include protection and security, co-operation and competition.

Societies are selective in pursuing and cherishing these values. Some societies prefer to pursue one or the other and lay more emphasis on that. For example, America, England and other countries give more importance to competition while Russia and China stress the importance of the value of co-operation.

The Pre-requisites to Effective Planning

As *Ogburn* and *Nimkoff* have mentioned, the pre-requisites to effective planning include the following— (*i*) the existence of a modern as opposed to a traditional society, including a monetised economy, considerable urbanisation, a technical and scientific intelligentia, and a well ordered system of information gathering and analysis. (*ii*) The existence of an adequate system of information gathering and analysis. (*iii*) The existence of favourable public attitudes towards planning. (*iv*) The existence of progressive economic and political leadership. (*v*) More important at first are the development of responsible organs of public administration and an educated elite followed by popular enlightenment. (*vi*) To carry out a plan successfully, a high degree of organisation (as in the case of army) with good discipline is required. (*vii*) Concentration of authority is needed for the successful formulation and prosecution of a plan. Otherwise, the programme is likely to be subject to fluctuations and modifications due to the pressure of diverse interests.

Limitations of Social Planning

Social planning has its limitations also. Social planning activities emanating from centralised government evoke many negative responses. This is true in democracies where the great concentration of power may be misused. *Example*: America. In such democratic countries social planning may serve to further the interests of elite individuals or groups, rather than the common good of society. There is traditional suspicion often exploited for political reasons. In a highly competitive society dominated by private groups and individuals with private interests, it is difficult to develop techniques for voluntary and co-operative planning.

Further, the planners may try to demonstrate that "*for their own good*" people should co-operate in this or that programme only. Still, the people who would be benefited from the plans may show their indifference and apathy or even resistance. When the entire people of a community undertake planning on their own they often lack the technical skill to develop a practical scheme. They may even fail to face the challenges at the hands of more alert and better-informed vested interests.

The experience of some societies such as Nazi Germany and Stalinist Russia, has shown that social planning can serve the interests of a totalitarian state also. Here it is more used to curtail individual freedom of choice. Elite direction of social planning is characteristic of communist societies. "Decision making has been highly centralised and plans have been exceedingly intricate and detailed". Recently there has been-some decentralisation of decision-making in Russia. Less attempts are made to specify all details. "Planning which attempts to programme practically all the activities of a society is less successful than planning that is limited to only one, or small number of activities or goals".

Obstacles of Social Planning

Social planning has been there in all the countries. But it is not free from obstacles. Three related factors make the task of social engineering very difficult. They are: (*i*) *the complexity of modern culture and society*, (*ii*) *the rapidity of contemporary social and cultural change*, (*iii*) *the large number of people in interlocking relationship*.

(*i*) Complexity of modern society and its culture. Modern technology has made the present- day society more complex. Changes that take place in any one of the institutions such as political, economic, social, etc., would affect the other. Due to the development in the means of transport and communication people's world view has changed a great deal. Science and technology have been helping man to lead a pleasurely life. "Pleasure–seeking" has become a "life-policy" of many. Such people look towards planning only as a means for enjoyment and not as a means for improvement with concerted efforts. Everyone tries to look at planning from individual point of view and not from the view point of the entire group or community. Further, due to the interdependence of various social institutions, it is difficult to tackle any one with planning without affecting the other.

***(ii)* The rapidity of socio-cultural change:** The modern complex society is undergoing fast change. A single change is capable of bringing about a series of changes. A change in one aspect of culture may also lead to changes in other aspects also. Radical changes have taken place in values. The speed of socio-cultural change in general has vitally affected stability of society. In a state of instability and rapid social change, social planning is difficult to be made, if not, impossible.

***(iii)* An increase in population:** Social planning is quite easier and more effective in small communities with limited population than big communities with vast population. In many Asian and African countries population is increasing at a very fast rate. At the same rate of growth means of subsistence are not growing. Hence social planning has become quite challenging in such countries. This is particularly true in countries such as China, India, Bangladesh, Indonesia, etc. Similarly, planning in cities where population is increasing beyond control is also difficult.

Applications of Social Planning

It has been observed that the tools and concepts of planning have so far had their greatest impact in the private business sector. Almost every large business corporation or firm has a man or a department in charge of planning the company's future. The planners devise alternate course of action, collect required knowledge about the possible effects of each course, and suggest choices. After a decision has been made, they collect feedback on its success and effectiveness. It could be said that partly in response to this development in private business sector planning has now spread to government agencies. This is especially true in democratic nations. Despite the opposition to planning from vested interests the planning movement has been gaining ground. "The great debate about planning is no longer concerned with the question as to whether it is possible or whether it can be reconciled with democracy, but rather with the question of how planning may be improved. Planning is inherent in the conception of modern society".— *Ogburn and Nimkoff*

Sociology in Action

Social planning, in a way can be understood as the application of social scientific knowledge to help solve social problems. In the studies of early sociologists such as Comte, there was a great stress on the application of sociological knowledge. In the 19th and early 20th centuries a good number of sociologists distinguished themselves as social reformers and tried to change society through their knowledge of its workings. Neither did they have sufficient knowledge. of the society nor could they attain success in their efforts. Sociologists with this point of view got discouraged and in turn, switched over to research and to the development of sociology as a science. "In the last several decades, sociology has once again begun to seek practical applications of its knowledge and the pure and applied branches of the discipline work more closely together to contribute to the solution of social problems".—*David Popenoe*.

It is true that overall planning of all social development is beyond the ability of people to accomplish in the present state of development of social sciences. *Ogburn* writes: "*Planning is likely to be more effective where it is most needed, at the level of social problems on which practical social engineering can be brought to bear*".

REVIEW QUESTIONS

1. What is applied sociology? Write in brief about the scope of applied sociology.
2. What is distinction between applied sociology and social work?
3. Examine the role of a sociologist in applied sociology.
4. What is social policy? Evaluate the contribution of sociology to social policy.
5. What do you mean by social planning? Write the objectives of social planning.
6. What are the limitations and applications of social planning? Discuss in brief.
7. Write short notes on the following:
   (a) Definitions of social planning
   (b) Pre-requisites to effective planning
   (c) Obstacles of social planning

⌘⌘⌘⌘⌘⌘⌘⌘⌘⌘⌘

52

SCIENCE, TECHNOLOGY AND SOCIETY

CHAPTER OUTLINE

- MEANING OF SCIENCE AND TECHNOLOGY—DEFINITION OF SCIENCE
- NATURE OF SCIENCE
- DEFINITION OF TECHNOLOGY
- DIFFERENCES BETWEEN SCIENCE AND TECHNOLOGY
- INSTITUTIONALISATION OF SCIENCE—SCIENCE AS THE MODERN INSTITUTION
- EFFECTS OF INSTITUTIONALISATION OF SCIENCE
- THE NORMS OF SCIENCE—NORMS OF UNIVERSALISM–COMMUNALISM AND ITS CONSEQUENCES–NORM OF DISINTERESTEDNESS AND ORGANISED SKEPTICISM
- SOCIAL PROCESS OF INNOVATION— COMPETITION IN SCIENCE
- RESISTANCE TO SCIENTIFIC INNOVATIONS
- INFLUENCE OF SOCIAL FACTORS ON SCIENTIFIC INNOVATIONS
- INFLUENCE OF FOUR FACTORS AS SUGGESTED BY KINGSLEY DAVIS
- TECHNOLOGY AND SOCIETY—TECHNOLOGICAL DETERMINISM—OGBURN AND HIS TECHNOLOGICAL DETERMINISTIC THEORY
- TECHNOLOGY AND THE RATE OF SOCIAL CHANGE
- THE SOCIAL CONTROL OF SCIENCE AND TECHNOLOGY: PROBLEMS ARISING OUT OF THE LACK OF SYSTEMATIC CONTROL OVER SCIENTIFIC AND TECHNOLOGY
- DIFFICULTIES INVOLVED IN ESTABLISHING SYSTEMATIC CONTROL OVER SCIENCE AND TECHNOLOGY
- CONDITIONS FOR THE SUCCESS OF SCIENCE AND TECHNOLOGY IN THE SERVICE OF SOCIETY
- SCIENCE AND TECHNOLOGY SHOULD BE MADE THE SERVANTS OF SOCIETY?

We are living in an era of science and technology. Both have received ascendancy in almost all the modernised nations of the world. Even in the economically backward countries the longing for science and scientific achievement persists. Scientific and technological achievements have become the measuring rods to assess the economic strength of a nation today. In fact, the control of information, especially scientific and technical information, is a source of prestige and power in all post-industrial societies. Especially in the beginning of this 21st century, nations that are doing well in the fields such as computers, and super computers, information technology, electronics, biotechnology, telecommunications, etc., are normally regarded as the *"most modern"* and *"technologically and scientifically most advanced nations."* India which is regarded as a fast developing nation too has started giving more importance to these subjects of great scientific importance in its educational system during the recent years especially after 1995. In fact, in the newly established engineering colleges, these subjects are introduced and greater number of students are getting attracted towards them. Thus, *"science is a major institutional sector of modern societies; a hallmark of the modern social order is the conduct of scientific research in universities and other research organisations"*[1]. The study of science and technology, has, therefore, become an increasingly important sociological speciality.

Science has become a part of modern life. Any modern society's existence today depends very much on the advanced scientific knowledge and its technological applications to fields such as computers, telecommunications, satellite launching, aircraft, antibiotics, life saving drugs, skyscrapers, synthetic fabrics, automobiles and so on. Not only our physical existence

[1] William Kornblum *Sociology—In A Changing World*, P. 469.

depends on science and technology but even our world view has radically changed over the past century by scientific thought. Our very conception of subjects such as physics, biology, psychology, medicine, astronomy, sociology, etc., has been altered. Our vision of the future life also rallies round science and technology and the question how they will be able to transform our future way of life. In contrast with this modern situation a century or two ago, the value of science was not considered that important, and science as such was *"The private hobby of wealthy gentlemen of leisure. Hence, throughout the Napoleonic Wars, scientists travelled freely between France and England in spite of the political rivalry between the nations to show their harmless conversations."*

Unlike in the past, science has become a central institution in the life of all modern societies. *Science itself is institutionalized.* Science is recognised as very essential and important. *It is standardized*; scientists throughout the civilised world follow the same basic methods and procedures. There is no capitalist or communist or Christian or atheist way to conduct a scientific experiment or to programme a computer.

MEANING OF SCIENCE AND TECHNOLOGY

The two terms *'Science'* and *'Technology'* are very often used interchangeably in our ordinary speech. Though these are very much interrelated they are distinct phenomena as such. Hence the difference in the meaning of both must be properly understood.

Definition of Science

Science is essential knowledge. The word *"science"* is derived from the **Latin** word ***Scientia*** which means *"knowledge"*. But science is a particular kind of knowledge, that is, knowledge that has been obtained through the *'scientific method'*. One or two definitions of science may be cited here.

1. ***In a more general sense,*** science refers to *"any systematic study of physical or social phenomena."*[2]
2. ***In a more restricted sense,*** science can be understood as *"The study of physical and social phenomena where this involves observation, experiment, appropriate quantification and the search for universal general laws and explanations."*[3]
3. ***From a sociological stand point,*** *"Science is a body of knowledge about the natural world and a method for discovering such knowledge and a social institution organised around both."*[4]
4. ***In simple words,*** *"Science is a systematic body of knowledge".*

Two Main Branches of Science

Science is customarily divided into two branches namely *"pure sciences"* and *"applied sciences"*. (*i*) ***Pure Science*** is concerned mainly with the acquisition of knowledge and not its application. It is scientific investigation that is devoted exclusively to the pursuit of knowledge for its own sake. It has no immediate concern or pressure for using that knowledge to solve practical problems. ***Examples***: Physics, Chemistry, Biology, Sociology, Anthropology, Political Science, Economics, Psychology, etc., are all pure sciences. (*ii*) ***Applied Science***, in contrast, is the application of known scientific principles to a practical problem, and the outcome in many cases is new technologies. It may thus be stated that if pure science is interested in the acquisition of theoretical knowledge, applied science is concerned more with the task of applying the theoretical knowledge, for human utility and service. Each pure science, however, may have one or more applied fields. *Engineering* is an applied field of physics, *pharmacology* is the applied field of chemistry, *social work* is the applied field of sociology, and so on.

Nature of Science

1. ***Science is Concerned with Knowledge***: The ultimate objective of science is acquisition of knowledge. Exploring the different horizons of knowledge is not only a challenge but also a matter of great intellectual delight to a scientist. Knowledge is as vast as an ocean. The more a scientist acquires it, the more it remains to be acquired. A scientist is not only more interested in acquiring knowledge but also is better equipped to do so.
2. ***Division of Sciences into Two Types or Branches***: The sciences are conventionally divided into two main branches: (1) *natural sciences*, and (2) *social sciences*.

The Natural Sciences study physical and biological phenomena. They are said to be more precise, exact, and objective. ***Examples***: Physics, Chemistry, Geology, Biology etc. ***The Social Sciences*** refer to *"a related group of disciplines that*

[2] *Collins Dictionary of Sociology*, p. 576.

[3] *Collins Dictionary of Sociology*, p. 576.

[4] A.G. Johnson in *The Blackwell Dictionary of Sociology,* 2000, p. 244.

study various aspects of human behaviour".[5] They are mainly concerned with man, his social life and society. *Examples:* Sociology, Economics, Political Science, Anthropology, etc.

Characteristics of Science

1. ***Factuality***: Science is not based on imagination. It is based on facts. *"A fact is an observed phenomenon itself".*[6] It may be about a thing, an event, a measurement, etc. *"Any statement which is true can be described as a fact."*[7] ***Example:*** (1) Stone is a solid substance. (2) Hindus constitute a major religious community in India.
2. ***Causality***: Science tries to find out the causal relationship between the events or things. In other words, it explores causation. Causation states that *"the occurrence of events is determined by cause-and- effect relationships."* Causation assumes that events do not occur in a random fashion. It also assumes that events are associated in a one-way relationship. ***Example:*** (1) Harmful bacterias cause diseases. (2) Poverty is one of the causes of economic backwardness. The function of science is to uncover the laws of cause and effect relationships.
3. ***Universality***: Scientific findings or truths or laws are expected to have universal validity. They are not supposed to be limited to any race, nationality, religion or region, social class or political ideology. It means scientific laws or findings must allow themselves to be evaluated purely in terms of their scientific worth. ***Examples***: (1) Fire burns, water flows, wind blows, etc..., (2) Hindus are polytheistic, Muslims and Christians are monotheistic, and so on.
4. ***Predictability***: Prediction refers to the *"foretelling of an event or set of events."*[8] Prediction is generally understood as *'foretelling' or 'making' "statement about the future"*. It is an estimation of what the future will look like. Making prediction is one of the tasks of science. ***Example***: (1) Physical scientists make predictions about earthquake, rainfall, cyclones, eclipses, and so on. (2) Though predictions are difficult, if not impossible, in the field of social sciences, attempts are being made to make predictions. Predictions are being made about demographic trends, rate of economic growth, rate of increase in literacy, and so on.
5. ***Verifiability***: Science is based on verification principle. According to this principle, a proposition or hypothesis or statement can be accepted as *"scientific"*, only if it is verifiable. *"Verification refers to any procedure regarded as establishing the truth of a proposition or hypothesis".*[9] To verify a statement is to provide evidence generally of an empirical or observational kind for believing it to be true. ***Examples:*** (*i*) Earth revolves round the Sun, and the Sun is bigger than the Earth, (*ii*) All men are mortal.
6. ***Objectivity and value neutrality***: Science expects scientists to be objective. Objectivity implies *"an absence of bias in making or interpreting observations."*[10] Objectivity means interpreting the facts in such a way that our personal judgements are eliminated from them. A scientist should allow facts to speak for themselves. He should not attribute his personal views to them.
   - ***Value-neutrality*** is closely connected with objectivity. This concept was first explored by **Max Weber.** He insisted that a scientist / researcher should not choose methods and interpret data in ways that favour his values or ideological stance. The principle of value neutrality implies that the researcher must control whenever possible the influence of values on his studies or research.

   In fact, it is highly challenging for a social scientist to become objective and value-free in his studies. He must try to guard against his own views and values affecting the study of topics such as role of love in marriage; consequences of racism, sexism, improvement of worker productivity in work place, role of communism in economic development, and so on.
7. ***Insistence on the scientific method***: A branch of knowledge can be called a *science* only if it relies on the scientific method. **Francis Bacon** who laid the foundations of modern scientific method insisted that science should follow a systematic method in its studies. As **Karl Pearson** has remarked, *"The unity of all science consists alone in its method, not in its material. The man who classifies facts of any kind whatever, who sees their mutual relation and describes their sequences, is applying the scientific method and is a man of science."*[11]

---

[5] Ian Robertson in his *Sociology, p.* 10.

[6] William.P. Scott in his *Dictionary of Sociology,* 1988, p. 144.

[7] *Oxford Dictionary of Sociology,* 1998, p. 217.

[8] William Scott in his *Dictionary of Sociology,* p. 310.

[9] Collins Dictionary of Sociology, p. 718.

[10] *The Blackwell Dictionary of Sociology,* 2000, p. 193.

[11] Karl Pearson as quoted by Horton and Hunt in *Sociology,* p. 27.

While scientific methods are more or less same for all sciences, *scientific techniques differ.* These techniques refer to the particular ways in which scientific methods are applied to a particular problem. Each science must therefore, develop a series of techniques which fits the body of material it studies.

- ***Scientific method*** can be understood as a systematic and organised series of steps that ensures dependable results in researching a problem with maximum objectivity.
- ***Scientific method*** refers to *"the building of a body of scientific knowledge through observation, experimentation, generalisation and verification."*[12]

Definition of Technology

1. **Horton and Hunt:** *"Technology is the use of scientific discoveries to solve practical problems".*
2. **William Kornblum:** Technology which is an aspect of culture can be defined as - *"the use of tools and knowledge to manipulate the physical environment in order to achieve desired practical goals."*: [Page - 469].
3. Technology refers to *"The practical application of knowledge and use of techniques in productive activities."* - *Collins Dictionary of Sociology* - Page: 678.
4. In simple words, *"technology refers to the practical application of knowledge about nature."*

DIFFERENCES BETWEEN SCIENCE AND TECHNOLOGY

Science and technology though interlinked, are distinct. Main differences between the two can be noted below.

The Goals of Science and Technology are not One And The Same

Science is concerned with the pursuit of knowledge about nature, whereas technology is concerned with putting the knowledge of nature to some use. When the scientific knowledge is applied to the problems of human life, it becomes technology. Technology is systematic knowledge which is put into practice, that is, to use tools, and run machines, and to do such other things to serve human purposes. *Science is theoretical knowledge whereas technology is practical knowledge.*

1. Basic Research and Applied Research

Difference between science and technology is also expressed in terms of the differences between *basic research* and *applied research*. ***Basic Research*** which corresponds to "science" aims at merely increasing the quantum or sum of knowledge. In the previous centuries most of the scientists were involved primarily in basic research. But the trend has reversed in favour of applied science. In America, for example, during the 1970-80's hardly 14% of the scientists were engaged in basic research.

Applied research which corresponds to *"technology"* on the contrary, aims at finding technological applications for scientific knowledge. The modern governments and industries are concerned more with useful technologies than with the pursuit of knowledge. The determination of how money should be allocated for what type of research has little to do with what scientists themselves regard as the most pressing social or scientific priorities.

2. Technology is much older than Science

Every society has at least a simple technology, even if it is limited to such techniques as making stone implements, bows and arrows, fire building, making crude boats such as canoes, etc. All primitive people have somebody of practical knowledge on which their technology is based. But this kind of knowledge is not virtually science. On the contrary, such knowledge is derived from earlier trial-and-error experience, and not from an understanding of the abstract principles involved. The cave dweller, for example, does not know why fire burns, and why some substances burn while others do not, how water or sand extinguishes fire, and so on.

3. Technological Innovation may Precede The Scientific Investigations

People in all societies whether they have scientific knowledge or not, have always needed to find out better ways of doing things or ways of making their lives more comfortable. Technological innovations have met these needs for thousands of years. *"In fact, technological change proceeded without the benefit of scientific knowledge for the bulk of human history".*[13]

[12] William P. Scott in his *Dictionary of Sociology,* p. 370.

[13] William Kornblum in his *Sociology—In a Changing Society*, p. 469.

4. Science or Scientific Knowledge is not Universal

Science is not the inborn trait or inherited quality of all persons. Hence all the societies may not have the tradition of science. On the contrary, technology however crude, is found in all societies. Even the stone age people had their own crude technique of using stone implements and sharpening them. Science, very rarely appeared in human societies in the past. Because, scientific knowledge requires a proper and a systematic understanding of the principles that underlie natural events. Advanced technology is possible only by a proper scientific understanding of the world. Understanding of science and its principles is not that simple. Satellites cannot be launched, atomic reactors cannot be built, and nuclear bombs cannot be manufactured, for example, without the precise knowledge of the relevant scientific principles.

5. Science and Technology together Support Modernisation

Only the close link between scientific and technological development can accelerate the process of modernisation. In fact, the close link between science and technology which we normally take for granted today, is a relatively recent development. Accelerated by the discoveries of modern science, technology rapidly expanded the human capacity to live in and exploit different habitats. In the past two - three centuries it has changed the face of the earth. Heavy industries, big dams, international airports, supersonic rockets, super computers, satellites, skyscrapers, big ports, oil refineries, super highways, atom bombs, etc., are all the products of technology that have transformed the surroundings in which human beings live and work. *"It is this interrelationship between science and technology that is responsible for the breath-taking speed for technological change in our century."*

THE INSTITUTIONALISATION OF SCIENCE

Though science was hardly recognised as an important aspect of man's socio-economic life, its practical importance began to be felt over the years. Today, science is institutionalised. Throughout the civilised world, science is recognised as highly important and useful. It is standardised. Scientists throughout the civilised world follow the same basic methods and procedures. Scientists in governmental, industrial or university laboratories work in predictable ways to bring about unpredictable discoveries.

Institutionalisation of Science: A Recent Development

Though science and scientists have been in existence since centuries, science has emerged as a major social institution relatively recently.

The Background of Institutionalisation

Two-three thousand years ago, a few ancient people such as the Indians, the Arabs, the Greeks, the Mayans accumulated considerable amount of scientific knowledge especially in the fields of mathematics and astronomy. They made some practical use of their knowledge in such fields as agriculture, architecture and navigation. But they had hardly any specialised scientific roles, and *they made no efforts to link science to technology.*

The beginning of the modern science was marked by the rebirth of learning in the 16th and 17th centuries. Even at this stage there were no specialised scientific roles.

Until the 20th century, science was practised primarily by gentlemen equipped with intellectual curiosity and private wealth. The activity was not of great importance from the societal point of view, for its practical purposes were not widely recognised. Virtually, there were no full time professional scientists. The field of science was dominated by people who are understood in today's language as *"gifted-amateurs"*. Though universities were gradually admitting science to the curriculum, they continued to give more importance to the more prestigious traditional subjects such as classical languages and philosophy. Specialised scientific roles existed mainly in the universities and scientific research was largely confined to the ivory towers of the academic world.

Science as the Modern Institution

It is in the 20th century the relationship between science and technology has become fully recognised and exploited. This development has made the science to become a full-fledged and a well-developed institution. Science which was referred to in the previous centuries as *"little science"* has now become the *"big science"*. It is now firmly associated with big organisations, big money, big industries and big politics. The number of scientists in the world has grown very rapidly. In fact, the 20th century produced more than 90% of the scientists who ever lived on earth. [Price, 1963]. At the fag end of the 20th century (1980), more than one lakh scientific journals were in circulation and more than 2 million individual scientific papers appear each year. In America, for example, by 1980s, there were more than 5.66 lakh full-time scientists. Most of these scientists were employed by large formal organisations, universities, industry and the government. Of these, the universities constituted the largest single employer. The scientists had considerable freedom to choose the area of research in a university, provided it got the financial assistance from some agency. As far as the industry and government are concerned, the scientist's specific tasks are usually set by the organisation in accordance with its own political, military, commercial or other purposes.

Effects of Institutionalisation of Science

The institutionalisation of science has important effects especially on the scientific community. Some of them are mentioned below.

Firstly, science no longer remains a field to be occupied by the *"gifted-amateur"*; or a field of *"respectable leisure activity"* to serve *"the needs of gentlemen equipped with intellectual curiosity and private wealth."*

Secondly, scientists must spend many years in training for scientific careers and can rarely expect to make a significant contribution until they have mastered a specific sub-section of some scientific field.

Thirdly, scientific disciplines have become more and more specialised. Even the super specialists in the scientific field may find it difficult to keep up with the literature that gives report about the developments taking place in that field.

Fourthly, scientists in order to face these realities form social organisations of various kinds. These organisations may be either as large formal organisations as the international organisations or small informal, *"invisible colleges"* consisting of a small number of scientists working in the same field. These organisations are of great help to the individual scientists to keep themselves in touch with the latest developments taking place in the field. These are also of help to find answers to specific questions, to sense new trends and to seek critical remarks about their own work.

Fifthly, competition among the formal scientific organisations has become almost inevitable. *"One consequence of this unplanned growth of scientific organisations in universities, government, the military and the private sector,* ***Bell*** *concluded, is that it became impossible to create a single set of policies for the support of science. The various organisations must compete for resources and are vulnerable to changing national needs as well as new demands for scientific knowledge by business and industry. This makes scientific institutions even more intense and competitive."*[14]

Finally, conflicts between scientists and the sponsors of the scientific researches have almost become inevitable in the modern complex socio-political situations. Since many resort to scientific career as professional, scientists are to be paid for their work. The more their research is on *"pure"* sciences [that is, basic research] the more it is to be supported by the institutions like the government or the university. If they resort to *"applied research"* which aims at finding technological applications for scientific knowledge, the chances of getting financial support by the institutions such as industries, and commercial establishments, are brighter.

Neither the educational institution nor the formal scientific organisation itself, is able to support continuously all the research projects that the scientists want to take up. *"This dependence of science on other institutions continually subjects scientists to pressure to make their work relevant to the needs of business or the military. Conflicts between scientists and their sponsors thus have been a feature of science since its origins"*.[15] In fact, a glance at the norms of science or scientific institutions help us to understand more fully the nature of this conflict.

THE NORMS OF SCIENCE

It is quite known that every social institution develops its own norms that specify how its special functions are to be carried out. The institutions of science not an exception to this.

"The norms of science, like the norms in any other social system are the set of rules that govern how scientists do their work."[16]

Members of the scientific community have developed a set of norms to control and govern their own work. Those norms are not made very much public, but they are implicitly followed by most of them. These who violate these norms are tackled by the community members in their own way. **Robert K. Merton** (1942) identified four principal norms that constitute the *"moral imperatives"* of science. They are: (*i*) *universalism*, (*ii*) *communalism,* (*iii*) *disinterestedness* and (*iv*) *organised skepticism.*

---

[14] William Kornblum, pp. 471-472.

[15] Ibid., p. 472.

[16] Allan G Johnson in *The Blackwell Dictionary of Sociology,* p. 245.

1. Norm of Universalism

One of the basic norms of scientific institutions is universalism. This norm emphasises the universal nature of the scientific enterprise and its findings. This norm requires scientists to evaluate findings solely on their objective scientific merits rather than on such subjective criteria as the personal or social characteristics of the scientists who report them. It means *the truth of the scientific knowledge must be determined by the impersonal criteria of the scientific method, not by the criteria related to race, nationality, religion, social class, or political ideology.* In brief, this norm suggests that research findings must be evaluated purely in terms of their scientific worth.

2. Norm of Communalism

This norm of science refers to the *"common ownership of scientific findings."* The principle behind communalism is that *"scientific knowledge should not be the personal property of the discoverer."* This norm of *"communism"* or *"communalism"* has nothing to do with the economic or political systems for it only requires scientists to share results freely with one another in order to further the scientific discovery. All science rests on a shared heritage of past discoveries and no individual can claim property rights over the outcome of research. *Any new work of any scientist for that matter is only the continuation of what others have already done in that field.* This fact was acknowledged with all humility and humbleness by **Sir Issac Newton** when he reacted about his scientific achievements in the following manner. *"If I have seen any farther, it is by standing on the shoulders of giants."*

The scientific findings are not the property of any individual although in some cases they may bear the name of the person who first published them as in *"Darwin's Theory of Evolution", "Raman's Effects", "Einstein's Theory of Relativity", "Boyle's Law", "Newton's Laws of Motion",* etc. These discoveries in actualities are common property. Technology, in contrast, can become private or corporate property through the use of patents.

Consequences: The Norm of Communalism Leads to Two Consequences

(*i*) This particular norm may, however, give rise to frequent conflicts over scientific priority, that is over *who was the first to discover* or *publish a particular item of scientific knowledge.* For example, there is the continual controversy over who discovered the differential calculus - **Newton** or **Leibniz**. But there are no limitations or restrictions on the use of the calculus.

(*ii*) Yet another consequence of the norm of common ownership is *the norm of publication.* The scientists are required to give full and open communication relating to their scientific findings in journals, and periodicals which are accessible to all. Theoretically, secrecy is thus, out of place in science. Though theoretically scientific findings are required to be made public, they are not often done so. Scientific research is often conducted in the interests of national defence, or under the sponsorship of private firms that hope to profit from applications of the findings. The norms of common ownership and publication are often suspended. Situations like this have led to innumerable conflicts in scientific circles.

3. Norm of Disinterestedness

According to this norm, the scientists should be free from self-interests in their professional roles. Scientists are expected to act in the best interests of science. The scientist is not supposed to allow the desire for personal gain to influence the reporting and evaluation of results. Further, fraud and irresponsible claims are outlawed. Scientific research is subject to the scrutiny of others. In fact, this is a part of the research itself. The results of the research are to be verified by others. Scientists who falsify research results in order to make a name for themselves clearly violate this norm and threaten the credibility of scientists in general. *Science is, in a sense, 'self-policing'.*

The norm of disinterestedness, however, does not imply that scientists cannot and should not hope to profit from their findings. On the contrary, scientists may legitimately hope that their work will be recognised and praised by the scientific community. There are many instances in which scientists have held lucrative patents for their discoveries. Though he is entitled to obtain the reward in terms of recognition or in other approved means, his main interest should be to contribute to the sum of scientific knowledge. In other fields, for example, say in business or politics it is almost expected that people will distort the facts to serve their own ends. *But in the scientific community, the dishonest manipulation of the data or any other fraudulent practice is intolerable.*

The norm of disinterestedness has also been violated. Some instances of scientific fraud have become notorious. Some states have taken advantage of the general public's lack of scientific knowledge to spread scientific misinformation on such matters as racial purity as in the case of Nazi Germany.

4. Norm of Organised Skepticism

The norm of organised skepticism requires scientists to always question their results, to resist the temptation to conclude that any idea about how things work, is once and for all proven to be true. There are no *"sacred"* areas in science that should not be critically investigated, even if political or religious dogma forbids it. No theory, however ancient and respected, or new or old or revolutionary, can be uncritically accepted. *"The skepticism of the scientific community is "organised" in the sense that is built into the scientific method itself and is binding on all members of the scientific community."*[17]

The norms that are described above, are well established aspects of modern science These norms make science become clearly differentiated from other institutions such as religion or state. These norms have added dignity and prestige to the institution of science. But the emergence of these norms in the institution of science, is only a recent phenomena. Hence, science was not always viewed as a legitimate institution or a respectable occupation. Science in its early history was often regarded as a dangerous activity with the potential to threaten the existing social order. The repression of the scientific activities of **Galileo** by the Holy Court Inquisition is an example in this regard.

Norms of Science are not Always Obeyed!

Commenting on the norms of science, sociologist **R. K. Merton** says that as long as these norms are obeyed so long the scientific knowledge will accumulate. If norms are violated, scientific inquiry will suffer. But the bitter fact is that norms of science, like any other type of norms, are sometimes broken. Some examples in this regard are cited below.

1. *The norm of universalism* for example, was blatantly violated in Nazi Germany which attempted to distinguish between *"Jewish"* and *"Aryan"* science. This distinction is associated with racial discrimination which resulted in the suppression of the Jews.
2. *The norm of communalism* is often violated particularly when research is conducted for military purposes and commercial interests that hope to profit from a monopoly over some item of knowledge.
3. *The norm of disinterestedness* is also violated for the scientists may prove to be as greedy or ambitious as anyone else.
4. *The norm of organised skepticism* is also violated, probably more frequently than the other types of norms. Scientists after all, are human beings, they have their own private values and prejudices, and may be unwilling to give up old ideas or to accept new ones.

SOCIAL PROCESS OF INNOVATION

Science is a part of the aspect of modern life. Science is not stagnant. It is ever growing. Science is after knowledge. Scientists are always at work to explore the new horizons of knowledge. Scientific inquiry is an unending process .The object of scientific inquiry is ***innovation***, that is, *the discovery of new knowledge*. This innovation is neither automatic nor accidental. It is product of deep thinking, careful observation and systematic activity. Innovation does not simply occur in a random fashion. Science is not just the creation of a few curious and inquisitive individuals. *It is a social institution that is subject to the influence of social forces, both within and beyond the scientific community.* The social forces that influence science not only govern the growth of science but also strongly affect both the rate and the direction of scientific innovation.

Science is not a matter of a steady accumulation of knowledge. All scientific inquiries need not necessarily lead to success. New theories are proposed, some of the existing ones are still used while some others are abandoned. The existing knowledge at any period is only provisional, never final and irrefutable. In fact, **Karl Popper** (1959), one of the philosophers of science, is of the opinion that it is never possible to prove anything in science with absolute finality. He asserts that there is always a possibility that an exception will be found to every scientific law. *"All that we can do is disprove hypotheses, and our scientific knowledge consists entirely of theories that are not yet disproved, although one day they might be."*[18]

Competition in Science

Scientist's Desire for Recognition

Competition is one of the factors involved in the social process of innovation. Scientists are also caught in a competitive race like any other individuals because of their longing for recognition. Those who arrive at first in a discovery naturally obtain name, fame and honour. The scientist who gets there second by independent work is ignored, no matter how meritorious

[17] Ian Robertson in *Sociology,* p. 395

[18] Ibid., p. 397.

his or her work consists in. Scientists are also socialised to do original research. Importance is laid on this aspect. Because, researchers get no credit or recognition for following in the footsteps of others. Since professional recognition is of great importance to the scientists they normally prefer to follow their own path and break away from that of others.

Functional Effects of the Desire for Recognition

The desire for recognition on the part of scientists may have its own undesirable effect by encouraging secrecy. But such a desire is not always dysfunctional. It has several functional effects such as the following:

Firstly, *desire* for recognition encourages scientists to publish their findings and communicate their results to others as soon as possible.

Secondly, competition reduces wasteful duplication of efforts for scientists are motivated to tackle problems that the others are not working on.

Thirdly, competition encourages scientists to explore new specialities or even to find new disciplines in the existing areas of ignorance.

Resistance to Scientific Innovations

Innovation is an essential aspect of science. Growth of science hinges more and more on innovations. But the history of development of science reveals that innovation has not always been encouraged and welcomed. On the contrary, it is often resisted. As **Thomas Kuhn**[19] points out, *"Resistance to radical innovation has been the norm rather the exception in the scientific community."*

Examples **:** (*i*) **Galileo's** colleagues, for example, refused *to look through his telescope to the moons of Jupiter.* (*ii*) Scientist **Giordano Bruno** was burnt at the stake for having proclaimed that *the earth revolved round the sun.* (*iii*) **Louis Pastuer's** *germ theory* was ignored by the surgeons of his time, who could have saved countless lives by washing their hands and instruments before operating on the patients. (*iv*) **William Harvey's** *theory of the circulation of blood* was greeted with hootings and derisive laughters when he presented a paper on the subject in a gathering of the physicians. (*v*) **Sigmund Freud**, was shouted down by his furious fellow psychologists when he proposed his theory of childhood sexuality. In fact, a contemporary biologist **Edward Wilson** made an attempt to launch a new science namely, *"socio-biology"* -(the unified study of all social animals, including human beings) which was severely opposed by scientists in several fields.

In the same manner, various discoveries of modern physics, such as - *the laws of gravitation, theory of relativity, wave theory,* and *quantum theory*, were vigorously resisted for years after they were first announced.

Influence of Social Factors on Scientific Innovations

The examples cited above give rise to a pertinent question : *"Why so many of these scientists themselves are reluctant to accept scientific innovations ?"*

Scientists during the early days were reluctant to accept new scientific theories or innovations mostly due to the following reasons :

Firstly, most of the scientists used to follow the existing norm of the day that is rejecting as unacceptable any new theories or discoveries that deviated from or undermined the existing one.

Secondly, scientists might be reluctant to give up the ideas that have proved useful in the past, and particularly when their reputation is very much tied to their work.

Thirdly, scientists were reluctant to admit fresh evidence that would upset their tidy theories, or make them look foolish in the eyes of the public.

Fourthly, the scientific community was under the heavy influence of the society especially during the early times. As it could be observed in the 17th and 18th centuries, and also earlier, scientists were blinded to the facts by the religious dogma of the time. By the late 19th and 20th centuries, the religious world view was no longer uncritically accepted. Further, there was growing faith that the science could unlock the mysteries of nature. Hence, new theories started getting quick acceptance.

Factors Contributing to Quick Acceptance of Innovations

It is significant to note that the time lag between an innovation and its final acceptance was far greater in the past than it is today. For example, it took centuries for the scientists to accept the evidence of the earth's age, but it took only decades before most of them accepted the evidence for the evolution of the species. Scientists have become today more open minded. They are mentally equipped to accept new facts and give up the old ones, if they are proved to be wrong. *Why is this change in their approach? Why the scientific innovations are much more readily accepted today?*

[19] Thomas Kuhn in his *The Structure of Scientific Revolutions,* 1962.

Influence of Four Factors as Suggested by Kingsley Davis

According to *Kingsley Davis,* there are four factors which make the modern society more or less willing to accept comparatively quicker the scientific innovations. They are as follows:-

Firstly, *society's attitude towards change* very much influences its preparedness or unpreparedness to accept innovations. Most of the modern societies are no longer suspicious of change. Those societies which believe in *"progress"* and acknowledge the role of scientific innovations in bringing about that progress, normally have a readiness to accept novel ideas, new findings and innovations.

Secondly, *the factor of institutionalisation of science* affects also influences the acceptance of innovations. *The process of institutionalisation of science leads to the primacy of science.* In a society where science is institutionalised, science becomes a central activity rather than a marginal one. In such societies, scientists are socially rewarded for new discoveries. Needless to say, innovations take place much faster in them.

Thirdly, *the factor of specialisation* also affects the tempo of innovations. We are living in an amazing world where life is short and intellect is limited. If scientists are amateurs in several fields, they are less likely to make discoveries than highly specialised practitioners. These practioners are intimately acquainted with a particular field. They delve deep into that field and try to know a small topic. They become specialists in their respective fields. They are the ones who take initiative in innovations and who invite and encourage innovations.

Fourthly, *the factor of the methods and means of communication* not only influences innovation but also contributes to its diffusion. If new ideas can be conveniently stored and quickly transmitted, information becomes more accessible and can more readily be put to use. The modern means of communication such as computer networks, internet, e-mail, etc, have added to the process of diffusion of innovations.

As **Kingsley Davis** has pointed out the four factors mentioned above, have been operating in most of the well developed modern societies to make them accept rather than resist innovations.

TECHNOLOGY AND SOCIETY

Technology and technological developments have reached their heights in the modern society which is often picturised as a technological society. Though technology has assumed importance in the present world it is yet to acquire a prominent place in the sociological thinking . In spite of it, there are a number of sociologists who argue for its importance especially in understanding the course of history and social change. Major types of societies such as - hunter-gather society, horticultural society, agrarian society, industrial society, or post industrial society- are mostly distinguished by differences in technology. The industrial revolution, which produced enormous social change, was based to a great extent on technological innovations.

Technological Determinism

Science in the modern world is more and more tending towards developing sophisticated technology. Much of the scientific knowledge that is required in the modern industrial society has been used to create an extremely sophisticated technology. It is indisputable that technological innovations have immense social significance. Our way of life and social behaviour are influenced by technologies available to us; from kitchen gadgets to automobiles.

The influence of technology on society seems so powerful that some sociologists have adopted a position of *technological determinism*. They are of the view that the technology available to the society is an important determinant of its nature and character.

"Technological determinism is an assumption that technology is both autonomous and has determinate effects on society. Technology is seen as political and as independent variable in social change."[20]

There is a strong element of technological determinism in the work of **Karl Marx** also. He drew attention to the technologies of economic production that affects the social order. In fact, Marx's famous phrase- *"the handmill gives you society with feudal lord; the steam mill, society with the industrial capitalism."* - is sometimes used (mistakenly) as an example of technological determinism. Marx, however, saw technology as intimately related to the social relations of production.

Technological determinism is associated with neo-evolutionary theories which give technology primacy in the analysis of social change.

Several American social scientists such as **Thornstein Veblen** (1922) and **William Ogburn** (1950), have also stated that the specific historical developments and culture traits are the direct result of particular technologies.

Ogburn and his "Technological Deterministic Theory"

Ogburn made technology a powerful factor of social change. He even tried to explain specific social or historical events

[20] *Collins Dictionary of Sociology,* p. 678.

in terms of suggesting that the self starter in the motor-car had something to do with the emancipation of women in the American and Western Europe. Similarly, he gave us illustrations of the labour saving devices in the kitchen and the use of new fuels like gas and electricity which reduce the toil of the woman in the kitchen. Ogburn in his attempts to trace connections between historical events and technological developments stated that the invention of cotton gin in 1793 promoted the institution of slavery in America. The cotton gin greatly increased the productive capacity and thus the profitability of the textile industry. As a result, many more slaves were needed to work on the new cotton plantations that had emerged.

Ogburn divided human culture into *material* and *non material* elements. He stated that normally changes occur in the material culture first. People accept new tools and implements much more readily than they accept new ideas, values, norms, or institutions. These technological innovations invariably lead to changes in the non material culture. As a result, there is always a *cultural lag* as the non material elements attempt to *"catch up"* with changes in the material elements. Ogburn argued that this culture lag is a continuing source of social disorganisation and social problems.

Ogburn's argument has its own limitations. It is very difficult, if not impossible, to isolate the technological factor from the others as the main cause of social change. Technological change, such as the introduction of cotton gin, always occurs in the context of other changes. Technology cannot operate independently.

Moreover, the precise effect of technological innovation depends on the culture into which it is introduced. Thus, different cultures will accept, reject, ignore, or modify an innovation in accordance with their existing norms, values, and expectations.

It is thus argued that the theory of technological determinism cannot be pushed too far. It is better to see technological innovation as a part of social system along with other elements in society such as religious, political, economy, military, educational, familial, and so on.

Technology and the Rate of Social Change

Technology has established itself as a powerful agent of social change. The more the society is advanced, the more it encourages technology, and, as a result, the more it gets changed due to technology. And the more rapid the technological change, the more rapid is the social change that it generates.

Significant technological changes have taken place in the past 70-80 years. For a long period in history, people lived in a world little different from that of their parents. Parents expected their children and grand children to live much the same lives as they did. The *traditional societies* assume an almost unchanging social world and are typically very suspicious of change. On the contrary, in the *modern societies*, however, people accept change as the norm. They look for novelty, new experiences and new ventures. People expect constant improvements in their material environment. This fact has been beautifully explained by **Alwyn Toffler** (1970) in his famous book *"Future Shock"* .He has argued that *"we are living in a permanent state of "future shock". The future, he contends, continually intrudes into the stability of the present. Ours is a "throwaway" society in which change takes place faster than our ability to adjust to it."*[21]

The technological change has its implications on almost every aspect of society. Some examples may be cited here.

1. *Advancement in the medical field has lengthened life expectancy and brought down the death rate and this has radically altered the population structure.*
2. *Innovations in the field of industry have turned thousands of workers as unemployed persons. Old manufacturing machineries have become obsolete within a few years.*
3. Cultural activities of the people have undergone revolutionary changes due to such innovations as radio, television, cinema, computer and phonograph records.
4. The socialisation process has become more complex in the modern society. The elderly people can no longer pass on safely the age old culture to their children. **Margret Mead** hints at it in a curious way. She suggests that *"the pace of technological change is now so great that the old and the young live in quite different worlds- so much so that, in a sense, the parents have no children and the children no parents. For the first time in history, she points out, the old are no longer the main source of wisdom and knowledge in the community. The young often know far more relevant information about the modern world than their parents."*[22]

It is, indeed, beyond our imagination to say with certainty about the direction, dynamics, and dimensions of technology. It is bound to grow with ever greater speed. Since technology is a part of society, it is sure to affect and influence the course of our social life. People in the days to come would find it more and more difficult to adjust and accommodate themselves to the ever growing technology.

[21] Views of Alwyn Toffler as expressed in the words of Ian Robertson in his *Sociology*, p. 403.

[22] Views of Margret Mead as expressed in the words of Ian Robertson in his *Sociology*, p. 403.

THE SOCIAL CONTROL OF SCIENCE AND TECHNOLOGY

Science and technology have become today two formidable forces. Both are changing fast and are making other institutions to undergo fast changes. Interaction of other social institutions with science and technology is a great challenge of our time.

Science and technology are advancing so fast that they have irresistible effects on other institutions. Commercial establishments, business firms, industries, etc., stand to lose heavily unless they use the latest technology. Technical changes often alter the problems of the government. Religion is forced to adopt its teachings to meet new scientific interpretations. Education seeks to prepare students for scientific and technical developments.

Problems Arising Out of the Lack of Systematic Control Over Scientific and Technological Innovations

As it is made clear, science and technology have been undergoing relatively fast changes. These changes do not always guarantee beneficial results to the society and people. These changes may often give rise to some special problems also. At the same time, we have not been able to develop a system to exercise control over scientific and technological innovations. Our failure in this regard has further added to these problem. Three main problems in this regard are worth citing here.

1. Problem Related to the Nature and Qualities of the Environment

Environment has been the first casualty as far as scientific and technological innovations are concerned. A relatively unsystematic and uncontrolled scientific and technological advance may have many unforeseen social effects particularly on the quality of the environment. ***Examples;*** (*i*) Due to excessive use of chemicals and artificial fertilisers soil impoverishment has taken place in nations such as South Italy, Greece, Palestine, Egypt and Morocco, (*ii*) There have been fears that food additives may contribute to human cancers, blood pressure, diabetes, nervous weakness and such other diseases. (*iii*) Atmospheric pollution caused by man may lead to climatic changes that could cause a new ice age, (*v*) Gases sprayed through aeroplanes may interfere with the planet's ozone layer and allow dangerous radiation to reach the surface of the earth. Many more examples of this kind could be cited.

2. Distortion of the Priorities of the Research Matters and Efforts

Society should take up the responsibility of fixing priorities for making scientific researches and technological findings. If such priorities are not fixed then the innovations may not take place in accordance with the defined social goals. The haphazard way in which the scientific and technological advances take place not only cause unforeseen effects but also distort the priorities of techno-scientific development. Critics are of the opinion that under the present conditions, the scarce natural resources are to be judiciously handled and conserved; and they must be used for serving important human needs such as - *producing more effective life-saving drugs, predicting more effectively and well in advance the probable dangers of earthquakes, cyclones, and such other natural calamities; for producing more effective instruments to increase the efficiency of physically and mentally handicapped children and so on.* Scarce resources, for example, need not be wasted just for producing new types of cosmetics

3. Highly Technological Society Posing a Possible Threat to Democracy?

In a participant democracy ordinary people and their elected representatives take part in the decision making process. In a highly technological society such decision makers may unknowingly cause great dangers to the society by taking unscientific and wrong decisions. ***For example,*** *they may take decisions to build nuclear reactors near urban-settlements, to issue licenses to industries that cause environment pollution of the worst type; to issue such licenses to the industries without considering, the "sustaining power" of that particular environment, and so on.* Due to their ignorance of scientific and technical matters, such representatives may invite dangers to the society.

Further, there is another danger caused by what is known as *technocracy.* **Galbraith** (1967) and others have warned about technocracy, that is, rule by technical experts who play their role behind the scenes. In modern corporations, big companies and government departments, the real decisions are often made by the so called experts The decision makers normally rely upon the specialised knowledge and recommendations of these technical experts. Sometimes, societies will have to pay a heavy penalty for the erroneous technical advises given by these experts.

DIFFICULTIES INVOLVED IN ESTABLISHING SYSTEMATIC CONTROL OVER SCIENCE AND TECHNOLOGY

It is clear from the above analysis that there exists a need for establishing a systematic control over scientific and technological developments. But the establishment of social control over science and technology is not an easy task. According to **Ian Robertson**, such an attempt itself involves some difficulties or problems [Page: 405] which may be briefly examined here.

1. Problem of the Conflict of Values

The task of establishing social control over science and technology gives rise to the problem of conflict of values. The ultimate object of science *is the pursuit of knowledge.* Any real scientist for that matter expects an atmosphere of complete intellectual freedom. **Albert Einstein,** one of the greatest scientists of the 20th century, points to this conflict in the following words. *"There arises at once the question; should we consider the search for truth... as an autonomous objective of our work? Or should our search for truth be sub-ordinated to some other objective, for example, to a " practical one?" This question cannot be decided on a logical basis. The decision, however, will have considerable influence upon our thinking and our moral judgement, provided that it is born out of deep and unshakable conviction.."*[23] He further writes "*.... any thinking individual would find it impossible to have a conscious, positive attitude towards life"* unless he is allowed to have independent objectives.

Einstein also states that *"... intellectual individualism and the thirst for scientific knowledge emerged simultaneously in history and have remained inseparable ever since..."* - [Page: 2]. Should a scientist be allowed to have intellectual liberty and freedom to do research, even if his research or findings would bring disastrous effects on the society? This is virtually a question related to *value conflict.*

2. Problem of Non-Scientists Dictating Terms to Scientists Regarding Science and Technology

There is the problem of non-scientists giving orders or directions as to what scientists should do, and should not do, what researches to pursue and what to drop out, and so on. If it is a question of imposing restrictions on research, it again becomes difficult to decide the nature of restriction. It becomes impossible for the scientists with conscience to receive such orders or commands at the hands of unqualified persons.

3. Dilemma Created by the Shifting of Priorities

The issue of establishing social control over science and technology gives rise to yet another conflict of values, particularly if society attempts to shift its priorities in applied research from one set of goals to another. ***For example,*** if a manufacturing company which has been encouraging scientists to produce new types of packed food, suddenly changes its priority towards producing cosmetics, it may lead to heavy loss in terms of infrastructure. It may also mean interference in the intellectual freedom of the scientists. In a capitalist system like America, such shifts in priorities are often resisted by the scientists.

4. The Question of Owning Moral Responsibility for the Research

Scientific and technological innovations or researches may not always bring about positive results. They may often lead to deadly and disastrous consequences. The problem that arises here is, -*who should own the moral responsibility for having taken decisions about research that may have far-reaching consequences ?* The manufacture of atomic bomb, and later the development of hydrogen bomb, are but examples of many such cases. In these cases, for example, technical and moral issues are not easily separated in practice.

5. The Problem of the Scientists not having any Control over their Own Research

The present day scientists in most of the countries are not able *"to control the uses to which their work is put"*. Many scientists are very much disturbed about this situation. **Albert Einstein** points out at the helplessness of the scientist in the following words. *"What then, is the position of today's man of science as a member of society? He obviously is rather proud of the fact that the work of scientists has helped to change radically the economic life of men by almost completely eliminating muscular work. He is distressed by the fact that the results of his scientific work have created a threat to mankind since they have fallen into the hands of morally blind exponents of political power........... the concentration of economic and political power in the hands of small minorities which has not only made the man of science dependent economically, but also threatens his independence from within.......... He even degrades himself to such an extent that he helps obediently in the perfection of the means for the general destruction of mankind"*[24]

6. The Necessity of International Science Court

Who should take decisions regarding new technology and new researches? This question has assumed to be an important one. Moneyed people with greediness, scientifically ignorant people with political power, and common people who conspicuously lack genius - can never take such important decisions. It is, in this context, establishment of an international

[23] Albert Einstein in his article The Scientist: His Responsibility and Dignity, published in Bangalore University's publication entitled *Thoughts on Science and Society,* 1975, p. 1.

24. Albert Einstein in his article, p. 3-4.

controlling agency such as an *"international science court, with full legal powers to restrict certain dangerous or risky research seems to be the need of the hour. Many thinkers and scholars* have already made proposals of such a *'science court'*." It is left to the community of scientists, technologists of international standard, and the formal organisations of scientists to take a final decision about this proposal. **Ian Robertson** has warned that *"The question is a very important one, for scientific and technological advance in the years ahead may change our material and social environment in ways that many people might consider undesirable."*[25]

CONDITIONS FOR THE SUCCESS OF SCIENCE AND TECHNOLOGY IN THE SERVICE OF SOCIETY

Science and technology are an inseparable aspect of the modern life and hence progress without science and technology is inconceivable. Research in the scientific and technological field is a sine quo non for economic advancement. Industry and society must provide the necessary environment for research to flourish. Effective utilisation of research is equally important. Knowledge can be a real *"power"* only when there are able and efficient people to use it. From the society's point of view, scientific and technological research is useless in a practical sense unless it is properly tapped or exploited. Such exploitation, however, requires more successful, aggressive, forward looking and efficiently organised mechanism for development.

Science and technology cannot assure progress or service to humanity by themselves. They depend on certain conditions to make available for the society and people, their utilisation. The conditions for the success of science and technology in service of society and people, may briefly be examined here.

1. ***Presence of scientists and technologists***: The first requirement for the success of science and technology is the very presence of scientists and technologists. Technology can be imported, but the scientists cannot be. Import of research results cannot assure progress. A nation which is interested in quick progress must have its own natural resources, raw materials, and finally its own scientific personnel. It must pay proper attention to develop its own scientific community.
2. ***Institution to support research***: Research work is supported, sponsored, organised and directed by a well established institution. The tasks of the institutions are- *to identify the areas of research, select problems which need immediate solutions, arrange resources, and fix priorities relevant to country's economic growth.* Constant attention should be paid to the way in which the expected results can be made technologically and economically more practicable. *It is necessary to sell the results of research in a profitable manner.* The capacity to succeed depends more on the strategy and efficiency of the management than on the research potential.
3. ***Presence of the potential user***: Success of technological and scientific researches depends upon the presence of the potential users and their capacity to appreciate and actually utilise the relevant technology made available by research. There has to be a proper communication line between the sender and the receiver. Research result can be sold only within the limited circle of the people, such as industrialists who can take the actual benefits out of it.
4. ***Proper market and enterprise***: Applied research is most effective when it is coupled with a proper market and enterprise. Creation of market, identification of needs and demands and an appropriate environment are thus important.
5. ***Strong government support***: Science and technology can hardly flourish in the modern situation in the absence of strong government support. As far as India is concerned, the Indian Government is highly supportive of science and technology. India has gone ahead of many of the developed nations especially in the fields of computer software and space research because of the strong government backing. The nation has now a firm commitment to science and a strong will to achieve results through the application of science and technology.
6. ***Enlightened public opinion in support of scientists*** : Another major prerequisite for science to succeed is a public opinion sufficiently well informed and enlightened to give every support to scientists. Well-informed public opinion can be got only through education. In this fast changing world of science, we need to focus our emphasis on the development of attitudes towards creativity, scientific method, critical thinking, devotion to the sense of values and ideals and individual excellence. Superstition, ritualism, and prejudice must give way to rational thinking, questioning attitude, spirit of adventure and scientific temper.
7. ***Proper identification of problems and issues relevant to economic growth***: Benefits of scientific and technological research will largely depend upon the proper identification and definition of problems that are relevant to economic growth. Researches and technologies are to be oriented towards the national priorities and the felt-needs of the people. Raw material resources and the genius of the land must be properly utilised. Proper facilities must be created

25. Ian Robertson in his *"Sociology"*, p. 405.

for the designing and engineering establishments of the research. Industry, society and government must provide a necessary atmosphere and economic environment for research to grow.

Thus, the research yields differ from country to country differing at the levels of incomes, levels of technology, in industrial structure, size, technical and skilled manpower, the rate of expenditure on research and development.

8. ***Proper co-ordination between research industry and society***: Research and industry are partners to promote and catalyse the progress of the country. The support for science and technology from the side of society should be an act of faith. Industries must turn towards science and scientific research not only for finding solutions that crop up in their process of productive activity, but also to develop their intrinsic strength and efficiency.

"As it stands now, research and industry in India are running parallel like the two banks of a river, so near yet so far. What is most needed is the creation of common industry-research culture. The research and the industrialist must each live in both the worlds in such a manner that the worlds of research and industry become a single world."[26] Further, the society should create a proper social and economic environment that is favourable for the growth of science and technology. Science and technology, in turn, must support each other and contribute to the progress of society and industry.

SCIENCE AND TECHNOLOGY SHOULD BE MADE THE SERVANTS OF SOCIETY?

As it is already made clear, science and technology are growing at a very fast rate in the modern world. Changes taking place especially in the technological world force changes in the society. Science influences technology and in turn, gets influenced by technology. Both are changing and both contribute to changes in other fields as **Horton** and **Hunt** have pointed out, *"Science and technology have irresistible effects on other institutions. Business concerns face bankruptcy unless they use the latest technology, governments find that technical change has altered the problems which they face, religion must adapt its teachings to meet new scientific interpretation, and education seeks to prepare students for scientific and technical developments."*[27]

The Irresistibility of Science and Technology

Science and Technology have become a powerful force now. It is very difficult, if not impossible, to resist their temptation. Once set in motion, they cannot be stopped. Any attempt to prohibit new scientific and technological research would soon put us in the backwaters of history. Because all sciences are interrelated and interdependent, and discoveries in one field open new vistas in others. As **Horton** and **Hunt** have said, *"Marx may have been wrong in making the economic institutions dominant over all the others. It may be that science and technology have greater effect upon our social relationships than any other institution."*[28]

Science and technological advancements spread very fast. In fact, it is very difficult to maintain secrecy in the realm of science and technology. Anything that scientists and engineers or technicians in industry, corporation or nation can do, the scientists, engineers and technicians of any advanced country can duplicate. Given a little time and a lot of money techniques involved in the new innovations are often stolen illegally. The findings of science and technology can never be secret for long.

Is Humanity at the Mercy of Science and Technology?

Science and technology are considered two important means for socio-economic progress. When we speak of science and technology, we speak in terms of their practical utility and convenience, and neglect their impact on human satisfaction for it cannot be demonstrated. When we evaluate the effects of science and technology, we normally do not examine them in terms of the totality of human experience. We say this or that invention is valuable because it generates other inventions. Because, it is a means to some other means not because it achieves an ultimate human end and we undermine the *"side effects"* which often completely negate all the alleged benefits. The advantages of all technological progress will be totally outweighed the moment nuclear war breaks out.

It is true that once a new technology is accepted, its hidden consequences may be unavoidable. For example, automobiles pollute environment, mass production promotes monotony and alienation, sophisticated technology produces technological unemployment, birth control techniques augment instances of sexual immorality, pesticides cost human health, war weapons make international peace a casualty, and so on. These, and many more examples of these kind, make us believe that we are becoming helpless victims of technology.

[26] Y. Nayudamma in an article Research, Industry and Society, published in the book *Thoughts on Science and Society*, Published by Bangalore University, p. 159.

[27] Horton and Hunt in their *Sociology,* p. 309.

[28] Horton and Hunt, p. 309.

Science and technology have developed far faster than have social mechanisms to control them. A century ago, science was struggling to secure recognition and technology was relatively undeveloped. Today, they have brought about socio-political upheavals. They have the potentiality of causing wholesale destruction of human life. These undesirable consequences of science and technology were never anticipated previously.

The question of controlling science and technology: Now the question before us is - *can people control science and technology* - ? The answer to this question is an emphatic *"yes"*. It is 'yes' only if there are other values which are more important and precious. When people make reckless use of technology, science gets blame. As we see it today, political control of scientific and technological research is increasing. The autonomy of science diminishes as the domination of the Government grows. Popular skepticism is also increasing about science and technology especially after the two World Wars and the recent war between Iraq on the one hand, and America and the European Union, on the other. Hence, there is an urgent social challenge to find some means of ensuring that science and technology continue to develop in the direction of serving humanity rather than destroying it.

Einstein's call to the scientist to face the challenges with courage: **Albert Einstien** who analyses the role of a scientist and his responsibility in an article - [Page: 4] also gives a call to the scientist to face the challenges of the modern situations in a courageous manner. According to him, no one should feel that *"there is really no escape for the man of science..."*, and he should not *"tolerate and suffer all the indignities"* perpetrated on him. He cautions that no scientist should allow himself to be *"enslaved or used as a blind tool."* He writes; *"If the man of science of our day could find the time and the courage to think honestly and critically over his situation and the tasks before him and if he would act accordingly, the possibilities for a sensible and satisfactory solution of the present dangerous international situation would be considerably improved.*[29]

Conclusion: Science and technology have not only become major institutions of modern times, but also posed big challenges to the present world. The advances in these fields carry along with them latest consequences, which are difficult, if not impossible, to control. Still both can be directed at human welfare rather than human destruction. **Horton** and **Hunt** conclude this discussion in the following words: *"Those who really understand science have always been in the minority. Science may even go into temporary eclipse in one region, as in Hitler's Germany in the 1930s or in the People's Republic of China in the 1950s, but barring the worldwide destruction of civilization in a nuclear holocaust - which is not at all impossible - science and technology will continue to promote both innovation and change."*[30]

REVIEW QUESTIONS

1. Define science. What are the main branches of science? Explain.
2. Highlight the nature of science. Bring out its characteristic features.
3. What do you mean by technology? Distinguish between science and technology
4. Write a detailed note on the institutionalisation of science. Discuss its effect on the scientific community.
5. What are the norms of science? Explain.
6. Assess the influence of social factors on scientific innovations.
7. Show the relation between science, technology and society.
8. Examine the role of science and technology in social control.
9. Technology is a powerful agent of social change Analyse.
10. Examine the difficulties involved in establishing systematic control over science and technology.
11. Highlight the conditions for the success of science and technology in the service of society.
12. Science and technology should be made the servants of society. Comment.

⌘⌘⌘⌘⌘⌘⌘⌘⌘⌘⌘⌘

[29] Albert Einstein in his article in the book *Thoughts on Science and Society* published by the Bangalore University, p. 4.

[30] Horton and Hunt in their *Sociology,* p. 310.

53

Social Work, Social Security and Social Welfare: Conceptual Overviews

Chapter Outline

- Social Work—Confusion Regarding the Definition of Social Work—Some Definitions of the Concept—Assumptions of Social Work—Essential Values in Support of Social Work—Characteristics of Social Work—A Brief Historical Background of Social Work—Evolution of Social Work
- Social Work as Individual Charity, As Organised Activity and as a Professional Service —Scope of Social Work—Methods of Social Work
- Social Case Work, Social Group Work, Community Organisation
- Social Action, Social Welfare Administration and Social , Work Research
- Social Work As A Profession: Requirements of a Profession, the Beginning of Social Work as a Profession, the Beginning of Social Work As an Academic Discipline in India
- Social Work and Other Related Concepts
- Social Service, Social Services, Social Reform, Social Education
- Social Work : Relations With Some Other Social Sciences
- Social Work and Sociology, Economics, Psychology and Psychiatry
- Social Security: Definition of Social Security—Main Components of Social Security—Scope and Forms of Social Security
- Social Insurance, Public Assistance and Public Service—Origin and Development of Social Security
- Development of Social Security in India
- Social Security Legislations in India
- Social Welfare—Definition of Social Welfare—Vast Scope of Social Welfare—Two Characteristics of Social Welfare—Main Objectives of Social Welfare
- Purposes of Social Welfare Programmes in the Indian Context—Functions of Social Welfare
- Social Welfare and Social work—Differences Between Social Work and Social Welfare

SOCIAL WORK

Social work is one of the applied fields of sociology. It consists of the application of sociological and psychological principles to find solutions to the specific problems of the community or society or the individual. Social work can be stated as a "*recent branch of knowledge which deals with the scientific solution and treatment of the psycho-social problems.*"[1]

Social problems have been in existence in every society since times immemorial. Attempts to find solutions to these problems in the name of "*social service, social reform*" or "*charity*" have also been a part of every society. People with religious fervour or humanitarian outlook have been lending a helping hand to people in distress, destitution and deprivation. Love for one's fellowmen, feeling of brotherhood, urge for service to members of one's own community, giving charity to

[1] Sanjay Bhattacharya in *Social Work: An Integrated Approach*, 2004, p. 1.

the poor, etc., also functioned as inner driving forces to be at the service of the distressed and the disturbed people. Not only individuals but also some voluntary groups and organisations were engaged in such type of charitable or service activities. The charitable work and service activities taken up by individuals, groups and voluntary organisations came to be termed as "*social work*" in due course. This social work has now attained the status of a profession.

Confusion Regarding the Definition of Social Work

The term "*social work*" has not been properly defined by the scholars. Like the Monalisa smile, it means many things to many people. There are many misconceptions about it and to make an exhaustive inventory of them itself would be a difficult task. Since the very development of social work has not been uniform in all the countries the task of providing a satisfactory definition to the concept has become still more difficult. **Walter Pettit** [1925] in this context regrets that "*in social work we are still in the twilight zone of undefined terminology*". **Philip Klein** too complains (1934) that "*no satisfactory definition of the term* [*social work*] *has been achieved.*" The term is often confused with other similar terms such as - "*social welfare*", "*social service*", "*social security*", "*welfare work*" and so on.

Some Definitions of Social Work

In spite of the confusions prevailing regarding the term social work, scholars have ventured to find their own definitions for it. Some such definitions may be cited here.

1. ***Radhakamal mukerjee:*** Social work consists of "*the entire body of public and voluntary welfare activities that seek to assure every citizen a desirable minimum standard of living, freedom and security.*"
2. ***Friedlander:*** "*Social work is a form of professional service based upon scientific knowledge and skill in human relations which assists individuals alone or groups to obtain social and personal satisfaction and independence. It is usually performed by a social agency or a related organisation.*"
3. ***Indian conference of social work [1957]:*** "*Social work is a welfare activity based on humanitarian philosophy, scientific knowledge and technical skills for helping individuals or groups or community to live a rich and full life.*"
4. ***William P. Scott [in dictionary of sociology]:*** Social work refers to "a specialised professional field concerned with the application of sociological and psychological principles to the solution of specific community problems and the deviation of individual distress."
5. ***Collins dictionary of sociology:*** Social work refers to "*the organised provision of personal welfare services to people in need, including the poor; the physically and mentally disabled, the aged, children in need, etc.*"
6. ***Prof. Stroup:*** "*Social work is the art of bringing various resources to bear on individual, group and community needs by the application of a scientific method of helping people to help themselves.*"
7. ***Prof. Sushil Chandra:*** "*Social work is a dynamic activity undertaken by public or private efforts in the implementation of social policy, with a view to raise the standard of living and to bring about social, economic, political and cultural wellbeing of the individual family and the group within a society irrespective of its stage of social development.*"

Assumptions of Social Work

Social work as a profession seeks to enhance the social functioning of individuals, singly and in groups. By resorting to various types of activities it focuses upon their social relationships which constitute the interaction between man and his environment. Social work essentially involves certain assumptions[2] among which the following may be noted.

1. Like all other professions social work has problem - solving functions.
2. The practice of social work is an art with a scientific and value foundation.
3. Social work as a profession came into being and continues to develop because it meets human needs and aspirations recognized by society...
4. Social work practice takes its values from those held by the society of which it is a part. However, its values are not necessarily, or altogether those universally or predominantly held or practised in society.
5. The scientific base of social work consists of three types of knowledge : (*a*) *tested knowledge,* (*b*) *hypothetical knowledge that requires transformation into tested knowledge, and (c) assumptive knowledge (or "practice wisdom") that requires transformation into hypothetical and thence into tested knowledge...*

[2] Werner W. Boehm, *Objectives of the Social Work Curriculum of the Future* Curriculum Study, 1. New York: Council on Social Work Education, 1959, p. 54 as quoted by Rex A. Skidmore and Milton G. Thackery in their *introduction to Social Work*, Second Edition, p. 3.

6. The knowledge needed for social work practice is determined by its goals and functions and the problems it seeks to solve.
7. The internalization of professional knowledge and values is a vital characteristic of the professional social worker since he is himself the instrument of professional help.
8. Professional skill is expressed in the activities of the social worker...

Essential Values in Support of Social Work

Social work assumes importance because it is backed by some values. The essential values of social work that are very significant in defining this profession may be mentioned below[3]

1. Each person has a right to self-fulfilment.
2. Each person, as a member of society, has the obligation to seek ways of self-fulfilment that contribute to the common good.
3. Society has the obligation to facilitate the self-fulfilment of the individual and his right to righteous enrichment.
4. For the harmonious development of his personality each person requires opportunities for satisfying his basic needs in the physical, psychological, economic, cultural, aesthetic, and spiritual realms.
5. As society becomes more complex and interdependent, increasingly specialised social organisation is required to facilitate the individual's efforts at self-realisation.
6. To facilitate "*self-realisation*" on the one hand, and "*contribution to society by the individual*" on the other, the social organisation must make available all the socially important devices so as to satisfy the human needs and promote general welfare.

The values mentioned above, constitute the minimum commitment for the social worker. The goal of social work is the enrichment of social functioning wherever the need for such enhancement is felt or experienced socially or individually.

CHARACTERISTICS OF SOCIAL WORK

Social work aims at creating conditions for the individuals and groups under which they are able to utilise their potentialities to the maximum extent. It also aims to make use of the existing resources to remove some of the handicaps and to overcome them by proper adjustment. Social Work as such exhibits some general characteristics which are mentioned by the **United Nations** in an "*International Survey of Training for Social Work*".[4] These three general functions as mentioned by the U.N. are as follows-

1. ***Social work is a helping activity***: Social work is designed to help the individual in adjusting to his present circumstances. It intends to give assistance to individuals, families and groups which are prevented from achieving a minimum desirable standard of social and economic well being.
2. ***Social work is basically a social activity***: It is carried on not for personal profit by private practitioners. It is, however, carried under the auspices of government or non-governmental organisations or both which are established for the benefit of members of the community.
3. ***Social work denotes liaison activity***: It is a liaison activity through which disadvantaged individuals, families and groups may tap all the resources in the community available to meet their unsatisfied needs.

Distinguishing Characteristics of Social Work

The concept of 'social work' may better be comprehended by consideration of some of its distinguishing characteristics[5]

1. ***Focus on the total person***: In social work there is focus on the wholeness and stability of the person. It stresses the total person in the total environment.
2. ***Emphasis on the importance of the family***: Social workers are aware of the fact that most social problems are the results of imbalanced family relationships. They consider family as a case in social work. They attempt to emphasise the importance of the family in moulding and influencing behaviour.
3. ***Utilisation of community resources***: Social Workers have a knowledge of community resources and are able to tap them to meet the needs of their clients.

[3] W.H. Boehm's views as quoted by R.A. Skidmore and M.G. Thackery, p. 5.

[4] D. Paul Chowdhry in *Introduction to Social Work*: *History Concept, Methods and Fields*, pp. 23-24.

[5] R.A. Skidmore and M.G. Thackery, pp. 9-1 l.

4. ***Use of the supervisory process***: Social work provides supervision both in academic study and in practice by qualified, professional personnel to help the worker to grow professionally. The supervisor is available regularly to help the worker do a better job and increase his or her understandings and skills in working with people.

5. ***Relationship is a key factor in social work process***: Everything that is a part of interview is important here. As far as the social worker is concerned, the feeling tones between the worker and client are particularly important. The social worker attempts to help the client to face and solve his or her problems by sharing knowledge and skills. The worker tries to establish an "*emotionally supportive relationship*" with the client.
   - Significant principles from sociology, social psychology and group dynamics are woven into the art of social work. These are utilised in understanding relationships of people and in helping them to resolve their conflicts.

6. ***Social work involves basic knowledge of psychiatry also:*** Social worker gives importance to the understanding of people. He intends to know how the client feels about himself or herself and his or her relationship with others. The worker is supposed to have a basic knowledge of the concepts of psychiatry and dynamic psychology which assists him or her in dealing with human behaviour.

7. ***Social work recognises that most of the social problems are rooted in social institutions***: Hence, in order to understand these problems and behaviour, it is necessary to understand the institutions of man. Social problems may be reduced by working with individual personalities or by changing social institutions. ***For example***, a particular boy may be helped to give up delinquent behaviour through individual therapy. Social work also recognises that thousands of delinquent acts may be prevented through sensible changes in political or economic institutions.

8. ***Traditional social work emphasises three basic processes***: (*i*) *Case work* involves a close, face-to-face relationship in working with people and their problems. (*ii*) *Group work* utilises the group as the tool to bring about desired changes in social functioning with troubled persons. (*iii*) Community Organisation is the intergroup approach toward facing and solving social pathologies.

9. ***Social work and agency settings***: Most social workers are employed in agency settings. Those who operate within the framework and policies of agencies Obtain the structural backing and support that strengthen their services in many ways. They get, for example, many positive resources such as supervision, consultation, and collaboration that are inherent in agency settings.

10. ***Effectiveness of social work depends on team work***: A social worker is particularly effective in developing and using the team approach and bringing about co-ordination of services and activities. The social worker often acts as co-ordinator and integrator for the team effort.

11. ***Social work consists of educational programme also***: Social work involves both classwork and practical field work experience which go hand in hand. To get a Master of Social Work [MSW] degree one requires to undergo two years of training course in any recognised university of India. It includes both academic classes and live field experiences in working with clients, which gives an integrated combination of theory and practice. Provision is also there for undergraduate course in social work. Graduates with B.S.W.- [Bachelor of Social Work] degree are recognised as beginners qualified to start the profession of social work.

It is clear from the above explanation that the basic aim of social work is to help the client to help himself or community to help itself. Social worker is not a person who never listens to his clients but prescribes a "*social-psychological pill*" even though most clients ask for it. On the contrary, he tries to help a person to improve his or her understanding of himself or herself. He assists the person to improve his/her relationships with others and to tap his or her own and community resources in solving personal problems. Social work endeavours to emphasise and utilise the strengths and resources of both the individual and community to effect desired changes.

A Brief Historical Background of Social Work

Social work as a profession is a product of the 20th century. It has however, its roots well established in history. It has been in existence from the time when people first began to think and take responsibility towards others, that is, their neighbours, fellow caste-members, community-members or fellow citizens by way of indulging in activities which were called "*charity*", "*poor relief*", "*philanthropy*", "*social reform*" and so on. Social work as we call it today attained professional status not until the second decade of the 20th century.

Evolution of Social Work

Social work as a profession is found in several nations of the world today. But it didn't develop in these nations in the same Way. It has undergone different stages of development in dificrent countries. The stages through which social work has passed in many of the countries in which it is today most fully developed may be divided into three major categories namely:

(*a*) *Social work as individual charity*,

(*b*) *Social work as organised activity*, and

(*c*) *Social work as a professional service*.

(a) Social Work as Individual Charity

Many countries consider charity, especially alms-giving as social work. Helping the poor and the needy persons by voluntary spirit on the part of a few individuals has been regarded as social work. Giving alms or giving something as charity has been a conventional way of helping poor people to meet their material needs. Further, the inspiration for rendering this kind of charity originally came from religious teachings. Individuals are inspired either by humanitarian motives or religious teachings to do volunteer service. Social work as individual charity serves two purposes, namely.

(*i*) *catering to the material needs of an underprivileged destitute class*," and (*ii*) *fulfilling the self assumed social or religious obligations of a privileged upper or middle class*.

Though some people in some countries still cling to this concept of social work, its meaning has radically changed today. Informed people now believe that social work is not just poor relief. Charity can never remove poverty. Charity given unscrupulously, or without any discrimination, encourages beggary. Unlike social work, charity aims to the spiritual welfare of the donor, rather than at the welfare of the recipient. Social workers are not concerned with poverty but their main interest is in the personality of the individuals concerned.

It is indeed, true that social work understood as individual charity has throughout the centuries and throughout the world, frequently paved the way for organised governmental and non- governmental action in the social field. Realisation of the evils of indiscriminate alms-giving led to the recognition of the need for organised effort not only to mitigate poverty but to seek and remedy its causes. It was also realised that preventive and curative work in this area requires trained minds as well as sympathetic hearts. Thus, social work as individual charity was only an initial phase in the development of social work as a scientific method. But in many countries, many people still continue to regard social work as a charitable activity concerned entirely with the relief of the poor and the destitutes.

(b) Social Work as Organised Activity

There are many countries which believe that social work deals with economic dependency which includes destitution. From this point of view, social work is regarded as "*a systematic method of providing for the support and / or rehabilitation of economically dependent groups, that is, the unemployed, the sick, the aged, the handicapped, the mentally ill, widows and dependent children, etc*."

Social work as an attempt to deal with economic dependency and distress has taken many different forms both public and private. In some countries, the prevention and treatment of destitution has become a recognised responsibility of the government. The social work activity in this regard both governmental and non-governmental has generally taken three forms namely; (*i*) *palliative*, (*ii*) *protective*, and (*iii*) preventive.

(*i*) ***Palliative activity***: Social work as palliative activity has the purpose of relieving the already existing economic distresses or problems. This activity includes measures such as - giving assistance in terms of cash or kind, institutional care for the destitutes, relief work projects etc. Here the intention is to provide maintenance for the persons who are temporarily or permanently without other means of support.

(*ii*) ***Protective activity***: Social work as protective or rehabilitative activity includes all types of protective services being rendered to the orphans, neglected children, mentally and physically handicapped people and so on. Here, the intention is to protect economically disadvantaged groups and assist them to become self-sufficient.

(*iii*) ***Preventive activity:*** Social work as preventive activity is "*directed towards the elimination of those factors in the environment or those deficiencies in personality development that prevent the individual from achieving a minimum desirable standard of socialised economic well being.* "[6] *Preventive activities include - family case work, industrial welfare services, housing welfare services, vocational guidance and vocational training. They also include the development of broad social welfare measures such as social insurance, wages and hours of work, legislation; slum clearance programmes, compulsory school attendance, child labour legislation, etc*. One of the objectives of social work as understood at this stage is to contribute to the development of sound social policy and progressive social welfare programmes. It is regarded as the task of the social work to provide its expert knowledge to the state to frame appropriate social policies and legislations in order to meet the challenges of social and economic mal-adjustment.

[6] G.R. Madan, p. 6.

(c) Social Work as Professional Service

This is the third and also the present stage in which social work is considered as a professional service under governmental or non-governmental auspices. It is now available to every member of the community irrespective of the means at his disposal. Its purpose is to assist the individual in achieving his full potentialities for productive and satisfactory living. Social work in the present sense, begins as a professional service available to any member of the community who may be in need of help in removing obstacles to productive living. This shift of emphasis widens the scope of social work and it is extended far beyond the provision of assistance to economically dependent groups. For example, in England, "*Citizens Advice Bureaux*" were established as a war time service to civilians in personal or environmental difficulties. Similarly, in the Union of South Africa, the "*State Administration of Railways and Harbours*", employs and trains social workers to serve its employees and their families. The service is considered as necessary and desirable for the promotion of the health and welfare of individuals and families. Thus, "*welfare services in relation to industry have also been widely accepted throughout Europe and Latin America as a means of maintaining or improving the social well-being of industrial workers and their families*."[7]

Social work as a kind of social service is very old, but as a profession it is definitely a new venture. It evolved into a professional discipline within universities in the beginning of the 20th century. The first academic institute, namely, "*the Newyork School of Social Work*" of Columbia University was established in 1904 in America and since then number of schools of social work have been established to provide systematic training for the candidates to pursue social work as their profession. As far as India is concerned, the "*Tata Institute of Social Sciences*", Mumbai, established in 1936 with its original name "*Sir Dorabji Tata Graduate School of Social work*", is the earliest institution in this regard.

Scope of Social Work

The basic philosophy of social work is to reduce individual and social problems and assist the advancement and welfare of both. The scope of social work is being extended to more areas. Its scope depends upon the special needs and problems of each society which are constantly changing because of various socio-economic factors. It is now international and inter-racial in scope. The methodology of social work is useful in solving the human problems of the unhappy as well as the handicapped and those who are deprived of the happiness.

Friedlander classifies the major activities in the field of social work as follows according to the type of service they render, that is. - *public assistance, social insurance, family services, child welfare services, health and medical services, mental hygiene services, correctional services, youth leisure time services, employment services, housing services, community welfare services and international services* [8]

In the book "*Social Welfare of India*" issued on behalf of the Planning Commission, Government of India, these services have been mentioned as follows: - "*Child welfare services, youth welfare services, women welfare services, composite services or family social service, community welfare services, services for the handicapped, services for the unadjusted, services for the maladjusted, specialised or applied services such as medical social work, socio-psychological and mental hygiene problems, psychiatric social work, services for the backward or under - privileged groups, activities of international welfare agencies, etc.*"

In the modern society such as ours, the main task of social work is to provide various types of services to the people, that is, especially for children, women, handicapped, destitutes, dependents, disabled persons and so on. For the benefit of these people, various programmes of social work are carried out through the following services.[9]

1. ***Public assistance***: Public assistance is a kind of help which is given to the applicant depending upon his social and economic needs. The amount of public assistance given is based on legal provisions. It includes assistance given to old, blind, disabled and destitute persons. To some needy persons institutional care is also provided.
2. ***Social insurance***: Social insurance covers such contingencies as old age, unemployment, industrial accidents and occupational diseases. Social insurance covers certain risks such as - pension in old age after retirement, pension during inability, medical care in times of illness, medical care and cash allowances during the employment injury, cash allowances to wife and dependents in case of death and allowances during the period of unemployment. Benefits under social insurance are granted only to those persons who pay a certain amount of contribution. It is partly financed by the state.

---

[7] As quoted by G.R. Madan in *Indian Social Problems*, Vol. 2, p. 7.

[8] Friedlander W.A. in "*Introduction to Social Welfare*, 1959, p. 13 as quoted by G.R. Madan in *Indian Social Problems*, Vol. 2, Second Edition, 1973, p. 24.

[9] *Social work, An Integrated Approach* By Sanjay Bhattacharya Deep and Deep Publications Pvt. Ltd., New Delhi, 2004, p. 38.

3. ***Family services***: In the sphere of family organisation also social work has a great role to play. It gives assistance and counselling towards family and individual relation, marriage, health and economic problems. Here, the social worker has the responsibility of establishing hamronious relationship between the individual and his family. He renders his service by way of assistance and advice to the family organisation.
4. ***Child welfare services***: These include residential institutions for the protection, care, education and rehabilitation of socially handicapped children such as orphans, destitutes, children born to unmarried mothers and so on. Child welfare service includes temporary homes for children day care centres, recreational and cultural centres and holiday homes for children of low income families.
5. ***Welfare services for handicapped***: Social work provides for the physically and mentally handicapped persons also. In this context, the services include institutions for the protection and care of physically and mentally handicapped; hostels for the working handicapped and small and simple production units for the handicapped and so on. To promote their welfare, special schools for mentally retarded children and orthopaedically handicapped children are also maintained.
6. ***Women welfare services***: Social work includes women welfare activities also. In the Indian context, it was realised even before freedom that the problems of women must be solved so as to enable them to lead a comfortable life and to take an active role in the political emancipation of the country. Raja Ram Mohan Roy, Keshava Chandra Sen, Dayananda Saraswathi, Ishwar Chandra Vidyasagar, Swami Vivekananda, M.G. Ranade, Pandit Rama Bai and many others had made pioneering efforts in the emancipation of Indian women. Gandhiji was able to impress upon women to take part in the freedom struggle. Many women came to understand their role not only in freedom struggle but also in national reconstruction.

   After independence, efforts were made to identify and tackle the problems of women. It was also considered necessary to initiate specific measures for the welfare of women.
7. ***Labour welfare service***: Labour welfare includes may types of service activities. According to the report of the I.L.O., workers' welfare includes such services, facilities and amenities which enable the employed persons to perform their work in healthy and congenial surroundings. "*Labour welfare includes anything done for the intellectual, physical, moral and economic betterment of the workers whether by employer, or by government or by other agencies...* "[10]
8. ***Community welfare services***: These include the establishment of urban community centres including - welfare aspects of slum improvement, clearance and prevention, short term specialised courses for women seeking employment, dormitories and night shelters and holiday homes for children and community welfare services in rural areas.
9. ***International social services***: Social work at the international level includes the direction, supervision and administration of welfare services. Some of the organisations rendering social services at the international level are - *the World Health Organisation, International Red Cross Committee, The world Federation for Mutual Health, the U.N. Technical Assistance Programme, the International Conference of Social Work*, and so on.

Methods of Social Work

Social work which is regarded as a profession has developed certain methods and techniques which have been tested over time. These methods and activities have also become areas of social Work. In our discussion of social Work three terms such as - "*social work methods*", "*social work activities*" and "*social work processes*" are often used interchangeably. All social work activities or methods are classified into six major categories which are as follows.

Of these six methods, the first three are direct helping methods while the last three are sometimes called secondary ones. They are social work methods in the sense they are systematic and planned modes of helping people.

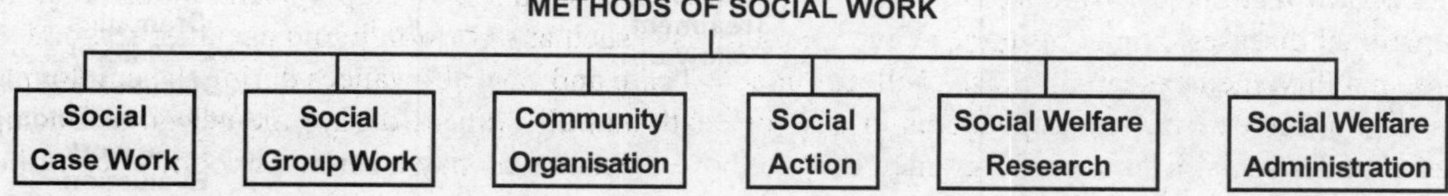

1. Social Case Work

Social case work is the most developed social work method which deals with the problems of an individual in his adjustment to his total environment or to any part of it. It is primarily related with the psycho-social problems. It consists of the study of mental, emotional and social factors.

10 *Labour Investigation Committee* as quoted by **Sanjay Bhattacharya,** p. 41.

- As **Friedlander** points out, social case work is a method "*which helps by counselling the individual client to effect better social relationships and a social adjustment that makes it possible for him to lead a satisfying and useful life*."

This method involves the study of individual problem in its total setting. It is concerned with the understanding of individuals as whole personalities and with the adjustment of these personalities to socially healthy life. This method or technique is applicable in the following situations. - (*i*) *Delinquent children*, (*ii*) *Rehabilitation and diversional therapy for TB*., *V.D.* or *other patients*, (*iii*) *Beggary*, (*iv*) *Unmarried mothers*, (*v*) *Family maladjustments*, (*vi*) *Marriage guidance*, (*vii*) *Youth Counselling*, *and* (*viii*) *Psychiatric social work*. Its method involves stages such as - (*i*) *Case study*, (*ii*) *diagnosis* and (*iii*) *treatment*.

2. Social Group Work

Social group work is an important area of social work which deals with individuals as members of group. Its central focus is a group rather than individual. Since the principle aim of this method is to develop the entire group much emphasis is given on social adjustment of collectivity.

- According to **Freidlander**, social group work is an activity "*which helps people to participate in the activities of a group of their intellectual, emotional and physical growth and for the attainment of desirable goals of the group*".

In social group work, the group itself is utilised by the individual, with the help of the worker, as primary means of personality growth, change and development. "*The worker is interested in helping to bring about individual growth and social development for the group as a whole as a result of guided group interaction.*"[11] Group Work as such-is a method by which the group worker enables various types of groups to function in such a way that both group interaction and programme activities contribute to the growth of individual and the achievement of desirable social goals.

In the group work, the group is fruitfully used for helping the individual members in their social relationships. Group work also gives people agreeable leisure time experiences. In the social group Work, *the group members, the agency and the social worker - are the main constituents*. It is necessary that the group be properly formed. The agency should also provide adequate facilities to the group. But the key to successful group work lies with the role of the intelligent and the professionally mature group worker who seeks to bring out desirable changes in groups members' attitudes, values and behaviour. He helps the group to make its decisions and never imposes his will on the group. The worker tries to guide the interaction of the group members in a non-manipulative way. He tries to obtain maximum participation of the members in-the planning and execution of its programme.

The group process is used in - *leisure time activities, Bal Bhavan, holiday homes, youth hostels, hospitals, institutions, community welfare work, school social work, etc*.

Casework Versus Group Work

A comparative study of the case work and group work methods clearly reveals the distinction between the two. The table give below reflects this comparative analysis.

COMPARATIVE REFERENCES	SOCIAL CASE WORK	SOCIAL GROUP WORK
1. FOCUS	Individual group as a whole	Individual and the
2. POINTS OF CONTACT	At breakdown or maladjustment	Effective functioning of the group
3. GOALS	Re-adjustment to society	(*i*) Develop personality (*ii*) Social Action
4. METHODS AND ACTIVITIES	Interviewing observation Investigation Diagnosis Recording Treatment Follow-up	Group Games Arts and Crafts Picnics Social Education Literacy Dramatics Visits Discussions Audio-Visual aids Case work Evaluation

3. Community Organisation

Community organisation refers to the adjustment of the needs and resources of a community. Community organisation as a process implies all those welfare measures which are undertaken by the members of a community in accordance with their needs and resources. This method is meant to be applicable to the whole community.

[11] Prof. Tracker in *Social Group Work*, p. 9 as quoted by Paul Chowdhry in *Introduction to Social Work*, 1983, Third Edition, *Atma Ram* and *Sons*, *Delhi*, p. 38.

- According to **Friedlander**, "*community organisation is the process of planning and developing social services in order to meet the health and welfare needs of a-community or larger unit.*"[12]

As **Mildred Barry** points out "*community organisation in social work is the process of creating and maintaining a progressively more effective adjustment between community resources and community welfare needs. This adjustment is achieved through the help of the professional social worker and through the participation of individuals and groups in the community. It involves the articulation of problems and needs, the determination of solutions and the foundation and conduct of a plan of action.*"[13]

Community organisation is a process by which a sustained and systematic attempt is made to improve the relationships in a community. It is a deliberate attempt at adjusting the welfare needs and resources of a community. Community organisation, in simple words, implies the following work.[14]

Firstly, it involves a conscious attempt to find out the needs of a given community which can be done by a scientific survey, by studying the history of the community, or by a combination of these methods.

Secondly, when once the needs are identified, they have to be arranged according to their priority, and accordingly the urgently-felt needs should be given first attention.

Thirdly, the community's resources must then be properly tapped, mobilised and multiplied. The community organisation must help the community to discover and utilise its own unused and untapped resources. He is also of help in taking the assistance of external human and material resources.

Fourthly, a suitable action programme must be planned on the basis of this knowledge of needs and resources.

Finally, two precautions be taken in community organisation work. (*i*) The organiser must know and make it clear that the purpose of community organisation is to help the community stand on its own feet. (*ii*) The community organisation programme must always seek to develop harmony, Co-operation, good will and a sense of sharing and solidarity in the community. The development of these co-operative attitudes is as important as the planned attempt to satisfy the unmet felt needs.

Community organisation is basically a democratic process and hence much effort is to be made in eliciting people's willing participation in community activities. This gives the community a sense of belonging, identification and achievement. It is wrong to suppose that community development programme is only confined to the rural communities. On the contrary, it is a technique which can be successfully used in the development of all communities - it may be rural community, urban community in a slum or a congested area, a Harijan or tribal community, etc. The basic principles are the same but programmes may differ from community to community according to local needs.

***Example of fields of work in the process of community organisation*:** The following table reveals some of the fields of work in community organisation.[15]

4. Social Action

Social action has now been considered as a separate technique of social work. It aims at desirable social change and social progress. It is a method that demonstrates the profession's commitment to environmental changes. It makes social worker to take definite stands on controversial issues.

SOME EXAMPLES OF FIELDS OF WORK IN THE COMMUNITY ORGANISATION

Economic Field	Educational Field	Medical Field	Cultural Field	Community Life
• Improvement of agriculture	• Adult Literacy	• Health Education	• Bhajans Mandalis	• Cultural and Recreational Activity
• improvement in local crafts	• Primary Education	• Opening Dispensaries	• Kirtans	• Starting of Community Centre
• Promotion of cottage industries.	• Promotion of Reading Rooms and Libraries	• Family Planning and Population Education	• Dramas	• Mock Elections
• Vocational guidance and exhibitions	• Social Education	• Care of Physically and Mentally Handicapped	• Folk Songs	• Public Meetings
	• Special Education for the handicapped		• Kathas	• Participation in National Life
			• Kavi Sammelana Organisations	• Improving Panchayats
			• National Days and Festivals	

12 Friedlander as quoter by G.R. Madan in *Indian Social Problems*, Vol. 2, *Second Edition*, p. 17

13 Mildred Barry as quoted by Prof. G.R. Madan, p. 17.

14 S.K. Kindulka in *Social Work in India*, *Kitab Mahal Pvt, Ltd.*, 1965, pp. 18-19.

15 Paul Chowdhry's *Introduction to Social Work*, pp. 46-48.

- According to **Witmer H.L.** "*The term social action refers to organised and legally permitted activities designed to mobilise public opinion, legislation and public administration in favour of objectives believed to be socially desirable.*"

She [Witmer] also points out that many groups other than those composed of social workers engaged in social action such as political parties, labour unions and the like may have this as one of their main objectives. Social action can be understood as a mass approach in a most peaceful manner used for changing or modifying existing social and economic institutions which do not function properly and which has made social work ineffective.

Social action may be described as a group effort to solve mass problems or to further socially desirable objectives by attempting to influence or change basic social and economic conditions or practices. Social action is made possible by the application of some methods or techniques among which the following may be noted.[16] *Research and collection of data about the mass problem, planning solutions and arousing public opinion, meeting key-persons, groups and agencies, public meetings, propaganda, discussions enlisting public support, co-ordinating the work of different groups and agencies, presentation of the proposal to those in authority, use of press and meeting members of legislature, social legislations, enforcement of legislation, case work, and so on*.

Through the application of the 'social action' approach some of the social problems could be solved. ***Example***: *Untouchability, dowry problem, zamindari system, removal of caste hatred, religious prejudices, purdah system, child marriage, restrictions on widow remarriage, illiteracy through compulsory primary education, etc*. Problems such as these could be tackled through social action approach.

5. Social Welfare Administration

Social welfare administration refers to "*the process of organising and directing a social agency*".[17] The administrative aspects of social work include the organisation and management of social agencies, public and private. This virtually includes every activity in a social agency that is necessary to the giving of service to the clients and communities. Social welfare administration is a process of organisation and direction of a social institution.

Social welfare administration in order to become successful must set up some realistic and attainable objectives before the agency. These objectives are to be shared by the agency personnel. In order to achieve these goals plans are formulated, programmes developed and resources mobilised. Proper organisation and co-ordination of different activities of the agency are equally important. The agency is able to render good services only if the competent and efficient staff are recruited to it. Much administrative efficiency and expertise is needed for financing and budgeting a programme.

Periodic evaluation lot the type and quality of service rendered helps to improve administrative efficiency. The administrator of the agency has to maintain good public relations. Social welfare administrators should also guard themselves against bureaucratisation.

In the broader context, it could be said that "*the aims of social welfare administration are the progressive achievement of the justice, protection against disease and insecurity, the adjustment and compromise of conflicting groups and their interest. In short, it aims at the attainment of good life*."[18]

- ***Functions of administration*** : According to **Paul Chuwdhary**, the main functions of administration can be listed out in the following way :

1. *Determining the purposes, aims and objects of the organisation,*
2. *Establishing the structure of the organisation and keeping the organisation strong.*
3. *Directing the work of the organisation, selecting and developing efficient and adequate staff.*
4. *Working with boards and committees.*
5. *Evaluating accurately the results achieved in relation to established purposes.*
6. *Looking ahead and forecasting, so that services are kept consistent with changing needs and resources.*
7. *Providing financial administration - securing and handling finances.*
8. *Maintaining effective public relations and proper cooperation with the other agencies.*

[16] Paul Chowdhry in *Introduction to Social Work*, pp. 49-50.

[17] Friedlander as quoted by G.R. Madan, p. 17.

[18] Sanjay Bhattacharya in *Social Work*, p. 20.

6. Social Work Research

- "*Social work research is the systematic critical investigation of questions in the social welfare field with the purpose of yielding answers to problems of social work, and of extending and generalising social work knowledge and concepts.*"[19]
- "*Social work research is a methodical inquiry undertaken to find new facts, test old hypothesis, verify existing theories and discover the causal factors of phenomena in which social workers are interested*"

Social research can be one of the important tools in our attempt to assess social problems of the community, the type of people affected by the problem and the methods used in trying to solve the problem. Social planning would be ineffective without proper research which will enable the planners to assess the needs of the community.

Social research and social work research are not one and the same. In comparision with social research, the social work research is narrower in scope; while the former aims at the advancement of any of the social sciences like sociology, anthropology, psychology, economics, political science, etc., the latter is limited to the problems of social help, social adjustment, social work techniques and other areas of use and interest to social workers in general.

Even though the scope and objectives of social research and social work research are different, the tools, techniques and methods that are used are mostly common. The methods applied in social work research have been to a large extent derived from those used in sociology and social psychology, as well as in history and anthropology. Sampling, schedules, interviews, observations and other research methods are employed in social work research and in social research. The difference between the two consists mainly in the focus and function of the two.

As far as the area of social work research is concerned, it is really very vast. There are as many areas of social work research as there are areas of social work interest. But for obvious reasons social work research has lagged behind other social work methods. Though research is very costly, judged even from the utilitarian point of view, it is a highly rewarding investment. In a country like India, there is a vast scope and need for social work research. A few areas of research may be mentioned here - "*The role of social work in helping people solve their economic problems; the use of casework and group work in India; the various human relations, aspect of community development; themes pertaining to social legislation, correction, labour welfare, youth welfare, child welfare, welfare of the socially, physically and mentally handicapped, welfare of the backward classes and tribes; problems related to administration, organisation and co-ordination of social work agencies in India, including their personal practices and financial conditions; growth and development of professionalism in social work; and patterns and problems of social work education - these are some of the broad and general areas on specific aspects of which research may fruitfully be undertaken.*"[20]

5. Social Work as a Profession

Social work is not a science, nor is it a branch of any of the social sciences. Though it has its close links with social sciences like sociology, psychology, psychiatry, etc., it is not regarded as a science as such. Social work is no more considered as a leisure time activity of a few social service - minded individuals. It has developed into a full-fledged profession with definite knowledge, techniques and skills, which are acquired by a social worker. Though social work is very old as a service, it is definitely new as a profession.

Social work as a profession has definite ameliorative and creative functions in society. It is a professional service which used scientific techniques to alleviate economic, social and emotional distresses, among individuals, groups and communities. It uses knowledge to meet human needs and it is, in this sense, an "*applied science*." Knowledge, understanding and skills are all inseparable parts of this profession.

Requirements of a Profession

According to **Dr. Abraham Flexner**, a true profession should fulfil the following requirements.[21]

1. There should be some intellectual thinking followed by individual responsibility.
2. The members of any profession must constantly resort to laboratory and seminar for a fresh supply of facts. They must keep on updating their knowledge.
3. The profession is not merely academic and theoretical but is definitely practical in its aims.
4. It has its own techniques possessed through a highly specialised educational discipline.

---

[19] G.R. Madan in *Indian Social Problems*, Vol. 2, p. 18.

[20] S.K. Khindulka in *Social Work in India*, p. 21.

[21] Dr. Abraham Flexner as quoted by G.R. Madan, pp. 25-26.

5. It has its own activities, duties and responsibilities which completely engage its participants and develop group consciousness.
6. The profession is likely to be more responsive to public interest than are isolated individuals. It tends to become increasingly concerned with the achievement of social ends.

As **Prof. Brown** has pointed out social work fulfils all the above mentioned requirements and specially the last one. Social work as a profession has definitely made progress over the last several decades. Unfortunately, it has not been able to convince the community that those who possess professional skill definitely deliver a superior service than those who do not. Hence, the belief that good men and women with good intention will be able to render good service to the society [even though they do not possess the required professional skill] continued to prevail for years. What is to be noted is that mere good intention and dedication are not sufficient. *The social worker requires a peculiar combination of temperament, intelligence, training and experience*.

There is another problem faced by the social workers. Within social work itself there are conflicts regarding the justifiable boundaries of the field. "*Opinions range all the way from seeing social work as a network of services to social work as a unique method and process, to social work as a policy*"[22] Social work shares with related professions an interest in promoting human welfare. If one views the objective from this point the line between social work and other related fields would appear to be blur. Similarly, social work method does not always make for an easy differentiation from such related fields as - health, education, religion, recreation and labour.

The Beginning of Social Work as a Profession

The first educational programme in social work was organised in America as early as in 1898 by the *New York Charity Organisation Society* in the form of a simmer institute. It later on got transformed into ***New York School of Social Work of Columbia University*** in 1904. Since then schools of social work have been steadily increasing in America, Canada, Britain, France and other countries. In these Western countries, social work education is greatly recognised as having reached a high state of development. Western societies consider social work education as a graduate professional discipline within universities which grant a master's degree [M.S.W.] after completion of a two year educational programme. Some of these social work schools even offer advanced educational programmes which lead to the doctoral degree.

During the recent years, the university pattern of social work is getting increasing acceptance in Asia, and in some places of Latin America and Africa. The United Nations also has strongly recommended that steps must be taken to promote social work education. For the promotion of the same it has introduced international fellowships, consultant services, required seminars and a variety of special studies and training projects.[23]

The Beginning of 'Social Work' as an Academic Discipline in India

As early as in 1936, the first institute of social work known as "*Sir Dorabji Tata Graduate School of Social Work*" which is presently known as "*Tata Institute of Social Sciences*" came to be established. Since then number of institutions imparting education and training in social work have come into being. Though their number is increasing they suffer from certain drawbacks among which the following may be noted.

(*i*) Most of these institutes are influenced by the American model rather than by the utmost requirements of Indian society. However, during the recent years some attempts have been made to make social work more relevant to the needs and resources of the country.

(*ii*) Further, almost all of these schools prepare graduates for administrative jobs rather than to take up classical social work roles. The education and training given to them is not attuned to the actual social work practice by social work professionals.

(*iii*) Trained social workers do not have many job opportunities. Some of them are employed as factory inspectors, labour welfare officers in supervisory positions where the knowledge, skills and attitudes are not identical with those of social workers.

(*iv*) Unlike the Indian Medical Council and Indian Bar Council, all India level institutions concerned with social work such as - "*Indian Council of Social Welfare*", "*Indian Association of Trained Social Workers*", "*Association of Schools of Social Work*" - do not exercise any control on the profession or the schools of social work.

[22] G.R. Madan, p, 26.

[23] "The International Conference of Social Work, the International Association of Schools of Social Work, and the International Federation of Social Workers bring together the practitioners affiliated with national associations of social workers. Each of these organisations has also been granted consultant status by the Economic and Social Council of the United Nations." Dr. D.R. Sachdeva in *Social Welfare Administration in India*, 2000, p. 14.

(*v*) Finally, the social work profession is not provided with the necessary public recognition nor the required prestige. **Radhakamal Mukherjee** in this context regretted "*Social work is the youngest, yet unhonoured and unacknowledged profession in India... it has obtained neither social recognition nor developed a code of ethics grounded in a philosophy of social work and welfare.*"[24]

6. Social Work and other Related Concepts

Ordinary people in their daily talks and discussions make use of terms such as social service, social security, social welfare, social reform, etc., interchangeably. The indiscriminate usage of these terms has created a good deal of confusion about the correct meaning of these terms. For example, a doctor, a teacher of a nursery school, or a school for the mentally handicapped, a warden of poor boys hostel, a magistrate of a juvenile court, a labour officer in a factory, a probationary officer in a firm, a block development officer, a *gram sevak, anganawadi teacher*, etc., are all referred to as social workers in one or the other contexts. It is necessary, therefore, to clarify the appropriate usage of these terms at this stage.

1. Social Service

The "*term 'social service' is used to denote help given by o volunteer to an individual or group at the time of need.*"[25] Social service is not an activity taken up by an individual to help himself. A person inspired by the feeling of rendering help to other person may do social service. It does not involve any trained work of any professional worker. Professional techniques and methods are not involved in it. ***Examples*** **:** Providing drinking water facility to a family or group of families during summer, helping a blind or the aged or handicapped to cross a road, rescuing people from a house on fire, helping people encircled by floods to move to safer places, and so on.

2. Social Services

Harry M. Cassidy defines social services as, "*those organised activities that are primarily and directly concerned with the conservation, protection and the improvement of human resources*." [26] Social services also include social assistance, social insurance, child welfare, mental hygiene, public health, education, recreation, labour protection and housing.

- According to "*Collins Dictionary of Sociology", the term social services refers to "any state- provided services which have a bearing on the quality of life of all citizens*."

As it is already made clear, the primary function of social work however is to help members of a community to make effective use of social services so that they achieve a minimum desirable standard of social and economic wellbeing. It means mere rendering health services or organising educational programmes for the economically backward, as such is not social work.

3. Social Reform

"*Social reform*" refers to socio-political activities whose object is to modify or change a socio-political practice or some aspects of social legislations without changing the fundamental political structure. Social reform aims essentially at a change in the basic values and social institutions in a community. It requires pioneers and leaders of public opinion. Its intention is not to provide just a temporary relief but to trigger lasting changes in the society. In modem India, for example, Raja Ram Mohan Roy took the lead in social reform movement. He pledged himself to the task of the abolition of the "*sati*" system. He was instrumental in pressurising the British government to introduce the *Prevention of Sati Act in 1829*. Thereafter, number of other leaders like Ishwarchndra Vidyasagar, Maharshi Karve, Maharshi Dayananda Sarswathi, Swami Vivekananda, Dadahhai Navaroji, Annie Besant, Ramabai Ranade, Gopallcrishna Gokhale, Mahatma Gandhiji, Sarojini Naidu and others took the lead in the field of social reforms. These reformers never tried to transform the Hindu society and its basic structure as such, but only struggled to reform or repair it from inside.

Social work, on the other hand, is related to the welfare activities undertaken within the limits set by existing resources, values and institutions. Its purpose -is to meet the needs of individuals and groups. Social work activities are carried on not through pioneers and leaders but professionally trained workers.

As far as the modem social work in India is concerned, it has developed out of the social reform movement of the 19th century. An uncompromising struggle to get equal rights for women, a concerted attempt towards the abolition of the outmoded and harmful practices such as child marriage, sati, untouchability, human sacrifice, etc., come under the term "*social reform*". On the contrary, running a rescue home for women, a community centre for the Harijans, special homes

---

[24] Radhakamal Mukherjee in an article Social Welfare Administration, *Indian Journal of Social Work*, July 1965, p. 179.

[25] D. Paul Chowdhry in *Introduction to Social Work*, p. 30.

[26] H.M. Cassidy as quoted by G.R. Madan in his *Indian Social Problems*, p. 14.

for the juvenile deliqunts, institutions for the care and protection of the mentally handicapped children, etc., represent some of the instances of social work activities. Sometimes, social reform programmes involve the use of social work techniques.

4. Social Education

The fields of social work and social education are very much overlapping though they have different roles to play. *Social education is a learning process through informal methods the art of making satisfactory adjustment to the changing needs and demands of life*. This involves acquiring knowledge of social life and social habits which help in making life more meaningful and satisfactory. Social education is more a preventive programme than a curative one. It is more akin to public health programmes.

On the contrary, social work is both preventive and ameliorative. Social work and social education, are not however, contradictory. They often go together. ***Example*** : Community organisation is both a technique and a field of social work. Here, social education plays a vital role in helping the community to understand its needs and problems so that a self-help programme can be successfully run.

Social Work: Relations With Some other Social Sciences

Though 'social work' is not one among the social sciences it has meaningful relations with many of these sciences. But it is not exclusively related to any of the social sciences such as sociology, economics, history, philosophy, political science or psychology. With each of these, social work maintains cordial relations but its function is something other than that of any one of them. At the same time, all of these social sciences contribute to the enrichment of this profession. **Prof. Friedlander** points out, "*Social work has drawn its knowledge and insight from political science, psychology, sociology, economics, medicine, psychiatry, anthropology, biology, history, education and philosophy, but by synthesis it has developed into a science of its own. As a profession social work depends upon the body of knowledge based upon these other social sciences...* "

Social Work and Sociology

Social work is often regarded as "*applied sociology*". Despite the historic ties between the two there is no exclusive relationship between them as such. Social work draws its insights and skills from many fields of knowledge within the social sciences and sociology is one among them.

Sociology and social work are both interested in people, their interactions and understanding these interactions. Both sociology and social work look to society as essentially a network of social relationships. Sociology provides a scientific analysis of society and its problems whereas social work provides the most scientific and suitable means and methods for scientific solution. It is in this way, sociology inspires social work.

The sociologist is particularly concerned about *how, when* and *why* people behave as they do in association with others. He is also interested in studying social problems, conducting research, collecting facts about the social realities and doing everything possible to understand interaction in human associations.

The social worker, on the contrary, is more interested in helping the people to solve social problems they have and to improve their social functioning. He attempts to establish adjustment between the individual and his social environment. In the spheres of community organisation, social co-ordination, provides for co-operation and makes possible synthesis between various social programmes and welfare activities. Social work represents socially oriented services.

Social Work and Economics

Economics as one among the social sciences, is concerned with wealth. It deals with the way in which man cams wealth, distributes it and finally enjoys it. Economics, as **Prof. Marshal** *points out. studies on the one hand, material wealth and on the other, human happiness*. It tends to study how man satisfies his wants, what economic problems he faces and what material resources he has at his disposal to solve them.

Social work tries to find out the best course of action towards the solution of the social problems. Social problems never occur in vaccum. Of the various factors that contribute to social problem, economic factors are the chief ones. They are at the root of many social problems. Social problems such as crime, poverty, unemployment, beggary, bonded labour, child labour, prostitution, exploitation, etc., are by and large, based on unsatisfactory economic conditions. Individual happiness is often dependent upon economic factors. Hence, social worker cannot afford to forget the role "of economic factors in influencing human problems on the one hand and human happiness on the other. Both study the general principles of human relation.

Social Work and Psychology

Psychology is the science of human behaviour. A psychologist is always interested in understanding the individual and his/her behaviour. As **Silverman** suggests "*psychology is the science that seeks to measure, explain, and sometimes change the behaviour of man and other animals*."

A psychologist and a social worker are often members of the same professional team. Pscyhology and social work operate in some common grounds. Both are interested in the behaviour of people, although the psychologist focuses mainly on individual behaviour and social worker on social functioning. Both of them seek the thinking and feeling processes of the people.

As far as the differences are concerned, the psychologist is particularly interested in the individual attributes of people and aims to understand their characteristics and behaviour. However, some psychologists [particularly clinical psychologists] go beyond the study phase and work directly with the people in the helping process. Though some of these activities overlap with social work, the focus of both the sciences seems to be different. The psychologist usually works with individuals on a rather intensive basis. He often becomes a psychotherapist even. The social worker, on the other hand, is interested particularly in the social functioning and relationships of his clients. He is equally concerned with the idea of utilising community resources to meet their personal and social problems.

Social Work and Psychiatry

- Psychiatry is that "*branch of medicine dealing with the genesis, diagnosis and treatment of mental disorders*"[27]
- In simple words, psychiatry is that branch of knowledge which deals with the "*treatment of the mentally ill by medically trained practioners*".[28]
- "*Psychiatry is a branch of general medicine using drug treatment as a clinical resource, and also other physical methods such as surgery and ECT [Electro Convulsive Therapy]*".[29]

Social work and psychiatry are interrelated. They have many things in common. Both of them work with people who possess personal and social problems. They help people to improve their relationships with others. They have considerable interest in sensitivity and ability to understand and direct feelings and emotions.

Social work and psychiatry have some differences between them. As someone has commented the psychiatrist deals mainly with *depth* in regard to personal and social problems, and the social worker with the *breadth*. The psychiatrist in his studies delves deep into intrapersonal dynamics, he goes into the depth of the role of unconscious motivations and related factors. The social worker, on the contrary, operates within the conscious level of behaviour. He also tends to utilise environmental and community resources to achieve his purposes. In order to improve the social relationships he is compelled to tap many material resources economic and otherwise.

The psychiatrist is busy in dealing with patients on a medical basis. He prescribes medication and hospitalisation, and if needed, he even tends to focus on the unconscious and intrapsychic factors. Sometimes, social workers use psychiatric understandings in diagnosis and treatment of social diseases and some other times work directly with the seriously disturbed individuals and families.

Finally, it could be said that psychiatry tends to focus on pathology and the healing of illness. The psychiatrist is particularly interested in the internal dynamics of individual behaviour. The social worker, on the other hand, is more concerned about social functioning involving social and community factors and interactions.

SOCIAL SECURITY

Concept of Social Security

The term "*social security*" is a very wide term and it has acquired a global character. But unfortunately, the term has not aquired any standard or uniform definition. The term is given economic as well as social interpretations. Let us consider some of the explanations and definitions offered to the concept.

Social security is the protection furnished by society to its members through a series of public measures against social and economic distresses such as unemployment, under employment, invalidity, destitution, social disability, old age, backwardness, death, employment injury, sickness, maternity, and so on. During these contingencies, it becomes difficult

[27] William P Scott in *Dictionary of sociology*, p. 320.

[28] *Collins Dictonary of sociology*, p. 533.

[29] Ibid., p. 533.

for the person concerned either to work or to obtain work. People are often forced to face a number of contingencies or socio-economic and personal distresses like these. Social security is an attempt to meet such hardships. Thus, it is said that "*the idea of social security has arisen out of the deep and eternal need of man for some measure of security for his immediate future.*"

The concept of social security is based on ideals of human dignity and socio-economic justice. The concept connotes a strong desire to give protection to its citizens to contribute to a country's total welfare against certain hazards of life.

8. Definitions of Social Security

1. **Prof. Friedlander:** "*Social security is a programme of protection provided by society against those contingencies of modern life - sickness, unemployment, old age dependency, industrial accidents, and invalidism against which the individual cannot be expected to protect himself and his family by his own ability or foresight.*"
2. **Ronald Mendelson:** Social security system refers to "*any form of organisation designed to ensure income security for the whole or for the substantial portion of community by means of compensation to persons for lack of income from their own efforts or those of their bread winner, and also of health services designed to restore the sufferer to full earning capacity and to prevent him and his dependents from incurring under costs of maintenance of health.*"[30]
3. **Laxicon Universal Encyclopaedia** gives the following meaning to the term social security. "*Social security consists of public programmes intended to protect workers and their families from income losses associated with old age, illness, unemployment or death. The term is sometimes also used to include a broad system of support for all those, who, for whatever reasons are unable to maintain themselves.*"
4. **The National Commission on Labour** defines the concept in the following manner - "*Social security envisages that the members of the community shall be protected by collective action against social risks causing undue hardship and privation to individuals whose private resources can seldom be adequate to meet them. The concept of social security is based on ideals of human dignity and social justice. The underlying idea behind social measures is that a citizen who has contributed or is likely to contribute to his country's welfare should be given protection against certain hazards.*"
5. **Collins Dictionary of Sociology:** Social security refers to "*a system of income maintenance provided by the state. Most systems have two components; a contributory system, which in the U.K. is labelled "National Insurance", and a contributory "safety net" which usually has some connection with conceptions of a poverty line.*"
6. **International Labour Organisation:** "*Social security is the security that society furnishes, through appropriate organisation, against certain risks to which its members are exposed. These risks are essentially contingencies against which the individual of small means cannot effectively provide by his own ability or foresight alone or even in private combination with his fellows.*"

It is clear from the above definitions that the general goal of social security is to provide social protection to the needy people. This social protection is secured through various forms of public assistance, social insurance and frequently preventive health and welfare services. The term social security, in general, does not embrace private social welfare activities which are, however, an important part of the system of social welfare in most countries.

Main Components of Social Security as per the Aforesaid Definitions

The above mentioned definitions highlight the following components of social security.

1. Main purpose of social security is to give socio-economic protection and relief to the workers or other members of the society against any type of unfortunate eventualities.
2. Though social security includes mainly economic considerations, it also involves social and physical aspects.
3. The concept of social security includes statutory enactments which are enforced at the local, state and national level for the purpose of providing financial assistance to the persons who have become victims of socio-economic distresses and hardships.
4. The concept of social security includes in itself social assistance and social insurance.
5. It is necessary for the worker or other person to establish his financial need to obtain financial assistance under the scheme of "*social assistance.*"

[30] Definition quoted by P.C. Sikligar in *Social Security*, Published by Mangal Deep Publications 2000, p. 12.

6. In order to claim the benefits under the scheme of "social insurance", the worker/ person has to discharge the burden of having fulfilled all the requisite conditions specified under the law.
7. Social security also includes schemes enforced and regulated by the government or some public authority on its behalf for the purpose of workers and their families.
8. Under the social security schemes financial protection is provided to the workers or their dependents in case of loss of employment, injury, old age, invalidity or death.
9. The benefits generally covered by social security schemes as reflected from the above mentioned definitions are - *medical care, sickness benefit, unemployment benefit, old age benefit, maternity benefit, invalidity benefit, survivor's benefit and so on.*

Social security provisions constitute one of the multifarious activities of the state. Any state which makes for such provisions is regarded as a "*welfare state*". A welfare state is one in which Government assumes basic responsibility for the well-being of its citizens by making sure that people have access to basic resources such as housing, health care, education, and employment.

Scope and Forms of Social Security

Social security is given to the needy people in different ways. **Professor Hassan** speaks of three main types or forms of social security. They are as follows :

(*a*) *Social insurance*, (*b*) *public assistance*, and (*c*) *public service.*

(a) Social Insurance

Social insurance aims at granting adequate benefits to the insured on compulsory basis in times of unemployment, sickness and other emergencies. It is used in cases of those contingencies which are predictable, namely, old age, death, sickness, maternity, work-injury and unemployment. It also involves the setting aside of sums of money in order to provide compensation against loss resulting from particular emergencies.

In the case of social insurance, contributions are made by the insured persons, and sometimes by their employers and the government also. Hence, the benefits are paid as a matter of right on the fulfilment of certain prescribed conditions according to a fixed scale.

(b) Social or Public Assistance

Social or public assistance is o kind of help which depends upon certain conditions and legalities between the worker and the state. It is generally a matter of government gesture. It is granted only if certain prescribed conditions are fulfilled. It is given by the government on the basis of actual existence of need. No previous contributions will have to be paid. The existence of the need is the only condition irrespective of the causes or circumstances of need. For example, it is given to the old and blind people who are economically poor.

It is also given in the form of family allowances, unemployment allowances, old age pension allowances to the needy and the helpless.

(c) Public Service

"*The term public service is used for those benefits and services which may be provided by government on a general basis to all the members of a group based on age, sex, or other considerations for example, children's allowances and mental health service.*"

It must however be noted that these three forms of social security are not exclusive categories. Any particular programme of social security may combine the characteristics of more than one of three forms.

Origin and Development of Social Security

Historically speaking, social security in the modern sense, first originated in **Germany** in 1881 when the Emperor William I urged upon the Govt. to adopt social insurance schemes. Thus was passed in Germany the first compulsory Insurance *Act in 1883* as per which old age security was provided to the working classes. On the same model, Unemployment Insurance was initiated in the year **1925**. The example of Germany was later on emulated by various European nations. In the second half the 20th century, the International Labour Organisation **[I.L.O.]** of the United Nations Organisation **[U.N.O.]** played a vital role in the field of social security. The **[I.L.O.]** adopted conventions on *maternity benefits*, *workmen compensation, sickness insurance, minimum wages, unemployment insurance, income security, medical care, and so on*. These conventions had a great impact on the member-nations of the U.N.O. After Second World War, social security schemes and ideas made worldwide progress.

Development of Social Security in India

As far as India is concerned, during the olden days, the joint family system, caste system, village community system, the monarchical ruling system and individuals with pious and philanthropic attitude used to provide social security to the needy people in an informal and unorganised manner. In fact, taking care of the needy and the helpless has always been regarded as a pious duty in India. Due to the impact of the Western civilisation and industrialisation, these institutions have fallen into decay and are no longer able to meet the situation satisfactorily. In spite of that some institutions to help orphans, widows, blind, deaf and other handicapped persons were started by voluntary organisations. These however had only limited range of operations.

During the British rule, the British overlords were not in favour of introducing social security schemes in the beginning. Even the *Royal Commission of Labour* did not permit the introduction of a permanent social security scheme, although various committees and commissions recommended the same. But gradually, the British had to follow the example of the other European nations in matters of social security.

The system of social security made its appearance in India at a relatively later stage than in many of the industrially developed countries mainly due to her slow growth in industrialisation. The British Government had to initiate a few legislations in the field of social security, though it was not very serious about their rigorous implementation. Thus, a beginning in the social security programme was made in 1923, when the *Workmen's Compensation Act* was passed in that year. It also passed a few other social security legislations such as "*The Industrial Employment Standing Orders Act, 1946*", etc. However, after independence. the Indian Government retained many of these legislations introduced by the British after making suitable modifications in them. The Government also introduced on its own a number of social security legislations in order to promote the welfare of the people in general.

Social Security Legislations in India

At present, we have a number of social security legislations covering various aspects of our socio-economic life. The major objectives in the form of specified risks and the laws under which they are covered are shown in the following chart.[31]

RISKS COVERED UNDER SOCIAL SECURITY ACTS IN INDIA

Risks		Laws under which covered
1. Death	(*i*)	Workmen's Compensation Act, 1923.
	(*ii*)	Employees State insurance Act, 1948.
2. Disablement	(*i*)	Workmen's Compensation Act, 1923.
	(*ii*)	Employees' State Insurance Act, 1948.
	(*iii*)	Industrial Employment Standing Orders Act, 1946. (Medical aid in case of accident).
3. Maternity	(*i*)	Central Maternity Benefit Act, 1961.
	(*ii*)	State Maternity Benefits Acts.
	(*iii*)	Employees' State Insurance Act, 1948.
4. Sickness	(*i*)	Employees' State Insurance Act, 1948.
5. Old age	(*ii*)	The Payment of Gratuity Act, 1972.
	(*iii*)	Coal Mines Provident Fund and Bonus Scheme Act, 1948
	(*iv*)	Employees Provident Fund Act, 1952.
	(*v*)	Assam Tea Plantation Provident and Linked Insurance Fund Scheme Act, 1955. Assam Tea Plantation Provident and Pension fund and Deposit Linked Insurance Fund Scheme Act. 1955.
	(*vi*)	Seaman's Provident Fund Act, 1966
6. Funeral	(*i*)	Employees' State Insurance Act, 1948.

[31] P.C. Sikligar in *Social Security*, pp. 7-8.

SOCIAL WELFARE

Concept of Social Welfare

The term "*social welfare*" is very popularly used though it is steeped in controversy and contradictions. People disagree about its goals, methods, and consequences. What some perceive as a great "*welfare state*", others view as disgracefully inadequate compensation for continuing social and economic injustice. Services that some groups consider as a promise of restoration and rehabilitation, others brand as warehouses of misery and the graveyard of hope. Programmes that impress some citizens as symbols of the highest humanitarian values, others brush it aside as nothing but disguised agents of social control. Endless contradictions are also there within the social welfare system These contradictions are not unique to social welfare. They are the reflections of the value conflicts that are found in any society.

"*The important question is: Should social welfare simply reflect or at best, somewhat compensate for societal imperfections? Or does it have a responsibility for striving toward social justice and equality ? If the farmer role is sufficient, the mere existence of a network of benefits and services, however inadequate, irrational, or maldistributed, may bring a sense of accomplishment. But if the latter is paramount, then social welfare must be judged against standards of equality and social justice and by its success in translating humanitarian values into living realities.*"[32]

Broader Meaning of the Term "Social Welfare"

The term 'social welfare' denotes the well- being of the individual and the community. The primary objective of social welfare is to secure for each individual the basic economic necessities, high standards of health, decent living conditions, equal opportunities with his fellow-citizens and self-respect. The extent to which provision should be the responsibility of the state or the individual is a central issue running through many debates in modern society.

The term social welfare includes various social welfare programmes launched for the benefit of the individual or the community. Social welfare programmes signify "programmes of formal agencies, either governmental or private, designed to aid poor and disadvantaged individuals...[33]

Definition of Social Welfare

1. **Prof. Friedlander:** "*Social welfare is an organised system of social services and institutions, designed to aid individuals and groups, to attain satisfying standards of life and health. It aims at personal and social relationships which permit individuals the development of their capacities and the promotion of their well-being in harmony with the needs of community.*
2. **Elizabeth Wickenden:** "*Social welfare includes those laws, programmes, benefits, and services which assure or strengthen provisions for meeting social needs recognized as basic to the well- being of the population and the better functioning of the social order.*[34]
3. **Collins Dictionary of Sociology :** The concept of "*social welfare refers to "the general state of health, wellbeing and happiness of individuals or a society...*"
4. The term social Welfare has come to be defined as - "*a set of social services intended to meet the special needs of individuals and groups who because of social, economic, physical and mental handicaps, are unable to make use of services in the community, or have traditionally been denied the use of these services.*[35]
5. ***As Per United Nations Document*** **:** "*For Planning purposes, the field of social welfare can be defined as a body of organised activities which are basically meant to enable individuals, groups and communities to improve their own situation, adjust to changing conditions and participate in the tasks of development.*[36]
6. ***Social Welfare in the Indian Context*** **:** "*The term is rather given a narrow meaning in the Indian context. Thus, in a restricted sense, social welfare includes - the provision of social welfare services for the socially underprivileged groups, scheduled castes, scheduled tribes, denotified communities, orphans, widows. unmarried mothers, women in moral danger; aged and infirm, women and children, socially maladjusted', beggars, prostitutes, delinquents,*

---

[32] Winfred Bell in *Contemporary Social Welfare*, Second Edition, Macmillan Publication, p. 1.

[33] *Dictionary of Sociology* by William P. Scott, p. 396.

[34] As quoted by Winfred Bell in *Contemporary Social Welfare*, p. 2.

[35] As quoted by D.Paul Chowdhary in *Handbook of Social Welfare*, p. 5.

[36] As per the document prepared by the United Nations on *Social Welfare Planning in the Context of National Development Plans*, as quoted by Dr. D.R.Sachadeva in *Social Welfare Administration in India*, pp. 5-6.

physically and mentally disabled, diseased, mentally retarded or ill and economically underprivileged such as destitutes and unemployed, and social welfare programmes are therefore directed to ameliorate their conditions."[37]

Vast Scope of Social Welfare

The above mentioned definitions point out that social welfare covers a very wide area of human service. It embraces a long list of *income maintenance benefits and educational, developmental, medical, rehabilitative, urban renewal, housing, vocational, recreational, protective, and counselling services.*

Social welfare programmes provide direct services to individuals, groups and neighbourhoods. They serve people of all ages. They are organized by all levels of government and under voluntary auspices. They are administered by many federal, state, and local agencies. They include community- based and institutional services. Some are national and some regional in scope; many are concentrated in large cities. Directly and indirectly, they affect every citizen in the nation.

Referring to the usage of the term social welfare in the Indian context, **Smt. Durgabai Deshmukh** points out : "*The concept of social welfare is distinct from that of general social services like education and health etc. 'Social welfare is specialised work for the benefit of the weaker and more vulnerable sections of the population and would include social services for the benefit of women, children, the physically handicapped, the mentally retarded and those specially handicapped in many ways*."[38]

Durgabai Deshmukh further says that "*social welfare was the result, and social work was the process employed to secure it. Social workers were the people working through social work and welfare... If the process was understood, the attendant skills were appreciated... the social policy makers, social planners, social administrators, professionals and lay social workers were properly equipped, then the quality of social welfare services would improve and expansion of social welfare programmes and services would be less difficult...* "[39]

Two Characteristics of Social Welfare

According to **Wayne Vasey**, the definition of social welfare includes two main characteristics. They are as follows :

(*a*) ***The utilisation of welfare measures to support or strengthen the family as a basic social institution through which needs are met.*** These welfare measures include the well-being and interests of large number of people which comprises their physical, mental, emotional, spiritual and economic needs of the family members.

(*b*) ***Welfare measures have the intention of strengthening the individual's capacity to cope with his life situation.*** The social welfare system has the objective of creating the basic conditions that will enable all the members of the community in realising their potential for growth and self- fulfilment. Regardless of physical, psychological or social handicaps, person should be enabled to live, work and develop in a normal environment.

Main Objectives of Social Welfare

1. In the widest sense of the term "*social welfare*", *it may be said that social welfare has the basic object of promoting the welfare and well—being of all the members of the society.*

   Social welfare has the intention of serving all income classes. But unfortunately, as **Winfred Bell** points out, "..... *the most frequent misconception about social welfare is that it serves, only the poor. Nothing could be further from the truth.*" Around the world, as nations grow in complexity, people have recognised that collective efforts are necessary to satisfy social needs and to resolve social problems. In pre-industrialised societies, the initial focus of social welfare is on public health measures and education. As industrialisation spreads, *income maintenance programme* tends to assume importance. People of different classes make use of the benefits of such programmes.[40]

   When the provision of social welfare programmes spread benefits over all income classes, such programmes come to be known as "*universal programmes*". When they are designed solely for the poor they are called "*selective programmes*". It is quite interesting to note that "*contrary to a widespread assumption, for more is spent worldwide.... on universal programmes than on programmes limited to the poor*."[41]

---

[37] As per the U.N.O. Document as referred to above

[38] As quoted by G.R. Madan, p. 14.

[39] Smt. Durgabai Deshmukh in her preface to *Encyclopaedia of Social Work in India*, 1968, Vol. l, p. VIII as quoted by G.R. Marian, p. 14.

[40] For example, by 1933, not less than 130 nations had social security systems to assure minimum income when workers retire, become disabled, or die, while 136 had workers' compensation plans providing medical care and cash benefits for work-related illnesses or accidents. Eight-five nations had short-term sickness and maternity insurance, and forty insured workers in the event of involuntary unemployment. [Source: Winfred Bell, p. 2].

[41] In the American context, for example, by 1982, 1/6th of public social welfare expenditures were for "selective programmes". while the other 5/6th were spent on "universal programmes" like public education, social insurance, etc...—Winfred Bell, pp. 2 and 3.

2. ***Purposes of Social Welfare Programmes in the Indian Context***: Objectives of welfare programmes are to be understood in two senses in the context of the Indian social situations. ***Firstly,*** in a ***comprehensive sense***, the purpose of social welfare includes the satisfaction of the basic needs like food, clothing and shelter as well as the normal satisfaction of family life, enjoyment of physical and mental health, opportunities for the expression of skills and recreational abilities and active and pleasurable social participation. ***Secondly***, in a ***narrow sense***, the purpose of the social welfare programmes is to cater to the physical, mental and social needs of the weaker sections of the society including the handicapped and the traditionally underprivileged groups like backward classes. Who are unable to avail themselves of, or are traditionally denied the amenities and services provided by the community.

   The above idea is echoed by the views of **Pandit Nehru**, the first Prime Minister of India when he observed : "... *the welfare must be a common property of every one in India and not the monopoly of a privileged group, as it is today. In particular; those who are underprivileged today and have no opportunities of growth and progress must be brought within its fold.*" Pandit Nehru also stressed that the welfare of women, children and handicapped should have the first place in order of priority.

Functions of Social Welfare

Social welfare programmes serve both individual and societal functions. In fact, **Wickenden** in her definition, refers to the dual functions of social welfare : (*a*) *to meet the social needs of the population*, and (*b*) *to promote the better functioning of the social order.* In her literary works also she has emphasised the point that social welfare serves societal as well as individual needs or goals.

1. ***Social welfare to serve individual needs***: Social welfare is generally Understood as some organised means of protecting the interests and promoting the well-being of the poor, needy, downtrodden, underprivileged, backward, mentally, physically or otherwise handicapped. In the Indian context, it is meant to provide services to the Under previleged, disadvantaged and backward sections of the society. The most advanced and developed countries regard social welfare as *guaranteeing minimum standards of living for their citizens*. The developing countries, on the contrary, consider it to be *providing basic needs to their population*.
2. ***Social welfare to serve societal needs***: Social welfare programmes have the purpose of promoting the smooth functioning of the social order. This function or purpose is mostly underscored or neglected by most of the people. Thus, many citizens seem to believe that social welfare is a one- way traffic for conveying their hard - earned money to the poor and helpless with no hope of return. But over the last several decades it has become clear that social welfare is not just a reflection of altruism. Instead, programmes of this nature are just as vital to the host society as to individual recipients.

Social welfare programmes, especially all "*income maintenance programmes*" provide not only necessary funds to families but also support the capitalist economies, democratic set ups, by reinforcing the work ethic, instilling administration for the promoters of industry, and helping to maintain law and order. It has been observed that when great civic unrest erupts, public welfare programmes tend to increase, and soon the poor and the afflicted are "*cooled off*" by their more generous help. The generous welfare programmes and schemes make the afflicted people to understand the "hard realities" and to accept their "lot in life", however miserable it may be.

SOCIAL WELFARE AND SOCIAL WORK : COMPARED

According to **Miss Witmer**, there are many differences between the terms such as social work and social welfare; social work and social services, and so on. She says that social welfare is basically secured through the institutional organisation of society, and its activities are directed towards the improvement of that organisation. On the other hand, the activities of social work are directed towards assisting individuals in their use of social institutions. She is of the opinion that "social welfare" embraces programmes of public works, agricultural relief, resettlement, flood control, labour laws, etc., which are not immediately concerned with the client group. Whereas social work is an activity that seeks to secure for an individual or a family or a community some concrete help to come out of a distressing situation or to attain a better position.

Social welfare activities are to be distinguished from other types of social activities. ***For example***, establishment of a building and a financial company, widening of roads, forming of co-operative for a village, etc., cannot be considered social welfare activities. On the contrary, establishment of a juvenile court, parole system for the adult criminals, orphanage, home for the aged and the infirm, a beggar home, etc., are all examples of activities designed to use social welfare resources to meet social welfare needs.

Differences between Social Work and Social Welfare

Social work and social welfare are not one and the same though these terms are often used synonymously. The main differences between the two may be noted below:

1. ***Difference in the scope*** : Social welfare has a broader meaning than that of social work. It includes all social work and other related programmes and activities undertaken with the intention of promoting the well-being of the individuals, groups or community.
2. ***Difference in the orientation*** : The orientation of social work and social welfare is not one and the same. Social work is normally undertaken by highly trained practitioners for it is a profession. On the contrary, most of the voluntary workers in social welfare agencies are untrained. Social work cannot be taken up systematically by ordinary people for it has become formalised and has emerged into a specialised profession.
3. ***Unlike in the case of social welfare, social work is not imposed upon its beneficiaries***: A social worker respects the autonomy and personal worth of his client in trouble but he never imposes his ideas or programmes on him even if they are considered to be good and beneficial. On the contrary, a social welfare worker feels obliged to make available programmes and activities when once he is convinced of their utility or benefit.
4. ***Social worker always expects the client to approach him for help and guidance but not the social welfare worker***: A social worker normally mobilises the resources of his profession to help the client to help himself only after being approached by the client. Unless his help is sought in terms of counselling or material aid, the social worker does not start his work. A social welfare worker is not constrained by such things. However, in our country, social workers often go to the needy clients and enlist their co-operation in bringing about necessary changes either in the institution or in the individual, or both.
5. ***Difference between the process and the end result***: Finally, it can be stated that social work is only the process whereas social welfare is the end result of social work.

REVIEW QUESTIONS

1. Define social work. What are assumptions of social work? Discuss.
2. Bring out the distinguishing features of social work.
3. Discuss the development of social work at different stapes.
4. Write the scope of social work. Discuss the methods and techniques of social work.
5. Write in brief about social welfare administration.
6. What are the requirements of a profession. Is social work a profession? Examine.
7. Bring out the relations of social work with sociology, economics, psychology and psychiatry.
8. Explain the concept of social security. Discuss the scope and forms of social security.
9. What are the main components of social security? Describe.
10. Discuss the origin and development of social security.
11. Explain the concept of social welfare. Write the scope and characteristic features of social welfare.
12. Write the objectives and functions of social welfare.
13. Compare social welfare and social work.

⌘⌘⌘⌘⌘⌘⌘⌘⌘⌘⌘

PART ELEVEN

Sociological Thought

Contributions of:

- Auguste Comte
- Herbert Spencer
- Emile Durkheim
- Max weber, and
- Karl Marx

54

INTRODUCTION TO SOCIAL THOUGHT

CHAPTER OUTLINE

- Meaning and Nature of Social Thought
- Development of Social Thought
- Sociology and Social Thought
- Importance of the Study of Social Thought.

MEANING AND NATURE OF SOCIAL THOUGHT

Man is not only a "Social Being", but also a Reasoning Animal

Man is not like other animals. He is an animal of extra-ordinary abilities and capacities. He is the final product of organic evolution and as such has greater capacities to adjust himself to the environment. He not only adjusts himself to the environment, if need arises, he even modifies the environment to suit to his conveniences. Other animals cannot do this; they can only adjust to the existing environment and their failure to do so would ultimately result either in their death, or in their running away from the situation. Man's life is many-sided. Hence, he claims himself to be a "*social animal*", a "*political animal*", a "*cultural being*" and so on. He is also called a "*thinking animal*" or a "*reasoning animal.*" Man with the help of his more evolved brain and greater intelligence has been thinking about a number of things. The physical world itself posed a big puzzle for him. In the beginning, various natural phenomena such as birth and death, day and night, health and ill-health, rotation of seasons, etc.... constituted the content of his thinking process. In course of time, he shifted his attention towards various non-physical things. It is impossible to prepare an exhaustive list of things which man's mind today is pre-occupied with. No such attempt is made in this book either.

Social Thought as a By-product of Social Interaction

Man does not live in isolation. He is social in nature and always prefers to live in the company of other men. Sociality or sociability has become an essential and inextricable aspect of his life. The individual and society are hence inseparable. Man's life is interwoven with society. Sociality or sociability has been the central problem in sociological discussions. "*Why man depends on society*?" — is a pertinent question for which we have different and even contradictory explanations. Each aspect of man's social life must have been the result of at least some people's experiences, mutual adjustments, and experiments. People must have been directly or indirectly, and explicitly or implicitly thinking about the ways in which they could share their feelings and emotions, problems and challenges, miseries and maladies, etc., from the very beginning. They must have also tried on their own the ways of facing the problems and challenges of life, to secure some amount of stability for their social life and contentment for their individual mind. The thought that they have entertained in this regard, no matter how irrational and unscientific it is, could be referred to as "*social thought.*"

Definition of the term "Social Thought"

In simple words, it can be said that "*social thought*" *essentially refers to the thought concerning the social life and activities of man.* Sociologists have given their own definitions of social thought among which the following may be cited.

- **Bogardus:** "*Social thought is thinking about social problems by one or a few persons here and there in human history or at the present.*"
- **Rollin Chambliss:** "*Social thought is concerned with human beings in their relations with their fellows.*"
- **H. E. Jenson:** Social thought is "*the totality of man's thought about his relationship and obligations to his fellowmen.*"
- **William P. Scott:** "*Social thought refers to any relatively systematic attempt to theorise about society and social life, whether it be classical or modern, scientific or unscientific.*"

CHARACTERISTICS OF SOCIAL THOUGHT

1. *Social Thought is Societal Thought*

Social thought is basically the thought regarding societal issues or matters. It is concerned with the ways in which people live together and face collectively their problems and challenges. These thoughts may themselves have solutions to these problems.

2. *Social Thought is not the Sum Total of the Thoughts of all the Members of Society*

Social thought has evolved out of the capacity for critical and analytical thinking of a few scholars, rationalists, scientists and philosophers. People of average intelligence can hardly enrich the existing social thought. Only a handful of people can delve deep into the social matters, events, and problems and form opinions and theories about them. **Bogardus** thus comments: "*However, the developing and perfecting of new ideologies are usually the work of scholars, somewhat removed from the turmoil of the hour. Social thought thus is the product of social crisis and of scholarly analysis and synthesis.*"[1]

3. *Social Thought need not Necessarily be Scientific Always*

Social thought touches upon various aspects of our social life, experiences, conclusions, opinions, assessments, valuations, etc. All these cannot be put to scientific tests to assess their validity and dependability. In spite of this deficiency they have their own practical importance.

4. *Social Thought is not the Same Everywhere*

Social thought has been immensely influenced by factors such as time, place, environment and conditions. Social thought normally arises in part from the nature of the prevailing social conditions. To understand it properly the student must know the times which furnish the setting for it. "*A thorough going knowledge of the culture and of the social, economic, political and religious standards of a people is a minimum essential for a social thought.*"

5. *Every Human Community has given its own Contribution to the Development of Social Thought*

Social thought is not the monopoly of any particular community. At the same time all the nations or communities have not contributed equally to its enrichment. For example, the ancient Indian, Chinese, Egyptian, Babylonian, and Hebrew civilisations of the East and the ancient Greek and the Roman civilisations of the West, have given commendable contributions to the realm of social thought. The rural and the tribal people also have played their role in the enrichment of social thought.

6. *Social Thought is Continuous in its Development*

Social thought has been found to be consistent in its development. As **Bogardus** has pointed out, "*the history of social thought rises out of the beginnings of human struggle on earth and with jogged edges extends along the full sweep of the changing historical horizons.*"

7. *Social Crises or Hardships have Always Provided Motivation for the General Social Thought*

Social thought usually finds its initial expression during social crises. When "*prosperity*" reigns and people are, in general, satisfied, new social thought is at ebb tide. But when social conditions are marked by gross injustices or when social changes come rapidly due to inventions, wars, or other basic disturbances, the thinking about social life and problems is highly stimulated and new ideas or systems of ideas, that is, ideologies, are originated.

8. *Other Characteristics*

(*i*) *Social thought though continuous is very slow and gradual* in its development. We do not find fast developments taking place in this field as in the realm of physical sciences.

---

[1] Bogardus in *The Development of Social Thought* 1960, p. 8.

(*ii*) *Major portion of the social thought is not found to be preserved in the form of books* but in the unwritten forms such as folklores, folksongs, legends, myths, folktales and so on.

(*iii*) "*Social thought is abstract*" - says **Bogardus.** All thinking is abstract and social thought is no exception to this general rule.

(*iv*) *Social thought has not always been utilitarian and beneficial* to mankind. It has been, at times, abused by some people to subserve their own ends. **Ex:** (*i*) The theory of inborn superiority of the Aryan Race advocated by Nazis of Germany. (*ii*) The ideologies such as Gandhianism, socialism, secularism, etc. are being abused by different people in India today for different purposes.

DEVELOPMENT OF SOCIAL THOUGHT

Social thought is not something that emerges suddenly or abruptly. Its development is slow and gradual. Old thoughts form the basis for the new ones. New thoughts do not completely negate the old ones. Many a times we find the combination of the old and the new. Social thought in its historical development can be stated to have undergone at least four important stages namely: (1) *Stage of folklore*, (2) *Stage of Social Philosophy*, (3) *Stage of Social Theory*, and (4) *the Stage of Social Sciences.*

1. The Stage of Folklore

Pre-literate people were also inquisitive. They thought about the dramatic phases of life, and they sought their own explanation. Their imagination worked out only supernatural explanations. They reasoned about the daily occurrences of life in concrete and personal terms. Archaeological records indicate that the pre-literate people had a simple and crude awareness which had its own social implications. Early mythologies speak of the importance of social bonds which early people had developed among themselves. The proverbs of the primitive people give us some idea about social property and social responsibility. Folktales, folksongs, etc., give us ideas about the primitive man's family, life, his religious beliefs, social organisations such as clans and so on.

There are enough proofs to say that primitive man's mind entertained social thinking. Communal property was the outcome of communal thinking. Group dances, feasts, festivals, building enterprises, celebrations, etc., denote a social spirit. Warfare, which they engaged in, indicate tribal loyalty and group spirit. Folkways of these people mirror their notions of societal welfare. All these things reveal the beginnings of social thought. Though it appears premature today, it had its own prominence then.

2. The Stage of Social Philosophy

Just as human society proceeded from simplicity to complexity, human thinking also started becoming more complex. Early people started thinking in terms of facing the challenges in a better manner, and finding solutions to the social problems more efficiently. In their efforts to do so, their thinking style underwent a change. It got ascended from the stage of folklore to the stage of social philosophy. In the stage of social philosophy, large number of poets, philosophers, moralists, spiritual leaders, metaphysical thinkers, social visionaries, social reformers and others expressed their views, and enriched human thought. Their views influenced the ways of life then and also of the future generations. The views of Manu on Varnashrama system, the opinions of Kautilya on politics, the beliefs of Confucius on ideal family, and practical morals, etc., could be cited here as examples.

3. The Stage of Social Theory

In the stage of social theory, there is scope for discussion, logic, analysis, appreciation, acceptance, rejection and so on. The views or ideas expressed or advocated by a philosopher or scholar need not necessarily be accepted by all as though it is "*divine*", "*unchangeable*" and "*ultimate.*" The views of Manu, Aristotle, Cicero, Confucius and others were taken for granted in the beginning. As years passed on, social theoreticians like John Locke, Thomas Hobbes, Rousseau, Karl Marx, Adam Smith, Ferguson, Machiavelli, Montesquieu, and a host of others established their own theories regarding human society and its dynamics. Jeremy Betham's "*Utilitarianism*", Thomas More's "*Utopianism*", Spencer's "*theory of social evolution*", Marxian "*theory of classless society*", Huntington, Lombroso and other social geographer's "*theory of geographic determinism*" can be mentioned here as examples.

4. The Stage of Social Sciences

It is very difficult to say when exactly the stage of social sciences began, because different social sciences emerged at different times. ***Example***: Political science and history are pretty old social sciences, whereas anthropology, psychology and sociology are quite new. The success attained and the progress registered in the field of natural sciences also provided inspiration for the social thinkers to emulate the same in the field of social sciences. The methods that helped the physical sciences to attain success were also borrowed to understand and analyse the social world in a scientific manner. This new approach added precision, credibility and dependability to the social sciences. Most of the social sciences have now obtained a stage in which they stand on their own, have their own field of study, and pursue their own approach. They have modified the scientific method and procedure to suit to their needs and conveniences. Sociology, which has joined the family of social sciences at a later stage has also made an impressive beginning and progress in its studies.

SOCIOLOGY AND SOCIAL THOUGHT

The terms such as "*social thought*", "*sociology*" or "*sociological thought*" or "*social theory*", "*sociological theory*"[2], though are not one and the same, are closely interrelated. It is true that roots of sociology are to be found in social thought and social philosophy. Social thought itself provided the stimulus for the establishment of sociology. Further, the pioneers of sociology, like Comte, Durkhiem, Spencer, Weber, Marx and others were more recognised during their lifetime as social thinkers than as sociologists. In spite of the affinity between social thought and sociology or sociological thought they are not one and the same. The main differences between the two can be briefly examined here.

1. Sociology and Social Thought: Difference in Meaning

"Sociology" is the science of society. Its main purpose is to study human life, activities and relations in a scientific way. It is an independent science by itself and applies scientific method to its studies. Whereas *social thought* is nothing but societal-thought; it is the totality of man's thought about his relationships with his fellowmen. According to **Bogardus,** it is co-equal with social problems. As and when social problems cropped up, the social thought sprang up. Social thought is a kind of thought and it need not necessarily be classical or systematic in its nature.

2. Sociological Study is more Scientific whereas Social Thought is more General in Nature

Sociology has become a relatively well established social science. It is able to make a scientific analysis of human society, its structure, function, organisation, institutional network, changes, challenges, problems and so on. Sociology is now recognised as an empirical and a rational science. It tries to be "*value-free*" in its approach and objective in its findings.

Social thought, on the contrary, is bound by the values, norms and the expectations of the people of a particular epoch. There is no insistence on it to be scientific. Plato's "*idealism*", Hindus' concept of "*Rama Rajya*", Marx's "*Communism*", Bentham's "*Utilitarianism*" or Gandhiji's "*Sarvodaya*", etc. for example, represent high thoughts, but they are not considered as scientific. They are either regarded as value-based or imaginary or even ideological. Social thought is more based on logic, imagination, intuition, and capacity of creative thinking, whereas sociology is based on science, rationality, empiricism and reality.

3. Sociology has a Limited Range while Social Thought is more Pervasive

Sociological thoughts or theories have limited range. They are applicable to limited contexts. They contain issues or themes which are basically social in nature. On the contrary, the scope of social thought is wider. It is all-inclusive, because it may incorporate in itself knowledge that is not only social but also spiritual, moral, political, economic, psychological, philosophical, and so on.

4. Social Thought is ancient whereas Sociology is Modern

Social thought is old when compared with either sociology or sociological thought. The history of social thought is very ancient and it begins from pre-historic times, whereas the history of sociology and sociological thought is very short; it begins from the time of Auguste Comte.

---

2. **Terminological Clarifications**

(a) ***Social Theory***: "Social Theory" is a term often used to refer to all or any general theoretical accounts of social relations, whatever their disciplinary base or origin.

(b) ***Sociological Theory:*** This term is used in a narrow sense to the theory produced by those fully identified with, and working within, paradigms clearly located within disciplinary sociology.

The distinction between the two is not a hard-and-fast one. Many sociologists prefer to work with whichever theories appear most relevant, whatever their disciplinary source might be in doing this as "social theorists" — *Collins Dictionary,* pp. 625-626.

(c) ***Sociological Thought:*** The thought that has emanated from the scientific study of social life and social ideas, that is, the thought process that began with such thinkers as Comte, Durkhiem, Weber and others. In this sense, sociological thought is more akin to sociological theory.

5. Other Differences

(*a*) *Social thought adopts no scientific criterion of validity* whereas in the case of sociology or sociological thought there is definite validity criterion.

(*b*) Only the *people with specialised skills and training can make contributions to the realm of sociology* whereas, any knowledgable person whether he is a scientist or an artist, a philosopher or a social reformer, a psychologist or an educationist, an uneducated man or an educated one, an ordinary man or a genius, can enrich the field of social thought.

(*c*) Thinkers who contributed to the realm of social thought were known as social reformers, social philosophers, social visionaries, social revolutionaries and so on, but *not as sociologists.* The era of sociology and sociologists began only in the middle of the 18th century.

George Ritzer thus writes: "*In any case, none of the thinkers associated with those eras thought of themselves, and few are now thought of, as sociologists ..... It is only in the middle and late 1800s that we begin to find thinkers who can be clearly identified as sociologists.*"[3]

IMPORTANCE OF THE STUDY OF SOCIAL THOUGHT

Social thought is the product of human thinking. Man has been thinking about society, social environment, social events, happenings, developments, problems, etc. from the beginning. Even the primitive man had his own thinking about society. With the progress of civilisation, man's thinking became more and more complex. The study of social thought assumed importance in various respects.

1. Social Thought Provides Information about the Present Social Scene

Study of social thought is important because it gives an idea about contemporary social science, environments and circumstances of a particular society. It mirrors the environment of a society at any particular point of time or during a particular period.

2. Social Thought Throws Light on Social Problems

No society is free from problems. Any society experiences many types of problems. Social thought usually finds its initial expression during social crisis. When "*social conditions are marked by gross injustices or when social changes come rapidly due to inventions, wars or other basic disturbances, then thinking about social life and problems is highly stimulated and new ideas or systems of ideas, that is, ideologies are originated.*"[4]

3. Social Thought Helps Solve Social Problems

Social thought not only provides information about social problems encountered in different societies and different times but also about the efforts made by these people to solve them. This knowledge can be of great help in solving the problems of our own age. Indeed, no contemporary social problem can be grasped fully without an extensive knowledge of the social history of thought.

4. Social Thought Helps Common People also

It is true that "*the developing and perfecting of new social ideologies are usually the work of scholars somewhat removed from the turmoil of the hour.*" [**Bogardus** - 8.] But in our practical life, the common people are also involved in fighting against the social problems [such as corruption, divorce, dowry, environment pollution, youth unrest, etc.]

5. Social Thought has Lessons to Teach

Social thought helps man in rectifying the blunders committed in the past. Both man and society are falliable. Mistakes are committed both at the individual and social level. These misdeeds or erroneous acts can be rectified by experience. Neither an individual nor any collective group can have all types of experiences. Social thought, indeed, is nothing but a narration of the experience of societies at different points in history.

6. Social Thoughts Influence Our Life, Our Thoughts, Values and Ideologies

Thoughts have tremendous impact on our life and doings. Hence **Plato** said long back "*ideologies rule the world.*" **J.M. Keynes** had recognised this fact when he said: "*The ideas of economists and political philosophers, both when they*

---

[3] George Ritzer in *Contemporary Sociological Theory*, p. 4.

[4] Bogardus in *The Development of Social Thought*, p. 8.

are right and when they are wrong, are more powerful than is commonly understood. Indeed, the world is ruled by little else......" It is an acknowledged fact today that social thinking has its impact on religious, philosophical, psychological and even physical thinking.

7. The Unfading Influence of the Old Thoughts

In the realm of the physical world normally new knowledge completely dominates the old knowledge and sometimes its traces are washed away. Such a thing does not happen in the realm of social thought. Age old thoughts relating to the subtle topics such as God, ideal conditions of the state, man's ultimate purpose in life, role of spirituality in life, etc., still hold their sway. Very often we make references to them in our discussions and debates.

8. Old Social Thoughts may Give Rise to New Ones

Progress in the field of social sciences does not automatically and inevitably lead to the destruction of the old social thoughts. On the contrary, many a times, old thoughts may trigger new ones, or new interpretations are given to the old ones. No society finds it relevant to reject outrightly the old thoughts to accept new ones.

REVIEW QUESTIONS

1. What do you mean by social thought? Explain the nature of social thought.
2. Man is not only a social being, but also a reasoning animal? Comments.
3. Highlight the characteristic features of social thought.
4. Elaborate on the development of social thought.
5. Describe the various stapes of the development of social thought.
6. Differentiate between sociology and social thought.
7. Assess the importance of the study of social throught.

⌘⌘⌘⌘⌘⌘⌘⌘⌘⌘⌘

55

AUGUSTE COMTE AND HIS THOUGHTS

CHAPTER OUTLINE

- BRIEF BIOGRAPHIC SKETCH OF AUGUSTE COMTE
- MAIN WORKS OF COMTE
- COMTEAN POSITIVISM—MEANING OF POSITIVISM
- POSITIVISM AS A DOCTRINE AND AS A METHOD—CRITICISMS AGAINST POSITIVISM
- LAW OF THREE STAGES —THEOLOGICAL STAGE—METAPHYSICAL STAGE POSITIVE STAGE—STAGES IN SOCIAL ORGANISATION AND PROGRESS
- CLASSIFICATION OF SCIENCES —SPECIAL FEATURES OF COMTEAN CLASSIFICATION—CONCLUDING COMMENTS
- COMTE'S VIEWS REGARDING SOCIOLOGY
- RELIGION OF HUMANITY—SOME SALIENT FEATURES OF COMTEAN RELIGION
- AN ESTIMATE OF COMTE'S ACHIEVEMENTS.

BRIEF BIOGRAPHIC SKETCH OF AUGUSTE COMTE

Auguste Comte [1798-1857] was a great French thinker, a famous social philosopher and the first sociologist. It was he who laid the foundations of sociology and is acclaimed as the "*father of sociology*". He insisted that the science of society, that is, sociology, should be treated on par with other sciences. Sociology has gone far ahead in the scientific tradition about which Comte had insisted. The community of sociologists remains ever grateful to Comte for his pioneering works to make sociology a science.

Comte was born at Montpellier, France, on 19th Jan. 1798, a decade after the French Revolution. His parents were very humble, law-abiding and highly religious. His father was a government servant and a royalist and a traditionalist. From the very beginning, Comte exhibited extra-ordinary mental ability, a strong character, and a tendency to go against authority. He was often described as "*brilliant and recalcitrant.*" He was a voracious reader and had an excellent memory power. In school, he won many prizes and led the students who used to call him "*the philosopher.*"

Auguste Comte
[1798-1857]

Comte received his primary education at the Imperial Lycee and joined the famous "*Ecole Polytechnique*" in Paris at the age of 16. Here he was taught by professors of physics and mathematics who had no interest in the study of human affairs and society. But unlike them, Comte developed great social and human concern.

As a youth, Comte was critical of Napoleon's administration and disliked both parental and religious authority. He even led a group of students in demanding the resignation of one of his instructors at the school. Though Comte was a bright student he never received a college-level degree. This had a negative effect on his teaching career. In 1818, he became secretary to **Saint Simon, [1760-1825]** a philosopher, forty years senior to Comte. Saint Simon was a great socialist thinker of the day, and was often referred to as a socialist dreamer. Comte became his secretary for which he was getting 300 francs per month as salary. In course of time, Comte became his co-worker, co-writer and co-thinker. The friendship between the two lasted only for a few years, that is, up to 1824 only. They jointly published the work "*Plan of the Scientific Operations Necessary for the Reorganisation of Society*" - 1822; [also known as "*The Prospectus of the Scientific Works Required for the Reorganisation of Society*"] and thereafter their partnership dissolved. Comte believed that Saint Simon was not giving him adequate credit for his contributions.

Comte married in the year 1825 but within 17 years, that is, in 1842, his wife deserted him. He almost led an isolated life for a long time due to his personal disappointments and quarrels with others. He had to face economic crisis also. A small group of his admirers invited him to deliver a series of private lectures on positive philosophy. Good number of learned men including scientists and economists were attending his lectures. His lecture notes were later published (between 1830-42) in six volumes running to 4800 pages which constituted his masterly work called "*Course of Positive Philosophy*". This treatise fetched him a sizeable number of admirers even outside France. **J.S. Mill** of England, a famous philosopher, for example, was impressed by his work.

In 1826, Comte thought of a scheme of presenting a series of 72 lectures on his philosophy of life. The course drew a distinguished audience. It was, however, halted after three lectures when Comte suffered a nervous breakdown. He was unhappy with his wife whom he had married in 1825 [and who deserted him in 1842]. At one stage in 1827 he sought to commit suicide by throwing himself into the Seine river.

Comte had taken to teaching at the Ecole Polytechnique. During this period Comte worked on the famous six volume work-running to 4800 pages, known as "*Positive Philosophy*" ["*Cours de Philosophie Positive*"]. In that work Comte was the first to use the term ***"sociology"***. He also outlined his view that sociology was the ultimate science. This book fetched him a sizeable number of admirers even outside France.

By 1851, Comte had completed the four Volume book entitled "*System of Positive Politics*" ["*Systeme de Polytique Positive*"]. This book proposed to offer a grand plan for the reorganisation of society. Here Comte tried to apply the findings of theoretical sociology to the solutions of social problems.

Comte had a series of bizarre ideas. He believed in "*cerebral hygiene*", and to preserve his mental health he stopped reading the works of other writers. He wanted to suggest proposals for the improvement of society. But in his attempts to do so he deviated from the path and established the "*religion of humanity*" claiming himself to be its high priest.

Comte, whose life was beset with stresses and strains, conflicts and controversies, poverty and isolation, breathed his last on 5th Sept. 1857. The religion which he started died along with him but the science he set out continues to flourish.

MAIN WORKS OF AUGUSTE COMTE

1. "*The Prospectus of the Scientific Works Required for the Reorganisation of Society*", 1822 - A joint work of Comte and Saint Simon.
2. "*Positive Philosophy*", 1830-1842 - in six volumes.
3. "*Positive Polity*", 1851-54 - in four volumes.

COMTEAN POSITIVISM

The acknowledged founder of "*positivism*" or "*positive philosophy*" is no other than the French philosopher Comte himself. "Positivism" is nothing but a "*philosophy of science.*" It has its roots in the "*empiricist tradition.*" It rejects metaphysical speculation in favour of "*positive*" knowledge based on systematic observation and experiment. Though Comte is regarded as the founder of positivism, he was influenced by the writings of **David Hume** and **Claude H. Saint-Simon.**

Meaning of Positivism

- Positivism refers to "*the doctrine formulated by Comte which asserts that the only true knowledge is scientific knowledge, that is, knowledge which describes and explains the co-existence and succession of observable phenomena, including both physical and social phenomena.*"[1]
- Positivism denotes "*any sociological approach which operates on the general assumption that the methods of physical sciences (example, measurement, search for general laws, etc.) can be carried over into the social sciences.*"[2]

Nature of Comtean Positivism

Comte used the term "positivism" in two distinctive ways: (*i*) *positivism as a* "*doctrine*" and (*ii*) *positivism as a* "*method*".

[1] *Collins Dictionary of Sociology*, p. 506.
[2] Ibid, p. 507.

Positivism as a Doctrine

***Positivism as a way of thinking*:** As developed by Auguste Comte, positivism is a way of thinking based on the assumption that it is possible to observe social life and establish reliable, valid knowledge about how it works. Such knowledge can be used to affect the course of change and improve the human condition.

Positivism of Comte which represents a philosophical position states that knowledge can be derived only from sensory experience. Metaphysical speculation, subjective or intuitive insight, and purely logical analysis, are rejected as outside the realm of true knowledge. The methods of the physical sciences are regarded as ***the only accurate means*** of obtaining knowledge, and therefore, the social sciences should be limited to the use of these methods and modelled after the physical sciences.

Positivism as a Method

***Positivism implies the use of scientific method*:** By the concept of "*positivism*", Comte meant the application of scientific methods to understand society and its changes. Applying this concept to the modern societies, Comte emphasised that sociology must depend on careful observation, usually based on statistical measures of social statics and social dynamics. He also recognised that sociology would have to be less experimental than the physical sciences because of the ethical and practical difficulties intervening in people's lives.

Comte believed that social life is governed by underlying laws and principles that can be discovered through the use of methods most often associated with the physical sciences. In choosing the term "positivism", Comte conveyed his intention to repudiate all reliance on earlier religious or speculative metaphysical bases of knowledge' (see Law of Three Stages). However, Comte regarded scientific knowledge as *'relative knowledge'*, not absolute. Absolute knowledge was, and always would be unavailable.

Positivism would essentially mean a method of approach. The methods of science can give us knowledge of the laws of co-existence and succession of phenomena, but can never penetrate to the inner "*essence*" or "*nature*" of things. As applied to the human social world, the positive method yields a law of successive states through which each branch of knowledge must first pass, that is, the *theological,* then *metaphysical,* and finally *positive* [or *scientific*] state. Since the character of society flows from the intellectual forms which predominate in it, this gives Comte a law of the development of human society itself.

***Positivism deifies observation and classification of data*:** According to Comte, positivism is purely an intellectual way of looking at the world. He believed that the mind should concentrate on the observation and classification of phenomena. He believed that both theological and metaphysical speculations as he used the terms, were as likely to be fiction as truth, and that there is no way of determining which is the cause. Thus, it would be more profitable if a person would direct his thoughts to the lines of thinking which are most truly prolific, namely to observation and classification of data. Comte even took the position that it is futile to try to determine causes. We can observe uniformities, or laws, but it is mere speculation to assign causes to these uniformities. *Positivism deified observation and classification of data.* Its weaknesses should not hinder the student, however, from seeing the importance of its emphasis upon the scientific procedure of observing and classifying data in an age when dogmatism and speculation were rife.[3]

Comte's work was much admired by **John Stuart Mill**, amongst others, and positivism became something of a popular movement in the latter part of the nineteenth century. But Comte's views shifted later in his life, under the influence of Clotilde de Vaux. He came to see that science alone did not have the binding force for social cohesion, as he had earlier supposed. He argued that *the intellect must become the servant of the heart, and advocated a new 'Religion of Humanity'*.[4]

Impact of Positivism on Social Thinking

Comte's "positivism" has its own impact on the world of social thinking. Today, positivism signifies adherence to an empiricist view of the nature of science. It also projects a scientific approach to the study of social life on the empiricist model. As far as the social sciences are concerned, this would mean modelling of the methods of social sciences on those of natural science. It also signifies an attempt to discover social laws similar to the law-like regularities discovered by natural sciences and an absolute insistence on the separation of facts and values.

Criticisms Against Positivism

1. ***Positivism is not influential at present*:** Positivism has had relatively little influence in contemporary sociology for several reasons. Current views argue that positivism encourages a misleading emphasis on superficial facts without

3. Bogardus in his *The Development of Social Thought,* p. 235.
4. *Oxford Dictionary of Sociology*, p. 510.

any attention to underlying mechanisms that cannot be observed. ***For example,*** we cannot observe human motives or the meaning that people give to behaviour and other aspects of social life, but this does not mean that meaning and motive are nonexistent or irrelevant. Some argue that the nature of social life is such that the methods used in the physical sciences are simply inapplicable and must be replaced with a less rigid approach.[5]

2. *Methological gulf between the physical and social sciences*: "Criticisms of positivism commonly focus on the inappropriateness of natural-scientific methods in the human or social sciences. Consciousness, cultural norms, symbolic meaning, and intentionality, etc., are variously held to be distinctive human attributes which dictate a methodological gulf between natural science and the study of human social life."[6]

3. *Problem of verification*: "Methodologically, a central problem of positivism arises from the so-called '*problem of empiricism*'; the lack of any conclusive basis for *'verification'* in '*inductive logic*'. A further telling criticism - the so-called 'paradox of positivism' - is that the verification principle is itself unverifiable.[7]

In spite of the criticisms levelled against the term "positivism", it is still used [more usually as logical positivism][8] to refer to the radical empiricism and scientism advanced in the early decades of the 20th century by the "*Vienna Circle.*" This is usually considered to be the major influence on modern 20th century sociological positivism.

LAW OF THREE STAGES

The theory of "*The Law of Three Stages*" constitutes one of the main contributions of Comte to the field of sociological thought. The influence of Charles Darwin and his "*theory of organic evolution*" had its own impact on Comtean views including his law of three stages.

Auguste Comte organised and classified the social thought prevailing before his times. Comte gave birth not only to a specific methodology of studying knowledge but also analyzed the evolution of human thinking and its various stages. The principle evolved by Comte in the study of human thinking presumes gradual evolution and development in human thinking and is known as *the law of three stages of thinking.*

Affinity between the Development of Human Knowledge and the Development of Society

Comte who was busy in laying the foundations of a new social science, began his task with an analysis of types of thinking. Comte elaborated the Law of Three Stages of human thought (or the Law of Human Progress): *theological, metaphysical* and *positive.* These Stages, he thought, characterised the development of both human knowledge and of society, which correspondingly developed from a military to a legal, and finally to an industrial stage. According to Comte, the evolution of the human mind has paralleled the evolution of the individual mind. Just as an individual tends to be a staunch believer in childhood, a critical metaphysician in adolescence, and a natural philosopher in manhood, so mankind in its growth has followed three major stages. Comte believed that each field of knowledge passes through three periods of growth namely:

(*i*) First stage: Theological or Fictitious Stage

(*ii*) Second stage: Metaphysical or Abstract Stage

(*iii*) Third stage: Positive or Scientific Stage

Theological Stage

The primitive persons everywhere tend to think in supernatural terms. They believe that all phenomena are "*produced by the immediate action of supernatural beings.*" They believe in all kinds of fetishes in which spirits or supernatural beings live. Hence, "*fetishism*" as a form of religion started and it admitted of no priesthood, because its gods are individuals, each residing in fixed objects.

When the mind of primitive man became better organised, fetishism became cumbersome. Too many fetishes created confusion. Hence, they started believing in several gods. Thus arose *polytheism.* They created the class of priests to get the goodwill and the blessings of these gods. The presence of too many gods also created for them mental contradictions. Hence, they arranged the gods, in the form of hierarchy. Finally, they developed the idea of one god, or of *monotheism.* They started believing in the superhuman power of only one god. Slowly feelings and imaginations started giving place to

5. *The Blackwell Dictionary of Sociology*, pp. 207-208.
6. *Oxford Dictionary of Sociology*, p. 510
7. *Collins Dictionary of Sociology*, p. 507.
8. Logical positivism refers to the philosophical viewpoint of a group of philosophers in the 1920s and 30s known collectively as the *Vienna Circle*, whose ideas were in part based on Comte but presented as giving Comte's positivism a more secure logical basis. The Central doctrine of the Vienna Circle, the verification principle, states that the only valid knowledge is knowledge which is verified by sensory experience. — *Collins Dictionary of Sociology*, p. 506.

thinking and rationality. Monotheism is the climax of the theological stage of thinking. *This kind of thinking was suited to the military society.*

Metaphysical Stage

The metaphysical thinking is almost an extension of the theological thinking. Rationalism started growing instead of imagination. Rationalism states that God does not stand directly behind every phenomenon. Pure reasoning insists that God is an *Abstract Being.* Reasoning helped man to find out some order in the natural world. The continuity, regularity and infallibility found in the natural order were attributed to some "*Principles*" or "*Power*". Thus, principles and theories gained ascendency over feelings and speculations. Even these metaphysical explanations were unsatisfactory to the mind. Still *this kind of thinking corresponded with the legal type of society,* Comte maintained.

Positive Stage

The positive stage represents the scientific way of thinking. As Comte stated, "*In the final, the positive stage, the mind has given over the vain search after Absolute notions, the origin and destination of the universe, and the causes phenomena, and applies itself to the study of their laws - that is, their invariable relations of succession and resemblance.*"

Comte developed his concept of positivism, which is a purely intellectual way of looking at the world. He stressed the need for observation and classification of phenomena. He even said that it is futile to try to determine causes. "*We can observe uniformities, or laws, but it is mere speculation to assign cause to these uniformities*" - he stated. Positivism actually glorified observation and classification of data. *The positive thinking suits the needs of the industrial society.*

STAGES IN SOCIAL ORGANISATION AND PROGRESS

Comte not only identified three stages in the development of human thinking but also observed three stages in the development of society or social organisation. Each of these modes of thinking - *the theological, metaphysical and the positive* - determines and corresponds to a type of social organisation. This explanation of Comte could be regarded as another major contribution of his to social thought.

Comte declared that *theological thinking* leads to a *military* and monarchical social organisation. Here the God would be there as the head of the hierarchy as King of Kings and a mighty warrior. The human beings would be arranged in a military organisation. Divine sanction rules. This divine sanction could hardly be questioned or challenged. Dogmatism would prevail here and its challengers would be punished or threatened with severe punishments.

"*Metaphysical thinking* produces a government nominated by doctrines of abstract rights." It corresponds to a *legalistic* social organisation. The Medieval social organisation clearly represented this kind of society. Here the natural rights were substituted for divine rights. A priesthood is furthered. Society becomes legalistic, formal and structural. In Europe nation-states emerged during this stage.

Positive thinking produces a society dominated by industrialists. It leads to an *industrial society* in which men inquire into the nature and utilisation of the natural resources and forces. Here the main stress is on the transformation of the material resources of the earth for human benefit, and the production of material inventions. In this positive or scientific stage the great thought blends itself with the great power.

Comte's ideas concerning the law of three stages could be presented in the following way:

Concluding Comments

Comte has made it abundantly clear that the intellectual evolution is the most important aspect in human progress. Still, he was aware of the importance of factors such as increase in population, division of labour, etc. in determining the rate of social progress. As **L.A. Coser** writes, "*It can hardly be questioned that Comte's Law of Three Stages has a strongly materialistic or idealistic bias.*"

According to **Prof. N.S. Timasheff,** "*Comte's law of the three stages in the meaning ascribed to it by its inventor is clearly invalid.*" *As he opines,* "*neither of the later approaches (metaphysical and scientific) wholly supersedes the religious approach*; *rather, there has been accumulation and often admixture of the three.*" He further writes, "*Comte's law of the three stages could not stand the test of facts known today.*"

Three Stages:	*Theological Stage*	*Metaphysical Stage*	*Positive Stage*
Nature of Society:	Military Society	Legal Society	Industrial Society
Unit of Society:	Family	Nation	Entire Humanity
Basic Principle: or Type of Order	Love of Family or Domestic Order	Mutual Co-Existence or Collective order	Universality or Universal Order

Prevailing Sentiment:	Affection or Attachment	Mutual Respect or Veneration	Kindness or Benevolence

E.S. Bogardus writes, "*Comte failed to postulate a fourth mode of thinking, namely, socialised thinking, or a system of thought which would emphasise........ the purpose of building the constructive, just, and harmonious societies.......*" He adds, "*Comte, however, should be credited with opening the way for rise of socialised thinking.*"

CLASSIFICATION OF SCIENCES

Comte's theory relating to the "*classification of sciences*" is directly related with his "*Law of Three Stages.*" Just as mankind progresses only through certain determined stages, so also scientific knowledge passes through similar stages of development. But all the sciences do not attain progress with the same rate of speed. Hence, he felt the need to provide a hierarchy of sciences. The classification of the sciences with sociology as the latest and greatest of the group, occupies the third phase in the Comtean system of thought.

Existence of *"Classification of Sciences"* — Prior to Comte

The idea of the "classification of sciences" did not originate with Comte. It did exist prior to Comte. From times immemorial thinkers have been trying to classify knowledge on some basis. The early **Greek thinkers** undertook to classify all knowledge under three headings: (1) *physics,* (2) *ethics,* and (3) *politics.*

Later on, **Bacon** made the classification on the basis of the faculties of man namely, (*i*) *memory,* (*ii*) *imagination,* and (*iii*) *reason.* The science based upon memory is *history*; the science based upon imagination is *poetry*, and the knowledge based upon reason is *physics, chemistry,* etc. Comtean classification of sciences has its own specialities among which the following may be noted

Special Features of Comtean Classification of Sciences

1. *Linkage with the "Law of Three Stages"*

Comtean classification of sciences, as it is already stated, is linked with his famous contribution to the social thought namely, the law of three stages. The logic of the link is that - as with individuals and societies, so with the sciences themselves - they all pass through the same stages.

2. *The Main Purpose of the Classification*

It could be inferred that Comte had a specific purpose in providing a classification of sciences. The main aim of the classification of knowledge by Comte was to prepare the background and the basis for the study of "*sociology*", a new science founded by him. On the basis of this principle he also determined the methodology of sociology. It also helped him in establishing the relation between sociology and other sciences. It tried to establish the fact that by discovering some general principles, it is possible to establish relationship among various sciences.

3. *Classification of Knowledge on the Basis of the Principle of Increasing Dependence*

Comte chose "*the order of increasing dependence*" as his principle of classifying knowledge. Comte "arranged the sciences so that each category may be grounded on the principal laws of the preceding category, serve as a basis for the next ensuing category. *The order, hence, is one of increasing complexity and decreasing generality. The most simple phenomena must be the most general - general in the sense of being everywhere present.*"[9]

This principle could be stated in simple words in this way: The facts pertaining to different sciences differ in complexity. Some facts are simple while others are complex. The complex facts being dependent on simple facts are, general and are present everywhere. The sciences based upon complex sciences are, in turn, dependent upon simple sciences. Thus, each science is, in some measure, dependent upon some other science and by itself forms a basis of some other science. On this basis Comte presented a serial order of sciences.

Comte was of the opinion that the more complex sciences in the course of their development will ultimately attain the positive stage. He thus stated: "*Any kind of knowledge reaches the positive stage early in proportion to its generality, simplicity and independence of other departments.*"[10] "*Hence astronomy, the most general and simple of all natural sciences, develops first. In time, it is followed by physics, chemistry, biology, and finally sociology. Each science in this series depends for its emergence on the prior developments of its predecessors in a hierarchy marked by the law of increasing complexity and decreasing generality.*" [L.A. Coser, p. 9].

9 Bogardus in his *The Development of Social Thought,* p. 236.
10. Comte in his Positive Philosophy as quoted by Coser, p. 9.

4. *Classification of Sciences begins with Mathematics*

Comte considers mathematics the basic tool of the mind. "*With mathematics as its chief tool, the mind of man can go anywhere in its thinking. Mathematics is the most powerful instrument which the mind may use in the investigation of natural laws.*"[11]

According to Comte, *mathematics occupies the first place in the hierarchy of the sciences.* Mathematics, in the Comtean scheme, *is not a constituent member of the group of sciences. It is the basis of them all.* It is the oldest and most perfect of all the sciences.

Comte gives importance to mathematics for yet another reason. He says that mathematics is "*the science.*" It is the science that measures precisely the relations between objects and ideas. It ascertains the relationships between things, a process which is basic to scientific thinking in all fields. Comte confidently asserts: "*Education that is based on any other method is faulty, inexact, and unreliable. It is only through mathematics that we can understand sciences.*"[12]

5. *The Design of the Classification of Sciences*

In the Comtean design of the hierarchy of sciences mathematics occupies the lowest rung and the topmost, rung is occupied by sociology. The hierarchy of this classification is as follows: (1) *Mathematics,* (2) *Astronomy,* (3) *Physics,* (4) *Chemistry,* (5) *Biology,* and (6) *Sociology* or *Social Physics.* This classification makes it clear that the simplest and the least dependent science is at the bottom and the most complex and dependent of the sciences is at the top of the hierarchy.

Comtean Scheme of Hierarchy of the Sciences

Sociology and the Moral Sciences	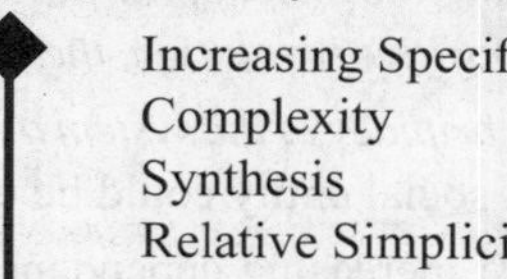	Increasing Specificity
Physiology (Biology)		Complexity
Chemistry		Synthesis
Physics		Relative Simplicity
Celestial Physics (Astronomy)		Generality
Mathematics		"Analytical"

Hierarchy of Sciences: According to this view of the sciences, first proposed by Comte, the sciences can be arranged in ascending order of complexity, with sciences higher in the hierarchy dependent, but not only dependent, on those below. Thus, sociology makes assumptions about the physical and biological world, but at the same time also involves an "*emergent*" level of analysis different from and not reducible to those below.[13]

6. *Classification of Sciences into Inorganic and Organic*

Comte stated that the classification of knowledge could be done in another manner by making use of mathematics as the tool. Thus all natural phenomena could be categorised into two grand divisions: *inorganic* and *organic.* Comparatively speaking, ***inorganic sciences*** [for example, astronomy, physics, chemistry] are simpler and clearer. ***Organic sciences*** such as biology are more complex. "*It involves the study of all life and the general laws pertaining to the individual units of life.*"[14]

7. *Social Sciences Including Sociology at the Apex of the Hierarchy*

In the Comtean scheme, social sciences are at the apex of the hierarchy for they enjoy "*all the resources of the anterior sciences.*" Social sciences are the most complex and the most dependent for their emergence on the development of all the other sciences. Social sciences offer "*the attributes of a completion of the positive method. All others are preparatory to it. Hence, they occupy the highest place in the hierarchy.*" Social physics or sociology according to Comte, is the last and the greatest of the sciences. Although sociology has special methodological characteristics that distinguishes it from its predecessors in the hierarchy, it is dependent on them too.

8. *The Emphasis on Holistic Approach in Social Sciences*

According to Comte, inorganic sciences proceed from simple to compound and the organic sciences move the reverse way from compound to simple. Hence, the inorganic sciences pursue what is known as individualistic approach whereas organic sciences [including sociology] stress upon the importance of the "*holistic approach.*"[15] The holistic approach is the

11. Comte in his Positive Philosophy, p. 237.
12. Comte as quoted by Bogardus, p. 237.
13. *Collins Dictionary of Sociology,* p. 283.
14. Bogardus, p. 238.
15. *Holism:* Holism refers to "*any form of sociological theory which emphasises the primacy of "social structure", "social system", etc., in determining social outcomes, and in sociological explanations. The opposite position is methodological individualism.........*" — *"Collins Dictionary of Sociology."* p. 290.

natural direction of the progress of sciences. All sciences progress towards the positive method. Sociology is the crowning glory of all sciences. The holistic approach starts with biology and culminates with sociology. Biological approach is virtually the holistic approach and it proceeds from the study of the organic wholes.

The stress on the organic unity**:** Comte in his approach towards society stressed on the organic unity of society. Comte has thus stated: "In the organic sciences, the elements are much better known to us than the whole which they constitute; so that in that case we must proceed from the simple to the compound. But the reverse method is necessary in the study of man and society..... Just as biology cannot explain an organ or a function apart from the organism as a whole, sociology cannot explain social phenomena without reference to the total social context. This idea of organic unity or the primacy of the system over elements has important theoretical implications" - **[Abraham** and **Morgan.** Page : 10.**]** Comte's faith in the holistic approach was very firm. In the words of Comte, "*There can be no scientific study of society either in its conditions or its movements, if it is separated into portions, and its divisions are studied apart.*"

Concluding Comments

1. Though the classification of sciences presented by Comte is not free from certain limitations, it still holds some importance today. In this scheme of classification *Comte found an appropriate place for sociology and gave that discipline its name.*

2. Comte successfully established through his classification of sciences that *sociology is also a positive science.* He also stressed that sociology must be a theoretical discipline. "*The conversion of sociology into a positive science completed the system of positive philosophy thus marking the onset of the positive stage of development of the human mind and human society. It meant, in Comte's view, the real* "*positive revolution, the victory of science over the scholasticism of past epochs.*"[16]

3. Comte's "*idea of organic unity or the primacy of the system over element,* has important theoretical implications. Comte has repeatedly asserted that one element of social entity could be understood only in terms of the entity as a whole......."[17]

4. Comte's assertion of the principle of increasing dependence in the classification of sciences has today culminated in what is being called "*interdisciplinary approach.*" This approach is quite popular at the academic level. In this regard **Bogardus** writes: "*Comte urged that no science could be effectually studied without competent knowledge concerning the sciences on which it depends. It is necessary not only to have a general knowledge of all the sciences but to study each of them in order - this is Comte's dictum to the student of sociology. Comte insisted that one general science could not develop beyond a given point until the preceding has passed a given stage.*"[18]

COMTE'S VIEWS REGARDING SOCIOLOGY

Comte is acclaimed as the *'father of sociology'*. First he named the science which he set out to establish as "*social physics*". But later he came to know that the Belgian statistician by name **Adolf Quentelet** had already used that term in his "*An Essay on Social Physics.*" Hence, Comte dropped that term and in its place used the term '*Sociology*' in 1839.. This term is a combination of two words - the Latin word '*socius*', meaning '*society*', and the Greek word *'logos'* meaning *'science'* or study. Etymologically 'sociology' means, "*science of society*".

As stated earlier, according to COMTE, sociology represents the culmination of the development of science. It is based on mathematics and is dependent on biology, chemistry, physics and astronomy. These sciences have taken time to become free from theological and metaphysical speculation and thinking. Hence, Comte argued that sociology too would require some time to attain the full status of the positive science. Comte believed that sociology would be helped to become scientific by means of his writings.

Social Statics and Social Dynamics

According to Comte, there are two divisions in sociology: *Social statics* and *social dynamics*. The distinction between these two does not refer to two classes of facts, but they represent two aspects of the same theory. The distinction corresponds to the double conception of order and progress. Order and progress, or statics and dynamics, are hence always correlative to each other.

Social statics

Social statics refers to "*the study of the laws of action and reaction of the different parts of social order..*" It studies the balance of mutual relations of elements within a social whole. It deals with the major institutions of society such as

16. *A History of Classical Sociology,* Edited by Prof. I.S. Kon, p. 25.
17. Abraham and Morgan, p. 10.
18. Bogardus, p. 239.

family, economy or policy. It inquires into the co-existence of social phenomena. Comte stressed that there must always be a "*spontaneous harmony between the whole and the part of the social system.*" The parts of a society cannot be studied separately, "*as if they had an independent existence*". When the harmony between the parts is lacking a pathological situation may prevail. *Social statics emphasises the unity of society or social organisation.*

Social Dynamics

If statics examines how the parts of societies are interrelated, social dynamics focuses on whole societies as the unit of analysis, and reveals how they developed and changed through time. Social dynamics was equated by Comte with human progress and evolution. It inquires as to how the human civilisation progresses in different stages. Comte was convinced towards ever increasing perfection.

Nature and Features of Sociology — Comte's Views

Comte defined sociology as the science of social phenomena "subject to natural and invariable laws the discovery of which is the object of our investigation". He mentioned the following features of sociology in some or the other context - 1. *Sociology is the objective analysis of social phenomena.* 2. *Sociology is an abstract science*. 3. *Sociology is a synthetic science*. It synthesises the knowledge of all the other sciences. 4. Like all the other sciences, sociology can also provide the knowledge of the future in the sense, *it can make predictions*. 5. Sociology is not just a science. *It is a science committed to social reconstruction and moral rejuvenation.*

RELIGION OF HUMANITY

Comte's "*theory of religion of humanity*" though can be considered one of his contributions to the realm of social thought, it has only an insignificant place in the study of sociology or sociological thought. Comte after successfully establishing the intellectual supremacy of positivism in his earlier works, devoted his later writings to moral and religious considerations rather than to scientific and sociological inquiries.

Religion of Humanity as a Product of Comte's Idealistic Imaginations

Comte's focus on sociology as a scientific enterprise could be clearly understood by a glance through his masterpiece "*Positive Sociology.*" But, Comte, the promising scientist too had his own normative ideas which figured prominently in his "*Positive Polity*" published in 1852. An important change had taken place in his thinking by this time. Comte purported to establish a new religion, a "*scientific religion*", or *a religion of humanity.* The irony is, Comte sincerely believed that he was trying to establish such a religion on a firm scientific foundation.

The *"Theory of Religion of Humanity"* Represents a Radical Change in the Development of Comte's Rational Thinking

It is surprising to note that Comte, a great champion of science or positivism, could transform himself into an advocate of a new religion, a religion of humanity. Comte during his younger days used to say that a scientist requires the thirst for knowledge and not the divine grace. He was an atheist. But he turned out to be a champion of a religion because of several upsets that he had to undergo in his personal life. His own wife deserted him; his lady love Clotilde de Vaux died; he had no friends worth calling by that name, to share his thoughts; the lonely life that he was leading became unbearable; he stopped reading the works of others, he alienated himself from other intellectuals of the day. These biographical accidents did play an important role in this transformation in his thinking.

Some Salient Features of Comtean Religion

1. A Religion Without God

Comte's "*religion of humanity*" is based upon morality and religion, and not upon a belief in a divine force. Comte was opposed to the theological type of religion. According to Comte, God lives in the ignorance of man. The object of worship should be mankind and not God. Hence, the main slogan of the Comtean religion thus reads: "*We should have religion but not God.*"

2. Sociologist-Priests Constitute the Moral Guides of the Comtean concept of a New Society

Comte was of the opinion that a society which was built upon scientific principles needed a religion which he termed as religion of humanity. Comte conceived of a society directed by the spiritual power of priests of the new positive religion and leaders of banking and industry. These scientific sociologist-priests would be the moral guides and controllers of the community. They use their "*superior knowledge to recall men to their duties and obligations.*" They would be the directors of education and the supreme judges of the abilities of each member of the society. They "*would sternly hold men to their collective duty and would help suppress any subversive ideas of inherent rights.*"

3. New Religion Destined to Begin a New Epoch

Comte claimed himself to be the high priest of this new religion committed to "*institute a reign of harmony, justice, rectitude, and equity.*" The new positivist order, Comte claimed, "*would have Love as its Principle, Order as its Basis, and Programme as its Aim.*" The egoistic tendencies of mankind as evidenced in all the previous history "would be replaced by altruism, and by the command, "*Live for Others*". Individual men would be imbued with love for their fellows. Comte at this stage made '*love*' and *'affection'* the central points of life. "*We tire of thinking and even of acting, he asserted, but we never tire of loving.*" "*The Comtean ideals became a disinterested love of mankind.*"

4. Religion of Humanity - a Social Religion Based upon Morality

It is clearly ascertainable that during his later years, Comte "considered himself not only a social scientist but also, and primarily, a prophet and founder of a new religion that promised salvation for all the ailments of mankind." Comte, thus tried to create a purely "*social religion.*" He made mankind an end in itself.

5. Comte - Not in Favour of Traditional Christianity

Comte's contact with Christianity gave him the belief that it is chiefly ecclesiastical. "*He was of the opinion that Christianity employed the instruments of political pressure and tyranny in order to gain allegiance of people to Christian religion.*"[19] **Bogardus** writes: "Comte did not see in Christianity a social keynote. Hence, he attempted to create a purely social religion."[20]

6. Comtean Religion is Virtually a Religion of Human Unity

As **Raymond Aron** has pointed out, "*Comte is the sociologist of human unity and one of possible, if not inevitable, results of this "sociology of humanity is the religion of human unity. Comte wanted men,...... to be united by common conviction and by a single object of their love.*"[21]

Critical Comments

1. Comte's religion of humanity is widely criticised. Christian scholars say that the religion of humanity is *nothing more than a mixture of science and catholic religion.*

2. Some have commented that *it is not at all a religion but primarily a code of morality.* Its architect Comte was, indeed, "*morally-intoxicated*" !

3. **J. S. Mill** rightly remarked that Comtean ideas of religion, instead of protecting his mental health made him lead an isolated life and develop strange thoughts.

4. **Thomas Huxley** called Comte's religion "*Catholicism minus Christianity.*" Some others criticised it as a highly "*egoistic religion.*" A few others considered it utopian in character.

5. **L. A. Coser** has remarked that the normative aspects of Comte's thought may be of importance for the historian of ideas; but they are of little importance for the sociologist. Viewed in the social and intellectual contexts from which Comte's thoughts emerged, his religious ideas have their own place in social thought.

AN ESTIMATE OF COMTE'S ACHIEVEMENTS

It is not out of place to make a brief review of Comte's contributions to the growth of sociology and social thought. Though some of Comtean ideas have been bitterly criticised one should not underestimate the achievements of Comte. It would be unjust to say that Comte only introduced the term "*sociology*" and did nothing to develop it. In fact, various thinkers have given Comte a glowing tribute. Some such expressions of appreciation are mentioned below:

(*i*) **John Stuart Mill** referred to Comte as one among the first of European thinkers; and by his institution of a new social science, in some respects, the first.

(*ii*) **George Henry Lewis** called Comte the greatest of modern thinkers.

(*iii*) **John Morley,** the English statesman and author, says of Comte: "*Neither Franklin, nor any man that has ever lived, could surpass him in the heroic tenacity with which, in the face of a thousand obstacles, he pursued his own ideal of vocation.*"[22]

19. R.N. and R.K. Sharma in *History of Social Thought,* p. 145.
20. Bogardus, p. 243.
21. Raymond Aron in *Main Currents in Sociological Thought* Vol. I, p. 109.
22. Bogardus in *The Development of Social Thought,* p. 234.

Comte's Achievements

1. *By giving a name and laying the foundations of a newly emerging social science Comte filled in the vacuum.* The name that he gave is quite apt to the science, *i.e.*, sociology, which is all comprehensive in nature.

2. Comte's *insistence on positive approach, objectivity* and *scientific attitude* contributed to the progress of social sciences in general.

3. Comte's ideas relating to the Law of Three Stages reveal that man became more and more rational and scientific in his approach by gradually giving up speculations, imaginations, etc. *He also showed that there is a close association between the intellectual evolution and the social progress.*

4. Even though his classification of sciences is not perfect, it has shown *how and why sociology depends heavily on the achievements of other sciences.* Comte has shown that any broad-based science will grow only after the growth of sciences that have emerged prior to that.

5. Comte's writings reveal an enormous wealth of ideas. He has made a number of propositions concerning the scope and method of sociology. He has shown the way towards the modern definition of sociology and its basic divisions. "*With the decline of evolutionism, however, sociology returned, though with modifications, to Comte's view about its subject-matter*" – **Prof. Timasheff.**

6. The division of sociology into *social statics* and *social dynamics, i.e.*, into *social order* and *social change* or *progress* - which Comte made, is quite appropriate. Even the present-day sociologists speak of the same divisions.

7. Comte gave maximum importance to the *scientific method.* He criticised the armchair social philosophers and stressed the need to follow observation, classification of data and experimentation of the main steps involved in the scientific method. *This stress on the scientific method provided a boost for the growth of science.*

8. Comte argued that sociology was not just a *'pure'* science but an *'applied'* science also. He believed that sociology, "the science of his creation" would help to solve the problems of the society. He "*invented the new science as a necessary instrument of social reform.*"

9. Though one can charge Comte as a "*morality-intoxicated*" man, one cannot reject Comte's attempts to uphold the "*moral order*" in society as highly unwanted. In fact, *by highlighting the importance of* "*morality*" *he became a guide and a source of inspiration for Arnold Toynbee and Pitirim A. Sorokin.*

10. Finally, by doing a lot of descriptive work *Comte contributed to the growth of theoretical sociology.*

Comments Against Comtean Views

Comte has been severely criticised by different writers. Some such critical comments made against Comtean views are stated below.

1. It is commonly asserted that *Comte made very few original contributions.* It is also stated that Comte merely elaborated a programme of sociology and did not construct a sociological theory as such.
2. Though, Comte claimed to be the father of "*positivism*" or "*scientific approach*" *he himself was not committed to it.*
3. "Comte believed in the existence of a prepotent factor in social change - the development of ideas. *Therefore, he could be considered one of the ideological determinants.* The basic premise of his theory, *the faith in evolution towards progress,* was faulty."
4. As far as his sociological theories are concerned, as **Prof. Timasheff** opines, they represent "*a premature jump from the level of observation and inferences...... to the level of theory.*"
5. Comte at the fag end of his life forgot his role as a scientist and played the role of a social reformer. He even believed himself to be a prophet, a high priest of a new religion.
6. "*Comte was a poor religious thinker though he firmly believed that religion was one of the pillars of society*" - writes **Prof. Timasheff.**
7. As **J.S. Mill** felt, Comte's religion does not stand the test of rationalism for it is a strange thing that can never be put into practice. As someone has criticised, his religion was born out of his "*moral intoxication.*" *People wanted him to give a science of religion, but instead of that he made the science, a religion.*
8. Finally, as **Rollin Chambliss** has opined Comte wanted to build a science of social phenomena. But instead of doing that he struggled to provide his own projects and programmes of social reorganisation. *He built a* "*utopia*" *instead of science.*

To conclude, as **Chambliss** has said, we can speak of two Comtes, so to say: Comte a brilliant scientist; and Comte, an ordinary saint. Of the two, we at present, need Comte, the brilliant scientist.

REVIEW QUESTIONS

1. Write the biography of Auguste Comte in brief.
2. What are the main works of Comte? Explain.
3. What is positivism? Explain its nature.
4. Examine the impact of positivism on social thinking.
5. What are the criticisms against positivism?
6. Throw light on the law of three stapes.
7. Discuss comte's theory relating to the classification of sciences.
8. What contributions did Auguste Comte make to Sociology? Explain.
9. Discuss the features of Comtean religion.
10. Make an estimate of comte's achievements.
11. Write short notes on the following:
    (a) Comtean positivism
    (b) Comte's view regarding the nature and features of Sociology

⌘⌘⌘⌘⌘⌘⌘⌘⌘⌘⌘⌘⌘

56

HERBERT SPENCER AND HIS THOUGHTS

CHAPTER OUTLINE

- Brief Biographic Sketch of Spencer : Main Works of Spencer
- Spencer's Theory of Evolution: Meaning of Evolution—General Theory of Evolution
- Theory Social Evolution
- Some Observations Relating to Spencer's "Theory of Social Evolution
- Critical Remarks
- Spencer's Theory of Organic Analogy: Similarities and Differences Between Organism and Society as Visualised by Spencer
- Critical Comments
- Social Darwinism: Meaning of the Concept of Social Darwinism
- The Principle of the Survival of the Fittest
- The Principle of Non-Interference
- Critical Remarks
- Types of Society: Classification and Comparision: Military Society and Industrial Society
- Concluding Remarks
- A word About Spencer's Contributions.

BRIEF BIOGRAPHIC SKETCH OF HERBERT SPENCER

Herbert Spencer [1820-1903] was a prominent British social thinker of the 19th century. He is often called "*the second founding father of sociology*". He is known to the world as a great social philosopher, a famous evolutionist, a strong defender of individualism and a prolific writer. It is said that Spencer undertook to create what Comte envisaged to do. He made sociology an all encompassing science.

Spencer who is considered one of the most brilliant intellects of modern times was a British engineer and an editor, a philosopher and a sociologist. Spencer was a self-taught man and hence his learning was highly selective.

Spencer was born on April 27, 1820, in Derby in England in a middle-class family. He was the oldest of the nine children and the only survivor in George Spencer's family. Due to his ill-health he could not go to any conventional school. He received some education from his father. His family members were highly individualistic in their outlook and Spencer also inherited the same tradition. At the age of 13, he went to the home of his uncle from whom he received his further education. The education which he received from his father and the uncle was more scientific than anything else. Hence, Spencer decided to pursue his scientific interest. In 1837, he joined the staff of the London and Birmingham Railway as an engineer. But he gave up the work within a short time and returned home to Derby.

Herbert Spencer
[1820-1903]

Spencer shifted his attention to journalism and became an editor of the *Economist*, one of the greatest English publications. During the five years of his stay within '*Economist*', he developed relations with a number of people in the world of advanced journalism. Even while working as a journalist, he found time to finish his first book, *'Social Statics'* - 1851. The book was well received by the radical public. In 1853, he resigned from his post and decided to earn his living as an independent writer. A sizeable sum of money which he got from his uncle soon after his death, also provided him the courage to take risk of resigning from his job. He remained all through his life a private scholar without regular job or institutional attachment. He also remained a lifelong bachelor with strict discipline.

Spencer slowly resorted to writing career. By 1850, he had completed his first major work "*Social Statics*". During the writing of this book, Spencer began to suffer from insomnia. His physical and mental problems mounted over the years. He continued to suffer from a series of nervous breakdowns throughout the rest of his life.

Spencer never earned a university degree or held an academic position. Surprisingly, Spencer's productivity as a scholar increased in spite of his isolation and physical and mental illness. In 1855, Spencer published his second book "*The Principles of Psychology*". This, however, did not become popular In the meantime, Spencer suffered from a nervous illness. He could hardly overcome it completely. He had to remain as a psychic cripple throughout his life. He used to take often a heavy dose of opium to overcome his insomnia. Since then he could read and write only for a few hours a day. In spite of his unfavourable mental conditions he produced scholarly books such as - *First Principles, Principles of Biology, Principles of Ethics, Principles of Sociology, The Study of Sociology*, etc.

Spencer earned international reputation for his scholarly writings. Leading thinkers of the day such as J.S. Mill, Thomas Huxley, Tyndall, Charles Darwin and others had great appreciation for his writings and thoughts. Like his predecessor Comte, he too was unwilling to read the works of other people in order to preserve the purity of his thought. He even ignored those ideas that did not agree with his. His contemporary, Charles Darwin said of Spencer: "*If he had trained himself to observe more, even at the expense of.... some loss of thinking power, he would have been a wonderful man*".[1]

Spencer also wrote on the most controversial issues of the day such as - *opposition to Boer War, proposal for the introduction of the metric system in England etc.* He used to write on political issues also. Due to his deteriorating mental conditions Spencer had to live the last few years in almost complete isolation from human society. He died on December 8, 1903, at the age of 83.

MAIN WORKS OF SPENCER

On Philosophy and Religion

1. *The Nature and Reality of Religion, 1885* [withdrawn from publication].

Series of Books on Synthetic Philosophy

2. *First Principles, 1862.*
3. *The Principles of Biology, 2 volumes, 1864-67.*
4. *The Principles of Psychology, 1855.*
5. *The Principles of Sociology, 3 volumes, 1876-96.*
6. *The Principles of Ethics, 2 volumes, 1892-93.*
7. *Descriptive Sociology, 2 volumes, 1873-94.*

On Political and Social Matters

8. *The Proper Sphere of Government, 1843.*
9. *Social Statics, 1851.*
10. *Education: Intellectual, Moral, Physical, 1861.*
11. *The Study of Sociology, 1872.*
12. *The Man Versus The State, 1884.*
13. *Data of Ethics, 1893.*
14. *Facts and Comments, 1902.*

Other Works

1. *Essay: Scientific, Political and Speculative, 3 volumes, 1891.*
2. *Autobiography, 1904, an intellectual rather than a personal autobiography.*

[**Source:** *The New Encyclopaedia Britannica,* Vol.11, p. 83].

SPENCER'S THEORY OF EVOLUTION

"*Evolutionary Theory*" or "*The Laws of Evolution*" is often regarded as the greatest contribution of the British sociologist Herbert Spencer to the realm of social thought. Spencer's ideals have left an indelible impression on the succeeding writers.

1. Quoted by George Ritzer in *Contemporary Sociological Theory*, p. 43.

It is true that his social theories have caused more controversy than those of any other writer in the sociological field. The controversies that his ideas created, of course, will not obscure the important role that he had played in enriching the field of social thought.

"Evolution" — The Most Exciting Concept of the 19th Century

"Evolution" was one of the most exciting ideas of the 19th century. Its most influential sponsor was the naturalist Charles Darwin. Darwin developed the concept of "*Evolution*" in his "*Origin of Species - 1859.*" Spencer, the sociological giant of the second half of the 19th century, was enamoured by the idea of evolution. He applied the principle of evolution to the social world and called it "*social evolution.*" He saw social evolution as "*a set of stages through which all the societies moved from simple to the complex and from the homogenous to the heterogeneous.*"

Meaning of the Concept of *"Evolution"*

The term "evolution" comes from the Latin word "*evolvere*" which means "*to develop*" or to "*unfold.*" It closely corresponds to the Sanskrit word "*Vikas*". Evolution literally means gradual "*unfolding*" or "*unrolling.*" It indicates changes from "*within*" and not from "*without*"; it is spontaneous, but not automatic. It must take place on its own accord. It implies continuous change that takes place especially in some structure. The concept applies more precisely to the internal growth of an organism.

Meaning of *"Social Evolution"*

The term "*evolution*" is borrowed from biological science to sociology. The term "*organic evolution*" is replaced by "*social evolution*" in sociology. Whereas the term "organic evolution" is used to denote the evolution of organism, the expression "*social evolution*" is used to explain the evolution of human society. Here the term implies the evolution of man's social relations. It was hoped that the theory of social evolution would explain the origin and development of man. Anthropologists and sociologists wanted to find a satisfactory and significant explanation of how our society evolved. They wanted an explanation in this regard rather than a description. They were impressed by the idea of organic evolution which could convincingly explain how one species evolves into another, and wanted to apply the same to the social world. Hence the concept of social evolution is quite popular in sociological discussion. It was Herbert Spencer who made the concepts of "*evolution*" and "*social evolution*", the central concepts in his sociological theories.

Spencerian Interpretations Relating to Evolution

As **L.A. Coser** has pointed out the "*evolutionary principle*" or "*the law of evolution*" constitutes the very basis of Spencerism. Spencerian interpretations relating to "evolution" could be divided into two parts: **(1)** ***General Theory of Evolution,*** and **(2)** ***Theory of Social Evolution.*** In his book "*First Principles*" *- 1862* we get his views about the first theory, and information and interpretations about the second theory, are available in his sociological treaties namely, "*The Study of Sociology*" and "*The Principles of Sociology.*"

General Theory of Evolution

Spencer's "*Theory of Social Evolution*" is grounded in his "*General Theory of Evolution.*" But the evolutionary perspective as such, Spencer borrowed from **Charles Darwin's** "*Theory of Organic Evolution*".

Spencer's Concept of "Universal Evolution"

Spencer made "evolution" a universal principle in his treatise "*First Principles.*" The fundamental principle behind every phenomenon or every development whether it is physical or social in nature, there is the supreme law of evolution operating. The law of evolution, according to him, is the supreme law of every becoming.

According to **Spencer,** "*evolution is a change from a state of relatively indefinite, incoherent homogeneity to a definite coherent heterogeneity.*"

For Spencer, this law of evolution was universal in character for it was applicable to the physical, organic and the social world. Spencer was of the opinion that this universal process of evolution would explain the "*earliest change which the universe at large is supposed to have undergone.......*" It also explains the law of evolution "*as a master key to the riddles of the universe.*"

Three Basic Laws as Proposed by Spencer

Within the framework of universal evolution, Spencer developed his "*three basic laws*" and his "*four secondary propositions*" - each building upon each and all upon the doctrine of evolution.

The Three Basic Laws

1. *Law of persistence of energy or force*: There is a persistence of force in the world. There is the persistence of some sustaining energy in which all phenomena are rooted and upon which all phenomena rest. But this force or energy itself lies beyond our knowledge. This is a major, irreducible fact which we cannot explain, but which we are obliged simply to accept.

2. *The law of indestructibility of matter*: The basic elements of matter and energy in the world are neither created nor destroyed, but conserved. It means there is a basic "*indestructibility*" of the elements of matter.

3. *The law of continuity of motion*: There is a continuous motion in the world. All things continue in motion. As it is in the case of matter, motion also cannot be stopped or destroyed. When the form of the matter changes, motion also changes. Though energy passes from one form to another, it always persists, and never disappears nor does it get extinguished.

Four Secondary Propositions or Laws

In relation to the evolutionary process, Spencer has mentioned four secondary propositions or laws in addition to the three basic laws. They are as follows.

(*a*) *Uniformity of law*: There is a persistence of certain relationship among the forces in the world. The world is an order of elements. Recurring manifestations of events in the natural world, the forces, elements of matter, and relations of motion existing among them have a definite regularity.

(*b*) *Law of transformation and equivalence of forces*: The force, the elements of matter, the motion, are never lost or dissipated entirely in a process of change. They are merely transformed into the manifestation of some other event or some other form of existence.

(*c*) *The law of least resistance and great attraction*: There is the tendency of every thing [all forces and elements] to move along the line of least resistance and of greatest attraction.

(*d*) *The principle of alteration or rhythm of motion*: All phenomena in nature have their own particular rate and rhythm of movement, of duration and development. Force, matter and motion, each of these, has its appropriate pattern of transformation.

Evolutionary Theory — A Joint Product of the Seven Laws

It is significant to note that Spencer derived from these basic propositions his "law of evolution." According to Spencer, when we examine the nature of both order and change in any kind of phenomena in the world we find that the pattern of transformation is the same, and could be formulated in the following words.

"*Evolution is an integration of matter and concomitant dissipation of motion, during which the matter passes from relatively indefinite incoherent homogeneity to a relatively definite coherent homogeneity.*"

"According to Spencer, all the phenomena of nature, the stars and planetary systems, the earth and all terrestrial phenomena, biological organisms and the development of species and all the changing psychological and sociological process of human experience and behaviour - followed this pattern of change. All process of change are similar, in that they emerge out of the physical stuff of the world........... in this condition of organised complexity; from a condition of indefiniteness to a condition of definiteness..........."[2] This was how Spencer made evolution a universally applicable system of analysis. Spencer thus made applicable the laws of evolution to analyse the development and evolution of the human society. It is in this context he gave birth to "*the theory of social evolution.*"

Theory of Social Evolution

Two of the main books written by Spencer namely, (*i*) "*The Study of Sociology*", (*ii*) "*The Principles of Sociology*", provide us more details about his "*theory of social evolution.*" Just as "*the theory of organic evolution*" analyses the birth, development, evolution and finally death of the organism, in the same manner "*the theory of social evolution*" analyses the genesis, development, evolution and finally the decay (?) of the society.

2. Ronald Fletcher in his *The Making of Sociology*, Vol. I, p. 259.

Spencer was of the opinion that the evolutionary principle could be applied to the human society for he treated human society as an organism. Both the organism and the society grow from simple to complex and from homogeneous to heterogeneous.

As **Abraham** and **Morgan** have pointed out "*Spencer's Theory of Evolution*" involves two essential but interrelated trends or strains of thought:

(*i*) Change from simplicity to complexity or movement from simple society to various levels of compound societies; and
(*ii*) Change from military society to industrial society.

Change from Simplicity to Complexity, or Movement from Simple Society to Various Levels of Compound Society

As Spencer repeatedly argued all phenomena in all fields proceed from simplicity to complexity. Societies also undergo evolutionary stages of development. Spencer identified four types of societies in terms of stages of their evolutionary development - *simple*, *compound*, *doubly compound* and *trebly compound.*

(*a*) ***Simple society*:** This is *the most primitive society* without any complexities and consisting of several families.

(*b*) ***Compound society*:** A large number of above mentioned simple societies make a compound society. This is *clan society.*

(*c*) ***Doubly compound society*:** These consist of several clans compounded into tribes or *tribal society.*

(*d*) ***Trebly compound society*:** Here the tribes are organised into *nation states.* This is the present form of the world.

The master trend in this process of universal evolution is the *increased differentiation of social structures* which leads inevitably to better integration and adaptation to environment.

Change from Military [Militant] Society to Industrial Society

According to **Spencer,** evolution proceeds from military society to industrial society. The type of social structure depends on the relation of a society to other societies in its significant characteristics.

(*i*) Thus while the military society is characterised by compulsory co-operation, industrial society is based on voluntary co-operation.
(*ii*) While the military society has a centralised government, the industrial society has a decentralised government.
(*iii*) Military society has economic autonomy whereas it is not found in industrial society.
(*iv*) There is the domination of the state over all other social organisations in the military society whereas in the industrial society the functions of the states are very much limited;

Some Observations Relating to Spencer's "Theory of Social Evolution"

1. ***Social evolution is also as rigid as organic evolution*:** It can be said that Spencer had a belief in the unilinear evolution of mankind. It means "*The mankind's progress through stages of development is as rigidly determined as the evolution of individuals from childhood to maturity.*" "As between infancy and maturity there is no short cut..... so there is no way from the lower forms of social life to the higher, but one passing through small successive modification....... The process cannot be abridged and must be gone through with due patience" - Spencer wrote in his "*Study of Sociology.*"

2. ***Is evolution bound to move towards progress*:** It could be questioned whether Spencer believed that evolution, the law of becoming, was directed towards progress. Spencer had claimed that the ever-present process of evolution was inevitably leading towards progress. He believed that "*man by nature was pre-destined to progress.*" Spencer in his earlier writings pictures the process of evolution as unremitting, unrelenting, and ever present. "*The change from the homogeneous to the heterogeneous is displayed in the progress of civilisation as a whole, as well as in the progress of every nation; and it is still going on with increasing rapidity.*"

Though Spencer very strongly asserted in the beginning that evolution is inevitably and unremittingly heading towards progress, the political developments that took place in England at the fag end of the 19th century made him suspect the power of evolution to promise progress always. He felt that "*Evolution is not endless progress......... There is a limit to it after which disintegration and death take place. Moreover, disintegration is also gradual and involves a process of evolution in reverse. Evolution is thus cyclical in nature.*"[3]

3. *The process of equilibrium involved in evolution*: According to Spencer, evolution is a process heading towards equilibrium. He wrote: "*A social organism like an individual organism, undergoes modifications until it comes into equilibrium with environing conditions; and thereupon continues without further change of structure.....*"[4] The so called equilibrium will be established through what Darwin called "*The struggle for existence.*" Once the equilibrium is established societies will obtain greater freedom and peace. Since societies and institutions are subject to the "*automatic process*" of evolution they do not have the capacity to alter the conditions but will have to adjust to the conditions.

Critical Remarks

Comments in appreciation:

1. As **Bogardus** has pointed out, "*Spencer emphasised the laws of evolution and natural causation. He described social evolution as a phase of natural evolution.*"[5]

2. Spencer has made the principles of evolution universal in character. It is indeed, a remarkable intellectual exercise.

3. Spencer's work inspired the British social thought to a great extent. "*L.T. Hobhouse, G.C. Wheeler, and in later generation, Morris Ginsberg continued work in his general evolutionary tradition while rejecting his anti-reformist individualism. In America, W.G. Sumner........ may be said to have been a disciple of Spencer, Ward, Cooley, Veblen, Giddings, Ross, and Park, whether agreeing with his ideas or using them as a springboard for dissent, were all in Spencer's debt.*"[6]

4. According to **Bogardus,** "*Spencer deserves credit, however, for developing the concept of social evolution as a phase of natural evolution and for stressing the idea of natural sequences in soceitary matters.*"[7]

5. **Abraham** and **Morgan** have rightly commented: "*No one after Spencer ever matched either the sheer volume of sociological writing nor made more significant contributions to the science of human society.*"[8]

Comments against spencer's views:

1. No modern sociologist subscribes to the "*theory of social evolution*" in its original form as put forward by Spencer. *His attempt to equalise evolution with progress is totally rejected.* But its modified form known as "*Theory of Neo-Evolutionism*" advocated by the anthropologists like, **Leslie A. White, V. Gordon Childe** and others, is getting some publicity in the anthropological circles.

2. **Bogardus** is unhappy with Spencer's theory of social evolution for *it underestimates the importance of man.* He writes: "*The emphasis upon 'man' as a primary unit neglects the importance of the 'group' in the social evolutionary process. Moreover, Spencer underrated the intellectual nature of primitive man; he denied to early man the qualities involving exclusiveness of thought, imagination, and original ideas.*"[9]

3. Spencer had spoken of uniformity in the process of evolution. He "*did not realise that societies at the same stage of evolution do not necessarily possess identical politics, ethics, art and religion.*"[10]

4. "*While Spencer believed that social part exists for the social whole, today, society is believed to exist for the welfare of the individuals.*"[11]

SPENCER'S THEORY OF ORGANIC ANALOGY

Spencer is popularly known for his treatment of the organic analogy. The evolutionary doctrine was no doubt the foundation of Spencer's sociological theory. He, however, presented the organic analogy, as a secondary doctrine which

---

3. Samuel Koenig in *Sociology — An Introduction to the Science of Society*, 1970, p. 24.
4. L.A. Coser as quoted in his "*Masters of Sociological Thought,* p. 96.
5. Bogardus in his *Development of Social Thought*, p. 295.
6. L.A. Coser in Masters of Sociological Thought, p. 126.
7. Emory S. Bogardus, p. 292.
8. Abraham and Morgan in *Sociological Thought,* p. 71.
9. E.S. Bogardus in *The Development of Social Thought*, p. 292.
10. R.N. and R.K. Sharma in *History of Social Thought,* p. 204.
11. R.N. and R.K. Sharma, p. 204.

also played a vital role in his thought system. "*He established the hypothesis that society, is like a biological organism and then proceeded to defend it against all objections with great logical force.*" But his logic proved to be his sociological downfall, for it spoiled his scientific insight.

Herbert Spencer came to sociology via biology. Therefore he drew analogy between the society and the biological organism. "*So completely is society organised on the same system as an individual that we may perceive something more than an analogy between them, the same definition of life applied to both [biological and social organism].*"[12]

Spencer believed that the social structure is a living organism. He took great pains to elaborate in great detail *the organic analogy which is the identification of society with a biological organism.* Indeed, he regarded the recognition of similarity between society and organism as a major step towards a general theory of evolution. He concentrated on bringing forth wonderful parallels between organic and social evolution, between similarities in the structure and evolution of organic and social units. In fact, biological analogies occupy an important role in all of Spencer's sociological reasoning.

Similarities between Biological and Social Organism — As visualised by Spencer

Spencer wanted to explain the nature of social structure by the help of the organismic theory. He observed some similarities between biological and social organisms.

1. ***Similarity in visible growth***: Both society and organism are distinguished from inorganic matter by means of their visible growth. Thus both society and the organism are subject to growth. ***Example***: *A child grows up to be a man; a tiny community becomes a metropolitan area; a small state becomes an empire, and so on.*

2. ***An increase in the complexity of structure***: As both society and organisms grow in size they also increase in complexity of structure. Primitive organisms [like amaeba] are simple whereas the highest organisms [like the mammals] are very complex. Primitive community was very simple whereas the modern industrial society is highly complex.

3. ***Differentiation of structure leading to differentiation of functions***: In societies and in organisms progressive differentiation of structure is accompanied by progressive differentiation of functions. It is quite obvious. The primitive living organism was a unicellular creature; but with the increase in the cells, differentiation of organs resulted, at the highest levels of evolution the structure of the body is quite complex. Similar is the case with society. In the case of an organism that has very complex organs, each organ performs a specified function. Similarly, in the case of complex society subdivided into many different organisations, each organisation carries on a specified function.

4. ***Change in structure leads to change in functions***: When change takes place in the structure of organs and communities, there results a change in their functions. The function becomes more and more specialised. This applies to the body of a living creature as well as to the society.

5. ***Differentiation as well as harmony of organs***: Evolution establishes for both societies and organisms, differences in structure and function that make each other possible. Evolution leads to development of greater differentiation of the organs of society as also that of an individual. Along with this differentiation there is also the harmony between various organs. Each organ is complementary to the other and not opposed. This holds true both in the body of a living organism and society.

6. ***Loss of an organ does not necessarily result in the loss of organism***: Both society and the individual are organisms. It is common to both that a loss of one organ or the other does not necessarily result in the death of an organism. *For example*, if an individual loses his leg he does not necessarily meet with his death. Similarly, in society if some association or a political party disintegrates it does not invariably lead to the decay of the society.

7. ***Similar process and methods of organisation***: In discussing the organic analogy further Spencer compared—

(*i*) The **alimentary system** of an organism to the productive industries, or the **sustaining system** in the society.

(*ii*) There is a strong parallelism between the **circulation system** of an organism and the **distributing system** in society with its transportation lines and with its commercial classes and media of exchange.

(*iii*) In both the cases there are developed ***regulating systems***. In society, there is the *social control mechanism* to fulfil

12. Spencer as quoted by R.N. and R.K. Sharma in *History of Social Thought,* p. 193.

the regulative function. In an organism there are *dominant centres and subordinate centres*, the senses, and a neural apparatus to perform the tasks of the regulating system.

These parallelisms throw only a small measure of light upon the nature of society. But they become ridiculous when carried to an extreme.

Differences between Organism and Society — As Visualised by Spencer

Spencer had recognised important differences between societies and organisms. He said, "*the parts of an animal form a concrete whole, but the parts of society form a whole which is discrete. While the living units, composing the one are bound together in close contact; the living units composing the other, are free, are not in contact, and are more or less widely dispersed.*" In simple words, *the organism is a concrete, integrated whole whereas society is a whole composed of discrete and dispersed elements.*

The main differences between the society and a living organism which cannot be overlooked were noted by Spencer. They are listed below:

1. Organs are organised, but parts of society are independent: As Spencer has observed various organs of the body are incapable of independent existence, whereas various parts of society can exist independently. ***Example*** : Limbs of the organism such as legs, hands, face, etc., cannot have existence outside the physical body of the organism. But the parts of society such as family, school, army, police, political parties, etc., are relatively independent and are not organically fixed to the society. The movement of the parts is relatively free here.

2. Society does not have a definite form as does the organism: Unlike organisms, societies have no specific external form, such as a physical body with limbs or a face. Organisms have an outward form or shape [for example, dog, donkey, monkey, deer and so on] whereas societies such as Indian society or American society do not have any definite and externally identifiable form. Society is only a mental construct. It is abstract and exists in our mind only in the form of an idea.

3. Manner of difference in the dependence of organs or parts on the organism or society: According to Spencer, parts or organs of the body [such as legs, hands, nose, eyes, head, etc.] of the organism are dependent upon the body itself. They exist for the sake of the body. On the other hand, in the case of society the parts [such as individuals, families, groups, etc.] are more important than the society. In fact, society exists for the benefit of its parts, that is, individuals. Spencer as a champion of the philosophy of individualism very strongly felt that the state and society exist for the good of the individual and not vice versa.

4. Difference regarding the centrality of "consciousness": In an organism, there exists what is known as "*consciousness*" and it is concentrated in a small part of the aggregate. The parts of the body do not have this. But in the case of the society consciousness is diffused throughout the individual members.

5. Differences regarding the structure and functions: In the case of organism each of its parts performs a definite and fixed function. The parts perform their functions incessantly. This certainty relating to the functions of the parts, we do not find in society. Functions of the parts of society such as institutions, often get changed. Some of the functions of family, for example, have changed. On the contrary, the eyes, heart, nerves, ears, tongue and other organs of the organism cannot change their functions.

It is quite interesting to note that Spencer made an elaborate effort to establish the similarities and differences between organic and social life. He persistently endeavoured to establish the organic analogy as the central theme of the second part of his "*Principles of Sociology.*" But at one stage he denied that he held to this doctrine of organic analogy. Replying to critics he made statements such as the following: "*I have used analogies, but only as a scaffolding to help in building up a coherent body of sociological induction. Let us take away the scaffolding: the induction will stand by themselves.*"[13]

Critical Comments

1. *Spencer used his organic analogy in a ridiculous manner* when he compared the King's Council to the medulla

13. Herbert Spencer as quoted by Nicholas S. Timasheff in *Sociological Theory — Its Nature and Growth*, p. 36.

oblongata, the House of Lords to the cerebellum, and the House of Commons to the cerebrum. He failed to understand the limitations of his analogy.

2. *Spencer used his analogy in a very dogmatic manner*, but later referred to it as merely a scaffolding for building a structure of deductions. He actually proceeded as if the scaffolding were the real building,. "*Unfortunately, he consistently and conspicuously used the terminology of organicism. Moreover, one chapter of Principles of Sociology is entitled "Society is an Organism.*"[14]

3. The organic analogy was used by thinkers in their discussions even prior to Spencer. But Spencer was the first to give to that analogy the value of scientific theory. *But he was very definitely taken a prisoner by the ghost he had evoked.*

4. If a society is like an organism, it experiences a natural cycle of birth, maturity, old age, and death. *But the death of a society does not come with organic inevitableness.* A society need not die.

5. Whether we accept or reject Spencer's comparisons between the human society and the organism, we are bound to acknowledge the fact that he popularised the concept of "*system*" in our sociological discussion. Present-day sociology profusely uses Spencer's concept of "*system*", of course, in a modified form.

SOCIAL DARWINISM

Meaning of the Concept of *"Social Darwinism"*

"Social Darwinism" *a 19th century adaptation of Charles Darwin's theory of evolution, is a theoretical explanation of human social life in general and social inequality in particular.*"[15]

"*The term Social Darwinism refers to any doctrine which makes use or misuse of Charles Darwin's biological evolutionary principles to explain or justify the existing forms of human social organisation.*"[16]

Herbert Spencer of Britain and **W.G. Sumner** [1840-1910] of America can be considered the two priminent advocates of the theory of "*Social Darwinism.*" There is an attempt in this theory to extend the principles of evolution to explain the developments taking place in the social world.

Spencer's "*Social Darwinism*" centred around two fundamental principles:

1. The Principle of "Survival of the Fittest"

According to Spencer, nature is endowed with a providential tendency to get rid of the unfit and to make room for the better. It is the law of the nature that the weak should be eliminated for the sake of the strong. He believed that the rapid elimination of unfit individuals from society through natural selection would benefit the race biologically. It is for this reason that the state should do nothing to relieve the conditions of poor, whom Spencer assumed to be "*less fit.*" By less fit, Spencer meant less healthy and less intelligent than the social norm. According to Spencer, stupid persons, people with vices and idleness, people who become victims of sickness and deformity and such other persons belong to the category of *less fit.* Due to the operation of the laws of evolution only the ***"more fit"*** persons will survive and the ***"less fit"*** ones will decline on their own. By this, Spencer did not, however, mean that "*widows and orphans should be left to struggle for life or death.*" He was only opposed to governmental assistance to the "*less fit.*" But he did not oppose individual philanthropy. As a strong supporter of individualism Spencer maintained that "*the economic system works best if each individual is allowed to seek his own private interests and that consequently the state should not intervene in the economy.*"[17]

2. The Principle of Non-Interference

Spencer who championed the ideology of Social Darwinism also became a very strong advocate of individualism and laissez-faire politics. Spencer opposed almost all forms of state interference with private property. "He insisted that the state

14. N.S. Timasheff, p. 37.
15. *Blackwell Dictionary of Sociology* by Allan G. Johnson, p. 258.
16. *Encyclopaedia of Anthropology* by Hunter and Whitten, p. 357.
17. Abraham and Morgan, p. 64.

had no business in education, health and sanitation, postal service, money and banking, regulation of housing conditions or the elimination of poverty. Money used for such activities could better be spent "*to support labourers employed in new productive works - land - drainage, machine building, etc.*"[18] According to Spencer, state was just like a joint stock company, whose primary business was protection of the rights of individuals and defending the interests of its citizens against external aggression.

Views of Comte were different in this regard. He was of the opinion that the sociologist-priests should be actively involved in the social world - "*to reform and to change it.*" Spencer on the other hand, argued - "*sociologists should convince the state and the citizens not to intervene in the natural process of selection operative in society. Nature is more intelligent than man, he argued, and* "*once you begin to interfere with the order of nature there is no knowing where the result will end.*"[19] The good society, according to Spencer, is thus, based completely upon contracts between individuals pursuing their respective interests unhindered by the state interference.

Critical Remarks

1. The theory of "*Social Darwinism*" got wide publicity during the second half of the 19th century especially in Europe and America. The theory was being used to justify the imposition of the politico-economic domination of the whites over non-whites. It thus became an ideological theory for justifying the exploitation of exploiters and for protecting the vested interests of the imperialists.

2. This theory "*had racial overtones with the belief that some races, being innately superior, were bound to triumph over inferior ones.*"[20]

3. The principle of the "*survival of the fittest*" *indirectly supports the status quo, inactivity and idleness.* As per this principle, nature itself plays the role of the selector. It supports the fittest and leaves the less fit to decadence.

4. The theory *does not take into account an enormous increase in the population* especially in the Asian nations like India, China, Bangladesh and the like. In these nations, we find a large number of people being born in the category of poor, and the labour class. Why the principle of the "*survival of the fittest*" is not operating in these nations - ? There is no answer.

5. This theory does not take into account that people in the category of the poor and labour class are suffering from problems and seem to be "*less fit ones*", not because they are basically incapable and less fit, but *they have become the victims of socially organised coercions.*

6. "*As an argument, Social Darwinism is deeply flawed and has little, if any, credibility among contemporary social scientists........ As such, it could always be used to justify the status quo, beginning with racial and other forms of social oppression and imperialism.*"[21]

7. In the circle of social theorists, the theory of Social Darwinism, exists only pejoratively.

8. The views of "Social Darwinism", however, are occasionally continued in the form of "*socio-biology.*"

TYPES OF SOCIETY: CLASSIFICATION AND COMPARISON

Spencer's clear conception of the nature of society helped him develop models to classify and compare societies. Two models which he followed could be identified from this analysis.

1 Classification of Societies on the Basis of the "Degree of Composition"

Spencer's evolutionary law suggested that societies could be classified on the basis of their "*degree of composition.*" On this basis he classified societies into four types.

(*i*) Simple Society,

(*ii*) Compound Society,

18. Ibid, p. 65.
19. Ibid, p. 65.
20. N. Abercrombie and Others in "*The Penguin Dictionary of Sociology.*"
21. *Blackwell Dictionary of Sociology,* p. 258.

(*iii*) Doubly Compound Society,

(*iv*) Trebly Compound Society.

2. Classification Based on the Method of Constructing *"Models"* or *"Types"* of Society

According to **Ronald Fletcher,** Spencer also classified societies into (*i*) *Military Society*, and (*ii*) *Industrial Society*, on the basis of the relative preponderance of one or the other of the "*Regulating*", "*Sustaining*" and "*Distributive*" systems.

Military Society and Industrial Society

Spencer thought of constructing two extremely dissimilar "*types*" or "*models*" to classify societies into two categories. He called the types as "*militant societies*" and "*industrial societies.*" The first was a type in which the "*Regulating System*" was dominant over all the other aspects of society. The second was one in which the "*Sustaining System*" was emphasised, and all the other aspects of society were subordinated to its service. Spencer developed the construction of "*two polar types*" mainly for the sake of a clear understanding of societies which possessed a relative preponderance of one or other of the two systems.

Spencer described his "two types" of society as follows:

1. *The Militant [Military] Society*

Military Society is any form of society in which the military exerts a dominant or pervasive role. Its main characteristics may be noted below:

(*i*) *Organisation for offensive and defensive military action*: The militant society is a type in which organisation for offensive and defensive military action is predominant. It is the society in which the army is the nation mobilised and the whole nation is regarded as a silent army. Here, the entire structure of society is moulded into military structure. It reflects a military organisation.

(*ii*) *Centralised pattern of authority and social control*: Here the military head is also the political head. He has a despotic control over life and property of all his subjects. Absolute control of the ruler makes necessary a clear, precise and rigid hierarchy of power throughout society. The officials at each level are completely subservient to that above. Spencer wrote: "*All are slaves to those above and despots to those below.*"[22]

(*iii*) *Rigid social classes*: This rigid hierarchy of power necessarily involves a rigid grading of social statuses. Hence it gives rise to rigid social classes in economic life. The distribution of property, and the distribution of material rewards in society, are meticulously linked with the order of social ranks.

(*iv*) *Religious beliefs and doctrines relating to the hierarchical power of gods*: This authoritarian and hierarchical nature of the society is also reflected in the prevailing system of ideas and beliefs. There exists a set of doctrines, myths, and rituals which portray a supernatural authority and government. The gods are also pictured in terms of a hierarchy of power. The religion itself, is a hierarchical organisation, and the Ecclesiastical Head himself possesses supreme, despotic authority. In such a society, the despotic head is, at the same time, not only the military and political head, but also the Ecclesiastical one. His central power over government, army, and all civil and economic affairs, is sanctified and given justification by religion. Here, the societies are normally in antagonism with other societies. Thus Spencer said: "*Ever in antagonism with other societies the life is a life of enemity and the religion a religion of enemity.*"[23]

(*v*) *Life is subject to rigorous discipline*: The whole tenor of life in a military society is characterised by rigorous discipline. Virtually there is no difference between the public life and the private life. No element of the private life of the citizen is closed to the state. The state can invade and interfere in the private lives of citizens whenever it is felt necessary or desirable to do so. There is the lack of individual rights in the relationship between individual and the state. Thus the prevailing belief is - "*that its members exist for the benefit of the whole and not the whole for the benefit of its members.*"[24] The loyalty of the individual to the state has to be unquestioning.

---

22. Spencer as quoted by Ronald Fletcher in *The Making of Sociology*, Vol. I, p. 284.
23. Spencer as quoted by Ronald Fletcher, p. 284.
24. Ronald Fletcher, p. 284.

(vi) Human relationship based on compulsory co-operation: Human relationships are characterised in this kind of society by a state of "*compulsory co-operation.*" Spencer, however, has not elaborated this point much.

It is clear from the above description that Spencer's "*Militant type*" of society could be used as a basis of interpretation not only to the despotic societies of the ancient world, but also to the totalitarian societies in the contemporary world. As **Ronald Fletcher** says, as a "*type*", the "militant society" could be seen to be of wide use for the purpose of comparative societies. It is relevant to the societies of both the past and the present.

2. THE INDUSTRIAL SOCIETY

The concept of "*Industrial society*" *refers to* "*that form of society or any particular society, in which industrialisation and modernisation have occurred.*"[25]

The general term "*industrial society*" originates from **Saint Simon** who chose it to reflect the emerging central role of manufacturing industry in 18th century Europe, in contrast with the previous pre-industrial society and agrarian society.

Spencer's "*Industrial Society*" is one in which military activity and organisation exists but it is carried on at a distance. It takes place in the periphery of the society and the greater part of the social organisation is peaceful. It concentrates upon the increase and improvement of all aspects of human production and welfare; upon economic and civil activities.

The characteristics of "industrial society" in this way contrast strongly with those of the "militant type." They are briefed below.

(i) Recognition of personal rights: In the industrial society the members hold "*personal rights*" as citizens of the community. There is also an active concern on the part of the members for the maintenance of these rights. Hence they insist upon an effective means of representative government. Any dispute or mutual claims and counter-claims relating to the rights are to be resolved here through an impartial procedure or institutional arrangement.

(ii) "Sustaining system" possessing a large degree of freedom: In this society, the "*sustaining system*" possesses a large degree of freedom from the "*regulatory system.*" Here the control and governance of the economic affairs is deliberately separated from the political government. It is assumed here that the intelligent individuals concerned with their own economic activities are more capable of making their own decisions than the administrative officials. They are not only *allowed*, they are actively *encouraged*, to do so.

(iii) Opportunity for the growth of free associations and institutions: The growth of agr culture, commerce and industrial manufacture within a fixed geographic territory is given military security. The peaceful atmosphere leads to the growth of free associations and institutions. In all such associations, forming committees, laying down rules and procedures, conducting elections, etc. become a common practice.

(iv) A less rigid class structure: "*These factors bring about a much less rigid and less tyrannical class structure........*" [**Ronald Fletcher** - 285]. In this type of class structure human relationships become contractual and free. Further, the gradations of status and rank are less precisely marked. As Spencer puts it "*There is a growth...... of* "*combinations of workmen and employers*" *to resolve, particular disputes, quite separately from central authority of law.*"[26]

(v) In the industrial society, religious organisations and religious beliefs lose their hierarchical structure and power: Individual faith and sectarian discrimination, enters into religion. Religion instead of working as a means of social control remains only as a matter of individual faith and commitment. Religious institutions and practices become more and more secular in nature.

(vi) Here the members of the society do not exist for the good of the state; but the well-being of the individuals becomes the supreme objective of the government: The doctrine that the members of the society exist for the good of the state slowly disappearing. The idea that the will and the well-being of the individual citizens which is of supreme importance in the society, prevails upon the previous one. Hence all forms of governmental control, exist merely to manifest their wishes and to serve them.

25. *Collins Dictionary of Sociology,* p. 318.
26. Ronald Fletcher, p. 85.

***(vii) Awareness of the duty to resist irresponsible government*:** In such a society the despotic government is considered to be irrelevant and wrong. It becomes a positive duty on the part of the citizens to **resist** the irresponsible government. "*There is always a tendency to disobedience amongst minorities and individuals, and such a critical tendency is positively encouraged.*"

***(viii) Dominance of free and contractual type of human relationships*:** It is clear from the above explanation that the "*Human relationships in the industrial society are, therefore, wholly different from those in the militant society. Free, responsible, contractual relationships between individuals require voluntary co-operation, not the compulsory co-operation which characterises relationships in the militant type.*"[27]

Characteristics of Military and Industrial Societies: A Contrast

Concluding remarks: It must be noted that "Spencer did not believe that societies actually existed in the world with the sharp clarity of distinction that he described in drawing these "*models.*" [**Ronald Fletcher** - 286].

Spencer was aware that he was presenting those *two "models" to help comparison of societies.* Spencer was of the opinion that this mode of classification would help to interpret and understand some of the crucially important trends of social evolution. These trends, according to him were of great importance as the traditional societies get radically transformed by the process of industrialisation.

This mode of classifying societies helped Spencer in undertaking a very detailed comparative study of each major social institution within each "*type*" of society. "*This gave him a picture of what, in the whole field of social institutions had actually occurred in the past, and what was happening in the present.*"[28]

Characteristics	*Militant Society*	*Industrial Society*
Dominant Function or activity	Corporate defensive & offensive activity for preservation and aggrandizement	Peaceful, mutual rendering of individual services
Principle of social coordination	Compulsory cooperation; regimentation by enforcement of orders; both positive and negative regulation of activity.	Voluntary cooperation; regulation by contract and principles of justice; only negative regulation of activity.
Relations between state and individual	Individuals exist for the benefit of state; restraints on liberty property, and mobility.	State exists for benefit of individuals; freedom; few restraints on property and mobility.
Relations between state and other organizations	All organizations public; private organizations excluded.	Private organizations encouraged.
Structure of state	Centralized	Decentralized
Structure of social stratification	Fixity of rank, occupation, and locality; inheritance of positions	Plasticity and openness of rank, occupation, and locality; movement between positions
Type of economic activity	Economic autonomy and self-sufficiency; little external trade; protectionism trade.	Loss of economic autonomy; interdependence via peaceful trade; free trade
Valued social and personal characteristics	Patriotism; courage; reverence; loyalty; obedience; faith in authority; discipline	Independence; respect for others; resistance to coercion; individual initiative; truthfulness; kindness.

Militant and Industrial Societies: Spencer's contrasts between militant and industrial societies. This table (from **Smelser,** 1968) is derived from Herbert Spencer, *The Principles of Sociology* 1897 as quoted in *Collins Dictionary of Sociology*. Page-415.

In this classification of societies, it appears that Spencer was too optimistic about the industrial society. **Bogardus** thus points out: "*In the coming industrial order Spencer foresaw an era in which the main business of society will be to defend*

27. Ibid., p. 286.
28. Ibid

the rights of "Individuals." Spencer forecast an epoch of industrial states which have abolished war."[29] Experience would tell us that the wars have not yet become the things of the past.

Bogardus further writes: "*Spencer's industrialism, however, had fundamental wea nesses. It implies that social organisation is more important than social process. It neglects to provide sufficiently for inherent psychical changes. It assumes that an industrial society, as such, will be peaceful. It underestimates the importance of socialising motives*" [**Bogardus,** p. 293.]

A WORD ABOUT SPENCER'S CONTRIBUTIONS

1. Spencer's contributions to social thought are not negligible, but recognisable. Unlike those of Comte, Spencer's views were widely accepted during his lifetime. They dominated the minds of many scholars and others from 1865 to 1895. During the three decades the leading thinkers and philosophers of the West had come under the influence of Spencer.

2. Spencer's theories had a special appeal because they catered to the two needs of the day, (*a*) *the desire for unifying knowledge*, and (*b*) *the need for scientific justification for the* "*laissez-faire*" *principle.*

3. Spencer emphasised the laws of evolution and natural causation. He described social evolution as a phase of natural evolution.

4. He strongly supported the principle of "*individualism*", for he himself was individualistic. He attacked the idea that the State is a master machine to which all the citizens must submit automatically.

5. Spencer formulated an integral theory of all reality. "His law of evolution is a cosmic law. His theory is, therefore, essentially philosophical not sociological. Strictly speaking, philosophers should check its validity" **- L.A. Coser.**

6. Spencer's organismic theory highly influenced the later sociologists like **Paul Von Lilienfeld, Jacques Novicow, Ward, Sumner** and **Giddings.**

7. Spencer in his organic analogy suggested likenesses and differences between biological organisms and human society.

8. He made the role of social structures, or institutions stand out distinctly.

In conclusion, it could be said that "........ *Spencer spoke in his writings to the needs of his time. Times have changed, but once again his work seems to commend itself to our age as it searches for answers to age-old questions about how to live in community while maintaining individuality.*"[30]

REVIEW QUESTIONS

1. Write in brief the biography of Herbert spencer.
2. Give an account of the main works of Herbert spencer.
3. Highlight the contribution of Herbert spencer to sociology.
4. Explain spencer's theory of evolution.
5. Discuss spencer's theory of social evolution.
6. Spencer's theory of evolution is a joint product of the seven law. Analyse.
7. Describe spencer's theory of organic analogy.
8. Highlight the similarities and dissimilarities between the biological and social organisms as visualised by Herbert spencer.
9. Explain the concept of social darwinism.
10. Critically analyse the theory of social darwinism.
11. Discuss the types of society.
12. Classify and compare societies.

⌘⌘⌘⌘⌘⌘⌘⌘⌘⌘⌘

29. Bogardus in *The Development of Social Thought,* p. 293.
30. Abraham and Morgan in *Sociological Thought,* p. 71.

57

DURKHEIM AND HIS CONTRIBUTIONS

CHAPTER OUTLINE

- A Brief Biographical Sketch of Spencer : Main Works of Spencer
- A Brief Biographical Sketch of Emile Durkheim
- Main Works of Durkheim
- Theory of Social Facts : Meaning of the Concept of Social Facts
- Two Main Characteristics of Social Facts
- Critical Comments
- Durkheim's Theory of Division of Labour: Meaning of Division of Labour
- The Link Between Division of Labour and Social Solidarity
- Division of Labour and Anomie
- Concluding Remarks
- Durkheim's Theory and Typology of Suicide: Definition of Suicide
- Social Forces are the Real Causes of Suicide
- Durkheim Egoistic, Altruistic and Anomic Suicides
- The Elementary Forms of Religious Life
- An Estimate of Durkheim's Works.

A BRIEF BIOGRAPHICAL SKETCH OF EMILE DURKHEIM

Emile Durkheim [1858-1917] was the most prominent French sociologist of the 19th century. He was an erudite scholar, a deep thinker, a progressive educationist, an effective writer and a strict disciplinarian. Unlike Spencer, Durkheim acknowledged Comte as his master. He borrowed from Comte the positivistic stress on empiricism. But he went far ahead of Comte to establish sociology as an empirical science. He insisted that sociology too should follow the scientific method for it to be considered a science.

Emile Durkheim
[1858-1917]

Durkheim was born in a Jewish family at Epinal in the eastern French province of Lorraine on 15th April, 1858. He studied Hebrew language, the Old Testament, and the Talmud at an early age. In spite of this background he remained an agnostic throughout his life.

Durkheim had a bright student career in the College at Epinal and won several prizes. He was not happy with the conventional subjects taught at the school and college level. He longed for schooling in scientific methods and in the moral principles needed to contribute to the moral guidance of society. Although he was interested in scientific sociology there wasn't one at that time. He graduated from the famous college of Paris "*Ecole Normale*". Between 1882 and 1887 he taught philosophy in a number of provincial schools in Paris and surrounding area.

Durkheim's love for education took him to Germany where he was exposed to the scientific psychology being pioneered by Wilhelm Wundt. After his return from Germany he went on publishing several articles based on his experiences there. These publications earned him a prominent place in the department of philosophy at University of Bordeaux in 1887. He was later asked to head the newly created department of "*Social Science*". Thereafter Durkheim and his writings became famous.

The years that followed were characterised by a series of personal success for Durkheim. In 1893 he published his French doctoral thesis, "*The Division of Labour in Society*". His other famous works were also published in due course: "*The Rules of Sociological Method*" in 1885, "*Suicide*" in 1897 and "*The Elementary Forms of Religious Life*" in 1912. In the meantime [in 1902] he was invited to the famous French University, the Sorbonne. In 1906, he was named the professor of the science of education and his title was subsequently changed in 1913 to professor of the science of education and sociology.

Durkheim was actively concerned with French politics throughout his life. He was respected as a political liberalist. The most prominent area of his interest was moral education. He was particularly concerned to discover values and moral principles that would guide French education. In these matters he inherited the collectivist tradition of social thought represented by di Maistre, St. Simon, and Comte. He reacted sharply against the individualist ideas of Spencer and English Utilitarians. He wanted to reverse the moral degeneration he saw around him in French society. He urged people "*to achieve victory in the struggle against public madness.*"

Durkheim had evinced interest in socialism. His conception of socialism was markedly different from that of Marxian socialism. Durkheim labelled Marxism as *a set* of "*disputable and out-of-date hypotheses.*"[1] He did not see the proletariat as the salvation of society, and he was greatly opposed to agitation or violence.

Durkheim was relatively unhappy during his last days. The moral degeneration of the French society brought him great disappointment. In this state of disappointment he died in his 59th year in 1917. His influence on sociology is a lasting one. The journal which he started "*Anne Sociologique*" [in 1896] still continues to serve, as one of the leading journals of sociological thought. Though Durkheim is no more, *functionalism, sociology of education, sociology of law, sociology of religion etc.* started by him, are still alive.

MAIN WORKS OF DURKHEIM

1. *'The Division of Labour in Society', 1893.*
2. *'The Rules of Sociological Method', 1895.*
3. *'Suicide', 1897.*
4. *'Collective and Individual Representations', 1899.*
5. *'Judgements of Reality and Judgements of Value', 1911.*
6. *'The Elementary Forms of Religious Life', 1912.*
7. *'Professional Ethics and Civic Morals'.*

THEORY OF SOCIAL FACTS

The concept of "*social facts*" assumes importance in Durkheimian sociology. In fact, Durkheim has even defined *sociology as a science of social facts.* Social facts and events constitute the fundamental bases of his sociological thought. He tried to analyse and explain social phenomena and social life by making use of this concept as his basic concept. Durkheim's views about social facts are extensively dealt with in his second major treatise namely "*The Rules of Sociological Method*" (1895).

Main Intentions of the *"Theory of Social Facts"*

Durkheim was in part a positivist and a believer in applying the methods of physical science to the study of social facts. Durkheimian conception of sociology is based on a theory of social fact. Durkheim's aim is to demonstrate that there is a science called "*sociology*" which is an objective science conforming to the model of the other sciences and whose subject is the social fact.

Meaning of the Concept of *"Social Fact"*

1. "*A Social fact is a phase of behaviour [thinking, feeling or acting] which is subjective to the observer and which has a coercive nature.*"[2]

2. Social facts represent "*a category of facts*" *with distinctive characteristics,* "*consisting of ways of acting, thinking and feeling, external to the individual and endowed with a power of coercion by means of which they control him.*"[3]

---

1. Lukes as quoted by George Ritzer in *Contemporary Sociological Theory*, 2nd Edition p. 81.
2. E.S. Bogardus in *The Development of Social Thought,* p. 413.
3. Durkheim [1895] as quoted in *Collins Dictionary of Sociology,* p. 608.

The Two Requirements of Durkheimian Sociology

According to **Raymond Aron,**[4] the requirement of Durkheimian sociology is twofold:

(*i*) The subject of sociology must be *specific,* it must be distinguished from the subjects of all the other sciences; and

(*ii*) This subject must be such that it is to be observed and explained in a manner *similar* to the way in which facts are observed and explained in other sciences.

When we begin to analyse the subject of study of sociology, that is, "*social facts*" in the light of these two requirements, we will come to know about the two important characteristics of social facts. The twofold requirements mentioned above throw light on the two important characteristics of social facts.

Two Main Characteristics of Social Facts

Durkheim has emphatically stated that social facts must consist of the following two characteristics.

1. *Social facts must be regarded as* ***"things"****, and*
2. *Social facts are* ***"external"*** *and* ***"exercise constraint"*** *on individuals.*

1. Social Facts must be Regarded as "Things"

According to Durkheim, social facts must be treated as ***"things",*** *as empirical facts* from the outside, we must discover them as we discover physical facts. "Precisely because we have the illusion of knowing social realities, it is important that we realise that they are not immediately known to us. It is in this sense that Durkheim maintains that we must regard social facts as things because things, he says, are all that is given, all that is offered to - or rather forced upon - our observation."[5] Durkheim also warns that we have to "*get rid ourselves of the preconceptions and prejudices which incapaciate us when we try to know social facts scientifically.*"

Social facts are not reducible to individual facts: Durkheim, thus writes: "*Social facts are inexplicable in terms of and irreducible to either psychological or physiological analysis.*" Distinguishing between psychological and social facts Durkheim says: "The former are elaborated in the individual consciousness and then tend to externalise themselves; the latter are at first external to the individual, whom they tend to fashion in their image from without."[6] Thus, Durkheim's orientation towards the study of society requires that economic and psychological reductionism be eschewed in the light of the "sui generis" quality of social facts.

2. Social Facts are External to the Individuals and Exercise a Constraint on Them

This characteristic feature involves two elements:

(*a*) *Social facts are external to the individuals,* and

(*b*) *Social facts exercise a constraint on them.*

(a) Social facts are external to the individuals

Durkheim has emphatically stated that *society is a reality* "*sui generis*" *above and apart from the individuals.* He provides four evidences in defence of this assertion. **H.E. Barnes**[7] has listed those four evidences and they are mentioned below.

(i) Heterogeneity of individual and collective states of mind: Durkheim says that there is a difference in the states of mind of an individual and a group. **Ex.** In times of national danger the intensity of the collective feeling of patriotism is much greater than that of any individual feeling. Further, society's willingness to sacrifice individuals is much greater than the willingness of individuals to sacrifice themselves.

(ii) Difference in individual attitudes and behaviour which results from the group situation: Individual, for example thinks, feels, and acts in a different fashion when in a crowd. This means that a new reality is created by the association of individuals and this reality reacts upon the sentiments and behaviour of the individuals. It can even change them.

(iii) Uniformities of social statistics: Many types of social facts like crimes, marriages, suicides, etc., show a surprising degree of numerical consistency from year to year. This consistency cannot be explained from personal motives or characteristics. According to Durkheim, this could be explained only in terms of "*certain real social currents which form a part of the individual's environment.*

(iv) The fourth evidence is based on analogy and on the philosophical theory of emergence: Just as the phenomenon of life cannot be explained by the physiochemical properties of the molecules which form the cell, but by a particular

4. Raymond Aron in his "*Main Currents in Sociological Thought*" Vol. II. p. 70.
5. Raymond Aron, p. 71.
6. Durkheim in his *Rules of Sociological Method,* p. 102.
7. H.E. Barnes in *An Introduction to the History of Sociology*, Abridged Edition, pp. 211 - 212.

association of molecules, so also we must assume that society is not reducible to the properties of individual minds. On the contrary, society constitutes a reality sui generis which emerges out of the interaction of individual minds.

(b) Social facts exercise constraints on the individuals

According to Durkheim, social facts have a constraining effect on individuals. Social facts so condition human beings that it makes them behave in a particular manner. Durkheim gives a series of examples such as moral laws, legal rules, penal system and the crowd behaviour in support of this view. ***Examples***:

(1) In a *crowd situation* an individual feels constrained to behave in a particular manner. Laughter, for example, is communicated to all. Such a phenomenon is social because, its basis, its subject is the group as a whole and not the society.

(2) Similarly, *fashion is social in nature*. Everyone dresses in a certain manner in a given year because everyone else does so. It is not an individual who is the cause of fashion, it is society itself which expresses itself in these ways.

(3) The institutions of *education, law, beliefs* also have the characteristics of being given to everyone from without and of being imperative for all.

Critical Comments

(*i*) According to **L.A. Coser,** Durkheim's *theory of social facts completely ignores the importance of the individual* and places too much premium on society.

(*ii*) Durkheim's attempts to analyse and study "*social facts as things*" is criticised by **H.E. Barnes.** He says that Durkheim has not made it clear anywhere as to what he means by the term "*things*" in the context of social facts. The term can mean many things to many people.

(*iii*) Durkheim recommended indirect experiment that is, the *comparative method as the only appropriate method suited to study social phenomena.* He made comparative sociology .... not a branch of sociology, *but sociology itself.*

(*iv*) **Gabriel Tarde** criticises that it is difficult to imagine and appreciate Durkheimian analysis of society bereft of individuals.

In spite of these criticisms, Durkheim's theory of social facts has its own importance in Durkheimian sociology. "Durkheim's general interest in *social order* and *social constraint* led him directly to a study, not only of affluence and labour, but of suicide and religion. His theory of social fact further inspired him to lay the foundation for the "*functional approach.*"

DURKHEIM'S THEORY OF DIVISION OF LABOUR

Durkheim's "*Theory of Division of Labour*" is often regarded as his major contribution to the field of sociological thought. Durkheim's doctoral thesis, "*Division of Labour in Society*" - 1893, is his first major book. In this, the influence of Auguste Comte is clearly evident. The theme of this book is the relationship between individuals and society or the collectivity. *It is indeed a classic study of social solidarity.* In this book he reacted against the view that modern industrial society could be based simply upon agreement between individuals motivated by self-interest and without any prior consensus. He agreed that the kind of consensus in modern society was different from that in simpler social systems. But he saw both of these as two types of social solidarity.

In his famous work "*The Division of Labour in Society*" Durkheim tried to determine the social consequences of the division of labour in modern societies. A major theme in all Durkheim's writings is *the importance of shared social norms and values in maintaining social cohesion and solidarity.* He argued that the nature of this social solidarity depends on the extent of the division of labour.

Meaning of Division of Labour

The concept of "*Division of Labour*" has been used in three ways:

(*i*) in the sense of the ***technical division of labour,*** it describes the production process;

(*ii*) as the ***sexual division of labour,*** it describes social divisions between men and women;

(*iii*) as the ***social division of labour,*** it refers to differentiation in society as a whole.[8] [It is in the third sense, that Durkheim uses this term.]

In a general sense, the term division of labour involves the *assignment to each unit or group a specific share of a common task.*

8. *The Penguin Dictionary* by Abercrombie and others, p. 74.

As used by the early classical economists such as **Adam Smith** (1776), *the term describes a specialisation in workshops and the factory system, and explains the advantages accruing in terms of the increased efficiency and productivity from these new arrangements.*[9]

Durkheim's Optimistic View of Division of Labour

"While Marx was pessimistic about the division of labour in society, Durkheim was cautiously optimistic. Marx saw the specialised division of labour trapping the worker in his occupational role and dividing society into antagonistic social classes. Durkheim saw a number of problems arising from specialisation in industrial society but believed that *the promise of the division of labour outweighed the problems.*"[10]

Two Main Types of Social Solidarity

As it is made clear that the main theme of the book "*Division of Labour in Society*" by Durkheim, is the relationship between the individual and society. The nature of this relationship could be stated in the form of two questions: (*i*) *How can a large number of individuals make up a society-*? and (*ii*) *How can these individuals achieve 'consensus' which is the basic condition of social existence-*?

In his attempts to answer these vital questions Durkheim drew up a distinction between two forms of solidarity namely: (*i*) *mechanical solidarity* and (*ii*) *organic solidarity,* respectively. These two types of solidarity were found in the traditional tribal societies and in the modern complex urban societies.

The Link between Division of Labour and Social Solidarity

Meaning of the concept of solidarity

- "*Social solidarity*" *is synonymous with social cohesion or social integration.*
- Social solidarity refers to "*the integration and degree or type of integration, manifest by a society or group.*"[11]
- Social solidarity refers to "*the condition within a group in which there is social cohesion plus co-operative, collective action directed towards the achievement of group goals*"[12]

The basis of social solidarity are different in simple societies and complex societies.

Durkheim made comparisions between the primitive and the civilised societies in terms of his concept of solidarity. According to him, the primitive society is characterised by "*mechanical solidarity*" based on the "*conscience collective*"; and the advanced society is characterised by "*organic solidarity*" based on the "*division of labour.*"

1. *Mechanical Solidarity*

As defined by Durkheim, mechanical solidarity refers to "*social solidarity based upon a homogeneity of values and behaviour, strong social constraint, and loyalty to tradition and kinship. The term applied to small, non-literate societies characterised by a simple division of labour, very little specialisation of function, only a few social roles and very little tolerance of individuality.*"[13]

As Durkheim has stated *mechanical solidarity is a solidarity of resemblance.* It is rooted in the similarity of the individual members of a society. In the society where this kind of solidarity prevails individuals do not differ from one another much. They are the members of the same collectivity and resemble one another because "*they feel the same emotions, cherish the same values, and hold the same things sacred. The society is coherent because the individuals are not yet differentiated.*" Here we find the strong states of the "*Collective Conscience.*" Collective conscience refers "*to the sum total of beliefs and sentiments common to the average members of the society.*" This prevails mostly in primitive societies. The common conscience completely covers individual mentality and morality. "*Here social constraint is expressed most decisively in repressive, severe criminal law which serves to maintain mechanical solidarity.*"

2. *Organic Solidarity*

As defined by Durkheim, organic solidarity refers to "*a type of societal solidarity typical of modern industrial society, in which unity is based on the interdependence of a very large number of highly specialised roles in a system involving a*

9. *Collins Dictionary of Sociology,* p. 172.
10. M. Haralambos in *Sociology — Themes and Perspectives*, p. 237.
11. *Collins Dictionary of Sociology,* p. 621.
12. W.P. Scott. *Dictionary of Sociology*, p. 406.
13. Ibid., p. 407.

complex division of labour that requires the co-operation of almost all the groups and individuals of the society.......... This type of solidarity is called ***organic*** *because it is similar to the unity of a biological organism in which highly specialised parts or organs, must work in co-ordination if the organism [or any one of its parts] is to survive*"[14]

Organic solidarity is almost the opposite of mechanical solidarity. According to Durkheim, increasing density of population is the major key to the development of division of labour. Organic solidarity emerges with the growth of the division of labour. This especially is witnessed in the modern industrial societies. Division of labour and the consequent dissimilarities among men bring about increasing interdependence in society. The interdependence is reflected in human mentality and morality and in the fact of organic solidarity itself. In organic solidarity, consensus results from differentiation itself. The individuals are no longer similar, but different. It is precisely because the individuals are different that consensus is achieved. *With the increase in division of labour the collective conscience lessens.* Thus, *criminal law tends to be replaced by civil and administrative law.* Here the stress is on restitution of rights rather than on punishment. *An increase in organic solidarity would represent moral progress* stressing the higher values of equality, liberty, fraternity, and justice. Even here, the social constraints in the form of contracts and laws continue to play a major role.

Differences between Mechanical and Organic Solidarities

Durkheim formulated the distinction between the two types of solidarity by identifying the demographic and morphological features basic to each type. He also identified the typical forms of law, and formal features and content of the conscience collective, which ought to be associated with each type Table 1.

Mechanical and Organic Solidarity: A Summary of Durkheim's Ideal Types [from Lukes, 1973] as Quoted in *Collins Dictionary of Sociology,* p. 406.

Table 1

	Mechanical Solidarity	*Organic Solidarity*
(1) Morphological (structural) basis	based on resemblances (predominant in less advanced societies) Segmental type (first clan- based, later territorial) Little interdependence (social bonds relatively weak) Relatively low volume of population Relatively low material and moral density	based on division of labour (predominant in more advanced societies) Organized type (fusion of markets and growth of cities) Much interdependence (social bonds relatively strong) Relatively high volume of population Relatively high material and moral density
(2) Type of norms (typified by law)	Rules with repressive sanctions Prevalence of penal law	Rules with restitutive sanctions Prevalence of cooperative law (civil, commercial, procedural, administrative and constitutional law)
(3) (a) Formal features of conscience collective	High volume High intensity High determinateness Collective authority absolute	Low volume Low intensity Low determinateness More room for individual initiative and reflexion
(3) (b) Content of conscience collective	Highly religious Transcendental (superior to human interests and beyond discussion) Attaching supreme value to society and interests of society as a whole Concrete and specific	Increasingly secular Human-orientated (concerned with human interests and open to discussion) Attaching supreme value to individual dignity, equality of opportunity, work ethic and social justice Abstract and general

Division of Labour is Different from Disintegration: Durkheim

Durkheim distinguishes between division of labour and disintegration. Disintegration is illustrated by industrial failures, crises, conflicts and crimes. All these are pathological in nature. "In these forms the division of labour ceases to bring forth

14. Durkheim as quoted by W.P. Scott in *Dictionary of Sociology,* p. 407.

solidarity hence represents an "*anomic division of labour*" so to say. Division of labour in society is actually different from occupational division of labour in the factory as pointed out by Marx.

In his earlier work Durkheim stated that a society with organic solidarity needed fewer common beliefs to bind members to the society. But later he changed his view and stressed that even the societies in which organic solidarity has reached its peak, needed a common faith, a "*common conscience collective.*" This would help the men to remain united and *not to* "*disintegrate into a heap of mutually antagonistic and self-seeking individuals.*"

Division of Labour and Anomie

Division of labour, though an essential element of society can do great harm to the society if carried to the extreme. Durkheim was quite aware of this and hence had cautioned against the adverse consequences of unregulated division of labour. ***"Anomie"*** is one such adverse consequence. In fact, Durkheim was the first to use this concept.

The Greek term **"Anomie"** *literally means* "*without norms*" *or* "*normlessness.*" "Anomie" is *the outcome of clash in one's own values and those of the society* and one is not clear in what way to go, how to behave and how to come upto the expectations of the society and also how to mould the environment to suit his expectations.

"*Anomie is the strict counterpart of the idea of social solidarity. Just as solidarity is a state of collective ideological integration, anomie is a state of confusion, insecurity, normlessness. The collective representations are in a state of decay.*"[15]

State of Anomie Leading to Personal and Social Disorganisation

The essential problem of modern society, Durkheim argued, is that the division of labour leads inevitably to feelings of individualism, which can be achieved only at the cost of shared sentiments or beliefs. The result is *anomie* - a state of normlessness in both the society and the individual. Social norms become confused or break down, and people feel detached from their fellow beings. Having little commitment to shared norms, people lack social guidelines for personal conduct and are inclined to pursue their private interests without regard for the interests of society as a whole. Social control of individual behaviour becomes ineffective, and as a result the society is threatened with disorganisation or even disintegration.

Durkheim was probably correct in his view that the division of labour and the resulting growth of individualism would break down shared commitment to social norms, and it seems plausible that there is widespread anomie in modern societies. Yet these societies do retain some broad consensus on norms and values, as we can readily see when we compare one society with another, say, the United States with China. Although this consensus seems much weaker than that in preindustrial societies, it is probably still strong enough to guide most individual behaviour and to avert the social breakdown that Durkheim feared. Durkheim's analysis remains valuable, however, for his acute insights into the far-ranging effects that the division of labour has on social and personal life.

Concluding Remarks

Durkheim's views regarding division of labour could be summed up in the words of **Raymond Aron** in the following way:

According to Raymond Aron, the philosophical idea which underlies the theory of "division of labour" could be summed up like this: "The individual is the expression of the collectivity itself...... It is the structure of the collectivity that imposes on each man his peculiar responsibility." "Even in the society which authorises each man to be himself and know himself, there is more collective consciousness present in the individual consciousness than we imagine." *Collective imperatives and prohibitions, collective values and things held sacred are needed to bind individuals to the social entity.* Hence Durkheim felt that only if all the members of a society were tied to a common set of symbolic representations or to common set of beliefs about the world around them, the moral unity of the society would be safe. "Without them, Durkheim argued, any society, whether primitive or modern, was bound to degenerate and decay."[16]

DURKHEIM'S THEORY AND TYPOLOGY OF SUICIDE

Durkheim's third famous book ***"Suicide"*** published in 1897 is in various respects related to his study of division of labour. "*Suicide*", the act of taking one's own life, figures prominently in the historical development of sociology because it was the subject of the first sociological data to test a theory. Durkheim's theory of suicide is cited as "*a monumental landmark in which conceptual theory and empirical research are brought together.*"[17]

15. D. Martindale as quoted in W.P. Scott *Dictionary of Sociology*, p. 12.
16. Raymond Aron in his *Main Currents in Sociological Thought,* Vol. II.
17. Abraham and Morgan in "*Sociological Thought*, p. 114.

Durkheim's book "*Suicide*" is an analysis of a phenomenon regarded as pathological, intended to throw light on the evil which threatens modern industrial societies, that is, "*anomie.*" Suicide is an indication of disorganisation of both individual and society. Increasing number of suicides clearly indicates something wrong somewhere in the social system of the concerned society. Durkheim has studied this problem at some length.

Durkheim's study of suicide begins with a definition of the phenomenon. He then proceeds to refute the earlier interpretations of suicide. Finally, he develops a general theory of the phenomenon.

Definition of Suicide

According to **Durkheim,** suicide refers to "*every case of death resulting directly or indirectly from a positive or negative death performed by the victim himself and which strives to produce this result.*"

It is clear from the definition of Durkheim that suicide is a conscious act and the person concerned is fully aware of its consequences. The person who shoots himself to death, or drinks severe poison, or jumps down from the 10th storey of a building, for example, is fully aware of the consequences of such an act.

Two Main Purposes Behind this Study

Durkheim used a number of statistical records to establish his fundamental idea that *suicide is also a social fact* and social order and disorder are at the very root of suicide. As **Abraham** and **Morgan** [Page - 114] have pointed out, Durkheim made use of statistical analysis for two primary reasons. They are stated below:

(*a*) *To refute theories of suicide based on psychology, biology, genetics, climate, and geographic factors,*

(*b*) *To support with empirical evidence his own sociological explanation of suicide.*

Durkheim Displays an Extreme Form of Sociological Realism

Durkheim is of the firm belief that suicide is not an individual act or a private and personal action. It is caused by some power which is over and above the individual or "*super-individual.*" *It is not a personal situation but a manifestation of a social condition.* He speaks of suicidal currents as collective tendencies that dominate some vulnerable persons. The act of suicide is nothing but the manifestation of these currents. Durkheim has selected the instance or event of suicide to demonstrate the function of sociological theory.

Durkheim Choses Statistical Method to Know the Causes of Suicide

Durkheim wanted to know why people commit suicide, and he choose to think that explanations focussing on the psychology of the individual were inadequate. Experiments on suicide were obviously out of question. Case studies of the past suicides would be of little use, because they do not provide reliable generalizations, about all suicides. Survey methods were hardly appropriate, because one cannot survey dead people. But statistics on suicide were readily available, and Durkheim chose to analyze them.

Durkheim Rejects Extra-Social Factors as the Causes of Suicide

Durkheim repudiated most of the accepted theories of suicide. (1) His monographic study demonstrated that heredity, for example, is not a sufficient explanation of suicide. (2) Climatic and geographic factors are equally insufficient as explanatory factors. (3) Likewise, waves of imitation are inadequate explanations. (4) He also established the fact that suicide is not necessarily caused by the psychological factors.

Social Forces are the Real Causes of Suicide : Durkheim

Suicide is a highly individual act, yet the motives for a suicide can be fully understood only by reference to the social context in which it occurs. In his attempts to substantiate this fact he came to know that the incidence of suicide varied from one social group or set up to another and did so in a consistent manner over the years. Protestants were more likely to commit suicide than Catholics; people in large cities were more likely to commit suicide than people in small communities; people living alone were more likely to commit suicide than people living in families. Durkheim isolated one independent variable that lay behind these differences: *the extent to which the individual was integrated into a social bond with others.* People with fragile or weaker ties to their community are more likely to take their own lives than people who have stronger ties.

Durkheim's Threefold Classification of Suicide

Having dismissed explanations of extra-social factors, Durkheim proceeds to analyse the types of suicide. He takes into account three types of suicide:

(*a*) ***Egoistic Suicide*** which results from the lack of the integration of the individual into his social group.
(*b*) ***Altruistic Suicide*** is a kind of suicide which results from the over-integration of the individual into his social group.
(*c*) ***Anomic Suicide*** results from the state of normlessness or degeneration found in society.

Having analysed the above mentioned three types of suicide, Durkheim concludes that "*suicide is an individual phenomenon whose causes are essentially social.*"

Suicide: An Index to Decay in Social Solidarity

Durkheim has established the view that there are no societies in which suicide does not occur. It means suicide may be considered a "*normal*", that is, a regular, occurrence. However, sudden increase in suicide rates may be witnessed. This, he said, could be taken as "*an index of disintegrating forces at work in a social structure.*" He also came to the conclusion that different rates of suicide are the consequences of differences in degree and type of social solidarity. *Suicide is a kind of index to decay in social solidarity.*

Brief Evaluation of Durkheim's Theory of Suicide

Comments in Appreciation of the Theory

1. As **L.A. Coser** stated, Durkheim's study of ***"suicide"*** could be cited as a monumental landwork study in which conceptual theory and empirical research are brought together in an imposing manner."
2. As **Abraham** and **Morgan** have said "the larger significance of suicide lies in its demonstration of the function of sociological theory in empirical science" [Page - 114].
3. A successful attempt is made in this theory to establish logically the link between social solidarity, social control and suicide.
4. Durkheim has thrown light on the various faces of suicide. He is, indeed, the first person in this regard.

Critical Comments

1. Durkheim has given importance only to social factors in suicide. In doing so, he has neglected the role of other factors, especially the psychological. Hence this is a one-sided view.
2. The theory is based upon a very small sample of data concerning suicide.
3. As criminologists have pointed out, economic, psychological and even religious factors may lead to suicide. But Durkheim did not give any importance to these factors.

THREE TYPES OF SUICIDE

On the basis of the analysis of a mass of data gathered by him on many societies and cultures, Durkheim identified three basic types of suicides. They are as follows:

(*i*) Egoistic Suicide
(*ii*) Altruistic Suicide
(*iii*) Anomic Suicide.

According to Durkheim, all these occur as an expression of group breakdown of somekind or the other. These three types of suicide reveal different types of relations between the actor and his society.

1. Egoistic Suicide

Egoistic suicide is a product of relatively weak group integration. It takes place as a result of extreme loneliness and also out of excess individualism. When men become "*detached from society*", and when the bonds that previously had tied them to their fellow beings become loose - they are more prone to egoistic suicide.

According to Durkheim, egoistic suicides are committed by those individuals who have the tendency to shut themselves up within themselves. Such individuals feel affronted, hurt and ignored. Introvertive traits gain upper hand in them. Egoistic persons are aloof and cut off from the mainstream of society and do not take full interest in social matters. Such persons get alienated and find it difficult to cope with social alienation and feel impelled to commit suicide.

Durkheim's belief is that lack of integration of the individuals into the social group is the main cause for egoistic suicide. Durkheim studied varying degrees of integration of individuals into their religion, family, political and national communities. He found that among the Catholics suicides were comparatively less than among the Protestants. He also found that Catholicism is able to integrate its members more fully into its fold. On the other hand, Protestantism fosters spirit of free inquiry, permits great individual freedom, lacks hierarchic organisations and has fewer common beliefs and practices. It is known that the Catholic church is more powerfully integrated than the Protestant church. It is in this way the Protestants are more prone to commit suicide than the Catholics. Hence, *Durkheim generalised that the lack of integration is the main cause of egoistic suicide.*

2. *Altruistic Suicide*

This kind of suicide takes place in the form of a sacrifice in which an individual ends his life by heroic means so as to promote a cause or an ideal which is very dear to him. It results from the over-integration of the individual into his group. In simple words, *altruistic suicide is taking off one's own life for the sake of a cause.* It means that even high level of social solidarity induces suicide.

Examples:

(*i*) In some primitive societies and in modern armies such suicide takes place.

(*ii*) Japanese sometimes illustrate this type of suicide. They call it "*Harakiri.*" In this practice of Harakiri, some Japanese go to the extent of taking off their lives for the sake of the larger social unity. They consider that self-destruction would prevent the breakdown of social unity.

(*iii*) The practice of "*sati*" which was once in practice in North India, is another example of this kind.

(*iv*) The self-immolation by Buddhist monks, self-destruction in *Nirvana* under the Brahmanical influence as found in the case of ancient Hindu sages represent other variants of altruistic suicide.

Wherever altruistic suicide is prevalent, man is always ready to sacrifice his life for a great cause, principle, ideal or value.

3. *Anomic Suicide*

The breakdown of social norms and sudden social changes that are characteristic of modern times, encourage *anomic suicide.* When the collective conscience weakens, men fall victim to anomic suicide. "*Without the social backing to which one is accustomed, life is judged to be not worth continuing.*"

Anomic suicide is the type that follows catastrophic social changes. Social life all around seems to go to pieces. According to Durkheim, at times when social relations get disturbed both personal and social ethics become the casualities. Values of life come down and outlook of some persons changes radically. There are then certain dangerous developments in the society. A sudden change has its vibrations both in social life and social relationship, which paves way for suicide. If the change is sudden, adjustment becomes difficult and those who do not get adjusted to changes commit suicide. It is this social disruption which leads to suicide. According to Durkheim, not only economic disaster and industrial crisis but even sudden economic prosperity can cause disruption and deregulation and finally suicide.

Concluding Remarks

These three kinds of suicide understood as social types also correspond approximately to psychological types. ***"Egoistic suicide** tends to be characterised by a kind of apathy, an absence of attachment to life; **altruistic suicide,** by a state of energy and passion; **anomic suicide** is characterised by a state of irritation or disgust*" **- Raymond Aron.**

Raymond Aron pointed out that Durkheim in his study of "*suicide*" has been successful in establishing a social fact that there are "*specific social phenomena which govern individual phenomena. The most impressive, most eloquent example is that of the social forces which drive individuals to their deaths, each believing that he is obeying only himself.*"[18]

THE ELEMENTARY FORMS OF RELIGIOUS LIFE

This book "*The Elementary Forms of Religious Life - 1912*" seems to be the last of Durkheim's major works. In this book he brings his analysis of collective or group forces to the study of religion. It could be very well identified that Durkheim's concern about religion lay in the fact that it was one of the main agencies of solidarity and morality in society.

Durkheim, one of the earliest functionalist theorists, was the first sociologist to apply the functional approach to religion in a systematic way. His theory of religion got its proper form in his famous book "*The Elementary Forms of Religious Life, 1912.*" It is, indeed, his significant contribution to the field of "*sociology of religion.*"

Durkheim in his study stressed the social role or functions of the most simple form of religion called ***totemism*** of Australian Aborigines. *The totem, denotes a common object such as an animal, or a plant, and a symbol representing that it is sacred.* Each tribal clan is organised around totem. The totem, then, is sacred but it is also the symbol of society itself. From this fact Durkheim concluded that when people worship religion, they are really worshipping nothing more than their own society: "*divinity is merely society transformed and symbolically conceived.*"

---

18. Raymond Aron in *Main Currents in Sociological Thought,* Vol. II, p. 45.

What happens, Durkheim argued, is that the members of the clan gather periodically. They participate in some group functions with emotional excitement and feel great ecstacy and elation of a kind which they would never feel alone. Now, the "*Men know well that they are acted upon, but they do not know by whom.*" They pick on some nearby item such as a plant or animal, and make this the symbol of both their clan gathering (or society) and their experience of fervour and ecstacy (or religion). Their shared religious belief arises from the society and, in turn, it helps to hold the society together." - **Robertson.**

The unity and solidarity of the community is further increased by the rituals that are enacted on religious occasions. These rituals also have the capacity of bringing people together and reaffirming the values and beliefs of the group. They also help to transmit the cultural heritage from one generation to the next. The rituals maintain taboos and prohibitions and those who violate them are punished. The disobedient or violators of norms may even be required to undergo ritual punishment or purification. The rituals have another function also. In times of individual distress or group crisis the rituals provide help and comfort. "*The social function of shared religious beliefs and the rituals that go with them is so important, Durkheim argued,-that every society needs a religion or at least some belief system that serves the same function*" - **Ian Robertson.**

Durkheim rejected theories of '*Animism*', '*Naturism*' and '*Totemism*' for he regarded them to be inadequate to explain the main distinction between the *sacred and the profane*. According to him, the group life is the generating force or source or cause of religion. The religious ideas and practices always symbolise the social group. The distinction which Durkheim has made between the sacred and profane has important implications for social life as a whole. According to him, the main function of religion is "*the creation, reinforcement, and maintenance of social solidarity. So long as society persists so will religion.*"

According to Durkheim, much of the social disorder in modern times is due to the fact that people no longer believe deeply in religion and that they have found no satisfying substitute for that. Lacking commitment to a shared belief system, people tend to pursue their private interests without regard for their fellows.

In this book on religion, Durkheim tried to provide an explanation of the basic forms of classification and the fundamental categories of thought itself. In this speculative exploration Durkheim laid the foundation for another specialised field of sociology called "*sociology of knowledge*".

Concluding Remarks

It is true that much of Durkheim's work on religion was *purely speculative.* His account of the origins of religion could not be accepted by most of the modern sociologists. **Goldenweiser**, for example, criticised Durkheim's theory as one-sided and psychologically untenable. He argued that a "*society possessing the religious sentiment is capable of accomplishing unusual things, but it can hardly produce that sentiment out of itself.*" Some others have stated that "by making the social mind, or collective representations the sole source of religion, Durkheim resorted to something quite mysterious in itself and, hence failed to give a satisfactory explanation." But the real merit of his analysis is his recognition of the vital social functions that religion plays in society.

AN ESTIMATE OF DURKHEIM'S WORKS

1. *Contribution to sociological theory*: Durkheim never wrote any specific treatise on sociology as such. But his writings on various sociological topics provide relatively convincing answers to many problems in sociological theory.

2. *Stressed the inseparable relationship between society and individual*: Durkheim's discussions on "*collective representations*" and "*collective conscience*" throw light on the relationship between the individual and society. They also "call attention to the ways in which social interaction and relationships significantly influence individual attitudes, ideas, and sentiments." For Durkheim, the reality of society preceded the individual life.

3. *Emphasised the application of scientific methods in the study of social facts*: Durkheim, in a way was a positivist and *strongly recommended the application of the methods of physical science to the study of social facts.* As a believer in scientific method he sought to deal chiefly with empirical data and to avoid value-judgements. Like Spencer and Karl Marx he did not subscribe to an individualistic theory of society as such.

4. *Stressed the importance of morals, values and social integration in social life*: Durkheim was, however, able to prove convincingly that *social facts are facts* "*sui generis.*" His explanations regarding the social and cultural importance of the division of labour and his analysis of the consequences of social solidarity are quite impressive. He indicated the role of *social pressure* in areas of human activity, which was not stressed upon by others till then. He has sufficiently emphasised the significance of values and ideals in social life. He also demonstrated the need for empirical research for the science of society.

5. *Durkheim a great moralist*: Durkheim was a man of character. Throughout his life he was passionately engaged in the moral issues of his time. He probably considered it to be his life task to contribute to the moral regeneration of his

French society. He made number of proposals for the improvement of the moral climate of his society. Durkheim's deep concern for order and unity in the body social has often made his critics brand him as a thinker with conservative bias opposed to the creative functions of conflict. He, of course, found it impossible, even in theory, to escape "*the limits of the contemporary social life.*"

6. *Durkheim gave priority only to the society and not to the individual* - ?: He has made "social facts" central in his methods. A social fact is a phase of behaviour - thinking, feeling or acting - which has a coercive nature. Social facts involve rules and regulations, systems of procedure, and sets of customary beliefs. They have super-individual value. It appears that in his treatment of social facts and collective conscience. Durkheim almost completely neglected the social importance of individual decision. "*Society, is real, to be sure, but so is the individual and the two, it should be remembered, are always in interaction. Giving priority to one or the other, is misleading in the long*" **- L.A. Coser.**

REVIEW QUESTIONS

1. Give a biographical sketch of Emile Durkheim in brief.
2. Throw light on the main works of Emile Durkheim.
3. What is Durkheimian sociology? Bring out its salient features.
4. Discuss the theory of social facts. Highlight the main characteristics of social facts.
5. Critically analyse Durkheim's theory of social facts.
6. Explain the concept of division of labour.
7. Explain Durkheim's theory of division of labour.
8. What is social solidarity? Discuss its main types.
9. Differentiate between mechanical and organic solidarities.
10. Division of labour is different from disintegration. Critically analyse.
11. Define suicide. Given its classification.
12. Critically evaluate Durkheim's theory of suicide.
13. Elaborate on the types of suicide.
14. Throw light on the elementary from of religious life.
15. Make an estimate of Durkheim's works.

⌘⌘⌘⌘⌘⌘⌘⌘⌘⌘⌘

58

MAX WEBER AND HIS THOUGHTS

CHAPTER OUTLINE

- A BRIEF INTRODUCTION OF MAX WEBER
- MAIN WORKS OF MAX WEBER
- WEBER'S THEORY OF IDEAL TYPES: DEFINITION AND CHARACTERISTICS
- CRITICAL COMMENTS ABOUT IDEAL TYPES
- WEBER'S THEORY OF RELIGION OR SOCIOLOGY OF RELIGION: WEBERS MASTERLY WORK: "THE PROTESTANT ETHIC AND THE SPIRIT OF CAPITALISM"
- ESTABLISHMENT OF THE THEORY OF RELIGION IN THREE STAGES
- WEBER'S THEORY OF BUREAUCRACY: DEFINITION AND CHARACTERISTICS OF BUREAUCRACY
- FACTORS CONTRIBUTING TO THE DEVELOPMENT OF BUREAUCRACY
- FUNCTIONAL AND DYSFUNCTIONAL ASPECTS OF BUREAUCRACY
- A BRIEF EVALUATION OF WEBER'S CONTRIBUTIONS.

A BRIEF INTRODUCTION OF MAX WEBER

Max Weber [1864-1920] is a memorable thinker in sociology for he has left a deep imprint upon sociology. He was a profound scholar, a voracious reader and a prolific writer. He entered the field of sociology through law and remained as one among the great sociologists of the 20th century.

Max Weber was born in a comparatively rich Protestant family on 21st April 1864 in Erfurt in Germany. He lived most of his early life in Berlin. Weber's father was a bureaucrat who rose to a very high political position. He was a part of the political establishment and was more a hedonist than a Protestant. In sharp contrast to him, Weber's mother was a devout Calvinist, a woman who sought to lead an ascetic life. These sharp differences between the parents led to marital tensions. Growing conflicts and increasing tensions between the parents affected Weber's feelings and sentiments deeply.

Max Weber
[1864-1920]

Weber after completing his basic education joined the University of Heidelberg at the age of 18 to study law. Here he gravitated towards his father's way of life of enjoyment. He became addicted to beer. Though he was basically a student of law, he studied Roman institutions, theology, attended lectures in economics, showed interest in medieval history and philosophy.

Weber in his life earned varied experiences as a soldier, a professor, a politician, a legal expert and also as a sociologist. When his military service was over in 1884, he joined the University of Berlin for studies. For 8 years he stayed along with his parents and was financially dependent on his father. He disliked his father's bullying behaviour towards his mother. At one stage [in 1900] he clashed violently with his father and asked him to quit the house. The father upon quitting the house died within a month and due to this Weber suffered a complete mental breakdown. He could not recover from that shock for about five years.

After recovering from his mental breakdown Weber travelled extensively. He even visited America. Between 1900-1918, he was almost out of teaching work. He lectured in the last three years of his life - 1918-1920 in the universities of Vienna and Munich. Two of his lectures: "*Science as a Vocation*" and "*Politics as a Vocation*" - were very famous. During the last three years of his life he was actively engaged in political activity. He died at a time [14th June 1920] when his talent had reached full maturity.

Sociology remains ever grateful to Weber for his memorable contributions such as - "*Economy and Society*", "*The Protestant Ethic and the Spirit of Capitalism*", "*The City*", "*Bureaucracy*", "*The Organisation*", "*The Theory of Social and Economic Organisation*", etc. He laid the foundations of *German Sociological Society* in 1910. He published a number of study reports, essays and articles in the leading social science journal "*Archiv fuer Sozial wissenschaft*".

Although Weber repeatedly entered the political field, he was not just a politician, he remained a great intellectual. His home became a centre for a wide range of intellectuals, including sociologists such as **George Simmel, Robert Michaels,** and **George Lukas.** With all this, "*he was first and foremost his own man*".

"There was a tension in Weber's life, and more important, in his work, between the bureaucratic mind as represented by his father, and his mother's religiosity. This unresolved tension permeates Weber's work as it permeated his personal life."[1]

MAIN WORKS OF MAX WEBER

1. "*General Economic History*" - London: Allen and Unwin - 1927.
2. "*The Protestant Ethic and the Spirit of Capitalism*" - New York (NY) Scribner - 1930.
3. "*Max Weber on Law in Economy and Society*" - Cambridge MA: Harward University Press - 1945.
4. "*From Max Weber: Essays in Sociology*" - NY Oxford University Press - 1946.
5. "*The Theory of Social and Economic Organisations*" - NY Oxford University Press - 1947.
6. "*The Methodology of Social Sciences*" - NY: Free Press - 1949.
7. "*The City*" - NY: Free Press - 1958.
8. "*The Sociology of Religion*" - Boston - Beacon Press - 1963.
9. "*On Charisma and Institution Building*" - Chicago: The University Press - 1968.
10. "*Economy and Society*" - in Three Volumes - Totwa, M.J. Bedminister - 1968.

Other Main Works

1. *The Religion of China - The Religion of India - Ancient Judaism.*
2. *Science as a Vocation and Politics as a Vocation [Two Lectures].*
3. *Bureaucracy.*

WEBER'S THEORY OF "IDEAL TYPES"

The concept of "*ideal type*" is one of the major concepts in Weberian sociology. In fact, it has an important place in his methodology. In methodology, it is known as "*typological analysis.*" It is said that the inspiration which Weber had derived from the writings of Plato and Immanuel Kant enabled him to make use of the concept of "*ideal type.*"

Weber's Definition of *Ideal Type*

"An ideal type is an analytical construct that serves the investigator as a measuring rod to ascertain similarities as well as deviations in concrete cases."

Some other definitions of ideal types * are given in footnote.

General Background of the Emergence of the Concept of *"Ideal Type"*

At the fag end of the 19th century, philosophical discussions in Germany were focused on the question of the place of science in human studies. It was felt by the idealist philosophers that scientific method could not be used for studying

1. George Ritzer in *Contemporary Sociological Theory*, p. 27.

*** Some Other Definitions of Ideal Types**

- *"An ideal type is simply an abstract description, constructed by the sociologist from observations of a number of real cases in order to reveal their essential features."* – Ian Robertson
- *"Any type, however, being an abstraction, is ideal and not real in the sense that a given material object is real."* – Duncan Mitchell
- *"Ideal type or pure type refers to any conceptualisation [idealisation] of a general or particular phenomenon which, for analytical and explanatory purposes, represents this phenomenon only in its abstract or "pure" [hence 'idealised'] forms."* – Collins Dictionary of Sociology

cultural subjects. The main argument was "*that social phenomena are unique and do not, therefore, allow generalisations.*"

Weber did not accept this view. He was of the opinion that scientific categories could be used in the field of human studies or cultural objects. Weber's belief that scientific method was relevant to social studies encouraged him to offer a set of operational definitions and to construct concepts such as "*ideal types*" which could be used. "*The idea behind the concept of ideal type is that social phenomena in virtue of their manifold and fluid nature, can be analysed solely in terms of the extreme forms of their characteristics, which can never be observed in their purity.*"[2]

"Ideal Types" as Conceptual Tools and Standards of Comparison

Sociologists make use of "ideal types" as *measuring rods* or as *means to find out similarities and differences in the actual phenomena.* In fact, it is one of the methods of comparative study. Weber used the concept as an abstract model, and when used as a standard of comparisons, it enables us to see aspects of the real world in a clearer, and more systematic way. ***Ex***: *Socialism and free market capitalism, for example, can be described as "ideal types: by identifying their essential characteristics, their essence - in a pure somewhat exaggerated form, that is, unlikely to actually exist anywhere other than in our minds.* Socialist and capitalist societies differ in many ways, from their respective ideal types. ***For example,*** socialist states usually have been authoritarian and never reflect workers' interests. In the same way, capitalist markets are increasingly controlled by oligopolies rather than being freely competitive.

What is to be understood here is that, it is not the purpose of ideal types to describe or explain the world. Instead, *they provide us with points of comparison from which to observe it.* By comparing the ideal type of socialism with actual socialist societies, for example, we can highlight their characteristics by seeing how they match or depart from the ideal type. Sociologists use many ideal types in this way, including "*primary and secondary groups*", "*bureaucracy*", types of authority such as "*charismatic, traditional and legal-rational*" and so on.

"*Ideal Types* are to be Constructed and Used with Care" - *Cautions Weber*

Max Weber cautions that the "ideal-type" is to be constructed and used with great care. As he has stated,

(*i*) The ideal types are *not hypotheses;*

(*ii*) They do not state or imply an *ethical ideal;*

(*iii*) they do not state an "*average*" type;

(*iv*) they *do not exhaust reality;* i.e., they do not correspond exactly to any empirical instances.

Main Characteristics of "*Ideal Types*"

Main characteristics of "ideal types" can be briefly examined in the following manner

1. *Ideal types are mental constructs or subjective in nature*: As Weber has stated more positively the ideal types are mental constructs which are ideal in the "*logical sense*", that is, they state a logical extreme. They depend on our capacity for comprehension and imagination. **Example:** *We may have ideal type regarding "perfect health", church, state of equilibrium, perfect religion, democracy, etc.*

2. *Since ideal types are mental constructs they do not exactly correspond to the reality*: Ideal types are constructed in such a way that they are kept at a distance from the real world. Though they are constructed out of many actual facts, they themselves do not exactly correspond to the actual facts in each and every respect. Because, they are mental constructs created to understand reality and they themselves do not have actual existence. Differences are found between ideal constructs and actual situations. Thus, "*not all the characteristics will always be present in the real world, but any particular situation may be understood by comparing it with the ideal type. For example, individual bureaucratic organisations may not exactly match the elements in the ideal type of bureaucracy, but the type can illuminate these variations. Ideal types are therefore hypothetical constructions, formed from real phenomena, which have an explanatory value.*"[3]

3. *Ideal types as theoretical tools*: Though "ideal types" are not actualities and remain as our mental constructs they function as theoretical tools to understand the reality. "*Its function is the comparison with empirical reality in order to establish its divergences or similarities, to describe them with the most unambiguously intelligible concepts and to understand and explain them causally.*"

4. *Ideal types are not the instruments to denote statistical average*: The ideal type is "*not a description of those factors or laws which are thought to be found "on the average" in that kind of configuration.........*"[4] For example, the Protestant

2. Duncan Mitchell's *Dictionary of Sociology*, p. 94.
3. Abercrombie and others in *The Penguin Dictionary of Sociology*, p. 117.
4. Ronald Fletcher in " *The Making of Sociology*" Vol.II - Page : 429.

Ethic does not indicate the average behaviour of all the Protestants. (ii) Similarly, *'honesty'* does not indicate the average behaviour of all the honest people that the society has witnessed.

5. *Ideal types signify "pure" or "abstract" types and do not indicate anything that is normatively desirable*: As Weber himself has stated the ideal types have "no connection at all with value-judgements, and it has nothing to do with any type of perfection there than a purely logical one." There are thus all sorts of ideal types "*of brothels as well as religions*" [Weber]. Totalitarianism is no less an ideal type than democracy, for example, for both are abstract constructs with which we can compare and contrast actual political systems in order to see their various characteristics more clearly. It is a "*methodological device*", that is all. "*It is not ideal in the sense of ethically good or right.*"[5]

6. *Ideal types are not hypotheses*: Ideal types are not hypotheses and hence the question of proving or disproving them and establishing general laws does not arise here. **Ronald Fletcher** writes: "*It is not a basis of comparative experiment for the purpose of setting up "general laws.*" On the contrary, it is a limiting case for the explanation of a specific configuration. Comparative tests are always such as to throw light upon the specific configuration and check the adequacy of the specific ideal type. Thus, Weber in his very wide studies in the sociology of religion, examined the relationship between the religious ethics in various societies and elements of economic development there. But this was **not** to establish general laws about the relationships between "*religious ethics*" and "*economic development;* it was essentially to check the sufficiency and validity of his ideal type of the relationship between the Protestant [Calvinist] Ethic and the emergence of industrial capitalism of the Western Europe" [Page - 430].

7. *It is essentially a "one-sided model"*: It is one-sided in the sense it deliberately emphasises those imputations thought to be worth postulating and testing. In this sense, it is purely selective, and of the nature of experiment.

8. *Ideal types do not provide an exhaustive description of a social phenomenon*: The nature of ideal type is such that it does not provide an exhaustive description or an account of a social phenomenon or an entire social configuration. "*Many ideal types can be constructed about any specific configuration, each selectively emphasising "one point of view" and submitting its particular imputations to test.*" [**Ronald Flethcer** - 430].

9. *Ideal types are not rigid and fixed things, but are subject to change*: Ideal types are abstract in nature and they reside in our imagination. They are changeable and subject to consideration from time to time. They are affected by social thinking and social environments and hence cannot be permanent. "*Weber did suggest that major discrepancies between reality and an ideal type would lead to the type being redefined.*"[6] Thus redefinitions of ideal types can also take place.

Critical Comments About "Ideal Types"

Though Weber's concept of "ideal type" has been well appreciated by scholars it is not free from criticisms. Some of the criticisms levelled against the concept are briefed here,

1. Though the ideal type is a "*mental construct*" many a times it is confused to be the "*actual reality*" itself.
2. There is also the possibility of considering the "*ideal type as a procrustean bed*[7] *into which data are forced in.*"
3. The "ideal type" is often made a theory and the ideas or things that it represents are often taken to be the ideas and things that are very much found in the real world.
4. It is commented that *the concept of "ideal type" is very complex* and **only** an expert sociologist can understand and make use of it efficiently.
5. Though "ideal types" are very significant in the study of social sciences, *their usage is somewhat limited because they cannot be used in all types of social analysis.*
6. There are critics who argue that "*ideal type analysis should be dropped as utterly inappropriate to sociological analysis once this is seen as involving the meaningful understanding of specific cases and* **not** *the development of general concepts and general theories.*"[8]
7. Weber himself had argued that "*ideal types were not models to be tested. However, other sociologists treat them as testable models of the real world. Further confusion may arise since Weber himself often implicitly used ideal types as testable models.*"[9]

---

5. Ibid., p. 429.
6. Abercrombie and others in *Penguin Dictionary of Sociology,* p. 117.
7. Procrustes was "a fabulous Greek robber, who stretched or cut his captives' legs to make them fit the bed" — Chamber's 20th Century Dictionary.
8. *Collins Dictionary of Sociology,* p. 305.
9. Abercrombie and Others, pp. 117-118.

Finally, it can be said that if the above mentioned dangers and deficiencies are averted, the *ideal type* can become an extremely useful instrument to confront reality.

RELIGION AND SOCIETY OR WEBER'S THEORY OF RELIGION OR SOCIOLOGY OF RELIGION

Sociologists have been discussing the intimate relationship between society and religion, social change and economic factors, social change and religious factors from the very beginning. Marx and Weber have written extensively about the relationship between society and religion on the one hand and the role of religion in socio-economic changes on the other. Their views, however, differed significantly. "*The theory of religion*" or "*sociology of religion*", established by Max Weber clearly indicates that there is a close relationship between the religious beliefs of the people and their economic activities.

Weber's Masterly Work : *"The Protestant Ethic and the Spirit of Capitalism"*

As it is stated above, Weber wrote extensively on the subject of religion. Nothing contributed more to Weber's fame than his essay on "*Protestant Ethic and the Spirit of Capitalism.*" He observed a close connection between religious and economic forces. His concept of religion is more ethical than theological. Religion is a vital influence in everyday life. Weber wanted to examine its influence on the life of people. In his studies in the sociology of religion, Weber was trying to answer one fundamental question: "*To what extent the religious conceptions of the world and of existence have influenced the economic behaviour of various societies?*"

Weber's Purpose was not to Attack: *"The Economic Deterministic Theory"* of Karl Marx

It is often said that Weber wanted to test the basic contention of Karl Marx according to whom, "*all cultural phenomena, including religion, are fundamentally determined by the evolution of economic forces.*" It is further argued that instead of explaining religious and other cultural behaviour in terms of economic forces as Marx did, Weber wanted to explain economic behaviour in terms of religion

It is wrong to say that Weber undertook the study of religion with the sole intention of disproving or attacking the economic deterministic theory of Marx. Max Weber partially disagreed with the Marxian view. He, however, accepted that Marx's approach was useful and might be correct in many instances, but he maintained that under certain circumstances religious or other ideas could influence social change. Like Marx, he never developed single factor theory. For him, economic factor is not the only factor which influences religion. On the other hand, religion itself gets influenced by social system, ethics of a community and the economic system.

Impressive Growth of Western Capitalism

Weber was very much fascinated by the growth of modern capitalism of the West which was rapidly transforming the European and American societies of his time. But why had capitalism first emerged in Europe rather than in, say, China or India, was a question for which Weber wanted to find a suitable answer. Weber undertook a massive study of the major world religions and the societies in which they were found and concluded that the answer lay in specific religious beliefs - say, **Calvinism** and other forms of Puritanism. In other words, Weber's studies helped him to establish a correlation between the Protestant Ethic and the development of modern Capitalism in Europe.

Two Main Propositions of Weber.........

According to **Raymond Aron,** Weber wanted to establish two main propositions in this work.

(*i*) The behaviour of men in various societies could be understood only in the context of their general conception of existence or world view. Religious dogmas and their explanations also form a part of the world view. *Hence, the religious outlook of the people can help one to understand the behaviour of individuals and groups, including their economic behaviour.*

(*ii*) Religious conceptions are actually *a determinant of economic behaviour* and hence one of the causes of economic changes.

Modern Capitalism is Different from the Previous Ones

Weber pointed out that modern capitalism is not like traditional commercial activity. Previously consumption of wealth was regarded as a thing of the higher value than the earning of it. *Modern capitalism, on the other hand, requires rational, calculated procedures (such as accounting) in a methodical attempt to accumulate money.* Hard work and making money are regarded as high values in themselves, but the spending of money in luxurious living is disreputable. Instead, the capital must be reinvested to earn yet more capital. Weber felt that *some new approach towards wealth must have been the source of inspiration for the rapid growth of capitalism in modern Europe.*

Protestant Ethic Provides Motivation for Hardwork

Weber argued that this approach stemmed from the **Protestant Ethic**[10] of hard work and deferred gratification. Weber made two observations: (*i*) *Great material achievements have resulted from the work of monastic orders,* and (*ii*) *Specifically, ascetic Protestant sects were noted for their economic success.* Therefore, Weber projected a hypothesis: *"There appeared to (be) a paradoxically positive relationship between ascetic religious belief and economic enterprise."*[11] The "*religious belief*" refers to Protestant Ethic and "*economic enterprise*" denotes capitalism.

On the basis of his historical study Weber asserted that modern capitalism emerged not simply by inner economic necessity, but by the religious ethic of Protestantism, and particularly of Calvinism. The early Calvinists[12] believed that they had been predestined by God to salvation in heaven or damnation in hell. No one could do anything to change his or her fate, and only a small minority were among the elect who would go to heaven. The duty of the believers was to abstain from pleasure and to spend their lives working for the glory of God. Thus, the Calvinists looked for "*signs*" that they were among the elect - and found these signs in their worldly success. The more successful a person was at work, the more likely he or she was to be among the elect. Since profits could not be spent on pleasure, they had to be reinvested. Modern capitalism was born, thus, argued Weber.

It is interesting to note that the very people who rejected material comforts unwittingly created industrial capitalism. By a further supreme irony, industrialism encouraged the development of modern, rational, scientific world view. In this world view, religion has virtually no place. Modern capitalists, however, have retained the "*Protestant Ethic*" on which their success is largely found.

Establishment of the Theory of Religion in Three Stages

As it is made clear Weber observed that capitalism was growing very fast in the West. He felt that capitalism of the Western type was growing more in Protestant societies than in others. This observation made him advance the hypothesis that - "*a certain interpretation of Protestantism has created some of the motivations favourable to the formation of the capitalistic regime.*" As **Raymond Aron** has pointed out Weber set out to establish this hypothesis or thesis in three stages:

1. *Collection of statistics in Support of his idea*: Weber collected statistics to support the following observation: In regions of mixed religions in Germany, Protestants and particularly Calvinists occupied economically dominant positions. This did raise the question *whether the religious ideas influence the economic activity.*

2. *Establishment of a correlation between the spirit of protestantism and the spirit of capitalism*: Weber made an analytical study of Protestantism to establish an intellectual or spiritual affinity between the spirit of the Protestant Ethic and the spirit of capitalism. It means, he established a correlation between "*a religious way of thinking in the world and an attitude towards economic activity.*"

3. *Study of other religions to find out the relevance of the religious variable used*: Finally, Weber tried "*to discover whether, or to what degree, in other civilisations - in China, in India, in primitive Judaism, and in Islam - social conditions were favourable or unfavourable to the development of capitalism of the Western type.*" The religious variable which Weber used could explain why capitalism of the Western type could not develop anywhere outside the Western civilisation.

---

10. Weber identified the following values in "Protestantism" which were in harmony with the spirit of capitalism.

(*i*) *Changed attitude towards work:* Protestantism considers work as a kind of virtue. Hardwork contributes to the glory of God.

(*ii*) *Concept of "Calling":* In order to achieve salvation every individual must pursue a calling [or a job or vocation] and must engage himself in hardwork and become successful. Those who become successful in their enterprises are marked for salvation.

(*iii*) *Wealth is to be used for productive purposes:* The Ethic insists on strict moral life. It says that the acquired wealth and profit are not meant for enjoyment but for further production of wealth.

(*iv*) *Strictures on alcoholism:* The Ethic prohibits the consumption of alcohol. Extravagance and merriment are discouraged ,saving and investment are encouraged.

(*v*) *Encouragement to literacy and learning:* This stress on literacy helped mass education among the Protestants.

(*vi*) *Rejection of holidays:* Work is important to achieve the glory of God. Hence time should not be wasted under the pretext of observing "*holidays.*"

(*vii*) *New attitude towards the collection of interest on loan:* The ethic permits the collection of interest on loans for it multiplies capital and encourages new investment.

(*ix*) *Honesty in one's "Calling":* One must be true to oneself in one's business or work or profession. God always supports and selects the honest ones for his Kingdom and not the dishonest ones.

- Weber was of the opinion that the ethical principles contained in Protestantism provided lot of encouragement for the development of Capitalism of the modern type.

11. *Robert Bierstedt* as quoted by R.N. and R.K. Sharma in *History of Social Thought,* p. 322.
12. Calvinism represents a sect within Protestantism.

Other religions, Weber argued, did not provide the same incentive for this kind of social and economic change. **Catholicism** stresses rewards in heaven and encourages people to be satisfied with their lot on earth. **Hinduism** threatens a lower form of life after reincarnation to anyone who tries to leave his or her caste status. It glorifies spiritualism and not materialism. **Buddhism** stresses mysticism, far removed from earthly goals. **Taoism** requires the believer to withdraw from worldly temptations. **Confucianism** emphasises a static social structure as a part of the natural order. **Islam,** though an activist religion, lacks the emphasis on thrift and hardwork. All these religions, according to Weber, served to discourage the growth of capitalist industrialism.

Weber's Thesis is Misunderstood?

Ian Robertson is of the opinion that Weber's thesis is often misunderstood and misinterpreted. Weber never tried to disprove Marx's view that *society usually shapes belief systems rather than vice versa.* Nor did he mean to prove that the "Protestant Ethic" was the "*cause*" of capitalism. He only said that it exerted an important influence. Weber did not believe that he had proved this hypothesis. He offered it *only as a tentative hypothesis.*

Weber's Study Went Wrong in Certain Respects ....

It is certainly possible that Weber was wrong about the origin of capitalism. Capitalism did not occur in some Calvinist societies, and it sometimes occurred in non-Calvinist societies. England, the birthplace of the Industrial Revolution, was not Calvinist; Scotland, which was Calvinist, failed to develop early capitalism. There is no way of proving that the "*salvation panic*" of the Calvinists led them to become capitalists. They may have done so for other reasons, such as the fact that they were more likely than Catholics to live in urban areas, or that their religion encouraged hard work, or even that they were not so wedded to tradition as were Catholics of the time. "*Weber's hypothesis is one of the most provocative in all sociology, but its subject is so vast and complex that his argument is probably unverifiable. Weber simply bit off more than he or anyone else could chew.*"[13]

Weber's Study of Religion and Society has its Merits

According to **Raymond Aron,** the study of Weber has its own merits among which the following may be noted,

(i) *Weber never attempted to establish any kind of causalty as such.* In his study nowhere had he claimed that the Protestant Ethic (*i.e.,* the Calvinist Ethic) was the *sole cause* of the rise of capitalism. Weber interpreted Protestantism in one way but *he did not rule out other kinds of interpretations.* He required only the totality of interpretations.

(ii) Weber could make "*the affinity between a religious attitude and an economic commandment credible.*"

(iii) "He has raised a sociological problem of considerable importance: *the influence of world views upon social organisation or individual organisations.*"

(iv) It is not right to say that Weber maintained a thesis exactly opposite to Marx's. It means, Weber never explained "*the economy in terms of religion instead of religion in terms of the economy.*"

WEBER'S THEORY OF BUREAUCRACY

The term "*bureaucracy*" finds its origin from the French word "*bureau*" which means *desk, and a government which is run from table is called a bureaucratic government.* The word implies a particular system of administration. Historically, it has been associated with the rule of government and governmental officials. In this form of the government there is concentration of power in the hands of departments. Sociologists regard bureaucracy as a form of administration that is found in formal organisations pursuing a wide variety of goals.

As a technical term in sociology, "*bureaucracy*" is associated with Max Weber. He gave it a precise definition and suggested that it was the best administrative form for the rational pursuit of organisational goals.

Definition of Bureaucracy

1. **Max Weber:** Bureaucracy is "*a type of hierarchical organisation which is designed rationally to co-ordinate the work of many individuals in pursuit of large scale administrative tasks.*"
   - **Weber** also said that "*bureaucracies are organised according to rational principles, officials ranked in a hierarchical order and operations are characterised by impersonal rules.*"
2. **Talcott Parsons:** "*The relatively large-scale organisations with specialised functions...... loosely tend to be called bureaucracies.*"

---

13. Ian Robertson in *Sociology,* p. 377.

3. **Wallace and Wallace:** "*Bureaucracies are large-scale formal organisations which are highly differentiated and organised through elaborate policies and procedures in a hierarchy of authority.*"

Weber: The Prime Architect of the *"Theory of Bureaucracy"*

Weber is the first sociologist to analyse the functioning of bureaucracy from the sociological point of view. Weber's theory of bureaucracy is a significant contribution to the field of sociology. Weber's interest in the nature of power and authority and his realisation of the inevitability of rationalisation in the operation of large-scale modern organisations - led him to establish a "*theory of bureaucracy.*" Weber felt that the operation of modern large-scale enterprises or organisations in the political, administrative, and economic fields would be impossible without bureaucracy. Bureaucratic co-ordination of activities is the distinctive mark of the modern era, he maintained.

According to Weber, bureaucracy refers to an instrument that has become indispensable "for the rational attainment of the goals of any organisation in industrial society." *Bureaucracies can be understood as large-scale formal organisations of the modern society with specialised functions.* Bureaucratisation and rationalisation go together, because bureaucracies are organised according to rational principles.

Characteristics of Bureaucracy

Max Weber was the first to give a detailed sociological account of the development of bureaucracy. According to him, bureaucracy reveals the following characteristics.

1. *Fixed official jurisdiction area*: Bureaucracies normally have their own official fixed jurisdiction. Bureaucracy consists of various statuses each of which has its own fixed official duties. There are clear cut written rules governing each status.

2. *Hierarchy of authority*: Bureaucracy has its own hierarchy of statuses. Officials who occupy these statuses are governed by the principle of super-ordination and subordination. There is the supervision of the lower offices by the higher ones.

3. *Clear-cut division of labour*: The entire task of the bureaucratic system is governed by a stipulated system of division of labour. Who should do what work and who should shoulder what responsibility is decided by this system.

4. *Appointment based on eligibility*: Bureaucracy has its own system of selecting employees and giving them promotions on the basis of seniority, technical competence, specialised knowledge or skill.

5. *Fixed salary, allowance and pension*: The officials of the bureaucracy are paid monthly salary and other types of allowances and pensions as per the written rules.

6. *Office and maintenance of files*: Bureaucracy as an organisation functions through an office wherein all the matters and transactions relating to its area of operation are maintained in the form of files. It has a system of written documents defining its procedures and manner of functioning.

7. *Appointment of officials on full time and long term service basis*: Appointment of officials in a bureaucracy is normally made by the higher officials and not by election. Normally the position of the bureaucrat is held for life as specified by the contract or order.

8. *Difference between private matter and official issues*: The officials of the bureaucracy are expected to make a clear distinction between the official issues and pure private or personal matters. They are not entitled to make use of official facilities for personal needs except as defined by written rules.

9. *Supervision of work by higher officials*: Officials of the bureaucracy are expected to work according to the written rules. Still there is the system of supervision of the work of lower officials by the higher officials.

10. *Systematisation of official relations with officials*: The officials of bureaucracy maintain contact and communication among themselves in a particular way. Orders and communications among them always proceed through "*proper channels.*"

11. *Political neutrality*: Officials of bureaucracy are expected to be very objective in the official discharge of business. They are expected to be politically neutral in their dealings.

12. *Guidance by past procedures*: Bureaucrats are mostly guided by the past procedures. A good bureaucrat is one who always tries to be up to date with the subject with which not only he is dealing at present but he may be required to deal at any subsequent stage.

The characteristics stated above, cannot be found in any existing bureaucracy in their true or complete form. Never before in history such bureaucracies existed. As Max Weber has said, the concept of bureaucracy associated with these rules represents the **"ideal types."** The existing bureaucracies or any particular instance of a bureaucracy can only be compared with or evaluated in relation to this ideal type. Weber was quite aware of the increasing importance of the bureaucracies in the modern world.

Factors Contributing to the Development of Bureaucracy

Bureaucracies did exist in the ancient world in the great empires of India, China, Rome, Greece, Egypt and so on. They are found today. As Weber has rightly prophesied the importance of bureaucracy has reached immeasurable proportions in the modern world.

According to Weber, following factors contributed a great deal to the development of modern bureaucracy.

(*i*) The *development of money economy* guarantees a constant income for maintaining bureaucracy through a system of taxation.

(*ii*) Modern industries and states which require a big army of administrative officials necessitated bureaucracy.

(*iii*) *Qualitative changes in the administrative tasks also led to bureaucratisation.* Modern states which claim themselves to be "*welfare states*" have to maintain an elaborate system of transport and communication including mass media. They naturally tend towards bureaucratic system.

(*iv*) Bureaucracy as a form of organisation seems to be technically superior to any other form of organisation.

(*v*) *Demand for objective experts*: The modern culture demands "*the personally detached and strictly objective experts.*" This nature of the modern culture encourages the development of bureaucracy.

(*vi*) *Mass Democracy*: Modern political parties are functioning on a mass scale which necessitates bureaucracies.

(*vii*) *Concentration of material means*: The development of big capitalist enterprises and the giant public organisations such as the state or army require the modern bureaucratic system.

(*viii*) *Rational interpretation of law*: Modern states guarantee to their citizens equality before law. It is a guarantee against arbitrariness. This has given rise to the bureaucratic form of administration and judiciary.

Functional and Dysfunctional Aspects of Bureaucracy

Positive or Functional Aspects of Bureaucracy

1. *Bureaucracy provides opportunity for division of labour*: Some of the modern organisations consist of lakhs and millions of members. Such organisations are institutionalised through bureaucracies.

2. *Performance of complicated tasks*: Some of the complicated tasks of the modern society such as, *conducting census, capturing criminals, collecting taxes, arranging for voting in elections,* etc. are more efficiently undertaken in bureaucracy.

3. *Performance of repetitive tasks*: Some of the modern bureaucracies, for example, industrial corporations, universities, advertising agencies, etc. regularly repeat their work. Modern bureaucracies have been able to perform that work without much difficulty.

4. *Maintenance of law and order*: There are certain organisations [such as police, court, army, temple or church, religion, college, etc.] that deal with people's actions in a normative manner. Here the right type of behaviour is to be encouraged and the wrong type is to regulated. Bureaucratic method is better suited to do this.

5. *Mobilisation of resources and their rightful usage*: The heads or the leaders of the state could mobilise and centralise material resources and make necessary arrangements for their most effective use only through bureaucracy.

In feudal times, for example, power was dispersed in a variety of centres. Only through bureaucratic machinery at present economic resources are being mobilised while in the pre-modern age they remained untapped or improperly managed. "*Bureaucratic organisation is to Weber, the privileged instrumentality that has shaped the modern polity, the modern economy, the modern technology.*" Just as a machine production is superior to hand-made articles so the bureaucratic types of organisation are technically superior to all other forms of administration.

6. *Control of the waste of time*: In comparison with any other type of organisation bureaucracy has been found to be less expensive, less conflicting and more efficient and useful.

Negative Aspects or Dysfunctional Aspects of Bureaucracy

Bureaucracy has its own ugly face. It has its own demerits and Weber, the champion of the theory of bureaucracy, was aware of this. **Abraham** and **Morgan**[14] have stated: "*Having granted its virtues and its unquestionable advancement of modern society, Weber was the first to concede the vices of bureaucracy.....*"

Some of the main drawbacks or dysfunctions of bureaucracy may be enlisted here.

1. *Static rules for dynamic situations*: The unchanging static rules of bureaucracy many a time fail in its very purpose of serving the human needs. Bureaucracy becomes dysfunctional when the rules remain static even while the social situations undergo fast changes.

2. *Unnecessary waste of time and redtapism*: Since there is a hierarchical arrangement in this system every paper or file is to pass through several stages before a final decision is taken. This delay leads to waste of time and sometimes to unwanted consequences.

3. *Quarrel among officials*: As **Dahrendorf** has pointed out junior and senior officials of bureaucracy always quarrel among themselves lowering its dignity and efficiency. In fact, this quarrel among these officials has necessitated the beginning of trade unions.

4. *Blind rules and uncreative officials*: Officials of the bureaucracy become rule bound and extremely formal. They act according to the written rules, and verbally stick on to them. "*The uniform and rational procedures of bureaucratic practice largely prevent spontaneity, creativity and individual initiative. The impersonality of official conduct tends to produce "specialists without spirit."*[15] Weber also wrote: "*It is horrible to think that the world would one day be filled with little cogs, little men clinging to little jobs and striving towards the bigger ones.*"[16]

5. *Ever expanding army of employees*: Bureaucracy goes on expanding and new members are recruited regularly whether there is a need for the same or not. Hence it becomes expensive at one time, officials who become lethargic give more importance to their salary, promotion, increments, allowances, facilities, etc. rather than to the services.

6. *Human Relations are made to become Mechanical*: Too much of bureaucratisation leads to depersonalisation. As a result, human relations become extremely mechanical devoid of human touch. Weber too had foreseen "*the possibility of men trapped in their specialised routines with little awareness of the relationship between their jobs and the organisation as a whole.*"

7. *Bureaucracy unsuited to face emergencies*: Officials of the bureaucracy find it difficult to face an emergency situation. They search for solutions only within the framework of existing rules and procedures and do not take the risk of facing the challenges.

8. Other disadvantages or deficiencies:

***(a) Bureaucracies become corrupt and puppets in the hands of the vested interests*:** Since bureaucrats have vast powers, vested interests try to corrupt them and provide them all temptations to get decisions in their favour. **Ex.:** The Tehalka Dotcom episode which has rocked the Indian Parliamentary discussions during the recent days is an example in this regard.

***(b) Bureaucracies tending to exist even after the achievement of their goals*: Ex.:** Bureaucratic committee formed to offer famine relief or flood relief, or earthquake relief to the people may continue to exist even after the settlement of the problem.

***(c) New despotism*:** It is said that bureaucracts are new despots. Since they have knowledge and expertise, they wish that even decision should be taken to suit their whims and wishes.

***(d) Superiority complex*:** Usually bureaucrats come from educated families and enjoy certain social prestige and economic privileges. After joining services they enjoy more of it. They thus suffer from superiority complex.

Weber who had recognised some of the dysfunctions of bureaucracy also knew about its inevitability. Bureaucracy today has come to stay. We have to find out ways and means of making it more efficient and less problematic. In the absence of any other alternative, it seems that the present bureaucracy will reign supreme in the years to come.

Weber argued that the bureaucratisation of the modern world has led to its *depersonalisation.* The more fully it is realised the more it depersonalises itself. The bureaucrats may function as "*emotionally detached*" "*professional experts.*"

---

14. Abraham and Morgan in their *Sociological Thought,* p. 188.
15. M. Haralambos and R.M. Heald in *Sociology — Themes and Perspectives,* p. 284.
16. Quoted by Haralambos, p. 284.

The bureaucrat functions to the exclusion of feelings and sentiments, of love and hatred in the execution of official tasks. According to Weber, bureaucratisation and rationalisation are almost an "*inescapable fate.*" Like a reformist, Weber hoped that some charismatic leader might arise in future to provide some relief to mankind which is gripped by the tentacles of bureaucracy. Like Marx, he never visualised an emancipatory struggle or revolution that would help them to become free from the shackles of bureaucracy. Weber thought it more probable that "*the future would be an 'iron cage' rather than a Garden of Eden.*"

A BRIEF EVALUATION OF WEBER'S CONTRIBUTIONS

Weber's contribution to the development of sociology and social thought has been enormous. He wrote on several issues and topics of sociological interest. In all his writings he has tried his level best to maintain his objectivity, neutrality, analytical approach, historical insight and scientific fervour.

The fundamental elements of sociological investigation for Weber are, "*typical social actions.*" Social action or even the single individual is the basic unit of society according to Weber. He never entangled himself with the problem of the relationship between the individual and society. "*He convincingly denied the existence of any predominant determinant of social change.*" He laid emphasis on "*rational action*" and stressed "*the role of ideas in social life.*"

According to **Prof. Timasheff,** Max Weber could be considered one of the greatest sociologists of the 20th century for the following reasons:

(1) He has made "painstaking study of concrete social situations and processes that must form the foundation of any adequate *sociological theory.*" He has furnished vast wealth of material in his writings which are of great help to any sociologist.

(2) Weber has helped "*to make clear the significant role of values in social life.*" He also emphasised the necessity of keeping social science value-free.

(3) He has "demonstrated that much can be achieved by using the "*ideal type*" procedure in social science."

(4) He has contributed greatly "*to the understanding of social causation*" in human affairs.

It would be in the fitness of things to call Max Weber our contemporary. The books he wrote, the problems he raised, the issues he interpreted and the propositions he established would continue to be points of references for the students of sociology in the generations to come. As **Raymond Aron** has pointed out, "*whether one considers comprehension,* or the ideal type, or the distinction between value-judgement and value-reference, or subjective meaning as a proper subject for the sociologist's curiosity, or the contrast between the way writers have understood themselves and the way the sociologist understands them, one is tempted to multiply the questions, if not the objections."

As **Raymond Aron** has remarked Weber was a man who was asking to himself the ultimate questions - "*the relations between knowledge and faith, science and action, the church and prophecy, bureaucracy and charismatic leader, rationalisation and personal freedom......*" *More than that he was a man with great historic erudition who* "*searched all civilisations for the answers to his own questions.......*"

Weber has also been Criticised.........

(*i*) Weber's tendency "*to explain social reality in terms of individual motivation blurred the line between sociology and psychology.*"

(*ii*) As **Prof. Timasheff** has regretted, despite his achievements, Weber did not leave a "*school of followers*". Probably Weber was not bothered about it. "*In keeping with the norms of science and scholarship, he sought the truth, not followers.*"

(*iii*) As **Raymond Aron** has pointed out one cannot be sure whether Weber's practice always corresponded to his theory. In the same way, as Aron says: "*It is doubtful that Max Weber refrained from all value-judgement.......*" It is still more doubtful that "*Value reference*" and "*Value judgement*" are radically separable - as he made them so.

In spite of the criticism made on Weber and his ideas, Weberian sociology is still alive. Though Weber did not leave behind him a school or a set of followers, Parsons and his followers in America have become his unclaimed followers. Parsons has translated some of Weber's works into English and in his theories one easily notices the strong impact of Weberian thoughts.

REVIEW QUESTIONS

1. Give a brief introduction of Max Weber.
2. Throw light on the main works of Max Weber.
3. Define 'ideal type'. Explain Weber's theory of 'ideal types'.
4. Bring out the main features of 'ideal types'.
5. Cricially comment on Weber's theory of religion.
6. Define bureaucracy. Give its characteristic features. Discuss the factors contributed to the development.
7. Explain Weber's theory of bureaucracy.
8. Discuss the functional and dysfunctional aspects of bureaucracy.
9. What are the negative aspects of bureaucracy? Explain.
10. Elucidate the contribution of Max Weber to the development of sociology.
11. Bring out the relation between religion and society.

⌘⌘⌘⌘⌘⌘⌘⌘⌘⌘⌘⌘

59

Karl Marx and his Thoughts

Chapter Outline

KARL MARX: A BRIEF BIOGRAPHICAL SKETCH

Karl Marx: A Great Revolutionary Who Created History

Karl Marx
[1818-1883]

It is a paradox of history that Karl Marx, one of the most influential social thinkers of the 19th century was *"an improverished exile for most his life."* He is known to the world as the architect of socialism and the champion of communism. He was a good organiser, committed revolutionary, a voracious reader and an effective writer. He was a German scholar, a historian, an economist, a political propagandist, a journalist (editor of the "Rheinische Zeitung") a great humanitarian and a philosopher. Above all, he was a dreamer and a socio-political prophet. He committed himself to the cause of the exploited working class and declared a kind of an intellectual battle against the exploiting rich or the capitalist class. As a fearless fighter he was sincere enough to cling on to the views which he believed in, till his last. His views and thoughts were so powerful and influential that more than one-third of the world's population was under their grip until recently. Even today, in spite of the great set back of the recent times to the Russian Communism, his thoughts and the communist ideology, are still alive. His ideology of communism which retained its supermacy in many countries of the world for decades (for not less than 75 years in Russia itself) has virtually proved the Platonic saying *"ideologies rule the world"*. We consider Marx as one among the pioneering sociologists because his views and thoughts have a great sociological significance.

Family Background of Marx

Karl Marx, the eldest son of Neinrich and Henrictta Marx, was born on May 5th, 1818 in the Rhenish city of Trier in Germany. His father, a lawyer provided the family with a fairly typical middle-class existence. Both parents were from rabbinical families, but for business reasons the father had converted to Lutherianism.

Marx's Education

Marx had received his early education at Trier. In 1835, he joined the law faculty at Bonn University and ultimately took his law degree from Berlin University in 1836. In 1841, Marx received the doctorate in philosophy from the University of Jena. His thesis was on *"The Difference Between the Democritean and the Epicurean Philosophy"*, a dry philosophical topic. German Universities (particularly the Berlin University) at that time were under the heavy influence of the German philosopher Hegel and the *"Young Hegelians"*. Because of Marx's association with the Hegelian philosophy - which was considered dangerous by many authorities - he was unable to teach in a German University.

Marx as a Journalist

Marx started his career as a journalist in *"Rheinische Zeitung"* and later became its chief editor within ten months. However, because of his political positions the paper was closed shortly thereafter by the government. The early essays published in this period began to reflect his thoughts. *"They were liberally sprinkled with democratic principles, humanism and idealism. He rejected the abstractness of Hegelian philosophy, the native dreaming of utopian communists, and those activists who were urging what he considered to be political action."* [1]

Migration to Paris

In 1843, Marx married **Jenny Von Westphalen** from a family of Prussian nobles much against the wishes of her family men. He left the editorship of *Rheinische Zeitung* and migrated to Paris along with his wife where he expected to find a comparatively liberal atmosphere for his writing. Here he started publishing German - French Year book in 1844. As a Young Hegelin *"he encountered here two new sets of ideas - French socialism and English Political Economy. It was the unique way in which he combined Hegelianism, Socialism and Political Economy that shaped his intellectual orientation."* [2]

Friendship with Engels

Marx met Fredrick Engels in 1844 who became his closest friend, benefactor, and life-long collaborator. *"The son of a textile manufacturer, Engels had become a socialist critical of the conditions facing the working class. Much of Marx's compassion for the misery of the working class came from his exposure to Engels and his ideas."*

Marx Becomes a Writer

Marx's association with Engels provided him a new spirit for his writing works. He wrote in collaboration with Engels the famous books *"The Holy Family"* and *"The German Ideology"*. He also produced *"The Economic and Philosophic Manuscripts of 1844."*

Though Marx and Engels became the best friends who shared many ideas in common, there were differences between them. *"Marx tended to be a highly abstract thinker, a disorderly intellectual, and very much oriented to his family. Engels was a practical thinker, a neat and tidy business man, and a womaniser"* - (**George Ritzer**). In spite of these differences Marx and Engels had developed good union in which they worked jointly. They wrote books, published articles and worked together in radical organisations. Engels even helped Marx financially throughout the rest of his life so that Marx could devote himself to his intellectual and political endeavours. Still Engels was humble enough to regard himself as *"the junior partner"*. His own words express this feeling beautifully: *"Marx could very well have done without me. What Marx accomplished I would not have achieved. Marx stood higher, saw farther, and took a wider and quicker view than the rest of us. Marx was a genius"* - (**McLellan** - 1973).[3]

---

1. **George Ritzer** in his *Contemporary Sociological Theory*, p. 122.
2. Ibid.
3. As quoted by George Ritzer in his *Contemporary Sociological Theory*, p. 123.

Marx Leaves Paris and Participates in a Revolutionary Movement

Marx could not stay for long in Paris. In 1845, he was expelled from Paris at the insistence of the German Government for his writings in Silesian weavers uprising. He then moved to Brussels. His radicalism was growing, and he had become an active member of the international revolutionary movement. In 1846, Marx and Engels set up *"Communist Correspondence Committe"* in Brussels. (They completed the *"German Ideology"* at this stage). In 1847, Marx joined the "Communist League" and worked for its popularity. His another famous work *"The Poverty of Philosophy"* was published at this stage. He was elected Vice-President of the *"Brussels Democratic Society"*. Because of his close association with the Communist League he was asked to write a document (with Engels) expounding its aims and beliefs. The result was, he published in 1848 the programme of the Communist League, *"The Communist Manifesto of 1848"*, often hailed as the *"birth certificate of scientific socialism."* This work was "characterised by ringing political slogans" (for example, *"workingmen of all countries, unite"*) (G. Ritzer - Page: 123.)

Journey Towards London

Marx now started *"Neue Rheinische Zeitung"* and became its chief editor. He took active part in organising democratic upsurges in Vienna, Frankfurt and Berlin. He was tried in a court and deported from Germany. He came to Paris and after being expelled from there migrated to London where he lived till his death. He kept close contact with all revolutionary movements including the *Paris Commune* of 1871.

Writes the Famous *"Das Kapital"*

In London, Marx undertook a prolonged study of economics that focused on the development of industrial capitalism. The failure of the political revolutions of 1848 made him to withdraw from active revolutionary activity. He devoted much of his attention to a serious and detailed research on the workings of the capitalist system. These untiring works of Marx culminated in the publication his most famous work *"The Capital"*, (Das Kapital) the first volume of which came out in 1867. Two other volumes of this book were published posthumously.

Marx in the Midst of Poverty

During his stay in London Marx lived in poverty barely managing to survive on a small income which he was getting from his writings. Engels' financial support helped his survival, he became reinvolved in political activity. In 1864, he founded the *"international working men's association"*, known as *"First International"*. He soon gained dominance within the workers movement and devoted a number of years to it. He began to gain name and fame both as the leader of the *International* and as the author of *Capital.*

Marx's Concern towards the Developments in India

Marx very keenly observed the Indian developments. "His despatches on the *"Great Indian Revolt"* of 1857 in *"New York Daily"* Tribune; his Notes on Indian History, and other writings, and his prognosis of British rule - clearly depict his deep understanding of the Indian Society and the changes brought about by the British".

Marx—As a Theoretician

Marx, with the due help of his friend Engels, founded the *"Theory of Scientific Communism", enunciated the laws of "Dialectical and Historical Materialism" and discovered the "theory of surplus value."* These have great sociopolitical and economic significance. He is also the chief architect of *"The Theory of Class Conflict"* and *"The Theory of Alienation"*.

The Sad Demise of Marx

Marx, being a sensitive man, was greatly disappointed when he learnt that the *Paris Commune* of 1871 (a worker's upsurge to seize political power) met with failure. The disintegration of the *International* by 1876, the failure of various political movements, and added to all these things, his personal illness-contributed to his sad demise. He died in London on March 14, 1883 and cremated in *Highgate Cemetary.* His wife died in 1881, a daughter in 1882 and though Marx had his followers and admirers throughout the world, when he died in 1883 hardly a handful of people arranged for his funerals.

Engels Becomes the Spokesman for the Marxian Thought

After the death of Marx his trusted friend Engels became the spokesman for the Marxist thought. He sought to bring to light many of the unpublished writings of Marx. The second and third volumes of his *"The Capital,"* were published in 1885 and 1894 respectively.

The Lasting Influence of Marx and Marxian Thought

"Marx believed social scientists must be committed to political action as well as scholarship. He put much of his energy into efforts to bring about the communist society he dreamt of. Although his prediction of world-wide revolution of the working class has turned out to be wrong, his contribution to sociological thought - particularly in the area of social class and social change - have had lasting influence."[4]

The influence of Marx has been simply immense. "Millions of people accept his theories with most religious fervour, and modern socialist and communist movements owe their inspiration directly to him. It is important to realise, however, that Marxism is not the same as Communism. Marx would probably be dismayed at many of the practices of communist movements, and he can not be held responsible for policies pursued in his name decades after his death."[5]

Main Contributions of Marx

Marx nowhere called himself a sociologist. Still his social thoughts and ideas have a great sociological significance. During the recent years greater attention is being paid to Marxian thought and towards his contribution to the fields such as history, economics, political science and sociology. His theory of social class and class conflict, of social change and alienation - are of very great sociological significance. [**Note :** A list of major works of Marx is given at the end of the lesson.]

HISTORICAL MATERIALISM

The theory of *'historical materialism'* is very much associated with the names of Karl Marx and Engels, the champions of Communism. *The theory of historical materialism is also known as the materialistic interpretation of history.* The idea of historical materialism is derived from the most fundamental principle of Marx, namely, *"dialectical materialism."* This dialectical materialism is regarded as *"the consolidation of Marx and Engel's main ideas as a scientific philosophy."*[6] This theory can be regarded as a *"philosophical approach"* made use of by Marx and his followers to analyse the reality.

Marx—As a Prominent Champion of *"Dialectical Materialism"*

Dialectical Materialism is one of the basic principles of Marx. *"Dialectic"* literally means discussion. Dialectic is the study of contradicts, which lie at the very heart of existence. Marx and Engels learnt from Hegel, the famous German thinker, the general nature of the dialectic. They however, objected to and rejected Hegel's idealistic interpretation. They did not approve of the *"Hegellian idealism"*. They did not agree with the Hegellian principles that external reality was a mere reflection of something within the human mind. Unlike, the idealists [Hegel and his followers] who believed in the existence of mind, materialists [Marx and his followers] thought that nature or matter existed independent of and outside the mind. According to them, matter is primary and the mind [which is the mirror of matter] is secondary.

"Marx evolved the theory of philosophical materialism according to which the world is by nature material, and the different phenomena in the world are different forms of matter in movement. From this it follows that material life of society is primary and spiritual life is secondary. The material life of society depends upon the method of securing the means of livelihood and the way of producing material values."[7]

Essential Aspects of Dialectical Materialism. *Thesis-Anti-Thesis-Synthesis*

According to the argument of dialectical materialism, the opposite forces which are always present constitute the moving force of history. As it is already made clear Marx had borrowed this *"dialectical materialism"* from **Hegel.** Hegel "conceived of history as a dialectical process, or struggle of opposites, in which the dominant idea of each age assumed the role of a ***thesis.*** The thesis was soon confronted and eventually defeated by an ***anti-thesis*** or opposite. This contest finally resulted in the production of a ***synthesis,*** which incorporated the more value elements of both thesis and anti-thesis".[8] The opposite forces in society never balance each other; on the other hand one of them is stronger than the other. History presents the process of action and reaction between the forces. Capital, which represents one force is the thesis, and labour is the anti-thesis. **This leads to class struggle.**

---

4. N. J. Smelser in his *Sociology, Fourth Edition,* 1993, p. 391.
5. Ian Robertson in his *Sociology,* p. 13.
6. *Collins Dictionary of Sociology*, p. 165.
7. B. K. Gokhale in *Political Science—Theory and Governmental Machinery,* 1972, p. 42.
8. E. M. Burns in *Ideas in Conflict,* 1960, p. 148, as quoted by B. K. Gokhale. Page - 421.

Historical Materialism or the Materialistic Interpretation of History

Materialistic interpretation of history is another basic principle of Marxism. Marx applied the principle of dialectical materialism to the interpretation of history. As Marx has stated economic conditions determine historical phenomena. *"Human beings must eat and drink and obtain shelter and clothing before they can pursue politics, science, religion and art. Thus the stage of advancement of the production, distribution and exchange of goods and organisation of society resulting therefrom, determine in the final analysis, the political, social and cultural developments."*[9]

***Historical materialism is the economic interpretation of history*:** that is, all evolution is the result of the economic forces alone. Marx regarded the economic forces as the predominant dynamic agency of human society and its history. This kind of economic interpretation found in Marx's historical materialism consists of the following aspects:

Essential Aspects of the Economic Interpretation

1. According to Marx, *the material or economic conditions are more important than the ideological or the spiritual things.* He did not accept spiritualism and idealism, but based his concept of dialectics on materialism. With this pre-occupation of the materialistic ideas in his mind he declared that *"It is not the consciousness of the man that determines their existence, but their social existence that determines their consciousness."*
2. *The form and structure of every society is determined by its economic structure.* This economic structure is referred to as the *"infrastructure"* of society. This infrastructure consists of two things:
   (*a*) ***"material forces of production"**, and*
   (*b*) *the indispensable **"relations of production."***
3. *The economic infrastructure constitutes the basis* on which the social, political, religious, moral, educational, legal and other institutional network referred to as *"super-structure"* is built. The "social consciousness" which includes the thoughts, ideologies and philosophies of the people, is rooted in this institutional network.
4. The forces of conflict which are associated with the historical development within the society have brought about conflict within the economic infrastructure, that is, between the *"forces of production"* and *"relations of production."* It is through the ideological forms men become conscious of the conflict within the economic structure.
5. *The productive forces of the society determine its total conditions.* The modes of production determine the character of the social, political and intellectual life, in general. Change in the system of production brings about transformation in the social, political, legal and cultural institutions. Thus, according to Marx, the form of production is the cause of difference between the legal, political, intellectual and religious institutions of the pastoral, feudal and capitalist societies.

Relations between the Modes of Production and Social Structures

According to Marx, the nature of society and its structure depends very much on the mode of production. Marx spoke in terms of five stages in the development of society which correspond to five consecutive modes of production. They are:

(*i*) Primitive Society and *Primitive* [*Asiatic*] *Mode of Production,*
(*ii*) Ancient Society and *Ancient Mode of Production,*
(*iii*) Feudal Society and *Feudal Mode of Production,*
(*iv*) Capitalist Society and *Capitalist Mode of Production,*
(*v*) Communist Society and *Socialist Mode of Production.*

1. In the ***Primitive Communist stage,*** there is no private property and hence the productions are owned by the community.
2. In the ***Ancient stage,*** there is slavery in which one class owns and exploits the members of another. Owners of the slaves and of the means of production get everything substantial and the poor and the slaves receive very little.
3. In the ***feudal stage,*** the class of aristocratic landowners or barons exploit the mass of peasants or serfs.
4. In the ***Capitalist stage,*** the capitalists own all the important means of production and make the workers wage-slaves or tools. Here the owners of wealth exploit the mass of industrial workers.

   In the Ancient, Feudal and Capitalist stages, the structure of society is the result of conditions of production. Material conditions of life are so important that they determine the political and social conditions. Society develops a particular outlook

---

9. Quoted by Gokhale, p. 422.

owing to economic conditions. *The mental attitude of the people is the product of material conditions.* Religion and law are also determined by the same conditions. Society goes through these different stages to ultimately reach a stage of classless society. Each stage is better than the earlier one. Each of these modes or systems is more economically productive than its predecessor, but the tensions of class conflict lead to a revolution that results in the fifth stage, that is, socialism.

5. In the ***Communist society*** or the fifth stage, the mode of production is socialist. The socialist mode of production is based on social ownership. This stage is found when the industrial workers have finally revolted. This is the society aimed at the revolutionary overthrow of the capitalist society.

Comments Against the Historical Materialism

The theory of *"Historical materialism"* advocated by Marx has been widely criticised. Some such comments could be mentioned here.

1. *Marx unnecessarily limited the range of the theoretical scheme of Historical materialism.* Marx intended the theoretical scheme of historical materialism to have a universal character. But his own researches were limited almost entirely to the 19th century capitalist societies. He gave only a fragmentary accounts of the other types of societies. His scheme is not, for example, helpful when applied to the phenomenon of a caste system.
2. *Is the truth of historical materialism itself historically determined ? Or, is it valid for all history, past and present ?* These are pertinent questions here. But the explanations that we could find for these questions in the works of Marx and Engels are far from satisfactory. *"Both Marx and Engels declared that its truth was relevant only for class societies........ Does this mean that the leap from the kingdom of necessity to that of a freedom........." implies a condition in which man escapes the limitations of his earthly fate? There is no warrant for the belief that historical materialism justifies any such historical apocalypse."*[10]
3. *The materialistic interpretation of history is incorrect for it exaggerates the role of economic factors.* It fails to recognise the non-economic factors like political conditions, religion, language, art and science as something important. As **Seligman** has stated it is wrong to suppose that all the wars and conflicts recorded so far took place only because of economic factors.
4. Further, there is the problem of measuring the determining effects of economic factors. We do not have any precise measuring rods to prove or assess that interests, habits and motives of the social classes are determined by the economic factors. The statement of Marx that in *"the last instance" economic conditions determine social life, implies a theory of measurement. "So far, however, no theory of measurement for the social discipline has been evolved."*[11]
5. The constant association between economic ownership and political power which is a basic postulate of Marx's theory has been rejected as inconsistent by the thinkers like **Raymond Aron, C. Wright Mills, Ralf Dahrendorf** and others.

Concluding Remarks

In spite of various comments made against Marxian theory of historical materialism **Bottomore** points out at the two important contributions of Marx to sociological thinking. *"In the **first place,** Marx adopted and maintained very consistently in his work a view of human societies as wholes or systems in which social groups, institutions, beliefs and doctrines are interrelated, so that these have to be studied in their inter-relations rather than in isolation. **Secondly,** he viewed societies as inherently mutable systems in which changes are produced largely by internal contradictions and conflicts.*[12]

MARX'S THEORY OF SOCIAL CHANGE

Social Change Through Class Conflict

Marx's theory of social change is much interlinked with his concept of social classes and class conflicts. Marx's focus on the process of social change is so central to his thinking that its shadow pervades all his writings. The motor force of history for Marx is not to be found in any extra-human agency but in man himself. *"Marx insisted that men make their own history. Human history is the process through which men change themselves...."* (**Coser**).

10. Parimal B. Kar in *Sociology*, p. 356.
11. Ibid, p. 356.
12. Ibid, p. 357.

Marx declared that *"Violence is the midwife of history"*. In a similar tone, **Mao** who was one of the strong supporters of Marxian views, wrote that *"Change comes from the barrel of a gun"*. Marx who is the most prominent and eloquent exponent of the *"conflict theory of social change"*, holds that change is caused by tensions between competing interests in society.

Marx believed that the class struggle was the driving force of social change. **Marx** and **Engels** wrote in *"The Communist Manifesto"* (1848): *"All history is the history of conflict."* Marx believed that *"the character of social and cultural forms is influenced by the economic base of society specifically by the mode of production that is used and by the relationships that exist between those who own and those who do not own the means of production. History is the story of conflict between the exploiting and the exploited classes. This conflict repeats itself again and again until capitalism is overthrown by the workers and a socialist state is created. Socialism is the forerunner to the ultimate social form of communism"*[13] Thus it is clear that the Marxism theory of social change is essentially conflict-oriented. It is appropriately called the *"Conflict theory of Change"*. Marx as a conflict theorist considers society fundamentally dynamic, not static. He regards conflict as normal, not an abnormal process and he believes that *"The existing conditions in any society contain the seeds of future social changes."*

Marx conceived of four major successive modes of production in the history of mankind after the first stage of primitive communism: *The Asiatic, the Ancient, the Feudal, and the Modern bourgeoisie* form. Each of these came into existence through contradictions and antagonisms that had developed in the previous order. *"No social order ever disappears before all the productive forces for which there is room in it have been developed, and new higher relations of production never appear before the material conditions of their existence have matured in the womb of the old society"* (as quoted by **Lewis Coser**).

Free men and slaves, patricians and plebians, barons and serfs, guild masters and journey men, exploiters and the exploited, have confronted one another from the beginning of recorded times. The *"class antagonisms specific to each particular mode of production led to the emergence of classes whose interests could no longer be asserted within the framework of the old order.."* (**Coser**) However, "the bourgeoisie relations of production are the last antagonistic form of the social process of production." When they have been overthrown by a victorious proletariat, *"the prehistory of human society will have come to an end."* and the dialectical principle that ruled the previous development of mankind, ceases to operate, as harmony replaces social conflict in the affairs of men. These ideas portray Marx's wishful thinking rather than his dreams.

As a creative thinker Marx had very strongly supported social change. *"Philosophers have already interpreted the world; our present task is to change it"* - Marx used to say. He never depended on the status quo. But in his analysis of social change he placed high premium on economic factors and neglected religious, political and other factors. He made conflict the driving force of history and undermined the importance of harmony and consensus. Though Marx called man the main instrument of change, in his analysis of capitalism he reduced man to the level of a helpless creature. It is true that nobody can stop the future course of history. But it need not necessarily follow the particular course as expected and insisted upon by Marx and his followers.

MARXIAN THEORY OF SOCIAL CLASS

According to **Marx,** *"Class is the manifestation of economic differentiation."* **R. Bendix** and **S.M. Lipset** have stated: *"A social class in Marx's terms is any aggregate of persons who perform the same function in the organisation of production."*[14]

The above definitions make it clear that *"class"* according to Marx, is basically *economic in nature,* though it had great social importance. From the Marxian point of view, class is *not determined by the occupations or income* but by the position an individual occupies and *the function he performs in the process of production.* ***For example,*** if there are two blacksmiths of whom one is the owner of workshop and another a paid worker, they belong to two different classes though their occupation remains the same.

Thus, Marx defined a class as *all those people who share a common relationship to the means of economic production.* Those who own and control the means of production - *slave-owners, feudal landowners, or the owners of property such as factories and capital* - are the ***dominant class.*** Those who work for them - *slaves, peasants or industrial labourers* - are the ***sub-ordinate class.*** The relationship between the two classes, is not only one of dominance and subordination, but also of exploitation. The workers produce more wealth in the form of food, manufactured products, and services than is necessary to meet their basic needs. In other words, they produce *"surplus wealth"*. But they do not enjoy the use of the surplus they have created. Instead those who own the means of production are able to take this surplus wealth as *"profit"*

13. Ian Robertson, p. 546.
14. F. Abraham and J.H. Morgon

for their own use. This, in Marx's view, is the essence of exploitation and the main source of conflict between the classes that has occurred throughout history.

Marx linked this analysis to the idea that *"the economic base of society influences the general character of all other aspects of culture and social structure such as law, religion, education and government. The dominant class is able to control all of these institutions and to ensure that they protect its own interests. The laws, therefore, protect the rich, not the poor. The established religion supports the social order as it is, not as it might be. Education teaches the virtues of the existing system, not its vices. Government upholds the status quo rather than undermines it"* [15]

Five Variables That Determine The Marxian Concept of Class

Bendix and **Lipset** have identified five variables that determine a class in the marxian sense:

1. *Conflicts over the distribution of economic rewards between the classes*;
2. *Easy Communication between the individuals in the same class positions so that ideas and action programmes are readily disseminated*;
3. *Growth of class-consciousness in the sense that the members of a class have a feeling of solidarity and understanding of their historic role*;
4. *Profound dissatisfaction of the lower class over its inability to control the economic structure of which it feels itself to be the exploited victim*;
5. *"Establishment of a political organisation resulting from the economic structure, the historical situation and maturation of class-consciousness"* [16]

Marx stressed that mere organisation of production is not a sufficient condition for the development of social classes; *"there must also be a physical concentration of masses of people, easy communication among them, repeated conflicts over economic rewards and the growth of class conciousness."* For the very same reason, small peasants who constitute a vast mass and live in more or less similar conditions, but scattered over a big area, do not form a class group in the Marxian sense.

Only Two Major Classes: *'Haves'* and *'Have-Nots'*

From the Marxian point of view, in all stratified societies there are two major social groups; *a rich class and a poor class, or the 'Haves and Have-nots'*; or *a ruling class and subject class.* The key to understanding a given society is to discover which is the dominant mode of production within it. All the other relations stem out of it. From a Marxian view, a class is a social group where members share the same relationships to the forces of production. Thus during the feudal stage, there are two main classes distinguished by their relationship to land, the major force of production. They are the (*i*) *fedual nobility who own the land and,* (*ii*) *the landless serfs* who work the land. Similarly, in the capitalist stage, there are two main classes: (*i*) *the bourgeoisie or Capitalist class* which owns the forces of production and (*ii*) *the proletariat or working class* whose members own only their labour which they hire to the capitalists in return for wages.

Stages in the Evolution of Society and Development of Social Classes

Marx believed that human society evolves through different stages according to the means of production that is dominant at each stage: (*i*) the first is *primitive communism*, on which there is no private property (*ii*) The second is *slavery* in which one class owns and exploits the members of another; (*iii*) The third of *feudalism* in which a class of aristocratic landowners exploits the mass of peasants; (*iv*) The fourth is *capitalism* in which the owners of wealth exploit the mass of industrial workers. Each of these systems is more economically productive than its predecessor, but the tensions of class conflict lead to a revolution that results in the fifth stage. (*v*) the fifth stage, *socialism,* occurs when the industrial workers have finally revolted.

In the three stages, excluding the first, the labour power required for production was supplied by the subject class, that is, by *slaves, serfs*, and *wage labourers,* respectively. The subject class is made up of the majority of the population whereas the ruling or dominant class forms a minority. Marx mentions the case of the first stage, the stage of *'primitive communism'* as the only example of a *"classless society"*.

Development of Social Classes

According to Marx, classes did not exist during the era of primitive communism when the societies were based on a sort of socialist mode of production. In a hunting and food gathering stage, classes did not exist, since all members

15. Ian Robertson in his *Sociology*, p. 219.
16. As quoted by Francis Abraham and J.H. Morgon in their *Sociological Theories*.

of society shared the same relationship to the forces of production. Every member here was both producer and owner. This stage represents a subsistence economy which means that production only meets basic survival needs. *"Classes emerge only when the productive capacity of society expands beyond the level required for subsistence......"* This occurs in an agricultural economy where a few individuals are freed from food production to do other tasks. As agriculture developed, surplus wealth, that is, goods above the basic subsistence needs of the community, was produced. This led to an exchange of goods and trading developed within and between communities. This was accompanied by the development of a system of ***private property.***

"Private property and the accumulation of surplus wealth form the basis for the development of class societies. In particular, they provide the pre-conditions for the emergence of a class of producers and a class of non-producers. Some are able to acquire the forces of production and others are therefore obliged to work for them. The result is a class of non-producers which owns the forces of production and a class of producers which owns only its labour power. From a Marxian perspective, the relationship between the major social classes is one of neutral dependence and conflict."[17]

MARXIAN THEORY OF CLASS STRUGGLE OR CLASS CONFLICT

The Idea of Class Conflict is Central to Marxian Thought

The theory of class struggle or class conflict is central to Marxian thought. In fact, Marxian sociology is often called *"The sociology of class conflict."* The idea of class war emerges from the theories of *dialectical materialism, materialistic interpretation of history,* and *surplus value.* The main promise of the *"Marxian Class Theory"* is to be found in the opening sentence of his famous work *"The Communist Manifesto, 1848"* which reads as follows;

"The history of the hitherto existing society is the history of the class struggles. Freeman and slave, patrician and plebian, lord and serf, guild-master and journey man, in a word, oppressore and oppressed, stood in constant opposition to one another, carried on uninterrupted, now hidden and now open fight, a fight that each time ended in a revolutionary reconstitution of society at large, or in common ruin of the contending classes."[18]

It is clear from the above, that at every stage in history, there is war between the classes. The landowner exploits the landless, and the factory owner exploits the workers. Between classes, there is endless antagonism and hatred. Class conflict is the severest form of class antagonism.

War between Classes

Marx says that according to the relentless law of history, a particular class owns and controls the means of production, and by virtue of this exploits the rest of the people. The capitalist class makes use of the state as an instrument of oppression and exploitation. Thus at every stage there are broadly two classes: *the owners of means of production*, that is, *exploiters* on one side and the *exploited on the other.* History presents nothing but the record of a war between classes. Every exploiting class at each stage gives rise to an opposite class. Hence thesis and anti-thesis can be noted. Feudal barons and capitalists form the thesis, and the serf and the proletariat respectively constitute the anti-thesis. Marx gave a call to the workers to overthrow the thesis of capitalism by the antithesis of organised labour.

Essential Aspects of the Marxian Theory of Class Conflict

Marx developed his theory of class conflict in his analysis and critique of the capitalist society. The main ingredients of this theory of conflict have been enlisted by **Abraham** and **Morgan**[19] which may be briefly described here.

1. The Development of the Proletariat

Accentuation of capital is the essence of capitalism. In **Raymond Aron**'s words, *"The essence of capitalist exchange is to proceed from money to money by way of commodity and end up with more money than one had at the outset."* Capital is gained, according to Marx, from the exploitation of the masses of population, the working class. *"The capitalist economic systems transformed the masses of people into workers, created for them a common situation and inculcated in them an awareness of common interest. Through the development of class consciousness, the economic conditions of capitalism united the masses and constituted them into "a class for itself" .....* (**Abraham** and **Morgan.** Page: 37.)

---

17. M. Haralambos in *Sociology—Themes and Perspectives*, pp. 39-40.
18. Quoted in Gokhale's Political Science, pp. 423-424.
19. Abraham and Morgan in their *Sociological Thought*, pp. 36-41.

2. Importance of Property

According to Marx, the most distinguishing feature of any society is its form of property. *An individual's behaviour is determined by his relations to property.* Classes are determined on the basis of individual's relation to the means of production. Means of production or forces of production represent a type of property which in the capitalist society are owned by the capitalists. Here, an individual's occupation is not important but his relations to the means of production, are important. *"Property divisions are the crucial breaking lines in the class structure."*

3. Identification of Economic and Political Power and Authority

From a Marxian perspective, political power emerges from economic power. The power of the ruling class therefore stems from its ownership and control of the forces of production. The political and legal systems reflect ruling class interests. In Marx's words: *"The existing relations of production between individuals must necessarily express themselves also as political and legal relations."* The capitalists who hold monopoly of effective private property take control of political machinery. Their interests are clearly reflected in their political and ideological spheres. As **Raymond Aron** points out, *"Political power, properly so-called, is merely the organised power of one class for oppressing another."* The political power and ideology thus seem to serve the same functions for capitalists that class consciousness serves for the working class.

4. Polarisation of Classes

In the capitalist society there could be only two social classes: (*i*) ***The capitalists** who own the means of production and distribution,* and (*ii*) ***the working classes** who own nothing but their own labour.* Though Marx had repeatedly referred to the intermediate state such as the *"small capitalists", "the petti bourgeoisie",* and the *"lumpenproletariat",* he was of the firm belief that at the height of conflict these would be drawn into the ranks of the proletariat. **Raymond Aron** has termed this process as *"proletarianisation."*

5. The Theory of Surplus Value

Marx believed that the capitalists accumulate profit through the exploitation of labour. In fact, the relationship between the capitalists and workers is not only one of dominance and subordination, but also of exploitation. The workers produce more wealth in the form of food, manufactured goods and services than is necessary to meet their basic needs. In other words, they produce *"surplus wealth."* But they do not enjoy the use of the surplus they have created. Instead, those who own the means of production are able to seize this surplus wealth as *"profit"* for their own use. According to Marx, this is the essence of exploitation and the main source of conflict between the classes.

6. Pauperisation

Exploitation of the workers can only add to their misery and poverty. But the same exploitation helps the rich to become richer. As Marx says *"the wealth of the bourgeoisie is swelled by large profits with corresponding increase in the mass of poverty; of pressure, of slavery, of exploitation"* of the proletariat. In every mode of production which involves the exploitation of man by man, majority of people, the people who labour, are condemned to toil for no more than the barest necessities of life. With this, society gets divided into rich and poor. To Marx, *poverty is the result of exploitation not of scarcity.*

7. Alienation

The process of alienation is central to Marxian theory of class conflict. The economic exploitation and inhuman working conditions lead to increasing alienation of man. *Alienation results from a lack of sense of control over the social world.* The social world confronts people as a hostile thing, leaving them *"alien"* in the very environment that they have created. The workers caught in the vicious circle of exploitation find no way to get out of it. Hence they lose interest in work. Work becomes an enforced activity, not a creative and a satisfying one. The responsibility of the worker gets diminished because he does not own the tools with which he works, he does not own the final product too. He is *"a mere cog in a machine"* and nothing else. This situation of alienation ripens the mood of the worker for a conflict.

8. Class Solidarity and Antagonism

With the growth of class consciousness among the working class, their class solidarity becomes cystalised. The working class becomes internally more homogeneous and this would help to intensify the class struggle. Because of this class feeling and solidarity, the workers are able to form unions against the bourgeoisie. They club together in order to keep up the rate of wages. They form associations in order to make provisions beforehand for occasional revolts. Here and there contests break out into riots.

9. Revolution

When the class struggle reaches its height, a violent revolution breaks out which destroys the structure of capitalist society. This revolution is most likely to occur at the peak of an economic crisis which is part of the recurring booms, and repressions characteristic of capitalism. *"Marx predicted that the capitalists would grow fewer and stronger as a result of their endless competition; that the middle class would disappear into the working class, and that the growing poverty of the workers would spark a successful revolution."* (**I. Robertson.**) Marx has asserted, unlike other wars and revolutions, *this would be a historic one.*

10. The Dictatorship of the Proletariat

Marx felt that the revolution would be a *bloody one.* This revolution terminates the capitalist society and *leads* to the social dictatorship of the proletariat. Since the revolution results in the liquidation of the bourgeoisie, they will cease to have any power and will be reduced to the ranks of the proletariat. Thus, the inevitable historical process destroys the bourgeoisie. The proletariats, then establish their social dictatorship. But this expression *"social dictatorship of the proletariat"* has become a topic of controversy among the communists themselves. Many have abandoned that *"treacherous phrase"* particularly after the tyrannical Stalinist and post-Stalinist dictatorships. Marx himself had written that he differentiated himself from *"those communists who were out to destroy personal liberty and who wish to turn the world into one large barrack or into a gigantic warehouse."*[20]

11. Inauguration of the Communist Society

After attaining the success in the revolution, the workers in course of time, would create a new socialist society. In this new society the means of producing and distributing wealth would be publicly and not privately owned. This new socialist society would be a classless and a casteless society free from exploitation of all sorts. The state which has no place in such a society will eventually *"wither away"*. In this society *nobody owns anything but everybody owns everything. Each individual contributes according to his ability and receives according to his needs.*

MARXIAN CONCEPT OF CLASSLESS SOCIETY

Karl Marx has been regarded as the champion of communism and an advocate of *"classless society."* Marxism is often known as *"a philosophy of social revolution."* Marx never aspired for a revolution just for the sake of a revolution. He wanted to establish an egalitarian society known for equality and social coherence. He intended to see a *"classless society"* free from all types of exploitations. He believed that the class struggle would help the establishment of such a society. It is in this context, the nature of the classless society and the manner of establishing it assume importance. A brief analysis of the Marxian notion of classless society is provided here.

Classless Society : A Dream of Marx

In the Marxian thought, the concept of *"classless society"* remains as a figment of imagination of Marx. A classless society devoid of all kinds of exploitation and conflicts is only imaginary. Such a type of society never existed in the past, nor do we find it today. Marx, who had a deep historical insight was quite aware of this. In spite of this awareness, Marx was cherishing such a dream in his mind. Marx who had seen the pitiable lot of the workers in the initial stages of the Industrial Revolution, was helplessly aspiring for a classless society.

Marx was Sufficiently Aware of the Existence of Classes

"Classless society" means a society without the antagonistic classes or strata. It means a society in which the classes with opposing interests such as the land-owners and the landless, workers and management, freemen and slaves, the rich and the poor, exploiters and the exploited, capitalists and labourers, etc. are not found. Such a type of society never existed in the past. The very statement of Marx - *"The history of the hitherto existing society is the history of the class struggles"*[21] makes it evident that he knew that classes had been in existence from the very beginning of history.

Circumstances Favouring the Emergence of *"Classless Society"*

As Marx stated, when the human society in its historical development reaches the capitalistic stage of production it gets divided into only two classes namely *capitalist class* [or *the Bourgeoisie*] and the *working class* [or *the proletariats*]. The former one is the *"exploiting class"* while the latter is the *"exploited"* one. Their interests always clash and conflict arises. It is this class conflict which is always responsible for social movements and revolutions. When the class conflict reaches its final stage the workers gain upperhand in it. They become victorious in this struggle and establish their regime. In the initial stages *"the dictatorship of the proletariat"* will be established and thereafter it prepares the way for the transformation of the society. This transformation finally culminates in the establishment of the classless society.

20. Irwing Howe as quoted by Abraham and Morgan, p. 4.
21. The opening sentence in Marx's book *The Manifest of Communist Party*,. 1848.

Capitalist System is Sure to Fall - Marx

Marx was of the opinion that the capitalist system would not last long because it is sowing the seeds of its own destruction. Hence Marx felt that *"The prophecy of capitalism is the prophecy of doom or despair."* About the whole system of capitalism **Coser** said, *"Thus, the capitalist system enlarges the number of workers, brings them together into compact groups, makes them class conscious, supplies them with means of inter-communication on a world-wide scale, reduces their purchasing power, and by increasingly exploiting them, arouses them to organised resistance."* Marx wanted such an imperfect system to go at the earliest. Hence he gave a call for the workers to put an end to it. Hence his clarion call: *"workers of the whole world unite, you have nothing to lose, but your chains, you have a world to win."*

Marx was very sure of the fall of the capitalist system. Hence he wrote in the *"Communist Manifesto"*: *"The Bourgeoisie produces its own grave-diggers. The fall of the Bourgeoisie and the victory of the proletariat are equally inevitable."*

Establishment of the *Classless "Communist" Society*

When man has become aware of his loss, of his alienation, as a universal non-human situation, it will be possible for him to proceed to a radical transformation of his situation by a revolution. This revolution will be the prelude to the establishment of communism and the reign of liberty reconquered. *"In the place of old Bourgeoisie society with its classes and class antagonisms, there will be an association in which the free development of each is the condition for the free development of all."*

The Classless society, then in the Marxist thought, refers to *"the ultimate condition of social organisation, expected to occur when true communism is achieved."*[22] The classless society is thus *the final phase of communism* where there will be no classes and no class conflicts.

As per the imagination of Marx, in the communist society, that is going to be established after the revolution, the needs of the individuals will be taken proper care. The working principle of the communist society would be: *"From each according to his abilities and to each according to his needs."* This type of society provides opportunities which make the people feel that the entire society is at the back of everyone, because it is based on another noble principle namely: *"All for each and each for all."*

Political Principles of the Classless Society

What is the role of the state in a classless society-? This question is very significant in the Marxian thought. This question has given rise to confusions, disputes, controversies, and embarrasments within the circle of the communists or the Marxists. Marx was very much pessimistic about the state and had contempt for its role. He considered it nothing but the *"organised means of violence."* According to Marx, *"the state represents the dominant class in the society."* The state which is based on exploitation aims to protect the interests of the rich and of the ruling class. About the role of the state Engels writes: Arising out of class contradictions, *"the state becomes the state of the most powerful class, the class which rules in the economics and with its aid becomes also the class which rules in politics and thus acquires new means of holding down and exploiting the oppressed class."*[23] It is thus clear that the communists themselves regard the state as an instrument of exploitation. Then, what is to be done with the state now-?

***The "Withering away" of the State in the Socialist Society*:** The state in its historical development has always stood with the ruling class protecting its interests. Hence Engels stated that socialism should aim at not only removing the classes but also the state. *"After the class struggle has resulted in the victory of the proletariat and the establishment of a socialist society, however there will be no further need for such a repressive institution; theoretically, the state then, is expected to "wither away."*[24] All that is needed is, that the workers should unite and hasten the process of the revolution which will ultimately make the state disappear.

It is believed that after the proletarian revolution *"the dictatorship of the proletariat"* will bring about social and economic justice; then there will be no thesis, anti-thesis and class-war. One man will not exploit another man, and one class will not exploit another class. Thus the ground will be prepared for the disappearance of the state. *"The complete disappearance of the state marks the zenith of "Marxian socialism."*

***"The State is Not Abolished, it Withers Away"*:** In the words of Engels, *"the state is not abolished, it withers away."* He writes: *"The society that will reorganise production on the basis of the free and equal association of the producers will*

22. *The New Encyclopaedia Britannica,* Vol. 3, p. 356.
23. Engels as quoted by R.C. Gupta in his *Great Political Thinkers*, p. 421.
24. *The New Encyclopaedia Britannica*, Vol.3, p. 356.

put the machinery of the state where it will then belong: into the museum of antiquities by the side of the spinning wheel and the bronze axe." [25]

Transformation of Socialism into Communism under the *"Dictatorship of the Proletariat"*

Though the ultimate aim of the revolution is to establish a classless society, the proletariats are going to establish their dictatorship for some time. This dictatorship which will prevail for a short period will act to transform socialism into communism. In this transitional period, it will seize and centralise means of transport and communication. In the temporary phase, labour will be paid according to work, but the ultimate aim is to realise the principle *"from each according to his ability and to each according to his need."* The dictatorship of the proletariat will protect the needs of the working class and provide it socio-economic justice. Thus, *"under the loving care of the dictatorship of the proletariat, socialism will blossom into communism."* [26]

Main Economic Principles of the Classless Society

As it is stated, in the final phase of communism classless social system will appear. In such a social system there will be *"one single form of public ownership of the means of production and full equality of all members of society. Under it, the all-round development of people will be accompanied by the growth of the productive forces through continuous progress in science and technology."* [27] In a communist society *"the ability of each person will be employed to the greatest benefit of all the people."*

The classless society is one in which all the major industries, commercial establishments, banks, transport and communication systems will be *collectively owned and their profits collectively shared.* An increase in production or wealth or property will never result in an increase in inequality, but *will add to the prosperity of all.* Medical, educational, commercial, banking, transport, communication and other facilities are made equally available for all. Their main motto will be *"service"* and not *"profit making."* All landed property will be in the ownership of the society and cultivation will be carried out on co-operative basis. In the whole economic field there will be no scope for exploitation of any kind.

Society Meeting the Requirements of the People

Classless society ensures uninterrupted progress of society and provides for all the members material and cultural benefits according to their growing needs. People's requirements will be satisfied from public sources. Articles of personal use will be in the full ownership of each member of the society and will be at his disposal. *Every able bodied person will participate in the social labour and thereby ensure the steady growth of the material and spiritual wealth of society.* The communist classless society represents the highest form of organisation of public life.

Strengthening of the Societal Power Under the Classless Community Society

Classless society is virtually the stateless society. It does not mean that there will be nothing but chaos in such a society. It will by no means be a society of anarchy, idleness and inactivity. On the contrary, people's organisations will evolve on a voluntary basis to look into the needs of the masses. These organisations will have *"only a social base"* **and not** *a political one.* The rights, freedom, honour and dignity of the citizens will be closely protected by the society with the help of these organisations.

***Classless society is a homogeneous society*:** According to Marx, the elimination of the distinction between classes makes for greater homogeneity of society. All people will have equal status in society and will stand in the same relation to the means of production. All will actively participate in the management of public affairs for *there is no scope for the re-emergence of the class system.*

Marx was of the firm belief that in a classless communist society *"Harmonious relations will be established between the individual and society........ Classless communist society will, thus, constitute the highest form of organisation of the human community. For all their diversity, the requirements of people will express the sound reasonable requirements of the fully developed person."* [28]

Critical Evaluation of the Marxian *"Theory of Classless Society"*

1. ***Marxian theory of classless society is regarded as the weakest link in his thought system.*** Marx was a strong advocate of change. He had great convictions and faith in his thoughts. This faith made him project his own concept

25. Engels in *The Origin of the Family, Private Property and the State.*
26. R.C. Gupta in *Great Political Thinkers.*
27. A.C. Kapoor in *Principles of Political Science,* p. 672.
28. A.C. Kapoor. p. 672.

of an ideal society, *the communist classless society.* His view that the historic social revolution will take the people to *"the brave new world"* remains only a product of his wishful thinking. Establishment of socialism in a few of the countries [such as Russia, that is, U.S.S.R. of 1917-1990, China, Poland, etc.] does not reveal as yet any desire to move *"from the kingdom of necessity to the kingdom of freedom"* [Lenin]. It only remains as an unfulfilled desire of the communists such as Lenin.

2. ***Classless society of Marxian vision is not to be seen anywhere*** in the so called communist world even after more than 120 years of death of Marx. His prophecy relating to the *"withering away of the state"* has not come true. As a matter of fact, in the communist nations today, the state is increasing its power and authority day by day.
3. ***Marx's theory of a classless society is a kind of utopian dream.*** Marxian utopianism is also not regarded as his original ideal. According to Bogardus, Marxian communism is the result of the *Plato's communism and Moore's "Utopianism."*
4. ***Marxian concept of classless society remains only as a political instrument in the hands of the communists.*** This concept is being misused for gaining political benefits. It is thus reduced to the level of a tool of political propaganda.
5. ***"Like all dogmas, Marxism is strong in what it asserts and weak in what it denies."*** Marx was, *"at his best only when he was thundering as a prophet against the capitalists."*[29]
6. ***Durkheim considered Marxian socialism as the theory worthy of being rejected*:** Durkheim showed interest in Marxian socialism, but his concept of socialism was different from that of Marx's. *"He did not see the proletariat as the salvation of society, and he was greatly opposed to agitation or violence."* He regarded socialism as a movement worthy of being launched for the moral rejuvenation of society and not for obtaining temporary political gains through a violent revolution. He regarded Marxian socialism as *"a set of disputable and out-of-date hypothesis"* - [**Lukes**].

In spite of its failures and shortcomings, both theoretical and practical, the theory of the classless communist society makes an appeal to an increasing number. It has had a tremendous appeal to the people with a sense of social justice.

MARX'S CONCEPT OF ALIENATION

The concept of *"alienation"* has become very popular in modern literature, political philosophy, existentialist philosophy, psycho analysis, psychology and sociology. In the writings of Marx, *alienation* is a principal term, and hence it has dominated the history of sociological thought.

What is Alienation?

1. *"Alienation refers to the sense of powerlessness, isolation and meaninglessness experience by human beings when they are confronted with social institutions and conditions that they can not control and consider oppressive".* - (**Seeman**, 1959 - as quoted by **I. Robertson**)
2. *"Broadly speaking 'alienation' denotes a socio-psychological condition of the individual which involves his estrangement from certain aspects of his social existence".*[30]

It is difficult to provide an adequate analysis of this concept for it has been used differently by different scholar. But it was Karl marx who introduced to modern sociology *"the theory of alienation"*.

Due to Alienation Man No More Remains a Man, But Becomes an *"Improverished Thing"*

For Marx, the social arrangements which form the context of work in capitalist society alienated the worker. They failed to provide him with the opportunities for a *meaningful and creative existence.* The worker is alienated in that neither he receives satisfaction from his work nor receives the full product of his labour. The worker is accordingly alienated from *"the true nature of man"*. The conditions that characterise the modern industrial production prevent the worker from *"exercising his full creative powers and so releasing the full potentialities of his nature."* Thus, alienation is *"that condition when man does not experience himself as the active bearer of his own powers and richness, but as an improverished "thing" dependent on powers outside of himself* - (quoted by **Duncan Mitchell**)

---

29. Quoted by E. Asirvatham and K.K. Misra in *Political Theory*, p. 596.
30. **Duncan Mitchell's** *"Dictionary of Sociology"* - Page: 4.

No Control Over the Social World

According to Marx, alienation results from *the lack of a sense of control over the social world.* People forget that society and social institutions are constructed by human beings and can, therefore, be changed by human beings. The social world thus environs people as a hostile thing, leaving them *"alien"* in the very environment that they have created.

Economic Alienation is More Important

Marx applied the term *"alienation"* to many social institutions such as law, government, religion and economic life. But he gives more importance to alienation in the economic field. He writes *"religious alienation as such occurs only in the sphere of conciousness, in the inner life of man, but economic alienation is that of 'real life'. It therefore, affects both aspects (mind and action)"* [31]

Four Aspects of Alienation

Marx took more interest in analysing the process of alienation in capitalist society. Because of his close association with Engels, Marx became personally aware of the anguish and alienation of urban industrial workers.

According to Marx, alienated labour involves four aspects:

(*i*) *Worker's alienation from the object that he produces;*

(*ii*) *from the process of production;*

(*iii*) *from himself and*

(*iv*) *from the community of his fellowmen.*

According to Marx, *"alienation appears not merely in the result but also in the process of production, within productive activity itself."*

Alienation leads to Dehumanisation

Marx, was of the opinion that alienation would lead to dehumanisation and *devaluation of human beings*. The worker is a victim of exploitation in the world of capitalism. *"The more wealth the worker produces, the poorer he becomes. Just as labour produces the world of things it also creates the devaluation of the world of men. This devaluation increases in direct proportion to the increase in the production of commodities"*[32]

Extreme Division of Labour—A Source of Alienation ?

An important source of this alienation, in Marx's view, is *the extreme division of labour in modern societies*. Each worker has a specific, restricted and limiting role. He or she no longer applies total human capacities of the hands, the mind, and the emotions to work. The worker has very less responsibility. He does not own the tools with which the work is done, does not own the final product, does not have the right to make decisions. He becomes a minute part of a process, *"a mere cog in a machine"*. Work becomes *an enforced activity, not a creative and satisfying one.*

Alienation—At its Heights in a Capitalist Economy

This situation is aggravated in the capitalist economies, in which the profit produced by the labour of the worker goes to someone else. *"In short, the worker spends his life and produces everything not for himself but for the powers that manipulate him. While labour may produce beauty, luxury and intelligence, for the worker it produces only the opposite deformity misery and idiocy"* - (**Abraham** and **Morgan**)

"Alienation"—In the Words of Marx...

Marx's summary of the nature of alienation at work, written well over a century ago, seems as relevant today. It runs like the following[33]:-

*"What then, constitutes the alienation of labour? **First**, the fact that labour is **external** to the worker, that is, it does not feel content but unhappy, does not develop freely his physical and mental energy but mortifies his body and ruins his mind. The worker, therefore, only feels himself outside his work, and in his work feels outside, himself. He is home when he is not working, and when he is working he is not at home. His labour, therefore, is not voluntary, but coerced, it is **forced labour.** It is therefore, not the satisfaction of a need: it is merely a **means** to satisfy the needs external to it. Its alien*

31. As quoted by **Abraham** and **Morgan** from *"Karl Marx, Early Writings*
32. **Abraham** and **Morgan**, Page : 42-43.
33. originally published in 1844,quoted by **I. Robertson** in his *"Sociology"*

character emerges clearly in the fact as soon as no physical or other compulsion exists, labour is shunned like the plague. External labour, labour in which a worker alienates himself is a labour of self-sacrifice. Lastly, the external character of labour for the worker appears in the fact that it is not his own, but someone else's that it does not belong to him; that he belongs, not to himself but to another."

Concluding Remarks

The term alienation pervades the beginning works of Marx, but, it is not found in his later writings. On the basis, we cannot generalise as some commentators have done, that Marx abandoned the idea. The idea gets its expression again in the *"Das Kapital"*. As **Lewis Coser** points out, *"Explicitly stated or tacitly assumed, the notion of alienation remained central to Marx's social and economic analysis"*.

AN ASSESSMENT OF MARX'S CONTRIBUTIONS

Karl Marx was undoubtedly a great social thinker, profound scholar and a prolific writer. He was an idealist who committed himself to the cause of welfare of the working community. It is more appropriate to call him a social philosopher than a sociologist. Marx has almost no influence on the development of early sociology which was dominated by the evolutionists, particularly social Darwinists. The mid twentieth century witnessed the rebirth of Marxist sociology. He has exerted a tremendous influence on a large number of sociologists. He has made scholars discuss the problems which he had raised, and has opened up vast new areas of investigation. *"Most of the modern social sciences owe their existence in greater or lesser degree to Karl Marx"* - (**Duncan Mitchell**).

The Contributions of Marx

1. ***Marxism - An Influential Political Dogma***: The Marxian ideas still constitute the gospel of revolution and his *"Communist Manifesto"* still remains the handbook of the revolutionaries throughout the world. *"Marxism has become the state dogma and the creed of political orthodose in many countries."* His famous slogan, *"Workers of the world unite, you have nothing to lose but your chains; you have a world to win"* - still holds the sway over the working masses throughout the world. More than 1/3 of the world's population has been swept away by the most appealing Marxian ideology.
2. ***Marx has Provided a Comprehensive Theory of Social Change***: According to **T.B. Bottomore,** a leading expert on Marxist sociology, though Marx's theory of class cannot be treated as a theory of stratification, *it can definitely be treated as a comprehensive theory of social change.* It can be considered as a tool for the explanation of change in total societies. This is reflected by the Marxian view that *"Societies are mutable systems in which changes are produced largely by internal contradictions and conflicts...."* As **Abraham** and **Morgan** pointed out, *"even the worst critics argue that Marxian theory provides an excellent framework for the analysis of conflict and change in modern society."*[34]
3. ***Marx's "Conflict Theory" is a Good Alternative to the Western "Functional Theory"***: During the recent years, especially after sixties, due to the efforts of **C. Wright Mills** and others Marx's writings became quite popular in the West including America. There is one main reason for this. As **Bottomore** has pointed out, the *"conflict theory"* of Marx served in all respects as a *"counter theory"* to the *"functional theory"* which reigned supreme in the Western world. The functional theory stresses the importance of *social harmony, social equilibrium* and *social stability* but undermines the role of conflict elements within the society that would lead to the changes in the structure of society. Marx's theory of conflict removes this deficiency and thus provides an alternative to the functional theory. Further, Marx's influence on contemporary sociological theory is growing and *"Marxist Sociology"* has already become an established branch of the discipline. **[Abraham and Morgan - 50.]**
4. ***Marx has Enriched the Realm of "Sociology of Knowledge"***: On the basis of his philosophical writings one can reasonably say that *Marx has given a great contribution to the realm of "sociology of knowledge"*. Marx has said that there is a close relationship between ideas and philosophies on the one hand, and the social contexts and the social structures from where they emerged, on the other. He established this in his *"German Ideology"*. Marx extended this logic and said, *"'Ideas' must be traced to the life-conditions and the historical situations of those who uphold them"* - **(Lewis Coser).**
5. ***Marxian Approach is an "Integral Approach"***: Marx has time and again stressed that we should have an *"integral view"* of the society and not a partial one. According to him, society is the net result of the interwoven social groups, institutions, beliefs, practices, ideas, principles and ideologies. Hence, these constituent elements should

34. Abraham and Morgan in *Sociological Thought*, p. 50.

not be studied independently or separately but as interconnected ones. *This integral approach of Marx is of great sociological significance,* says **Bottomore.**

6. ***Marx's Views Served as Warnings to the Capitalists***: It can be said that the ultimate purpose of Marx was to achieve the welfare of the working community and to lay the foundations of a classless, casteless society based on social harmony and justice. He sincerely believed that his purpose could be realised by a historic class struggle and by the destruction of the capitalist class. His powerful writings, earnest efforts to save the labour community from exploitation, popularisation of socialist ideology, predictions of the future, and his clarion call to the working class to unite and fight against injustice, etc. - created a sort of awareness not only among the workers but also among the capitalists. They started taking Marx's predictions as *"warnings"* and his analysis of the capitalist regime as highly suggestive to correct themselves. As a result, they changed their approach towards them, brought out number of labour legislations to promote their interests and undertook many of the labour welfare programmes. Hence, we do not find that kind of exploitation of the labourers which Marx had witnessed during his lifetime.

Criticisms Against Marxian Views

Marx and his thoughts have been widely criticised. Probably, no other thinker's views have been as widely criticised as those of Marx.

1. ***Marxian Idea of the "Polarisation of Classes" and "Self-destruction of the Capitalist Class is too Simplistic***: Marx's theory of class conflict and his political ideas have been highly criticised. "His theory about capitalist society's inevitable tendency towards radical polarisation and self-destruction is too simplistic and fallacious. The most distinct characteristic of modern capitalism has been the emergence of a large, *"contended and conservative"* middle-class, consisting of managerial, professional, supervisory, and technical personnel. Marx neglected the importance of the role of this middle-class. *"Today's capitalism does not justify Marx's belief that class conflict is essentially revolutionary in character and that structural changes are always the product of violent upheavals....."*[35]
2. ***The Relationship between Revolution and Class Struggle is not Clearly Broughtforth in the Marxian Works***: As **Dr. N. Jayaram** has pointed out, *"the relationship between revolution and class struggle is problematic*. We are accustomed today to regard revolution as a sudden seizure of power, after which radical changes are made. However, the *"epoch of social revolution Marx refers to in the 'Preface' must mean the lengthy process of transformation of one mode of production (and treated social structure) into another. According to Marxist historians, the transition from fedualism to capitalism in Britain, took anything upto 500 years - a very long revolution....."*[36]
3. ***Too Much Emphasis on the Role of "Alienation"***: Marx *misjudged* and even *exaggerated* the extent of alienation of the average worker. *"The great depth of alienation and frustration which Marx "witnessed" among the workers of his day is not "typical" of today's capitalism or its worker...."* (**Abraham** and **Morgan.** Page - 46). Further, the workers tend to identify themselves not entirely and only with their working class groups, but also with a number of *"meaningful" groups - religious, ethnic, caste, occupational and local.* This does not mean that 'alienation' does not exist in the modern capitalist societies. It could rather be said that *"alienation" results more from the structure of bureaucracy.*
4. ***Marx has Neglected or Underestimated the Role of Non-economic Factors in Social Life***: Marx has been criticised *for the undue emphasis he laid on the economic forces or factors.* He has ignored other important sources of power. His assertion that economic forces play the determining role in bringing about social change and in leading to the historical class struggle, has compelled his critics to dub his theories as *"Theories of economic determinism"*. As we know all deterministic theories, in one way or the other, are one-sided and misleading.; Much against the assertion of Marx, Max Weber has established that even the religious beliefs and attitudes contribute to the development of capitalism.
5. ***Marx is Branded as a Political Propagandist***: More than being appreciated as an objective writer, *Marx has been criticised as an advocate of a revolution.* He has also been branded as a political propagandist and prophet. Marx's predictions about the downfall of capitalism have not come true. *"Contrary to his belief, socialism has triumphed in predominantly peasant societies such as Russia and China. Whereas capitalist societies show no signs of destructive class war."* Capitalism at the height of its growth is still strong in America.
6. ***The Bourgeoisie and the Proletariats in their Typical Form are not Found Anywhere***: It is also commented that the Marxist division of capitalist society in to two sections - the bourgeoisie and the proletariat is not seen anywhere. As

35. Abraham and Morgan in *Sociological Thought,* p. 46.
36. Dr. N. Jayaram in his *Sociology*: *Methods and Theories*, p. 70.

Raymond Aron has said, *"The analogy between the rise of proletariat and the rise of bourgeoisie is sociologically false. In order to restore the equivalance between the rise of bourgeoisie and the rise of the proletariat, the Marxists are forced to resort to something which they themselves condemn when practised by others, namely, 'myth'.*

7. ***Marxian Notion of Classless and Stateless Society is Utopian***: *Marxist theory of social classes is ambiguous and debatable.* His analysis of the rise of social classes may be applicable to the Western societies but not to Asiatic societies including the Indian society. And Marx's classless and stateless society is utopian. Nowhere in the world, including in the so called communist societies such as Russia, China Cuba, Poland and the like, such state of affairs exist. Thus, Marx has been proved to be a failure in many respects.
8. ***Different Versions of Marxian Thought are Confusing***: In the Marxist circles also *there is no consensus regarding Marxian thoughts.* In fact, there are different versions of Marxist doctrine - *the Soviet Version, the Chinese Version, the Western Version,* and the like. There is no way of knowing how Marx would have reacted to this development, had he been with us today. **Raymond Aron** observes: *"In all probability, Marx who had a rebel's temperament, would not be enthusiastic about any of the versions, any of the modalities of society which call themselves Marxist. But which would he prefer? An answer seems to me impossible and, in the last analysis, pointless"*[37]

Concluding Remarks

The contributions of Karl Marx to the development of social thought can hardly be exaggerated. He was undoubtedly a genius and a profound scholar. It is not an easy task to evaluate the contribution and influences of Karl Marx and his thoughts on his followers and opponents. **Abraham** and **Morgan** observe: *"That he has profoundly influenced Western thought, sociological, economic and political, cannot be denied. Although many of his predictions have not come true, the fact that those who have read his works have changed the world also cannot be denied. Even the worst critics agree that Marxian theory provides an excellent framework for the analysis of conflict and change in modern society. And Marx's influence on contemporary sociological theory is growing and Marxist sociology has already become an established branch of the discipline."*

MAIN WORKS OF KARL MARX

1. *The German Ideology, 1845,* with Friedrich Engels.
2. *The Poverty of Philosophy, 1847.*
3. *Manifesto of the Communist Party, 1848,* translated by S.Moore, New Edition - 1952.
4. *The Class Struggles in France, 1848 to 1850.*
5. *The Eighteenth Brumaire of Louis Bonaparte, 1852* with F Engels
6. *The Holy Family.*
7. *A Contribution to the Critique of Political Economy,* Translated by N.I. Stone, 1904.
8. *Das Kapital,* [Vol. I in 1867, Vol. 2 and 3 published by Engels in 1865 and 1894.]
9. (*a*) *The Economic and Philosophical Manuscripts of 1844* [1964] and (*b*) *Grundrisse - 1973* - These two manuscripts were published after the death of Marx that too very recently.

? REVIEW QUESTIONS

1. Give a biographical sketch of Karl Marx in short.
2. Karl Marx was great revolutionary who created history. Analyse.
3. Critically comment on Marx's theory of historical materialism.
4. Explain Marx's theory of social change.
5. Critically evaluate the Marxian theory of social class.
6. Explain the concept of social class. Discuss the development of social classes.
7. Discuss the Marxian theory of class conflict. Elaborate on its essential aspects.
8. Throw light on the Marxian concept of classless society. Discuss the political and economic principles of the classless society.
9. Explain Marx's concept of alienation. Throw
10. Make an assessment of Marx's contributions to sociology.

⌘⌘⌘⌘⌘⌘⌘⌘⌘⌘⌘

37. Raymond Aron in his *Main Currents in Sociological Thought*, Vol. I. p. 181.

60

TALCOTT PARSONS AND ROBERT K. MERTON: THEIR CONTRIBUTIONS

CHAPTER OUTLINE

- TALCOTT PARSONS : BIOGRAPHIC SKETCH OF PARSONS
- MAIN WORKS OF PARSONS
- MAIN CONTRIBUTIONS OF PARSONS TO SOCIOLOGY : PARSONS' THEORY OF SOCIAL ACTION A PARSONS' CONCEPT OF SOCIAL SYSTEM
- PATTERN VARIABLES
- FUNCTIONAL PRE-REQUISITES OF SOCIAL SYSTEM.
- ROBERT K. MERTON : A BRIEF BIOGRAPHIC SKETCH OF R. K. MERTON
- MAJOR CONTRIBUTIONS OF R. K MERTON: SOCIAL CONFORMITY AND DEVIANCE-MERTON'S THEORY OF ANOMIE OR DEVIANCE OR MERTON'S STRAIN THEORY
- MANIFEST AND LATENT FUNCTIONS
- CONCEPT OF DYSFUNCTION
- REFERENCE GROUP THEORY
- RELATIVE DEPRIVATION AND REFERENCE GROUP BEHAVIOUR.

TALCOTT PARSONS [1902—1979]

Talcott Parsons (1902-1979)

Talcott Parsons was the most influential American sociologist of the 20th century and the leading modern exponent of functionalism. For twenty to thirty years after the Second World War, Parsons was the major theoretical figure in America and in the English- speaking area, if not in the world of sociology. Being a theorist, he was not in the dominant tradition of American empirical research. As often criticized, as supported, Parsons' work was at the center of debate in sociological theory until the mid 1970's.

Although Parsons has relatively few followers among sociologists today, he is acknowledged as the greatest spokesman of functionalism and a mastermind in theoretical sociology. It was Parsons who first introduced the works of Durkheim and Max Weber to American readers and who laid the foundation for what was to become the modern "*functionalist perspective*." As a professor of sociology at Harvard University, he influenced a large number of students through his teachings and writings. Parsons was a prolific Writer, and with his varied writings, he has acquired an important place in the history of sociology.

Biographic Sketch of Parsons

Talcott Parsons was born in the year 1902 at Colorado Springs in America in a family having a good religious and intellectual background. His father was a congregational minister [chief of local religious board]. His father was also a professor who later became the president of a college. His father had instilled educational interest in him and helped him to develop work culture. Parsons completed his Pre-degree from Amherst College in 1924 and went to U.K. to join the famous London School of Economics where he wanted to continue his degree level education. During his stay in England, he came under the influence of Prof Hamilton, L.T. Hobhouse, Morris Ginsberg and B. Malinowski. Parsons intellectual contact with these people in a way made him develop greater interest in the functionalist method.

Intellectual Influence of Weberian Thoughts on Parsons

Parsons obtained his degree from the London School of Economics in the year 1926 and in the very next year he joined the Heidelberg University at Germany. Weberian influence was very dominant in this area though Weber had died 5 years prior to Parsons joining the Heidelberg University. Parsons was impressed by the efforts of Weber's wife who was taking all the pains to continue the intellectual tradition of her husband by way of convening discussions and debates at her own home. Parsons who attended such meetings at Weber's house unknowingly came under the influence of Weberian thought. In fact, he obtained his Ph.D. degree from the Heidelberg University and the subject of research was also related to Weber's works. The topic of his thesis was "*Max Weber and Sombart and Their School of Capitalism*". Within a few years, Parsons translated Weber's masterpiece namely; "*The Protestant Ethic and the Spirit of Capitalism*", from German to English.

Parsons' Professional Life

After receiving his Ph.D. degree from the Heidelberg University, Parsons joined Harvard University as an instructor in the year 1927. Harvard gave him the opportunity to study the works of the classical theorist of economics, Alfred Marshall. Within a very short span of time, Parsons came under the influence of the thoughts of Durkheim, Spencer, Pareto and a famous physiologist L.J. Henderson.

After joining Harvard, Parsons spent the whole of his professional life there till his death in 1979. Parsons' progress as a teacher in Harvard was not an impressive one in the beginning, for he had to work as an ordinary teacher till 1939. His first major volume in his cum right, "*The Structure of Social Action*" which was published in 1937, fetched him recognition as a theoretical sociologist.

Parsons was able to achieve quick professional progress especially after 1939. He became the Chairman of the Department of Sociology in 1944, and in 1946, he became the President of the Department of Social Relations. These positions gave him an opportunity to work in the wide circle of social scientists. His reputation spread far and wide when he became the President of the American Sociological Association in 1949. Between 1950 and 1960, Parsons brought out his famous books including "*The Social System*" (*1951*), "*Towards A General Theory of Action*" (1951) with Edward Shils,"*Economy and Society*"(1956) with Smelser, and so on.

Cold War Between Sorokin and Parsons

P.A. Sorokin was the Chairman of the Department of Sociology in the Harvard University, the department which he himself had established, when Parsons joined the department as an ordinary instructor. As long as Sorokin was the chairman of the department of sociology, Parsons could not come to prominence. In fact, Sorokin was a strong critic of Parsons views and there was a kind of cold war between the two. Parsons' favourite student R.K. Merton's comments regarding this so called cold war is worth mentioning here: "*Of the very first generation of graduate students coming to Harvard precisely none came to study with Talcott. They could scarcely have done so for the simplest reasons. At about 1931, he had no public identity whatever; as a sociologist... Although we students come to study with the renowned Sorokin, some of us stayed to work with the unknown Parsons*".[1]

Waves of Criticisms about Parsons Views and Thoughts

Parsons' theories and thoughts were subjected to criticism in the circle of slowly emerging radicals in the American sociology especially after 1960s. Parsons' "*sociological theory* [*most often labelled* '*structural-functionalism*' or '*normative functionalism*'] was commonly seen *as a product of modern, affluent American society, where structural social conflicts had been largely eliminated or were of a transient nature, and where there appeared to be a general social cohesion and shared adherence to democratic values. Parson' theory came under increasing criticism as the path-war consensus itself showed signs of dissolving, particularly under the impact of the Vietnam war*"[2]

Parsons was bitterly criticized as a political traditionalist and his theories were also branded as conservative. "*A number of criticisms have been levelled against Parsons: (1) his is a grand theory with little empirical use; (2) he gives too much importance to values and norms; (3) he does not pay enough attention to social conflict; (4) he is unable to reconcile action theory and system theory, and in effect sees individual action as structurally determined; (5) his functionalism involves teleology*".[3]

Death of the Epoch — Maker in Sociology

As an impressive professor, a famous theoretician, a prolific writer; and a trend-setter Talcott Parsons proved to be an epoch-maker in the realm of sociology. His contribution to the development of sociology has been immense. Even in

[1] Merton, l980:89 as quoted by George Ritzer in his *Contemporary Sociological Theory*, p. 331.

[2] Allan G Johnson in *Oxford Dictionary of Sociology*, p. 480.

[3] Abercrombie and others in the *Penguin Dictionary of Sociology*, p. 256.

his seventies, he was actively involved in various educational activities. He died at the age of 77 while he was engaged in furthering his own intellectual activities. In his death America lost one of its topmost sociologists. His death marked the end of an era in sociology which he himself had begun. Merton's words of tribute to Parsons are as follows: "*The death of Talcott Parsons marks the end of an era in sociology. When a new era does begin it will surely be fortified by the great tradition of sociological thought which he has left to us.*"[4]

Main Works of Talcott Parsons

1. *The Structure of Social Action (1937)*
2. *Essays in Sociological Theory (1954)*
3. *The Social System (1951)*
4. *Toward a General Theory of Action (1951), with Shils.*
5. *Working Paper in the Theory of Action (1953), with R. Bales and E. Shils.*
6. *Family, Socialisation and Interaction Process (1955), with R. Bales, J. Olds, M. Zelditch and R Slater*
7. *Economy and Society (1956), with N. Smelser:*
8. *Structure and Process in Modern Societies (1960)*
9. *Social Structure and Personality (1964)*
10. *Societies: Evolutionary and Comparative Perspectives (1966).*
11. *Sociological Theory and Modern Society (1967)*
12. *Politics and Social Structure (1969)*
13. *The System of Modern Societies (1971)*
14. *The American University (1973), with Gerald M. Platt and Neil J. Smelser.*

Critical assessments of Parsons' works have been published in two volumes of essays in his honour by sociologists who were his former students or colleagues:

(*i*) "*Stability and Change* " (1971) by Bernard Barber, Alex Inkeles.

(*ii*) "*Explorations in General Theory in Social Sciences*" (1971) by Jan J. Loubser, Rainer C. Baum.

[**Source:** "*The New Encyclopaedia Britannica Vol. 9. Page: 171 and "Dictionary of Sociology"* (Penguin) by Abercrombie and others]

MAIN CONTRIBUTIONS OF TALCOTT PARSONS TO SOCIOLOGY

(i) Parsons Theory of Social Action

As a theoretician, Parsons' aim was nothing less than to provide "*a conceptual structure for the whole of sociology which would serve also to integrate all the social sciences. This was to be accomplished by a synthesis between the analysis of individual action and analysis of large-scale social systems. His starting point is the theory of social action, the essential feature of which is the relationship between actors and features of their environment, social and natural, to which they give meaning*".[5]

Actor and Situation in the Social Action

The focus of attention of 'social action theory' is on the action of individual actors or of a group of actors. The behaviour of an individual or a group in a social context is called "social action". Social action has two main aspects: (*i*) *action* and (*ii*) *objective situation*.

(*i*) The "**actor**" refers to the subject of social action, that is, the individual through whom the actions are performed. Anyone who does the social action is called the *subject* or *actor*.

(*ii*) There is always a context or situation in reference to which the actor performs a social action. Social action cannot take place in a vacuum and there must be some objective situation or context under which social action takes place. The objective situation may be social or non-social. Social situation refers to individuals or groups while *non-social environment* refers to physical environment. The actor and situation of social action are mutually linked and they are interdependent. The actor, by his behaviour, in turn, is also affected by the situation.

[4] Merton, 1980-81 as quoted by George Ritzer, p. 331

[5] Abercrombie and others in the *Penguin Dictionary of Sociology*, p. 254.

Importance of Function in Social Action

Parsons is of the opinion that the main task of sociology is to describe, explain and analyse social action. Any assembly or congregation of individuals results in social action. Social action is not aimless or purposeless. In any social action, each individual performs a specific function. Social action is also guided by some goal or motivation. Social action is therefore, goal-oriented or motivational.

Types of Action

As Parsons has stated, action can be classified into three types depending upon the nature of motivational orientation. They are **cognitive, cathetic** and **evaluative**.

(i) ***Cognitive Action***: Cognitive action is social action with cognitive orientation. If a social action is dominantly rational it is said to have a cognitive orientation. In this kind of social act, feelings or emotions do not play any prominent role. This orientation refers to the knowledge aspects for, it is dominated by rational considerations.

(ii) ***Cathetic or Emotional Action***: Some social actions are found to be highly emotional. In an emotional social action, reason does not play any role and only emotions dominate. For example, under the influence of motherly love, a woman who does not know swimming may jump into the river to save her child who is drowning. In such social actions, orientation is said to be cathetic or emotional.

(iii) ***Evaluative Action***: Actions that are guided by values or moral standards are said to be "evaluative" in nature. Since values play an important role in society, different people act in different ways depending upon the inspiration of different values. Depending upon the nature of values people's actions are judged to be good or bad, and right or wrong. Such actions are obviously backed by evaluative orientation.

Critical Remarks

The theory of social action profounded by Talcott Parsons is one of the important theories in sociology. Despite its merits, it has been severely criticized by the scholars. According to some, it is not a comprehensive and self-sufficient theoretical orientation for sociologists. It is irreparably individualistic. Further, though individuals may perceive and orient themselves to some goals or purposes, social institutions cannot do that for, no one now subscribes to the existence of the "group mind". Social processes cannot be explained entirely in terms of the intentions, goals, or purposes of the individual people.

Parsons' concept of social system

Talcott Parsons can undoubtedly be regarded as "*the most outstanding exponent of the social system theory. In his "Structure of Social Action", Parsons focused on unit act but in "The Social System", emphasis shifted from unit act to institutional orders, and the system was the primary unit of analysis. However, it must be noted at the outset that Parsons' 'social system' 'is a constructed type, an analytical conceptual framework and not an empirical referent......*"[6]

Parsons takes 'social action' as the building block of the system. He prefers the term 'action' to behaviour because he is interested not in the physical events of behaviour for their own sake but in their patterning. Parson's sociological theories are largely based upon his conception of social action. Parsons has also given three configurations or systems of social action. Social actions according to him, are guided by the following systems: *personality system, cultural system and social system*. It can also be said that the scheme of three types of social action [or orientation] "*serves as a background for the construction of three analytical systems: the social system, the personality system and the cultural system*".

Meaning of System

Parsons has discussed the personality, the cultural and the social systems in his treatise "The Social System". It is thus necessary to know what a system is. "*A system is any collection of interrelated parts, objects, things or organisms*".

In Parsonian language, "*In general, system can be defined as a set of interdependent elements or parts that can be thought of as a whole. In this sense, we can think of a motor car or the human body as a system*"[7] As a general approach to understanding a variety of phenomena, systems theory is the study of how systems are organized, how they adopt to changing circumstances, how the interests of subsystems adjust or conflict with those of the whole, and so on.

1. ***Personality system:*** Parsons considers personality as the aspect of the living individual. Personality system is concerned with the total social actions of an individual. It must be understood in terms of the cultural and social content of all the learnt things that make up his behavioural system. Personality is autonomous as a distinct

[6] M.F. Abraham in *Modern Sociological Theory*, 1982, pp. 52-53.

[7] *The Blackwell Dictionary of Sociology*, p. 266

subsystem of action. Parsons also claims that the personality system is the primary meeting ground of the cultural system, the behavioural organism, and secondarily, the physical world. As **Abraham** [page-64] has pointed out, "*The main function of the personality system involves learning, developing, and maintaining through the life cycle an adequate level of motivation so that individuals will participate in socially valued and controlled activities. In return, society must also adequately satisfy and reward its members if it is to maintain the level of motivation and of performance*." This relationship constitutes socialization, the process by which individuals become social beings. Effective process of socialization is crucial to make the individual's value commitments link primarily with the cultural system. Parsons insists that "*in addition to rewarding conformity and punishing deviance, motivation must be furnished at different levels*."

2. ***Cultural System:*** When the individual system rises to the level of culture, it is known as cultural system. It is constituted of the normative patterns. It includes cognitive beliefs, values, norms, private moral obligations, expressive symbols which guide the choices made by the individuals. "*The main function of the cultural system is the legitimation of the society's normative order: Cultural value patterns provide the most direct link between the social and cultural systems in legitimizing the normative order of the society. They define what is appropriate and what is not, not necessarily in the moral sense but in accordance with the institutionalized order*." [**Abraham** — 63]. It could be said that the cultural system is said to be well organized if it actively influences, guides and controls the lives of the individuals.

3. ***Social System:*** The concept of "social system" has been used most explicitly, and self-consciously in modern 'functionalism'. But it was implicit as much in the 19th century social thought. "*A social theory which treats social relations, groups or societies as a set of interrelated parts which function to maintain some boundary or unity of the parts is based explicitly or implicitly on the concept of social system*."

The chief exponent of the 'most modern theory of 'social system' has been Talcott Parsons. Parsons has tried to give a more scientific and a rational explanation to the concept of social system in his books "*The Structure of Social Action*", and "*An Outline of the Social System*."

Meaning and Definition of Social System

Parsons uses the term 'social system' to refer to society whether it is the smallest or the largest collectivity. The social system is made up of the relationship of individuals. A simplified version of the definition of Parsons has been given by *W.F. Ogburn* and it is stated below

- "*A social system may be defined as a plurality of individuals interacting with each other according to shared cultural norms and meanings*."
  —**W.F. Ogburn**
- "*A social system consists of a plurality of individual actors interacting with each other in a situation which has at least a physical or environmental aspect, actors who are motivated in terms of a tendency to the "optimization of gratification" and whose relation to their situations, including each other, is defined and mediated in terms of a system of culturally structured and shared symbols*."[8]
- *In simple words, the term 'social system' "basically consists of two or more individuals interacting directly or indirectly in a bounded situation*".[9]

Elements or Units of Social System

The social system is constituted by the actions of individuals. It involves participation of an actor in a process of interactive relationships. This participation has two main aspects: (*i*) *the positional aspect and the processional aspect*. The positional aspect indicates the location of the actor in social system which may be called his "*status*". The processional aspect indicates the functional importance of the actor for the social system which may be called his "*role*".

(*i*) ***The act*** : Social act or action is a process in the social system that motivates the individual or individuals in the-case of a group. 'The orientation of action has a close relation with the attainment of satisfaction of the actor. The action is not an unexpected response to a particular situation or stimulus. It indicates that the 'actor has a system of expectations relative to his own need-arrangements. The need-arrangement system of the individual actor has two aspects: (*i*) *the gratificational aspect*, and (*ii*) *the orientational aspect*. The gratificational aspect refers to what the actor gets out of his interaction and what its costs are to him. The orientational aspect refers to the how he gets it. Both these aspects must be present in what is called a social act.

[8] Parsons' definition in his *Social System*, pp. 5-6 as quoted by M.F. Abraham, p. 60.

[9] Duncan Mitchell in *A Dictionary of Sociology*.

(*ii*) ***The actor***: fire actor is also a significant unit of social system. It is he who holds a status and performs a role. A social system must have a sufficient proportion of its actors. These actors must be sufficiently motivated to act according to the requirements of its role system. The social system must also be adapted to the minimum needs of the individual actor. The system must secure sufficient participation of its actors also. It means, it must motivate them sufficiently to the performances which are necessary for the social system to develop or to persist. The act and actor are complementary to each other. The actor has to act according to the roles assigned to him. This he learns through the process of socialization. The social system limits and regulates the needs and also actions of the actor. This, the social system does through social control.

(*iii*) ***The role and status***: The social system involves the participation of actor in a process of interactive relationship. This participation has two aspects : (*i*) *the role aspect*, and (*ii*) *the status aspect*. Role denotes the functional significance of the actor for the social system. Status denotes the place of the actor in the social system.

An actor may have a high or low status in a social system and he has a definite role to play. Different roles associated with the same status are properly integrated in the system. The actors are distributed between different roles. This process of distribution has been called by Parsons as "*allocation*". Proper allocation of roles between actors minimizes problems for the system. The allocation of roles is related to the problem of allocation of facilities. Problem of facilities is actually the problem of power because possession of facilities means to have power-economic or political.

Thus, a social system faces the problems of proper allocation of roles, proper allocation of facilities and rewards and proper allocation of economic and political power. If this allocation is properly done it may preserve itself, otherwise, it may disintegrate.

Mechanism of Social System

Social system is a system of interdependent action processes. But the tendencies of the individuals are such that they may alter the established status of social system. This may disturb the established interaction process of the system. It is, therefore, essential that some proper mechanisms are applied for maintaining the equilibrium between the various processes of social interaction. These mechanisms have been classified by Parsons into two categories:

(*i*) *Mechanisms of socialization*, and (*ii*) *Mechanism of social control.*

(*i*) ***Socialisation***: Socialisation is a process whereby an individual learns to adjust with the conventional pattern of social behaviour. He learns to adjust himself with the social situation conforming to social norms, values, and standards. This process is not confined to the child alone. It goes on throughout life. Some of the principal aspects of socialization are known as rearing, sympathy, identification, imitation, social teaching, suggestion, practice and punishment.

(*ii*) ***Social Control***: Social control consists of the mechanisms whereby the society moulds its members to conform to the approved pattern of social behaviour. According to Parsons, there are two types of elements, which exist in every system. These are *integrative* and *disintegrative*. The function of social control is to eliminate those elements, which cause disintegration and create problems for integration. Besides, in every society, there is a system of rewards for conformative behaviour and punishments for deviant behaviour. Deviant behavioural tendencies may also constitute one of the principal sources of change in the structure of the social system.

Pattern Variables

"Pattern Variables" is an important concept coined by Talcott Parsons and is closely associated with his theory of social action. As Parsons says we can analyse actions, social relationships, and whole systems according to what he calls "pattern variables" — or choices between pairs of alternatives. Parsons notes that social interaction has a systematic character and hence he refers to it as a "social system". The concept that bridges social action and social system is that of "pattern variables".

Definition of Pattern Variables

- The term "pattern variables" refers to "*the four [sometimes five] basic pattern-alternatives of value orientation for individuals and cultures, according to Parsons.*"[10]
- Pattern variables represent *"Five dichotomies or pairs of variables proposed by Talcott Parsons for the purpose of classifying types of social relationships. Each pattern variable provides two mutually exclusive alternatives, one of which must be chosen by an individual before he can act in a social situation.*"[11]

[10] *Collins Dictionary of Sociology*, p. 479

[11] W.P. Scott in *Dictionary of Sociology*.

- The concept of pattern variables introduced by Talcott Parsons "..... *is an attempt to supply a logically exhaustive list of action dilemmas on the highest possible level of abstraction*".

According to Parsons, the five pattern variables represent the basic dilemmas a person faces in orienting to another person. As per Parsons' analysis, "*cultures are seen as organizing action, and actors are faced with implicit 'choices' in relationships, in terms of four dichotomous alternative modes of orientation to 'social objects', including other actors*". In simple words, individuals are faced with some fundamental dilemmas in their interaction and social systems offer a combination of solutions for these dilemmas.

Five Pattern Variables

Five sets of pattern variables as stated by Parsons are as follows:

1. Affectivity versus affective neutrality
2. Diffuseness versus specificity
3. Universalism versus particularism,
4. Ascription versus achievement [also as quality and performance]
5. Self-orientation versus collectivity orientation

1. ***Affectivity Versus Affective Neutrality:*** Affectivity versus affective neutrality represents one of the pattern variables proposed by Talcott Parsons. The word 'affectivity' refers to feelings or emotions whereas "affective neutrality" signifies emotional neutrality or detachment. This is one of the dilemmas that the actors face. For the individual in a given situation, this is the dilemma of whether to give importance to an impulse or to the values and more distant goals. This is like the opposition between the demands of an impulse or immediate need and the possible benefits of restraint and discipline. Here, the individual has to decide whether he should opt for the immediate gratification of an impulse or need or he should abstain himself from doing it. **Example:** Eating a meal or watching a chess match compared with work that does not require one's emotional involvement, say, working in a garage. This pattern variable suggests that actors can either engage in a relationship for emotional reasons [affectivity] or in a relationship for instrumental reasons without the involvement of feelings [affectivity neutrality].

2. ***Diffuseness Versus Specificity:*** As per this dichotomy, actors in their relationship with others will have to choose in any situation between a totally wide range of activity [diffuseness] or a specific and a structured one [specificity]. 'Diffuseness' implies wide range of satisfying relationships while 'specificity' denotes a narrower range of relationships. In confronting an object [that is, another person], an actor must choose among the various possible ranges in which he will respond to the object.

   The dilemma here consists in whether the actor should respond to restricted range of them. ***Example*** : Mother-child relationship and family relationships, in general, represent "diffuseness" where relationships are not fixed or defined but spread about all aspects of life. On the other hand, bus conductor issuing tickets to the passenger; or the relationship between the doctor and patient- represent relationships which have only a specified and limited purpose.

3. ***Particularism Versus Universalism:*** This represents a "*dichotomy in social behaviour, that is concerned with the problem of whether a person in a given situation should be oriented to another person [or persons] in terms of generalized standards of behaviour or in terms of the special nature of their relationship to each other*". [**W.P. Scott**-449]. In simple words, actors have to decide whether to judge a person by general criteria [universalism] or criteria unique to that person [particularism]. **Example**, Mother's relationship with the child. A mother's relationship with her child may sometimes be particularistic but at other times, involve universalistic criteria as when the child's performance is appraised at school. '

4. ***Ascription Versus Achievement:*** This pattern variable has recently been called as the dichotomy between quality and performance. This pattern variable refers to the dilemma of whether to treat a person according to who he is or in terms of what he is doing, or may be expected to do in the given situation. As per this variable, actors have to decide whether to judge persons by what they do [performance] or by their personal characteristics [quality]. **Example:** In most societies, relationships based on inherent qualities [age, sex, caste, etc.] of the individual can be considered ascriptive; while his success in business or a cricket match or in a musical career involves achievement.[12]

[12] "Probably because of this difference from the usual distinction between ascribed and achieved status, this dilemma has more recently been called Quality versus Performance". —W.P. Scott in *Dictionary of Sociology*, p. 17.

5. ***Self-Orientation Versus Collectivity Orientation:*** Here the dilemma is between personal interests and group interests in social situations. For the individual in a given situation, this is the dilemma of whether to pursue his own personal interests and goals or sub-orient his private interests to the interests and welfare of a group or other individuals. This dichotomy is described by Parsons as the "dilemma of private values versus collective interests", or "the distribution between private permissiveness and collective obligation". This fifth variable, originally proposed by Parsons, was subsequently dropped as being of a different order from the other four.

Importance of Pattern Variables

According to Parsons, through pattern variables it is possible for us to understand the four dilemmas which the individuals face in orienting their relationship with others. In fact, all relationships between individuals and others can be brought under this scheme. "*The first four pattern variables namely, affectivity, diffuseness, particularism and ascription – bring out the broad norms of relationships among friends and close ones and they are primary in nature. By contrast, the second four variables – namely, neutrality; specificity, universalism and achievement [or performance] – bring out the broad norms of secondary relationships*".[13]

It appears that "Parsons" conception of pattern variables was presented by him as deriving from previous characterization of types of society such as Tonnies' distinction between Gemeinschaft and Gesellschaft."[14] Parsons saw his "*pattern variables as providing an exhaustive general statement of the fundamental dilemmas permanently facing all actors and involved in all social organizations*."

Functional Pre-requisites of Social System

The concept "*functional pre-requisites*" or "*functional imperatives*" constitutes an essential aspect of the functional theory. This concept refers to the basic needs of a society which have to be met if it is to continue to survive as a functioning system. Thus, from a functional perspective, societies survive and function only if certain tasks are accomplished. For example, without reproduction and socialization, there would be no supply of new members. Similarly, a system of social stratification is said to be necessary to ensure that the most able people are recruited to the most important positions, a requirement for an efficient society.

Functional theory looks upon society as a social system which is believed to perform certain functions. Parsons and his followers have given a list which they have called the "functional pre-requisites" of any social system. They can be grouped under four recurrent functional problems which every social system must solve in its attempt to adapt itself to the basic facts of life. As mentioned by Parsons, they are : (*i*) *pattern maintenance and tension management*, (*ii*) *adaptation*, (*iii*) *goal attainment*, and (*iv*) *integration*.

Pattern Maintenance and Tension Management

A social system has its own patterns which must be maintained. The units of the system, that is, role-occupants or sub-groups, must learn these patterns and develop an attitude of respect towards them.

Tension management: A human group cannot endure if it fails to meet the individual human needs of its members. The units of any system, i.e., individuals or sub-groups are subject to emotional disturbance and distractions. Man's emotional, spiritual, and cultural requirements are extremely complex. Still they must be met with or "managed" if the units are to be able to carry on effectively. All social systems provide for relaxation from tension by means of activities that allow a person to express his or her inner feelings. For example, dance and the arts do this task. All societies provide special structural arrangements for differences in sex and also for such crucial events as births and deaths. Wherever there is social life, there are structures or patterns of leisure and recreation, crafts, art, and some form of religion expressed in myths or elaborate ritual.

Adaptation

Any social system must be adapted to its social and non-social environment. For a society to survive it must have a technology adequate to provide food, shelter and clothing. The economy of the society meets this need. Every 'permanent' social system has its own division of labour. Because, for the production of goods and services, role differentiation becomes necessary. It is known that no one person can perform simultaneously all the tasks that have to be performed. The system must also provide care for the helpless young and protection against animal and human predators. Many of the structures existing in any society are designed to fulfil these essential functions.

---

[13] C.B. Damle and Richard Pais in *Sociological Thought from Comte to Merton*, p. 130.

[14] *Collins Dictionary of Sociology,* p. 480.

Goal Attainment

Every social system has one or more goals to be attained, through co-operative effort. 'National security' - can be cited here as the best example of a societal goal. Adaptation to the environment, social and non-social, is necessary if goals are to be attained. Further, in accordance with the specific nature of tasks of the system, the human and non-human resources must be mobilized in some effective way. For example, in any social system there must be a proper process for determining which persons will occupy what role at what time and for what purpose. The problem of allocation of members within the social system will be solved by such a process. The rules regulating inheritance, for example, get solved by such a process. The rules regulating inheritance, for example, solve this problem in part.

The allocation of members and the allocation of scarce resources are important for both adaptation and goal attainment. The economy of a society as a sub-system produces goods and services for various purposes. The government in complex societies, mobilizes goods and services for the attainment of specific goals of the total society. Example : A business firm may have the goal of producing steel. The goal is adaptive for the society because steel can be used for many purposes, including the purpose of other business firms. The steel company faces the adaptive problem. It means, it has to adjust to the government and to competing firms and provide itself with the necessary raw materials for its productive goals.

Integration

Since they live in groups, men and women must consider the needs of the group as well as their own needs. They must coordinate and integrate their actions. 'Integration' has to do with the interrelations of units of social system, that is, individuals and groups. "*To some extent, the members of a system must be loyal to one another and to the system as a whole. This is a problem of solidarity and morale*". Morale is important for both integration and pattern maintenance. It is closely related to common values. It is the willingness to give oneself to specific undertakings. In the routine living, the goals and interests of the whole society are not of much interest to the whole society and are not very much present in the minds of most of its members. That way, the interests of sub-groups are always remembered. But during the period of crisis such as war or revolution the goal and interest of the whole society must always dominate if the society is to survive as an independent group.

In almost every social system, some participants, including whole sub-groups, violate the norms. Since the norms fulfil some social needs, their violations are a threat to the social system. Thus, the need for "*social control*" arises. It is essential to protect the integrity of the system. "*Thus, the elaborate rules provide orderly procedures to determine who will occupy given sites, to control the use of force and fraud, to co-ordinate traffic, to regulate sexual behaviour, to govern the conditions of exchange, and so on*".

Since the individual members are often motivated by "*self-interests*", chances of clashes taking place between them cannot be ruled out. Sometimes, even with best morale we find threats to integration. Hence, there must be mechanism for restoring solidarity. Such mechanisms are normally operative most of the time. It must be noted that even with the well-institutionalized norms, instances of deviance do take place. The deviations may even become disruptive. Hence, there is the need for "secondary" mechanism of social control. *Example*: In the modern state, the whole apparatus of catching and rehabilitating the criminal represents such a kind of secondary mechanism.

ROBERT K. MERTON [1910-2003]

A Brief Biographic Sketch of Merton

Robert King Merton has been widely recognised as one of the leading figures in the 20th century American sociology. He has made an important contribution to the discipline by successfully combining theory and research. As a leading US sociologist, he became an influential voice of functionalist sociology in his own right. As a bright student of Pitirim.A.Sorokin and Talcott Parsons, he was highly influenced by both of them. In spite of his poor family background he rose to very great height and earned a good name for himself as an internationally reputed theoretical sociologist. He had a wide range of sociological interests among which - *sociology of science, sociology of professions, sociological theory and sociology of mass communications* - are very significant.

Robert K. Merton (1910-2003)

Merton's Educational and Professional Life

Merton was born on 5th July, 1910 to Slavic immigrant parents in Philadelphia under very poor circumstances. His father worked as a carpenter and truck driver. The economic backwardness of his family never deterred him from continuing his education. Soon after completing his high school education at Philadelphia he won a scholarship to Temple University, where he proved to be a brilliant scholar. After receiving his B.A degree from Temple University he got a chance to continue his post sociology. Merton also got the rare opportunity to study the subject his interest with the intellectual giants like Pitirim. A. Sorokin, Talcott Parsons and L.J.Henderson.

Merton served on the faculty of Tulane University, New Orleans [U.S] between 1939 and 1941 and later he moved to Columbia University on an invitation to work as a lecturer in sociology. He became a full professor in 1947 and thereafter served in the same post till l handed over the responsibility to professor Giddings in 1963. He served as an associate director of the Bureau of Applied Research at Columbia where he became the colleague of Paul Lazarsfeld, yet another great, scholar of the day.

Merton and Lazarsfeld Form the Brilliant Team at Columbia University

Lazarsfeld who had become the director of the above said bureau was a good guide to Merton in some fields and Merton too had his influence on Lazarsfeld in some other matters. Both influenced each other to a great extent. "*Lazarfeld's logic of concept clarification and his methodology of quantitative and qualitative research influenced Merton's orientation to historical studies, and Mertons' gift for theory influenced Lazarfeld's philosophic grasp of the discipline of sociology. They produced important research and writing on methods of improving standards of training for the social sciences .... Merton and Lazarfeld's formed a brilliant team at Columbia University [1941-76] and inspired many students*".[15]

Social Thinkers who Influenced R.K. Merton

As R.K.Merton has stated in his autobiography, Sorokin and Parsons exercised a great influence on him especially regarding the European social thought. Parsons in particular, influenced him greatly to develop the 'structural view' about society. Famous biochemist and often known as a sociologist **L.J. Henderson**, roused **Merton's** curiosity regarding what is known as "*disciplined investigation*". The intellectual influence of economic historian E.F.Gay and the dean of the History of Science, George Salton on Merton, was no less significant.

Though Merton had no contact with the famous pioneering sociologists like Durkheim and George Simmel, he was highly influenced by them. As Merton himself had acknowledged, sociologically sensitive humanists Gilbert Murray and Paul.F.Lazarsfeld played an important role in enkindling his intellect.

Major Contributions of Merton

Merton has made enduring contributions to the critical understanding of a variety of concepts including those of social structure, science, deviance, anomie, opportunity structure, mass communications, role theory and the analysis of relative deprivation and reference groups and bureaucracy.

Merton's "*doctoral dissertation on the development of science in the 17th century is generally credited with prompting a major shift in sociological approaches to science that has influenced work in the field ever since.*"[16]

Merton's most influential general work is the collection of essays entitled "*Social Theory and Social Structure*" *1949*, [subsequently enlarged and revised]. This book portrays the interrelationship between social theory and empirical research. This classical work contains a number of prominent essays including — "*Manifest and Latent Functions,*" and "*Social Structure and Anomie*". Two other concepts of significance as newly introduced and analysed by Merton in this book are — "*anomie*" and "*reference group theory* "

Throughout his career, "*Merton has been concerned with developing meaningful sociological theories that can be tested empirically with finding a middle range between what C. Wright Mills criticized as the untreatable abstractions of grand theory and the triviality of abstracted empiricism.*" [Allan G. Johnson — Page : 347.]

Major Works of Merton

Of the joint authored and edited books of Merton, the following are considered to be important;

1. *Mass Persuasion 1946*,
2. *Continuities in Social Research – 1950*,
3. *A Reader in Bureaucracy – 1952*,
4. *The Student Physician – 1957*,

[15] *The New Encyclopeadia Britannica,* Vol.8, 1988 Edition, p. 44.

[16] Allan. G. Johnson in the *Blackwell Dictionary of Sociology*, p. 347.

Other Prominent Works of Merton

Although all the above mentioned works have been very influential, Merton's doctoral dissertation on science "*Science, Technology and Society in Seventeenth Century England,*" was particularly a brilliant work. In fact, it was the work, which made his reputation. The following works of Merton have made him a memorable name in sociology.

1. *The Focused Interview: A Manual of Problems and Procedures (1956);*
2. *Science, Technology and Society in Seventeenth Century England. [1938; Reprinted 1970].*
3. *Social Theory and Social Structure. [1949; Revised Edition 1968].*
4. *On The Shoulders of Giants. [1965]*
5. *On Theoretical Sociology. [1967],*
6. *Social Theory and Functional Analysis. [1969] .*
7. *The Sociology of Science : Theoretical and Empirical Investigations : [1973]*
8. *Social Ambivalence and Other Essays. [1976] .*
9. *Qualitative and Quantitative Social Research. [1979 - Edited by Merton]*
10. *Sociological Traditions from Generation to Generation. [1980 - Edited]*

[**Source:** *The New Encyclopaedia Britannica* (1988). Vol. 8. Page: 44]

MAJOR CONTRIBUTIONS OF R.K. MERTON

Social Conformity and Deviance

Society maintains itself by a normative system. Normative system refers to the system of rules and regulations. All societies expect their members to follow some rules or norms and to avoid their violation. Acting or behaving in accordance with the norms is called 'conformity' and acting or behaving against them is known as "deviance". Conformity and deviance are common to all societies.

Functionalist Perspective of Deviance

According to functionalists, deviance is a common part of human existence, having both positive and negative consequences for social stability. Deviance helps to define the limits of proper behaviour. In fact, deviance is a necessary part of social organization. This point was made clear by Durkheim a century ago.

Durkheim's Functionalist Legacy

Durkheim in his pioneering study of deviance, made a major observation that there is nothing abnormal about deviance. In fact, it performs four essential functions.[17] They are:

(i) ***Deviance affirms cultural values and norms:*** There can be no good without evil and no justice without crime. Deviance is needed to define and sustain morality.

(ii) ***Clarification of moral boundary***: Attempts to respond to deviance, help to clarify moral boundaries. By defining some people as deviant, people draw a boundary between right and wrong.

(iii) ***Responding to deviance promotes social unity*** : People typically react to serious deviance with collective outrage. Example: Indians stood with the government when latter made efforts to suppress Pakistan's attacks. In Durkheim's language, we can say that people reaffirm the moralties that bind them.

(iv) ***Deviance encourages social change*** : As Durkheim said, today's deviance can become tomorrow's morality. Deviant people may suggest alternatives to the status quo and encourage change.

Durkheim's Theory of Anomie

Perhaps the oldest sociological explanation of deviance is Durkheim's theory of anomie. Durkheim applied this theory to his classic study of suicide. He found that one type of suicide seems to be rooted in a condition termed anomie [literally means, lack of regulation.] Anomie refers to a state of normlessness that typically occurs during a period of profound social change and disorder, such as a state of economic collapse. Durkheim used the term [originally in 1893] to describe the confused condition that exists in both individuals and society when social norms are weak, absent or conflicting. A society with high level of anomie, risks disintegration, for, its members no longer share common goals and values. During crises or drastic social changes, people become more aggressive or depressed, which results in higher rates of violence and suicide.

---

[17] John J. Macionis in *Sociology*, 10th Edition, p. 192.

During crises, people's life experiences no longer match the ideals represented in societal norms. As a result, these people experience confusion and disorientation. According to Durkheim, both depression and prosperity are "disturbances of the collective order". Social norms breakdown, people become disoriented, and deviant behaviour occurs. Individuals in a state of anomie lack guidelines for behaviour, for they feel little sense of social discipline over their personal desires and acts. *Robert Merton (1938, 1968) has modified this concept and applied it to deviant behaviour.*

Merton's Theory of Anomie or Deviance or Merton's Strain Theory

Gap between Cultural Goals and Institutional Means

Some deviance may be necessary for a society to function, but Merton argued that excessive deviance results from particular social arrangements. Merton believes that deviance is a result of a gap between the goals of a culture and the approved means of meeting those goals. To Merton, anomie is the situation that arises when there is a discrepancy between socially approved goals and the availability of socially approved means of achieving them.

Merton in his theory of deviance makes an analysis of the relationship between social structure and anomie. Among the several elements of social structure, Merton separates two: *cultural goals* and *institutional means*. The cultural goals are more or less integrated and constitute a frame of aspirational reference. They are the acknowledged desirables in any society such as – success, money, power, prestige, name, fame, etc. The institutionalized means are the acceptable modes of reaching these goals. These are not necessarily the most efficient means. But they are normatively regulated and approved by the social system. They are the standardized practices of the group found in the form of customs, traditions, institutions, laws, etc. For example, as Merton states, in America, success in life which is measured largely in terms of money or wealth, is set forth for the people as one of the cultural goals. American society also specifies the means of attaining it, that is, in terms of education, hard work, making adventures, taking advantage of opportunities and so forth.

Individuals Facing the State of Anomie

Merton proceeds to define anomie, as the disjunction between cultural goals and institutionalized means, Anomie according to him, is not the same thing as the absence of norms or even absence of clarity of norms. "*In the condition called anomie, norms are present, they are clear enough, and the actors in the social system are to some extent oriented to them. But this orientation, on the part of many, is ambivalent*; *it either leans towards conformity, but with misgivings, or leans towards deviation, but with misgivings*."

People who accept the goal of success but find accepted means to success blocked may fall into a state of anomie and seek success by disapproved methods. The strength of Merton's approach is that it locates the source of deviance mainly within culture and social structure, not in the failings of individual deviants. Society itself in this state of anomie [or disjunction between cultural goals and institutionalized means], exerts a definite pressure on some people to behave in deviant rather than conformist ways.

Five Types of Individual Adaptation

Individuals faced with the state of anomie may respond in one of the five different ways. Merton reasoned that people adapt in certain ways, either by conforming to or by deviating from such cultural expectations. His anomie theory of deviance mentions five basic forms of adaptation.[18]

A Typology of Modes of Individual Adaptation [OR Merton's Typology of Deviance]

Modes of Adapting	Accepts Culturally Approved Goals	Accepts Culturally Approved Means
Conformist	Yes	Yes
Innovator	Yes	No
Ritualist	No	Yes
Retreatist	No	No
Rebel	no (creates new goals)	No (creates new means)

Source *: Adapted from Robert K. Mertons', Social Theory and Social Structure [New York : Free Press, 1968] p. 194] as cited by Ian Robertson in "Sociology" - Page – 168]*

1. ***Conformity***: Conformity to social norms, the most common adaptation in Merton's typology, is the opposite of deviance. Conformity lies in pursuing conventional goals through approved means. Conformists accept both the approved goals and the approved means. Hence, to attain success and to obtain wealth, they work hard, save money,

[18] Harry M. Johnson in *Sociology: A systematic Introduction*. p. 557.

and generally use approved means of seeking the goals — even if they are unsuccessful.

2. ***Innovation***: A second possible response is innovation, which involves accepting the goals but rejecting the means. This is the most common form of deviance. It occurs, for example, when a student wants to pass an examination but resorts to cheating; when a candidate wants to win an election but uses 'dirty tricks' to discredit an opponent. The innovator would use new illegitimate means of obtaining wealth – racketeering, blackmailing or resorting to "white – collar crimes', and so on.

3. ***Ritualism***: A third response, ritualism, involves rejecting the goals while accepting [or even overemphasizing the means]. Here, people abandon the goals as irrelevant to their lives but still accept and compulsively enact the means. For example, low-level bureaucrats, knowing that they will achieve only limited financial success, stick closely to the rules in order to feel at least respectable. Ritualism is the mildest form of deviance and except in extreme cases, is not usually regarded as such.

4. ***Retreutism***: Retreatism occurs when a person rejects both goals and means. The retreatist is a "double failure" in the eyes of the society. Some alcoholics, drug addicts, the vagrants, street people are retreatists. The deviance of the retreatists lies in their unconventional lifestyle and perhaps more seriously in their apparent willingness to live in their peculiar ways. A retreat is the person who has lost commitment to both the goals and the means that society values.

5. ***Rebellion***: Like retreatism, rebellion involves rejection of both goals and means. But the rebel substitutes new goals and means for the old ones. He or she develops an ideology, which may be even revolutionary, that creates new goals and means. A rebel, for example, may advocate a system of socialist ownership that would put an end to private property. Similarly, some rebels, such as "radical survivalists" – go one step further by forming a counter culture and advocating alternatives to the existing social order. The rebels consider the new goals and means, which they are advocating, as more legitimate than the existing ones.

Critical Evaluation of Merton's Theory of Deviance

Comments in favour of the theory

1. Merton theory of deviance is an elegant, thoughtful, and an influential one.
2. It has been usefully applied to several forms of deviance, particularly that of delinquent juvenile gangs.
3. As pointed out by this theory — "*deviance reflects the opportunity structure of society*" — is a fact which has been confirmed by subsequent research. Sociologists like Cloward, Cohen, Miller and Anderson have endorsed this opinion.
4. The theory has the virtue of locating the cause of deviance in society. It provides a very plausible explanation of why people commit certain deviant acts, particularly crimes involving property.
5. Merton's theory is useful for it "*treats conformity and deviance as two ends of the same scale, not as either/or categories*."[19]
6. The theory also shows that *deviance is not a product of a totally negative, rejecting attitude, as people often assume. A thief does not reject the socially approved goal of financial success. He or she may embrace it warmly as any young person on the way up the corporate ladder A ritualistic bureaucrat does not reject the proper procedures but actually overdose them. Even so, both of these people are behaving in deviant ways*".[20]
7. Merton's "*theory helps us to understand deviance as a socially created behaviour rather than as the result of momentary pathological impulses.*" —**Richard Schaefer** [p. 187]

Comments against merton's theory

1. Merton's theory has comparatively limited applications. "*Little effort has been made to determine to what extent all acts of deviance can be accounted by his five modes... his formulation for fails to explain key differences in crime rates. Why, for example, do some disadvantaged groups have lower rates of reported crime than others... Merton's theory of deviance does not answer such questions easily.*"[21]
2. Merton's theory is "*less useful, however, for explaining other forms of deviance, such as homosexuality, exhibitionism, or marijuana use ....*" —**Ian Robertson** [p. 169]

[19] N.J. Smelser in *Sociology*, IV Edition, 1993, p. 130.

[20] Ibid.

[21] Views of Clinard and Miller 1993 as quoted by Richard Schaefer in *Sociology*, 6th Edition, p. 186.

3. All "*structural-functional theories imply that everyone who breaks the rules is labeled deviant. Becoming deviant is however; actually a highly complex process...*"[22]
4. Merton's strain theory has been criticized for explaining some kinds of deviance, for example, theft, far better than others, such as crimes of passion. Further, all people do not seek success in the conventional terms of wealth, as strain theory implies.

Manifest and Latent Functions

More than any other sociologist Robert Merton has contributed much to the codification and systematization of functional analysis. He reviewed the essential postulates in functional analysis and critiqued and modified them. In an attempt to eliminate some of the prevailing types of confusion, Merton sets out to redefine current conceptions of function. He defined "function" in terms of useful or 'system sustaining activity'. Merton also spoke in terms of the concept of "dysfunction".

According to Merton, "*Functions are those observed consequences which make for the adaptation or adjustment of a given system; and dysfunctions are those observed consequences which lessen the adaptation or adjustment of the system*."[23]

Two Major Contributions of Merton to Functional Analysis

Two of Merton's major contributions to functional analysis are to be found in his discussion of the (*i*) distinction between *manifest and latent functions*, and (*ii*) between *function and dysfunction*. These distinctions and Merton's clarification of them have made functional analysis of cultural patterns and social institutions both, more meaningful and scientific.

Distinction Between Latent and Manifest Functions

The functional theory presupposes that every element in a social system fulfils certain functions. But how does one determine what the functions of a given element in the social system are? The sociologist only asks what its consequences are, and not what its purposes are believed to be. The assumed purposes of some component can have consequences other than those that were intended. This fact has made **R.K. Merton** make a distinction between '*manifest functions*' and '*latent functions*'.

According to Merton, "*Manifest functions are those objective consequences contributing to the adjustment or adaptation of the system which are intended and recognised by the participants in the system*". "*Latent functions correlatively, being those which are neither intended nor recognised*"

—**M.F. Abraham**.

Manifest Functions

These are the functions "intended and recognised" by the participants in the system. These are functions which people assume and expect the institutions to fulfil. **Examples:** (*i*) Schools are expected to educate the young in knowledge and skills that they need. It is its manifest function. (*ii*) Economic institutions are expected to produce and distribute goods and direct the flow of capital wherever it is needed. (*iii*) Dating is expected to help the young men and direct young women to find out their suitability for marriage. (*iv*)The welfare system has the manifest function of preventing the poor from starving. (*v*) Similarly, incest taboos are expected to prevent biological degeneration. These manifest functions are obvious, admitted, and generally applauded.

Latent Functions

These are "*unrecognised and unintended*" functions. These are the unforeseen consequences of institutions. **Examples:** (*i*) Schools not only educate youth, they also provide mass entertainment and keep the young out of employment market. (*ii*) Economic institutions not only produce and distribute goods, but also promote technological, political and educational changes, and even philanthropy. (*iii*) Dating not only selects marriage partners, but also supports a large entertainment industry. (*iv*) The welfare system not only protects the starving, but it also has the latent function of preventing a civil disorder that might result if millions of people had no source of income. (*v*) Incest taboo has the latent function of preventing conflicts within the family. Another latent function is, it reinforces the sexual union between husband and wife.

Role of Latent Functions in Relation to Manifest Functions

Latent functions of an institution or partial structure may-(*i*) support the manifest functions, or (*ii*) be irrelevant to, or (*iii*) may even undermine manifest functions. These points may be clarified.

(*i*) ***Latent functions may support the manifest functions.*** *Example*: The latent functions of religious institutions in the modem society include-offering recreational activities and courtship opportunities to young people. All church

[22] J.J. Macionis in *Sociology*, 10th Edition, 2006, p. 195.

[23] M. Francis Abraham in *Modern Sociological Theory: An Introduction*, 1982, p. 84.

leaders agree that these activities help churches pursue their manifest functions.

(*ii*) ***Latent functions may be irrelevant to manifest functions.*** *Example*: It is very much doubtful that the sports spectacles staged by schools and colleges have much effect upon the manifest functions of promoting education. But, they seem to be largely irrelevant to this manifest function.

(*iii*) ***Latent functions sometimes undermine manifest functions.*** *Example*: The manifest function of civil service regulations is to secure a competent, dedicated staff of civil servants to make government more efficient. But the civil service system may have the latent function of establishing a rigid bureaucracy (consisting of bureaucrats with least concern), which may block the programme of an elected government. Such a bureaucracy may refuse to carry out the government programmes, which disturb the bureaucrats' routine procedures. This could be referred to as the 'dysfunctional' aspect of the civil service system.

Purposes and Importance of the Distinction between Manifest and Latent Functions

1. The distinction between manifest and latent functions helps us to understand that many social practices continue to persist even though their manifest purpose is clearly not achieved.
2. Through this kind of functional analysis we come to know that many of the ceremonials which people observe may fulfil the latent function of reinforcing the group identity by providing a periodic occasion on which the scattered members of a group assemble to engage in common activity.
3. The concept of latent function directs one's attention towards a range of consequences, which are normally not noticed or simply ignored.
4. Latent functions represent greater departures from common sense knowledge about social life. The distinction throws light on the complexity of social practices found in social life.
5. The concepts of latent and manifest functions are indispensable elements in the theoretic repertory of the social engineer. In this sense, both of these concepts are practical as well as theoretical."[24]

Interlink Between Latent and Manifest Functions

As H.M. Johnson has pointed out the distinction between manifest and latent functions is essentially relative and not absolute. A function may appear to be "manifest' for some participants in the social system and 'latent' for others. But the individuals, many times, are not aware of the latent, or manifest dysfunctions of most of the partial structures of society. Still the distinction between them is of some importance.

Firstly, if the sociologist is not aware of the possibility of latent functions, he might often think that some partial structures have no function at all. Further, he might become quite contented with discovering manifest functions only. It is here, that the sociologist in his investigation, has got ample chance to go beyond his "common sense" to find out explanation for certain social elements in terms of latent functions and dysfunctions.

Secondly, any social reformer must be sufficiently aware of the latent functions and dysfunctions of any partial structure which he wants to reform or change. His proposals for reform would become ineffective, if he is not conscious of these functions. In fact, "*knowledge of the way in which society actually "works" is the only sound basis of social planning. Naive moralising can be not only ineffectual but wasteful and otherwise harmful*". For example, mere launching a crusade against the so called 'corrupt' political machines in a city or a province in a blind manner is of no use if one is ignorant of the latent functions of "corruption".

Finally, the distinction will help one to know or estimate the effects of transformation of a previously latent function into a manifest function. The distinction also involves the problem of the role of knowledge in human behaviour and the problems of "manipulation" of human behaviour.

Concept of Dysfunction

The term dysfunction [or disfunction] refers to "*any social activity seen as making a negative contribution to the maintenance of effective working of a functioning social system.*"[25]

- '*Dysfunction' refers to "Any consequence of the existence or operation of an aspect of social system that is judged to be a disturbance or a hindrance to the integration, adjustment, or stability of the system.*"[26]

---

[24] R.N. Sharma and R.K. Sharma in *Contemporary Sociological Theories*, 1999, p. 104.

[25] *Collins Dictionary of Sociology,* p. 183.

[26] W.P. Scott in *Dictionary of Sociology*, p. 121.

Merton in his functional analysis makes a distinction between 'functions' and 'dysfunction' depending upon their consequences. Thus, speaking from Merton's point of view, "*consequences that interfere with the system and its values are called dysfunctional while those that contribute are called function.*"[27]

As Merton says functions increase the adaptation of adjustment of a given social system while dysfunctions lessen its adaptation and adjustment. The consequences of functions lead towards harmony and adjustment whereas the consequences of dysfunctions lead towards disintegration and maladjustment. Aspects of systems often have both functional and dysfunctional consequences. Divorce, for example, often has the dysfunctional consequence of interfering with family members material needs, but it also can have the functional consequence of providing a solution to destructive conditions such as family violence.

Latent Dysfunctions

Merton has also observed that a particular or some latent functions of an element or a particular structure may prove to be dysfunctional for the system as such. ***Example*** **:** The manifest function of the regulation of drugs by the government is to protect consumers against injurious substances. Its latent function may be to delay the introduction of new, life-saving drugs. This latent function, it is obvious, is dysfunctional for the social system. Similarly, the manifest function of western health institutions has been to reduce illness, premature death and human misery; the latent function has been to promote a population explosion and massive famine in the underdeveloped countries. These latent functions are definitely 'dysfunctional' in nature.

There are, therefore, many instances in which latent functions might precisely be called "*latent dysfunctions*". Because, they tend to undermine and weaken institution or to impede attainment of its manifest functions.

Different Perceptions of the Consequences of the Function

The same social arrangement can have, or may be perceived to have, both positive and negative consequences. It means – what may be judged dysfunctional for one part of a system may be judged functional for some other part. *For example*, in a particular class system, the prevalence of a certain belief [say, religion being considered as a means of salvation] may be functional for the upper class but dysfunctional for lower class. Similarly, the rain that saves a crop of thousands of farmers may spoil a marriage party or a picnic. What is in the best interest of the individual may be detrimental to the solidarity of the collectivity. What is functional for a particular group under certain circumstances may be dysfunctional for the same group under other circumstances. For example, what is functional for the elite in the short run, works towards their destruction in the long run.

Reference Group Theory

In the analysis of individual and group behaviour, and in the study of social mobility, both and group, "*reference group theory*" is of great help as an important tool. The term reference group "was coined by **Herbert Hyman** in "*Archives of Psychology*" (1942), to apply to the group against which an individual evaluates his own situation or conduct. R.K. Merton developed this concept into a theory known as "*reference group theory*". However, 'the concept of reference group' and 'the theory of reference group' are extensively used in the sociological studies of social stratification and mobility.

Meaning of the Concept of Reference Group

1. **R.K. Merton:** "*Reference group theory aims to systematise the determinates and consequences of those processes of evaluation and self-appraisal, in which the individual takes the values or standards of other individuals and groups, as a comparative frame of reference.*"
2. **Sherif** and **Sherif:** "*Reference groups are those groups to which the individual relates himself' as apart, or to which he aspires to relate himself psychologically. In everyday language, reference groups are those groups with which he identifies or aspires to identify himself*."[28]
3. **Ogburn** and **Nimkoff:** "*Groups which serve as points of comparison are known as reference groups*". They have further added that the reference groups are those groups from which "*we get our values, or whose approval we seek.*"
4. **Horton** and **Hunt** have pointed out "*A reference group is any group to which we refer when making judgements – any group whose value – judgements become our value-judgements.*" *They have further said,*" *groups which are important as models for one is ideas and conduct norms...* " *can* be called reference groups.

[27] *The Blackwell Dictionary of Sociology*, p. 117.

[28] Muzaffer Sherif and Carolyn W. Sher if in *An Outline of Social Psychology*, 1956, p. 175.

5. **John J. Macionis** says that "*reference group is a social group that serves as a point of reference in making evaluations and decisions*." *Example*: To a doctor, other physicians constitute the most important reference group. How high or low should he set his consultation fee? Is it acceptable to wear jeans when interacting with patients?" How much ongoing training should doctors receive after leaving medical college? If a doctor is incompetent should another doctor who is aware of this truth inform the medical and government authorities? Am I a competent doctor? — These are the kinds of questions that a doctor would most likely answer in relations to physicians as constituting a reference group.

Membership and Non-Membership Groups Playing the Role of Reference Groups

Merton's 'reference group theory' has drawn our attention towards the fact that both membership and non-memberships groups play the role of reference groups. The concept of 'reference group' arises essentially from the fact that any person acting in any situation may be influenced not only by his membership groups but also by his conception of other groups of which he is not a member. These other groups exert their influence as reference groups in a purely passive or silent way, that is, simply by being thought of. They do not, of course, entirely exist as reference groups. But they are called so only from the point of view of their capacity in exerting influence. The young child in the family is interested in the reactions of everyone in the family with whom it is in contact. The family is both a membership group and a reference group for the child. But when the child becomes mature he selects particular groups which are understood here as "reference groups" whose approval or disapproval he especially desires.

The concept, reference groups, as distinct from membership groups, has particular relevance in modern complex, heterogeneous society with its high rates of physical and occupational mobility. In such complex society, a person may be a member of one group but prefer membership or aspire for membership in another. In a small folk society, the distinction between membership group and reference groups is less common and may be nonexistent.

Impact of Multiple Reference Groups

As R.K. Merton has pointed out, reference groups are not necessarily one or two, they could be several. It is not uncommon to orient ourselves to more than one reference group at a time, especially when this involves reference groups to which we do not belong. Medical student, for example, use other students as one reference group in addition to the reference group of practicing physicians whose ranks students hope to join eventually.

In modern complex societies, individuals come into contact with various groups and it is not necessary for them to orient themselves to the values and standards of any one particular group. They may prefer to adopt the values and standards of different groups for guiding their behaviour in different sectors of life. *For example*, they may find one reference group in economic field another in religious field and yet another in political field, and so on.

Importance of Reference Group in Socialisation

The concept of reference group is important for understanding 'socialisation' and 'conformity', and how people perceive and evaluate themselves especially in relation to the "self". Our evaluation of ourselves are strongly influenced by the reference groups we choose. *For example*, if a student who obtains a "B Grade" in an examination, compares the result with that of 'A Grade' students, the self-evaluation will be very different than if the result is compared with that of "C" Grade students. Whether people are members of these groups or not, they refer to the norms and values of the groups in evaluating their own behaviour and personality no less powerfully than any other group to which a person feels loyal.

Anticipatory socialisation: Merton has introduced the concept of "*anticipatory socialization*"[29] to analyse the consequences of conforming to the norms of a group other than one's own. Anticipatory socialization may lead to two important consequences. (*i*) As the individual leans more towards anticipatory socialization he incurs the hostility of his in-group. This may compel the individual to develop increasing conformity to the out-group. As a result, the former out-group becomes the in- group now. (*ii*) Secondly, to prevent the members from going out of the group and to sustain the structure of authority in the group, greater rewards are offered for conformity.

Relative Deprivation and Reference Group Behaviour

R.K. Merton and Alice S. Kitt provide a systematic functionalist formulation of the concept of reference group in their classic "*Contribution to the Theory of Reference Group Behaviour*" [edited by R.K. Merton and RF. Lazarsfeld], "*Continuities in Social Research*: *Studies in the Scope and Method of the American Soldier*, 1950]. Merton was highly influenced by Samuel A. Stouffer's research study namely; "*The American Soldier* (*1949*)". Stouffer's study aims at understanding the

[29] R.K. Merton and Alice S. Kitt have introduced in the term "Anticipatory Socialisation" in *Continuities in Social Research*, Edited by R.K. Merton and RF. Lazarsfeld, 1950.

behaviour pattern among American soldiers. The study revels that "soldier's feelings of deprivation were less related to the actual degree of hardship they experienced, than to the living standards of the group to which they compared themselves."[30]

Stouffer's Research

Samuel Stouffer (1949) conducted a class study of reference group dynamics during World War II. Researchers asked soldiers to rate their own or any competent soldier's chances of promotion in their own army unit. Stouffer's study revealed that the soldiers measured themselves differently with different groups. *For example*, those having assignments with lower promotion rates looked around them and saw people making no more headway than they were. It means, although they had not been promoted they did not feel deprived, soldiers in units with a higher promotion rate, however, could easily think of people who had been promoted sooner or more often than they. With such people in mind, even soldiers who had been promoted were likely to feel shortchanged or even deprived.

It is true that we do not make judgements about ourselves in isolation, nor do we compare ourselves with just anyone. Regardless of our situation in absolute terms, we form a subjective sense of our well-being by looking at ourselves in relation to specific reference groups."[31]Thus, the millionaire can feel relatively disadvantaged among his multimillionaire friends, as can the man with only one air-conditioned car, or the one-star general[32] and so forth.

Conditions or Circumstances under Which a Group Functions as a Reference Group for a Particular Group

Only under certain circumstances a group may become reference group for the members of a particular social group. H.M. Johnson has mentioned four such circumstances.[33]

1. ***Striving for admission***: When some or all the members of a particular group aspire for membership in the reference group. *Example*: The ambitious upper-middle class people are always interested in joining the rank of upper-class people. In order to get an admission into upper-class, they may show their prejudice and even aggressiveness towards low-ranking groups.
2. ***Attempts at emulation***: When the members of a particular group struggle to imitate the members of reference group, or try to make their group just like the reference group at least in some respects. *Example* : The lower caste people in India who suffer from a sense of inferiority are found to be emulating some of the styles and practices of Brahmins to feel equal to them at least in some respect. Similarly, members of the minority groups may to incorporate in their personality dominant -group standards to help better their relationship with the dominant majority group.
3. ***Conferral of superiority***: When the members of the particular group derive some satisfaction from being distinctive and unlike the members of reference group in some aspects. Further, they may try to maintain the difference between the two groups or between themselves and the members of the reference group. *Example* : If Whites as a status group are a reference group for Negroes, so are Negroes a reference group for Whites because both want to retain their difference. Whites want to remain unlike the Negroes and so is the case with Negroes. Similarly, Muslims may be interested in maintaining their difference with the majority community, especially in the Indian context.
4. ***Simple comparison or standard for comparison***: When the members of a particular group consider the reference group or its members as a standard for comparison. Example: The teachers of a city college may always make references to the most prestigious college of the city as a measuring rod to assess their position, service condition, performance and so on. Such contemplation of reference groups may have some consequences for the moral of the group.

Critical Remarks

The concept of reference group behaviour or Merton's "theory of reference group" has been criticised on some grounds.

(*i*) This theory does not discover any new fact except giving some ideas about comparison of behaviour at individual and group level.

(*ii*) The theory only explains the behaviour but does not suggest any ways or means to control or direct it,

(*iii*) The theory reveals how an individual is influenced by a reference group. But it does not explain how the reference group is influenced by his entry, or admission into the group.

[30] *Oxford Dictionary of Sociology*, p. 556.

[31] *Views of Merton in the words of JJ. Macionis,* p. 168.

[32] "*One-star general*" refers to an army officer having one star as an army badge.

[33] H.M. Johnson in *Sociology—A Systematic Introduction*, pp. 39-43.

In spite of its shortcomings, the theory is of practical importance in understanding group behaviour and informs us of the directions which an individual's behaviour may take in a particular social environment.

The theory helps to explain the psychological stresses and strains which the individuals and groups undergo in the modern industrialised and complex society to model themselves after some other individual or group.

REVIEW QUESTIONS

1. Write a brief biographic sketch of Talcott Parsons.
2. Throw light on the main works of Talcott Parsons.
3. Evaluate the contribution of Talcott Parsons to sociology.
4. Critically analyse Parsons' theory of social action.
5. What do you mean by social system? Discuss its elements.
6. Throw light on the mechanism of social system.
7. Define pattern variables. Elaborate on the various sets of pattern variables as stated by Parsons.
8. What are the functional pre-requisites of the social system. Explain.
9. Write a biographic sketch of Robert K. Merton in brief.
10. Throw light on Merton's educational and professional life.
11. Assess the contribution of R.K. Merton to sociology.
12. Write the main works of Merton.
13. Critically evaluate Merton's theory of anomie or deviance.
14. What is Merton's strain theory. Explain.
15. Comment on Merton's strain theory.
16. Bring out the relation between the manifest and latent functions.
17. Critically analyse Merton's reference group theory. Assess the impact of multiple reference groups.

BIBLIOGRAPHY

1. Abercromabic, et al., ... *The Penguin Dictionary of Sociology.*
2. Abhraham, J.H. ... *Sociology* (*Teach yourself Book*).
3. Abraham, M.F.: ... *Modern Sociolological Theory,* 1982.
4. Ahuja, Ram ... *Indian Social System*
5. Ahuja, Ram ... *Social Problems in India*
6. Albert K. Cohen ... *Deviance and Control.*
7. Alex Inkeles ... *What is Sociology?*
8. Amitai Etzioni ... *Modern Organisations.*
9. Apte, B.P. ... *Student Power and Student Unrest.*
10. Barnes, H.E. ... *An Introduction to the History of Sociology*
11. Bates, A.P. and J. Julian ... *Sociology—Understanding Social Behaviour.*
12. Bhattacharya, Sanjay ... *Social Work [An integrated Work],* 2004.
13. Bogardus, E.S. ... *Development of Social Thought*
14. Bottomore, T.B. ... *Sociology—A Guide to Problems and Literature.*
15. C.B. Damle and Richard Pais ... *Sociologist Thought from Comte to Merton*
16. Chitambar ... *Rural Sociology.*
17. Chowdhry, D. Paul ... *Introduction to Social Work [History, Concept, Methods and Fields].*
18. David Dressler and Donald Carns ... *The Study of Human Interaction*
19. David Popenoe ... *Sociology.*
20. Demerath, N.J. and Gerald Marwell ... *Sociology—Perspectives and Applications.*
21. Desai, Neera and Usha Thakkar ... *Women in Indian Society,* National Book Trust of India, New Delhi.
22. Donald Light Jr. and Suzanne Keller ... *Sociology.*
23. Don C. Gibbons ... *Criminology*
24. Doshi, S.L. and P.O. Jain ... *Rural Sociology.*
25. Duncan Mitchell ... *A Dictionary of Sociology.*
26. Editor J. Gould and W.L. Kolb ... *Dictionary of Social Sciences*
27. Eldridge et al. ... *Fundamentals of Sociology*
28. Francis Abraham and John Henry Morgan ... *Sociological Thought.*
29. Friedlander, W.A. ... *Introduction to Social Welfare,* 1959.
30. George Ritzer ... *Contemporary Sociological Theory,* 2nd Edition.
31. Ghosh, Biswanth ... *Contemporary Social Problems of India.*
32. Gokhale ... Political Science
33. *Government of India* Parts I and II Report of the Commission for SCs and STs for 1975-76, 76-77, 24th Report.
34. Graham White ... *Socialisation* (*Aspects of Modern Sociology-Social Process*)
35. Grald R. Leslie, Richard F. Larson and Benjamin L. Gorman ... *Introductory Sociology*

36. Green, A.W. ... *Sociology—An Introduction to the Science of Society.*
37. Gupta, R.C. ... *Great Political Thinkers East and West.*
38. Haralambos M. and Heald R.M. ... *Sociology—Themes and Perspectives*
39. Harry M. Johnson ... *Sociology: A Systematic Introduction.*
40. Horton, P.B. and C.L. Hunt ... *Sociology*
41. Ian Robertson ... *Sociology*
42. Indra, R. ... *Mahile-Samaja Mattu Sanskriti,* Kannada Book.
43. James C. Coleman and William E. Broen, Jr. ... *Abnormal Psychology*
44. Jayaram, N. ... *Introduction to Sociology,* 1987.
45. Jayaram, N. ... *Sociology of Education in India,* 1990.
46. John J. Macionis ... *Sociology,* 10th Edition.
47. Kachroo, J.L. ... *General Sociology,* 1990.
48. Kar, P.K. ... *Indian Society,* 2000, Kalyani Publishers.
49. Kimball Young and Raymond W. Mack ... *Systematic Sociology—Text and Readings*
50. Kindulka, S.K. ... *Social Work in India,* 1965, Kitab Mahal Pvt. Ltd.
51. Kingsley Davis ... *Human Society*
52. Kon, I.S. ... *A History of Classical Sociology.*
53. Kuppu, Swamy B. ... *An Introduction to Social Psychology*
54. Kuppu, Swamy B. ... *Social Change in India*
55. Leah Levin ... *Human Rights,* National Book Trust of India New Delhi.
56. Leonard Broom and P. Selznick ... *Sociology*
57. Lewis A. Coser ... *Masters of Sociological Thought*
58. Louise Weston, et al. ... *The Study of Society,* 2nd Edition
59. Maciver and Page ... *Society: Introduction Analysis*
60. Madan, G.R. ... *Indian Social Problems,* Vol. II, 2nd Edition, 1973, Allied Publishers.
61. Madan, G.R. ... *Indian Social Problems,* Vol. I.
62. Madan, G.R. ... *Theoretical Sociology,* Vol. III.
63. Mamoria, C.B. ... *Social Problems and Social Disorganisation in India.*
64. Mathur, S.S. ... *A Sociological Approach to Indian Education*
65. Merrill, F.E. and H. Wentworth ... *Culture and Society—An Introduction To Sociology*
66. Metta Spencer and Alex Inkeles ... *Foundation of Modern Society*
67. Michael Harlambos (Editor) ... *Sociology—A New Approach*
68. Nagesh, H.V. ... *Samagika Chintaneya Ihihasa,* Kannada Version Book.
69. Neil J. Smelser ... *Sociology—An Introduction,* 1993.
70. Neil J. Smelser ... *Sociology—An Introduction.*
71. Nicholas S. Timasheff ... *Sociological Theory, Its Nature and Growth.*
72. Ogburn, W.F. and M.F. Nimkoff ... *A Handbook of Sociology.*
73. Oomen, T.K. and C.N. Venugopal ... *Sociology for Law Students*
74. Parimal B. Kar ... *Sociology—The Discipline and its Dimensions*
75. Pascual Gisbert ... *Fundamentals of Industrial Sociology.*
76. Pascual Gisbert ... *Fundamentals of Sociology.*
77. Peter Berger ... *An Invitation to Sociology.*
78. Peter Worsley ... *Introducing Sociology.*
79. Publication Division (Ministry of Information and Broadcasting) Government of India ... *Fair Deal for Backward Classes*

80. Quarterly Journal of Deendayal Research Institute, New Delhi ... *Manthan,* Vol IV, No. l. Feb. 1982.
81. Quinn ... *Urban Sociology*
82. Radcliffe Brown, A.R. ... *Structure and Function in Primitive Society.*
83. Rao, M.S.A. (Editor) ... *Social Movements in India*
84. Raymond Aron ... *Main Currents in Sociological Thought*
85. Rex A. Skidmore and Milton G. Thackery ... *Introduction to Social Work,* 2004.
86. Richard T. Lapiere ... *Social Change*
87. Robert Bierstedt ... *The Social Order*
88. Robin Fox ... *Kinship and Marriage*
89. Ronald Fletcher ... *The Making of Sociology,* Vol. I and Vol. II.
90. Roucek, J.S. and Warren R.L. ... *Sociology : An Introduction*
91. Sachadeva, D.R. ... *Social Welfare Administration in India,* 2011, Kitab Mahal.
92. Sachdev and Vidyabhushan ... *Introductory Sociology*
93. Scarpitti, F.R. and M.L. Andersen ... *Social Problems, 1989.*
94. Sen Gupta, Surajit ... *Introductory Sociology,* 1984.
95. Shamim Aleem ... *Women's Development Problems and Prospects,* 1996.
96. Shankar Rao, C.N. ... *Bharateeya Samaj*
97. Shankar Rao, C.N. ... *Samajashastra,* Vol. I and Vol. II.
98. Shankar Rao, C.N. ... *Sociology,* Vol. I and Vol. II.
99. Sharma, R.N. and R.K. Sharma ... *Contemporary Sociological Theories,* 1999.
100. Sharma, Ramnath ... *Principles of Sociology*
101. Sikligar P.C. ... *Social Security, 2000,* Mangal Deep Publications.
102. Sinha, Anjana Maitra ... *Women in Changing Society,* 1993.
103. Smauel Koeing ... *Sociology—An Introduction to the Science of Society.*
104. Sri Chandra ... *Tension in the Youth*
105. Srinivas, M.N. ... *Caste in Modern India and Other Essays.*
106. Sutherland, R.L. J.L. Woodward and M.A. Maxwell ... *Introductory Sociology,* 6th Edition.
107. Thomas F. D'Dea ... *The Sociology of Religion.*
108. NCERT ... *'Understanding Society' A Textbook on Sociology* for Class XI (Part I).
109. Wallace, R.C. and W.D. Wallace ... *Sociology*
110. William J. Goode ... *The Family*
111. William Kornblum ... *Modernisation of Indian Tradition*
112. Winfred Bell ... *Contemporary Social Welfare,* 2nd Edition, Macmillan Publications.

OTHER SOURCES

1. *Manorama Year Book*—1993 and 1994.
2. *India Year Book*—1987 and 1990.
3. *India Today.*
4. *Competition Success Review.*
5. *Collins Dictionary of Sociology.*
6. W.P. Scott's *Dictionary of Sociology*.
7. *Blackwell Dictionary of Sociology* by Allan G. Johnson.
8. *Oxford Dictionary of Sociology.*
9. *The New Encyclopaedia Britannica*, Vol. 3.
10. *Encyclopedia of Social Sciences*, Vol. 14.

UPSC Civil Services (Main) Examination Question Papers: 2014–2018

SOCIOLOGY (PAPER–I), 2014

SECTION A

1. Write short answer of the following in about 150 words each: (10 × 5 = 50)
   (a) How is objectivity different from value neutrality? Discuss with reference to Weber's views on methodology.
   (b) How did the emergence of industrial society change the family life in Western Europe?
   (c) How is sociological approach to human actions different from that of psychological approach?
   (d) In what way biographies could be used to study social life?
   (e) How can we use reference group theory to understand fashion in society?
2. (a) Which research technique would be most suitable for the study of consumer behaviour and its social correlates? Explain. 20
   (b) Identify the similarities and differences between Marx's theory of 'alienation' and Durkheim's theory of 'anomie'. 20
   (c) How could one use Merton's concept of deviance to understand the traffic problem in urban India? 10
3. (a) What do you understand by gender? How does it shape 'male' identity? 20
   (b) "According to Max Weber, 'class' and 'status' are two different dimensions of power." Discuss. 20
   (c) Using Merton's concepts of 'manifest' and 'latent' functions, explain the persistence of corruption in Indian society. 10
4. (a) How does Weber use the notion of 'ideal types' in his theory of bureaucracy? 20
   (b) In what way 'interpretative' method is different from 'positivist' approach in the study of social phenomena? 20
   (c) Using Mead's theory of symbolic interactionism, discuss the stages in the formation of gender identity. 10

SECTION B

5. Answer the following questions in about 150 words each: (10 × 5 = 50)
   (a) For Marx, class divisions are outcomes of 'exploitation'. Discuss.
   (b) What are the distinctive features of social organization of work in slave society? How is it different from feudal society?
   (c) Discuss T. H. Marshall's views on citizenship.
   (d) Distinguish between Political Parties and Pressure Groups.
   (e) "According to Durkheim, the essence of religion in modern society is the same as religion in primitive society." Comment.
6. (a) "Power is not a zero-sum game." Discuss with reference to Weber's and Parsons' views. 20
   (b) Critically examine the functionalist views on the institution of family. How do those help us in understanding family in the present times? 20
   (c) What do you understand by institutionalization of 'live-in relationship'? 10
7. (a) How is religious revivalism different from communalism? Elaborate with suitable examples from the Indian context. 20
   (b) Education is often viewed as an agency of social change. However in reality it could also reinforce inequalities and conservatism. Discuss. 20
   (c) According to Marx, capitalism transforms even the personal relationships between men and women. Critically examine with illustrations from the contemporary Indian context. 10
8. (a) How is the increasing use of technology changing the status of women in Indian society? 20
   (b) Write a short essay on the Latin American perspective on 'dependency'. 20
   (c) What do you understand by social movement? How has the mobilization by Scheduled Castes helped them in constructing a new identity? 10

SOCIOLOGY (PAPER–I), 2015

SECTION A

1. Write short answers of the following in about 150 words each: (10 × 5 = 50)
   (a) Is Sociology a Science ? Give reasons for your answer.
   (b) Discuss the relevance of historical method in the study of society.
   (c) What are variables ? Discuss their role in experimental research.
   (d) Which concepts did Weber use to analyse the forms of legitimate domination ?
   (e) "No society can either be absolutely open or absolutely closed." Comment.
2. (a) Discuss the role of Calvinist ethic in the development of Capitalism. 20
   (b) Examine the problems of maintaining objectivity and value neutrality in Social Science research. 20
   (c) "Self and Society are twin-born." Examine the statement of Mead. 10
3. (a) Why is random sampling said to have more reliability and validity in research? 20
   (b) Differentiate between Marxian and Weberian theories of Social Stratification. 20
   (c) How had Enlightenment contributed to the emergence of Sociology? 10
4. (a) "Non-positivistic methodology is essential for understanding human behaviour." Discuss. 20
   (b) How is social equilibrium maintained in Parsonian framework? 20
   (c) "Anomie is rooted in social structure." Explain with reference to R.K. Merton's contribution. 10

SECTION B

5. Write short answers of the following in about 150 words each: (10 × 5 = 50)
   (a) Distinguish between the social organization of work in feudal society and in capitalist society.
   (b) "Ideology is crucial for social transformation in a democracy." Discuss.
   (c) Distinguish between sects and cults with illustrations.
   (d) Is male authority absent in matrilineal society ? Discuss.
   (e) Explain the relevance of the idea of 'cultural lag' in understanding social change.
6. (a) "Education helps in perpetuating social and economic inequalities." Critically examine the statement. 20
   (b) Explain the conditions under which a collective action transforms into a social movement. 20
   (c) How do the rules of descent and alliance in kinship differ from each other? Illustrate. 10
7. (a) Define Secularisation. What are its major dimensions in the modem world? 20
   (b) The increasing importance of the tertiary sector has weakened the formal organization of work in recent times. Examine the statement. 20
   (c) Caste ideology appears to have strengthened democracy. Comment. 10
8. (a) "Globalization involves deterritorialization." Examine with reference to the nation-state. 20
   (b) Examine the dialectical relation between tradition and modernity in the study of social change. 20
   (c) Elaborate the views of Durkheim on "The Elementary Forms of Religious Life". 10

SOCIOLOGY (PAPER–I), 2016

SECTION A

1. Write short answers of the following questions in about 150 words each: (10 × 5 = 50)
   (a) "Sociology is pre-eminently study of modern societies." Discuss.
   (b) What is 'value-free sociology'? Clarify.
   (c) Analyze the importance of qualitative method in social research.
   (d) Evaluate Marx's ideas on mode of production.
   (e) "Vertical mobility brings structural change even in a closed social system." Comment.
2. (a) Elucidate the basic premises of Davis' structural-functional theory of social stratification. How far is it relevant in understanding contemporary Indian society? 20
   (b) Describe the functional prerequisites of social system as given by Talcott Parsons. Examine in the context of a university as a social system. 20
   (c) Is sociology common sense? Give reasons in support of your argument. 10
3. (a) Analyze the manifest and latent functions of 'security of the tenure of bureaucrats' in the light of Merton's theory. 20
   (b) Describe the basic postulates of scientific method. How far are these followed in sociological research? 20
   (c) "Hypothesis is a statement of the relationship between two or more variables." Elucidate by giving example of poverty and illiteracy. 10
4. (a) Examine Max Weber's method of maintaining objectivity in social research. 20
   (b) "Participant observation is the most effective tool for collecting facts." Comment. 20
   (c) Discuss the relationship between poverty and social exclusion. 10

SECTION B

5. Write short answers of the following questions in about 150 words each: (10 × 5 = 50)
   (a) Describe the nature of social organization of work in industrial society.
   (b) Discuss the importance of 'power elite' in democracy.
   (c) Is religion playing an important role in increasing fundamentalism? Give reasons for your answer.
   (d) To what extent is patriarchy a cause for the problems of women? Discuss.
   (e) "Social conflict is both a cause and a consequence of social change." Explain.
6. (a) "Globalization has pushed the labour into informal organization of work." Substantiate your answer with suitable examples. 20
   (b) "Social change can be brought about through development." Illustrate from the contemporary situation of India. 20
   (c) Examine the role of protest movements in changing the status of Dalits in India. 10
7. (a) "Religious pluralism is the order of present-day societies." Explain by giving suitable examples. 20
   (b) Discuss the contemporary trends in family as a response to social change in modern society. 20
   (c) To what extent revolution replaces the existing order of society? Discuss. 10
8. (a) "Education is a major source of social mobility in contemporary society." Explain. 20
   (b) How is Durkheim's theory of religion different from Max Weber's theory of religion? 20
   (c) Distinguish between family and household as sociological concepts. 10